APA UNDERGRADUATE LEARNING GOALS AND OUTCOMES   *PSYCHOLOGY* CONTENT

3 CRITICAL THINKING SKILLS IN PSYCHOLOGY

Respect and use critical and creative thinking, skeptical inquiry, and, when possible, the scientific approach to solving problems related to behavior and mental processes.

3.1 Use critical thinking effectively.
3.2 Engage in creative thinking.
3.3 Use reasoning to recognize, develop, defend, and criticize arguments and other persuasive appeals.
3.4 Approach problems effectively.

- **Ch 1**: Goals of Psychology, p. 3 Thinking Critically about Psychology, p. 4, 13, and 19
- **Ch 2**: Basic Concepts of Research, p. 25-7; Thinking Critically about Psychology, p. 40 and 43
- **Ch 3**: Thinking Critically about Psychology, p. 55, 61, 76, and 81
- **Ch 4**: Thinking Critically about Psychology, p. 98, 101, 104, 110, and 116
- **Ch 5**: Thinking Critically about Psychology, p. 124, 132, 136, 144, 147, and 157
- **Ch 6**: Thinking Critically about Psychology p. 166, 177, 181, and 188
- **Ch 7**: Thinking Critically about Psychology, p. 203, 214, 217, and 225
- **Ch 8**: Thinking Critically about Psychology p. 243, 251, and 256
- **Ch 9**: Thinking Critically about Psychology p. 269, 277, 282, and 298; Thinking and Problem Solving: Using Information to Reach Goals, p. 269-76; Intelligence: The Sum Total of Cognition, p. 282-94
- **Ch 10**: Thinking Critically about Psychology p. 310, 315, 325, 330, and 339; Adolescent Development, p. 325-9
- **Ch 11**: Thinking Critically about Psychology p. 357, 366, 375, 385, and 389
- **Ch 12**: Thinking Critically about Psychology p. 400, 410, 414, 418, and 422
- **Ch 13**: Thinking Critically about Psychology p. 436, 443, 447, and 454
- **Ch 14**: Thinking Critically about Psychology p. 465, 475, 487, 492, and 495
- **Ch 15**: Thinking Critically about Psychology p. 505, 508, 515, and 522
- **Ch 16**: Thinking Critically about Psychology p. 537, 548, 551, and 559; Groups and Social Influence, p. 527-36; Attitudes and Persuasion, p. 538-46
- **Ch 17**: Thinking Critically about Psychology p. 571, 587, 592, and 596

4 APPLICATION OF PSYCHOLOGY

Understand and apply psychological principles to personal, social, and organizational issues.

4.1 Describe major applied areas of psychology (e.g., clinical, counseling, industrial/organizational, school, health).
4.2 Identify appropriate applications of psychology in solving problems.
4.3 Articulate how psychological principles can be used to explain social issues and inform public policy.
4.4 Apply psychological concepts, theories, and research findings as these relate to everyday life.
4.5 Recognize that ethically complex situations can develop in the application of psychological principles.

- **Ch 1**: Goals of Psychology, p. 3; Contemporary Perspectives and Specialty Areas in Psychology, p. 13-18; What We Know about Human Behavior: Some Starting Places, p. 19-21
- **Ch 2**: Application of Psychology, p. 44-5
- **Ch 3**: Application of Psychology, p. 82-5
- **Ch 4**: Application of Psychology, p. 117
- **Ch 6**: Application of Psychology, p. 189-91
- **Ch 7**: Theoretical Interpretations of Learning, p. 217-24; Application of Psychology, p. 226
- **Ch 8**: Application of Psychology, p. 257-61
- **Ch 9**: Thinking and Problem Solving: Using Information to Reach Goals, p. 269-276; Application of Psychology, p. 299-301
- **Ch 10**: Application of Psychology, p. 341-4
- **Ch 11**: Application of Psychology, p. 390-1
- **Ch 12**: Personality Assessment: Taking a Measure of the Person, p. 419-21
- **Ch 13**: Coping With Stress, p. 444-447; Changing Health-Related Behavior Problems, p. 448-51; Human Diversity: Psychology and Women's Health, p. 451-4; Application of Psychology, p. 455-6
- **Ch 14**: Definition of Abnormal Behavior, p. 459-64; Sexual Dysfunction and Sexual Health, p. 492-4
- **Ch 15**: Psychoanalysis, p. 500-504; Humanistic Psychotherapy, p. 505-7; Cognitive Behavior Therapy, p. 508-14; Group and Family Therapy, p. 515-6; Medical Therapies, p. 518-21; Application of Psychology, p. 523-4
- **Ch 17**: Applied Fields of Psychology, p. 563; Psychology and Work, p. 571-86; Psychology and Law, p. 587-91; Psychology and Education, p. 592-5

eleventh edition

Psychology
An Introduction

Benjamin B. Lahey
University of Chicago

McGraw Hill

Connect
Learn
Succeed™

Connect
Learn
Succeed™

Psychology, 11e

Published by McGraw-Hill, an imprint of The McGraw-Hill Companies, Inc., 1221 Avenue of the
Americas, New York, NY 10020. Copyright © 2012 by The McGraw-Hill Companies, Inc. All rights
reserved. No part of this publication may be reproduced or distributed in any form or by any means,
or stored in a database or retrieval system, without the prior written consent of The McGraw-Hill
Companies, Inc., including, but not limited to, in any network or other electronic storage or transmission, or broadcast for distance learning.

This book is printed on acid-free paper.

1 2 3 4 5 6 7 8 9 0 DOW/DOW 9 8 7 6 5 4 3 2 1

ISBN: 978-0-07131575-3
MHID: 0-07-131575-6

For Megan, Ted, Erin, Clare, Eamonn, Riley, Hannah, Miller, Mollie, and Kate.

Brief Contents

Contents

part one
Introduction and Foundations

chapter one
Introduction to Psychology 1

chapter two
Research Methods in Psychology 24

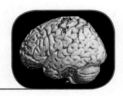

part two
Awareness

chapter five
Sensation and Perception 120

chapter six
States of Consciousness 162

part three
Learning and Cognition

chapter seven
Basic Principles of Learning 193

chapter eight
Memory 228

chapter nine
Cognition, Language, and Intelligence 263

part four
Developmental Psychology

chapter ten
Developmental Psychology 303

part five
The Self

chapter eleven
Motivation and Emotion 349

chapter twelve

Personality 394

part six
Health and Adjustment

chapter thirteen

Stress and Health 424

chapter fourteen
Abnormal Behavior   458

chapter fifteen
Therapies   497

part seven
Social Context

chapter sixteen
Social Psychology   526

chapter seventeen
Psychology Applied to the Environment and to Professions   561

Preface

Although the Preface is the first part of *Psychology: An Introduction* that you read, it is the last part that I write. It is my opportunity to reflect on the completed project in the hope that these reflections will help introduce you to the text. Over 11 editions, the unchanging goal of *Psychology* has been to teach. We (referring to the large group of talented psychologists, editors, consultants, and reviewers who have worked with me) have centered our efforts on giving you course material that fully captures the immense importance and fascination of the scientific study of ourselves. I have done my best to teach the concepts and facts of psychology in the clearest and most exciting manner possible. In addition, I worked very hard to make sure that the scientific basis of what is said is as strong as the science will allow. The gratifying responses of both instructors and students to the first ten editions of *Psychology* have been a wonderful source of encouragement for these efforts. In the three years since the last revision, the thousands of psychologists at work in research have given us an enormous amount of new information. The rapidity of scientific advance is always striking to me when I read the wide range of psychological literatures needed to keep up with the field. This progress is reflected in many changes in the content of the *Psychology*. Most of these changes reflect confirmations and relatively minor modifications of existing hypotheses, but there have been some notable advances in knowledge and theory. In addition, I have made a number of changes designed to teach psychology better.

Hallmark Features

While incorporating new material, the time-tested format of *Psychology* has not changed in the 11th edition. Students like the strong pedagogical format of the text, and research continues to support its use. As before, learning and memory are enhanced through the use of advance organizers followed by clearly written text, with explicit organizational cues, and repeated reviews.

Psychology offers thorough topic coverage and standard organization designed to fit courses as they are most commonly taught. But it differs significantly from other textbooks in two main ways: First, every effort has been made to create a writing style that is—as one former student kindly described it—friendly. *Psychology* does not attempt to impress students with the arcane complexities of the science of psychology. It was written to provide a clear, informative, challenging, exciting, and personal introduction to the science of psychology. All the necessary complexities are taught, but in the clearest manner possible. *Second, Psychology supports meaningful learning.*

In Support of Meaningful Learning

Psychology differs from other textbooks in its emphasis on meaningful learning. It contains many elements designed to enhance learning and remembering based on current models of semantic memory. The content of the first course in psychology can be thought of as a hierarchical organization of concepts and facts. Quite simply, this means that information about psychology is not a disorganized jumble of facts. Some information "goes with" other information, some concepts are detailed elaborations of more general concepts, and so on. To improve learning and memory of the contents of this course, students need to grasp the overall organization of the new information to better understand and retain the individual concepts and facts.

Based on what has been learned from years of research on learning from textbooks, five pedagogical supports help the student understand how new information about psychology is organized and to process that information:

1. Advance organizers. Considerable research indicates that students learn and retain information better when they have an advance understanding of the hierarchical organization of the new information being learned. To accomplish this, the student is given two kinds of advance organizers before reading the main body of the text. The student is first presented with a chapter outline of the major topics covered within the chapter, a device common to many textbooks. But to add to the effectiveness of this bare-bones overview, a prose organizer, called the Prologue, both piques the student's interest with exciting information and highlights the major concepts in the forthcoming chapter. Thus, the student is provided with two forward looks at the chapter to create a cognitive organization on which to "hang" new facts and concepts.

2. Questions to stimulate critical thinking. An important feature of *Psychology* is the set of questions designed to stimulate critical thinking. These critical thinking questions appear at the end of each section. They are designed to catch the student's attention and stimulate thought for two reasons. First, it is important that students do not passively absorb new information but, rather, critically evaluate and ponder what they are learning. Moreover, it may be more effective to teach critical thinking skills through the content of a specific course than in the abstract. And what course is more appropriate than psychology—in which human beings ponder themselves? Second, current research suggests that thinking about what you have just learned leads to deeper semantic processing and better retention. Thus, both as an aid to student reading and as a stimulus for classroom discussion, these high-interest questions at the end of each section are important pedagogical tools. To help students prepare to use these critical thinking questions, a discussion on critical thinking appears in the "Before You Begin" section.

3. Nested hierarchical reviews. The interrelationships among new concepts are highlighted further in review and summary sections. Following each major section within each chapter, the content of that section is briefly reviewed in prose. In addition, students can test their knowledge of each section in the Check Your Learning sections. At the end of each chapter, the main content of the chapter is again summarized, but this time in a hierarchical outline that visually highlights the *organization* of the material.

4. Visual organizational cues. Using hierarchical outlines in the end-of-chapter summaries is only one way in which the student is shown the organization of the new material. Close attention has been paid to the use of visual cues—such as typeface, type size, color of type, and indentations—to repeatedly indicate the organization of the text. The difference between this book and others is intentionally subtle at first glance, but it is powerful. Similarly, in diagrams and figures, colors were chosen not to be decorative but to show students which elements are related and which are different. In addition, lists—like the one you are reading now—have been frequently (but not excessively) used to show that each element in the list is at the same level of organization and is subordinate to the title of the list.

1. **Standardization.** Because intelligence tests are designed to compare the performance of one person with others, the test must be given in the same way to every person. If this were not so, differences in performance might be due to differences in the way the test is administered rather than to true differences in ability. For this reason, properly designed psychological tests contain detailed instructions telling the examiner how to administer the test to each person in the same *standardized* way.

2. **Norms.** To compare the individual's score with that of others, the developer of the test must give the test to a large sample of people who represent the general population. For example, you could not develop an intelligence test for adults by giving the test only to college students, because they are brighter ... sample used in evaluating the performance ... ed the *normative sample*. It must be large

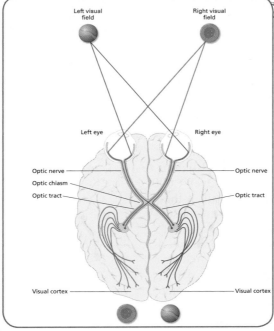

5. Verbal cues to organization. Another very important way to help readers see how concepts and facts are related is simply to tell them in words. Therefore, this textbook makes many references to the organization of the new information. This is done in two main ways: First, when a newly introduced concept is related to another concept that was discussed in an earlier section, this fact is specifically pointed out. Second, information that is subordinate to a concept is frequently introduced in a way that makes that relationship very clear (for example, "The two factors that cause forgetting in short-term memory are . . ."). Although these cues are subtle to avoid interrupting the flow of the discussion, they have been added to help improve the student's comprehension and memory.

higher general intelligence have better connected neurons. A greater ability to form neural connections is hypothesized to lead to better general intelligence in two ways:

1. Greater ability to form neural connections means that a person with high g is better able to learn from experience.

2. Greater interconnectedness of the neurons means that the brain can process information more quickly. Persons with higher g have faster reflexes, have faster reaction times, and take less time to make simple judgments (such as which of two lines is shorter). This greater speed of processing is thought to be the primary basis for greater general intelligence. As we will see in the next section, however, the fact that more intelligent people process information more quickly does not mean that they do everything more quickly in cognitive tasks. Sometimes taking our time leads to better problem solving.

The use of these pedagogical devices was chosen over two other pedagogical approaches after much consideration. I chose not to use the SQ3R (survey, question, read, recite, review) method of organizing the text because in SQ3R it is the author, not the student, who must ask the questions. Text that is written in SQ3R format reduces student involvement and discourages the student from critically evaluating and deeply processing the new information. It is much better for the *student* to use SQ3R than for the author to use it. Therefore, instructions to the student on the use of SQ3R are included in the Study Skills for Success section that follows the Preface. For those instructors who wish to use learning objectives, we have included them in the Instructor's Manual that *accompanies Psychology;* each question in each of the Test Banks is also keyed to one of the Learning Objectives.

Instructor and Student Resources

For the Instructor

Online Learning Center (OLC) www.mhhe.com/lahey11e

- **Instructor's Manual.** The Instructor's Manual provides a wide variety of tools and resources for presenting the course, including learning objectives, chapter outlines and summaries, ideas for lectures and discussions, critical thinking questions, current controversies, learning style activities, suggested readings, websites, and films, and handouts.

- **Test Bank.** By increasing the rigor of the Test Bank development process, McGraw-Hill aims to raise the bar for student assessment. Over 4,000 multiple-choice, 750 true/false, 340 fill-in-the-blank, and 70 essay questions across two test banks were prepared by a coordinated team of subject matter experts. Each question and set of possible answers were methodically vetted by a team of instructors for accuracy, clarity, effectiveness, and accessibility, and each is annotated for level of difficulty, Bloom's Taxonomy, APA Learning Outcomes, and corresponding coverage in the text. Organized by chapter, the questions are designed to test factual, applied, and conceptual understanding. The test banks are compatible with McGraw-Hill's computerized testing program EZ Test, and most Course Management systems.

- **PowerPoint Presentations.** The PowerPoint Presentations cover the key points of each chapter and include figures and charts from the text. The presentations serve as an organizational and a navigational tool integrated with examples and activities from an expert teacher. The slides can be used as is or modified to meet the needs of the individual instructor.

- **Image Gallery.** The Image Gallery features the complete set of figures and tables from the text. These images are available for download and can be easily embedded into instructors' PowerPoint slides.

Create

Craft your teaching resources to match the way you teach! With McGraw-Hill Create, www.mcgrawhillcreate.com, you can easily rearrange chapters, combine material from other content sources, and quickly upload content you have written like your course syllabus or teaching notes. Find the content you need in Create by searching through thousands of leading McGraw-Hill textbooks. Arrange your book to fit your teaching style. Create even allows you to personalize your book's appearance by selecting the cover and adding your name, school, and course information. Order a Create book and you'll receive a complimentary print review copy in 3–5 business days or a complimentary electronic review copy (eComp) via email in about one hour. Go to www.mcgrawhillcreate.com today and register. Experience how McGraw-Hill Create empowers you to teach your students your way.

Blackboard

McGraw-Hill Higher Education and Blackboard have teamed up. What does this mean for you?

1. **Your life, simplified.** Now you and your students can access McGraw-Hill's Create™ right from within your Blackboard course—all with one single sign-on. Say goodbye to the days of logging in to multiple applications.

2. **Deep integration of content and tools.** Not only do you get single sign-on with Create™, you also get deep integration of McGraw-Hill content and content engines right in Blackboard. Whether you're choosing a book for your course or building Connect™ assignments, all the tools you need are right where you want them—inside of Blackboard.

3. **A solution for everyone.** Whether your institution is already using Blackboard or you just want to try Blackboard on your own, we have a solution for you. McGraw-Hill and Blackboard can now offer you easy access to industry leading technology and content, whether your campus hosts it, or we do. Be sure to ask your local McGraw-Hill representative for details.

Tegrity

Tegrity Campus is a service that makes class time available all the time by automatically capturing every lecture in a searchable format for students to review when they study and complete assignments. With a simple one-click start and stop process, you capture all computer screens and corresponding audio. Students replay any part of any class with easy-to-use browser-based viewing on a PC or Mac.

Educators know that the more students can see, hear, and experience class resources, the better they learn. With Tegrity Campus, students quickly recall key moments by using Tegrity Campus's unique search feature. This search helps students efficiently find what they need, when they need it, across an entire semester of class recordings. Help turn all your students' study time into learning moments immediately supported by your lecture.

For the Student

Online Learning Center for Students

The Student Online Learning Center contains chapter-by-chapter quizzes, weblinks, key term flashcards, and learning objectives. The Multiple Choice and True/False quizzes ask questions to build on conscientious reading of the text. To access the Online Learning Center, go to **www.mhhe.com/lahey11e**

CourseSmart e-Textbook

This text is available as an eTextbook at www.CourseSmart.com. At CourseSmart your students can take advantage of significant savings off the cost of a print textbook, reduce their impact on the environment, and gain access to powerful web tools for learning. CourseSmart eTextbooks can be viewed online or downloaded to a computer. The eTextbooks allow students to do full text searches, add highlighting and notes, and share notes with classmates. CourseSmart has the largest selection of eTextbooks available anywhere. Visit www.CourseSmart.com to learn more and to try a sample chapter.

Supplemental Reading

Annual Editions: Psychology 10/11, edited by William Buskist, Auburn University. This annually updated reader is a compilation of carefully selected articles from magazines, newspapers, and journals.

Sources: Notables Selections in Psychology, 4e, edited by Terry Pettijohn of The Ohio State University. This book includes over 40 book excerpts, classic articles, and research studies that have shaped the study of psychology and our contemporary understanding of it.

Taking Sides: Clashing Views on Controversial Psychological Issues, 16e, edited by Brent Slife of Brigham Young University. This debate-style reader is designed to introduce students to controversial viewpoints on the field's most crucial issues. Each issue is carefully framed for the student, and the pro and con essays represent the arguments of leading scholars and commentators in their fields.

Acknowledgments

An undertaking of this scope could never be successful without the assistance of many people, and I would like to take this opportunity to express my thanks to all those who in large and small ways have made this 11th edition possible. Among the many McGraw-Hill team members who contributed their efforts and expertise are Editorial Director, Beth Mejia; Publisher for Psychology, Mike Sugarman; Senior Editor, Allison McNamara; Director of Development, Dawn Groundwater; Senior Development Editor, Cara Labell; Development Editor, Maureen Spada; Executive Marketing Manager, Julia Flohr; Editorial Coordinator, Sarah Kiefer; Senior Production Editor, Mel Valentín; Designer, Preston Thomas/Cadence Design; Lead Photo Research Coordinator, Natalia Peschiera; and Art Editor, Ayelet Arbel.

The following instructors helped tremendously by providing feedback that influenced this new edition of *Psychology: An Introduction.*

Ira Albert,
Community College of Baltimore County

Amanda Baldridge,
Murray State College

Julie Brooks,
Itawamba Community College

Yvonne Gardner,
Coahama Community College

Ethan Gologor,
Medgar Evers College

David Harrison,
Virginia Tech

Rebecca Henthorn,
Murray State College

Ron Kinsman,
Davenport University

Grant Leitma,
Washington Adventist University

Tammy Lochridge,
Itawamba Community College

Susan Long,
Central Methodist University

Clark McKinney,
Southwest Tennessee Community College

Lynn Michaluk,
Northern Oklahoma College

Regina Midgett,
Itawamba Community College

Donald Nichols,
Oakland Community College

Donna Owens,
Murray State College

Neophytos Papaneophytou,
Borough of Manhattan Community College

Mary Peoples,
Cerro Coso Community College

Donna Reed-Mathena,
Southwest Tennessee Community College

Debra Rundell,
Cerro Coso Community College

Robert Strausser,

Southwest Tennessee Community College

Joan Thomas-Spiegel,
Los Angeles Harbor College

Natasha Tokowicz,

University of Pittsburg

Cherine Trombley,
Los Angeles Valley College

JoAnne Uthe-Gibson,
Northeast Iowa Community College

Stefani Weber,
Northeast Iowa Community College

Choichiro Yatani,
Alfred State College

Many other talented contributors and team members also played essential roles. I particularly want to express my sincere thanks to Brian M. D'Onofrio and Lisa J. Thomassen of Indiana University for their wonderful contributions to the chapters on states of consciousness, developmental psychology, abnormal psychology, and social psychology. The results of our combined efforts are before you, and I hope that it will serve the needs of students and instructors even better than did the previous edition.

Content Changes

Many revisions are made simply to improve the clarity of the text over the previous edition. But, during the period since the previous edition, some scientific advances were important and basic enough to demand inclusion in the introductory course in Psychology. New findings have to be filtered to be certain that unnecessary complexity is not added to the text. The goal of this course is to help students to learn the fundamentals of the science. Nonetheless, some new discoveries are so important that they change the fundamentals of Psychology or change how they are applied to contemporary life.

Some of the most important changes in the 11th edition based on emerging research are:

Biological Foundations of Behavior (Chapter 3)

- New evidence that new neurons are generated in the brain from glial cells throughout life.

- Growing evidence on the surprising extent to which the brain is a developing and interactive system throughout life.

Interplay of Nature and Nurture (Chapter 4)

- Highly important and convincing evidence from a meta-analysis that the much-discussed gender difference in performance on tests of mathematics ability and achievement has disappeared since the early 1990s.

Sensation and Perception (Chapter 5)

- Recent evidence that playing videogames improves some aspects of visual perception.

- New information on complementary colors.

- Recent evidence on kinesthetic receptors.

- Description of a simple new way to control phantom pain.

- Recent research supporting the role of pheromones in sexual attraction.

States of Consciousness (Chapter 6)

- New material on the role of selective attention in consciousness.

- New evidence on the dangers of distraction when multi-tasking, such as texting while driving.

- Updated references reflecting newest research on the role of sleep in cognition and emotion.

- Information on the role of differences in metabolism in blood alcohol levels.

- Coverage of the growing problem of abuse of prescription stimulants by college students.

- New information on mindless reading.

- Coverage of negative consequences of shift work for physical health.

- Discussion of the use of stimulants in treatment of ADHD, FDA ban of Ephedra, addition of Crack to cocaine section, Adderrall and Ritalin in discussion of stimulants, legalization of medical marijuana.

Memory (Chapter 8)

- New material documenting major distortions in "flashbulb memories."

- Recent evidence on the nature of deep processing and its role in memory.

- Recent work on false memories.

- Corroborating evidence on the role of sleep in the consolidation of memories.

Cognition, Language, and Intelligence (Chapter 9)

- New findings on the importance of preparation and incubation in creative problem solving.

- Important new evidence on the association between breastfeeding and children's intelligence.

Developmental Psychology (Chapter 10)

- Emerging evidence on the importance of the prenatal environment to later health and development.

- New findings on adjustment to cochlear implants.

- Updated information on the impact of grandparents, day care, and divorce on child development.

- New section reviewing the importance of individual variation in development.

- Revised discussion of early deprivation to include findings on adopted individuals who were initially raised in institutions.

- Clarified definition of imprinting.

- Additional material on attachment and the parents who spank their children.

Motivation and Emotion (Chapter 11)

- Discussion of the surprising role of opponent-process motivational processes in friendship and love.

- New evidence on the complicated relationship between making money and happiness.

Personality (Chapter 12)

- New evidence on the strength of the association between personality traits and our future academic success, physical health, and longevity.

Stress and Health (Chapter 13)

- Coverage of the surprisingly strong links of depression and anxiety to cardiovascular health and early mortality.

- New research on the association between air pollution and depression.

- Discussion of ways to improve physical and mental health by advocating for sustainable energy sources.

- Coverage of the association between excessive alcohol use by college students and academic failure and accidental injuries and death, and how to prevent them.

Abnormal Behavior (Chapter 14)

- Advances in the field's understanding of post-traumatic stress disorder including research on combat-related problems and problems associated with terrorism and mass conflict.

- Updated definition of abnormal behavior that includes the differences between symptoms, syndromes, and diagnoses.

- Increased emphasis on how cultural and scientific changes influence our understanding of abnormal behavior.

- Increased description of the magnitude of the problems associated with abnormal behavior and the World Health Organization study on the mortality and morbidity associated with disorders.

- New references on the personal and societal costs associated with specific mental disorders.

- New references noting some of the downfalls of the current diagnostic system.

- Updated and clarified definitions of sexual disorders.

- Updated references and key findings related to prevalence estimates of stigmatization of mental disorders, rape, and sexual problems.

Social Psychology (Chapter 16)

- New coverage of recent events in the news that make research on the bystander effect relevant to today.

- New research on the experience of "choking" in front of others when trying to perform under pressure.

- Research on the exploding phenomenon of social networking over the Internet.

- Reorganized material reconciling social facilitation and social inhibition via arousal and attention.

- Incorporated findings on benefits of individual brainstorming.

- New coverage of "door in the face" technique to persuasion techniques, with example.

- Reorganized and added example to discussion of conformity.

- Updated cognitive dissonance references, with references for applications in preventing eating disorders in college students.

- New coverage of discrimination in discussion of prejudice and stereotypes, and classic the La Pierre study.

- Added research on: physical characteristics related to attraction, characteristics of others related to liking, repetition and familiarity with the message in persuasiveness, and how intergroup contact reduces prejudice.

- New discussion of Sternberg's theory of love.

Before You Begin
Study Skills for Success

You are about to begin your introduction to the science of psychology. Before you do that, I want to offer some suggestions to improve your chances of success in any college course. These suggestions are based on some of the psychological principles you will learn in this book. Psychology is a science that addresses a great many topics, most of which have some direct relevance to our lives. One topic that has long been of interest to psychologists is human learning—the ways in which we learn and remember new information. Much has been discovered about learning and memory that can help you become a more efficient learner in your college courses.

First and foremost, it is essential to know that people do not absorb information as a sponge absorbs water. We have to work at learning new information in college courses. Human beings are highly effective learners, but we learn better in some ways than others. By understanding how human beings learn, we can make far more efficient use of study time. Before you begin to study the science of psychology, take a look at the following helpful hints provided by psychologists for improving learning and recall.

I have kept this section brief because I know how busy the beginning of the term can be, but the information contained in this section is worth your attention. From my own experience as a student, and from teaching many students since that time, I know that adopting more efficient ways of studying can make the learning process more enjoyable, can increase the amount of information that you learn and retain, and can improve your grades. I hope that the following suggestions will help you.

Use the Aids to Effective Learning in the Text

This textbook includes several features that can help you learn more as you read the text. These features:

1. Focus your attention on the subject of the chapter

2. Give you an advance view of what you are about to learn

3. Show you how each fact and concept is related to the theme of the chapter

4. Help you review, so you can be sure that you understood the material and strengthen your newly formed memories

5. Help you think critically about information and relate what you have learned to your life.

Take a moment to notice each of the following features in the book and think about how they are designed to help you learn:

1. **Chapter Outline.** Each chapter begins with a brief outline that summarizes the key ideas in the chapter. Before starting to read each chapter, take a moment to see which topics will be studied and to think about them. This takes a few minutes, but it is time very well spent!

2. **Chapter Prologue.** Each chapter begins with a short essay that briefly introduces you to the content of the chapter. Research shows that having a general understanding of what is going to be learned improves learning and memory of the new information.

3. **Section Reviews.** Within each chapter you will find reviews at the end of each major section. The review section is made up of three parts:

   a. The Review paragraph summarizes the main ideas introduced in the section. This will help you keep the overall organization of the new material in your mind as you master the details.

   b. The Check Your Learning questions are designed to test your mastery of some of the material before you move on. The correct answers are provided to give you immediate feedback and guide you to the page where the material is covered if you need additional review.

   c. The section on Thinking Critically about Psychology is designed to stimulate more than just memorizing new ideas. The few minutes of active thought that each question provokes should help you personalize your new knowledge of psychology, making it "your own." It will also help you remember the content of the chapter.

4. **Visual Reviews.** At the end of some chapters, key illustrations are reprinted from the chapter, but this time you fill in the missing labels. This is a final check to ensure that you have mastered the visual material before you start the next chapter.

The SQ3R Method

Some ways of studying are more efficient than others. This means that you can learn more without studying more, but only if you use the right study methods. One popular method for studying textbooks is known as SQ3R. These initials stand for the following five steps in effective textbook study:

S: Survey. Look ahead at the content of the text before you begin to read. Flip through the pages and get a sense of what you are going to be learning to lay a foundation for effective learning.

Q: Question. Keep asking yourself questions about the material both before you read it and during the process of reading.

R: Read. Read through the material in the normal way.

R: Recite. Recite the new information that you are learning out loud or silently.

R: Review. Go over the material that you have just learned several times before you are tested on it in class.

Let's go through these steps in more detail to better understand them.

Survey

Most of us think there is just one way to read—you start at the beginning and read to the end. That is the best way to read a novel because you don't want to know about the next plot twist or the surprise ending until you get there. But a very different strategy is needed when reading a textbook. It's important to survey, or look ahead, at what you are going to read. In fact, you should try to find out as much as possible about the text material you are going to read *before* you read it.

The reason behind this strategy of surveying before reading is based on the way humans learn and store new information in memory. Speaking loosely, we "hang" new information on what we already know. If we learn a new fact about marijuana, we hang that information on what we already know about mind-altering drugs; and, the more organized knowledge we have of a topic, the better we are able to learn and to remember new information about it. In particular, the more general information we possess about a topic, the easier it is to learn and to remember new specific information about that topic There are several effective ways to survey this textbook. Begin by examining the general content of each chapter by reading the *headings* within it. For your convenience, the headings within each chapter of this text are placed in an outline on the chapter opening page (figure 1). Novels do not have headings, because there is no reason to survey their content in advance; textbooks have them because they greatly aid surveying and reviewing. For example, did you look ahead at the headings in this section before beginning to read it? If you did, you developed an overview of its content.

Chapter Outline

PROLOGUE 24 — *Level one heading*
Basic Concepts of Research 25
Research Methods 27
Ethical Principles of Research 40 — *Level two heading*
Human Diversity: Equal Representation in Research 42
Application of Psychology: Design Your Own Formal Experiment 44
SUMMARY 45 — *Page number*

Figure 1

Next, look at the prologue section at the beginning of each chapter. It gives you an advance look at the main points of the content you will be reading. Study this section carefully before going on—this will increase the amount of information you learn as you read. When surveying some textbooks, you may need to add to what you learn from the headings by briefly skimming sections and looking at illustrations, but in this text, the chapter outlines and prologues provide the best sources of advance information. Is it really worth the time and effort to read the prologue section of each chapter to get an overview of what is ahead? Actually, I spent a considerable amount of time researching this question before I started writing this book. I didn't want to waste my time in writing the prologues—and your time in reading them—unless they would actually increase what you learn. The value of prologues was tested by David Ausubel (1960) in a classic experiment conducted at the University of Illinois. One hundred twenty students were divided into two groups that read a long passage with and without a prologue section preceding it. The passage covered the properties of carbon steel and contained many facts that were new to the students. After both groups had read the passage on carbon steel, they took a brief multiple-choice test covering the facts presented in the passage. As predicted, the group that read the prologue first correctly answered approximately 20% more of the questions (the difference between an F and a B in most courses). A considerable amount of research over the years confirms this strategy for improving learning and memory (Dunlosky & others, 2004; Deese & Deese, 1979; Langan-Fox & others, 2000). That is why a prologue was written to precede each chapter in this text—and that is why giving them your close attention is worth the effort.

Question

After you have surveyed the material you will be reading by reading the prologue and looking over the headings, ask yourself questions. Do this before you read each section. These questions should be those raised during your survey and first reading. They should reflect your own personal struggle to understand and digest the contents of this book. For example, figure 2

Where is the thyroid gland located? What role does the thyroid gland play in metabolism? What are the effects of thyroxin?

The **thyroid gland,** located just below the larynx, or voice box, plays an important role in the regulation of **metabolism.** It does so by secreting a hormone called **thyroxin.** The level of thyroxin in a person's bloodstream and the resulting metabolic rate are important in many ways. In children, proper functioning of the thyroid is necessary for proper mental development. A serious thyroid deficiency in childhood will produce sluggishness, poor muscle tone, and a type of mental retardation called **cretinism.**

Figure 2

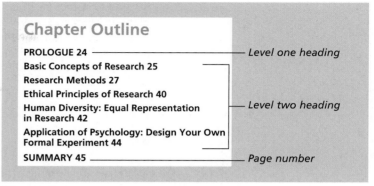

includes sample questions that you might ask while studying coverage of the thyroid gland in chapter 3, page 80. Asking such questions will help you to become actively involved in the learning process and will focus your attention on relevant information. As you locate the information that answers your questions, you may find it very helpful to underline or highlight it with a felt-tip pen.

Read

After the S (Survey) and Q (Question) steps, you are ready to begin reading in the usual way. Although you have put in a lot of time preparing for this step, your reading will be so much more efficient and enjoyable that it's worth the extra time. In fact, if you have the time to invest, you could improve the efficiency of your reading even more by skimming the material quickly before reading it more closely.

Recite

When you are studying, is it more beneficial to spend your time reading the material over and over again, or to read it and then practice reciting it (repeating it to yourself)? Reciting is definitely the most useful part of the study process. If nothing else, it alerts you to those things you do not really know yet (the things you cannot recite correctly), and makes learning more efficient. In the early days of psychology, A. I. Gates (1917) found that individuals who spent 80% of their time reciting lists and only 20% reading them recalled *twice* as much as those who spent all their time reading. These powerful benefits of reciting or other forms of testing our learning as we go have often been replicated in contemporary research (Roediger & Karpicke, 2006). The "Check Your Learning" questions at the end of most chapter sections will help you "recite" what you have learned. See figure 3 for some examples of these helpful questions. In addition, the list of key terms at the beginning of each chapter and the glossary of terms in the margins of each page can help you with this recitation. If you can recite the basic definitions of these terms, you will have learned the most important material.

Review

After you have learned the new information in the text by Reading and Reciting, you will need to add one final step that most students neglect: Review what you have learned several times before you are tested on it

To be sure that you have learned the key points from the preceding section, cover the list of correct answers and try to answer each question. If you give an incorrect answer to any question, return to the page given next to the correct answer to see why your answer was not correct.

1. Research on humans is considered to be ethical only when the following five conditions are met:

   a)

   b)

   c)

   d)

   e)

2. Research with nonhuman animals is considered to be ethical only when the following three conditions are met:

   a)

   b)

   c)

1. _____ are categories of things, events, or qualities that are linked by some common feature or features in spite of their differences.

2. The concept of *aunt* is an example of a _____ because it has two simultaneous defining characteristics (female and sibling of one of your parents).

   a) disjunctive concept   c) simple concept

   b) conjunctive concept   d) natural concept

3. By virtue of being born human beings, we are prepared to learn some concepts more easily than others. These concepts are termed _____ .

   a) simple concepts   c) natural concepts

   b) disjunctive concepts   d) conjunctive concepts

4. Cultural learning appears to play a role in the interpretation of emotion-causing stimuli and in the expression of emotions.

   a) True   b) False

Figure 3

by your instructior. The goal of the review process is to *over-learn* the material, which means to continue studying material *after* you have first mastered it. The learning process is *not* over when you can first recite the new information to yourself without error. Psychologists have long known that your ability to recall information later can be greatly strengthened by reciting it several more times before you are tested (Krueger, 1929). To aid you with the review step, this text provides you with a review section following each major heading within the chapter and a sentence outline summary at the end of each chapter (see pages 110 and 117–119 for examples). In addition, many chapters contain a Visual Review that follows the chapter summary, providing a visual overview of one or more key illustrations from that chapter to help you practice what you have learned in a different format (see pages 160–161 and 347–348 for examples).

Strategies for Studying

Although the SQ3R method can improve your ability to learn information from textbooks, several other study strategies also help you make efficient use of your study time.

Be Sure That You Are Actually Learning

The most common reason students "forget" information when taking tests is that they did not actually learn it in the first place. Because studying is an effort, even when you are efficient at it, it's far too easy to act as if you are studying when, in fact, you are really listening to the radio, thinking about your sweetheart, or clipping your nails. If you are good at acting as if you are studying—I didn't realize it at the time, but I was a master of it during my first two years of college—you can easily fool your roommate, your best friend, and even yourself. Do not fool yourself into thinking that you are studying when you are not really exerting the effort to become absorbed in the material. When you study, really study.

Find a Good Place to Study and Study Only There

One way to help you really concentrate on studying is to find a good place to study, and study only in that place. The goal is to associate that place only with effective studying. Begin by choosing a spot that is free from distractions. Some places in libraries are ideal for studying, but others are better for talking and making new friends. Avoid the latter when you are studying, but feel free to visit these places when you are taking breaks. After you find a good place to study, never do anything there except study. If a friend comes over for conversation, get up and move to another area to talk. Return only when you are ready to study. Similarly, if you are in your study place and find that your mind is wandering, leave it until you are ready to study again. If you do this consistently—if you only study when you are in your study place—this spot will "feel" like a place to study, and you will be more apt to study efficiently while you are there. This doesn't mean that you cannot also study in other places—such as on the bus when you have a 20-minute ride—but having a good place to study that becomes associated only with studying will help you study efficiently when you are there.

Space Out Your Study Time

As long ago as 1885, Hermann Ebbinghaus found that studying a list of new information once a day for several days resulted in better recall of that information than studying the list several times in one day. Since then, a great deal of research has shown that dividing study time into smaller sessions spaced at least a day apart results in better learning and memory than studying once for the same total amount of time (Bahrick & others, 1993; Rohrer & Pashler, 2007). This is why cramming (massing all your study time into one long session) is terribly inefficient. You can get much better grades by spacing the same amount of study time over time.

Use Mnemonic Devices

The suggestions given thus far concern how to study. The following suggestions are about how to memorize information when you are studying. Mnemonic devices are methods for storing memories so that they will be easier to recall. In each mnemonic device, an additional indexing cue is memorized along with the material to be learned. More is less with mnemonics; memorizing something more will result in less forgetting.

1. *Method of loci.* Loci is the Latin word for "places." In this method, the items in a list are mentally placed in a series of logically connected places. For example, if you are trying to remember a grocery list, you might think of a bag of sugar hanging on your garage door, a gallon of milk sitting in the front seat of your car, a carton of eggs perched on your steering wheel, and a box of donuts sitting in front of the grocery store door. Stanford University psychologist Gordon Bower (1973) found that persons who used the method of loci were able to recall almost three times as many words from lists as those who did not.

2. *Acronym method.* My favorite mnemonic device is the method of acronyms. Nearly every list of facts in psychology that I successfully memorized in college was memorized using acronyms that I made up. In this simple method, the first letters of each word in a list are combined to form an acronym. For example, the four stages of alcoholism, which are prealcoholic, prodromal, crucial, and chronic, can be memorized using the acronym PPCC. Acronyms are even more useful if they form a real word.

   A system closely related to acronyms takes the first letter of each word in an ordered series but uses them in a new sentence. My high school biology teacher taught me to remember the hierarchy of biological classification using the sentence "Kathy pulls candy on Friday, good stuff." Note that the first letter in each word of this sentence is the same as in kingdom, phylum, class, order, family, genus, species. As with acronyms, memory of a phrase or sentence is likely to spark recall of an entire list.

3. *Keyword method.* We will see later in chapter 8 on memory that it is easier to memorize information that you understand than information that you do not. Some of the things that you need to memorize for college courses will be meaningful to you if you take the time to think about them before you try to memorize them, but sometimes you will have to give additional meaning to the things you are memorizing. Raugh and Atkinson (1975) demonstrated the value of teaching students to do this in memorizing Spanish vocabulary words, using what they called the keyword method. They asked one group of students to memorize English translations in the standard way of rotely associating the English word with the unknown Spanish word. Another group was taught to increase the meaningfulness of the association between the English and Spanish word pairs. As shown in figure 4, students were told to think of an English word that sounded like the Spanish word (such as *charcoal* for the Spanish word for puddle, *charco*) and to form a mental image of the English sound-alike word and the actual English translation (charcoal grill sitting in a puddle). Students who learned the Spanish vocabulary in this more meaningful fashion were able to recall an average of 88% of the words, whereas the students who used rote memorization were able to recall an average of only 28% when tested later. By actively enhancing the meaningfulness of what was learned using the keyword method, the students were able to greatly improve its storage in memory.

Critical Thinking

Like most college courses, the goal of this course is to teach you a great deal of new information. But there is a second goal even more important than the first—to teach you to *think critically about human beings.* You are enrolled in a college or university to become well educated. This means, of course, that you want to learn more information, but it also means that you want to be better prepared to make decisions, to plan for the future, and to realize your goals. If we human beings are to be able to continue to inhabit this fragile planet, and if we are to make the most of our time here, we must all try to hone our intellectual skills.

Psychology provides an excellent vehicle for teaching critical thinking skills. By its very nature—as a *science* of human behavior—we will be looking critically at ourselves. As we discuss the many new facts and concepts that make up this course, we will describe many of the experiments that have helped psychologists reach tentative conclusions about the nature of our behavior and experience. *Psychological research is critical thinking in practice.* As you read about each experiment, take a moment to consider the logic that went into its design. Consider for a moment the thinking that helped the researcher decide between rival explanations for that facet of human life.

But more important than seeing how scientists use their critical thinking skills, a major goal of this course is to encourage you to improve your own critical thinking skills. Success in every walk of life and meaningful participation in democratic society require more than the simple knowledge of facts—they require using facts intelligently.

What, then, is critical thinking? There are many aspects of critical thinking, but the steps that I will describe are a good start. As you read this textbook or approach any other source of new information—from political speeches to newspaper articles— try the following steps:

1. ***What is the evidence?*** I will present you with many statements in this textbook, and I expect you to demand that I back up my statements with evidence. When I tell you that, unlike 20 years ago, women and men now place the same importance on love in marriage, you should look to see if I present evidence to support that conclusion. If I make a statement without supporting evidence, you should strongly question my statement.

2. ***How good is the evidence?*** Suppose I tell you that the reason that I believe that women and men place the same value on romance today is because my wife and my daughters say so. My wife and daughters are pretty smart people,

Figure 4

In the keyword method of learning Spanish vocabulary, the student visualizes the Spanish noun with a noun that sounds like it in English. For example, the Spanish words for *puddle, lizard,* and *clown* sound similar to the English words for *charcoal, log,* and *pie.*

but should you believe the opinions of just three people? Would you be more convinced if I cite a study of 20,000 men and women? Not only should we demand evidence to support statements of fact, we also should examine the quality of that evidence. In this book, I can tell you that I have thought carefully about the quality of evidence that supports every statement. But you should completely disregard this reassurance and think critically about the evidence yourself. You might very well decide that I am wrong on some key issues, but at the very least, you will sharpen your critical thinking skills.

3. ***What are the alternative interpretations of the evidence?*** Even if I do provide you with solid evidence to support every conclusion, critical thinking cannot stop there. Facts are meaningless until they are *interpreted,* and there is almost always more than one interpretation of every set of facts in psychology.

   Let's think about an example. There is strong evidence that, other things being equal, heterosexual women tend to be more strongly attracted to men as marriage partners if they are more intelligent, hardworking, and successful. Those are well-substantiated "facts," but what do they mean? One group of scholars believe that women have an *innate* need (part of every female in the human species) to guarantee the well-being of their children that leads them to prefer successful husbands who can help them provide for their children. Do you agree? Even if you think this is a reasonable explanation, are there alternative explanations of these facts that make better sense? Take a moment now to think about alternative explanations for these facts (really—I hope you will stop reading and try to think of alternative interpretations of these facts for a moment). Did you come up with any alternative explanations? It doesn't matter if you didn't come up with a brilliant explanation, but it is important that you see that alternative explanations of almost any set of facts are possible.

   So what do we do with facts that can be interpreted in several different ways? Critical thinking requires two approaches to this situation. The first and most important step is to look for *more facts* that will help you choose between the alternative explanations. For example, do women in *all* cultures find successful men to be attractive? Do highly successful women in our culture find the man's success to be unimportant? Do women who do not want to have children still find successful men to be attractive? If the answers to these questions are not all yes, you might be less likely to believe that the preference for successful men reflects an innate need shared by all women. There are many ways in which new facts can be sought that might allow you to decide between alternative explanations for facts. Indeed, that is what science is all about.

   The other way in which the critical thinker deals with alternative explanations of facts, however, is to learn to live with alternative explanations. At this point in the history of the science of psychology, there are many alternative explanations of facts that we cannot yet choose among. Indeed, one of the things that makes psychology exciting is that there is so much yet to learn. Many of the current disagreements among psychologists will be resolved ultimately through better experiments—the use of critical thinking to plan the logic of scientific studies. But in other cases, the different ways of viewing the same phenomena will prove to be equally valid conceptions. Therefore, the ability to consider more than one perspective on issues in psychology—as in all walks of life—is important. Moreover, the discussion of these differing views will help refine your critical thinking about yourself and the human race in general.

4. ***Go beyond this book.*** This book only scratches the surface of psychology, and it provides only a few examples of how the facts and concepts of psychology might apply to your life. The final step in critical thinking is to ask

questions about the information given in the textbook to expand its application to your experience. Critical thinking is not just an academic exercise—it is a part of life. The thinking and evaluative skills that you develop in this and other courses will also serve you well as you solve problems and confront the challenges of daily life.

If you are concerned that critical thinking takes time and might detract from your ability to memorize information that will be on tests, I have good news for you. Thinking critically about the information that you have just read will improve your memory for that information. In chapter 8, we will discuss the "deep processing" of information and present evidence that the more you think about information the more information you will remember. But don't take my word for it! Read the section on levels of processing in chapter 8 and think about it critically. Better yet, try your own experiment to see if thinking critically about the information presented in this book makes this course a better learning experience.

Notes for the First-Generation College Student

Are you the first member of your family to attend college? If so, this is an exciting time. You deserve to be proud of yourself. Still, being a first-generation college student can have its challenges. Let's look at the college experiences of a man named John who now works as a psychologist. He is from a poor family and was the first of 4 siblings and 16 cousins to finish college. He knew that his family was proud of him, but he sometimes felt that he had left his family and old friends behind in his quest for higher education. Sometimes these feelings interfered with his motivation to complete school.

Many first-generation college students struggle with similar feelings (Barry & others, 2009; Piorkowski, 1983; Whitten, 1992). They often perceive themselves, and are perceived by their families, as moving into a new social class. In some cases, this can be anxiety provoking for both the student and the family. Issues related to group loyalty arise as the student's interests, vocabulary, and worldview become different from those of his family and neighborhood friends. Family members sometimes accuse first-generation college students of "changing" or "thinking they are better" than the family. These issues are particularly challenging for members of ethnic groups that traditionally attended college infrequently. Not only do they face strained relationships with their families and friends, but they may not fit into the college community if they attend a majority-culture institution.

Many first-generation college students handle these conflicts very successfully. They recognize that they are part of both their college and home communities and develop strategies for moving comfortably from one to the other. They speak standard English on the college campus and speak the language of their home community, which might be Spanish, Creole, or Black English, when they are among friends. They reassure their family members by word and deed that they still feel a part of their home, even though they are changing in some ways. This is important because students who are able to integrate their old and new lifestyles more successfully make higher grades than do students who experience a high degree of conflict (Whitten, 1993b).

What is the climate like at your institution for first-generation college students and students who do not fit the mold in other ways? How effective is your college when it comes to addressing diversity issues? How do your family and friends feel about your decision to enter college? Thinking about these questions may help you identify sources of potential conflict in yourself or understand the experience of other students better.

Additional Information on Study Skills

If you are interested in learning more about study skills, you might want to consult two books that deal with the topic in more depth:

Ellis, D. B. (2006). *Becoming a master student* (11th ed.). Boston: Houghton-Mifflin.

Parrott, L. (1999). *How to write psychology papers* (2nd ed.). New York: Longman.

Barry, L. M., Hudley, M. et al. (2010). *Differences in Self-Reported Disclosure of College Experiences by First-Generation College Student Status*. Adolescence, 43, 55–68.

chapter **one**

Introduction to psychology

Chapter Outline

Psyche + Science = Psychology

Welcome to psychology! You are invited to learn about one of life's most interesting subjects—you. You enrolled in this course knowing that it had something to do with people. But what exactly is psychology?

The earliest origins of psychology are found in the writings of the ancient Greek philosophers about the nature of *life,* particularly in the work of Aristotle. Aristotle, who was born in 384 B.C.E., was broadly interested in the nature of living things. He collected and dissected plants and animals to see how their organs sustained life. He studied reproduction to see how life was recreated in each generation, and he studied the everyday actions of living people as they reasoned, spoke, remembered, and learned. In his later years, Aristotle discussed

1

Key Terms

Philosopher and early scientist Aristotle (right) with Plato.

psychology Science of behavior and mental processes.

science Approach to knowledge based on systematic observation.

behavior Directly observable and measurable actions.

mental processes Private psychological activities that include thinking, perceiving, and feeling.

philosophy with his students as they strolled the covered walks of his school, the Lyceum. Imagine what he said to them about the nature of life:

> You'll understand what life is if you think about the act of dying. When I die, how will I be different from the way I am right now? In the first moments after death, my body will be scarcely different in physical terms than it was in the last seconds of life, but I will no longer move, no longer sense, nor speak, nor feel, nor care. It's these things that are life. At that moment, the psyche takes flight in the last breath.

Aristotle used the term *psyche* to refer to the essence of life. This term is translated from ancient Greek to mean "mind," but it is closely linked in meaning to the word "breath." Aristotle believed that psyche escaped in the last dying breath. Modern psychologists study the same actions, thoughts, and feelings that fascinated Aristotle. Indeed, the term *psychology* comes from Aristotle's word *psyche* plus the Greek word *logos,* which means "the study of."

Aristotle was trained in philosophical methods by Plato, but he disagreed with Plato's belief that one could achieve a full understanding of anything simply by *thinking* about it. Aristotle believed that one must also *observe* the thing being studied—look at it, listen to it, touch it. Although Aristotle was not a scientist in the modern sense of the word, his emphasis on observation is the basis for the methods of contemporary science. Since Aristotle's time, modern scientists have developed only more precise and efficient ways of observing. Thus, Aristotle launched the study of life that eventually evolved into the modern science of psychology.

Definition of Psychology

In some ways, it would be correct to say that psychologists still define *psychology* as the "study of life." However, that definition is not specific enough to distinguish the modern discipline of psychology from the other sciences that also study life, such as biology. Therefore, **psychology** is defined as the *science of behavior and mental processes.*

Note that this definition contains three key terms—*science, behavior,* and *mental processes.* Consider each of these terms separately. Psychology is considered a **science** because psychologists attempt to understand people by thinking critically about careful, controlled observations. This reliance on rigorous scientific methods of observation is the basis of all sciences, including psychology. The term **behavior** refers to all of a person's overt actions that others can directly observe. When you walk, speak, throw a Frisbee, or frown, you are behaving in this sense. The term **mental processes** refers to the *private* thoughts, emotions, feelings, and motives that other people cannot directly observe. Your private thoughts and feelings about your dog catching a Frisbee in midair are examples of mental processes. Because mental processes are private, psychologists use observations of public behavior to draw inferences about mental processes.

What exactly does it mean to say that psychology is the science of behavior and mental processes? If you look carefully through this book, you will see that a wide range of topics are discussed, including love, violence, mental disorders, and sexuality. We also discuss emotions, ways of improving memory, relationships between employers and employees, compulsive gambling, and other important topics. Almost everything that you expected psychology to be about is in this course, even if more basic topics are there, too.

This text surveys the basic principles of psychology and shows you how they are related to significant human problems. Because this is a first course in psychology, we spend most of our time covering the basic principles, but to help you understand those principles, we discuss how they can be applied to key human issues throughout the text. Indeed, all the material in this book, even the most basic concepts, is relevant to human lives.

Goals of Psychology

Why do psychologists devote their professional lives to the study of behavior and mental processes? What are they trying to accomplish? The four *goals* of the science of psychology are to describe, predict, understand, and influence behavior and mental processes:

1. ***Describe.*** Information gathered in scientific studies helps psychologists describe behavior and mental processes accurately. For example, descriptive information gathered in a survey of the frequency of sexual behavior among college students without the protection of condoms would be an important first step in designing a program to prevent the spread of sexually transmitted diseases such as AIDS.

2. ***Predict.*** In some cases, research gives psychologists the tools to predict future behavior reasonably well. For example, psychologists have developed tests that enable employers to predict more accurately which job applicants will perform their jobs well.

3. ***Understand.*** We understand behavior and mental processes when we can *explain* them. Because there is always more to learn, our current explanations are always tentative. In other words, our explanations are not *truths*. They are **theories** that might be improved, or even rejected, by future studies.

4. ***Influence.*** Finally, psychologists hope to go beyond description, understanding, and prediction to influence behavior in beneficial ways. What can we do to help a teenage boy climb out of severe depression? How can we help parents raise a rambunctious child? What is the best way to help college students select their careers? It's not until we have identified ways to intentionally influence behavior that psychology completely fulfills its promise.

The term *behavior* refers to all of a person's overt actions that others can directly observe. When you walk, speak, throw a Frisbee, or show facial expressions, you are behaving in this sense.

theories Tentative explanations of facts and relationships in sciences.

Review

We have defined *psychology* as the science of behavior and mental processes. Behavior refers to all of your actions that other people can directly observe. Mental processes, in contrast, are private events, such as your thoughts and feelings. The goals of psychology are to describe, predict, understand, and influence behavior and mental processes. Using the methods of science, we think critically about systematic observations, which allows us to accurately describe psychological facts and relationships. When adequate descriptive information has been acquired, reasonably accurate predictions can be made and explanations proposed to help us understand these facts and relationships. Finally, when enough understanding and ability to predict have been acquired, we can sometimes intentionally influence people in ways that improve and enrich their lives.

Check Your Learning

One efficient way to learn information from textbooks is to be sure that you have mastered the key points in each major section before moving on to the next one. You can do this by asking yourself questions about the material you have just read. If you cannot answer some of the questions, you can go back to that part of the section and reread it. Then, when you can answer all your questions, move on to the next part of the chapter. This step of asking and answering questions takes a little time, but you will learn and remember much more information.

Check Your Learning (cont.)

To make it easier for you to check your learning in this way, I have written some questions at the end of each section. If you give an incorrect answer to any question, return to the page number given next to the correct answer to see why your answer was not correct. When you have mastered the information in this section, you will be ready to move on to the next section.

It is important for you also to ask *your own* questions, however, for two reasons. First, asking your own questions will help you personalize the course and make it a more worthwhile learning experience for you. Second, I have asked you questions only about some of the key points in each section. If you learn only what is emphasized in these few questions, you will miss a great deal of information. Therefore, use these questions only as a starting point in checking your learning.

1. The ancient Greek philosopher who wrote about *psyche* and first broadly defined the subject matter was _____.

   a) Plato   c) Hippocrates

   b) Aristotle   d) Epicurus

2. The modern definition of psychology is "the science of _____ and _____."

3. Mental processes are _____.

   a) directly observable   b) private

4. The four goals of the science of psychology are to (a) _____, (b) _____, (c) _____, and (d) _____ behavior and mental processes.

Thinking Critically about Psychology

Pause for a moment to *think* about and *evaluate* what you have just read. The following questions can help you do that. There are no right or wrong answers to these questions, but they should help you become an active reader and think critically about what you have just read. The next step is to ask your own critical questions. The more you think about and question the content of this book, the more you will learn and remember.

1. Is psychology really a science? Can human behavior and mental processes actually be studied using scientific methods?

2. How do your personal goals as a student of psychology relate to the four goals of the science of psychology? Do you think this course will be relevant to you?

Correct Answers: 1. b (p. 2), **2.** behavior and mental processes (p. 2), **3. b** (p. 2), **4a.** describe **b.** predict **c.** understand **d.** influence (p. 3)

Founding the Science of Psychology

There was no formal discipline of psychology during the time of Aristotle—and not for 2,200 years after he lived. In the 17th and 18th centuries, physics, biology, medicine, and other sciences accumulated enough knowledge and scientific methods to set them apart from other fields. The launching of the separate field of psychology is usually credited to Wilhelm Wundt for establishing the first laboratory of Psychology in Leipzig, Germany, in 1879. Some historians believe that William James deserves the honor for a less-publicized laboratory that opened in 1875 at Harvard University. Actually, no one person "founded" psychology. Psychology was founded by many groups of scientists. Their varied interests laid the foundations for the diverse field surveyed in this text. As you read about some of the most influential early psychologists, imagine how different their answers would be if you asked each of them: "What is the most important question that psychology must answer?"

Nature of Conscious Experience

The first topic studied by psychologists was private conscious experience. What are you thinking and feeling right now? Everything that you are aware of at this moment is your private conscious experience. The first psychologists wanted to understand the basic elements of consciousness and how they worked together.

Wundt, Titchener, and Structuralism. Wilhelm Wundt was a professor of biology in Germany who was fascinated by human consciousness (Wong, 2009). His work was expanded by his student Edward Titchener, who later taught at Cornell University. Just as chemists were trying to discover the basic elements that make up physical substances, Wundt and Titchener wanted to identify the basic elements of conscious experience. Because Wundt and Titchener were interested in the basic elements of the conscious experience and how those elements are organized, their viewpoint is known as **structuralism.**

Wundt and Titchener studied the elements of private consciousness using **introspection,** a method of looking inwardly at one's own conscious experiences. Wundt and Titchener trained themselves to observe the contents of their own minds as accurately and unemotionally as possible in an attempt to isolate the basic elements of the mind. What does that mean exactly?

Suppose I visit your school someday, and your instructor asks me to give a guest lecture on the history of psychology. If I am in a particularly dramatic mood, I might decide to give the lecture playing the role of Edward Titchener. Imagine that I arrive wearing a fake beard and the flowing black academic robes like the ones he always wore, and I choose you to be the subject of a demonstration of introspection. I ask you to close your eyes, and I place in your mouth a bit of apple that you have not seen. Then I ask you to describe the raw *sensations* that the apple creates in your mind. You hesitate a moment, then announce with a smile: "It's an apple!"

"*Nein! Nein! Nein!*" I shout, using the only word I can remember from German 101. "I asked you to tell me what you *sense*. Don't tell me what the thing is on your tongue. Describe the sensations that you experience!"

You hesitate again, regain your composure, and say: "Sweet?"

"Yes! Yes!" I cry. "What else do you sense?"

"A little bit of sourness, a grainy texture, and a wetness."

"Wonderful!" I shout, causing you to break into a grin. "Now you're introspecting. Now you're describing the elemental contents of your mind. Sweet, sour, grainy . . . those are some the building blocks from which consciousness is structured. Everything that you experience in life is based on a small number of these basic elements."

J. Henry Alston. Although Wundt and Titchener were the first structural psychologists to study conscious experience, other scientists soon joined the effort. One notable early structuralist was J. Henry Alston. Alston is best known for his studies of the sensations of heat and cold. He discovered that we feel cold when one kind of nerve ending in the skin is stimulated, and we feel warm when a different kind of nerve ending is stimulated. Most interestingly, Alston found that we feel intense heat only when *both* the warmth and the cold receptors in the skin are stimulated at the same time. Very hot objects—such as a hot iron—not only stimulate the warmth receptors but also stimulate the nerve endings that ordinarily respond only when it is cold.

Alston demonstrated this fact in a simple but elegant experiment in 1920. He constructed the apparatus shown in figure 1.1 (p. 6) by wrapping two water pipes together,

Wilhelm Wundt (1832–1920).

Edward Titchener (1867–1927).

structuralism (struk´tūr-al-izm) 19th-century school of psychology that sought to determine the structure of the mind through controlled introspection.

introspection (in"tro-spek´shun) The process of looking inward at one's own consciousness.

J. Henry Alston.

Warm   Cold
water water

Figure 1.1

When you grasp a coil made up of two twisted pipes, one carrying cold water and the other carrying moderately warm water, the sensation is one of extreme heat because the receptors for both cold and heat are stimulated.

Max Wertheimer (1880–1943).

Gestalt psychology School of thought based on the belief that human consciousness cannot be broken down into its elements.

Gestalt (ges-tawlt´) Organized or unified whole.

phi phenomenon (fī fe-nom´ĕ-nom) Perception of apparent movement between two stationary stimuli.

one carrying moderately warm water and the other carrying cold water. When people grasped these pipes, they felt the sensation of intense heat! Because both the warmth and the cold receptors in the skin were stimulated by the two twisted pipes, the individual in the experiment felt the sensation of intense heat.

J. Henry Alston is also a notable figure in the history of psychology because he was the first African American psychologist to publish a research paper in a journal of the American Psychological Association.

Max Wertheimer and Gestalt Psychology. Max Wertheimer, a professor of psychology at the University of Frankfurt in the early 1900s, was also interested in the nature of conscious experience. However, his ideas about consciousness were quite different from those of the structuralists. Wertheimer led a group of psychologists known as **Gestalt psychologists.** Their approach to psychology was based on the German concept of the **Gestalt,** or *whole.* The Gestalt psychologists thought that human consciousness could not be meaningfully broken down into raw elements, as the structuralists tried to do. As they were fond of saying: "The whole is different from the sum of its parts." To illustrate, the two examples in the left side of figure 1.2 are drawn from exactly the same angled lines, but their organization greatly changes our perception of them. Although the parts are the same in each example, the whole is seen as a triangle in one example and arrows in the other. Similarly, the second element in the two rows in the right side of figure 1.2 is exactly the same each time, but when we look at the two rows from left to right, it is perceived as a "13" in the first row and as a "B" in the second.

Gestalt psychologists also used the **phi phenomenon** to demonstrate that the whole is different from the sum of its parts. When two lights are presented in rapid sequence, the viewer sees an apparent movement in the stimuli. That is, rather than perceiving two stationary lights, the viewer sees one light moving from one position to another. This is a highly important phenomenon to Gestalt psychologists, because what is seen—a moving light—is not present in the two parts of the stimulus at all. Movement is a property of the whole perception—the gestalt—but movement is not part of the stimulus. Motion pictures are based on this phi phenomenon. A series of still images that change slightly in each frame is projected on the screen so quickly that the image appears to be moving. The Gestalt psychologists used such examples to make their point that perception has meaning only when it's seen as a whole rather than as a simple collection of elements, as the structuralists implied.

Functions of the Conscious Mind

While many of the early psychologists were studying the nature of conscious experience, another group was trying to understand the *survival value* of consciousness to us as a species. What useful *functions* does consciousness serve that help us survive as a species?

William James and Functionalism. In 1875, a young professor of biology and philosophy at Harvard University named William James taught the first "psychology" course, and in 1890 he published an influential early textbook of psychology. James was impressed with the work of biologist Charles Darwin. Darwin's theory of evolution stated that every physical characteristic evolved in a species because it served a purpose. James suspected that the same thing could be said about the characteristics of the human mind. He believed that thinking, feeling, learning, remembering, and other mental processes exist only because they help us *survive* as a species. Because we can think logically, for example, we are better able to find food, avoid danger, and care for our children—all of which help the human species survive. Because of its emphasis on the survival *functions* of consciousness, James' school of thought is known as **functionalism.**

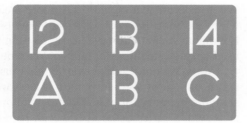

Figure 1.2
The organization of the lines in these two illustrations shows that only "whole" perceptions have meaning. The lines do not change, but their meaning does.

James criticized the structuralists for creating a barren approach to psychology. He compared human consciousness to a flowing stream; we could study that stream by isolating single molecules of water like the structuralists, but we would miss the nature and beauty of the whole stream. Moreover, studying the water molecules in a stream would tell us nothing about what the stream *does*—it erodes riverbanks, provides a home for fish, carries barges, and so on. Similarly, studying the elements of the mind tells us nothing about how the mind helps us adapt to the demands of life. The functions of the mind, not its raw elements, were the subject matter of psychology to the functionalists.

functionalism (funk´shun-al-izm) 19th-century school of psychology that emphasized the useful functions of consciousness.

Studies of Memory: Hermann Ebbinghaus and Mary Whiton Calkins.

One of the most useful mental processes is memory. In 1885, German functionalist Hermann Ebbinghaus published a book titled *On Memory*. This remarkable book gave a detailed account of a series of studies spanning six years in which Ebbinghaus served both as the scientist and the only subject. He memorized lists of information and measured his memory for them after different intervals of time. To be sure that the material he was learning was not affected by his prior experience with it, Ebbinghaus invented an entirely new set of meaningless items for his experiments called *nonsense syllables,* such as KEB and MUZ.

Ebbinghaus found that forgetting is very rapid at first but proceeds slowly thereafter. Almost half of his original learning was lost within 20 minutes, and almost all of the forgetting that was going to occur had occurred within about 9 hours (see figure 1.3).

William James (1842–1910).

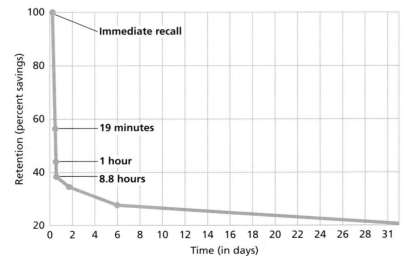

Figure 1.3
Herman Ebbinghaus published these findings in 1885 showing that most forgetting of nonsense syllables occurs rapidly, with almost half of the original learning being lost within 20 minutes.

Herman Ebbinghaus (1850–1909).

Mary Whiton Calkins (1863–1930).

cognition (kog-nish´un) Mental processes of perceiving, believing, thinking, remembering, knowing, deciding, and so on.

cognitive psychology Viewpoint in psychology that emphasizes the importance of cognitive processes, such as perception, memory, and thinking.

behaviorism (be-hāv´yor-izm) School of psychology that emphasizes the process of learning and the measurement of overt behavior.

social learning theory Viewpoint that the most important aspects of our behavior are learned from other persons in society—family, friends, and culture.

unconscious mind All mental activity of which we are unaware.

We now know that memories of more meaningful information are not always forgotten in the same way as nonsense syllables, but with his careful and detailed studies, Ebbinghaus set an important example of how rigorous experimental methods could be used to study functions of human consciousness.

Mary Whiton Calkins was another early functionalist who studied memory. She was a student of William James at Harvard University in the late 1800s. Rather than studying memory for lists of unrelated nonsense syllables, Calkins presented her subjects with a series of numbers, each paired with a different color. Later she showed the subjects the colors alone to see how many of the numbers they could recall. Variations on Calkins's method, called the *paired associates* method, dominated research on memory in the United States for more than 50 years (Madigan & O'Hara, 1992).

Cognitive Psychology. Functionalism is still important in contemporary psychology, but the terminology has changed. Rather than speaking about the functions of human consciousness, psychologists now use the term *cognition*. **Cognition** is a broad term that refers to all intellectual processes—perceiving, believing, thinking, remembering, knowing, deciding, and so on. Today's **cognitive psychology** is a modern version of functionalism—also strongly influenced by Gestalt psychology and structuralism. Although we only briefly mention cognitive psychology in this chapter, we return to it many times throughout the book. The chapters on sensation and perception, learning, memory, thinking and language, and intelligence are partly or wholly about key topics in cognitive psychology. In addition, the chapters on emotion, stress and health, abnormal psychology, therapy, social psychology, and other topics also refer to important topics in cognitive psychology. In many ways, cognitive psychology is the heart of modern psychology.

Behaviorism and Social Learning Theory

A third group of scientists working in the late 1890s contributed to the founding of psychology in different ways. Like William James, this group was influenced by Charles Darwin to study psychological processes that are useful in survival. Unlike James, they were not interested in the adaptive functions of consciousness. Their approach is known as **behaviorism** because they believed that it was not possible to study conscious experience scientifically. Instead, the behaviorists studied the adaptive value of *learning* from experience.

Ivan Pavlov. Russian biologist Ivan Pavlov and his coworkers were conducting research on digestion in dogs when they noticed a curious thing. They had surgically implanted tubes in the cheeks of the dogs to study the reflexive secretion of saliva during eating. Pavlov noticed that when they saw food being brought to them, not just when the food was placed in their mouths. He recognized that the dogs had learned to associate the sight of the food being brought with the food itself. Because the sight had immediately preceded the food on many occasions, the dogs came to respond to the sight of food by salivating. He demonstrated that this interpretation was correct by conducting experiments using a clicking metronome instead of the sight of food and small quantities of powdered meat. When the metronome and the meat powder were presented together, the dogs quickly learned to salivate to the metronome alone.

Although teaching dogs to salivate to the sound of the metronome is not important in its own right, Pavlov's accidental discovery was of tremendous importance to the new field of psychology. He had identified a simple form of learning—or *conditioning,* to use his term—in which an inherited reflex (salivating) comes to be triggered by a stimulus that has nothing to do with that reflex (the metronome). Pavlov had shown that even inherited reflexes could be influenced dramatically by learning experiences.

Ivan Pavlov (1849–1936).

Pavlov thought that conditioning was so important to the survival of species that he abandoned his research on digestion, for which he won the Nobel Prize, and spent the rest of his career studying conditioning.

John B. Watson and Margaret Floy Washburn. Pavlov's research and theories were not immediately accepted in the United States, but in the 1910s and 1920s the concepts were taken up in the writings of behaviorists John B. Watson and Margaret Floy Washburn. They agreed with Pavlov that the importance of conditioning went far beyond salivating dogs and that most human behavior was learned through classical conditioning. Until his death in 1990, B. F. Skinner of Harvard University was the leading exponent of behaviorism.

Social Learning Theory. Most contemporary behavioral psychologists endorse a broader version of behaviorism that integrates the study of behavior with the study of cognition. Albert Bandura of Stanford University is the leading spokesperson for this broader viewpoint, often referred to as **social learning theory.** This viewpoint states that the most important aspects of our behavior are learned from other persons in society—we learn to be who we are from our family, friends, and culture. The social learning viewpoint, which integrates aspects of behaviorism and the cognitive perspective, continues to be an important theoretical perspective today.

Nature of the "Unconscious Mind"

While most of the founders of psychology were focusing on the structure of the brain, or on conscious mental processes or overt behavior, others were moving in yet another different direction. They believed that the most important aspect of human psychology was neither the mental processes nor the behavior that we are aware of but, rather, the mental processes of which we are *unaware*. That is, this group of founders of psychology focused on the "unconscious" mind.

Sigmund Freud and Psychoanalysis. Sigmund Freud was an Austrian physician who practiced neurology, the treatment of diseases of the nervous system. Unlike the other founders of psychology, he was responsible for the day-to-day care of a large number of patients, many of whom had serious psychological problems. This fact, perhaps more than anything else, explains the enormous differences between his view of psychology and those of the other founders.

Beginning in the 1890s, Freud wrote a series of papers in which he argued that conscious mental processes were of trivial importance compared with the workings of the **unconscious mind.** Freud believed that the roots of the psychological problems he tried to treat were innate **motives,** particularly sexual and aggressive ones that reside in an unconscious part of the mind. He believed that these unconscious motives, and the conflicts that surround them, influence us, even though we do not know they exist.

Freud's theory of **psychoanalysis** has been revised numerous times since his death. Modern psychoanalysts still adhere to Freud's view that conflicts in the unconscious mind are the chief source of psychological problems. Few modern psychoanalysts accept all of Freud's ideas, however. Most believe that Freud made an important contribution in calling our attention to the role often played by unconscious sexual and aggressive motives in our emotional conflicts. Nonetheless, they think that other motives, such as the need to feel adequate in social relationships, are of even greater importance (Westen, 1998). Research continues on the possibility that sometimes people are unaware of their motivations (Winkelman & Berridge, 2004), but the psychoanalytic perspective has not been a dominant force in North American psychology for many years (Robins & others, 1999).

John B. Watson (1878–1958).

Margaret Floy Washburn (1871–1939).

motives Internal states or conditions that activate behavior and give it direction.

psychoanalysis (sī″kō-ah-nal′i-sis) Technique of helping persons with emotional problems based on Sigmund Freud's theory of the unconscious mind.

B. F. Skinner (1904–1990).

Sigmund Freud (1856–1939).

Carl Rogers (1902–1987).

humanistic psychology
Psychological view that human beings possess an innate tendency to improve and determine their lives by the decisions they make.

psychometrics Perspective in psychology founded by Binet that focuses on the measurement of mental functions.

neuroscience perspective
Viewpoint in psychology that focuses on the nervous system in explaining behavior and mental processes.

Humanistic Psychology and the Unconscious Mind. During the 1950s, another movement that focused on the role of the unconscious emerged—**humanistic psychology.** The founders of this movement, including Abraham Maslow, Carl Rogers, and Viktor Frankl, did not agree with Freud that only unconscious processes are important, however. Instead, humanists believe that human beings determine their own fates through the conscious decisions they make. Like Freud, however, the humanists believe that the unconscious mind often defeats our efforts to make good, conscious decisions.

To the humanists, our view of what we are like—our *self-concept*—is the key element of conscious decision making. If you think that you are intelligent, you may sign up for a difficult college course. If you think that you are caring and cool-headed, you might volunteer to work on a telephone crisis line. Humanists believe, however, that society makes it difficult to have an *accurate* self-concept. For example, we are constantly bombarded with information from society that says only witty, athletic, and attractive people are worth loving. So, what if you are like most of us and are a little dull, slightly clumsy, and not so attractive?

Humanists believe that we often push into the unconscious upsetting information, such as not living up to the ideals of society. This causes problems in two ways: First, it means that most of us have an inaccurate self-concept—because we push out of consciousness information about ourselves that doesn't match what society values. Second, this unconscious information sometimes threatens our self-concept and makes us anxious. Thus, although the psychoanalysts and humanists view the unconscious mind in very different ways, they both see it as the most important cause of human problems. As with the psychoanalytic perspective, few papers in core psychology journals are currently on humanistic themes (Robins & others, 1999).

Psychometrics: Alfred Binet

Alfred Binet was a founder of psychology who took the study of mental processes in a very different and highly practical direction. In the 1890s, the members of the Paris Ministry of Education were faced with a problem. They wanted to provide extensive education for all "intelligent" children and more practical, less academic kinds of schooling for less intelligent children. They not only wanted to be fair about choosing the children to be given advanced academic training but also wanted to make the decision when the children were still young. How could they measure something as intangible as a young child's intelligence?

The Ministry of Education turned for advice to Binet, who was a professor at the University of the Sorbonne. Binet and his collaborators were able to find a set of test questions (for example, arithmetic problems, word definitions, memory tasks) that could be answered by most children of a given age but not by most children who were younger. These questions were used to create an intelligence test that was later revised and translated in the United States to become the still widely used Stanford-Binet Intelligence Scale. Binet's work led to the modern branch of psychology that specializes in the measurement of intelligence, personality, and job aptitude. Binet's approach to psychology is known as **psychometrics,** meaning the measurement (*metric*) of mental functions (*psycho*). It continues to be an important and practical viewpoint in modern psychology.

Neuroscience Perspective

In 1894, Spanish scientist and physician Santiago Ramón y Cajal published the first description of *neurons*—the cells that make up the brain and the nervous system. His view that the brain was made up of a network of interacting neural cells laid the foundation for our modern understanding of the role of the brain in psychology. In 1906, Ramón y Cajal was awarded the Nobel Prize for his work on neurons.

Today, psychologists who approach the science from the **neuroscience perspective** are interested in the structures of the brain that play roles in emotion, reasoning, speaking, and other psychological processes. They also seek to determine the extent to which our psychological characteristics, such as intelligence and emotional stability, are influenced by heredity. Neuroscientists are influenced by Charles Darwin's theory of evolution, which says that all animal species are related through the process of evolution. For this reason, they study relations between biology and psychology in many different species, including humans and nonhuman animals. Like functionalism, the neuroscience perspective has become important in nearly every aspect of psychology. We examine the neuroscience foundations of behavior and mental processes in chapter 3, and we integrate references to the role of biological factors throughout the book.

Santiago Ramón y Cajal (1852–1934).

Figure 1.4

Historical time line describing the major schools of thought that have influenced psychology in the past and continue to directly or indirectly influence psychological thinking today. In addition, the neuroscience and sociocultural perspectives are increasingly integrated into current psychological theory and practice.

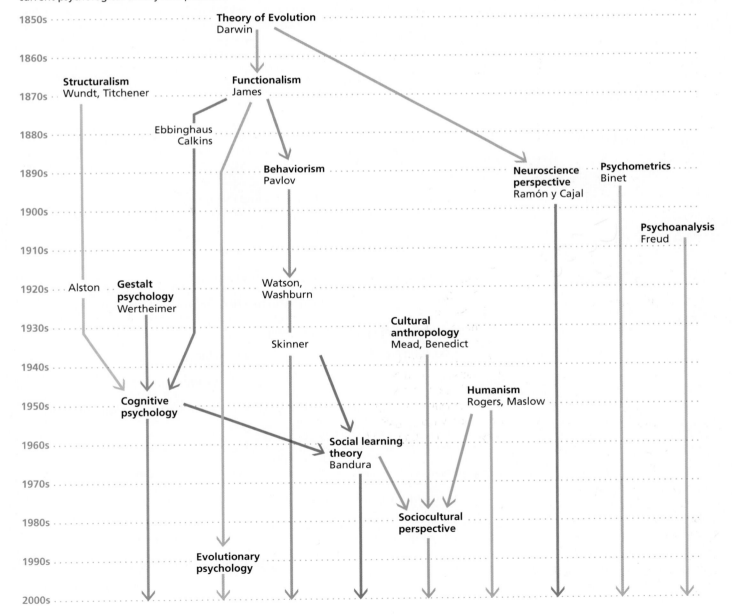

Review

There was no formal science of psychology for 2,200 years after the time of Aristotle. Then, in the late 19th century, a number of events led to the emergence of an independent discipline. Wilhelm Wundt founded his psychology laboratory in 1879. Wundt and his followers Edward Titchener and J. Henry Alston (known collectively as structuralists) engaged in controlled introspective studies of human consciousness. Max Wertheimer and his associates in Germany developed Gestalt psychology, which emphasized the need to study consciousness in whole, meaningful units rather than the artificial elements studied by the structuralists. William James founded the school of functionalism, which stressed the evolutionary significance of consciousness. Functionalists Hermann Ebbinghaus and Mary Whiton Calkins published influential studies of memory that showed how experimental methods could be used to study this useful mental process. Alfred Binet founded the psychometrics movement by developing an intelligence test for selecting children for advanced education in Paris. Russian biologist Ivan Pavlov founded the behaviorism movement, which advocated a science of psychology that included only overt behavior and made no attempt to study mental processes. Behaviorists John B. Watson and Margaret Floy Washburn introduced the United States to the research on classical conditioning conducted by Russian biologist Ivan Pavlov. The discovery of the neuron by Santiago Ramón y Cajal launched the neuroscience perspective in psychology. This lead to the work of many scientists on how the brain and other biological structures are related to behavior and mental processes. Physician Sigmund Freud published his observations on psychoanalysis and the unconscious, which were followed half a century later by the humanists' different perspective on the unconscious. Together these many founders of psychology launched a diverse science amid a storm of energetic controversy.

Check Your Learning

To be sure that you have learned the key points from the preceding section, cover the list of correct answers and try to answer each question. If you give an incorrect answer to any question, return to the page given next to the correct answer to see why your answer was not correct.

1. The early psychologist who first pioneered the introspective study of human consciousness and who generally is credited with founding the first laboratory of psychology in 1879 was _____.

   a) Ivan Pavlov

   b) William James

   c) Hermann Ebbinghaus

   d) Wilhelm Wundt

2. The early American psychologist who founded the school of functionalism, which emphasized the evolutionary importance of human consciousness, and who taught the first psychology course in a college was _____.

   a) Sigmund Freud

   b) William James

   c) Alfred Binet

   d) Wilhelm Wundt

3. The functionalist who developed the paired associates method to study memory was _____.

   a) Alfred Binet

   b) Max Wertheimer

   c) Mary Whiton Calkins

   d) Margaret Floy Washburn

4. The scientist who first discovered neurons (individual nerve cells in the brain) was _____.

   a) B. F. Skinner

   b) Ivan Pavlov

   c) Santiago Ramón y Cajal

   d) Margaret Floy Washburn

5. The physician who founded psychoanalysis and its study of the unconscious mind and abnormal behavior was _____.

a) Sigmund Freud

c) Alfred Binet

b) William James

d) Max Wertheimer

6. Modern cognitive psychology was influenced by which earlier schools of thought?

a) structuralism

c) Gestalt psychology

b) functionalism

d) all of these

There are no right or wrong answers to the following questions. They are presented to help you become an active reader and think critically about what you have just read.

1. Each founder of psychology focused on a different aspect of behavior and mental processes. Did he/she choose important questions? If you had been one of the founders, on which topic would you have focused?

2. Can the study of nonsense syllables tell us anything about human memory in everyday life? Did Ebbinghaus study something important?

Correct Answers: 1. d (p. 5), 2. b (p. 6), 3. c (p. 7), 4. c (p. 10), 5. a (p. 9), 6. d (p. 5–6)

Contemporary Perspectives and Specialty Areas in Psychology

Each of the founders of psychology who emerged in the late 1800s and early 1900s had different interests and assumptions about human nature, so each defined the methods and subject matter of psychology differently.

Where are we today in psychology? No single point of view from the early days has emerged as the "correct" way of viewing human behavior and mental processes. Although there are some strict adherents of some of the traditional schools of thought—such as behaviorism and psychoanalysis—contemporary psychology could be said to combine the best ideas from all its founders. In some ways, the effects of their intermingled ideas are even more important than the original schools of thought.

Before beginning our study of the methods and findings of psychology, we look at the sociocultural perspective, which is a more recent viewpoint that has profoundly influenced modern psychology. We also look at the divisions among modern psychology in terms of their area of focus.

Sociocultural Perspective

People are all the same in fundamentally important ways and yet different in other equally important ways. We are all the same in the sense that the principles of psychology apply equally to all of us. Your brain has the same working parts whether you are a woman of Chinese descent who was raised in Holland or a man of Swedish descent raised in Minneapolis. In the same sense, the principles of perception, motivation, learning, and personality also apply to all human beings. Even so, people also are different from one another. Their gender, culture, age, sexual orientation, and unique experiences all contribute to these differences. What is your age, gender, and ethnic heritage? How well educated are the members of your family? What is your political philosophy and your sexual orientation? If all these things about you were different, would you be a different person in important ways? I am not asking if you would be a

The *sociocultural perspective* in psychology emphasizes the importance of understanding people in the context of their ethnicity and culture.

sociocultural perspective Theory of psychology that states it is necessary to understand a person's culture and other social influences to fully understand him/her.

social anthropology (an´ thrō pol´´ e gee) Field of social science that studies the ways in which cultures are both similar and different from one another and how cultures influence human behavior.

cultural relativity Perspective that promotes thinking of different cultures in relative terms rather than judgmental terms.

better or a worse person, because we are not talking of value judgments here. I am asking only if you would be psychologically *different* from who you are presently.

Important questions such as these are addressed by the **sociocultural perspective** in psychology. This has been an important perspective in psychology since the 1980s. But the sociocultural perspective in psychology is actually derived from one of psychology's sister sciences—**social anthropology.** Pioneering social anthropologists, such as Margaret Mead and Ruth Benedict, visited many different cultures around the world in the 1930s and described how they were similar to and different from one another. The modern sociocultural perspective in psychology also was shaped by social learning theory within psychology. Like social learning theory, the sociocultural approach states that our personalities, beliefs, attitudes, and skills are learned from others.

During the past 20 years, many psychologists have come to believe that the basic course in psychology overemphasizes the ways in which people are the same and neglects the important message that the human race comes in a rainbow of sociocultural varieties. Therefore, almost all chapters in this book contain a *Human Diversity* section to further counteract the false impression that all human beings are the same in the eyes of psychology. These statements explore differences related to gender, ethnicity, age, physical disability, and other factors.

Therefore, it would be fair to say that this text takes a "sociocultural" approach. As you read this text, please keep in mind that human diversity is discussed in every chapter to help you understand the broad natural range of differences among human beings. These differences are never discussed in evaluative terms but simply as important aspects of the human condition. Although mentioning, for example, that males and females are different in some ways, those differences do not mean that one gender is superior to the other. The same holds for differences associated with ethnic groups and all other sociocultural factors.

Cultural Relativity. The sociocultural perspective not only encourages us to consider cultural and social factors when attempting to understand a neighbor or coworker but also requires that we not *misuse* that information. Two aspects of this perspective are particularly relevant to our discussion. First, the sociocultural perspective promotes **cultural relativity.** Although virtually every culture in the world views other cultures as inferior (Triandis, 1991), the sociocultural perspective encourages us to think of different cultures in *relative* terms rather than judgmental terms. That is, the sociocultural perspective promotes the view that different cultures, ethnic groups, genders, and sexual orientations are simply *different* from, rather than inferior to, others. Indeed, the sociocultural perspective encourages us to view differences among persons in our diverse world as rich sources of new ideas and ways of coping with the demands of human life.

Second, the sociocultural perspective reminds us that not all members of a given culture, ethnic group, or gender are *alike.* Some Asian men, for example, are tall and some are short; some are good at mathematics and some are not. The same is true of any sociocultural group. With most characteristics (moral beliefs, interest in music, willingness to work hard in school, or sports ability), there are usually more differences among persons *within* each group than *between* different groups.

The sociocultural perspective has become important in psychology in recent years, partly because psychologists who advise companies that conduct international business are in great demand during this era of globalization. To create solid personal and business relationships with persons from other cultures, one must understand cultural differences. For example, small gestures and ways of speaking that are perfectly acceptable in the United States can be insulting to members of another culture. Although international business has given the sociocultural perspective a strong push, the changing nature of Western countries continues to require close attention to this important perspective. The United States is a richly multicultural and multiethnic country. In 1989, 20% of all youth (up to 17 years of age) were members of minority ethnic groups. By the year 2000, that proportion had grown to more than 33%, and it is still on the rise. If the United States is to continue to succeed and prosper, we all must learn to understand one another better and to extend more opportunities to groups held at the bottom of the economic ladder by the kind of prejudice and discrimination that comes from lack of understanding (Comas-Díaz, 2000).

Sociocultural Factors in the History of Psychology. Because psychologists are people, too, sociocultural factors influence the thinking and behavior of psychologists. Psychology emerged at the close of the 19th century, when white males were expected to take positions of leadership, white females were expected to be stay-at-home homemakers, and people of color were expected to play roles of servitude. Although remnants of these prejudicial attitudes still affect us in important ways, they were far stronger in the 1890s than now.

The prejudices of the late 19th century were a sociocultural factor that played an important role in the thinking of the early psychologists (Minton, 2000). As just described, roles were played by women, African Americans, Hispanics, and others in founding psychology, but for many years the field of psychology was dominated by white males. Indeed, in textbooks as recently as 20 years ago, the contributions of women and ethnic minorities to founding psychology were largely ignored.

Although men in psychology greatly outnumbered women during the first 75 years of the profession, Christine Ladd-Franklin completed the doctoral program in psychology at Johns Hopkins University in 1882. She was one of only 10 women in the still-new science to do so before 1900. Women participated less in the early development of psychology than men did because sexual discrimination actively interfered with their ability to contribute. For example, although Christine Ladd-Franklin completed the doctoral program at Johns Hopkins, she was never given a degree, because Johns Hopkins was an all-male institution at that time and would not grant her one (Furomoto & Scarborough, 1986).

In the early days of psychology, even the most qualified women found it extremely difficult to obtain admission to graduate programs. When they did receive training, these women were rarely offered teaching positions at the male-dominated institutions that had the best-equipped laboratories.

Furthermore, around the turn of the century, a woman's decision to marry often meant the end of her career owing to the dominant stereotypes concerning a woman's role in the family (Furomoto & Scarborough,1986). One unmarried woman who is recognized for her important contributions during the pioneering days of psychology is Mary Whiton Calkins. When I described the history of Mary Whiton Calkins earlier, I said that she was "a student of William James at Harvard University in the late 1800s." She completed the requirements for the Ph.D. at Harvard but, like Christine Ladd-Franklin, was never awarded the degree. Like other all male institutions, Harvard did not confer degrees on women at that time.

Similar prejudicial roadblocks slowed the entry of African Americans, Latinos, and other ethnic minorities into psychology. Nevertheless, surprising numbers of people of color overcame the odds and became pioneers of the science of psychology. The first African American to be a professor of psychology in the United States was Gilbert Jones. Dr. Jones studied in Germany, where he obtained his Ph.D. in 1901 at the University of Jena. Inez Prosser was the first African American woman to receive a Ph.D. in psychology in the United States. Prosser obtained her master's degree and taught for many years before receiving her Ph.D. in 1933 from the University of Cincinnati. Tragically, she was killed in an automobile accident shortly after receiving her degree.

Inez Prosser (1897–1934).

Mamie and Kenneth Clark were among the first researchers to study the psychology of African American children.

George Sanchez (1906–1972).

The landmark research by Mamie Phipps Clark and Kenneth Clark (1939) on the self-concepts of African American children provided the scientific basis for the *Brown v. Board of Education* decision by the U.S. Supreme Court that ruled that segregated school systems could no longer be considered "separate but equal." The research of the Clarks showed that legally barring minority group children from all-white schools implied to the segregated children that they were inferior (Nyman, 2010). Thus, any segregated school system would be inherently unequal for the segregated ethnic group. In recognition of such research, in 1971 Kenneth Clark was the first African American to be elected president of the American Psychological Association. Similar important roles in psychology have been played by Hispanics, in addition to Santiago Ramón y Cajal. For example, George Sanchez's research discouraged the use of culturally biased tests for minority schoolchildren.

Although the number of women and ethnic minorities in psychology has grown dramatically in recent years, and all formal barriers against their entry into the field have long been dropped, prejudice still plays a negative role in psychology, as in all scientific and professional fields (Peterson, Brown, & Aronson, 1998; Vasquez & others, 2006). Although women now outnumber men among graduate students in psychology, men still outnumber women at advanced professorial ranks and in positions of authority (Peterson, Brown, & Aronson, 1998). The salaries of female psychologists must still be monitored to be sure that they receive equal pay for equal work. Furthermore, much remains to be done to provide child care and childbirth leave to facilitate the careers of women in psychology.

Basic and Applied Areas in Modern Psychology

Psychology is, as we have seen, a broad and diverse field. From the very beginnings of psychology, different founders studied different aspects of human behavior and declared their own theories and methods to be the correct way to look at psychology. Today, the most important divisions in psychology are not theoretical but are based on the kind of work that psychologists do. Even though a basic core of knowledge is shared by all psychologists, the interests and expertise of a psychologist who conducts basic research on sense of taste, for example, are distinct from those of one who evaluates employees in a large company for possible promotion to management positions, or those of one who works in a mental health clinic.

Contemporary psychologists can be roughly divided into two broad groups: those who study basic topics and those who work in applied areas of psychology (see figure 1.5).

Figure 1.5

The percentage of psychologists who received a doctoral degree in 1997 and who are employed in each of the major basic and applied subfields within psychology.

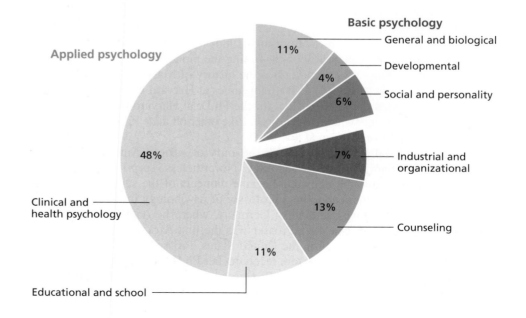

Basic Areas of Modern Psychology. About 20% of all psychologists work in the basic areas of psychology. They are broadly trained, but they tend to specialize in the study of a single psychological process. Most psychologists in the basic areas work in colleges and universities, where they teach and conduct research, but some work in research institutions, government agencies, or other settings. Their domain is the basic knowledge of psychology on which all applications are built. The largest specialties within the basic experimental areas of psychology are these:

1. *Biological psychology.* Biological psychologists study the ways in which the nervous system and other organs provide the basis for behavior and mental processes. They also study nonhuman animal behavior, both to compare it with human behavior and to gain a better understanding of other species.

2. *Sensation and perception.* This specialty is concerned with how the sense organs operate and how we interpret incoming sensory information.

3. *Learning and memory.* The ways in which we learn and remember new information and new skills are studied in this specialty area.

4. *Cognition.* **Cognitive psychologists** study thinking, perceiving, planning, imagining, creating, dreaming, speaking, listening, and problem solving.

5. *Developmental psychology.* This field of psychology is concerned with changes that take place in people during their life span, as we grow from birth through old age.

6. *Motivation and emotion.* In this specialty, psychologists study the needs and states that activate and guide behavior, such as hunger, sex, the need for achievement, and the need to have relationships with others.

7. *Personality.* The field of personality focuses on the relatively consistent ways of behaving that characterize our individual personalities.

8. *Social psychology.* Social psychologists study the influence of other people on our behavior; interpersonal attraction and intimate relationships; and attitudes and prejudice toward others.

9. *Sociocultural psychology.* Psychologists in this area focus on ethnic and cultural factors, gender identity, sexual orientation, and related issues.

Applied Areas of Modern Psychology. Eighty percent of psychologists use basic psychological knowledge to solve human problems (figure 1.5). Some **applied psychologists** teach and do research, but most work in mental health centers, industries, school systems, medical centers, and other applied settings. Following are the major subspecialties within applied psychology:

applied psychologists Psychologists who use knowledge of psychology to solve and to prevent human problems.

1. *Clinical psychology.* Clinical psychologists try to understand and treat serious emotional and behavioral problems.

2. *Counseling psychology.* Specialists in this field help people with personal or school problems and with career choices.

3. *Educational and school psychology.* Educational psychology is concerned with the ways children learn in the classroom and with the construction of psychological and educational tests. School psychologists consult with teachers about children who are experiencing learning or behavioral problems and test children to see whether they could benefit from special educational programs.

4. *Industrial and organizational psychology.* This field focuses on ways to match employees to jobs, to train and motivate workers, and to promote job satisfaction and good relationships among workers.

5. *Health psychology.* Health psychologists focus on the ways in which stress and other factors influence our health. They seek to prevent health problems such as heart disease by teaching people to relax, exercise, control their diets, and stop high-risk behaviors, such as smoking.

The distinction between the basic and the applied fields is not always clear. Often psychologists in the experimental fields work on important applied topics. For example, some developmental psychologists work with the producers of public television programs to insure that the content is appropriate for young children. Similarly, some social psychologists work on applied topics, such as helping businesses overcome prejudice based on gender or ethnicity in the workplace. There is something in psychology to interest or help just about everyone. If you glance ahead, you will see that the chapters of this book are organized to cover these experimental and applied facets of psychology.

Relationship between Psychology and Psychiatry

Psychology instructors are often asked about the similarities and differences between psychology and psychiatry. Psychiatrists have completed medical school and obtained the M.D. (doctor of medicine) degree and completed residency training in psychiatry. Because of their medical training, psychiatrists often prescribe drugs and use other medical treatments. Psychology is a much broader field than psychiatry. The specialty within psychology that is most similar to psychiatry is clinical psychology. Clinical psychologists have attended graduate school in psychology rather than medical school, have obtained the degree of Ph.D. (doctor of philosophy) or Psy.D. (doctor of psychology), and have completed an internship in clinical psychology. Psychologists are not licensed to prescribe drugs in most states.

Review

Since the founding of psychology, the sociocultural perspective has come to play an increasingly important role in defining the field. This perspective emphasizes the need to understand persons in the context of their cultures and other social influences. Generally, contemporary psychologists do not align themselves with one, single theoretical position, rather, they integrate the best contributions of each theoretical perspective into their own eclectic view. Modern psychologists both study basic psychological processes and apply what has been learned to meet important human needs. The basic and the applied areas of psychology can be further subdivided into the specific subject matter studied or the kind of human problems to which the application is addressed.

Check Your Learning

To be sure that you have learned the key points from the preceding section, cover the list of correct answers and try to answer each question. If you give an incorrect answer to any question, return to the page given next to the correct answer to see why your answer was not correct.

1. The approach that states a person can be understood only in terms of her or his culture and social influences is termed the _____.

   a) psychoanalytic theory   c) humanistic perspective

   b) cognitive perspective   d) sociocultural perspective

2. The basic area of psychology that studies intimate human relationships and prejudice is _____.

   a) neuroscience   c) clinical psychology

   b) health psychology   d) social psychology

3. The applied area of psychology that provides help for people with emotional and behavior problems is _____.

    a) neuroscience

    b) health psychology

    c) clinical psychology

    d) social psychology

There are no right or wrong answers to the following questions. They are presented to help you become an active reader and think critically about what you have just read.

1. Do you agree that sociocultural factors are important in our lives today? Can you think of barriers that exist today to the success of women and minorities in scientific and professional fields that psychologists could study and help eliminate?

2. In terms of helping solve an important social problem, such as crime, which basic or applied area of psychology do you think would be most useful?

Correct Answers: 1. d (p. 13), **2.** d (p. 17), **3.** c (p. 17)

What We Know about Human Behavior: Some Starting Places

Now that we have defined *psychology,* looked at the many beginnings of psychology around the turn of the 20th century, and have reviewed psychology's areas of specialization, we are ready to begin talking about the substance of psychology. Despite the complexity and diversity of this large field, psychology is a unified science with many shared assumptions and beliefs. Lest we overemphasize the differences among psychologists, let's identify some ideas that all psychologists have in common.

I have prepared a list of the most important things that contemporary psychologists believe about human lives. This is not a list of universally accepted "truths." There are sure to be differences of opinion among psychologists about this or any other similar list. My intent, though, is to come as close as possible to a summary of the most important concepts that all psychologists share. These are shared beliefs about the "true nature" of human beings. Because this section forms the foundation for the rest of the course, read this section carefully and think about it.

1. ***Human beings are biological creatures.*** We take our biological nature so much for granted that often we do not realize how much it influences our behavior. For example, we walk but we cannot fly because of our biological nature. Similarly, our biology limits the stimuli that we can hear and taste and even influences the emotions that we experience. Yet, even though our biology determines our behavior to a great extent, the limits it places on us are elastic—we can *stretch* them. The muscles given to us by heredity can be strengthened through exercise. Our native intelligence can be stretched by a stimulating home environment. We can even build airplanes to fly.

2. ***Every person is different, yet all people are much the same.*** Every human being is truly unique. With the exception of identical twins, each person's heredity is unique. And each person's

experiences are different from anyone else's. It's inevitable that we should differ from one another in significant ways. Psychologists devote much of their time to studying the ways in which our personalities, intellects, and interests differ.

Yet, as members of the human race, we are all similar in our capacities to think, feel, and remember. This similarity makes it possible to have a single science of human psychology. If we were not alike in these human qualities, we would have to develop a different psychology for each person. Fortunately, we are enough alike to be understood using one science of psychology, yet we are different enough to be interesting.

3. *People can be understood fully only in the context of their cultures and other social influences.* We are shaped by our experiences with other members of our culture. Our beliefs about right and wrong, our food preferences, our language, our religious beliefs, and many other facets of our lives come from cultural learning experiences. It is impossible to understand a person fully without understanding the sociocultural forces that influence him or her.

4. *Human lives are a continuous process of change.* From birth to death, humans are changing. We grow from helpless infants through the time of playing with toys, through the time of adult work and rearing children, into old age. Much of this developmental change is the inevitable result of our biological nature: Unless the process is disturbed, all creatures mature from infancy to old age. Other aspects of change come from our experiences in life. Every time we learn a new concept from a college course, make a new friend, or adjust to a tragedy in our lives, we change in some way.

5. *Behavior is motivated.* Human behavior is not aimless. Rather, most of our actions can be viewed as attempts to meet our needs. We work to earn money for food, shelter, and clothing. We go on dates for companionship and perhaps to satisfy our sexual needs. We tell a joke at a party because of the sweet feeling that laughter brings. However, not all our motives are simple and selfish. Some of us are willing to spend long hours tutoring children to see the joy of accomplishment in the children's faces. Others are motivated to express themselves in a painting or a poem.

6. *Humans are social animals.* Like hives of bees and flocks of geese, people gather in social groups. The survival of the human species has been possible only because people work together in groups for the benefit of all. From hunting large animals in the jungle to operating an assembly line, social groups are able to accomplish things that single individuals cannot. The social nature of human lives extends beyond mutual benefit, however. Most people need to have contact and relationships with one another. Most of us actively seek social support, friendships, and romantic relationships.

7. *People play an active part in creating their experiences.* Aristotle compared the mind of an infant to a blank clay tablet on which experiences leave their mark. In his view, we passively let experiences teach us about the world and become the person that they lead us to become. This is one of the few ideas of Aristotle that almost all contemporary psychologists reject. People play an active role in creating their experiences. Some people regularly choose relaxed, low-pressure situations; others get themselves into frenetic, exciting circumstances. We are shaped by these experiences, to be sure, but we play a role in choosing the experiences to which we are exposed. We are active participants in the flow of life, not passive, blank tablets.

8. ***Behavior can be adaptive or maladaptive.*** Humans have an amazing ability to adapt to the demands of life. We are flexible, capable creatures who generally use our wits to adjust to whatever life dishes out. Sometimes, however, we behave in ways that are harmful. Some of us have difficulty coping because we are too aggressive, whereas others are too timid. These maladaptive ways of behaving result from a combination of biological influences and our learning experiences. They are correctable, however, under the right conditions— such as good advice from friends, a change in life circumstances that encourages more adaptive ways to behave, or professional help.

These ideas serve as starting places for our study of psychology. As you read the following chapters, you may find it useful to glance back to these ideas to see how they relate to what you are studying.

Summary

Chapter 1 defines *psychology* and previews what psychologists have learned about human behavior.

 I. *Psychology* is defined as "the science of behavior and mental processes."

   A. Psychology is considered to be a science because—like all sciences—knowledge is acquired through systematic observation.

   B. The goals of psychology are to

   1. describe,

   2. predict,

   3. understand,

   4. and influence behavior and mental processes.

 II. Modern psychology developed from the pioneering work of many individuals during the late 19th and early 20th centuries.

   A. Early psychologists who studied the nature of conscious experience included

   1. Wilhelm Wundt (structuralism),

   2. Edward Titchener (structuralism),

   3. J. Henry Alston (structuralism),

   4. Max Wertheimer (Gestalt psychology).

   B. Founders of psychology who focused on the useful functions of conscious mental processes (functionalism) included

   1. William James,

   2. Hermann Ebbinghaus,

   3. Mary Whiton Calkins.

   C. Alfred Binet founded the practical perspective in psychology known as psychometrics, which focuses on the measurement of intelligence and other mental functions.

D. Early psychologists who focused on observable behavior and the importance of learning (behaviorism) were

   1. Ivan Pavlov,

   2. John B. Watson,

   3. Margaret Floy Washburn.

E. Pioneers of psychology who examined the "unconscious mind" were

   1. Sigmund Freud (psychoanalysis),

   2. Carl Rogers (humanistic psychology).

F. The neuroscience perspective began with the discovery of neurons (the basic cells of the nervous system) by Santiago Ramón y Cajal. This perspective emphasizes the need to understand the nature of the nervous system and other biological systems to understand our psychological nature.

G. Cognitive psychology is the modern viewpoint that is based on the early work of the functionalists, structuralists, and Gestalt psychologists and that emphasizes the importance of intellectual processes from perception to thinking. Social learning theory is the modern school of thought that is based on the earlier work of the behaviorists but incorporates cognitive psychology rather than rejecting it as the behaviorists did.

H. The sociocultural perspective, which states that people can be understood only in terms of their culture and other social influences, is a major contemporary influence in contemporary psychology.

I. Modern psychology can be divided into basic and applied areas.

   1. Psychologists working in the basic areas teach and conduct research on the biological basis of behavior, the processes of sensation and perception, learning and memory, cognition, human development, emotion, personality, social behavior, ethnic and gender identity, and sexual orientation.

   2. Applied psychologists put the basic knowledge of psychology to work in helping people. Then they specialize in applied fields, such as clinical treatment, personal or marital counseling, industrial or educational applications, or health psychology.

III. Most psychologists would agree that the following statements accurately describe human behavior and mental processes.

   A. Human beings are biological creatures whose structure and physiology influence and limit behavior.

   B. Each person is unique, yet enough similarities exist among individuals to allow a true science of behavior.

   C. People can be fully understood only in the context of their culture and other social influences.

   D. Human lives are in a continuous process of change, evolving from birth through old age.

   E. Behavior is motivated, not random or aimless.

   F. Humans are social animals who prefer to interact with others.

   G. People play an active part in choosing their experiences and constructing perceptions.

   H. Behavior can be either adaptive or maladaptive.

Visual Review of Historical Time Line

This visual review is designed to help you check your learning of the historical influences on modern psychology. Fill in the blanks with the names of the missing psychologists, historical and contemporary perspectives, or movements within psychology. (This information is summarized in figure 1.4 on p. 11.) Once you have the historical time line in mind, it is easier to organize additional ideas and facts within that structure. Be sure to ask your instructor how much of the historical information he or she expects you to learn. The names and dates are not the most important historical information in this chapter. Rather, the key point is that many psychologists with very different viewpoints founded the science of psychology over time. Beyond that concept, different instructors expect students to memorize different amounts of detailed historical information.

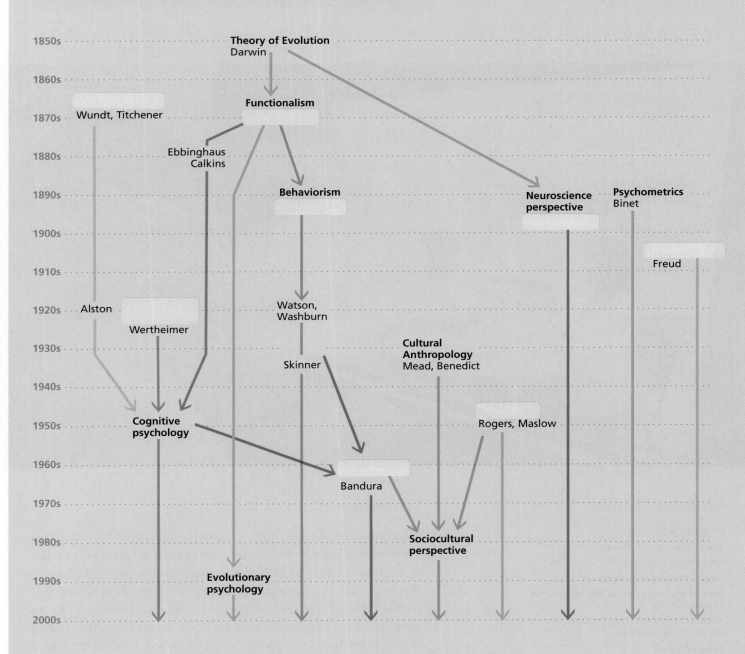

Figure 1.6
Visual review of historical time line

chapter **two**

Research methods in psychology

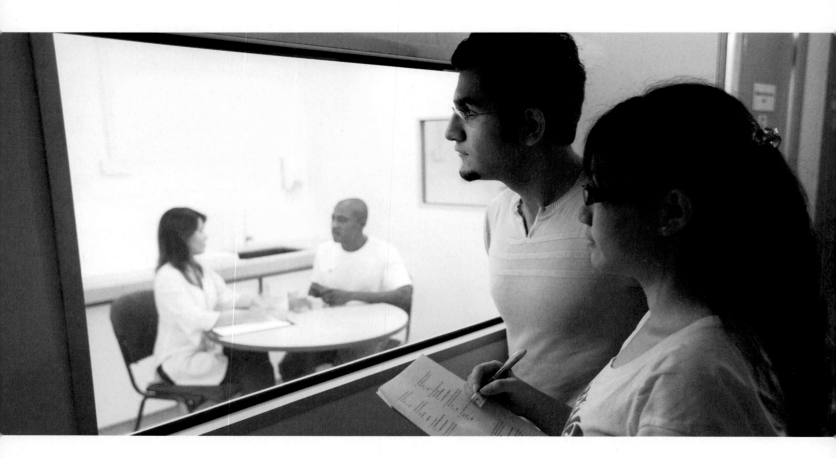

Chapter Outline

Prologue

All scientists believe that nature is orderly and lawful. If astronomers believed that the planets wandered aimlessly and randomly through space, they would have little reason to study their paths. The same is true of people. To have a science of psychology, we must believe that human behavior is at least somewhat predictable. Often, though, we see ourselves as capable of doing whatever we choose without being subject to the laws of nature. Psychologists believe that our behavior is much more orderly and predictable than most of us think.

I regularly begin teaching my own course in psychology with a disguised demonstration that human behavior is fairly predictable under some circumstances. It's a little corny, but it makes the point. After telling the students that I'm a very democratic fellow, I ask them to decide how they want to be evaluated in the course. I tell them that I require a cumulative final examination, but that everything else is open to a vote. I give them the option of doing a term paper (to give them a way of being evaluated that is free from the pressure of classroom testing), and I give them the options of having zero, one, two, or three tests plus the final examination. Then I take votes. In every class, a couple of students vote for the term paper (one student who writes well and one who thinks I'm too lazy to read them), but that option is always soundly defeated. A few students vote for no tests or one test, and about 20% vote for two tests, but about three-quarters always choose three tests plus the final.

When the voting is over, I thank the students for their judicious decision and hand out the course syllabus. Then I point out that I correctly predicted their behavior—that 250 copies of the syllabus had already been printed that include no requirement of a term paper and gives the dates of three tests plus the final examination. After the laughing, booing, and hissing have subsided, I say something like "The science of psychology rests on the assumption that your behavior is a good deal more predictable than you might think. That's not to take anything away from the mysteries and complexities of human existence; it's just to say that we're predictable enough to study scientifically."

In this chapter, we discuss how psychologists study human behavior and mental processes scientifically. We examine two general types of scientific methods used by psychologists—descriptive methods and formal experiments—and some of the specific strategies that researchers use in applying these methods. In many ways, this chapter covers the most important concepts in this course. Whereas the other chapters present what has been learned about behavior and mental processes, this chapter describes *how* we learn about ourselves in scientific terms. This is fundamentally important, because it is the use of scientific methods that allows psychology to move beyond mere speculation about the human condition. Science provides a set of methods for asking questions and rules for using evidence to answer them. To fully appreciate the value of scientific methods in psychology, however, you must understand these methods.

Key Terms

blind experiment 35
clinical method 29
control group 33
correlation coefficient 30
correlational method 29
dependent variable 33
descriptive statistics 36
descriptive studies 27
empirical evidence 25
experimental control 34
experimental group 33
experimenter bias 35
formal experiment 32
hypothesis 26
independent variable 33
mean 36
median 36
mode 37
naturalistic observation 28
normal distribution 37
operational definition 26
placebo effect 35
random assignment 34
replication 27
sample 26
scientific method 25
standard deviation 37
statistical significance 38
survey method 27
theories 26
variable 29

Basic Concepts of Research

The basis of the **scientific method** is making observations in a systematic way, following strict rules of evidence, and thinking critically about that evidence. Indeed, science is critical thinking in action. The psychological scientist asks: What is the evidence? How good is the evidence? What are the alternative explanations for the evidence? What needs to be learned next? In this chapter, we discuss several of the most important aspects of the scientific method in psychology.

scientific method Method of studying nature based on systematic observation and rules of evidence.

Empirical Evidence and Operational Definitions

Like other scientists, psychologists work with **empirical evidence**—evidence from *observations* of publicly observable behavior. All sciences require that their evidence come from observations of *public* phenomena so other scientists can confirm the observations. In the case of psychology, we observe public behavior and often use those observations to draw inferences about private mental processes that are not publicly observable.

empirical evidence Evidence based on observations of publicly observable phenomena, such as behavior, that can be confirmed by other observers.

operational definition Definition used in science that is explicitly based on the procedures, or operations, used to measure a scientific phenomenon, including behavior.

When scientists describe their empirical evidence, they are careful to use **operational definitions.** This means that they describe their observations in terms of the *operations of measurement.* The meaning of this abstract phrase will be clear if we consider a hypothetical example. Let's say a team of psychologists studied the causes of fatal accidents involving city buses. One statement of the conclusions of this hypothetical study uses an operational definition and the other does not:

A. Sixty percent of Chicago bus drivers daydream while driving their buses.

B. Sixty percent of Chicago bus drivers answered "yes" to the question "Do you ever daydream when driving your bus?"

Which statement uses an operational definition? Version B does, because it explicitly refers to the operation of measuring daydreaming (the question that was asked), whereas version A does not. Why is this important? It is an example of critical thinking in action. When you know the operation of measurement, you can easily evaluate the quality of the evidence. Are people (including bus drivers) able to accurately recall if they daydream? Would bus drivers be honest in reporting daydreaming while driving to a researcher? Would they believe the researcher's promise of confidentiality? Would some bus drivers be too embarrassed to admit to daydreaming even if they thought the researcher would keep their answer private? Is there a more accurate way to study daydreaming by bus drivers? Questions are not the only kind of operation of measurement used by psychological scientists. You will learn about many others during this course.

Theories and Hypotheses

theories Tentative explanations of facts and relationships in sciences.

Science deals in theories and not in "truths." **Theories** are tentative explanations of observations in science. The knowledge that any science provides is always tentative, because theories are always subject to change. They are revised frequently, because scientists are constantly testing them. A theory is tested by making a prediction based on that theory—called a **hypothesis**—and by conducting a study to see if the hypothesis is confirmed. For example, psychologist Terrie Moffitt (1993) published an influential theory stating that youth who become juvenile delinquents *before* puberty are quite different from individuals who do not commit any crimes until *after* puberty.

hypothesis Prediction based on a theory that is tested in a study.

I have tested one specific hypothesis based on that theory that states that juvenile delinquents who begin committing crimes during childhood are more violent than other juvenile delinquents. My study confirmed Moffitt's hypothesis (Lahey & others, 1998). Like other studies that have confirmed this hypothesis, my study provided a reason for the field to continue to use Moffitt's theory. However, confirming a hypothesis based on a theory does not mean that the theory is "true." It is always possible that other studies will fail to support it. If this were to happen often, Moffitt's theory would be either revised or abandoned.

Representativeness of Samples

sample Group of human or nonhuman research participants studied to learn about an entire population of human beings or animals.

Psychologists use human beings or nonhuman animals as the research participants. A group of participants—called the **sample**—is studied in hopes of learning something that applies to other human beings or animals. This means that studies are valid only if we select a sample that is *representative* of the group that we are interested in, such as all women and men living in the United States. For example, suppose psychologists wanted to test the hypothesis that people who are happy in their work tend to be happy in their marriages. A psychologist working in a marital therapy clinic might be tempted to use the clinic's clients as the sample. It would be convenient to ask them to complete some questionnaires about their happiness at work and in marriage. This would not give us a representative sample, however. People who are so unhappy in their marriages that they seek help for marital problems are hardly representative of *all* married persons. Using such an unrepresentative sample could lead to a biased and misleading test of the hypothesis.

Importance of Replication in Research

If I were to tell you that a hypothesis had been tested in five studies and the results were very similar, would you be more convinced that it is a sound hypothesis than if it had been tested in only one study? Researchers also are influenced by the **replication** of the findings in many separate experiments. Indeed, replication is an essential principle of science. Scientists doubt every finding until it has been replicated.

replication Repeating studies based on the scientific principle that the results of studies should be doubted until the same results have been found in similar studies by other researchers.

Research Methods

Many kinds of scientific methods are used in psychology, each with its own advantages and disadvantages. Each method is best suited for answering different kinds of questions, so they tend to be used by different specialties within psychology. However, all research methods are based on critical thinking about systematic observations.

Descriptive Studies

The simplest scientific studies are the **descriptive studies.** These involve studying people as they live their lives, so that we can *describe* their behavior and mental processes. We watch them shop in stores, listen to them during psychotherapy sessions, and observe them in many other ways. Three kinds of descriptive studies are widely used in psychology today: the survey method, naturalistic observation, and the clinical method.

descriptive studies Methods of observation used to describe predictable behavior and mental processes.

Survey Method. One of the most direct ways to describe human behavior or mental processes is simply to ask people questions. This is called the **survey method.** Surveys are widely used by psychologists to describe people's opinions about television programs, soft drinks, political candidates, and similar subjects (Zimbardo, 2004). Surveys are frequently used for many other purposes as well.

survey method Research method that uses interviews and questionnaires with individuals.

A survey conducted by a group of researchers at the National Institute of Mental Health (Kasper & others, 1989) provides an excellent example of the survey method. They were interested in describing variations in people's moods. Are you more likely to have bad moods during certain times of the year? Do they occur during the winter? A lot has been written about "winter blahs" and "cabin fever"—periods of depression experienced during the short, cold days of the winter—but, until recently, little hard evidence supported this idea. These researchers conducted a random telephone survey of 416 persons living in Maryland and Virginia. They asked an adult in each household to name the month during which he or she felt worst during the past year. As shown in the top section of figure 2.1 (p. 28), there was a strong tendency for the winter months, particularly January and February, to be the times when people reported they felt worst. The bottom sections show that moods tend to be worse when the temperature is the lowest and the number of minutes of sunlight each day is the shortest. Keep in mind as you read about this study that it does not imply *everyone* feels depressed during the winter. Many people thrive during cold weather. It simply suggests that more people feel lousy during the winter than during the summer. This study has been replicated many times (for example, Agumadu & others, 2004), lending support to the idea of winter blahs, but one study found that mood dips in the summer if the weather gets too hot and muggy (Keller & others, 2005).

Figure 2.1

Results of a telephone survey of 416 adults living in Virginia and Maryland who were asked the month during which they felt worst during the previous year. The authors plotted the 12 months twice to show more clearly the seasonal patterns of depressed feeling.

Source: Data from S. Kasper et al. 1989.

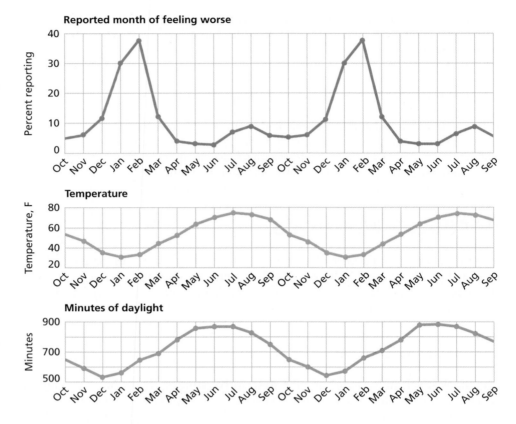

The primary advantage of the survey method is that you can collect a great deal of information in a relatively short time. The main disadvantage is that the results of surveys can be influenced by at least three factors:

1. The sample of people who are surveyed must be representative to avoid biased results. For example, if you asked people who logged onto a website on conservative politics if they favor tax breaks for the rich, you would probably get a different answer than if you asked a group of people who were typical of all adults in the United States.

2. You cannot always be sure that answers are completely honest, especially to questions about sensitive topics such as sex and drug use.

3. The way in which the survey is conducted can influence the results. For example, people are more likely to endorse feminist views when the interviewer is a woman (Huddy & others, 1997). Similarly, slight differences in how questions are worded can influence answers (Schwarz, 1999; Waenke, Schwarz, & Noelle-Neumann, 1995).

These considerations do not mean that surveys are not valuable; like all other methods of research, survey findings must be critically evaluated.

Naturalistic Observation. Another straightforward way to learn about behavior is simply to observe and to describe what naturally occurs. Careful observation in real-life settings is called **naturalistic observation.** When scientist Jane Goodall goes to Africa to observe a troop of apes, she is using naturalistic observation. She watches them in their natural habitat over long periods of time, taking careful notes of what she sees, until specific patterns of behavior become evident. Using this method, she and her coworkers have learned that the social behavior of apes is often strikingly similar to that of humans. She has even discovered that apes are capable of murder—ambushing and killing other apes in a way that looks intentional.

naturalistic observation Research method based on recording behavior as it occurs in natural life settings.

Naturalistic observation also is used to study human behavior. German scientist Irenaus Eibl-Eibesfeldt (1968) used naturalistic observation to study the gestures we use to greet other people. He found that smiling, nodding the head, and briefly raising the eyebrows are universal greeting behaviors across many diverse cultures. Naturalistic observation is also a method of studying such topics as the play and friendship patterns of young children, the leadership tactics of effective business managers, and the ways in which juvenile delinquents encourage antisocial behavior in one another.

Jane Goodall is a pioneer in naturalistic studies of ape behavior.

Clinical Method. An important variation on naturalistic observation is the **clinical method,** which simply involves observing people with psychological problems while they receive help from a mental health professional. Sigmund Freud, for example, developed his theories of abnormal behavior from years of observing his patients. He felt that he saw consistent patterns in what they did, thought, and felt during therapy. The clinical method is often used today for the preliminary evaluation of clinical treatment methods. For example, daily measures of anxiety might be taken on an individual before, during, and after treatment to evaluate a new method of treating excessive anxiety.

clinical method Method of studying people while they are receiving psychological help from a mental health professional.

correlational method (kor″ĕ-lā′shun-al) Research method that measures the strength of the relation between variables.

variable A factor that can be assigned a numerical value.

quantitative measures (kwon′ti-tā-tiv) Units of measure expressed in numerical terms.

Correlational Studies. The goal of the **correlational method** is simply to see if two observations are systematically related. To understand the correlational method, we'll use a topic that is often in the news—the possible effects of media violence on children and adolescents—as an example. Over the past 25 years, scientists and politicians have debated the effects of children's exposure to violence in television, movies, and electronic games. Does watching violence in the media make youth more likely to be violent themselves? The student who killed 32 people at Virginia Tech in 2007 was said to play highly violent video games. Did that help make him violent? Many psychologists believe that large increases in the amount of violence viewed by children during the 20th century have indeed caused an increase in violent crime (Anderson & others, 2001, 2003) and support legislation to curb violence in the media. Often such legislation is strongly opposed by the producers of violent television shows and films, by people who don't believe that media violence leads to real-life violence, and by others who believe that any form of censorship is a threat to the First Amendment right of free speech. This complex topic involves much more than just science, but see how correlational studies shed light on the issue.

Correlation: Statistical Relations between Quantitative Variables. Well over 200 studies have been published in psychological journals about exposure to media violence (Anderson & others, 2001; Huesmann, Moise, & Podolski, 1997; Konijn & others, 2007). Many of these studies used the **correlational method.** In such studies, researchers simply measure the two variables (viewing media violence and engaging in real-life violence, in this example) and see if they are statistically related. A **variable** is anything that can be assigned a *numerical* value. The primary difference between naturalistic observation and correlational studies is the use of **quantitative measures** in correlational studies. The two quantitative variables in many studies of media violence are the *amount* of violent movies or television programs viewed by each child (measured as the number of hours per week, for example) and the amount of violent behavior by the child (measured as the number of verbally or physically aggressive acts per week, for example).

Most published studies show that children who are exposed to more violence in movies, television, and video games are slightly more likely to be violent themselves in real life. That is, these two variables are *correlated.* Does this mean that viewing media violence makes children more violent? Not necessarily. We must consider two key issues to make sense of correlational studies: How *strong* is the relationship between watching media violence and engaging in violent behavior? And what do correlational studies tell us about cause and effect?

Correlation Coefficient. Correlational studies not only use quantitative measures of each variable but also measure the strength and the direction of the relationship between the two variables in quantitative terms. Is the *correlation* between watching media violence and engaging in violence strong? If the correlation is very weak, media violence is not likely an important factor in real-life violence. Researchers in psychology and other fields use the **correlation coefficient** to measure the strength of the correlation between two quantitative variables in *statistical* terms. You can see how this coefficient is calculated by turning to the *Appendix on Statistics* at the end of this book.

A correlation coefficient can range from $+1.00$ through zero to -1.00. A coefficient of $+1.00$ means a perfect *positive correlation* between the two variables, and a coefficient of -1.00 means a perfect *negative correlation* between the two variables. What does that mean? If two variables are *positively correlated,* participants who have lower scores on one variable will have lower scores on the other variable, and participants who have higher scores on the first variable will have higher scores on the other variable. If the correlation coefficient is $+1.00$, then we can predict with total accuracy each participant's score on one variable by knowing each participant's score on the other variable—they would be perfectly related in the positive direction. Look for a moment at figure 2.2. I have used hypothetical data to illustrate a coefficient of $+1.00$ between variable 1 and variable 2. Each participant in the study is represented by a dot and a letter of the alphabet in this figure. The dots are positioned at the points that represent each participant's score on the two variables. For example, the dotted lines show that participant C has a score of 4 on variable 1 and a score of 24 on variable 2. Because the correlation between these two variables is perfect, all the dots representing each participant lie on a perfectly straight line.

If two variables are *negatively correlated,* participants who have lower scores on one variable will have *higher* scores on the other variable, and participants who have higher scores on one variable will have *lower* scores on the other variable. If the correlation coefficient is -1.00, then we can still predict with total accuracy each participant's score on one variable by knowing each participant's score on the other variable—the variables would just be related in the negative direction. Look for a moment at figure 2.3, where I have again used hypothetical data to illustrate a

correlation coefficient The numerical expression of the strength and the direction of a relationship between two variables.

Figure 2.2 Hypothetical data illustrating a correlation coefficient of $+1.00$.

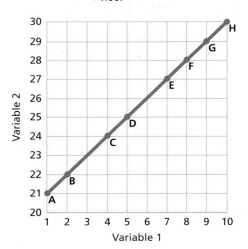

Figure 2.3 Hypothetical data illustrating a correlation coefficient of -1.00.

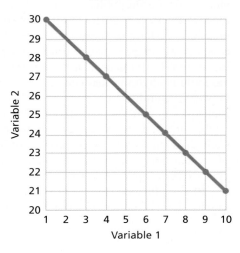

Figure 2.4 Hypothetical data illustrating a correlation coefficient of zero.

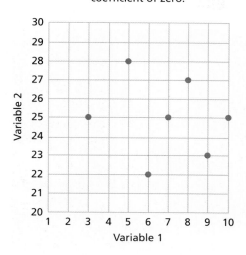

Figure 2.5 Hypothetical data illustrating a correlation coefficient of −.68.

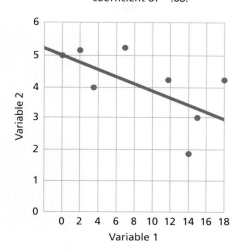

correlation coefficient of −1.00 between variable 1 and variable 2. Again, all the dots representing each participant's score on each variable lie on the straight line. Because the correlation is negative in this case, however, the direction of the line is opposite that of a positive correlation. It is common for students to be confused at this point and to think that a correlation coefficient of +1.00 is "better" than a coefficient of −1.00. Not so! Both are perfect correlations of equal strength—one just predicts in the positive direction and the other in the negative direction.

A correlation coefficient of zero, in contrast, means that there is absolutely no relationship between the two variables in either the positive or the negative direction. Again, I have used hypothetical data in figure 2.4 to illustrate a correlation coefficient of zero. Note that knowing a participant's score on one variable does not allow us to predict that participant's score on the other variable at all.

Very few correlation coefficients are perfect in actual correlational studies. Therefore, I have used hypothetical data to illustrate a correlation coefficient of −.68 in figure 2.5, which would be considered a fairly high correlation in most studies. This negative correlation tells us that participants with higher scores on variable 1 tend to have lower scores on variable 2. Note, however, that some of these data points lie quite far from the line that comes closest to connecting the dots representing each score. This means that we can only roughly predict each participant's score on one variable by knowing the other score.

Let's return to our example of media violence. Correlations between watching violence in the media and engaging in violence oneself tend to be relatively small, in the range of +.20 to +.30 (Anderson & Bushman, 2001; Anderson & others, 2003; Paik & Comstock, 1994). However, these small correlations *could* mean that 8 out of every 100 children viewing media violence are influenced to be more violent. A small increase in the number of violent children could be of great importance to society— particularly if you are one of their victims.

Correlation Does Not Necessarily Mean Causation. Finding that two variables are correlated tells us that they are related, but it does *not* necessarily mean that one of the variables influences the other variable in a causal way. For example, it is possible that viewing violence in the media causes some children and adolescents to become more violent, but it is equally likely that the *opposite* is true. That is, it is possible that youth who engage in more violence are more likely to enjoy violent shows than do less aggressive children. Correlations do not tell us which variable is the cause and which is the effect. In fact, correlations can exist between variables that are not causally related in either direction. For example, it is possible that viewing violence and engaging in

Figure 2.6   Example of a formal experiment. Incarcerated delinquent boys who were shown films depicting high levels of violence engaged in more verbal and physical aggression over the next 2 weeks than did boys in the same juvenile detention facility who were shown nonviolent films.

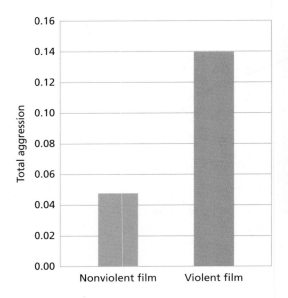

violence are both the result of another variable (such as having parents who do not supervise *either* the child's television viewing *or* the child's aggressive behavior).

Therefore, we must not reach conclusions about cause and effect based on correlational studies alone. They tell us only how strongly two variables are related. How, then, do we decide if one variable *causes* another? How do we decide if exposure to media violence causes an increase in violence? The next section describes another way to study the relationships between variables that can help us answer such questions.

Formal Experiments

formal experiment Research method that allows the researcher to manipulate the independent variable to study its effect on the dependent variable.

Formal experiments are particularly helpful in reaching psychology's goals of understanding and influencing behavior. This is because, unlike other scientific methods, a carefully conducted experiment allows the researcher to draw conclusions about cause-and-effect relationships.

In formal experiments, quantitative measures of behavior are compared under different conditions that the researchers create. For example, over 30 years ago, psychologist Jean-Pierre Leyens conducted a formal experiment of the effects of viewing violent films on the behavior of adolescent boys (Leyens & others, 1975). Boys who were in a detention facility because they had been convicted of juvenile crimes participated in the study. Over several days, half of the boys were shown several violent films (Westerns and war films), and half of the boys were shown neutral films that contained no violence. Observers (who did not know which films the boys had seen) recorded every instance of verbal or physical aggression among the boys at two times during each day. As shown in figure 2.6, the boys who viewed violent films engaged in more verbal and physical aggression over the next 2 weeks than did the boys who viewed the neutral films.

Later, Wendy Josephson (1987) conducted a similar formal experiment on the effects of media violence. In this case, 400 6–8-year-old boys who had not committed juvenile crimes participated. Prior to playing floor hockey, the boys were shown films. Half of the boys were shown a highly violent film depicting a police officer being murdered by a sniper and other police officers' vengeful beating and shooting of the sniper and his accomplices. The other half of the boys viewed a nonviolent film. To increase the boys' level of anger, all the boys were frustrated by being told that they would also see a "really neat" cartoon, but then the television monitor did not work. Later, when the boys played hockey, observers who did not know which film the boys had seen counted the number of acts of verbal and physical aggression. As in Leyens's study, the boys who had seen the violent film were more aggressive than were the boys who had seen the nonviolent film. Thus, the replication of Leyen's study by Josephson increases our confidence in the finding.

These formal experiments support the hypothesis that viewing media violence *causes* real-life violence (at least in boys, who, unfortunately, have been studied more than girls). Does this surprise you? After all, most college students have been exposed to a lot of media violence, but most have never committed a violent act. If media violence causes real-life violence, why hasn't it turned you into a violent criminal? In both the Leyen and Josephson studies, boys were divided into two groups on the basis of their levels of aggression *prior* to the study to see if the violent films affected the aggressive boys more than the nonaggressive boys. In both studies, the effect of the violent films was stronger for boys who tended to be aggressive, suggesting that media violence does not affect everyone in the same way. Rather, media violence might exert its strongest effect on boys who are already prone to violence. Over the years, many other formal experiments have been conducted on this topic almost always supporting the hypothesis that media violence causes real-life violence to a small extent, particularly among boys with a predisposition to violence (Anderson & others, 2001, 2003, 2010; Konijn & others, 2007). As I said at the beginning of this section, though, the scientific question is only part of this issue. Many political, philosophical, legal, and economic issues greatly complicate the debate.

Elements and Logic of Formal Experiments. How are formal experiments conducted to allow us to reach conclusions about cause and effect? Every formal experiment has at least two variables. The **independent variable** is what the researcher arranges to allow a comparison of the participants' behavior under different conditions. In the case of the two experiments on media violence, the independent variable was the type of film (violent or nonviolent). It is called the *independent* variable because the researcher has independent control over it—in this example, the researcher can choose which participants are shown each film. The **dependent variable** is the measure of the specific behavior of interest that may (or may not) be related to the independent variable. In the preceding examples, the dependent variable was the amount of aggression engaged in by the boys. It is called the *dependent* variable because its quantitative value could *depend* on which condition the participant is in.

In the simplest formal experiments, one group is placed in the condition that is hypothesized to influence the behavior of the participants (watches the violent film, in this case), and it is called the **experimental group.** A second group receives none of the supposedly "active" condition of the independent variable (watches a film containing no violence) and is called the **control group.** If the behavior of the participants in the experimental group differs from the behavior of the participants in the control group, the hypothesis that differences in the independent variable cause differences in the dependent variable is supported, but under only two circumstances:

1. Formal experiments are valid only when the participants are *randomly* assigned to the experimental or the control group. The experimenter must follow a random procedure, such as putting the names of all participants in a hat and drawing the names of the participants in the two groups without looking. If the researcher uses a method of assigning participants to the experimental and control groups that is not random, the experiment is invalid. For example, if boys were shown a violent film and girls were shown a nonviolent film, the researcher could not know if any differences in the behavior of the participants in the two groups were due to the violence

independent variable Variable whose quantitative value is independently controlled by the researcher.

dependent variable Variable whose quantitative value is expected to depend on the effects of the independent variable.

experimental group Group in an experiment that receives some value of the independent variable.

control group Group in simple experiments that is not exposed to any level of the independent variable and is used for comparisons with the treatment group.

random assignment Requirement that participants be assigned randomly to experimental conditions in formal experiments rather than in a systematic way.

experimental control Requirement that all explanations for differences in the dependent variable are controlled in formal experiments, except for differences in conditions of the independent variable.

in the films or the sex of the participants. Hence, formal experiments require **random assignment** to experimental conditions to roughly equalize the groups on all factors except the independent variable.

2. Formal experiments are valid only if all alternative explanations for the findings have been ruled out through strict **experimental control.** For example, in both of the formal experiments on media violence, both groups of boys were shown a film. If half the boys had been shown a violent film and half the boys had been shown no film at all, the unlikely possibility that watching *any* type of film causes increased aggression could not be ruled out. The boys in the control group had to be shown some kind of (nonviolent) film to rule out this alternative. In similar ways, all alternative explanations must be ruled out. For example, if the violent film had been shown in the morning and the nonviolent film had been shown in the afternoon, the researchers wouldn't know for sure if the violent content of the film or the time of day was important. All alternative explanations must be controlled in formal experiments to be sure that differences in the *dependent variable* between groups can be traced to just one factor—the *independent variable.* Look at figure 2.7 to review these important concepts in research.

Figure 2.7   Steps in conducting a formal experiment.

First **randomly select** a group of potential participants from the full population of interest and ask them to give informed consent to participate.

Randomly assign the participants to the experimental group and the control group.

Expose the two groups of participants to different conditions of the **independent variable. Control** other factors to keep the conditions of the two groups the same except for the independent variable.

Measure the **dependent variable** (in this example, violent behavior by the participants) to see if the groups differ.

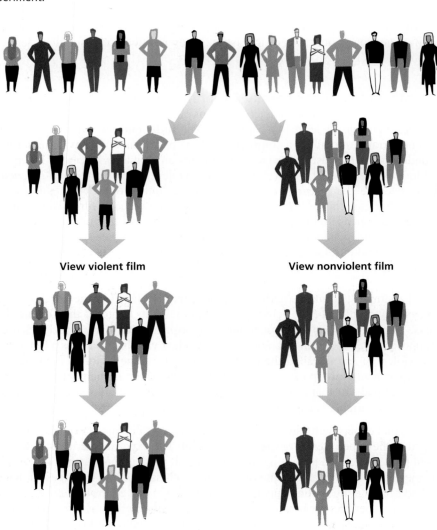

View violent film   View nonviolent film

Experimental group   Control group

Placebo Control in Formal Experiments. In this section, we focus on a type of experimental control that is important in psychological research. The simplest example of this type of control is in studies of medications. Suppose that after graduation you take a job with a pharmaceutical firm and want to test a new medication for the treatment of anxiety. You might conduct a formal experiment by randomly assigning participants, all of whom have high levels of chronic anxiety, to two groups. The experimental group would receive the medication each day for 5 days, and the control group would not receive the medication. On each of the 5 days, the participants would fill out a questionnaire on their anxiety symptoms. The hypothesis that you are testing is that the participants who receive the medication will show greater reductions in anxiety over the 5 days than will the participants who do not receive the medication.

Researchers have known for many years, however, that this kind of formal experiment does not yield valid findings. The problem is that many people who are given pills often feel better even when the pills contain no active ingredients. This is known as the **placebo effect.** To control the placebo effect in medication studies, participants in the control group are always given *placebo pills,* which are pills that are exactly like the active medication, but contain no active ingredients.

> **placebo effect** Changes in behavior produced by a condition in a formal experiment thought to be inert or inactive, such as an inactive pill.

Placebo effects are not restricted to pills, however. Suppose you take a job as a research assistant in a study of the effectiveness of a type of psychotherapy for treating fear of elevators. The method of psychotherapy involves the therapist going with the participants as they first walk up to an open elevator, then walk on and off the elevator, then ride up one floor in the elevator, and so on. If the experimental group is given this form of psychotherapy, the control group must be given some kind of "placebo" psychotherapy. In this case, the control group members would meet with a therapist and talk about their fears in a way that *seems* like psychotherapy but lacks the "active ingredient" of actually getting into elevators and riding them. In other words, the placebo is not effective psychotherapy, but it would *seem* like psychotherapy to the participants. If this were not done, it would be impossible to know if the improvements in anxiety in the experimental group were the result of the exposure to elevators or of just participating in something that *seems* like psychotherapy. In general, researchers must always create conditions in the experimental and the control groups that are as identical as possible, except for the active ingredient, which is the independent variable. This is the only way that valid conclusions can be reached about the causal effects of the independent variable on the dependent variable.

Blind Formal Experiments. Let's return to the example of formal experiments on the effects of media violence. Did you notice that the persons who rated the aggressiveness of the boys in the experimental and control groups did not know which boys were in which group? This is called a **blind experiment,** because the researchers recording the data (the dependent variable) did not know which participants had received which condition of the independent variable. Experimenters who measure the dependent variable are kept "blind" to rule out two factors that could contaminate the experiment:

> **blind experiment** Formal experiment in which the researcher who measures the dependent variable does not know which participants are in the experimental group or the control group. In double-blind experiments, the participants also do not know if they are in the experimental or the control group.

1. Researchers are kept blind to avoid their unintentionally recording the data in a way that would favor their hypothesis. In the studies of media violence, the researchers who rated boys on their verbal and physical aggression might be more likely to decide erroneously that ambiguous behaviors were aggressive among boys who they knew had seen the violent films—even if they did know they were doing so.

2. Researchers also are kept blind to rule out the possibility of **experimenter bias.** A number of studies show that researchers who are not blind can behave differently toward participants in the experimental and the control groups in ways that subtly but powerfully influence their behavior (Basoglu & others, 1997).

> **experimenter bias** Subtle but potentially powerful unintentional influences on the dependent variable caused by experimenters' interacting differently with participants in the experimental and the control groups.

Table 2.1   Comparison of Different Methods of Research in Psychology

Research Method	What Is Done?	What Are the Advantages?	What Are the Disadvantages?
Survey Method	Ask questions to a representative sample of persons	Relatively quick and inexpensive way to describe attitudes and behavior	Difficult to obtain truly representative sample; answers are not always truthful; subtle things like how questions are worded can influence results
Naturalistic Observation	Observe behavior in everyday life settings	Inexpensive and easy way to describe patterns of behavior	Cannot reach conclusions about causes and effects
Clinical Method	Observe behavior of people receiving therapy	Inexpensive and easy way to describe patterns of behavior	Cannot reach conclusions about causes and effects
Correlational Studies	Determine strength and direction of relations between variables	Useful way to determine what things are related to behavior and mental processes	Cannot reach conclusions about causes and effects
Formal Experiments	Randomly assign persons to different conditions to determine if the behavior or mental process is different in each condition	Can sometimes reach conclusions about cause and effect	Often complicated and expensive to conduct

The strongest formal experiments are *double blind.* This means that neither the researchers who measure the dependent variable nor the participants know who is in the experimental group and who is in the control group. In a later section, we discuss ethical limits on keeping research participants blind to their condition in some studies. In these two ways, "blind" experiments help researchers "see" what is going on. In research, blind is better.

See table 2.1 for a comparison of various methods of research in psychology that we have covered in this section. We revisit these ideas again in the *Application of Psychology* section at the end of this chapter.

Describing and Interpreting Data

Psychologists use the mathematical tool of *statistics* to help them describe the results of studies and to reach sensible conclusions based on the results.

Descriptive Statistics. The findings of most research studies are described in quantitative (numerical) terms. Because most studies involve many participants, it is impractical to present the numerical results for each participant. Instead, numerical results for large groups of people are almost always *summarized* using **descriptive statistics.** For example, in figure 2.8 data on the ages at which different mothers gave birth to their first child from a large study are presented from youngest to oldest. The findings are lined up horizontally according to the mother's age at the time of her first birth. The percentage of mothers who first gave birth at each age is shown by the vertical bar at that age. If we add up all the ages at which the mothers first gave birth and divide the total by the number of mothers, we find that the **mean** (or *average*) age of first giving birth was 26 years. If we start on the left side of the figure and add up the percentage of mothers who gave birth at each age, we find that half the mothers gave birth on or before age 26 years. This point is called the **median.** When a set of numbers is lined up from smallest to largest the median is middle point (the 50th percentile). The shape of the data in figure 2.8 happens to be fairly symmetrical, or balanced, with about equal numbers of scores on each side of the mean. The data in figure 2.8 roughly

descriptive statistics Statistics such as the mean and standard deviation that summarize the numerical results of studies.

mean The average of a set of scores.

median The middle of a set of scores that are ordered from smallest to largest where 50% have higher and 50% have lower scores.

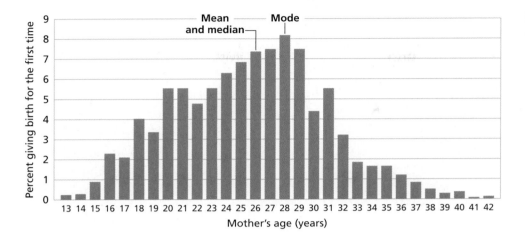

Figure 2.8
An illustration of descriptive statistics.

resemble what statisticians call a **normal distribution,** or a bell-shaped curve. If the scores were spread more evenly and were more closely bunched together around the mean, it would be a true normal distribution. When scores in studies are arranged from smallest to largest in this way, they often resemble normal distributions. Statisticians have used this fact as the basis for many statistical methods.

Another descriptive statistic that describes a distribution of scores is the **mode.** This is the most common score in a set of scores. Figure 2.8 shows that more women gave birth at age 28 than at any other age. So the most common (or *modal*) age at which women gave birth was 2 years older than the mean age and the median age.

Although the ordered distribution of ages at first birth in figure 2.8 is relatively symmetrical, the distribution of ages is quite spread out from the mean. This is significant, because the mean accurately represents more people in the sample when scores are tightly bunched around the mean—because more persons have scores *near* the mean. The degree to which scores in an ordered distribution are spread out is summarized using the **standard deviation.** The standard deviation of the ages of first birth is 5 years. This tells us that approximately two-thirds of the women gave birth in the range of 5 years above, or 5 years below, the mean of 26 years. That is, about two-thirds of the women first gave birth in the range of 19 through 31 years. That is a large span of ages! Knowing that the standard deviation is large tells us that many women gave birth at ages that were considerably younger or older than the mean.

Distributions of scores in psychological studies are often more complicated than in figure 2.8, however. Consider another finding from the same study: The 9- to 17-year-old children of these mothers were asked about the total number of different kinds of fears or anxieties they experienced during the last 6 months. This distribution of these anxiety scores is shown in figure 2.9 (p. 38). This distribution of anxiety scores is not symmetrical at all, so the mean, the median, and the mode are quite far apart.

The mode (the most common number of anxiety experiences) was 0 in this case. The median was 4, meaning that half the sample had 4 or fewer anxious experiences and half reported 4 or more anxious experiences. The mean number of anxious experiences was still higher at 6. This is because the mean is inflated by the very high anxiety scores of a small number of youth. Because the mean reflects the average of *all* scores, it can be strongly influenced by the presence of a *few* persons with extremely high (or low) scores. In this example, the mode (the most common number of anxious moments) and the median (the middle of the distribution of scores ordered from smallest to largest) provide better summaries of the number of anxious experiences than does the mean.

normal distribution Symmetrical pattern of scores on a scale in which a majority of the scores are clustered near the center and a minority are at the extremes.

mode The most common score in a set of scores.

standard deviation Mathematical measure of how spread out scores are from the mean score.

Descriptive Statistics in Everyday Life.
We are frequently called on to make decisions based on descriptive statistics, so it is essential to understand them. When I was a senior in college, the new governor of my state made a televised speech. He was

Figure 2.9
Number of anxiety experiences.

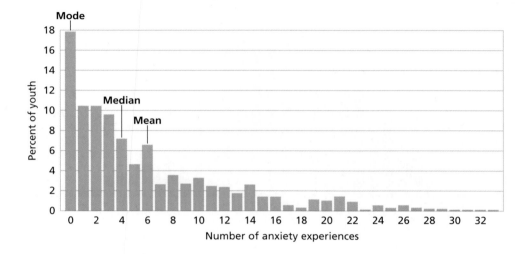

upset to learn that 50% of the graduating high school seniors failed the entrance test to state universities. He concluded that the state's high schools were doing a poor job of preparing students for college entrance. Was he right? What he did not understand was that the passing score for the test was set every year at the *median* of the scores for students taking the test, regardless of how many questions were answered correctly. When the passing score on a test is defined by the median score, by definition only 50% will pass each year. I often wondered if anyone took the governor aside after that broadcast and explained his error to him. When you're elected governor, that's one mistake you won't make.

Assume, though, that instead of going into politics, you become president of an automobile company that has developed an automobile that creates no air pollution. You want to sell as many cars in Los Angeles as you can to relieve the smog. You do some research and learn that the average new car buyer in California wants a car that will seat 4⅓ persons. How many people should you design your new car to hold? Since no family actually has ⅓ of a person in it, what do you do? In this case, the relevant descriptive statistic is the mode, not the mean. If the largest number of new car buyers—say 75%—wants a car that holds 4 persons, you might sell more cars if the model holds 4 persons.

Reaching Conclusions from Data. Suppose that a study finds a correlation coefficient between a measure of stress and blood pressure of +.40. Another study tells us that the mean score on a measure of depression of persons who have gone through a new type of psychotherapy is 22, compared to a mean of 26 for persons who had the usual type of psychotherapy. If these studies were perfectly designed and controlled, do their findings mean that stress is related to blood pressure and that the new therapy works better? In statistical terms, the question is whether the correlation and the difference between the means have **statistical significance.** This tells us if the magnitude of the correlation and the difference between the means are greater than would be expected by chance. Usually, if the finding would be expected by chance fewer than 5 times out of 100 studies, the finding is said to be statistically significant. This is an arbitrary standard, but it allows all researchers to make such decisions on the same basis. Two important issues to always keep in mind when interpreting tests of statistical significance are these:

statistical significance Decision based on statistical calculations that a finding was unlikely to have occurred by chance.

1. The same correlation or difference between means is more likely to be statistically significant when the size of the sample of persons in the study

is larger. This is logical, because it is less likely that an odd chance finding would be found in a large study than in a small study, but it means that a small study can fail to find a statistically significant result even when the hypothesis is correct.

2. Statistical significance does not equal *practical* significance. It is possible that a small difference between means could be statistically significant in a very large study, but the size of the difference is so small that the result is of little practical use.

Statistical significance is important, but it needs to be considered with good common sense. For a more detailed discussion of these and related topics, see the appendix about statistics at the end of the book.

Review

Psychology is a science, which simply means that it uses scientific methods to gather information and test hypotheses. Psychologists acquire new evidence through systematic observation and critically evaluate the evidence. All scientific methods are based on the assumption that behavior is lawful, orderly, and capable of being understood in scientific terms. Each scientific method has advantages and disadvantages and is best suited to answering a different type of question. The simplest scientific methods are descriptive methods. Information that allows us to describe a psychological phenomenon can be gathered by asking questions about it in surveys, by observing it in natural settings, or by acquiring extensive experience with it in clinical cases. When the scientific question concerns the relationship between two variables, correlational methods often are used. The variables are measured quantitatively, and the strength of the relationship between them is calculated. Correlational studies are useful, but they do not tell us about cause-and-effect relations between the variables.

To determine whether cause-and-effect relationships exist, formal experiments must be conducted. In formal experiments, scientists arrange conditions of the independent variable and rigorously control other aspects of the experiment, so that only one explanation for the results is likely. In the simplest experiments, one factor—the independent variable—is manipulated by the experimenter to see what effect it has on the dependent variable. Often, one group of participants—the control group—is not exposed to any level of the independent variable, whereas the experimental group is exposed to the active independent variable. In a study of the effects of alcohol on the memory of a list of words, for example, the alcohol is the independent variable. Alcohol is given to participants in the experimental group and not given to those in the control group, so its effects on the dependent variable, memory of the list, can be determined. In such a study, both groups of participants would need to be given drinks that look, taste, and smell identical, except that one contains alcohol and the other does not, to rule out placebo effects. In double-blind studies, neither the participants nor the researchers who measure the dependent variable know which condition of the independent variable each participant receives. The results of studies are often summarized using descriptive statistics. These include the mean, the median, the mode, and the standard deviation. Psychologists use statistical methods to determine if a correlation or a difference between two means is statistically significant (was very unlikely to have occurred by chance). Because statistical significance is influenced by the size of the sample and does not necessarily mean that the finding is useful, statistically significant findings should be interpreted critically.

Check Your Learning

To be sure that you have learned the key points from the preceding section, cover the list of correct answers and try to answer each question. If you give an incorrect answer to any question, return to the page given next to the correct answer to see why your answer was not correct.

1. The basis of all scientific methods is systematic and _____.

Check Your Learning (cont.)

2. A study that simply measured the strength of the quantitative relationship between intelligence scores and the number of illegal acts committed by teenagers would use which method?

   a) naturalistic   c) correlational

   b) clinical   d) formal experimental

3. The scientific method that allows the researcher to reach the strongest conclusions about cause and effect is _____.

   a) naturalistic   c) correlational

   b) clinical   d) formal experimental

4. In a double-blind study, who does not know which condition of the independent variable each participant received?

   a) the researchers who measure the dependent variable

   b) the research participants

   c) both a and b

5. The average of a set of scores found in a study is referred to as the _____.

   a) median   c) standard deviation

   b) mean   d) mode

Thinking Critically about Psychology

There are no right or wrong answers to the following questions. They are presented to help you become an active reader and think critically about what you have just read.

1. Is psychology as scientific as biology, chemistry, or other fields?

2. Are there some aspects of human behavior and mental processes that cannot be studied scientifically?

Correct Answers: 1. observation, rules of evidence (p. 25), 2. c (p. 29), 3. d (p. 32), 4. c (p. 36), 5. b (p. 36)

Ethical Principles of Research

Psychological research is conducted to advance knowledge and to improve the lives of all living things. It is a noble goal, but not so noble that any method of conducting research is justifiable. To be considered ethical, research conducted with people and with nonhuman animals must follow strict ethical principles.

Ethics of Research with Human Participants

Researchers have an obligation to protect the welfare of their participants. Research on humans is considered ethical only under the following five conditions:

1. *Freedom from coercion.* People cannot be coerced or pressured into participating in an experiment. Students in college courses, for example, cannot be required to participate. They must be given an alternative way to meet any course requirement. Similarly, in parole hearings it is unethical to offer special consideration to prisoners who volunteered to participate in psychological studies, because the promise of special considerations might coerce them into participating in a study that they would not otherwise choose. Furthermore, once the experiment has begun, participants must be informed that they are fully free to change their minds and withdraw from the experiment without penalty, such as embarrassment or loss of course credit.

2. *Informed consent.* The experimenter must, under most circumstances, give potential participants a full description of the procedures of the study and its risks and benefits in language they can understand before they are asked to participate.

3. *Limited deception.* Sometimes, however, it's necessary to conduct experiments without the participant's knowing the true purpose of the study. For example, the chapter on social psychology describes a study in which individuals were asked to make judgments about the relative lengths of three lines after other individuals (actually, employees of the experimenter who were acting out parts in the experiment) had given obviously wrong answers. The question was, would the real participants give the wrong answer, too, under these conditions? Obviously, it was necessary to deceive the participants into thinking that the other individuals really believed their erroneous judgments about the lines. Is it ethical to deceive participants in this manner? Deception can be used by research only if two conditions are met. First, the potential participants must be told everything they could reasonably be expected to need to know to make an informed decision about participation. That is, the deception can involve only aspects of the study that would not influence the decision to participate. Second, the nature of the deception must be fully revealed to individuals immediately after their participation in the experiment.

4. *Adequate debriefing.* Research participants have a right to know the results of the study. If a summary of the results is not immediately available, the participants have a right to receive them when they are available.

5. *Confidentiality.* Researchers have an obligation to keep everything they learn about the research participants absolutely confidential. This means that findings from the study must be published in a way that protects the anonymity of the participants (no names or detailed descriptions of individuals). In addition, data must be stored safely to protect against future abuses of the information.

All institutions where research is conducted now require that proposals for human experimentation be approved by a board of other scientists to protect individuals from potential abuses. These are not all the ethical issues raised by psychological research with humans, but they are the major ones. A complete discussion of the ethics of research with humans can be found on the American Psychological Association's website (www.apa.org/ethics).

Ethics of Research with Nonhuman Animals

A great deal of psychological research is also carried out using nonhuman animals as subjects. Why would some psychologists study animals when they could be studying people? Some kinds of studies are conducted using nonhuman animals because it would be unethical to do the research with humans. Studies of the brain, for example, sometimes require surgically removing a part of the brain to discover its role. In addition, it's possible to conduct experiments that are far more precisely controlled if animals rather than humans are used. A researcher can know and control almost every detail of a laboratory animal's life from birth: its environment, diet, and social experiences. This makes it possible to control a multiplicity of factors that must be left uncontrolled when using humans.

A great deal also can be learned about humans by studying nonhuman animals. For example, a number of insights into human aggression have come from studies of aggression in other animal species. Similarly, much has been learned about the brain structures involved in sleep by identifying animals that have differing sleep patterns

The use of animals in research has received a great deal of public attention in recent years due to the activities of animal rights groups.

and by comparing the evolutionary development of the sleep centers in these different species. However, many psychologists study animal behavior not to learn about humans but to learn more about the animals. If we are going to protect endangered species, we must understand their patterns of behavior. We must know, for example, how an endangered species hunts, mates, and raises its young before we can help it survive.

As with human participants, a number of principles govern the ethical conduct of research with nonhuman animal subjects in psychology. Research with animals is considered ethical by the American Psychological Association only when the following conditions are met:

1. *Necessity.* Studies of nonhuman animals are considered to be ethical only when they are necessary to significantly advance the understanding of human or animal behavior and mental processes.

2. *Health.* All animal subjects must be cared for in a manner that ensures their health.

3. *Humane treatment.* Every effort must be made to minimize the discomfort of the animal subject. Necessary surgery must be performed under anesthesia, and the animal's death must be as painless as possible. Studies that inflict pain or stress are ethical only when they are essential to worthwhile scientific aims.

The use of nonhuman animals in research has received a great deal of public attention in recent years owing to the activities of animal rights groups. However, humans have long been concerned with the protection of their fellow animals. For example, the Society for the Prevention of Cruelty to Animals was founded in 1824 in London, and the American Psychological Association formed its Committee on Precautions in Animal Experimentation in 1925 (Dewsbury, 1990). Today, oversight committees at all research universities closely monitor all uses of laboratory animals.

Human Diversity
Equal Representation in Research

The U.S. National Institutes of Health now require that all new research grants involving human subjects must study diverse samples that include both sexes and members of the major racial and cultural groups. There are necessary exceptions to this rule, such as not requiring participants of both sexes when studying a disease that is found only in one sex, such as cancer of the ovaries. The rule requires diverse samples for most studies, however.

Why is this important? The primary reason is that we do not presently know how many findings based on one group apply to other groups. Would a treatment for alcohol abuse that was found to be effective for men also work for women? It might or *might not.* The new rule requiring diverse samples ends decades of research conducted mostly by white men using white men as research participants. No one knows how many sex differences or cultural differences in key research findings will be discovered, but this new rule will finally allow us to find out.

Review

Although psychological research is important, the rights of research participants must be protected. Human research participants must not be coerced into participating and must be informed about the nature of the study before they are asked for their consent to participate. Human research participants may be deceived about a study only if (1) the information withheld is not relevant to their decision to participate and (2) they are informed about the true nature of the study immediately after it's over. Furthermore, the experimenter must keep all information learned about human research participants confidential.

Review (cont.)

Research with nonhuman animals is considered to be ethical only when (1) the research is necessary, (2) the health of the animals is protected, and (3) pain and suffering are minimized. Diverse samples are required to ensure that research findings apply to every group.

Check Your Learning

To be sure that you have learned the key points from the preceding section, cover the list of correct answers and try to answer each question. If you give an incorrect answer to any question, return to the page given next to the correct answer to see why your answer was not correct.

1. Research on humans is considered to be ethical only when the following five conditions are met:

   a) _____,

   b) _____,

   c) _____,

   d) _____,

   e) _____.

2. Research with nonhuman animals is considered to be ethical only when the following three conditions are met:

   a) _____,

   b) _____,

   c) _____.

Thinking Critically about Psychology

There are no right or wrong answers to the following questions. They are presented to help you become an active reader and think critically about what you have just read.

1. Although research on nonhuman animals has produced many findings that are beneficial to humans, not everyone agrees that it should be allowed. How do you think we should balance the welfare of animals against benefits to human society?

2. Are there some aspects of human behavior and mental processes that would not be ethical to study even if the participants freely consented to be studied?

Correct Answers: 1. freedom from coercion, informed consent, limited deception, adequate debriefing, and confidentiality (p. 40–41), **2.** the research is necessary, the health of the animal is protected, pain and suffering are minimized (p. 41–42)

Application of Psychology

Design Your Own Formal Experiment

Now that we have gone over the basic principles of scientific research in psychology, it's time for *you* to be the researcher. After I suggest a research question, you will design a formal experiment to answer that question. To help you along, I will pose a series of questions. I hope this will be fun and give you a chance to review what you have just learned in a new context. Because books do not allow for much interaction between the author and the reader, I will guide you more than I would ordinarily do. I hope, however, that you will think about each question on your own before you read my suggested answers.

Here is the topic for your study: For a long time, psychologists have thought that the simple act of telling someone about your private worries, disappointments, and agonies makes you feel better. In general, it often seems to help get negative feelings off your chest, whether you are venting your emotions to a friend, a relative, or a therapist.* More recently, psychologists have suspected that expressing your negative emotions can even improve your physical health. So here is the general hypothesis for your study: *Expressing negative emotions improves a person's physical health over the next 6 months.*

Who Will Your Research Participants Be?   For the conclusions of a study to be valid, a sample of subjects needs to be selected that is representative of some meaningful population of human beings. Because you are a student and have limited financial resources for conducting this study, you probably are going to use introductory psychology students as your participants. This means that you cannot be certain that your findings apply to anyone other than introductory psychology students at similar schools. What should you do to ensure the representativeness of your sample? For starters, select a sample that is typical in terms of the sex, age, race, and ethnic composition of college students in your school.

What Is the Independent Variable?   You are designing a study to test the hypothesis that expressing negative emotions improves physical health, so the independent variable is whether or not a person expresses negative emotions. How could you arrange the conditions of this independent variable? Take a moment to imagine how you would do it if you were really designing this formal experiment.

One reasonable experimental approach would be to ask half of the participants to express their feelings about the *saddest* thing that ever happened to them. This would be the *experimental group,* because the active condition of the independent variable is expressing negative feelings. The other half of the participants would be asked to describe the architecture of the buildings at their college. This would be the *control group,* because they do not express their negative emotions (unless the buildings at your school are really ugly). In this way, you could independently arrange for some participants to talk about their negative emotions and for other participants to talk about something else.

To protect everyone's confidentiality, you could ask all the participants to write a letter to someone they know. In this way, they could express their emotions (or describe the buildings) in a way that you do not hear. You could even ask them to destroy the letters at the end so there is no risk that your research participants would reveal some hidden feelings that they later wished they had kept private. The idea is to have half of the participants *express* their negative feelings, even if no one actually reads the letters. There are stronger ways of arranging this independent variable (you could actually have each person speak to a therapist a number of times), but writing this kind of letter can lead to some pretty intense emotional expression.

What Is the Dependent Variable?   Your study will test the hypothesis that expressing negative emotions improves physical health, so the physical health of the participants is the dependent variable. If you ask the research participants to write the letters during the fall, you could measure their health over the next 6 months. How do you want to measure their physical health? That is, what will your operational definition of health be? Please think about it for a moment.

If you had a large research grant, you could draw blood samples every month and directly measure each participant's immune system. Let's assume that you are doing this study on a shoestring budget, however, and can ask the participants only each month if they have had a cold or the flu during the past month. Then your quantitative dependent variable is the number of months in which each participant had a cold or the flu. Now you can make your hypothesis more specific: Writing a letter that expresses your emotions about the worst thing that had ever happened to you reduces your number of colds and the flu over 6 months relative to persons who wrote a letter not on their emotions.

How Do You Decide Which Participants Will Be in the Experimental or Control Groups?   Randomly! Remember that formal experiments allow valid conclusions only if the participants are *randomly assigned* to the different conditions of the independent variable. If you were to ask the students sitting in the front half of the classroom to express their negative emotions and the students sitting in the back half of the classroom to write neutral letters, the two groups of students might differ in a systematic way. It is possible that students with better health tend to sit in the front (or the back). If so, this would invalidate your experiment, because the health of the participants in the experimental and the control groups would differ prior to the start of the study. Therefore, you will need to do something like assigning an identification number to every participant and then using a computer to randomly assign each participant to one of the two groups.

What Kinds of Experimental Control Should You Use?
So far you have designed a formal experiment in which the participants will be randomly assigned to the conditions of the

---

*Of course, we always have to balance the benefits of expressing our negative feelings against the risks of hurting other people's feelings and alienating ourselves from friends and family members. There is a right time and situation for almost everything.

independent variable, and you have treated them all in the same way, except for the independent variable. The only way in which your procedures are different for the two groups is that one group will write letters that will evoke negative emotions and the other group will write letters that should contain much less negative emotion. What else should you control to rule out alternative explanations for any differences between the groups? Consider that question for a moment.

Because you will ask the participants in the two groups to write letters about different topics, you cannot have both groups of participants in the same room at the same time. If you separate the groups and have them write their letters in different rooms, what should you control? Would it be okay to have a female research assistant give the instructions to the participants writing about their negative emotions while a male gives the instructions for the architecture letter in another room? Is it okay to have one group in a cheerful, well-lighted room and the other group in a cold, messy, dim room? If you treat the participants in the two groups differently in any way, you will not reach valid conclusions. Maybe the participants who wrote their letters in the cold, messy room caught colds while they were there!

Can You Make Your Study "Double Blind"? Recall
what it means for a study to be double blind. In a double-blind experiment, neither the participants nor the researchers who measure the dependent variable know which participants received which condition of the independent variable. This is the same as saying that they do not know which participants were in the experimental or the control group. It would be an easy matter to keep the researchers who measure the dependent variable (ask the questions about having colds or the flu, in this case) unaware of which participants were in the experimental and control groups.

It is not clear that you could keep the participants completely unaware of who was in the experimental and the control groups. You would not tell them, of course, what your hypothesis is, but each participant would know if he or she wrote a letter about negative feelings or not. When you obtained informed consent from the participants who volunteered for the study, you could tell them that you were studying the relationship between "communicating with others about different topics through letters and physical health." It is possible that some of the participants who wrote about their emotions would guess the hypothesis from this information. Why is that a problem? If the experimental group that wrote letters about negative emotions reported fewer colds and flu over the next 6 months, that might be because the participants who guessed your hypothesis might intentionally or unintentionally tell you about fewer colds because they think that is what you want to hear. Alternatively, they might think your hypothesis is correct and intentionally or unintentionally remember fewer colds because they expect to be healthier. You would have to weigh this possibility carefully when interpreting your results and would need to continue thinking of better ways to control such alternative explanations in future experiments.

Formal Experiments Outside the Laboratory We have
gone through this exercise both to review the logic and concepts of formal experiments that you have just learned and to give you the experience of thinking through the logic of an experiment yourself. Formal experiments are not something that only professional researchers can perform. You can use the powerful logic of formal experiments to answer questions in business, education, government, and other areas that affect human beings. For example, if you want to know which of two methods of manufacturing a product will create less pollution and fewer defective products, don't *guess*—conduct a formal experiment. In the long run, it may be much wiser to compare the two methods in a formal experiment than to make a bad decision based on inadequate information. Similarly, it is not difficult for governments to conduct formal experiments that compare alternatives to housing the homeless, increasing the use of public transportation, or recycling waste. Formal experiments are just ways of using observation and critical thinking to answer important questions—and there are plenty of important questions in the real world that need good answers.

Summary

Chapter 2 describes the scientific methods that psychologists use to move beyond mere speculation about human behavior and mental processes.

I. The scientific method is to make systematic observations following rules for obtaining and using evidence to answer questions.

II. Psychologists use two major types of scientific methods to study human behavior and mental processes—descriptive methods and formal experiments.

    A. Descriptive methods allow researchers to study people as they live their lives.

1. Surveys are a descriptive method that involves asking questions of groups of persons who are representative of the entire population.

2. Naturalistic observation involves unobtrusive observations of behavior in real-life settings.

3. The clinical method involves observing people when they are receiving help from a mental health professional for psychological problems.

4. Correlational methods are used to describe systematic relations between quantitatively measured variables in statistical terms.

a. The correlation coefficient provides a standard mathematical method of measuring the strength of the relationship between two variables.

b. Like other descriptive methods of research, the correlational method does not allow researchers to reach conclusions about cause-and-effect relations between the variables studied. Correlation does not necessarily imply causation.

B. **Formal experiments often can be used to reach conclusions about cause-and-effect relationships between variables.**

1. In formal experiments, the independent variable is the one that the researcher independently arranges to see if different conditions of the independent variable have different effects on the dependent variable (usually the behavior or mental processes of the participants in the study).

2. Unlike descriptive methods of research, formal experiments involve arranging the conditions of the independent variable to study its effects on the dependent variable and carefully controlling other extraneous factors. In formal experiments, a key method of controlling alternative explanations for differences in the dependent variable is random assignment of participants to the various conditions of the independent variable (to reduce the likelihood that the participants in different groups do not differ from one another systematically in other ways).

3. In some types of experiments, placebo control is used to keep research participants unaware of which condition of the independent variable they are receiving. For example, in a study of a medication, half of the participants might receive a pill containing the active ingredient and half of the participants would receive a placebo pill that is identical in every way except it does not contain the active ingredient.

4. The most complete experimental control can be achieved in so-called double-blind experiments in which both the research participants and the researchers who measure the dependent variable are unaware of the condition of the independent variable that each participant is receiving.

5. The simplest kind of formal experiment involves one *experimental group,* which receives the active condition of the independent variable, and a *control group,* which receives none of the independent variable. The research can infer that differences between these groups on the dependent variable was likely caused by the independent variable when participants are randomly assigned to these two groups and stringent and complete experimental controls are used.

III. Statistics are used to describe the results of studies and to help researchers reach conclusions about their data.

A. Research findings on many participants can be summarized using the descriptive statistics of the mode, the mean, the median, and the standard deviation.

B. Tests of statistical significance are used (cautiously) to determine if correlations and differences between mean are large enough to be very unlikely to have been found by chance.

IV. Ethical research carefully protects the rights of participants in many ways.

A. Research using humans is considered to be ethical when the following conditions are met:

1. Individuals are asked to volunteer to participate without coercion.

2. Individuals are informed about the nature of the experiment before giving consent to participate.

3. Unnecessary deception of the participants is avoided, and deception is carefully regulated when required.

4. When deception is used, the true nature of the study is fully explained to the participant after the study is over.

5. All information learned about the participant is kept completely confidential.

B. Research involving nonhuman animals is considered ethical when the following conditions are met:

1. The study is necessary to understand an important issue concerning behavior and mental processes.

2. The health of the animal subjects is protected.

3. The animals are treated humanely.

chapter **three**

Biological foundations of behavior

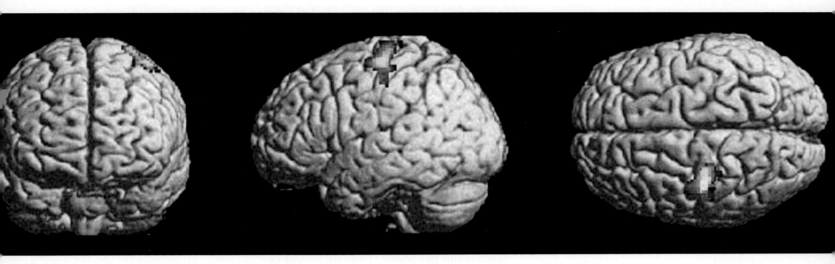

Chapter Outline

Prologue

Psychological life depends on biological life for its very existence. If humans did not have hands that grasp, we might never have learned to write, paint, or play racquetball. If we did not have eyes that could sense color, we would see a world that existed only in shades of black and white.

The brain is the part of the body most intimately linked to psychological life. A classic experiment conducted by Canadian brain surgeon Wilder Penfield in the 1930s dramatically illustrates this fact. Dr. Penfield was conducting surgery on the surface layer of the brain known as the cerebral cortex while the patient was awake under local anesthesia. When Penfield placed a small rod that carried a mild electric current against the brain, his patient experienced being in her

Key Terms

brain The complex mass of neural cells and related cells encased in the skull.

spinal cord The nerve fibers in the spinal column.

kitchen. In the background, she could hear the voice of her little boy playing in the yard and cars passing in the street. When another patient's brain was stimulated he recalled a small-town baseball game that included a boy trying to crawl under a fence. Penfield's experiment showed that the cerebral cortex is involved in our psychological experiences. This is just one of many ways in which we know that the brain and our psychological lives are intimately connected.

In this chapter, we discuss several aspects of human biology directly relevant to understanding behavior: the brain and nervous system, endocrine glands, and genetic mechanisms. We study these biological systems because we are psychological beings living in biological "machines." Just as electronic machines are built from wires, transistors, and other components, the nervous system is built from specialized cells called *neurons.* Billions of neurons in your nervous system transmit messages to one another in complex ways that make the nervous system both the "computer" and the communication network of the body. The biological control center of the nervous system is the brain. Although its many different parts carry out different functions, these parts operate together in an integrated way.

The human nervous system consists of two large parts. One part is the brain and the bundle of nerves that run through the spinal column. Because it is located within the skull and the spine at the center of the body, this part is called the *central nervous system.* The many nerves that lie outside the skull and the spine make up the second part of the nervous system. Because it reaches the periphery of the body, this part is called the *peripheral nervous system.*

The brain communicates with the body through the network of neurons that fan out to every part of the body. The brain also uses the endocrine glands to communicate with the body. These glands secrete chemical messengers, called *hormones,* that travel through the bloodstream. Hormones regulate the functions of many parts of the body and influence our behavior and experience. Hormones are powerful tools of the brain, but they influence us in diffuse rather than precise ways.

Nervous System: Biological Control Center

The nervous system is both a powerful computer and a complex communication network. Unlike a computer, however, the **brain** not only thinks and calculates but also feels and controls motivation. The brain is connected to the **spinal cord,** a thick bundle of long nerves running through the spine. Individual nerves exit or enter the spinal cord and brain, linking the brain to every part of the body. Some of these nerves carry messages from the body to the brain to inform the brain about what is going on in the body. Other nerves carry messages from the brain to regulate the body's functions and the person's behavior. Without the nervous system, the body would be a mass of uncoordinated parts that could not act, reason, or experience emotions. In other words, without a nervous system, there would be no psychological life.

Neurons: Primary Units of the Nervous System

Computers, telephone systems, and other electronic systems are made of wires, transistors, microchips, and other components that transmit and regulate electricity. The nervous system is similarly made up of components. The most important unit of the nervous system is the individual nerve cell, or **neuron.** Our discussion of the nervous system begins with the neuron and then progresses to the larger parts of the nervous system. As we discuss the neuron in biological terms, do not forget its importance to consciousness and behavior.

In the early 1900s, Santiago Ramón y Cajal, the scientist who discovered neurons, described them as "the mysterious butterflies of the soul, the beating of whose wings may someday—who knows?—clarify the secret of mental life." Since his time, much has been learned about these building blocks of the nervous system.

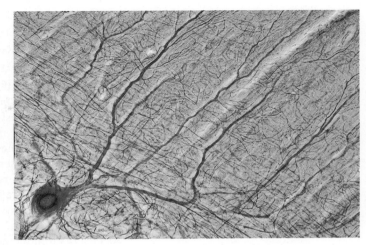

A neuron in the human brain.

Parts of Neurons. Neurons range in length from less than a millimeter to more than a meter in length, but all neurons are made up of essentially the same three parts (see figure 3.1):

1. The **cell body** contains the cell's *nucleus* and other components necessary for the cell's preservation and nourishment.

2. **Dendrites** are branches that extend out from the cell body and receive messages from other neurons. Other parts of the neuron receive messages from other neurons, but the dendrite is specialized for this purpose.

3. **Axons** are branches at the other end of the neuron that mostly carry neural messages away from the cell body and transmit them to the next neuron. It's easy to remember the difference between the functions of the dendrites and axons by remembering that the axon mostly *acts on* the next cell, but there is a catch. Although we long believed that neural transmission always flowed

neuron (nuron) Individual nerve cell.

cell body The central part of the neuron that includes the nucleus.

dendrites (den´drīts) Extensions of the cell body that usually serve as receiving areas for messages from other neurons.

axons (ak´sonz) Neuron branches that transmit messages to other neurons.

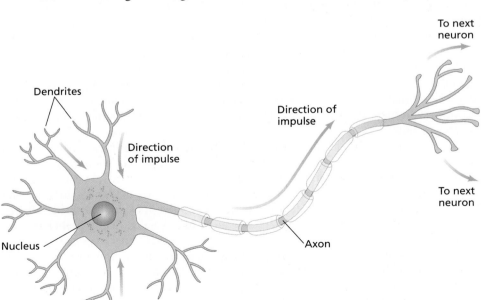

Dendrites

Direction of impulse

Direction of impulse

To next neuron

To next neuron

Nucleus

Axon

Figure 3.1

Neurons are typically composed of a cell body, which contains the nucleus of the cell, dendrites that typically receive impulses from other neurons, and an axon that passes the neural impulse on to the next neuron.

from dendrite to axon to the next neuron's dendrite, recent research has demonstrated that some neurons can carry messages in the opposite direction, from axon to dendrite (Bullock & others, 2005). The more we study the nervous system, the more complicated we realize it is.

Neurons are grouped in complex networks that make the largest computer seem like a child's toy. The human nervous system is composed of 100 billion neurons (Kandel, Schwartz, & Jessel 1995), about as many as the number of stars in our galaxy. Each neuron can receive messages from or transmit messages to 1,000 to 10,000 other neural cells. All told, your body contains trillions of neural connections, most of them in the brain. These numbers are not important in their own right, but they help us understand the incredibly rich network of neural interconnections that makes us humans.

Incidentally, be careful not to confuse the term *neuron* with the term **nerve.** A nerve is a bundle of many long neurons—sometimes thousands of them—outside the brain and spinal cord.

As described in the next two sections of this chapter, neurons transmit messages in the nervous system in two steps: (1) the transmission of the message from one end of the neuron to the other end (neural transmission), and (2) transmission from one neuron to the next neuron (synaptic transmission).

Neural Transmission. Neurons are the "wires" of the nervous system—messages are transmitted over the neuron much as your voice is transmitted over a telephone line. But neurons are *living wires,* with their own built-in supplies of electrical power. They are the "batteries" that power the nervous system, too.

Neurons can take on the functions of wires and batteries, because, like all living cells, they are *wet.* Neurons are sacs filled with one type of fluid on the inside and bathed in a different type of fluid on the outside. These fluids are "soups" of dissolved chemicals, including **ions,** the particles that carry either a positive or a negative electrical charge. More of the ions inside neurons are negatively rather than positively charged, making the overall charge of the cell a negative one. This negative charge attracts positively charged ions to the outside of the neuron, just as the negative pole of a magnet attracts the positive pole of another magnet. Thus, the outside of the cell membrane becomes cloaked in positive ions, particularly sodium ($Na+$). When neurons are in a resting state, there are 10 times as many positively charged sodium ions outside the membrane of the neuron than inside. This is the source of the neuron's electrical power—it is electrically positive on one side of the membrane and negative on the other.

If you have trouble remembering which side of the membrane has most of the positive sodium ions, remember that there is a lot of sodium in salty seawater. The fluid on the *outside* of neurons is very similar to seawater in its chemical contents, including the high amounts of sodium. Why is this so? According to the theory of evolution, as animals evolved and moved from the oceans onto the land, they brought the seawater with them *in their bodies.* This seawater-like liquid fills the space between the body's cells.

Many ions are able to move freely through the **cell membrane** of the neuron, but other ions, such as sodium ions, cannot. For this reason, the membrane is said to be **semipermeable** in its normal resting state—only some chemicals can permeate, or pass through, "holes" in the membrane. Therefore, a balance exists between the mostly negative ions on the inside and the mostly positive ions on the outside. Therefore, when neurons are in a resting state they are said to be electrically **polarized** (see figure 3.2).

When the membrane is stimulated by an adjacent neuron, however, the semipermeability of the neural membrane is lost for an instant. Positively charged ions, including the important sodium ions, rush into the neuron. This process is called **depolarization,** because the neuron is no longer mostly negative on the inside.

Depolarization creates the dramatic chain of events known as an **action potential** (Bean, 2007). During an action potential, a small section of the axon adjacent to the

nerve Bundle of long neurons outside the brain and spinal cord.

ions (i´ons) Electrically charged particles.

cell membrane The covering of a neuron or another cell.

semipermeable
(sem´´ē-peŕ-mē-ah-b´l) Surface that allows some, but not all, particles to pass through.

polarized (pō´lar-īz´d) Resting state of a neuron, when more negative ions are inside and more positive ions are outside the cell membrane.

depolarization Process during which positively charged ions flow into the axon, making it less negatively charged inside.

action potential Brief electrical signal that travels the length of the axon.

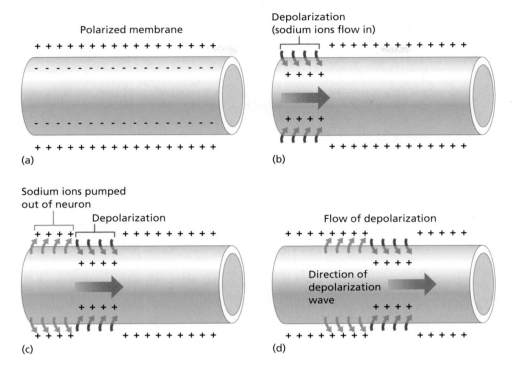

Polarized membrane

Depolarization
(sodium ions flow in)

(a)

(b)

Sodium ions pumped
out of neuron

Depolarization

Flow of depolarization

Direction of
depolarization
wave

(c)

(d)

Figure 3.2
Short sections of an axon illustrating neural transmission (an action potential). (a) When an axon is in its resting state, the number of positively and negatively charged ions along the membrane are in balance. (b) When the axon is sufficiently stimulated, the membrane allows positively charged sodium ions to pass into the cell, depolarizing that spot on the membrane. (c) This depolarization disturbs the adjacent section of the membrane, allowing sodium ions to flow in again while sodium ions are being pumped back out of the first section. (d) This process continues as the swirling storm of depolarization continues to the end of the axon.

cell body becomes more permeable to the positive sodium ions. Sodium ions rush in, producing a depolarization in that part of the axon. However, the membrane quickly regains its semipermeability and "pumps" the positive sodium ions back out, reestablishing its polarization. But this tiny electrical storm of sodium ions flowing in and out of the neuron—which lasts approximately one-thousandth of a second—does not stop there. It disturbs the adjacent section of the membrane of the axon, so that it depolarizes, which in turn disturbs the next section of the membrane, and so on. Thus, the action potential—the flowing storm of ions rushing in and out—travels the length of the axon. By the way, local anesthetics, such as the ones that dentists inject, stop pain by chemically interrupting this flowing process of depolarization in the axons of nerves that carry pain messages to the brain.

Ramón y Cajal believed that neural transmission always operated according to the **all-or-none principle.** This means he thought that neurons transmitted signals to other neurons only when depolarization was strong enough to trigger an action potential. He further believed that all action potentials are all the same once they get started. This idea dominated neuroscience for 100 years, but it is now known that neurons often transmit messages through *graded electrical potentials* that vary in magnitude (Bullock & others, 2005).

all-or-none principle Law that states that once a neural action potential is produced, its magnitude is always the same.

Myelin Sheath and Neural Transmission. Many axons are encased in a white, fatty coating called the **myelin sheath.** Wrapped around the axon like the layers of a jelly roll, this sheath insulates the axon and greatly increases the speed at which the axon conducts neural impulses (see figure 3.3 on p. 52). The myelin sheath continues to grow in thickness into late adulthood. Interestingly, from early childhood to late adulthood, the average thickness of myelin is greater in females than in males in some areas of the brain (Benes, 1998). This may indicate more efficient neural processing of some kinds of information by females. Sadly, the importance of the myelin sheath in neural transmission can be seen in victims of multiple sclerosis. This disease destroys the myelin sheath of many neurons, leaving them unable to operate at normal efficiency. As a result, individuals with multiple sclerosis have severe difficulties controlling their muscles; experience fatigue, dizziness, and pain; and suffer serious cognitive and vision problems (Morell & Norton, 1980).

myelin sheath (mī´ e-lin) Insulating fatty covering wrapped around the axon that speeds the transmission of neural messages.

Figure 3.3

Many neurons are wrapped like a jelly roll in a white, fatty substance called myelin. The myelin sheath insulates the axon and speeds neural transmission.

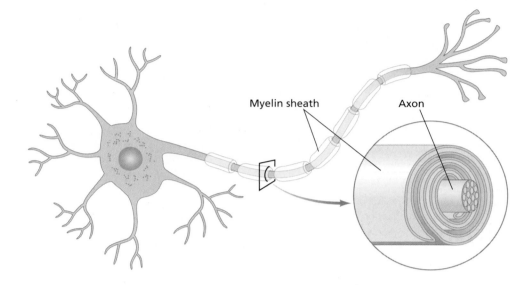

Myelin sheath   Axon

synapse (sin-aps´) Space between the axon of one neuron and another neuron.

synaptic gap The small space between two neurons at a synapse.

neurotransmitters (nu´rō-tranz´-mit-erz) Chemical substances, produced by axons, that transmit messages across the synapse.

synaptic vesicles Tiny vessels containing stored quantities of the neurotransmitter substance held in the synaptic terminals of the axon.

synaptic terminal (si-nap´tik) The knoblike tips of axons.

receptor sites Sites on the neuron that receive the neurotransmitter substance.

glial cells (glee-uhl) Cells that assist neurons by transporting nutrients to them, producing myelin sheath, and regulating the likelihood of transmission of messages across the synaptic gap.

Neurotransmitters and Synaptic Transmission. Neurons work together in complex chains, but they are not connected to one another. Rather, one neuron influences the next neuron through the **synapse.** The small space between two neurons is known as the **synaptic gap.** Neural action potentials cannot jump across this gap. Instead, the neural message is carried across the gap by chemical substances called **neurotransmitters.** The capacity of the brain to process information is multiplied many times by the fact that not all neurotransmitters are *excitatory.* Some axons transmit *inhibitory* substances across synapses, which makes it more difficult for the next neuron to fire. Thus, the brain is composed of a staggering network of digital "yes" and "no" circuits that process and create our experiences (Kandel & others, 1995; Snyder, 2009).

Neurotransmitters are mostly stored in tiny packets called **synaptic vesicles** located in the **synaptic terminals,** which are the knoblike ends of the axons. When an action potential reaches the axon terminal, it stimulates the vesicles to release the neurotransmitter into the gap. The neurotransmitter floats across the gap and "fits" into **receptor sites** on the adjacent neuron's membrane like keys fitting into locks (Gubernator & others, 2010). This changes the polarity of the receiving neuron, which either causes an action potential that continues the neural message on its way (see figure 3.4) or inhibits the receiving neuron from firing.

Hundreds of different neurotransmitter substances operate in different parts of the brain, carrying out different functions (Kandel, Schwartz, & Jessel, 1995). Because of this fact, the process of synaptic transmission in a particular portion of the brain can be altered through the use of drugs that chemically alter the function of one of these neurotransmitters. Our growing knowledge about neurotransmitters has made possible the use of psychiatric drugs to help control anxiety, depression, and other psychological problems. Some of these drugs have a chemical structure similar enough to a neurotransmitter to fit the receptor sites on the receiving neuron and cause action potentials. Other drugs block the receptor site and reduce the likelihood of neural transmission. Still another class of drugs reduces the amount of neurotransmitter that is reabsorbed by the axon, keeping it active in the synapse longer and increasing the likelihood of neural transmission. For example, Prozac, widely used for depression, operates by reducing the reabsorption of a neurotransmitter. (See table 3.1 on p. 54.)

Glial Cells

Neurons are not the only living cells in the nervous system. In fact, neurons are greatly outnumbered by a second class of cells called **glial cells.** Glial cells help the neurons carry out their functions in three ways:

Figure 3.4   Neural messages are transmitted chemically from the axon of the sending neuron to the receiving neuron. The neurotransmitter substance contained in the synaptic vesicles is secreted across the synaptic gap. The neurotransmitter is able to stimulate the receiving neuron because its chemical "shape" matches that of receptor sites on the receiving neuron.

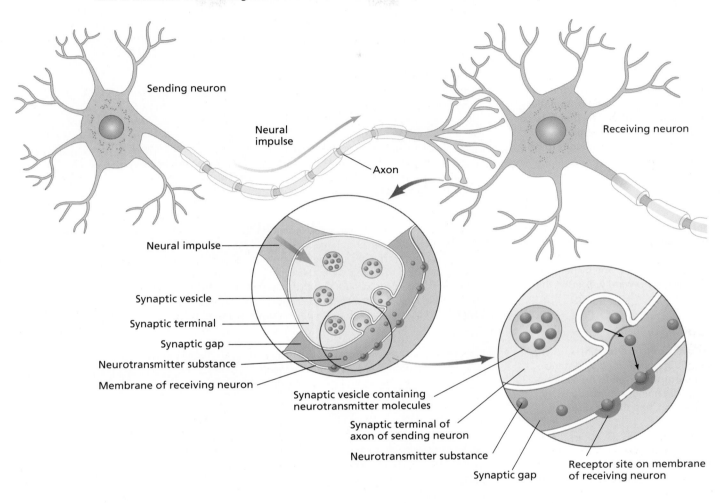

1. New neurons grow from glial cells throughout life (Malatesta & others, 2008).

2. Glial cells support neurons and transport nutrients from blood vessels to neurons.

3. Some glial cells produce the myelin sheath that surrounds and insulates axons.

4. Glial cells also influence the transmission of messages from one neuron to another across synaptic gaps (Fields, 2004). Some glial cells surround synapses and can increase or decrease chances of synaptic transmission. They do this by absorbing the neurotransmitter from the synaptic gap, releasing more of the neurotransmitter into the synaptic gap, or by chemically preparing the synapse for transmission (Eulenburg & Gomeza, 2010; Fields, 2004).

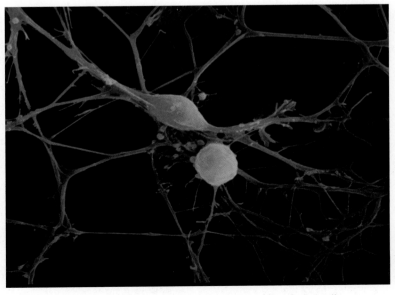

Neurons in central nervous system growing on a matrix of glial cells.

Table 3.1   Selected Neurotransmitters

The neurons of the nervous system use many different neurotransmitters to intricately manage its complex functions. Each year, new neurotransmitters are discovered and more is learned about their biological and psychological functions. A few of the many neurotransmitters are described here to provide examples of their diversity and to lay a foundation for later chapters (Cooper, Blum, & Roth, 2003; Snyder, 2009).

Acetylcholine

Acetylcholine is used by the somatic neurons that cause the body's large muscles to contract. Some poisonous snakes and spiders secrete venoms that disrupt the action of acetylcholine in the synapse, suffocating their prey by interfering with breathing. Similarly, some native peoples of South America put curare on the tips of blowgun darts to paralyze animals by blocking the action of acetylcholine. Acetylcholine also plays a role in regulating wakefulness and is one of the neurotransmitters believed to play a role in dreaming and memory. One source of problems for people with Alzheimer's disease is abnormal functioning of neurons that use acetylcholine (Chu & others, 2005).

acetylcholine (a˝suh-teel´koh˝leen) A neurotransmitter used by somatic neurons that contract the body's large muscles. Acetylcholine also plays a role in memory and is thought to help regulate dreaming.

Dopamine

One large group of neurons in the brain that uses **dopamine** as the neurotransmitter is involved in the control of large muscle movements. Persons with Parkinson's disease experience uncontrollable muscle tremors and other movement problems because of the depletion of dopamine in these circuits. A second group of dopamine neurons plays a central role in pleasure and reward systems in the brain and may be involved in schizophrenia and attention-deficit hyperactivity disorder. This second group of neurons appears to be stimulated by cocaine and other drugs of abuse.

dopamine (do˝pah´meen) A neurotransmitter substance used by neurons in the brain that control large muscle movements and by neurons in pleasure and reward systems in the brain.

Serotonin

Serotonin plays an important role in a number of seemingly unrelated psychological processes. Serotonin is one of the brain neurotransmitters believed to regulate sleep cycles and dreaming, appetite, anxiety, depression, and the inhibition of violence. The widely discussed drug Prozac increases the action of serotonin.

serotonin (se´ruh-to˝nin) A neurotransmitter used by systems of neurons believed to regulate sleep, dreaming, appetite, anxiety, depression, and the inhibition of violence.

Norepinephrine

Systems of neurons in the brain that use **norepinephrine** (also known as noradrenaline) as the neurotransmitter are believed to play a role in vigilance and attention to important events, such as the presence of rewards or dangers in the environment. It is also thought to be one of the neurotransmitters involved in anxiety and depression. Norepinephrine is also the neurotransmitter in many neurons of the sympathetic division of the autonomic nervous system and plays the role of a hormone when it is released by the adrenal glands.

norepinephrine (nor´ep-i-nef´rin) Neurotransmitter believed to be involved in vigilance and attention and released by sympathetic autonomic neurons and the adrenal glands.

Glutamate

Glutamate is the major excitatory neurotransmitter in the central nervous system, as virtually every neuron in the brain contains glutamate receptors. Glutamate plays a key role in the regulation of cognition and emotion (and their serious dysfunction in schizophrenia). Glutamate also plays a key role in the development and shaping of the neural structure of the brain over the life span.

glutamate (gloo-tuh-māt) The most widespread excitatory neurotransmitter in the brain.

Neuropeptides

The **neuropeptides** are a broad class of neurotransmitters that differ considerably in chemical composition from other transmitters. Often they are secreted by the same neurons that secrete other neurotransmitters. Neuropeptides are sometimes referred to as neuromodulators because they broadly influence the action of the other neurotransmitters released by their neuron. For example, some neurons that release acetylcholine into their synapses also release one or more neuropeptides. When the neuropeptide is released, it can increase or decrease the normal effects of the acetylcholine. Neuropeptides have longer-lasting effects than other neurotransmitters, are released through parts of the neuron other than the axon in many instances, and diffusely affect other nearby neurons. As will be discussed later in this chapter, some neuropeptides are also secreted by some endocrine glands.

neuropeptides (nur-o-pep-tidz) Large group of neurotransmitters sometimes referred to as neuromodulators, because they appear to broadly influence the action of the other neurotransmitters.

The nervous system is a "living computer" and communication system built of neurons. These specialized cells mostly transmit neural messages from their dendrites to their axons in a flowing swirl of electrically charged molecules produced by the changing semipermeability of their membranes. When the action potential reaches the tip of the axon, it is transmitted across the synaptic gap to the next neuron by a neurotransmitter substance. Many longer neurons are wrapped in an insulating layer called the *myelin sheath,* which increases the speed of neural transmission. Glial cells assist neurons by transporting nutrients to them, by producing the myelin sheath, and by increasing or decreasing the likelihood of transmission of messages across the synaptic gap.

To be sure that you have learned the key points from the preceding section, cover the list of correct answers and try to answer each question. If you give an incorrect answer to any question, return to the page given next to the correct answer to see why your answer was not correct. Remember that these questions cover only some of the important information in this section; it is important that you make up your own questions to check your learning of other facts and concepts.

1. The part of the neuron that most often receives messages from other neurons is called the _____.

   a) axon   c) dendrite

   b) cell body   d) myelin sheath

2. The part of the neuron that transmits the neural message to the next neuron by releasing a neurotransmitter across the synaptic gap is called the _____.

   a) axon   c) dendrite

   b) cell body   d) myelin sheath

3. During the process of conducting an action potential down the length of the neuron's membrane, the balance of positive ions on the outside of the neuron and negative ions on the inside is disturbed for a moment (called *depolarization*) when _____ are allowed to rush into the neuron through the semipermeable membrane of the cell.

   a) sodium ions   c) LSD ions

   b) neurotransmitters   d) negative ions

4. The fatty covering of some long neurons that insulates them and allows them to carry messages more rapidly is called the _____.

There are no right or wrong answers to the following questions. They are presented to help you become an active reader and think critically about what you have just read.

1. The neurons in the nervous system are not directly connected to one another, and messages must be transmitted across the synaptic gap using neurotransmitters. How would we be different if the neurons were simply connected like wires?

2. Some drugs that affect the nervous system are thought of as useful medications, whereas others are illegal because they are thought to be harmful. Why do such drugs have the potential to harm or to help?

Correct Answers: 1. c (p. 49) 2. a (p. 49), 3. a (p. 50), 4. myelin sheath (p. 51)

Divisions of the Nervous System

central nervous system The brain and the spinal cord.

peripheral nervous system (pě-rif´er-al) The network of nerves that branches from the brain and the spinal cord to all parts of the body.

interneuron Neurons in the central nervous system that connect other neurons.

As shown in figure 3.5, our complex nervous systems have many different parts, or divisions. The two major divisions of the nervous system are the **central nervous system** and the **peripheral nervous system.**

1. ***Central nervous system.*** The central nervous system consists of the brain and the spinal cord. As we discuss in detail in this chapter, the brain controls the functions of the nervous system. The spinal cord's primary function is to relay messages between the brain and the body, but it also does some rudimentary processing of information on its own. A simple reflex, such as the reflexive withdrawal from a hot object, is a good example. The hot object stimulates a neural message that reaches a neuron in the spinal cord, called an **interneuron.** The interneuron transmits the message to another neuron that stimulates the muscles of the limb to contract (see figure 3.6). Any behavior more complicated than a simple reflex, however, usually involves processing in the brain.

Figure 3.5   Organization of the human nervous system.

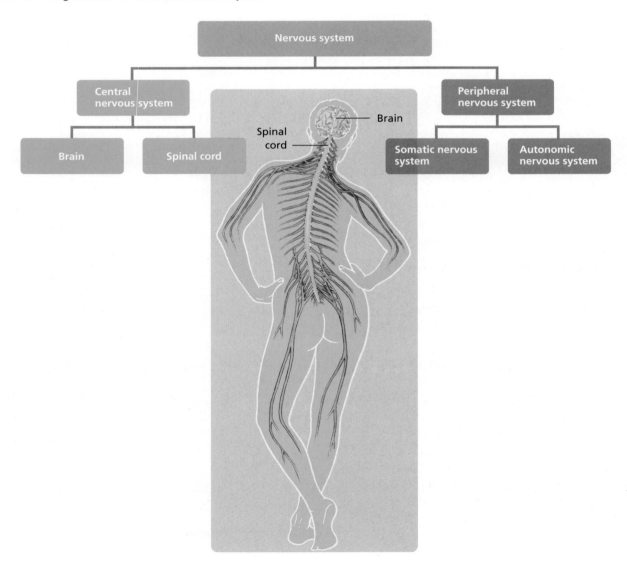

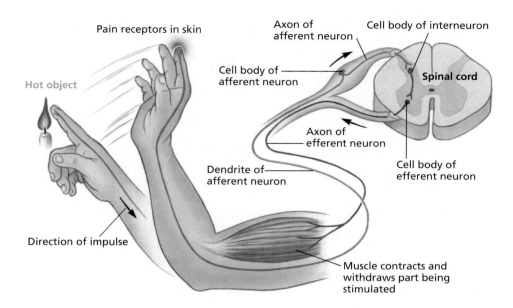

Pain receptors in skin

Axon of afferent neuron

Cell body of interneuron

Cell body of afferent neuron

Spinal cord

Hot object

Axon of efferent neuron

Cell body of efferent neuron

Dendrite of afferent neuron

Direction of impulse

Muscle contracts and withdraws part being stimulated

Figure 3.6

Some simple reflexes, such as the reflexive withdrawal of the hand from a hot object, are a result of a message's traveling along an afferent neuron from the hot spot on the hand to the spinal cord. In the spinal cord, the message travels across a short interneuron to an efferent neuron, which causes the muscles in the limb to contract.

2. *Peripheral nervous system.* The peripheral nervous system is composed of the nerves that branch from the brain and the spinal cord to the body. The peripheral nervous system transmits messages from the body to the central nervous system. It also transmits messages from the central nervous system to the muscles, glands, and organs that put the messages into action. Messages can travel across the synapse in only one direction, however. So messages coming from the body into the central nervous system are carried by one set of neurons, the **afferent neurons.** Messages going out from the central nervous system to the body are carried by a separate set of **efferent neurons.**

Divisions of the Peripheral Nervous System

The peripheral nervous system is further divided into two systems. The **somatic nervous system** carries messages from the central nervous system to the skeletal muscles that control movements of the body. These include voluntary movements, such as typing words on a computer keyboard, and involuntary movements, such as when the eyes maintain fixation on the computer screen in spite of small but frequent changes in the position of the head. The somatic nervous system also receives incoming messages from sensory receptors and transmits them to the central nervous system.

The **autonomic nervous system** is composed of nerves that carry messages to the glands and the visceral organs (heart, stomach, and intestines). The autonomic nervous system affects the skeletal muscles only by influencing general muscle tension. The autonomic nervous system plays a key role in two primary functions:

1. *Essential body functions.* The autonomic nervous system automatically regulates many essential functions of many organs. Heartbeat, breathing, digestion, sweating, and sexual arousal operate through the autonomic nervous system.

2. *Emotion.* The autonomic nervous system also plays a role in emotion. Have you ever wondered why you sometimes get a stomachache, diarrhea, a pounding heart, or a headache when you feel anxious? It's because the autonomic nervous system is activated during emotional states. When a person becomes very emotional, the autonomic system throws the internal organs that it

afferent neurons (af′er-ent) Neurons that transmit messages from sense organs to the central nervous system.

efferent neurons (ef′er-ent) Neurons that transmit messages from the central nervous system to organs and muscles.

somatic nervous system (sō-mat′ik) The part of the peripheral nervous system that carries messages from the sense organs to the central nervous system and from the central nervous system to the skeletal muscles.

autonomic nervous system (aw″to-nom′ik) The part of the peripheral nervous system that regulates the actions of internal body organs, such as heartbeat.

regulates out of balance in ways that create discomfort. As we see in chapter 13, prolonged emotional arousal can adversely affect the health of the organs controlled by the autonomic nervous system.

We do not consciously control the actions of the autonomic nervous system. It carries out its functions in an automatic way that does not require our awareness or intentional control.

Divisions of the Autonomic Nervous System

The autonomic nervous system is composed of two parts: the sympathetic and the parasympathetic nervous systems. These two systems work together closely to adjust and balance the functioning of the body according to the circumstances that the individual faces.

As shown in figure 3.7, the **sympathetic nervous system** prepares the body to respond to psychological or physical stress. In many cases, the sympathetic nervous system *activates* organs to improve our ability to respond to stress, but in other cases, it *inhibits* organs that are not needed during times of stress.

The sympathetic nervous system:

sympathetic nervous system (sim″pa-thet′ik) The part of the autonomic nervous system that prepares the body to respond to psychological or physical stress.

1. Dilates (opens) the pupils of the eyes to let in light

2. Decreases salivation

3. Speeds the beating of the heart

4. Dilates the passageways (bronchi) of the lungs to increase air flow

5. Inhibits the digestive tract (stomach, pancreas, intestines)

6. Releases sugar (glycogen) from the liver

7. Stimulates the secretion of epinephrine from the adrenal glands

8. Inhibits contraction of the urinary bladder

9. Increases blood flow and muscle tension in the large muscles (not shown in figure 3.7)

The **parasympathetic nervous system** acts in tandem with the sympathetic nervous system to maintain balanced regulation of the internal organs and the large body muscles. When levels of physical and emotional stress are low, it stimulates maintenance activities and energy conservation. The parasympathetic nervous system:

parasympathetic nervous system (par″uh-sim″pa-thet′ik) The part of the autonomic nervous system that promotes bodily maintenance and energy conservation and storage under nonstressful conditions.

1. Constricts (closes) the pupils of the eyes

2. Increases salivation to facilitate digestion

3. Slows the beating of the heart

4. Constricts the bronchi of the lungs

5. Activates the digestive tract

6. Releases bile from the liver to aid digestion of fats

7. Inhibits secretion of epinephrine from the adrenal glands

8. Contracts the urinary bladder

9. Reduces blood flow and muscle tension in the large muscles (not shown in figure 3.7)

Why do many people experience dry mouths and feel their hearts pound when stressed—and have digestive problems under prolonged stress? The answers are in the

Figure 3.7   The sympathetic and parasympathetic divisions of the autonomic nervous system regulate many of the body's organs.

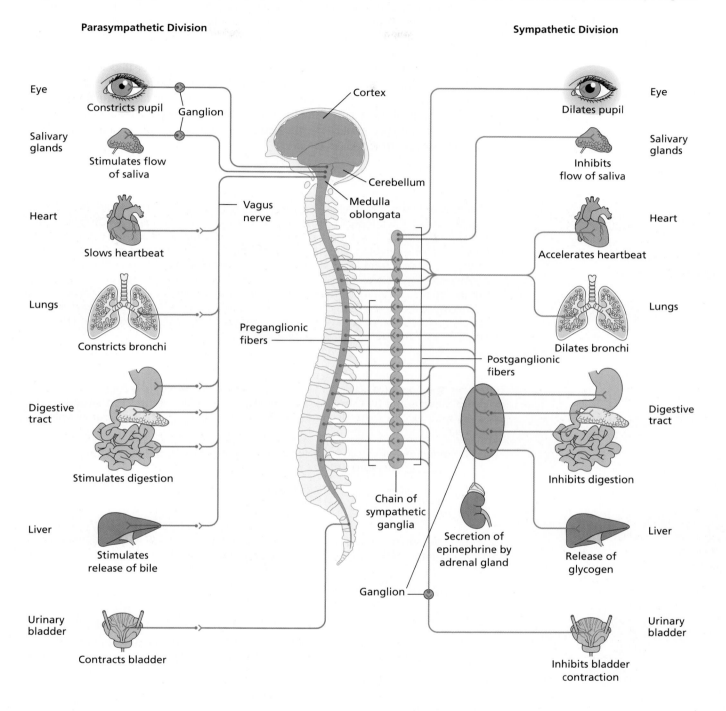

Parasympathetic Division

Eye
Constricts pupil   Ganglion

Salivary glands
Stimulates flow of saliva

Heart
Slows heartbeat

Lungs
Constricts bronchi

Digestive tract
Stimulates digestion

Liver
Stimulates release of bile

Urinary bladder
Contracts bladder

Cortex

Cerebellum

Medulla oblongata

Vagus nerve

Preganglionic fibers

Postganglionic fibers

Chain of sympathetic ganglia

Secretion of epinephrine by adrenal gland

Ganglion

Sympathetic Division

Eye
Dilates pupil

Salivary glands
Inhibits flow of saliva

Heart
Accelerates heartbeat

Lungs
Dilates bronchi

Digestive tract
Inhibits digestion

Liver
Release of glycogen

Urinary bladder
Inhibits bladder contraction

preceding list. Use this simple mnemonic device to remember the difference between the functions of the sympathetic and parasympathetic nervous system: **S** is for **s**ympathetic and **s**tress, and **P** is for **p**arasympathetic and **p**eaceful.

The structure and functions of these two divisions of the autonomic nervous system can be seen clearly in figure 3.7. Essentially, all organs that are served by the sympathetic division are also served by the parasympathetic division. Note also that the clusters of cell bodies of neurons—called **ganglia**—are organized in different

ganglia (gang′glē-ah) Clusters of cell bodies of neurons outside the central nervous system.

ways in the two divisions of the autonomic nervous system. The ganglia of the sympathetic division are all connected in a chain near the spinal column. This arrangement results in the sympathetic division's operating in a diffuse manner. That is, when the sympathetic division is aroused, it stimulates *all* of the organs it serves to some extent—because all of its parts are chained together through the ganglia. The ganglia of the parasympathetic division, in contrast, are separate and located near the individual organs. This allows the parasympathetic division to operate more selectively, which is particularly fortunate in some cases. For example, the parasympathetic division stimulates the flow of saliva and the flow of urine. If the parasympathetic ganglia that control the salivary glands and the urinary system were not separate, we would wet our pants every time we salivated!

Review

The nervous system can be divided into a central nervous system, composed of the brain and spinal cord, and a peripheral nervous system, composed of nerves that carry messages to and from the body. The peripheral nervous system is further divided into the somatic and the autonomic nervous systems. The somatic nervous system carries messages from the sense organs, muscles, and joints to the central nervous system and from the central nervous system to the skeletal muscles. The autonomic nervous system regulates the internal organs in response to changing demands. The autonomic nervous system has two working parts: the sympathetic nervous system, which prepares the body for stress or exertion, and the parasympathetic nervous system, which promotes bodily maintenance and energy conservation and storage during peaceful times.

Check Your Learning

To be sure that you have learned the key points from the preceding section, cover the list of correct answers and try to answer each question. If you give an incorrect answer to any question, return to the page given next to the correct answer to see why your answer was not correct.

1. The nervous system can be divided into two major parts, the peripheral and the _____ nervous system.

   a) autonomic   c) somatic

   b) afferent   d) central

2. The neurons in the somatic division of the peripheral nervous system that transmit messages from the sense organs to the central nervous system are called _____ neurons.

   a) efferent   c) sympathetic

   b) afferent   d) parasympathetic

3. The division of the peripheral nervous system that adjusts the functioning of the body according to the circumstances that it faces is called the _____ nervous system.

   a) autonomic   c) automatic

   b) somatic   d) central

4. During stress, the division of the autonomic nervous system that prepares the body for exertion or danger is called the _____ division.

   a) visceral   c) parasympathetic

   b) sympathetic   d) central

Thinking Critically about Psychology

There are no right or wrong answers to the following questions. They are presented to help you become an active reader and think critically about what you have just read.

1. Why do you think simple reflexes are "wired" into the spinal cord (connections of afferent neurons, interneurons, and afferent neurons) and do not involve the brain?

2. What are the advantages and disadvantages to human beings of an autonomic nervous system that operates largely automatically (that we do not voluntarily control)?

Correct Answers: 1. d (p. 56), 2. b (p. 57), 3. a (p. 57), 4. b (p. 58)

Structures and Functions of the Brain

The brain is the fundamental basis for psychological life. To begin our discussion of the brain, we look at the different functions performed by different parts of the brain. As we look at the parts of the brain, keep in mind that all mental functions require the *integrated* functioning of multiple parts of the brain. No function of the brain is carried out solely by one part. The brain can be viewed as having three major parts: the hind-brain, the midbrain, and the forebrain. These major parts of the brain are, in turn, divided into smaller parts. As we look at these parts of the brain, we start at the bottom of the brain and work our way up.

Hindbrain and Midbrain: Housekeeping Chores and Reflexes

The **hindbrain** is the lowest part of the brain, located at the rear base of the skull. Its primary responsibility is to perform routine "housekeeping" functions that keep the body working properly. The hindbrain has three principal parts: the medulla, the pons, and the cerebellum (see figure 3.8 on p. 62). The **medulla** is a swelling just above the top of the spinal cord, where the cord enters the brain. It controls breathing and a variety of reflexes, including those that enable you to maintain an upright posture. The **pons** is concerned with balance, hearing, and some parasympathetic functions. It is located just above the medulla.

The **cerebellum** consists of two rounded structures located to the rear of the pons. The cerebellum plays a key role in the coordination of complex muscle movements and plays an important role in types of learning and memory that involve coordinated sequences of information (Andreasen, 1999; Woodruff-Pak, 1999).

The **reticular formation** is a set of neurons that spans the medulla and pons. Neurons project from the reticular formation down the spinal cord and play a role in maintaining muscle tone and cardiac responsiveness to changing circumstances. More interesting to psychologists, rich networks of neurons arise in the reticular formation and end throughout the cerebral cortex. These networks influence our wakefulness, arousal, and attention. Although the reticular formation was originally thought of as a single neural system, it is now clear that it is composed of many neural systems that use different neurotransmitters, including serotonin, norepinephrine, and acetylcholine. These different parts of the reticular formation influence somewhat different areas of the brain (Guillery & others, 1998; Mesulam, 1995).

The **midbrain** is a small area at the top of the hindbrain that helps to control important postural systems, particularly those associated with the senses. For example, the midbrain controls the automatic movement of the eyes that keeps them fixed

hindbrain The lowest part of the brain, located at the base of the skull.

medulla (mĕ-dula´h) The swelling just above the spinal cord within the hindbrain responsible for controlling breathing and a variety of reflexes.

pons (ponz) The part of the hindbrain that is involved in balance, hearing, and some parasympathetic functions.

cerebellum (ser˝e-bel´um) Two rounded structures behind the pons involved in the coordination of muscle movements, learning, and memory.

reticular formation (reh-tiku-lur) Sets of neurons that project from the medulla and pons downward into the spinal cord to play a role in maintaining muscle tone and cardiac reflexes and also project upward throughout the cerebral cortex where they influence wakefulness, arousal level, and attention.

midbrain The small area at the top of the hindbrain that serves primarily as a reflex center for orienting the eyes and ears.

Figure 3.8
Important structures of the hindbrain and midbrain.

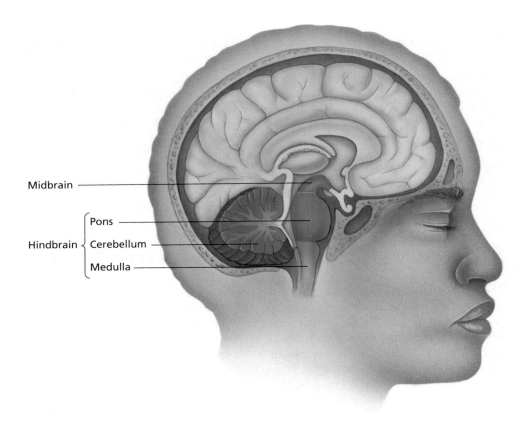

Midbrain

Hindbrain {
Pons
Cerebellum
Medulla

on an object as the head moves and controls automatic movements of the head that orient the ears to sources of sound.

Forebrain: Cognition, Motivation, Emotion, and Action

forebrain The parts of the brain, including the thalamus, hypothalamus, and cerebral cortex, that cover the hindbrain and midbrain and fill much of the skull.

By far the most interesting part of the brain to psychologists is the **forebrain.** Structurally, the forebrain consists of two distinct areas. One area, which contains the thalamus, the hypothalamus, and most of the limbic system, rests at the top of the hindbrain and midbrain (see figure 3.9). The other area, made up of the cerebral cortex, sits over the lower parts of the brain like the fat cap of an acorn covering its kernel. These two areas are not only distinctly different in terms of structure, but they also control very different functions.

thalamus (thal´-a-mus) The part of the forebrain that routes sensory messages to appropriate parts of the brain and works with other parts of the brain to process sensory information.

Thalamus, Hypothalamus, and Limbic System. The **thalamus** routes incoming stimuli from the sense organs to the appropriate parts of the brain and links the upper and lower centers of the brain. Recently, it has become clear that the thalamus plays a key role in processing incoming sensory information along with upper brain structures (Theyel & others, 2010).

hypothalamus (hī´´po-thal´ah-mus) The small part of the forebrain involved with motives, emotions, and the functions of the autonomic nervous system.

The **hypothalamus** is a small, but vitally important, part of the brain. It lies underneath the thalamus, just in front of the midbrain. The hypothalamus is intimately involved in our motives and emotions. It also plays a key role in regulating body temperature, sleep, endocrine gland activity, and resistance to disease; controlling glandular secretions of the stomach and intestines; and maintaining the normal pace and rhythm

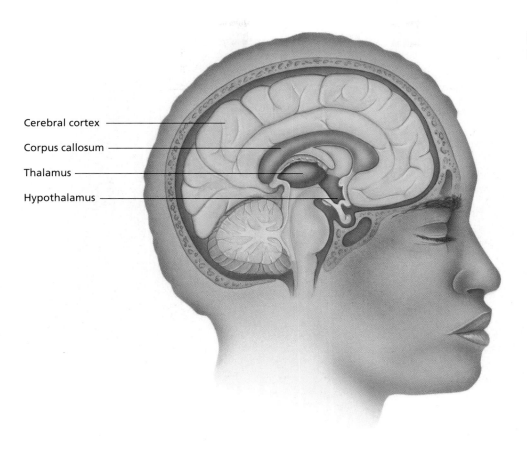

Figure 3.9
Key structures of the forebrain.

Cerebral cortex

Corpus callosum

Thalamus

Hypothalamus

of such body functions as blood pressure and heartbeat. Thus, the hypothalamus is the brain center most directly linked to the functions of the autonomic nervous system.

The hypothalamus works in close harmony with the **limbic system.** The limbic system is composed of three important parts (figure 3.10, p. 64):

1. The **amygdala** plays a key role in emotion and aggression (Phelps, 2006). The amygdala also plays a key role in the formation of memories about emotionally charged events (Buchanan, 2007; Kandel, 1999; Phelps, 2006).

2. The **hippocampus** brings important cognitive elements to the processing of emotion-related information (Zubieta & others, 2003). The hippocampus also plays a major role in the formation of new memories (Whitlock & others, 2006). It "ties together" the sights, sounds, and meanings of memories stored in various parts of the cerebral cortex (Jacobs & Schenk, 2003) and is particularly involved in spatial memory (how things are related in space). Interestingly, taxi drivers in London, who are known for their exceptional ability to navigate the city, have more neuron cell bodies in the hippocampus than people in general (Maguire & others, 2003). This may be the result of the drivers' practice recalling addresses. (On the other hand, a larger hippocampus might be necessary to learn the job.) The memory loss experienced by patients suffering from Alzheimer's disease (see p. 85) results in part from damage to the hippocampus.

3. The **cingulate cortex** works with the hippocampus to process cognitive information related to emotion (Zubieta & others, 2003). Both structures play a role in comparing current emotion-related information to information stored in memory.

limbic system A complex brain system, composed of the amygdala, hippocampus, and cingulate cortex, that works with the hypothalamus in emotional arousal.

amygdala (ah-mig′dah-lah) A part of the limbic system that plays a role in emotion.

hippocampus (hip″o-kam′pus) The part of the limbic system that plays a role in memory and the processing of emotion.

cingulate cortex A part of the limbic system, lying in the cerebral cortex, that processes cognitive information in emotion.

Figure 3.10

The structures of the limbic system play an important role in emotional arousal.

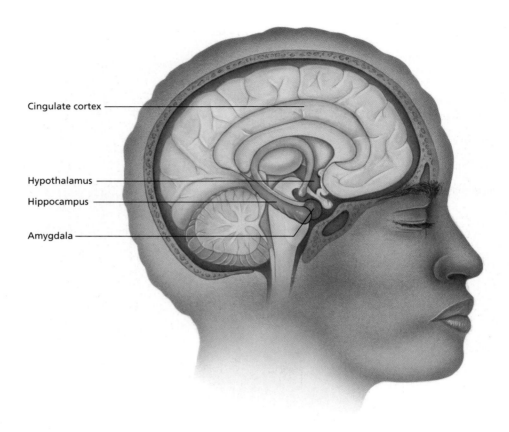

Cingulate cortex

Hypothalamus

Hippocampus

Amygdala

cerebral cortex (sere-bral) The largest structure in the forebrain, controlling conscious experience and intelligence and being involved with the somatic nervous system.

Cerebral Cortex: Sensory, Cognitive, and Motor Functions. The largest structure in the forebrain is the **cerebral cortex.** It is involved in conscious experience, voluntary actions, language, and intelligence—many of the things that make us human (Gazzaniga, 2000). As such, it is the primary brain structure related to the somatic nervous system. The word cortex means "bark," referring to the fact that the thin outer surface of the cerebrum is a densely packed mass of billions of cell bodies of neurons. The cortex has a gray appearance owing to these cell bodies and often is called the *gray matter* of the brain. The area of the cerebrum beneath the quarter inch of cortex is referred to as the *white matter,* because it is composed primarily of the axons of the cortical neurons. The fatty myelin coating of these neurons gives them their white appearance. The gray and white matter of the cerebral cortex can be seen clearly in the MRI image in figure 3.11.

Lobes of the Cerebral Cortex

Because of the importance of the cerebral cortex to our psychological functioning, let's look at it in more detail. The cerebral cortex has four sections, or *lobes* (see figure 3.12). Learning the names and locations of these lobes will help us discuss the major functions of the cerebral cortex.

frontal lobes The part of the cerebral cortex in the front of the skull involved in planning, organization, thinking, decision making, memory, voluntary motor movements, and speech.

1. Frontal Lobes. The frontal lobes occupy the part of the skull behind your forehead, extending back to the middle of your head. They play key roles in thinking, remembering, making decisions, speaking, predicting the future consequences of actions, controlling movement, and regulating emotions (Gray & Thompson, 2004; Krawczyk, 2002; Lieberman & others, 2007; Stuss & Levine, 2002).

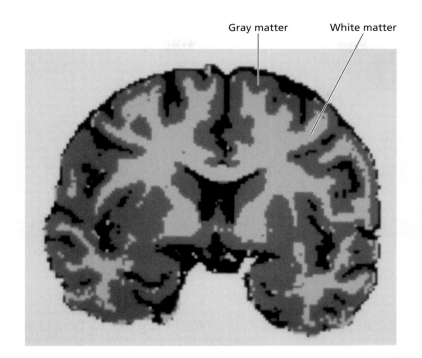

Gray matter   White matter

Figure 3.11
The gray matter and white matter of the cerebral cortex.

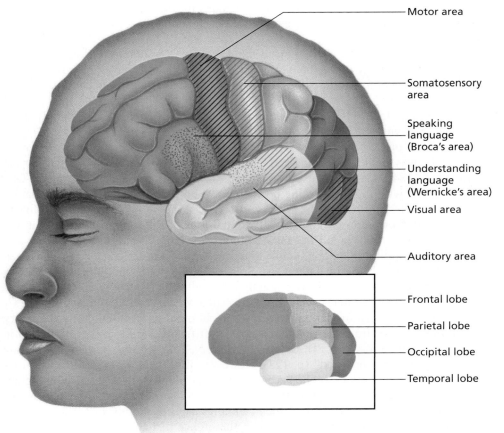

Motor area

Somatosensory area

Speaking language (Broca's area)

Understanding language (Wernicke's area)

Visual area

Auditory area

Frontal lobe

Parietal lobe

Occipital lobe

Temporal lobe

Figure 3.12
The four lobes of the cerebral cortex and the functions of key areas of the cerebral cortex.

Figure 3.13
A drawing of Phineas Gage's skull and the tamping rod that passed through his brain.

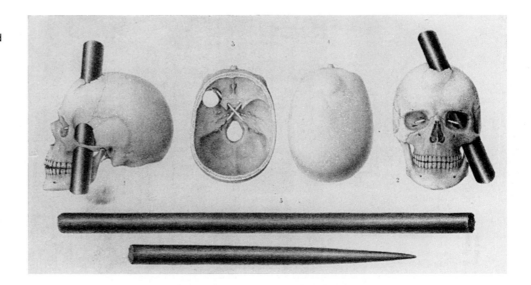

Broca's area Area of the frontal lobe of the left cerebral hemisphere that plays a role in speaking language.

expressive aphasia (ah-fā´ze-ah) Impairment of the ability to generate spoken language but not to comprehend language.

Area of damage to left frontal lobe

Right   Left

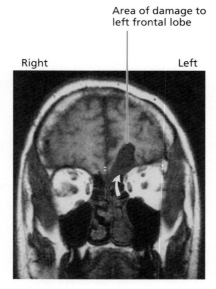

Figure 3.14
An MRI image of the brain of J. Z. (viewed from the front) shows the damage to the frontal lobe created when a tumor was removed.

The frontal lobe of the left cerebral hemisphere also contains **Broca's area,** which is involved in our ability to speak language (Hickok & Poeppel, 2007; McDermott & others, 2005). This area is named for French neurologist Paul Broca, who discovered its function in the late 1800s. He performed autopsies on persons who had had non-fatal strokes that damaged parts of their cerebral cortex and left them with a specific type of language disorder. Persons with **expressive aphasia** understand what is said to them but have difficulty speaking. The strokes of persons with expressive aphasia occurred in what is now known as Broca's area. He concluded that this area was involved in generating spoken language and that another area of the brain must be involved in understanding language.

The frontal lobes are also involved in the control of voluntary movements of the body. Near the middle of the top of the head, a strip called the *motor area* runs across the back portion of the frontal lobes. Damage to this area can result in paralysis or loss of motor control.

The frontal lobes also play a role in the regulation of emotion and socially inappropriate behavior (Lieberman & others, 2007; Yeates & others, 2008). These important functions of the frontal lobes were revealed by the dramatic case of Phineas Gage. Gage, who was known as a polite and hardworking man, worked as a foreman for the railroad. In 1848, Gage was excavating rock to lay railroad track in Vermont. One afternoon, he was packing blasting powder into a hole in the rock with a long tamping rod when a spark ignited the powder. As you can see in figure 3.13, the explosion shot the rod completely through his left frontal lobe. Gage's life was saved, but the destruction of part of his left frontal lobe took a terrific toll on him. He became irritable, publicly profane, and impossible to reason with. Gage also seemed to lose much of his ability to make rational plans. As a result, he had trouble holding a job and was regarded by his former friends as a "totally changed" man (Bigelow, 1850).

Nearly 150 years later, psychologist Christina Meyers and her colleagues (1992) described a strikingly similar case. A 33-year-old man, known as J. Z., had surgery to remove a tumor from the same area of the left frontal lobe that was destroyed in Phineas Gage (see figure 3.14). Before the surgery, J. Z. was an "honest, stable, and reliable worker and husband" (p. 122). However, after the surgery, he changed dramatically. Like Phineas Gage, he became irritable, dishonest, irresponsible, and grandiose. These dramatic changes in the behavior of Phineas Gage and J. Z. tell us that the frontal lobes play an important role in complex aspects of our social and emotional behavior. Indeed, many similar reports of the effects of damage to the frontal lobe have since been published (Koenigs & others, 2007).

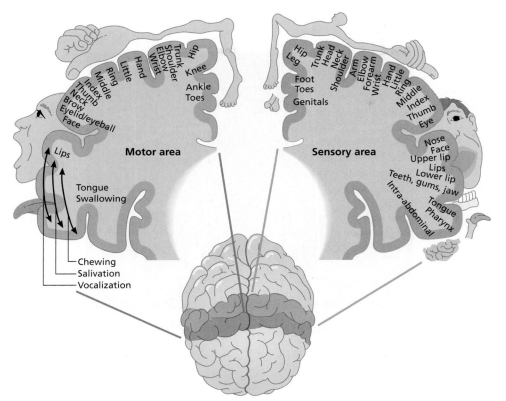

Motor area

Hip
Shoulder
Elbow
Trunk
Wrist
Little
Ring
Middle
Index
Thumb
Neck
Brow
Eyelid/eyeball
Face
Hand
Knee
Ankle
Toes
Lips
Tongue
Swallowing
Chewing
Salivation
Vocalization

Sensory area

Hip
Leg
Trunk
Head
Neck
Shoulder
Arm
Elbow
Forearm
Wrist
Hand
Little
Ring
Middle
Index
Thumb
Eye
Foot
Toes
Genitals
Nose
Face
Upper lip
Lips
Lower lip
Teeth, gums, jaw
Tongue
Pharynx
Intra-abdominal

Top view of cerebral cortex

Figure 3.15

A cross section of the cerebral cortex in the motor control area and the skin sense area showing the areas in the cortex serving each part of the body. The size of the body feature in the drawing is proportional to the size of the related brain area.

Source: Data from W. Penfield and T. Rasmussen, *The Cerebral Cortex of Man.* New York: Macmillan Publishing Co., 1950.

Do you recall my telling you in chapter 2 about studies that suggest that simply expressing our emotions in words can sometimes reduce emotional arousal and improve our health? A fascinating recent study used MRI to show that research participants who described the negative emotions that they saw in the faces of others in words showed both increased activation of part of the frontal lobes and reduced activity in the amygdala (Lieberman & others, 2007). This suggests that expressing our emotions may increase frontal lobe control of the amygdala, which processes negative emotions (Lieberman & others, 2007).

2. Parietal Lobes. The parietal lobes are just behind the frontal lobes at the top of your skull. The strip of the parietal cortex running parallel to the motor area of the frontal lobes is termed the **somatosensory area.** This area is important to the sense of touch and the other body senses that tell us, among other things, where our hands and feet are and what they are doing. It is not surprising, then, that the somatosensory area is located next to the motor area, because their functions are clearly related.

Different parts of the somatosensory and motor areas serve different parts of the body. The amount of area of the cortex devoted to a particular part of the body is not proportional to the size of that body part, however. Rather, it is proportional to the number of sensory and motor neurons going to and from that part of the body. Brain scientists have created amusing yet informative drawings of people with body features proportional to the space allocated to them in the somatosensory and motor areas (see figure 3.15).

3. Temporal Lobes. As suggested by their name, the temporal lobes extend backward from the area of your temples, occupying the middle area at the base of the brain beneath the frontal and parietal lobes. In both hemispheres, the temporal lobes contain

parietal lobes (pah-rī´e-tal) The part of the cerebral cortex that is behind the frontal lobes at the top of the skull and that contains the somatosensory area.

somatosensory area The strip of parietal cortex running parallel to the motor area of the frontal lobes that plays a role in body senses.

temporal lobes The part of the cerebral cortex that extends back from the area of the temples beneath the frontal and parietal lobes and that contains areas involved in the sense of hearing and understanding language.

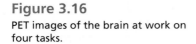

Figure 3.16
PET images of the brain at work on four tasks.

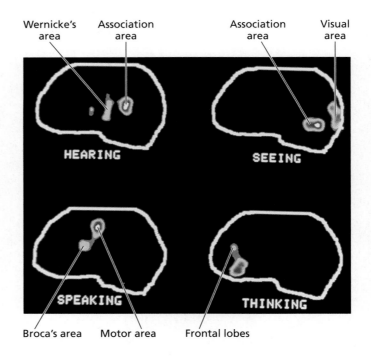

the auditory areas. These areas are located just inside the skull near the ears, immediately below the somatosensory area of the parietal lobes, and are involved in the sense of hearing.

Wernicke's area is located just behind the auditory area in the left hemisphere. This is the part of the cortex that plays a role in understanding spoken language (Hickok & Poeppel, 2007; McDermott & others, 2005). Wernicke's area further processes the messages arriving from the ears, which are first processed in the auditory area. Damage from strokes or injuries to this area of the cortex result in **Wernicke's aphasia.** Persons with this kind of aphasia cannot make sense out of language that is spoken to them by others. In addition, although they can make normal speech sounds, what they say typically makes little sense.

Wernicke's area The language area of the cortex that plays an essential role in understanding spoken language.

Wernicke's aphasia Form of aphasia in which persons can speak fluently (but nonsensically) and cannot make sense out of language spoken to them by others.

occipital lobes (ok-sip´ĭ-tal) The part of the cerebral cortex, located at the base of the back of the head, that plays an essential role in the processing of sensory information from the eyes.

4. Occipital Lobes. The occipital lobes are at the base of the back of the head. Although it is the part of the brain located farthest from the eyes, the most important part of the occipital lobes is the visual area (Amedi & others, 2007). The visual area plays an essential role in the processing of sensory information from the eyes. Damage to the visual area of the occipital lobes can result in partial or complete blindness, even though the eyes are able to function normally.

Note in figure 3.12 that the specific functions of some areas of each of the four lobes of the cerebral hemispheres have been left unlabeled. These unlabeled parts of the cerebral cortex are known as the **association areas.** The association areas play less specific roles in cerebral activities but often work closely with one of the nearby specific ability areas. This can be seen in the series of PET scan images presented in figure 3.16. The areas of the cerebral cortex that are yellow and red have the greatest amount of neural activity. Note that when the person is hearing words, there is activity in Wernicke's area and in the association areas just behind it. When the person is seeing words, the visual area in the occipital lobe is activated, along with nearby association areas. In contrast, when the person is speaking words, activation is found only in Broca's area and the motor area of the frontal lobes that controls speech movements; when the person is thinking, the frontal lobes are active.

association areas Areas within each lobe of the cerebral cortex believed to play general rather than specific roles.

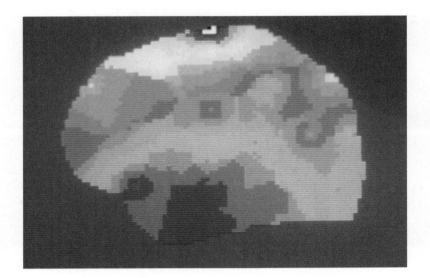

Figure 3.17
Image of the brain at work created by a computer from electrical recordings (EEG) of the activity of the brain. The image shows the activation of areas of the cerebral cortex of Dr. Monte Buchsbaum immediately after he administered a mild electric shock to his own arm.

Images of the Brain at Work

During the past 40 years, a number of exciting scientific tools have made the study of brain functions much easier. These techniques create images of the activities of the *living* brain by using computers to compile and interpret huge amounts of information from electrical activity, magnetic waves, and other forms of radiation. These computer-enhanced images of the brain are far more accurate and revealing than conventional X rays. In a very real sense, the advent of modern brain-imaging techniques is as important to the development of psychology and medicine's understanding of the brain as the invention of the telescope was to astronomy.

To study the brain's activity with an **electroencephalogram,** or **EEG,** the technician places electrodes on the surface of the person's scalp, and electrical activity from the brain is recorded. The EEG is commonly used to study the sleep cycle and to diagnose medical conditions, such as seizure disorder. Sometimes multiple EEG recordings are used to create computer-generated "maps" of brain activity. In this case, the person's head is covered with closely spaced electrodes to record brain activity. The computer converts these recordings into color images of the brain. The image in figure 3.17 shows the pattern of activity in the brain of psychiatric researcher Monte Buchsbaum moments after he administered a mild electrical shock to his arm. The area of greatest neural activity (red and orange) is at the top of the brain in the somatosensory area of the cortex that processes skin sensations (Buchsbaum, 1983).

A different kind of image is shown in figure 3.18 (p. 70). These images were created by computer interpretation of the activity of the brain obtained by **positron emission tomography,** or **PET** scanning. We see reduced activity in the outer portions of the brain beginning in image H and moving through image K as the powerful drug morphine (related to heroin) takes effect (London & others, 1990). In many similar experiments, the PET scan has given brain researchers extraordinary views of the living brain at work.

Perhaps the most amazing imaging technique is called **magnetic resonance imaging,** or **MRI.** This technique detects magnetic activity from the nuclei of atoms in living cells and creates visual images of the anatomy of the brain. Figure 3.19 (p. 70) shows an MRI of a living brain. Note the amazingly accurate picture of the anatomy of the brain provided by MRI. In addition, a type of MRI has been developed that allows researchers not only to image the anatomy of the brain but also to measure the *activity* of specific parts of the brain. **Functional MRI** measures changes in the use of oxygen by neurons that reflect their levels of activity (Baxter & others, 2003). This technique is safer than PET, because it does not involve exposure to radiation.

electroencephalogram (EEG)
(e-lek″trō-en-sef′ah-lo-gram)
Recording of the electrical activity of the brain obtained through electrodes placed on the scalp.

positron emission tomography (PET) Imaging technique that reveals the functions of the brain.

magnetic resonance imaging (MRI) Imaging technique using magnetic resonance to obtain detailed views of the brain structure and function.

functional MRI Type of MRI that measures the activity of parts of the brain by measuring the use of oxygen by groups of neurons.

Figure 3.18
Color-coded PET scans showing rates of glucose use, a measure of brain activity, in a human volunteer who received placebo (A–D) and then morphine, a drug related to heroin (H–K). These images are displayed in sequence from upper to lower levels of the brain (left to right). The lower images (H–K) show a reduction in brain activity in key areas when the subject received the drug.

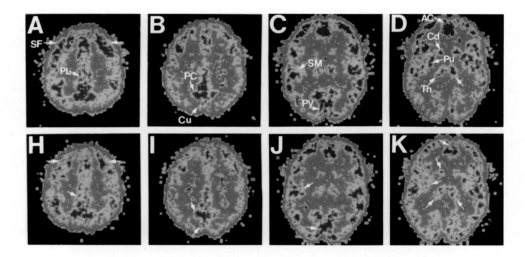

cerebral hemispheres The two main parts of the cerebral cortex, divided into left and right hemispheres.

corpus callosum
(kor´pus kah-lo´-sum) The major neural structure connecting the left and the right cerebral hemispheres.

Functions of the Hemispheres of the Cerebral Cortex

You now know that the cerebral cortex is composed of four lobes—each of which is involved in different psychological functions. Looking down at the cerebral cortex from the top reveals that it is made up of two halves called the **cerebral hemispheres.** These two separate hemispheres are linked by the **corpus callosum,** allowing communication between the two halves of the cortex (see figure 3.9). Many functions of the cerebral cortex are carried out jointly in both hemispheres, but the two hemispheres sometimes work together in surprising ways. There are some exceptions to this rule, but input from the senses of vision and touch, for example, generally goes to the *opposite* hemisphere. Stimulation of the skin on the left hand typically goes to the right cerebral hemisphere, visual stimulation falling on the right visual field of each eye goes to the left hemisphere, and wiggling the toes on your left foot is controlled by the right hemisphere. To accomplish this, the major sensory and motor nerves entering and leaving the brain twist and almost completely cross over each other.

Functions of the Left and Right Cerebral Hemispheres. The left and right cerebral hemispheres play different but complementary roles in processing information. For example, the areas that exercise the greatest control over language are located in the left cerebral hemisphere in over 90% of the population (Banich & Heller, 1998; Hopkins & Cantalupo, 2010). In particular, the left hemisphere plays the major role in analyzing the logical content of language (Beeman & Chiarello, 1998). The right cerebral hemisphere, in contrast, appears to play a greater role in processing information about the shapes and locations of things in space. For example, when you study a list of verbal items—such as memorizing the names of the four lobes of the cerebrum— there will be more activity in your left frontal lobe. However, if you study a drawing to memorize the shapes and the locations of the lobes of the cerebrum, there will be more activity in your right frontal lobes (Craik & others, 1999; Wheeler, Stuss, & Tulving, 1997). In general, the left side of the cerebral cortex tends to handle verbal information, and the right side tends to handle visual and spatial information.

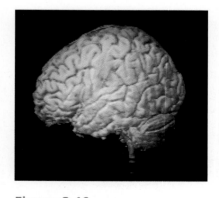

Figure 3.19
Three-dimensional image of the living brain based on computer-enhanced MRI.

Split Brains. Coordination of the shared functions of the two cerebral hemispheres is possible because they communicate through structures that connect them. The largest and most important bridge between the two cerebral hemispheres is the *corpus callosum.* It is sometimes necessary, however, to control the neurological disease of epilepsy by surgically cutting the corpus callosum to prevent seizures from spreading from one cerebral hemisphere to the other. When this is done, the right and left hemispheres have much less capacity to exchange information. Experiments performed on these "split-brain" patients provide a major source of our knowledge about the different functions of the two cerebral hemispheres (Franz, Waldie, & Smith, 2000; Gazzaniga, 1967, 1998, 2000).

What would be the result of cutting the primary line of communication between the two cerebral hemispheres? Surprisingly, people with a severed corpus callosum appear to change very little at first glance. Although it would be difficult for you—or even for the patient—to notice any difference in daily living, clever psychological experiments have revealed the effects of cutting the corpus callosum. In one experiment, the split-brain patient was seated in front of a screen and asked to stare at a spot in the middle. A slide projector briefly flashed a word on one side of the screen, so it was seen by only the left or only the right visual field of the eye. This was done because the left visual field sends information only to the right cerebral hemisphere, and the right visual field sends information only to the left hemisphere. The nerves from the eyes cross at the optic chiasm (see figure 3.20, p. 72), which is left uncut.

If the word *pencil* is presented in the right visual field of each eye, the information travels to the language control areas in the left hemisphere. In this situation, the patient has no difficulty reading aloud the word *pencil.* But, if the same word is presented to the left visual field of each eye, the split-brain patient typically would not be able to respond when asked what word had been presented. This does not mean that the right side of the brain did not receive or understand the word *pencil,* however. It means only that the patient cannot verbalize what she sees. Using the sense of touch, the split-brain patient can easily pick out a pencil as the object that matches the word from among a number of unseen objects—but only if she uses her left hand, which has received the message from the right cerebral cortex.

Nonetheless, if the split-brain patient holds an unseen pencil in her left hand, she cannot tell you what she is holding. It's not that the right cortex does not receive information about the pencil, but because it has no area controlling verbal expression, the person cannot say that it is a pencil. Such studies with split-brain patients clearly reveal the localization of language expression abilities in the left cerebral hemisphere (Gazzaniga, 1967, 1998).

Hemispheres of the Cerebral Cortex and Emotion. The cerebral cortex also plays important roles in the processing of emotional information. Just as there are differences in the cognitive functions of the two cerebral hemispheres, the two cerebral hemispheres also play different roles in processing emotions (Davidson, 1992; Verona & others, 2009). The right hemisphere plays a greater role in the expression and perception of negative emotions (fear, sadness, and anger), whereas the left cerebral hemisphere plays a greater role in the perception and expression of positive emotion (Pizzagalli & others, 2005; Stewart & others, 2010; Urry & others, 2004).

As long ago as 1861 physician Paul Broca noticed that patients who had suffered strokes were more likely to become depressed if the stroke was in the left cerebral hemisphere. This is apparently because a stroke on the left side of the cerebral cortex interferes with the processing of positive emotions but leaves the processing of negative emotion in the right cerebral hemisphere intact. Indeed, some patients with right-hemisphere damage are cheerful, happy, and not at all depressed by their disability (Kinsbourne, 1988). Since Broca's time, his observation has been repeated many times (Robinson & Starkstein, 1990; Vataja & others, 2001). For example, the images of the brains shown in figure 3.21 on p. 73 (obtained using computerized X rays) of persons who developed depression following strokes show clearly that the damage to their brains was primarily on the left side of the cortex (Starkstein, Robinson, & Price, 1988).

Similarly, Richard Davidson of the University of Wisconsin (Davidson & others, 1990) showed short films to college students—some entertaining films of playful

Figure 3.20   Studies of persons whose corpus callosum has been surgically cut to treat epilepsy tell us much about the different functions of the cerebral hemispheres and the important role that the corpus callosum normally plays in allowing communication between the hemispheres. When the word *pencil* is shown only to the right visual field, the information is sent only to the left cerebral hemisphere. The language areas in the left hemisphere allow the person to say that the word *pencil* has been seen. But, when the stimulus is shown only to the left visual field, the information is sent only to the right hemisphere, which does not have language areas. In this case, the person cannot confirm verbally that the word has been seen but can identify the pencil as the correct stimulus by the sense of touch.

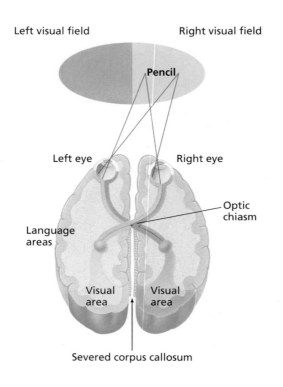

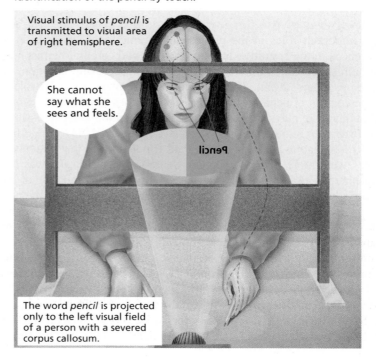

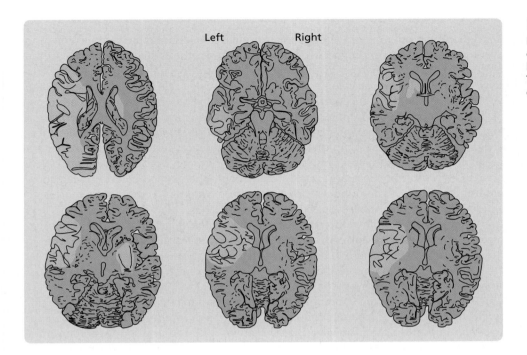

Figure 3.21
Drawings from computerized X rays of the brains of individuals who became depressed following a stroke. The shaded areas show the damaged cerebral tissue.

animals and some "quite gruesome" films of amputations and burn victims. As the students watched the films, their facial expressions were monitored. When they were smiling, EEG recordings indicated more activity in the left cerebral hemisphere, but when they showed disgust, their right hemisphere was more active. These and other studies strongly suggest that positive emotions are processed more in the left hemisphere and negative emotions more in the right hemisphere (Heller & others, 1998; Pizzagalli & others, 2005).

Plasticity of the Cortex. Severe damage to the cerebral cortex often results in the loss of important psychological functions. Fortunately, many of these functions can be recovered partially or fully, particularly if the damage occurs early in life. This is because the cortex, and some other parts of the brain, show a high degree of **plasticity** that allows other areas of the cortex to take over the functions of the damaged area (Mason, 2009; Yeates & others, 2008). For example, children with damage to the language areas of the left hemisphere often can relearn language, because areas in the right hemisphere take over the functions of the damaged area (Gazzaniga, 1992). Although many areas of the brain are specialized to perform certain tasks, they are not completely dedicated to those tasks. For example, blind individuals who read Braille show activation in the visual cortex when they "read" with their fingers (Cohen & others, 1997). Instead of using areas of the brain that usually serve the sense of touch, the tactile stimuli are interpreted in the area of the cortex that normally interprets visual stimuli.

plasticity Ability of parts of the brain, particularly the cerebral cortex, to acquire new functions that partly or completely replace the functions of a damaged part of the brain.

In chapter 4, we discuss evidence that men and women differ in a number of ways. Although these average differences are not large, there are meaningful differences in some areas of cognition, emotion, and social behavior. To build a foundation for our later discussion of this topic, we examine evidence of differences in the brains of men and women in this chapter. If men and women differ in behavior, it makes sense that the structure and organization of their brains may differ, too. **Continued on pg. 74**

Human Diversity
Sex Differences in the Cerebral Cortex

Human Diversity
Sex Differences in the Cerebral Cortex
cont'd from pg. 73

Continued from pg. 73 The average female brain is smaller but more complex than the average male brain (Lenroot & Giedd, 2010; Luders & others, 2004). In particular, the cerebral cortex of women tends to be more folded and have greater surface area, in spite of the smaller overall volume of the average female brain (Luders & others, 2004).

Other gender differences affect the way the brains of women and men are organized and function. For example, when men and women memorize verbal information and solve problems in their heads using that information, functional MRI studies show activation of the frontal and parietal lobes of the cerebral cortex in both sexes. However, men perform such tasks less accurately than women do on average and show greater activation in those areas in different hemispheres of the cortex. Men show greater activation in the right cerebral hemisphere, whereas women show more activation in the left hemisphere (Speck & others, 2000).

When men and women listen to speech, there are similar differences in the organization of the cerebral cortex. Language activates the frontal and temporal lobes in the left cerebral hemisphere in both men and women, but women are far more likely also to show activation in these areas in the right hemisphere (Baxter & others, 2003; Shaywitz & others, 1995).

Thus, on average, the structure and the organization of the human brain are different for females and males. In thinking about these differences, we must remember two very important facts, however: First, these studies tell us about *average* differences between the sexes. This does not mean that the brains of *all* men function differently from those of all women. Some men have brains that are structured and function more like the average female brain than the average male brain, and vice versa. Second, differences between the two sexes do *not* mean that one is superior to another. There is no best brain size or pattern of organization. Although male and female brains tend to differ, both are capable of working marvelously well.

The Brain Is a Developing System

The prevailing view until recently was that the anatomy of the brain changed little from birth through middle adulthood. Dramatic new evidence from MRI and other neuroimaging studies has radically changed our view of the brain, however. Now it is abundantly clear that the brain continues to change in structure throughout our lives (Lenroot & Giedd, 2006, 2010; Sowell & others, 2003; Yeates & others, 2008).

Developmental Changes in White and Gray Matter. The total weight of the brain does not change much after early childhood, but white matter (myelinated neural fibers) *increases* in the cerebral cortex (especially the frontal lobes and the corpus callosum that links the right and left hemispheres) from childhood through middle age. The increase in white matter is due to the continued growth of myelin through adolescence and into early adulthood (Durston & others, 2001). This growth in myelin insulates neurons and speeds the transmission of neural impulses. In contrast, gray matter (neural cell bodies) *decreases* in the cortex and some subcortical areas at about the same rate from childhood through middle age. Much of the decrease in gray matter (neural cell bodies) during this age span results from selective **neural pruning,** which is thought to improve the efficiency of neural systems by eliminating unnecessary neural cells (Durston & others, 2001). Thus, the increases in white matter and decreases in gray matter that occur into early adulthood appear to increase the efficiency of the brain. The volumes of both gray and white matter begin to decrease after the fifth decade of life, however, which is associated with reductions in working memory and cognitive speed (Abe & others, 2010; Bartzokis & others, 2001).

neural pruning Normal process of selective loss of gray matter in the brain over time, which is thought to improve the efficiency of neural systems by eliminating unnecessary cells.

The decline in white matter as people age is more rapid in men (Abe & others, 2010).

Neurogenesis. The brain also is a developing system in the sense that new neurons grow in many key areas of the brain well into adulthood, particularly the cortex and hippocampus, a process referred to as **neurogenesis** (Gould, Tanapat, Rydel, & Hastings, 2000; Lee & Son, 2009; Wandell & Smirnakis, 2009). These new neurons develop from a type of glial cell in the brain that can be transformed into neurons (Malatesta & others, 2008; Salomoni & Calegari, 2010). The growth of new neurons through neurogenesis apparently plays an important role in learning and the storing of new memories (Gould, 2007). For example, it has been shown that learning a new skill (juggling) causes an average increase of 3% in the number of neural cell bodies (gray matter) in areas of the cortex related to visual attention (Draganski, 2004).

"Young man, go to your room and stay there until your cerebral cortex matures."

The Brain Is an Interacting System

Even though it is convenient to think of the brain as being divided into many separate parts, the many parts of the brain work together in intellectual and emotional functioning. Consider, for example, the following situation. You are waiting at a bus stop late at night. A poorly dressed man approaches, smelling of alcohol. He asks if you can spare five dollars. In his pocket, you see the outline of what might be a gun. Your reaction to this scene would involve many parts of your brain working together. Parts of your cerebral cortex evaluate the possible threat to you and the alternative courses of action open to you. Your limbic system is involved in a process of emotional arousal. If you fight, run, or reach into your pocket to hand over the money, the motor areas of your cortex will work with your hindbrain and midbrain to coordinate the muscular movements involved.

Sometimes the many parts of the brain interact because one part of the brain sends a message to another part, which then sends it on to a third part of the brain, and so on. More often, however, several parts of the brain process different kinds of related information at the same time. That is, the brain often uses parallel processing (handling different information at the same time) rather than serial processing (handling one kind of information at a time) (Rumelhart & McClelland, 1986). The brain's amazing capacity for parallel processing magnifies its ability to use its 100 billion neurons to process our complex actions, emotions, and thoughts.

neurogenesis (nu´rō jen˝i sis) Hypothesized growth of new neurons in adult mammals.

Review

The brain is a complex system composed of many parts that carry out different functions but that work together in an integrated way. The hindbrain and the midbrain mostly handle the housekeeping responsibilities of the body, such as breathing, posture, reflexes, and other basic processes. The larger forebrain area carries out the more psychological functions of the brain: The thalamus integrates sensory input, and the hypothalamus plays roles in motivation, emotion, sleep, and other basic bodily processes. Most of the limbic system, which plays an important role in emotional experience, is located below

Review (cont.)

the cerebral cortex. The cerebral cortex provides the neural basis for thinking, language, control of motor movements, perception, and other cognitive processes, but it also processes emotional information. The cortex is composed of two cerebral hemispheres, which are connected by the corpus callosum. The right hemisphere plays a greater role in spatial and artistic cognitive processes, whereas the left hemisphere is more involved in logical, mathematical, and language-based processes. The left cerebral hemisphere also is more involved in processing positive emotion, whereas the right hemisphere plays a greater role in negative emotion. The brain continues to develop and to become more efficient through early adulthood and is capable of growing new neurons in some areas of the brain during adulthood.

Check Your Learning

To be sure that you have learned the key points from the preceding section, cover the list of correct answers and try to answer each question. If you give an incorrect answer to any question, return to the page given next to the correct answer to see why your answer was not correct.

1. The midbrain and the hindbrain play the greatest role in which functions?

   a) motivation and emotion   c) planning for the future

   b) learning and thinking   d) bodily housekeeping and reflexes

2. The small but vitally important part of the forebrain that plays a key role in the control of emotion, endocrine gland activity, blood pressure, and heartbeat (because it is the brain center most linked to the autonomic nervous system) is the _____.

   a) cerebrum   c) hypothalamus

   b) cerebellum   d) thalamus

3. Broca's area, which controls speaking, is located in the _____ lobe of the left cerebral hemisphere.

   a) frontal   c) parietal

   b) temporal   d) occipital

4. The area of the cerebral cortex that is primarily involved in vision is the _____ lobe.

   a) frontal   c) parietal

   b) temporal   d) occipital

5. Positive emotions are processed more by the _____ cerebral hemisphere.

Thinking Critically about Psychology

There are no right or wrong answers to the following questions. They are presented to help you become an active reader and think critically about what you have just read.

1. Imagine that you have put down this book and are taking a huge bite of your favorite kind of pizza. Think of the role that each part of the brain plays in this simple act.

2. Does what you have learned about the two cerebral hemispheres suggest that we should think of ourselves as having "two brains" or one? How about the autonomic nervous system—is that "another brain with a mind of its own"?

Correct Answers: 1. d (p. 61), 2. c (p. 62), 3. a (p. 66), 4. d (p. 68), 5. left (p. 71)

Endocrine System: Chemical Messengers of the Body

As we have just seen, the nervous system is the vital computer and communication system that forms the biological basis for behavior and conscious experience. Another biological system—the **endocrine system**—also plays an important role in communication and the regulation of bodily processes. This system consists of a number of **glands** that secrete two kinds of chemical messengers:

1. *Neuropeptides.* Many endocrine glands secrete **neuropeptides** into the bloodstream. When these neuropeptides reach other endocrine glands, they influence their functions. Thus, neuropeptides allow the endocrine glands to communicate with one another. In addition, some neuropeptides secreted by the endocrine glands reach the brain and influence neural systems. In this way, these neuropeptides play important roles in stress regulation, social bonding, emotion, and memory (Feldman & others, 2007; Kandel & Abel, 1995; Rosenkrantz, 2007; Skuse & Gallagher).

2. *Hormones.* The endocrine glands also secrete **hormones** into the bloodstream, through which they are carried throughout the body and influence many organ systems, including the brain (Forbes & Dahl, 2010).

The release of neuropeptides and hormones by the endocrine glands is regulated by several systems of the brain through the hypothalamus (Taylor & others, 2008). Thus, the endocrine gland gives the brain additional ways to control the body's organs. This is particularly true during physical stress or emotional arousal. At these times, neuropeptides and hormones influence such things as metabolism, blood pressure, blood-sugar level, and sexual functioning. As discussed more fully in chapter 4, hormones affect organ functioning by passing into their cell bodies and influencing how the genetic codes in their nuclei are expressed (Flint & others, 2007).

Let's look briefly at the seven endocrine glands that are most important to our psychological lives (see figure 3.22, p. 78).

endocrine system (en'dō-krin) The system of glands that secretes hormones.

glands The structures in the body that secrete substances.

hormones (hor'mōnz) Chemical substances, produced by endocrine glands, that influence internal organs.

Pituitary Gland

The **pituitary gland** is located near the hypothalamus, which directly controls its functioning. The pituitary is sometimes thought of as the body's master gland, because its secretions help regulate the activity of the other endocrine glands. Perhaps its most important function is regulating the body's reactions to stress and resistance to disease. The pituitary gland secretes hormones that control blood pressure, thirst, and body growth. Too little or too much of the pituitary's growth hormone make a person develop into a "dwarf" or a "giant." When the infant sucks the mother's nipples, a neural message is sent to the mother's hypothalamus, which sends a message to the pituitary gland through a neuropeptide. This causes the pituitary to secrete a hormone that releases breast milk for the baby.

pituitary gland (pǐ-tu'i-tār''ē) The body's master gland, located near the bottom of the brain, whose secretions help regulate the activity of the other glands in the endocrine system.

Adrenal Glands

The pair of **adrenal glands** sits atop the two kidneys. They play an important role in emotional arousal and secrete hormones important to metabolism. When stimulated either by a hormone from the pituitary gland or by the sympathetic division of the

adrenal glands (ah-drē'nal) Two glands on the kidneys that are involved in physical and emotional arousal.

Figure 3.22   Locations of major endocrine glands and their principal functions.

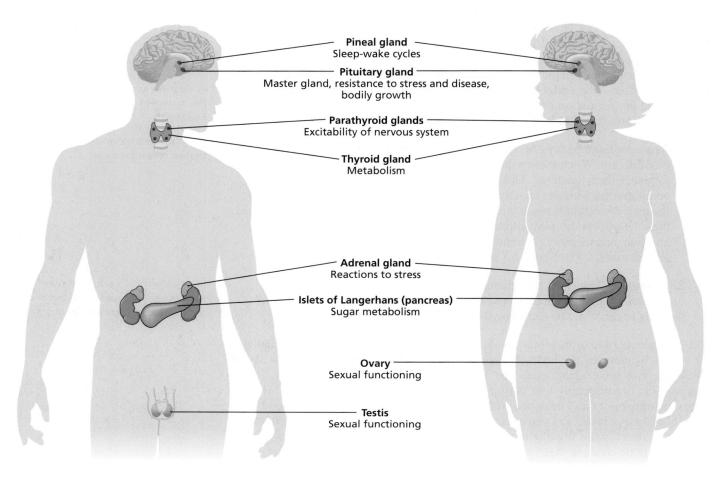

Pineal gland
Sleep-wake cycles

Pituitary gland
Master gland, resistance to stress and disease,
bodily growth

Parathyroid glands
Excitability of nervous system

Thyroid gland
Metabolism

Adrenal gland
Reactions to stress

Islets of Langerhans (pancreas)
Sugar metabolism

Ovary
Sexual functioning

Testis
Sexual functioning

epinephrine (ep″i-nef′rin) Hormone produced by the adrenal glands.

norepinephrine (nor″ep-i-nef′rin) Hormone produced by the adrenal glands.

cortisol Stress hormone produced by the adrenal glands.

autonomic nervous system, the adrenal glands secrete three hormones that are important in our reactions to stress. **Epinephrine** and **norepinephrine** (which also function as neurotransmitters in the brain) stimulate changes to prepare the body to deal with physical demands that require intense body activity, including psychological threats or danger. The effects of these two adrenal hormones are quite similar, but they operate differently. For example, at times of stress, epinephrine increases blood pressure by increasing heart rate and blood flow. Norepinephrine also increases blood pressure but does so by constricting the diameter of blood vessels in the body's muscles and by reducing the activity of the digestive system. The adrenal glands also secrete the hormone **cortisol,** which also activates the body's response to stress (Bandelow & others, 2000; Taylor & others, 2008) and plays an important role in the regulation of immunity to disease.

Let's look at a classic example of the action of the adrenal glands during stress. Does giving a speech in public make you tense? Most people find public speaking to be at least mildly stressful. German scientist Ulrich Bolm-Andorff collected blood and urine from 10 physicians and psychologists at two different times: (1) just after they gave an important public speech to their colleagues and (2) at the same time on another day when they had not given speeches (Bolm-Andorff & others, 1986). Three adrenal hormones (epinephrine, norepinephrine, and cortisol) were measured in these fluids. Look at figure 3.23 to see the dramatic increase in the secretion of adrenal hormones during the speech. Note, too, the corresponding increase in heart rate and blood pressure.

Figure 3.23   The stress of giving a public speech affects hormones secreted by the adrenal glands, increases the heart rate, and blood pressure.

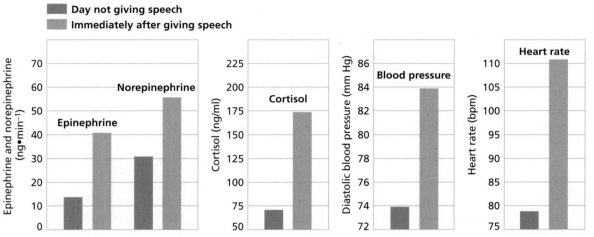

Source: Data from V. Bolm-Andorff, et al., "Hormonal and Cardiovascular Variations During a Public Lecture" in *European Journal of Applied Physiology, 54*:669–674. Copyright 1986 Springer-Verlag, New York, NY.

The changes in heart rate and blood pressure were caused by the action of epinephrine and norepinephrine on the heart and blood vessels, and by the direct action of the autonomic nervous system on these organs. Thus, the autonomic nervous system has two ways of activating the internal organs: (1) by directly affecting the organs and (2) by stimulating the adrenals and other endocrine glands that then influence the organs with their hormones. One reason it takes so long to feel calm after a stressful event has passed is because of this second route to activating the body. It takes quite a while for the hormones to leave the bloodstream, so their effects are rather long lasting.

Islets of Langerhans

The **islets of Langerhans,** which are embedded in the **pancreas,** regulate the level of sugar in the blood by secreting two hormones that have opposing actions. **Glucagon** causes the liver to convert its stored sugar into blood sugar and to dump it into the bloodstream. **Insulin,** in contrast, reduces the amount of blood sugar by helping the body's cells absorb sugar in the form of fat. Blood sugar level is important psychologically, because it's one of the factors in the hunger motive, and it helps determine how energetic a person feels.

Gonads

There are two sex glands—the **ovaries** in females, the **testes** in males. The **gonads** produce the sex cells—ova in females, sperm in males. They also secrete hormones important in sexual arousal (Eastwick, 2009) and contribute to the development of so-called secondary sex characteristics (for example, breast development in women, growth of chest hair in men, deepening of the voice in males at adolescence, and growth of pubic hair in both sexes). The most important sex hormones are **estrogen** in females and **testosterone** in males. Testosterone influences the tendency to be socially dominant in both sexes (Newman & Josephs, 2009). There is emerging evidence that sex hormones play a role in guiding the development of the brain and changes in social behavior during adolescence (Forbes & Dahl, 2010).

islets of Langerhans (i´lets of lahng´er-hanz) Endocrine cells in the pancreas that regulate the level of sugar in the blood.

pancreas (pan´krē-as) Organ near the stomach that contains the islets of Langerhans.

glucagon (gloo´kah-gon) Hormone produced by the islets of Langerhans that causes the liver to release sugar into the bloodstream.

insulin (in´su-lin) Hormone produced by the islets of Langerhans that reduces the amount of sugar in the bloodstream.

ovaries (o´vah-rēz) Female endocrine glands that secrete sex-related hormones and produce ova, or eggs.

testes (tes´tēz) Male endocrine glands that secrete sex-related hormones and produce sperm cells.

gonads (gō´nadz) Glands that produce sex cells and hormones important in sexual arousal and that contribute to the development of secondary sex characteristics.

estrogen (es´tro-jen) A female sex hormone.

testosterone (tes-tos´ter-ōn) A male sex hormone.

Thyroid Gland

thyroid gland (thī′roid) Gland below the voice box that regulates metabolism.

The **thyroid gland,** located just below the larynx, or voice box, plays an important role in the regulation of **metabolism.** It does so by secreting a hormone called **thyroxin.** The level of thyroxin in a person's bloodstream and the resulting metabolic rate are important in many ways. In children, proper functioning of the thyroid is necessary for proper mental development. A serious thyroid deficiency in childhood produces sluggishness, poor muscle tone, and a rare type of mental retardation called **cretinism.** In adults, people with low thyroxin levels tend to be inactive and overweight.

metabolism (me-tab′o-lizm) Process through which the body uses energy.

thyroxin (thīrok′sin) Hormone produced by the thyroid that is necessary for proper mental development in children and helps determine weight and level of activity in adults.

Parathyroid Glands

The four small glands embedded in the thyroid gland are the **parathyroid glands.** They secrete **parathormone,** which is important in the functioning of the nervous system. Parathormone controls the excitability of the nervous system by regulating ion levels in the neurons. Too much parathormone inhibits nervous activity and leads to lethargy; too little of it may lead to excessive nervous activity and tension.

cretinism (krē′tin-izm) Type of mental retardation in children caused by a deficiency of thyroxin.

parathyroid glands (par″ah-thī′roid) Four glands embedded in the thyroid that produce parathormone.

Pineal Gland

parathormone (par″ah-thor′mōn) Hormone that regulates ion levels in neurons and controls excitability of the nervous system.

The **pineal gland** is located between the cerebral hemispheres, attached to the top of the thalamus. Its primary secretion is *melatonin.* Melatonin is important in the regulation of biological rhythms, including the menstrual cycles in females and the daily regulation of sleep and wakefulness. Melatonin levels seem to be affected by the amount of exposure to sunlight and, hence, "clock" the time of day partly in that fashion. Melatonin also appears to play a role in regulating moods. Seasonal affective disorder, a type of depression that occurs most frequently in the winter months, is thought to occur because of the influence of the light on melatonin. Unfortunately, therapy involving exposure to bright light may not have lasting benefits, but current psychological treatments are effective in the long run in reducing seasonal affective symptoms (Rohan & others, 2009).

pineal gland (pin′e-al) The endocrine gland that is largely responsible for the regulation of biological rhythms.

Review

The endocrine glands influence one another by secreting neuropeptides. In addition, hormones are secreted by the endocrine glands to supplement the brain's ability to influence the organs of the body. These chemical messengers are involved in the regulation of metabolism, blood-sugar level, sexual functioning, and other functions. For example, epinephrine and norepinephrine are secreted by the adrenal glands. They activate body organs during stress in a diffuse and long-lasting way that is partially responsible for the length of time necessary for us to feel calm following a stressful event.

Check Your Learning

To be sure that you have learned the key points from the preceding section, cover the list of correct answers and try to answer each question. If you give an incorrect answer to any question, return to the page given next to the correct answer to see why your answer was not correct.

    1. The _____ secretes epinephrine, norepinephrine, and cortisol, which activate the body during stress (such as by increasing heart rate and blood pressure).

       a) adrenal gland   c) thyroid gland

       b) parathyroid gland   d) pituitary gland

    2. Sugar metabolism and hunger are influenced by the _____ in the pancreas.

Check Your Learning (cont.)

3. The _____ gland is called the "master gland," because its neuropeptide secretions influence many other glands.

a) adrenal

c) thyroid

b) parathyroid

d) pituitary

4. The excitability of the nervous system is regulated by parathormone, which is secreted by the _____.

a) adrenal gland

c) thyroid gland

b) parathyroid gland

d) pituitary gland

Thinking Critically about Psychology

There are no right or wrong answers to the following questions. They are presented to help you become an active reader and think critically about what you have just read.

1. In which ways does epinephrine resemble a drug such as caffeine?

2. When we are doing something stressful, such as speaking in public, how do the effects of hormones secreted by the adrenal glands help us—how are they adaptive? Or do you think they are only maladaptive?

Correct Answers: **1. a** (p. 77–78), **2.** islets of Langerhans (p. 79), **3. d** (p. 77), **4. b** (p. 80)

Application of Psychology

"Madness" and the Brain

We began this chapter by stating the obvious fact that the brain is the most important biological organ to psychology. We end the chapter by looking at two striking and sad examples in which the psychological lives of some people are seriously disturbed because the brain does not function normally—schizophrenia and Alzheimer's disease.

Schizophrenia and the Brain. Schizophrenia affects about 1% of the population. It is a severe psychological disorder that, unless successfully treated, renders normal patterns of living impossible. The central feature of schizophrenia is a marked abnormality in thought processes that leaves the person with schizophrenia "out of touch with reality." Persons with schizophrenia often hold strange and disturbing beliefs (such as that they receive telepathic messages from devils in another universe). In addition, they sometimes have strangely distorted perceptual experiences (such as hearing voices that are not really there that tell them to do dangerous things) and think in fragmented and illogical ways. At the same time, the emotions and social relationships of the person with schizophrenia are often severely disturbed.

Great strides have been made recently in understanding the link between schizophrenia and the brain. Although this evidence is strong and impressive, a word of caution might be wise before we look at this topic. Researchers tend to study very severe cases of any disorder, including schizophrenia, to make the difficult task of finding the cause of the disorder a little easier. Therefore, when we look at the striking images in this section of the very abnormal brains of persons with schizophrenia, keep in mind that these are the brains of severe cases. Individuals with milder schizophrenia may have more normal brains.

Images of the Brains of Persons with Schizophrenia. Whatever factors work along with heredity to cause schizophrenia, they produce marked changes in the brains of persons with severe schizophrenia (Henseler & others, 2010; Mata & others, 2009). An impressive number of studies using magnetic resonance imaging (MRI), PET, and other brain-imaging techniques show that the cerebral cortex and key structures of the limbic system are literally shrunken in persons with schizophrenia (Andreasen, 1999; Byne & others, 2001; Cannon & others, 1998; Mathalon & others, 2001). The easiest way to see the reduced size of the brain in persons with schizophrenia using MRI is to measure the size of structures called the *ventricles.* The ventricles are fluid-filled passageways located near the center of the brain that bathe the brain in fluid. If the underside of the cortex and nearby structures are shrunken, the ventricles are enlarged.

The enlargement of the ventricles in persons with schizophrenia is shown clearly in the two striking brain images in figure 3.24. These are MRI images of the brains of identical twins, only one of whom has schizophrenia (Horgan, 1993).

Figure 3.24   These are MRI images of the brains of identical twins viewed from the back. The twin on the right has schizophrenia, but the twin on the left does not. Notice that the open spaces inside the brain, called the ventricles, are enlarged in the schizophrenic because the interior regions of the brain are reduced in size.

Ventricles

Ventricles

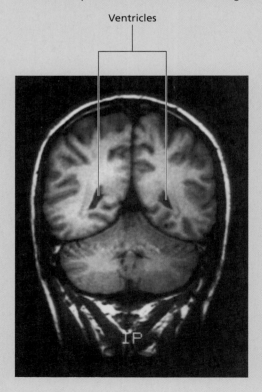
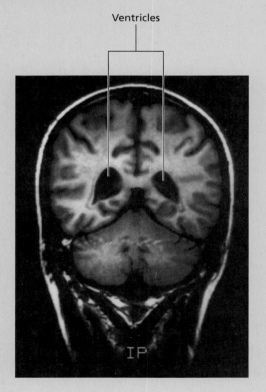

Figure 3.25   The brain of a person with schizophrenia (right) shows a shrunken hippocampus (in yellow) and enlarged, fluid-filled ventricles (gray) in comparison with the brain of a person without schizophrenia (left).

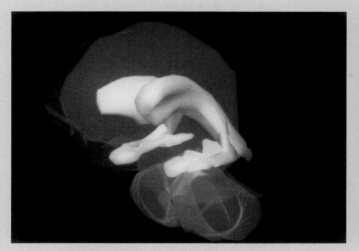 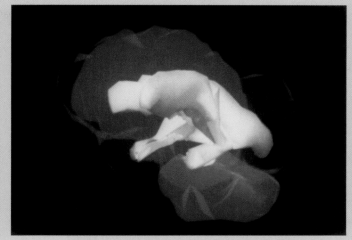

These images were made looking at the back of the head. The two lobes of the cerebral cortex can be seen at the top of the head, with the slightly darker cerebellum clearly visible at the base of the skull. The ventricles are two dark spots toward the bottom of the two hemispheres of the cerebral cortex. Can you tell which identical twin has schizophrenia? The brain of the twin with schizophrenia is on the right. Note that the ventricles are greatly enlarged, because the interior portions of the cerebral cortex and limbic system are reduced in size.

See an even more dramatic set of images in figure 3.25. These three-dimensional color photographs were constructed from computer-enhanced MRI images in the laboratory of Nancy Andreasen at the University of Iowa School of Medicine (from Gershon & Rieder, 1992). In these images, the brain is seen from an angle, looking at the head from the front on the left side. In these images, the ventricle closer to us is silver, and the ventricle in the cerebral hemisphere that is farther away is white. Both the cerebral cortex and the cerebellum are red. The image at the right is of a person with schizophrenia, whereas the image at the left is of a normal person. Note that the ventricles of the person with schizophrenia are enlarged in the middle and rear portions of the brain, showing smaller interior portions of the brain in these areas. Perhaps more interestingly, these color images also allow us to directly measure a key structure in the limbic system, the hippocampus, which is yellow. Recall that the hippocampus plays a key role in the regulation of both emotion and memory (see p. 63). In this image, the person with schizophrenia has a markedly smaller hippocampus.

The parts of the brain surrounding the ventricles are important in their own right, but they also are the source of neurons that activate the frontal lobes of the cerebral cortex (p. 64). The frontal lobes play important roles in emotional control and logical planning—two qualities that are quite disturbed in schizophrenia. Look at the two PET images of the cerebral cortex shown in figure 3.26 on p. 84, which reveal more about the level of brain activity than the size of the structures. We are looking at the brain from the top, with the frontal lobes shown at the top of these images. High levels of activity in an area of

the brain are shown in yellow and red, whereas cool greens indicate low levels of brain activity. Note that the level of activity in the frontal lobes of the normal person (the left image) is high during a task that requires close attention. In contrast, the person with schizophrenia in the image on the right shows little activity in the frontal lobes—they appear to be turned off.

Neurotransmitters and Schizophrenia.   These images, and many similar ones from other studies using brain imaging and autopsy studies of schizophrenics, strongly suggest that persons with schizophrenia experience life in abnormal ways partly because they have abnormalities in the hippocampus, the cerebral cortex, and other key brain structures. Interestingly, evidence shows that these abnormalities in brain structure also are reflected in abnormal levels of the neurotransmitter *dopamine* (Albert & others, 2002; McGowan & others, 2004). This neurotransmitter is involved in the activities of many parts of the brain, including the frontal lobe of the cerebral cortex.

Researchers long suspected that dopamine is involved in schizophrenia for two reasons: First, some drugs that Influence the neurotransmitter dopamine improve the symptoms of schizophrenia. The second kind of evidence that supports the dopamine hypothesis comes from experience with the side effects of the stimulant drugs called *amphetamines*. These drugs are widely abused because of the intense high and feelings of energy they produce. Excessive use of amphetamines can lead to amphetamine psychosis, which closely resembles paranoid schizophrenia. The fact that this condition resembles schizophrenia is important because amphetamines produce this psychotic reaction by altering dopamine transmission (Snyder, 1974). Furthermore, the best treatment for amphetamine psychosis is phenothiazine medication, which is also the best treatment for schizophrenia.

Causes of Schizophrenia.   A great deal of evidence suggests that the brains of persons with schizophrenia are abnormal in structure and function. There is evidence that a predisposition to schizophrenia is inherited, but it is also clear that some other factor or factors must play a role in causing schizophrenia,

Application of Psychology cont'd

Figure 3.26 These PET scans demonstrate how functioning of the cerebral cortex can be affected in schizophrenia. The level of activity in the brain is indicated by the colors on the scan. Yellow and red indicate high levels, whereas green signifies a low activity level. During a task that requires close attention, the frontal lobes of the cerebral cortex (at the top of each scan) are highly active in a person without schizophrenia (left). In contrast, a person with schizophrenia, shown on the right, has little activity in the same area during the same task.

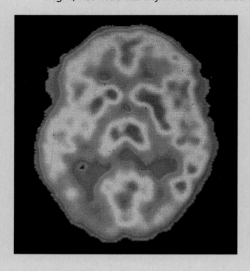 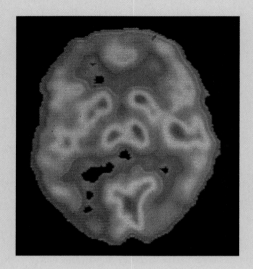

because not all identical twins both exhibit schizophrenia. What other factors cause schizophrenia in genetically predisposed persons? There is evidence that stress causes persons who are genetically predisposed to have episodes of schizophrenia (Meyer & Feldon, 2010; Ventura & others, 1989). However, because this chapter covers the biological foundations of behavior, we focus on evidence that the genetic predisposition is most likely to lead to schizophrenia if the predisposed person suffered some disturbance of the development of the brain before birth or during birth (Brown & others, 2004; Meyer & Feldon, 2010).

Studies by Sarnoff Mednick and others (Barr, Mednick, & Munk-Jorgensen, 1990; Cannon & others, 1993; Conklin & Iacono, 2002; Mednick & others, 1988) support the so-called *double strike theory of schizophrenia.* Mednick hypothesizes that schizophrenia is most likely in persons with (a) a genetic predisposition to schizophrenia and (b) some form of complication during pregnancy that alters the brains of individuals who are genetically predisposed to schizophrenia. According to this theory, a genetically predisposed individual who has no complications during pregnancy or birth would be unlikely to develop schizophrenia. Similarly, pregnancy complications would be unlikely to cause schizophrenia in individuals who are not genetically predisposed to it.

Emerging evidence suggests that brain development in genetically predisposed infants can be damaged by the dehydration of the mother if she takes diuretic medications for high blood pressure or contracts influenza during pregnancy (especially during the later months of pregnancy, the period of most rapid development of the nervous system of the fetus), by severe malnutrition of the mother during pregnancy, by an uncommon Rh incompatibility between the blood of the mother and the fetus, and by birth complications that deprive

the newborn of oxygen during birth (Kunugi & others, 1995; Susser & others, 1996; van Erp & others, 2002; Sørensen & others, 2003).

The clearest evidence in support of Mednick's double strike theory of schizophrenia comes from a long-term study (Cannon & others, 1993). Mednick's research team has been following a group of children of parents with schizophrenia in Denmark for many years and has detailed information on them from birth to adulthood. Some of the children had two parents with schizophrenia (and are considered to have an increased genetic predisposition to schizophrenia), whereas others had only one parent with schizophrenia. In contrast, a third group of children has been studied who have no parents with schizophrenia (and, therefore, are thought to be at low risk for this disorder).

Mednick's research team later obtained brain images of these children at age 29 years using computerized X rays and looked to see whether the persons with the highest genetic predisposition were most likely to have one of the kinds of brain abnormalities associated with schizophrenia (enlarged ventricles). Because Mednick believes that a person with a genetic predisposition to schizophrenia will develop the disorder only if a pregnancy or birth complication occurred, the researchers looked at birth complications as well.

Mednick found that the ventricles in the children of one parent with schizophrenia were significantly larger than those of the children of no schizophrenic parents, and the ventricles of the children with two parents suffering from schizophrenia were significantly larger than those of the children in either of the other two groups, but only when a birth complication had occurred. More recently, Mednick's double strike hypothesis of the origins of schizophrenia has been confirmed by a number of independent studies (Dalman & others, 1999; Kinney & others, 1998; Kirkpatrick & others, 1998). Thus, these studies

Individuals who develop Alzheimer's disease often rapidly fade, particularly in intellectual capacity, until they are no longer themselves.

strongly support the idea that both genetic predisposition and pregnancy and birth complications operate together to cause schizophrenia.

Alzheimer's Disease and the Brain. Few facts portray the intimate relationship between the brain and our psychological selves more vividly or more sadly than the decline of an individual with Alzheimer's disease (Wright & Harding, 2010). Fully functioning individuals who develop this disorder often fade

rapidly in emotional and intellectual functioning, until they are "no longer themselves." Like schizophrenia, Alzheimer's disease results from the deterioration of the cerebral cortex, the hippocampus, and other structures. In Alzheimer's disease, this deterioration is due to the death of neurons, the accumulation of protein deposits, and the development of tangles of neuronal fibers. In most cases, this deterioration can be seen clearly using brain-imaging techniques. Alzheimer's disease is a principal cause of what we commonly refer to as senility.

The loss of brain function results in loss of memory for recent and past events, confusion, and errors in judgment. The individual may no longer recognize close relatives, may forget to turn off the stove, may become lost in a familiar supermarket, and may often lose objects such as keys. Changes in personality are also common. A person who was formerly thought of as polite and socially inhibited may make coarse remarks, lewd jokes, and insulting sexual advances. A formerly shrewd businessperson may make extremely unwise investments. And a happy and loving parent may become apathetic, withdrawn, and unaffectionate.

Alzheimer's disease is uncommon before age 75, but it can develop as early as middle age. The cause of this massive deterioration of the brain is not known, but apparently there is an inherited predisposition to develop it. Close relatives of persons with Alzheimer's disease are four times as likely to develop the disorder by age 86 than are individuals without a relative with the disorder (Mohs & others, 1987). Recent advances in brain-imaging technology using magnetic resonance imaging make it possible to see the deterioration of portions of the cerebral cortex that results in Alzheimer's disease. The image on the left in figure 3.27 is of an older adult with few symptoms; the image on the right shows the dramatic deterioration in both hemispheres of the cortex that accompanies severe symptoms of Alzheimer's disease (Bondareff & others, 1990).

Figure 3.27   (Left) MRI scan of a normal older adult. (Right) MRI scan showing the deterioration of the cerebral cortex in both hemispheres (viewed from the top) in a patient with severe Alzheimer's disease.

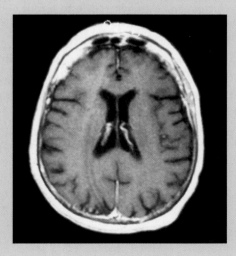

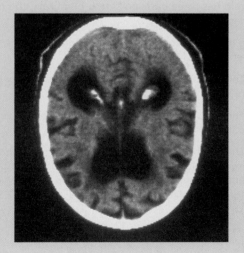

Summary

Chapter 3 describes people as psychological beings who live in biological bodies; it looks at the role played by the nervous system, the endocrine system, and genetic mechanisms in our behavior and mental processes.

I. The nervous system is a complex network of neural cells that carry messages and regulate body functions and personal behavior.

   A. Two kinds of cells allow the nervous system to carry out its functions:

   1. Neurons are the cells in the nervous system that transmit electrical signals along their length.

   2. Glial cells transport nutrients to neurons, provide insulation to some neurons, and regulate the likelihood that neural messages are transmitted from one neuron to the next.

   B. Chemical substances called *neurotransmitters* transmit neural messages from the axon of one neuron across the gap (synapse) to the next neuron.

   C. The central nervous system is composed of the brain and the spinal cord. The peripheral nervous system carries messages between the central nervous system and the rest of the body. It consists of the somatic nervous system and the autonomic nervous system.

   1. The somatic nervous system carries messages from the sense organs to the central nervous system, and it carries messages from the central nervous system to the skeletal muscles.

   2. The autonomic nervous system regulates the visceral organs and other body functions and plays a role in emotional activity.

II. The brain has three basic parts: the hindbrain, the midbrain, and the forebrain.

   A. The hindbrain consists of the medulla, the pons, and the cerebellum.

   1. The medulla controls breathing and a variety of reflexes.

   2. The pons regulates balance, hearing, and several parasympathetic functions.

   3. The cerebellum is chiefly responsible for maintaining muscle tone and coordination of muscular movements but also plays a role in learning and memory involving sequenced events.

   B. The midbrain is a center for reflexes related to vision and hearing.

   C. Most cognitive, motivational, and emotional activity is controlled by the forebrain, which includes the thalamus, hypothalamus, limbic system, and cerebral cortex.

   1. The thalamus is a switching station for routing sensory information to appropriate areas of the brain.

   2. The hypothalamus and limbic system are involved with motives and emotions.

   3. The largest part of the brain is the cerebral cortex, made up of two cerebral hemispheres that are primarily connected by the corpus callosum. The cortex controls conscious experience, intellectual activities, the senses, and voluntary functions.

   D. Each part of the brain interacts with the entire nervous system, and the parts work together in intellectual, physical, and emotional functions.

   E. The brain is an organ that is plastic to some degree—it changes over the course of development.

III. Whereas the nervous system forms the primary biological basis for behavior and mental processes, the endocrine system of hormone-secreting glands influences emotional arousal, metabolism, sexual functioning, and other body processes.

   A. Adrenal glands secrete epinephrine and norepinephrine, which are involved in emotional arousal, heart rate, and metabolism.

   B. Islets of Langerhans secrete glucagon and insulin, which control blood-sugar and energy levels.

   C. Gonads produce sex cells (ova and sperm) for human reproduction and estrogen and testosterone, which are hormones important to sexual functioning and the development of secondary sex characteristics.

   D. The thyroid gland secretes thyroxin, which controls the rate of metabolism.

   E. Parathyroid glands secrete parathormone, which controls the level of nervous activity.

   F. The pituitary gland secretes various hormones that control the activities of other endocrine glands and have important effects on general body processes.

Visual Review of Brain Structures

Because chapter 3 covered so much information on the structures of the brain and the endocrine system, a set of unlabeled illustrations (figures 3.28 through 3.32) has been prepared to help you check your learning of these structures. These reviews will be most helpful if you glance at the first one and then refer back to the illustration on which it is based to memorize the names of the structures. Then, return to the illustration in this review section and write in the names of the brain structures. Check your labels by looking at the original figure again. When you can label all the structures in one of the illustrations, move on to the next one.

This review section should help you learn the names of the structures of the many parts of the brain. Don't forget, however, to learn the function of each structure. After you have mastered the names and the locations of the structures, it should be easier for you to remember their functions.

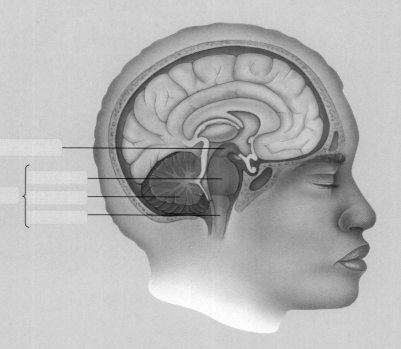

Figure 3.28
Key structures of the hindbrain and midbrain (based on fig. 3.8 on p. 62).

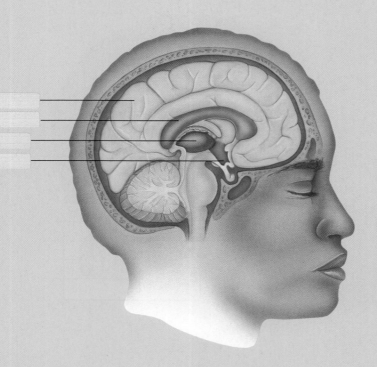

Figure 3.29
Key structures of the forebrain (based on fig. 3.9 on p. 63).

Figure 3.30
Key structures of the limbic system
(based on fig. 3.10 on p. 64).

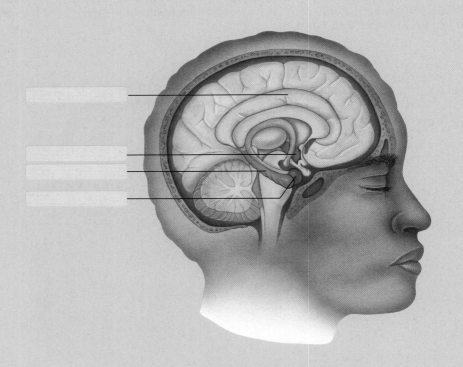

Figure 3.31
The four lobes of the cerebral cortex
(box on lower right) and areas with
specific functions (top area of illustration) in the cerebral cortex (based on
fig. 3.12 on p. 65).

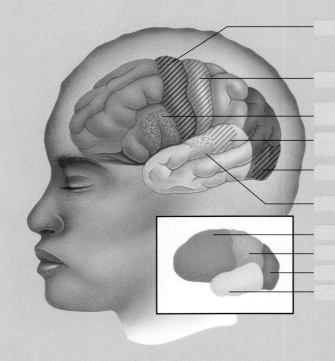

Figure 3.32 Endocrine glands (based on fig. 3.22 on p. 78).

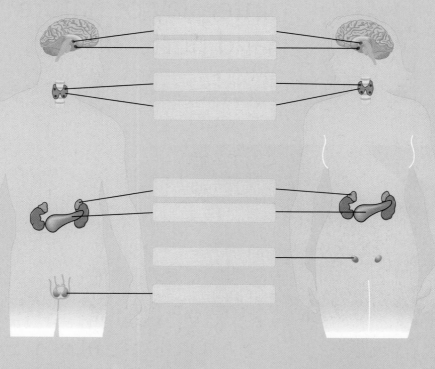

chapter **four**

Interplay of nature and nurture

Chapter Outline

Prologue

What are you like? Could you describe yourself well enough so I could pick you out from your classmates if I visited your class? Most students could easily do so, because you differ from other people in many ways. Indeed, one of the most striking things about human beings is their *diversity*. Especially if you live in a large U.S. city, you see people of different sexes, shapes, sizes, and skin colors every day. You hear some speaking English and others speaking a variety of other languages. Some people are friendly and kind, and others are downright hostile. Some are heterosexual, and others are gay or lesbian. We human beings are quite wonderfully and amazingly diverse.

This chapter is about human diversity and the factors that make one person different from another. Ironically, in order to understand our diversity, we first need to understand why we are more similar to some people than to others. In particular, why do some characteristics "run in families." During the 1970s, Felipe Alou and his younger brothers, Matty and Jesús, were all outstanding National League baseball players, and Filipe's son, Moisés Alou, is still a star outfielder. Ken Griffey senior and junior are another notable father-son pair of major leaguers. Negative traits also tend to run in families. Sixty years ago, Harvard University psychologists Eleanor and Sheldon Glueck compared boys who had committed juvenile crimes to public school boys. Two-thirds of the fathers of the delinquents also had been convicted of a crime, compared to only one-third of the school boys. Not everyone with an athletic or a criminal parent will share those characteristics, of course, but many studies show that people in families do resemble one another in many ways more than would be expected by chance. Why? If you are good in math like your mother, did you inherit her talent or did she create an environment that helped you learn math? The evidence is now clear that family resemblance is due to both inheritance (nature) and experience (nurture). This chapter describes the interplay of nature and nurture in determining family resemblance, but also in creating human diversity. To understand the role of "nature," we will study the structure and functions of genes. To understand the role of nurture, we will study the range of human diversity associated with being female or male, being a member of different race and ethnic groups, and living in different cultures.

Key Terms

chromosomes 94
culture 99
dizygotic twins 93
dominant gene 96
Down syndrome 97
ethnic group 99
ethnic identity 99
evolutionary psychology 111
fertilization 94
gender identity 104
gene expression 103
genes 94
monozygotic twins 93
nucleotides 94
polymorphic gene 94
recessive gene 96
social-role theory 114
zygote 94

Nature: Genetic Influences on Behavior

Do Genes Influence Our Behavior and Mental Processes?

It's obvious that children inherit many of their physical characteristics from their parents. Light or dark skin, blue or brown eyes, tall or short stature—these are all traits we routinely expect to be passed from parents to children. Inheritance is also important to psychology because many aspects of our behavior are influenced by our genes (Bouchard, 2004). Humans do not inherit specific patterns of behavior; rather, inheritance seems to influence *broad* dimensions of our behavior, such as general intelligence (Plomin, 1989; 1999). Although it was long suspected that positive and negative characteristics of our personalities also might be influenced by genetic factors, little solid evidence was available until the latter part of the 20th century. Evidence from many studies strongly suggests that heredity influences normal and abnormal aspects of broad dimensions of our personalities, including sociability, aggressiveness, alcohol and drug use, kindness, depression, and anxiousness (Bouchard, 2004). As we will discuss later in detail, heredity is never the sole cause of our behavior, however. Heredity always operates in conjunction with the effects of the environment.

Genetic Studies of Nonhuman Animal Behavior

Gregor Mendel was an Austrian monk who helped found the science of genetics in the 1860s. When he wanted to study genetic influences on the physical characteristics of pea plants, he was able to selectively breed plants with a particular characteristic, such as smooth skin, to see what the next generation would be like. Selective breeding

Figure 4.1

The findings of a study by Ebert and Hyde (1976) show that when the most aggressive female house mice in each generation were selected for breeding, each successive generation became increasingly more aggressive. Conversely, when the least aggressive female house mice in each generation raised under the same conditions were separately selected for breeding, each successive generation became less aggressive. These findings suggest that genes influence aggression.

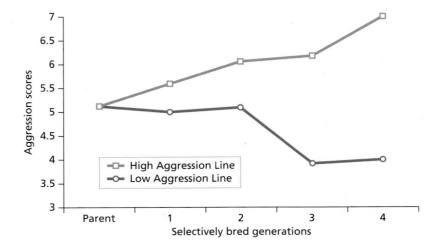

also has been used successfully with nonhuman animals, showing, for example, that aggressiveness and the ability to learn to find food in mazes in mice and emotionality in monkeys are influenced by genes (Petitto & others, 1999; Suomi, 1988).

For example, in a classic study, Patricia Ebert and Janet Hyde (1976) captured wild house mice and then began a program of selective breeding. In the first generation, females were tested for aggressiveness (when placed in a cage with another strain of mice) and divided into two lines based on their aggressiveness and bred with randomly selected unrelated males. In each generation, the 10 most aggressive female offspring in the high-aggression line and the 10 least aggressive offspring in the low-aggression line were bred with randomly selected males. The researchers predicted that each successive generation in the high-aggression line would be more likely to receive genes related to aggression from their mothers and would be more aggressive than previous generations. As shown in figure 4.1, the successive offspring of the selectively bred high-aggression line became increasingly more aggressive, and the offspring of the low-aggression line because less aggressive over successive generations. These findings suggest that genes influence aggression.

Is it possible, though, that the findings of Ebert and Hyde (1976) were actually caused by something other than genes? Perhaps the female mice in the aggressive line provided different rearing environments (or even different environments in the womb before birth) that caused each offspring generation to be more aggressive. A number of clever experiments have shown that such alternative explanations are unlikely, however (Gariepy & others, 2001). For example, an ingenious group of Dutch psychologists transplanted the embryos of aggressive females into the wombs of nonaggressive females, and vice versa, and allowed them to rear the "adopted" mice pups (Sluyter & others, 1996). If the increases in aggression across generations were being caused by the way in which aggressive females reared their young, the offspring should resemble their "adoptive" mothers more than their biological mothers. The results of the Dutch study were the same as in Ebert and Hyde's (1976) study, which provides strong evidence that genes influence aggression in female mice.

Genetic Studies of Human Behavior

For obvious ethical reasons, selective breeding experiments cannot be carried out with humans. Therefore, it's much harder to study the roles of nature and nurture in human behavior. Instead, researchers interested in genetic influences on humans must use research designs that allow them to separate genetic and environmental influences. These designs are based on unusual situations that are not arranged by the experimenter. Because such studies do not allow the same degree of experimental control as formal experiments, any conclusion drawn from them must be viewed cautiously until confirmed by other kinds of studies. The two most common types of "natural experiments" involve the study of twins and the study of adopted children (Bouchard, 2004; Rutter, 2006).

Studies of Twins. There are two kinds of twins that are formed in very different ways. In the case of *identical,* or **monozygotic twins,** a single fertilized egg begins to grow in the normal way through cell division in the mother's womb. Ordinarily, the growing cluster of cells develops over the course of about 9 months until the baby is born. Monozygotic twins result when the growing cluster of cells breaks apart into two separate clusters early in pregnancy. If conditions are right, each cluster grows into a baby and its twin. These twins are identical not only in appearance but also in genetic structure, because they came from the same fertilized egg.

Dizygotic twins, in contrast, are formed when the female produces two separate eggs that are fertilized by two different sperm cells from the father. These two fertilized eggs grow into twin babies who are born at about the same time but who are not genetically identical. Dizygotic twins are no more alike genetically than are siblings born at different times, because they come from two separate eggs and two separate sperm cells. Like other siblings, dizygotic twins share 50% of their genes on average.

Monozygotic and dizygotic twins provide psychologists with an informative "natural experiment," because both types of twins grow up in essentially the same home environment. They have the same parents, live in the same neighborhood, have the same sisters and brothers, and are raised during exactly the same time period in history. But the two kinds of twins differ in their degree of genetic similarity. If a characteristic of behavior is influenced to some degree by heredity, monozygotic twin pairs (who share 100% of their genes) will be more similar to each other than will dizygotic twin pairs (who share 50% of their genes, on average, like typical siblings born at different times).

The many experiments conducted using twins have revealed the influence of heredity on behavior. For example, studies of twins have suggested that intelligence, or IQ, is partly determined by heredity (Bouchard, 2009; Plomin, 1999). Figure 4.2 summarizes the findings of a number of studies indicating the degree of similarity in the intelligence test scores among various types of twins and siblings (Bouchard, 2004; Bouchard & McGue, 1981). Monozygotic twins who have identical genetic structures have almost identical IQ scores. Dizygotic twins and ordinary siblings share only half of their genes and have considerably less similar IQ scores than monozygotic twins. Similarly, there is evidence from other twin studies that aerobic fitness,

Identical, or monozygotic, twins are formed when a single fertilized egg breaks apart into two clusters of cells, each growing into a separate person.

monozygotic twins (mon″ō-zī-gotʹik) Twins formed from a single ovum; they are identical in appearance because they have the same genetic structure.

dizygotic twins (dī″zī-gotʹik) Twins formed from the fertilization of two ova by two sperm.

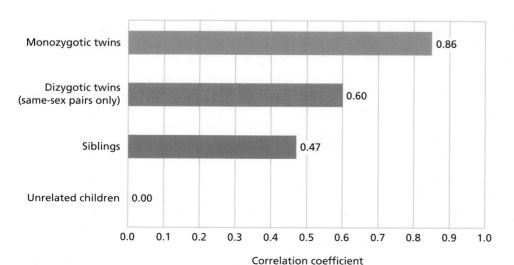

Figure 4.2
The degree of similarity among monozygotic twins, dizygotic twins, and other siblings on measures of intelligence.

Monozygotic twins 0.86
Dizygotic twins (same-sex pairs only) 0.60
Siblings 0.47
Unrelated children 0.00

Correlation coefficient

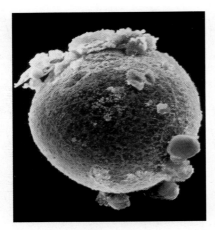

A human egg cell.

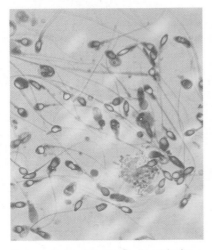

Human sperm, the tiny cells with the long tails.

chromosomes (krō´mō-somz) Strands of DNA (deoxyribonucleic acid) in cells.

nucleotides (noo´kli-uh-tīds) The four chemical compounds (adenine, thymine, guanine, and cystine) located on the double helix of DNA.

genes (jēnz) Segments of chromosomes made up of sequences of base pairs of adenine, thymine, guanine, and cystine, which are the basic biological units of inheritance, because they contain all the coded genetic information needed to influence some aspect of a structure or function of the body.

fertilization (fer´tī-li-zā´shun) The uniting of sperm and ovum, which produces a zygote.

muscular strength, and athletic ability are partly influenced by our genes (Silventoinen & others, 2008), and many other human behavioral and psychological characteristics are influenced partly by our genes (Rutter, 2006).

Studies of Adopted Children. Studies of adopted children also have shown that genes influence human behavior (Angoff, 1988; Plomin, 1994). Take the case of IQ again. Studies of adopted children have revealed that the IQs of adopted children are more similar to the IQs of their biological parents (with whom they share half of their genes) than to the IQs of the adoptive parents who raised them since infancy but are genetically unrelated to them (Plomin, 1994). Because the children spent no time living with their biological parents, the most likely explanation for the similarity in IQs is that genes play a role in influencing intelligence. Although we must be very cautious in interpreting naturally occurring experiments, the fact that many twin studies and many adoption studies consistently suggest that genes play a role in influencing intelligence is reassuring.

Molecular Genetic Mechanisms of Inheritance

In the past, it was believed that inherited characteristics were transmitted through the blood—hence old sayings such as: "He has his family's bad blood." We now know that inheritance operates through genetic material, called *genes,* found in the nuclei of all human cells. The existence of genes was guessed more than a century ago by Gregor Mendel. It has been only during the last half of the 20th century, however, that genes have actually been seen, with the aid of electron microscopes.

Genes, Chromosomes, and DNA. All cells of the body contain microscopic structures called **chromosomes** (see figure 4.3a). Chromosomes are long strands of deoxyribonucleic acid, or DNA for short. As shown in figure 4.3a, DNA usually takes the form of a curved ladder that doubles back on itself, known as a *double helix.* The outside rails of the ladder are composed of a type of sugar. Chemical compounds called **nucleotides** are located on the twin rails of the double helix. There are four different nucleotides in DNA: adenine (A), thymine (T), guanine (G), and cystine (C). The many possible sequences of A, T, G, and C carry the genetic code, much like the combinations of letters on this page convey verbal information to you. Segments of DNA on the chromosomes that contain the information needed to influence some aspect of the body are called **genes.** Thus, genes are the basic biological units of inheritance. Each of the chromosomes of a normal human cell contains thousands of genes.

Human chromosomes are arranged in 23 pairs (see photo in figure 4.3). When cells divide in the normal process of tissue growth and repair, they create exact copies of themselves. But, when sex cells (sperm or ova) are formed, the chromosome pairs split, so that the resulting sex cell has only 23 unpaired chromosomes. When a sperm unites successfully with an ovum in the process of **fertilization,** the new cell that is created is called a **zygote.** The zygote has a full complement of 23 pairs of chromosomes, with one member of each pair of chromosomes from the mother (ovum) and half from the father (sperm). If conditions are right, the zygote implants in the lining of the mother's uterus, and the embryo develops.

Polymorphic Genes. At various times in the long evolutionary history of human beings, small changes, called *mutations,* occurred in the DNA of sex cells. Most mutations damage the organism so much that it cannot live, but some mutations to genes help the organism survive and reproduce and, therefore, are passed on to future generations. Sometimes, more than one version of a gene is created by separate mutations and passed on. Genes with more than one version are called **polymorphic genes.**

Figure 4.3 **(a)** The nucleus of each human cell contains 46 chromosomes united in pairs, 23 from the sperm and 23 from the ovum. In this photograph, the 23rd pair is labeled X and Y. **(b)** DNA in cell bodies typically takes the form of the double helix, which resembles a curved ladder that doubles back on itself. The outer "rails" of the double helix are made of a type of sugar that provides structure to DNA. The rails are connected at intervals by bonded base pairs of adenine (A), thymine (T), guanine (G), and cystine (C). Different sequences of the base pairs of A, T, G, and C carry the genetic code.

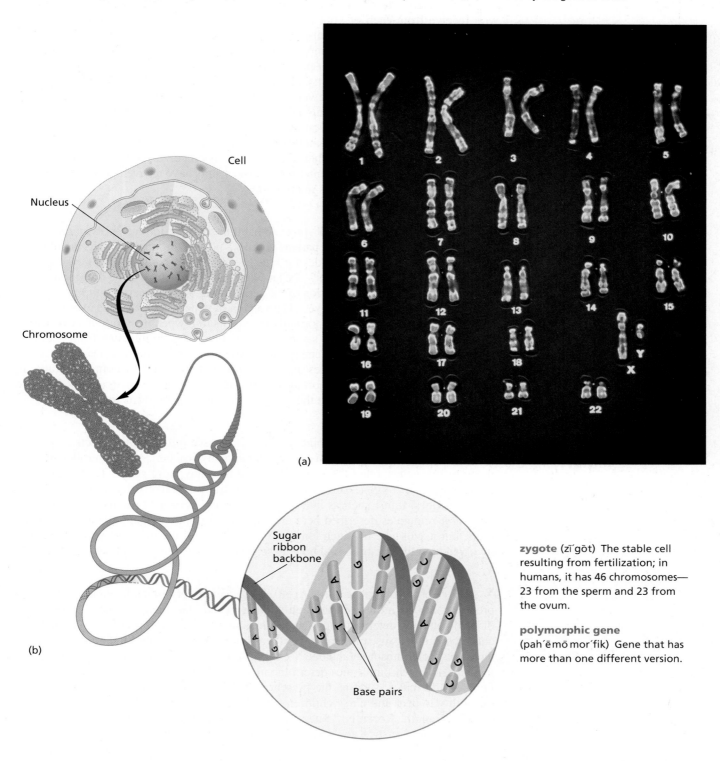

zygote (zī´gōt) The stable cell resulting from fertilization; in humans, it has 46 chromosomes—23 from the sperm and 23 from the ovum.

polymorphic gene (pah´ē mō mor´fik) Gene that has more than one different version.

There is only one version of about 99% of all human genes. The most interesting genes are the polymorphic genes, because different versions of some polymorphic genes are partly responsible for differences among people in their behavior and mental processes.

For example, think of each of the polymorphic genes influencing eye color that you receive from each of your parents as being labeled A and B. Three genes that influence eye color have been discovered, but to simplify our example, let's focus on the gene that influences whether you have blue or brown eyes, which is located on chromosome 15. The version of polymorphic genes that you receive from each parent is a matter of chance. That is why siblings can have substantially different genes. You might inherit two copies of one version of this gene, that we will call 15A, from both your mother and your father. In contrast, your sister might inherit two copies of 15B from your parents. Therefore, you and your sister would have no versions of this gene in common. A second brother might inherit one copy of 15A from your mother and one copy of 15B from your father. Because siblings receive versions of polymorphic genes randomly from each parent, brothers and sisters have an average of 50% of their entire set of polymorphic genes in common.

Dominant and Recessive Genes.

dominant gene Version of a polymorphic gene that produces a trait in an individual even when paired with a recessive gene.

recessive gene Version of a polymorphic gene that produces a trait in an individual only when the same recessive gene has been inherited from both parents.

Dominant and Recessive Genes. What if the two versions of a polymorphic gene that we inherit from each of our parents conflict? What if the version of a gene influencing eye color from the father codes for blue eyes and the version of the same gene from the mother codes for brown eyes? The answer depends on which is the **dominant gene.** In the case of eye color, the version of the gene coding for brown eyes is typically dominant over the version for blue eyes. The version of gene coding for blue eyes is said to be recessive. A dominant gene normally reveals its trait when it is present. A **recessive gene** is revealed only when the same recessive gene has been inherited from both parents and there is no dominant gene giving instructions to the contrary. Dark hair, curly hair, farsightedness, and dimples are other common examples of dominant traits. In contrast, blue eyes, light hair, normal vision, and freckles are recessive traits. To have these traits, persons must inherit the same version of the gene from both parents.

Polygenic Traits. To this point, we have discussed only simple aspects of genetic inheritance. Although traits such as eye color and physical height are controlled by only three or four genes, other traits are influenced by many more genes. Traits controlled by large numbers of genes are termed *polygenic* traits. It is likely that almost all important behavioral traits, such as intelligence traits and personality traits, are polygenic. The basic principles described here are the same for both simple traits and polygenic traits, but it will take us much longer to discover all of the many polymorphic genes involved in polygenic traits and how these genes work together (Jabbi & others, 2007).

X and Y Chromosomes and Sex. The diversity of human behavior and mental processes also is influenced through another genetic mechanism. The biological sex of each person is determined by the chromosomes that are referred to as "X" and "Y" chromosomes because of their shapes (see photo of chromosomes in figure 4.3). Males have one X chromosome (and one Y chromosome), whereas females have two X chromosomes. The chromosomes determine many profound physical differences between females and males, such as the presence of different glands (ovaries versus testes), the ability to bear and nurse children, and characteristic sex differences in height and muscle strength. Recently, geneticists have determined that sex differences in our physical characteristics are determined not only by the number of X chromosomes but also by sex differences in the *expression* of many genes on the other 22 chromosomes (Ellegren & Parsch, 2007). That is, the same version of the same gene can be expressed differently in females and males.

Although there is much to be learned about the origins and sex differences in our behavior and mental processes, these physical differences may directly and indirectly influence sex differences in our behavior.

Chromosome Abnormalities. Unfortunately, the genetic mechanisms of inheritance do not always work properly. When chromosomes are damaged or malformed, abnormalities of body and behavior often result. A common example is **Down syndrome,** which is caused by the presence of an additional 21st chromosome. Children with Down syndrome have obvious physical irregularities, including a thickened tongue and a skinfold at the corner of the eye. The most serious aspect of Down syndrome, as with many chromosomal abnormalities, is mental retardation. Other syndromes result from abnormal numbers of X or Y chromosomes.

Down syndrome Abnormality caused by the presence of an additional 21st chromosome.

Genes and Behavior

How can something as complex as our psychological lives be influenced by tiny segments of DNA located deep within our body's cells? This happens because genes code for the synthesis of specific proteins in our cells. It is those proteins that make up the structures and organs of the body that influence our behavior. When the cells that make up our neurons and endocrine glands differ in their constituent proteins, those structures often operate differently.

For example, some genes determine how protein structures on the axons of neurons operate. One kind of protein structure bring neurotransmitters back in from the synaptic gap between neurons after it has been released, influencing how much of the neurotransmitter reaches the next neuron. In this way, these genes influence how these neurons function and, therefore, indirectly influence our behavior and mental processes (Caspi & Moffitt, 2006). Ultimately, genes determine differences among people in the size and function of every area of the brain (Giedd & others, 2007; Gottesman & Hanson, 2005). Similarly, genes influence the structure and function of our endocrine glands (Jabbi & others, 2007). In turn, the hormones and neuropeptides secreted by the endocrine glands influence our behavior by influencing the functioning of our neurons and many organs (Flint & others, 2007).

Genes do not just influence our psychological lives through the structure of our neurons and endocrine glands, however. Genes influence many physical characteristics—such as our height, weight, and hair and skin pigmentation—that influence how we view ourselves and how others respond to us. This is not to say that we are not shaped by our experiences. We will have much to say about the role of the environment in the next section of this chapter and in later chapters.

Review

The effects of heredity on human behavior have been examined in studies using twins and adopted children. For example, the fact that monozygotic (identical) twins have exactly the same genes, whereas dizygotic twins share only about 50% of their polymorphic genes, can be used to study the role of heredity. Even though both kinds of twins grow up in essentially the same environment, monozygotic twins are more similar than dizygotic twins are on several dimensions of behavior, suggesting that genetics plays a role in influencing human behavior. Similarly, studies showing that adopted children resemble their biological parents on many psychological traits more than they resemble the adoptive parents who reared them indicate the role of inheritance.

The genetic codes that influence both our physical characteristics and our behavior are transmitted in our genes. Genes are segments of DNA on the chromosomes found in the nuclei of cells in humans. One version of each gene comes from each parent, giving us two versions of each gene. Sometimes these pairs of genes are in conflict—for example, when

Review (cont.)

a person inherits a gene for blue eyes from the mother and one for brown eyes from the father. When this happens, some genes are dominant, because they suppress the influence of the other conflicting gene for the same trait. Other genes are recessive and have an effect only when the same recessive gene is inherited from both parents. Genes indirectly influence our behavior and mental processes by coding for differences in the proteins that make up our neurons and endocrine glands. In turn, the ways in which our nervous systems and endocrine glands operate (and other physical characteristics that are influenced by heredity) influence our behavior and mental processes.

Check Your Learning

To be sure that you have learned the key points from the preceding section, cover the list of correct answers and try to answer each question. If you give an incorrect answer to any question, return to the page given next to the correct answer to see why your answer was not correct.

1. The genetic code is contained in segments of DNA called _____.

   a) genes   c) neurons

   b) mitochondria   d) hormones

2. A trait found in a child only when the child receives the same gene for the same trait from both parents is a _____ trait.

   a) recessive   c) Mendelian

   b) dominant   d) dizygotic

3. To study inheritance in humans, scientists often study twins, because one type of twins is genetically identical, whereas the other type shares only about 50% of the same genes; the type of twin that is genetically identical is called _____.

   a) Mendelian   c) monozygotic

   b) adopted   d) dizygotic

4. The results of a study of adopted children would indicate that a characteristic was influenced by inheritance if the children resembled their _____ parents more.

   a) adoptive   c) nonporous

   b) biological   d) dizygotic

Thinking Critically about Psychology

There are no right or wrong answers to the following questions. They are presented to help you become an active reader and think critically about what you have just read.

1. What are the social implications of research suggesting that intelligence is, to a considerable extent, inherited?

2. Does it make sense to you that some of the differences in psychological characteristics that characterize women and men, on average, could be related to something as simple as the number of X chromosomes and sex differences in gene expression?

Correct Answers: 1. a (p. 94), 2. a (p. 96), 3. c (p. 93), 4. b (p. 94)

Nurture: Environmental Influences

Although the influence of heredity on human behavior and mental processes is significant, the events that we experience in our environments play a profoundly important role as well. We are far from being rigidly programmed by our genes. Even highly heritable physical characteristics are influenced by environmental factors. For example, even though physical height is strongly influenced by heredity, the average height in some countries has increased by more than 3 inches since World War II owing to improvements in nutrition and medical care (Angoff, 1988). Even the strongest estimate of the role of genetics in the formation of our personalities leaves a major role to be played by our child rearing, the stresses and strains of our lives, our social relationships, and other psychological factors. Heredity and experience always work together to influence our psychological characteristics.

Physical Environments

When psychologists speak of the important role of the environment in shaping our lives, we are referring to both the physical and the psychological environment. One reason to be concerned about water and air pollution is that there is growing evidence that some of the chemicals we are exposed to can influence human behavior and mental processes. For example, a number of studies suggest that high levels of lead, mercury, and other heavy metals in the blood might influence neurotransmitter functioning and reduce the intellectual ability of children (Hubbs-Tait & others, 2005, 2007; Lanphear & others, 2005; Shih & others, 2006). There is even stronger evidence that greater exposure to alcohol during pregnancy has a causal impact on the level of aggressive and rule-breaking behavior later in childhood (D'Onofrio & others, 2007). Because it is possible that our physical environment is harming us in important ways, a great deal more research on the impact of environmental exposures to chemicals on human behavior and mental processes is needed.

Social Environments

Human beings are profoundly influenced by our social environments. Our parents, siblings, friends, and neighborhoods all influence us (Richter, 2006). The language that we speak, the foods that we eat, and the beliefs that we hold are all influenced by other people. For example, parents, siblings, friends, and neighborhoods all influence the likelihood that an adolescent will smoke cigarettes and suffer the health consequences caused by smoking (Picotte & others, 2006; Simons-Morton & others, 2004; van Lenthe & Mackenbach, 2006).

Culture, Ethnicity, and Identity. The culture and the ethnic group to which we belong are prime sources of the social influences that influence our behavior and make one individual different from another. Indeed, it is impossible to fully understand human diversity without understanding the role of culture, ethnic identity, and gender identity (Heine & Norenzayan, 2006; Lehman, Chiu, & Schaller, 2004; Miller, 1999).

Culture is defined as the patterns of behavior, beliefs, and values that are shared by a group of people. Culture includes everything—from language and superstitions to moral beliefs and food preferences—that we learn from the people with whom we live. During the 1990s, I lived and worked in Miami for three years. There I met several persons who were born in Cuba and had moved to the United States. They brought with them all of the beliefs, attitudes, and traditions of Cuban culture, but they had become a part of the culture of the United States. To fully understand my Miami friends, you would need to understand the ways Cuban and U.S. cultures are similar and different and how each has influenced their lives.

An **ethnic group** is composed of the descendants of a common group of ancestors, usually from a particular country or area. **Ethnic identity** refers to each person's sense of belonging to a particular ethnic group and of sharing that group's beliefs, attitudes, skills, music, ceremonies, and the like. Often members of less powerful ethnic

culture Patterns of behavior, beliefs, and values shared by a group of people.

ethnic group Group of persons who are descendants of a common group of ancestors.

ethnic identity Each person's sense of belonging to a particular ethnic group.

groups in a country also share a history of discrimination and repression by more powerful ethnic groups (French, Seidman, Allen, & Aber, 2006).

Members of an ethnic group often share racial characteristics, but there are many exceptions to this rule. My friend Maria is an immigrant to the United States from the Dominican Republic. She grew up speaking Spanish and learned English only after moving to the United States as a teenager. She sees herself as Hispanic, but she is of African descent and also identifies with her fellow African Americans. Her race is an important part of her ethnic identity, but it is only one part of it.

Culture and Parenting. Parents from all cultures want their children to be "well behaved," but they often define appropriate behavior differently and believe in different methods of child rearing. For this reason, we must understand cultural differences in parenting (Rubin, 1998). Consider one major difference among cultures: In collectivistic cultures, such as the Chinese, Japanese, and Indian cultures, the emphasis is on the well-being of the family and the larger culture, not on the well-being of each individual. In individualistic cultures, such as the mainstream culture in the United States, the emphasis is on the individual rather than the group.

The kinds of behavior that help a person succeed in collectivistic and individualistic cultures are different in some cases, and, therefore, parents raise their children differently in some ways. For example, in the United States, most parents believe that being shy and inhibited places children at a disadvantage—they would prefer for their children to be outgoing and assertive. This is because the individuals who assert themselves most confidently are most likely to succeed as individuals. In Chinese families, however, shyness and inhibition are viewed as advantages, because they help the child fit into the group and yield to its wishes. It is not surprising, then, that Chinese parents praise their shy children, whereas American parents disapprove of shy behavior and sometimes seek mental health treatment for their shy children (Rubin, 1998).

Another difference between Chinese and mainstream U.S. cultures reflects the relative emphasis on academic achievement in the two cultures and differences in how it is encouraged. In the United States, Chinese immigrant parents teach mathematics skills to their young children in more formal ways and structure their children's use of time more than European American parents do (Huntsinger, Jose, & Larson, 1998). Controlling for other factors, such as parental income and education, the parenting practices of Chinese American parents appear to lead to higher mathematics achievement among their children (Huntsinger, Jose, & Larson 1998). Importantly, the two groups of children do not differ in terms of personal adjustment, suggesting that the greater emphasis on academic achievement is not personally harmful to the Chinese American children. In these and many other ways, parenting reflects the varying goals and beliefs of people living in different cultures.

Review   Human lives are not just the product of our genes. On the contrary, our behavior and mental processes are profoundly shaped by our physical and social environments. There is growing evidence that exposure to some toxic chemicals early in life can influence neurotransmitter functioning and reduce intellectual ability. Most psychological studies of the environment are concerned with how we learn how to behave from others, however. To understand how we learn how the social environment shapes our lives, we must understand culture and ethnic identity. *Culture* refers to the patterns of behavior, beliefs, and values that are shared by a group of people. One important feature that distinguishes cultures from around the world is collectivism versus individualism. In collectivistic cultures, the emphasis is on the collective well-being of the family and the larger culture, not on the individual. In individualistic cultures, the emphasis is on the well-being of individual. *Ethnic identity* refers to each person's sense of belonging to a particular group and of sharing that group's beliefs, attitudes, skills, music, and ceremonies. Members of an ethnic group often share racial characteristics, but there are many exceptions to this rule.

Check Your Learning

To be sure that you have learned the key points from the preceding section, cover the list of correct answers and try to answer each question. If you give an incorrect answer to any question, return to the page given next to the correct answer to see why your answer was not correct.

1. The term _____ refers to all the patterns of behavior, beliefs, and values that are shared by a group of people.

   a) ethnic identity   c) culture

   b) race   d) sexual orientation

2. The term _____ refers to each person's sense of belonging to a particular group and sharing that group's beliefs, attitudes, skills, music, and ceremonies.

   a) ethnic identity   c) culture

   b) race   d) sexual orientation

3. Cultures that emphasize the well-being of the larger group are called

   a) ethnic groups.   c) individualistic cultures.

   b) mainstream cultures.   d) collectivistic cultures.

4. All members of an ethnic group are always of the same race.

   a) true   b) false

Thinking Critically about Psychology

There are no right or wrong answers to the following questions. They are presented to help you become an active reader and think critically about what you have just read.

1. How do your culture and ethnic identity influence your experiences as a college student?

2. Are there elements of both collectivism and individualism in your culture? If so, how is individualism expressed in your culture?

Correct Answers: 1. c (p. 99), 2. a (p. 99), 3. d (p. 100), 4. b (p. 100)

Interplay of Nature and Nurture

It is not enough to know that our psychological characteristics are influenced by both nature (our genes) and nurture (our environments). An even more important fact is that genes and environments work *together* in complex ways to influence our psychological characteristics. The two key aspects of this complex interplay of genes and environments are known as *gene-environment correlation* and *gene-environment interaction*.

Gene-Environment Correlation

The genes and environments that influence our psychological characteristics often are not independent of each other but are *correlated* (Plomin, DeFries, & Loehlin, 1977; Rutter, 2006). The term *gene-environment correlation* simply means that people who have a gene that influences a psychological characteristic also tend to have experiences that influence the same trait. How could our genes and environments become linked in this way? Genes and environments can become correlated in two ways:

1. *Passive gene-environment correlation.* The genes and environments that influence a person's behavior and mental processes often become linked, or correlated, "passively." This means that the person does not have to do anything to cause the genes and environments to become correlated. For example, college students like you almost always have above-average intelligence. Your intelligence is high partly because you inherited genes that foster high intelligence from your intelligent parents (Silventoinen & others, 2006). In addition, your intelligence is probably high because your intelligent parents created an intellectually stimulating environment at home. Therefore, you *passively* received both genes for high intelligence and a stimulating environment from your parents. You did not do anything to cause your genes and environment to be correlated. Nonetheless, you got a "double dose" of what it takes to be intelligent—the right genes and the right environment.

2. *Active gene-environment correlation.* Genes and environments also can become correlated though the actions of the individual. Let's consider young children who are genetically disposed to be antisocial as an example. It is clear from twin and adoption studies that antisocial behavior (aggression and disobedience) is moderately influenced by genes (Rhee & Waldman, 2002). Unfortunately, children who are genetically predisposed to be antisocial often behave in aggressive and disobedient ways that *create* experiences that make them even more likely to be antisocial. Parents and teachers often respond to this behavior with demeaning criticism and harsh punishment. Similarly, their well-behaved peers reject and avoid contact with aggressive and disobedient children. Furthermore, antisocial children often seek out the few classmates who are also aggressive and disobedient, and even may join antisocial gangs when they are older. As a result, the genes that increase the likelihood of antisocial behavior also lead to experiences that further increase risk for antisocial behavior. In order words, their genes and environments become *actively* correlated through their *actions*.

Gene-Environment Interaction

In addition to gene-environment correlation, there is a second highly important way in which genes and environments work together. Genes can influence how experiences operate, and experiences can influence how genes operate. This means that two people with different genes often respond differently to the same environment. In addition, the same genes can have different effects on the psychological experiences in two people who experience different environments. The phenomenon in which genes influence how environments work and environments influence how genes work is called **gene-environment interaction** (Rutter, 2006).

gene-environment interaction
The phenomenon in which genes influence how environments influence us and environments influence how genes influence us.

For example, children who are physically maltreated often engage in serious antisocial behavior when they grow up. Not all maltreated children are antisocial, however. What determines how different children are influenced by the experience of being maltreated? There is now strong evidence that gene-environment interaction provides part of the answer. Several studies show that maltreated children who have one version of a particular gene are more likely to engage in antisocial behavior than are maltreated children with the other version of this gene (Caspi & Moffitt, 2006; Kim-Cohen & others, 2006). The gene is important because it codes for the level of an enzyme that controls the amount of several neurotransmitters that are involved in our neural responses to stress. Children who have the version of the gene that results in low enzyme activity are at high risk for antisocial behavior, but *only* if they experience maltreatment (Caspi & Moffitt, 2006). This is an example of gene-environment interaction, because the effect on behavior of the experience of maltreatment depends on the version of the gene (which influences activity of several neural systems), and the influence of the version of the gene on behavior depends on the child's experiences. Apparently, the influence of maltreatment on behavior is different when the neural systems involved in stress response are more or less responsive due to the genetic difference (Caspi & Moffitt, 2006).

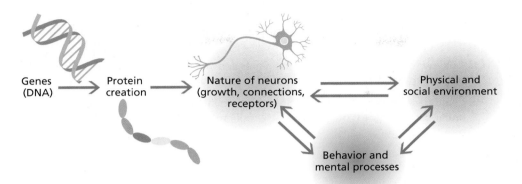

Genes (DNA) → Protein creation → Nature of neurons (growth, connections, receptors) ⇄ Physical and social environment

Behavior and mental processes

Figure 4.4
Genes influence our psychological lives by coding for the synthesis (or creation) of certain proteins, which influence the nature of our neurons, endocrine glands, and other bodily structures. The nature of our neurons and other structures, in turn, influences our behavior. Genes often operate through gene-environment correlations and gene-environment interactions. This means that (a) the genes that influence our behavior often become correlated with aspects of our environment that influence our behavior, and (b) the expression of genes depends on the environment, and the influence of the environment depends on our genes.

gene expression The physical chain effects through which genes determine which proteins are synthesized to create the structure of neurons, glands, and other bodily structures.

Sometimes, gene-environment interaction operates at the level of the gene itself. One of the most important developments in genetics in recent years has been the discovery that **gene expression** is *variable*. This means that the gene does not lead to the synthesis of proteins in the same way in different environments. For example, a gene might be expressed under conditions of extreme stress (resulting in protein synthesis), but remain silent (resulting in no protein synthesis) when life is easy (Caspi & Moffitt, 2006). In addition, there is revolutionary new evidence that some genes that influence neural functioning are "turned on" or "turned off" when new memories are formed (Levenson & Sweatt, 2005; Miller & Sweatt, 2007). Figure 4.4 illustrates the complex interplay of genes and the environment on our behavior and mental processes (Gottesman, 2001; Johnston & Edwards, 2002).

Review

Genes often operate through gene-environment correlations and gene-environment interactions. *Gene-environment correlation* means that the genes that influence our behavior often co-occur with aspects of our environment that influence the same aspects of behavior. This can happen passively, because we receive our genes from the same parents who create our childrearing environments, but it also happens when our behavior (which is influenced by our genes) actively changes our environment. *Gene-environment interaction* means that the expression of genes depends on the environment, and the influence of the environment depends on the genes.

Check Your Learning

To be sure that you have learned the key points from the preceding section, cover the list of correct answers and try to answer each question. If you give an incorrect answer to any question, return to the page given next to the correct answer to see why your answer was not correct.

1. Human behavior and mental processes are influenced by _____.

   a) heredity
   b) both factors in interplay
   c) the environment
   d) none of these

2. Gene-environment correlations can come about _____.

   a) actively
   b) passively
   c) both actively and passively
   d) intentionally

3. The same version of a polymorphic gene can be expressed in different ways under different conditions, such as under different levels of stress.

   a) true
   b) false

Correct Answers: 1. b (p. 101), 2. c (p. 101–102), 3. a (p. 103)

Sex, Gender, and Human Diversity

This chapter is about human diversity—how and why one person differs from another. Like ethnicity and culture, differences between people related to sex and gender are highly important sources of human diversity. There are both biological and psychological aspects of being female or male. A person's **sex** is defined biologically by his or her male or female genitals. Except in rare circumstances, genital structure is entirely determined by the "X" and "Y" chromosomes.

Gender, in contrast, is the psychological experience of one's sex (Gentile, 1993). It will help us to distinguish between gender identity and gender roles. **Gender identity** is the subjective experience of being female or male. **Gender role,** in contrast, refers to all the behaviors that are typically "masculine" or "feminine" in our culture (Money, 1987, 1988). Gender roles vary from culture to culture and provide a set of different expected behavior for persons of different sexes.

sex The distinction between males and females based on biological characteristics.

gender The psychological experience of being male or female.

gender identity One's view of oneself as male or female.

gender role The typical behaviors consistent with being male or female within a given culture.

androgynous Having both typically female and male psychological characteristics.

Gender Identity and Gender Roles

Gender identity develops early in infancy. The newborn is identified as either female or male based on her or his genitals. The parents select a name appropriate to the baby's sex and greet the newborn infant with all the culture's expectations for the behavior of boys or girls. Children quickly learn the gender behaviors that are expected of them through interactions with family members, peers, teachers, and others.

Gender roles are the behaviors that a culture expects of males and females based on their biological sex. Members of a culture classify behaviors as to whether they are appropriate and expected of males and females. *Feminine* behaviors are expected of females, and *masculine* behaviors are expected of males.

Masculinity and femininity are usually thought of as discrete categories (you are either masculine or feminine) that match a person's biological sex. In contrast, psychologists tend to view gender roles as being a graded continuum, with people displaying varying degrees of *both* masculinity and femininity (Bem, 1974; Spence & Helmreich, 1978). Masculinity and femininity are not polar opposites but, rather, are two separate dimensions. Therefore, people can display both masculine and feminine characteristics. Persons who have both masculine and feminine characteristics are referred to as **androgynous.** For example, in the United States today, a

"Jason, I'd like to let you play, but soccer is a girls' game."

Androgynous men and women combine the best characteristics of the stereotypical masculine and feminine roles.

woman or a man who is sensitive to others, nurturing, and emotionally expressive (traditionally feminine traits) and strong, independent, and competitive (masculine traits) would be considered to be androgynous. There is considerable evidence that androgynous people who possess both positive male and female characteristics are more likely to adapt well to a variety of situations, because they are more flexible in their approach to life's demands (Woodhill & Samuels, 2004).

Gender Similarities and Gender Differences

Do women and men differ in their psychological differences in important ways? This is not always an easy issue to discuss. Many people are concerned that information on differences between the sexes would encourage a sexist view of women. In contrast, psychologists Alice Eagly (1995) and Diane Halpern (2004) have argued that knowledge of gender differences is essential. They advocate the study and discussion of the psychological differences between females and males, as long as we remember that "different" does not mean "inferior."

In this section, we summarize hundreds of studies of gender differences. Only differences that have been replicated in multiple studies are presented. As you read this section, please note that *average* differences between females and males are being described in this section. This is an extremely important point, because many women and men differ considerably from the "average" for their genders. The only fair way to deal with people—males or females—is to evaluate them one person at a time without regard to what is average for their gender.

Gender Differences in Physical Characteristics. Only women can be pregnant, give birth, and breastfeed infants. In addition, on the average, men have greater upper-body strength than women. Men can throw objects farther, on average, and with greater accuracy (Buss, 1995; Hyde, 2007). Gender differences in strength and throwing are of little importance in contemporary life. Yet, as we will see later in this chapter, many psychologists believe that physical differences played an important role in the origins of psychological gender differences (Buss, 1995; Eagly & Wood, 1999; Wood & Eagly, 2002).

Table 4.1　Consistently Identified Gender Differences in Cognitive Ability and Achievement

On the Average, Women Score Higher than Men on Tests of:	On the Average, Men Score Higher than Women on Tests of:
Language skills	Spatial and mechanical reasoning
Reading comprehension	
Spelling	Science achievement
Verbal memory	Spatial memory
Perceptual speed	Social studies achievement
Fine motor skills	Electronics, automotive, and shop skills

Sources: Benbow & others, 2000; Buss, 1995; Eagly, 1995; Eagly & Wood, 1999; Else-Quest & others, 2010; Halpern, 1997; Hedges & Nowell, 1995; Herlitz & Rehnman, 2008; Hyde & Plant, 1995; Keenan & Shaw, 1997; Seidlitz & Diener, 1998; Steele, 1997; Stumpf & Stanley, 1998.

Gender Differences in Cognitive Ability and Achievement. Women and men are far more similar in terms of cognitive ability and academic achievement than they are different (Else-Quest & others, 2010; Hyde, 2007; see table 4.1). There are no gender differences in overall intelligence or achievement in most school subjects, from English literature to psychology, but there are some areas in which women excel and some in which men excel. On average, women perform better than men do in language skills, verbal memory, perceptual speed, and fine motor skills, whereas men perform *slightly* better than women in science and social studies on average (Else-Quest & others, 2010; Halpern, 2004; Hyde, 2007; Stumpf & Stanley, 1998). Most of these gender differences are very small, but on the average, men tend to receive higher scores on tests of spatial and mechanical reasoning, the ability to mentally rotate objects, estimates of the speed of moving objects, and navigation through three-dimensional space (Halpern, 2004; Hyde, 2007; Stumpf & Stanley, 1998).

Before the early 1990s, males performed slightly better on average than females on tests of mathematical ability and achievement (Benbow & others, 2000; Hedges & Nowell, 1995). However, several large studies conducted in the United States since 1990 have found no differences between females and males in mathematics (Hyde, Lindberg, Linn, Ellis, & Williams, 2008; Lindberg, Hyde, Petersen, & Linn, 2010). There are now no differences in either the average scores or the number of very high and low scores between females and males. This suggests that changes in U.S. culture have eliminated an important barrier to educational and occupational equality. Furthermore, women receive *higher* school grades in mathematics courses at all grade levels. This suggests that women are actually *better* prepared for careers that involve mathematics skills. Women, however, are less likely to be interested in careers based on mathematics (Ceci & others, 2010) and tend to attribute their success in mathematics courses to hard work, whereas men are more likely to attribute their success to their intellectual ability (Kimball, 1989). These differences in career interests and the way women and men think about their success in mathematics courses may play important roles in how they approach careers that involve mathematics (Ceci & others, 2010; Nosek & others, 2002).

Much the same thinking applies to differences in cognitive ability in which women have the advantage. Although men score only slightly lower on tests of reading and spelling on average, men are twice as likely to fall in the lowest 10% of reading scores (Hedges & Nowell, 1995). No one should assume that a given person is or is not proficient in reading and spelling on the basis of gender, of course.

Gender Differences in Emotion and Social Behavior. Gender differences in social and emotional functioning tend to be larger than gender differences in cognitive performance (Bjorklund & Kipp, 1996; Eagly & Wood, 1999; Hyde, 2007; Keenan & Shaw, 1997). On average, women are more likely than men to be nurturing, friendly,

On the Average, Women Are More Likely To	On the Average, Men Are More Likely To
Be nurturing and sympathetic	Be competitive and dominant
Be sociable and friendly	Be assertive
Be trusting and open	Commit most kinds of crimes (especially sex crimes)
Be cooperative and conciliatory	Be unafraid of risks
Engage in indirect verbal aggression	Engage in unprovoked physical aggression
Be anxious or depressed	Have high self-esteem
Be better able to hide their emotions	
Have a social and artistic interests	Have realistic and investigative interests

Sources: Bettencourt & Miller, 1996; Bjorklund & Kipp, 1996; Byrnes, Miller, & Schafer, 1999; Dindia & Allen, 1992; Eagly, 1995, 2009; Eagly & Wood, 1999; Feingold, 1994; Hyde & Plant, 1995; Keenan & Shaw, 1997; Kling & others, 1999; Knight, Fabes, & Higgins, 1996; Su & others, 2009.

Table 4.2 Consistently Identified Gender Differences in Emotion and Social Behavior

helpful, open, trusting, cooperative, and able to conceal their emotions (table 4.2). As a result, women are more interested in careers in which they can work with or help others (Diekman & others, in press). In contrast, men are more likely to be competitive, dominant, assertive and interested in careers in science, engineering, and mathematics (Diekman & others, in press; Eagly & others, 2004). Women tend to like one another more than men do (Rudman & Goodwin, 2004), but women are more likely to be anxious, depressed, and have low self-esteem. Men, in contrast, are more likely to engage in physical aggression and risky behavior and are more likely to commit most kinds of crimes (Bjorklund & Kipp, 1996; Eagly & Wood, 1999; Keenan & Shaw, 1997). Remember that these are just *average* differences. Even though most of these gender differences are moderately large, there are *many* exceptions to the rule. There are many nurturing and cooperative men and many highly competitive and aggressive women. Knowing a person's gender is not a reliable indicator of his or her cognitive abilities or personality.

Gender Differences in Mating and Sexual Behavior. Across many cultures, men think about sex more often, masturbate more often, and prefer to have sex more frequently than women do (Hyde, 2007; Peplau, 2003; Peterson & Hyde, 2010). As shown in table 4.3, women and men in many cultures also differ in other ways

On the Average, Women Are More Likely To	On the Average, Men Are More Likely To
Prefer an older mate	Prefer a younger mate
Prefer a mate who has high earning potential	Prefer a mate who is physically attractive
Prefer a partner of good character	Prefer a mate with good housekeeping skills
Be threatened more by emotional infidelity	Be threatened more by sexual infidelity
Restrict sex to potential long-term partners	Feel comfortable with the idea of casual sex for themselves
	Be sexually jealous and controlling of their partner

Sources: Bjorklund & Kipp, 1999; Bjorklund & Shackleford, 1999; Eagly & Wood, 1999; Oliver & Hyde, 1993; Peplau, 2003; Schmidt, 2003; Peterson & Hyde, 2010; Puts, 2010.

Table 4.3 Consistently Identified Gender Differences in Mating and Sexual Behavior

related to sexual behavior and the selection of a mate (Bjorklund & Shackleford, 1999; Buss, 1999; Eagly & Wood, 1999). On average, men prefer a mate who is younger and physically attractive and has good housekeeping skills. In addition, on average, men are sexually jealous and controlling of their partners but are more likely to feel comfortable with the idea of casual sex for themselves. Women, in contrast, tend to prefer mates who are somewhat older and who have good character and high earning potential. On the average, women say they are more threatened by the idea of their partner's emotional infidelity (loving someone else) than their sexual infidelity, and they are more likely to be sexually intimate only with potential long-term partners (Bjorklund & Shackleford, 1999; Eagly & Wood, 1999; Peplau, 2003; Schmitt, 2003).

All this research raises a perplexing question: If men have the characteristics listed in tables 4.2 and 4.3 (if they are aggressive, unfaithful brutes who are only interested in a woman's superficial beauty and cooking skills), how are women ever going to find men of good character? The answer is that this research, although technically accurate, exaggerates the differences in men and women in sexuality and mate selection. Although it is true that college men say that the number of different sexual partners that they would like to have over the next 30 years is higher on average than the number desired by college women, most college men (48%) and college women (66%) say that they want only *one* sexual partner over the next 30 years (Pedersen & others, 2002). The difference in the average number of desired sex partners comes from the fact that a few men say they want very high numbers of different sex partners (10 or more), whereas almost no women say they want such high numbers of sex partners. When married or in committed relationships, moreover, the overwhelming majority of both men and women are monogamous. Most of the gender difference in the number of sex partners is the result of a few males who prefer a very promiscuous lifestyle.

What about the assertion that men are more concerned with their partner's sexual infidelity than emotional infidelity (caring about someone else)? A study of adult men and women (both heterosexual and homosexual) found that although men said that emotional infidelity was less important to them, when they discussed actual acts of infidelity of their partners in the past, both women and men of both sexual orientations experienced both types of infidelity as upsetting but were even more upset by emotional than sexual infidelity (Harris, 2002; Miller, Putcha-Bhagavatula, & Pedersen & others, 2002).

Thus, although women and men differ in important ways, some of the prevailing views—even among scientists—of gender differences in mating behavior may exaggerate the facts (Miller, Putcha-Bhagavatula, & Pedersen, 2002).

Origins of Gender Differences

Why are women and men different in the ways previously described? Current thinking is dominated by two very different theories of gender differences. One view holds that inherited biological differences between women and men have evolved over thousands of years that are responsible for gender differences in behavior. A rival theory suggests that gender differences in behavior are the result of differences in social learning experiences associated with gender roles. We first consider current research on sex differences in the structure of the brain and then turn our attention to the two major theories of gender differences in the next section of this chapter.

Sex Differences in the Brain. There is now consistent evidence from many brain-imaging studies demonstrating that the brain structures of men and women differ in a number of ways, in addition to the gender differences in the brain that are related to reproduction (de Vries & Södersten, 2009; Schulkin, 1999). Also, considerable evidence from studies of both humans and nonhuman animals indicates that differences in levels of estrogen, testosterone, and other sex hormones during gestation play an important role in the creation of gender differences in the brain that are evident during adulthood (Dohanich, 2003; Halpern, 2004; Wisniewski, 1998). On average, the cerebral cortex of men is about 10% larger than that of women from childhood through late adulthood (Collaer & Hines, 1995; Giedd & others, 1997; Hopkin, 1995; Reiss & others, 1996). This difference is due to a greater volume of white matter (myelinated axons) in men, with no sex difference in the amount of "little gray cells" (the gray matter composed of the cell bodies of neurons) (Passe & others, 1997). The right cerebral hemisphere is slightly larger than the left hemisphere to the same degree in both sexes during childhood (Reiss & others, 1996), but by adulthood, the relative size of the right hemisphere is larger in men (Wisniewski, 1998). This is interesting, as most spatial abilities are mediated more by the right than the left hemisphere. Thus, the greater relative size of the right hemisphere in men is consistent with their better spatial abilities.

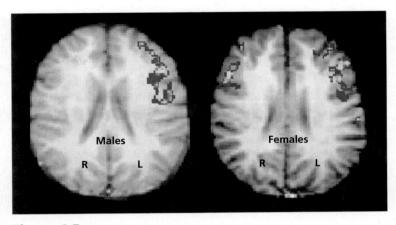

Figure 4.5

These composite magnetic resonance images show the distribution of active areas in the brains of males (left) and females during a "rhyming task." In males, activation is lateralized (confined) to the left interior frontal regions (following standard anatomic practices, left and right are reversed in these images). In females the same region is active both on the right and left.

In addition, there are sex differences in the corpus callosum. This band of 200 million neurons connecting the two cerebral hemispheres grows in size during childhood as its neurons become fully encased in the myelin sheaths that speed neural impulses. By adulthood, the corpus callosum reaches a larger size in women than men (Collaer & Hines, 1995), possibly indicating greater integration of the two hemispheres in women (Banich, 1998). Consistent with this possibility, a fascinating gender difference has been found in cortical activity during the performance of verbal tasks (Shaywitz & others, 1995). As shown in figure 4.5, when adult women and men performed a rhyming task, there was activation only in the verbal areas of the left hemisphere in men (note that left and right are reversed in the images shown in figure 4.5). In contrast, women showed activation in both cerebral hemispheres when they performed the same task. This suggests that the cerebral hemispheres function in a more integrated manner in women during some language tasks, perhaps because of the greater connectedness of their hemispheres through the corpus callosum. This difference is consistent with the superior language skills of women.

There are also interesting gender differences in subcortical areas of the brain. As children grow older, the amygdala increases in size more rapidly in males than females (Giedd & others, 1997) and is larger in adult men (Collaer & Hines, 1995). In contrast, the hippocampus increases in size more rapidly in female children (Giedd & others, 1997) and is larger in adult women (Collaer & Hines, 1995). These differences in the amygdala and hippocampus are tantalizingly consistent with some of the gender differences in behavior previously described. Although both the amygdala and the hippocampus play roles in both memory and emotion, the amygdala is more associated with the expression of aggression, whereas the hippocampus plays a key role in everyday memory and in the inhibition of previously punished behavior (Gray, 1988). Thus, the better memory performance of women and their greater inhibition and lower levels of aggression are consistent with gender differences in these key elements of the limbic system. There are also structural differences in the hypothalamus (Swaab & Hofman, 1995) that may be relevant to gender differences in emotion.

Although the similarities between sex differences in the brain and gender differences in behavior are provocative, we should not make too much of them. Both the human brain and human behavior are profoundly complex, and we are far from fully understanding the relationships between them. On the one hand, biological differences in the anatomy and physiology of the brain certainly could be the *cause* of gender differences in cognition and emotion. On the other hand, sex differences in the brain could be the *result* of gender differences in behavior and experience. The structure of the brain is not fixed at birth but changes throughout life, and it is well established that variations in experience can create changes in brain anatomy and physiology. Thus, it is possible that differences in the behavior and experience of females and males could produce sex differences in the brain. It is too early to choose between these two possibilities.

Review

The term *sex* refers to the biological characteristics of being male or female, whereas the term *gender* refers to the identity and behaviors associated with being a male or a female in a given culture. *Gender identity* is the sense of being either male or female. *Gender role* refers to the behaviors that society expects of males and females. Gender roles are typically classified as masculine or feminine, but a person may express high levels of both masculinity and femininity, a pattern referred to as *androgyny.* Males and females are far more similar than different in all psychological domains, but there are average gender differences in some aspects of cognitive performance, social and emotional behavior, sexuality, and mate selection. There also are sex differences in brain anatomy and physiology at both cortical and subcortical levels, but their meaning is not yet fully clear.

Check Your Learning

To be sure that you have learned the key points from the preceding section, cover the list of correct answers and try to answer each question. If you give an incorrect answer to any question, return to the page given next to the correct answer to see why your answer was not correct. Remember that these questions cover only some of the important information in this section; it is important that you make up your own questions to check your learning of other facts and concepts.

1. The set of behaviors that communicates to others the degree to which we are typically masculine or feminine is referred to as our _____.

   a) sex   c) gender role

   b) sexual orientation   d) culture

2. A person who has both feminine and masculine gender characteristics is referred to as _____.

   a) androgynous   c) bisexual

   b) polygamous   d) heterosexual

3. The theory of the origin of sex differences that views psychological gender differences as more likely to change in the near future is _____.

   a) evolutionary theory   b) social-role theory

Thinking Critically about Psychology

There are no right or wrong answers to the following questions. They are presented to help you become an active reader and think critically about what you just read.

1. What do you think has been more important in your choice of a major and in your plans for a career—your sex or your gender?

2. Are your abilities, emotions, and sexuality typical of your gender? Do you think these patterns of behavior are the product of evolution, of learned gender roles, or both?

Genetics and Psychological Theory
Darwin, James, and Functionalism

In 1859, Darwin published *The Origin of Species*, in which he proposed that the immense variety of plant and animal species in the world arose over many years from a few common ancestors through the process of *natural selection*. This process is often known by the phrase "survival of the fittest." Although Darwin wrote long before genes were understood in biological terms, he hypothesized that variations occur occasionally in the process of inheritance. Today, these variations are known to be based on spontaneous changes in a gene, known as mutations. Suppose a gene mutation produces a variation such as bright red feathers on a male bird's breast. If red feathers increase the likelihood that the bird will reproduce and its offspring will survive (because the red feathers attract healthy female mates), the mutant gene will be "selected" (passed on to the next generation), because male birds with red feathers are more "fit" in the competition to reproduce. In some cases, enough offspring of the red-breasted bird survive to eventually produce a stable new species. Usually, however, mutant genes produce a less healthy animal, and the mutation is lost when that animal fails to reproduce. Only the fittest new organisms based on genetic mutations survive. In evolutionary terms, *fitness* simply means reproducing offspring who pass the mutated gene on to future generations.

Evolutionary Psychology

Evolutionary psychology is the perspective in psychology that is based on the assumption that our evolutionary past holds the keys to understanding our current psychological characteristics (Buss, 1995, 1999; Confer & others, 2010; Puts, 2010). Evolutionary psychologists believe that the genes that influence human behavior and mental processes today were selected from the gene mutations that made some humans better able to survive in the past. For example, although humans learn to fear snakes and insects very readily, they are less likely to learn to fear other objects (potatoes, for example). Evolutionary psychologists argue that it was very important during our prehistoric past (when we lived outdoors) to avoid contact with snakes. People who avoided poisonous snakes lived to reproduce more often than those who did not. Thus, a mutation that made humans more likely to fear snakes was selected and passed on to their offspring. Over thousands of years, this trait became widespread in the human race, according to evolutionary psychologists, because it helped us survive. In the same way, evolutionary psychologists believe that many of our most important psychological characteristics evolved through natural selection (Kameda, Takezawa, & Hastie, 2005).

Does this sounds familiar? Recall from chapter 1 that, more than 100 years ago, William James based functionalism on the evolutionary theory of Charles Darwin. Although James speculated little about genetic influences on behavior, he believed that human psychological characteristics evolved because they helped the human species survive. In that sense, evolutionary psychology is a modern version of functionalism.

Evolutionary psychologists further believe that the *variations* in our genes that are one source of human diversity arose in our evolutionary past (Confer & others, 2010). A topic that is often discussed by evolutionary psychologists is gender differences in psychological characteristics (Buss, 1995; Finkel & Eastwick, 2009). Evolutionary psychologists believe that gender differences arose in our prehistoric past because evolutionary pressures on females and males were different. This means that evolutionary psychologists believe that psychological differences between women and men are hardwired—based on genetic influences. This view has made

evolutionary psychology The perspective in psychology that the psychological characteristics of human and nonhuman animals arose through natural selection.

evolutionary psychology highly controversial, in part because it appears to justify some behavior of males (such as marital infidelity) that is widely viewed as sexist (Confer & others, 2010).

Evolutionary Psychology and Gender Differences. Charles Darwin (1871) proposed that males and females in many species differ in physical appearance and behavior because past evolutionary pressures on the two sexes were different. That is, in Darwin's view, the natural forces that determine that some mutated genes survive (because the animal with those genes lives long enough to reproduce successfully), whereas other genes perish, are sometimes different for females and males. For example, some male hummingbirds may have long and symmetrical tails because they are sexually attractive to females, and being sexually attractive to females increases the likelihood that a male's genes will be passed on to the next generation. Female hummingbirds that find long feathers attractive may have become common over countless generations because long feathers are associated with genes that confer resistance to parasites (which increase the likelihood that a female's genes will be passed on) (Geary, 1999).

Darwin's idea of differences in natural selection for females and males has become the basis of one theory of the origin of human gender differences (Bjorklund & Shackleford, 1999; Buss, 1999; Geary, 1999; Puts, 2010). According to the **evolutionary theory of gender differences,** gender differences arose because *ancestral women and men faced different evolutionary pressures* during the Pleistocene era. This is when early humans survived by hunting animals with primitive weapons and by gathering wild plant foods. Evolutionary psychologists believe that there were different evolutionary pressures on the sexes primarily because mammalian reproduction involves a long period of gestation (pregnancy) followed by nursing and caring for the immature young. According to this theory, this pattern of reproduction had several implications that led to the evolution of the gender differences previously described:

1. *Evolutionary pressures associated with hunting.* Because women were physically slowed by their pregnancies and had to stay close to their infants during nursing, the work of hunting large animals largely fell to men. Evolutionary theorists believe that this meant that strong, fearless males who could throw weapons accurately were more likely to survive and reproduce. Because throwing weapons at moving animals requires good spatial abilities, males with this attribute were also more likely to survive and to reproduce. Eventually, men came to excel in this area, on average. There is some evidence that spatial ability is the basis of modern men's somewhat better average performance on tests of mathematical ability (Casey, Nuttall, & Pezaris, 1997; Casey & others, 1995), suggesting that the natural selection of the best hunters may have led to men's somewhat greater average mathematical abilities.

2. *Evolutionary selection of dominance and aggression.* Men could reproduce only if they could gain access to fertile women. One factor that increased the likelihood of mating with females during hunter-gatherer times was being stronger, more dominant, and more aggressive than male competitors (Buss, 1995; Puts, 2010). Thus, the evolutionary pressure to fend off male competitors selected these features in males. In contrast, no such pressures existed in our past that selected for aggression and dominance in females.

3. *Evolutionary pressures created by child care.* The care of young children had to fall to women during these ancestral times because nursing was the only reliable way to nourish infants. Evolutionary theorists suggest that women were more successful in raising young children when the women banded together in groups large enough to scare off predators that might kill their young (Bjorklund & Kipp, 1996; Buss, 1995; Geary, 1998). Because women who were sociable, cooperative, verbal, and nonaggressive were most likely to be accepted in such groups, the children of women with these traits were more likely to survive and pass their genes on to future generations of females. Thus, according to this theory, women's need to raise children in groups created evolutionary pressures that shaped their social, emotional, and cognitive functioning.

4. *Evolutionary pressures created by gender differences in parental investment.* Because ancestral women were pregnant and nursing for long periods with each child, their level of investment in each individual child was very high. That is, because women could give birth to only a relatively small number of children, it was important that each offspring survive if the mother's genes were to be passed on (Bjorklund & Kipp, 1996; Geary, 1998). In contrast, because the only contribution to reproduction that males were required to make was copulation, they could maximize the chances that *their* genes would be passed on by having sex with as many fertile females as possible.

According to evolutionary theory, men tend to prefer younger, attractive women because youthfulness and the facial, hip, and breast characteristics that men find attractive are associated with reproductive health and fertility (Geary, 1999). The fact that fertilization is hidden inside the female body also contributes to the different evolutionary pressures for the two sexes. Although a female always knows she is the mother of every child she gives birth to, a male cannot be certain that he is the father; the female could have had sex with another male without his knowledge. These facts of reproductive life meant that the level of parental investment of males in each offspring was lower than for females, according to evolutionary theorists (Bjorklund & Kipp, 1996; Buss, 1995; Geary, 1998).

Evolutionary theorists believe that this is why modern males evolved to be sexually jealous and controlling of women (to reduce the chances that they would bear the child of another man) but also to be comfortable with the idea of promiscuity for themselves (because this could increase the number of children with their genes).

5. *Evolutionary pressures in mate selection.* Because women are limited in their ability to gather food during some parts of pregnancy and child rearing, they and their offspring are most likely to survive if their mates help support them. Thus, women have evolved to prefer mates who have physical prowess and the social status and skills that come with age, who have financial resources, and who have good character (Buss, 1995; Geary, 1998; Puts, 2010). According to this view, women select such men because they will help them and their offspring survive. Because women depended on the help of men during ancestral times, evolutionary theory suggests that this is why they are more likely to be upset by emotional infidelity (which could mean that the male would help another female survive) than sexual infidelity.

Critique of Evolutionary Theory. What do you think of the evolutionary theory of gender differences? Some people find it to be highly revealing. Others feel that it is a self-serving attempt by men to justify their aggression, promiscuity, and shirking of child care. In addition, it is troubling to many that evolutionary theory implies that women and men are locked into gender differences by their genes.

Evolutionary theory has been criticized on a number of scientific grounds as well. First, evolutionary theories differ from most other psychological theories because they can never be directly tested. We can say anything we want about events that happened 10,000 years ago during the Pleistocene era, but we cannot conduct formal experiments to put our hypotheses to the test (de Waal, 2002). Thus, some psychologists believe that evolutionary theory is better thought of as intellectual frameworks for thinking about human behavior than as a fully testable theory. In addition, some of the specific arguments advanced by evolutionary theorists are debatable. For example, if women's need to band together for protection led to their greater sociability and cooperativeness, why did men's need to band together to hunt large animals in groups not lead to the same prosocial qualities? Since greater perceptual speed is an advantage in hunting, why do women outperform men in this area? If gender differences in sexuality are inherited, why are there large differences among hunter-gatherer societies that exist today in the extent to which men control women's sexual behavior (Eagly & Wood, 1999)? A cogent recent paper attempts to refute many of these criticisms (Confer & others, 2010).

Social-Role Theory of Gender Differences

social-role theory of gender differences The theory that the opportunities and restrictions inherent in women's and men's different social roles create psychological gender differences.

The major alternative to evolutionary theory is the **social-role theory of gender differences** (Abele, 2003; Bandura & Bussey, 2004; Bussey & Bandura, 1999; Wood & Eagly, 2002). Its primary hypothesis is that each society's division of labor, and the different social roles that it creates for women and men, is the force that creates psychological gender differences. That is, gender differences in behavior result from the different opportunities, challenges, experiences, and restrictions that social roles create for men and women in each culture.

In one important way, the two theories of gender differences are in agreement. Like evolutionary theory, social-role theory agrees that some biological gender differences led to a division of labor between the genders. Thousands of years ago, the biological realities of reproduction for women and the advantages of men's greater physical strength led most human societies to create social structures in which men had greater power and status. In turn, this difference in social status and roles—which still exists to varying degrees in virtually all human societies—led to social learning experiences that taught men to be dominant, assertive, and aggressive and taught women to be submissive, cooperative, and sociable. Similarly, the childbearing and nursing role fostered the learning of helpful and nurturing behavior among women.

Although social-role theory suggests that biological sex differences created the initial push for a gender-based division of labor in the past, gender roles are maintained today by current socialization practices, not by our genes. Now that hunting animals is no longer necessary and societies are governed by laws that have rendered physical aggression less advantageous (it mostly gets you put in jail), social-role theory posits that many gender differences are maintained today only by social pressures that are useless vestiges of past needs. Furthermore, they hypothesize that as gender roles change in contemporary societies, the psychological differences between women and men described above will also change (Eagly & Wood, 1999). Men may knowingly or unknowingly oppose social changes that threaten their position of power, however, and women may find patterns of behavior that are inconsistent with their internalized gender roles to be uncomfortable at first. Thus, although changes in outdated gender roles are to be expected, they may proceed slowly and bumpily at times.

Claude Steele (1997) of Stanford University addressed the influence of internalized gender roles on cognitive performance. He suggested that people succeed in school subjects only when achievement is part of their internalized gender role, but few North American women are socialized to view themselves as competent in mathematics and engineering. It is these differences in socialization, rather than biological differences, that he believes create differences in performance.

Empirical support for Steele's (1997) view comes from experiments in which expectations about performance were manipulated. In one study, women and men were asked to take a difficult test of mathematics skills and concepts. Half of the participants were told that it was a test on which males outperform females, whereas the remaining participants were told that it was a test that showed no gender differences. When the participants were led to expect gender differences in performance, men correctly answered three times as many questions as women. When they were led to believe that there would be no gender difference, however, there was none—the women and men performed equally well (Steele, 1997). Thus, *expectations* of gender differences apparently can create gender differences in cognitive performance.

Additional support for social-role theory comes from studies that have asked whether differences in cognitive performance are more closely related to a person's biological sex or gender identity. Kalichman (1989) found that performance on a spatial reasoning task (on which males tend to do better) was predicted better by each participant's degree of identification with the stereotypical masculine gender role than with being a member of the male sex. That is, both males and females who were more "masculine" performed better on this task than did less masculine participants. Similarly, a number of studies show that both men and women who are characterized by androgynous gender roles (high in both masculinity and femininity) perform more accurately on a wide range of cognitive tasks (Halpern, 1992; Nash, 1975; Signorella & Jamison, 1986).

Some social-role theorists have examined gender differences in mate selection to test their hypothesis that gender differences in behavior will change as social roles for women and men change (Eagly & Wood, 1999). Among 37 cultures around the world, the degree of equality between the genders (defined in terms of the percentage of women holding high-status jobs and political office and equity in incomes) varies widely. Among the cultures with the greatest degree of gender equality, the typical pattern of males preferring younger women with good domestic skills and females preferring older men with good earning potential is weakest (Eagly & Wood, 1999). Similarly, a study of 93 cultures found that girls are less likely to be socialized to be obedient and more likely to be socialized to be achievement-oriented in societies in which women can inherit property and hold political office (Low, 1989). The same study found that boys are most likely to be socialized to be competitive in societies that allow males to have multiple wives (Low, 1989). This suggests that changing social roles could produce changes in gender differences as hypothesized by social-role theory (Peterson & Hyde, 2010).

Critique of Social-Role Theory. What do you think about the social-role theory of gender differences? Is it consistent with your intuitions about women and men? Because it was proposed more recently, social-role theory is less well articulated than is evolutionary theory at this point. In addition, it has not yet fully addressed the significance of differences in the brain between women and men. It is possible that such differences could be integrated into social-role theory, however. As discussed in chapter 3, the brain is a plastic organ that changes with experience. Thus, female-male differences in brain structure and functioning could be the result of differences in the experiences of women and men. That is, it is possible that gender differences in the brain are actually the result of different social roles rather than the other way around. These and other issues have not yet been fully addressed by social-role theorists.

Review

Two major theories attempt to explain gender differences. *Evolutionary theory* posits that gender differences evolved over many generations owing to different evolutionary pressures on women and men. *Social-role theory* suggests that psychological gender differences arise from the different opportunities, experiences, and limitations associated with the female and the male gender roles in each society. In addition to gender identity and gender roles, persons also differ in how they express their sexuality in intimate relationships.

Check Your Learning

To be sure that you have learned the key points from the preceding section, cover the list of correct answers and try to answer each question. If you give an incorrect answer to any question, return to the page given next to the correct answer to see why your answer was not correct.

1. The theory of the origin of sex differences that views psychological gender differences as the result of genetic differences between the sexes is _____.

   a) evolutionary psychology   b) social-role theory

2. The theory of the origin of sex differences that views psychological gender differences as more likely to change in the future if the roles of women and men in society change is _____.

   a) evolutionary psychology   b) social-role theory

Thinking Critically about Psychology

There are no right or wrong answers to the following questions. They are presented to help you become an active reader and think critically about what you have just read.

1. Do you think the roles that your mother and father played in society shaped their psychological characteristics? Did they shape *your* psychological characteristics?

2. Do you find insights regarding gender differences in evolutionary psychology? Do they seem to have a strong scientific basis?

Correct Answers: 1. a (p. 111), 2. b (p. 114)

Application of Psychology

Genes, Environments, and the Cycle of Violence

One of the saddest realities that psychologists face is the fact that some children are physically maltreated. This sad fact is compounded by the knowledge that children who are mistreated by their violent parents often grow up to be violent themselves (Widom, 1989). Some maltreated children escape this cycle of violence, but many do not. Although reducing physical maltreatment for all children must be our goal, understanding why some maltreated children become antisocial adults and others do not would shed a great deal of light on the causes of antisocial behavior.

Avshalom Caspi, Terrie Moffitt, and their colleagues (2002) have provided remarkable evidence that maltreatment in childhood increases the likelihood, through a gene-environment interaction, that boys will grow up to be antisocial. These findings were treated with appropriate scientific skepticism when they were first published, but they have now been replicated by a number of other studies and have been shown to be reliable (Caspi & Moffitt, 2006; Kim-Cohen & others, 2006).

Caspi and colleagues (2002) obtained samples of DNA from a large sample of youth in New Zealand who had been studied multiple times since birth. They examined variations in a gene that is known to determine how much activity there is in the brain in the enzyme monoamine oxidase A (also referred to as MAOA). MAOA breaks down several important neurotransmitters, including serotonin, dopamine, and norepinephrine and makes them inactive. Thus, persons with low levels of MAOA activity have fewer of these neurotransmitters in their neurons, affecting neural transmission in parts of the brain known to play key roles in emotion and aggression. Caspi and colleagues then used data obtained during childhood that indicated if the child had been physically maltreated. As shown in figure 4.6, they found striking evidence that boys who were severely maltreated in childhood were much more likely to engage in antisocial behavior as adults, but particularly if they had the version of the gene that codes for low activity of MAOA in the

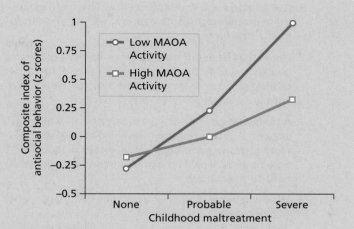

Figure 4.6
Evidence from Caspi & others (2002) that boys who are severely maltreated in childhood are more likely to engage in antisocial behavior when they grow up if they have the version of the gene that codes for low levels of activity in a key enzyme involved in neural transmission (MAOA). This illustrates a likely gene-environment interaction.

brain. Stated conversely, the gene for low activity of MAOA increased risk for later antisocial behavior only if the boy had been maltreated as a child. Thus, this study provides evidence for a gene-environment interaction.

The findings of Caspi and colleagues (2002) may help us understand why adopted children who may have an increased genetic risk for antisocial behavior because their biological parents were antisocial are much less likely to be antisocial if they are raised by well-adjusted adoptive parents (Bohman, 1996; Cadoret & others, 1995). It seems likely that genes such as the one coding for low activity of MAOA in the brain are less likely to be expressed in antisocial behavior when children are raised by well-adjusted adoptive parents who do not mistreat them. This suggests that the cycle of violence can be broken to a considerable extent if our society succeeds in preventing child abuse by parents.

Summary

Chapter 4 provides an overview of how genes and environments work together in complex ways to promote human diversity.

I. Genetic influences on behavior and mental processes are studied in different ways in nonhuman animals and humans.

  A. In nonhuman animals, methods such as selective breeding can be used to determine if an aspect of behavior is influenced by genetic factors.

  B. In humans, "natural experiments" must be used to separate genetic and environmental influences on behavior and mental processes.

1. Because identical and fraternal twins share the same home environments, but differ in the extent to which they share the same genes, studies of twins can be used to study genetic influences.

2. Studies of adopted children can determine if they resemble their biological parents (from whom they received their genes) or their adoptive parents (from whom they received their home environments) more on a psychological trait.

  C. Sequences of DNA (genes) on chromosomes in the cells of our body provide the genetic mechanism of inheritance.

1. Genes determine which proteins will be synthesized; these proteins constitute neurons, glands, and other bodily structures.

2. Genes that have different forms or versions (polymorphic genes) code for different proteins and, hence, differences in neurons and other structures that influence our mental processes and behavior.

3. A dominant gene normally reveals its trait when it is present. A recessive gene is revealed only when the same recessive gene has been inherited from both parents and there is no dominant gene giving instructions to the contrary.

4. Most of our psychological characteristics are thought to be polygenic, meaning that they are influenced by many different genes, each of which makes only a small difference in the trait.

5. Males have one X chromosome (and one Y chromosome), whereas females have two X chromosomes. The chromosomes determine physical differences between females and males, such as the presence of different glands (ovaries versus testes), the ability to bear and nurse children, and characteristic sex differences in height and muscle strength.

6. Some differences in behavior and mental processes are caused by chromosomal abnormalities that involve many genes on that chromosome.

D. Genes code for the synthesis of specific proteins in our cells. Those proteins make up the structures and organs of our body that influence our behavior. When the cells that make up our neurons and endocrine glands differ in their constituent proteins, those structures often operate differently.

II. Diversity in behavior and mental processes is not just the result of genetic variations, of course; differences in the environments in which we live also play important roles.

A. Variations in our biological environments, such as exposure to alcohol when the fetus is in the womb and exposure to lead and other toxins after birth appear to influence our behavior and mental processes.

B. Variations in our social environments, from our families, friends, and cultures, have profound influences on our behavior and identities.

III. Not only do both genetic factors (nature) and our environments (nurture) influence our behavior and mental processes, nature and nurture work together in complex interplays that result in the vast diversity that characterizes the human race.

A. Gene-environment correlation refers to situations in which certain genes and certain environments occur together more often than would be expected by chance.

1. Passive gene-environment correlations often arise passively, usually because the parents from whom you received your genes are the same people who create your childrearing environment.

2. Active gene-environment correlations occur because the individual actively selects one environment over another or creates differences in the environment by evoking reactions from others.

B. Gene-environment interactions occur when genes influence how experiences operate and experiences influence how genes operate.

C. The complex interplay of nature and nurture in gene-environment correlations and interactions results in a nearly infinite diversity of human behavior and mental processes.

IV. To fully understand human diversity, we must consider both sex and gender.

A. A person's biological sex is defined by having female or male genitals, which is determined by the presence or absence of a Y chromosome.

B. Gender identity is the psychological experience of being female or male and is influenced both by one's biological sex and one's experiences.

C. Gender roles are the behaviors that are expected for females and males in a culture. Persons who show a healthy combination of masculine and feminine characteristics (androgyny) may be better able to cope with the complex demands of life than persons who are exclusively feminine or masculine.

D. Although females and males are far more similar than different, some psychological differences between women and men have been consistently found in many studies.

1. Many psychologists believe that physical differences played an important role in the origins of psychological gender differences.

2. On the average, women perform slightly better than men do in verbal skills, memory, perceptual speed, and fine motor skills; men perform slightly better than women do in mathematics, science, and social studies. Only one gender difference in cognitive functioning is even moderately large: on the average, men score considerably higher on tests of spatial and mechanical reasoning.

3. These gender differences are more strongly related to gender identity (masculinity, femininity) than to biological sex.

E. On the average, women are more likely than men to be nurturing, friendly, helpful, open, trusting, cooperative, able to conceal their emotions, anxious, or depressed; to have low self-esteem; and to engage in indirect verbal aggression. In contrast, men are more likely to be competitive, dominant, assertive, physically aggressive, risk taking, and the perpetrator of most kinds of crimes.

F. On the average, men prefer younger mates who are physically attractive and have good housekeeping skills. Men tend to be sexually jealous and controlling of their partners but feel comfortable with the idea of casual sex for themselves. On the average, women prefer mates who are older and have good character and high earning potential. Women tend to be more threatened by their partner's emotional infidelity than their sexual infidelity and are more likely to be sexually intimate only with potential long-term partners.

G. In spite of these differences, there is much more variation within each gender than between the genders, and many persons of each gender do not resemble the average.

V. Two theories dominate current thinking about the origins of psychological gender differences.

A. A principal hypothesis of evolutionary theory is that gender differences became coded in our genes in the distant past, because ancestral women and men faced different pressures as a result of their different roles in reproduction and hunting that selected different genetic mutations.

B. The social-role theory of gender differences is that the nature of women's role in reproduction required each society to create some kind of division of labor based on sex. According to this theory, the different social occupational roles created for women and men—and the different opportunities, experiences, and restrictions associated with these different roles—create experiences that foster gender differences in psychological characteristics.

chapter **five**
Sensation and perception

Chapter Outline

Prologue

Last night I saw the University of Connecticut play University of Notre Dame in basketball—while listening to the radio. The play-by-play announcer watched the game, and he translated what he saw into a kind of information (words) that could be transmitted over the radio. Then I used that information to form a mental picture of the game. I did not see with my eyes, yet I was able to "watch" the game in my head.

I realized this morning that my way of seeing the game last night was not very different from how I see games in person. We don't "see" with our eyes alone. We use our eyes to gather information and translate it into a form that can be transmitted to the brain. It's in the brain that visual perception is created out of the incoming sensory information. I similarly created a visual picture of the game from what I heard.

We usually assume that we simply "see" what is "out there." The processes of seeing, smelling, or touching seem so straightforward. In reality, however, perception is based on a complex chain of receiving, transmitting, and interpreting sensory information. Each step of this process actively changes the information in significant ways. Because we know "reality" only through our sensations and perceptions, we must understand the sense organs and the ways in which the processes of sensation and perception change sensory information.

In this chapter, we study the five major senses: vision, hearing, the body senses, taste, and smell. In vision, the eye collects, translates, and transmits energy from light to the brain. The ear—the sense organ for hearing—accomplishes the same for the energy in vibrating molecules of air. The body senses provide the brain with information from the skin about temperature, touch, and pain; and information from receptors in the inner ear, joints, and muscles tells us about the position and movement of the body—where we are and where we are going. The chemical senses use receptor cells in the nose and on the tongue to provide information to the brain about the chemicals in the air we breathe and in the things we drink and eat.

Raw sensations have little meaning until they are organized and interpreted in the process of perception. In most cases, the ways in which the brain interprets information in the process of perception appear to be inborn. Our perceptions of reality are also colored by individual expectations, cultural learning experiences, and needs, however. As a result, different people sometimes have rather different views of the same world.

Human life would be very different without our ability to sense and perceive. Take friendships as an example. How could we have friends if we could not distinguish one person from another by sensing their differences? How could we communicate with our friends if we could not hear their words properly or read their notes accurately or notice the expressions on their faces? How could we let them know that we cared if they could not feel a pat on the back?

Sensation: Receiving Sensory Messages

We are aware of the world only because we have a number of **sense organs** able to receive messages. These organs enable us to see, hear, taste, smell, touch, balance, and experience such feelings as body stiffness, soreness, fullness, warmth, pleasure, pain, and movement. Sense organs operate through **sensory receptor cells,** which *receive* outside forms of energy (light, vibrations, heat) and *translate* them into *neural impulses* that can be *transmitted* to the brain for interpretation. Sense organs do the job of the basketball announcer who translates what he or she sees into words that can be transmitted on the radio. The process of receiving information from the outside world, translating it, and transmitting it to the brain is called **sensation.** The process of interpreting that information and forming images of the world is called **perception.**

Stimuli: What Messages Can Be Received?

The term **stimulus** refers to any aspect of the world that influences our behavior or conscious experience. The term *stimulus* comes from the action of *stimulating* sensory receptor cells.

Key Terms

sense organs Organs that receive stimuli.

sensory receptor cells Cells in sense organs that translate messages into neural impulses that are sent to the brain.

sensation (sen-sā´-shun) Process of receiving, translating, and transmitting messages from the outside world to the brain.

perception (per-sep´-shun) Process of organizing and interpreting information received from the outside world.

stimulus (stim´ ū-lus) Any aspect of the outside world that directly influences our behavior or conscious experience.

What humans see

What bees "see"

Figure 5.1
The visual receptor cells of bees allow them to transduce ultraviolet light better than we can with our normal visual receptor cells. Therefore, bees "see" more of this form of energy. The top flower is as the human sees it; the bee, however, is able to see an ultraviolet "landing strip" on the flower that we do not see. If you are color blind, you may not be able to see the blue marks on the red flower—more on color blindness later.

transduction (trans-duk′shun) Translation of energy from one form to another.

absolute threshold The smallest magnitude of a stimulus that can be detected half the time.

difference threshold The smallest difference between two stimuli that can be detected half the time.

sensory adaptation Weakened magnitude of a sensation resulting from prolonged presentation of the stimulus.

Virtually anything that can excite receptor cells can be a stimulus. When you take a seat at a dinner party, the chair is a stimulus through your senses of sight and touch. When you eat, the food becomes a stimulus through your senses of taste, smell, and sight. The compliments you lavish on your hosts are also stimuli for them. Whenever a person is aware of, or in some other way responds to, a part of the outside world, she or he receives a stimulus.

When I say that any part of the outside world can be a stimulus, I am using the term *outside* broadly. Even parts of the internal world of the body can be stimuli. If you ate too much at the dinner party, the bloated stretching of your stomach would be a very noticeable stimulus.

Transduction: Translating Messages for the Brain

Energy from stimuli cannot go directly to the brain. Light, sound, and other kinds of energy from the outside world are not able to travel through the nerves. To reach the brain, sensory messages must be translated into neural impulses carried by neurons to the brain. The translation of energy in the environment into neural impulses is called **transduction.**

Energy is transduced into neural impulses in the sense organs by *sensory receptor cells.* These are specialized neurons that are excited by specific kinds of sensory energy and transmit neural impulses along their axons. Some sensory receptor cells respond to sound waves, some to light waves, some to chemicals, and so on. Note that we can be aware of a stimulus only if we have receptor cells that can transduce it (see figure 5.1). For example, we cannot see radio waves or hear some high-frequency sound waves, and we find some chemicals to be "tasteless" and "odorless," because we do not have receptors that can transduce those stimuli. Although a radio wave is just as real as a light wave reflected to our eyes from an apple, we cannot transduce the radio wave. We know that radio waves exist only because radios physically transduce them into sound waves, which are in turn transduced by our ears into neural messages to the brain.

Sensory Limits: How Strong Must Messages Be?

Even when we have receptor cells that can transduce a form of energy, not every signal is strong enough to be detected. The term *threshold* refers to the lower limits of sensory experience. The two primary kinds of thresholds are (a) the smallest *magnitude* of a stimulus that can be detected and (b) the smallest *difference* between two stimuli that can be detected.

The **absolute threshold** is the smallest magnitude of a stimulus that can be detected. Measuring such thresholds is no simple matter. People differ considerably in their sensitivity to weak stimuli, and each person's sensitivity differs from time to time. For this reason, absolute thresholds are defined as the magnitude of a stimulus that subjects can detect *half* the time. The smallest difference between two stimuli that can be detected half the time is called the **difference threshold.** For example, the smallest change in intensity of your stereo that you can distinguish as "louder" 50% of the time is your difference threshold for that stimulus. Detailed knowledge of absolute and difference thresholds has, in fact, been used by the electronics industry to design better stereo systems.

Sensory Adaptation. Recall that an individual's sensitivity to a stimulus differs from time to time. There are many reasons why this happens, such as inattention, but **sensory adaptation** is one of the major causes. When a stimulus is continuously present or repeated at short intervals, the sensation that the same amount of sensory energy causes becomes gradually weaker, in part because the receptor cells become fatigued.

When I was a teenager, I frequently went skin diving in an extremely cold spring in central Florida. At first the water was almost unbearably cold; when I jumped in from the dock, the intensity of the cold grabbed my attention so totally that for a moment I felt like only the cold skin of a person rather than a whole person. But after a few minutes the water felt comfortably cool. The water did not change in temperature, of course, but the sensation changed considerably because the temperature receptors in the skin adapted to the temperature of the water. This is sensory adaptation. It happens to some extent in all the senses; loud sounds and offensive odors, fortunately, also seem less intense as time goes by.

At first, cold water bombards us with sensations. After being in cold water for a while, receptors in the skin adapt to changes in temperature and lessen the sensation of coldness.

Psychophysics. The specialty area within the field of psychology that studies sensory limits, sensory adaptation, and related topics is called **psychophysics.** The subject matter of this field is the relationship between the *physical* properties of stimuli and the *psychological* sensations they produce. Psychophysics is an important field, because frequently there is not a direct or simple relationship between stimuli and sensations.

Because our knowledge of the outside world is limited to what we sense, we need to understand that under some conditions our sensations do not directly reflect the physical nature of the stimulus. Sensory adaptation is one process that alters the relationship between stimuli and sensations, but numerous other circumstances provide examples of this lack of a one-to-one relationship. The concept of the difference threshold provides another good example.

Psychophysicists have been fascinated since the 19th century with the fact that the difference threshold increases as the strength of the physical stimulus increases. When a stimulus is strong, changes in it must be bigger to be noticed than when the stimulus is weak. You can see this for yourself the next time you turn on a three-way light in a dark room. Many three-way bulbs provide light energy in three approximately equal steps (such as a 50-, 100-, and 150-watt bulb). The greatest difference in brightness in the room is noticeable after the first click of the switch—the sofa that you just tripped over in the darkness is now plainly visible. Turning up the light to the 100-watt level adds a less noticeable increase in perceived brightness, and the third level adds even less in apparent brightness. At each level of increasing illumination, the difference threshold is greater, so the perceived increase in brightness is smaller. If you were to turn on another 50-watt bulb at this point—with the three-way bulb at its highest illumination—you might not see any increase in apparent brightness because your difference threshold is so high.

The ability to detect small changes in the intensity of weak stimuli, but only large changes in the intensity of strong stimuli, was first formally noted by German psychophysicist Ernst Weber. Today this phenomenon is known as **Weber's law.** Interestingly, the amount of the change needed to be detected half the time (the difference threshold) is almost always in direct proportion to the intensity of the original stimulus. Thus, if a waiter holding a tray containing four glasses were just able to detect the added weight of one glass, he would just be able to feel the added weight from *two* more glasses if the tray already held eight glasses. The amount of detectable added weight would always be in the same proportion, in this case 1/4.

What is the relevance of this bit of information? Weber's law tells us that what we sense is not always the same as the energy that enters the sense organ. The same magnitude of physical change in intensity can be obvious one time, yet go undetected under different circumstances. This fact has important practical implications. Suppose, for example, that you are chosen to help design the instruments for a new airplane. The pilot wants an easier way to monitor the plane's altitude, so you put in a light that increases in intensity as the plane nears the earth—the lower the altitude, the more intense the light. That way, you assume, the pilot can easily monitor changes in altitude by seeing changes in brightness. Right? According to Weber's law, this would be a dangerous way to monitor altitude. At high altitudes, the intensity of the light

psychophysics (sī′′kō-fiz′iks) Specialty area of psychology that studies sensory limits, sensory adaptation, and related topics.

Weber's law Law stating that the amount of change in a stimulus needed to detect a difference is in direct proportion to the intensity of the original stimulus.

would be low, so small changes could be detected easily; at low altitudes, however, the intensity would be so great that large changes in altitude—even fatal ones—might not be noticed. That is why the people who design instruments for airplanes and cars need to know about psychophysics. We now know that Weber's law is slightly incorrect mathematically but is correct in concept.

Review

The world is known to us only indirectly because our brains are not in direct contact with the outside world. Sensory receptor cells transduce physical energy into neural messages sent to the brain (sensation), where they are interpreted (perception). Not all forms of physical energy can become part of our perception of the world: we must have sensory receptor cells that can transduce that form of energy, and the stimulation must be strong enough to exceed the sensory threshold. Our perception of external reality is complicated, because there is no simple and direct relationship between the properties of physical stimuli and our conscious sensations. For example, a small change in the intensity of sound from a stereo is noticeable when the stereo is being played softly, but the same size change might go unnoticed if the stereo were at high volume. The complicated relationship between physical stimuli and conscious sensations is the subject matter of psychophysics.

Check Your Learning

To be sure that you have learned the key points from the preceding section, cover the list of correct answers and try to answer each question. If you give an incorrect answer to any question, return to the page given next to the correct answer to see why your answer was not correct. Remember that these questions cover only some of the important information in this section; it is important that you make up your own questions to check your learning of other facts and concepts.

1. The _____ is the smallest magnitude of a stimulus that can be detected half the time.

   a) absolute threshold

   b) visual threshold

   c) difference threshold

   d) relative threshold

2. When a stimulus is continuously present or repeated at short intervals, the sensation gradually becomes weaker. This is termed _____.

   a) sensory adaptation

   b) psychophysics

   c) desensitization

   d) none of these

3. According to _____, the amount of the change in a stimulus needed to be detected half the time is in direct proportion to the intensity of the original stimulus.

   a) psychophysical dualism

   b) McGurty's law

   c) Weber's law

   d) threshold variation

4. The specialty area within the field of psychology that studies sensory limits, sensory adaptation, and related topics is called _____.

Thinking Critically about Psychology

There are no right or wrong answers to the following questions. They are presented to help you become an active reader and think critically about what you have just read.

1. How would life be different if human beings had a much higher absolute threshold for the chemicals involved in the sense of taste?

2. What is the difference between sensation and perception? Can you have a perception without a sensation?

Correct Answers: 1. a (p. 122), 2. a (p. 122), 3. c (p. 123), 4. psychophysics (p. 123)

Vision: Sensing Light

In 1950, psychologist George Wald wrote an important paper comparing the eye to a camera. Although cameras and eyes differ in many ways, it is a good analogy to help us think about some aspects of the eye. Both the eye and a camera are instruments that use a lens to focus light onto a light-sensitive surface on which the visual image is registered. The gross anatomy of the human eye shown in figure 5.2 makes the resemblance to a camera very apparent. This intricate and efficient instrument transduces the physical properties of light into elaborately coded neural messages.

Light: What Is It?

We need to have some knowledge of the nature of light to understand vision. Light is one small part of the form of energy known as **electromagnetic radiation,** which also includes radio waves and X rays. Only a small portion of this radiation is visible—that is, our senses can transduce only a small part of it. For our purposes, light is best viewed as being composed of *waves* that vary in *frequency* and *intensity*. These two properties of light waves provide us with most of our information about vision.

The *intensity* of the light wave largely determines the *brightness* of the visual sensation. The light reflected by an apple that is lighted by a single candle is low in intensity, so we see the red of the apple as a dim rather than a bright sensation. Distinguishing between stimuli of different intensities is an important aspect of vision. It is very interesting, therefore, to learn that playing video games enhances this aspect of vision (Li & others, 2009).

The **wavelength** of the light largely determines the *hue* that we see—that is, light waves of different wavelengths are seen as different colors. Most light waves are not

electromagnetic radiation (e-lek´´trō-mag-net´ik) Form of energy including electricity, radio waves, and X rays, of which visible light is a part.

wavelength The frequency of light waves, which determines the hue we perceive.

Figure 5.2

Optical similarities between an eye and a camera are apparent in their cross sections. Both use a lens to focus an inverted image onto a light-sensitive surface. Both possess an iris to adjust to various intensities of light.

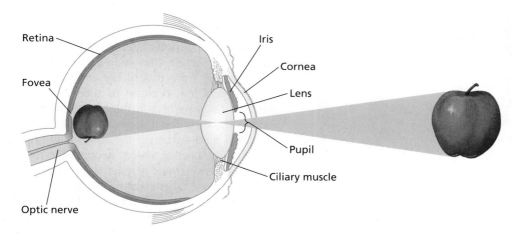

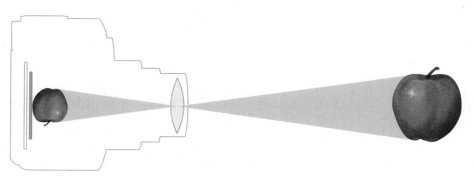

made up of a single wavelength and are therefore not seen as a pure hue. Rather, they are made up of light waves of more than one wavelength. The more wavelengths in a light, the less *saturated* (or pure) its hue is.

The Eye: How Does It Work?

The eye is an almost perfect sphere composed of two fluid-filled chambers. Light passes through the clear **cornea** into the first chamber. At the back of this chamber, the colored **iris** opens and closes to regulate how much light passes through the **pupil** into the **lens.** The lens is held in place by ligaments attached to the **ciliary muscle.** This muscle focuses images by controlling the thickness of the lens, so that a clear image falls onto the light-sensitive **retina** at the back of the second chamber (see figure 5.2). When the ciliary muscle is uncontracted, the tension of the ligaments stretches the lens relatively flat. When the ciliary muscle contracts, it lessens the tension of the ligaments and the lens thickens. The lens must be thickened to focus on close objects; that is why reading for long periods—which involves prolonged contraction of the ciliary muscle—makes your eyes feel tired. When the shape of the eye is not spherical, the lens cannot focus light on the retina, resulting in near sightedness or far sightedness.

The real business of transducing light waves is carried out in the retina by two types of receptor cells named the **rods** and the **cones** because of their shapes (see figure 5.3). The cones are far less numerous than the rods—about 6 million cones compared with 125 million rods in each eye (Pugh, 1988; Solomon & Lennie, 2007). Cones are concentrated in the center of the retina, with the greatest concentration at a central spot called the **fovea.** In good light, **visual acuity** (the clarity and sharpness of vision) is best for images that are focused directly on the fovea, partly because of the high concentration of cones (Rossi & Roorda, 2010).

The rods are located throughout the retina, except in the center (the fovea). Their role in vision differs from that of the cones in four main ways. First, because of their location, they are largely responsible for peripheral vision—vision at the top, bottom, and sides of the visual field—whereas the cones play little role in this aspect of vision. Second, the rods are hundreds of times more sensitive to light than the cones. This means that they play a more important role in vision in dim light than do the cones. Third, the rods produce sensations that are perceived with less visual acuity than do cones. This is largely because neurons leading from several rods often converge, so that their impulses are sent to the brain on a single nerve fiber (shown in figure 5.3). In contrast, cones more commonly send their messages to the brain along separate nerve fibers, giving the brain more precise information about the location of the stimulation on the retina.

The fourth difference between the rods and the cones concerns color vision. Both types of receptors respond to variations in light and dark (in terms of the number of receptors that fire and the frequency with which they fire), but only the cones can code

cornea (kor′nē-ah) Protective coating on the surface of the eye through which light passes.

iris (ī′ris) Colored part of the eye behind the cornea that regulates the amount of light that enters.

pupil (pyoo′pil) Opening of the iris.

lens Transparent portion of the eye that adjusts to focus light on the retina.

ciliary muscle (sil′ē-ar″e) Muscle in the eye that controls the shape of the lens.

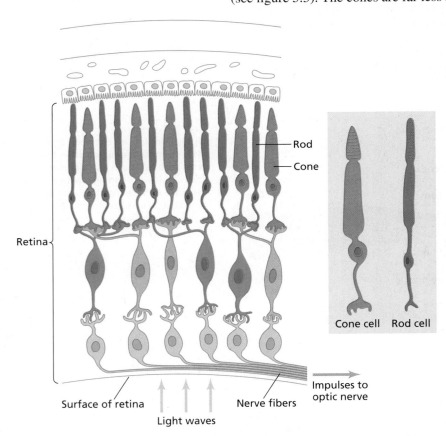

Figure 5.3

Diagram of the microscopic structure of a section of the retina showing the rods and cones and their principal neural interconnections. The blowup shows individual rod and cone cells.

Figure 5.4 You can demonstrate to yourself the existence of the blind spot in the following way below: Hold your book at about arm's length with the word *Spot* in front of your eyes. Close your right eye and stare at the word *Spot*. Move the book in slowly until the word Blind disappears. At this point, its image is falling on the spot in the retina where the optic nerve is attached and there are no receptors. We are not normally aware of the existence of this blind spot because we "fill in" our perceptions to compensate for the missing information. In this case, we see the dotted line as continuous after the word *Blind* disappears.

▢ ▢ ▢ Blind ▢ ▢ ▢ ▢ ▢ ▢ ▢ ▢ ▢ ▢ ▢ ▢ ▢ Spot ▢ ▢

information about color. Because the rods do not detect color, and because the cones can respond only in bright light, we can see only indistinct forms of black and gray in an almost dark room.

Would you be surprised to learn that you are partially blind in each eye? The spot near the center of the retina where the **optic nerve** is attached contains no rods or cones. Because there is no visual reception at this point, it is known as the **blind spot.** We are not normally aware of this blind spot because we "fill in" the missing information during the process of seeing by using information coming in from the other parts of the retina. However, look at figure 5.4 for a demonstration of its existence.

Neural messages from the rods and cones are processed in a preliminary way in the neurons of the retina and are then sent to the visual areas of the left and right occipital lobe of the cerebral cortex for interpretation. Recall from chapter 3 that the neural messages from the eyes is transmitted to the visual areas in a complicated fashion. As shown in figure 5.5 (p. 128), stimuli that are on your right fall on the left side of each eye. Information from the right visual field of both eyes is sent to the visual area in the occipital lobe of the left visual hemisphere after the optic nerves cross over at the **optic chiasm** in the brain. Information from stimuli on your left falls on the right side of each eye and is sent to the visual area in the right cerebral hemisphere. It's a bit confusing when you read about it for the first time, but the brain manages to keep it all straight.

Dark and Light Adaptation

When you walk into a dark movie theater from the daylight, you are "blind" at first; your eyes can pick up very little visual information. Within about 5 minutes, however, your vision in the darkened room has improved considerably, and very slowly it improves over the next 25 minutes until you can see fairly well. When you exit the theater from the matinee performance, you have the opposite experience. At first the intense light "blinds" you. You squint and block out the light, but in a little while you can see normally again. What is going on? How can you be sighted one moment and blind the next just because the intensity of light has suddenly changed?

The phenomena are called *dark adaptation* and *light adaptation.* Here is what happens in the retina during **dark adaptation.** In a lighted room, the rods and cones are being used frequently, so they are not very sensitive. When we enter darkness, the rods and cones are not sensitive enough to be stimulated by the low-intensity light. This gives the receptors a "rest," so they begin to gain sensitivity by making a fresh

retina (ret′i-nah) Area at the back of the eye on which images are formed and that contains the rods and cones.

rods The 125 million cells located outside the center of the retina that transduce light waves into neural impulses, thereby coding information about light and dark.

cones The 6 million receptor cells located mostly in the center of the retina that transduce light waves into neural impulses, thereby coding information about light, dark, and color.

fovea (fō′vē-ah) Central spot of the retina, which contains the greatest concentration of cones.

visual acuity (vizh′u-al ah-ku′i-tē) Clarity and sharpness of vision.

optic nerve Nerve that carries neural messages about vision to the brain.

blind spot Spot where the optic nerve attaches to the retina; it contains no rods or cones.

optic chiasm Area in the brain where half of the optic nerve fibers from each eye cross to the opposite side of the brain.

dark adaptation Increased sensitivity of the eye in semidarkness following a reduction in overall illumination.

In dim light, the color of this red apple hasn't changed, but its color appears to fade. Cones in the eye pick up color, but they do not work well in dim light.

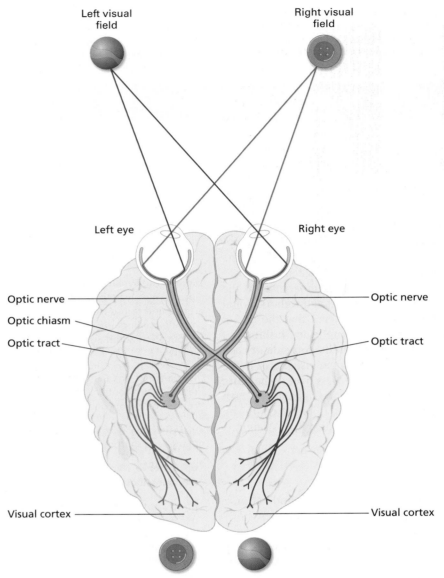

Figure 5.5

Images of objects in the right visual field are focused on the left side of each retina, and images of objects in the left visual field are focused on the right side of each retina. This information is conveyed along the optic nerves to the optic chiasm and the thalamus. The thalamus then relays the information to the visual cortex of the occipital lobes. Note that images of objects in the right visual field are processed by the left occipital lobe and images of objects in the left visual field are processed by the right occipital lobe.

light adaptation Regaining sensitivity of the eye to bright light following an increase in overall illumination.

supply of the chemicals used in light reception, which have been "bleached out" by the intense light (Wang & others, 2009).

At first, both the rods and the cones are recovering their sensitivity, so improvement is fairly rapid. But the cones become fully sensitive (remember, they are not very sensitive in weak light) within about 5 minutes, so the rate of improvement slows after that. The rods continue to improve in sensitivity slowly, reaching a level of sensitivity to light that is an amazing *100,000 times greater* than in bright illumination after about 30 minutes in the dark.

In **light adaptation,** eyes that have been in the dark for a while become very sensitive to light, partly because they have built up a full supply of chemicals used in light reception. When we are suddenly exposed to intense light, the rods and cones are highly responsive and, in essence, "overload" the visual circuits. It's not until the intense light has had a chance to reduce the sensitivity of the receptors—partly by bleaching out some of the receptor chemicals—that we can see comfortably again. Fortunately, this process takes place in about a minute.

Color Vision

Energy of any wavelength within the spectrum of visible light evokes a sensation of color when it stimulates the human visual system. But light energy is just that—energy; it has no color of its own. Color is the experience that results from the processing of light energy by the eye and nervous system.

It's obviously useful to be able to discriminate among different wavelengths of light: blueberries are ready to be eaten; green berries are not. A blueberry reflects the wavelength of light that we perceive as blue and absorbs the rest, but how does the human visual system produce the sensation of blue? It has taken psychologists and other scientists more than 150 years to reach the current understanding of the complex mechanisms of color vision.

In the early 1800s, Thomas Young and Hermann von Helmholz observed that any color can be created by shining different combinations of the wavelengths of light for red, blue, and green on a single spot. For example, as illustrated in figure 5.6, the combination of red and green light produces yellow. Based on this observation, Young and Helmholz guessed that there are three kinds of cones in the retina that respond mostly to light in either the red, green, or blue range of wavelengths. Their theory is referred to as the **trichromatic theory** of color vision. According to this theory, all sensations of colors result from different levels of stimulation of the red, green, and blue receptors in the retina.

Over the years, many types of studies have confirmed that there are indeed three kinds of cones (Solomon & Lennie, 2007; Mancuso & others, 2009). As shown in

Figure 5.6

The trichromatic theory of color vision is based on the observation that all colors can be produced by various combinations of red, blue, and green light (and that all three lights together create white).

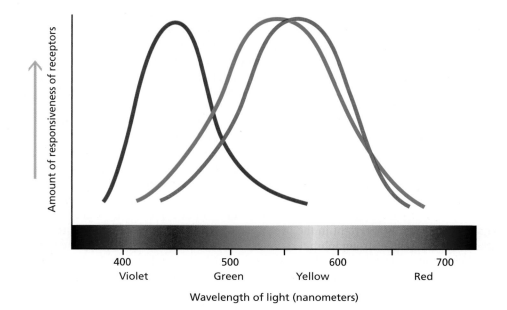

Figure 5.7

Our ability to see color is partly based on the fact that three kinds of cones contain pigments that respond mostly to light in the wavelengths for blue, green, and red. Note, however, that each type of cone also responds to other nearby wavelengths of light. This means, for example, that light in the yellow range stimulates both the red and the green cone receptors, but not as strongly as light in the red or green ranges, respectively.

trichromatic theory (trī˝krō-mat´ik) Theory of color vision contending that the eye has three different kinds of cones, each of which responds to light of one range of wavelength.

figure 5.7, each kind of cone contains pigments that mostly absorb light of the wavelengths that correspond to red, green, and blue. Does that mean that the trichromatic theory of Young and Helmholz was correct? Yes and no. Color vision is fascinatingly complex.

Soon after Young and Helmholz stated the trichromatic theory, other scientists pointed out that it could not explain the intriguing phenomenon of *color afterimages:* If you stare at a patch of color for a while and then shift your eyes to a white surface, you will see a ghostly afterimage of the patch in the color that is *complementary* to that of the original patch.[1] For example, stare intensely for about 30 seconds at the white dot in the center of the word *red* that is printed in the color red in figure 5.8. Then

Figure 5.8

Stimulus used in the demonstration of afterimages. Stare at the white dot in the center of the word *red* for 30 seconds. Then look at the white space above the word. What do you see?

---

[1] Note that complementary colors are different to artists. In art, a complementary color of a primary color (red, blue, and yellow) is the one you get when you mix the other two primary colors. Hence, orange is the complement of blue because mixing yellow and red yields orange. Don't be confused by these two different meanings of the term *complementary color.*

Figure 5.9

The modern theory of color vision combines the three kinds of cone color receptors of trichromatic theory with the two processing mechanisms of opponent-process theory. When light in the red wavelengths stimulates the red receptors, the receptors send a strong excitatory message to the red-green (R-G) opponent mechanism, which stimulates rapid firing of neural signals to the brain. Light in the yellow wavelengths stimulates both the red and the green receptors somewhat. They both send weak excitatory messages to the yellow-blue (Y-B) opponent mechanism, but together they are strong enough to stimulate it to send fast signals to the brain. When light is in the blue wavelengths, it stimulates the blue receptors, which send strong inhibitory messages to the Y-B opponent mechanism, leading it to fire slowly. Light in the green wavelengths leads to slow firing of the R-G opponent mechanism in a similar fashion.

opponent-process theory Theory of color vision contending that the visual system has two kinds of color processors, which respond to light in either the red-green or yellow-blue ranges of wavelength.

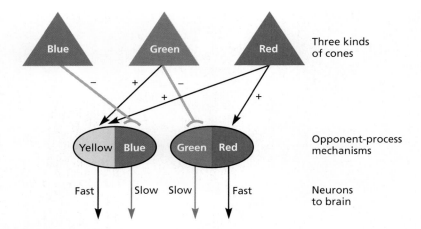

stare at the blank white space above it. You will see an afterimage of the word *red*, but it will be green. The same thing occurs for all four of the complementary colors.

The **opponent-process theory** was developed to explain phenomena that cannot be explained just by the existence of three kinds of cones. The opponent-process theory states that there are also two kinds of *color-processing mechanisms,* which receive messages from the three kinds of cones (see figure 5.9). These two color-processing mechanisms respond in *opposite* ways that correspond to the two pairs of complementary colors. For example, suppose you look at a lemon (and light in the yellow range of wavelength reflects from the lemon onto your retinas). Light of this wavelength stimulates both the red and green receptors, but not the blue receptors (see figure 5.7). The rate of firing of the *yellow-blue (Y-B) processing mechanism is increased* by signals from the red and green receptors but is *slowed down* by inhibitory signals from the blue receptors. Therefore, light in the yellow wavelengths leads the Y-B mechanism to send a high-frequency message along the visual system to the brain. This signal is the primary information used by the brain to produce the sensation of yellow on the peel of the lemon. However, the rate of firing of the *red-green (R-G) processing mechanism is increased* by signals from the red receptors but is slowed by signals from the green receptors. When light in the green wavelengths stimulates the green receptors, the receptors send a strong inhibitory message to the red-green (R-G) opponent mechanism, which causes it to send low-frequency neural signals to the brain. In similar ways, combinations of signals from the opponent-processing mechanisms supply the brain with the information necessary for all color sensations.

Note that opponent-process theory explains the phenomenon of color afterimages, because the R-G and Y-B mechanisms cannot signal both of their opponent colors at the same time. Staring at the red stimulus reduces the sensitivity of the red receptors (through sensory adaptation), leading the R-G system to send a signal to the brain that is interpreted as the sensation of green. Perhaps the strongest evidence for the opponent-process theory, however, is that we now know that neurons throughout the visual system—from the retina to the cerebral cortex—respond to light in an opponent-process fashion (Engle, 1999; Solomon & Lennie, 2007). For example, if a specific neuron in the retina is excited by green light, then it is inhibited from firing by red light.

Thus, the trichromatic theory accurately describes events very well at the first level of neurons in the visual system—the cones within the retina—but the opponent-process theory best describes the activities of neurons in the rest of the visual system. In other words, they are both correct when combined (Gegenfurtner, 2003).

Color Blindness. Few people are completely unable to distinguish among all colors, but partial color blindness affects about 8% of males and 1% of females. Most people with partial color blindness have difficulty distinguishing only between two colors. Usually they cannot tell the difference between red and green, but they see yellow and blue normally (see figure 5.10). In rare cases, they cannot distinguish yellow from blue. Note that the colors that look the same to a color-blind person are always complementary colors.

Red-green color blindness occurs because a genetic defect causes the pigments to be absent from the cones that respond to the wavelengths of light that we sense as red or green. Yellow-blue color blindness is the result of an absence of blue pigment in the cones. The absence of input from the cones that respond to light in the blue range of wavelengths gives incomplete information to the opponent processors, resulting in a failure to distinguish blue from its complementary color of yellow.

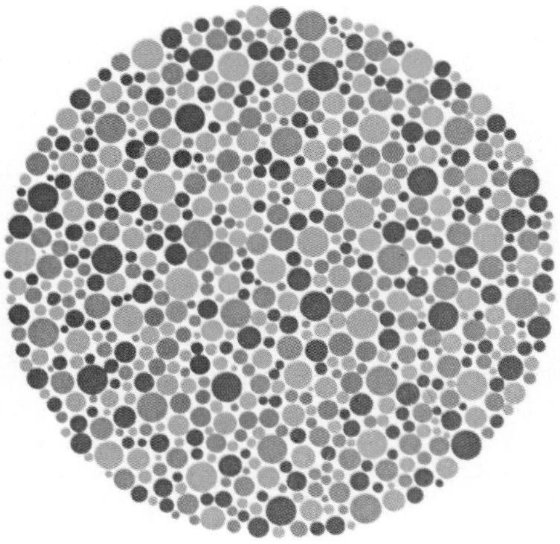

Figure 5.10 Individuals with normal color vision can see the number as 8. Most red-green color-blind individuals see a 3 here, and in rare cases, they do not see a number at all.

Source: This has been reproduced from *Ishihara's Tests for Colour Blindness* published by KANEHARA & CO., LTD., Tokyo, Japan, but tests for color blindness cannot be conducted with this material. For accurate testing, the original plates should be used.

Review

The lens of the eyes focuses a visual image on the retina, which contains two kinds of sensory receptor cells, the rods and cones. These transduce the wavelength, amplitude, and complexity of the light waves into neural messages. The two kinds of receptor cells perform their jobs somewhat differently. Cones work best in intense light, provide good visual acuity, and transduce information about the wavelength of light that result in the perception of color. Rods work well in weak light, do not provide good acuity, and do not code information about color. The eye does not function well when the intensity of light suddenly changes, but it quickly regains its sensitivity through the processes of light and dark adaptation. There are two major theoretical explanations for how the visual system transduces color. One states that three different kinds of cones are most sensitive to light of different wavelengths. The other suggests that two kinds of color-processing mechanisms in the visual system process complementary colors. Each theory is "correct" at different stages of the information processing about the wavelength of light.

Check Your Learning

To be sure that you have learned the key points from the preceding section, cover the list of correct answers and try to answer each question. If you give an incorrect answer to any question, return to the page given next to the correct answer to see why your answer was not correct.

1. The hue that we sense is largely determined by the _____ of the light.

   a) intensity   c) saturation
   b) amplitude   d) wavelength

2. Light waves are transduced into neural messages by two types of receptor cells, named *rods* and *cones,* in the _____ of the eye.

   a) ciliary structure c) retina
   b) pupil   d) iris

3. Cones are concentrated in the _____.

   a) periphery of the eye c) iris
   b) fovea   d) blind spot

Check Your Learning (cont.)

4. The _____ theory of color vision proposes that there are three kinds of cones in the retina that respond primarily to light in either the red, green, or blue range of wavelengths.

a) opponent-process

c) psychophysical

b) trichromatic

d) sensory adaptation

Thinking Critically about Psychology

There are no right or wrong answers to the following questions. They are presented to help you become an active reader and think critically about what you have just read.

1. If cones give us the best visual acuity, what is the advantage of having rods as well?

2. How can the two different theories of color vision both be correct?

Correct Answers: **1.** d (pp. 125–126), **2.** c (p. 126), **3.** b (p. 126), **4.** b (p. 128)

Hearing: Sensing Sound Waves

Without hearing and vision, there would be no spoken languages, and without languages most of the cultural and scientific accomplishments of human beings probably would have been impossible. The sense of hearing depends on the ear, a complex sensory instrument that transduces the physical properties of sound waves into neural messages that are sent to the brain. Neural messages from the ears are first interpreted in the temporal lobe's auditory area and then forwarded to other parts of the brain for additional interpretation (King & Nelken, 2009; Recanzone & Cohen, 2010).

Sound: What Is It?

audition (aw-dish´-un) Sense of hearing.

sound waves Cyclical changes in air pressure that constitute the stimulus for hearing.

frequency of cycles Rate of vibration of sound waves; determines pitch.

hertz (Hz) Measurement of the frequency of sound waves in cycles per second.

intensity Density of vibrating air molecules, which determines the loudness of sound.

pitch Experience of sound vibrations sensed as high or low.

decibel (db) (des´i-bel) Measurement of the intensity of perceived sound.

Hearing, or **audition,** is the sense that detects the vibratory changes in the air known as **sound waves.** When an object, such as a tuning fork, vibrates back and forth, it sets in motion successive waves of *compression* (increased density) and *rarefaction* (reduced density) of the molecules of the air (see figure 5.11). When the waves reach the ear, the reception of sound begins. The sound waves in the air cause a chain of small structures in the ear to vibrate in a way that is eventually translated into a neural message to the brain.

Because not all sound waves are alike, the nature of a sound wave determines to a great extent how we sense it. For one thing, sound waves differ in the **frequency of cycles** of compression and rarefaction of the air (see figure 5.11). Objects that vibrate slowly create low-frequency sound waves, whereas rapidly vibrating objects produce high-frequency sound waves. The frequency of sound waves is measured in **hertz (Hz)** units, the number of vibratory cycles per second. The human ear is sensitive to sound waves in the range of 20 to 20,000 Hz. Sound waves also differ in **intensity,** or how densely compacted the air molecules are in the sound wave.

The frequency of a sound wave largely determines its **pitch,** or how high or low it sounds to us. For example, striking a glass with a spoon causes a higher-frequency sound wave—which we hear as a higher pitch—than striking a bass drum. The loudness of a sound is largely determined by its intensity. Gently tapping a bass drum produces less dense compression and rarefaction, and a quieter sound, than striking it hard. Intensity is measured in **decibel (db)** units. This scale begins at zero at the absolute threshold for detecting a 1,000 Hz tone (and increases by 20 db as the intensity of the stimulus is multiplied by 10). Normal conversation averages about 60 db, whereas sounds of 120 db or more are quite painful (see figure 5.12). Protect yourself from prolonged exposure to sounds over 85 decibels, because they can lead to permanent loss of hearing and ringing in the ears. Even brief exposure to loudness of 150 decibels can permanently damage hearing, and most rock concerts exceed these levels.

The **timbre** of a sound (its characteristic quality) is determined by the complexity of the sound wave—that is, the extent to which it is composed of many waves of different frequency and intensity. The voices of different people sound different to us largely because of their unique timbres.

The relationship between the physical properties of sound waves and the sensation of sound is not as simple as I have just made it seem. Take loudness, for example. Two tones of equal intensity may not be heard as equally loud if they are not equal in frequency. Loudness seems greatest for tones of about 3,000 to 4,000 Hz; higher- or lower-frequency sounds of the same intensity seem less loud to us.

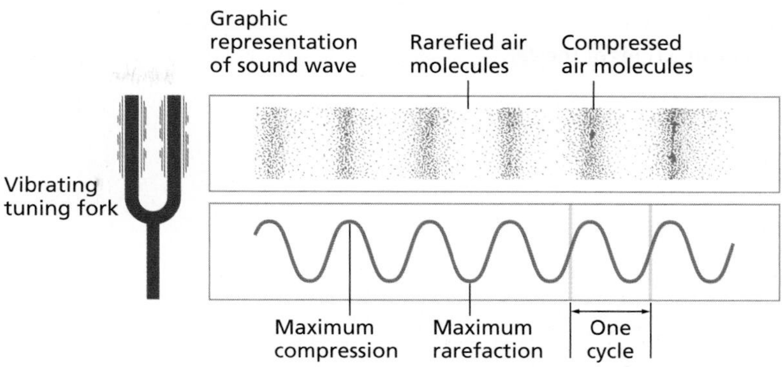

The Ear: How Does It Work?

The ear is a sensitive sensory instrument that transduces sound waves into neural impulses to the brain. It is composed of three major sections: the outer ear, the middle ear, and the inner ear (see figure 5.13, p. 134).

Outer Ear. The external part of the ear, or **pinna,** which we think of as the "ear," is useful as a sound collector and is helpful in locating the origins of sounds. The shape of the pinna is especially important in sound localization, as shown by the fact that temporarily smoothing the pinna with putty impairs sound localization. Connecting the outer ear and the middle ear is the hollow **external auditory canal.** It's the part that gets waxy and the part through which sound waves reach the eardrum (also known as the *tympanic membrane*), the first structure of the middle ear.

Middle Ear. The outermost structure of the middle ear is a thin membrane known as the **eardrum,** because it resembles the skin on a drum. Sound waves in the air cause the eardrum to vibrate. The vibrating eardrum passes the vibration on to a series of three movable, interconnected bones: the **hammer,** the **anvil,** and the **stirrup,** so

Figure 5.11
Vibrating objects, such as a tuning fork, create a sound wave of successive compression and rarefaction (expansion) in the air, which can be represented graphically as shown.

timbre (tam′br) Characteristic quality of a sound as determined by the complexity of the sound wave.

pinna (pin′nah) External part of the ear.

external auditory canal Tube connecting the pinna to the middle ear.

eardrum Thin membrane that sound waves cause to vibrate; a structure of the middle ear.

hammer, anvil, stirrup Three linked bones of the middle ear, which pass sound waves to the inner ear.

Figure 5.12   The loudness of common sounds as measured in decibel units.

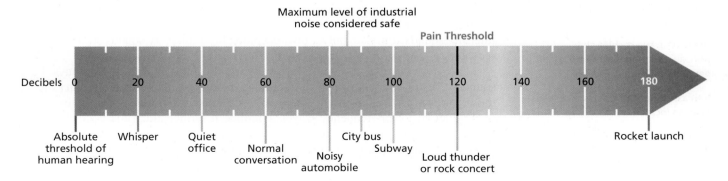

Figure 5.13
Major structures of the ear.

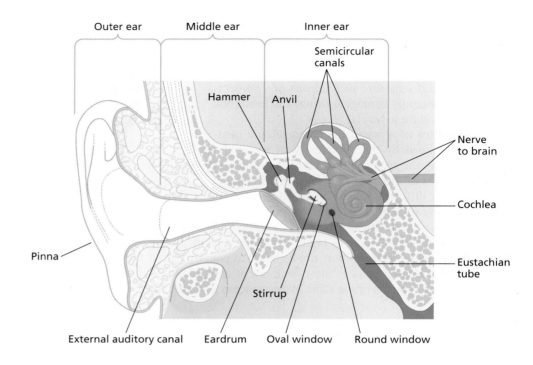

named because of their shapes. These middle-ear structures amplify the vibrations and pass them on to the inner ear.

Inner Ear. The vibrating stirrup shakes another eardrum-like structure called the **oval window** into motion. This membrane is at the end of a long, curled structure called the **cochlea,** which is filled with fluid. The vibrating oval window creates waves in the fluid of the cochlea (see figure 5.14). The cochlea contains two long tubes that double back on themselves and are connected only at the tip end of the spiral. The pressure of the vibrating waves is relieved by a third eardrum-like membrane at the other end of the cochlea called the **round window.** Running almost the entire length of the cochlea are several layers of membranes that separate the two tubes. The lower membrane, called the **basilar membrane,** forms a floor on which the ear's sensory receptors sit. Hairlike receptor cells are contained in the **organ of Corti.** Vibrations in the cochlear fluid set the basilar membrane in motion. This movement, in turn, moves the organ of Corti and stimulates the **hair cells** it contains. These receptors transduce the sound waves in the cochlear fluid into coded neural impulses sent to the brain (Meyer & others, 2009). The hair cells are sensitive to loud noises and aging. When they die, hearing declines. To date, there is no medical treatment for restoring them (Groves, 2010).

How does the organ of Corti code neural messages for the brain? The *intensity* of a sound wave is coded by the number of receptors in the organ of Corti that fire. Low-intensity sounds stimulate only a few receptors; high-intensity sounds stimulate many receptors.

The *frequency* of the sound wave is apparently coded in at least two ways. First, sound waves of various frequencies stimulate receptor cells at different *places* along the organ of Corti. Higher-frequency waves stimulate the organ of Corti close to the oval window; lower-frequency waves stimulate it farther along the cochlea (except for very low frequencies). Second, the frequency of the sound waves is duplicated to some extent in the *frequency* of the signals sent to the brain by the auditory receptors.

oval window Membrane of the inner ear that vibrates in response to movement of the stirrup, creating waves in the fluid of the cochlea.

cochlea (cok´lē-ah) Spiral structure of the inner ear that is filled with fluid and contains the receptors for hearing.

round window Membrane that relieves pressure from the vibrating waves in the cochlear fluid.

basilar membrane (bas´-ĭ-lar) One of the membranes that separate the two tubes of the cochlea and on which the organ of Corti rests.

organ of Corti (kor´tē) Sensory receptor in the cochlea that transduces sound waves into coded neural impulses.

hair cells Receptor neuron cells for hearing located on the organ of Corti.

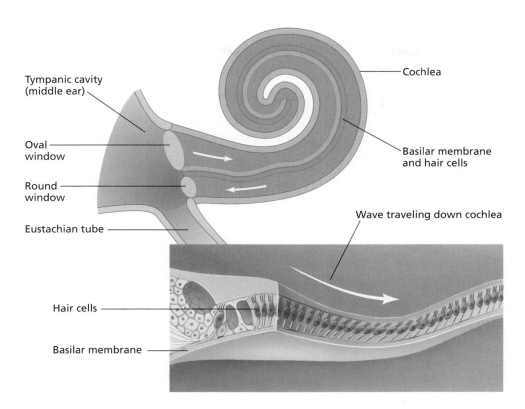

Tympanic cavity (middle ear)

Oval window

Round window

Eustachian tube

Cochlea

Basilar membrane and hair cells

Wave traveling down cochlea

Hair cells

Basilar membrane

Figure 5.14
Vibrations from sound waves enter the cochlea through the oval window and travel the length of the cochlea, where they are transduced into neural messages by hair cell receptors in the organ of Corti. Two factors tell the listener the location of sounds. First, a sound wave that originates from the side reaches the closer ear slightly sooner than it reaches the farther ear. Second, the head blocks some of the sound wave that reaches the farther ear, reducing the intensity of stimulation to the ear that is farther away from the source of the sound.

Only at lower frequencies is each neuron able to signal at the same frequency as the sound wave. At higher frequencies, the coding of frequency is achieved by *volleys* of neural impulses by different groups of neurons, which reflect the frequency of the sound wave.

Not all sounds travel this complete route from outer ear to cochlea. Some sounds are transmitted through the bones of the head directly to the cochlear fluid. We hear ourselves speak (and eat) largely through bone conduction hearing. This is an important consideration in diagnosing hearing problems. People who have suffered damage to the hearing apparatus of the middle ear can hear bone-conducted sounds fairly well, but not airborne sounds. People with damage to the auditory nerve—nerve deafness—have difficulty hearing either type of sound.

One more thing about ears deserves mentioning. Ever wonder why people have two of them? For one thing, having a pair of ears gives us a spare in case something goes wrong with one, but the fact that we have two ears also serves an important function in *locating* the origin of sounds. The ears locate sounds in two ways. First, when a sound wave is coming from straight ahead or from straight behind us, the sound reaches both ears simultaneously. When a sound is coming from the sides or from an angle, it reaches each ear at a slightly different time. The ears are sensitive enough to this difference that they allow us to locate the direction of sounds, especially high-frequency sounds. The reason you know that the person to the left of you is blowing her nose again is because your left ear hears it before your right

The barn owl hunts at night, often inside dark barns and other structures that block the light. It uses its extraordinary sense of hearing to locate its prey in the darkness. The same cues used by humans to localize the source of sounds (differences in sounds reaching the two ears) enable the barn owl to find its scampering prey.

ear does. Second, cues for the location of high-frequency sounds are also produced by the fact that your head dampens some of the sound reaching the more distant ear, creating a difference in the intensity of the sound waves that reach each of the ears.

Review

Sound is a physical stimulus made up of successive waves of densely and sparsely compressed air. The ear is composed of a series of structures that transmit the sound wave from the outer ear to the inner ear, where it produces vibrations in the fluid of the cochlea. The vibrations of the cochlear fluid are transduced by the receptor cells in the organ of Corti. Coded neural messages are sent to the auditory sensory areas of the brain, where frequency, intensity, and complexity are interpreted as pitch, loudness, and timbre. Differences in the timing and intensity of sound waves reaching the two ears allow us to determine the location of the source of the sound.

Check Your Learning

To be sure that you have learned the key points from the preceding section, cover the list of correct answers and try to answer each question. If you give an incorrect answer to any question, return to the page given next to the correct answer to see why your answer was not correct.

1. Objects that vibrate slowly create low-frequency sound waves, which we hear as having _____.

     a) low pitch   c) simple timbre

     b) high pitch   d) complex timbre

2. The sound wave is amplified by the hammer, anvil, and stirrup in the _____.

     a) outer ear   c) inner ear

     b) middle ear   d) pinna

3. The sound wave is transduced into neural impulses in the _____, which is located in the cochlea in the inner ear.

     a) auditory nerve   c) organ of Corti

     b) cochlear fluid   d) pinna

4. Even with your eyes closed, you know that the person speaking to you is on your left because _____.

     a) the sound reaches your left ear slightly before it reaches your right ear

     b) the sound wave that reaches your left ear is slightly more intense than the sound wave that reaches your right ear

     c) both of these

     d) neither of these

Thinking Critically about Psychology

There are no right or wrong answers to the following questions. They are presented to help you become an active reader and think critically about what you have just read.

1. In terms of human adaptation and survival, what are the advantages and disadvantages of having our ears located on the sides of our heads rather than somewhere else on the body?

2. Juan and Patrick are close friends. Juan hears normally, but Patrick is totally deaf. How might this difference in the way they experience life influence their friendship?

Correct Answers: 1. a (p. 132), 2. b (pp. 133–134), 3. c (p. 134), 4. c (pp. 135–136)

Body Senses

The body senses tell us how the body is oriented, where it is moving and what it is touching. Information about orientation and movement comes from a sense organ located in the inner ear and from individual receptors spread throughout the body. The sense of touch and temperature is based on receptors located just below the surface of the skin. Information about pain comes from receptors in the skin and inside the body. Although we usually are not aware that we are using them, the body senses play an important role in keeping us standing upright, moving straight ahead, and literally out of hot water. Information from all of the body senses is sent to the somatosensory area of the parietal lobe of the cerebral cortex.

Orientation and Movement

Messages about the orientation, balance, and movement of the body come to us from the skin senses (pressure on different parts of our body) and from two kinds of sense organs (Lackner & DiZio, 2005). A complicated set of sensory structures called the **vestibular organ** is located in the inner section of the ear, where it provides the cerebral cortex with information about orientation and movement. Individual sensory receptors, called **kinesthetic receptors,** located in the muscles, joints, and skin provide additional messages about movement, posture, and orientation.

Vestibular Organ. The vestibular organ is composed of two sets of small sensory structures: the *semicircular canals* and the linked *saccule* and *utricle* (see figure 5.15). The **saccule** and **utricle** are fluid-filled sacs in the inner ear that contain sensory receptors that keep the brain informed about the body's orientation. The part of the vestibular organ that provides the most sensitive messages to the brain about orientation, however, is the **semicircular canals.** This organ constitutes a marvelous bit of natural engineering perfectly suited to its purpose. The semicircular canals are composed of three nearly circular tubes (canals) that lie at right angles to one another, providing information on orientation of the body in three planes—left and right, up and down, and front to back. Think of the semicircular canals as the corner of a room, with one in the plane of the floor and the other two in the planes of the walls. At the base of each canal is an enlargement that holds the sensory receptors. A tuft of these hairlike receptor cells is formed in a gelatin-like structure called the **cupula,** which sticks out into the enlargement of the canal. As the head is tilted, the fluid flows through the canal in the opposite direction. This bends the cupula and causes its receptors to fire, sending a message of "tilt" to the brain. Although the vestibular organ provides the brain with vital information about orientation and movement, it can turn from a friend to an enemy at times. When overwhelmed by rocking boats, turbulent airplane flights, or twisting circus rides, it can produce nausea. Why does that happen? Why would tilting the vestibular organ cause nausea and vomiting—as in seasickness? Experts think it is because

vestibular organ (ves-tib′ū-lar) Sensory structures in the inner ear that provide the brain with information about orientation and movement of the head and body.

kinesthetic receptors (kin′es-thet′ik) Receptors in the muscles, joints, and skin that provide information about movement, posture, and orientation.

saccule, utricle (sak′ūl ū′tre-k′l) Fluid-filled sacs of the vestibular organ that inform the brain about the body's orientation.

semicircular canals (sem″ē-ser′kū-lar) Three nearly circular tubes in the vestibular organ that inform the brain about tilts of the head and body.

cupula (ku′-pu-lah) Gelatin-like structure containing a tuft of hairlike sensory receptor cells in the semicircular canals.

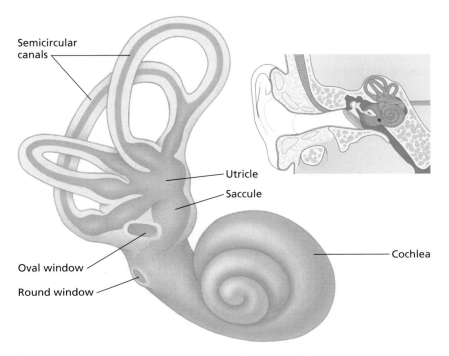

Figure 5.15
Major structures of the vestibular organ.

The vestibular organ and kinesthetic receptors help orient us, even in unusual situations.

the disorientation and dizziness of seasickness resemble the dizziness caused by poisoning. The body apparently vomits in response to dizziness regardless of the cause, just in case it is due to poisoning (Stern & Koch, 1996).

Kinesthetic Sense. Throughout the skin, muscles, joints, and tendons are kinesthetic receptors, that signal when they are moved. As the body walks, bends, and writes, these receptors provide information about the location and movement of each part of the body. Close your eyes, take off your shoes, and wiggle your toes. You can tell they are wiggling because of your kinesthetic sense. Unlike the vestibular organ, the kinesthetic receptors are individual receptors that are not clumped together into sense organs. The kinesthetic receptors provide detailed information on the orientation of the head and body, differences in pressure due to gravity and movement on different parts of the body, the movement of each body part, and a host of other kinds of information (Gray, 2008; Sholl, 2008). As reflected in the skilled movements of a musician, painter, or discus thrower, they are remarkably sensitive, allowing fine and complicated patterns of movement.

Skin Senses

free nerve endings Sensory receptor cells in the skin that detect pressure, temperature, and pain.

basket cells Sensory receptor cells at the base of hairs that detect pressure.

tactile discs (tak´til) Sensory receptor cells that detect pressure.

specialized end bulbs Sensory receptor cells that detect pressure.

We usually do not think of the skin as a sense organ, yet it's capable of picking up many different kinds of sensory information. The skin can detect *pressure, temperature,* and *pain.* Feeling a kiss on the cheek, cold in the winter, and all other sensations involving the skin are made up of combinations of these three skin sensations. Although the skin can detect only three kinds of sensory information, it has at least four types of receptors: the **free nerve endings,** the **basket cells** wound around the base of hairs, the **tactile discs,** and the **specialized end bulbs.** These are shown in figure 5.16. It appears that all four types of receptors play a role in the sense of touch (pressure), with the free nerve endings being the primary receptors for temperature and pain (Hole, 1990).

Figure 5.16
Diagram of the skin showing the major skin receptor cells.

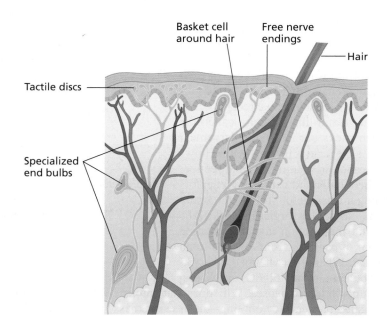

Pressure and Sensitivity. The skin is amazingly sensitive to pressure, but sensitivity differs considerably from one region of the skin to another depending on how many skin receptors are present. In the most sensitive regions—the fingertips, the lips, and the genitals—a pressure that pushes in the skin less than 0.001 mm can be felt, but sensitivity in other areas is considerably less (Schiffman, 1976). Perhaps the most striking example of the sensitivity of the skin is its ability to "read." Many blind people can read books using the Braille alphabet, patterns of small raised dots that stand for the letters of the alphabet. An experienced Braille user can read up to 300 words per minute using the sensitive skin of the fingertips (see figure 5.17).

Temperature. When it is hot or cold outside, how do you sense this fact? It seems to most of us that the entire surface of the skin is able to detect temperature, but we actually sense skin temperature only through sensory receptors located in rather widely spaced "spots" on the skin. One set of spots detects warmth and one detects coldness. The information sent to the brain by these spots creates the feeling of temperature across the entire skin surface.

When the skin is warmed (for example, by air, sunlight, or water), the receptors in the warm spots send messages about warmness to the brain; when the skin is cooled, the cold spots send messages about coldness. Recall from chapter 1 (p. 6) that the sensation of intense heat is created by stimulation of *both* the warm and cold spots. Although the cold receptors are generally responsive only to cold temperatures, extreme heat also makes them fire. Therefore, high temperatures stimulate the receptors in both sets of spots to send messages simultaneously to the brain, which are interpreted as hotness.

Pain

Everyone experiences pain some of the time. Toes get stepped on, fingers are cut, and ankles are twisted from time to time. Even though it is unpleasant, pain is the useful signal that something bad has happened to a part of the body and it needs our attention. What are the neural systems that underlie the experience of pain?

Free nerve endings throughout the body serve as **nocioceptors**—receptors for stimuli that are experienced as painful (Perl, 2007). Neural messages from the nocioceptors are transmitted to the brain along two distinct nerve pathways—*rapid* and *slow* neural pathways. This is why we often experience "first and second pain" (Melzack & Wall, 1983; Sternbach, 1978). The first pain sensation is a clear, localized feeling that does not "hurt" much, but it tells us what part of the body has been hurt and what kind of injury occurred. The second pain is a more diffuse, long-lasting pain that hurts in the emotional sense. When you cut your finger with a knife, an initial sensation tells you that you have been cut and where the cut has occurred, followed a moment later by a more diffuse and painful sensation. The first sensation makes you drop the knife and grab your finger; the second makes you jump up and down and scream!

There are two reasons that we experience these two somewhat separate pain sensations in sequence. First, the two sensations travel on different neural pathways that have different speeds of transmission. The rapid pathway neurons are thicker and sheathed in myelin (see p. 51), which speeds transmission. The slow pathway neurons, in contrast, are smaller and slower, unmyelinated neurons. The second reason that we experience first and second pain is that the two neural pathways travel to different parts of the brain. The rapid pathway travels through the thalamus to the somatosensory area. If you recall from chapter 3 (p. 62), this is the part of the parietal lobe of the cerebral cortex that receives and interprets sensory information from the skin and body. When the information transmitted to this area on the rapid pathway is interpreted, we know what has happened and where it has happened, but the somatosensory area

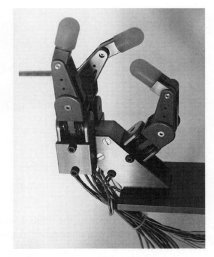

Robots are increasingly important in industry. Using what is known about the sense of touch, the inventors of the "Salisbury Hand" have given it kinesthetic sensors that simulate tension on the tendons of the hand and stimulation of the fingertips.

(Photo of Salisbury Hand at MI AI lab courtesy of David Lampe, MIT)

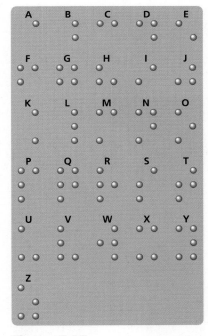

Figure 5.17
Raised dots used in the Braille alphabet are "read" with the fingertips.

nocioceptors (nō″-see-oh-sep′-turs) Receptors for stimuli that are experienced as painful.

does not process the emotional aspects of the experience of pain. Information that travels on the slower pathway is routed to the limbic system (p. 63). Here, in the brain system that mediates emotion, the emotional "ouch" part of the experience of pain is processed.

Pain Gates. Pain involves much more than the simple transmission of neural messages from nocioceptors to the brain. There is not a direct relationship between the stimulus and the amount of pain experienced. Under certain circumstances, pain messages can even be suppressed. For example, a football player whose attention is focused on a big game may not notice a painful cut until after the game is over. The pain receptors transmit the pain message during the game, but the message is not fully processed by the brain until the player is no longer concentrating on the game (Keefe & France, 1999).

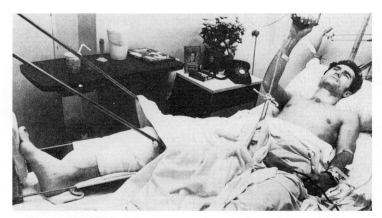

Guy Gertsch, who finished the 1982 Boston Marathon in a respectable 2 hours and 47 minutes, discovered at the finish line that he had run the last 19 miles with a broken thigh bone.

Pain signals are regulated in three parts of the nervous system: the brain stem, the spinal cord, and in the peripheral pain receptors (Melzack, 1999; Perl, 2007):

1. ***Regulation of pain in the brain stem.*** A matrix of neurons in the brain stem regulates the transmission of impulses from the nocioceptors to the cerebral cortex (see figure 5.18) (Christie & Mallet, 2009; Melzack & Wall, 1983). All messages from the body's nocioceptors travel to the brain through the brain stem. The slow-pain neural fibers pass through "pain gates" in the brain stem that can be either "opened" or "closed." That is, the pain gates can make us more or less sensitive to stimulation of the nocioceptors. The pain gates can be influenced to allow more slow-pain neural transmission along the slow-pain pathways to the limbic system. When pain messages are received from nocioceptors—say, from a bruised toe—they sensitize the pain gates and make them transmit slow-pain impulses more readily. This is because the neuropeptide involved in slow-pain transmission—called *substance P* (for pain)—sometimes diffuses across to nearby neurons in the brain stem that ordinarily do not carry pain messages, causing them to transmit pain impulses, too (Hopkins, 1997; Kobayashi & others, 2010).

Fortunately, the pain gates also can be "closed" to make them less likely to transmit slow-pain impulses to the limbic system. For example, placing a sore foot in warm water helps close the gate on pain from the toe. Similarly, sweet tasting liquids and sweet aromas associated with them can reduce the sensation of pain (Prescott & Wilkie, 2007). Even looking at the part of the body that hurts in a mirror reduces the sensation of pain by closing the pain gates (Longo & others, 2009).

A woman is being treated for pain by an acupuncturist. One theory for the effectiveness of acupuncture is that the needles stimulate the release of pain-blocking endorphins.

The pain gates appear to be operated by specialized neurons that block transmission in the neurons that carry "second pain" messages to the brain. As shown in figure 5.18, the *gate neurons* inhibit the pain neurons using substances called *endorphins.* When signaled by other sensory neurons or by neural fibers from the cortex to close the pain gate, the gate neuron inhibits the pain neuron and stops the pain message from reaching the brain.

Some pain-killing drugs, such as the opiate morphine, operate by duplicating the effects of the endorphins in inhibiting pain neurons (Perl, 2007). Indeed, the term *endorphin* means *endogenous* (produced inside the body) morphine.

The endorphins may explain why acupuncture is successful for some individuals. Pain often can be reduced by this procedure. In acupuncture, needles are inserted in the skin at special points and then twirled or heated. There is little doubt that some persons receiving acupuncture experience less pain, but the question is why. One possibility is that the needles indirectly stimulate the production of endorphins, which block the pain in the pain gates (Goldman & others, 2010). To test this

Figure 5.18 The operation of inhibitory pain gates. Secretion of endorphins by inhibitory gate neurons inhibits the firing of the axon of the neuron that transmits the pain message. Pain gate neurons regulate only the transmission of slow-pain fibers and are located primarily in the brain stem and spinal cord. Unfortunately, other pain gate neurons can make transmission of slow-pain messages to the limbic system more likely under some circumstances.

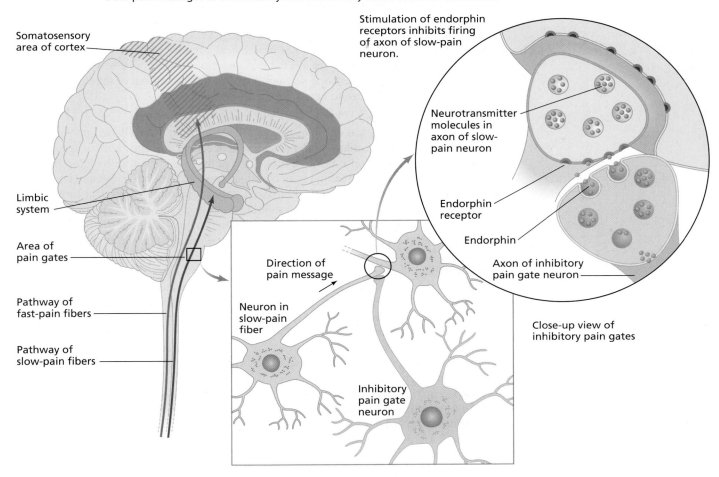

hypothesis, the drug naloxone, which blocks the action of endorphins, was administered to persons undergoing acupuncture. While the endorphin-blocking drug was active, the person receiving acupuncture experienced the normal level of pain (Price, 1988). This suggests that acupuncture may close the pain gates by stimulating the endorphins.

2. *Regulation of pain in the spinal cord.* Linda Watkins and Steven Maier (2003) of the University of Colorado have provided evidence that glial cells regulate the transmission of pain messages in the spinal cord. As described in the last chapter, some glial cells surround the synaptic gap and influence the likelihood that a neural signal will cross the gap. One function of glial cells is to regulate the transmission of pain signals in this way. For example, glial cells increase the transmission of pain signals when viral or bacterial infections are in the body (causing you to ache when you have the flu). In addition, several neurotransmitters cause glial cells to increase the transmission of pain signals, raising the possibility that stress may influence pain sensations in this way (Watkins & Maier, 2003).

3. *Peripheral regulation of pain.* Under some circumstances, nociceptors outside the spinal column can be made more sensitive to the stimuli that we sense as painful. If you have been cut on the hand, you may notice that even a light touch near the cut feels painful. The inflammation (swelling) around the cut leads to the sensitization of nociceptors near the cut, which results in the light touch being experienced as painful. This occurs in two ways: First, inflammation makes nociceptors themselves so sensitive that they fire even when stimulated by a light touch. Second, the release of substance P can turn nearby nerve endings that normally play a role in the sense of touch into nociceptors (Hopkins, 1997). Usually, this sensitization of nerve endings reverses itself as the wound or bruise heals, but for persons with arthritis and other chronic inflammatory diseases, the phenomenon of peripheral sensitization can be debilitating. Researchers hope that our growing understanding of the three levels of pain regulation will lead to new ways to control pain.

Phantom Limbs. A sad and curious phenomenon often occurs when persons have lost limbs. Amazingly, many amputees experience their missing arm or leg as if it were still there. They feel a missing arm, for example, as if it were hanging by their side when they sit still, and swinging in coordination with their other arm and legs when they walk. This *phantom limb* is experienced not as a memory of the lost limb but as a clear and realistic sensation that the missing limb is actually there (Melzack, 1992). Over 60% of amputees experience pain in the phantom limb (Bosmans & others, 2010). Phantom-limb pain is especially common in women and when the limb was an arm (Bosmans & others, 2010). A friend of mine recently wrote to say: "My mother, who lost her left leg to polio in her early 20s, is now 73, and sometimes when I ask how her arthritis is, she often responds, 'the foot I don't have aches as much as my good one.'" Fortunately, phantom-limb pain often improves over time (Bosman & others, 2010).

How is it possible to feel sensations from a limb that does not exist and, therefore, cannot be transmitting sensations to the brain? A team of researchers from Germany and the United States appears to have provided the answer: When sensory and pain neurons from one part of the body have been cut, the area of the somatosensory cortex that served that part of the body becomes sensitive to input from parts of the body that activate *nearby* portions of the somatosensory cortex (Flor & others, 1995). For example, in a woman whose left arm was amputated, the portion of somatosensory cortex that formerly served her left arm may begin to receive input from her face. (Look back to figure 3.15, p. 67, to see that the area of the somatosensory cortex that serves the face is next to the area that receives input from the arm.) In addition, cutting sensory neurons from one part of the body tends to reduce the efficiency of the pain gates. This suggests that phantom pain that is perceived as being in a missing arm may come from minor irritations to the face that are allowed through the pain gate and are perceived to be pain in the missing limb, because the neural message stimulates the part of the cortex that used to serve input from the arm. The phantom-limb experience is another illustration of the fact that our conscious experience is not always a direct and simple representation of the sensory information that reaches the brain.

Human Diversity
Culture and Pain

In this chapter, we examine the ways in which neural impulses from the sense organs are experienced as sensations and perceptions. Although much of this process is determined by the biological nature of the sense organs and neurons, learning experiences in our cultures apparently can influence even basic sensations such as pain.

Let's consider an example of the impact of culture on the perception of pain. Members of the Bariba society in Benin, West Africa, appear to be able to tolerate pain more easily than members of most cultures. Bariba folklore includes many examples of honored people who showed strength in the face of pain, and this calm response to pain is seen as an integral part of Bariba pride (Sargent, 1984). For example, pregnant women are expected not to reveal to others that they are experiencing labor pains. When labor becomes advanced, they leave the company of others to go through labor and childbirth alone, calling for help only with cutting the umbilical cord.

Continued on pg. 143

Continued from pg. 142 To the Bariba, letting other people see that they are in pain is cause for great shame. When discussing pain, many quote a Bariba proverb that translates to "Between death and shame, death has the greater beauty." According to a Bariba physician, an individual who displays pain lacks courage, and cowardice is the essence of shame. Rather than live in shame, a Bariba would rather die (Sargent, 1984). In this cultural context, one would do everything possible to avoid displaying signs of pain.

Human Diversity
Culture and Pain
cont'd from pg. 142

Do Bariba women who are in labor actually experience less pain than women in other cultures do, or have they simply learned not to let the pain show? It is difficult to answer such questions, partly because of the difficulties involved in describing pain to another person. Because pain is a private experience, language must be used to communicate the experience to others, and language is shaped by culture. It is not surprising that there is a more limited vocabulary for describing pain in the Bariba language than in most other languages. When the Bariba discuss the experience of pain, therefore, it is difficult to know how much their description is influenced by their language.

There is some reason to believe that the cultural emphasis on not showing reactions to pain might actually reduce the amount of pain that the Bariba experience. As noted in chapter 11, there is evidence that facial expressions are an important part of the experience of pain (Izard, 1977). Apparently, sensory feedback to the brain from facial muscles supplies part of the neural input for the perception of pain (along with input from the part of the body that is cramped or injured). Indeed, persons who were given electrical shocks reported less pain when they were told to make no facial reactions than when they let their emotions show in their faces (Colby, Lanzetta, & Kleck, 1977). Maybe the calm face of a Bariba woman in labor results in the experience of less pain than does the agonized grimace of women in other cultures.

According to Linda Garro (1990), medical professionals who work with people in pain must understand the impact of culture on the expression of pain. If culture is not taken into account, the physician may overestimate or underestimate the amount of pain patients experienced. However, professionals must also remember that not all members of a culture are the same: as in all other aspects of human diversity, one must be aware of variation within cultures.

What did you learn about pain in your own culture? Were you taught to minimize pain because it is important to be tough? Did you learn that no one will pay attention to your pain unless you exaggerate it? How do you respond when a parent or your friends are in pain? Such questions help you think about cultural influences on perception.

Review

The body contains a number of sense organs that provide vital information about the body's movement and orientation in space and about the world that contacts our skin. Information about posture, movement, and orientation is coded and sent to the somatic sensory area of the cortex by the vestibular organ in the inner ear and by kinesthetic receptors spread throughout the body. Skin receptors send information about temperature, pressure, and pain to the same area of the brain. We experience the pain from cuts and other injuries in two steps: a first sensation of pain tells us what has happened and where it has happened, followed by a second, more emotional pain. These two aspects of the pain experience travel on different neural pathways to different parts of the brain. The phenomenon of pain provides a good example of the lack of direct relationship between physical stimuli and conscious sensations in that a number of factors increase or decrease the experience of pain. The phantom limb experience also provides compelling evidence that conscious experiences are constructed in the brain and do not always have a direct relationship to incoming sensations. Even our culture-based learning experiences influence our perception of pain.

Check Your Learning

To be sure that you have learned the key points from the preceding section, cover the list of correct answers and try to answer each question. If you give an incorrect answer to any question, return to the page given next to the correct answer to see why your answer was not correct.

1. Sensory receptors located in the muscles, joints, and skin provide the brain with messages about movement, posture, and orientation of the body. These are called _____ receptors.

   a) vestibular   c) ciliary

   b) semicircular   d) kinesthetic

2. Which is not one of the four types of receptors in the skin?

   a) vestibular cells   c) tactile discs

   b) basket cells   d) specialized end bulbs

3. The sensation of intense heat is created by the stimulation of _____ on the skin.

   a) warm spots   c) both warm and cold spots

   b) cold spots   d) vestibular cells

4. According to the _____ theory of pain, placing a sore foot in warm water blocks pain signals on the slow-pain pathway by closing neural gates in the spinal cord and brain stem.

Thinking Critically about Psychology

There are no right or wrong answers to the following questions. They are presented to help you become an active reader and think critically about what you have just read.

1. In what ways is the experience of pain both a psychological and a physical event?

2. Have you had experiences in your life that are consistent with the gate-control theory of pain?

Correct Answers: 1. d (p. 137), 2. a (p. 138), 3. c (p. 139), 4. gate-control (p. 140)

Chemical Senses: The Flavors and Aromas of Life

gustation (gus-tā´-shun) Sense of taste.

olfaction (ōl-fak´-shun) Sense of smell.

The senses of **gustation** (taste) and **olfaction** (smell) differ from the other senses in that they respond to chemicals. The chemical senses tell us about the things we eat, drink, and breathe.

Taste

taste cells Sensory receptor cells for gustation located in the taste buds.

papillae (pah-pil´ē) Clusters of taste buds on the tongue.

We are able to taste food and other things because of the 10,000 *taste buds* on the tongue. Each taste bud contains approximately a dozen sensory receptors, called **taste cells,** grouped together much like the segments of an orange (figure 5.19). These taste cells are sensitive to chemicals in our food and drink (Bartoshuk, 1988). The taste buds are further bunched together in bumps, called **papillae,** that can easily be seen on the tongue.

Collectively, the taste buds respond to thousands of chemicals, but all our sensations of taste apparently result from the stimulation of different *combinations* of a small number of different types of taste receptors, which are most responsive to only one class of chemicals each. There are taste buds that respond primarily to chemicals that give rise to the sensations of *sweetness* (mostly sugars), *sourness* (mostly acids), *saltiness* (mostly salts), and *bitterness* (in response to a variety of chemicals that have no food value or are toxic). In addition, there is evidence that there is a fifth type of taste bud, which gives rise to the sensation of *fattiness* in response to fats (Schiffman & others 1998). Some scientists believe that there is yet another kind of taste bud that give rise to the sensation called *umami* (the savory taste of meat stock, cheese, and mushrooms), but this has been shown to arise from the same taste buds that give rise to the sensation of sweetness (Li, & others, 2002).

Interestingly, the taste buds that are most sensitive to these five classes of chemicals are not evenly distributed over the tongue. They are bunched together in different parts of the tongue, as shown in figure 5.20. This means that different parts of the tongue are sensitive to different tastes. We do not usually notice this, because the differences in sensitivity are not great and because our food usually reaches all parts of the tongue during the chewing process anyway. But, if you ever have to swallow a truly bitter pill, try placing it in the exact middle of the tongue, where there are no taste receptors at all.

We lose taste buds as we age, especially over 45 years of age. Babies have the most taste buds and are very sensitive, whereas older adults are less sensitive to the chemicals that give rise to taste sensations (Schiffman & others, 1998).

Our perception of food also includes sensations from the skin surfaces of the tongue and mouth: touch (food texture and thickness), temperature (cold coffee tastes very different from hot coffee), and pain (as in jalapeño peppers). The sight and aroma of food also greatly affect our perception of food.

Smell

Chemicals in the air we breathe pass by the olfactory receptors on their way to the lungs. These receptor cells are located in a dime-sized, mucous-coated sheet at the top of the nasal cavity called the **olfactory epithelium** (see figure 5.21 on p. 146). Until recently, scientists believed that we could smell only a limited number of primary odors (Ackerman, 1991; Amoore, Johnston, & Rubin, 1964). In 2004, however, Linda Buck and Richard Axel received the Nobel Prize in Medicine and Physiology for demonstrating that hundreds—perhaps thousands—of different receptors detect a multitude of different chemicals in the air we breathe (Buck, 1996; Dulac & Axel, 1998; Liberles & others, 2009).

Interestingly, nearly all the chemicals that humans can detect as odors are organic compounds, meaning they come from living things. In contrast, we can smell very few inorganic compounds, such as rocks and sand. Thus, our noses are useful tools for sensing the qualities of plants and animals—necessary, among other things, to distinguish between poisonous and edible things.

The sense of smell is important in and of itself, of course, sometimes bringing messages of sweet perfumes to the brain and other times warning of dangerous and foul odors. But the sense of smell contributes to the sense of taste as well. Not only do we smell foods as they pass beneath our noses on the way to our mouths, but odors also rise into the nasal passage as we chew. We are usually unaware of the impact of smell on the sense of taste, until a head cold makes everything taste like paste. The contribution of smell to taste is important because of the greater sensitivity of the sense of smell. The nose can detect the aroma of cherry pie in the air that is 1/25,000th of the amount required for the taste buds to identify it (Ackerman, 1991).

Pheromone Detection

There is growing evidence that an additional chemical sense plays important roles in the regulation of reproductive behavior in many species, including humans. Many mammals have receptors for detecting chemicals known as **pheromones.** Pheromones

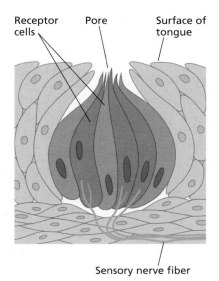

Figure 5.19
Taste buds contain clusters of taste (gustatory) receptor cells.

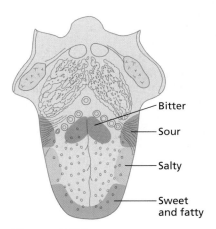

Figure 5.20
Areas of the tongue that are most sensitive to the five primary qualities of taste: sweet, fatty, salty, sour, and bitter.

olfactory epithelium (ōl-fak′to-rē ep′′i-thē′lē-um) Sheet of receptor cells at the top of the nasal cavity.

pheromones Chemicals that stimulate receptors in the vomeronasal organ in some animals, influencing some aspects of reproductive behavior.

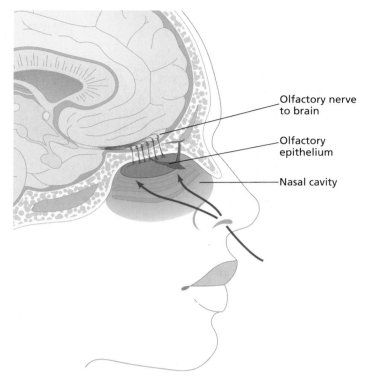

Olfactory nerve
to brain

Olfactory
epithelium

Nasal cavity

Figure 5.21
Olfactory receptor cells are located in
the olfactory epithelium at the top of
the nasal cavity.

released in the sweat, saliva, or urine of one animal are
sensed by these chemical receptors. The pheromone receptor
cells send neural messages to several areas of brain, including the hypothalamus, which stimulates the release of sex
hormones, initiates ovulation in some nonhuman species,
and influences sexual motivation and behavior (Savic, 2002).

There is evidence that when women inhale adrostadi-
enone, a male sex hormone found in high concentrations on
the skin, their attention is shifted to emotion-relevant stimuli,
such as facial expressions (Hummer & McClintock, 2009)
even when the women are unaware of the hormone. There
also is evidence that smelling chemicals in human breast
milk increases the sexual motivation and sexual fantasies of
women (Spencer & others, 2004). When men smell T-shirts
worn by women who are fertile (ovulating) they experience a greater increase in testosterone than when the woman
who wore the T-shirt was not ovulating (Miller & Maner,
2010). So when we say that sexual attraction is partly based
on "chemistry," maybe we are literally correct. Chemical
pheromones may be part of sexual attraction. We discuss this
topic more when we discuss sexual motivation in chapter 11.

In addition, researchers at the University of Chicago
have discovered pheromones that influence human female
reproductive cycles (Stern & McClintock, 1998). It has been
known for some time that women who live together, such as
in military barracks, soon find that they are on similarly timed menstrual cycles. It was
not clear until recently, however, that this was due to the influence of pheromones. Psychologists Kathleen Stern and Martha McClintock (1998) collected sweat from women at
different times in their menstrual cycles and identified at least two distinct pheromones.
When other women inhaled sweat collected during the early phase of the menstrual cycle,
lutenizing hormone was secreted by most of the women, and their menstrual cycles
were accelerated. When sweat collected during the later stages of the menstrual cycle
was inhaled by other women, it had the opposite effect. Because these pheromones have
no odor (that is, they do not stimulate receptors in the olfactory epithelium itself), and
because the receptors for pheromones send their neural messages to subcortical structures
rather than to the cortex, the women were not consciously aware of their influence.

Review   Chemicals in the air we breathe and in the things we eat and drink are sensed by the
gustatory receptors (taste buds) on the tongue and the olfactory receptors in the nose.
For both chemical senses, combinations of a relatively small number of primary sensations
apparently make up the entire variety of our experiences of taste and smell. Pheromones
influence reproductive behavior in many animal species. Increasing evidence suggests that
pheromones also influence human reproductive behavior, menstrual cycles, and mood.

**Check Your
Learning**   To be sure that you have learned the key points from the preceding section, cover the list
of correct answers and try to answer each question. If you give an incorrect answer to any
question, return to the page given next to the correct answer to see why your answer was
not correct.

1. Approximately a dozen sensory receptors called taste cells are found on each of the
10,000 _____ on the tongue.

2. All our sensations of taste appear to result from five basic sensations of taste:
sweetness, fattiness, sourness, saltiness, and _____.

Check Your Learning (cont.)

3. The olfactory receptors are located in a dime-sized, mucous-coated sheet at the top of the nasal cavity called the _____.

   a) gustatory center

   c) olfactory cortex

   b) olfactory epithelium

   d) thalamus

4. Chemicals that influence reproductive behavior in many animals are called _____.

   a) pheromones

   c) astringents

   b) olfactory bulbs

   d) stereochemicals

Thinking Critically about Psychology

There are no right or wrong answers to the following questions. They are presented to help you become an active reader and think critically about what you have just read.

1. Why do you think some people love the smell of coffee but other people dislike it?

2. Why do you think there is an uneven distribution of the five types of taste buds on the tongue?

Correct Answers: 1. taste buds (p. 144), **2.** bitterness (p. 145), **3. b** (p. 145), **4. a** (pp. 145–146)

Perception: Interpreting Sensory Messages

Neural messages from sensory receptors transmitted to the brain have little meaning of their own. They must be organized and interpreted in the process we call *perception*. The process is pretty much the same in all of us. If this were not the case—if each of us were to interpret sensory input in a unique way—there would be no common "reality" in the sense of a perceived world that we all share. However, some aspects of perception are unique to members of different cultures. In addition, our learning experiences, motives, and emotions also can influence our perceptions. For example, we all perceive the visual stimuli of a knife in pretty much the same way because of the inborn ways we organize visual information. But a knife also has unique perceptual meaning to each individual, depending on whether the person has been cut by a similar knife.

In this section, we examine the inborn organizational properties that all humans share and briefly discuss some of the ways in which each individual's perceptions are unique. Keep in mind as we discuss perception that, although it's easy to distinguish between sensation and perception in theory, it's very difficult to do so in practice. Visual perception, for example, begins in the complex neural structures of the eye before sensory messages are transmitted to the brain (Hochberg, 1988; Solomon & Lennie, 2007). The distinction between sensation and perception, then, is largely an arbitrary one, but it makes our discussion of information processing by the sense organs and brain easier to understand.

Visual Perception

In the discussion that follows, we look at the major ways in which sensory information is interpreted into meaningful perceptions. The key point is that what we perceive is often based more on how sensory information is processed in our brains than what is in front of our eyes (Long & Toppino, 2004). For example, what do you see in figure 5.22? This stimulus can be perceived as a young woman facing away or as an older woman

Figure 5.22
This drawing can be viewed as a younger or an older woman, depending on the viewer's figure-ground organization.

Figure 5.23
The distinction between figure and ground in visual perception is clearly illustrated by this vase prepared for Queen Elizabeth of England. Do you see a vase, or do you see the profiles of Queen Elizabeth and Prince Philip? It depends on whether the dark space on each side of the vase is the figure or the ground in your perceptual organization of the stimulus.

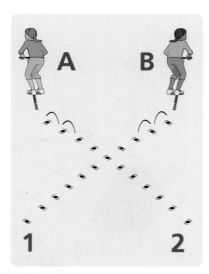

Figure 5.24
At which point did girl B start jumping on her pogo stick? According to the principle of continuity, we would tend to perceive point 1 as her starting point, although either 1 or 2 would be equally possible.

facing forward and downward. Which image you see depends on how the visual information is processed.

Our discussion of perception focuses on visual perception, rather than on all of the perceptual systems, for several reasons: Visual perception is a highly important sensing system; scientists understand how it works better than they do other systems; and it is representative enough of other systems to tell us something about the process of perception in general.

Perceptual Organization. Raw visual sensations are like the unassembled parts of a washing machine: they must be put together in an organized way before they are useful to us. Some of the fundamental ways in which the eye and the brain organize visual sensations were described about 75 years ago by Gestalt psychologists in their pioneering writings on perception (see chapter 1). These principles of perceptual organization are still worthy of our attention (Palmer, 2002; Prinzmetal, 1995). The following are five of the so-called Gestalt principles of perception.

1. *Figure-ground.* When we perceive a visual stimulus, part of what we see is the center of our attention, the figure, and the rest is the indistinct ground. The vase in figure 5.23 shows that this way of seeing can reorganize the nature of reality. The figure and ground of this photo can be reversed to perceive either a vase or two opposing faces. This principle of perception is very useful in showing us that what we perceive is often based more on what goes on in our brains than what is in front of our eyes. The remaining Gestalt principles amplify this point.

2. *Continuity.* We tend to perceive lines or patterns that follow a smooth contour as being part of a single unit. In figure 5.24, at which point did child B start bouncing her pogo stick? We tend to organize our perceptions of the tracks so that it appears that girl B started at point 1, but both girls could have made sharp turns in the center and headed off at right angles. We do not naturally organize sensations in this way, however; we tend to perceive continuity in lines and patterns.

3. *Proximity.* Things that are proximal (close together) are usually perceived as belonging together. In figure 5.25, we see three vertical columns of blocks on the left side and three horizontal rows on the right side, owing to proximity.

4. *Similarity.* On the left side of figure 5.26, we perceive two vertical columns of apples and two vertical columns of pears, even though they are evenly spaced. On the right side, in contrast, a different arrangement results in the perception of two horizontal rows of each fruit. Similar things are perceived as being related.

5. *Closure.* Incomplete figures of familiar things, such as in figure 5.27, tend to be perceived as complete wholes. Again, missing sensory information is automatically "filled in" in the process of perception to create complete and whole perceptions (Kellman & others, 2005).

Our perceptions are actively organized according to these and other, similar inborn principles.

Perceptual Constancy. We perceive the world as a fairly constant and unchanging place. Tables, lamps, and people do not change in size, shape, or color from moment to moment. Yet, the sensations that tell us about these things do change considerably from moment to moment. The size of the image that falls on the retina changes as a person walks away from us, but we do not perceive the person as shrinking in size. The shape of a pot seen from different angles is different on the retina, but we do

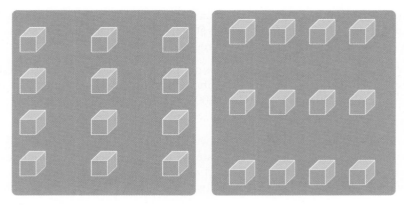

Figure 5.25   Do you see vertical columns or horizontal rows? The principle of proximity determines how these stimuli are organized perceptually.

Figure 5.26   Do you see vertical columns or horizontal rows? The principle of similarity suggests that we organize the figure on the left into vertical columns and the one on the right into horizontal rows, even though the objects are equally spaced.

figure-ground principle Gestalt principle of perception that states that part of a visual stimulus will be the center of our attention (figure) and the rest will be the indistinct ground. In many cases, the figure and ground can be reversed in our perception of the same stimulus.

continuity principle (kon´ti-noo´´i-tee) Gestalt principle of perception that states that lines or patterns that follow a smooth contour are perceived as part of a single unit.

proximity principle (prok´sim´´-i-tee) Gestalt principle of perception that states that parts of a visual stimulus that are close together are perceived as belonging together.

similarity principle Gestalt principle of perception that states that parts of a visual stimulus that are similar are perceived as belonging together.

closure principle (klo´zhur) Gestalt principle of perception that states that incomplete figures of familiar objects tend to be perceived as wholes.

Figure 5.27
We see a face rather than unrelated lines because of the perceptual principle of closure.

perceptual constancy Tendency for perceptions of objects to remain relatively unchanged in spite of changes in raw sensations.

not believe that the pot is changing shape. This characteristic of perception is called **perceptual constancy.**

There are several types of perceptual constancy:

1. *Brightness constancy.* A piece of white paper does not change in perceived brightness when it moves from a dimly lit room to a brightly lit room, even though the intensity of the light reaching the eye changes considerably. Fortunately for our ability to cope with the world, our perception corresponds to the unchanging physical properties of the paper rather than to the changing sensory information about its brightness. When you stop to think about it, this is a remarkable accomplishment, but one that we take so much for granted that you may not have been aware that it was happening until you read this paragraph.

2. *Color constancy.* Colors do not appear to change much in spite of different conditions of light and surroundings that change incoming visual information.

3. *Size constancy.* A dollar bill seen from distances of 1 foot and 10 feet casts different-sized images on the retina, but we do not perceive it as changing in size. Familiar objects do not change in perceived size at different distances.

4. *Shape constancy.* A penny seen from straight ahead casts a circular image on the retina. When seen from a slight angle, however, the image it casts is oval, yet we continue to perceive it as circular.

The process of perceptual constancy means our perceptions are automatically adjusted to correspond with what we have learned about the physical world, rather than relying solely on changing stimulus input (Graf, 2006).

Depth Perception. The retina has a two-dimensional surface. It has only an up and a down, and a left and a right. How are we able to perceive a three-dimensional world with depth using a two-dimensional retina? The eye and the brain accomplish this remarkable feat by using a number of two-dimensional cues to create a perceptual distance.

The **monocular cues** to depth perception can be perceived by one eye (see figure 5.28). We use these monocular cues in everyday life and artists manipulate them to create images in art that appear to have depth on flat surfaces and to bring Shrek and other computer-animated figures to life. The eight monocular cues are these:

1. *Texture gradient.* The texture of objects is larger and more visible up close and smaller when far away. On curved surfaces, the elements of texture are also more slanted when the surface does not squarely face us. For example, we see figure 5.29 (p. 152) as three-dimensional even though it is a flat image on the page, because we perceive the black circles to be slanted when the surface curves away from us (Todd & others, 2004).

2. *Linear perspective.* Objects cast smaller images on the retina when they are more distant. As a result, parallel lines, such as railroad tracks, appear to grow closer together the farther away they are from us. In paintings, objects with larger relative size appear to be closer than objects with smaller relative size.

3. *Superposition.* Closer objects tend to be partially in front of, or partially cover up, more distant objects.

4. *Shadowing.* The shadows cast by objects and highlights of reflected light suggest their depth. For example, figure 5.30 (p. 152) has no real depth on this flat page, but you perceive it as three-dimensional because of the shadowing and highlighting (Norman, Todd, & Orban, 2004).

5. *Speed of movement.* Objects farther away appear to move across the field of vision more slowly than do closer objects. A dog running through a distant field appears to move slowly, but it moves more quickly when the dog runs right in front of us.

6. *Aerial perspective.* Water vapor and pollution in the air scatter light waves, giving distant objects a bluish, hazy appearance compared with nearby objects.

7. *Accommodation.* As discussed earlier in the chapter, the shape of the lens of the eye must change to focus the visual image on the retina from stimuli that are different distances from the eye. This process is called *accommodation.* Kinesthetic receptors in the ciliary muscle, therefore, provide a source of information about the distance of different objects. This information is useful, however, only for short distances up to about 4 feet.

8. *Vertical position.* When objects are on the ground, the farther they appear to be below the horizon, the closer they appear to be to us. For objects in the air, however, the farther they appear to be above the horizon, the closer they appear to be to us.

Perceptual constancy helps us recognize this vase as unchanging, even though we are viewing it from different angles and from different distances.

monocular cues (mon-ok′ū-lar) Eight visual cues that can be seen with one eye and that allow us to perceive depth.

Figure 5.28   Texture gradient, linear perspective, shadowing, superposition, and aerial perspective are monocular cues used in depth perception.

Texture gradient

Linear perspective

Shadowing

Superposition

Aerial perspective

Binocular cues in depth perception can only be perceived using two eyes. The two binocular cues:

1. *Convergence.* When both eyes are looking at an object in the center of the visual field, they must angle inward more sharply for a near object than for a distant object (see figure 5.31, p. 152). Information from the muscles that move the eyes thus provides a clue as to the distance of an object from the viewer.

2. *Retinal disparity.* Because our two eyes are a couple of inches apart, they do not see the same view of three-dimensional objects, especially when the object is close. This disparity, or difference, between the images on the two retinas is a key factor in depth perception. Retinal disparity is the principle behind the old-fashioned stereopticon. As shown in figure 5.32 (p. 153), the individual looks at two pictures of the same scene in a viewer that lets each

binocular cues (bīn-ok´ū-lar) Two visual cues that require both eyes to allow us to perceive depth.

Figure 5.29

This figure creates an illusion of depth even though it is a flat image on a two-dimensional page. We perceive it as a three-dimensional figure with depth because we interpret the black circles as being slanted because they are on a surface that curves away from us.

Figure 5.30

This figure has no depth on this flat two-dimensional page, but you perceive it as three-dimensional because the shadowing and highlighting create an illusion of depth.

Figure 5.31   The degree to which the eyes must look inward (convergence) to focus on objects at different distances provides information on the distance of that object. It's a binocular cue in depth perception because it requires the use of both eyes.

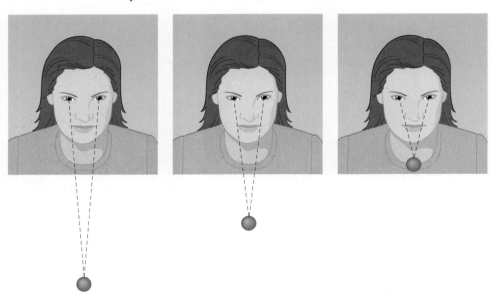

eye see only one of the two images. The images have been photographed from two slightly different spots to duplicate the disparity between two retinal images. When seen in the stereopticon, the two images fuse into a single scene perceived in startlingly good three dimension. Try placing your hand edgewise between the two pictures and the bridge of your nose to allow each eye to see only one of the pictures. Look at them for a while to see if they fuse into a single, three-dimensional scene. Recent studies have revealed that there are specific neurons in the visual areas of the cerebral cortex that process cues from the left and right eyes that contribute to depth perception (Parker, 2007).

Through a combination of these monocular and binocular cues, we are able to perceive our three-dimensional world using only two-dimensional information.

Figure 5.32 Two photos taken from slightly different angles are used in a stereopticon to create an illusion of depth through retinal disparity.

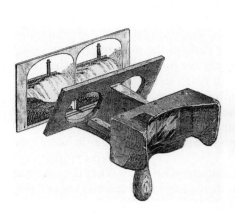

Figure 5.33
The Ponzo illusion. Are the horizontal lines the same length?

Figure 5.34
This figure often produces an illusory judgment of length. Which line is longer, the horizontal or the vertical line? Actually, they are the same length.

Visual Illusions. Instructors of introductory psychology have long enjoyed amazing their classes with **visual illusions.** These illusions intentionally manipulate the cues that we use in visual perception to create a false or illusory perception. They are instructive, therefore, in showing us more about the process of perception and for showing us in yet *another* way that what we see is not always the same as the visual information that enters the eyes. For example, are the two horizontal lines in figure 5.33 (the Ponzo illusion) the same size? (They are, even though the upper line looks longer.) How about the two lines in figure 5.34 (the vertical-horizontal illusion)—most people see the vertical line as longer, even though they are the same length. The white square that you see in figure 5.35 (p. 154) does not exist in the drawing, which is just four circles with missing quarters. My personal favorite is the Zollner illusion, shown in figure 5.36 (p. 154). Believe it or not, the diagonal lines are parallel. Even after you cover all but two lines or measure the distance between the diagonal lines for yourself, this illusion is amazing.

How do these illusions fool us? They do so by using monocular depth cues to create an illusion. Consider the Müller-Lyer illusion: the two vertical lines on the left

visual illusion Visual stimuli in which the cues used in visual perception create a false perception.

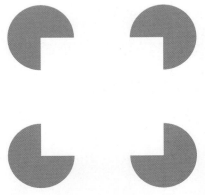

Figure 5.35

Do you see a white square? Most of us perceive the illusory "Kanizsa square" in front of four orange circles, in spite of the fact that there is no square actually depicted in the drawing—just four circles with missing quarters. What we see is often not literally what is "out there."

Figure 5.36

The Zollner illusion. Are the diagonal lines parallel?

Figure 5.37

The Müller-Lyer illusion. Most people see the vertical line on the right as being longer, even though they are the same length. The shorter lines give an illusion of depth, as in the two books on the right.

of figure 5.37 (p. 154) are of different lengths—or are they? Actually, they just look different because of the context they are in. Ordinarily, the short lines at the end of the longer lines would be cues to depth, as in the two booklets shown on the right side of figure 5.37. We see the vertical line as longer when the cues suggest that it is farther away. In the Ponzo illusion (figure 5.33), the two vertical lines appear to be converging in the distance, like railroad tracks, suggesting that the horizontal line at the top is farther away, so we see it as longer. Perhaps the most impressive visual illusion ever created in a psychology laboratory is the *Ames room.* When this room is viewed through a peep-hole made in one wall (used to restrict the availability of binocular cues), the room appears to be a normal square. Actually, however, the room is much deeper on one side than the other, but many cues of depth perception have been altered to give the illusion of equal depth for all sides of the back wall. The effect this room has on perception is startling when people are in the room (see figures 5.38 and 5.39).

Not all visual illusions are laboratory demonstrations, however. They are common in everyday life. Few sights are more beautiful than a huge full moon on the horizon. Have you ever stopped to wonder why it always looks *bigger* on the horizon than overhead? It doesn't really grow, you know; it's an illusion. In fact, it's an illusion that still puzzles scientists. There is no widely accepted theory of the moon illusion (Reed, 1984; Rock & Kaufman, 1972), but it is based partly on the misperception of depth.

As shown in figure 5.40 (p. 156), an object that our senses tell us is *farther away* is perceived as being larger than an object that casts the same-size image on the retina but appears to be closer. The two triangles in this figure are the same size, but the one at the top is perceived as *larger* because it appears to be farther away. Ordinarily, the top triangle *would* be larger if it were farther away, but it could still cast as large a retinal image as a closer object.

The moon illusion is based partly on the same principle. When the moon is overhead, not only does it appear closer owing to its vertical position, but we have no distance cues, so depth cues do not accurately influence our perception of the moon's size. When it's near the horizon, however, it appears to be farther away because of its vertical position. In addition, we can see the moon is farther away than objects such as distant trees and buildings, which we know to be large but which cast a small image on the retina. When the size of the moon is perceived in comparison with these objects, it looks much bigger.

And then there is the dreaded Poggendorf illusion! Look at the diagonal line that appears to pass behind the blue bar in figure 5.41 (p. 156). Which line on the right is the continuation of the diagonal line? Most persons choose the middle line. Now place the edge of a piece of white paper along the line. Which line on the right do you think is the continuation of the line on the left now? In the Poggendorf illusion, lines that appear to pass behind solid objects at an angle appear to be "moved over" when they emerge. You can demonstrate this phenomenon again by drawing a straight line with

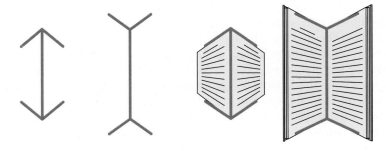

Figure 5.38
The Ames room, which was constructed to illustrate how the monocular cues used in depth perception can be used to create illusions. Is the child on the right really taller than the adult on the left?

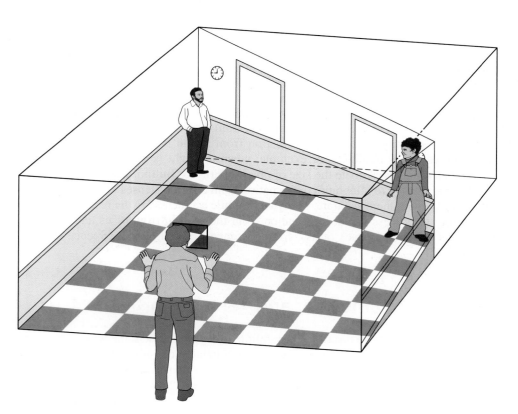

Figure 5.39
Although not apparent to the viewer, the right side of the Ames room is one-half as deep as the left, the floor is higher and the ceiling is lower on the right, and the window on the right is smaller. All of these cues create the impression that the person on the right is much larger than the person on the left in the Ames room.

a ruler on a piece of paper and then covering it with a 25-cent piece. The line now emerges from the quarter in the wrong place.

The Poggendorf illusion is not only interesting, it can be downright *dangerous* (Coren & Girgus, 1978)! Consider the dilemma that might be faced by a surgeon, as illustrated in figure 5.42. Suppose the surgeon views a bullet that lies next to a bone

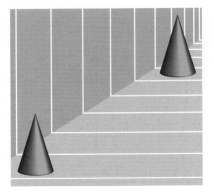

Figure 5.40
When two objects of the same size are perceived as being at different distances, the one that seems farther away is perceived as being larger.

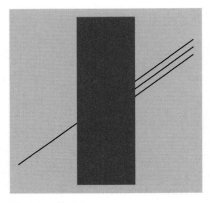

Figure 5.41
A demonstration of the Poggendorf illusion. Which line on the right is the continuation of the diagonal line on the left?

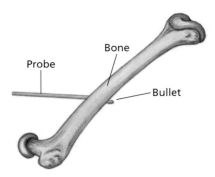

Figure 5.42
An example of the danger of the Poggendorf illusion. Will the surgeon's probe touch the bullet?

on an X ray and lines up a probe to remove it. Will the probe touch the top of the bullet? Is it lined up correctly? If you place the edge of a piece of paper along the line of the probe, you can see that it misses the bullet. The Poggendorf illusion may even be involved in some air accidents. In 1965, two airplanes heading for a landing field near New York City passed on opposite sides of a cloud. Apparently because of the Poggendorf illusion, their paths seemed to be on line for a collision where they were estimated to emerge from the cloud. Tragically, the pilots changed course and collided, killing 4 persons and injuring 49 more (Matlin, 1988).

Color Perception. As important as the cones and the opponent processors are to color perception, they are not the whole story. The perception of color is based on more than the information that reaches the brain about the wavelengths of light that reach the cones. Like other perceptual processes, visual information is *interpreted* in the brain. For example, the orange circle on the right side of figure 5.43 is brighter than the orange circle on the left. Or is it? Actually, the ink is exactly the same in both circles, but it looks more or less bright in the context of the surrounding colors (Hong & Shevell, 2004). In this and many other ways, color perception is influenced by other nearby (contextual) cues.

Multisensory Integration

We do not perceive the world using one sense at a time. Rather, we integrate and interpret information from multiple senses at the same time (Ernst & Bulthoff, 2004). When you eat an apple, what senses are involved? Your perception of eating an apple is the result of an integration of sensations from gustatory and olfactory receptors, temperature and pressure sensations from the lips and mouth, auditory sensations from biting and chewing, and kinesthetic feedback from the moving structures of the mouth and throat. In many situations, information from vision is more important than the other senses for us humans. For example, when the light is good, we rely more on vision than touch to estimate the size of objects (Ernst & Bulthoff, 2004).

We are so used to integrating information from different senses that we have great difficulty keeping them separate. Many automobile accidents are the result of our limited ability to process visual information from the road in front of us and hear conversations beside or in back of us—from passengers or cell phones (Spence & Read, 2003).

Motivation, Emotion, and Perception

Up to this point, we have discussed perception as if it works the same way all the time. That is not always the case because our motivational and emotional states influence our perceptions. For example, hungry people are more sensitive to tastes of sweetness and saltiness than they are when they are full (Zverev, 2004), and when people are wearing a heavy backpack they estimate the distance they would need to walk to a distant object to be farther (Proffitt, 2006). Similarly, sexually aroused males perceive females as being more physically attractive (Stephan, Berscheid, & Walster, 1971) and more sexually interested than they actually are (Maner & others, 2005). Similarly, our emotions can strongly influence perception. Persons who are afraid of heights who are standing on a balcony estimate the distance to the ground to be greater than do people who are less afraid (Proffitt, 2006). Similarly, persons who are anxious because they have experienced traumatic stress perceive the faces of other people as

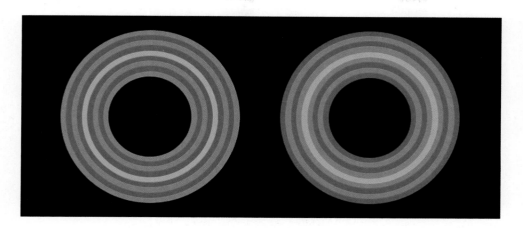

Figure 5.43
Is the orange circle brighter on the right or left? The orange circle on the right appears to be brighter than the one on the left, but the ink is exactly the same in both circles. You perceive the circle on the right to be brighter in the context of the surrounding stimuli.

showing more fear (Shin & others, 2005). Unfortunately, U.S. college students who are more concerned about the risk of terrorism conducted by Arab individuals perceive Arab faces as expressing more anger than do people less concerned about such terrorism (Maner & others, 2005). Perception is not a "cold" mechanical process. It is can be influenced strongly by the "heat" of our emotions. This provides more evidence that there is not a simple one-to-one relation between the physical stimulus and what we perceive.

Thinking Critically about Psychology

Perception is the interpretation of sensations. It's an active process in which perceptions are created that often go beyond the minimal information provided by the senses. Many of the ways in which we organize and interpret sensations are inborn and common to all humans. The Gestalt principles of perceptual organization, perceptual constancies, depth perception, and visual illusions provide examples of the active, creative nature of perception. Other factors that enter into the process of perception are unique to the individual, such as emotional and motivational states and cultural learning experiences. These factors ensure that we perceive the world in a way that is largely universal among humans, but with a great deal of individuality owing to differences in motivation and emotion.

Check Your Learning

To be sure that you have learned the key points from the preceding section, cover the list of correct answers and try to answer each question. If you give an incorrect answer to any question, return to the page given next to the correct answer to see why your answer was not correct.

1. When we perceive a visual stimulus, the center of our attention is termed the *figure* and the rest of the visual stimulus is perceived as the indistinct *ground.* Is it possible to change our perception of the same stimulus so that the figure becomes the ground and the ground becomes the figure?

   a) yes   b) no

2. The cues used in depth perception that require both eyes are called _____.

   a) constant   c) binocular

   b) monocular   d) dichromatics

Check Your Learning (cont.)

3. The shape of the lens of the eye must change to focus the visual image on the retina from stimuli that are different distances from the eye, providing a cue used in depth perception. This process is called _____.

   a) superposition

   b) aerial perspective

   c) convergence

   d) accommodation

4. Visual perception can be influenced by _____.

   a) motivation

   b) learning

   c) both a and b

   d) neither a nor b

Thinking Critically about Psychology

There are no right or wrong answers to the following questions. They are presented to help you become an active reader and think critically about what you have just read.

1. What is the point of studying perceptual illusions? What can we learn from them?

2. What is the value of knowing that our perception is influenced by our emotions and motives?

Correct Answers: 1. a (p. 148), **2. c** (p. 151), **3. d** (p. 150), **4. c** (p. 157)

Summary

Chapter 5 describes how we live in a physical world that we experience through our sense organs and perceive by processing sensory information in our nervous systems.

I. We are aware of the outside world because we have specialized sensory receptor cells.

   A. Sense organs transduce sensory energy into neural impulses and send neural messages to the brain where they are organized and interpreted in the process of perception.

   B. Psychophysics is the field of psychology that studies the complex relationships between physical stimuli and psychological sensations and perceptions.

II. The rods and cones of the eye transduce light energy into neural signals.

   A. The intensity of light waves largely determines brightness, whereas the wavelength (frequency) largely determines hue.

   B. The eye is the primary sense organ for seeing.

   1. Light enters the eye through the cornea (with the iris regulating the size of the pupil) and the lens into the retina.

   2. Rods and cones in the retina transduce light waves into neural impulses that are transmitted to the brain.

   3. The 125 million rods, located throughout the retina except for the fovea, are active in peripheral vision

and vision in dim light, but they do not play a role in color vision.

   4. The 6 million cones, clustered mostly near the fovea, respond to differences in the wavelength of light and play a role in color perception.

   5. Both trichromatic theory and opponent-process theory are helpful in understanding color vision.

III. The sense of hearing is based on the transduction of sound waves.

   A. The frequency of sound waves determines the sensation of pitch, whereas the intensity determines loudness.

   B. The ear is the primary sense organ involved in hearing.

   1. The outer ear functions as a sound wave collector.

   2. Sound waves vibrate the eardrum, which is connected to a series of three movable bones (hammer, anvil, stirrup) in the middle ear.

   3. The inner ear, containing the cochlea and the organ of Corti, transduces the sound wave energy into neural impulses for transmission to the brain.

IV. Internal stimuli are also transduced by the bodily sensory system.

   A. The vestibular organ provides information about the orientation of the body relative to the pull of gravity, whereas the kinesthetic sense reports the position and movement of the limbs and body.

B. The various skin senses can detect pressure, temperature, and pain.

1. Neural impulses that give rise to sensations of pain reach the brain at slightly different times because they travel on different neural pathways.

   a. The first sensation of pain is based on neural impulses that reach the somatosensory area quickly on myelinated neurons.

   b. The more emotional sensation of pain is based on neural impulses that reach the limbic system more slowly on unmyelinated neurons.

2. Many factors can block the pain gates for the emotional aspect of pain.

V. Chemical senses transduce chemicals in the environment.

A. In the sense of taste, different classes of chemicals are experienced as sweet, sour, bitter, salty, and fatty.

B. In the sense of smell, many different classes of chemicals are experienced as different odors, because we have hundreds or thousands of distinct odor receptors in the olfactory epithelium.

VI. Sensory neural impulses, when transmitted to the brain, are interpreted in a process called *perception;* examining visual perception demonstrates the general nature of the process of perception related to all of the senses.

A. Perception is an active mental process in the sense that what we perceive often goes beyond limited information from the sensory receptors.

B. Gestalt principles explain many of the ways in which humans tend to organize sensory information.

Visual Review of the Sense Organs

A great deal of new information was covered in chapter 5 on the structure of the sense organs. A set of unlabeled illustrations (figures 5.44 through 5.47) has been prepared to help you check your learning of these structures. These reviews will be most helpful if you glance at the first one and then refer back to the illustration on which it was based to memorize the names of the structures. Next, return to the illustration in this review section and try to write in the names of the key structures of the sense organs. Then check your labels by looking at the original figures once again. When you can label all the structures in one of the illustrations, move on to the next one.

Figure 5.44
Key structures of the eye
(based on fig. 5.2 on p. 125).

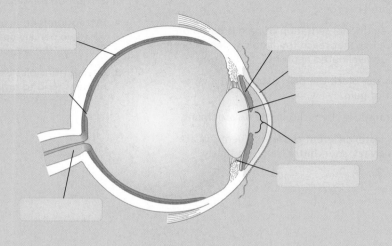

Figure 5.45
Key structures of the ear
(based on fig. 5.13 on p. 134).

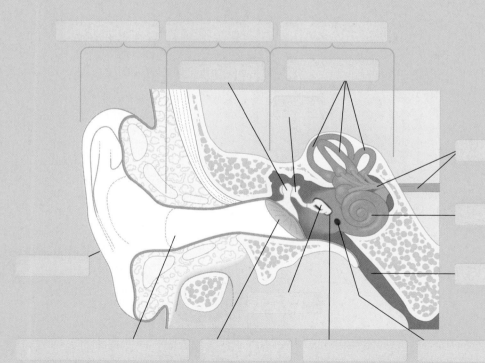

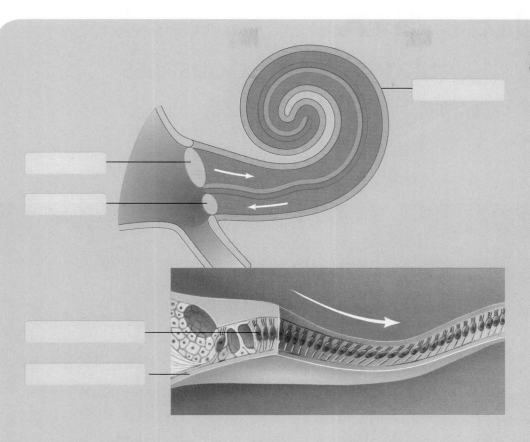

Figure 5.46
Key structures of the cochlea
(based on fig. 5.14 on p. 135).

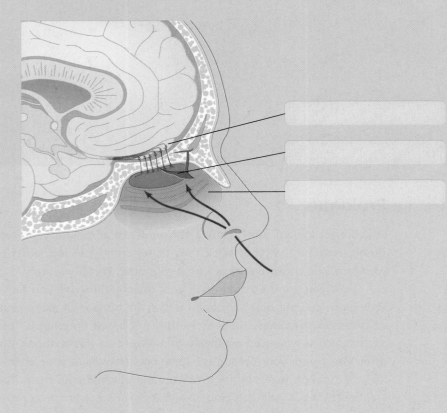

Figure 5.47
Key structures of the olfactory
receptors (based on fig. 5.21
on p. 146).

chapter **six**

States of consciousness

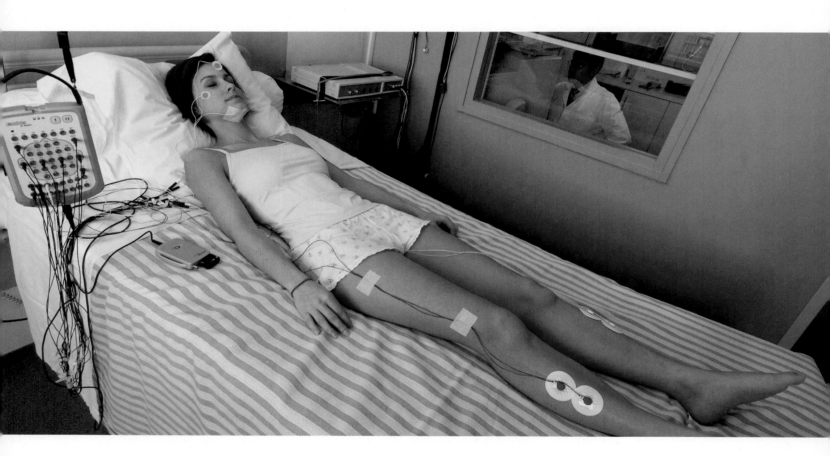

Chapter Outline

Prologue

Stop for a moment after reading this sentence and, with your eyes closed, imagine that your book rises slowly from your lap, drifts to your face, and closes, lightly pinching your nose. Try it—seriously.

Could you see the book rise in your imagination? Did you feel a little pinch on your nose? My point is this: life is made of many kinds of conscious awareness. Sometimes they are based on what is "out there," such as when you are aware of the words in this textbook. But often you create your conscious experiences entirely in your brain—like the floating textbook that rose up and pinched your nose. You create realities in your consciousness that never were and may never be. You do so every time you imagine, daydream, or dream.

Nancy Kerr of the Georgia Mental Health Institute conducted a classic study that illustrates this point beautifully (Foulkes, 1989). Kerr studied the dreams of adult men and women who had lost their eyesight as young children. She found that when they dreamed about friends their dreams were very much like those of sighted adults. Indeed, when they dreamed about people they had met as blind adults—friends they had never seen—they dreamed about them in visual images. They could "see" what their friends looked like in their dreams, even though they had never seen them with their eyes. They created these visual images entirely in their brains.

In this chapter, we define consciousness as a state of awareness—awareness of the outside world, of our own thoughts and feelings, and sometimes even of our own consciousness. Consciousness is not a single state. There are many different states of conscious awareness. When the waking day ends, we do not cease to be aware; rather, we experience other kinds of consciousness. As we drift off to sleep, we often pass through a dreamlike "twilight" phase, and even amid the shifting stages of sleep itself we experience the strange reality of dreams.

Other states of consciousness are experienced less frequently. Some states of altered awareness occur spontaneously, as do hallucinations and other distorted perceptual experiences. Other altered states of consciousness are achieved in part through deep concentration and relaxation, such as during meditation and hypnosis. Still other altered states can be induced by taking certain drugs. As you read about each form of consciousness, ask how much of the awareness comes through the sense organs that you studied in chapter 5, and how much comes from within.

Key Terms

attention 163
circadian rhythm 170
consciousness 163
day residue 174
daydreams 173
depersonalization 180
divided consciousness 164
dreaming 168
hallucinogens 182
hypnagogic state 166
hypnosis 179
inhalants 182
insomnia 176
latent content 175
manifest content 175
meditation 178
mindfulness 178
myoclonia 166
narcolepsy 176
night terrors 175
opiates 185
psychotropic drugs 181
REM sleep 168
sleep apnea 176
sleepwalking 175
transcendental state 178
unconscious mind 164

Wide Awake: Normal Waking Consciousness

Conscious thought plays a crucial role in helping us function in human societies (Baumeister & Masicampo, 2010). But, what exactly does it mean to be conscious? When conscious, we are aware of the sights and sounds of the outside world, of our feelings, and our thoughts. When unconscious, we are not aware of these things. **Consciousness,** simply defined, is *a state of awareness*. There is more than one kind of conscious state. The qualities of conscious awareness that people experience when they are focused on a task, daydreaming, hypnotized, high on drugs, or dreaming are so different from one another that we need to think of consciousness as being many different states of awareness. To understand consciousness fully, we need to explore its many varieties and the conditions under which they occur. In this chapter, we speak of dreams, trances, highs, and the like, both to understand the nature of these states and to help us better understand the conscious experience of being awake.

We are limited in how much we can focus on or attend to at any one time. Psychologists use the term **attention** to refer to the process of responding to some things in the environment, to the exclusion of others (Dijksterhuis & Aarts, 2010). The limitations of our attention are demonstrated in a classic study where participants focusing their attention on players passing a basketball did not notice someone in a gorilla suit walking across the court, pounding on its chest (Simons and Chabris, 2009). The limits

consciousness (kon´shus-nes) A state of awareness.

attention Selective focus on some things in the environment, to the exclusion of others.

of our attention are apparent when we look at instances when we divide our consciousness or engage in numerous activities simultaneously, often referred to as multitasking.

Divided Consciousness: Being Two Places (Mentally) at the Same Time

"I'm sorry dear, I must have lost consciousness. What were you saying?"

divided consciousness The splitting off of two conscious activities that occur simultaneously.

unconscious mind Mental processes that occur without conscious awareness.

I was once invited to watch a friend record a demo tape of a song he had written. It was my first time in a studio and I was fascinated—they even let me record a few bars using my friend's guitar (I was less than excellent). As I drove home, my thoughts raced about my own long-forgotten fantasies of making hit records. When I got home, I was horrified to realize that I had no recollection whatsoever of the five-mile drive! Obviously I had negotiated several stoplights and made a couple of turns, but I was so lost in my thoughts that I was driving on "autopilot." Stanford University psychologist Ernest Hilgard (1975) describes such phenomena as moments of **divided consciousness.** He believes that our conscious awareness becomes "split," and we simultaneously perform two activities requiring conscious awareness (in my case, driving and thinking about recording songs).

We are better at handling multiple tasks when they are automatic. Walking and chewing gum at the same time is pretty easy for most of us, but few of us can walk and juggle at the same time. Driving is usually fairly automatic through practice and requires less conscious attention, until we are trying to find a street in an unfamiliar city during rush hour. That's when we want our friends to stop talking to us, because we are trying to drive. Of course we have been driving all along, but what we mean is that we need to focus our attention on our driving, on checking rearview mirrors, etc. Trying to give attention to that and a conversation is just too much.

What are the limitations to our attention and how much does our performance suffer when we multitask? How about driving and talking on a cell phone at the same time? Can we successfully allocate conscious awareness to two tasks at the same time? We usually believe we're good at this, but the research says otherwise (Schlehofer & others, 2010). Studies of cell-phone use show that even with a hands-free headset, cell-phone conversations distract drivers, causing errors and accidents (Strayer & Johnston, 2001). Even it you don't answer it, a ringing cell phone distracts us (Shelton & others, 2009). Texting while driving receives a lot of publicity, and laws are being passed against it, due to train, bus, and car accidents. But how about just walking and talking on a cell phone? Surely that's easy enough to do, while paying attention to both. Yet in one study, people talking on a cell phone while walking failed to notice a clown on a unicycle (Hyman & others, 2009)! Clearly there is a cost to dividing our consciousness. Probably you have experienced "mindless reading" (Reichle & others, 2010), the frustrating experience of reading your textbook, only to realize pages later that you haven't paid attention to a single word and you must go back and re-read it all again, because your mind had wandered even though your eyes moved across the page.

Would you notice this? Perhaps not, if you were talking on your cell phone.

The Concept of the Unconscious Mind

In discussing conscious experience, we need to compare the term *conscious* with the term *unconscious.* Many people beginning to study psychology expect to learn about the **unconscious mind.** Until recently the term was not even mentioned in most introductory psychology textbooks. Psychology is taught in most American colleges and universities from a scientific viewpoint, and historically the term *unconscious* was used primarily by psychologists who took a more philosophical approach to understanding people and their problems. Today, however, most scientists agree that it's useful to apply scientific thinking to the study of the unconscious (Bargh & Morsella, 2008; Dijksterhuis & Nordgren, 2006). As psychologists now know, many of our cognitive operations and mental processes occur unconsciously, without our awareness.

Consider this: when you are in a room where more than one person is talking, most of the time you pay attention to one voice and "tune out" the other voice. Usually you are focused on your instructor's lecture in class, but sometimes you may listen to what your neighbors are whispering. This has been called the *cocktail party phenomenon,* because it happens so often at parties where you focus your attention on the person you are talking with, to the exclusion of all of the other voices around you. What becomes of the other voices—the ones we do not listen to? These, too, reach the brain, though we are not *consciously* aware of it—that is, it is unconscious. If someone across the room happens to mention your name (or your teacher calls on you in class!), you usually look up and re-focus your attention, even if you were doing something else at the time. Hearing your own name makes it through to your consciousness, and you change the focus of your attention from your conversation.

Andrew Mathews and Colin MacLeod (1986) studied this phenomenon experimentally. Participants in their study listened to two messages presented simultaneously over different earphones. They were instructed to ignore one of the messages but to repeat the other message aloud. Some of the time, the words presented to the ignored earphone were nonthreatening words, such as *friend* and *concert,* whereas threatening words, such as *assault* and *emergency,* were presented at other times. As the participants repeated the message, they also kept their eyes on a computer screen and pressed a key as quickly as they could after the word *press* appeared on the screen (see figure 6.1).

To be sure that the threatening words would have a great deal of emotional impact on the participants, researchers selected only highly anxious persons who were receiving treatment for their problems. The participants reported that they were not consciously aware of any of the ignored words because they focused all of their attention on the message they had to repeat; yet when threatening words were being presented, the anxious individuals pressed the key significantly less quickly than when nonthreatening words were presented. Apparently, the ignored words were being processed without conscious awareness, and the emotional impact of the threatening words disrupted performance on the reaction-time task. Careful experiments of this sort lead to a better understanding of the mental processes that affect us without our conscious awareness.

Figure 6.1

Participants in Mathews and MacLeod's study of unconscious information processing listened to two different messages presented simultaneously through different earphones. They were able to completely ignore one message and repeat the other one. At the same time, they pressed a key as quickly as they could when the word "press" appeared on the computer screen. Although not consciously perceived, threatening words disrupted the reaction time of highly anxious individuals, suggesting they had unconsciously processed the emotional meaning of the threatening words.

Review

Consciousness is composed of many different states of awareness, and from moment to moment we change the focus of our attention. During each day, we shift many times between everyday consciousness and daydreams. At times, our consciousness appears to "do two things at once," in what Hilgard refers to as divided consciousness. We also process information unconsciously; these unconscious processes can be studied scientifically.

Thinking Critically about Psychology

There are no right or wrong answers to the following questions. They are presented to help you become an active reader and think critically about what you have just read.

1. Why do you think we typically fail to notice the limitations to our attention? Can you think of a time when you suddenly became aware of something?

2. Can you think of any instances when you've experienced divided consciousness?

Correct Answers: 1. a (p. 163), 2. b (p. 164)

Sleep and Dreams: Conscious while Asleep

Most nights, we slip gently from wakefulness into sleep, only to return from our nocturnal vacation the next morning. Is that all there is to sleeping? Is it merely a gap in awareness that consumes one-third of our lives? How important, really, is getting a good night's sleep? Why do we dream? Sleep is actually not a single state. Instead, it's a complex combination of states that we move through throughout the night, some involving conscious awareness. This means that we do not completely leave consciousness behind when we sleep. Rather, we enter worlds of awareness with properties that are very different from those of the wide-awake world.

Stages of Sleep

As we fall asleep, we pass from waking consciousness into a semiwakeful state, then into four states of progressively deeper sleep. Intermittently, we shift from the four stages of sleep into a stage in which dreaming is common, which brings a kind of conscious awareness with a reality all its own. Let's consider each of these parts of the sleep cycle.

Hypnagogic State. We do not always go directly from wakefulness to sleep. Often, we pass into a "twilight" state that is neither daydreaming nor dreaming. This is the **hypnagogic state** (Vaitl & others, 2005). In this state, we begin to lose voluntary control over our body movements; our sensitivity to outside stimuli diminishes; and our thoughts become more fanciful and less bound by reality. For most, it's a highly relaxed, enjoyable state. Occasionally, however, we are rudely snapped out of the peaceful hypnagogic state. We suddenly feel as if we are falling, and our bodies experience a sudden jerk called a **myoclonia.** These jerks are completely normal, caused by brief seizure-like states of the brain as sleep commences.

hypnagogic state (hip´´nah-goj´ik) Relaxed state of dreamlike awareness between wakefulness and sleep.

myoclonia (mī´´o-klō´nē-ah) An abrupt movement that sometimes occurs during the hypnagogic state in which the sleeper often experiences a sense of falling.

Stages of Light and Deep Sleep. After making the transition from the hypnagogic state to sleep, we pass through four stages of progressively deeper sleep. The
four levels of sleep are defined by **electroencephalogram (EEG)** measures of electrical brain activity. The depth of sleep alternates changes many times during the night.
Indeed, young adults show an average of 34 shifts in the depth of sleep during the first
6 hours (Webb, 1968). Sleep, then, is not a single, continuous state; it is an almost
constantly changing state, with deeper, slower frequencies of wavelength occurring
during the later stages (see figure 6.2).

electroencephalogram (EEG)
(e-lek´´trō-en-sef´ah-lo-gram) A
measure of electrical brain activity.

Figure 6.2

Each night we pass through the four stages of sleep and the phase of rapid eye movement (REM) sleep. The irregular pattern of shifting
from one stage or phase of sleep to another is shown in the graph at the bottom half of the illustration. You'll see that in the first hour of
sleep, this student passed through each of the four phases of sleep and then began the cycle again.
  The top half of this figure shows records of electroencephalograph (EEG) recordings of brain activity (in blue) and eye movement activity
(in red) from one night of sleep of a male college student. Look at recording "f" or "REM, or paradoxical sleep" and note the slow, rolling
eye movements that give REM sleep its name. Except for the amplitude of the EEG tracings (displayed as distance up and down the black lines
across the bottom of each recording), the EEG during REM sleep in recording "f" paradoxically resembles wakefulness in recording "a."

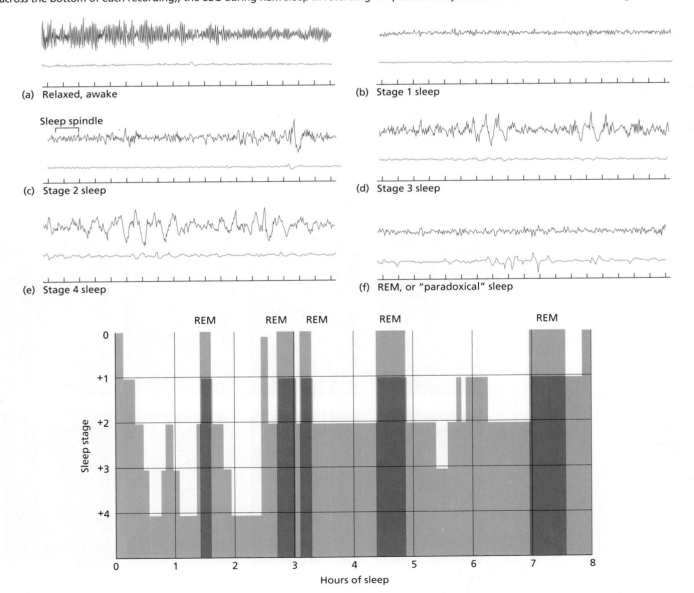

Source: Records provided by T. E. LeVere. Used by permission.

REM Sleep and Dreams

The year was 1952. University of Chicago graduate student Eugene Aserinsky was spending a sleepless night watching a child sleep in Dr. Nathaniel Kleitman's laboratory. Kleitman was interested in the slow, rolling eye movements that occur during sleep in infants. The child was connected to a complicated network of wires that led from instruments to monitor many aspects of the body's functioning (such as brain waves, heartbeat, breathing) and an instrument to measure eye movements.

As Aserinsky dutifully watched the instruments, he often saw periods in which the child's eyes moved rapidly. Half a dozen times during the night, the child's eyes darted back and forth rapidly and irregularly under his closed eyelids. When Aserinsky looked at the electroencephalograph (EEG) readings, he saw something startling. When the child's eyes were moving, his brain activity looked more like he was awake than asleep. Each time the rapid eye movements returned, the same brain pattern resembling wakefulness returned.

When Aserinsky showed his professor the unexpected findings, the hypothesis was almost inescapable: did the child's EEG look like he was awake because he was **dreaming** when his eyes were moving? During the next several years, Aserinsky and Kleitman awakened many sleeping adult and child participants when they entered this peculiar stage of sleep characterized by rapid eye movements. When awakened during rapid-eye-movement sleep and asked if they were dreaming, more than 80% said yes. The era of the scientific study of dreams began with Aserinsky and Kleitman's surprising discovery of the relationship between dreaming and movements of the eyeballs (Kleitman, 1960). Their discovery that dreams are very common during a period of sleep marked by rapid eye movements and brain-wave activity suggests the presence of conscious awareness. This provided a convenient way for scientists to know when dreams were occurring so that they could study them. Because of the characteristic eye movements, this phase of sleep is referred to as *rapid-eye-movement sleep,* or **REM sleep.**

dreaming Conscious awareness during sleep that primarily occurs during rapid-eye-movement (REM) sleep.

REM sleep Rapid-eye-movement sleep, characterized by movement of the eyes under the lids; often accompanies dreams.

Electroencephalograms and eye muscle monitors allow psychologists to study dreams scientifically.

Autonomic Storms. Six decades of study have revealed the eyeballs are not the only parts of the body that are busy during REM dreams. Pioneer sleep researcher Wilse Webb (1968) likened dream sleep to an "autonomic storm." The autonomic nervous system and other parts of the peripheral nervous system (see chapter 3) are very active during dreams, causing noticeable changes in many parts of the body: blood flow to the brain increases; the heartbeat becomes irregular; the muscles of the face and fingers twitch; and breathing becomes irregular. Interestingly, voluntary control of the large body muscles is largely lost during REM sleep, perhaps to keep us from acting out our dreams. Anyone who has watched a sleeping beagle twitch, make miniature running movements, and rasp muffled barks (at dream rabbits?) knows about these autonomic storms and knows that REM sleep is not limited to humans. This fact has been confirmed in many laboratory studies of sleeping mammals.

REM sleep is like an autonomic storm, causing marked changes in many parts of the body—human or animal. Beagles provide an interesting sight during REM sleep as they twitch and sometimes even make muffled howls.

In addition, females experience vaginal lubrication and erection of the clitoris, and males experience erection of the penis during REM sleep. Because of erections that begin during REM sleep, the penis of an adult male is erect during one-fourth to one-half of an average night's sleep. This fact can be used in the diagnosis of conditions in which some males are unable to have an erection (known as *erectile dysfunction*). By having the patient spend a night in a sleep laboratory to see if he has erections during REM sleep, clinicians can determine if the cause of the problem is psychological (he would have erections during REM sleep) or physical (he would not have REM erections).

Time Spent Dreaming. How often do you dream? In a survey of college-aged adults, about 15% thought that they dreamed every night, and another 25% thought that they dreamed on most nights during the week. But almost a third of young adults said that they rarely or never dream (Strauch & Meier, 1996). How often do you *actually* dream? Even if you think you dream every night, you probably greatly underestimate the frequency of your dreams. We spend much more time in the world of dream consciousness than most of us realize.

Studies of dreaming show the average college student spends about two hours a night in REM sleep, divided into about four to six separate episodes. Based on the reports of sleepers who were awakened during REM sleep, we know that we dream during at least 80% of these episodes of REM sleep (Strauch & Meier, 1996). The length of our REM dreams vary, but the longest REM dream, generally about an hour in duration, usually occurs during the last part of the sleep cycle (Hobson, 1989; Webb, 1982).

Therefore, young adults have 30 to 40 REM dreams per week. We do not remember dreaming nearly this often when we are awake, because we forget dreams quickly unless we awaken during or soon after the dream. But we spend about two hours each night in the conscious state of REM dreams. There is much more to the story of consciousness while sleeping, however. REM sleep is not the only part of the sleep cycle that contains dreams.

Non-REM Sleep and Dreams

Initially, sleep researchers believed that dreams were uncommon during the non-REM parts of the sleep cycle (Kleitman, 1960). Subsequent studies showed, however, that the number of dreams that occur during non-REM deep wave sleep is much higher

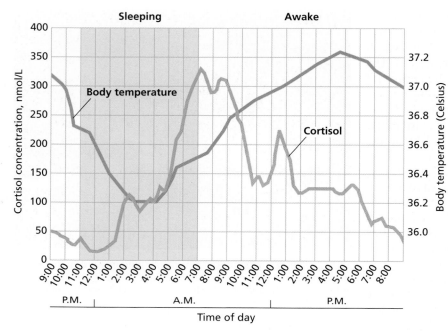

Figure 6.3

The concentration of the adrenal hormone cortisol in the blood follows a circadian rhythm, reaching its peak just before a person wakes from sleep, whereas the circadian rhythm for body temperature follows a different pattern.

Source: Data based in part on J. Puig-Antich & others, "Cortisol Secretion in Prepubertal Children with Major Depressive Disorder," *Archives of General Psychiatry*, 46:801–812, 1989.

circadian rhythm (sur-kā´dē-un) Internally generated cycles lasting about 24 hours a day that regulate sleepiness and wakefulness, body temperature, and the secretion of some hormones.

than suspected. When people are awakened during non-REM phases of sleep, they report dreaming about half of the time (Strauch & Meier, 1996; Vaitl & others, 2005). On the average, non-REM dreams are less bizarre and filled with less negative emotion than REM dreams are (McNamara & others, 2005), but in most ways, recent research suggests that dreams that occur during REM and non-REM stages of sleep are more similar than different (Vaitl & others, 2005).

When both REM and non-REM dreams are considered, we spend a surprising amount of time in states of consciousness during sleep. In addition to the two hours of REM dreaming per night, non-REM dreaming occurs two to three hours per night on average.

Circadian Rhythms

When is it time to go to sleep? Drowsiness may take over when it gets dark. Others, particularly adolescents, are night owls, awake until the wee hours of the morning, preferring to sleep in (Crowley, Acebo and Carskadon, 2007).

We are all on a biological cycle of approximately 24 hours, called the **circadian rhythm** (*circa* = about; *dia* = day), that regulates our pattern of wakefulness and sleep (Bratzke & others, 2007). Parts of the brain stem and hypothalamus play important roles in the body's internal "clock" (Sakurai, 2007). Its activity increases and decreases in a regular pattern that lasts about 24 hours. In addition, variations in the hormone *melatonin* that fluctuate on a 24-hour pattern appear to be one key factor in regulating sleepiness (Gilbertini, Graham, & Cook, 1999).

The body has many other circadian rhythms, most of which roughly follow the pattern of the sleep-wake cycle. For example, an important hormone of the pituitary that plays a key role in body growth and repair, *growth hormone,* is secreted mostly during the first two hours of sleep, with little secreted during the waking hours of the day. Apparently, this reflects the role that sleep plays in normal growth and the maintenance of health.

Body temperature also follows a circadian rhythm linked to the sleep cycle. As you can see in figure 6.3, body temperature falls just as you are beginning to feel sleepy and continues to fall until the middle of the sleep period. Figure 6.3 also shows that the adrenal stress hormone *cortisol* follows a circadian rhythm that is tied to the sleep period in yet another pattern. Cortisol secretion begins to rise shortly after you fall asleep and continues to rise through the night. This is another indication that REM sleep is not a calm period for the body. Cortisol secretion peaks just before awakening, during the longest period of REM sleep. Thus, the autonomic storm (p. 169) that takes place during REM dreams is accompanied by activation of the adrenal glands. A good night's sleep is healthy, but not all of it is a "restful" time for the body.

The circadian sleep-wake cycle is influenced by the level of light. Some clever experiments have shown, however, that the circadian sleep rhythm continues even when individuals are isolated in chambers that are always kept lighted. Surprisingly, the rhythm quickly changes to a 25-hour cycle when the level of light does not change

Figure 6.4   It generally takes longer to adjust to local sleep schedules and get over jet lag when traveling west to east.

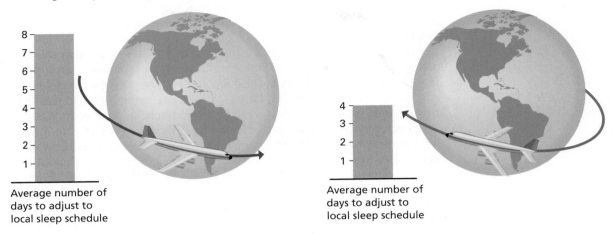

Average number of
days to adjust to
local sleep schedule

Average number of
days to adjust to
local sleep schedule

Source: Data from M. C. Moore-Ede, F. M. Sulzman, and C. A. Fuller, *The Clocks That Time Us.* Harvard University Press, Cambridge: 1982.

(Aschoff, 1981; Horne, 1988). Apparently, the body's clock runs on a schedule that is a little longer than 24 hours, but is reset each day by daylight.

We dramatically became aware of the importance of circadian rhythms when we disrupt them during trips. Flying west from Atlanta to Hawaii, for example, means you experience a much longer period of daylight, and you generally stay awake longer than usual on the first day. If you fly to Paris, however, you will have a very short first night. Both trips will disrupt your circadian rhythms and make you inefficient and out of sorts—a phenomenon known as "jet lag." People differ in how much they are affected by jet lag, but interestingly, the time required to readjust to local time is generally longer when traveling from west to east (Moore-Ede, Sulzman, & Fuller, 1982; see figure 6.4). Thus, you shouldn't expect to tour the entire Louvre museum the morning after arriving in Paris. You'll be lucky to have the energy to break your French bread. Data from 10 years of major league baseball showed that teams with the circadian advantage won more games than predicted by chance, due to the other team's jet lag, gaining almost as much as the home team advantage (Winter & others, 2009)!

People who rotate the times of their work shifts also find it hard to ignore circadian rhythms (Wilkinson & others, 1989). It is less disruptive to rotate from the night shift (midnight to 8 A.M.) to the day shift (8 A.M. to 4 P.M.) or from the day shift to the swing shift (4 P.M. to midnight) than to rotate in the opposite direction, since you stay awake longer on the first day of each rotation. It is apparently better to move from night to day shift and to travel from east to west, because these changes are consistent with our natural tendency to lengthen our circadian rhythms (Moore-Ede & others, 1982). Jet lag and work-shift rotations have been the subject of considerable study because of their effect on second and third "graveyard" shift workers, such as airplane mechanics, the scheduling of airline pilots, nurses, and other key employees, as well as the timing of travel for diplomatic, business, and military purposes, and for athletes and performers. Recent studies point to the dangerous effects of disrupting our circadian rhythms, with negative consequences for physical well-being, including not only more accidents, but also increased risk of cancers (Erren & others, 2008; Megdal & others, 2005; Davis & Mirick, 2006) and heart disease (Elliott, 2001).

Sleep Deprivation, the Need for Sleep, and Health

We have to sleep to function well and be healthy. When our sleep is less than normal, we create what is called a "sleep debt." Many years ago, students at the University of

Florida participated in a now-classic sleep experiment in which their sleep was limited to two hours for one night. The next day they were irritable, fatigued, inattentive, and inefficient; the next night they fell asleep more quickly and slept longer than usual (Webb & Bonnet, 1979).

In the early days of sleep research, it was not clear that sleep was important to maintaining good health. For example, sleep researchers made much of the fact that teenager Randy Gardner set a world record by staying awake for 264 hours as a science project. Although he felt fatigue, sleepiness, irritability, and was hallucinating by day 4, he suffered no obvious short-term effects on his health. When a group of volunteer college students gradually reduced their sleep from 8 to 4 hours a night for a period of 2 months, there were no detectable short-term effects (Webb & Bonnet, 1979). We now know, however, that sufficient sleep is essential to maintaining good physical health (Cappuccio & others, 2010; Grandner & others, 2010). Rats deprived of sleep die as a result of extended sleep deprivation (Rechtschaffen & Bergmann, 1995). In humans, sleeping less than average is associated with high blood pressure (Knutson & others, 2009) and heart disease (King & others, 2008), and death rates from all causes (controlling for age and other factors) increase as the number of hours of sleep decrease (or increase) from 7 hours per night (Kripke & others, 2002). This finding is especially important at this time in history, because the average amount of sleep has declined from 9 hours per night in 1960 to 7 or 8 hours in 2000 in the United States among people who are employed (Knutson & others, 2010). Fortunately, only the shortest durations of sleep are associated with large differences in death rates. For example, men who sleep less than 4.5 hours per night and women who sleep less than 3.5 hours per night have a 15% higher death rate (Kripke & others, 2002).

Why does sleeping less than average harm our health? Sleep deprivation disrupts the healthy functioning of the body in many ways. It alters the efficiency of brain activity (Gujar & others, 2010), increases the activation of the sympathetic nervous system, increases levels of stress hormones secreted by the adrenal glands, influences levels of insulin and alters the metabolism of sugar, and slows the body's immune system (Grandner & others, 2010; Motivala & Irwin, 2007).

Another likely cause of death related to sleep deprivation is accidental death. Even small amounts of sleep deprivation can decrease alertness and increase the risk of accidents. For example, each spring, when we lose an hour of sleep because of daylight savings time, a temporary increase occurs in the rate of deaths due to injury in the United States (Coren, 1996, 2004). A review of the scientific findings on short-term sleep deprivation reveals that the strongest impact is on simple attention, although there are other cognitive deficits resulting from short-term lack of sleep, too; all of these factors likely contribute to the accidents and injuries resulting from sleep deprivation (Lim & Dinges, 2008, 2010).

Not only do we need sleep, we specifically appear to "need" REM dreams during sleep. In a number of experiments, sleeping individuals were awakened when they entered REM sleep. They were otherwise allowed to get a normal amount of sleep each night. Depriving participants of approximately two hours of REM sleep each night had the same effects as much longer deprivations of sleep in general. The participants deprived of REM sleep were irritable, inefficient, and fatigued. On subsequent nights, they showed an increase in the amount of REM sleep, suggesting that they had a need to catch up on REM sleep. REM sleep is not the only important phase of sleep. Deprivation of the deepest part of non-REM sleep has much the same effect as loss of REM sleep (Hobson, 1989; Webb & Bonnet, 1979). Memory consolidation, which allows us to form good memories, seems to occur in deep-wave sleep, as synapses between the hippocampus and prefrontal cortex synchronize (Mölle and Born, 2009).

REM sleep may also play a role in the consolidation of newly learned information from the day before (Hu & others, 2006; Ribeiro & others, 1999; Walker & Stickgold,

2006). REM sleep plays this important role by influencing the rate of neurogenesis (Lucassen & others, 2010; Mirescu & others, 2006) and by activating the expression of genes that control changes in the connections between neurons that are involved in memory (Ribeiro & others, 2002). So allow time to get a good night's sleep before your exams, so that your studying will pay off. If you pull an "all nighter" or do not sleep long enough after you study, you may not remember as much, because you haven't given your memories a chance to consolidate as you sleep. It would be a shame to waste all that effort!

Sleep also enhances memory of emotional information (Payne & others, 2008), and REM in particular appears important for processing emotion, and the link between the memory of an event and the emotional experience (Walker & van der Helm, 2009).

Student pulling an all-nighter—studying late into the night.

Dreams

Daydreams are a commonly experienced conscious state of thinking and feeling, not bound by logic or reality. Deams during sleep are one of the most fascinating aspects of human consciousness. At least since the time of the Egyptian pharaohs, people have attempted to decipher the meaning of dreams—and some psychologists are still trying. Let's begin our discussion of dreams by looking at psychological studies of what people dream about. Because dreams are private, it is interesting to compare your dreams with those of others.

Daydreams Conscious dreamlike states of wishful fantasizing.

The first systematic study of dreams was conducted by Mary Whiton Calkins, who is noted in chapter 1 as a founder of psychology. Calkins was a pioneer in the study of memory, but she was also the founder of scientific dream research. Over 100 years ago, Calkins and her partner wrote down a verbatim description of every dream they recalled over several months—often writing by candlelight in the middle of the night (Calkins, 1893). Because many researchers have since studied spontaneously recalled dreams, and those from research participants awakened in sleep labs, we can confidently describe the content of the "average" human dream.

The Nature of Dreams. Most of the conscious experience in dreams is visual. If you dream about washing dishes, you often experience a visual image of dishwashing but are less likely to "hear" the clatter of the dishes or "feel" the wet dishwater. Only about one-fourth of dream images include auditory sensations, and about 20% include body sensations. About half of the dreams that involve body sensations are sexual—10% of all dreams. Less than 1% of dreams include tastes or smells (Hall, 1951; Strauch & Meier, 1996).

Do you dream in black and white or in color? Most people dream in something that is in between. The visual images in dreams are usually as bright and clear as waking images, but they are drab in color. Dreams usually include few intense colors, and most have blurry backgrounds (Rechtschaffen & Buchignami, 1983). Who are the characters in your dreams? Because we are the "author" of our dreams, it is not surprising that we have an active role in nearly three-fourths of our dreams (Strauch & Meier, 1996). About half of the other characters are friends, acquaintances, or family members, but the other half are people we don't recognize. The characters in dreams are about an even mixture of men and women (Hall, 1951; Strauch & Meier, 1996).

Sweet Dreams: The Emotional Content of Dreams. Are your dreams mostly happy or sad or scary? When people are asked about the emotional content of their dreams as soon as they spontaneously wake up, they say that about 60% of their emotional dreams contained negative emotions (Strauch & Meier, 1996). When researchers awaken people during REM sleep, however, most of the emotional dreams they report are positive (Fosse & others, 2001). So why don't we remember all of our sweet dreams in the morning? Although we dream mostly of positive things, negative dreams are more likely to wake us up, so we are more aware of them. It's reassuring to know that usually we are happy in our dreams.

There are gender differences in the emotional qualities of the dreams that we usually recall, with men being a little more likely to recall positive dreams than women. When verbal or physical aggression occurs in dreams, both men and women are more likely to dream that they are the victims rather than the perpetrators, but this tendency is stronger for women than men (Strauch & Meier, 1996).

Creative and Bizarre Aspects of Dreams. Dreams fascinate us because they can be amazingly creative and bizarre. About three-fourths of our dreams contain at least one bizarre and unrealistic element, mixed into an otherwise realistic dream. However, 10% of our dreams involve mostly nonsensical story lines, while another 10% of our dreams are almost completely fantastic and bizarre (Hall, 1951; Strauch & Meier, 1996).

Meaning of Dreams

Why do we dream about the things that fill our heads during sleep? What do they mean? A century of research suggests that some of the content of dreams relates to our waking experiences.

day residue Dream content that is similar to events in the person's waking life.

Day Residue. A large part of the content of dreams is directly related to things going on in our lives during the day—what Sigmund Freud called **day residue.** Most dreams contain at least one character or event from the preceding day. For example, half of all dreams reported by research participants in sleep laboratories include the researchers or parts of the laboratory (Strauch & Meier, 1996). The role of day residue in dreaming was clearly demonstrated in a well-designed study conducted at the Max Planck Institute of Psychiatry in Munich, Germany (Lauer & others, 1987). Participants slept in the laboratory after being shown either a neutral film or an upsetting film depicting violence, humiliation, and despair. They were awakened during their first REM stage and asked if they were dreaming. After viewing the upsetting film, the participants' REM dreams contained considerably more aggressive and anxious content than on the night following the neutral film. Furthermore, about one-third of the dreams contained images or themes directly related to the content of the upsetting film.

On October 17, 1989, a major earthquake took place in the San Francisco area, causing more than $5 billion in damage, and killing 62 people. A team of researchers (Wood & others, 1992) had students at two universities in the San Francisco area track the number of upsetting dreams they had during a three-week period immediately following the earthquake. As a control group, students at the University of Arizona, far from the earthquake, also kept track of their dreams. Not surprisingly, 40% of the students in the San Francisco area reported at least one dream about earthquakes, compared with 5% of the students in Arizona (Wood & others, 1992). Similarly, persons exposed to highly stressful events, such as wars, sometimes have nightmarish dreams about them for many years afterward (Neyland & others, 1998). Clearly, day residue (events and concerns in our daily lives) is a common part of our dreams.

Dream Interpretation. Some of the content of dreams is the day residue (events and concerns of daily life), but what about the rest? What do the other dream images mean? There are many different views of the meaning of dreams, ranging from the opinion that they mean virtually nothing to the belief that they provide a rich source of information about hidden aspects of our personalities that cannot be revealed easily in other ways.

Sigmund Freud believed dreams were the "royal road to the unconscious," allowing us to travel deep into the unconscious mind, viewing hidden conflicts and motives cloaked only by the symbols of dreams. Freud divided the content of dreams into two levels, manifest and latent. The events that we experience in dreams are their **manifest content.** Freud believed it was necessary to get beyond the surface and find out what the manifest content of the dream symbolized to discover its true meaning, or **latent content.** For example, the manifest content of a young woman's dream might involve riding on a train and becoming frightened as it enters a tunnel. On the surface, the dream is about trains and tunnels. This is the manifest content—the actual content of the dream. But what does this mean? The classic Freudian interpretation is that the train symbolizes a penis and the tunnel symbolizes a vagina. Hence, the hidden, or latent, content of the dream might concern the young woman's conflicts about having sex.

Such interpretations are provocative, but are they accurate? Psychologists do not agree on this issue, as symbols can be interpreted in infinite ways, varying by culture, or even being unique to each person. We can never be sure that our interpretations are correct. It is also extremely difficult to test scientifically. Psychologists today place much less emphasis on dream interpretation than did Freud.

manifest content According to Freud, the literal meaning of dreams.

latent content According to Freud, the true meaning of dreams that is found in the symbols in their manifest content.

Nightmares and Other Sleep Phenomena

We have all had terrifying dreams known as **nightmares.** The content of these dreams, which mostly occur during REM sleep, can be exceptionally frightening, sad, or uncomfortable. They are often upsetting enough to wake us up during the dream, so we often remember our nightmares, even though they account for only a small proportion of our dreams (Hartmann & others, 1987). Disturbing nightmares are more common in people under psychological stress, particularly if they have a tendency to respond to stress with high levels of negative emotion (Levin & Nielsen, 2007).

Night terrors are a less common but perhaps even more upsetting nocturnal experience. The individual awakens suddenly in a state of panic, sometimes screaming, usually with no clear recollection of an accompanying dream. A sense of calm usually returns within a few minutes, but these can be terrifying experiences. Unlike nightmares, they do not occur during REM sleep but during the deepest phases of non-REM sleep. Night terrors are most common in preschool-age children, but sometimes adults also experience them (Hartmann & others, 1987).

Sleepwalking is another interesting phenomenon occurring primarily during the deepest parts of non-REM sleep. It is not an abnormal behavior. Sleepwalkers get up and carry on complicated activities, like walking from room to room, even though they are sound asleep. Sleepwalking is most common in children before the age of puberty but is not unusual in adults, usually reappearing in adults only during periods of stress.

Sleeptalking is a fairly common phenomenon that can occur during any phase of the sleep cycle. In this, the soundly sleeping person says words, sometimes making fairly coherent statements for a brief period of time. It's most common in young adults but occurs at all ages.

nightmares Dreams that occur during REM sleep and whose content is exceptionally frightening, sad, angry, or in some other way uncomfortable.

night terrors Upsetting nocturnal experiences that occur most often in preschool-age children during deep non-REM sleep.

sleepwalking Walking and carrying on complicated activities during the deepest part of non-REM sleep.

sleeptalking Talking during any phase of the sleep cycle.

Sleep Disorders

Although we all sleep, some experience serious difficulties with the sleep process. The term **sleep disorders** is often used to refer to these troublesome but highly treatable disorders.

sleep disorders Disturbances of sleep.

People with sleep-onset insomnia have difficulty falling asleep.

insomnia Sleep disorder in which the person has difficulty falling asleep or staying asleep.

narcolepsy Sleep disorder in which the person suddenly falls asleep during activities usually performed when fully awake, even when the person has had adequate sleep.

sleep apnea Sudden interruption of breathing during sleep.

Insomnia refers to a variety of difficulties in which individuals report that they sleep less than they wish. There are two major varieties of insomnia. In *sleep-onset insomnia*, individuals have difficulty falling asleep at the hour at which they would like, but sleep is normal after it begins. In contrast, *early-awakening insomnia* is characterized by waking up earlier than desired, either several times in the middle of the night or early in the morning. Both are found in individuals experiencing no other psychological problems but are more common in individuals undergoing periods of stress, anxiety, or depression. Insomnia is particularly common among individuals with little education and lower income, perhaps because they experience more stress in their lives (Gellis & others, 2005).

Narcolepsy is a rare sleep disorder, occurring in less than one-half of 1% of the general population, but its impact can be quite serious. The narcoleptic often unexpectedly falls into a deep slumber in the middle of work or even during conversations with others, especially when upset or stressed. Often, the individual experiences loss of muscle tone and shows a lack of body movement, as if suddenly falling into dream sleep, but laboratory studies show that this is not REM sleep. Narcolepsy is not just intense sleepiness. It occurs in individuals who get adequate sleep. Narcolepsy often causes serious difficulties with the use of dangerous machines and other job-related activities.

Sleep apnea is the sudden, temporary interruption of breathing during sleep. Brief interruptions are normal, but people with sleep apnea have more of these, and of longer duration, sometimes occurring for 10 to 20 seconds at a time, hundreds of times per night. Sleep apnea is common, often in older or heavier adults who snore. It is caused either by too much relaxation of the muscles of the throat or by a temporary cessation of brain signals for breathing. Sleep apnea can lead to serious medical problems, but even moderate sleep apnea can have an impact on waking life, including tiredness, irritability, impaired cognitive functioning, and falling asleep while driving. One study found that people with sleep apnea with just 5 episodes per hour had a 7 times higher incidence of automobile accidents (Findley, Unverzagt, and Suratt, 1988).

Review

Each night, we depart the world of waking consciousness and enter another world that we scarcely remember the next morning. Alternating among periods of sleep that contain no conscious experience, we live a life of dreams. When studied systematically, much of the content of dreams is found to reflect daily events and concerns. The meaning of dreams has long fascinated us and played a major role in Freud's attempts to understand the hidden workings of the mind, although current psychological research usually focuses on the physiological workings of the brain in explaining the dream experience. Sleep eludes some of us for part of the night, or we are troubled by sleep disorders. The daily rhythm of sleep and wakefulness is only one of numerous natural rhythms that tend to follow daily, weekly, or annual patterns.

Check Your Learning

To be sure that you have learned the key points from the preceding section, cover the list of correct answers and try to answer each question. If you give an incorrect answer to any question, return to the page given next to the correct answer to see why your answer was not correct.

1. Research suggests that _____ may be the most important components of sleep, because subjects deprived of them were irritable, inefficient, and fatigued.

    a) hypnagogic sleep periods   c) REM sleep and deep sleep

    b) myoclonia and REM sleep   d) naps

Check Your Learning (cont.)

2. According to Freud, the _____, or true meaning of dreams, reveal(s) hidden conflicts and motives in the unconscious mind.

   a) latent content   c) events

   b) manifest content   d) colors

3. _____ is a rare sleep disorder in which the person suddenly falls asleep during activities usually performed when fully awake, such as during conversations with others.

   a) Sleep apnea   c) Epilepsy

   b) Insomnia   d) Narcolepsy

4. Body temperature and hormones such as cortisol follow a _____, or daily cycle linked to the sleep cycle.

Thinking Critically about Psychology

There are no right or wrong answers to the following questions. They are presented to help you become an active reader and think critically about what you have just read.

1. What patterns have you noticed in the content of your dreams?

2. What does research on sleep-wake cycles suggest about being at your best when taking a test?

Correct Answers: 1. c (p. 168), 2. a (p. 175), 3. d (p. 176), 4. circadian rhythm (p. 170)

Altered States of Consciousness

We all know what it feels like to think about a problem, to daydream, and to dream. Next we turn to more unusual and less familiar realms of conscious experience, the so-called *altered states of consciousness*. We will begin by looking at some general characteristics of altered states of consciousness.

Altered states of consciousness may occur during meditation, during drug use, during an unusually intense sexual orgasm, or during a moment of religious conversion. They differ from one another in important ways, but they share the following common characteristics (Deikman, 1980; Pahnke, 1980; Tart, 1975).

1. **Distortions of perception.** In altered states of consciousness, distortions often occur in what is seen, heard, and felt. Time passes differently, and the body may seem distorted—indeed, the body may even seem to have been left behind and to be observed from the outside.

2. **Intense positive emotions.** People who have experienced altered states of consciousness frequently describe them as joyful, euphoric, loving, or profoundly tranquil experiences.

3. **Sense of unity.** Individuals often experience a sense of being unified with nature, blended with the universe, or one with a spiritual force.

4. **Illogical.** Many of the experiences and revelations of the altered states of consciousness do not make sense by the standards of everyday logic. For example, the experience that "I exist as a separate person, yet I am one with the universe" is typical of altered states.

5. **Indescribable.** Individuals who have experienced altered states of consciousness usually feel that words cannot adequately express the nature of their experience. Our languages may not have words for many of the qualities of

Many persons achieve altered states of consciousness and deep relaxation through meditation.

the experience, but the difficulty also may come from trying to use language to describe illogical experiences.

6. *Transcendent*. The altered states are experienced as transcending—going beyond—what is normally experienced. In particular, the individual may experience a new perspective that goes beyond ordinary conceptions of space and time limitations.

7. *Self-evident reality*. New revelations and insights are experienced that concern "ultimate reality" and are felt to be "real" in a way that requires no proof. The insight is intuitively and immediately understood as the truth; it requires no explanation or justification.

Given these qualities—particularly the euphoric emotionality of experiencing self-evident revelations—our evaluation of the insights obtained through altered states of consciousness depends on the perspective we take. From the standpoint of science, we can say only that altered states of consciousness are different from everyday waking consciousness. No scientific claims can be made that one "reality" is more "real" than another.

Meditation

meditation (med˝i-tā-shun) Several methods of focusing concentration away from thoughts and feelings and generating a sense of relaxation.

Many people seek a different, more perfect state than usual waking consciousness. One method of attaining an alternative to waking consciousness that has its roots in Buddhism is **meditation.** Of the many varieties of meditation, some are very difficult to master and others much simpler. In its simplest form, meditation involves assuming a relaxed sitting or lying position and breathing deeply, slowly, and rhythmically (Vaitl & others, 2005; Walsh & Shapiro, 2006). Attention is directed only at the breathing movements of the diaphragm, and all other thoughts and feelings are gently blocked from consciousness. Although difficult to accomplish at first, if you do not pressure yourself this becomes easier with practice. In some forms of meditation, the individual also silently repeats a sound or word, which have special religious meanings (**mantras**), but research indicates that any pleasant sound or word (such as *calm* or *one*) has the same effect, focusing attention away from thoughts and feelings (Benson, 1975).

mantras (man´trahz) Words or sounds containing religious meaning that are used during meditation.

Once mastered, meditation can produce what many describe as a desirable altered state of consciousness—the so-called **transcendental state**—that is very different from normal consciousness. If nothing else, meditation generally produces a relaxed state (Beiman & others, 1976; Walsh & Shapiro, 2006). Because the state of meditation often involves a reduction in the arousal of some brain systems and the sympathetic autonomic arousal nervous system (Cahn & Polich, 2006; Wallace & Benson, 1972), meditation has been prescribed for many years as a natural remedy for stress-related medical problems ranging from high blood pressure to insomnia (Walsh & Shapiro, 2006). Thousands of individuals practice meditation in the belief that it counteracts the physiological effects of stress. Emerging evidence supports this view, but the scientific community has not reached clear conclusions (Walsh & Shapiro, 2006).

transcendental state Altered state of consciousness, sometimes achieved during meditation, that is said to transcend normal human experience.

Mindfulness

mindfulness The state of focusing conscious awareness completely on what is going on at the present moment.

Mindfulness is another practice with roots in Buddhism. Rather than achieving a state in which one's awareness is focused away from everyday life, mindfulness training seeks the *opposite*. Mindfulness is the state of focusing one's conscious awareness completely on what is going on at the present (Brown & Ryan, 2003). For example, a father returning home from work would be taught to focus entirely on his children, who greet him at the door, rather than on thinking about the complaints he got from his biggest customer that afternoon or his plans to pay bills that evening. In mindfulness training, one is taught to acknowledge that thoughts about things that are not present are constantly entering one's consciousness, but to calmly leave those thoughts and return one's complete awareness to the present moment. The goal is to experience life as it unfolds to the fullest extent and minimize concerns about the future and past.

There is now strong evidence that mindfulness training can reduce mood disturbances in persons going through stressful experiences (Brown & Ryan, 2003; Chambers & others, 2008; Hofman & others, 2010). If you decide to look into meditation or mindfulness training because you think it may help your emotional functioning, do so by consulting a trained mental health professional who also has experience with this discipline (Ma & Teasdale, 2003).

Hypnosis

A person who has been hypnotized can sometimes be so convinced that she is standing in a snowstorm without a coat that she shivers. Similarly, a hypnotist can tell a hypnotized person he is going back to his 4th birthday party and watch him act as if he is playing with other 4-year-olds. People who have been hypnotized often tell us that they actually feel the cold wind or believe that they are reexperiencing their childhood birthday party. What is it about this state of **hypnosis** that makes it so different from waking consciousness?

The person becoming hypnotized focuses all attention firmly on the hypnotist's voice and is talked and lulled into an altered state of consciousness. This hypnotic state differs from individual to individual but typically has the following characteristics (Vaitl & others, 2005):

hypnosis (hip-nō′sis) Altered state of consciousness in which the individual is highly relaxed and susceptible to suggestions.

1. *Relaxation.* A sense of deep relaxation and peacefulness exists, often accompanied by changes in the way the body feels, such as floating or sinking.

2. *Hypnotic hallucinations.* When told to do so, the person may see, feel, or hear things in altered ways or may even experience things that are not there, such as smelling a flower that does not exist.

3. *Hypnotic analgesia.* When told to do so, the person may lose the sense of touch or pain in some region of the body. This is one of the best validated aspects of hypnosis and has led to the use of hypnosis in surgery, dentistry, and childbirth (Milling & others, 2006; Patterson & others, 2006; Price & Barber, 1987).

4. *Hypnotic age regression.* The person can sometimes be made to feel that he or she is passing back in time to an earlier stage of life, but most experts do not believe that hypnosis improves the recall of childhood events (Kirsch & Lynn, 1995).

5. *Hypnotic control.* The actions of hypnotized individuals sometimes seem as if they are out of their own control. When told that her arm can float, a hypnotized person's arm may seem to float up as if it were lifted by invisible balloons rather than by her own muscles (Bowers, 1976).

What is the nature of this altered state of consciousness? Let's look briefly at the fascinating history of hypnosis.

Mesmer and Mesmerism. Franz Anton Mesmer was a practicing physician in Paris in the late 1700s. Although trained in medicine, his medical practice was

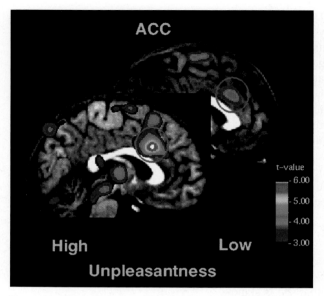

These are PET scan images of the brain of a hypnotized person whose hand is immersed in a hot water bath. When the image on the right was made, the hypnotized person had been told that the water was comfortable. When the image on the left was made, the person had been told that the water was painfully hot. Notice the large differences in activity in the cingulate cortex—a part of the limbic system that plays a key role in the perception of the emotional aspect of pain transmitted by slow-pain fibers. Apparently, hypnosis reduced the emotional experience of pain in this person.

decidedly unusual—so unusual that he was driven from his native Austria by the medical establishment for alleged quackery. Mesmer believed that all living bodies were filled with magnetic energy and that diseases resulted when these magnetic forces were out of balance. His treatment, called *magnetic séances,* consisted of passing his hands, which he believed had become magnetized, over the afflicted part of the patient's body and having the patient touch metal rods that protruded from a large tub filled with water, chemicals, ground glass, and iron filings—a mixture that Mesmer thought created magnetism.

It is likely that what Mesmer actually created, however, was a hypnotic trance. He entered the darkened and silent room wearing flowing lilac-colored robes. He lulled his patients into a deep state of relaxation and made them believe deeply in his healing powers. That is, Mesmer *hypnotized* them. He told them that their problems would go away, and some of them did. The process of putting people into hypnotic trances came to be known for many years as *mesmerism.* Only much later was it referred to as hypnosis. It took psychologists a long time to decide that it was respectable to study a phenomenon with such a shady and controversial past, but in the past 30 years, hypnosis has finally seen the hard light of scientific inquiry (Allen & others,1995; Benham & others, 2006; Kirsch & Braffman, 2001). For example, it is now clear that when hypnotized persons are told to "see" a gray stimulus as having color, areas of the brain involved in color perception are actually activated (Kosslyn & others, 2000), indicating that they are not merely faking the report of seeing color.

Psychologists are still not in agreement on how to characterize hypnosis, however. Some (Barber & Wilson, 1977; Kirsch & Lynn, 1995) suggest that hypnosis should not be thought of as a trance but as a highly relaxed state in which the person's conscious awareness is highly focused, the person's imagination is intensified, and the person is highly susceptible to the instructions of the hypnotist. Viewed in this way, hypnosis has gained limited acceptance by the physicians and psychologists for the relief of pain (Harmon, Hyan, & Tyre, 1990; Patterson, 2004).

Depersonalization

depersonalization
(dē-per´´sun-al-izā´shun) The perceptual experience of one's body or surroundings becoming distorted or unreal.

Not all altered states of consciousness occur when we are striving to attain them; some occur spontaneously. This section describes one of the most common of these experiences. The term **depersonalization** refers to the perceptual experience of one's body becoming distorted or unreal in some way, or the sense of strange distortions in one's surroundings. Although very bizarre, these occasional spontaneous experiences are not necessarily abnormal or even uncommon. British researchers interviewed 891 university students and found 76 who had experienced depersonalization (Myers & Grant, 1972).

astral projection (as´tral)
Depersonalization that includes the illusion that the mind has left the body.

Suppose that this afternoon you feel as if your mind is leaving your body and floating up to the ceiling, where it watches you. Does this mean you have gone crazy? Have you had a psychic or religious experience? Depersonalization experiences sometimes include the illusion that the mind has left the body and traveled about in a so-called out-of-body experience, or **astral projection.** Recurrent experiences may be an indication of psychological or medical problems, but isolated experiences seem to be quite normal, if somewhat unnerving (Myers & Grant, 1972).

Sometimes a kind of consciousness is experienced that is greatly different from normal waking consciousness. Some altered states of consciousness may be unwelcome and upsetting occurrences (as with depersonalization), but others are intentionally induced through meditation, mindfulness training, and hypnosis. Meditation produces a transcendent sense of relaxation in which consciousness is focused away from everyday life. Mindfulness training seeks the opposite—to teach people to focus conscious awareness fully on the present moment. Hypnosis creates an altered conscious state and has been found to be useful in relieving pain under some circumstances.

Check Your Learning

To be sure that you have learned the key points from the preceding section, cover the list of correct answers and try to answer each question. If you give an incorrect answer to any question, return to the page given next to the correct answer to see why your answer was not correct.

1. _____ is the focusing of conscious awareness away from thoughts and feelings and the generation of a sense of deep relaxation.

   a) Sleep   c) Hallucination

   b) Depersonalization   d) Meditation

2. _____ was one of the first persons to use what is now called hypnosis; he used it while treating patients in so-called magnetic séances.

   a) Ernest Hilgard   c) Sigmund Freud

   b) Franz Mesmer   d) David Holmes

3. _____ is the perceptual experience of one's body becoming distorted or unreal in some way, or the sense of strange distortions in one's surroundings.

   a) Meditation   c) Depersonalization

   b) Psychosis   d) Hypnosis

4. _____ involves training the individual to focus conscious awareness fully on the present moment.

   a) Transcendental meditation   c) Mindfulness

   b) Hypnosis   d) Mesmerism

Thinking Critically about Psychology

There are no right or wrong answers to the following questions. They are presented to help you become an active reader and think critically about what you have just read.

1. In your opinion, why isn't hypnosis more widely used in our society as a substitute for anesthesia in surgery?

2. Have you experienced altered states of consciousness? How would you describe them?

Correct Answers: 1. d (p. 178), 2. b (p. 179), 3. c (p. 181), 4. c (p. 178)

Drugs and Altered Consciousness

So far we have been discussing altered states of consciousness that are natural in that they can be experienced by anyone without artificial inducements. Perhaps the most distinctly different types of altered consciousness involve taking chemicals into the body—using drugs. Specifically, we are talking about **psychotropic drugs,** a class of

psychotropic drugs
(sī″ko-trōp′pik) The various classes of drugs, including stimulants, depressants, and hallucinogens, that alter conscious experience.

depressants Drugs that reduce the activity of the central nervous system, leading to a sense of relaxation, drowsiness, and lowered inhibitions.

stimulants Drugs that increase the activity of motivational centers in the brain, providing a sense of energy and well-being.

hallucinogens (hah-lū´si´´no-jenz) Drugs that alter perceptual experiences.

inhalants (in-hā´lants) Toxic substances that produce a sense of intoxication when inhaled.

drugs that alter conscious experience. These drugs influence specific neurotransmitters in the brain or alter the action of neurons in other ways. The range of effects of psychotropic drugs is enormous, from mild relaxation to vivid hallucinations. Perhaps even more enormous than the range of their effects, however, is the frequency of their abuse in contemporary society (Carroll, 2000). Drugs vary not only in their effects on the mind and body, but also in the legal consequences for use or misuse.

Psychotropic drugs can be divided into four major categories. **Depressants** reduce the activity of inhibitory centers of the central nervous system, leading to a sense of relaxation and lowered inhibitions. **Stimulants** increase the activity of the motivational centers and decrease action in inhibitory centers of the central nervous system, providing a sense of energy and well-being. **Hallucinogens** produce dreamlike changes in perception. **Inhalants** are common, often readily available chemicals that are put to dangerous use when inhaled to produce feelings of intoxication. Marijuana does not fit easily into this classification. It induces a relaxed sense of well-being in most persons. Common members of these classes of drugs are summarized in table 6.1. We begin by focusing on illegal drugs and frequently abused prescription drugs. The *Application of Psychology* section at the end of this chapter covers the most commonly used legal consciousness-altering drugs: caffeine, nicotine, and alcohol.

Table 6.1   Commonly Abused Legal and Illegal Psychotropic Drugs

Depressants	Stimulants	Hallucinogens
Tranquilizers	Amphetamines	LSD (lysergic acid diethylamide-25)
Equanil (meprobamate)	Adderall, Ritalin, Concerta	Mescaline (peyote)
Librium (chlordiazepoxide)	Benzedrine (amphetamine)	PCP (phencyclidine hydrochloride)
Miltown (meprobamate)	Dexedrine (dextroamphetamine)	Psilocybin (psychotogenic mushrooms)
Valium (diazepam)	Methedrine (methamphetamine)	Salvia divinorum (Diviner's Sage)
Xanax (alprazolam)	Cocaine	
Narcotics	MDMA (ecstasy)	
Opiates (opium and its derivatives)	Caffeine (in coffee, tea, and colas)	
Codeine	Nicotine (in tobacco)	
Heroin		
Morphine		
Opium		
Synthetic narcotics		
Demerol	**Inhalants (Volatile Hydrocarbons)**	**Marijuana Family**
Methadone	Cleaning fluids	Marijuana
Percodan	Gasoline	Hashish
Sedatives	Glue	
Alcohol (ethanol)	Nail polish remover (acetone)	
Barbiturates	Paint thinner	
Nembutal (pentobarbital)		
Quaalude (methaqualone)		
Seconal (secobarbital)		
Tuinal (secobarbital and amobarbital)		
Veronal (barbital)		

Drug Use: Basic Considerations

In the sections that follow, we look at the psychological effects of a number of widely used drugs. In discussing these effects, we must keep in mind that the effects that drugs have on each individual are far from perfectly predictable. Five sets of factors influence the individual's response to a drug:

1. ***Dose and purity.*** Obviously, the amount of the drug taken influences its effect, but drugs purchased on the street often are cut (mixed) with other substances altering the effects of the drug.

2. ***Personal characteristics.*** The weight, health, age, and personality of the person taking a drug can influence the drug's effect.

3. ***Expectations.*** The effect that a person *expects* a drug to have partly determines the effect of the drug.

4. ***Social situation.*** Others influence a person's response to a drug. Someone may respond differently if a drug is taken alone rather than in the midst of a loud and upbeat party.

5. ***Moods.*** The mood someone is in at the time of taking the drug can dramatically alter its effects. Alcohol, for example, can make a happy person happier or a sad person more depressed, or even unleash violence in an angry individual.

Psychotropic Drugs

The drugs described in this section are powerful in their effects, often powerfully addictive and dangerous, and are typically used illegally.

Stimulants. **Amphetamines** (trade names: Dexedrine, Benzedrine, and Methedrine) are stimulants that generally produce a conscious sense of increased energy, alertness, enthusiasm, and a euphoric high. Because they produce rapid and intense psychological dependence, the possibility for abuse is very high. Amphetamines are dangerous physically, particularly increasing risk for cardiac disease, including debilitating strokes (Westover & others, 2007). Psychologically, the greatest risk is known as **amphetamine psychosis**—a prolonged reaction to excessive use of stimulants characterized by distorted thinking, confused and rapidly changing emotions, and intense suspiciousness.

The use of amphetamines in the United States was on the decline until the late 1980s, particularly use of the extremely dangerous form of amphetamine known as *methamphetamine,* or *speed.* Apparently word had gotten around on the street that "speed kills." Unfortunately, when the street name for methamphetamine was changed to "crystal," "crystal meth," "crank," and "ice," the bad reputation that speed had earned for highly serious psychological and medical side effects was lost. Unfortunately, this white powder, which is usually inhaled but is also swallowed or injected, is now used in virtually epidemic proportions in most areas of the United States.

Cocaine is a stimulant much like an amphetamine that is made from the leaves of the coca plant. It is taken in many forms but is most commonly inhaled as a powder, injected, or smoked in the dangerously powerful form known as *crack.* Cocaine produces alertness, high energy, optimism, self-confidence, happiness, exhilaration, and talkativeness. It raises body temperature, breathing and heart rate, and reduces the desire for food and sleep.

Because a cocaine high lasts only a matter of minutes, cocaine is often used repeatedly. Binges of repeated cocaine use sometimes last for hours or even days, until a state of exhaustion is reached. At this point, the cocaine user *crashes,* feeling

amphetamines (am-fet′ah-minz) Powerful stimulants that produce a conscious sense of increased energy and euphoria.

amphetamine psychosis (sī-kō′sis) Prolonged reaction to the excessive use of stimulants, characterized by disordered thinking, confused and rapidly changing emotions, and intense suspiciousness.

immensely tired, hungry, and in need of long periods of sleep. In the first few days following a cocaine binge, the user is absolutely miserable. Depression, agitation, confusion, paranoia, anger, and exhaustion are all part of the cocaine crash (Weddington & others, 1990).

Cocaine use can rapidly lead to intense addiction (Martinez & others, 2007) and is dangerous even to the occasional user. Because a person's tolerance for cocaine varies considerably, it is dangerously easy for experienced occasional users to overdose accidentally. Even the first dose can lead to a fatal heart attack. Ironically, cocaine was once a legal drug in the United States. Coca-Cola, originally marketed as a "nerve tonic," initially contained cocaine as part of its "secret formula." In 1906, the cocaine was replaced by the milder stimulant, caffeine.

"Crack" is a solid form of cocaine that is smoked to produce an immediate and intense experience. It is particularly dangerous because it enters the brain quickly and is even more highly addictive than other forms of the drug.

ephedra Herbal stimulant that may suppress appetite but may cause serious emotional disturbance.

Ephedra, also known as *ma huang,* is a herbal stimulant sold as a dietary supplement to aid weight loss. Like other stimulants it tends to suppress appetite. As with other stimulants, however, the benefits of ephedra are small compared to the potential harmful side effects. Ephedra can increase the likelihood of psychotic experiences, severe mood disturbances, violence to others, and suicidal acts (Maglione & others, 2005), as well as the well-documented risk of death due to heart disease and cardiovascular emergencies, leading to the FDA's ban on ephedra in 2006.

Some stimulants are prescribed by physcians, including those commonly used to treat ADHD, such as trade names Adderrall, Ritalin, and Strattera. There has been an alarming increase in the sharing of these drugs, as they are increasingly taken recreationally or used as performance boosters or study aids. As a result, increasing numbers of people are experiencing the negative consequences associated with amphetamine use, discussed above.

Depressants. Tranquilizers, sedatives, and narcotics and alcohol are all depressant drugs. As we discuss at the end of this chapter, alcohol is the most widely used depressant of all.

sedatives Depressants that in mild doses produce a state of calm relaxation.

Sedatives and Tranquilizers. **Sedatives** are depressants that in mild doses generally produce a state of calm relaxation. Some types of sedatives are prescribed in the United States to treat sleep problems. Common trade names for these drugs are Ambien, Halcion, and Restoril. Because they can be addictive and overdoses are dangerous—and even small doses are dangerous when taken with alcohol—they are prescribed by physicians less frequently now than in the past. However, these and other depressants are still widely abused through illegal drug markets.

Tranquilizers are milder drugs similar to sedatives that typically produce a sense of calm relaxation for a period of time. As such, often they are prescribed to reduce anxiety. Common trade names are Xanax, Valium, Librium, Ativan, Miltown, and Equanil. Like sedatives, most are dangerously addictive, often difficult to withdraw from, and very dangerous when mixed with alcohol. Also like sedatives, these types of downers are widely sold illegally.

narcotics Powerful and highly addictive depressants.

Narcotics. **Narcotics** are powerful and highly addictive depressants. The use of the narcotic drug opium, derived from the opium poppy, dates back at least 7,000 years in the Middle East. The derivatives of opium—morphine, heroin, and codeine—are powerful narcotic drugs that dramatically alter consciousness. They generally relieve pain and induce a sudden, rushing high, followed by a relaxed, lethargic drowsiness. Narcotics create a powerful physiological addiction very rapidly. With prolonged addiction, the physical effects on the body are profoundly damaging. Compared with the use of other drugs, narcotics use in the United States is not high. The dramatic effects of opiates include crimes that addicts commit to maintain increasingly expensive habits, making it a significant drug abuse problem. It was an especially difficult problem during the Vietnam War. Perhaps as the result of a combination of the availability of heroin and the stress of war, an estimated 20% of all Vietnam veterans tried heroin at least once (Harris, 1973).

Opium and its derivatives (the **opiates**) are not the only kinds of narcotic drugs. In recent years, synthetic narcotics have been artificially produced in drug laboratories. These synthetic narcotics include widely used painkilling drugs with trade names such as Demerol, Percodan, and OxyContin. These drugs are heavily abused today.

opiates (ō′pē-ats) Narcotic drugs derived from the opium poppy.

Inhalants. Substances that produce a sense of intoxication when inhaled are called *inhalants.* To produce a high, toxic substances such as glue, cleaning fluid, and paint are typically placed in paper bags and inhaled (called "huffing"). Since the materials are relatively easy to obtain, this type of intoxication is common among children. Inhalants are highly addictive and extremely dangerous. These toxic fumes often cause permanent brain damage and other serious complications. In addition, many of these compounds are highly flammable, resulting in accidental burns and death.

Hallucinogens. The drugs that most powerfully alter consciousness are hallucinogens, such as lysergic acid diethylamide (LSD), mescaline (derived from the peyote cactus), psilocybin (derived from a kind of mushroom), and salvia divinorum (a member of the mint family). These drugs typically alter perceptual experiences, but only large doses cause vivid hallucinations. In these states, the drugged individual experiences imaginary visions and realities that, ironically, sometimes seem more "real" to the drug user than waking consciousness. This fact, however, may be more attributable to the drug taker's dissatisfaction with everyday life than to the drug itself.

Hallucinogens are generally not physiologically addictive, but individuals can quickly become psychologically dependent on them. In addition, although many of the drug-induced states ("trips") produced by hallucinogens are pleasant, bad trips—frightening and dangerous drug responses—are not uncommon (McWilliams & Tuttle, 1973). Individuals frightened about taking a drug but doing so because of peer pressure are more likely to experience bad trips. These trips can sometimes recur in "flashbacks" that happen without the use of the drug. About 25% of all regular LSD users experience flashbacks, sometimes several months after the original trip (Matefy & Kroll, 1974). Most (about 65%) flashbacks are bad trips, apparently triggered by stress or anxiety. Another type of hallucinogenic drug has particular dangers. Developed as animal tranquilizers, the drugs phencyclidine, or PCP (angel dust), and Ketamin (special "K") have come into use, especially among adolescents. The effects of these drugs typically last from 4 to 6 hours. In some cases, the individual experiences auditory or visual hallucinations, but more likely he or she experiences feelings of numbness, lack of muscular coordination, anxiety, and a sense of detachment from the environment. Euphoria, a sense of strength, and dreaminess may also be present, and people may engage in unconventional behavior, such as going into public places nude. Violent behavior toward others, suicide, and psychotic episodes are other possible reactions to drugs of this type (Petersen & Stillman, 1978).

Marijuana. Marijuana, a popular consciousness-altering drug, often produces a sense of relaxation and well-being, and may alter sensory experiences and the perception of time. Not since Prohibition has any drug been so hotly debated or so widely used in spite of being illegal, and in some parts of the United States, medical marijuana is available legally with a prescription, because it provides pain relief and reduction of nausea. While not physically addictive, regular users experience uncomfortable psychological

Not since Prohibition has any drug been as hotly debated as marijuana.

withdrawal symptoms when they stop using marijuana (Budney & others, 2001). There is growing evidence that prolonged marijuana use decreases the efficiency of cognitive processing, weakens the body's immune response, decreases the action of male sex hormones, and increases risk for developing serious mental health problems (Henquet & others, 2006; Pope & others, 2001; Skosnik & others, 2006; Wallace & Fisher, 1983). In particular, there is evidence that marijuana use may increase the risk of schizophrenia and psychotic symptoms in predisposed individuals (Caspi & others, 2005; Compton & others, 2006). Moreover, as does any type of cigarette, marijuana greatly increases the risk of lung cancer. Driving an automobile or using any other form of machinery when intoxicated by marijuana (or any other substance) is also obviously dangerous.

Designer Drugs. Chemists often design new drugs, called *designer drugs.* For example, the designer drugs MDA and MDMA (*ecstasy*) are derivatives of amphetamines that produce a dreamlike, hallucinatory high lasting for up to 8 hours. There is now strong evidence from studies of humans and other animals that ecstasy causes lasting damage to neurons, which results in declines in verbal memory (Reneman & others, 2001; Rodgers & Ashton, 2004; Schilt & others, 2007).

Drug Abuse and Dependence

There are two major ways in which mind-altering drugs can be harmful—abuse and dependence.

Drug Abuse. A drug is being abused if its use causes physical or psychological harm to the individual. This harm could range from liver damage from excessive alcohol use to declines in school performance as the result of frequent marijuana smoking. Other kinds of potential harm include brain damage from inhalants, heart attacks and strokes caused by stimulants, loss of control of automobiles caused by depressants, violence when intoxicated, and the increased risk of infection with hepatitis or human immuno-deficiency virus (HIV) from sharing needles used for drug injection. Some researchers believe that drugs change neural functioning in ways that increase risk for serious mental health problems. For example, early marijuana use may increase the risk of suicide (Holden & Pakula, 1998; Lynskey & others, 2004) and later schizophrenia (Arsenault & others, 2004; Veen & others, 2004).

Drug Dependence. Many people who use psychoactive drugs find that they come to crave them intensely and suffer intense withdrawal symptoms when they do not take the drug. Why does this happen? How does something that feels so good come to control a person's life? There are three reasons why people become addicted to psychoactive drugs, regardless of which drug it is (heroin, cocaine, alcohol, marijuana, nicotine, and so on):

    1. *Sensitization of pleasure and reward systems in the brain.* Each class of drug influences different neurotransmitter systems in the brain. For example, nicotine increases the firing of acetylecholine neurons (Brody & others, 2006; Rose & others, 2003) and increases alertness. MDMA (ecstasy) decreases inhibition by reducing transmission in neurons that use serotonin as the neurotransmitter (Buchert & others, 2004).

In addition, however, *all* addictive drugs also stimulate the systems in the brain that use the transmitter dopamine and mediate pleasure and reward (Cromberg & Robinson, 2004; Self, 2004; Zubieta & others, 2005). These centers play a role in everyday life, such as by mediating the pleasurable effects of food and sex, but can be powerfully stimulated by highly addictive drugs. Drugs permanently alter the action of dopamine neurons in the pleasure and reward systems by *sensitizing* them, making the people who take them increasingly more vulnerable to the rewarding effects of drugs. This increased sensitivity to the pleasurable effects of the drug helps maintain the addiction and makes relapse more likely when addicted individuals try to quit.

2. *Reduction of negative feelings.* The positive effect on mood created by taking an addictive drug is quite temporary. Unfortunately, when the positive effect wears off, the individual often feels worse than before taking the drug. The more the person takes the drug, the stronger the negative feeling (withdrawal) is after the drug wears off. This aspect of addiction may result from even a single experience of some drugs (Baker & others, 2004). When the person takes another dose of the drug again, the drug taking is rewarded by reducing this negative feeling of withdrawal (Baker, 2004; Baker & others, 2004).

3. *Classical conditioning.* When taking a drug is rewarding, through positive effects on the brain pleasure systems, or reducing negative withdrawal symptoms, the stimuli that are present when the drug is taken (other people, or the environment) become associated with the effects of the drug. If these stimuli are repeatedly present when the drug is taken, they become potent cues that increase craving for the drug. It is important to know that even the drug itself (such as the first sip of beer or drag of a marijuana joint) is a cue that increases craving for more of the drug (Siegel, 2004).

Human Diversity
Substance Abuse and Diversity

Drug and alcohol abuse is a major problem in the United States, and increasingly, abuse of prescription medications is a big part of the problem. A large-scale study of the U.S. population (Kessler & others, 1993) found that 25% of adolescents and adults have had a substance abuse problem at some time in their lives—that's one person out of every four! Who abuses drugs and alcohol in our society? Our gender, ethnicity, and income level are factors that influence the likelihood of substance abuse. Substance abuse is very serious among women, but it is twice as common among men.

In terms of ethnicity, American Indians living on reservations have very high rates of alcohol abuse and are at increased risk for death from its complications (Spillane & Smith, 2007). In contrast, African Americans have been found to be less likely than whites to abuse drugs, tobacco, and alcohol (Breslau & others, 2001; Kessler & others, 1993). Apparently, there are cultural traditions in the African American community that protect against substance abuse. The lower rates of substance abuse among African Americans, which has been found in several U.S. surveys, are even more striking when findings for education and income level are considered. Persons with less education who earn less money in the United States are more likely to abuse substances than are persons with more money. However, even though African Americans tend to earn less money, on the average, than white Americans in the United States right now, their rates of substance abuse are much lower. Thus the protective influence of ethnicity is so strong that it counters the trends associated with income and education.

We will not fully understand the causes of substance abuse until we understand why women, African Americans, and the affluent are so much less likely to abuse drugs and alcohol. It is equally important to remember to treat everyone as an *individual*, however. Although African American women from high-income families are at the lowest risk for substance abuse, some members of this select group have serious substance-abuse problems. Similarly, most low-income white males and American Indians have no difficulties with drugs and alcohol whatsoever.

Review

Altered states can be induced by taking psychotropic drugs that alter conscious experience by influencing the action of neurons in the brain. These drugs produce changes in consciousness ranging from mild alterations of mood to vivid hallucinations. The effect of drugs on consciousness depends on a variety of factors, including dose and purity; the weight, health, age, and personality of the person taking the drug; expectations about the effects of the drug; the social situation; and the mood that the person is in at the time of taking the drug. Psychotropic drugs have great potential for being abused, which means that their use causes physical or psychological harm. Use of most psychotropic drugs can lead to dependence, meaning the person craves the drugs, develops increased tolerance for the drug, and experiences aversive withdrawal symptoms when the drug is not taken regularly.

Check Your Learning

To be sure that you have learned the key points from the preceding section, cover the list of correct answers and try to answer each question. If you give an incorrect answer to any question, return to the page given next to the correct answer to see why your answer was not correct.

1. Many factors influence an individual's response to a drug, such as the dose and the purity of the drug, expectations about the drug, and one's mood, making the response somewhat unpredictable.

   a) true　　　　　　　　　　b) false

2. Psychologically, the greatest risk of amphetamine abuse is known as _____, which is a prolonged reaction to an excessive use of stimulants characterized by distorted thinking, confused and rapidly changing emotions, and intense suspiciousness.

   a) schizophrenia　　　　　　c) phobia
   b) amphetamine psychosis　　d) withdrawal

3. A long-lasting drug, originally developed as an animal tranquilizer, that typically produces numbness, a lack of muscular coordination, a sense of detachment from the environment, euphoria, and a sense of strength and that sometimes results in unconventional, psychotic, or violent behavior is _____.

   a) phencyclidine (PCP)　　　c) cocaine
   b) amphetamine　　　　　　d) ecstasy (MDMA)

4. The drugs that most powerfully alter consciousness are _____ such as lysergic acid diethylamide (LSD), mescaline (derived from the peyote cactus), and psilocybin (derived from a kind of mushroom).

   a) inhalants　　　　　　　　c) hallucinogens
   b) stimulants　　　　　　　　d) depressants

5. Drug dependence is thought to be the result of _____.

   a) associating the effects of the drug with stimuli in the environment
   b) reduction of negative feelings
   c) sensitization of dopamine neurons in pleasure and reward centers
   d) all of these

Thinking Critically about Psychology

There are no right or wrong answers to the following questions. They are presented to help you become an active reader and think critically about what you have just read.

1. Why do millions of people abuse drugs despite the publicity regarding the harmful effects of drug abuse?

2. Our society makes a distinction between drugs such as alcohol and caffeine, which are legal to use, and others, such as marijuana and cocaine, that are not. Does this distinction make sense?

Application of Psychology

The Legal Consciousness-Altering Drugs

Each day, many of us use consciousness-altering drugs, usually without even being aware that we are taking drugs. Coffee contains the stimulant drug caffeine, cigarettes contain the stimulant drug nicotine, and alcohol is a powerful depressant drug. Millions of individuals who would never consider using drugs use, abuse, or are addicted to these drugs. What are these drugs' consciousness-altering effects (and side effects)?

Caffeine. Eighty-five percent of Americans ingest caffeine daily (Hughes & others, 1992), consuming an average of 300 milligrams of caffeine from all sources per day—the equivalent of more than two cups of coffee (Gray, 1998). Many people are addicted to caffeine enough to experience uncomfortable withdrawal symptoms when they do not consume it (Juliano & Griffiths, 2004).

You've seen the ads on television: the attractive woman, frazzled by the day's hassles, is restored to peaceful balance with a cup of coffee. Is that a good way to cope with our emotions when they have been bent and abused by life? Is caffeine good medicine for our nerves? Because caffeine is a stimulant, it does produce an increase in alertness, which helps explain the popularity of coffee, tea, colas, and other beverages that contain caffeine. But does it make you feel *better*?

Physicians and psychologists have long suspected that caffeine actually produces negative changes in emotions in many persons. David Veleber and Donald Templer (1984) conducted a classic study of the effects of caffeine on emotions using volunteer college students and businesspeople in the San Joaquin Valley of California. The participants completed a psychological test that measured the degree of depression, anxiety, and hostility that the individual was experiencing at the time of

Figure 6.5

Change in measures of emotion after drinking either decaffeinated coffee or coffee containing small or large amounts of caffeine.

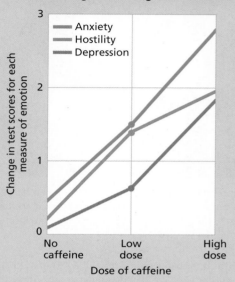

Source: Data from D. M. Veleber and D. T. Templer, "Effects of Caffeine on Anxiety and Depression," *Journal of Abnormal Psychology*, 93,120–122, 1984. 1984 by the American Psychological Association.

the test. They took the test before and one hour after drinking a cup of coffee. Some of the participants drank decaffeinated coffee, whereas others received the equivalent of either one cup (low dose) or two cups (high dose) of strong brewed coffee (the individuals did not know how much caffeine they were drinking). As shown in figure 6.5, the caffeine produced small but significant changes in all three emotions. Most of us feel no ill effects from small amounts of coffee, but a modest amount of caffeine is an invitation to a lousy mood.

Unfortunately, several health risks are associated with the overuse of caffeine. Although caffeine produces relatively small changes in consciousness, it has powerful effects on the body. Caffeine also increases blood pressure, particularly during times of stress (Pincomb & others, 1987). Moreover, drinking five or more cups of coffee per day over a period of years is associated with a two to three times greater risk of coronary heart disease, at least in men (LaCroix & others, 1986). Caffeine use quickly leads to physiological addiction with intense withdrawal symptoms when caffeine is not consumed (Hughes & others, 1992; Gray, 1998). Symptoms of withdrawal can be experienced even by moderate caffeine users if they suddenly stop drinking coffee, tea, caffeinated soft drinks, and other sources of caffeine. These withdrawal symptoms include drowsiness, headaches, and mildly depressed mood.

Nicotine. Nicotine found in tobacco is another widely used drug. A survey of more than 4,400 individuals in the United States found that half of all persons aged 15 to 54 years of age had smoked daily at some time in their life (Breslau & others, 2001). In any one year, 13% of the U.S. population is addicted to nicotine (Grant & others, 2004). About half of the persons who are dependent on nicotine are depressed, anxious, or have

On average, Americans drink 36 gallons of coffee each year.

The life expectancy of a person who never smoked is 8 years longer than that of a person who smokes two packs of cigarettes a day. Consequently, the average cost of the smoker's life insurance is 25 percent higher.

other mental health problems (Grant & others, 2004; Schmitz, Kruse, & Kuglar, 2003). Recent evidence suggests that smoking increases a person's risk for developing such mental health problems (Morissette & others, 2007; Zvolensky & Bernstein, 2005).

Rates of tobacco use remain surprisingly high, given the clear evidence that cigarette smoking is highly dangerous. The life expectancy of regular smokers is reduced, because smoking *greatly* increases the chances of dreadful diseases such as lung and mouth cancer, heart attacks, pneumonia, and emphysema. In addition, cigarette smoking during pregnancy greatly increases the risk of lower birthweight, premature delivery, and death of the infant. Over all, nearly half a million people die of a disease caused by tobacco every year in the United States (Cepeda-Benito, Reynoso, & Erath, 2004). Around the world, 4.9 million people die tobacco-related deaths each year (Centers for Disease Control and Prevention, 2005). That means that one-third to one-half of all persons who smoke die prematurely from a painful disease (Cepeda-Benito, Reynoso, & Erath, 2004; Rose & others, 2003). Altogether, a person aged 25 who never smokes has a life expectancy that is more than *8 years longer* than that of a person who smokes two packs a day.

Why, then, do people smoke? The answer seems to have several parts. First, virtually all smokers begin during their teenage years, when they are especially vulnerable to peer pressure and to advertisements that portray smoking as something that strong, sexy adults do. Second, because teenagers usually know that their parents do not want them to smoke, smoking becomes attractive forbidden fruit and an easy way to rebel against adults. (Few teenagers are mature enough to realize that some adults *want* them to start smoking—the mega-rich owners of tobacco companies are happy to sell them an addictive drug that will kill one out of four of them.)

Third, regardless of why smokers begin to smoke, nicotine dependence soon takes over for most regular smokers (Stein & others, 1998). Nicotine is highly addictive because it mildly stimulates the pleasure centers in the limbic system and increases alertness to a small degree by stimulating the frontal lobes of the cerebral cortex (Rose & others, 2003; Stein & others, 1998). But more important, when smokers have not had nicotine for a while, they become uncomfortable (Piper & Curtin, 2006). The next cigarette is highly reinforcing because it brings the smoker's discomfort back down (Baker & others, 2006; Parrott, 1999).

Unfortunately, water pipes, also known as hookas or shishas, imported from Eastern Mediterranean countries, are popular with college students. Water pipes deliver a potent dose of nicotine but also deliver a shocking 36 times the cancer-causing tar as a cigarette (Primack & others, 2006; Shihadeh, 2003)! Therefore, they are many times more likely to cause cancer than cigarettes.

Alcohol. Are beer, wine, and liquor drugs? Although we do not generally think of alcohol as a drug, it's a powerful and widely abused psychotropic drug that happens to come in liquid form. Alcohol works principally as a depressant, but it is experienced as a drug that "stimulates" sociability and exuberant activity ("partying"), as it depresses inhibitory mechanisms in the brain. Alcohol seems to stimulate the person, because it makes the drinker less inhibited. Alcohol also reduces tension and anxiety and increases self-confidence and self-esteem by erasing doubts about ourselves (Steele & Josephs, 1990). Alcohol also impairs visual judgment and motor control and induces sleepiness (Matthews & others, 1996), and can worsen negative moods, particularly increasing the likelihood of abusive aggression and deepening depression (Eckhardt, 2007; Steele & Josephs, 1990).

Many states consider an individual legally intoxicated when alcohol accounts for .08% of the volume of circulating blood. At this level, sensory and motor performance are noticeably impaired. But much lower blood-alcohol levels increase the risk of accidents when driving or operating other dangerous machinery, so in some states drivers under the age of 21 with *any* detectable blood alcohol are considered to be driving under the influence.

Translating drinks into blood-alcohol levels is difficult because many factors influence blood-alcohol levels, including drinking on an empty stomach, drinking carbonated alcoholic beverages, drinking quickly versus sipping, drinking higher-proof beverages—all lead to higher levels of blood alcohol, even when the same amount of alcohol is consumed (Chruschel, 1982).

Women's stomachs and livers metabolize alcohol more slowly due to differences in alcohol-metabolizing enzymes, consequently, regardless of size, women have higher blood alcohol levels relative to men who have the same number of drinks (Freza & others, 1990). This remains constant for women, but slows in men, too, as they age, and in alcoholics (Seitz & others, 1993).

Except for nicotine, alcohol is the most widely abused addictive drug in the United States. Assessing the exact extent of alcohol abuse is difficult mainly for two reasons: First, the amount of alcohol consumption that can lead to harmful effects varies markedly from person to person and from situation to situation. Someone having four drinks on New Year's Eve is an alcohol abuser if they drive themselves home when intoxicated; a pilot having two drinks a day may be an alcohol abuser if he drinks before a flight. Second, the potential harmful effects of alcohol abuse are so varied. Heavy drinking can affect job performance, disrupt marriages, and harm one's health. It is

Many factors affect blood alcohol levels.

involved in about half of all fatal fire and automobile accidents, one-third of all suicides, and two-thirds of all murders (Marlatt & Rose, 1980). Alcohol abuse frequently leads to highly stressful consequences, such as divorce and loss of employment; these stressful consequences then take a toll on health. In addition, alcohol has directly harmful effects on the liver, brain, and circulatory system. As a result, the life span of the addicted alcoholic is 12 years shorter than average (National Institute on Alcohol Abuse and Alcoholism, 1987). Even moderately high levels of alcohol consumption create a health risk (Hennekens, Rosner, & Cole, 1978; R. W. Jenkins, 1988).

In addition, drinking during pregnancy has been linked to a form of combined physical defects and mental retardation in infants known as *fetal alcohol syndrome* (Briggs, Freeman, & Yaffe, 1986). Although heavy drinking is most likely to lead to birth defects, no safe level of alcohol consumption during pregnancy has been established—and there may not be one.

Because of its powerful mood-altering qualities, alcohol can rapidly result in psychological dependence and physiological addiction (*alcoholism*). It is not always harmful, however. One survey (Calahan & Room, 1974) found that more than half of all the drinkers reported no harmful side effects. Indeed, under some conditions, small amounts of alcohol may be beneficial to the health of some individuals. Those who drink an average of one drink per day or so live longer than individuals who do not drink.

Summary

Chapter 6 explores human awareness and attention, normal waking consciousness, sleeping and dreaming, and altered states of consciousness.

I. Consciousness is defined as a state of awareness and is experienced in a variety of states.

  A. There are limitations to our attention, and we focus on some things at any moment, to the exclusion of others.

  B. It appears to us that consciousness may be divided, with different conscious activities occurring simultaneously, but there are limitations.

  C. Psychologists have conducted studies that suggest that it makes sense to say that unconscious mental processes operate in our lives.

II. Approximately one-third of our lives is spent in sleep, but not all sleep is unconscious.

  A. Sleep begins with a semiwakeful, hypnagogic state and moves through stages of progressively deeper sleep.

  B. Dreams occur mostly during the phase of sleep known as REM sleep, but dreams that tend to be somewhat less bizarre and emotional often occur in non-REM sleep.

  C. Sleeping and dreaming seem important to health. Even brief periods of sleep deprivation cause fatigue, inefficiency, and irritability.

  D. Nightmares, night terrors, sleepwalking, and sleeptalking are fairly common sleep phenomena.

  E. Disorders of sleep include insomnia (inability to get sufficient sleep), narcolepsy (falling asleep during daily activities), and sleep apnea (breathing stops briefly during sleep).

III. We sometimes experience more unusual altered states of consciousness.

  A. Many individuals practice meditation to achieve a highly relaxed state that is focused away from daily existence, whereas others use mindfulness training to learn to focus consciousness completely on the present moment.

  B. Hypnosis is sometimes used to alter consciousness, relieve pain, and enhance performance in sports.

  C. Altered consciousness is sometimes experienced in the form of depersonalization.

IV. Consciousness can also be altered through the use of various psychotropic drugs.

  A. Psychotropic drugs can be classified as stimulants, depressants, hallucinogens, and inhalants; the drug marijuana does not fit easily into this classification.

  B. Though risks differ by drug, drug use can lead to abuse, dependence, or addiction. Prescribed drugs are often abused.

  C. Commonly used legal drugs (caffeine, nicotine, alcohol) produce definite physical and psychological effects and can be quite harmful.

D. The more powerful drugs cause radical changes in consciousness, they can lead to serious physical and psychological problems, and many are illegal.

1. Stimulants produce psychological dependence and they can be dangerous, particularly in their effects on the heart.

2. Sedatives and tranquilizers are highly addictive and can be highly dangerous, particularly when taken in large doses or with alcohol.

3. Narcotics are powerful and dangerous depressants; physiological addiction occurs rapidly. Prolonged use has profoundly damaging effects on the body.

4. Inhalants are usually toxic and often cause permanent brain damage.

5. Hallucinogens radically alter perception, cause hallucinations, and are often associated with bizarre or even violent behavior. Although hallucinogens are not physiologically addictive, psychological dependence is common.

6. The drug marijuana produces a sense of well-being in most people, sometimes altering perception.

chapter **seven** | Basic principles of learning

Chapter Outline

Prologue

You behave the way you do largely because you *learned* to act that way. Imagine that you had been adopted as an infant by a family in a distant part of the world. You would speak a different language, eat different foods, and act in ways that are characteristic of a different culture. You would be a different person in all these ways simply because your *learning* experiences were different.

In 1934, a young scientist named Ruth Benedict published a book about remote cultures that were profoundly different from one another. In the 1930s, the Dobu were a competitive people living on Papua New Guinea who typically did everything they could to acquire more possessions than anyone else. Theirs was a very violent culture, with high rates of assault and murder. The Zuñi people (pictured on

Key Terms

p. 193), who are a tribe of Native Americans who once flourished in the Southwest, were very different. The Zuñi people found greed and ambition to be repugnant. Instead, they valued generosity and modesty. They shared wealth equally with one another and actively avoided doing anything that would bring them individual fame. Perhaps as a result, violence among the Zuñi was rare. Benedict's book tells a remarkable story about the power of learning experiences in shaping human lives. She argued that if there were some cultures in which greed, ambition, and violence were rare, then these could not be inborn traits in all humans—they were traits learned from other people in one's culture.

Are you still not convinced of the power of learning in shaping personalities? Benedict used courtship and marriage as another example of the great differences among different cultures due to learning. In Zuñi society, male and female children were strictly separated until adolescence, allowing almost no contact before marriage. If a female and a male interacted in any way, their parents quickly arranged their marriage. Courtship often consisted of no more than the male's asking a young woman he had never met for a drink of water as she returned from the stream with a water jug. If she gave him a drink, they were soon married.

Courtship among the Dobu was dramatically different than among the Zuñi. In Dobu society, male and female children were not only allowed to play with each other, but sex play among children was common and approved of by adults. When children reached puberty, frequent sex was common among the unmarried males and females, with the lovemaking generally occurring openly in the one-room home of the girl's parents.

By showing scholars in the Western world that not all people were like us, Benedict helped convince many scholars that learning is extremely important in shaping human behavior. In this chapter, you learn about three kinds of learning. As you learn the details about these kinds of learning, try not to lose sight of the overall importance of the topic. Learning is one of the important forces that make you the person you are.

Definition of Learning

learning Any relatively permanent change in behavior brought about through experience.

Life is a process of continual change. From infancy to adolescence to adulthood to death, we are changing. Many factors produce those changes, but one of the most important is the process of **learning.** Through our experiences, we learn new information, new attitudes, new fears, and new skills. We also learn to understand new concepts, to solve problems in new ways, and even to develop a personality over a lifetime. And, in the course of reading textbooks, we learn new definitions for words such as *learning:* In psychology, the term *learning* refers to any relatively permanent change in behavior brought about through experience.

As the definition states, not *all* changes in behavior are the result of learning. The term is restricted to the relatively permanent, as opposed to temporary, changes that are the result of experience, rather than changes due to biological causes such as drugs, fatigue, maturation, and injury. If a baseball pitcher throws the ball differently this season because his pitching coach has demonstrated a new way to pitch, learning has occurred—a relatively permanent change in pitching owing to the experience of the coach's demonstration. But if the pitcher's changed style is due to an injury, fatigue from throwing too much before each game, an arm strengthened by weight lifting, or biological maturation (if the pitcher is a Little League pitcher), we would not refer to the change in pitching as learning.

The *change in behavior* that is created by learning is not always immediately obvious. If you watch a film on the proper way to hit backhands in tennis this winter, the change will not be evident until you are back on the tennis court again next spring. Note also that the definition of learning does not restrict its usage to intentionally produced changes in behavior or even to desirable changes in behavior. For instance, if you begin to loathe fish sandwiches because you got sick after eating one, learning has occurred. The new disgust for fish sandwiches is undesirable and certainly unintentional, but it's still the result of learning.

Over the years, psychologists have isolated and studied a number of ways that learning takes place. As a result, we

Learning is any relatively permanent change in behavior brought about through experience.

now understand a number of different principles of learning. In the following sections, we describe these principles of learning and indicate some of the ways that they can influence us in our daily lives.

Classical Conditioning: Learning by Association

The scientific study of learning began in Russia around the turn of the 20th century with an accidental discovery made in the laboratory of Ivan Pavlov. Pavlov was a Russian physiologist who received the Nobel Prize for his work on the role of saliva in digestion. To study salivation, Pavlov surgically implanted tubes in the cheeks of his dogs. This allowed him to measure the amount of saliva produced when food was placed in their mouths (see figure 7.1). Pavlov noticed that after a few days dogs in the experiment started salivating when the attendant entered the room with the food dish—*before* food was placed in their mouths. The sights (and probably sounds) of the attendant had come to *elicit* (evoke or produce) a reflexive response that only the food had originally elicited. This fact would have gone unnoticed had the saliva-collection tubes not been placed in the dogs' cheeks—that is the accidental part of the discovery. Noticing that a dog salivates whenever it sees the laboratory attendant who brings food may not seem like a great step forward for science at first glance. But Pavlov recognized that an inborn reflexive response to food, which was biologically "wired into" the dogs' nervous systems, had come under the control of an *arbitrary* stimulus—the sight of the attendant.

Figure 7.1

Apparatus originally used by Pavlov to study the role of salivation in digestion, and later in his studies of classical conditioning.

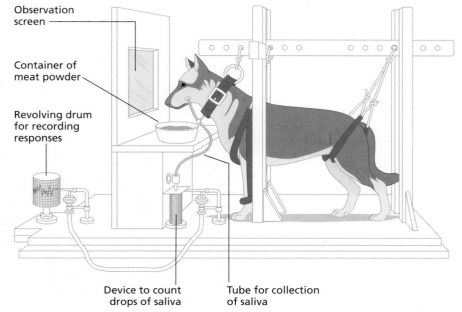

Observation screen

Container of meat powder

Revolving drum for recording responses

Device to count drops of saliva

Tube for collection of saliva

Stated in a different way, Pavlov knew he had witnessed a form of learning based on the repeated association of two stimuli. A *stimulus* is anything that can directly influence behavior or conscious experience. Because the dogs' experience of food was linked to the sight of the attendant, the dogs' behavior changed—the dogs now salivated to the stimuli of the approaching attendant. That is, the stimuli elicited a *response.* When you were born, you could respond to the outside world with only a limited repertoire of inborn reflexes, but now you are a marvelously complex product of your learning experiences. Pavlov wanted to understand this process of learning, so over his colleagues' objections, he hastily completed his studies of digestion and devoted the rest of his career to the study of this form of learning (Watson, 1971). Today, it is known as *classical conditioning,* because it was the first (classical) form of learning studied in the laboratory. Because it was first studied by Pavlov, classical conditioning is also often referred to as *Pavlovian* conditioning.

Association: The Key Element in Classical Conditioning

Although Pavlov conducted the first scientific studies of classical conditioning, Aristotle noted that two sensations repeatedly experienced together become *associated* more than 2,000 years before the time of Pavlov. Association is the key element in classical conditioning. If you visit the seashore with a friend, visiting the seashore by yourself may trigger memories of that friend. If you got sick the last time you ate a hot dog, you will likely feel nausea the next time you see one. Learning through association is a common part of our lives.

Pavlov considered classical conditioning to be a form of learning through association—the association in time of a neutral stimulus (one that originally does not elicit the response) and a stimulus that does elicit the response. Pavlov used an apparatus that was already constructed in his laboratory to measure the progress of learning, and he used food as the stimulus to elicit the response (of salivation).

Specifically, Pavlov presented (as the neutral stimulus) a clicking metronome that the dog could easily hear. After a precisely measured interval of time, he would blow a small quantity of meat powder into the dog's mouth to elicit salivation. Every 15 minutes, the same procedure was repeated, and soon the dog began salivating when the metronome was presented without the meat powder. By continuously measuring

Ivan Pavlov (*middle of photo*) accidentally discovered that dogs learn to associate the sounds of food being prepared with the food itself.

Hank Ketcham, Dennis the Menance © North America Syndicate.

the amount of salivation through the tube in the dog's cheek, the strength of the new learning was accurately monitored throughout the process of classical conditioning.

Again, the key element in classical conditioning is the *association* of the two stimuli. The more frequently the metronome and the food are associated, the more often the metronome elicits salivation (see figure 7.2). The *timing* of the association of the two stimuli is also highly important. Pavlov found, for example, that he obtained the best results when the metronome preceded the food powder by about a half a second. Longer time intervals were less effective, and almost no learning occurred when the metronome was presented at the same time as the food or when the food was presented slightly before the metronome.

Thus, Pavlov took advantage of a chance observation and began a systematic study of one aspect of the learning process. Although learning had been studied before Pavlov's time, his experiments were highly influential because of their extensiveness and precision. Pavlov's true genius lay in seeing that this simple form of learning had important implications far beyond clicking metronomes and salivating dogs. Pavlov's writings became an important part of American psychology when they came to the attention of John B. Watson, who expanded on and popularized Pavlov's views in English.

unconditioned stimulus (UCS) Stimulus that can elicit a response without any learning.

unconditioned response (UCR) Unlearned, inborn reaction to an unconditioned stimulus.

conditioned stimulus (CS) Stimulus that comes to elicit responses as a result of being paired with an unconditioned stimulus.

Terminology of Classical Conditioning

Before we can proceed much further in our understanding of classical conditioning, we need to learn some new terminology. Although these terms are a bit awkward at first, they will help us expand our discussion of classical conditioning to topics more relevant to your life than salivating dogs. First we use each of these four terms to refer to the specific stimuli and responses in Pavlov's experiments; then we use them with new examples. The terms are as follows:

1. *Unconditioned stimulus.* The meat powder was the **unconditioned stimulus (UCS)** in Pavlov's experiment. This is a stimulus that can elicit the inborn response without any learning.

2. *Unconditioned response.* Salivation was the **unconditioned response (UCR).** It's an unlearned, inborn reaction to the unconditioned stimulus.

3. *Conditioned stimulus.* Originally the metronome did not elicit the response of salivation, but it acquired the ability to elicit salivation, because it was paired with the unconditioned stimulus. It was the **conditioned stimulus (CS)** in Pavlov's studies.

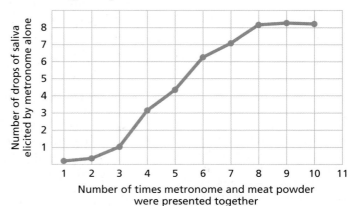

Figure 7.2

In Pavlov's studies, the more often the metronome was associated in time with meat powder, the more effective it was in eliciting salivation.

conditioned response (CR)
Response that is similar or identical to the unconditioned response that comes to be elicited by a conditioned stimulus.

4. *Conditioned response.* When the dog began salivating to the conditioned stimulus, salivation became the **conditioned response (CR).** When a response is elicited by the conditioned stimulus, it's referred to as the conditioned response.

To summarize: the meat powder was the unconditioned stimulus (UCS); the metronome was the neutral stimulus that became the conditioned stimulus (CS); salivation was the unconditioned response (UCR); and when the salivation was elicited by the conditioned stimulus, it became the conditioned response (CR). Because these terms are difficult to keep straight at first, I have provided two diagrams to walk you through their use in classical conditioning. Figure 7.3 reviews the meaning of these terms as used in Pavlov's original experiments with salivating dogs. Figure 7.4 (p. 200) provides a similar example based on a contemporary study of classical conditioning (Vervliet, Vansteenwegen, & Eelen, 2004). In chapter 3 you learned that your sympathetic nervous system is activated when you face a threat. In figure 7.4, you see how activation of this part of the nervous system could be classically conditioned to an arbitrarily chosen neutral stimulus.

Now that you have read through figures 7.3 and 7.4—you'll get lost if you don't read them carefully—let me tell you another dog story as a further example of classical conditioning. One of my all-time best friends was a beagle named Lester. Lester had a number of fine qualities; he was affectionate, warm, and genuinely loyal. But, in all candor, Lester was also a profound coward. I will never forget taking him to the veterinarian for the first of a weekly series of shots. Lester stood perfectly still with a friendly beagle smile on his face until the first time the needle was stuck into his hindquarter. At that point, he produced a flinching, lurching, terrified yelp. After a few injections, Lester began yelping before the injection when he saw the veterinarian with the needle in her hand.

Now, to be completely honest, I cannot criticize Lester too much for his cowardly behavior, because I also yelp when I see a needle coming my way. Why do you suppose that is so? Why should both of us, a grown man and a grown dog, react emotionally to the sight of a needle? After all, the sight of the needle cannot hurt you; only its stab can do that. The answer, of course, is that we have been classically conditioned to yelp at the sight of needles.

Stop for a minute and read back through the previous paragraph describing Lester's fear of needles and see if you can identify the CS, UCS, UCR, and CR. The sight of the needle is the CS because it originally did not elicit the yelp; the painful stab of the needle is the UCS, because it elicited the yelp; the yelp after the stab is the UCR; and, when the CS comes to elicit yelping, the yelp is the CR. I feel a little better knowing that my yelping at needles is simply a CR to a CS, but not a whole lot better. I still hate the things.

Definition of Classical Conditioning

classical conditioning Form of learning in which a previously neutral stimulus (CS) is paired with an unconditioned stimulus (UCS) to elicit a conditioned response (CR) that is identical to or very similar to the unconditioned response (UCR).

We have finally covered enough terminology to be able to give a precise definition of classical conditioning. **Classical conditioning** is a form of learning in which a previously neutral stimulus (CS) is followed by a stimulus (UCS) that elicits an unconditioned response (UCR). As a result of these pairings of the CS and UCS, the CS comes to elicit a conditioned response (CR) that, in most cases, is identical or very similar to the UCR.

For classical conditioning to take place, a CS must also serve as a reliable signal for the occurrence of the UCS (Domjan, 2005; Woodruff-Pak, 1999). An emergency siren that goes off only in a real emergency (no tests or false alarms) generates more fear responses than sirens routinely tested once a month. Similarly, if the sound of a metronome is always followed by food, salivation will be stronger than if the metronome is followed by food only some of the time.

Figure 7.3
Diagram of classical conditioning.

Before classical conditioning

Initially, the metronome is a neutral stimulus that does not elicit the response of salivation:

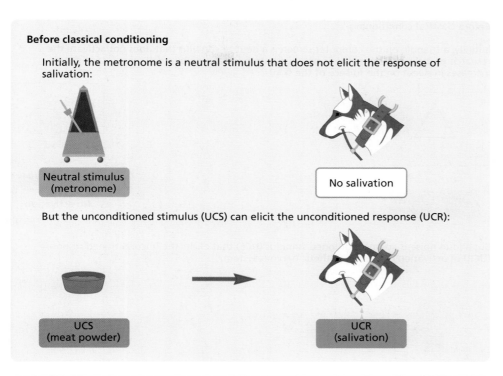

Neutral stimulus
(metronome)

No salivation

But the unconditioned stimulus (UCS) can elicit the unconditioned response (UCR):

UCS
(meat powder)

UCR
(salivation)

Conditioning procedure

During the classical conditioning procedure, the neutral stimulus is presented in association with the unconditioned stimulus (UCS) to elicit the unconditioned response (UCR):

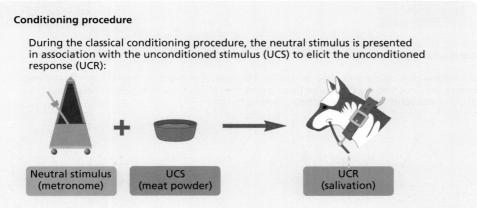

Neutral stimulus
(metronome)

UCS
(meat powder)

UCR
(salivation)

Test of conditioning

After classical conditioning, the neutral stimulus has become a conditioned stimulus (CS) that elicits the conditioned response (CR) of salivation:

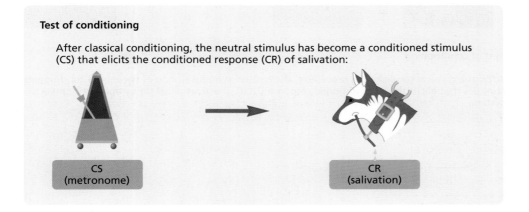

CS
(metronome)

CR
(salivation)

Figure 7.4

Diagram of classical conditioning in which activation of the sympathetic nervous system is conditioned to a triangle.

Before classical conditioning

Initially, a triangle on the computer screen is a neutral stimulus that does not activate the research participant's sympathetic nervous system (measured by small sensors that detect increases in sweat on the surface of the skin).

But a loud noise is an unconditioned stimulus (UCS) that elicits the unconditioned response (UCR) of activation of the sympathetic nervous system.

Conditioning procedure

During the classical conditioning procedure, the neutral stimulus (triangle) is presented just before the unconditioned stimulus (loud noise) that elicits the unconditioned response (UCR) of activation of the sympathetic nervous system.

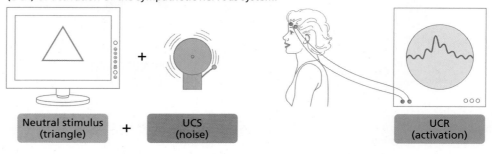

Test of conditioning

After the classical conditioning procedure, the neutral stimulus (triangle) becomes a conditioned stimulus that elicits the unconditioned response (UCR) of activation of the sympathetic nervous system.

Note that classical conditioning is considered to be a form of learning not because a new behavior has been learned but because old behavior can be elicited by a new stimulus. Behavior is "changed" only in that sense. It's important to notice also (for reasons that will be clear to you later in the chapter) that the process of classical conditioning *does not depend on the behavior of the individual being conditioned.* The metronome and the meat powder were paired whether the dog salivated or not, and the sight of the needle was followed by the stab whether Lester yelped or not. The critical element in classical conditioning are that the CS and UCS are closely associated in time. As we will see later, if the behavior of the individual can determine whether the stimulus is presented or not, the process is not classical conditioning.

Importance of Classical Conditioning

The concept of classical conditioning would not be so widely studied by psychologists if it applied only to salivating dogs. On the contrary, classical conditioning is helpful in understanding a number of important and puzzling aspects of human behavior.

In 1920, behaviorist John B. Watson and his associate Rosalie Rayner published what is probably the most widely cited example of classical conditioning in psychology. Watson was convinced that many of our fears were acquired through classical conditioning and sought to test this idea by teaching a fear to an 11-month-old child, the now famous Little Albert. Albert was first allowed to play with a white laboratory rat to find out whether he was afraid of rats: he was not at that time. Then, as he played with the white rat, an iron bar was struck with a hammer behind Albert's head. As might be expected, the loud noise caused Albert to cry fearfully. After seven such associations of the rat and the loud noise, Albert showed a strong fear response when the rat was placed near him. He had learned to fear the rat through classical conditioning.

Watson's own words provide the best description of the experiment's outcome: "The instant the rat was shown the baby began to cry. Almost instantly he turned sharply to the left, fell over on his left side, raised himself on all fours, and began to crawl away so rapidly that he was caught with difficulty before reaching the edge of the table" (Watson & Rayner, 1920, p. 3).

For understandable reasons, this experiment would not be considered ethical today. It is particularly distressing that Watson and Rayner did not reverse the conditioning of Albert's fear (Watson & Rayner, 1920). In a subsequent study (Jones, 1924), however, Mary Cover Jones and Watson successfully reduced fear of rabbits in another young child by gradually pairing the rabbit (CS) with cookies (UCS). This method of reversing a classically conditioned response by pairing the CS (the rabbit) with a UCS (cookies) for a response (eating the cookies) that cannot occur at the same time as the undesirable CR (crying fearfully) is called **counterconditioning.** As in the present example, the UCS for the incompatible response is typically presented first (Mary Cover Jones initially let the child start eating the cookie); then the CS (the rabbit) for the undesirable CR (fearful crying) is introduced only briefly. Over time, the CS for the undesirable response can be presented for longer periods of time, until it no longer elicits the undesirable CR.

Classical conditioning also plays a role in our physical health (Ader & Cohen, 1993). When the body is exposed to threats to health, such as a virus, specialized blood cells that attack the invading virus are produced. As strange as it may seem, the body's immune system responses can be classically conditioned (Bovbjerg, 2003). In the classic experiment, Robert Ader (1981) administered a drug (the UCS) to rats that suppressed the activation of their immune system cells (the UCR). The drug was given at the same time that the rats drank saccharin-sweetened water (the CS). After several pairings of the drug and the sweetened water, the rats showed a suppression in immune cell production (the CR) just from drinking the sweetened water.

This photo shows behaviorist John Watson and his graduate student assistant Rosalie Rayner with Watson's most famous subject, Little Albert. In this early study on the classical conditioning of fear reactions, Watson was able to demonstrate the importance of the environment in the development of human emotions.

Courtesy of Prof. Benjamin Harris, Ph.D., Univ. of New Hampshire.

counterconditioning Process of eliminating a classically conditioned response by pairing the conditioned stimulus (CS) with an unconditioned stimulus (UCS) for a response that is stronger than the conditioned response (CR) and that cannot occur at the same time as the CR.

Sexual arousal has also been shown to be influenced by classical conditioning (Zamble, Mitchell, & Findlay, 1986). Male rats were placed in a distinctive cage with a sexually receptive female rat. A screen prevented sexual intercourse, but the presence of the sexually receptive female (UCS) led to sexual arousal (UCR) in the male. The question was, would the pairing of the receptive female with the distinctive cage (CS) lead to classical conditioning of sexual arousal to the cage? This was shown by placing the male rats in the same cage later with another receptive female—but this time without the dividing screen. Compared with male rats who had not had the classical conditioning experience, males for whom the cage was a CS for sexual arousal became aroused and engaged in intercourse considerably more quickly. The fact that sexual arousal can be classically conditioned has been used to explain the origins of unusual *sexual fetishes.* Humans sometimes find that they have become classically conditioned to be sexually aroused by nonsexual objects, such as shoes or leather gloves (Rachman, 1966).

Classical conditioning also plays a role in our learning to fear stimuli that are not inherently dangerous, intense fears called *phobias* (Tamminga, 2006). Classical conditioning is a simple concept, but it helps us understand some of the complex puzzles of our lives.

Review

Your behavior is not static; it changes continually as a result of your experiences. This process of behavior change is called *learning.* Learning is defined as any relatively permanent change in behavior brought about by experience (rather than by biological causes). The prominence of the study of learning in American psychology can be traced in part to studies of a simple but important form of learning launched around the turn of the last century by Russian medical researcher Ivan Pavlov. Pavlov was studying salivary reflexes when he noticed that, after a few days in the study, his dogs began salivating before the food was placed in their mouths. He reasoned that they had learned to salivate at the sight of the attendant bringing the food, because this stimulus was always associated with (immediately preceded) the food. Pavlov tested this explanation in a series of studies in which a clicking metronome was repeatedly paired with the presentation of meat powder. As a result, the metronome soon came to elicit the response of salivation. In general, when a neutral stimulus is repeatedly paired with another stimulus that elicits an unlearned response, the previously neutral stimulus will begin to elicit the same or a very similar response. This form of learning is called *classical conditioning.*

Check Your Learning

To be sure that you have learned the key points from the preceding section, cover the list of correct answers and try to answer each question. If you give an incorrect answer to any question, return to the page given next to the correct answer to see why your answer was not correct. Remember that these questions cover only some of the important information in this section; it is important that you make up your own questions to check your learning of other facts and concepts.

1. The term learning refers to _____.

2. The critical element in classical conditioning is that the UCS and the _____ be closely associated in time.

    a) CS   c) UCR

    b) CR   d) REM

3. A(n) _____ is a response that is similar or identical to the unconditioned response that comes to be elicited by a conditioned stimulus.

    a) unconditioned stimulus   c) conditioned stimulus

    b) unconditioned response   d) conditioned response

Check Your
Learning (cont.)

4. Ivan Pavlov first studied classical conditioning, but in the United States _____ popularized the idea that classical conditioning and other forms of learning were important to the development of our personalities.

   a) B. F. Skinner   c) Albert Bandura

   b) John B. Watson   d) Karen Horney

Thinking Critically about Psychology

There are no right or wrong answers to the following questions. They are presented to help you become an active reader and think critically about what you have just read.

1. How might a student develop a classically conditioned fear response to a specific college classroom?

2. Is our ability to learn through classical conditioning generally an advantage or a disadvantage? How would Little Albert answer that question?

Correct Answers: 1. any relatively permanent change in behavior brought about through experience (p. 194), **2. a** (p. 201), **3. d** (p. 198), **4. b** (p. 201).

Operant Conditioning: Learning from the Consequences of Your Behavior

If you were to start parking your car in a parking space marked "For the President Only" and your car were towed away every day as a consequence, you would probably stop parking there. Similarly, if you were to move to a new seat in class and an interesting and attractive person spoke to you, you would probably choose to sit in that seat again. To a great extent, the frequency with which people do things increases or decreases depending on the *consequences* of their actions. Learning from the consequences of our behavior is called *operant conditioning*. The term is derived from the word *operate*. When our behavior "operates" on the outside world, it produces consequences for us, and those consequences determine whether we will continue to engage in that behavior. We can define **operant conditioning,** then, as the form of learning in which the consequences of behavior lead to changes in the probability of its occurrence (Dragoi & Staddon, 1999; Schultz, 2006).

Operant conditioning was first described by American psychologist Edward Thorndike (1911). Thorndike was interested in the question of animal intelligence, which he investigated using an apparatus called a "puzzle box." A hungry cat was placed inside a box with a closed door, food was placed outside, and the cat's efforts to escape were observed. With each trial, the cat became more efficient at opening the door of the box. Based on these observations, Thorndike formulated the "law of effect," which states that the consequences of a response determine whether the response will be performed in the future. Thorndike's law of effect formed the basis for subsequent study of what is now referred to as *operant conditioning* in contemporary psychology. In the sections that follow, we examine three ways in which the desirable and undesirable consequences of our behavior influence our future behavior:

1. Positive reinforcement

2. Negative reinforcement

3. Punishment

operant conditioning (op´e-rant) Learning in which the consequences of behavior lead to changes in the probability of its occurrence.

Figure 7.5

Increasing the amount of time that a child spends playing with other children through the use of positive reinforcement.

Source: Data from K. Eileen Allen, et al., "Effects of Social Reinforcement Isolate Behavior of a Nursery School Child" in *Child Development, 35:*511–518, 1964. Copyright 1964 The Society for Research in Child Development.

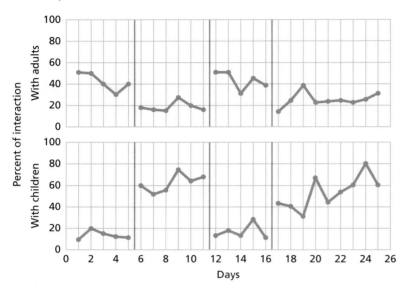

Positive Reinforcement

We say that **positive reinforcement** has occurred when a consequence of behavior leads to an increase in the probability that we will engage in that behavior in the future. In *positive reinforcement,* the consequences of a behavior are *positive,* so the behavior is engaged in *more frequently.*

In the early 1960s, a team of preschool teachers conducted a classic study in which they helped a young girl overcome her shyness that has become a widely cited example of the principle of positive reinforcement (Allen & others, 1964). The teachers were worried, because the girl spent little time playing with the other children and too much time with her adult teachers. They decided to encourage peer play through positive reinforcement. They knew that she enjoyed receiving praise from the teachers, so they decided to praise her only when she was playing with another child. The results of this use of positive reinforcement are shown in figure 7.5. To be able to evaluate the results of their positive reinforcement program, the teachers first counted the frequency with which the little girl interacted with other children and with adults before anything was done to help her. Then they started to positively reinforce (praise) her for playing with other children, but otherwise they paid very little attention to her (so that she would get positive reinforcement from her teachers only for playing with peers). As can be seen in the second segment of figure 7.5, the little girl's frequency of playing with peers increased markedly when the teachers reinforced her. To be sure that the positive reinforcement and not some other factor was responsible for the changes, the teachers stopped reinforcing her for playing with peers in the third segment (the *reversal* phase) of figure 7.5 and then reinforced her again during the fourth phase. As can be seen, the frequency of peer play dropped when the positive reinforcement was discontinued but increased again when it was resumed in the fourth phase. Thus, the teachers were able to intentionally teach this child a more adaptive pattern of play by using positive reinforcement.

Many other applications have been made of the principle of positive reinforcement, ranging from teaching hospitalized adults with schizophrenia more normal patterns of behavior to teaching employees to reduce the amount of damage sustained when sorting boxes for airfreight delivery. In each case, the behavior that becomes more frequent is termed the *operant response,* and the positive consequence of that response is called the *positive reinforcer.*

Two important issues in the use of positive reinforcement should be noted:

positive reinforcement
(rē′in-fors′ment) Any consequence of behavior that leads to an increase in the probability of its occurrence.

delay of reinforcement The passage of time between the response and the positive reinforcement that leads to reduced efficiency of operant conditioning.

1. *Timing.* The positive reinforcer must be given within a short time following the response, or learning will progress very slowly, if at all. The greater the delay between the response and the reinforcer, the slower the learning. This phenomenon has been referred to as the principle of **delay of reinforcement.**

2. *Consistency in the delivery of reinforcement.* For learning to take place, the individual providing positive

reinforcement must consistently give it after every (or nearly every) response. After some learning has taken place, it's not always necessary, or even desirable, to reinforce every response, however. As we will see later under "Schedules of Positive Reinforcement," consistency of reinforcement is essential in the beginning of the learning process.

Positive reinforcement is not something that occurs only when it's intentionally arranged. Rather, the natural consequences of our behavior can be reinforcing as well. For example, we learn that some ways of interacting with our friends or supervisors just naturally lead to happier relationships, and that is positively reinforcing. We are *always* affected by the consequences of our behavior and, hence, are always in the process of learning to adjust to our world through operant conditioning.

Primary and Secondary Reinforcement. Two types of positive reinforcement should be distinguished: primary and secondary reinforcement. **Primary reinforcers** are innately reinforcing and do not have to be acquired through learning. Food, water, warmth, novel stimulation, physical activity, and sexual gratification are all examples of primary reinforcers.

Secondary reinforcers (which play a very important role in operant conditioning) are learned through classical conditioning. Remember that classical conditioning involves the association of two stimuli: a neutral stimulus can be turned into a secondary reinforcer by pairing it repeatedly with a primary reinforcer. Consider an example from dog training. In teaching dogs to perform complex acts, such as those required of Seeing Eye dogs, primary reinforcers such as pieces of food are used extensively. It's much more convenient, however, to reinforce the dog for good behavior simply by saying, "Good dog!" than by lugging around a pocketful of dog biscuits. Unfortunately, dogs do not know what you are saying when you praise them and would not care much if they did—not until you *teach* them to care. So, how would you go about making praise into a secondary reinforcer? Actually, it's quite simple. You would only need to say, "Good dog," to the dog every time you give the dog a biscuit. After enough pairings of these two stimuli, the praise will become a secondary reinforcer and will be effective in reinforcing the dog's behavior. How many of the things that motivate us—such as school grades, prize ribbons, money, applause—were acquired through pairing with primary reinforcers? Learning plays a key role in turning these things into powerful reinforcers for some people.

Secondary reinforcers, such as praise, are learned from primary reinforcers, such as gentle physical contact.

primary reinforcers Innate positive reinforcers that do not have to be acquired through learning.

secondary reinforcers Learned positive reinforcers.

fixed ratio schedule Reinforcement schedule in which the reinforcer is given only after a specified number of responses.

Schedules of Positive Reinforcement. Up to this point, we have talked about positive reinforcement as if every response were always followed by a reinforcer, a situation known as *continuous reinforcement*. The world is not always so simple, however. In addition to continuous reinforcement, psychologists have described four types of schedules of reinforcement and have shown us the effects of each on behavior (Ferster & Skinner, 1957):

1. *Fixed ratio.* On a **fixed ratio schedule** of reinforcement, the reinforcer is given only after a specified number of responses. If sewing machine operators were given a pay slip (to be exchanged for money later) for every six dresses that were sewn, the schedule of reinforcement would be called a fixed ratio schedule. This schedule produces a fairly high rate of response, because many responses need to be made to get the reinforcer, but there is typically a pause after each reinforcer is obtained (see figure 7.6 on p. 206).

Gold medals or other similar rewards are powerful secondary reinforcers.

Fixed ratio

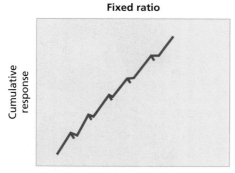

Cumulative response

Time

Figure 7.6

Pattern of behavior typically produced by a fixed ratio schedule of reinforcement. The hash marks show the delivery of reinforcement. In figures 7.5 to 7.8, steeper slopes indicate higher rates of responding.

Variable ratio

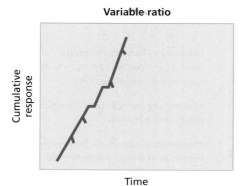

Cumulative response

Time

Figure 7.7

Pattern of behavior typically produced by a variable ratio schedule of reinforcement.

Casino operators may not claim to use variable ratio schedules of reinforcement, but they know that an occasional jackpot will keep players at the slot machines.

2. *Variable ratio.* On a **variable ratio schedule** of reinforcement, the reinforcer is obtained only after a variable number of responses have been made (see figure 7.7). These schedules produce very high rates of responding, and the learning is rather permanent. For example, why do successful sales representatives hustle so? They know from experience that, on the average, they will make a sale, for example, after every sixth presentation. But the fact that they cannot predict which presentation will make the sale—this one? the next one?—keeps them hopping. Another good example of reinforcement on a variable ratio is gambling. Slot machine players are reinforced for putting money into the machine and pulling the lever just often enough in an unpredictable fashion to addict many individuals to gambling.

3. *Fixed interval.* Here, the schedule of reinforcement is not based on the number of responses but on the passage of *time*. The term **fixed interval schedule** is used when the first response that occurs after a predetermined period of time is reinforced. This produces a pattern of behavior in which very few responses are made until the fixed interval of time approaches and then the rate of responding increases rapidly (see figure 7.8). A fellow psychology professor provided this great example of a fixed interval schedule: while in graduate school, he worked as a guard at night in a steel mill. He was paid for walking around the mill each hour and punching in at the time clock each time as he passed it on his rounds. He confessed that this schedule of reinforcement led to 40 minutes of sitting around each hour, followed by a brisk 20-minute walk around the mill to the time clock! Members of Congress also are on a fixed interval schedule for the response of visiting with the voters in their districts. Making a visit back home to talk to the people is of little value to the politicians until the fixed 2-year interval between elections starts to elapse and they could be rewarded by votes. Then visits back home are reinforced by votes, so the rate of visits rises dramatically.

4. *Variable interval.* Finally, there is a schedule of reinforcement in which the first response made after a variable amount of time is reinforced. Like the variable ratio schedule, this **variable interval schedule** produces high rates of steady response (see figure 7.9), and although it's not a good schedule for initial learning, it produces highly stable performance when the response has already been partially learned through continuous reinforcement. In Florida, where I grew up, lots of people sat on docks and bridges with fishing poles in their hands because of variable reinforcement. You can't tell when fish are going to bite—they're unpredictable. But, for some people, catching a fish every now and then is strong enough variable interval reinforcement to keep their lines in the water as much as they can.

Thus, different schedules of positive reinforcement result in distinct patterns of behavior. It is very important for anyone responsible for managing another person's behavior, such as teachers, parents, or supervisors, to make informed choices regarding the type of reinforcement schedule to be used.

Shaping. In many situations, the response that we want to reinforce never occurs. For example, let's say you want to begin positively reinforcing your 3-year-old child for helping to clean her or his room. You might have to wait a long time for that behavior to occur! If left to their own devices, most children would never clean their room. What we need to do in this case is to reinforce responses that are progressively more *similar* to the response that you finally want to reinforce (the target response of cleaning the room). In doing so, you gradually increase the probability of the target response and can then reinforce it when it occurs. This is called **shaping,** or the *method of successive approximations,* because we "shape" the target response out of behaviors that successively approximate it.

Before considering the practical applications of the concept of shaping, let's go back to the animal learning laboratory where so many of the principles of learning that are useful to humans were first carefully researched. Suppose you wanted to teach a rat to press a lever in a learning apparatus called the **Skinner box,** named after its creator, B. F. Skinner (see figure 7.10 on p. 208). If you continue to take psychology courses, you may be given this assignment in a lab course: "Here's a rat and here's a Skinner box; do not come back until you have taught him to press the lever!" What do you do? If you have not read the section on shaping in your textbook, you might program the Skinner box to drop a little pellet of rat food into the food tray every time the lever is pressed and then wait—and wait and wait—for the rat to press the bar. This strategy might work in time—the rat *might* accidentally press the lever enough times to get reinforced by the food pellets enough to make this a frequent response; but I wouldn't bet on it. Rats generally do not go around pressing levers. When placed in a Skinner box, they groom themselves, bite the Plexiglas walls, explore, urinate, defecate, and sniff a lot, but they do not press levers. How, then, do you teach the uncooperative rodent to press the lever?

You use shaping. First, whenever the rat (we'll call him "B. F." in honor of B. F. Skinner) gets up and *moves toward the lever,* give him a food pellet. After you do that a few times, the rat will move toward the lever frequently. Then you can wait until B. F. *touches* the lever in some way to reinforce him. Do that a few times and then wait until he *touches it with a downward pushing movement* (if at any time you have failed to reinforce him enough, you can go back a step in the shaping process). Then, after he is reliably touching the bar in a downward motion, B. F. should have quite a high probability of pushing it down enough to activate the automatic feeder, which will reinforce him for the complete response of lever pressing.

The principle of shaping has great importance outside the rat lab. For example, most beginning skiers cannot be reinforced for making perfect post turns because they just are not able to do them yet. They can be reinforced for successive approximations to good turns, however, and thereby shaped into good skiing. In programs for children with developmental handicaps, shaping is used to teach basic skills such as brushing teeth, performing useful jobs, and using public transportation. And how about shaping 3-year-olds to clean their rooms? At first you have to reinforce them for putting one toy away even though the rest of the room is littered with junk. After doing that a couple of times, reinforce them for putting several toys away, and then for an *approximately* clean room, and so on until the target response occurs and can be reinforced.

Negative Reinforcement

As we have just discussed, positive reinforcement results when a positive event occurs after our behavior and makes that behavior more likely. Reinforcers are not always positive events, however. Sometimes the consequence that makes a behavior more likely in the future is the *removal or avoidance of a negative event.* Suppose the fellow in the apartment next door plays his stereo so loud that it has kept you awake every night this week. If you assertively ask him to turn it down and the loud music stops, you will be more likely to act assertively in the future. Operant learning based on negative reinforcement plays an important, but often unnoticed, role in influencing our behavior.

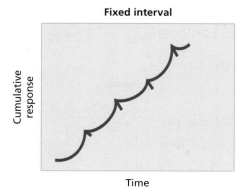

Figure 7.8
Pattern of behavior typically produced by a fixed interval schedule of reinforcement.

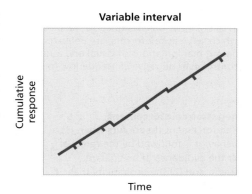

Figure 7.9
Pattern of behavior typically produced by a variable interval pattern of reinforcement.

variable ratio schedule
Reinforcement schedule in which the reinforcer is given after a varying number of responses have been made.

fixed interval schedule
Reinforcement schedule in which the reinforcer is given following the first response occurring after a predetermined period of time.

variable interval schedule
Reinforcement schedule in which the reinforcer is given following the first response occurring after a variable amount of time.

shaping Strategy of positively reinforcing behaviors that are successively more similar to desired behaviors.

Skinner box Cage for animals, equipped with a response lever and a food tray dispenser, used in research on operant conditioning.

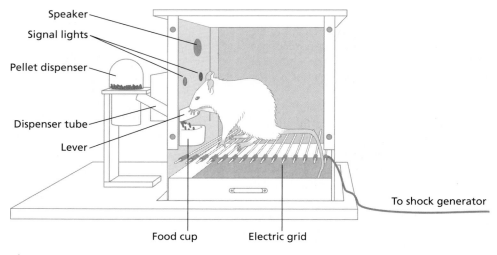

Speaker
Signal lights
Pellet dispenser
Dispenser tube
Lever
Food cup   Electric grid
To shock generator

Figure 7.10

In this Skinner box designed for rats, the response under study is lever pressing. Food pellets, which serve as reinforcers, are delivered into the food cup on the left. The speaker and light permit manipulations of visual and auditory stimuli, and the electric grid gives the experimenter control over negative consequences (mild shock) in the box.

negative reinforcement
Reinforcement that occurs when (1) a behavior is followed by the removal or the avoidance of a negative event, and (2) the probability that the behavior will occur in the future increases as a result.

escape conditioning Operant conditioning in which the behavior is reinforced, because it causes a negative event to cease (a form of negative reinforcement).

avoidance conditioning Operant conditioning in which the behavior is reinforced, because it prevents something negative from happening (a form of negative reinforcement).

The concept of negative reinforcement is one that students frequently find confusing for two reasons. First, to many students, the name implies that a negative or undesirable *behavior,* such as a bad habit, is being reinforced. That is not the case, since the behavior that is negatively reinforced could be either desirable or undesirable. Second, even more students find the term *negative reinforcement* confusing because it sounds like a new term for punishment, which it is not. When we look at the concept of punishment later in this chapter, you will see that it is quite different.

What the term **negative reinforcement** *does* mean is this: a behavior is reinforced (and, therefore, becomes more likely to occur), because something negative (or unpleasant or aversive) *is removed* by the behavior or does not happen at all because of the behavior. In the previous example, the loud music was the negative thing that your assertive behavior got rid of. Your asking him to turn down the volume was reinforced through negative reinforcement (stopping the loud music), and you probably would be more likely to be assertive in the future as a result.

Two types of conditioning are based on negative reinforcement:

1. *Escape Conditioning.* In **escape conditioning,** the behavior causes the negative event to *stop.* For example, if a young boy has been confined to his room for five minutes as a punishment, that is probably a pretty negative situation to him. If he starts to cry softly and murmur pitifully that no one loves him, and if this causes his parent to relent and let him out of his room early, then negative reinforcement may occur. Which behavior would be strengthened? Probably he will be much more likely to act pitifully the next time he is sent to his room, because it made something negative—the confinement—stop. Escape conditioning, therefore, is a form of negative reinforcement, because something negative is removed. It's called escape conditioning because the individual *escapes* from something negative (in the sense of causing it to stop).

2. *Avoidance Conditioning.* In the other form of negative reinforcement, called **avoidance conditioning,** the behavior has the consequence of causing something negative *not to happen* when it otherwise would have happened. Suppose you are terrified of pit bull dogs, but the route that you walk to campus takes you past a yard where a particularly vicious pit bull is penned up. If you find a new route to school that does not take you past a single pit bull, you will probably continue to take this route because it causes the negative event of passing the pit bull not to occur. Even if it does make you feel a bit like a coward, finding a new route is a highly reinforcing consequence. This is an example of avoidance conditioning, because the behavior of taking a new route is reinforced by *avoiding* something negative (the pit bull).

Negative reinforcement is a very powerful method of reinforcement, so we learn patterns of behavior quickly and easily from it. Unfortunately, what we learn are often immature ways of dealing with unpleasant situations rather than mature ways of facing them directly. The child in our first example would have been better off taking his punishment and learning how not to get into trouble next time, and the college student would have been better off getting over the fear of the penned pit bull. It's often too easy to learn a quick and easy, though inappropriate, solution through negative reinforcement.

Incidentally, when the parent let the child who was acting pitifully out of his room, the parent was probably reinforced for that lapse in discipline, too. Through what principle of operant conditioning was the parent reinforced? Because the act of letting the child out of his room caused the child's unpleasant whining to stop, the parent was reinforced through escape conditioning. Negative reinforcement of inappropriate behavior is a frequent occurrence that we need to be aware of and avoid.

Punishment

Sometimes the consequence of behavior is negative, and as a result, the frequency of that behavior decreases. In other words, the behavior has been *punished*. For example, if you buy a new set of pots and pans with metal handles and pick up a hot pan without a pot holder, a negative consequence will surely occur. And you will probably not try to pick up your new pans in that way again. **Punishment** is a negative consequence that leads to a reduction in the frequency of the behavior that produced it (Church, 1969; Tarpy & Mayer, 1978). When appropriately used, punishment can be an ethical and valuable tool for discouraging inappropriate behavior. In our society, however, *physical* punishment is still used with children by parents, teachers, and others in authority. In addition to the obvious ethical issues in using physical punishment, there are serious dangers inherent in the use of any form of physical punishment that must be weighed against its potential benefits.

punishment A negative consequence of a behavior, which leads to a decrease in the frequency of the behavior that produces it.

Dangers of Punishment. Five dangers are inherent in punishment:

1. The use of punishment is often *reinforcing to the punisher*. For example, if a parent spanks a child who has been whining and the spanking stops the child from whining, the parent is reinforced for spanking through negative reinforcement. This, unfortunately, may mean that the frequency of spankings, and perhaps their intensity, increase, thereby increasing not only the amount of physical pain the child endures but also the dangers of child abuse.

2. Punishment often has a *generalized inhibiting effect* on the individual. Repeatedly spanking a child for talking back to you may lead the child to quit talking to you altogether. Similarly, criticizing your bridge partner for mistakes may lead him or her to stop playing with you.

3. We commonly react to physical punishment by *learning to dislike* the person who inflicts the pain, and sometimes by *reacting aggressively* toward that person. Thus, punishment may solve one problem but only lead to a worse problem— namely, aggression.

4. What we think is punishment is not always effective in punishing the behavior. In particular, most teachers and parents (and many supervisors, roommates, and so on) think that *criticism* will punish the behavior at which it's aimed. However, in many settings, especially homes and classrooms filled with young children, criticism is often a *positive reinforcer* that increases the rate of whatever behavior the criticism follows.

This has been called the **criticism trap** (Madsen & others, 1968). For example, some teachers and parents see a behavior they do not like and criticize to get rid of it. But children's actions are sometimes reinforced by the attention they receive when criticized. In this way, the criticism reinforces rather than punishes the behavior, and

criticism trap An increase in the frequency of a negative behavior that often follows the use of criticism, reinforcing the behavior it is intended to punish.

Comparison of the types of operant conditioning: positive reinforcement, negative reinforcement, and punishment. The two types of reinforcement, positive and negative, are called *reinforcement* because the response is strengthened by the consequence.

Notice that the terms *positive* and *negative reinforcement* and *punishment* have nothing to do with the nature of the response that is strengthened or weakened. This example uses a very negative response; however, a positive response could have been used to illustrate the same results in each case.

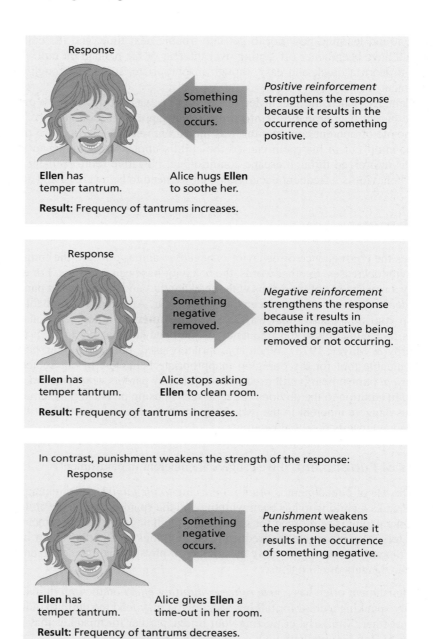

Response

Positive reinforcement strengthens the response because it results in the occurrence of something positive.

Something positive occurs.

Ellen has temper tantrum.

Alice hugs **Ellen** to soothe her.

Result: Frequency of tantrums increases.

Response

Negative reinforcement strengthens the response because it results in something negative being removed or not occurring.

Something negative removed.

Ellen has temper tantrum.

Alice stops asking **Ellen** to clean room.

Result: Frequency of tantrums increases.

In contrast, punishment weakens the strength of the response:

Response

Punishment weakens the response because it results in the occurrence of something negative.

Something negative occurs.

Ellen has temper tantrum.

Alice gives **Ellen** a time-out in her room.

Result: Frequency of tantrums decreases.

the criticized behavior increases in frequency. The adult then uses more criticism in an effort to quell this misbehavior. This reinforces the behavior even more and increases its rate in an upwardly spiraling course.

5. Even when punishment is effective in suppressing an inappropriate behavior, it does not teach the individual how to act more appropriately. Punishment used by itself may be self-defeating; it may suppress one inappropriate behavior only to be replaced by another one. It's not until appropriate behaviors are taught to the individual to replace the inappropriate ones through positive reinforcement that any progress can be made.

Guidelines for the Use of Punishment. The preceding list is an indictment of punishment as a method of changing behavior. It should not be considered as a total condemnation of punishment. In some situations, punishment is a necessary method of changing behavior. For example, in teaching a young child not to run out into a busy street, punishment may be the only method that makes sense. In these instances, however, every effort should be made to minimize the negative side effects of punishment by following some guidelines for its use:

1. Do not use *physical* punishment. Taking away TV time from a 10-year-old or giving a 4-year-old a time-out in a chair in the corner for 3 minutes is *more* effective than spankings, and certainly more humane. Indeed, physical punishment usually backfires and causes children to behave worse rather than better (O'Leary, 1995).

2. Punish the inappropriate behavior immediately. Immediately using a firm voice to tell a child that is bad to let go of your hand when walking on the sidewalk might punish that behavior, but waiting 5 minutes to do so will be much less effective.

3. Make sure that you positively reinforce appropriate behavior to take the place of the inappropriate behavior you are trying to eliminate. Punishment is not effective in the long run unless you are also reinforcing appropriate behavior.

4. Make it clear to the individual what behavior you are punishing and remove all threat of punishment as soon as that behavior stops. In other words, it might be okay to punish a certain behavior, but it does more harm than good to become generally angry at the other person for doing something inappropriate. *Do not punish people; punish specific behaviors.* And stop punishing when the inappropriate behavior ceases.

5. Do not mix punishment with rewards for the *same* behavior. For example, do not punish a child for fighting and then apologetically hug and kiss the child you have just punished. Mixtures of consequences of this sort are confusing and lead to inefficient learning.

6. Once you have begun to punish, do not back down. In other words, do not reinforce begging, pleading, or other inappropriate behavior by letting the individual out of the punishment. It both nullifies the punishment and reinforces the begging and pleading through negative reinforcement.

Contrasting Classical and Operant Conditioning

We have just talked about a number of forms of learning (conditioning). This blitz of new concepts can be confusing. However, if you can understand the distinction between classical and operant conditioning, the rest will be easy.

Classical and operant conditioning differ from each other in three primary ways:

1. Classical conditioning involves an association between two stimuli, such as a tone and food. In contrast, operant conditioning involves an association between a response and the resulting consequence, such as studying hard and getting an A.

2. Classical conditioning usually involves reflexive, involuntary behaviors that are controlled by the spinal cord or autonomic nervous system. These include fear responses, salivation, and other involuntary behaviors. Operant conditioning, however, usually involves more complicated voluntary behaviors, which are mediated by the somatic nervous system.

3. The most important difference concerns the way in which the stimulus that makes conditioning "happen" is presented (as the unconditioned stimulus, or UCS, in classical conditioning or the reinforcing stimulus in operant conditioning). In classical conditioning, the UCS is paired with the conditioned

stimulus (CS) independent of the individual's behavior. The individual does not have to do anything for either the CS or UCS to be presented. In operant conditioning, however, the reinforcing consequence occurs *only if* the response being conditioned has just been emitted. That is, the reinforcing consequence is *contingent* on the occurrence of the response.

Stimulus Discrimination and Generalization

Most responses do not have an equal probability of occurring in any situation. They are more likely to occur in some circumstances than in others. For example, schoolchildren are more likely to behave well when the teacher is in the room than when the teacher is not. Similarly, you are more likely to clean up your apartment when your new girlfriend or boyfriend says "I'll be over after class" than when no one is coming. Most responses are more likely to occur in the presence of some stimuli than in the presence of others. This phenomenon is called **stimulus discrimination,** meaning that we discriminate between appropriate and inappropriate occasions for a response.

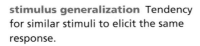

stimulus discrimination Tendency for responses to occur more often in the presence of one stimulus than others.

Let's go back to the rat lab and see one way in which stimulus discrimination might be learned. The last time you were in the lab, you taught your rat, B. F., to press the lever through shaping and positive reinforcement for lever pressing. Let's suppose that you want him to press the bar only in the presence of a specific stimulus, such as a light. That is, you want B. F. to learn a stimulus discrimination. We start by turning on a light over the lever, letting B. F. press the lever and receive the reinforcer several times. Then we turn off the light for a little while, and we do *not* reinforce lever presses when the light is out. Then we turn the light back on and reinforce responses, turn it off and do not reinforce responses, and so on many times. The stimulus in which the response is reinforced is called S^d (short for *discriminative stimulus*), and the stimulus in which the response is never reinforced is called S^{delta}. Soon, if we follow the teaching program just outlined, B. F. will begin pressing the lever almost every time the light comes on, and almost never press it when the light is off. He has learned a stimulus discrimination.

stimulus generalization Tendency for similar stimuli to elicit the same response.

Humans have to learn stimulus discriminations, too—lots of them. We have to learn to say "car" only to the stimulus of a car and not to a toy wagon; we have to learn to say "dog" to the stimulus of the printed letters D-O-G and not to other letters; and so on. Stimulus discrimination does not occur only in operant conditioning, however. Let's say that your lab instructor wants you to use classical conditioning to teach B. F. to stop moving in the presence of a slow-ringing bell but not a fast-ringing bell. First you need to know that rats explore freely in dim light but freeze in bright light. You would start classical conditioning in the normal way, by pairing the slow ring with the UCS (bright light) for the response of freezing. After several pairings, B. F. should be freezing whenever the slow-ringing bell is sounded. If we now begin presenting the fast ring sometimes, B. F. will respond to that by freezing, too. But, if we continue to present both the slow and fast rings, *but pair the bright light only with the slow ring,* B. F. will freeze only to the slow ring and not the fast one. That is, he will have learned a stimulus discrimination through classical conditioning.

Stopping for a stop sign is one stimulus discrimination drivers must learn.

The opposite of stimulus discrimination is **stimulus generalization.** This term indicates that people (as well as rats and other creatures) do not always discriminate between stimuli that are similar to one another. Stated another way, the more similar two stimuli are, the more likely the individual is to respond to them as if they were the same stimulus. A person who is afraid of Siamese cats may also be afraid of tabby and alley cats.

As with everything else, let's go back to the lab to demonstrate stimulus generalization based on similarity in the color of the stimulus. This time, however, we use a pigeon as our laboratory animal instead of a rat, because rats are color blind and pigeons are not. For example, we can reinforce the pigeon only for responding in the presence of a *yellow-green* light whose wavelength is 550 nanometers (a unit used to measure the wavelength of light). In a while, the pigeon emits lever presses only when the S^d of the light is present. In this part of our study of the pigeon's learning, however, the fact that it presses the lever only in the presence of the light is important to us only because it gives us a tool for carefully studying stimulus generalization. If we begin changing the wavelength of the light stimulus, we will be able to see that the more we change the wavelength, the less likely the pigeon will be to respond to it. If we carefully change the wavelength many times in small gradations, we will be able to make a graph that shows us this fact about stimulus generalization. The results of such a study appear in figure 7.11. Note that the more similar stimuli are, the more likely the pigeon is to respond to them as if they were the same; the less similar they are, the less likely they are to be responded to as the same.

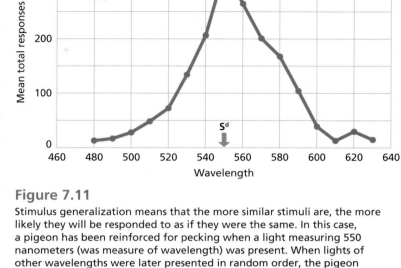

Figure 7.11

Stimulus generalization means that the more similar stimuli are, the more likely they will be responded to as if they were the same. In this case, a pigeon has been reinforced for pecking when a light measuring 550 nanometers (was measure of wavelength) was present. When lights of other wavelengths were later presented in random order, the pigeon pecked most frequently to lights similar to the S^d (discriminative stimulus of 550 nanometers).

Before we leave this concept, let's look at one more example of stimulus generalization; in this case, generalization involving classical conditioning. Recall the famous experiment with Little Albert, in which Albert was classically conditioned to fear a white laboratory rat by pairing a loud noise with the rat. In addition, the fear generalized to other similar objects. Five days later, Albert reacted fearfully to a white rabbit, a white dog, and a white coat. He even showed mildly fearful reactions to balls of cotton and a Santa Claus mask.

Review

We learn from the consequences of our behavior. If our behavior leads to a positive consequence, we are more likely to engage in that behavior again, with the specific pattern of behavior depending in part on the schedule with which reinforcement is delivered. The events that serve as positive reinforcers are both inborn (primary reinforcers) and learned (secondary reinforcers). Positive reinforcement can even increase the probability of behaviors that initially never occur by reinforcing successive approximations to that behavior (shaping).

Behavior can be reinforced not only when the consequence is positive but also when the behavior removes or avoids a negative consequence (negative reinforcement). Actually, two slightly different forms of learning are based on negative reinforcement: (a) escape conditioning, in which the behavior removes a negative event, and (b) avoidance conditioning, in which behavior causes the negative event not to occur at all. Punishment, which is different from negative reinforcement, is a negative consequence of behavior that reduces the probability of its future occurrence.

Behavior that is reinforced only in the presence of a specific stimulus tends to occur only in the presence of that stimulus (stimulus discrimination). However, there is a strong tendency to respond to similar stimuli as if they were the same (stimulus generalization). The phenomena of stimulus generalization and discrimination also occur in classical conditioning.

Check Your Learning

Check Your Learning

To be sure that you have learned the key points from the preceding section, cover the list of correct answers and try to answer each question. If you give an incorrect answer to any question, return to the page given next to the correct answer to see why your answer was not correct.

1. Learning from the consequences of our behavior is called _____.

   a) operant conditioning

   b) classical conditioning

   c) environmental learning

   d) cognitive learning

2. Slot machine players are on a _____ of reinforcement.

   a) variable interval schedule

   b) variable ratio schedule

   c) fixed ratio schedule

   d) fixed interval schedule

3. Negative reinforcement is another term for punishment.

   a) true

   b) false

4. The more similar two stimuli are, the more likely the individual is to respond to them as if they were the same stimulus. This is termed _____.

   a) stimulus discrimination

   b) generalized responding

   c) stimulus generalization

   d) stimulus conditioning

Thinking Critically about Psychology

There are no right or wrong answers to the following questions. They are presented to help you become an active reader and think critically about what you have just read.

1. Do your friends ever reinforce you for behaving in ways that are not good for you? In what ways?

2. What kinds of behaviors does our culture encourage? Is this done more through positive reinforcement, negative reinforcement, or punishment?

Correct Answers: 1. a (p. 203), 2. b (p. 206), 3. b (p. 210), 4. c (p. 212)

Extinction: Learning When to Quit

The process of learning is essential to human life. Through it we learn to cope with the demands of the environment. But the world is apt to change at any time, so people have to change their behavior, too. If we were able to learn only once and never change, we would not be able to survive changes in the environment. For example, if we were Stone Age people who learned to get oranges from the tops of orange trees by shaking the trees, that learned behavior would be very useful—that is, it would be positively reinforced. But the learned behavior of shaking orange trees would no longer be useful after all the oranges had been shaken out of the tree. At that point, we would need to quit shaking orange trees! If changes in the environment did not lead to changes in our learned behavior, we would be in big trouble.

If a learned response stops occurring because the aspect of the environment that originally caused the learning changes, **extinction** has occurred. The process of extinction is similar in many respects for both classical and operant conditioning.

extinction (eks-tink´-shun) Process of unlearning a learned response because of the removal of the original source of learning.

Removing the Source of Learning

Extinction occurs because the original source of the learning has been removed. In classical conditioning, learning takes place because two stimuli are repeatedly paired together. If Pavlov's dog were to stop receiving meat powder with the sound of the metronome, the dog would eventually stop salivating to the metronome. Or if you are hurt a couple of times when you are in a clumsy dentist's chair, the dentist's chair will elicit the response of fear by itself (because of the pairing of pain with the previously neutral chair). Let's suppose, however, that the clumsy dentist sells his practice to a new, truly painless dentist and you no longer get hurt in that chair. In this case, the cause of learning to fear the dentist's chair is removed. Eventually (classically conditioned fears are difficult to extinguish), the fact that the conditioned stimulus is presented alone (the dentist's chair is never again paired with pain) will lead to the extinction of the response of fear to the dentist's chair (Davis & others, 2005). In essence, you will have learned that the chair no longer predicts pain. Thus, using the terminology of classical conditioning, a CR will be extinguished if the CS for that response is presented repeatedly but the UCS for that stimulus is no longer paired with it.

In the case of operant conditioning, extinction results from a change in the consequences of behavior. If a response is no longer reinforced, then that response will eventually decline in frequency. If Skinner's rat were no longer given food pellets for bar presses, the bar pressing would eventually stop. Similarly, when there are no longer any oranges in the tree, the response of shaking it will no longer be reinforced and shaking will eventually stop.

The schedule of reinforcement and the type of reinforcement greatly influence the speed with which the extinction of operant conditioning takes place. This phenomenon is known as the **partial reinforcement effect.** Responses that have been continuously reinforced are extinguished more quickly than responses reinforced on variable ratio or variable interval schedules. Perhaps this is so because it's easier to see that the reinforcement is not going to come again if it used to come after every response. It may not be a bad thing that parents, employers, teachers, and others are often too busy to reinforce every good response; a variable pattern of reinforcement makes the good response more resistant to extinction.

The most difficult responses of all to extinguish, however, are responses learned through avoidance learning. Extinction of an avoidance response should result when the negative event ceases to occur. However, if you continue to perform avoidance responses, you will never see that the situation has changed. For example, if you continue to avoid the pit bull by taking the longer route to school, you will never learn that the owner and his dog have moved to another neighborhood.

Avoidance responses can be extinguished rapidly, however, using a technique called **response prevention.** This technique does exactly what its name implies. Avoidance responses are simply *prevented* to be sure that the individual sees that the negative consequence does not occur. The technique of response prevention has useful applications in treating disorders such as obsessive-compulsive disorder (see chapter 15). When compulsive behaviors, such as frequent hand washing, are physically prevented, the individual has an opportunity to discover that the feared consequences, such as terrible illness, are not really going to happen (Steketee & Cleere, 1990).

partial reinforcement effect Phenomenon whereby responses that have been reinforced on variable ratio or variable interval schedules are more difficult to extinguish than responses that have been continuously reinforced.

response prevention Prevention of avoidance responses to ensure that the individual sees that the negative consequence will not occur to speed up the extinction of avoidance responses.

Spontaneous Recovery and Disinhibition

The course of extinction is not always smooth. Normally, the learned response occurs many times before extinction is complete. Consider again the fear of the dental chair:

Figure 7.12
The course of extinction of a classically conditioned fear of dental chairs.

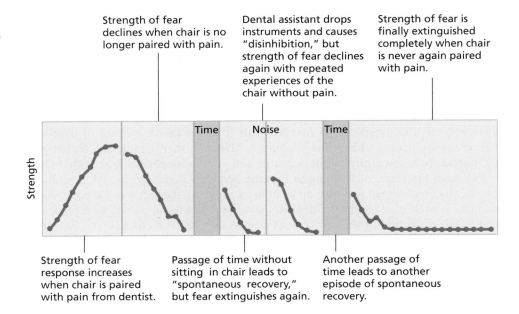

Strength of fear declines when chair is no longer paired with pain.

Dental assistant drops instruments and causes "disinhibition," but strength of fear declines again with repeated experiences of the chair without pain.

Strength of fear is finally extinguished completely when chair is never again paired with pain.

Strength of fear response increases when chair is paired with pain from dentist.

Passage of time without sitting in chair leads to "spontaneous recovery," but fear extinguishes again.

Another passage of time leads to another episode of spontaneous recovery.

spontaneous recovery Temporary increase in the strength of a conditioned response, which is likely to occur during extinction after the passage of time.

The strength of the response gradually decreases because the CS (chair) is never again paired with the UCS (pain). If, however, there is a long period of time between presentations of the CS (such as a year between visits to the dentist), the fear can reappear the next time the CS is presented (see figure 7.12). This is termed **spontaneous recovery.** It may occur several times during the course of extinction, but as long as the stimulus continues to be presented alone, the recovered response will be extinguished more quickly each time until the response no longer recovers.

In some cases, the strength of the extinguished response returns for a reason other than spontaneous recovery. If an intense but unrelated stimulus event occurs, it may cause the strength of the extinguished response to return temporarily. For example, if the dentist's assistant drops a tray of dental instruments while you were sitting in the chair, your fear response might come back for a while. This phenomenon is called **disinhibition.** That term will not seem to fit the phenomenon unless you understand that Pavlov, for theoretical reasons, believed that no response was ever really un-learned, just "inhibited" by another part of the brain. He termed this temporary increase in the strength of the response "disinhibition," because he believed that noise temporarily reduced the inhibition of the response. Both spontaneous recovery and disinhibition occur during the course of operant as well as classical extinction (Redish & others, 2007).

disinhibition (dis˝in-hi-bish´un) Temporary increase in the strength of an extinguished response caused by an unrelated stimulus event.

Review

To adapt fully to a changing world, we must be able to unlearn as well as learn. The process of extinction begins as soon as the source of the original learning is removed.

In classical conditioning, this means that no longer pairing the UCS with the CS will produce extinction of the CR. In operant learning, no longer reinforcing the response will extinguish the response. The course of extinction is often irregular, with the strength of the response often spontaneously recovering after long periods of time or when a strong disinhibiting stimulus occurs.

Check Your Learning

To be sure that you have learned the key points from the preceding section, cover the list of correct answers and try to answer each question. If you give an incorrect answer to any question, return to the page given next to the correct answer to see why your answer was not correct.

1. The process of unlearning a learned response because of a change in the aspect of the environment that originally caused the learning is termed _____.

   a) repression

   b) forgetting

   c) extinction

   d) terminating

2. The most difficult responses of all to extinguish are responses learned through _____.

   a) avoidance learning

   b) operant conditioning

   c) classical conditioning

   d) experience

3. _____ is a temporary increase in the strength of an extinguished response caused by an unrelated stimulus event.

   a) Spontaneous recovery

   b) Disinhibition

   c) Revival

   d) Learning

There are no right or wrong answers to the following questions. They are presented to help you become an active reader and think critically about what you have just read.

1. What makes some behaviors more difficult to extinguish than others?

2. Have you personally tried to eliminate unwanted behaviors using extinction?

Correct Answers: 1. c (p. 214), 2. a (p. 215), 3. b (p. 216)

Theoretical Interpretations of Learning

What is learned? When an individual's behavior changes as the result of classical or operant conditioning, what exactly has happened to the individual? One view dating back at least to the time of Pavlov is that neural *connections* between brain regions associated with specific stimuli and specific responses are acquired during the learning process. For example, when a rat is reinforced for pressing a lever in the presence of a light, a connection is believed to be automatically created between brain regions associated with the light and the specific pattern of muscle movements of the lever press. The next time the light is turned on, the neural connections to the muscles will cause the lever press to occur. Research based on the connection approach emphasized readily observable changes in behavior and basically ignored internal mental processes.

Other psychologists argue that internal mental processes play a central role in the learning process and are therefore deserving of study. For these psychologists, learning involves changes in cognitions rather than specific neural connections. As noted earlier in the text, the term *cognition* refers to the intellectual processes of thinking, expecting, believing, perceiving, and so on. Adherents to this view consider that the individual (rat or human) changes cognitions about a given situation during the learning process. For example, you flinch when a light comes on that has previously been paired with an electric shock, because you *expect* it to be followed by a shock. A rat turns left in a maze because it *knows* that the food was down that way the last 10 times it ran through the maze.

Cognition or Connection?

A considerable amount of research has been conducted through the years to evaluate the connectionist and cognition theories of learning. Although most of it has been carried out using animals as subjects, what has been learned about the nature of learning is relevant to us human animals, too.

Place Learning. An ingenious experiment to test the cognitive view of learning was designed by the late Edward C. Tolman of the University of California at Berkeley (Tolman, Ritchie, & Kalish, 1946). Rats were initially trained to run down the elevated path shown in figure 7.13. They started at point A, made a series of turns (left, right, right), and ran to point B, where food was provided. In the connectionist view of learning, the rats learned to do this by learning connections between the stimuli of the alley and the particular muscle movements of running and turning. Tolman took a cognitive view, however. He believed that the rats had learned a **cognitive map** of where the food was located relative to the starting place. They did not acquire a fixed pattern of muscle movements; they acquired knowledge of the location of the food.

How can we distinguish between the cognitive and the connectionist interpretations? Tolman's experimental test was ingenious. Suppose we give the rats a chance to take a shortcut directly to the food; will they take it? Or will they be unable to recognize it as a better path, because all they had learned were connections between maze stimuli and patterns of muscle movements? Tolman and his colleagues answered this question by blocking the old path (as shown in figure 7.14) and providing a variety of new choices.

Interestingly, the greatest number of rats chose the path that led directly to where the food had been. Tolman interpreted this as meaning that they had learned a new cognition, knowledge of the location of the food. Recent research has shown that the hippocampus, which you studied in chapter 3, plays an essential role in learning such "cognitive maps" (McGregor & others, 2004).

Latent Learning. Another clever experiment developed by Tolman evaluated the cognitive interpretation of learning in a rather different way (Devan & others, 2002; Tolman & Honzik, 1930). Suppose we allow a rat to run around in a complex maze of alleys, like the one shown in figure 7.15. Would the rat learn anything? The connectionist view would say no: learning would occur only if reinforcement were delivered at the end of the maze to "stamp in" a connection between the stimuli of the maze and a specific series of movements leading from the starting box to the box containing the food. Tolman, in contrast, thought that the rat would learn a cognitive map of the maze, but we would not be able to see that the rat had learned it until it was given a good reason (such as food) to run to the food box.

In Tolman's experiment, three groups of hungry rats were placed in the maze and timed to see how long it took them to reach the food box. One group was reinforced each time it reached the food box, so it gradually learned to run to the food box. A second group was never reinforced, so they wandered aimlessly in the maze (never decreasing the time it took to reach the food box). The third group of rats was the interesting one, though. This group was not reinforced for going to the food box for the first 10 days but was reinforced from then on. Look at figure 7.16 (p. 220) to see what happened. These rats suddenly decreased the time it took to reach the goal, catching up almost immediately to the group that had been reinforced every time. Tolman

Most of us have learned that good grooming usually elicits compliments from our friends. Is this a learned behavior involving a new stimulus-response connection or a change in cognition?

cognitive map (kog´ni-tiv) Inferred mental awareness of the structure of a physical space or related elements.

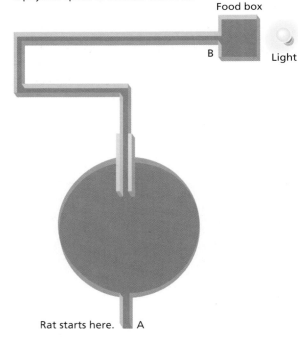

Food box

B   Light

Rat starts here.   A

Figure 7.13

The initial part of the apparatus used in Tolman's study of cognitive aspects of learning in rats. The rat begins at point A and receives food when it has reached point B.

Source: E. C. Tolman, B. F. Ritchie, and D. Kalish, "Studies in Spatial Learning I: Orientation and the Short-Cut," *Journal of Experimental Psychology*, 36:13–25, 1946.

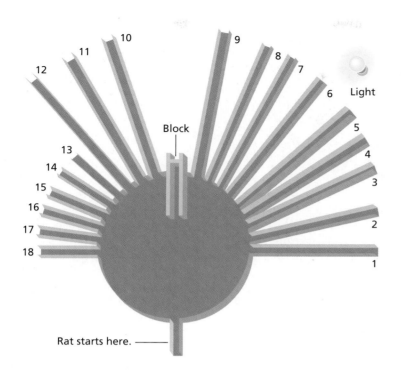

Figure 7.14

The modified apparatus used in the second part of Tolman's study of cognitive aspects of learning in rats.

Source: E. C. Tolman, B. F. Ritchie, and D. Kalish, "Studies in Spatial Learning I: Orientation and the Short-Cut," *Journal of Experimental Psychology*, 36:13–25, 1946.

interpreted these results as showing that the unreinforced rats had learned just as much about the location of the food box as the reinforced group, but they showed their learning only when given a reason to do so (the food). If learning were a matter of reinforcement strengthening connections between stimuli and responses, no learning would have been expected prior to the introduction of reinforcement.

Insight Learning and Learning Sets. Perhaps the most striking evidence for the cognitive view of learning comes from a series of experiments conducted by a German Gestalt psychologist during World War I. Wolfgang Köhler was visiting the island of Tenerife (in the Canary Islands) when the war broke out and was interned for the duration of the war. He took good advantage of a poor situation, however, by conducting learning experiments with chimpanzees native to the island. Köhler presented the caged chimps with a number of problems to see how they learned to solve them. For example, he hung a bunch of bananas out of reach on the ceiling. At first, the chimps tried to reach the bananas by jumping. When that failed, they sat down, looking annoyed. In time one of the chimps picked up the wooden boxes in the cage, stacked them, and climbed up to reach the bananas. From that time on, the chimps always reached bananas hung from the ceiling of the cage by stacking the boxes.

Köhler conducted many similar experiments with other chimps. For example, he placed another chimp in a cage with bananas hung from the ceiling. In this case, there were no boxes in cage, but there were two bamboo poles that could be fitted together to make a pole long enough to reach the bananas. At first, the chimp tried to reach the bananas by jumping and then by throwing the bamboo poles at the bananas, but it soon gave up. Later, the chimp suddenly picked up the sticks, put them together, and used the new pole to knock down the bananas. Again, when presented with the same problem later, the chimp immediately solved it every time by putting the sticks together.

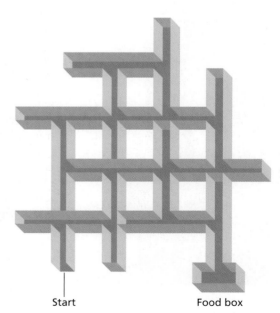

Figure 7.15

The maze used in Tolman's study of latent learning in rats.

Source: E. C. Tolman and C. H. Honzik, "Introduction and Removal of the Reward, and Maze Performance in Rats," *University of California Publications in Psychology,* 4: 257–275, 1930.

Figure 7.16

The results of Tolman's study of latent learning in rats. A group of rats that was never reinforced for reaching the food box did not improve in the amount of time required to reach it. But a group of rats that was reinforced each time gradually improved. A third group of rats was not reinforced for the first 10 days but was reinforced from then on. These rats' rapid improvement indicated that they had latently learned about the maze before they were reinforced.

Source: E. C. Tolman and C. H. Honzik, "Introduction and Removal of the Reward, and Maze Performance in Rats," *University of California Publications in Psychology*, 4:257–275, 1930.

insight (in´sīt) Form of cognitive change that involves recognition of previously unseen relationships.

learning set Improvement in the rate of learning to solve new problems through practice solving similar problems.

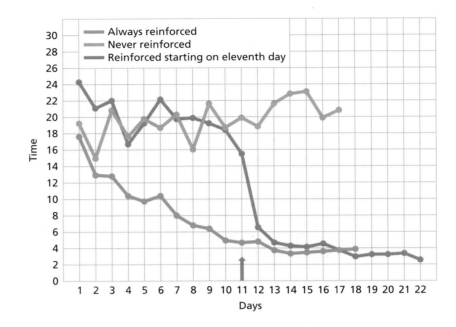

In Köhler's view, this chimp did not learn to stack the boxes to reach the bananas on the ceiling through a gradual learning process but, rather, through a process of sudden cognitive change involving a new understanding of the uses of the boxes.

In both cases, Köhler concluded that the chimps had not learned to solve the problem by gradually strengthening neural connections between stimuli and responses but, rather, had learned through **insight**—a sudden cognitive change that solved the problem. The chimps did not gradually improve their ability to reach the bananas but, rather, suddenly went from being unable to reach the bananas to being able to reach them easily using their new solution. Connection theorists have a great deal of difficulty explaining this type of insightful learning, but a series of classic experiments conducted by Harry Harlow (1949) at the University of Wisconsin took some of the mystery out of the chimps' insightful behavior. Harlow showed that the ability to solve problems insightfully is itself partially learned.

The apparatus shown in figure 7.17 was used in Harlow's study. A tray was presented to the monkey with two objects on it. Although the objects differed from problem to problem, food was always located under one of the objects. The monkeys had six chances to solve each problem. The monkeys in Harlow's experiments solved a total of 312 different problems, because Harlow's interest was in whether the monkeys' ability to solve the problems improved with experience. As can be seen in figure 7.18, their problem-solving ability improved dramatically. Look first at their performance on the first group of problems (problems 1 through 8). While their percentage of correct performance improved gradually over the six trials, they were still choosing the correct object only about 75% of the time by the sixth trial. In contrast, look at their performance on problems 257 through 312. On the first trial, they had to guess which object the food was under, so they were correct only 50% of the time. But note that if they did not get it right the first time, they "insightfully knew" that it must be under the other object, and they made the correct choice from the second trial on.

In Harlow's terms, the monkeys had acquired a **learning set;** that is, they had learned to learn insightfully. Harlow's point was that the insightful performance of Köhler's apes was not characteristic of all learning; rather, one must *learn* how to solve a particular class of problems insightfully. Further supporting Harlow's contention is a follow-up study of Köhler's banana-and-stick problem (Birch, 1945). Chimpanzees that had no previous experience playing with sticks could not solve the problem. However, after these chimps had been allowed to play with the sticks for only 3 days, they were able to solve the banana-and-stick problem easily. Evidently, they had learned something in their play that enabled them to learn insightfully.

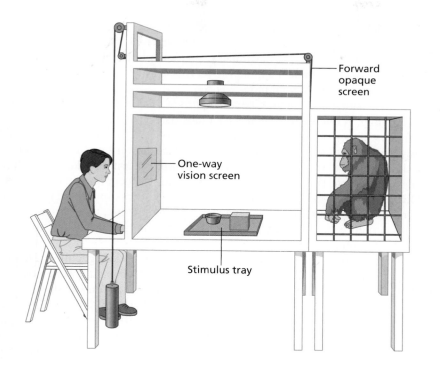

Figure 7.17
The apparatus used by Harlow to study learning sets (learning to learn insightfully) in monkeys.

Forward opaque screen

One-way vision screen

Stimulus tray

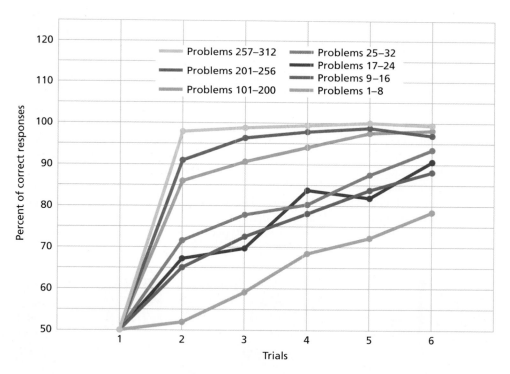

Figure 7.18
Monkeys learn which object is hiding food very slowly the first few times they are given this type of problem (problems 1–8). But they learn quickly (insightfully) after they have had a great deal of experience with such problems (problems 257–312).

Source: H. F. Harlow, "The Formation of Learning Sets," *Psychological Review,* 56:51–56, 1949.

Problems 257–312
Problems 201–256
Problems 101–200
Problems 25–32
Problems 17–24
Problems 9–16
Problems 1–8

Percent of correct responses

Trials

Modeling: Learning by Watching Others

Stanford University psychologist Albert Bandura is one of the most influential contemporary proponents of the cognitive view of learning. One of his many important contributions has been to emphasize that people learn not only through classical and operant conditioning but also by observing the behavior of others. Bandura (1977)

Albert Bandura's views about modeling predict that this boy will learn good work habits from watching his father work on home projects.

modeling Learning based on observation of the behavior of another.

vicarious reinforcement (vī-kar´ē-us) Observed reinforcement of the behavior of a model, which also increases the probability of the same behavior in the observer.

vicarious punishment Observed punishment of the behavior of a model, which also decreases the probability of the same behavior in the observer.

Bandura found that children who observed adult models play aggressively with a Bobo doll played more aggressively themselves.

calls this **modeling.** For example, in countries where grasshoppers are considered to be a delicacy, people learn to eat them partly by watching other people enjoy themselves while eating grasshoppers. Similarly, patterns of speech, styles of dress, patterns of energy consumption, methods of rearing children, and myriad patterns of behavior are taught to us through modeling.

Bandura considers modeling to be an important demonstration of the role of cognition in learning. A child who watches his older sister play baseball for several years is able to come pretty close to playing the game properly. He knows how to hold the bat, how to swing, and where to run if he hits the ball the very first time he is allowed to play. In Bandura's view, a great deal of cognitive learning takes place through watching, *before* there is any chance for the behavior to occur and be reinforced. But we can learn more than skills through modeling. Bandura has suggested that modeling can also remind us of appropriate behavior in a given situation, reduce our inhibitions concerning certain behaviors that we see others engaging in, or suggest to us which behaviors lead to reinforcement.

In Bandura's ground-breaking laboratory studies of modeling, children learned to be more aggressive or less fearful as a result of simply observing the behavior of models in films. In one study (Bandura, Ross, & Ross, 1963), one group of children saw an adult kick, hit, and sit on a blow-up Bobo doll. When these children were placed in a playroom and then frustrated by having all toys except the Bobo doll taken away, they were significantly more aggressive toward the Bobo doll than were a group of children who had not seen the film—they learned to act more aggressively through modeling. In a similar study with a more uplifting conclusion, research participants who were initially strongly afraid of snakes gradually learned to be less fearful by imitating a series of actions of the model, ranging from looking at a caged snake to holding it (Bandura, Blanchard, & Ritter, 1969). Modeling can be an important and powerful form of learning.

We are not equally likely to imitate all behavior of all models, however. We are considerably more likely to imitate a model whose behavior we see reinforced (**vicarious reinforcement**) than when we see that behavior punished in the model (**vicarious punishment**) (Carnagey & Anderson, 2005). In the absence of direct knowledge of vicarious reinforcement and punishment, we are more likely to imitate the behavior of models that are high in status, attractive, likable, and successful, perhaps because we assume their behavior often leads to reinforcement (Bandura, 1977).

In recent years, a great deal of debate has centered on the types of models presented to children on television and videogames. Unfortunately, solid experimental evidence seems to confirm these fears. It appears that television and videogames do teach youth to prefer sugary foods, engage in sex-stereotyped roles, initiate sexual relationships

during adolescence (Martino & others, 2005), and be violent and antisocial (Anderson, Lindsay, & Bushman, 1999; Sheese & Graziano, 2005).

Biological Factors in Learning

Learning is a powerful process that quite literally shapes our lives. But we must not overstate the importance of any psychological process, even learning. We must keep in mind that our ability to learn from experience is not limitless; it's influenced in a number of ways by biological factors. We know that it's impossible to teach goldfish to fly and owls to swim, but has it ever occurred to you that our biological nature influences what people can learn?

For example, it appears that people are biologically prepared to learn some kinds of fears more readily than others (Öhman & Mineka, 2001). It's far easier to classically condition a fear of things that have some intrinsic association with danger (snakes, heights, blood, and so on) using electric shock as the UCS than it is to condition a fear of truly neutral things such as lunch boxes and skate keys (Cook, Hodes, & Lang, 1986; Mercklebach & others, 1988; Öhman, Erixon, & Löfberg, 1975). Apparently, the process of evolution has prepared us to learn some potentially useful fears, through classical conditioning, more readily than useless ones. Interestingly, we are prepared to learn to fear only the things that would have been dangerous to our evolutionary ancestors. For example, fears cannot be easily conditioned to modern dangerous stimuli, such as electric outlets (Hugdahl & Karker, 1981).

John Garcia and his associates discussed another form of learning that exemplifies the role of biological factors in learning (Garcia, Hankins, & Rusiniak, 1974). An example of their experiments can be shown through one of my own experiences as a child. On one fateful evening, I ate eight hot dogs. Two hours later, I became more than just a little nauseated. As a result, it was many years until I ate another hot dog. This experience of learning to dislike hot dogs is an example of a **learned taste aversion.** Such learned taste aversions provide another good example of the role of biological factors in learning. Note that I learned to dislike the hot dogs through classical conditioning: The hot dogs were the CS and the nausea was the UCS. But think about two facts: the two stimuli were paired only *once,* but I learned a dislike that lasted for years. Moreover, there was a time interval of 2 hours between the conditioned and the unconditioned stimuli. Normally a gap of more than a couple of seconds between the conditioned stimulus and the unconditioned stimulus is enough to make classical conditioning impossible. For learning to take place under these conditions, we must be highly "prepared" for such learning. Indeed, this makes good sense from an evolutionary perspective; animal species that quickly learn to avoid foods that make them sick (and hence may be poisonous) are species that are more likely to survive. A species that does not quickly learn to avoid poisonous foods is likely to perish (Kehoe & Bass, 1986).

A particularly sad outcome of our readiness to acquire classically conditioned taste aversions can be seen in the treatment of cancer. Some effective forms of chemotherapy and abdominal radiation therapy have the side effect of causing the patient to be nauseated for a while after treatment. Individuals undergoing these treatments not only are quite uncomfortable but also tend to lose their appetite, causing weight loss, which complicates their health problems. Ilene Bernstein (1978, 1985) of the University of Washington reasoned that the loss of appetite may be caused in part by learned taste aversions produced by the frequent nausea. To test her hypothesis, a group of children with cancer were given mapletoff ice cream, an unusual mixture of maple and black walnut flavorings, immediately before their regular chemotherapy treatment. Later they were offered the ice cream again. Compared with a group of children given the ice cream just before a different kind of treatment that does not produce nausea, far fewer of the children who had become nauseated after eating the ice cream wanted the ice cream again. Similarly, a group of children who underwent the

learned taste aversion (ah-ver′shun) Negative reaction to a particular taste that has been associated with nausea or other illness.

same nausea-inducing chemotherapy but had not been given the ice cream just before the treatment showed no aversion to it.

Apparently, nausea from chemotherapy can create learned taste aversions for foods that are eaten prior to therapy and, over a period of time, can lead cancer patients to avoid many foods (Batsell, 2000). Fortunately, Bernstein and her colleagues (1982) have developed some strategies to avoid this problem. First, fasting before the chemotherapy reduces the chances of developing any taste aversions. Second, eating a novel and distinctive-tasting food (such as the mapletoff ice cream) with the meal preceding chemotherapy often results in a conditioned aversion only to the distinctive food. Nutritionally unimportant food, therefore, can be used as shields against aversions to more important foods. In addition, Redd and others (1987) have found that allowing children to play videogames just before chemotherapy is distracting enough to disrupt the conditioning of the nausea.

On a more positive note, a creative and useful application of our knowledge of learned taste aversions has been made by John Garcia and his colleagues in the area of wildlife preservation (Gustavson & others, 1974). A serious conflict exists in some western states between the interests of sheep ranchers and those of wildlife preservationists. Because coyotes kill many of the ranchers' sheep, the ranchers kill so many coyotes every year that they endanger the coyotes' survival as a species. Garcia's research group developed an alternative plan, which keeps the coyotes from killing sheep without being killed themselves. These researchers demonstrated that, if the sheep ranchers place on the range sheep meat containing a chemical that will make the coyotes nauseated, the coyotes will develop an aversion to the taste of sheep and no longer hunt them. Through this method, sheep and coyotes can peacefully coexist.

Review   Some psychologists believe that learning is based on the strengthening of neural connections between stimuli and specific patterns of muscle movements. Others suggest that learning involves changes in cognition (knowing what to do, where food is located, what to expect next, and so on). Research on place learning, latent learning, and insight learning provides strong support for the cognitive view of learning. Perhaps the most important learning phenomenon thought to be based on cognitive change is modeling; a great deal of our behavior is learned simply by observing the behavior of others. Although learning is a powerful force that shapes our lives, our biological characteristics place limits on it, making us better prepared to learn some things more than others.

Check Your Learning   To be sure that you have learned the key points from the preceding section, cover the list of correct answers and try to answer each question. If you give an incorrect answer to any question, return to the page given next to the correct answer to see why your answer was not correct.

1. _____ is a sudden change in behavior that results from a recognition of previously unseen relationships.

   a) Insight   c) Operant learning

   b) Modeling   d) Conditioning

2. Harry Harlow's work on learning sets shows that insightful learning is _____.

   a) learned   c) only possible in humans

   b) innate   d) all of these

3. Learning by observing the behavior of others is termed _____ by Albert Bandura.

   a) stimulus discrimination   c) operant conditioning

   b) classical conditioning   d) modeling

4. Learned taste aversions, in which humans and nonhuman animals learn to avoid foods that make them sick, are interesting because the time interval between the CS (the taste of the food) and the UCS is much _____ than in most instances of classical conditioning.

   a) longer   b) shorter

There are no right or wrong answers to the following questions. They are presented to help you become an active reader and think critically about what you have just read.

1. Why are place learning, latent learning, and insight learning all considered to support cognitive theories of learning?

2. Whom do you model your behavior after? What events or personal qualities have made them your models?

Correct Answers: 1. a (p. 220), 2. a (p. 220), 3. d (p. 222), 4. a (p. 223)

Application of Psychology

Learning to Be Superstitious

Operant conditioning helps us adapt to the realities of life. If our behavior is effective in bringing us good things, it will be positively reinforced, and we will be more likely to engage in these behaviors. However, ways of behaving that do not bring good things will be extinguished, and behaviors that bring negative consequences will be punished. We are always in the process of learning to adjust to our world through operant conditioning. But, *sometimes,* unfortunately, we learn the wrong things.

Are you superstitious? Did you ever wonder why? B. F. Skinner suggested that some of our superstitions are learned through flukes in positive reinforcement. Skinner was working with pigeons that were being reinforced for pecking at a small disk when he noticed that some of them had learned "superstitions." Sometimes a pigeon would turn around just before pecking the disk. The food pellet would reinforce the pigeon both for pecking and for the irrelevant response of turning. If the pigeon then happened to turn around again before another reinforced response, it would probably begin turning before every peck, even though turning had nothing to do with the delivery of the food. In Skinner's terms, the pigeon had learned a *superstitious behavior* because the reinforcer accidentally followed the response several times.

You can also see superstitious behavior acquired in this way by carefully watching a discus thrower just before he or she starts to throw. Many of them go through odd little rituals, such as touching a shoulder, each time they step in the ring. As odd as it looks, these gestures are probably just another form of superstitious behavior. When the discus thrower uncorks a really long throw (a big reinforcer for a discus thrower), any of the random behaviors that were occurring just before the long throw will be reinforced. These behaviors are called *superstitious* because

Athletes often learn superstitions from reinforcing stimuli that accidentally follow a response.

the reinforcement of the good throw had nothing to do with any gestures prior to the throw. Baseball players often develop similar superstitious behaviors before batting or pitching. Many other everyday superstitions are probably learned in much the same way. Do you have any superstitions like this?

Summary

Chapter 7 examines the psychological study of learning. The emphasis is on classical conditioning, operant conditioning, and extinction. The last section of the chapter explores theoretical interpretations of learning.

  I. Learning refers to any relatively permanent change in behavior brought about through experience.

 II. Classical conditioning is a form of learning in which a previously neutral stimulus (conditioned stimulus, CS) is paired with an unconditioned stimulus (UCS) that elicits an unlearned or unconditioned response (UCR). As a result, the CS comes to elicit a conditioned response (CR) that is identical or very similar to the UCR. Classical conditioning occurs because of the association in time of a neutral stimulus that already elicits the response. The CS becomes a signal that predicts the occurrence of the UCS.

III. Operant conditioning is a form of learning in which the consequences of behavior lead to a change in the probability of the behavior's occurrence.

  A. In positive reinforcement, a positive consequence of behavior leads to an increase in the probability of the occurrence of the response.

   1. Primary reinforcers are innately reinforcing.

   2. Secondary reinforcers are learned through classical conditioning (association of a neutral stimulus with a primary reinforcer).

   3. Four schedules of reinforcement that result in different patterns of behavior are fixed ratio, variable ratio, fixed interval, and variable interval.

4. Shaping is the process of positively reinforcing responses that are progressively more similar to the response that is wanted.

B. Negative reinforcement occurs when the reinforcing consequence is the removal or avoidance of a negative event.

1. The type of negative reinforcement in which the response causes an aversive stimulus to cease is called *escape conditioning.*

2. The type of negative reinforcement in which the response prevents the occurrence of the aversive stimulus is called *avoidance conditioning.*

C. Punishment is the process through which an aversive consequence of behavior reduces the frequency of a behavior.

D. A stimulus discrimination has been learned when a response is more likely to occur in the presence of a specific stimulus than in its absence.

E. Stimulus generalization has occurred when an individual responds in the same way to a stimulus that is similar to the original stimulus.

IV. The process of unlearning a learned response because of the removal of the aspect of the environment that originally caused the learning is termed *extinction.*

A. During extinction, the strength of the response sometimes increases after a period of time since the last extinction trial; this is termed *spontaneous recovery.*

B. An extraneous stimulus sometimes causes an extinguished response to recur; this is called *external disinhibition.*

V. Some psychologists view learning as resulting from changes in neural connections between specific stimuli and specific responses, whereas others think about learning as a change in cognition.

A. Research that supports the cognitive view includes Tolman's studies of place learning and latent learning, Köhler's studies of insight learning, and Bandura's work on modeling.

B. The ability of humans to learn from experience is not limitless; it is influenced in a number of ways by biological factors.

chapter **eight**
Memory

Chapter Outline

Prologue

Where were you on September 11, 2001? What were you doing when you first heard that terrorists had flown passenger airplanes into the World Trade Center? Were you still a child then? Take a moment before reading on to recall that moment.

On the morning of September 11, 2001, I was alone in my car, driving past the University of Chicago International House. I had just turned on National Public Radio, and the announcer, Robert Siegel, was saying that a second aircraft had just crashed into the other tower. I remember him saying that the second collision was clearly not an accident and might be the work of terrorists, but at that point, very little was known. I vividly recall the tone of profound shock and sadness in his voice, something that is rarely heard in professional news reports. Later, I watched videotapes of the collisions and the collapse of the towers on television at work, and I fell into a state that was both deeply sad and anxious.

At least I *think* that's what happened. Our memories give us the ability to store a remarkable amount of information about the past, but it can play tricks on us, too.

On September 12, 2001, 54 Duke University students wrote brief descriptions of where they were, what they were doing, and who told them about the terrorist attacks on the day before. They were asked to give complete descriptions, mentioning any distinctive details. In addition the students were asked to provide the same kind of detailed description of an *ordinary* event that had happened on that same September 11. The students agreed to be randomly assigned to one of three groups that would later be asked to recall these same events again after 1, 6, or 32 weeks had elapsed to test their memories of both events. When tested, the students were also asked to rate the vividness of their recollections and their level of confidence that their memory of each event was accurate (Talarico & Rubin, 2003).

Over time, the details of the students' recollections of both the events surrounding learning about the terrorist attacks and the everyday event became less accurate. Descriptions of each event contained 50% more accurate details after 1 week than after 32 weeks. Although one event clearly "made more of an impression" on the students than the other, there were no differences in the rates of decline in accuracy of their memories of the two events. In contrast, however, as time passed, the students rated their recollections of learning about the terrorist attacks as being more vivid than those of the everyday event and they were more confident that their recollections of learning about the attacks were more accurate than their recollections of the everyday event.

Memories of intense and dramatic events are often referred to as *flash-bulb memories.* For many years, most psychologists assumed that we recall highly emotional events more accurately than everyday events. In reality, our recollections of highly emotional events are vivid and *seem* more accurate than those of everyday events, but they often are inaccurate (Brainerd, Stein, & others, 2008; LeBar, 2007).

This chapter describes the ways in which memory works and the reasons why we forget. New information that we learn can be thought of as passing through three stages in the human memory. The first stage holds information for very brief intervals—often less than a second. The next stage retains information longer, but only a little longer—up to about half a minute. The third stage seems to hold information indefinitely. These three stages of memory operate according to different rules and mostly serve different functions. But because information must pass through each stage to reach the most permanent memory store, they work together as three linked stages in the memory process.

Key Terms

anterograde amnesia 254
decay theory 243
encode 230
engram 251
episodic memory 235
interference theory 244
levels of processing model 240
long-term memory (LTM) 234
procedural memory 235
recall method 238
recognition method 238
reconstruction (schema) theory 245
rehearsal 231
relearning method 238
retrograde amnesia 254
semantic memory 235
sensory register 230
serial position effect 239
short-term memory (STM) 231
stage theory of memory 230
synaptic facilitation 251

Three Stages of Memory: An Information-Processing View

Psychologists have developed theories of memory using the computer as a model. These *information-processing* theories of memory are based on the apparent similarities between the operation of the human brain and that of the computer. This is not to say that psychologists believe that brains and computers operate in exactly the same way. Clearly they do not (Rubin, 2006), but enough general similarity exists to make the information-processing model useful. Before looking at specific theories, let's look briefly at the general information-processing model and its terminology.

In the information-processing model, information can be followed as it moves through the following operations: input, storage, and retrieval. At each point in the process, a variety of *control mechanisms* (such as attention, storage, and retrieval) operate. Information enters the memory system through the sensory receptors. This is like your entering a term paper into your computer by typing on the keyboard. Attention operates at this level to select information for further processing. The raw sensory information that is selected is then represented—or **encoded**—in a form (sound, visual image, meaning) that can be used in the next stages of memory.

Other control mechanisms might then transfer selected information into a more permanent memory storage, like saving your term paper on a computer disk. When the stored information is needed, it is *retrieved* from memory. Before printing out your paper, you must first locate your file on the disk and retrieve it. Unfortunately, with both computers and human memory, some information may be lost or become irretrievable.

Some information needs to be stored in memory for only brief periods of time, whereas other information must be tucked away permanently. When we look at a cookbook to see how much tomato paste to add to chicken cacciatore, we need to remember that bit of information for only a few seconds. However, we must remember our Social Security numbers and our siblings' names for our entire lifetimes. The influential **stage theory of memory** (Atkinson & Shiffrin, 1968; Baddeley, 1999) assumes that we humans have a three-stage memory that meets our need to store information for different lengths of time. We seem to have one memory store that holds information for exceedingly brief intervals, a second memory store that holds information for no more than 30 seconds unless it's "renewed," and a third, more permanent memory store. Each of these memories operates according to a different set of rules and serves a somewhat different purpose. Because information must pass through each stage of memory to get to the next, more permanent one, these memory stores are best thought of as three closely linked "stages" of memory, rather than three separate memories. The three stages are known as the sensory register, short-term memory, and long-term memory (see figure 8.1).

Sensory Register

The first stage of memory—the **sensory register**—is a very brief one, designed to hold an exact image of each sensory experience until it can be fully processed. We apparently retain a copy of each sensory experience in the sensory register long enough to locate and focus on relevant bits of information and transfer them into the next stage of memory. For visual information, this "snapshot" fades very quickly, probably lasting about one-quarter of a second in most cases. For auditory information, a vivid image of what we hear is retained for about the same length of time, one-quarter of a second (Cowan, 1987), but a weaker "echo" is retained for up to 4 seconds (Tarpy & Mayer, 1978).

encode (en′cōd) To represent information in some form in the memory system.

stage theory of memory A model of memory based on the idea that we store information in three separate but linked memories.

sensory register The first stage of memory, in which an exact image of each sensory experience is held briefly until it can be processed.

A postal worker needs a good memory. According to the information-processing model, memory is a process involving attention, encoding, and transfer to storage from which information can be retrieved.

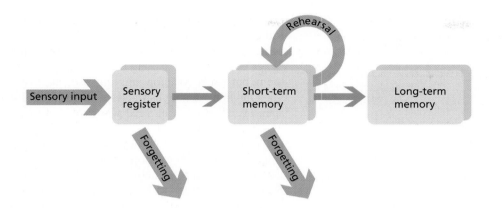

Figure 8.1
Stage model of memory.

The information stored in the sensory register does not last long, but it's apparently a complete replica of the sensory experience. This fact was demonstrated in an important experiment by George Sperling (1960). Sperling presented research participants with an array of 12 letters arranged in three horizontal rows of four letters each (see figure 8.2). He showed the participants these letters for 1/20 of a second and then asked them to recall all of the letters in one of the three rows. He did not tell them ahead of time which row he would ask them to recall. Instead, he signaled to them using a tone. A high-pitched tone indicated the first row, a medium tone indicated the second row, and a low tone indicated the third row. If the tone was presented very soon after the presentation of the array of letters, the participants could recall most of the letters in the indicated row. But if the delay was more than one-quarter of a second, the participants recalled an average of just over one letter per row, indicating how quickly information is lost in the sensory register.

Visual information in the sensory register is lost and replaced so rapidly with new information that we seldom are aware we even have such a memory store. Sometimes the longer-lasting, echolike traces of auditory information can be noticed, though. Most of us have had the experience of being absorbed in reading when a friend speaks. If we divert our attention from the book quickly enough, we can "hear again" what was said to us by referring to the echo of the auditory sensation stored in the sensory register.

Figure 8.2
Array of letters like that used in the sensory register experiments conducted by Sperling (1960).

Short-Term Memory

When a bit of information is selected for further processing, it's transferred from the sensory register into **short-term memory,** or **STM.** It's not necessary to intentionally transfer information to STM; generally, just paying attention to the information is enough to transfer it. You might not intentionally try to memorize the price of your dinner, but you will be able to recognize that you were given the wrong amount of change. Once information has been transferred to short-term memory, a variety of control processes may be applied. Rehearsal and chunking are two important examples of these control processes.

short-term memory (STM) The second stage of memory, in which five to nine bits of information can be stored for brief periods of time.

rehearsal Mental repetition of information to retain it longer in short-term memory.

Rehearsal in Short-Term Memory: Overcoming STM's Limited Life Span. As the name implies, short-term memory (STM) is good for only temporary storage of information. In general, information is lost from STM in less than half a minute unless it's "renewed," and it is often lost in only a few seconds (Ellis & Hunt, 1993; Unsworth & Engle, 2007). Fortunately, information can be renewed in STM by mental repetition, or **rehearsal,** of the information. When a grocery list is rehearsed regularly in this way, it can be held in STM for relatively long periods of time. If

Figure 8.3

The accuracy of recall for a single group of three consonants declines rapidly when subjects are prevented from rehearsing by being asked to count backward.

Source: R. L. Peterson and M. J. Peterson, "Short-Term Retention of Individual Items," in *Journal of Experimental Psychology 58*:193–198, 1959.

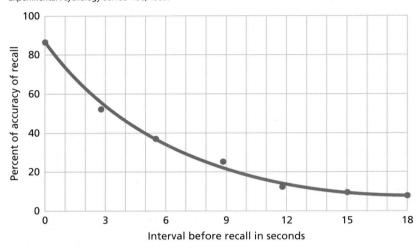

Interval before recall in seconds

the list is not rehearsed, however, it's soon lost. Rehearsing the information stored in STM has been compared to juggling eggs: The eggs stay in perfect condition as long as you keep juggling them, but when you stop juggling, they are lost.

Our first reliable estimate of the limited life span of information in STM was provided by an experiment conducted by Lloyd and Margaret Peterson (1959). The participants were shown a single combination of three consonants (such as LRP) and asked to remember it as they counted backward by threes to keep them from rehearsing the letters. The individuals counted backward for brief intervals (0 through 18 seconds) and then were asked to recall the letters. As shown in figure 8.3, the participants were able to remember the three consonants less than 20% of the time after only 12 seconds had passed. These findings make it clear that memories are impermanent in STM unless kept alive by rehearsal.

The information stored in STM can be of many different types of memories: the smell of a perfume, the notes of a melody, the taste of a fruit, the shape of a nose, the finger positions in a guitar chord, or a list of names (Rubin, 2006). But we humans have a preference for transforming information into sounds, or *acoustic codes,* whenever possible for storage in STM. If I asked you to memorize a list of letters (B, P, V, R, M, L), you would most likely memorize them by their "names" (bee, pee, vee, and so on) rather than by the shapes of the letters. We know this, because most people say they do it this way and because the errors people make are most likely to be confusions of similar sounds (recalling *zee* instead of *bee*) rather than confusions of similar shapes (recalling O instead of Q, or R instead of P) (Reynolds & Flagg, 1983). We probably use acoustic codes in STM as much as possible, because it's easier to rehearse by mentally talking to ourselves than by mentally repeating the images of sights, smells, and movements. Nonetheless, STM can store any form of information that can enter the brain through the senses (Rubin, 2006).

Chunking in Short-Term Memory: Overcoming STM's Limited Capacity.

Perhaps the most important thing to know about STM is that its storage capacity is quite limited (Fougnie & Marois, 2006). Psychologist George Miller (1956) referred to the capacity of STM as the *magic number seven plus or minus two.* Measures of the capacity of STM are obtained by asking research participants to memorize simple lists (of randomly ordered numbers, letters, and unrelated words) of different lengths. The length of the list that the participants can recall half the time is considered to represent the capacity of STM (Miller, 1956). Rarely are we able to hold more than five to nine bits of information in STM, regardless of the nature of that information. This is a very limited capacity, indeed, but more recent studies suggest that the capacity could even be smaller for some kinds of information (Alvarez & Cavanaugh, 2004; Cowan, Chen, and Rouder 2004).

In addition to temporarily storing information, STM serves another important function, which further limits its already small capacity—it serves as our *working memory* (Baddeley, 1992, 1999). This means that space in STM is used when old memories are temporarily brought out of long-term memory to be used or updated. Space in STM is also used when we think about this information (Morris, 1986). This is why you cannot remember the telephone number of the hardware store, which you just looked up, if

When we dial a number that we have just looked up in the telephone book, we are generally using information that has been stored only in short-term memory.

you begin thinking about your purchase before you dial—thinking takes up space in STM and forces out the numbers. The fact that thinking uses STM also explains why it's difficult to think about problems that involve more than 7 ± 2 bits of information. We keep forgetting some of the aspects of complex problems because they exceed the limited capacity of STM. In such situations, writing out all the issues on paper helps keep them straight while you are thinking.

One advantage of the small storage capacity of STM is that it's easy to "search" through it. When we try to remember something in STM, we apparently examine every item that is stored there. Experiments conducted by Saul Sternberg (1969) confirm that we exhaustively search STM every time we try to recall something. Sternberg's experiments even give us an estimate of how long it takes us to examine each bit of stored information. Participants were asked to memorize lists of numbers of different lengths. They were then shown a number and asked if it was in the list they had just memorized. When individuals had just memorized a long list of numbers, it took them longer to respond than when they had memorized a short list. In fact, the amount of time required to respond increased by a rather constant .04 of a second for each item in STM. Apparently, that's how long it takes to examine each item in STM.

Fortunately, there are some effective ways to get around the limited capacity of STM. One way is to learn the information well enough to transfer it into long-term memory, which, as we will see shortly, has no real space limitation. Another way is to put more information into the 7 ± 2 units of STM.

George Miller (1956) calls the units of memory **chunks.** Although it's true that we can hold only five to nine chunks in STM, we can often put more than one bit of information into each chunk. If you were to quickly read the following list of 12 words once,

STM holds 7 ± 2 bits of information. This shopper probably needs a written list.

chunks Units of memory.

east	winter
spring	lateral
fall	north
dorsal	ventral
west	summer
medial	south

you probably would not be able to recall it perfectly 10 seconds later, because 12 chunks normally exceed the capacity of STM. But, if you reorganized the words into 3 chunks (points of a compass, seasons, and anatomical directions) and memorized those, you could remember the list quite easily. This strategy would work for you only if you were able to regroup the list into meaningful chunks, however. If you did not know the four anatomical directions, it would do you no good to memorize these terms because you could not generate the four directions when you recalled them.

Other chunking strategies can also be used to expand the amount of information that can be stored in STM. It's no accident that Social Security numbers (as well as bank account numbers and telephone numbers) are broken up by hyphens. Most people find it easier to remember numbers in chunks (319-555-0151) than as a string of single digits.

In summary, STM is a stage of memory with limited capacity in which information—often stored in acoustic codes—is lost rapidly unless it's rehearsed. The capacity of STM can be expanded by increasing the amount of information in each chunk to be learned. But, no matter how good a job we do of chunking and rehearsing, STM is not a good place to store information for long periods of time. Such information must be transferred to long-term memory for more permanent storage.

Long-Term Memory

long-term memory (LTM) The third stage of memory, involving the storage of information that is kept for long periods of time.

Long-term memory, or **LTM,** is the storehouse for information that must be kept for long periods of time. But LTM is not just a more durable version of STM; the stage model of memory suggests it's a different kind of memory altogether.

LTM differs from STM in four major ways: (1) the way in which information is recalled, (2) the form in which information is stored in memory, (3) the reasons that forgetting occurs, and (4) the physical location of these functions in the brain. Let's look at each of these four differences between STM and LTM separately:

1. Because the amount of information stored in LTM is so vast, we cannot scan the entire contents of LTM when we are looking for a bit of information, as we do in STM. Instead, LTM has to be *indexed.* We retrieve information from LTM using cues, much as we use a call number to locate a book in the library. This retrieval can be an intentional act (such as "What was the name of the secretary in Accounts Receivable?") or an unintentional act, as when hearing a particular song brings back memories of a lost love. In either case, only information relevant to the cue is retrieved, rather than the entire contents of LTM.

2. LTM differs from STM in the kind of information that is most easily stored. You will recall that information is usually stored in STM in terms of the physical qualities of the experience (what we saw, did, tasted, touched, or heard), with a special emphasis on acoustic codes. Although sensory memories can be stored in LTM, information is stored in LTM primarily in terms of its meaning, or *semantic codes* (Cowan, 1988).

3. LTM also differs from STM in the way forgetting occurs. Unlike STM, where information that is not rehearsed or processed appears to drop out of the system, information stored in LTM is not just durable but actually appears to be permanent. In a dramatic demonstration of LTM, Bahrick (1984) tested memory for Spanish using individuals who had studied the language in high school 50 years ago. Bahrick's participants retained much of their knowledge of Spanish, even after a period of 50 years. Not all psychologists agree that memories in LTM are permanent, but there is a great deal of evidence supporting this view. If memories in LTM are indeed permanent, this means that "forgetting" occurs in LTM not because the memory is erased but because we are unable to retrieve it for some reason (Baddeley, 1999).

4. Each stage of memory is largely handled by a different part of the brain. STM is primarily a function of the frontal lobes of the cerebral cortex (Buckner & Barch, 1999; Fuster, 1995; Williams & Goldman-Rakic, 1995), whereas information that is stored in LTM is first integrated in the hippocampus and then transferred to the areas of the cerebral cortex involved in language and perception for permanent storage (Martin, 2005; Nadel & Jacobs, 1998; Squire, 2009). We describe these differences in more detail in the final section of this chapter.

Hearing an old favorite song can bring back memories of the earliest times you heard the song. We can use cues like old songs to intentionally retrieve long-term memories.

Types of Long-Term Memory: Procedural, Episodic, and Semantic. Tulving (1972, 2002) has proposed the existence of three kinds of long-term memory storage, each with distinctly different properties, and each probably based on different brain mechanisms. I think I can best explain the differences among these kinds of LTM by telling you another of my stories. Recently, I came across a photograph taken of me on my 14th birthday in my home in St. Petersburg, Florida. I was holding my birthday present—my first guitar. I took guitar lessons for a while and played in several mediocre rock bands until my junior year in college. Then I sold my guitar and concentrated on my studies. Later, I bought another guitar, and playing guitar once again became a part of my life. That's the story; now for the three types of LTM:

1. When I picked up my new guitar in the music store, I found that I could still play the basic chords, even though I had not played them in years. That is a long-term **procedural memory**—memory for skills and other procedures. Memories of how to ride a bicycle, to cook, or to kiss are procedural memories.

   procedural memory Memory for motor movements and skills.

2. Although I did not stop to think about it, I also obviously remembered what a guitar was. I knew what it was when I saw it, knew what it was used for, and so on. In other words, I had not forgotten the **semantic memory** of the meaning of guitar. Semantic memory is memory for meaning. When you remember what a father is, what pudding is, and what the phrase "peace of mind" means, you are recalling meaning from long-term semantic memory.

   semantic memory (se-man'tik) Memory for meaning without reference to the time and place of learning.

3. Until my memory was jogged by finding the old photograph, however, it had been years since I had remembered when and where I had gotten my first guitar. **Episodic memory** is the kind of LTM that stores information about experiences that took place at specific times and in specific places.

   episodic memory (epĭ-sodik) Memory for specific experiences that can be defined in terms of time and space.

The LTM mechanisms are apparently able to store procedural and semantic memories quite effectively, but LTM handles episodic information much less well. I immediately knew what a guitar was (semantic) and how to play it (procedural), but it took a photograph to recall the time and place of getting my first guitar (episodic). A great deal of research has been done to show the greater ability of LTM to store semantic than episodic memories. A clever study of the memorization of sentences by J. D. S. Sachs (1967) clearly illustrates this point. The experimenter had research participants listen to passages containing a number of different sentences. After intervals of different lengths, she asked the individuals to listen to more sentences and tell her whether they were exactly the same as one of the sentences in the passage. Some of the test sentences were the same, but some were changed either in physical form or in meaning. For example, an original sentence in the passage such as "Jenny chased Melissa" might be changed to "Melissa was chased by Jenny" (change in physical structure but not meaning) or to "Melissa chased Jenny" (change in both physical structure and meaning). Sachs found that the participants could tell quite well if a sentence had been changed in either way, as long as the test interval was within the span of STM (about 30 seconds). However, at longer intervals, they were accurate only in detecting changes in meaning. Apparently, the meaning of the sentences (semantic memory) was held in LTM, whereas details about their physical structure (episodic memory) were forgotten when they were lost from STM.

In spite of these apparent differences, some psychologists group semantic memory and episodic memory together under the heading **declarative memory** (see figure 8.4 on p. 236). Semantic and episodic memories are quite different, but they are alike in an important way as well: they are easily described (declared) in words. For example, I would have no difficulty telling you what a guitar is. This is in contrast to *procedural memory,* which can be accessed only through performance—as in when I play a song on my guitar (Squire, 1987). It is difficult, if not impossible, to describe verbally how to play a song on the guitar without playing it. This distinction between procedural and declarative memories will be important to our discussion of amnesia later in the chapter.

declarative memory Semantic and episodic memory.

Figure 8.4

Semantic and episodic memory are sometimes grouped together under the term *declarative memory* because both kinds of memory can be easily described (declared) in words. In contrast, procedural memories are difficult to describe in words because they involve such skills as playing the guitar, which can be seen only when the task is performed.

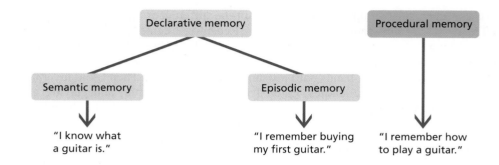

Declarative memory

Procedural memory

Semantic memory

Episodic memory

"I know what a guitar is."

"I remember buying my first guitar."

"I remember how to play a guitar."

Like a library, LTM organizes information to facilitate retrieval.

Organization in Long-Term Memory. We noted earlier that it's possible to make more efficient use of the limited capacity of STM by organizing information into larger chunks (Miller, 1956). Organization of information is also important for LTM, but it's probably not related to a need to save capacity, because LTM has essentially unlimited capacity. Rather, organization helps to facilitate the retrieval of information from the vast amount stored in LTM. The retrieval task in LTM is vastly different from that in STM: Instead of 7 ± 2 items that can be easily searched, LTM stores such an extensive amount of information that it almost certainly must be *organized* in some fashion. For instance, it's sometimes inconvenient that the 60-odd books in my office are not organized on my bookshelves, but I can still find what I am looking for by searching long enough. It would be impossible, however, to find the same book in the university library if the books were as unorganized and randomly placed on the shelves as mine. Like LTM, the library needs an organized way of storing and retrieving a huge amount of information.

Evidence for the organization of LTM has been available for some time. When research participants memorize new lists of items that could be categorized, they tend to recall them in related groups. For example, Weston Bousfield (1953) asked individuals to memorize a list of 60 words that could be conceptually grouped into four categories: animals, vegetables, names, and professions (*muskrat, blacksmith, panther, baker, wildcat, Howard, Jason, printer,* and so on). Even though the words were presented in random order, participants recalled them in categorical groupings significantly more often than would be expected by chance. Apparently, the words were stored in LTM according to organized categories.

In addition, there is clear evidence that recall from LTM is better when we impose more organization on the information that is stored there. Gordon Bower's Stanford University research group (Bower & Clark, 1969) asked participants to memorize 12 lists of 10 words, such as the following list:

boy	rag
boat	wheel
dog	hat
wagon	house
ghost	milk

Half of the individuals were given the usual instructions to memorize the lists of words in any order, but the others were asked to make up stories containing all of the words in the list—to organize them into a single story. For example, the previous list could be memorized as "The boy with the hat pulled his dog and his boat in his wagon with the crooked wheel. He saw a rag hanging on a house that he thought was a ghost. It scared him so much that he spilled his milk." The group that organized the words into stories recalled an amazing 90% of the words, whereas the other group recalled only 15%!

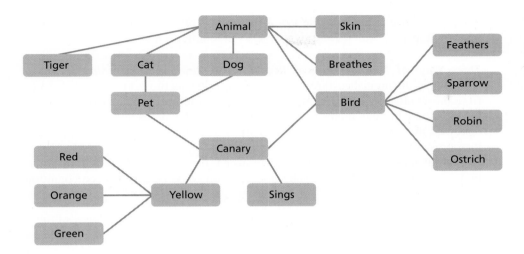

Figure 8.5

An example of the associative links that are hypothesized to exist among bits of information stored in long-term memory in the spreading activation theory.

The organization of memory in LTM has been characterized as an *associative network* by some theorists (Ellis & Hunt, 1993; Raaijmakers & Shiffrin, 1992). According to this view, memories are associated, or linked together, through experience. Your experience forms links between that special song and memories of your summer vacation, or between algebra and that unbearable teacher. Researchers have studied the operation of associative networks by asking research participants to answer general knowledge questions. For instance, suppose you were asked to answer the question: "Is a canary a bird?" How do you access your store of information to answer correctly? An influential network model known as the *spreading activation model* (Collins & Loftus, 1975) attempts to explain this process. According to Collins and Loftus, we form links between various concepts and their characteristics based on our experience. When we are asked a question, representations of the concepts or characteristics are activated. As shown in figure 8.5, the question would activate separate memory representations of *canary* and *bird*. The model then assumes that this activation spreads out along previously formed links to other representations. In the case of *canary* and *bird,* which are very closely associated for many people, the lines of activation spreading from these representations meet quickly, and a decision can be made. If representations are not as closely associated, it takes a longer time to respond. If you were asked whether or not a penguin is a bird, your answer would probably be slower than in the canary example.

Experimental support for the spreading activation model can be seen in a classic study (Meyer & Schvaneveldt, 1971). Research participants watched while groups of letters were flashed on a computer screen. Some of the letter groups spelled out real words, but others (such as *plime* and *blop*) just *looked* like words. The participants were asked to respond by hitting a "yes" button when a real word was shown and a "no" button when a made-up "word" was shown. The important part of this study is the time it took them to hit the button each time a real word was shown. The researchers found that the participants' reaction times were much faster for words that had been shown immediately preceded by a related word (*bread-butter*) than by an unrelated word (*nurse-butter*).

What does this mean for the spreading activation model of long-term memory? According to this theory, activation of *bread* would spread along the network to related items, including *butter*. Therefore, *butter* would be partially activated even before the word appeared on the screen, producing a very fast reaction time. Thus, these results support the spreading activation model.

Retrieval of Long-Term Memories. Students are very familiar with the frustration that comes from knowing that they know something but are totally incapable of retrieving it (until, of course, they step outside the exam room!). Research on methods

"Hey, good buddy!"   "Can't kick, big fella."
"How you doin'?"   "What's shakin'?"

recall method A measure of memory based on the ability to retrieve information from long-term memory with few cues.

recognition method A measure of memory based on the ability to select correct information from among the options provided.

relearning method A measure of memory based on the length of time it takes to relearn forgotten material.

of testing retrieval and on the tip-of-the-tongue phenomenon provide us with important insights into the retrieval process in long-term memory.

Three Ways of Testing Retrieval: Recall, Recognition, and Relearning. Psychologists have distinguished three ways of measuring memory retrieval that differ from one another in important ways. In the **recall method,** you are asked to recall information with few, if any, cues: Whom did Barack Obama defeat for the presidency of the United States in 2008? This is a recall method of assessing your memory for that fact.

In the **recognition method,** you are asked to recognize the correct information from among alternatives. The same question could be asked as a recognition question:

In 2008, Barack Obama defeated _____ for the presidency of the United States.

a. George W. Bush   **c.** John Kerry

b. Al Gore   **d.** John McCain

Generally, we can "remember" more when tested by the recognition method rather than the recall method, because recognition tasks provide more cues for retrieving information from long-term memory. Our greater ability to recognize rather than to recall remembered information was demonstrated vividly in a classic experiment on everyday memory to which we can all relate (Bahrick, Bahrick, & Wittlinger, 1975). Two years after graduation from high school, college students were found to be able to *recall* an average of 60% of the names of the students in their class when looking at their photographs. However, when they were shown their yearbook pictures and asked to *recognize* the corresponding names from a list, they could match names correctly 90% of the time.

The **relearning** (or *savings*) **method** is the most sensitive of the three methods of evaluating memory. Even when you can neither recall nor recognize information, you might be able to measure some memory of the information using the relearning method. In this method, you relearn previously memorized information. If the relearning takes less time than the original learning, then the information has been "remembered" in this sense. For instance, at some point in your life, you probably learned how to find the area of a right triangle. You might be unable to remember how to do that now, but you could relearn the method much faster than it took you to learn it the first time. Your enhanced ability to relearn the technique shows that the memory was never completely "lost."

The Tip-of-the-Tongue Phenomenon. We have all had the maddening experience of trying to recall a fact that we can *almost* remember—it's on the "tip of my tongue." Fortunately, there is a lesson in this on the nature of retrieval from LTM. The tip-of-the-tongue phenomenon was investigated by Harvard University psychologists Roger Brown and David McNeil (1966) by giving definitions of uncommon words to college students and asking them to recall the words. For example, they might be read the definition of *sampan* ("a small boat used in shallow water in Asia that is rowed from behind using a single oar"). Often, the students could recall the word *sampan*. Sometimes, though, they could not quite recall the word, and the researchers were able to create the tip-of-the-tongue sensation in these students. When this happened, the students found that they were able to recall some information about the word ("It starts with *s*" or "It sounds like *Siam*") or recall something about

It is easier to retrieve long-term memories using recognition than to try to recall the information.

the thing the word referred to ("It looks a little like a junk"), even when they could not retrieve the word. Then, moments later, the word would pop into memory for some students, proving that it was there all the time but just could not be retrieved for the moment. Studies suggest that about half of the things that we can't remember, but are on the tip of our tongues, are recalled within a minute or so (Schachter, 1999), but you can drive yourself nuts for hours trying to remember the other half!

Serial Learning. Sometimes the order in which we memorize a list is as important as the items in the list. It would be useless to memorize the steps in defusing a bomb if you were not able to remember them in the right order! When psychologists have studied memory for serial lists (lists of words, numbers, and the like that must be recalled in a certain order), a surprisingly consistent finding has emerged. The recall of items in the serial lists is often better for items at the *beginning* and *end* of the list than in the middle. This is called the **serial position effect.** Many explanations have been suggested for this effect (Laming, 2010; Oberauer & Lewandowsky, 2008), but it's perhaps best explained in terms of the differences between short-term and long-term memory. The last items in a list are remembered well because they are still in STM, whereas the first items in a list are remembered well because they can be rehearsed enough times to transfer them firmly into LTM.

Two experiments provide strong support for this explanation. First, Vito Modigliani and Donald Hedges of Simon Fraser University (1987) have shown that better recall for items at the beginning of lists is indeed related to greater opportunities for rehearsal. Second, in an experiment on the serial position effect (Glanzer & Cunitz, 1966), research participants attempted to memorize a list of 15 items. As shown in figure 8.6, the serial position effect was clearly found when the individuals were asked to recall the list immediately after learning it. That is, recall was better for items at both the beginning and the end of the list. But, when the participants were asked to recall the list after a delay of 30 seconds—just beyond the limits of STM—the serial position effect was only half there. Recall was better at the beginning of the list— presumably because those items were rehearsed more and stored in LTM—but not at the end of the list, probably because the participants did not hold the last items in STM that long. The serial position effect shows that we are simultaneously using both STM and LTM in an attempt to soak up and retain as much of what's going on as possible.

It is possible that all information stored in long-term memory is still there but cannot always be retrieved.

serial position effect The finding that immediate recall of items listed in a fixed order is often better for items at the beginning and end of the list than for those in the middle.

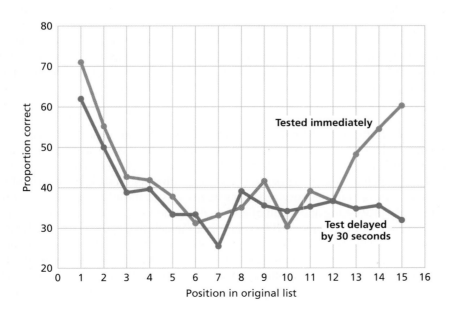

Figure 8.6

When recall of a serial list of 15 items is tested immediately after the presentation of the last item, participants recall the first and last items better than the middle items. But when the test is delayed by 30 seconds, fewer of the last items are recalled, suggesting that at least some of the last items in the list were stored only in short-term memory.

Sources: Data from M. Glanzer and A. R. Cunitz (1966), "Two Storage Mechanisms in Free Recall," *Journal of Verbal Learning and Verbal Behavior,* 5:351–360, 1966 Academic Press; and R. M. Tarpy and R. F. Mayer, © 1978 *Foundations of Learning & Memory,* Scott, Foresman.

Levels of Processing: An Alternative to the Stage Model

levels of processing model An alternative to the stage theory of memory stating that the distinction between short-term and long-term memory is a matter of degree rather than different kinds of memory and is based on how incoming information is processed.

The model suggesting the three separate stages of memory (sensory register, STM, and LTM) has been enormously helpful in making sense of the complex phenomenon of memory. Fergus Craik and Robert Lockhart (1972) have proposed an alternative **levels of processing model,** however, suggesting that the distinction between short-term and long-term memory is a matter of *degree* rather than separate stages. In brief, Craik and Lockhart believe that there is only one memory store beyond the sensory register. The durability of stored information depends on how well it is processed as it is being encoded for memory. Information will be kept only briefly if it's processed at a *shallow* level, but it will be kept much longer if it's processed at a *deeper* level. Thus, the differences that we have just examined between STM and LTM are not, in this view, differences between two different memory systems operating according to different principles. Rather, these differences are the results of different levels of processing during the encoding process. Furthermore, according to Craik and Lockhart, there is a continuum of levels of processing, ranging from very shallow to very deep, rather than just two types of storage (short and long).

What is the difference between deep and shallow processing? One way of putting it is to say that shallow processing involves the encoding of superficial perceptual information, whereas deep processing encodes meaning (Ellis, 1987). Consider the following list of adjectives:

soft
swift
warm
sharp
witty
bright
clean
beautiful

If you were to ask 10 classmates to process this list in a superficial way ("Look at each word for 5 seconds; then circle the adjectives containing the letter i") and ask 10 other acquaintances to process it in a deep way ("Look at each word for 5 seconds; then circle the adjectives that describe you"), which group do you think would remember more of the words if, without warning, you asked them to recall the list 10 minutes later? Craik and Lockhart's levels of processing view correctly predicts that the individuals who processed the words deeply by thinking about their meanings (the second group) will recall more of the words—not because they had stored the words in a different memory (LTM vs. STM) but because information processed more deeply is stored more permanently and is more easily retrieved.

Deep Processing and Survival Value. We have many experiences each day, but we don't remember most of what we experience. What determines which information is remembered later? One theory is that we deeply process some events more than others, which increases the likelihood of remembering them. One version of this theory suggests that our memory processes have evolved through natural selection to favor the deep processing and recall of information relevant to our survival and reproductive fitness (Nairne & others, 2008; Nairne & Pandeirada, 2008, 2010). In the past, if our ancestors were more likely to deeply process information about the location of food and water, edible and inedible plants, the location and characteristics of potential mates, and the identity of threatening rivals, they would be more likely to survive long enough to pass on their genes. Consistent with this theory, several studies have shown that our recall of words related to survival and reproduction is better than our recall of words with less relevance to survival (Nairne & others, 2008; Nairne & Pandeirada, 2008).

Similarly, there is evidence that recall is improved if we deeply process lists of words by thinking about their relevance to our survival needs (Nairne & others, 2008; Nairne & Pandeirada, 2008). In one study, two groups of research participants were given different instructions before being shown the same list of words:

1. *Survival instructions:* "In this task we would like for you to imagine that you are stranded in the grasslands of a foreign land, without any basic survival materials. Over the next few months, you'll need to find steady supplies of food and water and protect yourself from predators. We are going to show you a list of words, and we would like you to rate how relevant each of these words would be for you in this survival situation. Some of the words may be relevant and others may not—it's up to you to decide."

2. *Moving instructions:* "In this task we would like for you to imagine that you are planning to move to a new home in a foreign land, without any basic survival materials. Over the next few months, you'll need to locate and purchase a new home and transport your belongings. We are going to show you a list of words, and we would like you to rate how relevant each of these words would be for you in accomplishing this task. Some of the words may be relevant and others may not—it's up to you to decide."

Later, they were asked to recall as many words from the list (e.g., *stone, meadow, chair*) as they could. Consistent with the theory, participants given the survival instructions recalled more words than those given the moving instructions, possibly because they processed the words more deeply (Nairne & Pandeirada, 2008).

Elaboration and Deep Processing. For most of us, getting a good grade on psychology tests is not clearly related to our survival and reproductive fitness. If you don't recall everything that you are supposed to have memorized about memory, you probably won't starve or perish at the hands of your predators. Good grades help us get good jobs, and economic success is one factor in attracting desirable mates for many people, but that link may not be clear to you as you study for tests. If our brains are tuned by evolution to deeply process earthy and sex survival-related information, how can we remember the drier material in college textbooks? Fortunately, you can deeply process any kind of information by *elaborating* it.

Elaboration, in this sense, means creating more associations between the new memory and existing memories through deep processing (Ellis, 1987; Ellis & Hunt, 1993). We have already seen that the associative network model views these links as vital to your ability to use stored information. Therefore, deeply processing the information in this paragraph by linking the new information to your existing memories will improve your memory of the paragraph and your ability to use the information later. In contrast, simply going through the motions of rereading this paragraph several times without really thinking about it is a much less successful study technique. What is also interesting about this view of deep processing is that even superficial perceptual information can be richly elaborated, such as by relating a new telephone number to existing memories about the person you are calling.

Many studies suggest that one of the best ways to promote the elaboration of new memories to improve their later recall is to relate the new information to *your self* (Symons & Johnson, 1997). Because your perceptions of yourself are well elaborated and accessible in memory, linking new information to yourself is an excellent way to improve memory through deep processing (Symons & Johnson, 1997).

elaboration (e-lab″or-rā′shun) The process of creating associations between a new memory and existing memories.

decay theory The theory that forgetting occurs as the memory trace fades over time.

The levels of processing view probably has not replaced the STM/LTM stage model. This is not to say that the levels of processing view of memory is unimportant, however. It has proven to be an important complement to level-of-processing models of memory. It is a useful reminder to us that information learned in a shallow, rote manner will not be around in our memories very long. If you want to retain information for a long time and have the ability to retrieve it easily, you need to take the time and effort to understand and elaborate the information as you learn it.

Review

We can think of human memory as being composed of three different, but related, stages of memory. The sensory register holds a replica of the visual, auditory, or other sensory input for a very brief interval while relevant information is selected for further processing. Short-term memory holds information, generally as acoustic codes, for about a half minute unless it's renewed through rehearsal. The capacity of short-term memory is quite limited unless information is organized into larger chunks. Long-term memory stores information primarily in terms of its meaning, or semantic codes. Its capacity is very large, and memories stored there seem to be permanent. The store of information in LTM is so vast that it must be organized to facilitate retrieval of information. Current theories suggest that the organization is primarily in terms of categories of meaning or associative networks.

The division of memory into a distinct STM and LTM has been questioned by some theorists, however. They suggest, instead, that the duration that information can be held in memory depends on the depth at which it's processed, not the stage of memory in which it's held. Information that is processed deeply—more richly elaborated—during the encoding process is stored more permanently than information that is processed in a shallow way. Memory for information directly relevant to survival and reproductive fitness may have been favored by natural selection.

Check Your Learning

To be sure that you have learned the key points from the preceding section, cover the list of correct answers and try to answer each question. If you give an incorrect answer to any question, return to the page given next to the correct answer to see why your answer was not correct. Remember that these questions cover only some of the important information in this section; it is important that you make up your own questions to check your learning of other facts and concepts.

1. The _____ assumes that we humans have a three-stage memory, which meets our need to store information for different lengths of time.

   a) lateral processing theory of memory   c) psychoanalytic theory of memory

   b) stage theory of memory   d) progression theory of memory

2. The first stage of memory is the _____, which holds an exact image of each sensory experience for a very brief time until it can be fully processed.

   a) short-term memory   c) sensory register

   b) primary store   d) initial memory store

3. The _____ is used to store information temporarily and to think (sometimes termed "working memory").

   a) short-term memory   c) sensory register

   b) long-term memory   d) primary store

Correct Answers: 1. b (p. 230), 2. c (p. 230), 3. a (p. 231), 4. b (p. 234), 5. levels of processing model (p. 240)

Forgetting and Why It Occurs

So far we have talked about remembering and forgetting in terms of the three stages of memory. We have noted that forgetting is different in STM than in LTM, but we have skirted the issue of the causes of forgetting. Why do some memories become lost or irretrievable? What causes forgetting to occur? There are four major theories of forgetting that should be discussed in some detail: *decay theory,* which states that time alone causes memory traces to fade; *interference theory,* which suggests that other memories interfere with remembering; *reconstruction (schema) theory,* which proposes that information in memory becomes distorted when we attempt to recall it; and the *theory of motivated forgetting,* which suggests that we forget information that is unpleasant or threatening.

Decay Theory

According to **decay theory,** memories that are not used fade gradually over time. This theory has been around for a long time and fits our commonsense understanding of forgetting. But it had been discarded by psychologists as being wholly incorrect until recent years. As we will see in a moment, forgetting is more complicated than the mere fading of memory traces and involves factors other than time. The acceptance by most psychologists of some version of the three-stage conception of memory has brought the decay theory back into limited favor, however. It appears that the simple passage of time is a cause of forgetting, both in the sensory register and in STM (White, 2002). It does not appear that decay due to the passage of time is a cause of forgetting in LTM, however. Memory "traces" appear to be "permanent" once they make it into LTM. Forgetting does not seem

Forget the combination? According to the decay theory, forgetting occurs because time passes.

to happen in LTM because of disuse over time but because other factors, particularly *interference*, make memories irretrievable.

Interference Theory

Interference theory is based on strong evidence that forgetting in LTM does not occur because of the passage of time but, rather, because other memories interfere with the retrieval of what you are trying to recall, particularly if the other memories are similar to the one you are trying to remember. Suppose you take an interest in French impressionist painters and you read a book about the painting techniques of Degas, Monet, and Matisse. It would be no great feat to memorize each painter's techniques and keep them straight, but suppose you then learn about the techniques of three more French impressionists, and then three more. Pretty soon, recall becomes difficult, partly because the similar memories interfere with the retrieval of one another. This also happens when you try to remember a lot of telephone numbers, grocery-list items, or math formulas.

The fact that the other memories must be similar to the one you are trying to recall in order to interfere with its retrieval was demonstrated in a classic experiment by Delos Wickens and his associates (1963). They asked one group of research participants to memorize six lists of three-digit combinations (such as 632, 785, 877). As can be seen in figure 8.7, these individuals became progressively worse at recall as they memorized more and more lists. The previously memorized lists interfered with the recall of each new list. By the sixth list, their performance was quite poor. A second group of individuals was asked to memorize five lists of combinations of three letters, and then to memorize a list of three-digit combinations like those used in the first group. As can also be seen in figure 8.7, these participants became progressively less successful at recalling the letter combinations owing to the buildup of interference. But when they memorized the list of digit combinations instead of a sixth list of letters, their memory performance shot up, showing that the letters were too dissimilar to the digits to interfere with their recall. Interference comes primarily from *similar* memories.

In the experiment by Wickens and others (1963), the interference came from memories that were formed *before* learning the last list. The prior memorization of similar material caused interference with the recall of newly learned material. Interference can also come from memories that are formed *after* memorizing the material in question. If the individuals in the Wickens study had tried to recall the first digits they had learned after memorizing five additional lists, they would have found that a great

Figure 8.7

As two groups of participants memorized additional lists of letter combinations (L) or number combinations (N), interference built up from the earlier lists, and memory declined. When one group shifted from memorizing letters to memorizing numbers, their recall improved dramatically. The interference affected only memory for very similar material; the previously learned letters did not affect memory for numbers.

Source: Data from D. D. Wickens, D. G. Born, and C. K. Allen, "Proactive Inhibition Item Similarity in Short Term Memory," in *Journal of Verbal Learning and Verbal Behavior*, 2:440–445, 1963. © 1963 Academic Press.

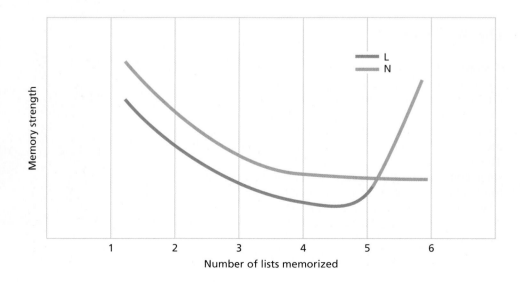

deal of interference had been created. Psychologists refer to the interference built up by prior learning as **proactive interference** and to interference created by later learning as **retroactive interference.**

Suppose you meet two interesting people, Rolf and Kate, on your vacation at the beach. Rolf tells you his room number and you listen carefully and commit it to memory. The next day, Kate tells you her room number and you memorize it. Later, you try to go to Kate's room and, oops, you can't remember the number. You are the victim of *proactive interference.* The recall of Kate's number was blocked by interference from the memorization of the number that *preceded* it. But if you had tried to recall Rolf's number rather than Kate's, you might not have been able to remember it owing to *retroactive interference.* The prefix *retro* means "going back." Hence, in retroactive interference, the second memorization interferes with recall of what was memorized *before* it.

Proactive Interference

Rolf's number **8136**

Kate's number **6213**

Try to recall Kate's number **8136**

Retroactive Interference

8136 Rolf's number

6213 Kate's number

8136 Try to recall Rolf's number

Today, interference is viewed as an important cause of forgetting (Wixted, 2004), but it appears to operate in different ways for different kinds of memory. Up to this point, we have talked about interference as a cause of forgetting, or retrieval failure, in LTM. Interference is also a cause of forgetting in STM, but it may operate in a different way to disrupt memory. Whereas interference appears to confuse the process of retrieval in LTM, interfering memories seem to disrupt STM either by overloading its capacity or by weakening or completely knocking an item out of storage (Klatzky, 1980). If you look up the telephone number 689-2354 and someone says, "Maybe it's 698-5423," before you can dial, you may experience interference in STM. In LTM, interference appears to play much less of a role in disrupting semantic memory than in disrupting episodic memory. Tulving (1972) reminds us that, in a memory experiment, it is a very different matter to forget that the list we were supposed to memorize included the word *frog* (an episodic memory) than to forget what a frog is (a semantic memory).

Reconstruction (Schema) Theory

First presented in 1932 by Sir Fredric Bartlett, the theory that is known as **reconstruction theory,** or *schema theory,* suggests that information stored in LTM is not forgotten in the usual sense but sometimes is recalled in a distorted, incorrect manner (Schachter, 1999). *Schemas* are associative networks consisting of beliefs, knowledge, and expectations. Our recollection of information in long-term memory often becomes distorted, because we recall it in ways that are more consistent with our schemas. For

proactive interference (pro-aktiv) Interference created by memories from prior learning.

retroactive interference (ret´rō-ak´tiv) Interference created by memories from later learning.

reconstruction (schema) theory The theory that information stored in LTM sometimes changes over time to become more consistent with our beliefs, knowledge, and expectations.

example, imagine that you hear a story about a guy named Max, whom you believe is a rotten person. The story is favorable to him on most points but contains some negative information about him. The next day, when you tell this story to a friend, you will tend to recall the negative points about him and minimize the positive points. Because your schema for Max is negative you may unknowingly add a few fictional details that embellish the negative parts of the story or "explain away" the positive things that were said about him. Would you trust someone who doesn't like you to recall accurately a story about you?

The distortion of recollections to fit our schema was demonstrated in a classic experiment (Carmichael, Hogan, & Walter, 1932). Researchers showed the participants ambiguous line drawings, as shown in the middle column (labeled stimulus figures) of figure 8.8. The participants were given verbal labels, telling them what

Figure 8.8

Individuals were shown the list of stimulus figures presented in the middle column along with one of the two word lists. As can be seen in the left and right columns, the figures they drew later were reconstructed to fit the labels they had learned for them.

Source: Redrawn from L. Carmichael, H. P. Hogan, and A. A. Walter, "An Experimental Study of the Effect of Language on the Reproduction of Visually Perceived Form" in *Journal of Experimental Psychology, 15*:78–86, 1932.

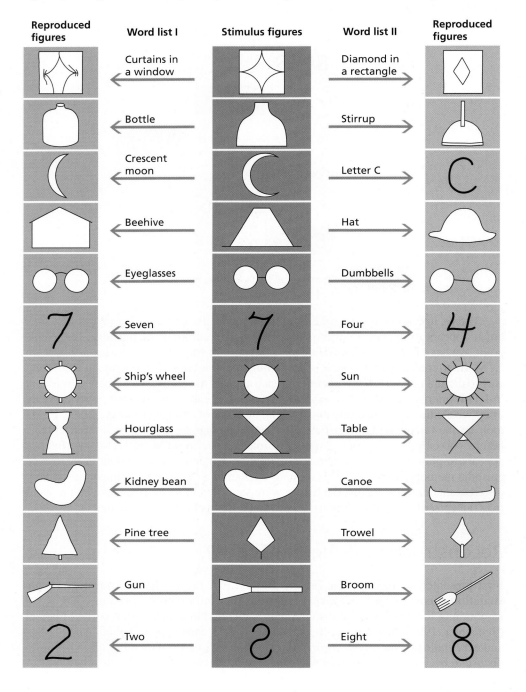

each figure represented, but two groups of individuals were given different labels for each figure (shown in the figure as "word list I" and "word list II"). For example, half of the participants were told that the second figure in figure 8.8 was a bottle, whereas the other half were told that it was a stirrup. Later the participants were asked to draw from memory the figures that they had seen. As predicted by schema theory, the drawings were distorted to fit the labels that they had been given for the ambiguous figures.

The distortion of memories to fit our schemas does not occur gradually over time but occurs during the process of retrieval itself (Reynolds & Flagg, 1983). Indeed the distorting effect of the labels is even more dramatic when research participants are given the labels (*bottle, stirrup,* etc.) *just before* they are asked to draw the shapes (Hanawalt & Demarest, 1939; Ranken, 1963).

Over the past 25 years, however, reconstruction theory has become an important focus for memory researchers. Recent versions of reconstruction theory are based on the distinction between episodic and semantic memory. The theory is that some information in LTM becomes distorted because LTM stores *meaning* better than episodic details. When we retrieve information from LTM, we are likely to remember the gist—the general idea—of the event, but we may unknowingly distort some details, or even invent details to be consistent with the general idea of the memory (Brainerd & others, 2003; Schachter, 1999).

This version of reconstruction theory has been tested in a clever experiment (Johnson, Bransford, & Solomon, 1973). Research participants listened to passages such as these:

> It was late at night when the phone rang and a voice gave a frantic cry. The spy threw the secret document into the fireplace just 30 seconds before it would have been too late

> Later, the participants were asked if they had heard the following sentence.

> The spy burned the secret document 30 seconds before it would have been too late.

Note that this is not a sentence that they had previously heard; the original sentence said nothing about actually burning the document (there might not have been a fire in the fireplace). Most participants, however, said that they had heard the second sentence. According to Bransford and colleagues, the meaning of the sentence, which strongly implies that the document was burned, was retrieved from LTM, but the details were distorted to fit the gist of the story.

Let's look at reconstruction theory from a different angle. Take a moment right now to participate in a memory experiment based on the work of Henry Roediger and Kathleen McDermott (2000). It will take a little mental effort, but it will help you to understand a very important aspect of memory and forgetting.

First read the words in the Study List. Read each word only once (spend 1 or 2 seconds reading each word). Then immediately cover the Study List and follow the instructions below under the heading of Test List.

Study List

bed	doze
rest	slumber
awake	snore
tired	nap
dream	peace
wake	yawn
snooze	drowsy
blanket	

Without looking back, find the words in the Test List that were not in the Study List:

Test List

nap	doze
snore	sleep
jump	peace
snooze	drowsy
blanket	yawn
dream	football
tired	rest
awake	

Which words were not in the Study List? Most college students identify *jump* and *football* as not being in the list that they studied. Did you notice that the word *sleep* was not in the Study List? College students "remember" the word *sleep* as being in the Study List about 50% of the time, even though it was not there. This is impressive, because the words that actually *were* in the Study List are recalled with only about 50% accuracy (Roediger & McDermott, 2000)!

Students who recall the word *sleep* as being in the Study List (perhaps including you) constructed a **false memory**—they remembered something that did not happen. Why did this happen? Recall that reconstruction theory states that information is stored and retrieved from LTM using schemas called *associative networks*. (Looking at figure 8.5 again will jog your memory of this theory if it is not yet easy to retrieve from LTM—or not yet there.) Although the word *sleep* was not in the Study List, it is so strongly *associated* with the words that were actually in the list that memory for the list is often reconstructed to include the word *sleep*. A false memory is the ultimate type of reconstruction error—a memory that is not a distortion of something that happened, but a memory of an event that never happened.

false memory Remembering an event that did not occur or that occurred in a way that was substantially different from the memory of the event.

Thus, forgetting or distorting memories of events is not the only kind of "forgetting." Our memories often play tricks on us both in the sense of incorrectly recalling events that actually occurred and remembering events that did not occur (Geraerts & others, 2008; Roediger & McDermott, 2000). Interestingly, children are less likely to have false memories than adults, perhaps because adults have more complex associative networks built up over many years (Brainerd, Holliday & others, 2008).

We saw in chapter 5 that the human brain actively constructs complete perceptions out of the limited sensory information provided by the senses, such as filling in the "blind spot" in visual perception. Reconstruction theory suggests that we also sometimes construct complete memories from minimal information, or distort memories to make them more consistent. As Bartlett (1932) said, memory is partly an "imaginative reconstruction" of experience that is guided by schemas. Unfortunately, these creatively distorted memories often take on the appearance of "facts." For example, I realized after writing the Prologue to this chapter that I could not have heard Robert Siegel report the news of 9/11, because he is on the air in the afternoon. Perhaps my memory was distorted, because I usually listen to the radio in the afternoon when he is on.

According to the principle of motivated forgetting, we may be more likely to forget details of an unhappy event like a car accident than details of a happy event.

Motivated Forgetting

Many years ago, Sigmund Freud suggested that we forget some information, because it's threatening to us in some way. We will have much more to say about the theory of **motivated forgetting** in chapter 12 on personality. Freud believed that the conscious mind often dealt with unpleasant or dangerous information by pushing it into unconsciousness, by an act of repression.

It now appears, however, that the relationship between emotion and memory is more complex than first assumed by Freud. Emotional arousal does not always lead to poor memory—sometimes it has little effect and sometimes emotional arousal improves memory in some ways.

A series of well-controlled laboratory studies by psychologist Michael Bock (1986; Bock & Klinger, 1986) examined the relationship between emotional arousal and memory. When individuals were shown a list of words and asked to recall them later, they were better able to recall words with positive emotional impact (such as *kiss* and *prize*) than words with negative emotional impact (such as *disease* and *loss*). However, words with neutral emotional impact were recalled least well in Bock's studies. Thus, mild levels of either positive or negative arousal appear to enhance memory.

As we learned in the Prologue to this chapter, memories of extremely emotional events (flashbulb memories) seem to be more vivid and accurate to us but can be less accurate than memories for everyday events (Brainerd, Stein, & others, 2008). Another interesting aspect of the complicated relationship between emotion and memory is that emotion focuses memory on some aspects of the situation and away from others.

motivated forgetting Forgetting that is believed to be based on the upsetting or threatening nature of the information that is forgotten.

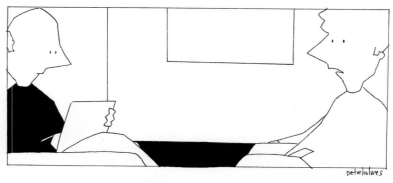

"I think I accidentally repressed my good memories."

Human Diversity
Cultural Circumstances and Memory

Does culture influence even basic intellectual skills, such as memory? Some psychologists believe that our cultural circumstances have a powerful impact on many fundamental aspects of intelligence. For example, psychologist Judith Kearins (1986) hypothesized that Australian aboriginal peoples possessed better visual memory skills for objects than white Australian children. She reasoned that excellent visual memory skills had allowed the aboriginal people to thrive in the challenging desert environments in which many of them live.

In Kearins' experiments, aboriginal and white adolescents were given 30 seconds to memorize the location of objects arranged on a rectangular grid. The experimenter then mixed up the objects, and each adolescent was asked to replace them in their original positions. Two of the tasks involved manufactured objects (match-box, ring, eraser) and two involved natural objects (twig, seed pod, feather, bone). The aboriginal adolescents performed significantly better than the white Australians on all of the tasks. The white adolescents performed better when the task material was manufactured objects than they did when the objects were natural, but this distinction did not affect the performance of the aboriginal children.

Kearins found that the aboriginal and white Australian adolescents used different memory strategies to approach the task. The aboriginal adolescents sat very still, were silent, and appeared to concentrate deeply. They were slow and methodical in replacing the objects. Most of the white adolescents, on the other hand, tended to fidget and mutter and replaced the first few objects **Continued on pg. 250**

Australian aboriginal youth perform better on average than white Australian youth on tests of visual memory for objects.

Human Diversity
Cultural Circumstances and Memory

cont'd from pg. 249

Continued from pg. 249 hurriedly. Kearins speculated that the white children were muttering the verbal labels of the objects in an effort to remember them, whereas the aboriginal children were more likely to memorize the arrangement of the objects in visual terms. Perhaps the different cultures emphasized verbal or visual approaches to memorization because of the importance of those skills in each culture.

Think about your own approach to memorization. How would you have approached the memory task in Kearins' experiment? Would you have memorized the placement of the objects in visual terms, or would you have memorized verbal labels for the objects ("The feather in the top-left, then moving clockwise, the stick, the weird-looking bone. . .")? What type of information is most important for you to remember to survive in your ethnic group? What cultural differences have you noticed between your community and other ethnic communities in terms of their approach to intellectual skills? Finally, has your ethnic community influenced your approach to memorization and other intellectual skills—and, if so, how has it done so?

Review

There are four major causes of forgetting, each with different relevance to the three stages of memory. Forgetting in the sensory register seems to occur primarily because of simple decay of the memory over time. Forgetting in short-term memory can be attributed to decay over time but also to interference from other similar information stored in memory. Interference from other memories explains some forgetting in long-term memory, but information also appears to be recalled inaccurately from LTM, because it is distorted to be more consistent with our schemas (beliefs, knowledge, and expectations) about that information (reconstruction errors). In addition to forgetting events from the past, we also sometimes have false memories of events that never occurred. This is thought to be caused by reconstruction errors based on the associative nature of LTM. Recall of information about positive events appears to be better than recall of information about negative events. Therefore, Freud may have been partially correct that some memories may be less accessible because they are associated with negative emotions (motivated forgetting). Overall, however, both positive and negative emotional arousal appear to facilitate memory. Memories of intensely emotional events tend to be particularly vivid but often became distorted over time. Like other important human characteristics, our cultural circumstances influence our memory skills and what and how much we forget.

Check Your Learning

To be sure that you have learned the key points from the preceding section, cover the list of correct answers and try to answer each question. If you give an incorrect answer to any question, return to the page given next to the correct answer to see why your answer was not correct.

1. According to _____ theory, forgetting occurs simply because the _____ memory trace fades as time passes.

    a) decay   c) diminishing

    b) disintegration   d) decline

2. _____ theory states that forgetting occurs because similar memories block the storage or retrieval of information.

    a) Disruption   c) Disturbance

    b) Interference   d) Freudian

3. _____ theory suggests that some long-term memories become so distorted over time that they are unrecognizable.

   a) Reconstruction (Schema)   c) Retrieval

   b) Destruction   d) Distortion

4. Forgetting that occurs because the memory is upsetting or threatening is termed _____.

5. Remembering an event that never happened is called a _____.

There are no right or wrong answers to the following questions. They are presented to help you become an active reader and think critically about what you just read.

1. Suppose you have started a company that manufactures cameras. Design an experiment to see if teaching the same employees to do two different assembly tasks produces proactive interference.

2. Based on your understanding of the four major causes of forgetting, what improvements could you make in your general study habits to improve your test performance?

Correct Answers: 1. a (p. 243), 2. b (p. 244), 3. a (p. 245), 4. motivated forgetting (p. 248–249), 5. false memory (p. 248)

Biological Basis of Memory

A great deal has been learned about memory in recent years through the study of the role of the brain in the storage and retrieval of information (Thompson, 2005). This boom in knowledge not only gives us a better understanding of the brain but also helps us to understand memory.

Synaptic Theories of Memory: Search for the Engram

It's obvious that some physical change must take place in the nervous system when we learn something new (Kandel, 2009). If some physical change did not occur, how would we be able to recall the new learning at a later time? The "something" that remains after learning—the **engram,** as early memory researcher Karl Lashley called it—is the biological basis of memory. Although neuroscientists have searched for the engram for a long time, there is only recently an emerging consensus about the neural processes involved in memory.

A theory stated many years ago by Canadian researcher Donald Hebb (1949) is still considered to provide a generally accurate model of the biological processes responsible for memory (Jeffrey & Reid, 1997; Tsien, 2007). According to Hebb, each experience activates a unique pattern of neurons in the brain. This activity causes structural changes to occur in those neurons near the synaptic gaps that link them. These often long-lasting changes in neurons make firing in the same loop of neurons more likely in the future. To Hebb, these changes in the functioning of synapses in the brain, which he termed **synaptic facilitation,** is the biological basis of memory.

engram (en´gram) The partially understood memory trace in the brain that is the biological basis of memory.

synaptic facilitation The process by which neural activity causes structural changes in the synapses that facilitate more efficient learning and memory.

Aplysia, the sea snail that opened new vistas to understanding the cellular basis of learning and memory.

consolidation (kon sol´ ah day´´ shun) The gradual strengthening of chemical changes in synapses following learning experiences.

Eric Kandel won a Nobel Prize in Medicine and Physiology for his research on the role of changes in neural synapses in memory. In a series of clever experiments conducted on sea snails (*Aplysia*), Kandel and his associates (Dale & Kandel, 1990; Kandel 2009; Kandel & Schwartz, 1982) strongly supported Hebb's synaptic theory. Sea snails were chosen for study of memory for a classically conditioned response because they have very simple nervous systems composed of very large neurons that are easy to study (Castelluci & Kandel, 1976). The sea snails were used to being handled and did not reflexively withdraw their gills and water siphons when touched. During classical conditioning, each snail's siphon was gently touched (CS); then the snail was given a mild electric shock (UCS), which caused reflexive withdrawal of the gill and siphon (UCR). Later, when the snail was touched (CS), the gill and siphon were withdrawn (CR). (See pp. 197–198 if you don't remember what the terms CS, UCS, UCR, and CR mean.)

The change in neurons at the synapses caused by classical conditioning was studied by measuring the amount of neurotransmitter in the neuronal connections involved in the withdrawal of the gills and siphons. After classical conditioning, the amount of neurotransmitter in the synapse increased. Consistent with this finding, drugs that interfere with protein synthesis block the formation of memories through classical conditioning in sea snails (Kandel, Schwartz, & Jessel, 1995). Thus, it seems that Hebb was right. At least for some simple forms of memory, the learned response is "remembered" in changes in neurons at the synapse.

Consolidation. Other evidence suggests that the chemical changes in neurons at the synapses that are the basis for memory are fragile at first. If nothing happens to disrupt the process, however, they grow more permanent over the course of a few minutes or hours. This process is referred to as **consolidation** (Dudai, 2004; Kandel, 2009; Wixted, 2004). Recall from our discussion of sleep in chapter 6 that there is convincing evidence that a period of sleep following learning (e.g., after studying for a test) helps consolidate and protect new memories (Rasch & Born, 2008; Scullin & McDaniel, 2010). This is one reason why overnight study sessions before a test are not efficient.

DNA and Memory. Recently, it has become clear that part of the biological basis of memory involves rapid changes in the expression of genes that influence neurons in the brain. A number of studies have shown that some genes are "turned on" or "turned off" when new memories are formed (Levenson & Sweatt, 2005; Miller & Sweatt, 2007). Experiences do not change our DNA, but as noted in chapter 4, experience can change how DNA is expressed. These changes in DNA expression are now believed to be part of what happens in the brain when a memory is created (Kandel, 2009; Tronson & Taylor, 2007).

Stages of Memory and the Brain

The results of research on the brain's role in memory reveals two ways in which STM and LTM differ: (1) There is extensive evidence that physical changes in neural synapses are involved in LTM but not in STM (Ezell, 1994; Kwon & others, 2001; Milner, Squire, & Kandel, 1998). (2) There is evidence that different brain structures are involved in different ways in the three stages of memory.

I have illustrated the major brain structures involved in the three stages of memory in figure 8.9. This description is an oversimplification, but it gives you an overview of current knowledge of how the brain stores and retrieves information. Consider this example: In 1990, I visited the Rocky Mountains for the first time, and I still

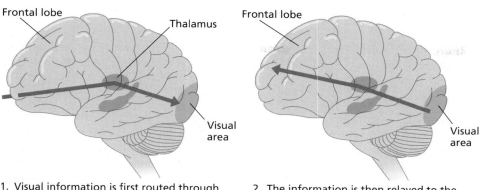

Figure 8.9
Stages of memory and the brain.

1. Visual information is first routed through the thalamus to the visual area of the cerebral cortex. This neural activity is the basis for the sensory register.

2. The information is then relayed to the frontal and parietal lobes, where it can be held in short-term memory.

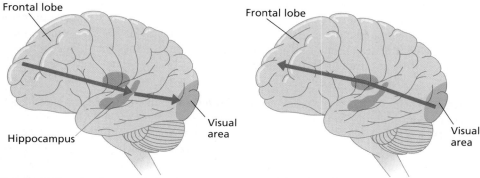

3. Information that is stored in long-term memory is then held in the hippocampus for weeks or months, and then transferred to the area of the cerebral cortex near where it was originally processed for long-term storage.

4. When we recall information from long-term memory, it is routed again to the frontal and parietal lobes, where it is held in short-term (or "working") memory.

have a clear recollection of one part of the trip. As we drove up to the mountain that the Shoshoni people named "Going to the Sun," the amazing visual stimuli from the mountain pass traveled from my eyes to the thalamus, where it was routed to the visual area of the occipital cortex (part 1 of figure 8.9). This neural activity briefly held the trace that we call the sensory register (Harrison & Tong, 2009). If I had closed my eyes at that time, I would have been able to recall the visual image from the sensory register and could have kept the memory active in STM for a while in the frontal and parietal lobes of the cerebral cortex (part 2 of fig. 8.9; D'Esposito, 2000; Goldman-Rakic, 1992; Ranganath, 2010). In this stage of STM, the frontal lobes play a key role in focusing attention away from distracting stimuli (Nee & others, 2008).

Because I can still recall this scene today, it must have been temporarily stored and processed in the hippocampus (Nadel & Jacobs, 1998; Dudai, 2004; Squire, 2009) then transferred to the occipital lobe of the cerebral cortex, where it was first processed (part 3 of figure 8.9). As I think about this memory now in working memory, my frontal lobes play the key role (part 4 of figure 8.9; Hempel, Giesel, & Caraballo, 2004; Schachter, 1999; Smith, 2000).

Thus, it appears that the three stages of memory involve a variety of different brain structures as information is stored and retrieved. Nonetheless, some scholars believe that the neural differences between different kinds of memory have been exaggerated or even misunderstood (Nee & others, 2008).

Amnesia: Disorders of Memory

Major disorders of memory deserve our attention, both because they are important conditions in their own right and because of what they tell us about the biological basis of memory.

retrograde amnesia (ret′rō-grād) A memory disorder characterized by an inability to retrieve old long-term memories, generally for a specific period of time extending back from the beginning of the disorder.

Retrograde Amnesia. In 1997, Diana, Princess of Wales, and two companions were killed in a high-speed automobile accident in Paris. It is still not completely known what happened, partly because the only survivor of the accident suffered a concussion and cannot remember what happened in the minutes before and during the accident. This condition is referred to as **retrograde amnesia.** In retrograde amnesia, there is typically little or no disruption of STM and the individual can create new long-term memories during the period after the amnesia. Usually, the period of memory loss is not for the individual's entire lifetime but extends back in time for a period of minutes or days (Kapur, 1999). Retrograde amnesia can be caused by seizures, brain damage of various sorts, a blow to the head, or highly stressful events. Most researchers believe that retrograde amnesia occurs because the stressful event or insult to the brain disrupts the process of consolidation (McGaugh, 1983), but some believe that the event creates an intense form of retroactive interference that blocks retrieval (Riccio, Millin, & Gisquet-Verrier, 2003).

anterograde amnesia (an′-terō-grād) Disorder of memory characterized by an inability to store and/or retrieve new information in long-term memory.

Anterograde Amnesia. **Anterograde amnesia** is a disorder of memory characterized by an inability to store and retrieve *new* information in LTM. Anterograde amnesia can be understood by reviewing the case history of the famous surgical patient known as "H. M." (Milner, Corkin, & Teuber, 1968). H. M. began suffering major epileptic seizures at the age of 10. The seizures increased in frequency to about once a week by age 27, despite the use of antiseizure medications, leading his neurosurgeon to conclude that surgery must be performed to stop them. The surgery destroyed several brain structures important in memory. The procedure dramatically reduced the incidence of the seizures but left H. M. with severe anterograde amnesia. He retained his above-average intelligence and had nearly normal memory for anything that had been stored in LTM *prior* to the surgery, but he had severe memory deficits for events that occurred *after* the surgery.

H. M.'s STM was normal after the surgery. Like most people, he could retain verbal information in STM for about 15 seconds without rehearsal and could retain it for longer intervals if he was allowed to rehearse it. However, H. M. had serious problems in storing new information in LTM and then retrieving it. He had almost no knowledge of current events, because he forgot the news as soon as it slipped out of STM. He could read the same magazine over and over, because it was "new" to him each time. He had no idea what time of day it was unless he had just looked at a clock; and generally he could not remember that his father had died since H. M.'s operation.

The most dramatic disruption caused by his memory problems, however, was to his social life. Although he could recognize friends, tell you their names, and relate stories about them, he could do so only if he had met them before the surgery. People that H. M. met after the surgery remained, in effect, permanent strangers to him. Each time a person came to his house, he had to learn the person's name again, but he could remember it for no more than 15 seconds or so unless he continued to rehearse it. This effectively meant that H. M. was incapable of forming new social relationships—a poignant but dramatic lesson in how important a basic cognitive function such as memory is to our lives.

H. M.'s inability to make new use of LTM was not total, however. His ability to learn and retain perceptual and motor skills in LTM (procedural memory) remained good, allowing him to learn to perform employable skills under supervision. But he had to be reminded each day what new skills he had learned to perform; if he left his job for a short while, he could not remember what kind of work he did. Similarly, when other individuals with anterograde amnesia have been taught to play a simple tune on the piano, they have been able to play it the next day but are surprised by their ability to do so, because they have no recollection of being taught to play the tune the day before (Hirst, 1982). These cases illustrate the differences between *procedural memory,* on the one hand, and *episodic memory,* on the other hand. Anterograde amnesia usually does not affect the ability to acquire procedural memories but disrupts the ability to form new long-term episodic memories (Squire, Knowlton, & Musen, 1993; Squire, 2009). Thus, the difficulties experienced by the anterograde amnesia patient in using LTM are highly selective; some kinds of long-term memories are affected, whereas others are not.

Drew Barrymore, the co-lead in the movie *50 First Dates,* portrayed a character with a memory disorder similar to that of H. M.

What caused H. M. to have this peculiar and sadly debilitating form of memory disorder? What happened to him during the surgery that damaged his ability to make new use of LTM? The key biological structure that was damaged in H. M.'s surgery, and is often damaged in anterograde amnesia, is the **hippocampus** and related structures (Kandel & Hawkins, 1992; Scoville & Milner, 1957; Squire, 2009). As noted earlier in this chapter, this brain structure is believed to govern the transfer of memories from STM to LTM. The case of H. M. also suggests that the hippocampus plays an important role in episodic memory but not procedural memory (Squire, 1987; Squire, Knowlton, & Musen, 1993). Damage to the hippocampus spares both new and old procedural memories but prevents the formation of new long-term declarative memories.

hippocampus (hip''o-kam'pus) The part of the limbic system that plays a role in emotional arousal and long-term memory.

Both anterograde and retrograde amnesia are experienced by individuals with **Korsakoff's syndrome,** a brain disorder caused by prolonged loss of the vitamin thiamine from the diet of chronic alcoholics. Because of their extreme degree of memory loss, individuals with Korsakoff's syndrome often engage in *confabulation*—when they cannot remember something that is needed to complete a statement, they make it up. Generally, they are not being knowingly dishonest but are engaging in an exaggerated version of normal reconstructive distortion.

Korsakoff's syndrome (Kor-sak'ofs) A disorder involving both anterograde and retrograde amnesia caused by excessive use of alcohol.

Review

The memory trace, or engram, must be stored in the brain in some form after learning; otherwise, recall at a later time would not be possible. Recent evidence supports theories about the specific nature of the engram, suggesting that it's most likely a change at the level of the neural synapse. The changes to the synapse are fragile at first but become more permanent over time through the process of consolidation. The three stages of memory appear to differ at the biological level. Synaptic change appears to be important in LTM, but not STM. In addition, the sensory register, STM, and LTM appear to involve different regions of the brain.

A group of disorders involving memory loss, known as amnesia, is instructive to study. The memory disorder known as retrograde amnesia involves a loss of memory, usually for a specific period of time extending back from the cause of the amnesia, such as a blow to the head, a stressful event, or a seizure. In anterograde amnesia, there is normal STM and a normal ability to recall information that was in LTM prior to the onset of the amnesia. But the individual with anterograde amnesia has an impaired ability to create new long-term memories. This condition is almost always caused by brain damage, generally involving the hippocampus. Chronic alcoholics sometimes experience such extensive brain damage owing to nutritional deficiencies that they develop Korsakoff's syndrome, which is marked by both anterograde and retrograde amnesia.

Check Your Learning

To be sure that you have learned the key points from the preceding section, cover the list of correct answers and try to answer each question. If you give an incorrect answer to any question, return to the page given next to the correct answer to see why your answer was not correct.

1. Scientists study the brain in hopes of discovering the _____, which is the change in the brain that occurs when a memory trace is stored.

2. The neural basis of memory formation may be the process of _____, which can produce long-lasting changes in synapses.

   a) electroconvulsive shock   c) synaptic facilitation

   b) anterograde amnesia   d) operant conditioning

3. A disorder of memory characterized by an inability to store and/or retrieve new information in LTM is _____.

4. The inability to remember a specific period of time before and during a stressful event or blow to the head would be called _____.

Thinking Critically about Psychology

There are no right or wrong answers to the following questions. They are presented to help you become an active reader and think critically about what you just read.

1. What would life be like without your long-term memory? What role do memories play in your life?

2. Why is research on the biological basis of memory important?

Correct Answers: 1. engram (p. 251), **2.** c (p. 251), **3.** anterograde amnesia (p. 254), **4.** retrograde amnesia (p. 254).

Application of Psychology

Eyewitness Testimony and Memory

No evidence is more convincing to a jury than the testimony of an eyewitness to a crime. If you were a juror and you heard an intelligent, credible witness say that she saw Professor Plum murder the victim in the conservatory with the candlestick, wouldn't you be convinced that Plum was the murderer? In many cases, of course, eyewitnesses provide accurate descriptions of crimes. But eyewitness testimony is based on *memories* of the crime, and as we have seen in this chapter, what goes into memory is not always the same as what comes out.

The three men pictured in figure 8.10 were involved in an actual case of double mistaken identity by eyewitnesses to a crime. Lawrence Benson (left) was mistakenly arrested for rape, and George Morales (right) was erroneously arrested for robbery. Both men were arrested because they had been identified in police lineups by eyewitnesses to the crimes. Benson was cleared of the charges, however, when Richard Carbone (center) was arrested and more convincingly implicated in the rapes. After his conviction for rape, he cleared Morales by confessing to the robbery as well (Buckhout, 1974).

Consider another case of mistaken eyewitness testimony (Thomson, 1988). A woman was raped in her home. Later, she was able to give the police a detailed description of the rapist. Her description led to the arrest of Donald Thompson, who perfectly fit her description. Charges against Thompson were quickly dropped, however, as he had an airtight alibi. He was appearing live on television at the time of the rape and could not have committed the rape. In fact, the victim was watching him on television just before the rape occurred. As discussed earlier in this chapter, events that create intense negative emotional arousal—and few experiences could be more intensely negative than being raped—leave memories that are vivid but very subject to distortion. In this traumatic circumstance, the woman recalled a vivid image of the man on the television screen, but her recollection of the event was so distorted that she incorrectly recalled the man on the television as being the rapist. Donald Thompson is a respected psychologist known for his research on memory; ironically, he was discussing memory distortions on television at the time.

It is frightening to think that these mistaken eyewitness identifications could have occurred, but at least these incorrectly accused individuals were not convicted. Now that DNA evidence is routinely used to investigate crimes, a considerable number of imprisoned persons—many on death row—have been found to be innocent on appeals based on DNA evidence. In one study of 40 such individuals, 90% of the cases of mistaken conviction involved erroneous eyewitness testimony (Wells & others, 1998, 2006).

We certainly should not conclude that eyewitness testimony is always incorrect—it's often quite accurate. Still, it is both important and revealing to consider the conditions under which eyewitness testimony is sometimes incorrect. By doing so, psychologists will be able to help law enforcement personnel obtain and use eyewitness testimony in ways that will minimize its inherent flaws (Kassin & others, 2001; Schachter, 1999; Wells & others, 1998, 2006).

Inaccurate Recall Due to Biased Questioning. Several researchers have looked at factors that lead to inaccurate recall of information by eyewitnesses (Zaragoza & Mitchell, 1996). A number of studies suggest that information contained in questions asked of the eyewitness can be a potent source of distortion. When a lawyer or a police investigator asks questions about the crime, the questions may contain cues that influence retrieval to a great extent. Elizabeth Loftus (2004) has conducted several important studies that look at the effect of the questions asked of eyewitnesses. In one study (Loftus & Palmer, 1974), individuals were shown a film of an automobile accident. Later, half of the research participants were asked the first question and half were asked the second question:

1. "About how fast were the cars going when they smashed into each other?"

2. "About how fast were the cars going when they hit each other?"

The speed was estimated to be considerably faster by individuals who were asked the first version of the question ("smashed") than by those asked the second question ("hit"). One week later, all of the participants were asked the same question:

"Did you see any broken glass?"

Although the film showed no broken glass, 32% of the participants who had been asked how fast the cars were going when they "smashed" into each other "remembered" seeing broken glass, compared with only 14% of the participants who were asked the more neutral version of the question.

Figure 8.10

Mistakes in eyewitness testimony led to the arrest of the man on the left and the man on the right for separate crimes. Both were cleared following the conviction of the man in the middle for both crimes.

Application of Psychology cont'd

The reconstruction theory of forgetting that we studied in this chapter would suggest that they remembered seeing broken glass when it was not there because broken glass would be consistent with two cars "smashing" together. Apparently the memory was reconstructed to include broken glass to make it more consistent.

Another researcher interviewed a large number of people who had witnessed a real-life drama. A high school football player went into cardiac arrest and apparently died (but, fortunately, was revived after he was taken from the field). Later, errors in recalling what had happened were common among the spectators. When some of them were intentionally questioned in a way that suggested that there might have been blood on his jersey, more than 25% of the spectators "remembered" seeing it there (Abhold, 1992).

Vicki Smith and Phoebe Ellsworth (1987) of Stanford University conducted a similar experiment, in which college students watched a videotape of a bank robbery in which the robbers were not wearing gloves and did not carry guns. Later, some of the students were asked neutral questions, such as:

"Were they wearing gloves?"

"Did the other guy have a gun?"

The other students were asked misleading questions, such as:

"What kind of gloves were they wearing?"

"What did the other guy's gun look like?"

As in Loftus' original studies, the misleading questions cued inaccurate recall of nonexistent gloves and guns. Interestingly, this happened only when the questioner was thought to be knowledgeable about the crime. Apparently, the memory was reconstructed to include gloves and guns only when the question implied that gloves and guns were present. Thus, the way in which an eyewitness is questioned can greatly affect the accuracy of the information recalled. This means that we must be extremely careful to allow only neutral questions in legal proceedings, particularly if the witness believes the questioner has actual knowledge of the crime—as is often the case with attorneys in trials.

"What did the other guy's gun look like?"

Are you losing your confidence in eyewitness testimony? Consider some more experimental findings. A simulated crime was staged in the early 1970s at California State University at Hayward, in which a student "attacked" a faculty member (Buckhout, 1974). The staged crime was videotaped to have a record of what happened and was then compared with the eyewitness accounts of 141 students who saw the attack. Overall, the witnesses were accurate on an average of only about 25% of the facts that they recalled. By now, you know that eyewitness testimony is frequently inaccurate. But the more interesting part of this experiment is that the eyewitnesses were later asked to pick out the "attacker" from a set of six photos of similar-looking college men. Half of the eyewitnesses were shown the photos under unbiased conditions: all the photos were head shots facing front, and the witnesses were asked if the attacker was pictured. The other half of the eyewitnesses were shown the photos in a biased fashion: the photo of the actual attacker was different in head angle and was tilted slightly in the presentation. In addition, the eyewitnesses were told that one of the photos was the attacker and were asked to pick him out. Under these biased conditions, 50% more of the eyewitnesses chose the attacker. In this case, the presentation was biased against the actual attacker, but the same kind of subtle bias could be unintentionally introduced when an investigator was questioning a witness about a suspect that the investigator falsely believed was guilty. Unfortunately, a number of subtle factors in the questioning of victims and eyewitnesses have been shown to influence their testimony (Bruck & Ceci, 2004; Kassin & others, 1989; Loftus, 2004).

A growing number of studies indicate that children and adolescents are particularly suggestible when they are interviewed by adults. Although their memories are often quite

The way questions about a past event are phrased can affect people's memories of the event. For example, after seeing a football player collapse with heart trouble, over a fourth of spectators recalled seeing blood on his jersey when questioned in a way that suggested he had been bloody.

accurate, they sometimes provide convincing descriptions of events that never happened. This complicates the investigation of allegations of sexual abuse, but when interviews are conducted without the use of leading and suggestive questions (such as telling the child that the suspect "does bad things"), it is possible to obtain accurate information in many cases (Bruck & Ceci, 2004).

Stereotypes and Eyewitness Testimony.
Do our stereotypes and prejudices influence the accuracy of eyewitness testimony? Unfortunately for the cause of justice, there is considerable reason to believe that they do.

Gordon Allport of Harvard University conducted a classic experiment some years ago that demonstrated the extent to which our memories can be distorted by our prejudices (cited in Buckhout, 1974). Allport had individuals look briefly at the picture shown in figure 8.11. Look carefully to see who is holding the straight razor. Now be prepared for a shock when you learn that an amazing 50% of Allport's subjects later recalled that the African American man was holding the razor. Allport's study was conducted many years ago. Does prejudice play less of a role in the United States today? Sadly, no. In a more recent series of studies, participants were shown a list of male names of famous criminals and were asked if they remembered seeing any of them mentioned in the news media. Half of the names were common names in the African American community and half were typical European names. Although none of the names was actually a name of a criminal, the research participants "recognized" significantly more African American names as famous criminals in several studies (Banaji & Bhaskar, 1999).

How do our prejudices influence what we remember? This probably represents distortions of memories to fit our schemas. People who believe that African Americans are more likely to be criminals will be more likely to "recall" information that is consistent with that schema. In the case of eyewitness testimony in the courtroom, this could lead to inaccurate testimony.

Recall of "Repressed Memories" of Sexual and Physical Abuse.
The most compelling eyewitness testimony is from victims themselves. Many court cases have been in the news in which women and men recall that they had been abused as children, but they had not been able to remember the abuse for many years. Some psychologists believe that memories of sexual and physical abuse are often suppressed. Other psychologists who specialize in the study of memory believe that it is difficult to know when so-called repressed memories of abuse are accurate. This issue poses a serious dilemma for psychologists (Frankel, 1995). On the one hand, no psychologist wants to discourage anyone from reporting sexual abuse. The sexual abuse of children is a sadly common occurrence, and any victim with the courage to report it should be supported in every way. On the other hand, there is reason to believe that not every adult who recalls that sexual abuse occurred in childhood is recalling something that actually occurred (Gleaves & others, 2004; Loftus & Davis, 2006; Spanos, 1996).

What is the evidence on the repression of upsetting memories, such as sexual abuse? One study of 590 persons who had been in automobile accidents found that 14% of the accident victims did not remember being in the accident one year earlier (Loftus, 1993, 2006). Similarly, in a study of adult women who reported that they were sexually abused as children, 18% reported that they went through a period in which they lost their memory of the sexual abuse and then recovered it later (Loftus, Polonsky, & Fullilove, 1993). These data suggest that it is possible that some people who experienced sexual abuse as a child may not remember it during parts of their adulthood.

However, it is well known that information that adults recall from childhood can be very inaccurate. The most famous example is that of Jean Piaget's false memory of his childhood "kidnapping." As you will learn in chapter 10, Piaget was a well-known Swiss child psychologist. For a large part of his adult life, he remembered in some detail an incident in which someone attempted to kidnap him when he was a young child. His nanny,

Figure 8.11

Psychologist Gordon Allport showed individuals this picture for a very brief period of time to test the accuracy of their "eyewitness" testimony in a situation in which racial prejudice might influence their perception.

Allport, G.W. & Postman, L. (1947). *The Psychology of Rumor.* Copyright © 1947 Henry Holt & Company. Illustration © Graphic Presentation Services.

however, was able to chase off the would-be kidnapper and save young Jean. Many years later, however, the nanny confessed that she had made up the entire incident to gain attention. She confessed because she felt guilty about the watch she had received as a reward. Piaget concluded that he must have heard a description during early childhood of the kidnapping attempt that never occurred and formed a memory from his visual images of what he imagined had taken place. Later those visual images seemed like a memory of a real event to Piaget.

Was Piaget's experience just a fluke, or can anyone remember experiences in childhood that never happened? Ira Hyman and his colleagues conducted a series of studies that sheds light on this question (Hyman & Billings, 1998; Hyman & Pentland, 1996). The research participants were college students whose parents had agreed to complete a questionnaire about events that had happened in the student's childhood. The researchers told the college students that they had looked over the information about childhood events provided by their parents and asked the college students to attempt to recall and describe several events. Some of the events were ones reported by the parents, but the researchers deceived the participants by asking them to describe some completely fictitious childhood events that their parents confirmed had not happened. For example, students were asked if they remembered running around with other kids at age 5 at a wedding reception, bumping into a table and spilling punch on the parents of the bride. In the first interview, the college students remembered almost 90% of the events that had actually happened in childhood, but almost no one remembered events that had never happened—not at first. Later, however, when the students were tested again, about a fourth of them "remembered" completely fictitious events from their childhood. The students were particularly likely to remember the false event if they were instructed to try to form mental images of the fictitious childhood event that the researchers led them to believe they had forgotten between testing sessions. They had constructed fictional memories of things that had never happened based on the suggestive questions asked by the researchers.

Many psychologists now believe that some memories of traumatic childhood events that some people "discover" in psychotherapy are false memories created by a combination of suggestive questioning and distortions of actual events (Loftus & Davis, 2006; Porter & others, 2000). As we struggle to understand our emotional problems, we could be unintentionally influenced to recall ambiguous moments in our childhoods (such as a bath given by a babysitter or an accidental encounter with a relative who was changing clothes) as an incident of sexual abuse. A well-meaning psychotherapist might say something like: "There is a lot of evidence that people with problems like yours have been sexually abused as children but have repressed the memory. Do you have any trace of a memory from childhood that might indicate that you were abused?" (Loftus, 1997). Could being asked such a question lead a person to unknowingly construct a distorted memory of an ambiguous event—or even recall an event that never happened?

In summarizing many similar research studies, memory researcher Elizabeth Loftus put it this way:

There are hundreds of studies to support a high degree of memory distortion. People have recalled nonexistent broken glass and tape recorders, a clean-shaven man as having a mustache, straight hair as curly, and even something as large and conspicuous as a barn in a bucolic scene that contained no buildings at all. Clearly, then, inaccurate memories of traumatic childhood events are possible as well. Perhaps as psychologists learn more about memory we will be able to play a more effective role in helping others distinguish between real and imagined memories. (Loftus, 1993, p. 530)

Improving the Accuracy of Eyewitness Testimony. Psychologists have conducted more than a thousand experiments since the 1970s to understand why persons who see a crime being committed can be wrong about the perpetrator of the crime (Loftus, 2004; Wells & others, 2000). These psychological studies raised concerns, but little was done to improve the use of eyewitness information in courts until recently. When DNA became accepted as evidence in criminal courts, it led to the overturning of many convictions of innocent persons. These innocent persons—some of whom were on death row awaiting execution—were mostly convicted on the basis of eyewitness testimony. These mistakes created enough concern about the problem of faulty eyewitness testimony to promote attempted solutions. In the late 1990s, the U.S. Department of Justice assembled a group of psychologists, police officers, prosecutors, and defense attorneys to discuss eyewitness testimony. In 1999, their recommendations for obtaining and using eyewitness testimony were released (available at www.ojp.usdoj.gov/nij/pubs-sum/178240.htm). This remarkable document is important for its positive approach to the issue. Whereas most of what had been written about eyewitness testimony focused on its shortcomings, these guidelines help police obtain and use information from eyewitnesses in the most accurate ways possible. Here is a summary of the recommendations:

1. *Establish good rapport—a friendly and comfortable relationship—with the eyewitness before questioning begins.* Eyewitnesses are more likely to relax and invest their time and effort when this is done, especially if they are frightened or distrustful of the police.

2. *Ask open-ended questions, do not lead the witness, and let the eyewitness speak.* Police investigators tend to ask many questions that have a fixed set of answers—yes or no, red or green, and so on. They often interrupt the eyewitness and cut off his or her answer after they have heard what they are seeking. As a result, eyewitnesses rarely have a chance to provide unsolicited information. This information can be critically important because it provides information that the investigator did not even know enough to ask about. It is similarly important for the investigator not to ask leading questions—questions that imply a certain answer is desired by the police. Such questions may influence some eyewitnesses to be "good citizens" and give the officer the information that is desired (whether it is entirely accurate or not) and may lead some hostile eyewitnesses to withhold information.

3. *Keep eyewitnesses from speaking to one another.* It is clear that eyewitnesses change their memories to make them more consistent with other eyewitnesses if they are allowed to speak with one another about what they saw and heard (Wright & others, 2009).

Police lineups are often used to test the ability of an eyewitness to identify a suspect by asking the eyewitness if the person who committed the crime is in the lineup. If the police know that the eyewitness said that the perpetrator had a moustache, having only one person in the lineup with a moustache could make a false identification more likely.

4. *"Fillers" in lineups should generally fit the witness's description of the perpetrator.* Police often bring suspects into the police station, where eyewitnesses behind a one-way mirror can view them in a line of persons. Some of the persons in the lineup are called *fillers,* because they are known to be innocent. Fillers who look very different from the suspect—different height, hair color, or race—increase the likelihood that the eyewitness will identify the suspect (whether the suspect is guilty or not). The same principle applies when eyewitnesses are viewing photographs—mug shots—of potential perpetrators. Defense attorneys often successfully attack photo identifications and lineups as biased if credible fillers were not used.

5. *When conducting lineup identifications of suspects, place only one suspect in each lineup.* If the police have more than one suspect for a crime, they often put all of them in a single lineup. The problem in this common practice can be seen in the simple arithmetic of the process. An eyewitness is more likely to mistakenly identify a suspect if there is more than one

suspect in the lineup. If the eyewitness identified perpetrators at random, and half of the people in the lineup were people suspected of committing the crime, the eyewitness would mistakenly select one of the suspects half the time.

6. *Instructions to eyewitnesses before viewing photos and lineups should not bias their choices.* They should be told that the person who committed the crime may or may not be in the photos or lineup. In addition, they should be told that it is just as important to clear innocent suspects as it is to identify the guilty person. This will reduce false identifications by making it clear to the eyewitness that it is okay to fail to select someone.

7. *Avoid giving feedback to eyewitnesses after they identify a photo or a person in a lineup.* Feedback can increase or decrease the eyewitnesses' confidence in their identification. This is important, because eyewitnesses are commonly asked how confident they are in their judgment during court proceedings.

Summary

Chapter 8 examines how we process information and how we remember or forget that information.

I. Human memory comprises three stages of memory.

  A. The sensory register holds an exact image of each sensory experience for a very brief interval until it can be fully processed.

B. Short-term memory holds information for about half a minute.

  1. Information fades from short-term memory unless it is renewed by rehearsal.

  2. Short-term memory has a limited capacity of 7 ± 2 items.

3. The capacity of STM can be increased by organizing information into larger chunks.

C. Long-term memory stores information primarily in terms of its meaning. Information is organized in LTM primarily in categories of related meanings and according to how frequently events have been associated in our experience.

1. Procedural memory is memory for skills and other procedures.

2. Episodic memory is memory for specific experiences that can be defined in terms of time and space.

3. Semantic memory is memory for meaning.

4. Declarative memory, which includes both episodic and semantic memory, is memory that is described easily in words.

D. The levels of processing model views the distinction between short-term and long-term memory in terms of degree rather than separate stages.

II. There are four major causes of forgetting, each with different relevance to the three stages of memory.

A. Decay theory states that forgetting occurs simply because time passes. This occurs in the sensory register and STM but probably does not occur in LTM.

B. Interference theory states that forgetting occurs when other memories interfere with retrieval. Interference can occur from memories that were formed in prior learning (proactive interference) or from memories that were formed in later learning (retroactive interference).

C. Reconstruction (schema) theory states that memories can be distorted as they are recalled from LTM to make them more consistent with our beliefs, knowledge, and expectations.

D. Freud believed that some unpleasant memories could not be recalled because they were repressed, but memory for events associated with either positive or negative emotional arousal is usually better than for emotionally neutral events, raising questions about Freud's theory. In addition, intense negative emotional arousal can produce vivid snapshot memories that are vivid, but are actually less accurate than memories of everyday events.

III. Much has been learned in recent years about the role of the brain in memory.

A. Synaptic theories view the engram as a change in the pattern or strength of synaptic linkages between neurons.

1. Changes in synapses related to memory are fragile at first but become more permanent in a matter of minutes or hours through the process of consolidation.

2. Rapid changes in the expression of DNA in the brain are part of the biological basis of memory.

B. The frontal lobes play a key role in STM, in encoding memories for long-term storage, and in the retrieval of information from LTM into working memory.

C. The hippocampus is a key structure in the organization and transfer of information between STM and LTM.

D. Amnesia is a major disorder of memory.

1. An inability to consciously retrieve new information in LTM is anterograde amnesia. Anterograde amnesia is caused by damage in the hippocampus and other brain structures.

2. The inability to recall things that happened just before and during stressful events or insults to the brain is known as retrograde amnesia. This is thought to occur because the event disturbs fragile memories that had not yet been consolidated.

chapter **nine**
Cognition, language, and intelligence

Chapter Outline

Prologue

Perhaps the most important reason that the human race has survived for more than 1.5 million years is that we are intelligent. We aren't the strongest, the fastest, or the most ferocious animals, but we are extremely good at solving problems. We survive cold weather by building shelters and making warm clothing; we invent wheels to move heavy objects; and we develop antibiotics when threatened by disease.

But we speak of human intelligence here not to praise it but to marvel at its quirks, foibles, and flaws! If human intelligence is a miracle of evolution, it's an amazingly flawed miracle. When our intellectual processes are examined carefully, it's sometimes amazing that we soft-skinned and slow-moving humans have been able to survive by our wits.

To help us understand the sometimes peculiar properties of human reasoning, Daniel Kahneman and Amos Tversky conducted a fascinating series of experiments. In one study, a group of physicians was presented with the following problem:

> Imagine that the United States is preparing for the outbreak of a rare disease, which is expected to kill 600 people. Two alternative programs to combat the disease have been proposed. Assume that the exact scientific estimates of the consequences of the programs are as follows: If Program A is adopted, 200 people will be saved. If Program B is adopted, there is a 1/3 probability that 600 people will be saved and a 2/3 probability that no people will be saved. Which of the two programs would you favor? (Kahneman & Tversky, 1982, p. 163)

What decision would you have made? The majority of physicians polled by Kahneman and Tversky chose Program A. The guarantee of saving 200 lives made it a better alternative than a long shot of saving all of the lives. But a fascinating thing happened when the researchers presented exactly the same problem in a different way. A second group of physicians was presented the following version of the same problem:

> Program A is adopted, 400 people will die. If Program B is adopted, there is a 1/3 probability that nobody will die and a 2/3 probability that 600 people will die. (pp. 163–164)

Would framing the problem in this different manner have influenced your decision? It did influence the physicians. When the problem was presented in the latter way, the majority chose B. The sure death of 400 people was too difficult to accept when stated this way. There is actually no logical difference between the two ways of asking the question. Stated either way, 200 people would live and 400 people would die if Program A were adopted. But the physicians' decision making was strongly influenced by the way the question was framed. Cold logic is sometimes less important than the way in which the problem is stated.

Perhaps the best way to view human intelligence is to recognize its amazing capacity and importance to our survival and to understand the shortcomings of our cognitive abilities and try to compensate for them. In this chapter, we examine both the advantages and the limitations inherent in human reasoning.

We use the term *cognition* to refer to all the intellectual processes through which we obtain information from the world, change it to meet our needs, store it for later use, and use it to solve problems. Although we focus on cognition in this chapter, it is a broad topic that is important in nearly every chapter in this book. We first mentioned cognition in chapter 1 and discussed important aspects of cognition when we studied perception, learning, and memory. In later chapters, we discuss cognition in many other contexts. But in this chapter we discuss several fundamental aspects of cognition—thinking, language, and intelligence.

Definition of Cognition

Cognition can be defined as the intellectual processes (such as perception, memory, thinking, and language) through which information is obtained, transformed, stored, retrieved, and used. Let's consider each of the three aspects of the definition of cognition:

1. ***Cognition processes information.*** Information is the *stuff* of cognition: the stuff that is obtained, transformed, kept, and used. Much of this information is dealt with in the form of categories or concepts, which is the subject of the next section.

2. ***Cognition is active.*** The information that the world gives us is actively changed, kept, and used in the process of cognition. In cognition, information is

   a. Obtained through the senses;

   b. *Transformed* through the interpretive processes of perception and thinking;

   c. *Stored and retrieved* through the processes of memory;

   d. *Used* in problem solving and language.

3. ***Cognition is useful.*** It serves a purpose. We think because there is something we do not understand. We use language when we need to communicate something to others. We create when we need something that does not exist. Humans use cognition to survive physically and to live in a social world.

cognition The intellectual processes through which information is obtained, transformed, stored, retrieved, and otherwise used.

Cognition involves intellectual processes through which information is obtained, transformed, stored, retrieved, and put to use.

Concepts: The Basic Units of Thinking

Concepts are the basic units of thinking. Concepts are general categories of things, events, and qualities that are linked by a common feature or features, in spite of their differences. About an hour ago, I went for a ride on my new bicycle. My bicycle is a specific object, but *bicycle* in general is a concept. I passed several people on bicycles as I rode—each bicycle was different in some ways from every other one, but I knew that they were all bicycles because they shared a list of common characteristics (two wheels, pedals, and handlebars). I also passed a lot of things that were not bicycles (cars, trucks, and barbecue grills), but being a clever fellow, I knew in a flash that they were not bicycles because they did not have the features shared by all bicycles. Keep in mind that concepts are categories of more than just concrete things—the terms *vacation, romance,* and *generosity* refer to concepts as well.

Adults take for granted that all these objects belong to the concept *bicycle*.

Nearly all productive thinking would be impossible were it not for concepts. Consider the following syllogism:

All human beings are mortal.

I am a human being.

Therefore, I am mortal.

When I reason in that way, I am using the general concepts of *human beings* and *mortality.* Without concepts, we would be able to think only in terms of specific things and acts. Concepts allow us to process information in more general, efficient ways. In this way, concepts are the basic units of logical thinking.

concepts (kon´septs) Categories of things, events, and qualities that are linked together by a common feature or features in spite of their differences.

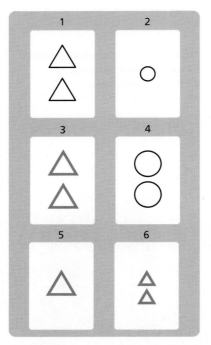

Figure 9.1
Cards like those used in laboratory studies of concept formation.

conjunctive concepts (kon-junk″tiv′) Concepts defined by the simultaneous presence of two or more common characteristics.

disjunctive concepts (dis-junk″tiv′) Concepts defined by the presence of one of two common characteristics or both.

Simple and Complex Concepts

We humans try to categorize things in simple ways and move to more complex concepts only when necessary (Feldman, 2003, Love, Medin, & Gureckis, 2004). Simple concepts are based on a single common feature, such as the concept *red*. If a thing is red, it belongs to the concept *red* regardless of its other characteristics. Red apples, red balls, and red T-shirts are all examples of the concept *red,* in spite of the other ways in which these objects differ. Other concepts are more complex. **Conjunctive concepts** are defined by the simultaneous presence of two or more common characteristics. The concept of *aunt* is an example of a conjunctive concept because it has two simultaneous defining characteristics (female and sibling of one of your parents). To be considered an aunt, a person must have both characteristics. **Disjunctive concepts** are defined by the presence of one common characteristic or another one, *or both*. For example, a person might be considered to be schizophrenic if he persistently has distorted perceptual experiences (such as hearing strange voices that are not there) or persistently holds distorted false beliefs (such as believing he is a king or a CIA agent), *or both*. The concept *schizophrenic person* is a disjunctive concept because it is defined by the presence of either of two characteristics or both of them.

Suppose the six cards in figure 9.1 were presented to you in the order shown (left to right). The odd-numbered cards are members of the concept and the even-numbered cards are not. What is the concept—and is it a simple, conjunctive, or disjunctive concept?[1]

Natural Concepts

Some concepts are easier for humans to learn than others because they are more *natural* (Ashby & Maddox, 2005; Rosch, 1973). This idea is an important extension of the notion discussed in chapter 7 that we are biologically prepared to learn some things more readily than others. Eleanor Rosch (1973) suggests that, by virtue of being born human beings, we are prepared to learn some concepts more easily than others. According to Rosch, natural concepts have two primary characteristics: they are *basic* and *prototypical*. Let's define these terms.

Natural Concepts Are Basic. A *basic concept* is one that has a medium degree of *inclusiveness*. Inclusiveness simply refers to the number of members included in a concept. Three levels of inclusiveness have been distinguished by Rosch:

1. ***Superordinate concepts are very inclusive.*** Therefore, they contain a great many members. For example, *vehicles* is a superordinate concept that contains all of the many cars, boats, planes, wagons, and so on that carry loads (see figure 9.2).

2. ***Basic concepts are of a medium degree of inclusiveness.*** *Cars* is an example of a basic concept because it is less inclusive than the superordinate concept *vehicles;* yet this category still includes many members.

3. ***Subordinate concepts are the least inclusive level of concepts.*** For example, the subordinate concept *sports car* includes far fewer members than the basic concept *cars* or the superordinate concept *vehicles*.

Rosch suggests that basic concepts are more natural and, hence, easier to learn and to use. She offers an observation on the way in which young children learn concepts as evidence. Children generally learn basic concepts, such as *cars,* before they learn

---

[1] The concept illustrated in this example is large triangles, which is a conjunctive concept.

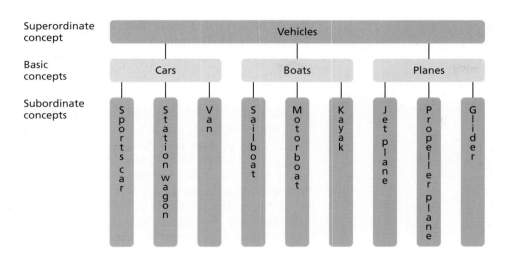

Superordinate concept

Basic concepts

Subordinate concepts

Vehicles

Cars | Boats | Planes

Sports car · Station wagon · Van · Sailboat · Motorboat · Kayak · Jet plane · Propeller plane · Glider

Figure 9.2
Basic concepts, which include neither the most nor the least other concepts under them, are easier to learn than superordinate or subordinate concepts.

superordinate or subordinate concepts, such as *vehicles* or *sports cars*. Why is this so? Why are basic concepts easier to learn than either superordinate or subordinate concepts? Rosch suggests that the explanation lies in several characteristics of basic concepts that "fit" the human intellect very well (Matlin, 1983; Rosch & others, 1976).

1. ***Basic concepts share many attributes.*** For example, the members of the basic concept *screwdriver* are all used to turn screws, have a metal protrusion, have a handle, are usually 4 to 10 inches long, and so on. Members of the superordinate category of *tools* have far fewer characteristics in common. Although the members of the subordinate category of chrome-plated screwdrivers have many common characteristics, only a few of them are not also common to the basic concept of screwdrivers (Jones, 1983).

2. ***Members of basic concepts share similar shapes.*** All screwdrivers (a basic concept) are shaped about the same, but the same cannot be said about all tools (a superordinate concept). The shapes of all chrome-plated screwdrivers (a subordinate concept) are also similar, but they are distinguishable from other screwdrivers on the basis of only one difference—the chrome plating—that has nothing to do with shape.

3. ***Members of basic concepts often share motor movements.*** The motor movements associated with members of basic-level concepts are similar (turning screwdrivers), but the same cannot be said for superordinate concepts (the motor movements for using different kinds of tools are very different). Members of subordinate concepts like chrome-plated screwdrivers also share motor movements, but they are generally the same as or similar to the basic concept to which they belong (see figure 9.3 on p. 268).

4. ***Basic concepts are easily named.*** If you were asked to name a half-dozen objects in your classroom, most of the words that you would use probably would refer to the basic concepts to which the objects belong. When referring to a chrome-plated screwdriver, we tend to say *screwdriver* instead of *tool* or *chrome-plated screwdriver*.

Medium-degree inclusive concepts such as *cars* are called basic concepts; the broader concept of *vehicle* is a superordinate concept; and the narrower concept of *luxury sedan* is a subordinate concept.

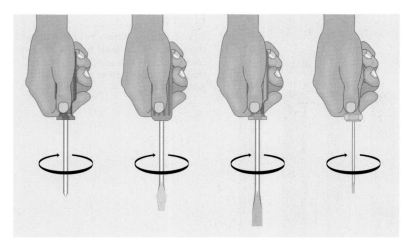

Figure 9.3
Members of the basic concepts like *screwdrivers* often share the same motor movements in spite of other differences.

Rosch believes that these four characteristics of basic concepts make them more "natural"—easier to learn and use in the human information-processing system.

Natural Concepts Are Good Prototypes. The second defining characteristic of natural concepts is that they are good examples, or *prototypes* (Ashby & Maddox, 2005; Rosch, 1975). If you were asked to give the best example, or the prototype, of the superordinate concept *toy,* you might say *doll* or toy *fire truck,* but you would be unlikely to say *sandbox.* Similarly, you might think of *chair* or *sofa* as prototypes of the superordinate concept of *furniture,* but you would not think of *carpet.* Rosch suggests that natural concepts tend to be both basic and good prototypes.

In her research with the Dani tribe of New Guinea, Rosch (1973) has provided intriguing evidence to support her notion that natural concepts are good prototypes. This tribe, which possessed a very limited technology in the 1970s, has only two color concepts in its vocabulary: *mola* for light colors and *mili* for dark colors. Hence, these people were ideal individuals for research on learning new color concepts.

Rosch's Dani research participants were taught to give a label to members of a color category that corresponded to both "pure" primary colors (wavelengths that are near the middle of the range described as red or blue, for example) and intermediate colors (such as bluish-green). Both kinds of color names are basic concepts (with the superordinate concept being *color*), but the Dani learned the names of the primary colors more easily.

In the last chapter, you learned that memory for details of an experience fades more rapidly than memory for the gist—the general idea. Consistent with Rosch's research, memories fade to make them consistent with basic concepts (Pansky & Koriat, 2004). Basic concepts are central to many aspects of cognition.

Review   Concepts are the basic units of thinking. They allow us to reason because they permit us to think in general categories. Concepts are categories that have one or more features in common in spite of differences among members of that concept. All red things belong to the concept of red even though apples, fire trucks, and red balls differ from one another in many ways. Some concepts are defined by a single characteristic, whereas others are defined by multiple characteristics in complex ways. Not all concepts are equally easy to learn; apparently, some concepts are more "natural" than others. These natural concepts are easy to learn because they are of a medium degree of inclusiveness and are good prototypes.

Check Your Learning   To be sure that you have learned the key points from the preceding section, cover the list of correct answers and try to answer each question. If you give an incorrect answer to any question, return to the page given next to the correct answer to see why your answer was not correct. Remember that these questions cover only some of the important information in this section; it is important that you make up your own questions to check your learning of other facts and concepts.

1. _____ are categories of things, events, or qualities that are linked by some common feature or features in spite of their differences.

Check Your
Learning (cont.)

2. The concept of *aunt* is an example of a _____ because it has two simultaneous defining characteristics (female and sibling of one of your parents).

a) disjunctive concept

c) simple concept

b) conjunctive concept

d) natural concept

3. By virtue of being born human beings, we are prepared to learn some concepts more easily than others. These concepts are termed _____.

a) simple concepts

c) natural concepts

b) disjunctive concepts

d) conjunctive concepts

4. Which of the following statements is *not* true?

a) Basic concepts share many attributes.

b) Basic concepts share similar shapes.

c) Basic concepts often share motor movements.

d) Basic concepts are difficult to describe in words.

Thinking Critically about Psychology

There are no right or wrong answers to the following questions. They are presented to help you become an active reader and think critically about what you have just read.

1. What is your favorite kind of thing (think of a concept, not a specific thing)? Try to describe in words the prototype of that concept.

2. Recall what you learned earlier about the role of the cones in color vision. Does this suggest why primary colors are "natural" color concepts?

Correct Answers: 1. Concepts (p. 265), **2. b** (p. 266), **3. c** (p. 266), **4. d** (p. 267)

Thinking and Problem Solving: Using Information to Reach Goals

Without concepts, sophisticated thinking would be impossible. Understanding concepts gives us insight into the *content* of thinking. Let's look now at an important example of the *process* of thinking—the question of how we use concepts to solve specific problems.

What should you do when you think you upset your boss with the hotly political statement that you made at last night's cocktail party? Do you tell her you were just joking? Do you talk to her again tomorrow in the hope that you can agree to disagree without animosity? Do you forget about it on the assumption that she will not let politics interfere with her evaluation of your job performance? Do you wait and see if she acts as if you really did offend her—remember you only *think* you upset her—before you do anything further? What do you do?

Fortunately, no one really expects textbook writers to answer such knotty questions but merely to discuss the general process through which we solve such problems!

Problem solving can be defined as the cognitive process through which information is used to reach a goal that is blocked by some kind of obstacle. Let's examine that process. What cognitive operations do we follow in trying to solve problems and reach our goals?

problem solving The cognitive process through which information is used to reach a goal that is blocked by some obstacle.

There are three steps in the cognitive operations involved in problem solving that apparently must be performed in sequence. First, we have to formulate the problem to decide what kind of problem we face. Second, we need to evaluate the elements of the problem to decide what information and tools we have to work with. Finally, we often need to generate a list of solutions and evaluate them.

Formulating the Problem

Before we can solve a problem, we must be able to define it in clear and specific terms. Sometimes the problem we face is obvious. For example, I want to drive to Key West, but I don't have enough cash to buy gas; what do I do? At other times, the nature of the problem is not at all clear. For example, you may know that the goal of being promoted in your job is not being reached, but you may not know what is preventing you from being promoted. You wonder: Do I need to perform my job better? Do I need to get along with my superiors better? Do I need to be more assertive in requesting a promotion? To solve a problem, *you have to know what the problem is.*

As Michael Posner (1973) pointed out, the key to effective problem solving is often our initial formulation of the problem. Take the problem illustrated in figure 9.4, for example. If you know the radius of the circle, what is the length of line *l*? See if you can figure it out. The trick is in *not* thinking of it as a problem involving the triangle *l, d, x.* Formulating the problem in *that* way blocks our being able to see what solution is called for. As can be seen in figure 9.5, the problem can be easily solved by thinking of *l* as the diagonal of the rectangle with sides *x* and *d.* The radius of the circle, then, is the other diagonal of the rectangle (dashed line in figure 9.5), and because our geometry teachers taught us that the two diagonals of a rectangle are equal, it's easy to determine that line *l* is the same length as the radius.

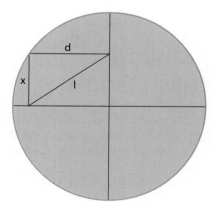

Figure 9.4

If you know the length of the radius of the circle (distance from the center to any side), what is the length of line *l*? This problem shows the importance of formulating a problem in the correct way.

Source: After W. Kohler, *The Task of Gestalt Psychology.*
Copyright 1969 by Princeton University Press.

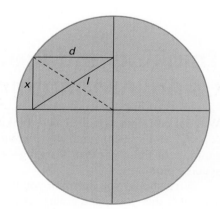

Figure 9.5

The problem given in figure 9.4 can be easily solved if it's viewed in the right way. Its solution requires you to think of line *l* as one of two diagonals of a rectangle rather than as part of a triangle. Line *l* is equal to the other diagonal (dotted line), which is the radius of the circle.

Source: After W. Kohler, *The Task of Gestalt Psychology.*
Copyright 1969 by Princeton University Press.

Understanding and Organizing the Elements of the Problem

After formulating the problem, we must make an inventory of the elements of the problem—the information and other resources available to us. Often, effective problem solving requires that we *flexibly* interpret the meaning and utility of these elements. Many of life's problems require an insightful reorganization of the elements of the problem: when you lock your keys in your car, a bent coat hanger becomes a door opener. One of the ways in which human problem solving is rather predictably fallible, however, is that we are often *not* flexible enough in evaluating the elements in problems. Consider the following situation. Karl Duncker (1945) has provided a problem for you to solve. See in figure 9.6 that you are given three candles, some thumbtacks, and a box of matches. Your problem is to put one of the candles on the wall in such a way that it will not drip wax on the floor or table when burning. Check out figure 9.7 on p. 272 when you have come up with an answer.

The limitations most of us experience in evaluating the elements of problems is that we get stuck in "mental ruts," or, in psychological terms, we get stuck in mental sets. The term **mental set** refers to a habitual way of approaching or perceiving a problem. Because problems often require a novel or flexible use of their elements, a habitual way of looking at the elements of a problem can interfere with finding a solution. If you had trouble with the Duncker candle problem, it was probably because you—like most people—thought of the box in the habitual way; the box is not immediately thought of as part of the solution because it is merely seen as an incidental item that holds the matches.

Generating and Evaluating Alternative Solutions

Very often a problem has more than one solution. Our task then is to generate a list of possible solutions, evaluate each one by attempting to foresee what effects or consequences it would produce, choose the best solution, and then develop an effective way of implementing it.

We use two general types of cognitive strategies to solve problems, algorithmic and heuristic. **Algorithms** are systematic cognitive strategies that (if followed) virtually guarantee a correct solution. Computers generally use algorithms, because they can quickly consider the many alternatives required by complex algorithms. In contrast, **heuristic reasoning** is based on strategies that increase the probability of finding a correct solution but do not guarantee it. Indeed, heuristic reasoning often leads to poor solutions.

Cognitive theorists believe that we use heuristic shortcuts in our reasoning because our capacity to keep information in working memory and process it logically is limited (Chun & Kruglanski, 2006; Hogarth & Karelaia, 2007). The concept of heuristic reasoning is derived partially from research that attempts to simulate human intelligence using computers. Efforts to program computers to play the game of chess, for example, were originally frustrated by the enormous number of possible solutions that would have to be considered before making each move. To avoid such extensive algorithmic programs, heuristic programs were written. For example, the program is written to maximize protection of the queen or to control the center of the board. Moves that meet these goals are executed, but the long-range negative consequences of each move are not always considered.

Heuristic reasoning is very efficient but is subject to error. We need to understand the flaws inherent in heuristic reasoning because we solve problems heuristically far more often than algorithmically (Evans & Thompson, 2004). Many graduate programs

Figure 9.6
A Duncker candle problem. How can you mount the candle on the wall so that it will not drip wax on the table or floor when it's burning? See figure 9.7 for a good solution.

mental set A habitual way of approaching or perceiving a problem.

algorithms (al´go-rith´mz) Systematic patterns of reasoning that guarantee finding a correct solution to a problem.

heuristic reasoning Way of thinking based on strategies that increase the probability of finding a correct solution but do not guarantee it.

In solving a problem, we perceive and formulate the problem; we evaluate the elements; and we generate a list of possible solutions.

Computer programs have been written to mimic human heuristic reasoning in playing chess—but human experts can often beat them.

representativeness heuristic The strategy of making judgments about the unknown on the assumption that it is similar to what we know.

in business administration devote a great deal of time to helping future managers avoid such heuristic decision making. For example, we tend to make judgments about the unknown on the assumption that it is similar to what we know (Tversky & Kahneman, 1974). This strategy is known as the **representativeness heuristic.** For example, if I describe "Lou" as shy and withdrawn, neat and tidy, and passionate about detail, what job would you guess he holds? Did an occupation come to mind—like librarian or some other occupation that you associate with those characteristics? We tend to make judgments in such situations on the basis of the similarity of the person to (our stereotypes about) most people with the same characteristics (Chun & Kruglanski, 2006). In other words, we play the odds and make decisions based on what is typically true (Hahn & Oaksford, 2007). Reasoning on the basis of similarity is valid to some extent—people in different occupations do tend to differ in personality characteristics *on the average*—but it can lead to false conclusions. Many librarians and accountants don't have these characteristics and most people with personalities like Lou's are not librarians or accountants.

Emotional Factors in Decision Making

We think of problem solving as solely a cognitive process, but it is often not based in cold, hard logic. Our emotions play important roles in our problem solving, as well (Blanchard-Fields, 2007; Blanchette & Richards, 2004). For example, suppose you are a stock broker. One morning, your boss gives you a pep talk on the opportunities to earn money for your clients, citing several examples of fortunes made. On another morning, your boss gives a sincere talk on your obligation to protect the hard-earned savings of your clients, providing examples of investors whose retirement nest eggs were wiped out. Would your investment decisions be different on those two days? Studies have shown that brief talks that change our moods can influence risk-taking behavior (Vikas & Ross, 1998). Consider the following experiment: College students were first asked to view either a sad film clip about the death of a boy's mentor or a neutral film about tropical fish. The experimenters asked the students to complete a scale of their current emotions and found that the students who had seen the sad film felt, as expected, much sadder than those who had seen the neutral scene about fish. Then the students were given a high-quality highlighter set and asked to select the price for which they would sell it back to the experimenter—anywhere from 50 cents to $14. Students who had seen the neutral film set an average price of $4.50 for the highlighter set. Students who had seen the sad film set a price of only $3.20—perhaps because they valued the highlighter set less during their brief sad mood. As the authors put it, a film that tugged at the students' heart strings influenced a decision that affected their purse strings (Lerner, Small, & Lowenstein, 2004). Emotions trumped logic in their selection of a fair price.

In other situations, emotional and cognitive factors work together to determine our perceptions of risk (Naqvi & others, 2006). Do you feel safer driving in an automobile or flying on a commercial airplane? If you are like most people, the flight feels riskier than the drive to the airport, but statistically speaking, you are *much* safer in the air. The website of the U.S. National Transportation Safety Board reported that U.S. commercial airlines carried 629 million passengers in 2000, with only 92 fatalities. These statistics are similar to those for other years, indicating that each time you

Figure 9.7

One solution to the Duncker candle problem. The candle problem requires a new perception of the function of the box in which the matches came. Tacked to the wall, the box becomes a candle holder.

fly on a U.S. commercial aircraft your chances of arriving without a fatal accident are better than 10 million to 1. This means that if you were to fly from one city to another on U.S. commercial aircraft once every day, on the average, you would have to fly for 29,348 years before being involved in a fatal accident! According to the National Safety Council (1998), air travel is many times safer than automobile travel—1 out of every 5,000 automobiles in the United States is involved in a fatal accident every year.

Why do many of us misjudge the safety of air travel? One reason is that airline accidents are given far more publicity than auto accidents because more people die when an aircraft crashes. Another likely reason is that images of falling from the sky into a flaming crash have a great deal of emotional impact on our thinking. The idea of an automobile crash is just less frightening to most people, even if airline crashes are far less common.

So how important is it that our emotions lead us to misjudge risks? After terrorists aligned with Osama bin Laden intentionally crashed three passenger jets in 2001, many people decided to make trips by automobile instead of by plane. As a result, the number of deaths from auto accidents increased by 317 in the U.S. during the months following September 11 (Gigerenzer, 2004).

In the Prologue of this chapter, we found that physicians were more likely to adopt a medical strategy that would save 200 out of 600 people than a medical procedure that would result in 400 deaths out of 600 people (Kahneman & Tversky, 1982). Although there was no logical difference between the benefits of the two strategies, the emotional pull of the strategy that was framed as saving lives was stronger than the strategy that was framed in terms of deaths. Emotion can have dramatic effects on the decision making of even highly intelligent persons.

Creative Problem Solving: Convergent and Divergent Thinking

Creativity is highly valued in our culture but is a difficult concept to define. No specific scientific definition has been widely accepted among researchers, and a wide gulf exists between the ways in which scientists define **creativity** and the way it's thought of by those in the arts. We can define creativity in general terms, however, as the ability to produce "products" (such as plays, solutions to social problems, poems, sources of energy, symphonies) that are both novel and valued by others (useful, aesthetically beautiful, informative, and so on).

creativity The ability to make human products and ideas (such as symphonies or solutions to social problems) that are both novel and valued by others.

We typically view creativity as an individual ability or attribute, similar to intelligence. What, then, determines whether a particular individual is creative? Guilford's (1950, 1967) concepts of convergent and divergent thinking provide an excellent framework for understanding creativity. **Convergent thinking** is logical, factual, conventional, and focused on a problem until a solution is found. When you are asked to solve an algebra problem, you use your convergent thinking skills to provide the answer. If this type of thinking sounds familiar, it should. Most formal education emphasizes the teaching and assessment of convergent thinking. Students are encouraged to discover the "right" answers. In contrast, **divergent thinking** is loosely organized, only partially directed, and unconventional. Unlike convergent thinking, divergent thinking produces answers that must be evaluated subjectively. If we were asked to list many possible uses for a brick, it is likely that some of our answers would be unique and the "correctness" of these answers would be unclear. In this example, individuals who list the most novel uses for common objects, whether they are "sensible" uses or not, are considered to be the most divergent thinkers. Divergent thinkers, in other words, more easily break out of mental sets that limit our thinking. In our culture, people who are good divergent thinkers tend to be thought of as creative (Butcher, 1968).

convergent thinking Thinking that is logical and conventional and that focuses on a problem.

divergent thinking Thinking that is loosely organized, only partially directed, and unconventional.

An individual's creativity might also be a result of intelligence. Most of the individuals that we think of as being highly creative are also highly intelligent (Kuncel,

Architects need to use divergent thinking when creating the design and convergent thinking to be sure the building is structurally sound.

Hezlett, & Ones, 2004). However, most researchers in the area of creativity believe that creative thinking is to some extent separate from general intelligence. Raaheim and Kaufmann (1972) provide evidence that people who successfully solve novel problems are different from unsuccessful problem solvers in the amount of effort they make rather than their basic intelligence. Successful problem solvers attempt more solutions to the problem before giving up. In her classic studies of creativity, Anne Roe (1946, 1953) found that a group of creative scientists and artists shared only one common characteristic—the willingness to work very hard. It is possible to be highly creative without being highly intelligent, and vice versa, especially if you love your craft enough to work hard at it.

Regardless of individual ability, how does the creative process occur? Many years ago, Wallas (1926) suggested that creative problem solving typically proceeds in four steps. The first step, *preparation,* includes initial attempts to formulate the problem, recall relevant facts, and think about possible solutions. The second step, *incubation,* is a period of rest. Wallas used the term *incubation* to compare the creative solution to an egg that needed to be incubated for a while before it is "hatched." People trying to solve difficult problems that require creative solutions generally feel the need to set the problem aside for a while after the initial preparation period. Wallas believed that the creative solution needed this time to "incubate." A substantial body of research shows that devoting time to both preparation and incubation improves creative problem solving (Helie & Sun, 2010; Sio & Omerod, 2009). The third step, called *illumination,* refers to a sudden insight pertaining to the solution. The final step, *verification,* involves the necessary but sometimes anticlimactic step of testing the solution.

A creative solution to important human problems does not always emerge in this way, but many anecdotes in history show how difficult problems have been creatively solved in a burst of insight following periods of preparation and incubation (Siegler, 2000). For example, the creative problem-solving abilities of the ancient Greek scientist Archimedes were challenged by his king. The king was suspicious that his beautiful new crown was not truly made of solid gold but was actually made of a thin layer of gold plate over wood or some other inexpensive substance. Archimedes was asked by the king to determine if the crown was solid gold. This would not ordinarily be a difficult problem, as Archimedes could easily cut through the crown or melt it and examine its contents, but the king loved the crown and instructed Archimedes not to harm it. After much initial thought (preparation), Archimedes gave up on the problem for a while (incubation) and took a bath. While floating in the bath he achieved illumination. He realized that he could solve his problem by placing the crown in water and measuring the amount of water it displaced (how much water rose in the container). Because he knew how much water was displaced by gold and less dense substances such as wood, he easily could determine the gold content of the crown without scratching it (only giving it a nice bath). Archimedes was so thrilled by the moment of insight that he reputedly ran through the town, shouting, "Eureka!"— Greek for "I found it!"

Human Diversity
Cultural Influences on Inferential Reasoning

Why is one fish swimming ahead of the others in the photograph on p. 275? I am asking you to engage in the cognitive process of inferential reasoning—to reach a conclusion that goes beyond the information presented by using the information that you have and what you know about fish and other creatures. Is the **Continued on pg. 275**

Continued from pg. 274 fish in front leading the other fish, or is the fish in front being chased by the other fish? Which do you think is happening in the picture?

Do you think your culture played a role in your thinking about this question? Although people from different cultures are far more alike than they are different, psychological research has revealed some important ways in which people raised in different cultures think differently. Using pictures of fish like this one, Morris and Peng (1994) found that Chinese participants were more likely than North American participants to infer that the fish in front was being chased by the group. Morris and Peng suggested that this tendency may reflect the greater influence of groups on individual behavior in collectivist cultures such as China. In contrast, individualistic North Americans are more likely to think of individuals—even individual fish—acting alone to take the lead. That is, Americans tend to see the lone fish as the "leader of the pack."

This kind of research has also been used to study bicultural persons. Some people are raised in two cultures at the same time. For example, because Hong Kong was a British colony for 100 years, many residents were raised in a culture containing many western and east Asian elements. Similarly, many young people who migrate from China to the United States have had the Chinese culture instilled in them, but they are influenced by their adopted American culture as well. Psychologists such as Ying-yi Hong of the Hong Kong University of Science and Technology (Hong & others, 2000) believe that bicultural individuals switch back and forth between their two cultural mind-sets as they move between Chinese and western cultures. For example, an immigrant to the United States might think and act in ways that fit the American culture at work, but shift to a more Chinese way of thinking at home with her husband and parents. Hong and colleagues examined this possibility by randomly dividing bicultural research participants into three groups and "priming" them to orient to either Chinese or western culture. One group was shown pictures that are representative of the United States (such as the U.S. Capitol building). The second group was shown pictures that evoke Chinese culture (such as the Great Wall of China). The third group was shown abstract geometric figures that represent neither culture. Later, in a part of the experiment that the participants thought was unrelated, they were shown the picture of the fish. The bicultural individuals who were primed to think in terms of Chinese culture were more likely to see the lone fish as being chased by the others than were the bicultural individuals who were primed to think of American culture (they were more likely to see the lone fish as the leader). Individuals who were not primed to think of either culture (those shown the geometric figures) were in between in their inferential reasoning.

Consider another example of cultural differences in thinking. Which two objects in figure 9.8 go together? In problems like this, North Americans tend to group the bird and the snake because they are both animals. People from several other cultures, including the Kpelle people of Africa and the Chinese, group the **Continued on pg. 276**

Continued on pg. 276

Is the fish on the left leading the other fish, or being chased by them? People from different cultures tend to give different answers.

Figure 9.8
Which two objects go together? People from different cultures tend to give different answers.

Human Diversity
Cultural Influences on Inferential Reasoning
cont'd from pg. 275

Continued from pg. 275 bird and the tree because birds live in trees (Ji, Zhang, & Nisbett, 2004; Sternberg, 2004). In these cultures, relations among objects is more important than classifications based on the characteristics of the objects.

Much remains to be learned about the influence of culture on cognition, but these studies suggest that culture can significantly influence thinking. What do these studies suggest we must do to improve relations among the many cultures of the world? How can we best communicate with someone who thinks a little differently than we do? How should they communicate with us?

Review

Problem solving is the process of using information to reach a goal that has been blocked by some obstacle. We use cognitive operations to solve problems. Key steps in this process are the initial formulation of the problem, the understanding of the elements of the problem (the information and resources available for problem solving), and the generation and evaluation of alternative strategies. Problem solving can fail at any of these levels. We can be unsuccessful because we define the problem incorrectly, because we reason heuristically, because we get stuck in mental sets in perceiving the elements of the problem, or because we fail to fully evaluate the consequences of alternative solutions. In some cases, emotional factors influence logical problem solving. Creative problem solving requires the ability to think in flexible and unusual ways (divergent thinking), but the most useful creative solutions are ones that have also been thought out logically (convergent thinking). Fortunately, some intelligent people excel in both divergent and convergent thinking. Although we tend to think of reasoning as universal, culture influences our reasoning.

Check Your Learning

To be sure that you have learned the key points from the preceding section, cover the list of correct answers and try to answer each question. If you give an incorrect answer to any question, return to the page given next to the correct answer to see why your answer was not correct.

1. _____ can be defined as the cognitive process through which information is used to reach a goal that is blocked by some kind of obstacle.

   a) Concept formation
   b) Problem solving
   c) Inductive reasoning
   d) Natural logic

2. The limitation most of us experience in evaluating the elements of problems is that we get stuck in "mental ruts," or _____, which refers to a habitual way of approaching or perceiving a problem.

   a) sets
   b) gemütlichkeits
   c) algorithms
   d) divergent thinking patterns

3. _____ an efficient cognitive strategy that does not guarantee finding a correct solution and often leads to incorrect solutions.

   a) Algorithms are
   b) Problem-solving strategies are
   c) Concepts are
   d) Heuristic reasoning is

4. _____ thinking is unconventional, loosely organized, and only partially directed.

   a) Algorithmic
   b) Semantic
   c) Divergent
   d) Convergent

There are no right or wrong answers to the following questions. They are presented to help you become an active reader and think critically about what you have just read.

Thinking Critically about Psychology

1. Could a computer be programmed to solve complex problems as a human does? What kinds of programs would be needed?

2. In solving problems, do you consider yourself to be more a convergent thinker or a divergent thinker? How does this affect the way you formulate and solve problems?

Correct Answers: 1. b (p. 269), **2. a** (p. 271), **3. d** (p. 271), **4. c** (p. 273)

Language: Symbolic Communication

Language is one of the most significant cognitive achievements of the human species. Without language, human beings and human civilization would be a pale shadow of what they are (Corballis, 2004). **Language** is a symbolic code used in communication. Without an efficient means of communication, it would not be possible to coordinate the efforts of many people in a division of labor, to regulate their behavior for the common good through laws, or to amass the wisdom learned through experience by previous generations and pass it on through education. And perhaps the most keenly felt loss of all is that psychology textbooks could be neither written nor read!

Semantics: The Meaning of What Is Said

The function of language is to say something to someone. The "something" is the meaning (the **semantic content**) that is communicated through language. Suppose you want to communicate to your child that *the bananas are on the top shelf.* That idea must be translated into the language code and expressed to your child, who must receive and comprehend it by translating it back into the same idea. Thus, meaningful ideas are sent from person to person via the system of symbols that we call language.

The fact that *semantic content* and language codes are not the same thing can easily be seen in a number of ways. For example, it is possible to express the same meaning in more than one way. *The bananas are on the top shelf* and *it's on the top shelf that the bananas are located* are physically very different patterns of sounds, but they express exactly the same meaning. Furthermore, it would be possible to express the same proposition in Chinese, Latin, French, or sign language. This distinction was made by linguist Noam Chomsky (1957), who called the superficial spoken or written structure of a statement its **surface structure** and the underlying structure that holds the statement's meaning its **deep structure.**

Generative Property of Language: Elements and Rules

Human language is a highly *efficient* system. It's particularly efficient in accomplishing so much while putting so little demand on our memories. Stop for a second and think about the sheer magnitude of language. Consider how many different things

language A symbolic code used in communication.

semantic content The meaning in symbols, such as language.

surface structure The superficial spoken or written structure of a statement.

deep structure The underlying structure of a statement that holds its meaning.

you have said in your lifetime. If we could accurately estimate the number, it would be staggering. Now let's imagine that human language were not an efficient system. Imagine that we had to learn and remember a different utterance for everything we wanted to say. Although it would be theoretically possible to store that many utterances in long-term memory, we would have to spend every waking hour of our lives doing nothing but memorizing utterances. Obviously, we do not spend anywhere near that amount of time learning language. More important, humans do not speak using a fixed stock of utterances. We could get by in a crude and uninteresting way if we talked like that, but fortunately we do not. Every day you say utterances that no one has ever said before.

If we do not memorize our utterances, where do they come from? We make them up as we go along. In more precise terms, we "generate" language from a set of elements and a set of rules for combining them into speech. When we say that language is **generative,** we mean that an infinite set of utterances can be made using a finite set of elements and rules (Chomsky, 1957). What are these elements and rules?

generative (jen´e-ra´´tiv) The ability to create an infinite set of utterances using a finite set of elements and rules.

Phonemes. One way of looking at the elements of language is to consider its individual sounds. **Phonemes** are the smallest units of sound in a language. In English, everything we say, and everything that we will ever say, is made up of only 44 phonemes (there are more phonemes than letters of the alphabet in English, because some letter combinations such as *ch* and *th* stand for separate phonemes). Different languages have different numbers of phonemes, but the principle is the same in every language: Every utterance is generated from a surprisingly small number of sounds.

phonemes (fō´nēm) The smallest units of sound in a language.

Morphemes. When most people think about the individual building blocks of language, they have in mind something like morphemes. The **morphemes** are the smallest units of meaning in a language. Morphemes are closely related to but are not the same as words. Some morphemes stand alone as words. *Word, stand,* and *fast* are each single freestanding morphemes. Other morphemes can exist only if they are bound to other morphemes. Examples are the morpheme for past tense in push*ed,* the plural morpheme in car*s,* and the prefix morpheme *anti* meaning "against" in the word *antibiotic.* The average person knows thousands of morphemes but can speak an infinite number of utterances using a finite set of morphemes and rules for combining them.

morphemes (mor´fēm) The smallest units of meaning in a language.

Syntax. The rules of a language that allow an infinite number of understandable utterances to be generated are called **syntax.** There are rules for the ways in which phonemic sounds can be combined in morphemes and rules for how morphemes can be combined in utterances. For instance, in English, we learn that the suffix *-ed* communicates past tense and that the *-s* suffix denotes a plural. We learn the importance of word order. For example, we wouldn't say "this an interesting class is." These rules of syntax are the heart of generative language, for without them, only a finite number of things could be said with the finite set of morphemes. These rules allow us to make new sentences that will immediately and effortlessly be understood by all speakers who speak normally in the same language.

It is interesting to consider, however, the differences between rules of syntax and the *prescriptive rules* of grammar that are usually taught by authorities, such as parents and teachers. Everyone who speaks a language in a way that can be understood by others knows the syntax of that language, but not everyone uses "proper" grammar. Winston Churchill, an undisputed master of the English language, provided a humorous example of the artificiality of prescriptive rules when he wrote the awkward but

syntax (sin´taks) The grammatical rules of a language.

grammatically correct "this is the kind of language up with which I will not put." It is also interesting to note that few cultures emphasize prescriptive rules of syntax as much as Western European cultures. Other cultures believe that speaking in an understandable way is all that matters.

Language and Thought: The Whorfian Hypothesis

Language and thinking are closely related phenomena. Although we often think in visual images, sounds, and images of movements—and some thought may involve no conscious images at all—much of our thinking takes place in the form of silent conversations with ourselves. If this is true, does language exert any influence on our thinking? If so, it is possible that people who speak different languages might think somewhat differently (Maass & others, 2006).

This hypothesis was stated by Benjamin Whorf (1956) and is known as the *Whorfian* hypothesis, or **linguistic relativity hypothesis.** Although Whorf was most concerned with the impact of different languages on the thinking of people from different cultures, his concrete examples of how this might happen generally concerned the relationship between language and perception. For example, Eskimos have several words for snow and can discriminate among different kinds of snow better than, say, lifelong residents of Florida. Does the fact that Eskimos have more words to describe different kinds of snow—and can notice small differences among different kinds of snow—mean that their additional words improve their perception of snow? Whorf proposed that the presence of these words in the Eskimo vocabulary improved visual perception. It seems at least as plausible to assume that the Eskimos first learned to perceive slight differences among various kinds of snow and *then* invented a vocabulary for talking about them to others.

A test of the Whorfian, or linguistic relativity, hypothesis was performed by an experiment based on the fact that each language contains terms referring to "personality types" that are important in each culture. For example, most of us understand that the "artistic type" is a person who is interested in the arts, imaginative, intense, moody, and unconventional. Each language contains such terms, but not every language has terms to describe the same personality types. For example, the Chinese language does not have a term for the artistic type, but it contains labels for other personality types that are not found in the English language. For example, the "shēn cáng bū lòu" type is recognized by speakers of Chinese to be a very knowledgeable person but one so shy that he or she is reluctant to reveal knowledge and skills unless it is absolutely necessary.

The Whorfian hypothesis suggests that these labels for personality types influence how we think about people. Do they? Fluent speakers of English were compared in their memories for, and reasoning about, hypothetical persons whose personality types were described by the experimenters. Individuals whose language contained a label for the particular personality type described by the experimenter were able to recall the hypothetical people more easily and thought about them in ways that were more consistent with the personality type. For example, English-speaking research participants recalled the characteristics of the hypothetical person described as artistic more often and reasoned about the artistic type in ways that reflected the description of his or her personality more accurately than Chinese-speaking participants did. The opposite was true of the shēn cáng bū lòu type. In this sense, the words in our language do seem to influence our cognition.

Linguistic relativity has led us to reexamine some of our common language usage. Persons concerned about gender equity have lobbied for the substitution of gender-neutral terms for unnecessarily masculine terms, as in the case of changing *chairman*

We learn language by first learning phonemes, then morphemes, followed by syntax.

linguistic relativity hypothesis
The idea that the structure of a language may influence the way individuals think.

"I understood each and every word you said but not the order in which they appeared."

These people from different cultures have different words to describe water. According to Benjamin Whorf, the vocabulary of a language can influence the way speakers of that language think.

to *chairperson.* If Whorf is correct, using *chairman* might subtly affect the way we think about the capabilities of females to serve in leadership roles. Although some of the changes seem initially odd to some people (*server* instead of *waiter* or *waitress*), they seem to be rapidly taking over common usage.

Animal Languages: Can We Talk to the Animals?

Although humans have the most flexible and symbolic language for communicating propositions, we are not the only species that can communicate. Bees, for example, use a simple but elegant system to communicate messages such as *flowers containing a nectar supply are about 200 meters away on a line that is 20 degrees south of the angle of the sun.* The bee who discovers the nectar tells the other bees about it not through speech or written memos but through a symbolic dance.

If the nectar is within 100 meters of the hive, the bee does a *round dance* (see figure 9.9), first turning a tight circle in one direction and then reversing and circling in the opposite direction. This dance does not communicate the direction of the nectar find, so it sends swarms of bees flying out in all directions within 100 meters of the hive looking for the nectar. If the nectar is 200 to 300 meters from the hive, the "speaker" bee gives better directions to his attentive audience. The bee does a *tail-wagging dance.* This dance is in the form of a tight figure eight. The direction of the nectar is communicated through the angle of the middle part of the dance relative to the sun. The distance is communicated by the rate of turning, the rate of tail wagging, and the sound made by the vibration of the wings. Distances between 100 and 200 meters are communicated through much looser figure-eight patterns in the tail-wagging dance (von Frisch, 1953).

Using these dances, bees are able to communicate rather complex messages very efficiently. Unlike humans, however, they have a limited vocabulary and can communicate only in a way that is firmly limited by inheritance. Human language, in contrast, must be learned through interactions with fluent speakers. In addition, human languages are more flexible. Animal communication can be varied little, whereas humans can generate an infinite number of unique and novel utterances.

These differences between human and animal languages have led some psychologists to assume that only humans can ever acquire a human language, because we alone have the mental abilities needed for a generative language (Lenneberg, 1967). Until recently, this was an assumption that was difficult to challenge. Using the principles of operant conditioning, parrots have been taught to use English surprisingly well (Pepperberg, 2002). A parrot named Alex can name colors, label categories of objects (such as "apples"), and refer to the number of a group of objects. Even more impressive accomplishments have been made with chimpanzees and apes. Because they are less able than parrots to learn to vocalize sounds, however, another mode of communication has been used in these studies.

Beatrix and Allen Gardner (1971) raised a young chimpanzee named Washoe to whom they taught American Sign Language (ASL), a language made up of hand signals used by the deaf. Washoe acquired a limited but useful command of the ASL version of English. She was able to use more than 250 signs and used them in such combinations as GIMME SWEET DRINK.

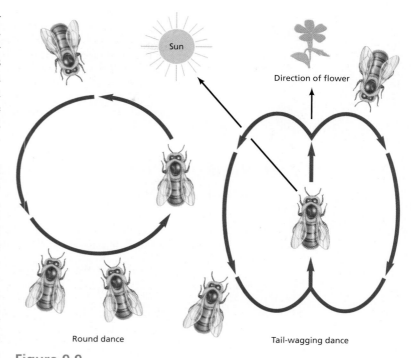

Figure 9.9

The language dances of honeybees. The round dance indicates that nectar is within 100 meters of the hive. The tail-wagging dance points in the direction of the nectar when it's over 200 meters away. Distances between 100 and 200 meters are signaled by a third dance.

Washoe has not been the only ape to learn a human language. Penny Patterson (1977) has taught more than 600 signs to Koko, a gorilla who may be showing even more spontaneous and generative use of language than Washoe. Koko signs THAT KOKO when she sees herself in the mirror; she once called a ring, a sign she had not been taught, a FINGER BRACELET; and she once replied to the question "How are you feeling?" by signing I WAS SAD AND CRIED THIS MORNING.

The linguistic accomplishments of even the most advanced adult chimpanzees and apes is limited compared with that of human 3-year-olds, however. Chimpanzees use language mostly to ask for something (food, tickling games, and so on). They rarely comment on their world or ask questions to gain information (Rumbaugh & Gill, 1976; Slobin, 1979). More important to scientists, their use of signs does not appear to show syntax. For example, Washoe was as likely to request a tickling game by signing ROGER TICKLE as TICKLE ROGER. To a human, these orders of signs have different meanings, but to Washoe they appeared to be interchangeable (Reynolds & Flagg, 1983). This has led some researchers to conclude that chimpanzees have not mastered true human language (Terrace, 1987).

Although it may be technically accurate to conclude that Washoe and other primates have not mastered human syntax, this criticism misses an important point. Washoe clearly learned to communicate with people and other chimpanzees using a form of human language. Even if her grammar was not perfect, some of her statements spoke volumes about the cognitive and emotional lives of our primate next-of-kin (Fouts, 1997).

Review

Language is the efficient symbolic code used in human communication. It utilizes a finite set of sounds, units of meaning, and rules for combining them to convey a limitless set of meanings. The question of whether our language influences our cognition has not been satisfactorily answered, but current evidence suggests that it does in some ways. Although no animals have learned to use human language in the same ways as humans, surprisingly complex two-way conversations can occur between humans and apes who have been taught sign language—we can talk to some of the animals.

Check Your Learning

To be sure that you have learned the key points from the preceding section, cover the list of correct answers and try to answer each question. If you give an incorrect answer to any question, return to the page given next to the correct answer to see why your answer was not correct.

1. While language is the term used to describe the symbolic code used in communication, the meaning of the code is termed _____.

   a) surface structure   c) semantics

   b) heuristics   d) syntax

2. Human language can be referred to as _____ in that an infinite set of utterances can be made using a finite set of elements and rules.

   a) divergent   c) semantic

   b) conceptual   d) generative

3. _____ refers to the rules of a language for the ways in which morphemes can be combined in that language to allow an infinite number of understandable utterances to be generated.

   a) Semantics   c) Phonemics

   b) Syntax   d) Morphemics

4. According to the _____ hypothesis, the vocabulary and structure of a language can influence the way speakers of that language think.

Thinking Critically about Psychology

There are no right or wrong answers to the following questions. They are presented to help you become an active reader and think critically about what you have just read.

1. Does it make sense to you to say that apes are not capable of using language in a human way?

2. The Greek language has three different words for different kinds of love. Would that influence the way Greeks think about and understand love?

Correct Answers: 1. c (p. 277), 2. d (p. 278), 3. b (p. 278), 4. linguistic relativity (or Whorfian) (p. 279)

Intelligence: The Sum Total of Cognition

intelligence (in-tel´i-jens) The cognitive abilities of an individual to learn from experience, to reason well, and to cope with the demands of daily living.

Intelligence refers to the cognitive abilities of an individual to understand complex concepts, learn from experience, to reason well, and to cope effectively with the demands of daily living (Gray & Thompson, 2004). Intelligence has been the subject of intense study since the founding of the science of psychology and there are many different views of it.

Differing Views of Intelligence

Psychologists still do not agree on how many kinds of intellectual ability exist. Other psychologists believe that, instead of trying to answer that question, we should work to identify the basic cognitive processes underlying intelligence.

Intelligence: General or Specific Abilities? In one view, intelligence is a single *general factor* that provides the basis for the more specific abilities that each of us possesses. According to this view, if we are generally intelligent, we are more likely to have strong mechanical, musical, artistic, and other kinds of abilities. This view that a general factor of intelligence underlies each of our more specific abilities was formalized by Charles Spearman (Spearman & Wynn-Jones, 1950), who used the term **g** to refer to the general factor of intelligence. Spearman based his opinion on complex mathematical analyses of intelligence test scores that support, but do not prove, his theory of general intelligence (Gray & Thompson, 2004).

Other psychologists have argued that intelligence is not a single general factor but a collection of many separate specific abilities (van der Maas & others, 2006). They point out that most of us are much better in some cognitive skills than others, rather than being generally good at everything. Louis Thurstone (1938), for example, developed an alternative to tests of general intelligence, called the *Primary Mental Abilities Test,* that measures seven intellectual abilities.

Howard Gardner (2000) also has argued that there are many kinds of intelligence. Gardner became convinced that there are many separate kinds of intelligence partly by studying patients who had suffered brain damage to only some parts of the cerebral cortex. He found that these individuals lost some kinds of intellectual abilities while other kinds of intelligence were left intact. This suggested to him that different types of intelligence are mediated by different parts of the brain. As a result of his investigations, Gardner has suggested that there are *eight independent types of intelligence:*

1. Linguistic (verbal)

2. Logical-mathematical

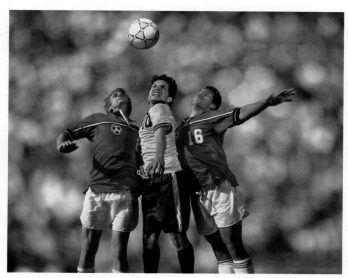

Howard Gardner's definition of intelligence is much broader than the traditional one. He believes great skill in music or sports reflects intelligence as much as great skill in mathematics.

3. Musical

4. Spatial (artistic)

5. Kinesthetic (athletic)

6. Interpersonal (social skills)

7. Intrapersonal (personal adjustment)

8. Naturalistic intelligence (understanding nature)

Gardner's definition of intelligence is much broader than the traditional one, because he believes that skill in music and good emotional adjustment should be said to reflect intelligence just as much as skill in mathematics. Most tests of intelligence focus on just verbal and logical-mathematical areas of intelligence.

Most contemporary psychologists believe that there is truth to both views. That is, it is probably correct that a general factor underlies all intelligence, but people can be strong in one specific area of intelligence and weak in another (Gray & Thompson, 2004; Kuncel, Hezlett, & Ones, 2004).

The Biological Basis of General Intelligence. Recently, a great deal has been written about the nature of g, or general intelligence. Consistent with the idea of general intelligence, it is clear that the same genes influence all the many specific aspects of cognitive intelligence to a considerable degree (Plomin & Spinath, 2004). This means these genes could influence biological characteristics of the nervous system that underlie the general intellectual factor (g) that is the basis for each of these specific mental abilities.

What might the biological nature of g be? One theory is the anatomy and functioning of the frontal lobes is strongly related to g (Gray & Thompson, 2004). A second theory is that persons with high g have a greater ability to form neural connections between axons and dendrites in the brain (Anderson, 2001; Garlick, 2002). That is, when stimulated by the environment, some people—those with high g—are more likely to form new neural connections than are other people. As a result, adults with higher general intelligence have better connected neurons. A greater ability to form neural connections is hypothesized to lead to better general intelligence in two ways:

1. Greater ability to form neural connections means that a person with high g is better able to learn from experience.

2. Greater interconnectedness of the neurons means that the brain can process information more quickly. Persons with higher g have faster reflexes, have faster reaction times, and take less time to make simple judgments (such as which of two lines is shorter). This greater speed of processing is thought to be the primary basis for greater general intelligence. As we will see in the next section, however, the fact that more intelligent people process information more quickly does not mean that they do everything more quickly in cognitive tasks. Sometimes taking our time leads to better problem solving.

Cognitive Components of Intelligent Behavior. A promising way of conceptualizing and studying intelligence has been proposed by psychologist Robert Sternberg (Sternberg, 1979, 1981; Sternberg & Gardner, 1982) and others. This approach suggests that the basic nature of intelligence can be illuminated by applying what we have learned in research on cognition, particularly research carried out using an information-processing model of cognition.

Sternberg has proposed a tentative theory of intelligence that specifies the cognitive steps that a person must use in reasoning and solving some kinds of problems—or in simple terms, the cognitive components of intelligence. For example, consider the following analogy problem (Sternberg, 1979):

LAWYER is to CLIENT as DOCTOR is to?

a. MEDICINE

b. PATIENT

To solve this problem, Sternberg believes that we must go through a number of cognitive steps. Among these steps, the person must:

Robert Sternberg proposes six steps in reasoning. Expert chess players seem to perform the first step, encoding information about the positions of the pieces, more effectively than beginners.

1. *Encode* (mentally represent in the memory system in some usable form) all relevant information about the problem. In this case, the person might encode information related to the term *lawyer* that includes that a lawyer knows the law, represents others before the courts, is paid fees for providing services, and so on. For the term *client,* the information that this is an individual who obtains professional assistance and pays a fee for those services would need to be encoded, and so on for all the attributes of all the terms in the problem.

2. *Infer* the nature of the relationships between the terms in the problem. In this case, it is essential to see that *lawyer* and *client* are related because a lawyer provides a service for a fee and a client obtains a service by paying a fee.

3. *Map* or identify common characteristics in relevant pairs of elements. In this case, the person must see that both lawyers and doctors provide services for fees and that both clients and patients obtain services by paying fees.

4. *Apply* the relationship identified between lawyer and client to the relationship between doctor and patient.

5. *Compare* the alternative answers.

6. *Respond* with an answer—in this case, "patient."

Sternberg suggests that this way of looking at intelligence does more than provide us with a convenient way of describing the steps in intelligent reasoning. It gives us a framework for discovering which components are most important in determining whether one person is "more intelligent" than another. For example, several initial studies have provided a finding that is, at least at first glance, rather surprising (Sternberg, 1979). Better reasoners take *more* time to complete the encoding component than poor reasoners do, but they are *faster* at all of the other stages. Sternberg explains this finding by drawing a parallel to a lending library. A library that invests more time in carefully cataloging books (like the encoding component) will be more than repaid for this investment of time in terms of more rapid access to the books. Such findings hold promise in identifying the key cognitive elements in effective intelligence and may even allow us to improve intelligence in the future by training people to carry out those key components more effectively.

Fluid and Crystallized Intelligence. As we think about intelligence, we must distinguish between *fluid intelligence* and *crystallized intelligence* (Hunt, 1995). **Fluid intelligence** is the ability to process information quickly and devise strategies

fluid intelligence The ability to learn or invent new strategies to deal with new problems.

crystallized intelligence The ability to use previously learned information and skills to solve familiar problems.

for dealing with new kinds of problems. **Crystallized intelligence** is the ability to use previously learned information and skills to solve familiar problems.

It is important to note that the distinction between fluid and crystallized intelligence is not just a logical one. It is well supported by research on how intelligence changes with age. Crystallized intelligence—facts and knowledge—improves throughout the years that adults work (Garlick, 2002). That is one reason most leadership jobs are held by persons over age 40 (Hunt, 1995). In contrast, fluid intelligence—the ability to learn new skills for new problems—declines from middle age on. To some extent, it really is harder to "teach an old dog new tricks," but we old dogs do pretty well with our still-growing crystallized intelligence!

Measuring Intelligence: The IQ Test

Intelligence would be too vague a concept to be of much use to psychologists if it were not for the reasonably accurate and meaningful tests that have been developed to measure it. A measure of intelligence makes it possible to use the concept of intelligence in both research and clinical practice. As noted in chapter 1, the first person to develop a useful measure of intelligence was Alfred Binet. In 1903, he began working on developing a test that he hoped would distinguish intellectually normal from subnormal Parisian schoolchildren. In the United States, Binet's test was refined by Lewis Terman of Stanford University, as the still widely used *Stanford-Binet Intelligence Scale.* Similar tests were also developed by David Wechsler, known as the *Wechsler Intelligence Scale for Children* (4th ed.), or *WISC-IV,* and the *Wechsler Adult Intelligence Scale, Revised,* or *WAIS-R.* Some *WISC-IV* items are oral questions, such as the following:

Subject	*Examples of Items*
Information:	"How many wings does a bird have?"
Similarities:	"In what way are a lion and a tiger alike?"
Arithmetic:	"If two buttons cost $.15, what will be the cost of a dozen buttons?"
Comprehension:	"What is the advantage of keeping money in a bank?"

From *Wechsler Intelligence Scale for Children—Fourth Edition.* Copyright © 1990 by Harcourt Assessment, Inc. Reproduced with permission. All rights reserved. Other *WISC-IV* items ask the child to assemble puzzle parts, to match symbols, and to arrange pictures in an order that tells a logical story.

How is it possible to develop a test that measures intelligence when psychologists cannot decide what intelligence is? Intelligence tests are no more than a small sample of some of the cognitive abilities that constitute intelligence. These tests are considered useful not because we are sure they measure the right things but because they do a fairly good job of *predicting* how people will perform in situations that seem to require intelligence, such as in school or on the job. This state of affairs has led some psychologists to say—only slightly in jest—that intelligence should be defined as whatever intelligence tests measure. We cannot be very confident that intelligence tests are very good at measuring "intelligence," whatever that turns out to be. But intelligence tests are fairly good at picking out those individuals who perform well on tasks that seem to require intelligence.

Construction of Intelligence Tests. We can perhaps better understand the nature of intelligence tests and the meaning of the related term IQ by taking a brief look at how intelligence tests were originally constructed. Binet constructed his test by looking for a large number of items related to cognitive efficiency that differentiated children of various ages. That is, he looked for items that he thought about half the children of one age could answer but that nearly all older children could answer and very few younger children could answer. He did this based on the assumption that intellectual abilities improve with age during childhood.

Once Binet had compiled a list of items, he gave them to a large number of children of different ages to determine exactly how many children at each age level could answer each question. Then he arranged the order of the questions in the test from the least to the most difficult.

In simplified terms, the score obtained on Binet's intelligence test is equal to the number of questions answered correctly, but it's expressed in terms of the age of the children for which that score is the *average*. For example, if a child correctly answers 18 items, and the average number of items answered by children 8 years and 6 months in age is 18, then the score on the test would be expressed as "8 years 6 months." Binet called this score the *mental age*. If your mental age is higher than your actual age (*chronological age*), then you are considered bright because you answered the average number of items for older children. If your mental age is lower than your chronological age, then you are considered below average in intelligence because you could answer only the average number of questions answered by younger children. This is all that an intelligence test is: a measure that compares your performance with the performance of individuals of different ages on items believed to reflect intelligence.

Is a child with a mental age of 9 years 4 months and a chronological age of 7 years 2 months brighter than a child with a chronological age of 8 years 5 months and a mental age of 10 years 3 months? Because it's difficult to compare the mental ages of children of different chronological ages, a more easily used score than the mental age was later developed for intelligence tests. This score is called the **intelligence quotient,** or **IQ.** The intelligence quotient is obtained by dividing the mental age (MA) by the chronological age (CA) so that children of different chronological ages can be directly compared. To remove the decimal point, the result is multiplied by 100. Thus, IQ 5 MA/CA 3 100. For example, if a child's MA is 6 years 6 months and his chronological age is also 6 years 6 months, then his IQ is 100.

IQs that are over 100 indicate that the person is more intelligent than average (the MA is greater than the CA). For example, if a child obtains an MA of 10 years, but her CA is only 8 years, then her IQ is 10/8 $\times$ 100 = 125. Conversely, IQs less than 100 indicate that the individual is less intelligent than average. A child who is 10 years in CA but obtains an MA of only 7 years has an IQ of 7/10 $\times$ 100 = 70.

Actually, Binet's approach to calculating the intelligence quotient from the ratio between the child's mental age and chronological age—called the **ratio IQ**—is no longer used in contemporary intelligence tests. There are several technical reasons that the ratio IQ is no longer used, but the most important reason to understand is that there are some significant limitations to the concept of mental age. For example, a very bright 4-year-old with an IQ of 150 has the mental age of the average 6-year-old but would not handle many situations demanding intellectual ability as well as the 6-year-old. Conversely, a child with low intelligence will often seem less competent than an average younger child with the same mental age.

For these reasons, a new approach to the measurement of intellectual ability, termed the **deviation IQ,** was developed. The deviation IQ is based on an intriguing mathematical property of measurements of many phenomena, including intellectual ability. As shown in figure 9.10 on p. 288, the scores of large numbers of persons on tests of intelligence fall in a **normal distribution.** This means that most people will obtain the average score, or scores that are close to the average, on the test. As scores *deviate* from the average in either direction (either higher or lower than average), the scores become progressively less common. Thus, scores a few points above or below average are common, but scores that are many points above or below average are very uncommon.

Instead of defining an average IQ as one in which the mental age and chronological age are the same (IQ of 100), the average score on the intelligence test (the midpoint of the normal distribution) is assigned an IQ score of 100, and based on

intelligence quotient (IQ) A numerical value of intelligence derived from the results of an intelligence test.

ratio IQ The intelligence quotient based on the ratio between the person's mental age and chronological age.

deviation IQ The intelligence quotient based on the degree of deviation from average of the person's score on an intelligence test.

normal distribution The symmetrical pattern of scores on a scale in which a majority of the scores are clustered near the center and a minority are at either extreme.

Figure 9.10

The normal distribution of scores on a test of intellectual ability.

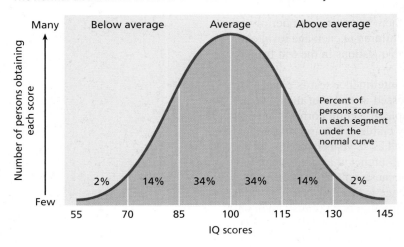

the shape of the curve, scores above the average are assigned IQ scores above 100 and below average scores are assigned IQ scores below 100. The exact IQ score is based on how much the score deviates from the average. Look carefully again at figure 9.10 to see how this works.

Deviation IQ scores work very well for adults. They also work well for children, but children's scores have to be compared with different normal distributions for each age group because their scores increase as children grow older. The same concept of deviation from the midpoint of the normal distribution is also used in many other tests of human characteristics. Scores on the tests of academic achievement that you took in school, some of the tests of specific job skills that you will take when you apply for employment, and some tests of personality are based on the same concept as the deviation IQ.

Characteristics of Good Intelligence Tests. When you measure the size of a window with a yardstick before buying drapes, you don't have to ask how good yardsticks are for measuring length. For the purpose you are using it, yardsticks are good measuring instruments. However, for something as important, yet difficult to define, as intelligence, it makes sense for us to ask how accurate the measuring instrument is. The following are five criteria that an intelligence test must meet before we accept it as an adequate measuring instrument. In chapter 12, in the section on personality tests, you will see how these criteria apply equally to all psychological tests.

standardization Administering a test in the same way to all individuals.

1. **Standardization.** Because intelligence tests are designed to compare the performance of one person with others, the test must be given in the same way to every person. If this were not so, differences in performance might be due to differences in the way the test is administered rather than to true differences in ability. For this reason, properly designed psychological tests contain detailed instructions telling the examiner how to administer the test to each person in the same *standardized* way.

norms Standards (created by the scores of a large group of individuals) used as the basis of comparison for scores on a test.

2. **Norms.** To compare the individual's score with that of others, the developer of the test must give the test to a large sample of people who represent the general population. For example, you could not develop an intelligence test for adults by giving the test only to college students, because they are brighter than the general population. The sample used in evaluating the performance of individuals given the test is called the *normative sample.* It must be large enough to validly represent the general population and must contain approximately the same proportion of each subgroup in the general population to be a valid standard of comparison for anyone taking the test. For example, a normative sample that contained no Hispanic children would not have the same validity when used to evaluate young Hispanics.

objectivity Lack of subjectivity in a test question so that the same score is given regardless of who does the scoring.

3. **Objectivity.** An intelligence test must be constructed so that there is little or no ambiguity as to what constitutes a correct answer to each item. If there is ambiguity, and the scoring is subjective rather than *objective,* then factors other than the individual's performance might influence the scoring, such as the examiner's mood or prejudices.

reliability A test's ability to produce similar scores if the test is administered on different occasions or by different examiners.

4. **Reliability.** To be useful, an intelligence test must be *reliable.* This means that the scores obtained would be approximately the same if administered on

two different occasions or by two different examiners. If the scores change a great deal from one testing to the next, no faith can be put in the scores.

5. **Validity.** Most important, an intelligence scale must be *valid;* that is, it must measure what it's supposed to measure. Validity can be evaluated in a number of different ways, but for intelligence tests, the most important issue is the degree to which the test *predicts* performance on other tasks that most people agree require intelligence. This is referred to as *predictive validity.* For example, the Wechsler and Stanford-Binet intelligence tests are considered valid in part because they are fairly good predictors of performance in school. About 25% of the differences in school performance among a group of high school students can be predicted from IQ scores. Similarly, the Scholastic Aptitude Tests (SATs) predict about 20% of the variation in grades among college students at all levels of socioeconomic status (Sackett & others, 2009). This is not a high level of predictability. As you are well aware, many factors besides intelligence, such as motivation and personality, contribute to school performance. But intelligence test scores are better predictors of school performance than any other measure that psychologists or educators now possess. So in this sense, intelligence tests are valid.

validity The extent to which a test measures what it's supposed to measure.

Tacit Intelligence

We have said that intelligence tests are considered to be useful because they allow psychologists to predict how well individuals will perform in situations that require intelligence. The predictions are not very precise, but they are accurate in extreme cases. That is, children with an IQ of 120 will almost always perform better in school than children with an IQ of 80, but we could not predict with much confidence that children with an IQ of 105 will perform better than children with an IQ of 95. Still, in spite of their lack of precision, intelligence tests are useful predictors.

It is important to understand that general intelligence tests such as the Stanford-Binet and the Wechsler scales are limited in what they predict. They are most useful in predicting success in school and complex occupations. General intelligence tests are not useful in predicting competence in specific areas that are generally not taught in school. For example, if a general intelligence test were given to all the adults who live in your city, the scores would not be very useful in predicting who would be the best at fishing, growing vegetables, maintaining their cars, taking photographs, picking horses at the race track, painting with watercolors, or shopping for food within a budget. Some researchers have referred to these competencies as "everyday intelligence," or tacit intelligence, and have developed tests to measure **tacit intelligence** (Galotti, 1990; Schmidt & Hunter, 1993; Sternberg & Wagner, 1993).

According to Kathleen Galotti (1990) of Carleton College, a useful test of tacit intelligence must assess practical knowledge and skills in getting things done. Sternberg and Wagner (1993) developed a measure of tacit intelligence consisting of scenarios describing work-related situations in particular areas of employment. Persons taking the test are asked to rate the quality of a number of different solutions to the problems. Because different areas of employment—from plumbing to selling insurance—pose different kinds of problems, tests of tacit intelligence that are specific to a given area are most useful in predicting who will perform well in that domain (Sternberg & Wagner, 1993).

tacit intelligence The practical knowledge and skills needed to deal with everyday problems that are usually not taught in school.

Although tacit intelligence is rather distinct from the cognitive competencies measured by general tests of intelligence, there are three ways in which tacit intelligence is related to general intelligence. First, at very low levels of general intelligence, it is rare to find individuals with highly developed tacit intelligence. Second, it is unlikely that persons of limited general intelligence will succeed in highly complex areas of tacit knowledge, such as amateur astronomy. Third, although persons with higher general intelligence are not more likely to have highly developed knowledge and skills in any particular area of everyday functioning, persons with higher general intelligence are more likely to have good practical knowledge across *many* different areas. In one study of a representative sample of U.S. high school students, students were administered a test of practical knowledge in 25 areas that are not taught in most schools (health, fishing, art, mechanical systems, law, and so on). The high school students with the highest general intelligence scores were much more likely to possess high levels of practical knowledge across many of the areas tested (Lubinski & Humphreys, 1997). Some students with lower general intelligence scores had high levels of practical knowledge in one area (for example, fishing or mechanical systems), but few had high levels of practical knowledge in many areas. That is, general intelligence is a better predictor of the breadth of knowledge than the depth of knowledge in any one area. Persons who are highly motivated to learn about a particular practical topic are not greatly limited by their level of general intelligence, unless the topic is very complex or their level of general intelligence is very low. Persons with higher intelligence scores are more likely to master many areas of practical knowledge, however.

Individual Differences in Intelligence: Contributing Factors

Why is one person more intelligent than another person? After many years of research, it is now clear that both our heredity and our experiences combine to determine our level of intelligence (Bouchard, 2004; Petrill & others, 2004). In chapter 4, we described how studies of twins and persons adopted at birth point to clear genetic influences on intelligence. The IQ scores of genetically identical monozygotic (identical) twins are considerably more similar than the scores of dizygotic twins, even though both kinds of twins are reared in essentially the same intellectual environment. Dizygotic twins, who are no more alike genetically than siblings born at different times, are no more similar in IQ than any other siblings. Furthermore, it makes little difference whether monozygotic twins grew up in the same home or were adopted and raised in separate homes. In both cases, their IQs are very similar (Erlenmeyer-Kimling & Jarvik, 1963; Hunt, 1995; Lewontin, 1982).

Adoption studies have similarly indicated that heredity is one of the more important factors determining IQ. A large number of studies have shown that the IQs of adopted children are more similar to the IQs of their biological parents with whom they never lived than those of their adoptive parents who raised them. Taken together, the twin and adoption studies make a strong case that heredity is one of the determinants of IQ.

The intellectual environment in which a child is reared is also an important factor in intelligence, however (Petrill & others, 2004). The exposure that children have to the world of adult intelligence through interactions with their caregivers seems essential to normal intellectual development. Children who have been so severely neglected by their parents as to be deprived of this stimulation show very slow intellectual development but usually develop more rapidly when placed in good foster homes (Clarke & Clarke, 1976). Michael Schiff and Richard Lewontin (1986) studied a group of children of poorly educated mothers who put one of their children up for adoption but raised their other children themselves. The children were adopted shortly after birth by much better educated families. Years later, the IQs of the adopted children averaged 109, whereas those of their nonadopted siblings averaged 95.

Recent evidence suggests that it is possible to intentionally increase intelligence scores by enriching young children's intellectual environments. In a well-designed formal experiment, infants from low-income families were randomly assigned to either

The amount of cognitive stimulation provided to infants is one factor in determining level of intelligence.

environmental enrichment or a control group that received no intervention (Burchinal, & others, 1997). The environmental enrichment program consisted of a free early educational preschool, access to a lending library of educational toys, and home visits from child development experts who taught parents how to provide responsive and stimulating child care at home. The enrichment program produced consistently higher intelligence scores from 2 years of age to 12 years of age. At age 12, 42% of the control group had Wechsler intelligence scores of 85 or below, compared with only 13% of the early enrichment group (Campbell & Ramey, 1994). At age 15, the youths who had received early intellectual enrichment scored higher on measures of reading and mathematics achievement, had failed fewer grades and were less likely to have been assigned to special education classes (Campbell & Ramey, 1995).

The beneficial influences of the environment on intelligence test scores are not limited to early childhood, however. Well-designed studies show that increased amounts of education result in improved scores on tests of both crystallized and fluid intelligence. Both attending more years of schooling and participating in extended year-round educational programs produce increased scores on measures of intellectual ability and academic achievement (Frazier & Morrison, 1998; Williams, 1998).

From a practical perspective, it seems very likely that investments in improving the level of intellectual stimulation of children from low-income families by providing free educational day care and assistance in parenting and by extending schooling throughout childhood and adolescence would pay off in terms of significant improvements in both intellectual ability and school achievement.

The Importance of Intelligence in Modern Society

Intelligence test scores are important because they predict to some extent how well we will do in life. Persons with higher intelligence tend to learn more in school, get better grades, and complete more years of education (Brody, 1997; Hunt, 1995). In addition, more intelligent individuals solve real-life problems better and tend to hold more complex and highly paid jobs (Brody, 1997; de Bruin & others, 2007; Galotti, 2007; Hunt, 1995). The average IQ score of truck drivers is a little under 100, whereas the average IQ of doctors and lawyers is 125 or higher (Hunt, 1995). At the other end of the IQ spectrum, persons with IQs below 85 (about 15% of the population) are very likely to have dropped out of high school, to live below the poverty line, to be unemployed for long periods, to be divorced, to receive aid for dependent children, to have health problems, and to have a criminal record. Indeed, the correlation between IQ and success in education and occupations is about as high as the correlation between people's heights and weights (Hunt, 1995).

Why does intelligence predict how well we will do in our jobs? There appear to be three major reasons:

1. Many occupations are available only to persons with college or graduate degrees, and persons with higher intelligence are more likely to qualify for advanced education (partly because admission tests largely measure intelligence) and are more likely to complete advanced degree programs once they are admitted (Brody, 1997).

2. It takes less time to train persons with higher intelligence to a high level of job knowledge and skill than persons with lower levels of intelligence (Gottfredson, 1997; Hunt, 1995). However, if the job skills are relatively well specified and not complex, one's level of intelligence does not influence job success very much after those skills have been learned (Hunt, 1995).

3. Persons with higher intelligence tend to perform better in complex jobs, particularly if they involve making judgments in changing situations and require

constant updating of job skills (physicians, lawyers, scientists, engineers; and computer programmers, and so on; Gottfredson, 1997). Even in nonprofessional occupations, persons with higher levels of intelligence are more likely to be promoted into more complex jobs than are persons with lower levels of intelligence (Wilk, Desmarais, & Sackett, 1995).

Are People Becoming More Intelligent?

James Flynn (1998, 2003, 2007) of the University of Otago in New Zealand has shown that average scores on intelligence tests have been increasing for several generations. These increases in test scores are known as the "Flynn effect." In many countries around the world, there is strong evidence that intelligence scores have risen dramatically over the past few generations. When tested at the same age using the same test, people born in earlier years answered fewer questions correctly than persons born more recently. Therefore, when the raw scores of persons born in different years are converted to deviation IQ scores using the norms for the group born in the earliest years, persons born more recently have higher average IQs than persons born earlier on the average (Flynn, 1998, 2003; Kanaya, Scullin, & Ceci, 2003).

The rate of increase in scores on tests of general adult intelligence (that measure both fluid and crystallized intelligence) such as the Stanford-Binet and Wechsler intelligence scales is shown in figure 9.11 (Neisser, 1998). These increases are surprisingly large, but data on tests that measure only fluid intelligence show even larger gains of about 20 points per generation (every 30 years; Neisser, 1998; Williams, 1998). The strongest evidence of changes in fluid intelligence comes from the Raven Progressive Matrices Test (Carpenter, Just, & Shell, 1990). In this test, the person is presented with a number of increasingly difficult nonverbal matrix problems to solve, like the simple item in figure 9.12.

The Raven test has been administered to representative samples of young adults each year in some countries over many years, with the best data coming from Holland. James Flynn (1999) asked us to imagine a Dutch woman with a score of 110 at age 25 years on the Raven test who taught teenagers in school from the time she was 25 until she was 55 years old. Her raw score (the number of questions answered correctly) on the Raven test did not change over that part of her life span, but her score's standing relative to her pupils' scores changed dramatically. In 1952, her score on the Raven was higher than those of 75% of her students. By 1967, however, her score was equal to the average score of her students, and by 1982, 75% of her students had higher Raven scores than she! Her raw score did not change over time, but the raw scores of her students increased markedly over time.

Is it really possible that the students of our hypothetical Dutch teacher surpassed her in fluid intelligence to such a great degree over a span of only 30 years? On the average, are we really that much smarter than our parents? Few psychologists doubt that large changes in raw intelligence test scores have occurred since the early 1900s (Hunt, 1995; Neisser, 1998; Nijenhuis & van der Flier, 2007), but we are all frankly shocked by these data. What do they mean? Has each generation really surpassed the previous generation so much in the wide range of competencies and cognitive skills that we call intelligence? In many ways, my grandparents

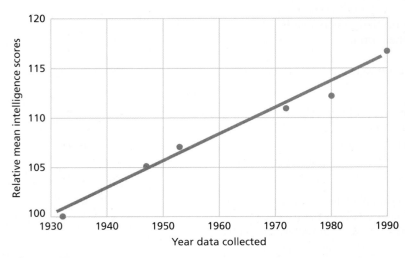

Figure 9.11

Intelligence scores of individuals born in different years (who were tested in different years when they reached the same age) when their scores are converted to intelligence scores based on 1932 norms.

seemed to be as intelligent as my children seem to be. My grandparents were very successful, but they succeeded in a much less complex world than the present world. It is simply not possible to know if they would have not been successful in coping with today's computerized, mathematics-based world.

What is the cause of these increases in scores on intelligence tests? There are at least four plausible explanations for why intelligence may have actually risen over successive generations:

1. Nutrition and health have improved dramatically in many parts of the world. Indeed, in the same countries that show increases in intelligence, the rates of increase in average height, weight, and life expectancy scores have been almost identical to the rate of increase in intelligence scores shown in figure 9.11 (Martorell, 1998). Because nutrition and body size are positively correlated with intelligence (Alaimo, Olson, & Frongillo, 2001; Sigman & Whaley, 1998), it is possible that much of the increase in intelligence scores is due to improvements in nutrition and health. Indeed, in several studies, when families of children in very poor parts of the world have been randomly assigned to an experimental group that received nutritional supplements or to a control group that did not receive supplements, the children who received nutritional supplements were found to have higher intelligence scores (Sigman & Whaley, 1998). Similarly, children with intestinal parasites are robbed of nutrition by the parasites. In economically deprived parts of the world, treating intestinal parasites (at a cost of 15 cents per child) has produced dramatic improvements in school and test performance (Williams, 1998). It seems unlikely that nutritional supplementation beyond the U.S. recommended daily allowances of nutrients improves intellectual or academic growth, however (Martorell, 1998). Vitamins are not "smart pills" for adequately nourished persons. On the other hand, breast-feeding infants is associated with a small increase (2 to 5 IQ points) in the children's IQ scores (Bartels & others, 2009).

2. Increases in levels of education may have produced increases in intelligence test scores. This could work in two ways—indirect effects through the parents of each generation and direct effects on each generation of children. Since the beginning of the 20th century, each successive generation has had better educated parents. Indeed, in the United States, there has been a 10-fold increase in the number of highly educated parents during the 20th century (Greenfield, 1998). This is important because the level of education of parents is correlated with the intelligence scores of their children (Flynn, 1998). It is possible that better educated parents provide a more intellectually stimulating home environment, which increases the intelligence test scores of their children (Greenfield, 1998). At the same time, each successive generation of children has received more education than the last. In the 1930s, the mean number of years of education in the United States was 9 years; by the 1990s, the mean had risen above 14 years (Williams, 1998). It is possible that these increases in education over the years are responsible for some of the increase in intelligence test scores. In particular, schools place more emphasis on teaching skills associated with fluid intelligence today than in the days of our grandparents, when memorization of facts was the focus of education (Williams, 1998). Thus, it may make sense that scores on measures of fluid intelligence have increased more than scores on tests of crystallized intelligence over time.

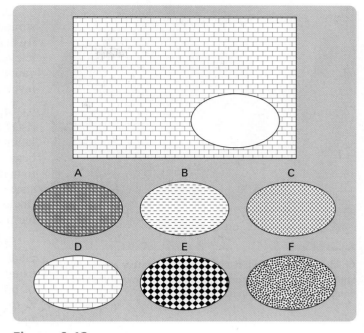

Figure 9.12

An example of a simple item on the actual Raven Progressive Matrices Test. Which of the eight figures presented at the bottom best completes the figure at the top? The correct answer is D.

Children born in the late 20th and 21st century are stimulated and challenged by a degree of environmental complexity unknown in earlier generations.

3. Children born in the latter part of the 20th century were stimulated and challenged by a degree of environmental complexity that was unknown in the 1930s (Neisser, 1998). Educational television, computers, learning toys, preschools, and other innovations may have increased intelligence by increasing children's levels of intellectual stimulation (Williams, 1998).

4. During the same time period that intelligence scores have risen, there has been a break-up of the small regional subpopulations from which people used to choose mates. When people began to move more within and between countries, they tended to mate with less genetically similar people. Some theorists have speculated that this has resulted in what is termed "hybrid vigor" (including higher intelligence scores), owing to less influence of harmful recessive traits (Mingroni, 2007).

But there are important reasons we must be cautious in concluding that genuine increases in intelligence have occurred. For example, children have much more exposure to the specific kinds of problems on tests of fluid intelligence today than did children at the start of the last century (Neisser, 1998). Does the item in figure 9.12 remind you of "brain teasers" on the back of cereal boxes or in "happy meals" from your favorite restaurant in childhood? If scores on tests of fluid intelligence are higher only because people born more recently are more familiar with such problems, the improved test scores may not reflect actual changes in intelligence at all. Scores on intelligence tests may have risen only because people born more recently have greater familiarity with the test items. Even though the greatest increases have been found in measures of fluid intelligence such as the Raven test, large increases over generations have occurred in many kinds of measures of intelligence, including aspects of intelligence not "tested" on cereal boxes or restaurant place mats (Neisser, 1998).

Race-Ethnic Differences in Intelligence and Achievement: The Narrowing Gap

Data gathered since the 1930s have consistently shown that the average intelligence and academic achievement scores of African Americans are about 15 points lower than those of white Americans, with children of Hispanic/Latino heritage having average scores that fall between those of whites and African Americans. Asian Americans, however, have average intelligence scores that are about 5 points higher than those of whites (Williams & Ceci, 1997). If people in general have become more intelligent over successive generations, what has happened to the difference between groups that differ in race and ethnicity?

Between 1970 and 2002, some of the gap in intelligence tests scores and reading and mathematics achievement scores between African American and non-Hispanic white Americans has been closed (Dickens & Flynn, 2006; Flynn, 1999; Mandara & others, 2009). These important trends reflect greater improvements in intelligence tests and academic achievement test scores among African American youths than among white youth.

Why have intellectual test scores improved more rapidly over time among African Americans? No one knows for sure, but marked changes in the environment seem to be the most plausible answer. Since the end of official segregation in the United States, the educational experiences of African Americans have changed dramatically. The timing of changes in schooling related to desegregation in different regions of the country closely parallel gains in academic achievement made by African Americans in those regions (Grissmer & others, 1998). From 1973 to 1990, the mean educational level of adults increased among white families by 70%, but the mean educational level of adults in African American families increased by 350% during the same period (Williams, 1998). Because the amount of schooling is related to scores on measures of both intellectual ability and academic achievement, the closing gap in ability and achievement may be due, in part, to the closing gap in educational opportunity.

Other factors probably also play a role in the narrowing gap between race-ethnic groups in the United States. For example, the average number of children in white families decreased from 4.7 to 2.4 from early 1970s to the mid-1990s, whereas the average number of children in African American families decreased from 6.0 to 4.2 (Huang & Hauser, 1998).

Group differences on intelligence tests between African Americans and white Americans appear to be dwindling as prejudice and economic barriers weaken.

Because the family size and birth order is inversely correlated with intelligence (Sulloway, 2007; Zajonc & Mullally, 1997), the decline in the number of large African American families may be another factor associated with improved scores. Although the average number of children in white families also declined, they had smaller families to begin with and may have benefited less from the decline in family size. Changes in health and nutrition and other factors also may have contributed to the greater increase in test scores among African Americans than among whites (Flynn, 2007). Unfortunately, much less information is available on trends in ability and achievement among Hispanic/ Latino children and other groups.

The Bell Curve: Policy Implications of Differences in Intelligence

In 1994, psychologist Richard Herrnstein and sociologist Charles Murray published a controversial book entitled *The Bell Curve*. They made assertions about genetic differences between race-ethnic groups that gained little scientific support, but they raised some important questions about the role of intelligence in society that deserve serious debate. Herrnstein and Murray reviewed many findings from studies of intelligence and occupational success and discussed their implications for public policy. They argued that North American society is moving toward a "meritocracy," in which opportunities for advanced education and favorable kinds of employment are determined solely by each person's ability. Although individual ability is certainly not the only factor that determines success today, it probably is more important than ever before. In the past, some occupations were open only to persons from wealthy families. Although such privileges endure today, laws regarding equal opportunity in education and employment have reduced their influence.

Although life in a meritocracy could be said to be more fair than in other social systems, Herrnstein and Murray argue that it poses new ethical problems as well. If we create a society in which the environmental contributions to intellectual ability are completely equalized (everyone has adequate nutrition, favorable intellectual environments, equal access to education, and so on), they believe that the influence of genetics on intelligence will increase. That is, if everyone's environment were essentially the same, heredity would be the only cause of differences in intelligence among people. Because intelligence in its various forms (fluid, crystallized, and tacit) plays an important role in determining occupational success, Herrnstein and Murray believe that the genes that influence intelligence will play an increasingly important role in determining each person's level of occupational success. Thus, if our society eliminates all barriers to equal opportunities to succeed, Herrnstein and Murray believe that the aspects of occupational success that are linked to intelligence will be determined by our genes from the moment of conception. This would be as unfair as an aristocracy that determined that only persons of royal families be educated or own property.

Is it fair for more intelligent persons to have a greater likelihood of occupational success than less intelligent persons? In the United States, the average income of persons in the top 10% of intelligence scores is 50% higher than that of persons with average intelligence scores (Ceci & Williams, 1997). Is that fair? Many people believe that allowing the most competent people to become wealthy is the engine that drives our successful economic system (to the benefit of everyone). What do you think?

If we as a society were to decide that we should minimize the effect of differences in intellectual ability on chances for occupational success, could we do so? Because intelligence is most strongly related to performance of complex jobs, and because complex managerial and professional jobs are the best paid, we likely could not eliminate the effect of intelligence on occupational success. The amount of influence, however, depends on how our society chooses to respond to differences in intelligence. If we were to make greater efforts to match each person's unique profile of intellectual strengths to her or his job, specify the requirements of each job as well as the military does, and provide each person with the amount of training needed to reach a high level of job performance, then we could reduce the impact of intelligence on occupational success (Brody, 1997). Society could even take the step of enriching the environments of children with lower intelligence to help level the intellectual playing field (Brody, 1997). Do any of these programs seem reasonable and appropriate to you?

It should also be said that differences in intelligence are only one of the factors that create inequalities in occupational success and income in North America. The difference between persons in the top 10% of incomes and persons earning average incomes is four times greater than would be expected on the basis of differences in intelligence scores alone (Ceci & Williams, 1997). Many factors contribute to the huge disparity in incomes in North America today. If equality is your goal, you will have to look at more than intelligence for solutions.

Extremes in Intelligence: Mental Retardation and Giftedness

Intelligence testing provides one of the main criteria for diagnosing mental retardation. To be considered mentally retarded, an individual must have a low IQ that causes serious deficits in the skills needed for everyday living. The usual line of demarcation is an IQ of 70 or below, which results in about 2% of the American population being diagnosed as retarded. In addition to IQ, an individual's ability in self-care activities and relating to others is considered in making a diagnosis. Degrees of retardation range from mild to profound: Individuals with IQs from 50 to 70 are said to be mildly retarded; 35 to 49, moderately retarded; 20 to 34, severely retarded; and under 20, profoundly retarded.

Retardation can result from a wide range of conditions. Genetic disorders, birth trauma, maternal infections, maternal use of alcohol, and sensory or maternal deprivation early in life are only a few of the possible causes of retardation. Since the 1960s educational efforts for those who have mental retardation have improved greatly. Because approximately 90% of the people who have retardation fall in the mild range, the vast majority of people with retardation can lead satisfying and productive lives (Tyler, 1965). People who have mental retardation have played featured roles in popular television shows, which has educated the general population by highlighting their abilities rather than disabilities.

At the other end of the scale, public school systems across the United States provide special educational programs for "gifted" children (Winner, 2000). "Gifted" is usually defined in terms of both high IQ scores and high levels of creativity. These programs are funded on two grounds: (1) that the nation needs to enrich the education of its brightest future leaders and (2) that these children are so bright that they sometimes need help to avoid developing psychological problems. This latter argument—that being more intelligent than one's peers causes problems—is not universally accepted. Is it true that being highly intelligent is a handicap, or is it an advantage, as we have heretofore assumed?

The best answer to this question comes from the research of Lewis Terman (1925), creator of the Stanford-Binet Intelligence Scale and expert on high intelligence. In the early 1920s, Terman identified more than 1,500 highly intelligent boys and girls living in California. They were mostly between the ages of 8 and 12 when identified and had IQs that averaged about 150. Terman studied these geniuses—affectionately nicknamed the "Termites"—both as children and later as adults. Many follow-up evaluations of Terman's Termites also have been conducted (Crosnoe & Elder, 2004; Holahan, Sears, & Cronbach, 1995; Holahan & others, 1999). When they were children, the gifted Termite group was functioning very well in every evaluated area of life. On average, they made better grades in school, were considered more honest and trustworthy, and were taller and stronger than their peers of average IQ. In their middle 40s, the Termites were still found to be highly successful. About 70% had graduated from college (compared with about 8% of their generation); 40% of the male graduates had earned law degrees, medical degrees, or Ph.D.s; and 85% were working as professionals or as managers in business. Their total family incomes were more than double the average for families from the same ethnic group and socioeconomic status. Perhaps reflecting the era during which they grew up, however, the educational and occupational success of the women was well behind that of the men. Physically, the gifted Termites were superior to their peers, in that they were very healthy adults and their death rate was one-third less than the national average (because more intelligent people do not smoke and take better care of themselves, Gottfredson & Deary, 2004). The Termites experienced no fewer minor emotional problems than average but showed lower rates of alcoholism and criminal convictions. The highly intelligent Termites are still doing far better than average in many ways during later life. These results clearly suggest that high intelligence is generally a good quality to possess. Other follow-up studies of other groups of highly intelligent children have similarly found that they tend to be open-minded, progressive, and highly successful in many spheres of life (Deary & others, 2008; Lubinski & others, 2006; Subotnik & others, 1993).

Review

The term *intelligence* refers to our ability to use cognitive processes to cope with the demands of life. This concept has found an important place in contemporary psychology because tests have been developed that predict with reasonable accuracy performance on tasks that require intelligence, particularly school performance. Scores on these intelligence (IQ) tests indicate whether an individual has correctly answered as many questions as the average person of his or her own age. Higher IQs indicate that the person has scored the same number of points as the average person of an older age; lower IQs indicate the opposite. Useful IQ tests must be standardized and evaluated against proper norms, objective, reliable, and valid.

Most psychologists think of intelligence both as a single general factor and as many independent facets of intellectual ability. Consequently, the most widely used IQ tests report both a general score and several more specific scores. Some facets of intelligence, however, particularly tacit intelligence, are not measured well by general tests of intelligence. It is

Review (cont.)

probable that both heredity and environmental factors help determine all aspects of an individual's level of intelligence. There is encouraging evidence that intelligence is rising around the world and that the gaps between different race-ethnic groups in North America are closing.

Check Your Learning

To be sure that you have learned the key points from the preceding section, cover the list of correct answers and try to answer each question. If you give an incorrect answer to any question, return to the page given next to the correct answer to see why your answer was not correct.

1. The term _____ refers to the cognitive abilities of an individual to learn from experience, to reason well, and to cope effectively with the demands of living.

2. Although the deviation IQ is now used in most modern intelligence tests, the original ratio IQ stated that IQ was equal to _____.

   a) mental age divided by chronological age

   b) chronological age divided by mental age

   c) mental age divided by chronological age × 100

   d) chronological age divided by mental age × 100

3. Heredity is the only factor that determines a person's intelligence.

   a) true   b) false

4. The size of differences in intelligence scores among ethnic groups in the United States is apparently _____.

   a) decreasing

   b) increasing

   c) remaining the same

Thinking Critically about Psychology

There are no right or wrong answers to the following questions. They are presented to help you become an active reader and think critically about what you have just read.

1. If psychologists do not agree about the nature of intelligence, how is it possible for them to agree on a test of intelligence?

2. Do you think the "Flynn effect" really means that your generation is more intelligent than your parents' generation? How do you think your parents would answer this question? Why?

Correct Answers: 1. intelligence (p. 282), 2. c (p. 287), 3. b (p. 290), 4. a (p. 294)

Application of Psychology

Improving Critical Thinking

It could be said that a successful person is not a person who has no problems—because all of us have problems—but is a person who is able to solve most of his or her problems. As I have discussed in this chapter, however, we human beings are not particularly good at using cognitive skills to solve problems. Our abilities to reason—as impressive as they may be compared with those of every other creature on earth—are not always equal to the problems that face us.

However, a great deal of evidence shows that we can improve our ability to cope with the demands of life by sharpening our critical thinking skills (Halpern, 1998). This section provides a brief overview of a number of ways to improve critical thinking. But it is not a solution by itself; if you are going to improve your *critical thinking skills,* reading this section must be only the first step in a long process.

Increase Mental Effort.
The first step in improving critical thinking skills is motivational, not cognitive. Critical thinking requires a willingness to engage in cognitive work (Halpern, 1998). It simply takes more time and effort to think carefully and critically about a problem than to make the first decision that pops into your head. On the other hand, the amount of effort needed to dig your way out of the consequences of some poor decisions is much greater. So, we either work hard to make good decisions, or we work hard to clean up the messes caused by our poor decisions—it's our choice.

Improve Problem Formulation.
Most of life's problems are not simple math problems that need no formulation. They are complex situations that must be stated in the form of specific problems. Experts on critical thinking recommend that we attempt to formulate all problems in at least two ways (Halpern, 1998). This forces us into the realization that there is more than one way to think about the problem—and some of those ways lead to better problem solving than other ways. As you work to formulate the problems that face you in the best way, think about the way in which each problem has been framed (or you have framed the problem yourself). Framing the problem in different terms can lead to different decisions. The way in which a problem is formulated and framed is sometimes as important as the problem itself.

Break Out of Unproductive Mental Sets.
As discussed in this chapter, mental sets are one of the most common barriers to effective problem solving. Sometimes we must break out of our habitual ways of viewing the elements of the problem to discover a solution. One of the most troublesome of these mental sets has been referred to as *functional fixedness.* Before we define this term, let's look at a problem in which it is encountered. Consider the Maier (1931) string problem. Figure 9.13 shows that you are in a room where two strings are hanging from the ceiling. Your job is to tie the strings together. The problem is that, when holding onto one string, you cannot reach the other. The only other thing in the room with you is a pair of pliers, but, even holding onto one string with the pliers, you cannot reach the other string. What do you do? Look at figure 9.14 on p. 300 for the solution. The difficulty that most people have in solving this problem is similar to the one in Duncker's candle problem. We are simply not accustomed to using pliers as a pendulum to move a string, just as we wouldn't ordinarily use a matchbox as a candle holder. Karl Duncker (1945) referred to the difficulty we have in seeing new uses for objects as functional fixedness. It's a kind of mental set that interferes with problem solving by focusing our thinking on the habitual uses of the elements in a problem. Often the key to effective problem solving is being able to break out of functional fixedness and other interfering mental sets when appropriate.

Let's look at another famous problem that was developed to illustrate the interference of mental set. Psychologist Karl

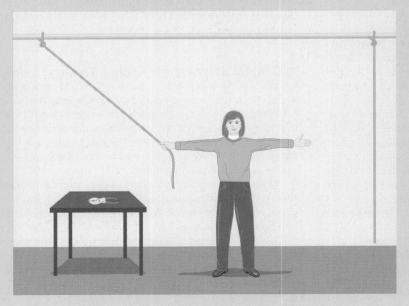

Figure 9.13

The Maier string problem. How do you tie the two strings together if you cannot reach them both at the same time? See figure 9.14 for the solution.

Application of Psychology cont'd

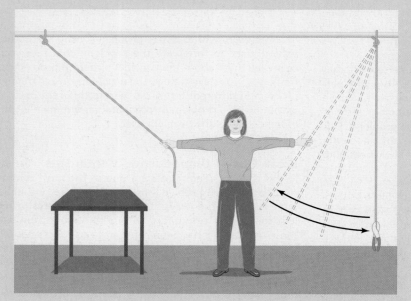

Figure 9.14
The solution to the Maier string problem is to use the pliers as a pendulum to bring the second string closer.

Luchins (1942) asked college students to imagine that they had three jars of different sizes. They then were asked how they would measure an amount of water that was different from that held by any single jar. For example, they might be asked to measure 5 quarts when the three jars held the quantities as shown here.

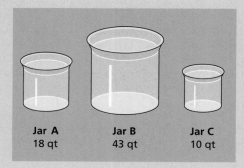

| **Jar A** | **Jar B** | **Jar C** |
| 18 qt | 43 qt | 10 qt |

How would you solve this problem? Five quarts can be measured by filling jar B, then pouring water from it until jar A is filled, leaving 25 quarts in jar B. Then jar C is filled twice from jar B, leaving 5 quarts in jar B. It's simple when you catch on to the method. In algebraic terms, the solution can be expressed as B − A − 2C.

After solving five more problems using jars of different sizes, all of which could be solved using the operation B − A − 2C, the subjects were given a problem like this: Measure 20 quarts when jar A contains 24 quarts; jar B contains 52 quarts, and jar C contains 4 quarts. This problem could also be solved using the operation B − A − 2C, but did you solve it that way? Or did you see that it could be solved more simply by subtracting one jar C from jar A (A − C)? In Luchins's study, more than three-fourths of his students solved the problem the long way.

Why did Luchins's students make a difficult problem out of a simple one? Do people just have a tendency to do everything the hard way? Luchins ruled out that unlikely possibility in his experiment by having another group of students skip the first six B − A − 2C problems and solve the seventh problem first. These students all used the simple A − C solution. The students who took the long solution to the seventh problem after solving six B − A − 2C problems simply had fallen into a "mental rut" or set. As we look for ways to improve problem solving in everyday life, we must be careful to examine our way of understanding the elements of the problem to avoid functional fixedness, prejudice, or other mental sets that may be interfering with optimal problem solving. The problem may be solvable if you look at it the right way.

Monitor Your Critical Thinking. People who are effective in critical thinking are aware that they are engaging in critical thinking (Halpern, 1998). That is, they are conscious of being critical thinkers and they monitor how well they are doing. When they catch themselves formulating problems in the first way that comes to mind or in getting stuck in mental ruts, they pull themselves back into a critical thinking mode.

A General Strategy for Critical Thinking. This section integrates the suggestions I have presented here with recommendations for generating and evaluating possible solutions to problems. These suggestions are presented in the form of a general strategy for critical thinking and problem solving (Goldfried & Davison, 1976; Halpern, 1998; Turkat & Calhoun, 1980). Even following this strategy will not solve all of life's problems, but it will give you a fighting chance.

You might try going through a hypothetical problem using this strategy just to see how it works. Suppose you run out of money for school—what would the best solution to this problem be for you? A loan? A part-time job? By trying this general outline for problem solving and the other ideas presented in this section, you may be better prepared to deal with the next curve ball that life throws at you.

Here is the general strategy:

1. What is the problem?

   a. Define the problem in clear, specific terms.

   b. Define the problem in at least one other way to find the best formulation.

   c. Be aware of the potential influence of framing and emotions.

   d. Think flexibly about the elements of the problem and avoid mental sets.

   e. Draw a diagram of the problem to see how the elements relate to one another.

   f. Make a list of the additional information you need to solve the problem, and then obtain that information.

2. Generate all possible solutions.

   a. At first, do not judge any solution—just keep thinking of alternative solutions.

   b. Wild ideas are welcome.

   c. See if some of your possible solutions can be combined to make a better possible solution.

3. Now, eliminate any possible solutions that are clearly poor choices.

   a. Alternatives with no chance of success should be dropped.

   b. Intuitive solutions based on heuristic reasoning should be eliminated in situations where logical (algorithmic) reasoning is possible.

   c. Select the solution with the greatest likelihood of more positive consequences than negative consequences.

4. Examine the likely consequences of the remaining possible solutions at one time.

   a. List all possible negative consequences of this option.

   b. List all possible positive consequences of this option.

   c. Eliminate the option if it is more likely to produce negative than positive consequences.

   d. Go on to the next option (and repeat steps a through c).

   e. Compare all remaining options in terms of likely consequences.

   f. Select the solution with the greatest likelihood of more positive consequences than negative consequences.

5. Generate all possible ways to implement the solution you have chosen. How can you best do this? Use steps 2 through 4 to select the best way to implement the solution.

6. Implement the solution.

Summary

Chapter 9 discusses cognition, language, the meaning of intelligence, and the measurement of intelligence.

I. In the process of cognition, information is obtained through the senses, transformed through the interpretive processes of perception and thinking, stored and retrieved through the processes of memory, and used in the processes of problem solving and language.

II. Concepts, the basic units of thinking, are categories of things, events, or qualities linked together by some common feature or features.

   A. Some concepts are categories based on a single common feature; others are more complex.

      1. Members of categories defined by conjunctive concepts all have two or more common characteristics.

      2. Members of disjunctive concepts have either one common characteristic or another one, or both.

   B. Not all concepts are equally easy for us to learn; some are more natural and easily learned than others.

1. Examine the likely consequences of the remaining possible solutions one at a time.

   a. List all possible negative consequences of this option.

   b. List all possible positive consequences of this option.

   c. Eliminate the option if it is more likely to produce negative than positive consequences.

   d. Go on to the next option (and repeat steps a through c).

   e. Compare all remaining options in terms of likely consequences.

III. In problem solving, information is used to reach a goal that is blocked by an obstacle.

   A. Cognitive operations are used to solve problems. After we decide what kind of problem we face, we evaluate the elements of the problem and decide what information and tools we have to work with. Then we generate a list of solutions and evaluate them.

B. Algorithmic and heuristic operations are two types of cognitive strategies used in solving problems.

1. Algorithmic thinking is systematic and logical.

2. Heuristic thinking is efficient but is not guaranteed to lead to a correct solution and often causes logic and relevant information to be ignored.

C. Emotional factors and the way in which questions are framed can influence our decisions in ways that are unrelated to the facts or the logic of the problem.

D. Creative problem solving requires the ability to think in flexible and unusual ways (divergent thinking); the most useful creative solutions are also thought out logically and realistically (convergent thinking).

IV. Language is a symbolic code used in human communication.

A. Semantic content is the meaning communicated through language.

B. We generate language from a set of elements and a set of rules for combining them into speech.

1. The phoneme is the smallest unit of sound in a language. The English language has only 44 phonemes.

2. Morphemes are the smallest units of meaning in a language.

3. Syntax is the rules of a language through which an infinite number of understandable utterances are generated.

C. Much of our thinking is in the form of language: the Whorfian, or linguistic relativity, hypothesis states that the structure of language influences how people think.

V. Intelligence refers to the cognitive abilities of an individual to understand complex concepts, to learn from experience, to reason well, and to cope effectively with the demands of daily living.

A. Intelligence is viewed as a single general factor by some psychologists and as many independent kinds of intellectual abilities by others.

B. Intelligence tests measure a small sample of the cognitive abilities that constitute intelligence.

1. Useful IQ tests must be standardized, objective, reliable, valid, and evaluated against proper norms.

2. In some cases, measures of tacit intelligence (knowledge and skills specific to a task that are usually not taught in schools) predict success better in specific everyday tasks than do measures of general intelligence.

C. Intelligence test scores are important in predicting occupational success because persons with higher scores are more likely to qualify for advanced education, take less time to train to perform job skills, and perform complex jobs better.

D. Intelligence is influenced by both genetic and environmental factors working in combination.

E. Scores on tests of intelligence and academic achievement appear to have risen considerably in many countries (possibly due to improvements in health and education), and the gap between race-ethnic groups has declined in recent years.

F. Contrary to widespread misperceptions, persons with very high levels of intelligence are taller, stronger, healthier, and more successful than persons of average intelligence.

chapter ten
Developmental psychology

Chapter Outline

Prologue

Jean Piaget was a notable Swiss scientist who studied the development of cognition in children until his death in 1980. His most important contribution was to show us that children of different ages understand the world in ways that are often very different from the ways adults understand it. Indeed, young children understand their worlds in ways that are so different from adults' that it is sometimes like trying to communicate with a creature from another galaxy!

A classic experiment by Piaget and his frequent collaborator Barbel Inhelder (1963) makes this point very well. Children of different ages were shown three small, three-dimensional replicas of mountains arranged on a table top. On the other side of the table, a doll

development The processes related to change and continuity in an individual's life.

developmental psychology The field of psychology that focuses on development across the life span.

was seated. The children were asked to look at the mountains and then to indicate which of two pictures showed the mountains as the doll would see them. Six-year-olds could not do it at all, some 7- and 8-year-olds could, and children 9 to 11 years of age had no more trouble with the task than an adult would.

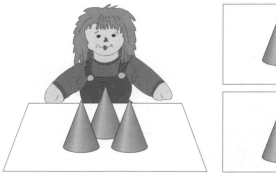 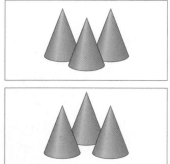

What does the doll see?

Life doesn't stand still. We are in a state of constant change throughout our lives. When we ask ourselves who we are, we think of ourselves in terms of who we are now. But we have been and will be many different people in our lifetime: an infant, a child, a teenager, a young adult, a mature person, and an aged person. The thread of continuity that runs through our lives is very real, but we change more than we realize. To understand ourselves fully, we must understand the processes of change and continuity in our lives that psychologists refer to as **development.**

Why do we change as we grow older? In previous times, psychologists differed on the question of how much of our development is biologically determined or shaped by the learning environment, but today psychologists agree that development is the product of the combined forces of "nature" (biology) and "nurture" (environment). **Developmental psychology** is the field of psychology that focuses on development across the life span. This chapter on developmental psychology is about the person that you were yesterday, *are today, and will become tomorrow.* Just as we cannot understand butterflies without understanding their metamorphosis from caterpillars, we cannot understand human beings without understanding how they change across the life span.

Basic Processes of Development

What forces cause us to change as we pass through life? What factors determine whether we grow up to be baseball players or umpires, musicians or opticians? In this section, we look at the factors that play key roles in the process of development. As you have probably already learned to expect, not all psychologists agree about these factors, so a variety of viewpoints are presented in this chapter.

Nature and Nurture

As was discussed in chapter 4, both nature and nurture combine to influence our actions, thoughts, and feelings. Language provides a good example of the rich interplay of nature and nurture in our lives. There can be no question that experience is important in language development. Children will learn to use language only if they are exposed to language, and they will learn to speak the language to which they are exposed. For example, a French child adopted by a Chinese-speaking family will grow up speaking Chinese, not French. But neither goldfish nor marmosets will learn to speak a human language when given the same amount of experience. One must have a human brain and throat to learn to speak a human language. In the absence of the right nature, nurture can accomplish nothing.

Other examples of the blending of nature and nurture abound in child development. Children cannot use a baseball glove correctly unless they have seen others play ball (nurture). But you cannot effectively teach children to do much with a glove until age 4 or so, after considerable physical development has taken place (nature). We are creatures of complex combinations of both our nature and nurture.

Both nature and nurture work together in development. Without getting some advice (nurture), a child cannot use a baseball glove correctly. But the child must be physically developed enough to use the glove (nature).

Maturation

In the study of development, the most important aspect of nature (biological factors) is **maturation.** This term refers to systematic physical growth of the nervous system and other bodily structures. A primary question for the psychologist specializing in the study of development is "How much of the change that we see occurring with age is the result of physical maturation?"

Although both experience and maturation are important in most developmental changes, maturation is surprisingly important in many specific contexts. For example, experience obviously plays an important role in toilet training—children must be taught to use the toilet—but maturation also plays a key role. Successful toilet training is difficult for most children before the age of 24 months. They are simply not *maturationally* ready to learn that task. After 24 to 36 months of age, however, most children learn to use the toilet fairly rapidly.

An experiment using identical twin boys illustrates the idea of maturational readiness beautifully. Toilet training was begun for one boy, Hugh, when he was only 50 days old. Training for Hilton, the other twin, did not begin until 700 days of age (almost 2 years). As shown in figure 10.1 (p. 306), Hugh made no real progress until about 20 months of age, whereas Hilton's progress was rapid from the beginning. Both children learned, but only when they reached the proper level of maturation (McGraw, 1940).

Maturation seems to function in much the same way in intellectual, social, and other areas of development. For example, children perform cognitive tasks more quickly and accurately as they grow older, largely because the myelin coating that speeds neural transmission in the cerebral cortex (see p. 000 to refresh your knowledge about myelin) continues to grow throughout childhood (Bjorklund & Green, 1992). It's unlikely that we could teach an 18-month-old to play cooperatively with other children, teach a 4-year-old the concept of physical mass, or teach the concept of justice to a 6-year-old. These behaviors and concepts generally cannot be learned until

maturation (mach″u-rā′shun) Systematic physical growth of the body, including the nervous system.

Toilet training, typical of many human behaviors, is learned more quickly when the child is maturationally ready.

Figure 10.1
The importance of maturational readiness is shown in McGraw's (1940) classic study of toilet training twin boys named Hugh and Hilton. Although Hugh's training was begun at 50 days of age, no progress was achieved until he was about 650 days of age. In contrast, Hilton's progress was rapid because training was begun when he was maturationally ready.

Source: Data from M. B. McGraw, "Neural Maturation as Exemplified in Achievement of Bladder Control," *Journal of Pediatrics, 16,* 580–590, 1940.

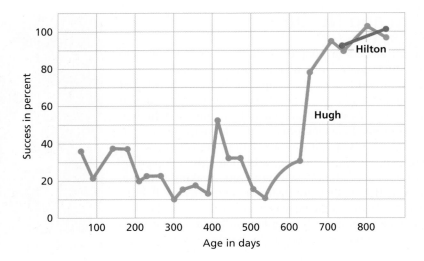

later ages, suggesting that maturation of the brain is one of the key factors involved in the development of cognition.

Early Experience and Critical Periods

When the Puritans came to America in the 1600s, they brought with them a belief about children that most of us still hold today—namely, that early childhood is the "formative period" for our personalities. We believe that the experiences that we have as young children powerfully and permanently shape our adult behavior. This is not just a belief held by laypeople; many psychologists hold it, too. But is it true that early experiences irreversibly form our personalities?

Imprinting. Supporting the view that our early experiences are of prime importance is a large body of research on nonhuman animals. German biologist Konrad Lorenz (1937), for example, extensively studied the behavior and development of the greylag goose. During one phase of his investigations, he wanted to know why young goslings followed their mothers in the little single-file parades that are the joy of farmers and park-visiting children everywhere. Do they follow the mother goose because of an inborn tendency or instinct (nature), or do they learn to follow their mother because of nurture? Lorenz found that goslings do have an inborn tendency to follow their mothers, but that they actually will follow any moving, noisy object that they are exposed to after hatching, not just mother geese. Furthermore, once they begin following something, they generally will not follow anything else but that object. If their mother is out to lunch when they hatch and a rooster should happen to strut by, they will follow him until they are mature geese—presumably much to the rooster's embarrassment.

imprinting (im´print-ing) A form of early learning that occurs in some animals during a critical period.

Lorenz called this special kind of early learning **imprinting.** He thought of it as a kind of learning that was highly constrained by maturation. The maturational control is seen clearly in the fact that imprinting can occur only during a brief, sensitive period of the bird's life called the **critical period.** If imprinting does not occur during the critical period, it probably will never occur. Still, the fact that imprinting is a kind of learning—part of nurture—is obvious because the birds will learn to follow anything that meets the biological requirements. Goslings have been imprinted on quacking duck decoys and footballs pulled by squeaking pulleys. A famous photo even shows Konrad Lorenz being followed by a flock of goslings that had imprinted on him. Nothing comparable to imprinting occurs in humans, although we do form attachments to our caregivers through prolonged experience with them.

Konrad Lorenz followed by some of his imprinted goslings.

critical period A biologically determined period in the life of some animals during which certain forms of learning can take place most easily.

early experiences Experiences occurring very early in development, believed by some to have lasting effects.

Early Social Deprivation. Studies conducted with monkeys, which are closer to humans on the evolutionary ladder than geese, also show the long-lasting effects of early experience in a way that seems more relevant to humans. Harry and Margaret Harlow (Harlow & Harlow, 1965; Harlow & Novak, 1973) carried out a number of studies of the role of early social experiences in development. Are our earliest social experiences especially important to the development of social behavior in childhood and adulthood? Sigmund Freud would have us believe that these **early experiences** are of the greatest significance, but until the Harlows, few researchers had experimentally tested Freud's claims.

The Harlows raised a group of infant monkeys in complete isolation for the first few months of life. Later they returned the monkeys, which had never lived with a mother, to regular group cages with other monkeys. When the monkeys reached adulthood (about 3 years of age), they were placed in breeding cages with another monkey of the other sex. It was then that the Harlows noticed that the social, sexual, and emotional behavior of these monkeys was distinctly abnormal. Females raised without early experience with a real mother appeared fearful and viciously attacked the male when a sexual advance was made. The males, however, alternated between fearfulness and overenthusiastic, clumsy sexual advances.

Although they had normal social experiences for 2½ years, these monkeys' abnormal experiences during the first 6 months of life had a continuing detrimental effect on their social behavior. Moreover, when a few of the females finally became pregnant and had offspring, the lasting effects of the early social deprivation were made more clear. When the mother-deprived monkeys became mothers themselves, they rejected, attacked, and some even killed their own infants before they could be protected by the researchers. The research provided insight into the possible consequences of early abuse and neglect for humans. The research also helped to start debates about the ethical treatment of animals in research, which remains a controversial topic (Blum, 2002).

The treatment of Harlow's monkeys started debates about ethical treatment of animals in research studies. The debate continues.

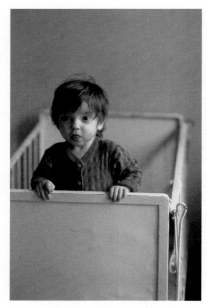

Orphaned children who are raised in inadequate orphanages that deprive them of normal contact with adults develop very slowly. Adoption by involved parents can often speed development.

Much less is known about the effects on humans of abnormal early experiences. Some psychologists believe that abnormal early experiences produce irreversible damage (e.g., Bruner, 1974), but others believe that, under favorable conditions, the early effects may not be permanent (Kagan, 1984; Parker, Barrett, & Hickie, 1992; Thompson & Nelson, 2001). A recent groundbreaking study has shed great light on the consequences of early deprivation (Rutter & others, 2010). In the late 1980s researchers began to study children who were adopted from profoundly depriving institutions in Romania (the conditions were described as appalling) into well-functioning households in England. The researchers found that children removed before they were six months old were generally functioning quite well later—being raised in good environments helped them overcome the early deprivation. In contrast, children who were raised in institutions past six months improved greatly but still had distinct deficits in forming close relationships with caregivers, attention/overactivity, cognitive abilities, and physical growth. This was in spite of the fact the children had spent an overwhelming majority of their lives in caring and supportive households. Another recent study found that deprivation from early institutionalization and from physical abuse was related to deficient immune system functioning during adolescence (Shirtcliff, Coe, & Pollak, 2009).

The research supports the importance of early nurturing experiences, especially the role of attachments (see Parenting and Attachment section at the end of the chapter). These findings suggest that children are quite resilient but that early risks, particularly those that are extreme and prolonged, can have significant implications for later psychological and physical development.

Human Diversity
Raising a Child Who Cannot Hear

All parents must make important decisions about raising children that can have a major impact on their child's emotional and intellectual development. The parents of children who are challenged by physical or sensory limitations, however, face a number of additional decisions. In the case of children with little or no hearing, for example, parents must first decide if the child will learn to speak orally (called "voicing") or will learn sign language. The parents of Montreal Expos team member Curtis Pride felt that he would always be an outsider if he did not learn to voice (Gildea, 1993). Other parents disagree, however. They feel that the child will not be able to enter the *deaf culture* (Rutherford, 1988) if sign language is not learned. Many deaf people consider themselves as part of a distinct cultural group rather than as having a physical disability. They feel that a deaf child who does not learn sign language will not fully join the only culture that will truly accept the child.

Another choice parents must make is whether to send their child to a residential school for deaf children or to a neighborhood school with hearing children. Some parents of deaf children feel that it is best for them to learn to be part of the mainstream culture. When deaf children attend local neighborhood schools, their parents are encouraged to work with the school to develop an individualized treatment plan that best suits the children's needs. The plan frequently needs to be updated, as children's needs change as they develop. Many deaf persons, however, feel that residential schools are better because they allow deaf children to be part of an accepting community. Unlike some other groups who are different from the majority of the population, many deaf persons object to being "integrated" into the hearing world. No matter how hard they might try to be part of the mainstream culture, they feel that they will remain separate because few hearing people know sign language. **Continued on pg. 309**

Parents of deaf children often decide to learn sign language along with their children.

Continued on pg. 309

Continued from pg. 308 Jan Hafer and Ellen Richmond (1988) encourage hearing parents of deaf children to learn sign language and to learn about deaf culture and history by interacting with successful deaf persons. But many deaf children live in families where no one has learned sign language. Sign language is a complex language, and it can take parents months or years to learn it. Often, financial and time constraints make it difficult for parents to attend sign language classes, but some experts believe that not doing so can lead to isolation of the child and slow his or her language development (Dolnick, 1993, p. 48).

Technology is continually progressing in ways that create new options for parents—and new difficult decisions to make. Some parents now have the opportunity to have a device implanted in the cochlea of their children's ears, referred to as a cochlear implant, that improves hearing. Some parents describe the operation as "a miracle of biblical proportions" (Dolnick, 1993, p. 43), but some controversy remains about the necessity of the surgery. An overwhelming majority of deaf children born to hearing parents now receive some medical intervention, such as hearing aids or a cochlear implant (Niparko, 2009), which greatly improve hearing and spoken language (Niparko & others, 2010).

Do you have any characteristic that sets you apart from other persons or has created barriers for you? Are you in the minority because of your height, weight, ethnicity, sexual orientation, religion, intelligence, attractiveness, or any other feature? Some of the ways in which human beings differ from one another are more challenging or lead to greater discrimination than others, but most of us are in the minority in some way. How has this influenced you? How do you think you would be different if you had a more challenging physical characteristic?

Human Diversity
Raising a Child Who Cannot Hear

cont'd from pg. 308

Review

Children change dramatically from birth to adulthood. This fact has led some theorists in the past to assert that developmental changes in behavior are biologically programmed to "unfold" with increasing age (nature). Other theorists have argued that changes in behavior occur because the learning environment "molds" our development (nurture). Today it's generally believed, however, that development results from a blend of both biological and environmental influences. Maturation provides an important example of this interaction between biology and environment: Some forms of learning (which clearly depend on the environment) can occur efficiently only when the child has reached a certain level of readiness through physical maturation.

Experiences during critical periods of early development can have lifelong effects on animal behavior. The Harlows' experiments with social deprivation during the infancy of monkeys also show long-lasting effects of abnormal early experiences. Studies of human infants who had abnormal early experiences but who were adopted by normal families during childhood, however, suggest that humans may be less permanently influenced by early experience than other animals and may be more open to environmental influences, particularly if they are provided with an adequate environment early, in the first year of life.

Check Your Learning

To be sure that you have learned the key points from the preceding section, cover the list of correct answers and try to answer each question. If you give an incorrect answer to any question, return to the page given next to the correct answer to see why your answer was not correct. Remember that these questions cover only some of the important information in this section; it is important that you make up your own questions to check your learning of other facts and concepts.

Check Your Learning (cont.)

1. In developmental psychology, the term *nurture* refers to _____ factors that influence development.

   a) biological   c) both of these

   b) environmental   d) neither of these

2. In the study of development, the most important biological factor is _____, the systematic physical growth of the body, including the nervous system.

   a) maturation   c) growth factors

   b) hormones   d) environment

3. A biologically determined period in the life of some animals during which certain forms of learning can take place most easily is called a _____.

   a) stage   c) critical period

   b) milestone   d) landmark

Thinking Critically about Psychology

There are no right or wrong answers to the following questions. They are presented to help you become an active reader and think critically about what you just read.

1. Is there any practical difference in implications of the "molding" and "unfolding" views of development for parents?

2. Do you think there are critical periods in human development?

Correct Answers: 1. b (p. 305), 2. a (p. 305), 3. c (p. 307)

Stage Theories of Development

stage One of several time periods in development that is qualitatively distinct from the periods that come before and after.

Although all psychologists agree that people change over time, they disagree considerably over how to conceptualize those changes. One group sees us as changing gradually with age; the other school of thought sees people as going through a series of abrupt changes or **stages.**

Stage theorists believe that the changes occurring from one stage to the next make children qualitatively different (different in "kind") rather than quantitatively different (different in "amount") from how they were at a previous stage. When a child learns to use simple words to express herself, for example, she has changed qualitatively; that is, she has become different from the kind of child she was when she could not use language. This qualitative change opens up new experiences and possibilities. Although stage theorists believe that changes between stages are qualitative, they believe that children also change quantitatively during each stage. For example, once the child has mastered some simple words, she will progress for a while by learning more simple words before the next qualitative change takes place (combining words syntactically).

Stage theorists also believe that all children must pass through the same qualitatively different stages in the same order. Stages are believed to be biologically programmed to unfold in a fixed sequence in all normal persons. In addition, they believe that a child cannot progress to the next stage until the current one has been mastered.

A close examination of the writings of even the staunchest stage theorists, however, shows that they recognize that the transition from one stage to the next is a gradual blending. In other words, a child may master one part of a new stage while still struggling with part of a previous stage. One gifted professor of psychology suggested to me that the stages of child development are like a rainbow: We can see that there are different colors in a rainbow, but it's not possible to see exactly where one color stops and the next one begins.

In the sections that follow, we discuss several major stage theories of cognitive development, moral development, and personality development. By taking a close look at each of these theories, we will better appreciate stage theories in general and will learn a little about the development of children in each of these three important areas.

Piaget's Stage Theory of Cognitive Development

Perhaps the best-known stage theory in psychology is that of Jean Piaget. Piaget was a Swiss scholar who wrote extensively about the development of cognition in children. Piaget distinguished four major stages of cognitive development. These four stages are summarized in figure 10.2 on p. 312. Note that the child's cognitive capacities develop rapidly until about the time of puberty but change little after that. Note, also, the magnitude of the changes in cognition that occur during the childhood stages. On the average, children progress from human beings who cannot reason in mental symbols to persons fully capable of adult reasoning in 11 short years, with many dramatic changes along the way.

We look more closely at each of the stages of cognitive development as we follow the course of normal development in detail later in the chapter.

Jean Piaget (1896–1980).

Stage Theories of Moral Development

Two theorists have provided us with stage theories of moral development that are related to Piaget's theory of cognitive development.

Kohlberg's Theory of Moral Development. Lawrence Kohlberg (1969) collected data for his stage theory of moral development by presenting boys with moral dilemmas and asking for evaluations of the people and actions involved. The following is an example of the type of dilemma used by Kohlberg in his research:

> In Europe, a lady was dying because she was very sick. There was one drug that the doctors said might save her. This medicine was discovered by a man living in the same town. It cost him $200 to make it, but he charged $2,000 for just a little of it. The sick lady's husband, Heinz, tried to borrow enough money to buy the drug. He went to everyone he knew to borrow the money. He told the man who made the drug that his wife was dying and asked him to sell the medicine cheaper or let him pay later. But the man said, "No, I made the drug and I'm going to make money from it." So Heinz broke into the store and stole the drug.

Did Heinz do the right thing? Kohlberg was interested in the logical process through which people arrived at their answers to moral dilemmas. He concluded that we pass through the three major levels of the development of moral reasoning shown in table 10.1 on p. 313. Nearly all children use only premoral reasoning at age 7, but conventional moral reasoning predominates after age 11. Thus, Kohlberg sees the first two major shifts in moral reasoning as occurring at the same times as the beginnings of the preoperational and concrete operational stages in Piaget's theory of cognitive development. According to Kohlberg, we engage in little principled moral reasoning until age 13, and very few of us ever make it to a stage in which we reason mostly in principled ways. He gives Mahatma Gandhi, Martin Luther King, Jr., and Eleanor Roosevelt as examples of persons at the principled stage of moral reasoning (Kohlberg, 1964).

Look carefully at the description of each of Kohlberg's stages of moral development and decide if Heinz did the right thing. At the premoral level, he did the wrong

Figure 10.2   Piaget's stages of cognitive development.

Formal operational stage: 11 years on

By the end of the stage of childhood, most individuals have progressed to full adult cognition, including the ability to reason using abstract concepts.

Concrete operational stage: 7–11 years

During middle childhood, the child has the ability to reason like an adult in every way except for reasoning about abstract concepts, such as justice, infinity, or the meaning of life.

Preoperational stage: 2–7 years

At this stage, the child is capable of symbolic thought—however, this thinking is still quite different from that of adults. It is often "illogical" in ways that reveal the unique nature of preoperational cognition.

Sensorimotor stage: Birth–2 years

The child deals with reality in terms of sensations and motor movements. At this stage, children are unable to reason in mental symbols.

thing because it would get him into trouble. At the conventional stage of moral development, Heinz would be judged to be wrong because he clearly broke the law (the conventions of right and wrong). However, from the perspective of principled reasoning, it could be argued that Heinz did the right thing. After trying to obtain the drug legally, he ignored the consequences of his action (imprisonment), disregarded the laws against theft, and followed what he thought was the higher moral principle of saving his wife's life.

Table 10.1   Kohlberg's Levels of Moral Development

Premoral Level	Conventional Level	Principled Level
Young children have no sense of morality as adults understand it. They make moral judgments to obtain rewards and avoid punishment.	At this stage, children make moral decisions on the basis of what they think others will think of them, particularly parents and other persons of authority. Because society's rules, or conventions, state what is expected of them, persons at the conventional level of moral development make moral decisions based on rules.	At this stage, we judge actions on the basis of ethical principles rather than the consequences to us (as in the first two stages). The most advanced moral reasoning within this stage, according to Kohlberg, is based on one's principles of morality, even if they differ from the rules of the larger community.

Does that evaluation bother you? Not everyone would agree that this use of principled reasoning is correct because it tends to place the individual above the law. Indeed, an individual could also explain why Heinz was wrong in terms of the principled stage of moral development. It is not the particular decision that differs at the different levels of moral development but the nature of moral reasoning involved.

Gilligan's Theory of Moral Development. Because Kohlberg and others used mostly boys in the initial studies that led to Kohlberg's theory of moral development, Carol Gilligan (1982) has suggested that Kohlberg's theory does not always accurately describe moral development in girls. She argues that female children pass through somewhat different stages progressing from self-interest toward a balanced concern for the welfare of self and others. Female moral reasoning, in other words, centers on the needs of people rather than on abstractions.

Specifically, Gilligan (1982) suggests that females progress through the three stages of moral development shown in table 10.2. How would the morality of Heinz's actions be judged at each of these stages of moral development? As in Kohlberg's

Table 10.2   Gilligan's Stage Theory of Moral Development

Morality as Individual Survival	Morality as Self-Sacrifice	Morality as Equality
The young child's first sense of what is "right" is what is good for him or her. Young children follow rules to obtain rewards for themselves and to avoid punishment.	The next stage of moral reasoning is attained after becoming aware of the needs of others. In this stage, the person believes that, to be good and to be approved of by others, they must sacrifice their own needs and meet the needs of others.	In the most advanced stage of moral development, the person views his or her own needs as equal to those of others. Persons at this stage of moral development have progressed from believing that they must always please others at the expense of their own wishes to a belief that everyone's needs should be met when possible and that sacrifices should be shared equally when the needs of different persons cannot all be met. This is a stage of advocacy of nonviolence—it is not right for anyone to be intentionally hurt, including the person himself or herself.

premoral stage, the kind of immature moral reasoning that Gilligan terms the morality as individual survival stage would judge Heinz to be wrong simply because he would be punished. At the morality as self-sacrifice stage, Heinz might be judged to be correct in sacrificing his own welfare to save his wife. At the morality as equality stage, one would have to equally balance the benefits to everyone in making a moral judgment.

Gilligan's contribution to our understanding of moral development has been acknowledged by Kohlberg and others (Levine, Kohlberg, & Hewer, 1985). However, considerable evidence suggests that Gilligan overemphasized gender differences in moral reasoning. Indeed, reviews of research on the subject (Jaffee & Shibley-Hyde, 2000; Walker, 1986) have shown that males and females are more similar in moral reasoning than they are different.

Erikson's Stage Theory of Personality Development

Erik Erikson provides us with a very different example of a stage theory of development. Erikson's stages are turning points, or *crises,* the outcome of which will partly determine the course of future personality development. In using the term *crises,* Erikson was not suggesting that these turning points are always experienced as emotionally difficult periods, although they certainly can be for some. Rather, Erikson chose this term to emphasize that they can be turning points with far-reaching implications.

The eight stages of Erikson's theory of personality development, which contain the crises, are presented in table 10.3. The name given to each stage by Erikson reflects the two possible outcomes of the stage. To a great extent, particularly in infancy and childhood, the outcome is influenced by the actions of children's parents and other significant people. For example, if infants' parents provide consistent, warm, and adequate care during their child's first year (stage of basic trust vs. mistrust), infants will learn to trust the world as a basically safe place. If infants are cared for inconsistently or are physically or emotionally abused, they will consider the world an unsafe place that cannot be trusted. Erikson believed that this basic sense of trust or mistrust is usually carried with the individual throughout life.

Erik H. Erikson (1902–1994).

Table 10.3　Erik Erikson's Stages of Personality Development

Age	Name of Stage	Developmental Accomplishments or Failures
0–1 year	Basic trust vs. mistrust	Learns to feel comfortable and trust parents' care; or develops a deep distrust of a world that is perceived to be unsafe
1–3 years	Autonomy vs. shame and doubt	Learns sense of competence by learning to feed self, use toilet, play alone; or feels ashamed and doubts own abilities
3–5 years	Initiative vs. guilt	Gains ability to use own initiative in planning and carrying out plans; or, if cannot live within parents' limits, develops a sense of guilt over misbehavior
5–11 years	Industry vs. inferiority	Learns to meet the demands imposed by school and home responsibilities; or comes to believe that he or she is inferior to others
11–18 years	Identity vs. role confusion	Acquires sense of own identity; or is confused about role in life
18–40 years	Intimacy vs. isolation	Develops couple relationship and joint identity with partner; or becomes isolated from meaningful relationships with others
40–65 years	Generativity vs. stagnation	Develops a concern with helping others and leaving children, products, and ideas to future generations; or becomes self-centered and stagnant
65–years on	Integrity vs. despair	Reaps benefits of earlier stages and understands and accepts meaning of a temporary life; or despairs over ever being able to find meaning in life

Stage theorists, such as Piaget (cognition), Kohlberg and Gilligan (moral reasoning), and Erikson (personality), see developmental changes as occurring in distinct steps, or stages, through which all children pass in the same order. Other psychologists tend to perceive these changes as being gradual and not marked by clear-cut stages. Many psychologists view development as occurring in something like stages, but ones that are not clearly separable from one another.

Review

To be sure that you have learned the key points from the preceding section, cover the list of correct answers and try to answer each question. If you give an incorrect answer to any question, return to the page given next to the correct answer to see why your answer was not correct.

Check Your Learning

1. _____ distinguished four major stages of cognitive development, the sensorimotor stage, the preoperational stage, the concrete operational stage, and the formal operational stage.

   a) Jean Piaget   c) Sigmund Freud

   b) John Bowlby   d) Harry Harlow

2. Kohlberg's theory of moral development was criticized by Gilligan primarily because _____.

   a) the data did not support   c) it was done so long ago his conclusions

   b) it was based on a study   d) his subjects consisted of urban of boys only children only

3. Gilligan suggests that moral reasoning in_____ centers on the needs of people rather than on abstractions.

   a) males

   b) females

4. In Erikson's stage theory of personality development, the stages are turning points, or _____, the outcome of which will partly determine the course of future personality development.

There are no right or wrong answers to the following questions. They are presented to help you become an active reader and think critically about what you just read.

Thinking Critically about Psychology

1. What are the similarities between the most advanced stages of moral reasoning described by Kohlberg and Gilligan?

2. What are the advantages of theories like Erikson's for understanding life-span development? What are their disadvantages?

Correct Answers: 1. a (p. 311), 2. b (p. 313), 3. b (p. 313), 4. crises (p. 314)

Normal Development across the Life Span

We now turn our attention to the normal course of development across the human life span. Our topic will be the typical physical and psychological changes that occur in people from birth to old age. This section is of *fundamental* importance to understanding human condition. Although we tend to think of ourselves as the persons we are right now, human lives are in a constant state of change. The person you are today is different in some ways from the person you were 10 years ago and from the person you will be 10 years from now.

Do you have any photographs that were taken of you as an infant? How about photos of you when you were in the first grade or just starting high school? If so, you can create an amazing learning experience by laying these photos out in a time line. My, how you have grown!

I thought it would help me write this chapter if I did the same thing. The six photos below show me from 5 months to my 50s. Look at the changes! The person in all the photos is me—the thread of continuity in my life is very clear—but the changes are certainly obvious, too. Look at that bewildered infant! It's amazing to me that I was ever that small—as an infant, I weighed less than 5% of what I weigh now—or that there was a time when I could neither walk nor talk. By the time I was 5 and was going off to kindergarten in that dashing sailor suit, I was walking, talking, and tying my shoes. But I could not yet read a book, let alone imagine that I would ever write one.

In high school, I played football and took the advice of my coach that the only proper way to cut hair was *off.* I learned how to play guitar about the same year that this photo was taken and played in some really bad high school rock bands. Later, in the 1960s, I grew more hair and sang and played a lot of folk songs (very badly). By the 70s, I was a young professor and clinical child psychologist, working hard to establish a career. I worked long hours and spent a great deal of time with my children. I was so busy that I did not even own a guitar for most of the 70s. Is that a bit of gray creeping into my shaggy head of hair?

In the 1980s, my hair was still long, but no longer brown. During this decade, I found time to play the guitar again. In fact, a friend of mine owned a recording studio and he let me live out a childhood fantasy of recording a song. That's me in the studio, listening intently to the advice of my bass player, who happens also to be my son. Many changes had taken place in my life by midlife, but when I listened to the recording I found that I still played the guitar badly and sang even worse! The last photo is me in my 50s—back to short hair and showing more than a few wrinkles. Once again, there is little time for the guitar, but considering my lack of talent, that's for the best.

Now, consider this question: which picture best represents me—the real me? The answer: all of them. And that is exactly the point of this section on the life span. We are all in a constant state of change—called development—throughout our lives. If you are going to understand human lives, you must understand that fundamental point.

We will now begin to tell the story of development across the life span. First, we will start with prenatal development. We then will follow the child from infancy through the stages of childhood, through adolescence, and finally through the stages of adult life.

Prenatal Development

The **prenatal period** is period of enormous development—more development occurred before our birth than will occur throughout our lifetime. This period is typically divided into three stages. The **germinal stage** starts at conception, when a sperm cell fertilizes an egg to form a zygote, which is a single cell. That cell then begins to divide and duplicate itself, over and over again. When the cells start to differentiate to specialize into different organs of the body two weeks after conception, the **embryonic stage** begins. During this stage all of the major organs begin to form and the heart begins to beat. The **fetal stage,** the last stage of prenatal development, begins 8 weeks after conception. The physical maturation of the organs occurs during the final stage, as the fetus grows rapidly in size.

Prenatal development is quite rapid and generally quite ordered. All of us went through similar developmental phases before we were born. But, different organs and biological systems begin developing at different times. For instance the heart begins development well before the eyes. This development does not happen by itself, however. During pregnancy an organ called the **placenta** develops to connect the mother and the developing fetus. The placenta transfers nutrients and oxygen to the fetus, removes waste from the fetus, and blocks some, but not all, harmful substances from reaching the fetus. As such, the placenta plays a critical role in prenatal development (Coe & Lubach, 2008).

But, why include prenatal development in a psychology textbook? Remember that who you are now depends in part on where you came from, and this includes your prenatal environment. The **developmental origins hypothesis** (Barker, 1992) states that prenatal factors influence the development of physical and psychological health. Research over the past couple of decades has supported this hypothesis—prenatal development appears to have profound implications for later development (Barker, 1992; Coe & Lubach, 2008). For example, prenatal exposure to harmful substances, such as maternal alcohol consumption (D'Onofrio & others, 2007), high levels of maternal stress during pregnancy (Seckl, 2008), and maternal infection during pregnancy (Brown & Derkits, 2010) have been associated with emotional, behavioral, and physical consequences across the infant's life span. Adequate prenatal nutrition is also necessary for normal intellectual development (de Rooij & others, 2010). These are just a few examples of prenatal risk factors that have been identified, but the processes through which many of these factors influence later development currently is not known (Thapar & Rutter, 2009).

prenatal period The time between conception and birth.

germinal stage The period of development right after conception, which lasts about two weeks.

embryonic stage The second period of prenatal development during which organs start to form.

fetal stage The final stage of prenatal development during which the organs mature.

placenta The organ that connects the fetus and the mother during prenatal development.

developmental origins hypothesis The belief that prenatal factors influence the development of physical and psychological health.

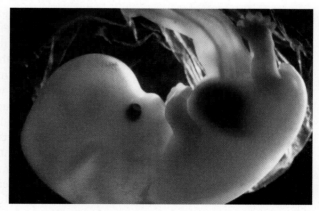

Researchers are beginning to understand the impact prenatal development has on the developing fetus.

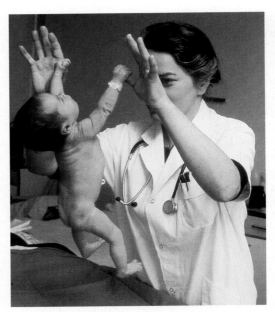

A neonate will reflexively grasp anything that is placed in its hand.

neonatal period (ne´´ō-nā´tal) The first two weeks of life following birth.

rooting reflex An automatic response in which an infant turns its head toward stimulation on the cheek.

Development in Infancy and Childhood

Dramatic developmental changes take place from birth to adolescence. The newborn becomes the infant, who becomes the toddler and then the child.

Neonatal Period: The Newborn

The first two weeks of life are termed the **neonatal period** and mark the transition from the womb to independent life. What is the world of the neonate like?

Physically, the neonate is weak and dependent on adults. It cannot raise its head or roll over by itself. The infant does have several useful reflexive behaviors, however. For example, when stimulated on one side of the mouth, the neonate turns its head toward the stimulation and begins searching and sucking until something is in its mouth. This **rooting reflex** enables the baby to take its mother's nipple in its mouth and nurse.

The sensory abilities of neonates are surprisingly well developed. Their hearing is fairly good, and they react differently to different odors and tastes (Santrock, 1998). Their vision is still limited, but they can see objects clearly that are 10 to 12 inches from their face. They have a distinct preference for staring at complex objects that have a lot of detail at the top (Cassia, Turati, & Simion, 2004). Fortunately for parents, this means that they spend a lot of time staring at the face of the adult who holds them. Neonates are quite sensitive to touch (Santrock, 1998). Few cognitive abilities are developed during the neonatal period, but neonates respond to faces in a way that suggests they recognize that they are a conceptual class distinct from other concepts of objects (Santrock, 1998). In most ways, however, the process of cognitive development is just beginning, and the neonate is just beginning to engage in social behavior during the intimate contact between neonate and parent in cuddling and nursing.

Infancy: 2 Weeks to 2 Years

Physical Development. At 2 weeks of age, the baby acquires the official title of infant. Much is going on developmentally during this period of rapid change. Physical development and growth are more rapid during the first year than at any other time after birth. By 2 months, many infants can raise their head and chest on their arms and can grasp an object that is held directly in front of their head and shoulders. Although young infants reflexively move to free their mouth and nose when something blocks their breathing, they increasingly rely on voluntary movements to keep their nose and mouth clear as they develop. During the transition period from reflexive to voluntary movements from 2 to 5 months, however, children are sometimes unable to free their airways. This is why using supports to keep infants sleeping on their backs for the first year has been successful in greatly reducing the number of infants that die of sudden infant death syndrome, or SIDS (Lipsitt, 2003).

By 6 months, many can roll over from back to front, sit, and begin to crawl. By 1 year, many can walk alone and grasp small objects with their fingers and thumbs. By 2 years, they are "getting into everything" and walking well.

From 2 weeks to 2 months, rapid change takes place in all senses. Clear vision increases to 12 feet during this period. By 6 months of age, their vision is 20/20 (normal). Young infants amuse themselves, and their families, by staring at interesting visual stimuli. They prefer to look at patterned stimuli with sharp contours (Banks & Salapatek, 1981), such as human faces.

Although we think of infancy as a single stage of development, a tremendous amount of change occurs from birth to 2 years. This photo illustrates the physical differences in infants from 2 through 18 months. Notice the differences in how they sit—the 2-month-old can only lie there, whereas the 18-month-old can lounge casually on the arm of the couch.

Cognitive Development (Sensorimotor Stage).

Infancy is the **sensorimotor stage,** according to Jean Piaget. During the early part of this stage, the infant begins to coordinate sensations and motor movements, such as voluntarily taking a nipple into the mouth and sucking. From about 2 months on, the infant begins to interact actively with its environment. It no longer passively stares at objects but takes great pleasure in pushing, pulling, and mouthing them. This kind of experience, in which the infant actively changes the sensations it receives by using its hands and feet to alter the environment (sensorimotor experience), is believed to be important in the development of motor behaviors such as crawling and cognitive development (Adolph & Berger, 2006; Held & Hein, 1963). By 4½ months, most infants respond positively to the sound of their names (Mandel, Jusczyk, & Pisoni, 1995).

From at least 2 months on, infants remember some of what they have experienced for a time (Ornstein & Haden, 2001; Pelphrey & others, 2004). Psychologist Carolyn Rovee-Collier (1999) developed a clever way to study memory in infants. Infants are placed in a crib with a distinctive mobile overhead. A ribbon is connected to one ankle, but at first it is not connected to the mobile. This is done to test the babies to see how much they kick spontaneously. Then they experience a "training period" in which the ribbon on their ankle is connected to the mobile—kicking causes movement of the mobile that the infants find to be positively reinforcing, so they kick more frequently. Later they are tested for their memory of this simple learning experience by placing them in the crib again and seeing how much they kick with the ribbon unattached. If they kick more than in their initial test, that suggests that they remember the learning experience. Infants of 6 months show memory for the task for as long as 2 weeks on average. The memory of older infants is tested by first having them learn to press a lever to move an electric train around a track. Later they are tested on their recall of this new skill. One-year-olds show recall of the train task for up to 8 weeks on average, whereas the average 18-month-old can remember this task for over 12 weeks.

During infancy, children develop the ability to form cognitive representations of the world. For example, by 6 to 9 months of age, the child begins to understand that objects exist even when they are out of sight. This is called **object permanence.** Before that time, if an object at which the infant is looking is hidden from sight by a card, the infant will not push the card aside to look for it. It's as if the infant does not know that the object is still there. After 6 to 9 months of age, however, the infant will search for the object behind the card, suggesting that the infant knows that it's back there somewhere. This is both a happy and a sad development for parents. Now that the 9-month-old knows that spoons still exist when thrown on the floor, the infant quickly masters the game of "dropsies" (McCall, 1979). Infants joyously fill

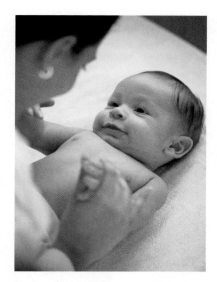

During the sensorimotor stage, infants stare at complex visual stimuli, including human faces.

sensorimotor stage In Piaget's theory, the period of cognitive development from birth to 2 years.

object permanence The understanding that objects continue to exist when they are not in view.

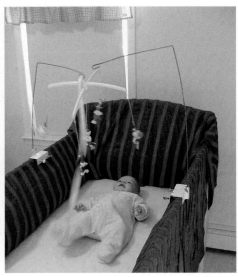

Psychologist Carolyn Rovee-Collier studies the memory of young infants using a clever adaptation of a mobile in a crib. At first (left), the infant is placed in the crib with a ribbon tied to her or his ankle to see how often the baby spontaneously kicks. Then (right) the ribbon is attached to the mobile to make it move when the baby kicks. On the average, the babies kick more often when the ribbon is attached because movement of the mobile is positively reinforcing. Later the babies are tested for their memory of this simple learning task by placing them in the crib again with the ribbon unattached. Babies who recall the task kick more than in the initial test.

Awareness that objects still exist after they are removed from view (object permanence) emerges between the ages of 6 and 9 months.

telegraphic speech The abbreviated speech of 2-year-olds.

their mealtimes with the game of throwing their spoons on the floor while Dad or Mom picks them up. By 14 months, infants even look for objects that were removed 24 hours earlier (Moore & Meltzoff, 2004), but although infants can represent parts of the world in mental images, they cannot yet use those images to reason.

By 9 months, too, infants begin to understand some nouns, such as *ball* and *cookie,* and can respond to *bye-bye* and other gestures. These changes mark the beginning of a far more complex level of cognitive functioning. By 12 months, most infants can say some words, and by 18 months the infant has a speaking vocabulary of 20 words. By 18 months, the average infant can also respond to prohibitions ("No, no . . . don't touch") and can respond correctly to "Show me your nose (ear, toe, mouth, etc.)." By age 2, the infant has a speaking vocabulary of 300 words and speaks in word combinations that fascinate adults because they accomplish so much by saying so little. It has often been referred to as **telegraphic speech,** because it leaves out the same words that would be left out of a brief telegram. Sentences like "Milk all gone" and "Daddy silly" say all that needs to be said.

Emotional and Social Development. Infants enter the world with a restricted range of emotions that grows more complex as they mature. Neonates are capable of only three emotional expressions: surprise, pleasure, and distress (National Advisory Mental Health Council, 1995a). By about 2 months, they show their first true social behavior—they smile at the faces of their caregivers. By 4 months, they have added a fourth emotion to their repertoire—anger. The infant's repertoire of emotions expands again between 6 and 9 months, when shyness around strangers and fear of being separated from their caregivers emerge for the first time. Before 6 to 9 months, infants are generally comfortable with any adult who will take care of them, but after that time they are often fearful of anyone but their mother, father, or

Figure 10.3
Eleanor Gibson and Richard Walk (1960) developed the visual cliff to test infant depth perception. The visual cliff consists of a thick sheet of glass placed on a table. The "shallow" end of the visual cliff has a checkerboard surface an inch or so below the glass. The "deep" end of the visual cliff has a checkerboard surface several feet below the glass. An infant who has reached the crawling stage will crawl from the center of the table across the shallow end, but not across the deep end, to reach his or her mother. This indicates that by at least the age of 6 months infants can perceive depth.

other caregiver (National Advisory Mental Health Council, 1995a). The emergence of social smiling at 2 months is a nice reward for parents, who change diapers and walk the floor at night, but the appearance of anger and fear between 4 and 9 months is not always welcome. Both are signs of normal, healthy development of the infant's emotions, however.

Cornell University psychologist Eleanor Gibson developed an interesting method of studying the development of the fear of heights (Gibson & Walk, 1960). When 6- to 9-month-old infants are placed on the "visual cliff" (see figure 10.3), they show fear and avoidance of the "deep" side. The visual cliff is made using a clear sheet of Plexiglas. Under one side, a patterned floor is right under the glass. On the other side, the pattern is several feet below the glass. When lighted properly, it appears to be a cliff from which the infant could fall. It's interesting to note that infants can perceive the depth of the visual cliff several months before they show any fear of it. They look puzzled when placed on the deep side of the visual cliff at 4 months but do not show fear until after they can crawl and have experienced stumbling and falling firsthand (Lewis & Rosenblum, 1978; Scarr & Salapatek, 1970).

Infants are richly social creatures who have formed strong **attachments** to their parents or other caregivers (Cassidy & Shaver, 2008; Lewis & Rosenblum, 1978). The strength of this attachment can be seen in three ways. First, infants often cling, grasp, grab, and do whatever else they can to stay close to their parents. Nothing short of the parents' physical closeness and undivided attention will suffice at times. Second, when infants 6 to 9 months or older are separated from their parents, they become anxious. This is known as **separation anxiety**—the crying and fussing that babysitters know so well when the child's parents are about to leave the child. Third, infants of this age sometimes also exhibit fear of strangers; no one but the adults to whom they are attached (parents, day-care workers, grandparents) has the same soothing effect. By 2 years, emotions grow even more complex. By this time, many infants act guilty after misbehavior and seem to feel ashamed after failure.

attachments The psychological bonds between infants and caregivers.

separation anxiety The distress experienced by infants when they are separated from their caregivers.

Strong attachments are formed between infants and caregivers during the first two years of life.

Early Childhood: 2 to 7 Years

According to Piaget, a qualitative change occurs as the child reaches the preoperational stage at about 2 years of age. Early childhood is still a period of rapid growth, but growth is far less explosive than in infancy and declines in rate annually. Great improvements in the coordination of small and large muscle groups take place during this period, which sees the emergence of hopping, skipping, throwing, and the other motor behaviors that are so much a part of early childhood.

preoperational stage In Piaget's theory, the period of cognitive development from ages 2 to 7.

Cognitive Development (Preoperational Stage). The **preoperational stage** begins at 2 years of age and is a time of dramatic change in cognition. By about 2 years of age, most children are first capable of thinking in mental images. The young child's ability to think is quite different from that of adults, however.

The preoperational child's thinking is often quite illogical by adult standards. Indeed, the name of this stage comes from the fact that the child still cannot perform logical mental operations. There are a variety of other ways in which the cognition of the preoperational child is wonderfully distinct. For example, the young child's thought is **egocentric,** or self-centered. Piaget does not mean by this term that the child is selfish but that the child is simply not able to see things from another person's perspective. Egocentrism also leads young children to believe that inanimate objects are alive, just as they are (known as **animism**). It's common for children of this age to believe that the moon is alive and actually follows them around when they are walking at night.

egocentric (e˝gō-sen´trik) The self-oriented quality in the thinking of preoperational children.

animism (a´-n -mizm) The egocentric belief of preoperational children that inanimate objects are alive, as children are.

The child's imagination is often very active at this stage, and because of the child's egocentrism, it's difficult at times for him or her to distinguish real from imaginary. Other errors of logic are quite common, too, giving young children a special kind of logic demonstrated in comments such as "Grandma, he's not your son; he's my daddy!"

transductive reasoning (trans-duk´tiv) Errors in understanding cause-and-effect relationships that are commonly made by preoperational children.

Transductive reasoning—errors in inferring cause-and-effect relationships—is also common in the preoperational child (Schlottman, 2001). For example, a preoperational child might conclude that spiders cause the basement to be cold. Indeed, the basement *is* cold and there *are* spiders in it, but young children often confuse the cause-and-effect relationships among such facts.

By the end of this period, the preoperational child begins to grasp logical operations and makes fewer cause-and-effect errors. At age 5, the child may be able to pick out all the blue marbles from a jar or all the big marbles, but thinking about two concepts at one time is still difficult. For example, picking out all the big blue marbles may still be too much.

During the preoperational period, children develop a sense of themselves as distinct from other persons and develop an "autobiographical" memory for the events that define their lives (Nelson & Fivush, 2004). As adults, we are able to remember little of our childhood experiences before the emergence of autobiographical memory.

Perhaps the most impressive developmental change during the preoperational stage is the growth in language. From a speaking vocabulary of 300 words at age 2, children in all cultures reach a vocabulary of more than 14,000 words by age 6, and 60,000 words by 18 years. This means that children must learn a phenomenal average of 10 new words per day from age 2 to age 18 (Bornstein & others, 2004; Ganger & Brent, 2004). From simple 2- or 3-word combinations at age 2, the child masters much of adult syntax during the same period. Seemingly, the child has finally achieved the maturational capacity to learn language and proceeds to do so without hesitation.

Emotional and Social Development. Both positive and negative emotions are fairly well developed by age 2, but they become considerably richer and more intricate during the preoperational stage. Most of this elaboration of emotion seems to be linked to cognitive development. For example, children do not develop fears of unexperienced things—such as fires, drowning, and traffic accidents—until well into the preoperational period, when they are capable of understanding the concepts behind the fears.

The most notable social changes during this period occur in relationships with peers. At age 2, most children engage in solitary play. That is, they play by themselves, even if other children are present. This type of play rapidly decreases in frequency from ages 2 to 5. At first, **solitary play** is replaced by **parallel play,** in which children play near one another in similar activities, but not with one another. By the end of the preoperational stage, **cooperative play,** which involves a cooperative give-and-take, has become the predominant type of play (Barnes, 1971).

The shifting pattern of play seems to parallel cognitive development. In the early part of the preoperational stage, when thinking is highly egocentric, it's not surprising that selfishness and lack of cooperation should prevail. Young children may not be able to understand any other type of play. As they reach the end of the stage, however, egocentric thinking declines and cooperative play increases.

About two-thirds of children have imaginary companions at some point between the ages of 2 and 7 years (Taylor & others, 2004). Not only are these imaginary playmates not harmful, children who have them tend to understand the emotions of others better. Apparently, they learn about others by imagining the playmate.

A similar shift occurs in emotional outbursts from the beginning to the end of the preoperational stage. Two- and 3-year-olds typically engage in temper tantrums that are directed at no one, whereas 4- to 7-year-olds direct their aggression at others (Sheppard & Willoughby, 1975). Although this kind of behavior is hardly "sociable," it's a more social, less egocentric form of emotion than temper tantrums.

By age 2, most boys and girls have begun to act in sex-typed ways. Males tend to play with trucks, airplanes, and blocks; girls play mostly with dolls, stuffed animals, and dress-up clothes (Fagot, 1974). At this early age, they seem to have a conscious awareness of their own sex (McConaghy, 1979) and understand the sex stereotypes of the culture concerning clothing, occupations, and recreation (Ruble & Ruble, 1980).

solitary play Playing alone.

parallel play Playing near but not with another child.

cooperative play Play that involves cooperation between two or more children.

The most notable social changes in the preoperational period are in peer relationships. Between the ages of about 2 and about 7, children go from mostly solitary play, through parallel play, and finally on to cooperative play.

Middle Childhood: 7 to 11 Years

These are the elementary school years. It's no accident that formal education begins in earnest during this period, because at this age most children are intellectually and socially ready for the demands of school. Physical growth proceeds at a fairly slow pace in middle childhood, but it's a healthy period in which most children experience little illness. Continued improvements in strength and coordination are the only notable advances.

Cognitive Development (Concrete Operational Stage). The opening of the **concrete operational stage** is marked by important cognitive changes. Children emerge as capable thinkers who use most adult concepts except those that are abstract. They can order objects (seriation) according to size, weight, and other dimensions. They understand the **reversibility** of logical operations; having added together $7 + 2 = 9$, they have little trouble reversing the operation to see that $9 - 2 = 7$.

One of the most fascinating acquisitions of the concrete operational child is the concept of **conservation.** When children younger than 7 are shown 2 wide beakers containing equal amounts of water, they have no trouble seeing that they contain the "same amount" of water. But, when the water from one beaker is poured into a tall, narrow beaker right in front of their eyes, they usually think the tall beaker contains

concrete operational stage In Piaget's theory, the period of cognitive development from ages 7 to 11.

reversibility (re-ver´sə bil-ə-tē) The concept understood by concrete operational children that logical propositions can be reversed (if $2 + 3 = 5$, then $5 - 3 = 2$).

conservation The concept understood by concrete operational children that quantity (number, mass, etc.) does not change just because shape or other superficial features have changed.

In the concrete operational stage, children learn to recognize that the volume of a liquid does not change when it is poured into a glass of a different shape.

decenter (dē-sen´ter) To think about more than one characteristic of a thing at a time; a capacity of concrete operational children.

"more" water because it's higher. Children over the age of 7 who are in the concrete operational period are not fooled by appearances in this way. According to Piaget, the concrete operational children are able to deal with conservation problems because their thought is more **decentered,** which means that they can think of more than one thing at a time. Consequently, the concrete operational child no longer has trouble picking out the big blue marbles from a jar; he or she can deal with both concepts at the same time. The rapid growth in cognitive ability during middle childhood is based on rapid increases in children's speed of processing information and expansions in the capacity of short-term memory (Fry & Hale, 1996).

Emotional and Social Development. Few changes of note occur in the expression of emotions during the concrete operational stage, but social relationships are markedly different than before. Children enter this period with close ties to their parents. Although these continue to be important, relationships with peers become increasingly significant during this period. Before age 7, children have friendships, but they generally are not enduring and typically are not close. After 7, peer friendships become more important to children and tend to last longer. Friendship groups, or *cliques,* also emerge during the concrete operational stage, and most friendships are with members of the same sex.

Review

When we look back over the explosive growth of the neonate into a child, it appears that there may be some utility in discussing development in terms of stages. Interrelated changes in several behavioral systems do occur that seem dramatic enough to justify the phrase "qualitatively different stage." However, the entrance to a new stage is not marked by abrupt changes. Developmental changes are gradual and inconsistent, and they take place both within and between stages. There is value, then, in thinking of human development in terms of stages, but there are limits on that value. The detailed picture of infant and child development presented in this section shows that human growth is both a series of landmark steps and a continuous, flowing process. There are no shortcuts to describing the marvelous complexities of human development.

Check Your Learning

To be sure that you have learned the key points from the preceding section, cover the list of correct answers and try to answer each question. If you give an incorrect answer to any question, return to the page given next to the correct answer to see why your answer was not correct.

1. Although an infant during the _____ (first two weeks of life) is weak and dependent on adults, it does have useful reflexive behaviors and has already begun to learn.

   a) trimester   c) toddler period

   b) neonatal period   d) prenatal period

2. By 6 to 9 months of age, a child begins to understand that objects exist even when they are out of sight. This is called _____.

   a) object permanence   c) constancy theory

   b) continuation   d) conservation

3. According to Piaget, the _____ stage (ages 2 to 7 years) is marked by a phenomenal growth in language.

   a) operational

   b) concrete operational

   c) infancy

   d) preoperational

4. _____ describes the concept understood by concrete operational children (ages 7 to 11 years) that quantity does not change just because shape or other superficial features have changed.

   a) Object permanence

   b) Conservation

   c) Quantity maintenance

   d) Continuity

Thinking Critically about Psychology

There are no right or wrong answers to the following questions. They are presented to help you become an active reader and think critically about what you just read.

1. If you were a teacher of kindergarten children, how would knowledge of the preoperational stage of cognitive development influence the way you teach?

2. If you were forced to choose, would you describe development in infancy and childhood as a series of stages or as a continuous process of change? How would you support your choice?

Correct Answers: 1. b (p. 318), 2. a (p. 319), 3. d (p. 322), 4. b (p. 323)

Adolescent Development

Adolescence is ushered in by the monumental physical changes of **puberty** through which the person who was a child only yesterday becomes sexually capable of being a parent. The adolescent period is marked by rapid physical growth, a heightening of sexual and romantic interest in others, and increases in the importance of peer relationships. The adolescent is capable of reasoning in abstractions for the first time. There is no clear-cut demarcation of the end of adolescence in our society. Rather than at any specific age, individuals pass from adolescence to adulthood when they establish adult social relationships and adult patterns of work.

adolescence The period from the onset of puberty until the beginning of adulthood.

puberty (pū′ber-tē) The point in development at which the individual is first physically capable of sexual reproduction.

Physical Development

A number of psychologically important physical changes occur during adolescence, particularly during puberty, which is the onset of adolescence. These changes alter physical appearance so much that—in what seems like a moment—girls come to look like women and boys like men. Height and weight increase sharply, pushing adolescents quickly to adult size. A look in the mirror changes forever the adolescent's image of himself or herself.

Puberty begins with the production of sex hormones by the ovaries in females and the testes in males. These hormones trigger a series of physiological changes that lead to ovulation and menstruation in females and the production of sperm cells in males. These are the **primary sex characteristics** that indicate that the adolescent has the ability to reproduce. These physical changes are accompanied by activation of sexual desire and corresponding increases in dating, kissing, petting, masturbation, and other sexual activities.

primary sex characteristics Ovulation and menstruation in females and production of sperm in males.

Activation of sexual desire occurs during adolescence.

menarche (me-nar´kē) The first menstrual period.

secondary sex characteristics
Development of the breasts and hips in females; growth of the testes, broadening of the shoulders, lowered voice, and growth of the penis and facial hair in males; and growth of pubic and other body hair in both sexes.

adolescent growth spurt The rapid increase in weight and height that occurs around the onset of puberty.

Menarche, or the first menstrual period, occurs on the average at about 12 years 6 months in American females, and the production of sperm begins about 2 years later in males (Matchock & others, 2004; Tanner, 1970). The age of menarche is younger today than in the past. In 1900, the average age of menarche in the United States was about 14 years (Tanner, 1970). Researchers believe that these differences are due to improved nutrition and health care but could also be caused by hormones in milk in the United States (Leenstra & others, 2005; Mandel & others, 2004).

The more obvious changes occurring during puberty are the development of the **secondary sex characteristics.** In females, the first change is an accumulation of fat in the breasts. There is also a growing accumulation of fat around the hips, resulting in a broadening that further gives the appearance of the adult female body shape. Finally, about the time of menarche, pubic hair begins to grow.

In males, the first secondary sexual change is the growth of the testes, followed by a broadening of the shoulders, lowering of the voice, and growth of the penis. Soon, pubic and facial hair grow, thus creating the physical image of an adult male.

Another outwardly obvious sign of puberty is the rapid increase in weight and height known as the **adolescent growth spurt.** Just before puberty, rapid weight gain is common, mostly in the form of fat. This can be a source of concern to both the adolescent and her or his parents, but soon most of this weight is redistributed or shed. At about the onset of puberty, the adolescent suddenly shoots up in height. As shown in figure 10.4, the rate of growth in height steadily declines after infancy, but it rises sharply for a little over a year in early adolescence. During the year of most rapid growth, many boys gain as much as 4 inches and 26 pounds, and many girls add as much as 3½ inches and 20 pounds.

Dramatic changes in the brain also take place in adolescence (Casey, Jones, & Hare, 2008; Spear, 2000). The structure and organization of the limbic system and frontal lobes change rapidly from childhood to adolescence in ways that promote risk taking, novelty seeking, and emotional response to stress. These changes are reversed in late adolescence as the brain takes on its adult organization (Casey, Jones, & Hare, 2008; Lewis, 1997). Spear (2000) has speculated that these changes, which are typical of many species of mammals, facilitate adolescents' leaving their families and breeding with members of other families to avoid inbreeding.

Figure 10.4

The adolescent growth spurt can be seen by the rapid increase in height that occurs in males and females at the beginning of puberty.

Source: Data from J. M. Tanner, R. H. Whitehouse, & M. Takaishi, "Standards from Birth to Maturity for Height, Weight, Height Velocity and Weight Velocity" in *Archives of Diseases in Childhood, 41,* 555–571, 1966.

Cognitive Development (Formal Operational Stage)

At about age 11, the shift from concrete operational to formal operational thought begins in some adolescents. Other individuals do not begin the shift as early or reach this advanced level of thinking until early adulthood, and some never reach it at all (Piaget, 1972; Santrock, 1998). The **formal operational stage** is characterized by an ability to use abstract concepts. The logic of formal operational thinking goes beyond the concrete details of each problem to the underlying abstract principles involved.

In a classic experiment conducted by Swiss developmental psychologists Barbel Inhelder and Jean Piaget (1958), children and adolescents of different ages were given two weights that could be hooked at different places on the arms of a scale; their job was to make the scale balance. Seven-year-olds— who were at the beginning of the concrete operational stage— were generally unable to balance the scale at all. They could understand that the two weights must be placed on opposite arms of the scale, but they did not seem to understand the importance of where the weights were hooked on the arms. By the end of the concrete operational stage, age 10, most children were able to balance the scale through trial and error, but they were not able to explain in words how it worked.

The ability to understand abstract concepts is a characteristic of formal operational thought.

By about age 14, many of the subjects had reached the stage of formal operational thinking and were able to explain that the farther a weight is placed from the center (fulcrum) of the scale, the more downward force it exerts. These children were able, without trial and error, to place a 5-kilogram weight twice as far from the fulcrum as a 10-kilogram weight on the other side. They could also easily deduce from this principle that weights of 3 and 6 or 2 and 4 kilograms would balance on the same hooks used by the 5- and 10-kilogram weights. They understood, in other words, the abstract principle that it's the ratio of weights and distances that matters, not the specific weights involved in any one example. They were able to think in abstract logical terms.

Individuals who have achieved formal operational thinking are able to use it in many areas of their lives. Piaget suggests, for example, that adolescents often seem preoccupied by concepts such as truth, justice, and the meaning of life partly because the capacity to think in such abstract terms is new to them.

Although most adolescents have reached the level of formal operational reasoning, their cognition at times often retains an immature quality. This is not really surprising; they have recently developed the ability to reason abstractly but have little experience on which to base their abstract thoughts. In particular, David Elkind (1967, 1981; Elkind & Bowen, 1979) has pointed out that adolescents often possess a form of egocentrism that, although different from the egocentrism of young children, similarly distorts their perception of reality. According to Elkind, there are four primary features of **adolescent egocentrism:**

1. *Imaginary audience.* Many adolescents act as though they believe that an audience is watching everything they do. If they stumble, stammer, or wear the wrong clothes, everyone will notice and talk about it.

2. *Personal fable.* The adolescent often believes that no one has similar problems or could possibly understand what he or she is going through.

3. *Hypocrisy.* It is often okay for the adolescent to copy someone else's homework, but a teacher who leaves class to take a short personal telephone call is irresponsible in the adolescent's eyes.

4. *Pseudostupidity.* Elkind believes that adolescents often use oversimplified logic. For example, when adolescents say, "If alcoholics know they are going to die of cirrhosis of the liver, why don't they just stop?" they fail to consider the many factors that contribute to an addiction to alcohol. Thus, their thinking is sometimes distorted a bit by their egocentrism, making their relationships with each other and with adults more difficult at times.

formal operational stage Period characterized by an ability to use abstract concepts.

adolescent egocentrism The quality of thinking that leads some adolescents to believe that they are the focus of attention in social situations, to believe that their problems are unique, to be unusually hypocritical, and to be "pseudostupid."

By adolescence, peers have become very important. The onset of puberty usually signals a dramatic increase in conformity to the ideas and judgments of the adolescent's peer group.

As you will readily notice, the thinking of fully mature adults is not always free of adolescent egocentrism. However, the four reality-distorting qualities are more characteristic of the adolescent stage than any other stage.

Emotional and Social Development

The shift from childhood to adolescence and from adolescence to adulthood is marked by changes in the emotional and social spheres of our lives.

Adolescent Social Development. Adolescents also show marked changes in their social relationships. Adolescence is a time of drifting away, and sometimes of breaking away, from the family. The onset of puberty particularly brings a distancing from parents (Arnett, 1999; Galambos, 1992). Adolescence peers, including intimate partners (Diamond, Fagundes, & Butterworth, 2010), often become the most important people in the adolescent's life. The shift in orientation from parents to peers can be seen in the dramatic increase in conformity to the ideas and judgments of the peer group that occurs at the beginning of puberty (around ages 11 to 13) but declines from age 15 on. In addition, young adolescents spend much more time with their peers than parents, even on weekends (Santrock, 1998).

Contrary to popular views of adolescence, current research suggests that about 80 percent of adolescents experience a relatively happy youth. However, risky behavior is common, and some adolescents do experience serious emotional and behavioral problems.

Adolescent Emotions. Since 1904, when the first American text on adolescent psychology was published by G. Stanley Hall, a debate has continued unabated about the nature of adolescent emotions. Is it a carefree period of happiness or, as Hall would have it, a time of "storm and stress"? Like many philosophical debates that are eventually settled by scientific evidence, the truth lies somewhere between the extreme viewpoints.

Contrary to popular views of adolescence, current research suggests that about 80% of adolescents are relatively happy and well adjusted (Arnett, 1999; Shaffer & others, 1996). In most areas, adolescents are as well adjusted as children and adults, but there are three areas in which adolescents have greater problems than both younger and older individuals:

1. *Parent-child conflicts.* Conflicts between parents and children increase during early adolescence and remain common until they decline in late adolescence (Arnett, 1999). These conflicts typically focus on dating, how long teenagers should be away from home, where they can go, and who they can be with (which often reflect differences in parent and adolescent views on sex, alcohol, drugs, delinquency, and safety).

2. *Mood changes.* Many studies now show that, compared with childhood and adulthood, adolescents experience more shifts of mood and more extremely positive and negative moods (Arnett, 1999; Roberts, Caspi, & Moffitt, 2001). Compared with children and adults, adolescents also are much more likely to feel self-conscious, embarrassed, awkward, lonely, nervous, and ignored.

3. *Risky behavior.* During adolescence, there is a sharp increase in the amount of behavior that exposes the child to danger. There is a marked increase in drinking to become drunk, use of drugs, reckless driving (and automobile accidents and fatalities), unprotected sex, aggression, and delinquent behavior, which does not decline until early adulthood (Arnett, 1999; Steinberg, 2009). Rates of suicide also increase dramatically during adolescence (but are still much lower than in adulthood).

Why do these unfortunate changes take place during adolescence? No one knows for sure, but it appears that adolescence is a tough time for many youths for a combination of reasons. Changes in the brain, surges in sex hormones, increases in social stress, and conflicts over autonomy during this natural period of transition all seem to be involved (Arnett, 1999; Casey, Jones, & Hare, 2008; Spear, 2000).

Review

In the span of about a decade, each individual passes from childhood to adulthood. This adolescent period of transition begins with the adolescent growth spurt and the emergence of primary and secondary sex characteristics (puberty) and ends with the assumption of adult patterns of work, living, and relationships. It's a period of dramatic physical changes. Considerable gains are made in height, weight, and strength; body fat is redistributed; and boys and girls come to look like men and women. These physical changes are often of considerable concern to self-conscious adolescents, particularly when irregularities and sex differences in physical development are obvious. Cognitively, most adolescents develop formal operational thinking, which gives them the ability to reason abstractly, but they often experience an adolescent form of egocentrism. Socially, they complete the shift from a focus on their families to a focus on peers. The great majority of adolescents are well adjusted, but adolescents are moodier and engage in more parent-child conflict and risky behavior than at any other period of their lives.

Check Your Learning

To be sure that you have learned the key points from the preceding section, cover the list of correct answers and try to answer each question. If you give an incorrect answer to any question, return to the page given next to the correct answer to see why your answer was not correct.

1. _____ is the period from the onset of puberty until the beginning of adulthood and is marked by rapid physical growth and change, as well as by a heightening of sexual and romantic interest in others.

2. The rapid increase in weight and height that occurs around the onset of puberty is known as the _____.

   a) maturation stage
   c) physical development stage
   b) adolescent growth spurt
   d) menarche

3. The _____ stage is characterized by an ability to use abstract concepts.

   a) concrete operational
   c) preoperational
   b) formal operational
   d) operational

4. We are more likely to experience which of the following during adolescence than at any other time in our lives?

   a) moodiness
   c) risky behavior
   b) parent-child conflicts
   d) all of the above

There are no right or wrong answers to the following questions. They are presented to help you become an active reader and think critically about what you just read.

1. Although adolescence is a time when peer influence often outweighs parental influence, most adolescents continue to hold values and attitudes that are similar to those of their parents. What factors might account for this?

2. What psychological changes mark the period called adolescence? Do they seem significant enough to be treated as a separate developmental period?

Correct Answers: 1. Adolescence (p. 325), **2.** b (p. 326), **3.** b (p. 327), **4.** d (p. 328)

Adulthood: Young Adulthood through Older Adulthood

Adulthood is the time of taking on adult responsibilities in work and social relationships. Adulthood is not a single phase of life. The challenges of adult love, work, and play change considerably during adulthood. The demands of maintaining a marriage are very different for newlyweds, parents of infants, parents of teenagers, or a couple in their 70s. Similar changes occur in the demands of work and play. In other words, adulthood is not the end of the process of development. Developmental changes *continue* throughout adulthood.

Physical Development

The life span is a continuous process of physical change. We continue to strengthen and grow well into early adulthood, but the body begins a slow process of physical decline after early adulthood. Physical speed and endurance decline gradually from early adulthood on. More and more of us need reading glasses for near vision with increasing age and have difficulty seeing in weak light and in the periphery of vision owing to a loss of rod cells in the retina after middle age. Our ability to hear high-pitched tones declines after age 20, with loss of ability to hear low-pitched sounds beginning in our 60s (Fisk & Rogers, 2002). Our sense of taste remains pretty much intact into later life, but many older adults report that food tastes more bland. This is due to declines in the number of taste buds and in the sense of smell with aging.

Cognitive Development

Cognitive development continues throughout adulthood, as some cognitive abilities improve whereas others decline. As shown in figure 10.5, fluid intelligence (solving logical problems, especially doing so quickly, reaches its peak in the early 20s and declines thereafter (Li & others, 2004; Salthouse, 2004). On average, fluid intelligence declines by a third by the late 80s, but different people decline at very different rates as they grow older. Much of the average decline in fluid intelligence is due to rapid declines in persons with Alzheimer's disease and other brain diseases, while healthy adults show much slower declines in fluid intelligence (Shimamura & others, 1995).

Crystallized intelligence (knowledge and skills) improves until the late 30s and then declines very slowly afterward (Li & others, 2004; Steinberg, 1995). Some aspects of crystallized intelligence follow a slightly different developmental course. Vocabulary increases until about age 65 and then holds steady (Salthouse 2004), and there are continued small increases across the adult years in our ability to solve problems of life in ways that are judged to be "wise" (Baltes & Staudinger, 1993). The rate and extent of these changes differ markedly from individual to individual, depending in part on the level of healthy exercise and activity that the individual maintains during adulthood (Lovden & others, 2010).

Emotional and Social Development

What about changes in our emotions, social relationships, and personalities? Do we go through developmental changes in these areas, too? The answer is a very interesting "yes and no." Imagine that a group of 1,000 18-year-old women and men took a test that measures their typical ways of responding emotionally and socially (a measure of their personalities, in other words) and then took the same test every 10 years until they were 90. How consistent would their personalities be across their adult lives? In one sense, their personalities would be very consistent over time. For example, people who scored higher than most other people at age 20 on a measure of emotionality would still score higher than most others at ages 30, 40, and so on. In this sense, the major dimensions of adult personality are very stable (McCrae & Costa, 1994; Moscowitz, Brown, & Cote, 1997; Roberts, Caspi, & Moffitt, 2001).

In another sense, however, predictable changes in personality occur during the adult part of the life span (McCrae & others, 1999). Although adults tend to keep their same rank order relative to others on most dimensions of personality over time (if they are higher or lower than others at 18, they still tend to be higher or lower than others at 40, and so on), the average personality trait scores of adults do change over time. On average, adults become less anxious and emotional, less socially outgoing, and less creative as they grow older, but they become more dependable, agreeable, and accepting of life's hardships (Helson & others, 2002; Kennedy, Mather, & Carstensen, 2004; Ross & Wilson, 2003; Vaidya & others, 2002). In addition, some gender differences in personality become muted over time: Women become more assertive, confident, and independent, and men become more aware of their aesthetic needs and their need for affection (Stewart & Ostrove, 1998).

How can our adult personalities be both stable and change at the same time? Although the average score of adults on, say, emotionality declines, people who are higher than others on emotionality at one age tend to stay higher than others at later ages, even though their emotionality declines along with the rest of the adult population. At 60, they are considerably less emotional than they were at 20 in absolute terms, but they are still more emotional than most other 60-year-olds (who have become less emotional in absolute terms, too). So, the key dimensions of our personalities change with increasing age, often in ways that make life more enjoyable, but people tend to stay in their same positions on each trait relative to other people.

It should be obvious, however, that most human lives are not "stable" in the strictest sense. Most of us experience periods of happiness and stability in alternation with periods of discontent and change. The woman who grows unhappy with her career in retailing after 20 years and returns to college to become a minister and the man who happily remarries after an unhappy 15-year marriage are but two examples.

There is much disagreement as to the way in which to think about such changes, however. Some psychologists believe that adulthood consists of a series of "stages of development," rather like the stages of child development proposed by Piaget and

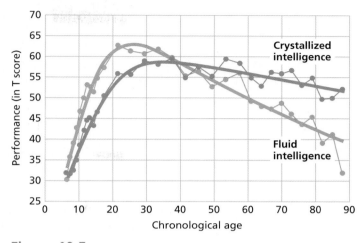

Figure 10.5

Fluid and crystallized intelligence increase with age into adulthood and then begin to decline. Note that fluid intelligence peaks earlier and declines more rapidly than crystallized intelligence.

(Adapted with permission from S.-C. Li, Lindenberger, Hommel, Aschersleben, Prinz, & Baltes, 2004.

Although personality traits remain relatively stable throughout adulthood, most adults can expect some personality changes in their middle and later years. Some of these are positive; for example, middle-age men often become more aware of their need for affection. Middle-age women often become more self-confident.

others. Erik Erikson (1963) and Daniel Levinson (1978, 1986) have each proposed a set of stages of adult life. These stages of adult development are different from the stages of infant and child development in three ways:

1. Not every adult is believed to go through every stage.

2. The order of the stages can vary for some individuals.

3. The timing of the stages is not controlled by biological maturation.

Although Erikson proposes three stages of adulthood and Levinson proposes nine stages, Levinson's theory can be thought of as an elaboration of Erikson's views. For this reason, we will discuss both stage theories together. Note that both theorists see adulthood as a series of alternating periods of stability and transition.

Stages of Adult Life

Early Adulthood: Intimacy vs. Isolation (17 to 45 Years). Erikson (1963) discussed his proposed stages of adult life in terms of the challenges faced at each stage and the consequences of successfully or unsuccessfully meeting those challenges. These adult stages are the continuation of the stages of child and adolescent development. He referred to early adulthood as the stage of *intimacy versus isolation.* The challenge of this stage is to enter into committed, loving relationships with others that partially replace the bonds with parents. If we are successful in this task, we will have the intimacy needed to progress in adult life; if not, we will become isolated and less capable of full emotional development, according to Erikson.

Levinson (1986) sees the transition to early adulthood as beginning sometime between the ages of 17 and 22 for most individuals (see figure 10.6). Early adulthood itself consists of three briefer stages. The *entry to early adulthood* lasts until approximately age 28. This is a time of creating an adult manner of working and living independently and often a time of marriage and young children. The *age 30 transition* (28 to 33) is a time of reevaluating one's start into adult life. Is this the right job for me? The right city? The right spouse? A sense of pressure often accompanies these decisions—they must be made "before it's too late."

The *culmination of early adulthood* is a time of working hard toward one's goals. It extends roughly from the early 30s to about age 40. During this phase, adults sometimes join the PTA Executive Board to improve the quality of their children's school, plant trees in the yard, and work long hours for promotion to a senior position at work. The individual is often aware of feeling like a full member of the adult generation at this time.

In general, the stage of early adulthood is a demanding one. The young adult often takes on the challenges of a career, a marriage, and parenthood during the same period. Frequently, large financial debts are incurred in anticipation of greater income, which has not yet arrived. As Levinson (1986) points out, crucially important decisions must be made concerning family and occupation before one has the maturity and life experience to make them comfortably. It is, at the same time, a period of vigorous health and sexuality, rich family rewards, and the potential for occupational advancement.

Middle Adulthood: Generativity vs. Stagnation (40 to 65 Years). During the transition to this phase of life, we often take stock of who we have become. This represents a marked shift from focusing on who we are *becoming* in our 20s and 30s to thinking about who we *are* during middle age (Carstensen, Isaacowitz, & Charles, 1999). For some people, this is a positive experience—they are happy with their adult selves at the transition to midlife. For many others, this is a time of at least some disappointment. Too many promotions have been missed, too many investments have gone bad, and too many elections have been lost to believe that we can still be

Figure 10.6   Daniel Levinson's periods of adult development.

Era of late adulthood: 60–?

Late adult transition: Age 60–65

Culminating life structure for middle adulthood: 55–60

Age 50 transition: 50–55

Entry life structure for middle adulthood: 45–50

Midlife transition: Age 40–45

Culminating life structure for early adulthood: 33–40

Age 30 transition: 28–33

Entry life structure for early adulthood: 22–28

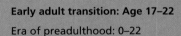

Early adult transition: Age 17–22

Era of preadulthood: 0–22

the unqualified success that we once dreamed of being. As a result of this appraisal of whom we have become, many people either redefine their goals (to fit their more modest accomplishments) or change directions during the transition to midlife. For example, one study of women in the baby-boom generation who attended a selective liberal arts college found that two-thirds made major changes in their educational or occupational work lives around the age of 40 (Stewart & Vandewater, 1999). Often

Erikson believed that to successfully navigate middle adulthood, people must develop a sense of generativity, or a devotion to endeavors that will last beyond their own life span. Mentoring others is an example of generativity.

climacteric (klī-mak´ter-ik) The period between about ages 45 and 60 in which there is a loss of capacity to sexually reproduce in women and a decline in the reproductive capacity of men.

menopause (men´o-pawz) The cessation of menstruation and the capacity to reproduce in women.

this involved pursuing studies or careers that had been set aside earlier in life when traditional conceptions of female roles were more dominant. Both men and women often make career changes, move geographically, adopt new fitness programs, divorce, or change course in other ways during the transition to middle adulthood. In many cases, this leads to an increased sense of identity, self-direction, and competence (Stewart & Ostrove, 1998).

Erikson refers to middle adulthood as the stage of *generativity versus stagnation.* The challenge is to find meaning in our "generative" activities (work, family life, community activities, religion). In part, this requires a shift away from ourselves to focus on others. People who successfully navigate middle adulthood develop a devotion to endeavors that live beyond their own life spans. This might take the form of building a family business, guiding one's children or grandchildren, or taking younger coworkers under one's wing as a mentor (Sheldon & Kasser, 2001). Generativity is a matter of "reaching out" rather than being self-centered. According to Erikson, a person who is self-absorbed will stagnate and find that life loses much of its meaning during middle adulthood.

Levinson describes four brief stages of middle adulthood. Middle adulthood opens with the *midlife transition.* This transitional stage reaches a peak in the early 40s. For some individuals, this transition is quite easy, but for others it's a period of anguish and turmoil. The majority of a sample of 40 men studied by Levinson—10 executives, 10 biologists, 10 factory workers, and 10 novelists—experienced at least some turmoil during their early 40s. Erikson described this stage as the early peak of the struggle between generativity and stagnation—can I find meaning in my life the way it's turning out? It's also a time to face growing evidence of biological aging.

The *entry to middle adulthood stage,* from about 45 to 50, is a period of calm and stability for most people who have emerged from the midlife transition. Individuals who are happy with themselves following the midlife transition often find this period to be one of the most productive and creative times of their lives. The illusory ambitions that were shattered during the midlife transition have often been replaced with more attainable goals that are pursued with vigor.

The *age 50 transition* is a stage that is similar to the age 30 transition. For many adults, this is a time to reassess the goals and lifestyle chosen during midlife and the entering middle adulthood stages. Another stable period from about age 55 to 65 follows the age 50 transition. Levinson refers to this stage as the *culmination of middle adulthood.*

Climacteric. Although many changes in adult development are timed by the "social clock" the climacteric is a biological event that has an impact for many persons. The **climacteric** is a period beginning at about age 45 when a loss of the capacity to sexually reproduce in women and a decline in the reproductive capacity of men occurs.

In women, the decrease in the level of sex hormones during this period eventually leads to the end of menstruation, or **menopause.** This event, which takes place at 46 to 48 years of age on the average (but can normally take place between the ages of 36 and 60) is sometimes an uncomfortable time for women. It's sometimes accompanied by hot flashes, anxiety, and depression, but most women do not find it as difficult as they were led to expect (Stewart & Ostrove, 1998).

The changes that accompany the male climacteric are generally less notable than in women. There is a decline in the number of sperm cells produced, and slight changes in the pattern of sexual arousal, but the decrease in sex hormones that occurs during the climacteric appears to have few psychological or sexual effects.

Later Adulthood: Integrity vs. Despair (65 Years On). Erikson refers to the late 60s and beyond as the stage of *integrity versus despair.* Levinson devotes little of his theory to the later adult years and adds little to Erikson's ideas. The older adult who sees meaning in her or his life when considered as a whole continues to live a satisfying existence instead of merely staying alive. The person who sees life as a collection of unmet goals and unanswered riddles may despair of ever achieving a meaningful life and will often withdraw from social interaction.

Far more older Americans find meaning rather than despair in their lives, however. This may come as a surprise to you. Just as most of us once thought that the process of development ended in childhood, many of us *still* think that there is little real life after age 65. Too often we think of older adults as leading colorless, joyless, passionless lives. It's surprising to some of us to learn that real *living* usually continues until death (Baltes & Staudinger, 1993). In fact, recent research has found that older Americans are the happiest age group in the United States (Stone & others, 2010)!

During the 20th century, the average life expectancy of North Americans increased dramatically. Persons born in 1900 had a life expectancy of less than 50 years, whereas persons born in 1955 can expect to live to be 70. A child born in 1999 can expect to live to be almost 80. As life expectancy has increased, our conceptions of old age have changed dramatically, too. Today, most people can expect to have many healthy years after the traditional retirement age of 65. As a result, many plan second careers, active political involvement, writing, or other engaging activities in their 60s, 70s, and 80s. Even so, older persons increasingly have a sense that time is running out on their lives. For some older people, this is a frightening realization, but in general, it is accompanied by a positive focusing on the meaningful emotional priorities of life (Carstensen, Isaacowitz, & Charles, 1999).

In the stage of integrity versus despair, older adults who see meaning in their lives when considered as a whole will continue to find life satisfying.

Evaluation of Stage Theories of Adulthood. Although they are thought-provoking and appealing in some ways, stage theories of adult development can be criticized on a number of grounds:

1. ***Gender differences.*** The theories of adult development offered by Erikson and Levinson clearly had men more in mind than women. Indeed, for many years, all of the participants in studies of adult development were men. However, a number of studies suggested that there are broad similarities between the patterns of adult development in women and men (Roberts & Newton, 1987; Stewart & Ostrove, 1998).

2. ***Cultural differences and historical change.***
   Early theories of adult development implied that they applied universally to all people born in all times. Very few studies have been conducted, however, to determine if the same patterns of adult development are found in different cultures. Indeed, we have data on only a very limited range of kinds of peoples—mostly white, college-educated, English-speaking adults. Much remains to be learned about the rest of the human race. Even within a given culture, it appears that historical change alters the course of adult development (Stewart & Ostrove, 1998). Consider the North American baby-boom generation born in the late 1940s and early 1950s after the end of World War II. They were born into a world of traditional gender roles but were young adults during the age of feminism and rapidly changing gender

Jimmy and Rosalynn Carter building a home for Habitat for Humanity.

"I was grinding out barnyards and farmhouses and cows in the meadow, and then, suddenly, I figured to hell with it."

roles. As children and teenagers, they experienced the civil rights movement and the assassinations of Martin Luther King, Jr., John F. Kennedy, and Robert Kennedy. Later, they took sides for or against the Vietnam War. As middle-aged adults, they lived through both the age of international terrorism and large rises and falls in North American economic prosperity. How have these events influenced the course of their adult development? How will the course of adult development be different for persons born in 1980 or 2000, who will have very different experiences?

3. **Inconsistent evidence.** Research has not always supported the specific predictions of the stage theories of adult development. For example, recent studies find that adults who are not successful in their work and romantic relationships in their 20s (during the *early adult transition*) often succeed in these areas later in life nonetheless (Roisman & others, 2004). This is good news to many college students!

4. *Questions about the idea of stage theories.* Finally, it is important to note that not all developmental psychologists believe that adulthood can be thought of as a series of crises or stages. Laura Carstensen believes that the processes that govern adult development are changeable and not tied to specific ages. Many psychologists (Stewart & Ostrove, 1998; Rossi, 1980) also have argued that the inevitability and negative impact of the midlife transition have been dangerously exaggerated. Some research suggests that the predictable changes do not take place at the times indicated by the stage theorists. For example, two studies found no evidence that "midlife crises" are common during the early 40s (Farrell & Rosenberg, 1981).

Causes of Aging and Predictors of Longevity. Aging is partly a biological process. Over the years, the body deteriorates—skin often sags and wrinkles, artery walls become less flexible, muscular strength is lost, cardiac and respiratory efficiency declines. And there are changes in the brain as well (Johnson & others, 2004; Mather & others, 2004). On the average, the total brain weight of persons in their 80s is about 8% less than that of a middle-aged person. For older persons with senile dementia, however, the brain weighs 20% less than in middle age (Emery & Oxmans, 1992).

Aging is not only a biological process; it involves many psychological aspects as well. Older people are different from younger people because they have experienced more. They have lived through eras that younger individuals have not, they have often retired from their jobs, they no longer have living parents, they often have children who are adults, and they have a host of other factors. Just as people experience biological aging at different rates, the psychological experience of aging also differs from person to person.

The key psychological variables that seem to be associated with happy aging and slowed intellectual decline are (a) whether one stays active and engaged in life's intellectual and social activities, (b) whether one believes the myths about old age, and (c) whether one avoids smoking and excessive drinking (Vaillant & Mukamal, 2001). Considerable research suggests that older individuals who continue to be actively engaged in meaningful activities are the happiest as older adults (Kim & Moen, 2001; Neugarten & Hagestad, 1976; Wilson & Bennett, 2003). These activities can involve family, hobbies, sports, politics, or employment. All that matters is that they be activities that are meaningful to the individual.

The other key to a satisfactory older adulthood seems to be in ignoring the restrictive myths and stereotypes of old age so prevalent in our society. Many older adults are active in sports and creative in the arts and sciences. In general, they do not behave like the passive, irritable "old people" of the stereotype. Philosopher Bertrand Russell, artists Marc Chagall and Pablo Picasso, political leaders Golda Meir and Mao Tse-tung, and psychologists Jean Piaget and B. F. Skinner continued to be creative and productive well into their 80s.

Not only have psychologists learned much about the factors that predict a well-adjusted older adulthood, we have recently learned something about psychological factors that predict how long people will live. In 1921, Lewis Terman began a study of 1,528 highly intelligent schoolchildren who were studied frequently across their life spans. As of the early 1990s, about half of the subjects had died and half were still living. Psychologist Howard Friedman and his colleagues (1995) have looked back at the records of the Terman study to determine whether psychological factors predicted the subjects' longevity. Because the subjects in Terman's study were all well above average in intelligence, we cannot be sure that the conclusions apply to the U.S. population in general. However, because college students and professors tend to be above average in intelligence, the results may well be relevant to us.

Friedman found that subjects in the Terman study lived longer if they were rated as having a "conscientious, dependable, and truthful" personality during childhood—they were 30% less likely to die during each year of life. But children who were rated as being "cheerful" tended to die earlier. This surprising finding is explained partly by the fact that cheerful children were more likely to take risks and were more likely to smoke and drink as adults, factors associated with early death. In addition, conscientious and dependable children were less likely to be involved in dangerous accidents and were more likely either to have a stable marriage or to remain single—and going through a divorce was linked to early death. If the parents of the children were divorced, the risk of early death was increased even more (by an average of four years). When Terman's subjects reached their 30s, they were interviewed about their emotions and behavior. Those with the most emotional difficulties also were more likely to die early (Peterson & others, 1998).

So, if you were a cheerful child with divorced parents, should you take out extra life insurance? No, but if you smoke, drink, take risks, and are thinking about leaving a good marriage just for a change of scenery, you might consider changing your behavior. We will return to the relationship between psychological factors and health in chapter 13.

Death and Dying: The Final "Stage"

The life cycle begins with the life of a single cell and ends with the death of the person who unfolded from that cell. In recent years, the topic of death and dying, particularly among the elderly, has received some long overdue scientific attention. This research has produced some interesting results.

Thoughts of death are an important part of the last stages of life for many individuals. Older adults spend more time thinking about death than do younger adults. Contemplating and planning for one's death is a normal part of old age (Kalish & Reynolds, 1976). Older adults tend to be less frightened by death than are younger adults. Older adults often come to accept its inevitability with little anguish. Indeed, it often helps them make the most out of the time remaining (Carstensen & Charles, 1998).

One's fear of death is related to other variables besides age, however. One significant factor is religious belief. Highly religious individuals experience the least fear of death. Nonreligious individuals experience moderate levels of anxiety about death,

Several variables affect how much we fear our own deaths. For example, highly religious people seem to have less fear of death than do nonreligious people.

whereas religious people who do not consistently practice their faith experience the greatest fear of dying (Nelson & Nelson, 1973).

Psychiatrist Elisabeth Kübler-Ross (1969, 1974) provided us with new and important insights into the process of dying through her interviews of hundreds of terminally ill patients. From these interviews, she developed a theory that people who learn of their impending death (and sometimes the impending death of their loved ones) tend to pass through five rather distinct stages:

1. **Denial.** At first, the individual strongly resists the idea of death by denying the validity of the information about his or her terminal illness. It's common at this stage for the terminally ill person to accuse his or her doctor of being incompetent or to look for a "miracle cure." Sometimes the denial is more subtle, with the individual simply acting as if the news of impending death was never revealed.

2. **Anger.** After the initial denial, the terminally ill person reacts to the fact of her or his impending death with anger: Why me? It's not fair that this should be happening to me! There is much hostility, envy of others, and resentment during this stage. As a result, the terminally ill person is often highly irritable and frequently quarrels with nurses, doctors, and loved ones.

3. **Bargaining.** The anger and denial of the impending death are largely gone by this third stage, and the terminally ill person realizes that death is coming. But death still is not accepted as inevitable. Instead, the person tries to strike bargains to prolong his or her life. These bargains may be in the form of willingness to undergo painful treatments to extend life, but they are more often silent deals with God, such as "I'll leave most of my money to the church if I can have six more months."

4. **Depression.** Eventually, the reality of impending death leads to a loss of hope. Bargains no longer seem possible; death is coming no matter what. The person often begins to feel guilty about leaving loved ones behind, feels incapable of facing death with dignity, and feels quite depressed.

5. **Acceptance.** In time, the depression lifts and the person finally achieves an acceptance of death. This generally is not a happy feeling of acceptance but a state of emotional exhaustion that leaves the individual peacefully free of negative emotions.

Kübler-Ross (1974) and others point out that not every terminally ill person passes through these stages. Reactions to impending death are highly individual (Feifel, 1990). If we go through the process of dying with a loved one, we must be careful not to impose on him or her our views of how the process of accepting death should proceed.

Review   Intelligence and personality remain relatively constant throughout the adult years in most healthy adults, but some change does take place. Most aspects of intellectual ability improve into early adulthood and then decline, with fluid intelligence declining more rapidly than crystallized intelligence. Most healthy adults experience only minor intellectual declines into old age and may improve in "wisdom." Although people tend to keep their same relative position on measures of personality relative to others throughout their lives, several positive changes in personality occur throughout adulthood. In particular, adults become increasingly less emotional, more agreeable, and more accepting of themselves as they age. Erikson and Levinson have outlined a series of stages of adult life, but we still have much to learn about adult development and not all psychologists agree that the changes in adulthood can be thought of as a series of stages.

Aging is partly a biological process of physical deterioration, but aging is also a psychological process that can be slowed to some degree by staying engaged in meaningful activities and by not believing the many negative myths about old age that are so prevalent in our society. Regardless of how the individual lives out the later adult years, the final "stage" of life is always death. Older adults tend to accept their impending deaths, especially religious adults, but individuals who must face the knowledge of their impending deaths earlier in the life span generally go through several stages of anguish before reaching a state of acceptance.

Review (cont.)

To be sure that you have learned the key points from the preceding section, cover the list of correct answers and try to answer each question. If you give an incorrect answer to any question, return to the page given next to the correct answer to see why your answer was not correct.

Check Your Learning

1. The challenge of the _____ stage is to enter into committed, loving relationships with others that partially replace bonds with parents.

   a) early adulthood   c) later adulthood

   b) middle adulthood   d) midlife

2. According to Erikson, a person in middle adulthood must be _____ (or productive) to find meaning in life.

   a) stagnant   c) generative

   b) divergent   d) flexible

3. Two keys to a satisfactory older adulthood seem to be ignoring the restrictive myths and stereotypes of old age and remaining actively engaged in life.

   a) true   b) false

4. _____ is one significant factor related to one's fear of death.

   a) Marital status   c) Success in life

   b) Local climate   d) Religious belief

There are no right or wrong answers to the following questions. They are presented to help you become an active reader and think critically about what you just read.

Thinking Critically about Psychology

1. How might the course of your adult development differ from that of your grandparents? How will your culture influence your development during adulthood?

2. Do you think that your personality has changed in the past 10 years? Do you expect it to change in the future?

Correct Answers: 1. a (p. 332), 2. c (p. 332), 3. a (p. 335), 4. d (pp. 337–338)

Variations in Development that Make US Unique

The majority of the information covered in this chapter has dealt with the more-or-less predictable changes in behavior that are associated with increasing age. These are the changes that all (or most) of us experience as part of our shared humanity. But, there are large **individual differences** in development. Individual differences refer to variations in development that make people different.

individual differences The variations in development that make people different.

Getting There at Different Times

It is very important to understand that it's normal for development to be highly variable—even when children are raised in typical conditions. This is true in two senses: (a) there are differences between children in their development, and (b) children vary in the rate of their own development from one period to the next.

It's normal for one child to walk or talk several months before another child. When we look at charts of the normal age at which children sit, walk, speak in sentences, and so on, we must remember that variations from those norms often mean nothing at all. Deviations from the average are not unusual. Variation is the rule, not the exception, in child development. Any large variation in development should be discussed with a pediatrician or child psychologist, but small variations should not be a cause for concern.

Some differences in the timing of development can be quite important, however. Because development is a dynamic process—we are always changing—variations in development at one point in time can lead to a series of cascading events, which can have profound consequences later (Smith & Thelen, 1993). To use just one example, females who reach puberty early often have different experiences and outcomes than females who sexually mature later (Burt & others, 2006; Mendle, Turkheimer, & Emery, 2007). Teachers, parents, the females themselves, *and* older male peers view these females quite differently. Many psychologists believe that early development places these females in social situations for which they are not developmentally ready (Ellis, 2004). As such, early maturers are at increased risk for a number of problems, including depression, substance abuse, early and risky sexual behavior, and antisocial behavior. Therefore, timing of development plays a role in making people different from others, including their own peers.

It's also normal for children to be variable in their own development. Development does not happen at a uniform pace. Children who are shorter than their age-mates for many years sometimes shoot up suddenly to become taller than most. A fussy baby can become a calm, happy child. And it's not unusual for a child who was above average on an IQ test at age 4 to be just average at age 9 or vice versa. Discontinuities in development, again, are the rule rather than the exception. Understanding this variability within individuals is also quite important for understanding what makes each person unique (Nesselroade & Molenaar, 2010).

Thus, understanding who we are now means understanding how everyone generally develops, as well the developmental processes that make us unique.

Application of Psychology

Parenting

During the important early stages of development—infancy, childhood, and most of adolescence—we typically live with our parents. They give us food and shelter, protect us from danger, and provide many of our early learning experiences. Parents play a key role in giving children a healthy start in life. But although parenting is important, we as a society provide parents with no training in how to raise their children. Our schools teach reading, writing, and arithmetic, but not parenting. For this reason, we will look carefully at the topic of parenting, with an emphasis on the styles of parenting that are best for children.

Parenting and Infant Attachment.
Let's begin with a look at the parents' role in helping their infant develop a secure relationship—or attachment—with the parents. The newborn in the hospital nursery seems equally happy to be rocked by anyone who has free arms, but sometime during the first year of life (usually by about 6 to 9 months) infants typically become closely attached to one or more of their caretakers. At this point in development, most infants develop a normal "stranger anxiety": They react fearfully and tearfully when strangers are present and cling to the safe fortress of the adult to whom they are attached (Ainsworth, 1979). By 18 to 24 months, however, most toddlers are better able to deal with stranger anxiety. They prefer to be near their primary caretaker when strangers are first encountered, but they are able to move out to explore the world and play, knowing that the safe caretaker is nearby. Infants who are able to deal with stranger anxiety in this way are said to be "securely attached."

Some infants and toddlers, however, are less securely attached to their parent. When separated from their caretaker, some "insecurely attached" toddlers cling excessively to the caretaker and become extremely upset when separated from the parent. Seemingly, the attachment is not secure enough to allow the toddler to turn her or his back on the parent for a moment. Other toddlers who are not securely attached rarely use the parent as a safe haven but, rather, seem to ignore or even avoid the parent. It is as if the attachment to the parent is too weak to be helpful to the toddler.

What leads to secure attachment? Part of the answer is the child's inborn temperament. Some children are simply calmer and more receptive to the parent from birth. But parents play an important role as well. Parents can help their infants form secure attachments by taking care of the infant's needs in a consistent way and by being warm, affectionate, and accepting. In this case, being an accepting parent means staying calm and loving (most of the time, at least) when the baby "acts like an infant"—crying in the middle of the night, wetting diaper

By age 18 to 24 months, "securely attached" toddlers are able to explore the world and play if they know a safe caregiver is nearby.

after diaper, and spitting every bite of cereal back into your hand (Goldsmith & Alansky, 1987)!

It is important for parents to help their infants develop the firm foundation of a secure attachment, but how worried should the parent of an insecurely attached infant be? The best answer is that the parent should be concerned enough to look at his or her parenting to see whether healthy changes can be made, but not overly concerned. It is not uncommon for an extremely clingy 2-year-old who receives consistent and loving parenting to grow into a happy and secure 5-year-old—I've personally seen it happen many times.

Parenting and Discipline Style.
Discipline style is one of the most important parts of parenting. As soon as the infant can move, the adult must attempt to regulate the child's behavior to protect the child and point the child in a healthy direction. In other words, the parent must provide guidance and discipline. What discipline style is the best for children? Psychologist Diana Baumrind (1983) extensively studied the discipline styles used by parents and has divided them into three types: authoritarian, permissive, and authoritative.

The *authoritarian* parent gives strict rules to the child or adolescent with little discussion of the reasons for the rules. It is the "because I say so" approach to rules. Authoritarian parents are openly critical of their children and frequently give them instructions on how to behave. Rules are enforced by punishing a child who does not obey, sometimes quite harshly.

In contrast, the *permissive* parent gives the child or adolescent few rules and rarely punishes misbehavior. The child is given great respect and autonomy but often too much independence at too early an age.

The *authoritative* parent (notice the difference in spelling between *authoritative* and *authoritarian*) is an authority figure to the child but provides good explanations for all rules and freely discusses them with the child. In allowing their children to freely state their opinions about rules, and sometimes being persuaded to alter the rules by a logical argument from them, authoritative parents give children a greater sense of involvement in their own rules. Authoritative parents emphasize reinforcement of appropriate behavior and affectionate warmth over punishment; indeed, they often do not use any physical punishment at all. They encourage independence, but within clearly defined limits that take the child's level of development into consideration. In short, authoritative parents show their children that they are loved and respected but provide the amount of authority that the child needs.

Which of these approaches to discipline works best? Research clearly indicates that children whose parents adopt

Our parents care for us from infancy through adolescence and provide us with many of our most important learning experiences.

an authoritative style are better behaved, more successful, and happier than the children of parents who use other styles of discipline, and their families are more harmonious (Baumrind, 1983, 1991; Querido, Warner, & Eyeberg, 2002).

Direction of Effect in Child Rearing: The Two-Way Street.

University of Virginia professor Richard Bell (1968) pointed out some time ago that we must be very careful in our interpretations of studies of parenting. I just said that children whose parents are authoritative are generally better behaved and happier than children whose parents use other styles of discipline. Does this necessarily mean that authoritative parenting causes good behavior in children? Most developmental psychologists think so, but it is very likely that something else is going on as well. It is probable that children who are happy and easy to get along with make it easier for their parents to adopt an authoritative style of discipline. A happy, reasonable child can be given a great deal of independence and needs little strict discipline. But would the same parent adopt a different style of discipline if the child were irritable, defiant, and aggressive? Several studies suggest that this might be the case—that children affect their parents as much as parents affect their children.

Hugh Lytton of the University of Calgary (Anderson, Lytton, & Romney, 1986) has compared parents of normal, well-behaved children to parents with children who were so disobedient and aggressive that they had been referred to psychologists for help. He observed these two groups of parents interacting with their children in a playroom in his laboratory. As in previous studies, Lytton found that the parents of the badly behaved children were less affectionate, less likely to reward positive behavior, more critical, and gave many more instructions to their children on how to behave than did the parents of the well-behaved children.

Generally, psychologists have concluded that it is exactly this pattern of authoritarian parenting that causes the children to behave badly (e.g., Baumrind, 1983). But Lytton provided a clever twist to his study. He exchanged parents and children—so that the parents of well-behaved children were matched with badly behaved children and vice versa—and observed their interactions again. When the parents of well-behaved children were faced with an aggressive, disobedient child, the formerly model parents behaved just like the parents of the badly behaved children. Quickly, they also resorted to the unpleasant, critical, authoritarian style of discipline.

So who influences whom in the family? Does the parent's discipline affect the child's behavior, or does the child's behavior influence the parent's discipline? Recent research has found that a great deal of both is going on (Schermerhorn & others, 2007, 2008). This is a very important point. Effective parenting is a very important influence on the child, but even the best parents know that different children will evoke different parenting responses from them. For instance, research suggests that parental behaviors, such as yelling and spanking, are partially provoked by the actions of children (Jaffee & others, 2004). When this leads to coercive cycles of children misbehaving and parents responding with angry outbursts, children are at a great risk of developing behavior problems (Granic & Patterson, 2006). Thus, the parents of temperamental, difficult children will have to resist the natural tendency to make authoritarian responses to their children's provocative behavior if they are going to help their children develop optimally.

A child's temperament may have as much effect on disciplinary style as the parents' choices. Lytton found that parents' who usually used the authoritative style tended to become more authoritarian when faced with an unruly child.

Common Discipline Mistakes. Psychologist Susan O'Leary (1995) has made a comprehensive study of the most common discipline mistakes made by ineffective parents. Parents of poorly behaved children often make the following mistakes:

1. *Lax parenting.* Ineffective parents often fail to enforce their rules for the children and give in to their children's demands to bend the rules or avoid punishment. Effective parents are consistent in the enforcement of rules.

2. *Reinforcement of inappropriate behavior.* Parents of poorly behaved children often provide positive reinforcement for inappropriate behavior. This is sometimes unintentional—such as only paying attention to their children when they misbehave—but is sometimes intentional—as in praising their child for giving another child a black eye. Effective parents provide positive reinforcement for good behavior, but not for inappropriate behavior.

3. *Verbosity.* Ineffective parents engage in lengthy arguments with their children about their misbehavior instead of simply enforcing the rules. Effective parents know that a brief explanation of why the rule is being enforced is much more effective than a lengthy debate. "I'm sorry, but you can't watch television tonight, because you did not do your homework" says all that needs to be said in most cases.

4. *Overreactivity.* Ineffective parents become angry, harsh, critical, and mean when their children misbehave. Effective parents stay cool and in control as they calmly enforce the rules.

Sociocultural Factors in Parenting.

Parents from all cultures want their children to be "well behaved," but they often define appropriate behavior differently and believe in different methods of child rearing. For this reason, we must understand cultural differences in parenting (Rubin, 1998). Consider one major difference among cultures: In collectivistic cultures, such as the Chinese, Japanese, and Indian cultures, the emphasis is on the well-being of the family and the larger culture, not on the well-being of each individual. In individualistic cultures, such as the mainstream culture in the United States, the emphasis is on the individual rather than the group.

The kinds of behavior that help a person succeed in collectivistic and individualistic cultures are different in some cases, and therefore, parents raise their children differently in some ways. For example, in the United States, most parents believe that being shy and inhibited places children at a disadvantage—they would prefer that their children be outgoing and assertive instead. This is because the individuals who assert themselves most confidently will be most likely to succeed. In Chinese families, however, shyness and inhibition are viewed as advantages, because they help the child fit into the group and yield to its wishes. It is not surprising, then, that Chinese parents praise their shy children, whereas American parents frequently disapprove of shy behavior and sometimes seek mental health treatment for their shy children (Rubin, 1998).

Another difference between Chinese and mainstream U.S. cultures reflects the relative emphasis on academic achievement in the two cultures and how it is encouraged. In the United States, Chinese immigrant parents teach mathematics skills to their young children in more formal ways and structure their children's use of time more than European American parents do (Huntsinger, Jose, & Larson, 1998). Controlling for other factors, such as parental income and education, the parenting practices of Chinese American parents appear to lead to higher mathematics achievement among their children (Huntsinger, Jose, & Larson, 1998). Importantly, the two groups of children do not differ in terms of personal adjustment, suggesting that the greater emphasis on academic achievement is not personally harmful to the Chinese American children. In these and many other ways, parenting reflects the varying goals and beliefs of people living in different cultures.

Myth of the Perfect Parent.

Loving and effective parenting is the greatest gift that a parent can give a child. But it is important to point out that *perfect* parenting is not as important as some of us seem to think. Many parents act as if their children are as delicate as spun glass. They are paralyzed in their attempts to be good parents by their fear that they will do the wrong thing and scar their children for life.

Actually, children are pretty resilient creatures. Within broad limits, they will grow up very well in spite of the fact that none of them has perfect parents. They will not be miserable forever if their parents sometimes lose their tempers and speak in harsh tones, and they will learn to play with other children without being coached in every step.

That is not to say that parents cannot harm their children. Unfortunately, children are hurt badly every day by neglectful and abusive parents. But most of the minor imperfections of parenting that are characteristic of every child's upbringing are of relatively little consequence.

Day Care, Divorce, and Parenting.

Until relatively recently, most children in the United States were cared for by one of their parents—almost always the mother—who stayed at home full-time to raise the children and care for the home while the other parent worked outside the home. And most of us felt that this way of raising children was the "natural" way of things. Indeed, the image of the "caretaker mother and breadwinner father" is so deeply embedded in our view of child rearing that many of us are shocked to learn that very few children are raised in that manner today. As long ago as 1991, one study found that less than 10% of all children in the United States were raised by two married parents through their entire childhood, with the mother not working outside the home (Silverstein, 1991).

In many families, both married parents have chosen—or have felt compelled by economic necessity—to be employed full-time outside the home. Indeed, the percentage of women with school-age children who work outside the home has risen by half since the 1970s (Marshall, 2004). In many other cases, divorce results in the custodial parent's (usually the mother) being more likely to work outside the home. About 40–50% of all marriages now end in divorce (Amato, 2010), and divorced women are more likely than married women to work outside the home (Scarr, Phillips, & McCartney, 1990).

Application of Psychology cont'd

All these changes in the nature of the American family over the past quarter century have resulted in mothers spending less time raising their children. Who cares for the children, then? The amount of time fathers spend in direct child care has increased in recent decades (Casper & Bianchi, 2002), and some of the job of child rearing has fallen to other family members, such as grandparents (Kreider & Elliott, 2009). But many children now spend a great deal of time in day care. As psychologist Sandra Scarr put it, "Child care is now as essential to family life as the automobile and the refrigerator" (Scarr & others, 1990, p. 26).

Have these changes in how our children are raised had a harmful effect on the children? This is an extremely controversial area of research. In spite of the great anguish of parents and psychologists alike, extensive research suggests that, in general, children who are in day care do not differ greatly from children who are raised by parents in their own homes in terms of physical health, emotional or intellectual development, or attachment. Early and prolonged child care has been associated with a slightly increased risk of behavioral problems but also for greater cognitive skills and academic achievement (Vandell & others, 2010). Again, the magnitude of the effects are modest, and it is unclear whether the exposure to day care actually caused the differences or whether other factors are responsible. The key elements in the successful adaptation of children to day care appear to be the *quality* of the day-care environment and the quality and quantity of time spent with parents in the evenings and on weekends. In general, the available research supports the conclusion that a poor day-care environment is harmful to children, whereas a positive day-care environment can be good for children, under some conditions (Marshall, 2004; NICHD Early Child Care Research Network, 2002; Vandell & others, 2010; Votruba-Drzal, Coley, & Chase-Lansdale, 2004).

The other common situation that reduces the amount of parenting is divorce. Is divorce harmful to children? There is little doubt that divorce is stressful and upsetting to all of the adults and children involved. Few children make it through the

In the words of one researcher, "Child care is now as essential to family life as the automobile and the refrigerator" (Scarr, 1990). A key element in children's successful adaptation to day care is the quality of care provided.

time of divorce without some emotional turmoil, which results in misbehavior and problems at school (Hetherington, 1979). Research has shown that parental divorce also is associated with an increased risk of problems throughout adolescence and adulthood, but a majority of children who experience the separation of their parents are resilient (Amato, 2010). The children who are most affected by divorce are the ones whose parents were openly conflictual after the divorce (Amato, 2010; Kelly & Emery, 2003) or whose parents have serious psychological difficulties (Lahey & others, 1988). Most children adapt well to divorce when their parents work out their differences after the divorce well enough to cease arguing in front of the children and cooperate in allowing each other to share in the duties and pleasures of parenting (Amato, 2010; Kelly & Emery, 2003).

Summary

Chapter 10 summarizes key concepts in developmental psychology and the major theories that explain the process of development. It describes the normal course of development from infancy and childhood, adolescence, adulthood, and later adulthood, to the time of death.

I. Some psychologists believe that developmental changes in behavior are biologically programmed to "unfold" with increasing age, whereas others believe that changes in behavior are "molded" by the environment that we experience.

    A. Maturation, the systematic physical growth of the nervous system and other parts of the body, is a key concept to "unfolding" theorists; learning is the key concept to "molding" theorists.

    B. Today, most psychologists believe that nature (biological factors) and nurture (environment) work together to influence our actions, thoughts, and feelings.

    C. Some theorists believe that early childhood is the "formative period" for our personalities.

        1. Research on imprinting in animals shows that experiences during critical periods of early development can have long-lasting effects on animal behavior, but there may not be such clear-cut critical periods in human development.

        2. Margaret and Harry Harlow's experiments with social deprivation during the infancy of monkeys show long-lasting effects of abnormal early experiences, but

human infants seem capable of recovering to a great extent from early abnormal experience.

D. Parents play a key role in fostering the development of their children, but the emotions and behavior of the child also influence the parents' choice of parenting styles.

II. Stage theorists believe that all children must pass through the same qualitatively different stages in the same order.

A. Piaget identified four stages of cognitive development from infancy to adulthood.

1. During the sensorimotor stage (birth to 2 years), an infant experiences the world in terms of sensory information and motor activities.

2. In the preoperational stage (2 to 7 years), children can think in mental images, but they sometimes think in ways that are illogical by adult standards.

3. The concrete operational stage (7 to 11 years) is marked by increased ability to reason logically, except for abstract reasoning.

4. In the formal operational stage (11 years on), an individual uses full adult logic and understands abstract concepts.

B. Kohlberg's theory of moral development is concerned with the logical process of arriving at answers to moral dilemmas.

1. At the premoral level, a child has no sense of morality as adults understand that term.

2. A child's moral view is based on what others will think of him or her as stated in laws and rules at the conventional level.

3. At the principled level, individuals judge right and wrong according to ethical principles rather than by rules or expected reward or punishment.

C. Carol Gilligan has provided a theory that she believes more accurately describes moral development in females than does Kohlberg's.

1. The young girl follows rules to obtain rewards and avoid punishment in the earliest stage, "morality as individual survival."

2. Later, in the "morality as self-sacrifice" stage, the girl believes that to be good she must sacrifice her needs at times to meet the needs of others.

3. In the most mature stage of "morality as equality," she believes that everyone's needs should be met when possible and that sacrifices should be shared equally when they are necessary.

D. Erik Erikson's theory of development focuses on the person's developing relationships with others in the social world.

III. Average ages at which changes in development take place are used to portray the pattern of age-related changes.

A. The neonatal period is the first two weeks of life and marks the transition from the womb to independent life.

B. Infancy (2 weeks to 2 years) is a time of rapid physical, perceptual, cognitive, linguistic, social, and emotional development.

C. During early childhood (2 to 7 years), growth is less explosive and rapid than during infancy.

D. Middle childhood (7 to 11 years) is characterized by slow physical growth, but important cognitive changes occur, such as the emergence of conservation.

IV. Adolescence is the developmental period from the onset of puberty until the beginning of adulthood.

A. The production of sex hormones in puberty triggers biological changes known as the primary sex characteristics.

1. Menarche, the first menstrual period, occurs at about 12 years 6 months in North American females.

2. Production of sperm begins about two years later in males.

3. Secondary sex characteristics appear in both sexes during puberty.

4. The adolescent growth spurt lasts for a little over a year in early adolescence.

5. For both sexes, different parts of the body grow at different rates, and weight and physique change in irregular ways.

6. Within each sex, there is wide variation in the age at which puberty begins. Girls tend to experience puberty about two years earlier than boys.

B. Piaget's formal operational stage—the ability to use abstract concepts—occurs in some individuals by about age 11.

C. Peers replace the family as the most important influence on the adolescent. Most adolescents are well adjusted, but adolescents are more likely to be moody and to engage in parent-child conflict and risky behavior than at any other time in their lives.

V. Adulthood is not a single phase of life. Some changes involving love, work, and play continue throughout adulthood.

A. Intelligence appears relatively stable throughout adulthood in healthy adults, with small declines beginning between ages 50 and 60, especially in the speed of intellectual processing. Some larger declines occur after age 70 in some aspects of intelligence, particularly in individuals with arteriosclerosis and other brain impairment.

B. Some relatively predictable personality changes that occur for many people during adulthood include becoming more insightful, dependable, controlled, and content. Most aspects of personality remain relatively constant across adulthood, however.

C. Some psychologists believe that we pass through "stages" of development during adulthood.

1. Developmental stages of adulthood appear to differ from those of childhood in that not every adult goes through each stage, the order of the stages can vary, and the timing of the stages is not controlled by biological maturation.

2. Erikson calls early adulthood the stage of intimacy versus isolation, during which many individuals enter committed, loving relationships.

3. Erikson calls middle adulthood the stage of generativity versus stagnation, during which many individuals find meaning in work and family lives.

4. Erikson calls the period from the late 60s on the stage of integrity versus despair; older adults who see meaning in their lives when considered as a whole continue to live a satisfying existence.

D. Although the stage theories of adult development are thought-provoking, many developmental psychologists are not convinced that we pass through predictable stages or a series of crises. Stage theories can be particularly criticized for their lack of attention to possible cultural, gender, and historical differences.

E. Psychological variables associated with happy aging are whether one stays engaged in life's activities and whether one believes the myths about old age. Older adults tend to be less frightened by death than are younger adults. Studies by Kübler-Ross suggest that younger adults who learn of their impending deaths tend to pass through five distinct stages: denial, anger, bargaining, depression, and acceptance.

Visual Review of Stage Theories of Development

The following visual reviews may help you consolidate your learning of some of the information presented in this chapter. Be sure not to limit your review to these diagrams, but because they are key to understanding some of the important concepts of the chapter, mastering them should help you master the entire chapter.

Figure 10.7

This is a diagram of Piaget's stage theory of child development. Fill in the missing labels for the names of the stages and the average age ranges for the stages and check them for accuracy by referring back to figure 10.2 on p. 312.

_____ stage: ____ years

By the end of the stage of childhood, most individuals have progressed to full adult cognition, including the ability to reason using abstract concepts.

_____ stage: ____ years

During middle childhood, the child has the ability to reason like an adult in every way except for reasoning about abstract concepts, such as justice, infinity, or the meaning of life.

_____ stage: ____ years

At this stage, the child is capable of symbolic thought—however, this thinking is still quite different from that of adults. It is often "illogical" in ways that reveal the unique nature of preoperational cognition.

_____ stage: ____ years

The child deals with reality in terms of sensations and motor movements. At this stage, children are unable to reason in mental symbols.

Visual Review of Stage Theories of Development cont'd

Figure 10.8

This is a diagram of the stage theory of adult development proposed by Daniel Levinson. Fill in the missing labels for the names of three major adult transitions and check them for accuracy by referring back to figure 10.6, page 333.

Era of late adulthood: 60–?

_____ transition: Age 60–65

Culminating life structure for middle adulthood: 55–60

Age 50 transition: 50–55

Entry life structure for middle adulthood: 45–50

_____ transition: Age 40–45

Culminating life structure for early adulthood: 33–40

Age 30 transition: 28–33
Entry life structure for early adulthood: 22–28

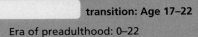

_____ transition: Age 17–22

Era of preadulthood: 0–22

chapter eleven

Motivation and emotion

Chapter Outline

Prologue

I love conducting research as part of my work. Still, I wonder if the great researcher, Walter Cannon, could have talked me into doing for science what he persuaded his colleague A. L. Washburn to do to understand the motive of hunger. Cannon and Washburn (1912) were trying to isolate the biological mechanism of hunger. They believed that the feeling of hunger was caused by contractions of the stomach wall. To determine whether this idea was correct, Cannon convinced Washburn to swallow a balloon that was attached to a long tube connected to an air pump. The balloon was then inflated to fill Washburn's stomach. In this way, stomach contractions could be mechanically detected because they squeezed the balloon and increased the air pressure in the tube (see figure 11.1 on p. 350). While the intermittent

Figure 11.1   Diagram of the device used in the experiment by Cannon and Washburn (1912) to find out if stomach contractions caused a conscious feeling of hunger. Note the balloon swallowed by Washburn to measure the contractions.

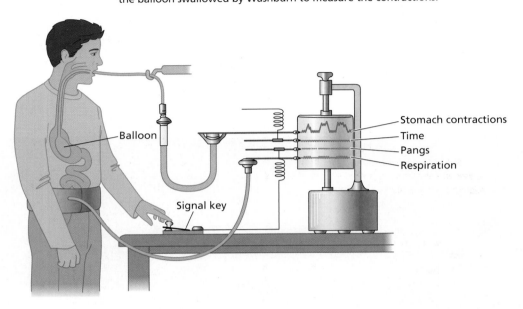

contractions were being measured, Washburn, who could not talk because of the tube gagging his mouth and throat, indicated when he felt a conscious sensation of hunger by pressing a key connected to a recording instrument. (History does not tell us, however, whether Washburn used his other hand to signal more negative feelings to Cannon during this unpleasant experiment.)

As predicted, Washburn did feel hungry when his stomach contracted, leading them to conclude that hunger was no more than the rumbling contractions of an empty stomach. Such contractions are still believed to be part of the feeling of hunger for many people, but, sadly, considering Washburn's selfless contribution to science, stomach contractions are only one factor in hunger, and one of the least important factors at that.

This chapter is about our motives and our emotions. Motives are states that make us active rather than inactive and lead us to do one thing rather than another. If I have just eaten, I may quietly read the newspaper; but if I am hungry, I will get up and fix food. The motive of hunger activates and directs my behavior. Some motives are based on the survival needs of the body for food, water, and warmth. These biological motives are regulated by intricate and sensitive mechanisms under the control of the hypothalamus that detect the body's needs.

Other motives—the so-called psychological motives—are not directly related to the survival needs of the body. The motive to maintain a moderate level of novel stimulation and activity, the motive to achieve and be successful, and the motive to have friendly relationships with others are examples of psychological motives. These motives are often strongly influenced by learning experiences and therefore differ from individual to individual and culture to culture. Sexual motivation is a special case with a number of unique characteristics.

Emotions are special states that often motivate us. Emotions are a complex mixture of three different but intimately related psychological processes. First, emotions involve a positive or negative conscious experience. Second, emotions are accompanied by physiological arousal of the autonomic nervous system, some endocrine glands, and other physiological systems. And third, they involve facial expressions, postural changes, and sometimes actions. When you are crossing the street and see a car driving toward you, you feel a negative conscious experience, your autonomic nervous system churns you up, and your face shows fear and you run. As we will see, some aspects of emotions appear to be inborn, whereas other aspects are shaped by our learning experiences.

Definitions of Motivation and Emotion

To people who are interested in human behavior, the key question is why? Carol wants to know why she continues to have sex with Michael when she knows she does not love him and is afraid of getting pregnant. The manager of the packing plant wants to know why two of her employees do not seem to care about doing a good job. A father wants to know why his son is not willing to work hard for good grades in school. Answers to questions like these often involve the concept of motivation.

The term **motivation** refers to an *internal* state that activates and gives direction to our thoughts. Marie was starting to feel a little hungry when an ad on television for tacos made her feel famished, reminded her that she had food in the refrigerator, and sent her scrambling to the kitchen. If her motive for hunger had not been activated, perhaps her motive to succeed in school might have led her in a different direction— maybe to read her psychology textbook. If no motives at all were activated, she would be doing nothing—just sitting around or maybe taking a nap. Motives are at the center of our lives—they arouse and direct what we think, feel, and do.

Some motives, such as hunger, are clearly based on internal physiological states. As we will see, several internal factors, such as the level of sugar in the blood, are important in feeling hunger. But other motives, such as the motive to succeed, are not based on simple internal physiological states. For all motives, however, *external cues* play an important role. Seeing the ad for tacos on television was an external cue that stimulated Marie's hunger motive; hearing her roommate worry aloud about passing her next psychology test would be an external cue that could have stimulated her motive to succeed.

Motivation is closely related to the topic of emotions. The term **emotion** refers to positive or negative feelings—generally reactions to stimuli—that are accompanied by physiological arousal and characteristic behavior. When we are afraid, for example, we experience an acutely unpleasant feeling: The sympathetic division of our autonomic nervous system is aroused and the fear generally shows in our behavior. The emotion of passion, in contrast, is a conglomeration of very different feelings, biological changes, and behavior.

Motivation and emotions are closely linked concepts for two reasons: (a) motives are often accompanied by emotions, (for example, the motive to perform well on a test is sometimes accompanied by anxiety; sexual motivation is generally blended with the emotions of passion and love); and (b) emotions typically have motivational properties of their own—because you are in love, you are motivated to be with your special person; because you are angry, you want to strike out at the object of your anger.

motivation The internal state or condition that activates and gives direction to our thoughts, feelings, and actions.

emotion Positive or negative feelings generally in reaction to stimuli that are accompanied by physiological arousal and related behavior.

Primary Motives: Biological Needs

Many human motives stem from the *need* for things that keep an organism alive: food, water, warmth, sleep, avoidance of pain, and so on. We consider these to be **primary motives,** because we must meet these biological needs or die. This section focuses on the biological motives of hunger and thirst, partly because they are the best understood of the primary motives.

primary motives Human motives for things that are necessary for survival, such as food, water, and warmth.

Homeostasis: Biological Thermostats

homeostatic mechanisms
(hō''mē-ō-stat'ik) Internal body
mechanisms that sense biological
imbalances and stimulate actions to
restore the proper balance.

Most of the primary motives are based on the body's need to maintain a certain level of essential life elements: adequate sugar in the blood to nourish cells, sufficient water in the body, and so on. These critical levels are regulated by **homeostatic mechanisms.** These mechanisms sense imbalances in the body and stimulate actions that restore the proper balance. The homeostatic mechanisms of the body are often compared to the thermostats of home heating systems. When the temperature of the house falls below a preset level, the thermostat senses that fact and signals the heater to produce heat until the proper temperature has been restored; then it signals the heater to turn off. The body's responses to imbalances include both internal reactions and overt behavior. For instance, when the water level in body cells falls below a safe level, a signal is sent to the kidneys to reabsorb additional water from the urine. At the same time, a signal is sent to the brain that leads the animal—human or otherwise—to seek out and drink liquids. Similar homeostatic mechanisms are involved in hunger and the maintenance of body temperature.

Hunger: The Regulation of Food Intake

hypothalamus (hī''pō-thal'ah-mus)
The part of the forebrain involved
with motives, emotions, and the
functions of the autonomic nervous
system.

The biological control center of hunger is not the rumbling stomach. It does play a minor part in the control of hunger, but the **hypothalamus** plays the controlling role in the motivation of hunger (Berthoud & Morrison, 2008; Seeley & Schwartz, 1997). This small but extremely important forebrain structure that we first discussed in chapter 3 is involved in the regulation of many motives and emotions (see figure 11.2). Hunger is regulated by three centers in the hypothalamus. Two of these hypothalamic

Figure 11.2

Three parts of the hypothalamus play a key role in the control of hunger: the lateral feeding center, the ventromedial satiety center, and the paraventricular nucleus. The lateral feeding center directly stimulates hunger and eating. The paraventricular nucleus controls hunger through the control of blood sugar. The ventromedial satiety center operates in a feedback loop with the body's adipose cells. Secretions of leptin lead the ventromedial satiety center to directly inhibit eating, stimulate the paraventricular nucleus, and increase the metabolism of fat cells through activation of the sympathetic nervous system (Ezell, 1995; Seeley & Schwartz, 1997).

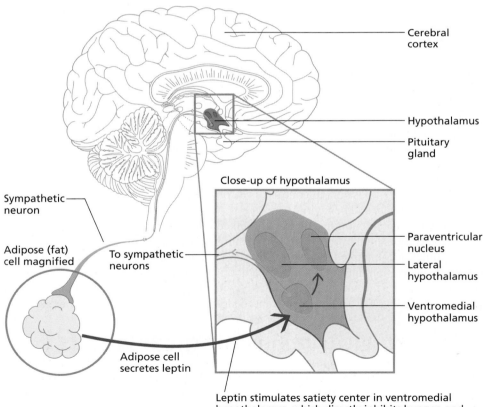

Leptin stimulates satiety center in ventromedial hypothalamus, which directly inhibits hunger, and sends message to adipose cells through sympathetic neurons and sends message to paraventricular nucleus, which controls blood-sugar levels.

control centers operate in opposing ways. A *feeding system,* which initiates eating when food is needed, is located in the **lateral hypothalamus,** and a *satiety system,* which stops eating when enough food has been consumed, is located in the **ventromedial hypothalamus.**

Studies of laboratory rats have shown that when the lateral hypothalamus (the feeding system) is electrically stimulated, rats that are too satiated (full) to eat will begin eating again. If this part of the hypothalamus is destroyed, on the other hand, rats will stop eating altogether and will starve to death if not artificially fed. Conversely, if the ventromedial hypothalamus (the satiety system) is surgically destroyed, the rats will overeat into a startling state of obesity (excessive fat). Figure 11.3 shows a normal rat and a rat with **hyperphagia** whose body weight tripled after surgical destruction of the ventromedial satiety center. These rats do not eat more times each day than normal rats, but they continue eating much longer each time they eat. Apparently, the destruction of part of the satiety system eliminates the homeostatic signal to stop eating when they have consumed enough food.

Alexander Reeves and Fred Plumb (1969) reported a clinical case study of a woman with tragic damage to the satiety center in the hypothalamus that bears a striking resemblance to hyperphagic laboratory animals. A 20-year-old bookkeeper sought medical help for her suddenly abnormal appetite and weight gain. X rays identified a tumor in the hypothalamus, but it could not be surgically removed. Until she died three years later, she regularly consumed 10,000 calories per day in an endless attempt to satisfy her hunger.

The third part of the hypothalamus that plays a role in the regulation of hunger is the **paraventricular nucleus.** This center both increases and decreases appetite by controlling the level of sugar in the blood (Martin, White, & Hulsey, 1991).

What information do the three centers of the hypothalamus use in regulating hunger? Apparently, two cues are used to regulate hunger on a daily basis, and a third cue is used to regulate body weight on a long-term basis:

1. *Stomach contractions.* The most immediate cue in the regulation of hunger does come from the stomach. Contractions signal the lateral hypothalamic feeding system, whereas a full stomach activates the ventromedial satiety system.

2. *Blood-sugar levels.* Eating is also regulated on a short-term basis by the amount of sugar (glucose) in the blood. The hypothalamus contains specialized neurons that can directly detect the level of glucose in the blood (Ribeiro & others, 2009), but two other organs provide most of the information to the hypothalamus. The liver, which is a storehouse for sugar, detects blood glucose levels, and the upper small intestine, or *duodenum,* detects sugar in food that has just been eaten. Both organs send chemical messages to the hypothalamus, which plays a role in initiating or stopping eating (Ezell, 1995; Petri, 1986).

Blood glucose levels are a key mechanism in the short-term control of hunger, so it is important to understand a simple fact about blood glucose and hunger. When you eat, it takes a few minutes for food to be digested and enter the bloodstream in the form of glucose. If you eat slowly, therefore, your brain will have enough time to detect the increase in blood glucose and make you feel "full" before you eat more than you need. In other words, the faster you eat, the more you will eat before you feel full.

3. *Body fat levels.* The long-term maintenance of body weight is managed by the ability of the hypothalamus to detect the level of a hormone secreted by the fat cells in the body (Farooqi & others, 2007; Friedman, 2004; Levin, 2010). The adipose (fat) cells that live on your waist, hips, and elsewhere secrete **leptin** into the bloodstream. The more full of fat the adipose cells are, the more leptin they secrete. When the circulating leptin reaches the hypothalamus, structures in and around the ventromedial hypothalamus detect it. This causes the hypothalamus to react in three ways to control body weight. First, the ventromedial satiety center sends a direct

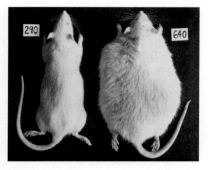

Figure 11.3
Destruction of the part of the hypothalamus that is involved in the satiety system causes rats to eat themselves into a state of extreme obesity called hyperphagia. A normal rat is shown on the left.

lateral hypothalamus A portion of the hypothalamus involved in feeling hungry and starting to eat (the feeding center).

ventromedial hypothalamus A part of the hypothalamus involved in inhibiting eating when sufficient food has been consumed (the satiety center).

hyperphagia (hī ˝per-fā′jē-ah) Excessive overeating that results from the destruction of the satiety center of the hypothalamus.

paraventricular nucleus A part of the hypothalamus that plays a role in the motive of hunger by regulating the level of blood sugar.

leptin (lep′tin) A hormone that plays a role in regulating hunger and metabolism.

Learning plays a role in eating habits. Many families encourage and model overeating.

metabolism (muh-ta´´buh-li-zim) The rate at which cells use energy.

incentives External cues that activate motives.

message to inhibit eating. Second, it signals the paraventricular nucleus to control hunger by regulating the level of blood sugar.

A third action taken by the ventromedial satiety center to control body weight in response to leptin also has been discovered. It provides a new and absolutely fascinating chapter on the sublime complexity of the human body. When leptin levels are high, the ventromedial hypothalamus activates the sympathetic nervous system. Tiny branches of this nervous system actually end on the adipose cells. Stimulation of the adipose cells by the sympathetic neurons increases their **metabolism,** causing them to burn off fat in the form of heat more quickly (Ezell, 1995).

Body Weight and the "Set Point." As we have just seen, the hypothalamus and related brain centers closely regulate hunger. This system must work differently for different people, however. Otherwise, we would all have more or less the same amount of body fat. This has led scientists to hypothesize that each of us has a different *set point* for body fat (Levin, 2010). The set point is thought to be like the point that you set on your home's thermostat to control the heater, but it determines the rate of the cells' metabolism rather than the rate at which your heater burns fuel.

It appears to be difficult to raise or lower body weight above or below this set point for very long (as we will see in the last section of this chapter, where we discuss losing weight). It is not known which step or steps in the feedback loop determine the set point, but researchers are very interested in understanding why the set point is so high for highly obese persons with medical complications.

Psychological Factors in Hunger. Although hunger is clearly a motive that is tied to biological needs, psychological factors are also involved in the regulation of food intake. Through maturation and learning, we go from an infant who drinks only milk to an adult with distinct food preferences that play an important role in our lives (Rozin, 1996). If you grew up in the American South, you might adore chitlins (deep-fried pig intestines) and stewed okra. If you grew up in another part of the world, however, the very idea of these foods might be disgusting. A Catholic woman might enjoy beef, pork, and shellfish, but eating these foods might violate deeply held religious beliefs of her Hindu, Muslim, and Jewish neighbors. Learning plays a powerful role in determining *what* we eat, *when* we eat, and even *how much* we eat (Ball & others, 2009).

Emotions also play a role in eating. People who are anxious often eat more than usual, and people who are depressed may lose their appetite for long periods of time. Ironically, though, individuals who get depressed after starting a new regime of healthy eating and exercise often lose the will to continue. If you are temporarily depressed enough to believe that nobody cares if you live or die, why would you bother to eat healthfully?

Perhaps the most troublesome psychological factors to those who are trying to control their eating, however, are **incentives.** How many times have you finished dinner at a restaurant or family gathering, feeling a bit overstuffed, only to be tempted into eating a seductive dessert? Incentives are external cues that activate motives. The smell of freshly baked bread makes you hungry; passing a fast-food joint on your way home from school creates a craving for french fries; and the sight of dessert creates a desire to eat even when you are way past the point of biological hunger. Incentives have their effect through the same brain mechanisms that regulate the biological aspects of hunger. The sight of food causes neurons in your hypothalamus to fire, particularly if it's a favorite food, and the smell of food triggers the release of insulin, which stimulates hunger by causing your blood sugar to drop (Rolls, Burton, & Mora, 1976).

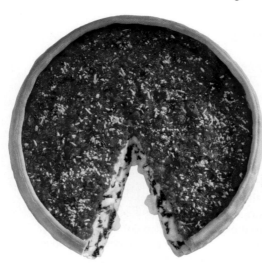

External incentives, such as the look or smell of a food, can increase our motivation to eat.

Laboratory research with animals has shown that incentives can be powerful enough under some circumstances to push weight above the natural set point. All rats will overeat to the point of obesity if they have easy access to large quantities of a variety of tasty high-calorie foods (National Advisory Mental Health Council, 1995b). Unless you are trying to gain weight, therefore, it is not a good idea to keep large quantities of a variety of tasty high-calorie foods in your kitchen. We talk about ways to control our weight for health reasons later in the chapter on Stress and Health.

Thirst: The Regulation of Water Intake

Just as we must control the intake of food to survive, we must also regulate the intake of water. What is the homeostatic mechanism involved in thirst? Actually, there are several mechanisms, as in the case of hunger; like hunger also, the key regulatory centers are in the hypothalamus.

Biological Regulation of Thirst. A *drink system* and a *stop drinking system* are regulated by different sections of the hypothalamus. Surgical destruction of the drink system causes the animal to refuse water; destruction of the stop drinking system results in excessive drinking. Although the control centers for thirst occupy much of the same areas as the centers for hunger, they operate separately by using different neurotransmitters (Grossman, 1960; Schulkin, 1999).

The hypothalamus uses three principal cues in regulating drinking: mouth dryness, loss of water by cells, and reductions in blood volume.

1. *Mouth dryness.* Dryness of the mouth is the thirst cue of which we are most consciously aware. In the 1920s, biologist Walter Cannon studied the role of mouth dryness in thirst, this time using himself as the subject. After drinking large amounts of water to be sure he was not thirsty, he injected himself with a drug that stops the flow of saliva. Very soon, he felt thirsty. Next, he injected his mouth with a local anesthetic that blocked all sensations from his mouth. This quickly eliminated the sensation of being thirsty. Cannon concluded that mouth dryness was the cue that led to the sensation of thirst, but he was only partially correct again. We know today that other factors play more important roles.

2. *Cell fluid levels.* When the total amount of water in the body decreases, the concentration of salts in the fluids of the body increases. Of particular importance to the regulation of thirst are *sodium salts* that exist primarily in the fluids outside the body's cells (because salts cannot pass through the semipermeable membranes of the cells). Decreases in the total body fluids of even 1% to 2% produce increases in the sodium concentration that are large enough to draw water out of the cells and *dehydrate* them (Hole, 1990; Petri, 1986). This happens to cells throughout the body, but when certain specialized cells in the drink center of the hypothalamus dehydrate and shrivel, they send multiple messages to correct the situation. In particular, they chemically signal the **pituitary gland,** which is located just below the hypothalamic drink center, to secrete the **antidiuretic hormone (ADH)** into the bloodstream. When ADH reaches the kidneys, it causes them to conserve water in the body by reabsorbing it from the urine. In addition, the hypothalamic center simultaneously sends a message of thirst to the cerebral cortex, which initiates searching for and drinking liquids (Pevtsova & others, 2009; Schulkin, 1999).

3. *Total blood volume.* The third cue used by the hypothalamus to regulate thirst is total blood volume. As the volume of water in the body decreases, the volume of blood—which is composed mostly of water—decreases as well. A decreased volume of blood is first sensed by the kidneys. The kidneys react in two ways. First, they cause blood vessels to contract to compensate for the lowered amount of blood. Second, in a series of chemical steps, they cause the creation of the substance **angiotensin** in the

pituitary gland (pĭ-tu´i-tār´´ē) The body's master gland, located near the bottom of the brain, whose hormones help regulate the activity of the other glands in the endocrine system.

antidiuretic hormone (ADH) (an´´tī-di´´ū-ret´ik) A hormone produced by the pituitary that causes the kidneys to conserve water in the body by reabsorbing it from the urine.

angiotensin (an´´jē-ō-ten´sin) A substance in the blood that signals the hypothalamus that the body needs water.

blood. When angiotensin reaches the hypothalamus, the drink center sends a thirst message to the cerebral cortex, which eventually leads us to seek fluids (Schulkin, 1999).

Psychological Factors in Thirst. Psychological factors also play a role in the regulation of drinking, although overall this role does not appear to be as large as in hunger. Learning influences *which* beverages we drink (the average citizen of Nepal prefers yak's milk to cow's milk) as well as *when* we drink them (an advertising campaign was recently mounted to convince us to drink colas for breakfast). Incentives, such as the sight of a glass of beer, may activate thirst in a person who is otherwise not thirsty. Stress and emotions seem to have little effect on drinking compared with eating, except in the case of beverages that contain alcohol or stimulants (coffee, tea, colas, and so on), which alter our moods.

Review

The term *primary motivation* refers to states based on biological needs that activate and guide behavior. Examples of primary motives include hunger, thirst, maintaining warmth, and avoiding pain. These motives must be satisfied if the organism is to survive. Primary motives are generally based on a complex number of biological factors. For example, the control centers for eating and drinking are located in the hypothalamus. The hypothalamus responds directly or indirectly to a number of body signals that food or water is needed. In the case of hunger, stomach contractions, levels of blood glucose, and hormones secreted by our adipose cells are all involved in the regulation of eating. Thirst is similarly regulated by a combination of mouth dryness, level of fluids in the body cells, and the total volume of blood in the body.

Although the primary motives are based on biological survival needs, psychological factors are involved in these motives as well. External stimuli, such as the sight of a highly preferred food or beverage, can act as an incentive that activates eating or drinking, even when the individual is satiated. Learning also influences what, when, and how much we eat and drink.

Check Your Learning

To be sure that you have learned the key points from the preceding section, cover the list of correct answers and try to answer each question. If you give an incorrect answer to any question, return to the page given next to the correct answer to see why your answer was not correct. Remember that these questions cover only some of the important information in this section; it is important that you make up your own questions to check your learning of other facts and concepts.

1. The term _____ refers to an internal state or condition that activates and gives direction to our thoughts, feelings, and actions.

   a) cognition   c) motivation

   b) incentive   d) physiology

2. A _____ is an internal mechanism that senses biological imbalances and stimulates actions to restore the proper balance.

3. The hunger and thirst motives are controlled by excitatory and inhibitory brain systems, with centers in the _____ playing key roles.

   a) cerebellum   c) thalamus

   b) hypothalamus   d) hippocampus

4. _____ refers to an external cue that activates primarily hunger motivation.

   a) Incentive   c) Catalyst

   b) Efferent   d) Stimulus

Psychological Motives

Psychological motives are motives that are not directly related to the biological survival of the individual or the species. They are "needs" in the sense that the individual's happiness and well-being depend on these motives. Even more than primary motives, psychological motives vary considerably in the degree to which they are influenced by experience. Some psychological motives are found in every normal member of a species and seem to be innate, whereas others seem to be entirely learned. In this section, we will look at three psychological motives: the need for novel stimulation, the need for affiliation with others, and the need for achievement.

psychological motives Motives related to the individual's happiness and well-being, but not to survival.

Stimulus Motivation: Seeking Novel Stimulation

Did you ever come home to an empty house and flip on the radio or television just to kill the silence? Have you ever spent all day Saturday writing a term paper and then felt you *had* to get up and take a walk or talk to someone just for sheer diversion? Most people get bored easily if there is little overall stimulation or if the stimulation is unchanging. We, and other animals, have an apparently inborn motive to seek **novel stimulation.**

novel stimulation New or changed experiences.

If you put a rat in a T-maze (see figure 11.4) in which it must choose between turning right into an alley painted gray or turning left into one painted with complex stripes, the rat will explore the more complex, more "interesting" alley first. But the next time it will be more likely to turn into the gray alley, which it has not seen yet, apparently because it is "curious" about it (Dember, 1965).

Monkeys that are kept in boring cages will similarly work hard pressing a lever to earn a chance to look at other monkeys or even to watch a model train run (Butler, 1953). Monkeys will also work manual puzzles for hours without any reward except finally getting them apart (Harlow, Harlow, & Meyer, 1950) (see figure 11.5a, b on p. 358). Watch a human infant play with her crib toys for a few minutes and you will see that humans, too, are motivated to manipulate, investigate, and generally shake up their environments. If we go without physical activity for a while, we will almost always begin to feel a need for activity.

Optimal Arousal Theory. Although no known homeostatic mechanism accounts for our need for novel stimulation, we clearly must have a certain amount of it to feel comfortable. But, just as too little stimulation is unpleasant and will motivate us to increase stimulation, *too much* stimulation is unpleasant and will motivate us to find ways to decrease it. Too many people talking at once, too much noise, or a room that contains too many clashing colors and patterns will send a person off in search of a few minutes of peace, quiet, and reduced stimulation. Apparently, an optimal level of stimulation exists, and we feel uncomfortable going either above or below this level (Korman, 1974).

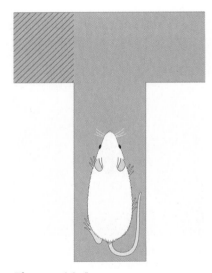

Figure 11.4
T-maze like those used to study stimulus motivation in rats.

Figure 11.5a   A monkey disassembling mechanical lock puzzles for no reward other than the activity and novel stimulation involved in the process.

Figure 11.5b   The need for novel stimulation motivated this monkey to learn to unlock the window that opens into the room with an electric train.

optimal level of arousal The apparent human need for a comfortable level of stimulation, achieved by acting in ways that increase or decrease it.

reticular formation (reh-tik´ū-lar) Sets of neurons in the medulla and pons from which neurons project down the spinal cord to play a role in maintaining muscle tone and cardiac reflexes and upward throughout the cerebral cortex where they influence wakefulness, arousal level, and attention.

Yerkes-Dodson law A law stating that effective performance is more likely if the level of arousal is suitable for the activity.

Some people always seem to need high levels of sensation. The optimal arousal theory would suggest that they are usually below their optimal level of arousal.

Our apparent "need" for an optimal level of stimulation has led psychologists to suggest that each individual strives to maintain an **optimal level of arousal** in the nervous system. Arousal, as used in this way, is a rather vague term, but it refers to the overall state of alertness and activation of the person. The individual who is sleeping is at a very low level of arousal; the relaxed person is at a somewhat higher level; the active, alert person is functioning at a moderate level; the anxious person is experiencing a high level of arousal; and the person in a frenzied panic is at an extremely high level. Arousal is linked to the activity of the brain's **reticular formation** and the sympathetic division of the autonomic nervous system. Optimal arousal theory does not suggest, however, that there is a biological need for a moderate or an optimal level of arousal. The individual can survive at high or low levels of arousal, but he or she is motivated to achieve a comfortable, optimal level of arousal by acting in ways that increase or decrease stimulation.

Arousal and Performance: The Yerkes-Dodson Law. Not only is arousal an important motivational concept, it's also linked to the efficiency of our performance in various situations. If arousal is too low, performance will be inadequate; if it's too high, performance may become disrupted and disorganized (Calabrese, 2008). This seemingly simple notion is often referred to as the **Yerkes-Dodson law,** and it's somewhat more complicated than it looks at first. The ideal level of arousal for different kinds of performance varies considerably. Football players "warm up" and "psych up" physically and emotionally to reach high levels of arousal for the game. It would be difficult to exceed the ideal level of arousal needed for highly physical contact sports. But the performance of a skilled artisan applying pottery glazes by hand would be most efficient at much lower levels of arousal (see figure 11.6). Too much arousal, as in the form of high levels of anxiety, would tend to disrupt the delicate, skilled performance of the potter.

Affiliation Motivation

Do you usually enjoy being with friends? Do you feel lonely during periods when you do not have many friends? Human beings are social creatures. Given the opportunity, we generally prefer to have regular contact with other people. In this sense,

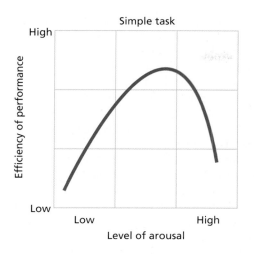

Simple task

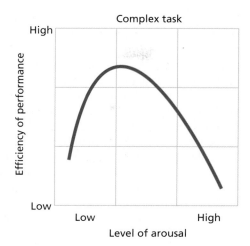

Complex task

Figure 11.6
The Yerkes-Dodson law describes the relationship between the amount of arousal and the efficiency of performance. In general, either insufficient or excessive arousal results in inefficient performance, but the optimal level of arousal is higher for simple, physically active tasks than for complex, highly skilled tasks.

it can be said that people have a **motive for affiliation** (Houston, 1985; Kuhl & Kazen, 2008).

The need for affiliation is present in all normal humans, but most research on this topic concerns differences between individuals who have different levels of this motive. Individuals who are high in the need for affiliation, for example, tend to prefer being with others rather than satisfying other motives. When asked to perform a clerical task with a partner, individuals who are high in the need for affiliation but low in the need for achievement choose to work with a friend, regardless of how competent the friend is. In contrast, individuals who are low in the need for affiliation but high in the need for achievement choose the partner who they believe is most competent (French, 1956).

Two theories have been proposed to explain our apparent need for affiliation (Houston, 1985). Some believe that affiliation motivation is an inborn need that is based on natural selection. A stone-age human who chose to hunt alone would have been less able to kill large animals for food and to avoid being the prey of other animals, and thus to survive, than a human who felt a need to live and hunt with others. Thus, the forces of nature may have selected those humans with a need for affiliation—because they were the ones who survived. Other psychologists, however, believe that each human learns the motive to affiliate through his or her own learning experiences. Because infants experience being fed, cleaned, tickled, kept warm, and other positive forms of nurturing in the presence of another human being, other human beings may become "positive stimuli" through classical conditioning. Similarly, because our actions that lead us to be in the presence of others—smiling, stretching out our baby arms for a hug, and the like—often lead to pleasant outcomes, then affiliative behaviors are likely to be positively reinforced (Houston, 1985).

That motive for affiliation may be related in some way to the greater chance that humans who affiliate—flock together—will survive receives some support from the fact that affiliation motivation appears to be stronger when we are frightened about our well-being. Stanley Schachter (1959) has conducted a number of experiments on the relationship between anxiety and the need for affiliation. In a typical experiment, female university students were brought to the laboratory in small groups. There they met a man dressed in a white coat who introduced himself as Dr. Gregor Zilstein, a professor of neurology and psychiatry. He told half of the research participants that they would be participating in an

motive for affiliation The need to be with other people and to have personal relationships.

The motive for affiliation is present in everyone to some extent, but people differ in the strength of their need to be with others.

experiment involving painful electric shocks—and they were shown the forbidding shock apparatus in the background. He told the other half of the participants that they would receive very mild shocks, which they would experience as a mere tickle. The first group was made far more anxious than the second group, as shown by the students' own ratings of their anxiety. Both groups were given the choice of waiting alone in individual waiting rooms or together in a group waiting room. As Schachter predicted, almost two-thirds of the subjects who were made to feel anxious chose to wait in groups, indicating a high level of need for affiliation. However, only one-third of the low anxiety group members chose to wait together.

Subsequent studies have similarly shown that everyday painful experiences—such as failing college tests—increase our motive to affiliate with others (Van Duuren & Di-Giacomo, 1997). As the saying goes, "misery loves company." However, some people tend to have more affiliation motivation than others under most circumstances, and when the chips are down—such as when they are fighting cancer—they are more likely to seek emotional support from family members (Manne, Alfieri, Taylor, & Dougherty, 1999). There is considerable evidence that higher levels of affiliation motivation predict better psychological adjustment throughout life, perhaps in part because the motive for affiliation promotes social support when times are tough (McAdams & Vaillant, 1982).

Achievement Motivation

achievement motivation The psychological need in humans for success.

Most high school senior classes vote on the female and male who are "mostly likely to succeed." Who was it in your high school class? Were they real go-getters who were willing to work hard to succeed? If so, they were probably high in achievement motivation. **Achievement motivation** is the psychological need to succeed in school, work, and other areas of life (Brunstein & Maier, 2005; Caldwell, 2010). The first scholarly works on achievement motivation portrayed it as a uniformly positive psychological force—the motivation that allowed many people to achieve the American dream of occupational and financial success. More recently, it has become clear that different people have different definitions of "success" and different motives for wanting to achieve their version of success.

We will focus our discussion of achievement motivation on a topic that is very relevant to you at this stage of your life—achievement in college—but the same ideas apply to achievement throughout life. Would you say that you are highly motivated to succeed in college? If so, how would you define success in college? Do you want to make good grades, or do you want to learn a lot of new and interesting information (or both)? Andrew Elliot and Marcy Church (1997) of the University of Rochester have conducted fascinating and important studies of achievement motivation among college students. Remember that motivation activates and directs behavior. They distinguished three key elements in the motivation to get out of bed, go to class, pay attention, take notes, ask questions, and set aside other activities to study for tests:

Achievement motivation is a complex psychological process. People differ both in their definitions of success and their reasons for being motivated to seek it.

1. *Mastery goals.* Persons with high mastery goals are intrinsically motivated to learn interesting and important new information. They enjoy challenging courses if those courses help them master new information, and they are disappointed by easy courses in which they get good grades but learn very little.

2. *Performance-approach goals.* Persons with high performance-approach goals are motivated to work hard to get better grades than other students do, to gain the respect of others.

3. *Performance-avoidance goals.* Persons with high performance-avoidance goals are motivated to work hard to avoid getting bad grades and looking unintelligent to others.

How would you rank the importance of these three sources of achievement motivation for yourself and your friends? Each will activate and direct work that will help you succeed, but Elliot and Church (1997) believe that they lead to rather different consequences. At the beginning of a college course on the psychology of personality, the students answered questions about their level of each of these three types of achievement motivation. At the end of the course, the students completed measures of how much they enjoyed and valued the course, and the researchers used their course grades to see how well they had performed on tests.

The different types of achievement motivation were associated with different outcomes at the end of the course. Not surprisingly, students with higher mastery goals reported enjoying the course more at the end. This was especially true if they were also low in performance-approach goals. This is because being motivated to make good grades to impress other people interferes with enjoyment of a course. Students with higher performance-approach goals made better grades, especially if they had low mastery goals. The desire to impress other people by making good grades does lead to better grades, but sadly, wanting to learn the material for its own sake sometimes gets in the way of making good grades. The students who made the lowest grades had either low performance-approach and low mastery goals (they had little positive motivation of either type to learn the material) or they had high performance-avoidance goals (they had only negative motivation to learn the material). Students with high performance-avoidance goals at the start of the course also reported that they enjoyed the course content less than other students. Working just to avoid failure rarely makes for a positive or fruitful experience.

Thus, to understand a person's achievement motivation for success in college, we need to understand both *what* people want and *why* they want it. Both our goals and our motives for attaining them have consequences for our success in college and enjoyment of the process. The same is true for success in other areas of life.

Solomon's Opponent-Process Theory of Acquired Motives

Richard Solomon (1980) proposed a theory that has important implications for our learning of *new* motives, particularly ones that are difficult to understand in any other way. Why do some people love to fight in karate matches or parachute out of airplanes? How do some people become so "addicted" to their spouses, boyfriends, or girlfriends that they cannot leave them, even when they *do not enjoy* being with them anymore?

Solomon provided an intriguing answer to these and other questions with his **opponent-process theory of motivation** (don't confuse this with the opponent-process theory of color vision). Solomon explained craving such diverse things as parachute jumping, drugs, and dysfunctional lovers by means of two concepts: (a) every state of positive feeling is followed by a *contrasting* negative feeling, and vice versa; and (b) any feeling—either positive or negative—that is experienced many times in succession loses some of its intensity.

opponent-process theory of motivation Solomon's theory of the learning of new motives based on changes over time in contrasting feelings.

The classic example is parachute jumping. When the novice jumper lands, he or she is generally in a mild state of shock but soon begins smiling and talking excitedly about the jump. That is, the negative state of fear is followed by the contrasting positive state of euphoria. The shift from negative fear to positive euphoria that reinforces the act of jumping is shown graphically in the left part of figure 11.7 (p. 362). But after many jumps, the fear becomes less intense. This change is shown in the right side of figure 11.7. There is a lessening in fear from the first experiences with jumping to later jumps. However, note that the amount of reinforcing *contrast* in the two parts of figure 11.7 stays the same. This means that, as the fear is reduced, the amount of euphoria produced afterward becomes even stronger. This is Solomon's explanation of the learning of new motives like the enjoyment of karate, motorcycle racing,

Figure 11.7
General illustration of Solomon's opponent-process theory of acquired motives as it applies to initially negative experiences, such as parachute jumping.

Source: Data from Richard L. Solomon, "The Opponent-Process Theory of Acquired Motivation," in *American Psychologist, 35,* 691–712. Copyright 1980 by the American Psychological Association.

Figure 11.8
General illustration of Solomon's opponent-process theory of acquired motives as it applies to initially positive experiences, such as taking euphoric drugs.

Source: Data from Richard L. Solomon, "The Opponent-Process Theory of Acquired Motivation," in *American Psychologist, 35,* 691–712. Copyright 1980 by the American Psychological Association.

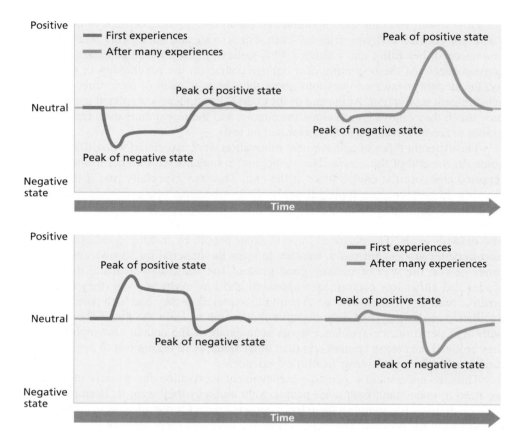

and jogging—even the use of saunas. Not only does the initial negative state diminish owing to repetition, but the person gets hooked by the contrasting shift to increasingly more intense levels of positive feeling. Graziano and Habashi (2010) have used opponent-process theory to explain how we sometimes develop positive attachments to people that we initially don't like.

The process of becoming addicted to things that feel good at first follows the opposite course. The wonderful, drug-like feeling that comes from being with that new guy that you have a crush on, for example, is followed by a contrasting feeling of missing him when he is not with you. Not only is being with him positive, but getting him back is doubly reinforcing because it stops the negative feeling of missing him. Furthermore, as the positive feelings diminish, as shown in figure 11.8, the feeling of missing—even needing—the loved one becomes more intense. If you stop seeing him because the positive feeling is gone, it is this negative feeling of missing him that motivates you to go back. If this sounds like a drug addiction, it's no accident. Solomon sees addictions to heroin and other drugs as forming in exactly the same way. First comes the pleasurable "rush," followed by the uncomfortable feeling of coming down. After frequent use, the pleasure of using the drug (cocaine, nicotine, and so on) in the same amount is greatly diminished, but the pain of withdrawal is much worse. It's the pain of withdrawal that powerfully motivates the addict to take more of the drug, not the diminished pleasure that the drug brings. Solomon's theory is not relevant to all motives, but it may help us understand the learning of some perplexing motives.

Intrinsic and Extrinsic Motivation

intrinsic motivation (in-trin´sik) Human motives stimulated by the inherent nature of the activity or its natural consequences.

It is important to distinguish between intrinsic and extrinsic motivation. We speak of **intrinsic motivation** when people are motivated by the inherent nature of the activity, their pleasure of mastering something new, or the natural consequences of the activity. For example, the monkeys that we mentioned earlier who will take apart mechanical puzzles for no reward other than getting them apart are intrinsically motivated to solve puzzles. People who read nonfiction books that are unrelated to their work just because it is fun to learn new things are intrinsically motivated. Similarly, people who donate anonymously to charity because they wish to help people without being recognized are intrinsically motivated. **Extrinsic motivation,** in contrast, is motivation that is external to the activity and not an inherent part of it. If a child who hates to do arithmetic homework is encouraged to do so by payment of a nickel for every correct answer, he is extrinsically motivated. That is, he works for the external payment rather than because of an intrinsic interest in math. Similarly, a person who works hard to be a good employee because she wants to be admired by others—rather than because of a genuine interest in the work—is extrinsically motivated. People who are intrinsically motivated tend to work harder and respond to challenges by working even harder. They enjoy their work more and often perform more creatively and effectively than people who are extrinsically motivated (Tauer & Harackiewicz, 2004). Not surprisingly, college students with high intrinsic motivation to learn consume less alcohol (Shamloo & Cox, 2010). Intrinsic motivation is shaped by our learning experiences. For example, children from families who emphasize the joys and importance of learning have more intrinsic motivation to learn in school (Fan & Williams, 2010; Gottfried, Fleming, & Gottfried, 1998).

Perhaps the most significant issue concerning the distinction between intrinsic and extrinsic motivation is the question of when extrinsic rewards should be supplied by parents, teachers, and employers in an effort to increase motivation. When is it wise to use extrinsic motivation in the form of positive reinforcement to increase the frequency of some behavior (such as completing homework, delivering packages on time, and so on)? Considerable evidence suggests that if a behavior occurs infrequently—and its intrinsic motivation can be assumed low for that individual—then extrinsic motivation can be successful in increasing the frequency of occurrence of the behavior. Children who hate to do their math homework often will do it diligently if rewarded with additional allowance money. However, if the individual is already intrinsically motivated to perform an activity, adding extrinsic motivation may detract from the intrinsic motivation. For example, when young children who like to draw pictures in school were given certificates for good drawing, they drew pictures less often than did children who had not received certificates (Lepper, Greene, & Nisbett, 1973). This study, and many subsequent studies (Ryan & Deci, 2000; Tang & Hall, 1995), suggest that we must be careful to avoid squelching intrinsic motivation by providing unnecessary extrinsic rewards.

What about praise? When we pat a child on the back for a job well done—whether it be homework or reading a book—does our praise increase the child's intrinsic motivation? Psychologists Jennifer Henderlong and Mark Lepper (2002) suggest that it depends on what we say and how we say it.

Praise increases intrinsic motivation when the praise:

1. Implies that the child was successful because of his or her effort and not because of the child's natural talent or abilities.

2. Is sincere and does not imply that the adult is controlling the child.

3. Does not compare the child to other children.

4. Implies that the adult has standards for the child's behavior that the child believes that he or she can attain with effort.

In contrast, praise that focuses on the child's abilities rather than effort, seems controlling rather than sincere, compares the child to others, or implies that he or she must reach standards in the future that seem impossible (or too low), may undermine intrinsic motivation according to Henderlong and Lepper (2002).

extrinsic motivation (eks-trin´sik) Human motives activated by external rewards.

For example, if a child writes a clever poem for her teacher, Henderlong and Lepper (2002) suggest that this might be effective praise that would increase the child's intrinsic motivation to write:

> "I really like this poem! I especially like the way you found so many ways to compare leaves and songs. That must have taken a lot of thought!"

But praise like this might reduce the child's intrinsic motivation:

> "This is brilliant! See, I told you that you were the only true genius in Mrs. Long's class. If you just write, write, write every night like your mother told you, you'll be great! Soon, Harvard and Yale will be fighting over you."

For many years, it was assumed that another good way to increase intrinsic motivation was to give people choices. When people have options, they will choose activities that they are intrinsically motivated to perform, and performing them will further enhance their intrinsic motivation. Research suggests that this is true, but only in individualistic Western societies (Iyengar & Lepper, 1999). American children of European ancestry show more intrinsic motivation for school tasks and other activities that they choose themselves. In contrast, Asian American children from collectivistic cultures that place greater emphasis on the well-being of the group than on the well-being of the individual have more intrinsic motivation for activities that were selected for them by trusted authority figures or friends (Iyengar & Lepper, 1999). As in many aspects of psychological life, sociocultural factors are important in motivation.

Maslow's Hierarchy of Motives

We have touched on only a few of the human motives, but it's already obvious that we are creatures of many and varied needs. Abraham Maslow (1970) put forward an interesting theory about our many motives. According to Maslow, we are not a crazy-quilt confusion of motives; rather, our motives are organized in a hierarchy arranged from the most basic to the most personal and advanced.

Maslow's hierarchy of motives (needs) is shown in figure 11.9. If lower needs in the hierarchy are not met for the most part, then higher motives will not operate. Higher needs lie dormant until the individual has a chance to satisfy immediately

Maslow's hierarchy of motives The concept that more basic needs must be met before higher-level motives become active.

Figure 11.9
Maslow's hierarchy of motives.

Source: Diagram based on data from Hierarchy of Needs from *Motivation and Personality* (3rd ed.), by Abraham H. Maslow. Revised by Robert Frager, et al., Harper & Row, Publishers, Inc., 1954, 1987.

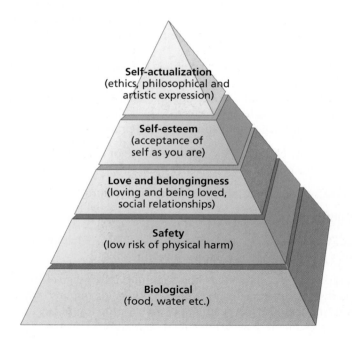

pressing lower needs, such as hunger, thirst, and safety. When the lower needs have been met, then motives to develop relationships with others, to achieve a positive self-esteem, and to realize one's full potential ethically, artistically, and philosophically (**self-actualization**) become important to the individual.

Maslow's hierarchy of motives helps explain such things as why starving peasant farmers are not particularly interested in the political philosophies of rival governments and why, throughout history, science, art, and philosophy have mostly been produced when a nation could afford to have a privileged class who did not have to work to eat. The concept of the hierarchy of motives also helps us understand why a person would give up a prestigious, but time-consuming, career to try to save a marriage with a much-loved spouse. Higher motives become unimportant when lower motives are unmet.

But, as helpful as Maslow's hierarchy of motives is, there are some obvious exceptions to it. The hierarchy does not explain why an individual would risk her or his life to rescue a friend from a burning building. Nor does it explain why imprisoned members of the Irish Republican Army intentionally starved themselves to death in 1981 to gain what might be seen by outsiders as minor changes in how political prisoners were treated. Similarly, the hierarchy fails to shed light on the common occurrence of an individual's ignoring spouse and children to pursue self-esteem in a career. Obviously, humans are sometimes willing to endure unmet lower motives to pursue higher ones. Still, Maslow's hierarchy appears to explain more facets of motivation than it fails to explain.

self-actualization According to Maslow, the seldomly reached full result of the inner-directed drive of humans to grow, improve, and use their potential to the fullest.

Review

Psychological motives help define and shape our lives, but unlike biological motives, they are not directly linked to the survival of the individual or the species. Some psychological motives are common to all normal members of a species and seem to be innate, whereas others appear to be primarily, if not entirely, learned. The stimulus motive—the need to maintain a moderate level of novel stimulation and activity—is an example of an apparently inborn psychological motive. The stimulus motive has led psychologists to speculate that individuals seek to maintain an optimal level of arousal in the nervous system by regulating stimulus input and activity levels. Other psychological motives appear to be influenced by social learning to a greater extent.

Most people have some need to affiliate with others, but people differ in the degree of their affiliation motivation. This motive appears to be strongest when times are tough—misery loves company, as they say. This is perhaps because people who affiliate with others during those tough times reap the benefits of social support.

Achievement motivation is the drive to be successful. This is a complex phenomenon, partly because it is a combination of desires to learn and succeed, fear of failure, and fear of the problems associated with success. In addition, people differ in both their definitions of success and their reasons for seeking success.

Some people acquire powerful new motives through learning. Richard Solomon provided a theory of acquired motives that attempts to explain diverse motives, from the desire to parachute to drug addictions, in terms of the contrasting feelings during and after experiences. For example, the first parachute jump is frightening, but the rush of relief afterward is highly reinforcing. In time, the relative strength of the fear declines and the potency of the rush increases, leading to motivation to parachute.

Some motives are intrinsic—inherent in the activity—whereas others are extrinsic to the activity. Both kinds of motives play a constructive role in our lives, but the unnecessary use of extrinsic rewards for an activity can backfire by reducing a person's intrinsic motivation for that activity. Giving persons a choice of activities improves intrinsic motivation in individualistic societies, but guidance from trusted persons improves intrinsic motivation in collectivistic societies.

Maslow suggests that our many motives are organized. Our higher-level psychological motives only become active when our biological and safety needs have been satisfied.

Sexual Motivation and Sexuality

It will come as no surprise to you to learn that human beings have a sexual motive, much as we have motives for hunger or thirst. Without a sexual motive, humans and other animals that depend on sexual reproduction would soon be extinct. Whereas hunger, thirst, and other primary motives are necessary for the survival of the individual, sexual motivation is a primary motive that is essential to the survival of the species.

Sexual Response Cycle

To understand the motive to engage in sexual activity, one must have a basic understanding of the sexual response cycle. The response of humans to sexual stimuli involves a predictable biological response known as the *sexual response cycle.*

Figure 11.10   The human sexual response cycle.

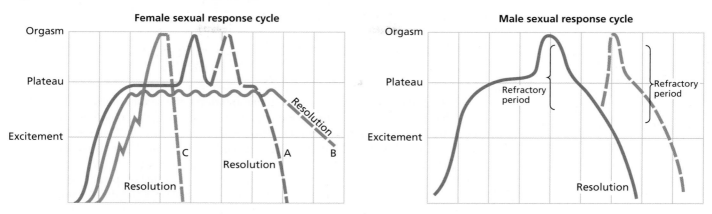

Although there are substantial similarities between the sexual response cycles of women and men, there also are some important differences. As shown in figure 11.10, William Masters and Virginia Johnson (1966) described four stages of the sexual response cycle:

1. ***Excitement phase.*** Both women and men show an initial increase in physiological arousal, called the **excitement phase.** This may begin from visual stimulation, physical contact, odors, fantasies, and the like. Blood flows to the penis and the vagina, erection and lubrication occur, the nipples become erect, the heart beats faster, blood pressure rises, and the body becomes aroused in other ways.

2. ***Plateau phase.*** If the sexual stimulation is intense enough, sexual arousal builds quickly to the **plateau phase,** which is characterized by high levels of arousal that are sustained for periods ranging from seconds to many minutes. The degree of sexual pleasure is very high, but not yet at a maximum.

3. ***Orgasmic phase.*** With sufficient stimulation, and under the proper psychological circumstances, the individual usually progresses to the reflexive stage of **orgasm.** A peak of physical arousal and pleasure is reached. Breathing is rapid, blood pressure and heartbeat reach high levels, the skin flushes, and the individual partially loses muscular control for a brief time and experiences involuntary spasms of many muscle groups. There is little variability in the orgasmic phase of men, but considerable variability in orgasms among women. Three common patterns of female orgasmic response were distinguished by Masters and Johnson (1966). Some women reach a single brief and intense orgasm, like that of men. Other women, depending on the circumstances, experience multiple intense orgasmic peaks. Other women experience a large number of smaller peaks of orgasm.

4. ***Resolution phase.*** Following orgasm, the body's level of physical arousal rapidly declines in the **resolution phase.** Within a few minutes, the body returns to a condition much like its original state prior to the beginning of the response cycle, although heightened relaxation and tiredness are common. In males, the resolution phase is accompanied by a period of time when the male is unresponsive to further sexual stimulation, termed the **refractory period.** Although a woman may briefly be too sensitive to enjoy further sexual stimulation during the resolution phase, with individual preferences determining her interest in further stimulation, there is no refractory period in which women are physically incapable of resumed sexual arousal.

excitement phase The first stage of the sexual response cycle, during which the penis becomes erect and the vagina lubricates.

plateau phase High levels of sexual arousal and pleasure that are maintained for variable periods of time.

orgasm The reflexive phase of the sexual response cycle accompanied by peak levels of arousal and pleasure and usually by ejaculation in males.

resolution phase The stage in the sexual response cycle following orgasm when arousal and pleasure diminish.

refractory period The period of time following orgasm during which males are incapable of sexual arousal.

Similarity of Sexual Motivation to Other Primary Motives

We will understand sexual motivation better if we compare it with other primary motives (p. 351). The sexual motive resembles hunger, thirst, and other primary motives in a number of important respects:

1. *Hypothalamic control.* Like hunger and thirst, the sexual motive is controlled by our hardworking friend, the hypothalamus. One center in the hypothalamus and related brain structures activates motivation and sexual behavior. This system is the equivalent of the hypothalamic feeding and drinking systems. If the hypothalamus is surgically destroyed, sexual behavior will not be initiated even in the presence of sexually provocative stimuli. A second system of the hypothalamus inhibits sexual behavior. If this inhibitory system is destroyed in laboratory animals, the animals become hypersexual; that is, they engage in unusual and unrestrained amounts of sexual behavior. These two centers act in balance to regulate sexual motivation.

2. *Role of external stimuli.* Like hunger, which can be stimulated by external stimuli, known as incentives, such as the sights and aromas of dessert stimulating the hunger of a well-fed person, sexual motivation is highly sensitive to external stimuli. The person who initially is not sexually aroused, whether male or female, will often be aroused by a seductive partner or romantic fantasies. Indeed, external stimuli play a very important role in arousing the sexual motive. One aspect of the role of external stimuli has been termed the *Coolidge effect.* Following intercourse, males of many animal species will have intercourse again with the same receptive female sometime after the refractory period has elapsed. Bermant (1976), for example, found that a ram (male sheep) will have sex an average of five times with the same ewe (female sheep) before seeming to lose interest. However, if a *different* receptive ewe is introduced after each mating, the ram will mate more than three times as often before losing sexual interest, and it will reach orgasm much more quickly than with the same ewe. Apparently, variety is a powerful external factor in sexual motivation for many mammalian species.

3. *Role of learning.* We have already seen that learning can play a powerful role in shaping the primary motives. What, when, and how much we eat, for example, is greatly influenced by our learning experiences. Sexual motivation is influenced by learning, at least to the same degree and probably to an even greater extent. The enormous variety in the sexual behavior of the members of any society at any point in history strongly points to the role of learning in sexuality. In North America today, for example, many individuals consider oral stimulation of the genitals to be a natural and loving part of a couple's sexual repertoire, whereas many others consider it to be a "crime against nature."

Differences in sexuality between cultures reveal the influence of learning experiences on sexual motivation. Contrast our own sexual behavior to the Polynesian residents of the island of Mangaia. Sexual pleasure is a principal concern of the Mangaians, young and old alike. Sex play among Mangaian children is common, with sexual intercourse usually beginning between the ages of 12 and 14. Most young males begin intercourse with an older, experienced woman, who teaches a variety of oral and genital sexual skills to him. Soon the frequency of masturbation drops and intercourse with age-mates becomes an every-night affair. This intense level of sexuality continues into married adulthood, with the average 20-year-old male reporting two to three orgasms per night, six nights per week. The quality of sexual intimacy is not overlooked in Mangaia, however, in spite of the quantity. There is a strong cultural emphasis on both partners' experiencing intense pleasure in intercourse. One of the worst insults that can befall a Mangaian male, in fact, is to be accused of reaching orgasm too quickly and not being interested in the pleasure of his female partner.

4. **_Role of emotions._** Like the other primary motives, especially eating, sexual motivation is influenced to a great extent by our emotions. Because stress, anxiety, and depression are accompanied by increased sympathetic autonomic arousal, and because sexual arousal is mediated by parasympathetic arousal, which is in opposition to sympathetic activity, these emotions generally result in a decrease in sexual motivation. Because the balance between the sympathetic and parasympathetic systems is complicated, however, anxiety sometimes result in an increase in sexual motivation. Just pointing to the obvious influence of strong negative emotions on our sexuality, however, does not begin to do justice to the intricate interplay of emotions and sexuality. Far more than any other motive, sexual passion is powerfully linked to even the delicate nuances of romantic love and other subtle emotions.

Differences Between Sexual Motivation and Other Primary Motives

Although sexual motivation is similar to the other primary motives in the many ways just mentioned, there are important differences as well:

1. **_Survival value._** We must satisfy the primary motives of hunger, thirst, need for warmth, and so on to survive as individuals and, collectively, to survive as a species. Although satisfaction of the sexual motive is essential to the survival of the species, it is not necessary for individual survival.

2. **_Increases and decreases in arousal._** We are motivated to _decrease_ the physiological arousal created by hunger and other primary motives. However, humans are motivated to both _increase_ and _decrease_ their sexual arousal. The intimate behaviors that we engage in to initiate the arousal phase of the sexual response cycle ("foreplay") obviously increase arousal. Yet the fact that Americans spend many millions of dollars each year on erotic videos and topless bars is strong testimony to our motive to both increase sexual arousal and then to decrease it through sexual activity.

3. **_Role of deprivation._** Motives such as hunger and thirst rather predictably rise and fall according to the length of time since they were last satisfied. A person who has just eaten a large meal will not be hungry, but a person who has been deprived of food for eight hours will be ravenous. To an extent, the same is true for sex. If you are used to a regular sex life, the two weeks that your lover goes home to visit family may lead to a noticeable increase in sexual interest. But sexual motivation is far less linked to deprivation than to the other primary motives. Except during the refractory period, humans are susceptible to sexually arousing stimuli and situations at almost all times. However, many individuals without a sexual outlet report going long periods of time without the arousal of sexual longings. Conversely, the more often we are sexually aroused and satisfied, the more sexual motivation we seem to have.

4. **_Decreases in energy._** The other primary motives lead to behavior that increases the body's store of energy and other bodily needs. In contrast, sexual behavior results in the use of stored energy.

Hormones and Other Biological Factors in Sexual Behavior

In nonhuman animals, hormones from the endocrine system play a major role in regulating sexual motivation (Blaustein, 2008). Female dogs, cats, and rats are receptive to sexual intercourse only when they are ovulating—a time referred to as being "in heat."

Males of these species are less influenced by hormones than females and are receptive to sexual stimulation at most times. In some species, however—mice, deer, and goats, for example—males will engage in sexual intercourse only during annual or biannual seasons ("ruts") when they are producing sperm. This means that sexual behavior in nonhuman animals is limited to those few times when fertilization and reproduction are highly likely.

The sexual motivation of humans is less influenced by hormonal factors than that of nonhuman animals (Geer, Heiman, & Leitenberg, 1984). Still, humans are more influenced by hormones than we think. Although intercourse among humans is not restricted to periods in which impregnation is possible, women tend to have greater sexual interest when they are ovulating and capable of becoming pregnant, including greater sexual interest in men who are not their current partners (Gangestad & others, 2005; Spiteri & others, 2010). Similarly, during ovulation, women tend to find men with more masculine faces and physiques, socially dominant men, and the scent of healthy males to be more sexually attractive, but show less of this preference during other parts of the menstrual cycle (Gangestad & others, 2005, 2007). Interestingly, women do not show this preference for virile males when they are judging men as potential marital partners, only as potential sex partners.

In addition, women are more sexually responsive to their male partner, and less likely to be attracted to other men, if their male partner has different genes related to immune system functioning (Garver-Apgar & others, 2006). This is thought to be because mating with a partner with different immune system genes creates healthier offspring. Although we are unaware of doing so, we are able to detect odors from phero-mones that reflect these genes and influence sexual attraction (Martins & others, 2005).

Patterns of Sexual Behavior

The first major surveys of human sexual behavior were conducted in the 1940s by Alfred Kinsey (1894–1956) and his colleagues at Indiana University. Their studies pioneered the study of human sexuality, but their methods were weak and led to some mistaken conclusions. More recently, a well-designed large-scale national survey of sexual behavior carried out by the University of Chicago (Michael & others, 1994) was conducted with some surprising findings. Are people as sexually promiscuous as they seem on television and in the movies? As shown on the left side of figure 11.11, the great majority of female and male Americans over the age of 18 have had either no sex partner or only one sex partner in the past 12 months. Few Americans of either sex have had more than one sex partner in a one-year span, and many of these individuals have had more than one partner only because one relationship ended and another

Figure 11.11

Number of sex partners in the past 12 months (left) and since age 18 (right) for males and females.

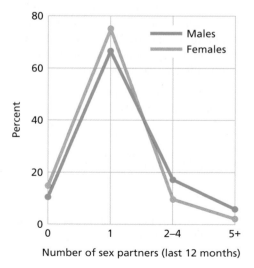
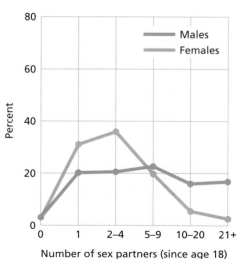

began during the past 12 months. Only 5% of males and 2% of females have had five or more sex partners in the past year. Among married individuals, 95% have had no sex partner other than their spouse in the past year. Indeed, about 85% of married women and 75% of married men never have sex with someone other than their spouse while they are married (Michael & others, 1994). Americans are much less promiscuous than we often think.

However, the average American does not have sex with only one partner in her or his lifetime. As shown on the right side of figure 11.11, less than one-fourth of adult males and less than one-third of adult females have had only one sex partner. Among females, a little more than 50% have had between two and nine sex partners in their lifetimes. Among males, one out of three men has had 10 or more sex partners in his lifetime. It is clear that we tend to be quite faithful when we are in a relationship but that we have many sex partners as we move from one relationship to another (Michael & others, 1994).

How often do Americans have sex with their partners? As shown in figure 11.12, most adult women and men have sex with their partners a little less than once a week. A little more than a fourth of us have sex two to three times a week, with fewer than 10% of Americans having sex four or more times a week. Most men and women say that they spend between 15 minutes and an hour making love each time. Some of you will be surprised (and some of you will not) to learn that people who are in committed relationships have sex more often than single persons do (Michael & others, 1994).

When heterosexual North Americans have sex with their partners, vaginal intercourse is the preferred practice but certainly not the only sexual practice that is enjoyed. About 95% of both women and men report that vaginal intercourse is "appealing." Over 75% of men 18 to 44 years old find both receiving and performing oral sex to be appealing. Relatively few men and fewer women (less than 5%) find anal sex appealing. By and large, our sexual practices match our preferences: the last time they had sex, 95% of men and women said they had vaginal intercourse, about 25% performed oral sex, and the same percentage received oral sex. Only 1% of women and 2% of males said anal sex was part of their last sexual encounter.

The University of Chicago sex survey found few differences in sexual behavior across levels of education, religion affiliation, or ethnic group. Hispanic men and women reported somewhat higher frequencies of sex, but the only large ethnic difference was in the age of first having sex. African American males reported an average age of first intercourse of about 15½ years. In contrast, all other men and women reported first having intercourse at about age 17 on average (Michael & others, 1994). Otherwise, there were fewer sociocultural differences in sexual behavior than might have been expected.

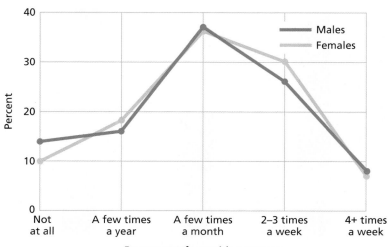

Figure 11.12

Frequency of having sex with a partner over the past year for females and males.

The best news from the survey is that most people who are having sex in committed relationships are enjoying it a great deal. Among 18- to 59-year-old adults, 95% of men and 71% of women say that they usually or always have an orgasm when they have sex with a partner. About 90% of persons in committed relationships say that they receive "great physical pleasure," and about 85% say they receive "great emotional satisfaction" (Michael & others, 1994). Not surprisingly, a happy sex life is strongly related to general happiness. In the University of Chicago sex survey, nearly everyone who was generally happy was also happy with their sex life—and almost all of these happy people were in monogamous, committed relationships.

As you read about the sexual behavior of Americans, I hope you will not fall into the trap of thinking that what is "average" is "normal." If you have sex less often or more often than average, and you and your partner are happy with your sex life, what could be more normal than that? The same is true for the average time spent making love, preferred sexual practices, and so on. Learning about norms and averages is useful, but the focus should be on what is happy and healthy for each individual.

Sexual Orientation

heterosexuality Romantic and sexual attraction to those of the different sex.

homosexuality Romantic and sexual attraction to those of the same sex, as distinguished from heterosexual.

An important aspect of sexual motivation is **sexual orientation.** Persons who prefer sexual and romantic relationships with members of the other sex are termed **heterosexual.** Persons who prefer sexual and romantic relationships with members of the same sex are termed **homosexual.** Most homosexual men use the term *gay*, whereas most homosexual women prefer the term *lesbian.* Other people are attracted to varying extents both to members of their same sex and members of the other sex, termed *bisexuality.*

A national survey of more than 3,000 adults conducted by the University of Chicago (Michael & others, 1994) provided the first reliable figures on sexual orientation and same-sex sexual behavior among Americans. As shown in figure 11.13, 9% of adult males report that they have had sex with another male since puberty. About half of these males who had an early same-sex experience continue to have homosexual experiences after age 18 (4% of all adult males), but only 2.8% of males identify themselves as either gay or bisexual.

Among women, 4% have had sex with another woman since puberty, with these experiences almost always occurring after age 18. About 1.4% of all adult women in the United States identify themselves as lesbian or bisexual. Thus, fewer women have

Figure 11.13

The percentage of males and females in the United States who have had a sexual experience with a person of the same sex since puberty, since age 18, or in the past 12 months. The percentage of persons who identify themselves as homosexual or bisexual is equal to the percentage who report having sex with a person of the same sex in the past 12 months.

(Based on figure 13, page 175, Michael, Gagnon, Laumann, & Kolata, 1994.)

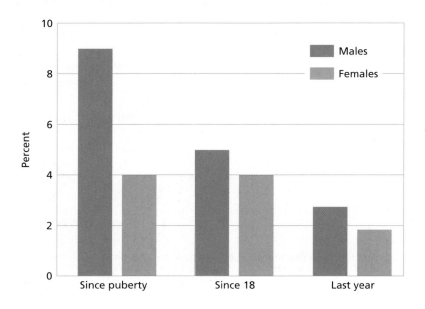

Heterosexual persons hold myths and stereotypes about gay men and lesbian women.

same-sex experiences than men (and women tend to have these experiences at later ages), and fewer women than men identify themselves as homosexual or bisexual. In contrast, more women than men report feeling sexually attracted to persons of both sexes (Chivers & others, 2004; Laumann & others, 1994; Savin-Williams, 2006). Similarly, women are more likely than men to have periods of time during which they identify as homosexual and then return to a heterosexual identity (Diamond, 2007). Women who report a high sex drive are more likely to be sexually attracted to both sexes than women with less sex drive; men with higher sex drives tend to be attracted just to one sex or the other (Lippa, 2006).

If you live in a large city, the percentages of homosexual and bisexual orientations reported by the University of Chicago study may seem low to you. That is because gays and lesbians tend to live in larger cities rather than in suburban or rural areas. In the 12 largest U.S. cities, over 9% of males consider themselves to be gay or bisexual—over three times as many as in the U.S. population as a whole. Among women who live in large cities, nearly 3% identify themselves as lesbian or bisexual, more than twice as many as in the general population. In rural areas of the United States, only 1.3% of males and virtually no females identify themselves as gay, lesbian, or bisexual, sometimes making life a lonely experience for the gay men and lesbian women who live in rural areas (Michael & others, 1994). Interestingly, the percentage of gay males among college graduates is double that of noncollege graduates, and the percentage of lesbian females among college graduates is nine times higher than that of noncollege graduates (Peplau, 2003).

Stigmatization, Stress, and Sexual Orientation. Although attitudes toward homosexuality are shifting toward greater acceptance, gays and lesbians are still harshly stigmatized around the world. In most cases, it is still difficult to be a gay or lesbian teenager who faces the threat of prejudice and ridicule from peers and possibly criticism from parents (Herek, 2000). Gays and lesbians often face discrimination when they live together as partners and have fewer legal and economic rights than heterosexual couples in most states (Peplau & Fingerhut, 2007). Gays also face a greater risk of AIDS and are far more likely than heterosexuals to experience the stress of living with HIV or taking care of a partner who is dying from AIDS (Irving, Bor, & Catalan, 1995). It is perhaps not surprising, therefore, that a number of studies have found bisexuals, gays, and lesbians to be at greater risk for depression, anxiety, suicide, and substance abuse (Balsam & others, 2005; Fergusson & others, 2005; Mills & others, 2004; Sandfort & others, 2001). Importantly, these findings are more complicated than they first appear. Women who have sex with only women are actually not at increased risk for these problems, whereas gay men, and particularly men who have sex with both men and women, are at highest risk (Bostwick & others, 2010).

Origins of Sexual Orientation. Why do some persons develop a homosexual orientation? Many people believe that a person's first sexual experiences are so reinforcing that they shape our sexual orientation. If our first sexual experience is with a person of the same sex, will we be more likely to develop a homosexual orientation? Anthropologist Gil Herdt (1984) of the University of Chicago has argued strongly against this idea by describing the sexual practices of the Sambian people of New Guinea. Sambian men believe that boys will become men only if they ingest the sperm of older males. Therefore, at 7 years of age, boys leave their family home and live in the men's lodge, where they are initiated into ritualized homosexuality. They regularly perform oral sex on older males for several years, and then receive oral sex from younger males when they reach sexual maturity. During this time, they have no sexual contact with females. Although Sambian males report enjoyment of their youthful homosexual activities, when they are old enough to marry, almost all Sambian males prefer to have sexual relationships exclusively with females. The experience of Sambian males suggests that one does not learn to be homosexual just by having homosexual experiences as a youth. Consistent with this view, only a minority of persons in the United States who have youthful sexual experiences with a person of the same sex develop a homosexual identity in adulthood (Michael & others, 1994).

Most psychologists today believe that social learning experiences are important in the development of homosexuality, but only in combination with important biological factors. Several kinds of studies have provided evidence that is consistent with (but does not prove) this hypothesis:

1. Twin studies suggest that genetic factors may predispose some individuals to homosexuality (Kendler & others, 2000; Santtila & others, 2008). If one twin is homosexual, the other is more likely to be homosexual if the twins are identical (they share the same genetic makeup) than if the twins are fraternal (they share half of their genes on average).

2. There is evidence that atypical levels of some sex hormones during prenatal development increase the likelihood of homosexuality (Lippa, 2003; Meyer-Bahlburg & others, 1995).

3. Many studies indicate that gay males are more likely to have more than one older male sibling (e.g., Blanchard & others, 1996a, 1996b; Bogaert, 2003). Because later-born males are exposed to lower levels of prenatal testosterone (Blanchard & others, 1996), this could reflect a hormonal influence on male homosexuality. Interestingly, however, birth order and the percentage of male or female siblings are apparently not related to the likelihood of female homosexuality (Bogaert, 1998).

4. There is evidence that homosexuals differ from heterosexuals in the same areas of the hypothalamus and other brain structures that are different among men and women (Allen & Gorski, 1992; LeVay, 1991; Swaab & Hofman, 1990, 1995). Thus, it seems that, in a few limited respects, the brains of homosexuals resemble the brains of heterosexual persons of the other sex more than heterosexual persons of their own sex.

Thus, it is possible that genetic factors and prenatal hormones organize the brains of some persons in a way that increases the likelihood that they will be homosexual. Since the differences in brain structure are not evident until early puberty (Swaab & Hofman, 1995), however, it is possible that differences in brain structure could be the result of differences in experiences.

Review

The sexual response cycle is similar for males and females, with the primary differences being that men have a longer refractory period between response cycles. Sexual motivation is similar to other primary motives, such as hunger, in that centers of the hypothalamus play an important role, external sexual stimuli can stimulate the sexual motive, and the sexual motive can be influenced by learning experiences and emotions. The sexual motive is different from other primary motives, however, in that it is not necessary to the survival of the individual, it does not always lead to decreases in arousal, it is not influenced by deprivation in the same way, and it leads to a decrease rather than an increase in energy. Sexual orientation directs a person's sexual arousal toward either other-sex (heterosexual) or same-sex (homosexual) partners, or both (bisexual). Researchers have not yet firmly established what leads to differences in sexual orientation, but both biological factors and learning appear to be important.

Check Your Learning

To be sure that you have learned the key points from the preceding section, cover the list of correct answers and try to answer each question. If you give an incorrect answer to any question, return to the page given next to the correct answer to see why your answer was not correct.

1. The four stages of the sexual response cycle were described by _____.

   a) Freud

   c) Kinsey

   b) Krafft-Ebing

   d) Masters and Johnson

2. Hormones have a greater influence on sexual motivation in humans than in other animals.

   a) true

   b) false

3. Most psychologists today believe that social learning experiences are important in the development of homosexuality, but only in combination with biological factors.

   a) true

   b) false

Thinking Critically about Psychology

There are no right or wrong answers to the following questions. They are presented to help you become an active reader and think critically about what you just read.

1. We will study the psychology of love in a later chapter. What can learning about sexual anatomy and the sexual response cycle teach us that is relevant to romantic love?

2. Why do you think that crimes of violence are so common against gay males (gay bashing)? What could be done to solve this problem?

Correct Answers: 1. d (p. 367), 2. b (p. 370), 3. a (p. 374)

Emotions

In 1899, Charles Darwin noted that many human emotions, such as fear and rage, can also be observed in dogs, birds, and other animals. What is the function of emotions in the lives of human and nonhuman animals? Since the time of Darwin, one widely held view has been that our emotions evolved over time through natural selection (Cacioppo & others, 1999). According to this view, two general classes of emotions were "sculpted by the hammer and chisel of adaptation and natural selection to differentiate hostile from hospitable stimuli" (Cacioppo & others, 1999, p. 840). Animals—including humans—who react to dangerous stimuli (like poisonous snakes)

Figure 11.14   Watson, Tellegen, and Clark's "map" of the structure and relationships among different emotions.

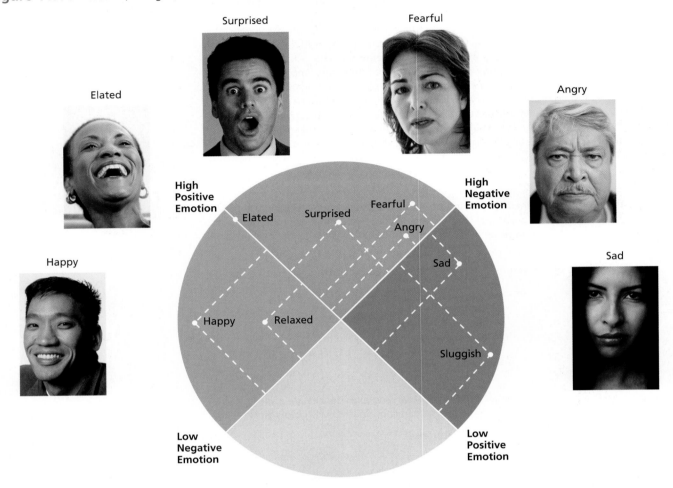

by experiencing negative emotions will avoid the dangerous stimuli and survive. By the same token, animals who react to helpful stimuli (such as friends or food) with positive emotions will approach them and be more likely to survive and reproduce (Damasio, 2001). Thus, positive and negative emotions are key to our survival.

Interestingly, there is reason to believe that positive and negative emotions are not the opposite of each other but are independent characteristics of emotions. Indeed, psychologists David Watson, Auke Tellegen, and Lee Anna Clark (1985; Tellegen, Watson, & Clark, 1999) have suggested that all of the many varieties of emotional experience arise simply from different combinations of positive and negative emotions. They suggest that all emotions can be placed on the "map" of emotions presented in figure 11.14. The map is created using two dimensions of emotion, each with two "poles"—much like the north-south and east-west dimensions on geographic maps. One dimension has high negative emotion at one pole and low negative emotion at the other pole. The second dimension has high positive emotion on one pole and low positive emotion on the other pole. For example, elation is viewed as a high level of positive emotion in combination with a neutral level of negative emotion. Surprise is a combination of moderately high positive and negative emotions, and sadness is a combination of high negative emotion and moderately low positive emotion. Where on this emotional map would you place the way you felt during the most emotional part of the past week? What word(s) would you use to describe that emotion?

A number of important points should be made about Watson, Tellegen, and Clark's emotional map. Although positive and negative emotions are separate dimensions on the map (rather than two ends of the same dimension), the specific emotions that we consider to be "opposites" (such as happy and sad or fearful and relaxed) are, in fact, in opposite positions on the emotional map.

Second, note that anger and fear are very close together on the emotional map. There are many reasons to believe that fear and anger are, in many ways, variants of the same emotion. This idea dates back to the "flight or fight" syndrome described in William James' first psychology textbook published in 1890. Intense negative emotion (which involves arousal of the sympathetic nervous system and the secretion of epinephrine and other endocrine hormones) prepares the individual either to run away in fear or to fight in anger. The two emotions are essentially identical at the physiological level, but many factors (How big is the scary person in front of me? Is that a gun? Do I remember my karate?) determine whether the emotion will be experienced as fear or anger. Third, did you notice that love is not on the emotional map? Many experts consider love to be distinct from the other emotions shown in figure 11.14 (National Advisory Mental Health Council, 1995a). Indeed, the experience of romantic love often involves *many* emotions that are all over the emotional map!

Three Theories of Emotion

What exactly is an emotion? Most psychological explanations of emotion distinguish the same basic elements of the experience of emotion: (a) There is a *stimulus situation* that provokes the reaction; (b) there is the *conscious experience*—the "emotion" that we feel; (c) there are changes that occur in the brain, the autonomic nervous system, and endocrine glands that create physiological arousal in the visceral organs; and (d) there is related *behavior* that generally accompanies emotions—the animal that is afraid cringes, trembles, then runs (Barrett & others, 2007; Lang, 1995).

Since the founding of psychology, however, psychologists have disagreed about the order in which the four elements of emotions (stimulus, conscious experience, physiological arousal, and behavior) are related to one another. Three main theories have been proposed to explain the workings of emotions. (It may help if you refer to figure 11.15 on p. 378 as you read the following theories.)

James-Lange Theory. The common sense view of emotions is that the stimulus of seeing a mugger makes us consciously feel afraid and that the conscious fear leads us to tremble and run. However, William James (1890) suggested that the elements of emotion occur in the opposite order. He believed that the emotional stimulus is routed (by the sensory relay center known as the thalamus) directly to the limbic system, which operates through the hypothalamus and sympathetic division of the autonomic nervous system to activate parts of the body to deal with the emergency (muscle tension, sweating, increased heart rate and breathing, and so on). Sensations from this arousal of the body are then sent back to the cortex and produce conscious feelings of emotion. According to James, "We feel sorry because we cry, angry because we strike, afraid because we tremble." A number of years later, Danish physiologist Carl Lange (1922) independently proposed the same theory, so it's known today as the **James-Lange theory of emotion.**

There is now substantial evidence that the afferent feedback from posture, muscle movement, and the slow-reacting visceral organs activated diffusely by the autonomic nervous system plays a key role in the conscious experience of emotion (Niedenthal, 2007). Interestingly, a very important part this sensory feedback comes from the *facial muscles* (Izard, 1972, 1991, 1997). Stop reading and smile for a few seconds. Did you feel a little bit happier when you smiled? Most people do—that's the idea behind Izard's version of the James-Lange theory. Part of what you feel when you

James-Lange theory of emotion
The theory that conscious emotional experiences are caused by feedback to the cerebral cortex from physiological reactions and behavior.

Figure 11.15   Illustration of three major theories of emotion: (1) the James-Lange theory, (2) the Cannon-Bard theory, and (3) the cognitive theory.

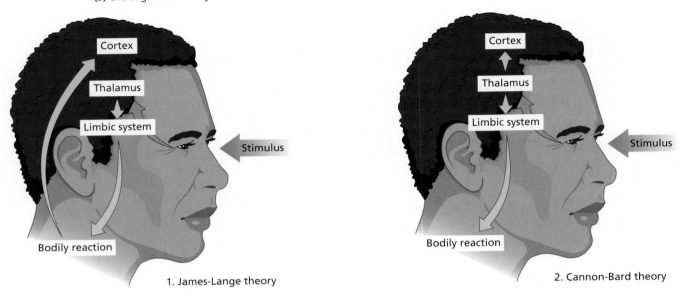

1. James-Lange theory

2. Cannon-Bard theory

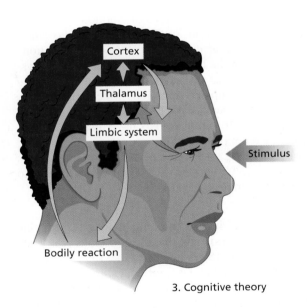

3. Cognitive theory

have an emotional experience is just sensory feedback from your facial muscles. Of the 44 muscles in the human face, 40 are devoted solely to emotional expression—the other 4 are for opening the mouth, speaking, and chewing (National Advisory Mental Health Council, 1995a). In a classic study, individuals who were given electric shocks reported less pain when they were told to make no facial reactions to the shock than when they let their emotions show in their faces. Perhaps the sensory feedback from their facial expressions made the difference in the amount of pain they experienced (Colby, Lanzetta, & Kleck, 1977). You might try that strategy the next time you have to experience minor pain at the doctor's office. A "stiff upper lip" (or, better yet, a relaxed facial expression) reduces the pain (a little).

Cannon-Bard Theory. Harvard University biologist Walter Cannon (1927) provided an alternative theory of emotion that is very different from the James-Lange theory of emotion. His theory was later revised by Philip Bard (1934) and is known as the **Cannon-Bard theory of emotion.** According to the Cannon-Bard theory, information from the stimulus that elicits the emotion goes first to the thalamus. From there, the information is simultaneously relayed *both* to the cerebral cortex, where it produces the emotional experience, and to the hypothalamus and autonomic nervous system, where it produces the physiological arousal that prepares the animal to fight, run away, or react in some other way. To Cannon and Bard, the conscious emotional experience and physiological arousal of the body are two simultaneous, but independent, events.

Cannon-Bard theory of emotion
The theory that conscious emotional experiences and physiological reactions and behavior are relatively independent events.

Cognitive Theory. A third, more contemporary theory of emotion views the *cognitive interpretation* of emotional stimuli—from both outside and inside the body—to be the key event in emotions. Although it is fair today to characterize the **cognitive theory of emotion** as a single theory (Lazarus, 1991; Leventhal & Tomarken, 1986; Scherer, 1997), a number of different individuals contributed different facets of the theory over many years (Arnold, 1960; Denson & others, 2009; Ellis, 1962; Schachter & Singer, 1962). According to the cognitive theory of emotion, the process of cognitive interpretation in emotions has two steps:

cognitive theory of emotion
The theory that the cognitive interpretation of events in the outside world and stimuli from our own bodies is the key factor in emotions.

1. The interpretation of stimuli from the environment.

2. The interpretation of stimuli from the body resulting from autonomic arousal and actions of the body.

We will look at these two steps individually:

Step 1: Interpretation of Incoming Stimuli. The cognitive perspective on the interpretation of stimuli relevant to emotions from the external world harkens back to the ancient Greek philosopher Epictetus, who said: "People are not affected by events, but by their interpretations of them." For example, if you receive a box in the mail that makes a ticking sound, will you be happy or afraid? If the return address says the box is from Violet, and Violet is your deadly enemy, you might think it contains a time bomb and feel afraid. If Violet is a loving friend, however, you would open the box feeling happy, expecting to find a clock. In this case, the interpretation of the stimulus, not the stimulus itself, causes the emotional reaction. Thus, in the cognitive theory of emotion, information from the stimulus travels first to the cerebral cortex, where it is both interpreted and experienced. Then a message is sent down to the limbic system and autonomic nervous system that results in physiological arousal.

Evidence supporting this aspect of the cognitive theory has been provided by an experiment in which four groups of college students were shown an upsetting film about circumcision-like operations conducted without anesthesia as part of the puberty ceremony of an Australian aborigine tribe (Speisman & others, 1964). One group of students saw the film without a soundtrack. A second group heard a soundtrack that emphasized the agony experienced by the boys. A third group heard a soundtrack that described the operations in a detached intellectual way. And a fourth group heard a soundtrack that ignored the painful operation by talking about irrelevant details.

Although all of the students saw the same film, the soundtracks influenced their cognitive interpretation of what they saw. The group who heard the soundtrack emphasizing the agony of the operations showed much greater autonomic arousal than did the group with no soundtrack. The soundtrack that emphasized the agony led to an interpretation of the film as a more upsetting stimulus. The groups who heard soundtracks that deemphasized the emotional nature of the events, either by intellectualizing or by ignoring it, showed less autonomic arousal. Apparently, the cognitive interpretation (encouraged by the soundtrack) altered the emotional meaning of the film considerably.

Step 2: Interpretation of Body Stimuli. The second step in the cognitive theory of emotion is the interpretation of stimuli from the body. Cognitive theory resembles the James-Lange theory in emphasizing the importance of afferent feedback from the body in the experience of emotion, but it goes further in suggesting that cognitive *interpretation* of these afferent stimuli is more important than the stimuli themselves.

Schachter and Singer's Classic Study. The role of cognitive interpretation of bodily stimuli caused by autonomic arousal in emotion was first studied by Stanley Schachter and Jerome Singer (1962). They believed that the arousal of the body during emotional experiences is not specific to the different emotions. That is, the body is aroused in the same global way regardless of which emotion is being experienced, especially the visceral organs. The afferent stimuli from the emotional arousal of the body play an important role in the experience of the emotion, but only through a cognitive interpretation of the arousal. For example, if you are all churned up inside after hearing gunshots in your neighborhood, you will interpret the feelings from your body as fear. But if you feel all churned up after a kiss, you will interpret the feelings as love.

Schachter and Singer's addition to cognitive theory helps explain such things as why sexual attraction is often mistaken for love and why frightened hostages often develop friendly feelings toward their captors if they are treated with even a slight amount of respect. Because the autonomic sensations produced in emotional situations are not distinctive, it's easy to misinterpret their meaning. Sexual arousal can be mistaken for love, and fear for friendship, if we interpret the arousal incorrectly.

Schachter and Singer (1962) tested this facet of cognitive theory in an important experiment. People were taken to a laboratory for what they thought would be a study of the effects of a vitamin on vision. They were given an injection of the supposed vitamin and asked to wait with another research participant for the experiment to begin. The other person was actually an actor who worked for the experimenters. The injection contained the hormone epinephrine, a substance that causes arousal of the heart and other organs. Schachter and Singer were interested in how the subjects would cognitively interpret this arousal under a number of different circumstances.

The actor behaved in a happy, silly manner with half of the participants; with the other half, he acted angry and walked out of the experiment. As predicted by Schachter and Singer, the behavior of the actor influenced the participants' cognitive interpretations of their own arousal. When they were with a happy actor, they rated themselves as happy; when they were with an angry actor, they interpreted their arousal as anger. Importantly, this effect was found only when the participants were not accurately informed about the true effects of the injection. When they were informed, the behavior of the actor did not influence their emotions—they simply attributed the arousal to the drug.

Falling in Love on a Suspension Bridge. A much more interesting test of Schachter and Singer's hypothesis about the interpretation of internal arousal in emotions was conducted by Donald Dutton and Arthur Aron (1974). This ingenious study is also now a classic. The research participants were unsuspecting males between the ages of 18 and 35 who were visiting the Capilano Canyon in British Columbia, Canada, without a female companion. An attractive female experimenter approached the men and asked them to answer questions as part of a survey that she was supposedly conducting on reactions to scenic attractions. The key item in the study required them to make up a brief story about an ambiguous picture of a woman. Their stories were later scored for the amount of sexual content, which was considered a measure of the amount of sexual attraction that the male participants felt toward the attractive interviewer. To provide a second measure of interpersonal attraction, the interviewer tore off a piece of paper from the survey and gave her name and phone number to a participant, inviting him to call her if he wanted to talk further.

Have I mentioned where the interviews took place? Half of the interviews were conducted in such a way as to create a high level of arousal (fear) in the male, and the other half were conducted to create a low level of arousal. The high-fear interviews were conducted while the males were *on* a 450-foot-long cable and wood suspension bridge with low handrails that stretched across the Capilano Canyon some 230 feet above rocks and shallow rapids. The authors reported that the bridge had "a tendency

The solid bridge over Capilano Canyon.

The swaying bridge over Capilano Canyon.

to tilt, sway, and wobble, creating the impression that one is about to fall over the side." I visited Capilano Canyon a few years ago and walked the suspension bridge, and I can personally attest to the fact that it wobbles, sways, and is generally fearsome! The low-fear interviews were conducted upstream on a solid wooden bridge that is not fear arousing.

The results strongly supported Schachter and Singer's (1962) theory that the autonomic arousal that accompanies all emotions is similar and that it's our cognitive interpretation of the cause of that arousal that is important. The participants who were highly aroused (confirmed by their own later reports) while on the high-fear, swaying suspension bridge made up stories that contained significantly more sexual imagery than did the low-fear participants. The high-fear group was also more than four times as likely to call the female interviewer later. Apparently, the high-fear group interpreted their autonomic arousal as a greater degree of attraction to the interviewer. Similar enhancement of attraction presumably occurs in other highly arousing situations, such as football games, emergency landings of airplanes, and the like. So be careful to separate all the possible sources of arousal when you are trying to decide if you are in love.

Role of Learning and Culture in Emotions

Most psychologists who specialize in the study of emotions believe that at least the most basic emotions are inborn and do not have to be learned. Cats do not have to be taught how to hiss and arch their backs in rage; dogs do not have to be trained to wag their tails; and people probably do not have to learn their basic emotions, either (Izard & others, 1997). Even children who are deprived of most normal learning experiences because of being born both deaf and blind show normal emotional reactions (Eibl-Eibesfeldt, 1973).

Comparisons of different cultures, however, suggest that learning does play an important role in emotions in two ways. First, cultural learning influences the *expression* of emotions more than what is experienced. For example, some cultures encourage free emotional expression, whereas other cultures teach people, through modeling and reinforcement, to reveal little of their emotions in public. Paul Ekman (1992) of the University of California at San Francisco, conducted a clever study of the influence of cultural learning on emotional expression. They showed Japanese and American participants films of unpleasant scenes involving pain and injury and videotaped their facial expressions. When the persons from the two cultures were alone, there were no differences in their facial expressions of emotion, but when an authority figure was also present in the room, the "Japanese more than the Americans masked negative

Culture influences the way we show emotions. For example, the Japanese culture tends to discourage the expression of negative emotions.

expressions with the semblance of a smile" (Ekman, 1992, p. 34). It seems likely that the Japanese cultural prohibition against the expression of negative emotions made the difference.

A colleague recently drew my attention to a deeply moving example of a similar cultural prohibition against the expression of some emotions in men. In the summer of 1993, one television network covered the evacuation of a few Muslims from war-ravaged Bosnia. As a young boy was handed up to his father on the truck, the boy began to weep. When the father saw this, tears began to roll down his own face. The father immediately turned away from the boy and rearranged the boy so that he could not see the tears on his father's face. The father then appeared to be attempting to distract himself so that he would no longer cry. Much in our cultural learning experiences influences the expression of emotions.

Second, there is accumulating evidence that people in different cultures tend to *interpret* differently those situations that create emotional reactions (Scherer, 1997). This makes perfect sense from the perspective of the cognitive theory of emotion. Recall that the same stimulus situation can elicit very different emotional reactions in two different people if they interpret the situation differently. It seems likely that these differences in our subjective interpretations are the result of different social learning experiences (Bandura, 1977, 1999). Therefore, it makes sense that people raised in different cultures might learn to interpret emotional stimuli differently.

Klaus Scherer (1997) of the University of Geneva conducted a truly international study of this topic by collecting data in 37 countries. In each country, 100 college students were asked to recall situations in which they had experienced each of seven emotions (joy, anger, fear, sadness, disgust, guilt, and shame). They were then asked a number of questions about how the events triggered those emotions. Scherer (1997) found many more similarities than differences across cultures, but there were some differences. For example, college students from African countries were more likely to view their negative emotions as being caused by the actions of other people and to interpret the actions that caused their negative emotions as immoral and unjust. In contrast, college students from Latin American countries were less likely to see their negative emotions as being caused by the immoral behavior of others.

Cultural differences in emotion is a new field of inquiry, but one that promises to tell us much about human emotions. If there are important cultural differences in how we interpret and give emotional meaning to the events in our lives, we must understand these differences if the citizens of the world are to fully communicate and cooperate with one another. Much research will be needed, however, to distinguish between the myths and stereotypes that we hold about one another and true cultural differences.

The Pursuit of Happiness

The Constitution of the United States says that everyone has a right to "life, liberty, and the pursuit of happiness." Feeling happy often is an important part of feeling that we are living a meaningful life (King & others, 2006). In addition, happiness leads to success and even to a longer life (Lyubomirsky & others, 2005; Pressman & Cohen, 2005). What makes the pursuit of happiness successful? What factors lead a person to be happy? Is it money, love, or something else? Psychologists have only seriously studied happiness since the last decade of the 20th century, but a great deal of valuable information has already been learned.

Does Money Buy Happiness? Almost three-quarters of students entering college say that being very well off financially is very important or essential to them (Myers, 2000). Does money make you happy? The answer is both yes and no. If we look at countries around the world, people in affluent countries are more likely to say that they are happier than people from poorer countries (Diener, Oishi, & Lucas, 2003; Plaut, Markus, & Lachman, 2002). The meaning of this correlation is not clear, however, for two reasons. First, the more affluent countries are also the countries with more stable, democratic governments that afford their citizens more rights and freedoms. So it is unclear whether happiness stems from wealth or rights—or both. Second, among the citizens of affluent countries, there is little correlation between a person's income and happiness. This is because, after a person's basic needs for food, shelter, and security are met, making a lot of money does not contribute very much to a person's happiness (Diener, Oishi, & Lucas, 2003). The exception is that having more financial resources can buffer us against the stress of life's major setbacks, such as becoming disabled in older life (Johnson & Krueger, 2006; Lucas, 2007; Smith & others, 2005).

Does making more money than other people make you happy? More important than the absolute amount of our income is the rank of our income relative to others (Boyce & others, 2010). It's a sad commentary on the human race, but most of us are happier if we make more money than others make.

Does having friends and a romantic partner make you happy? In general, people with many friends are slightly more likely to say that they are happy than are people with fewer friends. Similarly, both men and women who are married or are in a committed romantic partnership are a little more likely to report that they are happy than are adults who never have had a partner or spouse (Myers, 2000). It is possible, of course, that happier people are more likely to attract friends and romantic partners, but intimate relations contribute to the happiness of many people. Not all personal relationships make us happy, of course. Not surprisingly, studies show that some people become much happier after they marry, others become less happy, while most people become slightly happier (Lucas & others, 2003). It is likely that marriages foster happiness only when they are equitable and free of serious conflict.

Does work make you happy? Employment seems to be a major contributor to happiness. Being fired or laid off takes a toll on our happiness from which we are slow to recover (Lucas & others, 2004). In part, however, the happiness that we derive from work depends on our reasons for working. For people who become deeply involved in their daily activities (job, volunteer work, hobby, and so on), who are intrinsically motivated to engage in these activities, and who perceive the challenges as ones they can meet, work is a source of happiness (Kasser & Ryan, 1993; Massimini & Delle Fave, 2000) However, working hard only to make a lot of money and have material possessions often harms social and family relationships and leads to unhappiness (Nickerson & others, 2003).

Does religion make you happy? The evidence here is mixed. Some studies suggest that people with strong religious faith are happier than others (Myers, 2000), but other studies suggest that this is not the case (Diener & Seligman, 2002; Lykken & Tellegen, 1996). More research is needed on this topic.

Are some people inherently more likely to be happy? As the old adage goes, some people always see the glass as half empty, while others view the same glass as half full. Do some people just have a greater tendency to be happy regardless of their circumstances? While it is true that life could deal the most resiliently happy individuals enough tragedy to devastate their lives, there is strong evidence that some people have a knack for making the best of their lives almost regardless of the circumstances.

That is to say that happiness is linked to our personalities to a considerable extent (Diener, Oishi, & Lucas, 2003; Diener & Seligman, 2004; Heller, Ilies, & Watson, 2004). We study these personality traits in detail in chapter 12, but for the moment, note that people who score high on measures of "extraversion" (socially outgoing and uninhibited personality) tend to be happier than other people. Not surprisingly, people who score low on the personality trait of "neuroticism" (which means that they do not get upset easily and they recover quickly when they do get upset) also tend to be happy (Diener Oishi, & Lucas, 2003; Schimmack & others, 2002). Data from a large and important study of 2,310 middle-aged twins (Lykken & Tellegen, 1996) suggest that about half of the differences in happiness among people is due to genetic factors. This finding implies that much of our happiness depends on our genes, probably because of the considerable influence of genetics on our personality traits. Even if it is true that half of the differences in happiness among people is the result of genetics, however, the other half is in our hands!

Human Diversity
Cultural Differences in Happiness

Are people from different cultures equally happy? When measures of happiness are administered to people in different countries around the world, it is clear that the citizens of some countries are much happier than others (Diener, Oishi, & Lucas, 2003). These findings are sometimes difficult to interpret, however, as countries differ considerably in having enough income to cover basic needs and in the respect of human rights. There are clear differences in reported levels of happiness even between countries with stable democracies and high incomes, however. For example, the average level of happiness reported in Denmark is 33% higher than that reported in Japan (Diener, Oishi, & Lucas, 2003). This has led some psychologists to hypothesize that the collectivistic Japanese culture, which focuses on the welfare of the group rather than the individual, does not foster high levels of individual happiness (Diener, Oishi, & Lucas, 2003). On the other hand, there is evidence that the Japanese are less likely to exaggerate their level of happiness than people in Western cultures (Oishi, 2001). Perhaps we are not so different after all. In support of this view, the strong association between personality traits and happiness has been found to be very similar in many cultures (Diener, Oishi, & Lucas, 2003; Schimmack & others, 2002).

It is clear, however, that different things make people in different cultures happy (Diener, Oishi, & Lucas, 2003). For example, Asakawa and Csikszentmihalyi (1998) had students in the United States carry handheld computers that randomly signaled them to answer a few questions about their moods several times a day. Asian American students were most likely to say that they were happy when they were engaged in something related to their goals for the future (such as studying). In contrast, European American students said they were least happy when they were doing schoolwork or other serious tasks and happiest when doing something unimportant, but fun. In general, both people of European and Chinese ancestry living in the United States most enjoy highly aroused positive experiences, such as excitement, where as Chinese people living in Hong Kong generally prefer less aroused positive experiences, such as feeling calm (Tsai & others, 2006).

On average, the citizens of some countries are happier than others. For example, people in Denmark tend to be happier than most.

Review

Emotions are fascinating psychological states that are difficult to describe and define. Most definitions of emotion, however, contain four elements: (a) the stimulus that provokes the emotion; (b) the positively or negatively toned conscious experience; (c) the state of arousal and actions of the body produced by the autonomic nervous system and endocrine glands; and (d) the behavior that characteristically accompanies emotions. Three primary theories have been proposed to explain emotions: the James-Lange theory, the Cannon-Bard theory, and cognitive theory, each viewing a different relationship between stimulus, experience, arousal, and behavior. Many elements of emotions are apparently inborn in all humans, but learning seems to play a role in determining how much emotion will be displayed, how it will be displayed, and how the stimuli that evoke emotional reactions will be interpreted. After our basic needs are met, being married, affluent, and employed are important, but they do not guarantee happiness. Our happiness partly depends on our personality and partly on the quality of our relationships and the reasons that we work. Your culture may influence what makes you happy and perhaps even how happy you are overall.

Review (cont.)

Check Your Learning

To be sure that you have learned the key points from the preceding section, cover the list of correct answers and try to answer each question. If you give an incorrect answer to any question, return to the page given next to the correct answer to see why your answer was not correct.

1. _____ are the experiences that give color, meaning, and intensity to our lives.

2. The _____ theory of emotion is the theory that conscious emotional experiences are caused by afferent feedback to the cerebral cortex from visceral organs and muscles.

   a) Izard   c) James-Lange

   b) Cannon-Bard   d) cognitive

3. The _____ theory of emotion is the theory that the interpretation of the incoming stimuli and the interpretation of body stimuli together cause the emotional experience.

   a) cognitive   c) Cannon-Bard

   b) psychoanalytic   d) association

4. Cultural learning appears to play a role in the interpretation of emotion-causing stimuli and in the expression of emotions.

   a) true   b) false

Thinking Critically about Psychology

There are no right or wrong answers to the following questions. They are presented to help you become an active reader and think critically about what you just read.

1. Think of an intense emotion you have recently experienced and explain the sequence of events according to each of the three theories discussed in the text.

2. What is most important to your happiness?

Correct Answers: 1. Emotions (p. 375), 2. c (p. 377), 3. a (p. 379), 4. a (p. 381)

Aggression: Emotional and Motivational Aspects

We pride ourselves on being humane creatures who have left the brutal jungle to establish "civilized" societies. But the sad reality is that no other animal species even comes remotely close to our record of violent and harmful acts against members of our own species. Although fights to the death do sometimes occur over mates and territory in lower mammals, and apes do apparently "intentionally murder" other apes on rare occasions, no species rivals the frequency of human aggression. In my lifetime alone, a staggering number of people—hundreds of millions—have been killed by other humans in murders, wars, revolutions, and acts of terrorism.

Human beings are the most aggressive species on the planet. What can we do to curb violence in our society?

In the United States, in spite of recent declines, violence is the second most common cause of death among 15- to 24-year-olds after accidents, and it is the leading cause of death among African American males (National Center for Health Statistics, 2009). Perhaps most incomprehensible is the frequency of aggression toward members of one's own family. More than a third of the murders investigated by the FBI have been committed by one family member against another, and some 3% involve the murder of a child by a parent. Each year in the United States, 4 million husbands and wives violently attack each other, resulting in severe injuries in a quarter million of the cases. Each year, too, 2 million children are kicked, beaten, or punched by their parents.

Why are human beings so aggressive? Can we do anything to curb violence in our society? Aggression is a complex phenomenon with both motivational and emotional aspects that we should carefully examine. Like most important topics in psychology, aggression has been the focus of a great deal of research and theoretical speculation. One view holds that aggression is a natural instinct; another suggests that it's a natural reaction to adverse events such as frustration and pain; a third viewpoint considers aggression as learned behavior; and a fourth viewpoint sees our beliefs as a source of violence. We will look at these theoretical positions one at a time.

Freud's Instinct Theory: The Release of Aggressive Energy

Sigmund Freud suggested that all animals, humans included, are born with potent aggressive instincts. These instincts create a drive to commit aggressive acts that must be satisfied. In other words, they create an uncomfortable pressure that must be released. Freud's central point that aggression is instinctual has been echoed in modern times by a number of biologists (Lorenz, 1967). Robert Ardrey (1966) put it this way:

> Man is a predator whose natural instinct is to kill with a weapon. The sudden addition of the enlarged brain to the equipment of an armed, already successful, predatory animal created not only the human being but also the human predicament. (p. 332)

Freud's instinct theory The theory that aggression is caused by an inborn aggressive instinct.

catharsis The process of releasing instinctual energy.

The most controversial aspect of **Freud's instinct theory** of aggression is his belief that instinctual aggressive energy must be released in some way. The key to curbing violence, according to Freud, lies in finding nonviolent ways to release aggressive energy, such as competing in business or sports, watching aggressive sports, or reading about violent crimes. He calls the process of releasing instinctual energy **catharsis.** Freud's suggestion that societies should encourage the nonviolent catharsis of aggressive energy has been much debated. In particular, some psychologists believe that the ways that Freud and his followers have suggested as safe means of catharsis actually have the effect of increasing aggressions. A bit later in this section, we look at research bearing on this topic.

Frustration-Aggression Theory

frustration-aggression theory The theory that aggression is a natural reaction to the frustration of important motives.

Other psychologists believe, like Freud, that aggression is an inborn part of human nature, but they do not agree that it stems from an ever-present instinctual need to aggress. Instead, they believe that aggression is a natural reaction to the frustration (blocking) of important motives. This **frustration-aggression theory** (Berkowitz, 1993; Dollard & others, 1939) suggests, for example, that a child who takes a toy from another child may very well get a punch in the nose, or that a nation that frustrates another nation's desire for oil or for a seaport might become a target of war. People and nations who are frustrated react with anger and aggression.

In recent years, the frustration-aggression theory has been expanded to include aversive events other than frustration. Anything aversive—from pain to intense heat—is said to increase the likelihood of aggression (Berkowitz, 1989). For example, it is now clear that violent crimes are most common during periods of intense heat (Anderson & others, 1997; Cohn & Rotton, 1997; Hipp & others, 2004). Craig Anderson (2001) raised a cogent concern about global warming in this regard. If trends in world temperature continue upward, an increase of 8 degrees in average temperatures in North America could be associated with a 20% increase in serious and deadly assault.

Social Learning Theory

Freudian psychologists believe releasing aggressive feelings in a nonharmful way, like games, reduces the chance of violent behavior. However, social learning theorists believe that watching or practicing aggressive behavior, even in nonharmful ways, can actually increase the chances for violence.

To Freud, people have a need to aggress that must be relieved. According to the frustration-aggression hypothesis, people aggress only in response to frustrating or other aversive circumstances. In contrast, Albert Bandura (1973) and other social learning theorists believe that people are aggressive only if they have *learned* that it's to their benefit to be aggressive. Social learning theorists do not deny that frustration can make us more likely to be angry and aggressive, but they state that we will act aggressively in reaction to frustration only if we have learned to do so. We must see others be successful by being aggressive, or we must win victories of our own through aggression (make someone stop bothering us or take away someone else's possession) before we will become aggressive people.

Social learning theorists directly conflict with Freud on the topic of catharsis. Freudian psychologists believe that we must find cathartic outlets for our aggressive energy to keep it from emerging as actual aggression. They recommend such things as yelling when angry, hitting a punching bag, and vicariously experiencing aggression by playing violent electronic games. Social learning theorists argue that such activities will not decrease violence but instead will increase it by teaching violence to the person (Bandura, 1973).

Cognitive Theory of Aggression

In recent years, cognitive theories of aggression have been developed in an attempt to explain violence, suicide bombing, and the continual wars among nations. Cognitive theorists believe that our beliefs strongly influence the likelihood that we will commit violence or engage in war. Six beliefs that foster violence and wars are (Bushman & others, 2007; Eidelson & Eidelson, 2003):

1. *Superiority.* The belief that one group of people is superior to another group for religious, racial, or other reasons makes it easier to contemplate killing the supposedly "inferior" people.

2. *Victims of injustice.* Many groups of people believe that they are the victims of injustice. Although they may have good reason for believing that they have been victimized, this belief fosters war by justifying retaliation. These retaliatory acts make the other group feel that they are victims of injustice, too, which leads them to engage in new acts of aggression.

3. *Vulnerability.* The belief that your group is vulnerable to attack from another group is sometimes used to justify preemptive aggression.

4. *Distrust.* Some groups believe that other groups are not acting in good faith, but are hostile and intent on harming them. This belief is often used to paint the enemy as evil and justify violence or war against them.

5. *Helplessness.* Some groups of people feel that they cannot solve their problems through hard work and peaceful negotiation. Even powerful nations sometimes feel that there is no peaceful way to solve their problems with their enemies except for violence or war.

6. *Sanctions from God.* When people firmly believe that God wants them to kill members of another group and will reward martyrdom in heaven, they are more likely to engage in violence.

Violent Youth Gangs

The United States has long had a problem with crimes committed by urban adolescents who have joined together in gangs, but in recent decades there has been an increase in both the number of youths in gangs and the violence that they commit. Psychologist Ervin Staub (1996) has provided a plausible theory to explain the increase in gang violence in America that incorporates elements of both the frustration-aggression and social learning theories of aggression. According to Staub (1996), the problem begins in the homes of young adolescents who later join gangs. When parents use harsh physical punishment to discipline their children, they are modeling aggression for the child to imitate. In addition, the child is likely to react to the pain of the harsh punishment with even more aggressive misbehavior. This often leads the parent to write off the aggressive child as "no good" and to cease to supervise his or her activities—giving the child the freedom to spend time with older gang members.

This harsh and inadequate parenting creates children who act in aggressive ways toward their classmates at school, leading to rejection by most of their peers—most kids fear and dislike aggressive bullies. But gangs composed of other aggressive youths offer a place for aggressive kids to belong who have been rejected by their families and peers. The person most likely to respect an aggressive adolescent is another aggressive adolescent who has been rejected by family and peers.

Unfortunately, the gangs provide a place to belong at the cost of encouraging strong feelings of "us" versus "them." Gangs encourage their members to hate and demean the members of other gangs and to think of them as an "opposing army." Conflicts between rival gangs are made more frequent and intense because the sale of drugs by gangs gives poor adolescents their first opportunity to rise above the grinding frustrations of poverty.

Like all of us, youths in gangs live in a society that bombards them with the message that violence is an effective way to solve problems. They see it on television shows, at the movies, and just by observing violence in their homes and neighborhoods. If they watch the news on television, they see a nation that applauds violence when the "us" is the United States and the "them" is, for example, the army of Iraq. We give celebrations in honor of military leaders who organize the killing of hundreds of thousands of the enemy in wars, and we often encourage our war heroes to run for president. All of this provides a clear social learning experience that killing your enemies not only is okay but also is a source of great pride. Finally, the widespread availability of highly lethal automatic weapons in our society makes it easy for the small armies that we call "gangs" to be well armed. And guns in the hands of aggressive youths who believe that they are at war with other gangs often means death.

Review

Aggression is a topic of concern to everyone. Four major theories have been proposed to explain human aggression. Sigmund Freud proposed that aggression is the result of an inborn motive to aggress that needs to be released. The frustration-aggression theory suggests that aggression is an inborn reaction to frustration and pain. Social learning theory suggests that aggression is not an inborn behavior but that people will aggress only if they have learned to do so. Cognitive theorists believe that our beliefs determine our willingness to engage in violence. The most interesting conflict between these theories concerns Freud's prescription for reducing violence in society. Freudian psychologists suggest that an outlet—catharsis—must be found for the aggressive motive but that this can be a nonviolent outlet, such as playing violent video games or watching violence on television. Much research on this topic suggests that Freud was wrong and supports the social learning theory view that such supposed outlets merely teach people to be more violent.

Check Your Learning

To be sure that you have learned the key points from the preceding section, cover the list of correct answers and try to answer each question. If you give an incorrect answer to any question, return to the page given next to the correct answer to see why your answer was not correct.

Match each definition with one of the four terms below:

1. Aggression is caused by an inborn aggressive instinct.

2. Aggression is a natural reaction to aversive events, such as frustration, pain, and heat.

3. People act aggressively only if they have learned to do so.

4. Certain beliefs make people and nations more likely to engage in violence.

a) social learning theory

b) Freud's instinct theory

c) frustration-aggression theory

d) cognitive theory

Thinking Critically about Psychology

There are no right or wrong answers to the following questions. They are presented to help you become an active reader and think critically about what you just read.

1. In your opinion, which theory of aggression offers the best ideas for reducing gang violence?

2. Think of two countries or groups of people who are at war. How does each of the dangerous beliefs discussed by the cognitive theory of aggression relate to that war?

Correct Answers: 1. b (p. 386), 2. c (p. 386), 3. a (p. 387), 4. d (p. 387)

Application of Psychology

Date Rape

Date rape involves sexual motivation and coercion or even violence. Date is a common form of rape committed by a person who is on a date with the victim. Because the rapist is usually a male and the victim is usually a female, I speak of the rapist and victim in those terms. It is important to acknowledge, however, that both men and women commit rape, both women and men are victims, and rapes occur among both heterosexuals and homosexuals. No one is completely free of the threat of rape.

Most of us think of rapists as strangers lurking in the shadows with a knife. Such rapists certainly do exist, but more than 75% of rapists are acquaintances of the victim (National Victim Center, 1992; Cling, 2004). Indeed, many rapes are committed by a male who took the victim to a movie and drank a couple of beers with her afterward. Date rape is a common occurrence on college campuses across the United States. It is estimated that 33% of all college women have experienced unwanted sexual intercourse of this sort (Koss & Oros, 1982). Most often, the perpetrator is a trusted and well-liked male student who did not stop advancing sexual contact after protests from his date. In many cases, the date rapist became angry at the rejection and knowingly and brutally forced his date to have sex. In other cases, however, the date rapist had no intention of committing a rape and did not know that he was doing so. He didn't understand that she was saying "no," or thought that nice girls say "no" when they really mean "yes."

In many cases, date rapes begin with a miscommunication between the persons. Studies of dating have shown that it is common for men and women to miscommunicate their sexual interests to others. College males often misinterpret college women's behavior. When women think they are only being friendly and not expressing any sexual interest at all, men often think the woman is making a sexual advance (Abbey, 1982; Abbey & Melby, 1986; Buss, 2001). This occurs because males tend to misinterpret subtle aspects of friendly behavior, such as pleasant facial expressions, standing close to the male, and maintaining eye contact, as indications of sexual interest. Males engage in a lot of wishful thinking about sex and often see what they want to see in the woman's behavior.

One reason that men and women often miscommunicate about sex is that they differ in their beliefs and attitudes about sexuality. For example, if you were not in a relationship and you met someone that you really liked on Friday night, would it be okay to have sex with her or him on Sunday afternoon? When a large sample of college freshmen were asked about sex with someone that they had just met, 66% of the men said it would be okay, but only 38% of the women agreed (Astin, Korn, & Berz, 1991).

Alcohol is another aspect of dating related to date rape. Some men use alcohol to reduce the resistance of a date who has not previously consented to sexual activity. Sometimes this is done intentionally to trick the woman into agreeing to something that she would not agree to when sober. Most men, however, give the role of alcohol no thought and simply offer alcohol to their dates as part of the normal dating ritual. The problem is that these men believe that a woman who consents to sex when intoxicated is giving her consent (Koss & others, 1985).

Under some circumstances, alcohol lowers inhibitions and often increases interest in sexual activity (Cooper, 2006). Alcohol also makes it more likely that the male will do something—such as using force—that he would not do when he had not been drinking. Drinking may also lead the female to act in ways that are interpreted by her date as a sexual invitation.

What are the implications of these findings? Is there anything that you can do to prevent date rape? The ongoing discussion of what constitutes date rape is an important positive step. Everyone understands that an intentional and forceful rape is wrong under any circumstance, but the boundaries need to be clarified for some cases of date rape. Following are some simple guidelines that may help.

Guidelines for Men.

1. *It is always rape when she says "no."* Women do not mean "yes" when they say "no." Be clear about this—"no" means "no." The research of psychologist Charlene Muehlenhard suggests that men often think that "no" means "yes" in sexual situations, especially if it is not stated emphatically (Muehlenhard & Hollabaugh, 1988). Men need to be aware of their tendency to think wishfully about women's sexual availability and to realize that even an unclear statement of "no" is a clear warning sign that he may be committing the felony of rape if he does not stop his sexual advances.

2. *If it is not clear that she has consented to sex, she has not consented.* Just learning to take "no" for an answer is not enough to avoid committing date rape. What should a male do if his date does not say "no" to a sexual advance but says something like "I really don't know if this is a good idea"? Is it rape if he continues, anyway? Sexual situations are filled with pressures that make it difficult to communicate clearly, and men tend to misinterpret subtle signals. This means that the only appropriate decision is to discontinue sexual advances when it is not perfectly clear that they are wanted. If she really wants you to continue, she will tell you this when you stop, but if she was saying "no," you will have avoided becoming a rapist.

3. *If she is drunk or high, she cannot give consent to sex.* Whether a male is intentionally trying to loosen his date's inhibitions or not, a drunken (or unconscious or stoned or high) date cannot give consent to sex. Decisions made while drunk can be tomorrow's tragedy—both to the woman who finds that she has had sex with a man with whom she had no intention of having sex and to the man who is arrested for raping a woman who he thought had given consent. And remember, a male who has been drinking is more likely to do things that he would not otherwise have done. Like drinking and driving, drinking and dating is a dangerous combination.

Guidelines for Women.

1. *Communicate your wishes about sex clearly and early.* As noted earlier, men have a tendency to hear women say "yes" about sex more often than women say it, especially if

the communication from the woman is not crystal clear from the very start (Muehlenhard & Hollabaugh, 1988). This means that, to be safe, women who do not want sexual contact may need to communicate that fact in a way that leaves no room for doubt as soon as the first sexual advance is made. Our society teaches us to communicate about sexuality in subtle and indirect ways, but women who communicate their desires and limits clearly and assertively from the very beginning can reduce their chances of being the victim of a date rape.

   2. *The combination of alcohol and sexual situations is dangerous.* Alcohol and other drugs bring out the worst in people. When a male has been drinking, he will be more likely to disregard a clear "no" or to become angry and violent when frustrated than when he has not been drinking. Similarly, when a female has been drinking, she may be less likely to say "no" to unwanted sex or may even be unable to make a rational decision about sex if she is intoxicated. Even moderate drinking can create serious problems, but heavy drinking is an invitation to date rape.

   3. *Even "nice guys" can commit rape.* Because rapists are not characterized by any particular type of personality, it is not possible to predict who will commit rape. As stated earlier, most date rapists are men who seemed like nice guys to the victim before the rape. This is not to say that all men are potential rapists, but you should not assume that a male could not rape you under the wrong circumstances just because he seems nice. Try to avoid miscommunication and risky situations with all men. Finally, if you or someone you know has been raped or if you are concerned that you might rape someone, help is available. Most college campuses have come to recognize date rape as a serious problem. The majority of counseling centers and student development centers have methods for addressing the date rape problem. Student organizations often assemble meetings to discuss issues of dating and dating violence. Off campus, community resources, such as mental health centers and crisis lines, offer services to persons concerned about being a victim of sexual assault or about the possibility that one could become sexually assaultive. There are many possibilities for improving the present problem of date rape, but all require open and honest communication and a willingness to evaluate one's own behavior.

Summary

Chapter 11 defines motivation and emotion, discusses primary motives, psychological motives, and explores three theories of emotions. The topic of aggression is included in the chapter because of its close link to both emotion and motivation.

I. Motivation refers to those factors that activate behavior and give it direction. Emotions are positive or negative feelings usually accompanied by behavior and physiological arousal that are generally reactions to stimulus situations.

II. Primary motives are human motives that stem from the need for those things that keep a person alive.

   A. Homeostatic mechanisms in the body sense imbalances of essential life elements and stimulate actions that will restore the proper balance.

   B. Hunger is biologically regulated by three centers in the hypothalamus.

      1. Rats will not eat if their lateral feeding center is destroyed.

      2. Rats become hyperphagic (obese because of overeating) if the ventromedial satiety center is destroyed.

      3. The paraventricular nucleus of the hypothalamus regulates blood sugar levels.

   C. Cues for regulating hunger on a daily basis are stomach contractions and blood sugar levels; body fat is apparently involved in the long-term regulation of hunger.

   D. Learning influences when we eat, what we eat, and how much we eat. Hunger, as well as other motives, is affected by incentives—external cues that activate motives.

   E. The hypothalamus also controls thirst. Cues used to regulate drinking are mouth dryness, loss of water by cells, and reductions in blood volume.

   F. Learning influences drinking behavior, and incentives can activate thirst.

III. Psychological motives are "needs" in the sense that the individual's happiness and well-being, but not survival, depend on these motives.

   A. Humans and other animals have an inborn motive to seek an optimal level of arousal. The Yerkes-Dodson law states that if arousal is too low, performance will be poor, but if it is too high, performance may become disrupted and disorganized.

   B. Individuals high in affiliation motivation tend to prefer being with others.

   C. Achievement motivation is the psychological need for success. People are motivated to achieve by different combinations of:

      1. Desire to learn and master new topics and skills.

      2. Desire to do better than others.

      3. Fear of failure.

   D. Intrinsic motivation refers to motives stimulated by the inherent nature of the activity. External motivation is motivation stimulated by external rewards.

   E. According to Maslow, motives are organized in a hierarchy arranged from the most basic to the most personal and advanced.

IV. Sexual motivation

    A. Sexual motivation resembles other primary motives in a number of important respects.

        1. Like hunger and thirst, sexual motivation is controlled by opposing centers in the hypothalamus.

        2. Like hunger, which can be stimulated by external stimuli, known as incentives, sexual motivation is highly sensitive to external stimuli.

        3. Sexual motivation is influenced by learning, at least to the same degree as hunger and other primary motives.

        4. Like the other primary motives, especially eating, sexual motivation is influenced to a great extent by our emotions.

    B. Sexual orientation refers to our tendency to prefer romantic and sexual partners of the same or different sex.

        1. Persons are considered to be heterosexual, homosexual, or bisexual on the basis of the degree of romantic and sexual attraction to members of the same or other sex.

        2. It appears that both biological and social factors play a role in development of sexual orientation.

V. Emotions are the experiences that give color, meaning, and intensity to our lives.

    A. Theories that attempt to explain emotions include the James-Lange theory, the Cannon-Bard theory, and the cognitive theory.

    B. Most psychologists believe that many basic emotions are primarily inborn but that learning also plays an important role in emotions.

VI. Aggression is a complex phenomenon that is not yet fully understood.

    A. Freud suggested that all people are born with potent aggressive instincts that are released through catharsis.

    B. Other psychologists say aggression is a reaction to the frustration (blocking) of important motives or other aversive events (the frustration-aggression hypothesis).

    C. Social learning theorists explain aggression as learned behavior.

    D. Cognitive theorists believe that our beliefs are a key contributor to violence.

Visual Review of Theories of Motivation and Emotion

This visual review may help you consolidate your learning of some of the information presented in this chapter. Be sure not to limit your review to these diagrams, but because they are key to understanding some of the important concepts in this chapter, mastering them should help you master the entire chapter.

Figure 11.16
This is a diagram of Maslow's hierarchy of motives. Fill in the missing labels and check them for accuracy by referring back to figure 11.9, page 364.

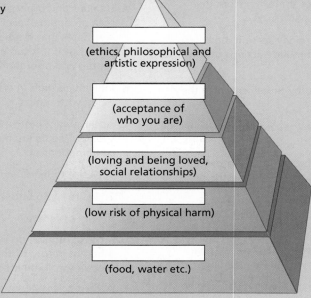

(ethics, philosophical and artistic expression)

(acceptance of who you are)

(loving and being loved, social relationships)

(low risk of physical harm)

(food, water etc.)

Figure 11.17 These three figures illustrate each of the three theories of emotion covered in this chapter. Write the name of the theory next to each illustration and check your answers for accuracy by referring back to figure 11.15, page 378.

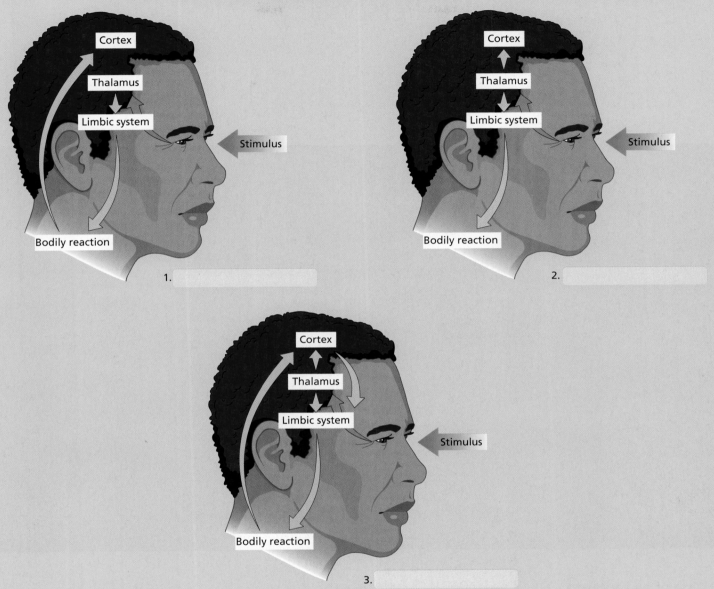

1. _____

2. _____

3. _____

chapter **twelve**
Personality

Chapter Outline

Prologue

In psychology, we use the term *personality* to refer to the typical ways of acting, thinking, and feeling that make one person different from another. How would you describe your personality? What are you typically like?

Many psychologists use just five basic concepts to describe our personalities. How would you rate yourself on the following five dimensions of personality? On the first dimension, if you tend to be very relaxed and secure, give yourself a "1"—but, if you tend to be very tense and insecure, give yourself a "3." If you are neither very tense nor very relaxed, give yourself a "2" on this dimension. You could even give yourself 1.5 if you think that you are somewhere between a 1 and a 2. Now, rate yourself on the other four dimensions in the same way.

	1	2	3
Relaxed and secure			Tense and insecure
Quiet and not social			Talkative and sociable
Down-to-earth and unadventurous			Imaginative and daring
Irritable and ruthless			Good-natured and kind
Careless and unreliable			Careful and reliable

Some psychologists believe that the enormous range of variation in human personalities can be thought of as just different combinations of high or low scores on these five basic dimensions of personality. How well do they capture your personality?

In this chapter, we discuss four theoretical approaches to the description and understanding of personality. These are trait theory, psychoanalytic theory, humanistic theory, and social learning theory. The last section describes several approaches to the measurement of personality.

Trait theory focuses on the best ways to *describe* the consistencies and organization of personality. In contrast, the other three theories are more concerned with *why* we behave as we do. Psychoanalytic theory was first stated by Sigmund Freud. Freud believed that your personality results from the struggle among opposing forces within your mind. We are born with selfish instincts, but our interactions with society give us the ability to think realistically and give us values and ideals that hold our selfish impulses in check. According to Freud, the particular way in which each of us balances these forces gives us our unique personality.

Humanistic psychologists view the development of personality in an almost completely opposite way. Humanists believe that, rather than entering the world full of selfish instincts, we are born with a healthy, positive drive to realize our full potential, but society often interferes with that drive. To humanists, an accurate self-concept is essential to healthy personality functioning. Humanists believe that society often sets such unrealistically high standards for what is "good" that it is difficult to see ourselves accurately, which interferes with personality functioning. The social learning theory of personality takes a simpler view of personality development. From this perspective, personality is simply something that is learned through our interactions with other members of society. People are not born with powerful negative or positive drives that collide with society. We simply learn our personalities from our interactions with others.

Definition of Personality

What do we mean when we use the term *personality*? It's no accident that the word *person* is in the word *personality*. Your personality defines you as a person rather than just a biological conglomeration of organs. One's **personality** is the sum total of all of the ways of acting, thinking, and feeling that are typical for that person and make each person *different* from other individuals.

The two key words in this definition are *typical* and *different*. An individual's personality is composed of all the relatively unchanging psychological characteristics that are *typical* for that person. Some people are typically generous; others are typically impulsive; others are typically shy. If people did not have at least some relatively

personality The sum total of the typical ways of acting, thinking, and feeling that makes each person different from other people.

Howard Stern's tendency to be flamboyant is a well-known aspect of his personality.

traits Relatively enduring patterns of behavior (thinking, acting, and feeling) that are relatively consistent across situations.

unchanging qualities, we would never know what to expect from them. Each time we encountered a friend, it would be like dealing with a stranger. We know what to expect from our friends because of the relatively unchanging psychological characteristics that make up each person's personality.

The second emphasis in the definition of personality is on the term *different.* Each person's unique pattern of typical ways of acting, thinking, and feeling sets him or her apart from each other person. Each of us is a unique person because no one else has exactly our combination of typical psychological qualities. Even if every person were exactly identical in every physical characteristic—eye color, height, weight, tone of voice—we would be able to distinguish one person from another because of their personality (their typical ways of acting, thinking, and feeling).

Trait Theory: Describing the Consistencies of Personality

What is the best way to *describe* an individual's personality? How can your entire personality best be reduced to mere words? We use many different words to refer to personality, such as *friendly, aggressive, flirtatious,* and *fearful.* We are so fond of describing people in such terms, in fact, that there are more than 17,000 words for them in the English language (Allport & Odbert, 1936). In psychological terms, these words refer to **traits.** Traits are defined as relatively enduring patterns of behavior that are relatively consistent across situations. When we say that a person has the trait of friendliness, for example, we mean that she is friendly to most people and that her friendliness does not change much as time goes by.

Some psychologists have developed their ideas about traits to the extent that they are considered to be theories of personality. Unlike the other theories that we discuss in this chapter, trait theories are more concerned with *describing* traits than *explaining* their origins. Although there are many important trait theories of personality, the best known are classic theories of Gordon Allport and the contemporary five-factor personality theory.

Allport's Trait Theory

Gordon Allport (1937, 1961) believed that the most important traits are those related to our *values.* Allport tells us that the best way to understand people and predict how they will behave in the future is to find out what they value—the things that they strive to attain. A person who values money more than family life, for example, can be expected to accept a promotion that would mean greater pay but would require spending more time away from home. A person who values family life over money, in contrast, could be predicted to make the opposite decision.

An important topic to all trait theorists is the ways that traits are related to one another and are organized. Allport (1961) believed that traits could be ranked in terms of their importance as *cardinal, central,* or *secondary.* Cardinal traits are those that dominate a person's life. The quest for knowledge could be said to be one of the cardinal traits that dominated Albert Einstein's life, whereas the desire for social justice dominated Mahatma Gandhi's behavior. Allport believed that relatively few people possessed such cardinal traits. Much more common, however, are the central traits. These also are important traits that influence and organize much of our behavior, but not to the extent of cardinal traits. For example, one person's behavior might mostly be aimed at obtaining intimacy and sexual gratification. Another person, however, may be relatively uninterested in intimacy but may strongly desire power and prestige. Secondary traits are much more specific (such as being rude to telephone salespeople) and much less important to a comprehensive description of a person's personality.

Gordon Allport (1897–1967).

Table 12.1   Brief Description of the Big Five Personality Traits

1. Neuroticism		4. Agreeableness	
Calm . . . versus . . . Worrying		Irritable . . . versus . . . Good-natured	
At-ease . . . versus . . . Nervous		Ruthless . . . versus . . . Soft-hearted	
Relaxed . . . versus . . . High-strung		Selfish . . . versus . . . Selfless	
Secure . . . versus . . . Insecure		Callous . . . versus . . . Sympathetic	
Comfortable . . . versus . . . Self-conscious		Vengeful . . . versus . . . Forgiving	
2. Extraversion		**5. Conscientiousness**	
Retiring . . . versus . . . Sociable		Negligent . . . versus . . . Conscientious	
Sober . . . versus . . . Fun-loving		Careless . . . versus . . . Careful	
Reserved . . . versus . . . Affectionate		Undependable . . . versus . . . Reliable	
Quiet . . . versus . . . Talkative		Lazy . . . versus . . . Hardworking	
Loner . . . versus . . . Joiner		Disorganized . . . versus . . . Well organized	
3. Openness			
Conventional . . . versus . . . Original			
Down-to-earth . . . versus . . . Imaginative			
Uncreative . . . versus . . . Creative			
Narrow interests . . . versus . . . Broad interests			

Five-Factor Model of Personality

Over the years, many trait models like those of Gordon Allport have been proposed, each stating that a different set of traits best describes our personalities. None of these models of personality was widely accepted, however, until recent years. There is now considerable consensus among trait theorists that five broad traits provide a complete description of our personalities (Ashton, Lee, & Goldberg, 2004; McCrae & Costa, 1987, 1999; McCrae & Terracciano, 2005).

The so-called *big five* personality traits are described in table 12.1. These descriptions elaborate on the five dimensions of personality discussed in the prologue to this chapter. The most important adjectives that describe each trait are listed under the label of the trait. Personality tests have been developed to measure these five traits. The goal is to use information that the person taking the test gives to determine whether the person is, for example, more "calm or worrying" or more "at ease or high-strung." Then an overall score is generated from these items to yield a description of the person on that trait and the other traits. For example, a person who revealed himself or herself as worrying, nervous, high-strung, insecure, and self-conscious would be considered to be high on neuroticism. A person who answered questions on the personality test indicating that she or he was calm, at ease, relaxed, secure, and comfortable would be considered to be very low in neuroticism. Most people, of course, would be somewhere in between. These five basic personality traits are influenced by both inheritance and our experiences (Bouchard, 2004).

By the way, are people the only animals with personalities? Does your dog or cat have a personality that makes it different from other animals? Since the time of Pavlov, there has been clear evidence that mammals have personality traits as humans do, and there is recent evidence that the five-factor model describes the personalities of dogs and other nonhuman mammals pretty well (Gosling, Kwan, & John, 2003).

Importance of Personality Traits

Measuring a person's personality traits is only worthwhile because it helps us understand important aspects of people's lives. Are personality traits useful in this way? A vast amount of research now makes it clear that our personality traits are substantially related with both our mental and physical well-being. In particular, people who are very high in neuroticism are less likely to be happy, are more likely to have mental disorders during their lifetime, are more likely to have serious health problems such as diabetes and heart disease, and are even expected to die somewhat earlier (Kotov & others, 2010; Lahey, 2009; Phillips & others, 2010; Roberts & others, 2009). Conversely, people who are high in conscientiousness are less likely to have health problems (Hampson, 2008; Lahey, 2009; Roberts & others, 2009).

Conscientiousness appears to influence health because it is associated with good nutrition, exercise, and health care (Lahey, 2009). It has been hypothesized that neuroticism is linked with physical and mental health for two main reasons (Lahey, 2009):

1. People who are high in neuroticism are sensitive to stress and show greater reactivity of the sympathetic nervous system and endocrine glands when stressed, which may adversely affect health. Furthermore, people high in neuroticism appear to behave in ways that create additional stress for themselves and to reduce the social support needed to buffer stress.

2. Neuroticism and physical and mental health problems appear to be influenced by some of the same genetic factors.

Personality traits are associated with more than just physical and mental health, however. For example, persons who are high in conscientiousness, agreeableness, and openness to experience achieve more in school. Indeed, when high school grades are controlled statistically, conscientiousness is as strong a predictor of college grades as is intelligence (Poropat, 2009). Thus, variations in personality traits are importantly related to many key aspects of our lives.

Human Diversity
Personality and Culture

Your introduction to psychology is occurring at an exciting time in the history of the field. Increasingly, psychologists are accepting the idea that sociocultural factors such as ethnicity, race, gender, sexual orientation, and physical challenges are important in understanding our personalities (Cross & Markus, 1999; Triandis & Suh, 2002). One focus of cultural psychology has been on the validity of North American concepts of personality traits when applied to other cultures. For example, many studies have confirmed the five-factor model of personality with minor variations in many Western and non-Western cultures (McCrae & Costa, 1997; McCrae & Terracciano, 2005). This means that when correlations among personality test items were examined in translated instruments, essentially the same personality traits emerged in many cultures. Does this mean that these five personality traits are a human universal and equally meaningful in all cultures? While it appears that personality traits like those in the five-factor model are important in all cultures, it is also clear that our experiences in our cultures shape our personalties in important ways.

Individualistic cultures, such as the United States and other western cultures, emphasize the rights and characteristics of the individual person. In contrast, collectivistic cultures, such as Japan, China, India, and other Asian cultures, understand the individual more in terms of the expectations, rights, and duties of being a member of a *group* (family, caste, country) (Cross & Markus, 1999; Triandis & Suh, 2002). Does growing up in an individualistic versus a collectivistic culture influence our personalities? Psychologists Harry Triandis and Eunkook Suh (2002) summarized research on this question. They found that persons in collectivistic cultures were **Continued on pg. 399**

Continued from pg. 398 more often characterized by terms such as friendly, having close feelings, and being respectful—characteristics that refer to relations with others. Persons in collectivistic cultures tend to be more motivated to work hard to meet goals set by respected authority figures than their own goals. When they have time off from school or work, they tend to spend it with family or friends. When they have conflict with others, they are less aggressive and more likely to say things that allow the other person to save face and avoid embarrassment (Triandis & Suh, 2002).

In comparison, persons in individualistic cultures are more likely to feel proud and superior—feelings that set them apart from the group. They tend to be more motivated to work hard to meet their own personal goals than the goals of others. They are more willing to prove themselves right even if it embarrasses others and are even more likely to resort to physical aggression when disputes arise. When they have free time, persons in individualistic cultures are more likely to spend it in solitary pursuits than in groups (Triandis & Suh, 2002). Thus, culture can powerfully influence personality.

Susan Cross of Iowa State University and Hazel Markus (1999) of Stanford University offered the following concrete example of the vast difference between individualistic and collectivistic cultures' views of the person. These four "personal ads" were published on the same day in two California newspapers (a general readership paper and a paper that has a readership of mostly immigrant families from India):

Many personality traits are similar in many different cultures, but some aspects of personality vary across cultures.

From the **San Francisco Chronicle:**

28 SWM, 6'1", 160 lbs. Handsome, artistic, ambitious, seeks attractive WF, 24–29, for friendship, romance, and permanent partnership.

Very attractive, independent SWF, 29, 5'6" 110 lbs., loves fine dining, the theater, gardening, and quiet evenings at home. In search of handsome SWM 28–34 with similar interests.

From the **India Tribune:**

Gujarati Vaishnav parents invite correspondence from never married Gujarati well settled, preferably green card holder from respectable family for green card holder daughter 29 years, 5'4", good looking, doing CPA.

Gujarati Brahmin family invites correspondence from a well cultured, beautiful Gujarati girl for 29 years, 5'8", 145 lbs. handsome looking, well-settled boy.

Note that these ads are similar in some ways (all refer to physical appearance and age) but very different in other ways. The ads in the general readership newspaper reflect the individualistic U.S. culture. They describe only the individual's characteristics and preferences. In contrast, the ads in the *India Tribune* reflect the collectivistic Indian culture by focusing on the individual's membership in *groups*. They were placed in the name of the families rather than the individual, and they refer both to the state in India from which the families came (Gujarati) and to the caste of the family (Vaishnav and Brahmin). It is this strong emphasis on the embeddedness **Continued on pg. 400**

Human Diversity
Personality and Culture
cont'd from pg. 399

Continued from pg. 399 of the individual in groups that have more importance than the individual that lies at the heart of collectivistic culture.

Thus, any personality theory must always consider the culture to which it is applied. People from different cultures tend to differ in some important ways. It is very important to remember, however, that there is also tremendous variation *within* cultures. Some people in individualistic cultures have traits that are typical of collectivistic cultures and vice-versa. If we forget this fact, the important findings of cultural psychology will backfire on us. If we think that everyone from an Asian culture has the same collectivistic personality traits, for example, we will stereotype them instead of using knowledge of culture to understand each individual better.

Review

Psychologists often describe the consistencies in personality in terms of traits. Traits are relatively enduring patterns of thinking, acting, and feeling that are relatively consistent across situations. Today, many psychologists believe that five basic dimensions of personality can be used to explain most of the variations among human—and even nonhuman mammals—personalities. The personality traits identified in the five-factor model have been found to describe personality well in a wide variety of different cultures, but culture clearly influences our personalities in important ways.

Check Your Learning

To be sure that you have learned the key points from the preceding section, cover the list of correct answers and try to answer each question. If you give an incorrect answer to any question, return to the page given next to the correct answer to see why your answer was not correct. Remember that these questions cover only some of the important information in this section; it is important that you make up your own questions to check your learning of other facts and concepts.

1. One's _____ is the sum total of all of the ways of acting, thinking, and feeling that are typical for that person and make that person different from other individuals.

2. _____ are defined as relatively enduring and consistent ways of behaving.

   a) States   c) Characteristics

   b) Traits   d) Conditions

3. Trait theories are more concerned with describing the nature and operation of traits than explaining their origins.

   a) true   b) false

4. Allport believed that the most important traits were those motivational traits related to our _____.

Thinking Critically about Psychology

There are no right or wrong answers to the following questions. They are presented to help you become an active reader and think critically about what you just read.

1. Does the five-factor model of personality leave out any important aspects of what makes you unique?

2. How would a police detective who was a proponent of trait theory attempt to catch a serial killer?

Correct Answers: 1. personality (p. 395), **2. b** (p. 396), **3. a** (p. 396), **4.** values (p. 396)

Psychoanalytic Theory: Sigmund Freud

Sigmund Freud was a young physician building a medical practice in Vienna in the late 1800s. He was particularly interested in treating patients with emotional problems but felt frustrated by the lack of knowledge that existed at that time. Although he had devoted many years of study to the disorders of the brain and nerves, Freud found that what he had learned was of little help to his patients. Thus, being a person of considerable confidence and intelligence, Sigmund Freud set out to develop his own methods of treatment. Freud also developed a general theory of personality, known today as **psychoanalytic theory,** to explain why people develop their unique patterns of typical behavior.

Freud's study of personality began with a very unusual and specific question. He wanted to understand the condition known today as *conversion disorder.* In this condition, the individual appears to have a serious medical problem, such as paralysis or deafness, for which there is no medical cause. To understand Freud's theory—which some of you will find quite shocking—we should begin with a description of one of Freud's first case studies. I think you will see the origins of his unusual ideas about what shapes our personalities in this description. The young woman was not treated by Freud, but he helped her physician publish a description of her—one that had a lasting impact on his theories.

Bertha Pappenheim's unusual problems began at age 21. After six months of caring for her dying father, the formerly healthy young woman suddenly became paralyzed in her legs, arms, and neck and lost the ability to talk, except in a meaningless garble. Nonetheless, her physician could find nothing physically wrong with her. In time, her speech and muscular coordination returned, only to be followed by other strange symptoms. She was plagued by hallucinations of writhing snakes and grinning skulls; she was deaf for a time; she experienced blurred vision; and she had difficulty swallowing water for 6 weeks. But, after 18 months of frequent therapy sessions with her physician, Joseph Breuer, she was free of these bizarre maladies.

Dr. Breuer terminated his relationship with Ms. Pappenheim partly because of her improvement and partly because he had developed strong emotional feelings for her, and he was worried that she had similar feelings for him. On the evening after his last session with Ms. Pappenheim, Dr. Breuer sat eating supper with his family when he was summoned back to Bertha's home by her maid. When Breuer arrived, he found Bertha writhing in bed, complaining of painful cramps in her lower abdomen. Suddenly, she shocked Breuer with the words "Now Dr. Breuer's baby is coming! It is coming!" She was giving birth to a completely imaginary baby. Because of his complicated emotional feelings toward Ms. Pappenheim, Dr. Breuer transferred her to the care of another physician.

In 1895, Breuer and Freud jointly published an account of Bertha Pappenheim's problems, giving different interpretations of her symptoms. To protect her identity, she was given the pseudonym of "Anna O." Freud's theory was shocking: Freud believed that six months of being alone with her father while he was sick in bed heightened the woman's unconscious sexual desires for her father to the point that they threatened to become conscious. The paralysis and other symptoms, according to Freud, served the purpose of making it impossible for her to express her sexual longings. Her symptoms held in check her nearly uncontrollable and wholly unacceptable desires. Later, these sexual feelings were transferred to Dr. Breuer, by whom she unconsciously wished to become pregnant.

Ms. Pappenheim left Dr. Breuer's care and her new physician attempted to treat her with morphine, to which she became addicted, and she had to be placed in a mental institution. However, by age 28, she had recovered and moved with her mother to Frankfurt. Although wealthy, Bertha began working in various ways

psychoanalytic theory Freud's theory that the origin of personality lies in the balance among the id, the ego, and the superego.

Bertha Pappenheim (1861–1936).

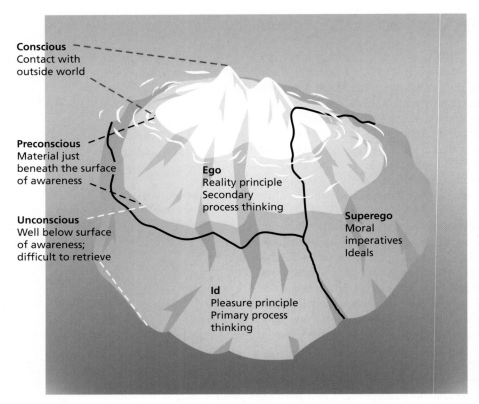

Figure 12.1

Freud's model of personality structure. Freud theorized that we have three levels of awareness—the conscious, the preconscious, and the unconscious. To dramatize the enormous size of the unconscious, he compared it to the portion of an iceberg that lies beneath the water's surface. Freud also divided personality structure into three components—id, ego, and superego—which operate according to different principles and exhibit different modes of thinking. In Freud's model, the id is entirely unconscious, but the ego and superego operate at all three levels of awareness.

"Good morning, beheaded—uh, I mean beloved."

to help illegitimate children and unwed mothers. She also played an important role in stopping the slave trade that exported impoverished Jewish girls to South America, where they were forced into prostitution. Many myths have grown up surrounding her later life, but the historical record makes it clear that she lived a highly productive life despite her earlier difficulties (Lorentz, 2007).

Freud's Mind: Three Levels of Consciousness

As Freud tried to understand complicated and atypical personalities, such as that of Bertha Pappenheim, he distinguished three levels of conscious awareness—the *conscious mind,* the *preconscious mind,* and the *unconscious mind.* To Freud, the mind is like an iceberg; the **conscious mind** is merely the tip visible above the surface, whereas the bulk of the important workings of the mind lurks mysteriously beneath the surface (see figure 12.1). Just below the surface is what Freud called the **preconscious mind.** It consists of memories that are not presently conscious but can be easily brought into consciousness. You are not thinking right now about your last meal, the name of your psychology instructor, or the taste of your favorite drink, but you could quickly bring those items into conscious awareness if you wanted to. The preconscious mind is the vast storehouse of easily accessible memories. The contents of the preconscious were once conscious and can be returned to consciousness when needed.

The **unconscious mind** stores the primitive instinctual motives, In addition, the unconscious mind contains memories and emotions that are so threatening to the conscious mind that they have been pushed into the unconscious mind through the process of **repression.** The contents of the unconscious mind, unlike the preconscious mind, are not normally accessible to consciousness. They can rarely be made fully conscious, and then only with great difficulty.

Freud's Mind: Id, Ego, and Superego

Freud also divided the mind into three parts in a *different* way. His theory of personality views the mind as being composed of three working parts, each with a different function: the *id,* the *ego,* and the *superego* (see figure 12.1).

Id: The Selfish Beast. When the infant is born, the mind has only one part, the **id.** The id houses two sets of instincts, *life instincts* and *death instincts*. Freud wrote relatively little about the death instincts, but he believed that aggression and even suicidal urges arose from these instincts. The life instincts, termed **libido** by Freud, give rise to motives that sustain and promote life, such as hunger, self-protection, and sexual desire. To Freud, the sexual and aggressive urges are by far the most important motives. As strange as it may seem, sex and aggression are used by Freud to explain a vast range of personality characteristics, from kindness to cruelty. Freud believed that from birth on, every person's life is dominated by these two motives— the desire to experience sexual pleasure and the desire to harm others. Because the id operates entirely at the unconscious level of the mind, however, we are generally not aware of these motives. Only safe, watered-down versions of our true sexual and aggressive urges ever reach conscious awareness.

Freud's view of the dark side of the human mind is not an easy one for most of us to accept. Freud tells us that a selfish, cruel beast lives with in each of us. The beast—the id—operates according to the **pleasure principle.** The id wants to obtain immediate pleasure and avoid pain, regardless of how harmful it might be to others. But the id's selfishness is not its most alien characteristic to most of us. According to Freud, the id seeks to satisfy its desires in ways that are totally out of touch with reality. The id, in fact, has no conception whatsoever of reality. The id attempts to satisfy its needs using what Freud calls **primary process thinking**—by simply forming a wish-fulfilling *mental image* of the desired object. We use the primary process when we daydream about having sex, think about eating chocolate fudge cake, or angrily plan how to get revenge on the person who embarrassed us yesterday. Dreams are also a primary process means of fulfilling motives. The primary process satisfies motives through imagination rather than in reality.

A person could not actually survive for long living by the pleasure principle (eventually you would get hurt if you fulfilled every selfish desire without regard for the feelings of others) or using only the primary process of wish fulfillment (forming a mental image of food will not meet the body's need for nutrition). Fortunately, during infancy, the period of time when we have only an id, we usually have adults around who see to it that our needs are realistically and safely met. As we grow up, our interactions with our parents and other parts of the real world lead us to convert part of the id into two other parts of the mind—the ego and the superego—that help us cope more effectively with the world. To borrow a phrase told to me by a skilled teacher, the ego and superego help us "keep a lid on the id."

Ego: The Executive of Personality. The **ego** is formed because the id has to find realistic ways of meeting its needs and avoiding trouble caused by the selfish and aggressive id. The ego operates according to the **reality principle.** This means that it holds the id in check until a safe and realistic way has been found to satisfy its motives. The ego's goal is to help the id fulfill its needs. It opposes the id's wishes only long enough to find a realistic way to satisfy them. The ego can be thought of as the *executive of the personality* because it uses its cognitive abilities to manage and control the id and balance its desires against the restrictions of reality and the superego.

Superego: The Conscience and Ego Ideal. The id and the ego have no morals. They seek to satisfy the id's selfish motives without regard for the good of others. The ego is realistic about how those motives are satisfied. But as long as the needs are *safely* and *effectively* met, it does not care if rules are broken, lies are told, or other people are wronged.

Restrictions are placed on the actions of the id and ego when the **superego** develops. The superego is the part of the mind that opposes the desires of the id by

---

conscious mind That portion of the mind of which one is presently aware.

preconscious mind That portion of the mind containing information that is not presently conscious but can be easily brought into consciousness.

unconscious mind The part of the mind of which we can never be directly aware; the storehouse of primitive instinctual motives and of memories and emotions that have been repressed.

repression Sigmund Freud's theory that unpleasant information is often pushed into unconsciousness without our being aware of it.

id According to Freud, the inborn part of the unconscious mind that uses the primary process to satisfy its needs and that acts according to the pleasure principle.

libido The energy of the life instincts of sex, hunger, and thirst.

pleasure principle According to Freud, the attempt of the id to seek immediate pleasure and avoid pain, regardless of how harmful it might be to others.

primary process thinking According to Freud, the attempt by the id to satisfy its needs by forming a wish-fulfilling mental image of the desired object.

ego (ē′go) According to Freud, that part of the mind that uses the reality principle to satisfy the id.

reality principle According to Freud, the attempt by the ego to find safe, realistic ways of meeting the needs of the id.

superego According to Freud, that part of the mind that opposes the desires of the id by enforcing moral restrictions and by striving to attain perfection.

enforcing moral restrictions and by striving to attain a goal of "ideal" perfection. Parents are the main agents of society in creating the superego. They teach moral principles to their children by punishing transgressions and rewarding proper behavior. These experiences become incorporated into the child's mind as two parts of the superego, the conscience and the ego ideal. According to Freud, parental punishment creates the set of moral inhibitions known as the **conscience,** whereas their rewards set up a standard of perfect conduct in the superego called the **ego ideal.** These two parts of the superego work together by punishing behavior that breaks the moral code through guilt and rewarding good behavior through pride. As the superego develops strength, children are able to control themselves and behave in ways that allow society to function smoothly. According to Freud's view, most of us do not steal, murder, and rape not because we do not want to or because our egos could not find relatively safe ways to do so, but because our superegos hold these desires in check.

conscience According to Freud, the moral inhibitions of the superego.

ego ideal According to Freud, the standard of perfect conduct of the superego.

Displacement and Identification: Becoming a Member of Society

displacement (dis-plās′ment) A defense mechanism in which the individual directs aggressive or sexual feelings away from the primary object to someone or something safe.

sublimation (sub′′li-mā′shun) According to Freud, a form of displacement in which a socially desirable goal is substituted for a socially harmful goal; the best form of displacement for society as a whole.

The ego is not always able to find ways to satisfy id motives that avoid trouble and stay within the moral boundaries of the superego. Sometimes the ego must settle for a *substitute* for the goal of the id. A child who would like to kick his father may have to settle for slugging his little brother instead. Or, if his superego prohibits hurting his brother, he may have to kick his teddy bear. The process of substituting a more acceptable goal for a selfish motive is called **displacement.**

In terms of the interests of society, the best kind of displacement is called **sublimation.** In this form of displacement, a socially desirable goal is substituted for a socially harmful goal. To Freud, competing in school is a sublimation of aggressive motives, painting nude portraits is a sublimation of sexual motives, and so on. Indeed, Freud believed that all the cultural and economic achievements of society were the result of sublimation. Thus, the individual who sublimates id energy not only is able to fit into society but contributes to its advancement as well.

identification The tendency to base one's identity and actions on individuals who are successful in gaining satisfaction from life.

Another process that allows individuals to learn to operate in society without friction is **identification.** This term refers to the fact that we tend to base the way we think, act, and feel on other individuals who are successful in gaining satisfaction from life. According to Freud, this is more than just a superficial act of imitation; we incorporate the other person's goals, actions, and values into our personalities. Thus, children come to be more like the adults they identify with. According to Freud, identification is the key step in the development of the superego. We do not fully incorporate the morals and goals of society until we identify with the parent and internalize his or her values and ideals.

Competition in sports is one way of sublimating unacceptable aggressive impulses, according to Freud.

Growing Up: The Stages of Psychosexual Development

Freud believes that our personalities are formed as we pass through a series of developmental stages from infancy to adulthood. Events that happen as the individual passes through these stages can be critical in the formation of personality. Excessive punishment or reward from parents or traumatically stressful events experienced during a period of development can leave the person's personality "stuck," or *fixated,* at that stage. This fixation of personality development will, according to Freud, have a lifelong effect on the personality.

To Freud, the developmental stages result from a shifting of the primary outlet of primarily sexually libido energy of the id from one part of the body to another. These parts of the body are termed **erogenous zones.** Because the developmental stages are based on changes in the release of sexual energy, Freud called them the **psychosexual stages.** According to Freud, the five stages of psychosexual development are as follows.

Oral Stage (Birth to 1 Year). The infant's earliest source of id gratification is the mouth. During the **oral stage,** the infant gets pleasure from sucking and swallowing. Later, when he has teeth, the infant enjoys the aggressive pleasure of biting and chewing. If the infant enjoys swallowing too much, however, she may fixate on this stage and become an **oral dependent personality** who continues to seek pleasure through the mouth by overeating and smoking and by being a gullible person who "swallows" ideas too easily.

If the infant's oral pleasures are frustrated, however, such as by a mother who sticks rigidly to a feeding schedule regardless of the infant's desire to eat, he may grow up to be a fixated **oral aggressive personality** who seeks aggressive pleasure through the mouth, for instance, by being verbally hostile to others. Similar fixations are possible at every stage of development.

Anal Stage (1 to 3 Years). When parents decide to toilet train their children during the **anal stage,** the children learn how much *control* they can exert over others with their anal sphincter muscles. Children can have the immediate pleasure of expelling feces before sitting on the toilet, but that may cause their parents to punish them. If they delay gratification until they are on the toilet, children can gain the approval of their parents. According to Freud, excessive punishment of failures during toilet training may create a fixated personality that is either stingy, obstinate, stubborn, and compulsive (**anal retentive**) or cruel, pushy, messy, and disorderly (**anal expulsive).**

Phallic Stage (3 to 6 Years). During the **phallic stage,** the genitals become the primary source of pleasure. According to Freud, the child begins to enjoy touching her or his own genitals and develops a sexual attraction to the parent of the opposite sex. Freud believed that the shift to genital pleasure goes on in the unconscious mind, so we are not consciously aware of the touching or the incestuous urges. Instead, the child merely feels an intense love for the opposite-sex parent: daughters become "daddy's girl" and sons become "mommy's boy." These sexual attractions bring about the intense unconscious conflict that Freud calls the *Oedipus complex* for boys and the *Electra complex* for girls.

Freud borrowed the term **Oedipus complex** from the ancient Greek play *Oedipus Rex* by Sophocles. It tells the mythical story of an infant who was abandoned by the king and queen of Thebes and grew up in a rival city. As a young man, not knowing his parents or who they are, Oedipus returns to Thebes, kills his father, and marries his mother. Freud believes that the play reveals a wish that is in all of us during the phallic stage of development.

According to Freud, all males unconsciously want to kill their fathers and sexually possess their mothers. Note that I said that this is an *unconscious* wish of which the boys are not consciously aware. Because such

erogenous zones A part of the body that releases sexual energy when stimulated.

psychosexual stages In the personality theory of Sigmund Freud, developmental periods during which the sexual energy of the id finds different sources of satisfaction.

oral stage According to Freud, the first psychosexual stage (from birth to 1 year), in which id gratification is focused on the mouth.

oral dependent personality A personality type in which the person seeks pleasure through overeating, smoking, and other oral means.

oral aggressive personality A personality type in which the person seeks pleasure by being verbally hostile to others.

anal stage According to Freud, the second psychosexual stage (from 1 to 3 years), in which gratification is focused on the anus.

anal retentive A personality type based on anal fixation, in which the person is stingy, obstinate, stubborn, and compulsive.

anal expulsive A personality type based on anal fixation in which the person is cruel, pushy, messy, and disorderly.

phallic stage (fal′ik) According to Freud, the third psychosexual stage (from 3 to 6 years), in which gratification is focused on the genitals.

Oedipus complex (ed′i-pus) According to Freud, the unconscious wish of all male children to kill their fathers and sexually possess their mothers.

castration anxiety (kas-trā′shun) According to Freud, the fear of a young boy that his father will punish his sexual desire for his mother by removing his genitals.

Electra complex (e-lek′-trah) According to Freud, the transfer of a young girl's sexual desires from her mother to her father after she discovers she has no penis.

penis envy According to Freud, the desire of a girl to possess a penis.

phallic personality (fal′ik) Personality type caused by fixation in the phallic stage in which the person is selfish, impulsive, and lacking in genuine feeling for others.

latency stage According to Freud, the fourth psychosexual stage (from about 6 to 11 years), during which sexual energy is sublimated and converted into socially valued activities.

genital stage (jen′i-tal) According to Freud, the psychosexual stage (from 11 years through adulthood) in which sexual and romantic interest is directed toward one's peers.

desires are unacceptable, they are blocked from consciousness. But the incestuous desires remain in the unconscious id, where they cause considerable discomfort. The child unconsciously senses that if these impulses ever become unleashed, he will enrage his father. A fear arises in the immature mind of the boy that his father will punish his sexual desires toward his mother by removing his genitals—a fear called **castration anxiety.** This fear eventually leads the boy to repress desires for his mother and to avoid angering his father by identifying with him. As previously noted, this step of identification with the father is crucial for the development of the superego to Freud, because the boy incorporates the moral values and ideals of the father when he identifies with him in the resolution that ends the Oedipal complex.

Freud believed that girls went through a process similar to the Oedipal complex, which was later named the **Electra complex** by Carl Jung. Jung selected this term based on the Greek myth of Electra who plotted the death of her mother when she learned that her mother had murdered her father. The Electra complex is one of Freud and Jung's most controversial doctrines, as contemporary readers find that it portrays women in an outrageously negative light.

In Freudian theory, the Electra complex begins with the girl's "upsetting" discovery that she does not have a penis but has an empty space instead. According to Freud, the girl unconsciously concludes that she has been castrated and blames the mother for letting this happen. As a result, she transfers her love and sexual desire from her mother to her father. In doing so, she hopes to share the father's valued penis because she has lost hers. The desire to possess a penis is termed **penis envy** by Freud.

However, the girl's sexual and emotional attachment to the father is too dangerous because of the prohibitions of society against her feelings. To resolve the Electra complex, therefore, Freud stated that her feelings for her father must be transformed into wholesome affection, and she must accept that she is "inferior," like her mother, and identify with her mother. In doing so, according to Freud, she will accept her role in society and develop her superego by incorporating the values of her mother.

According to Freud, failure to resolve the phallic stage results in a **phallic personality,** characterized by egocentric selfishness, impulsiveness, and lack of genuine feeling for others.

Latency Stage (6 to 11 Years). The **latency stage** is that period of life from about age 6 to age 11 in which sexual interest is relatively inactive. Sexual desire has been strongly repressed through the resolution of the Oedipal or Electra complex and is not a source of trouble at this time. Instead, sexual energy is being sublimated and converted into interest in doing schoolwork, riding bicycles, playing house, and participating in sports. To pass successfully through this developmental period, the child must develop a certain degree of competence in these areas.

Genital Stage (11 Years On). With the arrival of puberty and the **genital stage,** there is renewed interest in obtaining sexual pleasure through the genitals. Masturbation often becomes frequent and leads to orgasm for the first time. Sexual and romantic interest in others also becomes a central motive. But, because the parents have been successfully ruled out as sex objects through the Oedipus and Electra complexes, the new sex objects are peers of about the same age.

Although some interpersonal relationships are entered into merely to obtain selfish genital pleasure, individuals who have reached the genital stage also are able to care about the welfare of the loved one. This forms the basis for the more or less lasting relationships that characterize the genital stage and extend throughout adulthood. Sublimation continues to be important during this period as sexual and aggressive id motives become transformed into energy for marriage, occupations, and child rearing.

Theories Derived from Psychoanalysis

Psychoanalytic thinking continues to play a role in psychology, but mostly through revised versions of Freud's theory of personality. Some modern psychologists adhere to an orthodox version of psychoanalysis, but far more endorse somewhat newer versions that grew out of Freudian thinking but differ on several major points. Each of these revisions of psychoanalysis differs from the others in some ways, but they share the view that Freud placed too much emphasis on unconscious sexual motivation and aggression, gave too little importance to positive aspects of personality, underemphasized the importance of adequate social relationships, and was highly prejudicial toward women (Luborsky & Barrett, 2006; Westen & Gabbard, 1999).

Carl Jung (1875–1961).

Carl Jung. Carl Jung was a young physician working in a psychiatric hospital in Switzerland when he read Freud's work, *The Interpretation of Dreams.* Jung soon joined the inner circle of Freud's followers as an influential member. Jung published a number of works that used Freud's ideas to explain aspects of severe mental illness, but gradually Jung came to question Freud's emphasis on sexual motivation. Eventually, these differences in opinion led to a severing of their personal and professional relationship.

Jung felt that Freud took a one-sided negative view of human nature. Although Jung agreed that the unconscious mind contained selfish forces, he believed that it also contained positive, even spiritual, motives. In fact, a fundamental characteristic of the human mind to Jung was that all important elements of the mind came in the form of *opposites.* We possess the potential to be both good and evil, feminine and masculine, mother and father. The question is simply how much of each we manifest in our personalities.

Among Jung's most original and lasting contributions to the understanding of personality are the concepts of *extraversion* and *introversion.* Each of us possesses a desire to be friendly, open to the things happening in the world, and concerned about others **(extraversion),** but each of us also possesses a tendency to focus our attention on ourselves, to be shy, and to meet our own needs **(introversion).** As with all of the polar opposites, Jung felt that it was important to achieve a balance of these opposing tendencies. We should not be too much of an introvert or too much of an extravert.

Jung also modified Freud's view of the unconscious. He felt that we possess both a *personal unconscious* and a *collective unconscious.* The **personal unconscious** contains those motives, conflicts, and information that we have repressed into unconsciousness because they are threatening to us. The **collective unconscious** is the unconscious mind with which all humans are born. He used the term *collective* to

extraversion (eks´´tro-ver´zhun) According to Jung, the tendency of some individuals to be friendly and open to the world.

introversion (in-tro-ver´zhun) According to Jung, the tendency of some individuals to be shy and to focus their attention on themselves.

personal unconscious According to Jung, the motives, conflicts, and information that are repressed by a person because they are threatening to that individual.

collective unconscious According to Jung, the content of the unconscious mind with which all humans are born.

Each of us, according to Jung, is a blend of extravert and introvert. Jung felt that a balance of these two opposing tendencies is desirable.

Alfred Adler (1870–1937).

feelings of inferiority According to Adler, the feelings that result from children being less powerful than adults that must be overcome during the development of the healthy personality.

emphasize that its contents are the same for all humans. Much of his later career was devoted to blending his interest in psychology with his childhood interest in different cultures. He assembled evidence to suggest that every culture expresses the same sorts of unconscious motives in very much the same symbolic ways. For example, in Jung's view the sexual symbol of the phallus (the penis) has appeared in many cultures throughout history in the form of totem poles, scepters held by kings to symbolize authority, and structures such as the Washington Monument.

Alfred Adler. Alfred Adler agreed with Freud that the struggle to come to grips with one's sexual and hostile impulses was important to the development of personality, but not the most important factor. In his early career, Adler felt that the primary struggle in personality development was the effort to overcome **feelings of inferiority** in social relationships and to develop feelings of superiority. At first, he limited this view to individuals who were born with physical defects, as was Adler himself, but later he expanded this view to include physically normal individuals as well. Because we are all small and dependent on the protection of adults as children, we all begin life with feelings of inferiority in a sense. The task of personality development, according to Adler, is to outgrow the inferiority of childhood and to see ourselves as competent adults. Adler believed that the role of parents and other caretakers was so important in this crucial process that he devoted much of his time to the development of a preschool program that he thought fostered proper personality development. Even today, "Adlerian" preschools are popular in many parts of Europe and North America.

Later in his career, Adler deemphasized the importance of struggling to outgrow childhood feelings of inferiority. In fact, he thought that the effort to achieve feelings of superiority over other individuals was an essentially unhealthy motive. Instead, he focused on two other factors as the most important elements in personality development. First, Adler felt that all human beings are born with a positive motive, *social interest,* to establish loving, helpful relationships with other people. The full development of a healthy personality requires that the individual learn to express this motive fully in her or his relationships with others. This contrasted with Freud's belief that only selfish motives are inborn. Second, Adler believed that people's lives are governed by their *goals.* Often these goals are not realistic at all, but they regulate our actions anyway, as we strive to achieve them. Adler's emphasis on goals, by giving such importance to a cognitive ego function, was also in sharp contrast to Freud's approach.

Karen Horney. German-born physician Karen Horney became a leader in the revisions of psychoanalysis some 20 years after the first contributions of Jung and Adler. Perhaps in part because she continued to write into the 1950s, she remains the most influential of the three. Readers today generally find her ideas more contemporary than those of Freud, Jung, or Adler. Horney considered herself to be a "Freudian" throughout her career because she agreed that unconscious conflicts were the source of most human misery and maladjustment. Like Jung and Adler, however, Horney felt that Freud placed too much importance on sexual conflicts. Moreover, she believed that conflict was not the inevitable result of inborn motives in the id. She believed instead that conflicts developed only as the result of inadequate child-rearing experiences. If the child feels loved and secure, no conflicts will develop, and positive aspects of the personality will dominate. If, however, the child loses confidence in parental love—because of the parent's indifference, harshness, or overprotection or for other reasons—the child becomes anxiously insecure. And this anxious insecurity is the source of all future conflicts. For example, an insecure individual may develop a need to be "perfect" and feel tormented by all revelations that he is not. Another insecure individual may push away the affection of others out of fear that they, too, will not consistently love her, but pushing away others is in conflict with the underlying need to be loved.

Karen Horney (1885–1952).

Horney also was an important critic of Freud's view of women. She rejected Freud's notion that penis envy is the central feature of the feminine psychological makeup. She felt that the issue was not envy of the penis or of masculinity per se but of the power and privilege of the male role in society.

Most contemporary psychoanalytic psychologists have continued to revise the theories of Freud in much the same directions. Writers such as Erich Fromm, Harry Stack Sullivan, and Erik Erikson continued to develop the neo-Freudian view of personality. They revise Freud's image of women, deemphasize the importance of sexual and aggressive motives, emphasize positive aspects of personality, and assert the importance of adequate social relationships (Luborsky & Barrett, 2006).

Review

Sigmund Freud's theory of personality grew out of his early interest in the cause of the unusual symptoms of some of his patients. He decided that, since they had no conscious reason to have such symptoms, the cause must be unconscious, specifically repressed sexual or aggressive desires. Through the course of many years of treating patients with a variety of psychological problems, Freud came to believe that unconscious motives, particularly sexual and aggressive ones, were the source of most aspects of our personalities. Freud divided the mind into three levels of consciousness (conscious, preconscious, and unconscious) and into three parts with different functions (id, ego, and superego). The id is the storehouse of the unconscious sexual and aggressive instincts, and is the inborn, selfish part of the mind that operates according to the pleasure principle. The id seeks immediate satisfaction of its needs without concern for the welfare of others. The ego is the executive of the personality, which controls the id through adherence to the reality principle; it seeks to satisfy the needs of the id in ways that are both realistic and safe. The superego represents society's rules of right and wrong that often hold the id in check, not on the basis of what is realistic but on what is moral.

To Freud, the process of becoming an acceptable member of society is aided by the psychological processes of displacement and identification. When it's too dangerous to satisfy an id motive directly, the motive is displaced onto a safer, substitute goal. The most desirable form of displacement from society's perspective is sublimation, in which dangerous motives are transformed into socially desirable motives. The process of identification with social models further aids the individual's acceptance as a member of society by leading to the full development of the superego.

Sexual energy is transformed during the life span in yet another way. As the individual matures from infancy to adulthood, the principal means of obtaining sexual pleasure shifts from one part of the body to another. Abnormal experiences at any of these stages can lead to fixations that hinder the full development of an effective personality.

Following the lead of Jung, Adler, and Horney, who broke away from orthodox psychoanalytic views during Freud's lifetime, contemporary psychoanalysts generally deemphasize the importance of sexual and aggressive motives. They have revised Freud's view of the inferiority of women, have emphasized the importance of positive motives and social relationships in personality formation, and have stated that Freud overlooked important positive aspects of our personalities.

Check Your Learning

To be sure that you have learned the key points from the preceding section, cover the list of correct answers and try to answer each question. If you give an incorrect answer to any question, return to the page given next to the correct answer to see why your answer was not correct.

1. The _____ mind is the part of the mind containing information that is not presently conscious but can be easily brought into consciousness.

   a) conscious

   b) preconscious

   c) unconscious

   d) suppressed

Check Your Learning (cont.)

2. According to Freud, the _____ is the inborn part of the unconscious mind that uses the primary process to satisfy its needs and that acts according to the pleasure principle.

   a) id   c) superego

   b) ego   d) reality principle

3. To Freud, the five developmental stages represent a shifting of the primary outlet of id energy, particularly sexual energy, from one part of the body to another. For this reason, they are called _____.

4. Carl Jung disagreed with Freud's one-sided negative view of the human condition and proposed that all important elements came in the form of _____ such as introversion and extraversion.

   a) positive conditions   c) opposites

   b) synonyms   d) matches

Thinking Critically about Psychology

There are no right or wrong answers to the following questions. They are presented to help you become an active reader and think critically about what you just read.

1. Does Freud's theory describe human behavior only for Europeans and Americans of his era, or does it apply to people of any generation or culture?

2. Why do you think Karen Horney and Sigmund Freud had such different views of women?

Correct Answers: 1. b (p. 402), 2. a (p. 402), 3. psychosexual stages (p. 405), 4. c (p. 407)

Albert Bandura (1925–).

social learning theory The viewpoint that the most important parts of our behavior are learned from other persons in society—family, friends, and culture.

Social Learning Theory: Albert Bandura

The social learning view of personality is vastly different from that of the psychoanalysts. Little or no attention is paid to topics such as instincts, the unconscious mind, or the developmental stages that are of primary importance to psychoanalysis. Instead, social learning theorists focus on a psychological process that is largely ignored by psychoanalysts, *learning*. To the social learning theorist, personality is simply something that is learned; it's the sum total of all the ways we have learned to act, think, and feel. Because personality is learned from other people in society, the term *social learning* is used.

Social learning theory had its origins in the behavioral writings of Ivan Pavlov, John B. Watson, and B. F. Skinner. Each of these theorists argued that personality is no more than learned behavior and that the way to understand personality is simply to understand the processes of learning. To social learning theorists, the key concepts in the study of personality are not id, ego, and superego but classical conditioning, operant conditioning, and modeling. We will not repeat our discussion of these principles here, but it may be helpful for you to glance back over this material in the earlier chapter on learning.

Role of Learning in Personality

In the social learning view, a person develops an adequate personality if he or she is exposed to good models and is reinforced for appropriate behavior. An inadequate learning environment, in contrast, results in inadequate personality development.

The leading figure in social learning theory today is Stanford University psychologist Albert Bandura (1977, 1989, 1999). In one sense, Bandura's views are very similar to those of the behaviorists—Watson and Skinner. He agrees with the view that personality is the sum total of learned behavior. Bandura broke with traditional behaviorism in two main ways, however: (1) he sees people as playing an active role in determining their own actions, rather than being passively acted on by the learning environment, and (2) he emphasizes the importance of cognition in personality.

Bandura (1977) portrays us as playing an active role in our own lives by stating that social learning is an example of **reciprocal determination:** not only is a person's behavior learned but the social learning environment is altered by the person's behavior (see figure 12.2). The environment that we learn from, after all, is made up of people. If we behave toward them in a timid way, or a friendly way, or a hostile way, those people will react in very different ways to us—and will hence be teaching us very different things about social relationships. The aggressive, overconfident person will learn that the world is a cold, rejecting place; the friendly person will learn that the world is warm and loving. Personality is learned behavior, but it is also behavior that influences future learning experiences.

reciprocal determination (re-sip″ro-kal) Bandura's observation that the individual's behavior and the social learning environment continually influence one another.

Role of Cognition in Personality

According to social learning theory, our learned cognitions are the prime determinant of our behavior (Bandura, 1982, 1999; Cervone, 2004). People who believe that helping others only makes them less self-reliant will be stingy toward people in need; people who think that other people find them boring will act quiet and shy. Bandura places particular emphasis on the role our cognitions play about our ability to handle the demands of life. In his theory of personality, **self-efficacy** is the perception that one is capable of doing what is necessary to reach one's goals—both in the sense of knowing what to do and being emotionally able to do it. People who perceive themselves as self-efficacious accept greater challenges, expend more effort, and may be

self-efficacy According to Bandura, the perception of being capable of achieving one's goals.

Figure 12.2
Social learning theorists believe in reciprocal determination; we learn our behavior from interactions with other persons, but our behavior influences how other persons interact with us.

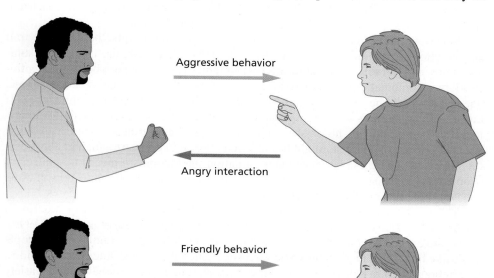

Aggressive behavior

Angry interaction

Friendly behavior

Warm interaction

more successful in reaching their goals as a result. A person with a poor sense of self-efficacy about social poise may not accept a promotion at work because it would involve giving many speeches and having to negotiate with dignitaries. Although our perceptions of self-efficacy are learned from what others say about us, from our direct experiences of success and failure, and from other sources, these cognitions continue to influence our behavior "from the inside out."

Bandura (1977, 1989) also emphasizes the importance of values and personal standards in personality. We learn personal standards for our behavior from observing the personal standards that other people model. We also learn our personal standards from the standards that others use when rewarding or punishing us. When we adopt those standards for ourselves and use them to evaluate our own behavior, we have developed what Bandura calls **self-regulation.** When we behave in ways that meet our personal standards, we cognitively pat ourselves on the back—we reinforce ourselves. We generally do not actually say to ourselves, "Good going; you did okay!" Rather, we feel a self-reinforcing sense of pride or happiness when we have met our standards (like Freud's ego ideal). Conversely, we punish ourselves (feel guilty, disappointed) when we fail to meet our personal standards (like Freud's conscience). In these ways, the process of self-regulation serves much the same purpose as Freud's superego.

Situationism and Interactionism

Are you usually cheerful or gloomy? It may well depend on the situations you typically are in. Some situations tend to make us cheerful and some make us gloomy. Behaviorist B. F. Skinner (1953) argued that behavior is determined by the situations in which people find themselves, not traits inside the person. This viewpoint, known as **situationism,** suggests that our behavior is consistent only as long as our situations remain consistent. A woman might be friendly most of the time when she is with her family, but cold and distant when she is with her gossipy coworkers, and stiff and formal with her boss. According to Skinner, people behave in ways that suit their situations, and—because situations are apt to change—behavior cannot be consistent enough to be adequately described in terms of personality traits.

Social learning theorists suggested a constructive compromise between the trait and situationism positions (Bandura, 1977, 1999; Mischel & Shoda, 1999). The solution, known as **person × situation interactionism,** suggests that our behavior is influenced by a combination of characteristics of the person *and* the situation. For example, one person might be relatively calm and relaxed when not frustrated or threatened. If this person encounters a stressful situation, however, such as interviewing for a new job after being laid off, he or she might react with intense anxiety and irritability. Another person, in contrast, might be calm and relaxed in both stressful and nonstressful situations. The concept of person × situation interactionism means that different people react to the same situation *differently*. It also means that the same person often behaves quite differently in different situations.

This is the essential point of interactionism: The only way to fully describe a person's personality is in terms of "if . . . then" statements (Mischel & Shoda, 1999). "If he feels liked by others, then he is cheerful and kind. If he thinks other people don't like him, then he is gloomy and sarcastic." Such if . . . then statements provide a description of our personalities that allows a prediction of future behavior in a variety of situations. Understanding *why* persons behave in different situations in the various ways that they do, however, requires a deeper level of analysis. To social learning theorists, the "person variables" in the person × situation interaction are the cognitive (beliefs, and so on), motivational (goals, and so forth), and emotional tendencies that we have acquired through social learning and that determine how we respond to different situations (Mischel & Shoda, 1999).

Person × situation interaction is even more complicated than it first appears. This is because people play an active role in choosing and even creating the situations that

---

self-regulation According to Bandura, the process of cognitively reinforcing and punishing our own behavior, depending on whether it meets our personal standards.

situationism (sit″ū-ā′shun-izm) The view that behavior is not consistent but is strongly influenced by different situations.

person × situation interactionism (in″ter-ak′shun-izm) The view that behavior is influenced by a combination of the characteristics of both the person and the situation.

they experience. For example, a very shy person may avoid social situations, whereas an aggressive person would tend to seek out challenging situations and might even provoke hostile encounters with others. Thus, the situations that interact with our personal characteristics do not just happen to us at random; we play an important role in selecting and creating many of the situations in which we live.

Review

Albert Bandura is the leading proponent of social learning theory. Although this approach to personality theory grew out of the behaviorism of Pavlov, Watson, and Skinner, Albert Bandura expanded behavioral thinking by emphasizing the importance of cognition in personality and the active role played by individuals in the social learning process (reciprocal determinism). To the social learning theorist, the process of learning is of central importance to personality development. Social learning theorists believe that people are influenced by the situations they are in too much for simple trait descriptions to be sufficient. They emphasize person × situation interactions to highlight the fact that different people are influenced by situations in different ways. Thus, personality can best be conceptualized in terms of multiple if . . . then descriptions that capture both characteristics of the person (patterns of cognition, motivation, and affect) and the influence of situations on that person.

Check Your Learning

To be sure that you have learned the key points from the preceding section, cover the list of correct answers and try to answer each question. If you give an incorrect answer to any question, return to the page given next to the correct answer to see why your answer was not correct.

1. _____ is the theory that our personalities are formed primarily through learning from other members of society and the theory in which the key concepts are classical conditioning, operant conditioning, and modeling.

2. Albert Bandura suggests that social learning is ____: not only is a person's behavior learned but the social learning environment is altered by the person's behavior.

   a) bilateral   c) bipolar

   b) reciprocally determined   d) interactive

3. According to Bandura, _____ is the perception that one is capable of doing what is necessary to reach one's goals.

   a) cognition   c) confidence

   b) self-regulation   d) self-efficacy

4. _____ suggests that our behavior is influenced by a combination of characteristics of the person (traits) and the situation.

   a) Situationism   c) Trait theory

   b) Learning theory   d) Person × situation interactionism

Thinking Critically about Psychology

There are no right or wrong answers to the following questions. They are presented to help you become an active reader and think critically about what you just read.

1. How might you use Bandura's theory of personality to help you better understand your own personality?

2. How would a police detective who understood the concept of person × situation interactionism attempt to catch a serial killer?

Correct Answers: 1. Social learning theory (p. 410), 2. b (p. 411), 3. d (p. 412), 4. d (p. 412)

Humanistic Theory: Maslow and Rogers

The **humanistic theory** of psychology is often referred to as the *third force* in psychology. Although it has deep historical roots in philosophy, it has been only since the 1950s that humanism has become a movement in psychology. This approach to personality is the least unified and well defined of the three major viewpoints. This lack of unity is probably due less to the newness of humanistic psychology than to its origins. Each of the other two schools of thought began with the ideas of a single person. Although the views of the original leaders were subsequently revised by later followers, the original writings of Pavlov and Freud gave a certain unity to the theories that followed. Humanistic theory, in contrast, emerged from the writings of a number of figures who shared only a few basic concepts.

The founders of humanistic psychology include Carl Rogers, Abraham Maslow, Viktor Frankl, Virginia Satir, Fritz Perls, and Rollo May, to name a few. It's impossible, therefore, to write a single statement that adequately summarizes the humanistic approach to personality. For this reason, we focus primarily on the views of Carl Rogers and secondarily on the views of Abraham Maslow, emphasizing the parts of their theories that are consistent with the views of humanists in general.

Inner-Directedness and Subjectivity

Humanists believe that humans possess an internal force, an **inner-directedness,** that pushes them to grow, to improve, and to become the best individuals they are capable of being. People have the freedom to make choices, and they are generally pretty good at making intelligent choices that further their personal growth. This inner-directedness is the primary force behind the development of personality.

Obviously, humanists have a positive view of the human species, but they are not blind to the fact that life is a struggle for everyone at some point and that many people consistently make a mess of their lives. We lose our ability to grow and to make good choices when we live with critical, rejecting people or when society tries to force us to be something that we are not. And, as Maslow has pointed out, the transition to higher motives is stunted when more basic motives are unsatisfied.

The personality that develops through the positive push of inner-directedness can only be understood "from the inside out," that is, from the perspective of the individual. To the humanist, the only reality is a **subjective reality.** Everyone views life in somewhat different, highly personal terms. What is real for you may not be real for me. You may see people as basically immoral, whereas I see them as basically moral. Each person's personality is a direct reflection of the individual's subjective view of reality. Our consistent ways of acting, thinking, and feeling reflect our unique perceptions of what life is all about. And, as we will see in the next section, no subjective view of reality is more important to humanistic theorists than our subjective view of ourselves.

The Self-Concept

The concept of the "self" is central to the personality theory of Carl Rogers and other humanists. Our **self-concept** is our subjective perception of who we are and what we are like. Of all of our subjective views of life, our view of ourselves is most important to our personalities. The concept of self is learned from our interactions with others: you might learn that you are a good athlete by seeing that you run faster than most other people, or by your parents' and friends' telling you how good you are at sports.

Rogers distinguishes between two self-concepts. There is the **self**—the person I think I am—and the **ideal self**—the person I wish I were. For example, I am pretty sure I can never be better than a "C" class racquetball player (self), but I would love to win tournaments in the "A" class (ideal self). On a higher plane, I see myself as a fairly nice person, but I wish I could learn to be less selfish at times. Rogers' concept of the ideal self is very similar to Freud's ego ideal.

Psychological problems can arise from three kinds of difficulties with the self and ideal self. First, excessive discrepancies between the self and the ideal self can be uncomfortable. It's okay for the ideal self to be slightly out of reach—that can stimulate us to improve ourselves. But if the ideal self is so unrealistically perfect that we know it can never be reached, then we feel like failures.

A study by Timothy Strauman (1992) at the University of Wisconsin tested this notion. Students in introductory psychology classes were interviewed and tested to determine if there were discrepancies between the way they view themselves (their concept of self) and the way that they think they would like to be or ought to be (two aspects of the ideal self). Students who saw themselves as different from the way that they would *like* to be were more likely to experience sadness over time, and students who saw themselves as different from the way they *ought* to be were more likely to be anxious.

Second, an inaccurate self-concept can also cause problems. If our view of our "selves" is not reasonably *congruent* (similar to the way we actually act, think, and feel), then we will develop an obscured view of ourselves. For example, if I see myself as totally free from prejudice, but I feel a twinge of resentment when someone from a minority group gets preference over me in a job promotion, then my feelings of resentment will not "fit" my self-concept. According to Rogers, I might deny those feelings that are incongruent with my self-concept by not admitting them to awareness. In Rogers' terms, we are aware of feelings and information only when they are mentally **symbolized.** The failure to symbolize parts of our experience is harmful not only because it leads to inaccurate concepts of self, but also because feelings can continue to influence us, often in conflicting or anxiety-provoking ways, even when we are not aware of them.

Third, we also deny awareness to some of our feelings and experiences as a result of our parents' and society's reactions to our behavior. By reacting with warmth and praise to some of our actions (sharing a toy with little sister), but with coldness and punishment to others (hitting little sister with the toy), our parents create **conditions of worth.** They let us know that they find us "worthy" under some conditions and "unworthy" under other conditions. We internalize many of these conditions and perceive ourselves as worthwhile only when we act and feel in accordance with those conditions. Furthermore, we often deny feelings that are inconsistent with the internalized conditions of worth. The child, for example, may not symbolize her hostile feelings toward her sister, robbing herself of a valuable bit of self-awareness.

Some psychologists believe that society's views of the ideal female and ideal male often create problems for us (Wood & others, 1997). When girls and boys internalize expectations for how they should ideally behave based on stereotypes of what females and males are like, conflict is created for those individuals whose actual behavior is different from their gender stereotype. Dominant females and shy males, for example, could have difficulties accurately symbolizing these characteristics that are inconsistent with gender stereotypes in their self-concept.

Rogers' concept of unsymbolized feelings is similar in some ways to Freud's view of repressed feelings. Both can continue to influence the person, often in a harmful manner. But Freud views some repression as a necessary part of life, whereas Rogers believes that lack of awareness is always harmful. According to Rogers, if we are to allow full expression to our inner-directed tendency to grow and be healthy, we must be fully aware of (symbolize) all of our feelings. Only in this way can we accurately understand and accept ourselves for exactly what we are.

Self-Actualization

A major tenet of humanistic psychology is that humans possess an inner drive to grow, improve, and use their potential to the fullest. Abraham Maslow calls the ultimate in completed growth **self-actualization.** According to Maslow, the self-actualizing

Carl Rogers (1902–1987).

symbolization In Rogers' theory, the process of representing experience, thoughts, or feelings in mental symbols of which we are aware.

conditions of worth The standards used by others or ourselves in judging our worth.

Abraham Maslow (1908–1970).

self-actualization According to Maslow, the seldom-reached full result of the inner-directed drive of humans to grow, improve, and use their potential to the fullest.

person is reaching the highest level of personal development and has fully realized her or his potential as a human being. What is a self-actualizing person like? Maslow (1967, 1970) gives the following description:

1. The self-actualizing person has reached a high level of moral development and is more concerned about the welfare of friends, loved ones, and humanity than self. The self-actualizing person is usually committed to some cause or task, rather than working for fame or money.

2. Self-actualizing people care deeply about others but are not dependent on their approval. They are open and honest and have the courage to act on their convictions, even if it means being unpopular. Self-actualizing individuals are not particularly interested in fads, fashion, and social customs and often appear unorthodox. They enjoy friends and are deeply caring, but they enjoy their privacy and independence.

3. They have an accurate, rather than a romanticized, view of people and life, yet they are positive about life.

4. Life is always challenging and fresh to the self-actualizing person. They are spontaneous and natural in their actions and feelings. Life is experienced in intense, vivid, absorbing ways, often with a sense of unity with nature.

Do not despair if you do not compare too well against Maslow's list. For one thing, self-actualization is at the end of a lifelong process of improvement, according to Maslow. You just may not have gotten there yet! Remember, too, from the chapter on motivation and emotion that all lower-level motives must be satisfied before a person can proceed toward self-actualization. If you are like most of us, you still have an unmet motive or two that is blocking your full development. Maslow felt that there are very few fully self-actualized individuals in the world. He identified a few that he thought probably were, including, Albert Einstein, Eleanor Roosevelt, and Ludwig van Beethoven.

Humanism Compared with Classic Psychoanalysis and Social Learning Theory

Humanism, psychoanalysis, and social learning theory differ from one another in their views of the basic nature of human beings and of society. In classic psychoanalytic theory, people are seen as selfish and hostile at birth; they are nothing but id. Society

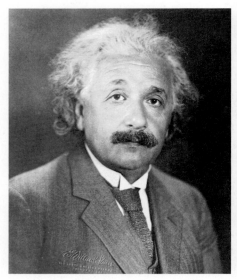

Albert Einstein (1879–1955).

Eleanor Roosevelt (1884–1962).

Ludwig van Beethoven (1770–1827).

Table 12.2 Comparison of Classic Psychoanalytic, Social Learning, and Humanistic Theories of Personality

	Classic Psychoanalytic	Social Learning	Humanistic
An "unconscious" or "unsymbolized" mind exerts a powerful influence on us.	Yes	No	Yes
We learn what is "good" and "bad" from our families and cultures.	Yes	Yes	Yes
Our internalized knowledge of what is "good" and "bad" is an important part of our personalities.	Yes (superego and ego ideal)	Yes (self-regulation)	Yes (ideal self)
People are inherently . . .	Selfish and evil	Neither good nor bad	Good
Society . . .	Usually teaches us to convert our selfish nature into positive behavior	Can influence us in either positive or negative ways	Often harms or destroys our inherent tendency to be healthy and good

is seen as a good force that instills the ego and superego into children, thus enabling them to behave realistically and morally enough to live in the social world.

To the humanist, the psychoanalytic view is exactly wrong. People possess a positive inborn drive to grow and improve. Instead of being born evil, the human is born basically good. Society, in contrast, is seen by the humanist as a frequently destructive force that leads people to deny their true feelings (of jealousy, insecurity, passion) and creates unattainable ideal self-concepts (for example, American society tells us that we should all be attractive, athletic, sexy, famous, and rich).

Social learning theorists differ from psychoanalytic and humanistic theorists in their evaluation of the basic nature of humans and society. Social learning theorists see humans as neutral at birth, having the potential to learn to be either good or bad. Similarly, society can be either destructive or constructive. A part of society that teaches inappropriate behavior to its children is destructive, whereas a part of society that teaches appropriate behavior is constructive.

All three theories, however, believe that we internalize society's standards of what is desirable and moral and guide our behavior accordingly. Freud spoke of the conscience and ego ideal of the superego, Bandura used the concept of self-regulation, and Rogers spoke in terms of the ideal self. Although they differ in important ways, these are highly similar ideas about why we tend to obey the rules and standards of society. For a comparison of all three theories, see table 12.2.

Review

Humanism is the least unified of the three movements, but several basic concepts about personality are shared by nearly all humanists. The most significant factor in the development of personality is the positive inner-directed drive to grow and improve. Unless our experiences with society interfere with this drive, it can be counted on to direct personal growth in positive directions. The personality that develops from this growth can be understood only from the point of view of the individual. Personality is seen as reflecting each person's subjective view of reality. We act, think, and feel in accordance with how we view reality. And the most important aspect of that view of reality is our subjective concept of self. The ways I view both the self that I think I am and the self I would like to be are powerful determinants of my personality. If my ideal self is unattainably perfect, I will always fall painfully short of my standards. If my self-concept is inaccurate, I will not be able to deal with information about myself that is incongruent with my self-concept. Incongruent information is not admitted to consciousness, a state of affairs that humanists view as unhealthy for the personality.

Humanists, psychoanalysts, and social learning theorists take very different views of the basic nature of people and society. Psychoanalysts view humans as wholly selfish and hostile ids at birth. Society, in contrast, is seen as a positive force providing experiences that create the ego and superego that allow humans to function effectively in society. Humanists view people as essentially good but see society as a negative force that often interferes with the individual's inner-directed growth. Social learning theorists see people as having the potential to develop in either positive or negative ways, depending on whether their personalities were learned from positive or negative aspects of society.

Check Your Learning

To be sure that you have learned the key points from the preceding section, cover the list of correct answers and try to answer each question. If you give an incorrect answer to any question, return to the page given next to the correct answer to see why your answer was not correct.

1. According to _____ theory, human beings possess an innate tendency to improve and to determine their lives by the decisions they make.

    a) social learning   c) humanistic

    b) psychoanalytic   d) conditioning

2. According to the humanists, the _____ is the person one wishes he or she were.

    a) real self   c) new self

    b) ideal self   d) self

3. Our _____ is our subjective perception of who we are and what we are like.

    a) self-concept   c) self-efficacy

    b) ideal self   d) actualized self

4. Humanists believe that humans are born neither good nor evil.

    a) true   b) false

Thinking Critically about Psychology

There are no right or wrong answers to the following questions. They are presented to help you become an active reader and think critically about what you just read.

1. If, as the humanistic perspective suggests, reality is subjective, how can individuals ever hope to agree on anything?

2. What are the best new ideas that you learned from this summary of the three theories of personality? What are the least helpful ideas to you?

Correct Answers: 1. c (p. 414), 2. b (p. 415), 3. a (p. 415), 4. b (p. 416)

Personality Assessment: Taking a Measure of the Person

Psychologists who work in business, schools, prisons, and clinics are frequently called on to make important decisions about people. Which employee should be promoted to sales manager? Should this person receive a parole from prison? What should be done to help a person out of a state of depression? Such questions can be answered only when the psychologist knows what the person is like—that is, how the person typically behaves in ways that distinguish him or her from other individuals. In other words, the psychologist must know a great deal about the person's personality.

You could probably describe the personality of your best friend, your sister or brother, or your parent fairly well. You have seen them in a variety of situations and know how they typically behave. But psychologists usually do not have the luxury of getting to know their clients over long periods of time. They must come up with a picture of their client's personality in short order. To do this, a number of ways of quickly assessing personality have been developed. These include interviews, structured observations of behavior, psychoanalytically inspired projective tests, and personality tests.

Interviews and Observational Methods

The most widely used method of personality assessment is the **interview.** Although few psychologists use it by itself, nearly every psychologist interviews the client by asking questions designed to reveal his or her personality. These interviews can range from the highly structured and formal to very unstructured.

Interviews are an essential part of getting to know the client, but they have serious limitations. For one thing, they are inherently subjective; different psychologists may evaluate the same behavior of the client during the interview in different ways. Second, interviews are artificial situations that bring into question the validity of the information obtained from them. Interviews are stressful events that may bring out atypical behavior. A person may feel very anxious when interviewing for a job but might ordinarily be a calm person when at work. In this way, interviews can be misleading. As a result, they are often supplemented by other methods to ensure a more complete and accurate view of the person's personality.

One alternative to interviewing is *observing* the person's actual behavior in a natural or simulated situation. **Observational methods** are particularly popular in business. For example, psychologists who consult with businesses on employee promotion often observe the employees being considered for promotion in situations that simulate actual managerial situations. Several employees might be given the problem of dividing up a limited budget for an employee health plan and then be observed as they negotiate a solution to the simulated problem.

To make observational methods more objective, a variety of observational rating scales have been developed. In these scales, the observer responds to specific items in describing the behavior observed. For example, the rating scale might include the item "Was friendly" and ask the observer to circle one of the following responses: "strongly agree," "agree," "disagree," or "strongly disagree." Most rating scales provide a comprehensive assessment of the person by using many such items. A commonly used type of rating scale for children takes advantage of the fact that teachers have learned a great deal about the children in their classrooms by observing them in the normal course of teaching. School psychologists who are assessing children's personalities frequently ask teachers to fill out rating scales about their students.

Projective Personality Tests

Another method of personality assessment is the **projective test.** These tests are based on the belief of psychoanalysts that the unconscious mind is the basis of personality. But, because the ego works hard to keep the contents of the unconscious mind out of awareness, a way must be found to slip past the censor of the ego to learn about the

interview A subjective method of personality assessment that involves questioning techniques designed to reveal the personality of a client.

observational methods Methods of personality assessment that involve watching a person's actual behavior in a natural or simulated situation.

projective test A test that uses ambiguous stimuli designed to reveal the contents of the client's unconscious mind.

Figure 12.3

The Thematic Apperception Test uses pictures like this to evaluate personality. The person is asked to make up a story based on such ambiguous pictures to allow the contents of the unconscious mind to be projected into the story.

Reprinted by permission of the publishers from Henry A. Murray, THEMATIC APPERCEPTION TEST, Plate 12F, Cambridge, Mass.: Harvard University Press, Copyright © 1943 by the President and Fellows of Harvard College © 1971 by Henry A. Murray.

unconscious. Psychoanalysts believe that the motives and conflicts of the unconscious mind can be revealed by projective tests. These tests are based on the theory that we tend to "project" our own feelings on to others (Kawada & others, 2004).

Projective tests ask the individual to interpret ambiguous stimuli so that unconscious feelings will be "projected" into the interpretation, much as a slide projector projects an image on a blank screen. For example, the *Thematic Apperception Test (TAT)* (Murray, 1938, 1951) asks the individual to make up a story about ambiguous pictures like the one in figure 12.3. What do you see in this picture? Is it an old woman happily remembering her youth? Is it a picture of the evil side of a young woman who is plotting the murder of her father? Psychoanalysts believe that, because the stimuli are ambiguous, the ego is not able to fully censor the unconscious thoughts and motives that are projected into the story made up about the picture.

Even more ambiguous stimuli are used in the *Rorschach inkblot test* (Rorschach, 1953). The test consists of 10 symmetrical inkblots like the ones in figure 12.4. The individuals tell what the inkblots look like and what parts of the inkblots they are focusing on. Do you see a vagina surrounded by a menacing spider? Are you projecting a fear of sex? Complex scoring systems are often used with the Rorschach inkblots (Exner, 1986), but many users interpret the responses subjectively. Projective tests are used less today than in the past, largely because research on their validity has been discouraging (Lilienfeld, Wood, & Garb, 2000).

Objective Personality Tests

A more recent development in personality assessment is the objective personality test. These tests have been widely used since World War II in an attempt to move away from the subjectivity of interviews and projective tests. The objective personality test consists of a number of written questions about the person. For example, there are several personality tests available that assess personality traits based on the five-factor model (McCrae & Costa, 1987, 1999).

Figure 12.4

In the Rorschach inkblot test, the individual is asked to explain what he or she sees in ambiguous stimuli such as these.

Evaluation of Personality Tests

It's obviously helpful for psychologists to be able to assess the personalities of the individuals with whom they are working. Not all psychologists agree, however, that personality tests are accurate enough to use for that purpose. A great deal of research has been done to determine whether personality tests are good at measuring what they are supposed to measure.

Research on the Rorschach, TAT, and other projective techniques suggests that these tests are generally not successful in predicting behavior (Garb, Florio, & Grove, 1998; Mischel, 1968). Objective tests based on the five-factor model of personality are far from perfect but are clearly valid in some important ways. A number of studies have found that tests based on the five-factor model of personality are useful in predicting our future behavior and outcomes. For example, the personality trait of conscientiousness is as good a predictor as intelligent test scores of future success in school and occupations, perhaps because more conscientious people applied themselves in a more disciplined way (O'Connor & Paunonen, 2007; Roberts & others, 2007). Conscientiousness even predicts how long we will live, perhaps because conscientious persons have fewer careless accidents and take better care of their health (Roberts & others, 2007). To take other examples, the combination of high neuroticism and low agreeableness predicts experiencing depression and having a marriage end in divorce (Chien & others, 2007; Roberts & others, 2007). Note that these personality tests are useful predictors of how groups of people with high or low scores will do on average, but they are not accurate enough to predict the future outcomes of specific individuals with a high degree of accuracy.

"It looks as if someone spilled ink on a piece of paper and then folded it in half."

Reprinted with permission of Tom Cheney.

Review

Psychologists have developed methods of quickly learning about a person's personality. The most widely used method of personality assessment is the interview, in which questions are asked that probe the nature of the individual's personality. Personality is often assessed by directly observing the individual in natural or simulated settings or by having people such as teachers or employers who have observed the person's behavior over a long period of time fill out checklists describing the pattern of behavior that they have observed. Psychoanalytically oriented psychologists often rely on projective tests to learn about the unconscious roots of personality. These tests ask the person to respond to ambiguous stimuli in the hope that the person will project important features of his or her unconscious mind into the interpretation of the stimuli. Psychologists who prefer less subjective methods of personality assessment often use objective tests. These utilize items that were objectively selected for the test by comparing the answers of groups of individuals who do or do not possess the personality characteristics in question. In general, objective personality tests based on the five-factor trait model have been shown to be reasonably accurate in predicting how groups of people with similar scores will function in the future, but it is difficult to predict the future functioning of specific individuals using the best objective personality tests.

Check Your Learning

To be sure that you have learned the key points from the preceding section, cover the list of correct answers and try to answer each question. If you give an incorrect answer to any question, return to the page given next to the correct answer to see why your answer was not correct.

1. An _____ is a widely used method of personality assessment that involves face-to-face questioning designed to reveal the personality of the client.

   a) observational method   c) objective personality test

   b) interview   d) essay test

2. A(n) _____ such as the TAT uses ambiguous stimuli designed to reveal the contents of the client's unconscious mind.

   a) objective test   c) subjective test

   b) interview   d) projective test

3. Objective personality tests are valid in the sense that their scores predict important outcomes, such as academic success, to some degree.

   a) true   b) false

Thinking Critically about Psychology

There are no right or wrong answers to the following questions. They are presented to help you become an active reader and think critically about what you just read.

1. How do the personality tests developed by psychologists differ from the "personality tests" that appear in popular magazines or on websites?

2. Could someone else really understand your personality based on your answers to a list of questions? Why or why not?

Correct Answers: 1. b (p. 419), 2. d (p. 420), 3. a (p. 421)

Summary

Chapter 12 defines personality, explores four major perspectives on personality—traits theory, psychoanalytic theory, social learning theory, and humanistic theory—and discusses several approaches to personality assessment.

I. Personality is the sum total of all of the ways of acting, thinking, and feeling that are typical for that person and make that person unique.

II. Some psychologists believe that one's personality can be described in terms of traits.

   A. Traits are defined as relatively enduring ways of behaving that are relatively consistent across different situations.

   B. The five-factor model is a widely endorsed description of the basic personality traits.

III. Psychoanalytic theory was developed by Sigmund Freud in the early 20th century.

   A. Freud distinguished three levels of conscious awareness—the conscious mind, the preconscious mind, and the unconscious mind. In his view, the mind is composed of three parts—the id, the ego, and the superego.

      1. The id operates on the pleasure principle. It seeks to obtain immediate pleasure and avoid pain.

      2. The ego operates on the reality principle. It seeks safe and realistic ways to satisfy the id.

      3. The superego opposes the id by imposing moral restrictions and by striving for perfection.

   B. When the ego cannot find ways to satisfy the id, it seeks a substitute.

      1. The substitution of a more acceptable goal is displacement, and displacement of a socially desirable goal is called sublimation.

      2. Identification is the tendency to sublimate by modeling our actions on individuals who are successful in life.

   C. Freud's theory is developmental in that it distinguishes five stages in the development of personality: the oral stage, the anal stage, the phallic stage, the latency stage, and the genital stage. During the phallic stage, boys experience the Oedipus complex, and girls experience the Electra complex.

   D. Alfred Adler, Carl Jung, and Karen Horney broke away from Freud primarily over the issues of sexual motivation, the presence of positive aspects of personality, and the importance of adequate social relationships.

IV. To social learning theorists, the key concepts in the study of personality are learning and cognition.

   A. Our personalities are learned from others, but Albert Bandura says that social learning is reciprocally determined by the actions of behavior on the environment, and vice versa.

   B. Behavior is self-regulated by our internalized standards for self-reward and by our perceptions of our own self-efficacy.

   C. Behaviorist B. F. Skinner believed that people were influenced by their situations too much for trait theories to be correct. This view is known as situationism.

   D. Social learning theorists have adopted the position of person × situation interactionism. This suggests that the behavior of different people is influenced by situations in different ways because our behavior reflects both situational influences and our personal characteristics.

V. Humanistic theory is based on a belief that humans possess an inner-directedness that pushes them to grow. To the humanist, reality is subjective.

   A. Self-concept is our subjective perception of who we are and what we are like. Carl Rogers distinguishes between the self (the person I think I am) and the ideal self (the person I wish I were).

   B. Problems result when the ideal self is unrealistic or when feelings and information that are incongruent with a person's self-concept are denied conscious awareness.

VI. Personality assessment is the use of psychological methods to learn about a person's personality.

   A. The most widely used method is the interview.

   B. Personality is also assessed by observing the person's behavior in a natural or simulated situation. Rating scales help make observational methods more objective.

   C. Another widely used method of personality assessment is the projective test, which psychoanalysts believe reveals the motives and conflicts of the unconscious mind.

   D. Objective personality tests consist of questions that measure different aspects of personality.

Visual Review of Personality Theory

Reviewing the figure below may help you consolidate your learning of some of the information presented in this chapter in a visual format. Be sure not to limit your review to these diagrams, but because they are key to understanding some of the important concepts in this chapter, mastering them should help you master the entire chapter.

An iceberg is often used to illustrate Sigmund Freud's theoretical structure of personality. Fill in the labels for the three levels of consciousness (along the left) and the three parts of the mind (on the iceberg).

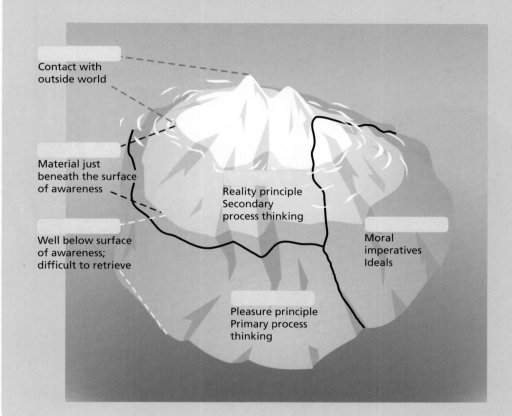

Contact with outside world

Material just beneath the surface of awareness

Well below surface of awareness; difficult to retrieve

Reality principle Secondary process thinking

Moral imperatives Ideals

Pleasure principle Primary process thinking

Figure 12.5

Illustration of Freud's theory of personality structure (from figure 12.1 on p. 402)

chapter **thirteen**
Stress and health

Chapter Outline

Prologue

No one's life is free of stress. Regardless of how sensible, intelligent, or privileged you are, you will be challenged at times by frustrations, losses, changes, and conflicts. Stress comes from negative events, such as failing a college course, but stress is part of many positive events, too, such as starting a new job or having a baby. Stress is as inescapable as death and taxes.

A certain amount of stress is probably healthy—it energizes us and challenges us to grow. But stress is generally experienced as an uncomfortable, unhealthy force that most of us would be happier without. Stress influences us at both psychological and biological levels (McEwen, 1998). Consider the following landmark studies.

Bengt Arnetz of Harvard University (Arnetz & others, 1987) conducted a classic study of the effects of psychological stress on the body's ability to fight disease. Arnetz studied a large group of Swedish women who had lost their jobs and been unemployed for many months. Compared with women with secure jobs, women who had lost their jobs had white blood cells that were less reactive to infections. Similarly, Janice Kiecolt-Glaser and colleagues (1987) of Ohio State University compared the immune system functioning of married and divorced women. The immune systems of recently divorced women functioned less well than those of married women, but with gradual improvements occurring over the first year after divorce. Within the group of married women, furthermore, immune functioning was poorest for those women with the unhappiest marriages.

Many other studies have confirmed findings that stress influences the functioning of the immune and cardiovascular systems (Chida & others, 2010; Cohen & others, 2007; Robles, Glaser, & Kiecolt-Glaser, 2005). These studies offer strong evidence for the intimate relationship between our psychological lives and our physical health. It now seems clear that psychological stressors can diminish the body's ability to fight disease.

If stress is inevitable, and if too much stress is a threat to our psychological and physical well-being, then *coping* well with stress is of paramount importance. A healthy and happy person is someone who can enjoy the good times and cope with the bad. Sometimes we can cope with stress by removing it—by changing jobs or filing a complaint against a sexually harassing boss. We cannot remove all the stress from our lives, however, and will inevitably have to cope with some of it (Davydov & others, 2010; Taylor & Stanton, 2007). Generally, we are better able to cope with the kinds of stress with which we have previous experience and that we can control somewhat. Good social support also improves our ability to cope with stress. Simply disclosing our negative experiences and feelings to friends (or to a psychotherapist) can improve immune system functioning and reduce need for medical care in many cases (Lyubomirsky & others, 2006; Richards & others, 2000).

Stress: Challenges to Coping

The stressful events that we all experience are sometimes important challenges to our health and happiness. **Stress** can be thought of as any event that strains or exceeds an individual's ability to cope (Ellis & Boyce, 2008; Lazarus, 1999). We discuss stress here to provide you with a new perspective on both stress and your health. The extent to which stress is related to many of our most serious medical conditions was greatly underestimated until research dramatically altered our perceptions of our own health. Leading causes of death and disability such as heart disease and stroke are almost certainly linked to stress (Aboa-Éboulé & others, 2007), and as we saw in the prologue to this chapter, immunity to infections is greatly affected by stress (Cohen & others, 2007; Robles & others, 2005). This makes the interface with psychology one of the most important frontiers in medicine today.

Sources of Stress

We need to begin our discussion of stress by looking at its causes. Most sources of stress are obvious to us all—they rip and tear at our lives—but other sources of stress

Key Terms

approach-approach conflict 429
approach-avoidance conflict 429
avoidance-avoidance conflict 429
conflict 428
coping 444
defense mechanisms 445
frustration 428
general adaptation syndrome (GAS) 432
health psychology 447
immune system 434
multiple approach-avoidance conflict 430
person variables 439
pressure 430
progressive relaxation training 447
social support 438
stress 425
Type A personality 439

stress Any event or circumstance that strains or exceeds an individual's ability to cope.

Figure 13.1

The percentage of women who experience serious levels of stress symptoms following the traumatic stress of assault is very high one month after the assault but declines gradually over the first year. Some women still show serious levels of stress symptoms a year after being assaulted, however, particularly if the assault was sexual.

(Foa & Riggs, 1995).

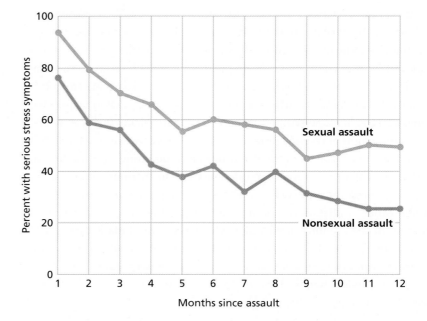

are quite surprising. Knowing what causes stress is the first step in understanding and coping with it. The major sources of stress include the following factors.

life events Psychologically significant events that occur in a person's life, such as divorce, childbirth, or change in employment.

Life Events. The most obvious sources of stress are major **life events** that create stress because they require adjustment and coping (Dohrenwend, 2006; Monroe & others, 2007). Although we mostly discuss negative life events in this section, keep in mind that even positive life changes, such as getting married or entering graduate school, also can be stressful.

Negative life events that create stress for us include such things as the loss of employment and being in an automobile crash. The most stressful negative life events that have been studied by psychologists include the following:

1. *Violence, war, and sexual assault.* Many studies document that being in a war (Bayer & others, 2007; Neuner & others, 2008; Ramchand & others, 2008; Vinck & others, 2007) and being the victim of a sexual assault or other violent crime are profoundly stressful experiences (Dohrenwend, 2006; Hedtke & others, 2008). For example, in a classic study Edna Foa and David Riggs (1995) interviewed a group of women who were the victims of assault. They asked them if they were experiencing high levels of irritability and anxiety, upsetting memories or dreams about the assault, and distressing flashbacks in which they had the illusion of being assaulted again. As shown in figure 13.1, the great majority of women experienced high levels of such stress symptoms one month after the assault, with the percentage declining gradually over the course of the first year. Over 40% of the women in this study who had been sexually assaulted still experienced serious levels of post-traumatic stress symptoms a year after the sexual assault.

2. *Loss of a family member.* The death of a spouse or a child can be tremendously stressful (Dohrenwend, 2006). For example, Sidney Zisook and Stephen Schuchter (1991) examined the stressful effects of the death of a spouse in a large sample of women and men. As shown in figure 13.2, widowed women and men were more likely to exhibit serious depression during the first year after the death of their spouse than were married women and men who had not lost their partners.

3. *Natural disasters.* Natural disasters also can be powerfully stressful negative life events (McFarlane & van Hooff, 2009). For example, the 1980 Mount Saint

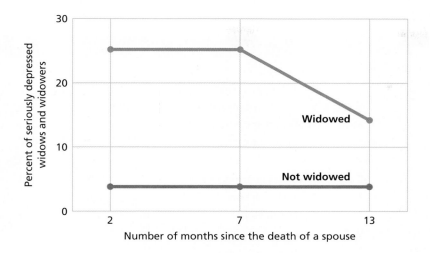

Figure 13.2
The death of a spouse is a severe stressor that leads to serious depression in some widowed men and women.

(Zisook & Schuchter, 1991).

Helens volcanic eruption was extremely stressful to the residents of nearby Othello, Washington. Compared with the preceding year, the residents of Othello had 200% more stress-related physical illnesses and psychological disorders, and the town police responded to 45% more reports of family violence. Indeed, the number of deaths in Othello increased by 19% in the year following the eruption (Adams & Adams, 1984). Similar effects have been reported for persons who were in the direct path of hurricanes, earthquakes, tsunamis, and other natural disasters (Asarnow & others, 1999; La Greca, Silverman, & Wasserstein, 1998; Roussos & others, 2005). For example, Hurricane Katrina in 2005 resulted in high levels of stress-related problems among the residents of New Orleans and nearby coastal areas (Galea & others, 2007).

4. *Terrorism.* For many years, people in many troubled parts of the world have had to cope with the stress of terroristic attacks. Since the close of the 20th century, terrorism has become a sadly common source of intense stress for Americans as well. The bombing of the federal building in Oklahoma City in 1995 killed 148 adults and 19 children. The attacks on the World Trade Center and the Pentagon on September 11, 2001, killed thousands more and shocked the world. Not surprisingly, many studies have found that anxiety, depression, sleep problems, and intrusive flashback thoughts about the disaster were common long after the attacks, particularly for those who were near the attack or who lost loved ones or possessions (Druss & Marcus, 2004; Holman & others, 2008; Ramchand & others, 2008).

5. *Daily hassles.* It is not surprising that major negative events are stressful, but the small *hassles* of daily life are also important sources of stress. The pressures at work, getting a speeding ticket, losing your glasses, having your friend arrive an hour late for dinner, and countless other daily irritants can grate abrasively on mind and body (Ben-Ari & Lavee, 2004; Monroe & others, 2007).

6. *Positive life events.* Even *positive life events* can be stressful under some circumstances (Dohrenwend, 2006; Shimizu & Pelham, 2004). College graduation, the birth of a child, job promotion, and the purchase of a house are examples of events that most people think of as positive, but they may also require stressful adjustments in patterns of living. Hence, positive life changes can be another source of stress of which we are typically unaware.

The relationship between life events and physical illness has been the subject of research for over 40 years. This research began when United States Navy physicians Thomas Holmes and Richard Rahe (1967) developed a scale to measure the amount of stress on sailors in terms of the "life change units." Table 13.1 (on p. 428) shows this scale of stress of events and the amount of stressful impact that Holmes and Rahe

Table 13.1　The Social Readjustment Rating Scale

Life Event	Mean Value	Life Event	Mean Value
Death of spouse	100	Son or daughter leaving home	29
Divorce	73	Trouble with in-laws	29
Marital separation	65	Outstanding personal achievement	28
Jail term	63	Spouse begins or stops work	26
Death of close family member	63	Begin or end school	26
Personal injury or illness	53	Change in living conditions	25
Marriage	50	Revision of personal habits	24
Fired at work	47	Trouble with boss	23
Marital reconciliation	45	Change in work hours or conditions	20
Retirement	45	Change in residence	20
Change in health of family member	44	Change in schools	20
Pregnancy	40	Change in recreation	19
Sex difficulties	39	Change in church activities	19
Gain of new family member	39	Change in social activities	18
Business readjustment	39	Mortgage or loan for lesser purchase (car, TV, etc.)	17
Change in financial state	38	Change in sleeping habits	16
Death of close friend	37	Change in number of family get-togethers	15
Change to different line of work	36	Change in eating habits	15
Change in number of arguments with spouse	35	Vacation	13
Mortgage or loan for major purchase (home, etc.)	31	Christmas	12
Foreclosure on mortgage or loan	30	Minor violations of the law	11
Change in responsibilities at work	29		

Reprinted from *Journal of Psychosomatic Research*, Vol. 11 by Thomas H. Holmes and R. H. Rahe, "The Social Readjustment Scale," 1967, with permission from Elsevier Science.

believed each event has on our lives. The individual filling out this scale indicates which events have happened to him or her during the past year and adds up the units of impact. Holmes and Rahe (1967) found that Navy personnel who had recently experienced unusually high levels of life stress were more likely to develop medical problems while on sea duty than were individuals with fewer life change units.

One lesson from studies of life events is to space out your life changes when you can. Try not to graduate from college, move to a new city, take a new job, buy a new house, get married, and have a baby all in one year. If you do, don't be surprised if you are moody, have stomachaches, and have more colds.

frustration The result of being unable to satisfy a motive.

Frustration. When we are not able to satisfy a motive, **frustration** results. You see frustration in the face of a child who cannot reach the toy he's dropped or in the exasperation of the college senior who finds that she cannot register for the one class she needs to graduate. When frustrations are serious, as in the case of underpaid workers who are denied raises, or when individuals experience the limits imposed by racial discrimination, they can be a major source of stress (Gallo & Matthews, 2003; Mays & others, 2007).

conflict The state in which two or more motives cannot be satisfied because they interfere with one another.

Conflict. Conflict is closely related to the concept of frustration. **Conflict** occurs when two or more motives cannot be satisfied because they interfere with one another.

Suppose you have been invited to spend a week skiing with friends, and then your car breaks down. You check your budget and find that you can afford either to fix your car *or* go skiing—that is a conflict. Psychologists use the terms *approach* and *avoidance* in discussing conflicts. In this sense, we "approach" things that we want and "avoid" things that we do not want. There are four major kinds of conflicts involving approach and avoidance (Lewin, 1931; Miller, 1944):

Frustration results when we are unable to satisfy a motive.

1. *Approach-approach conflict.* In **approach-approach conflict,** the individual must choose between two positive goals of approximately equal value. Suppose that when you finish school you are fortunate enough to be offered two attractive jobs. Both seem to offer good working conditions, good prestige, and reasonable salary. If both jobs are so good, why do you feel so anxious? Why are you having stomachaches and trouble sleeping? Even though both goals are positive—you would be happy with either job—the choice between these two goals can be very stressful. This is an example of a hidden source of stress. Because everything looks so positive, it's often difficult to see that you are in a serious conflict. The choice between two colleges, two roommates, or two ways of spending the summer can be similarly stressful.

2. *Avoidance-avoidance conflict.* This type of conflict involves more obvious sources of stress. In **avoidance-avoidance conflict,** the individual must choose between two or more negative outcomes. The person with a toothache must choose between the pain of the tooth and the anticipated discomfort of going to the dentist.

3. *Approach-avoidance conflict.* **Approach-avoidance conflict** arises when obtaining a positive goal necessitates a negative outcome as well. A student who is accepted to college in another state will be in a stressful conflict if she knows that it will mean being separated from her serious boyfriend, who works in his family's business in her hometown. Attending the college will have both positive and negative consequences, so she may experience considerable stress, especially as the time grows nearer for beginning school (Eyal & others, 2004).

Note that I said the student would especially experience stress *as the time grows nearer* for her to attend college. There is an important and interesting fact about approach-avoidance conflict behind that statement. As the positive and negative outcomes grow nearer (attending college and leaving the boyfriend, respectively), either in distance or time, the relative strength of the motives to approach and avoid them changes. This change has been described graphically in terms of the gradients of approach and avoidance. The strength of the motive to approach the positive goal of attending college increases slowly (has a gradual gradient). At any particular distance from the goal, the effective amount of motive to approach or avoid is the remainder when the motive to avoid is subtracted from the motive to approach.

At greater distances, there is a stronger motive to approach than avoid, so the net motive is to approach. At shorter distances, the motive to avoid is stronger than the motive to approach, so there is a net motive to avoid. Let's look at what this means in terms of our example.

The student who had been accepted to college began to experience a high level of stress about the time that the strength of the approach and avoidance motives were about equal. If the motives to approach and avoid were actually about equal in strength as diagrammed in figure 13.3 (p. 430), she might have even changed her mind and given up her admission to college as the time to attend college came nearer and the net motive switched strongly in favor of avoidance. After turning down her admission, however, she would have again been at a great "distance" from college.

approach-approach conflict
Conflict in which the individual must choose between two positive goals of approximately equal value.

avoidance-avoidance conflict
Conflict in which the individual must choose between two negative outcomes of approximately equal value.

approach-avoidance conflict
Conflict in which achieving a positive goal will produce a negative outcome as well.

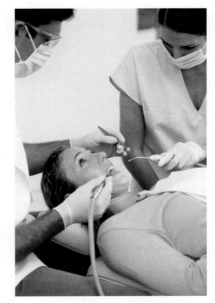

In an avoidance-avoidance conflict, the individual must choose between two or more negative outcomes, such as the pain of the tooth or the expected discomfort of going to the dentist.

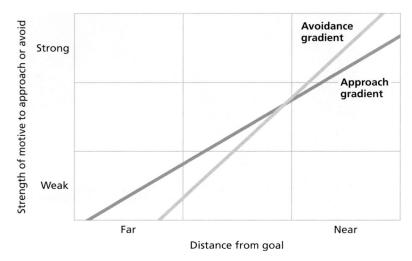

Figure 13.3

Gradients of approach and avoidance in an approach-avoidance conflict.

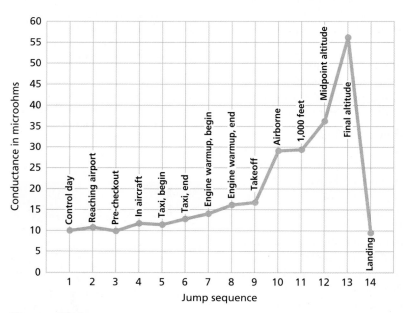

Figure 13.4

The amount of sympathetic autonomic arousal (as measured by changes in the electrical conductance of the skin caused by changes in skin sweat) in inexperienced parachutists at different "distances" from the approach-avoidance goal of jumping.

Source: Data from S. Epstein and W. D. Fenz, "Steepness of Approach and Avoidance Gradients in Humans as a Function of Experience: Theory and Experiment," *Journal of Experimental Psychology,* 70:1–12, 1965. Copyright 1965 by the American Psychological Association.

multiple approach-avoidance conflict Conflict that requires the individual to choose between two alternatives, each of which contains both positive and negative consequences.

pressure Stress that arises from the threat of negative events.

She might again feel a motive to approach and wish she had not decided against going.

Have you ever found yourself in such a conflict? Did you find yourself going back and forth on a decision? If so, you have had a very common human experience. The actual outcome of such a conflict depends on many factors, particularly the relative strength of the two motives.

Researcher Seymour Epstein vividly demonstrated the stressfulness of approach-avoidance conflicts in his classic study of parachute jumpers (Epstein, 1982). Epstein views parachute jumping as an approach-avoidance conflict because the jump entails both dangerous risks and exhilarating thrills. In his research, inexperienced jumpers were rigged with devices to measure the amount of sympathetic autonomic arousal by monitoring changes in skin sweat. As shown in figure 13.4, the autonomic reaction of the jumpers mounted dramatically to a peak at the moment of the jump, then returned to normal levels immediately after they landed. Although few of us face such obvious approach-avoidance conflicts, the more subtle conflicts in our lives affect us in similar ways.

4. *Multiple approach-avoidance conflict.* Sometimes the conflicts that we face are complex combinations of approach and avoidance conflicts. A **multiple approach-avoidance conflict** requires the individual to choose between alternatives that contain both positive and negative consequences. Imagine that you are a promising high school athlete and you have been offered athletic scholarships to two colleges. One is from a strong school that won its conference championship in basketball last season, but you dislike the coach and several of the players on the team. The other is from a weaker school that has had an embarrassing record of performance in recent years, but you like the coach and the players. What do you do? Do you go to the stronger college, where there are people you do not like, or do you go to the weaker school, where you like the people with whom you would be playing? This is a multiple approach-avoidance conflict because both choices involve both positive and negative outcomes.

Pressure. Does the pressure of working for good grades ever get to you? If you have been employed, was it a high-pressure job? Have you ever had problems paying your bills? The term **pressure** is used to describe the stress that arises from threats of negative events. In school, there is always the possibility that you will not perform well and you will fail. Some jobs are loaded with possibilities for making a mess of things and getting fired (Melamed & others, 2006). Some unhappy marriages are sources of pressure because one spouse always seems to displease the other, no matter how hard he or she tries to avoid it. Trying to balance the usual demands of our lives with the demands of taking care of a family member who needs special care also can be stressful for some people (Vitaliano, Young, & Zhang, 2004).

Environmental Conditions. There is growing evidence that aspects of the environment in which we live (temperature, air pollution, noise, humidity, and so on) can be sources of stress (Staples, 1996). For example, urban riots have occurred much more frequently on hot (mid-80s Fahrenheit) than cool days, although they have been rare on extremely hot days, perhaps because extreme heat leads to lethargic lack of energy (Baron & Ramsberger, 1978). Visits to the psychiatric emergency room of California's Sacramento Medical Center were found to be related to environmental conditions (Briere, Downes, & Spensley, 1983). Similarly, figure 13.5 shows that visits to emergency rooms in Canada for depression—usually involving a risk of suicide—are more common on days with greater air pollution. This increase in risk is greater in warm than cold weather and is greater among older adults (Szyszkowicz & others, 2009). The types of pollutants measured in this study come primarily from the unsustainable burning of oil and coal products in motor vehicles and power plants.

The term *pressure* is used to describe the stress that arises from threats, such as the possibility of poor performance on an exam.

General Aspects of Stress Reactions

Now that we have looked at the causes of stress, let's examine our reactions to it. When we are under stress, we feel it—we *react* to it. To fully benefit from the lessons that recent research has taught us about stress reactions, we must understand two important insights about stress:

1. First, we react to stress *as a whole*. That is, stress usually produces *both* psychological and physiological reactions—not one or the other, but both. If we remember from chapter 3 that several key aspects of the nervous system—the hypothalamus and the autonomic nervous system—control key aspects of both psychological functioning (emotions and motives) *and* body functioning, including the endocrine glands, this concept is easier to understand. It is through these joint systems that stress affects both our physical and psychological selves.

2. Second, our psychological and bodily reactions to stress are highly similar, whether the stress is physical or psychological. Although each source of stress evokes coping reactions that are specific to it, a *general* reaction to all types of stress also occurs, based largely on the interlinked responses of the hypothalamus, the sympathetic division of the autonomic nervous system, and the adrenal glands.

Psychological Reactions to Stress. Stress leads to changes in many aspects of our psychological states and process—changes in our emotions, motivations, and cognitions. Under stress, we feel some combination of the emotions of anxiety, depression, anger, and irritability (Cano & O'Leary, 2000). We experience changes in our energy, appetite for food, and interest in sex. Cognitive changes occur as well: we may have difficulty concentrating, lose our ability to think clearly, and find that our thoughts keep returning to the source of the stress. In most cases, these changes in our psychological states and processes are temporary. In some cases, however, stress leads to long-lasting changes in emotions, motivations, and cognition. We will have more to say on this topic in the next chapter, on abnormal behavior.

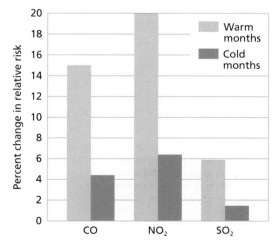

Figure 13.5

Visits to the emergency rooms for depression are higher on days when air pollution is higher, particularly during warm months (Szyszkowicz & others, 2009). CO = carbon monoxide; NO_2 = nitrogen dioxide; SO_2 = sulphur dioxide.

Physical Reactions to Stress and Health

Although nearly everyone knows that stressful events influence our emotions, they may be surprised to learn that stress can influence the physical functioning of our bodies. To understand the effects of stress on our health, we first examine general aspects of the body's response to stress, look at some specific ways in which stress affects health, and then see how psychological and social factors affect our responses to stress.

general adaptation syndrome (GAS) According to Selye, the mobilization of the body to ward off threats, characterized by a three-stage pattern of the alarm reaction, the resistance stage, and the exhaustion stage.

The General Adaptation Syndrome. Canadian medical researcher Hans Selye first gave us the insight more than 70 years ago that the body reacts to psychological stress in much the same way as it reacts to infection or injury. Regardless of the threat, the body mobilizes its defenses to ward off the threat in a pattern referred to by Selye as the **general adaptation syndrome (GAS).** Three stages can be distinguished in this syndrome, as shown in figure 13.6 (Ganzel & others, 2010).

1. ***Alarm reaction.*** As shown in figure 13.7, the body's initial response to any threat, including psychological stress, is to mobilize its stored resources. The sympathetic division of the autonomic nervous system increases heart rate and blood pressure, diverts blood away from digestion and into the skeletal muscles, increases perspiration, and in other ways prepares the body for a physical struggle. The endocrine glands pump epinephrine and other hormones into the bloodstream that aid the actions of the autonomic nervous system and increase levels of blood sugar. The immune cells in the body that fight infection also are activated by these hormones.

When stress is intense or prolonged, these body changes give rise to conscious feelings of general muscle tension, stomachaches, headaches, and other feelings of "sickness" (Maier & Watkins, 2000). In the early stages of the general adaptation syndrome, it's often difficult to know if you are catching a cold or stressed. During the alarm reaction stage, the rapid mobilization of resources leaves the individual temporarily less resistant to the stress than originally. This state of affairs is quickly changed as the next stage is entered.

2. ***Resistance stage.*** During the second stage of the GAS, the body's resources have been fully mobilized, and resistance to the stress is high (Segerstrom & Miller, 2004). This resistance is costly in terms of resources, however. If new stress is encountered, the body is less able to deal with it. Moreover, if the stress continues, the individual's resources will eventually become depleted, leading to the third stage of the GAS (Segerstrom & Miller, 2004).

Figure 13.6

Changes in resistance to stress during the three stages of the general adaptation syndrome. Note that a second stress produces a more rapid dissipation of resistance.

Source: Data from H. Selye, *The Stress of Life.* Copyright 1976 McGraw-Hill Book Company.

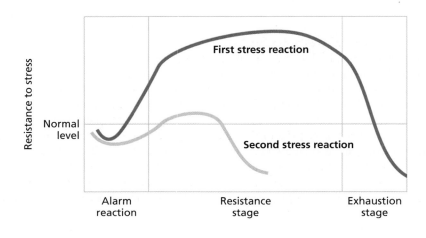

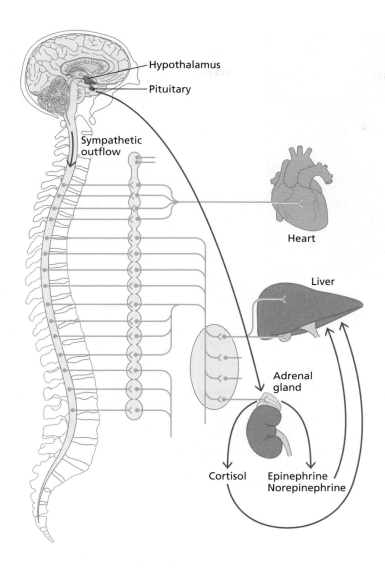

Figure 13.7
The body mobilizes its resources for "fight-or-flight" in the general adaptation syndrome in response to stress.

3. *Exhaustion stage.* If the stress continues, the individual's resources may become exhausted, and resistance to the stress and infection is lowered (Ray, 2004). In cases of prolonged exposure to severe physical stress (such as prolonged exposure to very cold temperatures), death can occur during the exhaustion stage. Psychological stress is rarely able to precipitate death, but it can severely disrupt body functioning (Selye, 1976).

Note in figure 13.6 that if a second stressor is encountered when the individual has already entered the GAS, the progress toward exhaustion is much more rapid. Keep in mind two additional points as you think about the GAS. First, not all stressors overwhelm and exhaust the body; obviously, we cope effectively with most stress. Second, emotional and other psychological reactions to stress follow roughly the same GAS pattern, sometimes resulting in "emotional exhaustion" when coping fails.

Healthy and Unhealthy Aspects of the GAS. As Selye (1976) helped us see, the general adaptation syndrome is the body's protective response to dangers. Without the GAS, we humans would be very frail creatures indeed. Then the body's complex reaction to stress—the GAS—is a blessing, right? Unquestionably, but it is a very mixed blessing. The GAS can be our best defense at times but our own worst enemy at other times (Ganzel & others, 2010).

Natural disasters can be potent sources of stress.

Modern-day stressors, such as preparing forms for tax deadlines, call for all of the body's reactions of the general adaptation syndrome. Although the GAS is a lifesaver in emergencies, it can be life-threatening if stress is prolonged.

immune system The complex body system of defenses to illness, such as white cells and natural killer cells of the blood.

The GAS does its best work during emergencies. Whether suddenly exposed to a deadly virus or being lost on a freezing ski trail, we need our bodies to respond with an alarm reaction to such emergencies. Our physical ability to endure such threats is enhanced for a while by the GAS.

Even our ability to cope behaviorally is helped by the GAS at times. I once narrowly missed stepping on a poisonous water moccasin, and my body responded with a GAS alarm reaction. My autonomic nervous system went into screaming sympathetic arousal and produced a multitude of changes in my body that prepared me to respond behaviorally to the snake. For purposes of simplicity, let's look only at changes in my cardiac system during the moments that followed. Sympathetic arousal of the autonomic nervous system caused my adrenal glands to pump epinephrine, norepinephrine, and other stress hormones into my bloodstream. These, in turn, increased my blood pressure and caused my blood to create substances that make the blood clot faster. My heart beat faster, rushing oxygen to my muscles, and blood flow was diverted from my liver and digestive organs to the muscles in my legs and arms. Those physiological changes that we call the alarm phase of the GAS were very welcome indeed as I jumped, turned tail, and ran from the water moccasin. My legs were supplied with the necessary oxygen to run to the next county, and I didn't mind one bit that my lunch was not being digested properly. Because blood flow to my liver was diminished during the GAS, it was not filtered as usual and my cholesterol levels probably rose, but I didn't mind that, either. And, if I had fallen and cut my knee, I would have been glad that hormones had prepared my blood to clot quickly.

Most of the stressors that we face in contemporary society, however, are not snakes, bears, or avalanches. More often, they are the day-to-day stresses of school, work, and families. Remember, however, that the body's reaction is much the same regardless of the source of stress. As a result, the GAS is not only unnecessary for some stressors, it can be dangerous if it is prolonged.

Take the example of preparing your income taxes—an annoying stress, but not one requiring speedy legs, high blood pressure, or fast-clotting blood. Nonetheless, a group of accountants was given repeated blood tests for several months and found to have normal levels of blood-clotting factors and cholesterol, until the April 15 deadline for filing tax returns grew near; then their cholesterol and clotting factors shot up (Friedman & Rosenman, 1974). Unfortunately, elevated levels of blood pressure, cholesterol, and blood-clotting factors are a potentially deadly combination, because they cause the formation of the "clots" of cholesterol inside arteries, called *plaque,* that clog and harden blood vessels. When the affected blood vessels are those that supply the heart muscles with oxygen, a heart attack can result. Since the time of this original study, many other studies have been conducted that suggest that many kinds of stressful life events affect blood clotting, blood pressure, and other aspects of the functioning of the heart that increase the risk of heart attack (Ganzel & others, 2010; Kubzansky & others, 2007; Matthews, 2005; Slavich & others, 2010; Taylor, 2010). Thus, although the GAS is a lifesaver in the face of emergencies, it can paradoxically affect the cardiac system in ways that can be quite dangerous to our hearts.

Stress, the GAS, and the Immune System. As we saw in the prologue to this chapter, another negative aspect of stress is that it decreases the effectiveness of the body's natural disease-fighting system, the **immune system.** Many studies now show that stress reduces the effectiveness of the immune system (Cohen & others, 2007; Robles, Glaser, & Kiecolt-Glaser, 2005; Segerstrom & Miller, 2004). For example, Sheldon Cohen (1996) conducted a classic experiment on the effects of stress on immunity to the common cold virus. Volunteers completed questionnaires that measured stressful life events and were interviewed about a variety of health practices. Then they were exposed to live cold viruses and were watched to see who developed a cold. Even after the effects of poor health practices (smoking, drinking, poor eating, poor exercising, and poor sleeping) were considered, life events were associated with less immunity to the cold virus. As shown in figure 13.8, more volunteers with above-average numbers of life events developed upper respiratory infections than did volunteers with below-average numbers of life events. I am sorry to tell you that even the stress of studying for college examinations temporarily suppresses the immune system (Segerstrom & Miller, 2004). Unfortunately, the older you become, the more stress takes a toll on your immune system (Segerstrom & Miller, 2004).

Depression, Anxiety, and Health. Stress gives rise to depression and anxiety in some persons (Beck, 2008; Monroe & others, 2007) and persons with high levels of depression and anxiety have impaired immune system functioning, poorer health, and higher rates of death from cardiac disease (Barnes & others, 2006; Irwin & Miller, 2007; Mykletun & others, 2009; Robles, Glaser, & Kiecolt-Glaser, 2005). Indeed, the increased risk for early mortality due to depression is as great as that caused by cigarette smoking (Mykletun & others, 2009). Depression influences health through its effects on inflammation, heart functions, and the immune system (Cohen & others, 2007; Padmos & others, 2008). Conversely, people who are generally happy people tend to be healthier (Cohen & Pressman, 2006; Roysamb & others, 2003).

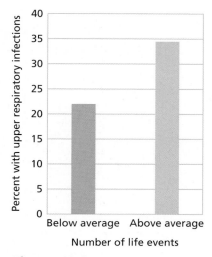

Figure 13.8
Volunteers with above-average numbers of stressful life events were more likely than volunteers with below-average numbers of life events to develop upper respiratory infections ("colds") after being experimentally exposed to live cold viruses.

Review

A human life that was completely free of stress would be pretty dull, but excess stress can take a toll. Stress comes from a variety of sources in our lives. Frustration over not being able to satisfy a motive, conflicts arising from mutually incompatible motives, pressure, and unpleasant environmental conditions are all sources of stress. Similarly, life events, both negative ones such as the loss of employment and positive ones such as marriage, can be potent sources of stress. These sources of stress lead to stress reactions. People react to stress in both psychological and physical ways. Stress brings anxiety, anger, and depression but also body changes such as increased appetite, headaches, and difficulty sleeping. Under some circumstances, stress even leads to high blood pressure, increased blood cholesterol, and decreased efficiency of the body's immune system. The body tends to react to all stressors, psychological and physical ones, in much the same way. This nonspecific response to stress has been called the general adaptation syndrome.

Check Your Learning

To be sure that you have learned the key points from the preceding section, cover the list of correct answers and try to answer each question. If you give an incorrect answer to any question, return to the page given next to the correct answer to see why your answer was not correct. Remember that these questions cover only some of the important information in this section; it is important that you make up your own questions to check your learning of other facts and concepts.

1. _____ can be thought of as any event that strains or exceeds an individual's ability to cope.

Check Your Learning (cont.)

2. In a(n) _____ , the individual must choose between two or more negative outcomes. For example, a person with a toothache must choose between the pain of the tooth and the expected discomfort of going to the dentist.

   a) approach-approach conflict   c) approach-avoidance conflict

   b) avoidance-avoidance conflict   d) simple conflict

3. A _____ is a psychologically significant event that occurs in a person's life that may create stress; it can be positive, such as marriage, or negative, such as divorce.

   a) pressure   c) life event

   b) repression   d) milestone

4. When a person experiences stress, the body's defenses are mobilized in a pattern referred to by Selye as the _____.

   a) alarm reaction   c) generalized stress response

   b) stress reaction   d) general adaptation syndrome

Thinking Critically about Psychology

There are no right or wrong answers to the following questions. They are presented to help you become an active reader and think critically about what you just read.

1. Using your knowledge of the stages of the general adaptation syndrome, what advice would you give someone who is experiencing a traumatic divorce or the breakup of a long-term relationship?

2. What are the major sources of stress in your life? Are they caused by things that you have much control over?

Correct Answers: 1. Stress (p. 425), **2. b** (p. 429), **3. c** (p. 426), **4. d** (p. 432)

Factors that Influence Reactions to Stress

Most of us will experience some kind of negative life event in our lives, but most of us will rebound quickly and go on with our lives (Bonanno & others, 2006). Why does stress sometimes lay us low and sometimes cause only temporary changes in our psychological and physical well-being? The answer lies in the fact that much more is involved in our reactions to stress than the source of stress itself. Much remains to be learned about the factors that influence our reactions to stress, but enough is currently known to outline some of the reasons for individual differences in reactions to it.

Prior Experience with the Stress

Stress reactions are generally less severe when the individual has had some prior experience with the stress event. For example, a soldier who is going into combat for the fourth time will usually be less stressed by it than a soldier facing combat for the first time. Studies of both humans and nonhuman animals suggest that prior exposure to stress can "inoculate" to the effects of future stress (Parker & others, 2004; Wilson & Gilbert, 2008).

Developmental Factors

The impact of stress is frequently rather different at different ages (Thompson & others, 2010). For example, younger widows and widowers (65 or younger) are more than twice as likely to still be depressed 13 months after the death of their spouse than are older widows and widowers. Perhaps the stress of the death of a spouse is less severe later in life, when widowhood is more common. Similarly, the effects of the stress of sexual abuse are more likely to leave victimized children with serious anxiety when the victim is younger (61% of preschool children compared with 8% of adolescents) but leads to more suicidal thinking in older children (41% of adolescent victims compared with no preschool victims) (Kendall-Tackett & others, 1993). Thus, the effects of stress depend, in part, on the developmental level of the person who is stressed.

Predictability and Control

In general, life events are less stressful when they are predictable than when they are not, and they are less stressful when the individual perceives that he or she can exert some degree of control over the stress (Folkman & Moskowitz, 2000). Let's look at several experiments that address the related issues of *predictability and control.*

Mild electric shocks are unpleasant stressful events that are often used in laboratory studies of stress. In one study, three groups of participants listened to a voice counting. At the count of 10, one group received an electric shock 95% of the time, the second group received a shock 50% of the time, and the third group received a shock only 5% of the time. A measure of sympathetic autonomic arousal (the amount of skin sweat) was taken during the counting. Which group do you think showed the strongest reaction? The shocks were least predictable for the group that received shocks only 5% of the time. Even though they received the fewest shocks, the higher degree of uncertainty resulted in greater sympathetic autonomic arousal than for the other two groups (Epstein & Roupenian, 1970). However, when the stress continues over long periods of time, predictable stress appears to become more stressful than unpredictable stress (Abbott, Schoen, & Badia, 1984).

A second line of research focuses on personal control over stress. In one study, two groups of participants participated in a difficult cognitive task in which errors were punished by electric shocks. One group could control this stressful situation by taking breaks whenever they wished, but the other group could take breaks only when told to do so. The amount of increase in blood pressure was significantly greater for the group that had no control over the stress (Hokanson & others, 1963).

Furthermore, lack of control over stress has been shown to have a variety of highly important consequences for health. Rats receiving uncontrollable shocks show a suppression in the proliferation of the white blood cells, which play an important role in the body's immune response (Laudenslager & others, 1983) and exhibit less immunity to cancer cells (Visitainer, Volpicelli, & Seligman, 1982). Importantly, only animals that were exposed to *uncontrollable* stress showed these ill effects; controllable stress did not take a detectable toll on the body in these cases.

The results of these studies are extremely important in the lesson they provide for personal stress management. Stress events in our daily lives that are not predictable or controllable are all the more stressful. It is highly important, therefore, that we seek ways to take control over our stressors. For example, working under a supervisor who often lashes out at you in unpredictable and uncontrollable ways may need to be dealt with by discussing the problem with the supervisor, by asking for assistance from your supervisor's boss, or by finding another job.

Unpredictable events over which we have little control, such as when the fire alarm will call this firefighter into action, can be unpleasantly stressful.

Social Support

In general, the magnitude of reactions to stress are less for individuals with good **social support** networks of friends and family members than for individuals with limited social support (Bolger & Amarel, 2007; Cohen, 2004; Lahey 2009). For example, persons who learn that they are infected with the human immunodeficiency virus (HIV), the virus that causes AIDS, react with less anxiety, despair, and depression if they have good social support (Dew, Ragni, & Nimorwicz, 1990). Similarly, children who have been sexually abused are less likely to experience anxiety and depression if they have good social support from their mothers (Kendall-Tackett & others, 1993).

It's not yet clear how social support functions to buffer us against stress, but there seems to be two aspects of social support:

1. *Someone to talk to.* One aspect of social support that has been studied experimentally is just having the opportunity to "get it off your chest" (Coman & others, 2009; Harris, 2006; Sloan & others, 2005). A clever experiment revealed the surprising extent to which this appears to be true (Pennebaker & Beall, 1986). College student subjects participated in a study in which they spent 15 minutes on each of four consecutive nights writing to the experimenter about a traumatic event in their lives—both a description of the event itself and their feelings about it. For purposes of comparison, another group of students wrote about unimportant topics assigned by the experimenter. Writing about the traumatic events, such as the death of a family member, understandably caused the students to feel sad and to have brief elevations in blood pressure immediately after venting their feelings. However, over the next six months, the students who "got it off their chest" reported being ill less often and making fewer visits to the university health center. Apparently, it is good for your health to share your negative feelings with someone else. Therefore, having someone to confide in seems to be one of the important benefits of social support.

There are risks associated with getting things off your chest, however. Sometimes revealing personal information has the effect of making us or other people look bad. It is wise to be selective in what you disclose, and to whom (Kelly, 1999). In addition, there is evidence that having a close relationship with someone with whom you mostly dwell on problems can lead to increased anxiety and depression in female youth (Rose & others, 2007).

2. *Receiving advice and solace.* There is interesting evidence that the most obvious kinds of social support may actually be harmful. Receiving explicit advice and support from others sometimes makes us feel incapable of handling our stresses and actually makes us more anxious and depressed (Bolger & Amarel, 2007). Just being there, being a good listener, or simply asking how things are going is often more supportive than offering advice or criticizing a friend or family member for how he or she is dealing with stress. This may particularly be true for persons from Asian cultures (Taylor & others, 2007).

Under some circumstances, the best "social support" comes from a trained psychotherapist. We will have much more to say about this in the chapter on therapies, but it is important to note here that receiving psychotherapy is associated with improvements in physical as well as emotional health (Mumford, Schlesinger, & Glass, 1981).

Person Variables in Reactions to Stress: Cognition and Personality

We have seen that our reactions to stress are influenced by a number of factors: our prior experience with the stressor, the degree to which we can predict and control the stressor, and the availability of social support. But our personal characteristics—the

The social support of friends and family helps buffer the effects of stress.

so-called **person variables**—are also important in determining our responses to stress (Asarnow & others, 1999; Smith, 2006).

As we saw in chapter 12, many personality theorists believe that the best way to understand behavior is to acknowledge that we are influenced by both the situations in which we find ourselves *and* some key characteristics we have as individuals. This view, referred to as *person × situation interactionism,* was described on page 412. In terms of stress, it means that our stress reactions are partly determined by the situation (the stressor, our social support, and so on) and partly determined by some of our personal characteristics (our personalities, how we think about the stressor, how "reactive" our bodies are to stress, and so forth).

person variables All characteristics of an individual that are relatively enduring, such as ways of thinking, beliefs, or physiological reactivity to stress.

Cognitive Factors in Stress Reactions. Two kinds of cognitive factors influence the extent to which people react to stress:

1. *Intelligence and stress.* People with higher intelligence scores are both less likely to be exposed to some kinds of stress (for example, violence) and are less likely to react severely to such stressors if they do experience them (Breslau & others, 2006).

2. *Appraisals of stress.* Another reason that different people react differently to the same stressor is that people think about these events differently (Beck, 1976; Bryant & Guthrie, 2005; Lazarus, 1999). Some individuals appear more likely than others to interpret events in stress-provoking ways. For example, suppose you are a graduate student in clinical psychology and your supervisor suggests a better way to help a client. She says: "You're doing very well with this client, but a better way to help him with his fear of automobiles might be to . . . ," and she proceeds to spell out her recommendations. Some individuals would be likely to interpret her statement as a combination of a nice compliment and a helpful bit of advice from a master therapist. Other individuals would interpret the same statement as a criticism and would expect to be dismissed from the graduate program. The interpretation of the event determines its stressfulness (Bryant & Guthrie, 2005).

Personality Characteristics and Stress Reactions. In addition to cognitive factors, differences among individuals in their personality traits prior to stress influence their reactions to stress (Folkman & Moskowitz, 2000). For example, persons who are high on the personality trait of neuroticism tend to react most to stressful events (Lahey, 2009; Smith, 2006). Similarly, military recruits who were more insecure and often sought reassurance from others before the stressor of basic training were more likely to be depressed afterward (Joiner & Schmidt, 1998). Thus, the effects of stress can be understood only in terms of a person × situation interaction. Stress (a situation variable) influences people with different cognitive and emotional characteristics before the stressor (person variables) in different ways.

Another personality characteristic that appears to be important in influencing the health consequences of stress has been termed the **Type A personality.** Some people simply react better than others to the stress of our pressured, competitive world. For some people, playing video games is a pleasant diversion, whereas for others it is a matter of life-or-death competition. A group of health psychologists watched subjects play a video game and took measures of the activity of their cardiovascular systems. Some subjects reacted to the game with large increases in heart rate, blood pressure, and cholesterol (Jorgensen & others, 1988). What is going on here? What kind of personality reacts even to trivial competitive stress with health-threatening sympathetic arousal?

Type A personality The pattern of behavior characterized most by intense competitiveness, hostility, overwork, and a sense of time urgency.

The classic work on Type A personality was done by Meyer Friedman and Ray Rosenman (1974), two physicians who specialize in heart disease. They were observant enough to look beyond their medical tests to see that many of their heart disease patients, particularly younger men aged 30 to 60, were often of the "same type" behaviorally. They were hard-driving, hostile individuals who rarely slowed down to smell the roses. They labeled this pattern of behavior *Type A personality*. The following characteristics more specifically describe the Type A personality (Diamond, 1982; Friedman & Rosenman, 1974; Matthews, 1982):

1. Is highly competitive, hard-driving, and ambitious in work, sports, and games

2. Works hurriedly, always rushing, has a sense of "time urgency," and often does two things at once

3. Is a workaholic, takes little time off for relaxation or vacation

4. Speaks loudly or "explosively"

5. Is perfectionistic and demanding

6. Is hostile, aggressive, and frequently angry with others.

If this description sounds like you, keep in mind that there is a little Type A behavior in most of us, and you should be concerned only if it's excessive. The most important characteristic appears to be *hostility*. Individuals who are hostile in the sense of reacting to frustration with verbal aggression (yelling, criticizing, insulting) or even physical aggression seem to be at slightly higher risk for coronary heart disease (Ben-Zur, 2002; Smith, 2006).

Why is Type A behavior associated with increased risk of coronary heart disease? Type A behavior appears to be indirectly linked to heart disease through two major risk factors: high blood pressure and cholesterol (Matthews, 2005). Researchers at Duke University Medical Center (Williams & others, 1982) classified a group of undergraduate males as Type A or normal. Both groups were asked to subtract 13 from 7,683, then subtract 13 from the answer, and so on, with a prize being given to the person with the fastest subtraction rate. In this competitive situation, the Type A individuals showed greater increases in epinephrine and norepinephrine in the blood. Because these changes are associated with the formation of cholesterol plaques, the greater responsiveness of the Type A individuals to competitive stress may indirectly lead to hardening of the arteries of the heart. Similarly, Type A individuals also have been shown to respond to stress with greater increases in blood pressure—another key risk factor for coronary disease (Matthews, 2005). Fortunately, there is evidence that hostility can be reduced through some types of psychotherapy (Suinn, 2001).

Person Variables in Reactions to Stress: Gender and Ethnicity

There is growing evidence that both gender differences and ethnic differences exist in stress and coping. As described in this section, we cannot fully understand stress and coping without understanding the role of these key person variables. When studying differences between genders or ethnic groups, however, one must remember that not all members of a group behave in the same way. In this section, we are speaking only of differences between groups *on average*. The large differences *among* both women and men, for example, in their reactions to stress are larger than the average difference *between* women and men.

Gender Differences in Response to Stress.
Women are more likely than men are to experience lasting reactions to traumatic events. That is, they are more likely to experience anxiety, depression, and sleep disturbances after a trauma (Fullerton & others, 2001; Tolin & Foa, 2006). This partly reflects a greater likelihood of women

being traumatized by spouse abuse, rape, and other highly stressful events, but it also reflects a gender difference in response to even the kinds of traumatic events experienced by both sexes (Tolin & Foa, 2006). For example, a study of women and men who had survived serious automobile accidents found that both women and men were affected by the trauma afterward, but women were more distressed emotionally and experienced more sleep problems than men did (Fullerton & others, 2001). Again, however, we are only speaking of average differences. Many women are resilient in their response to traumatic stress, and many men are seriously affected by trauma.

Gender Differences in the Benefits of Marriage. As discussed earlier in this chapter, social support buffers us against stress. Marriage and other committed relationships are important sources of social support for both sexes. For both women and

Having a committed partner, as in marriage, is beneficial to our health, particularly for men.

men, married people are healthier than people who are not in committed relationships. There is a huge difference in the benefits of marriage to women and men, however (Kiecolt-Glaser & Newton, 2001). Unmarried women have 50% higher mortality (death) rates than do married women, but unmarried men have 250% higher mortality rates than do married men. Similarly, losing a spouse through divorce or death is more detrimental to the health of men than women (Kiecolt-Glaser & Newton, 2001). Why is marriage more of a benefit to men than women? Janice Kiecolt-Glaser and Tamara Newton (2001) suggest two likely reasons. First, women tend to have more social support from close friendships than men do, so women tend to have social support whether married or not. In contrast, men tend to rely exclusively on their wives for social support to buffer them from the effects of stress. Second, women are more likely than men to urge their partners to take good care of themselves medically. Thus, marriage may help men to eat well, exercise, and seek medical advice more than marriage helps women in this way. In addition, many modern marriages are still not equitable, with women having more responsibilities but less authority than men. Thus, marriage is good for both sexes, but even better for men. Keep in mind that at least part of the correlation between marriage and good health may not be based on the beneficial effects of marriage, however. It may partly be that healthier men and women are more likely to marry than less healthy persons are.

Fight-or-Flight and Tend-and-Befriend. William James (1897) wrote about the fight-or-flight syndrome as the central aspect of emotion. When confronted with a stressful stimulus—such as a menacing person on a dark street—we respond with arousal of the sympathetic nervous system and the adrenal glands in preparation to flee the person or fight with him. Nearly everything that James wrote about emotion was based on this syndrome. And, to a great extent, modern psychologists have followed his lead.

Psychologist Shelley Taylor and her colleagues (2000) agree that the fight-or-flight syndrome is important to both men and women, but she argues that it omits the most important aspects of responses to stress in women. Taylor believes that women are more likely than men to respond to stress with what she calls the "tend-and-befriend" response. When faced with stress, such as a fire or natural disaster, women typically respond by tending to their children. They quickly locate their children and interact with them in ways that reduce their children's physiological response to the stressor, such as by holding or touching them. In studies of employed women and men, women who have had a particularly stressful day tended to be unusually nurturing with their children in the evening. Women withdrew from their children after work only if they had experienced overwhelming job stress that day. Fathers respond to stress in the workplace quite differently on average. Fathers tend to be grouchy or withdraw from family members if they have had even a moderately stressful day at work.

Taylor also hypothesized that if the threat is likely to recur, women tend to befriend others to create alliances. This process of bonding with other women serves two purposes. In some cases, the women create ways to defend against the threat, whether it is a predatory animal near their village or an unreasonable employer. In addition, creating alliances with other women provides social support to the women, which tends to reduce their own emotional and related physiological responses to the threat (Taylor, 2002; Taylor & others, 2000). Thus, according to Taylor, we cannot fully understand emotional responses to stressful events unless we recognize that there are profoundly important differences between women and men. Although it may be sufficient to study the balance between fight and flight in males, who tend to deal with threats as individuals, the social nature of the emotional response to stress in females requires study of the social aspects of their tending and befriending.

Ethnic Differences in Stress.   There is emerging evidence that members of race-ethnic groups that are in the minority in a society experience more stress than do members of the majority culture (Contrada & others, 2000). There are a number of reasons why this may be so. First, many members of ethnic minority groups tend to have fewer of the advantages (greater education, higher incomes, better health insurance, and so on) that shield us from stress. Second, members of minority groups often experience stressful interactions with the majority culture that are based on stereotypes, prejudice, and racism (Mays & others, 2007). Third, immigrant families often experience stress due to the more rapid acculturation of children into the new culture. Parents are sometimes stressed by their children's changing behavior, and children are sometimes stressed by pressure from their parents to maintain the language and standards of their culture. This new and important line of research for psychologists will bring many insights in the future, but it is a topic that many members of ethnic minority groups already understand very well.

| Review | The magnitude of the emotional, cognitive, and physical toll that stress takes on us varies from individual to individual and from time to time for the same individual. The factors that seem to be related to the magnitude of stress reactions are prior experience with the stress, age, gender, predictability and control over the stress, and social support.
The degree to which we react to stress also varies according to our personal characteristics. Different people react differently to stress partly because of cognitive factors. In addition, people with different personality traits react differently to stress. The hostility that often accompanies Type A behavior seems to be a factor in the degree of wear and tear on the body, particularly cardiovascular disease. In addition, females and males and members of different ethnic groups tend to react differently to stress. |
|---|---|

Check Your Learning	To be sure that you have learned the key points from the preceding section, cover the list of correct answers and try to answer each question. If you give an incorrect answer to any question, return to the page given next to the correct answer to see why your answer was not correct.

1. In general, stress events are _____ when they are predictable or controllable than when they are not.

   a) more stressful

   b) less stressful

   c) not stressful at all

   d) slightly stressful

2. Having _____, or someone to talk to, receive advice from, and be cheered and reassured by, is an important factor determining our reactions to stress.

3. _____ refers to all characteristics of an individual that are relatively enduring, such as ways of thinking, beliefs, or physiological reactivity to stress.

   a) Identity

   b) Person variables

   c) Individuality

   d) Superego

4. A person who exhibits a pattern of behavior characterized by intense competitiveness, hostility, overwork, and a sense of time urgency would be identified as _____.

   a) abnormal

   b) Type B personality

   c) Type A personality

   d) high-strung

5. On average, women derive more health benefits from marriage than men do.

   a) true

   b) false

There are no right or wrong answers to the following questions. They are presented to help you become an active reader and think critically about what you have just read.

1. Is there a stressful aspect of your college life that could be eased by better social support?

2. How does our society's emphasis on monetary success and power influence the Type A personality?

Correct Answers: 1. b (p. 437), 2. social support (p. 438), 3. b (p. 439), 4. c (p. 440), 5. b (p. 441)

Coping with Stress

We cannot always avoid stress in our lives. What are the best ways of coping with stress when we experience it?

Effective Coping

Effective methods of **coping** either remove the source of stress or control our reactions to it (Kramer, 2010):

1. ***Removing or reducing stress.*** One effective way of dealing with stress is to remove or to reduce the source of stress from our lives. If an employee holds a job that is stressful, discussions could be held with the employer that might lead to a reduction in the pressures of the job, or the employee could resign. If the stress stems from an unhappy marriage, either marriage counseling could be sought or the marriage could be ended. In a variety of ways, effective coping with stress can take the form of reducing it. For example, Taylor and her colleagues (1998) randomly assigned college students to two groups at the beginning of the term. One group was asked to imagine

coping Attempts by individuals to deal with the source of stress and/or control their reactions to it.

themselves beaming with success when they received high marks in the class. The second group was asked to think of practical steps they could take to avoid failure and get a good grade (getting the book, reading assignments, studying in advance, and so on). They actually studied more and received higher grades, and as a result of reducing the stressful threat of failure, felt less anxious (Taylor & others 1998).

2. *Cognitive coping.* Our cognitions are intimately linked to our reactions to stressful events and a number of effective methods of coping involve cognitive strategies. Three effective cognitive coping strategies involve changing how we think about the stressful event, focusing attention away from stressful events that cannot be changed, and religious coping:

reappraisal Changing how a person thinks about or interprets a potentially stressful event to reduce its stressfulness.

Reappraisal can be an effective method of coping. This refers to changing how we think about—or interpret—the stressful events that push and shove our lives. For example, I know a musician who had a successful first record, but his second album was a flop—the critics panned it and the public didn't buy it. At first, he saw this as a sign that the first record was a fluke and that he had no real talent. As a result, the failure of the second album was a huge stress. However, a veteran musician convinced him that having an unsuccessful second album is a common "sophomore slump" among musicians who go on to be very successful. This conversation changed his interpretation of his unsuccessful album and allowed him to view it as a challenge to do better next time. Finding an interpretation that is realistic and constructive minimizes the stressfulness of negative events (Folkman & Moskowitz, 2000; Richards, 2004; Taylor & Stanton, 2007).

In some cases, stressful events cannot be changed and reappraising their meaning is of limited help. For example, losing a spouse to death must be coped with in some other way. Focusing attention away from the death and moving on with life is associated with less depression and better physical health (Coifman & others, 2007).

Many individuals cope effectively by interpreting events in terms of their religious beliefs (Folkman & Moskowitz, 2000). For example, a study of Latinos with arthritis found that individuals who viewed their painful condition as being *en las manos de Dios* (in God's hands) experienced greater psychological well-being than did individuals who engaged in less religious coping.

3. *Managing stress reactions.* When the source of stress cannot realistically be removed or changed, another effective option is to manage our psychological and physiological reactions to the stress. For example, an individual may decide to start a new business, knowing full well that the first year or two will be hectic. She would be unwilling, then, to remove the source of the stress (the new business) but could learn to control her reactions to the stress. One strategy might be to schedule as much time as possible for relaxing activities, such as aerobic exercise, hobbies, or time with friends. Another would be to seek special training from a psychologist in controlling the body reactions to stress by learning to deeply relax the large body muscles (relaxation training is discussed more fully in a later section of this chapter).

Happily, psychological counseling that encourages all three methods of effective coping has even been successful in changing the Type A behavior pattern. Indeed, treated patients showed a 50% reduction in heart attacks and deaths compared with Type A individuals who did not receive treatment (Nunes, Frank, & Kornfeld, 1987).

Ineffective Coping

Unfortunately, many of our efforts to cope with stress are ineffective. They may provide temporary relief from the discomfort produced by stress but do little to provide a long-term solution and may even make matters worse. Three common, but ineffective, coping strategies are as follows:

1. *Withdrawal.* Sometimes we deal with stress by withdrawing from it. Many students encounter courses in college that are far more difficult than anything they

An ineffective method of coping with stress from an unhappy marriage is to withdraw to the refuge of a bar.

had experienced in high school. Attempting to study difficult material can be highly stressful, and that stress can lead to a withdrawal from studying—by playing electronic games, talking on the telephone, partying, and the like. Similarly, a husband may ineffectively cope with the stress of an unhappy marriage by withdrawing to the refuge of a bar every day after work.

Note that it is not *what* you do, but *how* and *why* you do it, that makes a coping strategy effective or ineffective. Spending your time playing electronic video games actually may be an effective coping strategy *if* you only do it for reasonable periods of time to relax. It becomes withdrawal if you use it excessively as a way to avoid the necessity for more effective coping (studying).

In this context, it is also important to recognize that there is a big difference between actually removing a source of stress and withdrawing from it. If you find that you have signed up for an extremely difficult course for which you are not prepared, dropping that class until you are ready to take it would be an effective way to *remove* the stress. However, simply not studying for the tests in that course because you have *withdrawn* to the refuge of long philosophical discussions with friends would obviously be an ineffective solution.

2. *Aggression.* A common reaction to frustration and other stressful situations is aggression. The woman who has tried unsuccessfully to create romantic interest in a man may suddenly become hostile toward him. The man who cannot get a screw to fit into a curtain rod may throw a temper tantrum and hurl the rod to the floor in disgust.

3. *Self-medication.* It appears that many individuals cope ineffectively with stress by using tobacco, alcohol, and other drugs to soothe their emotional reactions to stress. For example, a study in which participants' emotions were measured daily showed that higher levels of anxiety during the day increased the likelihood of drinking alcohol later that day (Swendsen & others, 2000). Although alcohol temporarily reduces anxiety for some people, it does nothing to remove the source of stress and often creates additional problems in relationships, studying, job performance, and health that make things worse in the long run. Self-medication with alcohol or street drugs is a very poor method of coping indeed. It does seem clear, however, that some individuals benefit from professionally prescribed medications that reduce anxiety and depression far more effectively and safely than from alcohol and street drugs. Perhaps because of the stigma associated with mental health "problems," far too many people self-medicate instead of seeking medication from a competent physician in conjunction with assistance from a psychologist in developing effective coping strategies.

4. *Defense mechanisms.* According to Freud, one of the key functions of the ego is to "defend" the person from a buildup of uncomfortable tension. Freud believed that the ego possesses a small arsenal of **defense mechanisms** that are unconsciously used to cope with tension. There is evidence that we use cognitive coping strategies that are very similar to the defense mechanisms described by Freud over 100 years ago (Simmon & others, 2004). When they are not overused, such defense mechanisms can effectively reduce stress (Coifman & others, 2007; Kramer, 2010), but they create problems when they are overused. The major defense mechanisms identified by Freud:

defense mechanisms According to Freud, the unrealistic strategies used by the ego to discharge tension.

Displacement: When it's unsafe or inappropriate to express aggressive or sexual feelings toward the person who is creating stress (such as a boss who pressures you), that feeling can be directed toward someone safe (such as yelling at your friend when you are really angry with your boss).

Sublimation: Stressful conflicts over dangerous feelings or motives are reduced by converting the impulses into socially approved activities, such as schoolwork, literature, and sports.

Projection: One's own dangerous or unacceptable desires or emotions are seen not as one's own but as the desires or feelings of others. A person who has

"You keep insisting that this isn't happening, Edwards, but in my opinion you're mistaken. I really believe myself to be firing you."

stressful conflicts about sex might perceive himself as having little sexual desire but might view other people as being "obsessed" with sex.

Reaction formation: Conflicts over dangerous motives or feelings are avoided by unconsciously transforming them into the opposite desire. A married man with strong desires for extramarital sex might start a campaign to rid his city of massage parlors and prostitutes. A woman who wishes her hateful mother would die might devote herself to finding ways to protect her mother's health.

Regression: Stress may be reduced by returning to an earlier pattern of behavior, such as a business executive who has a stomping, screaming temper tantrum when her company suffers a major setback.

Rationalization: Stress is reduced by "explaining away" the source of stress in ways that sound logical. A man who is rejected by his lover may decide that he is glad because she had so many faults or because he really did not want to give up the single life.

Repression: Potentially stressful, unacceptable desires are kept out of consciousness without the person being consciously aware that the repression is occurring.

Denial: The conscious denial of upsetting feelings and ideas. For example, in an argument, an obviously angry person may shout: "I am *not* angry at you!" Similarly, a cigar smoker who was shown widely endorsed research on the dangers of all forms of tobacco use would be using denial if he or she flatly rejected the validity of the evidence.

Intellectualization: The emotional nature of stressful events is lessened at times by reducing it to cold, intellectual logic. For example, the person who learns that he has lost a large sum of money in an overly risky investment may think about it in a detached way as a temporary debit in a successful lifelong program of investment, rather than as a painful financial mistake that should be avoided in the future through more careful planning.

When overdone, defense mechanisms can inhibit long-term solutions to stress if they *distort reality* (Kramer, 2010). For example, suppose that a student copes reasonably well with the stress of failing a course in college by deciding that her instructor graded her test papers unfairly because she asks too many questions in class. If her instructor is actually fair and competent, she would be distorting reality by using the defense mechanism of rationalization. A simple change in study habits or test-taking strategies might make a big difference in her grades, but she will never see the need for change if she distorts reality through rationalization. The other defense mechanisms can be harmful in similar, reality-distorting ways.

Review	Although some of us are exposed to more stress than others, we all face stressful events that require some form of coping. The most common sources of stress are frustration, the many forms of conflicts, pressure, and positive and negative life events. At times, we cope effectively with stress either by finding ways to remove the source of stress or by managing the stress reaction. At other times, however, we cope ineffectively through withdrawal, aggression, self-medication, and defense mechanisms.
Check Your Learning	To be sure that you have learned the key points from the preceding section, cover the list of correct answers and try to answer each question. If you give an incorrect answer to any question, return to the page given next to the correct answer to see why your answer was not correct.

1. The term _____ refers to attempts to deal with the source of the stress or control our reactions to it, or both.

   a) endurance   c) restructuring

   b) strategize   d) coping

2. Doing aerobic exercise to relax could be an effective coping strategy.

   a) true   b) false

3. Spending most of your time playing video games as a way to avoid the stress of studying would be considered to be _____.

   a) cognitive coping   c) withdrawal

   b) stress management   d) removal

4. According to Freud, _____ are unrealistic strategies, such as repression and denial, used by the ego to discharge tension.

   a) cognitive coping strategies   c) insights

   b) withdrawal   d) defense mechanisms

Thinking Critically about Psychology

There are no right or wrong answers to the following questions. They are presented to help you become an active reader and think critically about what you have just read.

1. What would you say are the main differences between effective and ineffective coping?

2. Have you had good and bad experiences when people tried to give you social support? What made the difference?

Correct Answers: 1. d (p. 444), 2. a (p. 445), 3. c (p. 445), 4. d (p. 446)

Changing Health-Related Behavior Patterns

As noted in chapter 1, one of the goals of psychology is to *influence* us in beneficial ways. The specialty field of **health psychology** seeks to improve the well-being of your body. A major goal of health psychology is to *prevent* health problems by helping individuals modify behaviors that create health risks through strategies such as learning to relax, not smoking or abusing other substances, and exercising and eating properly (Winett, 1995; Schneiderman, 2004).

health psychology The field of psychology that uses psychological principles to encourage healthy lifestyles and to minimize the impact of stress.

Learning to Relax

Is it easy for you to relax—really relax in a way that results in decreased sympathetic arousal? Relaxation is very difficult for a great many people. **Progressive relaxation training** teaches individuals to deeply relax their large body muscles (Lazarus, 2000).

In progressive relaxation training, the individual is first taught to sense the difference between tense and relaxed muscles. Stop reading for a few seconds and tense the muscles in your right hand and arm as tightly as you can. Focus your attention on the tension, carefully noticing how it feels. Then release the tension, letting your hand and arm

progressive relaxation training A method of learning to deeply relax the muscles of the body.

relax limply. Note how your relaxed muscles feel. Now try tensing the muscles in your neck while leaving the muscles in your shoulders relaxed. Now relax your neck. Can you do it? Many people cannot at first, but progressive relaxation training teaches you how.

The therapist slowly takes the individual through all the muscle groups, so that he or she becomes aware of how tension and relaxation feel. Over many sessions of practice, the individual becomes more able to achieve a very deep state of relaxation. As a result, progressive relaxation training has been found to be effective in the treatment of sleep problems, tension headaches, migraine headaches, ulcers, general anxiety, asthma, and high blood pressure (Lazarus, 2000; Smyth & others, 1999; Spiegler & Guevremont, 1998). In addition, programs that teach patients to relax and to cope with stress more effectively result in increases in immune system functioning (Schneiderman, 2004).

Eating Right, Exercising, and Doing Just What the Doctor Ordered

Health psychologists are very much involved in encouraging a variety of patterns of behavior that promote good health, including eating well and exercising to control weight and to prevent serious health problems (Kaplan, 2000; Schneiderman, 2004; Taylor, 1999).

Improved Eating Habits. It is clear that diet plays an important role in our health. Why, then, do most Americans still eat so poorly? Why don't we view a breakfast of eggs, bacon, biscuits, and butter as being as dangerous as eating asbestos? Our dietary behavior is unhealthy partly because of lack of knowledge—most of us are not aware of the importance of good diet. Even when people are given information on the importance of good nutrition, however, only about 20% eat better (Evers & others, 1987; Foreyt & others, 1979; Forster, Jeffrey, & Snell, 1988).

body mass index The ratio of a person's weight to that person's height.

Are you overweight to the extent that your weight poses a danger to your health? The answer depends on how much you weigh relative to your height and how much abdominal fat you carry. The ratio of your weight to your height is called the **body mass index.** The more you weigh relative to your height, the higher your body mass index. Fortunately, the National Institutes of Health provides an easy automatic calculator of your body mass index at www.nhlbisupport.com/bmi/. This website will tell you if you are overweight (and discusses limitations of the body mass index). The second key indicator of being overweight is waist size, because it is a measure of abdominal fat, which is more dangerous than fat elsewhere on the body. The risk of serious health problems increases with a waist measurement of over 40 inches in men and over 35 inches in women.

If you are overweight according to these measures, what should you do? For many people, the most effective solution is to make permanent lifestyle changes in eating and exercise. Consider the following suggestions for a healthy lifestyle:

1. Have reasonable goals. You do not need to be skinny to be healthy. Even modest reductions in weight yield large improvements in physical health if the reductions are maintained (Fabricatore & Wadden, 2006).

Michelle Obama's vegetable garden at the White House is used to educate children about healthy eating.

2. *Don't "diet."* Do not try to regulate your weight by eating low levels of calories for a brief period of time. In other words, do not go on a diet. Losing weight quickly can cause health problems, and weight that is lost quickly on diets will almost always be regained when you return to a more natural pattern of eating (Mann & others, 2007; Tomiyama & others, 2010).

3. *Eat differently.* First, instead of dieting, commit yourself to a lifelong pattern of eating *differently* that you can live with (Powell & others, 2007). Do not starve yourself! Rather, choose a moderate number of calories wisely. For example, replace high-calorie red meat and cheese with fish, lean meat, low-fat dairy products, and beans. Reducing the amount of saturated fat that you eat in the form of red meat and cheese makes terrific sense, because it reduces calorie intake and reduces your chances of cardiovascular disease and cancer. Cheeseburgers are extremely *dangerous* to your health!

Second, reducing the amount of simple carbohydrates that you eat (potatoes, white rice, and foods made from white flour and sugar) helps tremendously. Simple carbohydrates give you high numbers of calories with very little nutrition. Plus, eating simple carbohydrates actually increases hunger in the long run. When you eat simple carbohydrates, you feel an immediate drop in hunger, but they cause a sudden increase in insulin levels that typically purges the blood of more sugar than you ate, making you feel more hungry in an hour or two.

Another way to eat fewer calories and still feel satisfied with meals is to eat a smaller number of different foods in each meal. We need to eat a variety of foods to have a balance of nutrients, but the more different foods we put on our plate at each meal, the more we eat in each meal (Raynor & Epstein, 2001). Balance your selection of foods over several days, but instead of having three or four different foods on your plate for each meal, try two. You'll feel satiated (full) more quickly on two foods than when you have the variety of four foods to eat. You can also reduce calorie intake by slightly reducing the size of the portion of each food (Geier & others, 2006).

4. *Do not give up because of lapses in your healthy lifestyle.* We're only human; it's easy to commit to a lifestyle change in eating, but many things can knock you off your healthy course. A week spent with your family, a vacation trip, exams, and other things can disrupt your plans to exercise and eat right. This is inevitable, but it need not mean that your plans to eat better and exercise more are impossible dreams. Just start exercising again.

5. *Emphasize exercise.* As discussed in the next section of this chapter, increased exercise is beneficial in many ways. A pound of body fat is the equivalent of 3,500 calories, so if you cut down by 500 calories a day, you should lose a pound every week (7 days × 500 calories = 3,500 calories in a week). Right? That arithmetic works only if your metabolism does not *slow down* by 500 calories a day to offset the loss of calories taken in. The body does not like to lose fat. As a result, you must *increase* your metabolism by increasing your activity level (Golay & others, 2004; Thompson & others, 1982). If you burn calories through regular and moderate aerobic exercise, you stand a much better chance of losing weight than by restricting calories alone for two reasons. First, depending on your level of fitness and what is sensible for you, a good workout might burn 300 to 500 calories by itself. But, more important, *regular* moderate aerobic exercise keeps your metabolism from falling when you reduce your calorie intake (Wadden & others, 1997).

A routine of moderate exercise helps to promote good health.

Regular Aerobic Exercise. We all know that exercise is good for our health. But most of us would be surprised to see the large amount of evidence that links regular moderate aerobic exercise to both good health and a relaxed sense of well-being (Atlantis & others, 2004). Moderate aerobic exercise means at least 30 minutes of continuous exercise that raises the heart rate to 70% to 85% of maximum capacity at least three times each week (Taylor, 1986). Unless the individual has a preexisting medical problem that prohibits exercise, regular aerobic exercise has been shown to reduce high blood pressure, blood cholesterol levels, risk of coronary heart disease, and general health and well-being (Leon, 1983; Roy & Steptoe, 1991; Stiggelbout & others, 2004). Then why is it that so few of us exercise regularly?

Part of the answer seems to be a lack of information, but the number of us who know about the health benefits of exercise and still don't exercise regularly is very high. The real problem is *adherence* (Schwarzer, 2001). Far more of us begin exercise programs than stick with them. On the average, only half the individuals who begin a regular program of exercise are still at it only six months later (Dishman, 1982).

What, then, can a person do to help keep her or his commitment to a program of regular exercise? Social support from a friend who exercises with you, setting clear personal goals and providing reinforcement to yourself, finding a kind of exercise that you really enjoy, and avoiding excessively strenuous exercise all help long-term adherence (Taylor, 1986). A clear belief that regular exercise really will benefit *you* also seems to help, because individuals who believe that they should take charge of their own health and those who know they are at risk for coronary heart disease for other reasons are more likely to exercise regularly (Dishman, 1982). We all need to find a reason and a way to keep exercising.

Not Smoking. One of the most important things you can do to improve your chances of living a long and healthy life is not to smoke. Some people who smoke are able to simply quit. Many others are addicted to nicotine and need help. Fortunately, truly effective help is available. The National Institutes of Health provides information on effective methods to stop smoking at www.nlm.nih.gov/medlineplus/smokingcessation.html.

Medical Compliance. Psychologists have also found themselves called on by physicians to help solve a surprisingly difficult and widespread problem in health care delivery. Patients with chronic health problems, such as high blood pressure and diabetes, frequently do not take their prescribed medication. This is extremely unfortunate because proper use of medication can greatly reduce the risk of stroke and heart attack associated with high blood pressure and reduce the risk of blindness, amputation of limbs, and other complications of diabetes. Reasons for failing to follow prescribed treatments include not understanding the physician's instructions, concerns about cost, not wanting to experience the side effects of some medications, and simply denying the need to continue treatment. Some health psychologists, therefore, devote a substantial amount of their time to implementing programs to help patients comply most effectively with their doctors' orders (Brownlee-Dufek & others, 1987; Taylor, 1999).

Become an Advocate for Sustainable Energy. Working to reduce air pollution by using energy sources that do not burn carbon fuels (mostly oil and coal) will improve your health in at least three ways. First, air pollution directly harms our physical and mental health—the higher the pollution each day, the more people die (Ostro & others, 2010). Second, reducing the burning of carbon fuels will slow global warming, which will stress and kill millions (Takahashi & others, 2007). Third, joining the fight to promote life-saving sustainable energy use is an active form of adaptive coping that will reduce your stress.

A decade ago, psychologists Judith Rodin and Jeanette Ickovics (1990) summarized what psychologists know about the health and health care of women and issued a call for new research efforts in this area. Much still remains to be learned about the psychological factors that have an impact on women's health, but the National Institutes of Health in 2000 launched a large-scale effort to increase research on the health of women.

Human Diversity
Psychology and Women's Health

Health Concerns of Women. Many important health issues are unique to women (Clifford-Walton, 1998). Breast, ovarian, and cervical cancer; hysterectomy (surgical removal of the uterus); and menstrual dysfunction are concerns only of women, and osteoporosis (thinning of the bones), eating disorders, lupus, and rheumatoid arthritis are far more common in women than in men. In addition, two-thirds of all surgery in the United States is performed on women, mostly because of the high rates of cesarean deliveries and hysterectomies. Women are less likely to have medical insurance than men are, and when they are insured, their policies often do not cover essential preventive procedures such as Pap smears for early detection of cervical cancer (Taylor, 1999).

Women also have unique health concerns because they are sometimes prescribed the hormone estrogen. Estrogen is contained in birth control pills and is sometimes prescribed for women who have reached menopause to replace the natural supply that has diminished. Unfortunately, estrogen increases risk for some forms of cancer.

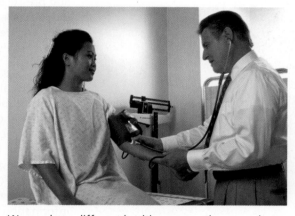

Women have different health concerns than men, but the medical profession is still dominated by men who are not properly trained to meet the needs of women.

In spite of these clear differences in the health concerns of women, women have been excluded from health research to a great extent in the past. This means that much of what has been learned in medical research may not apply to women. A decade ago, the National Institutes of Health mandated that women could no longer be excluded from research unless there is a strong reason. Although it took time for the new policy to affect research, there is now a greatly accelerated rate of research on the health and mental health of women.

Changes in High-Risk Behavior. The second reason that a focus on women's health is needed is that women are behaving more like men in terms of high-risk health behavior in recent years. The last century saw marked increases among women in risky behaviors that greatly increase the chance of illness, such as cigarette smoking, drug use, and excessive alcohol use. As a result, the death rates for men and women are growing more similar, particularly because of a large increase in the rates of cigarette-related lung cancer. Over the past 40 years, death due to lung cancer increased 85% in men but over 400% in women (Taylor, 1999).

Different Equation between Health Behaviors and Illnesses. Third, the equation relating health-related behaviors and illness is somewhat different for women than for men. For example, behaviors that create health risks for both women and men, such as cigarette smoking, moderate to excessive alcohol consumption, obesity, and high-fat diets are particularly dangerous for women who take birth control pills. Women need to be made aware of interactions among their risk factors that do not affect men.

Another way in which the health behavior equation is different for women can be seen in the example of AIDS. Men can and do acquire the HIV virus—which can lead to AIDS—from intercourse with women, but it is far more common for women to acquire the virus through either vaginal or anal intercourse with men. **Continued on pg. 452**

Human Diversity
Psychology and
Women's Health
cont'd from pg. 451

Continued from pg. 451 Whereas only 2% of men with AIDS acquired HIV through heterosexual intercourse, 31% of women with AIDS acquired HIV in this way. Thus, the risks for contracting HIV (and AIDS) from essentially the same behaviors are quite different for women and men (Rodin & Ickovics, 1990).

A third way in which the health behavior equation is different for women concerns the effects of employment. Women who are employed are generally healthier than women who are not, but women who are employed in demeaning, low-paying, and pressured jobs have much poorer health. Interestingly, women who have satisfying jobs, are married, and have children are the healthiest of all, in spite of the pressures involved in handling all of these roles (Waldron, 1991).

Other Sociocultural Factors in Women's Health. Gender is not the only sociocultural factor that plays a role in the health of women, of course. To understand the health behavior of women, we must also understand their ethnicity, sexual orientation, and other aspects of their sociocultural makeup (Gruskin, 1999). For example, African-American women have lower rates of breast cancer than non-Hispanic white women do, but when African-American women contract breast cancer, their survival rates are lower. Psychologist Beth Meyerowitz and her colleagues (1998) believe that ethnicity is related to survival from breast cancer, because African-American women tend to have fewer financial resources and have less access to quality health care and information about cancer. Sexual orientation also plays a role in women's health. Although lesbian women are at greatly reduced risk of contracting AIDS, they are more likely to have breast cancer. Having children reduces the risk of breast cancer, and although artificial insemination is on the rise, lesbian women are still less likely to become pregnant. In addition, lesbian women are less likely to have regular gynecological examinations and less likely to find cervical cancer early when it is most treatable. Each factor must be considered carefully in attempting to find ways to improve the health behavior of women.

Safety Management

When we think of promoting health, we quite reasonably think of preventing diseases like cancer or heart disease. But accidents are also a major cause of disability and death. In fact, they are one of the leading causes of death for children, adolescents, and young adults. Psychologists have tested a number of methods of reducing injuries and accidental deaths, particularly in the workplace and in automobiles (Cox & Geller, 2010; Geller, 1988).

Wearing seat belts greatly reduces the risk of death or injury in automobile accidents, but many people do not wear them. Does a simple reminder increase seat belt use? A classic study by Bruce Thyer and E. Scott Geller (1987) provided strong evidence in support of the use of such reminder signs. They asked 24 graduate students to wear seat belts when driving and to record for two weeks the percentage of times that passengers in the front seat of their cars wore seat belts. Then the drivers placed a sticker on the passenger-side dashboard for two weeks that said "SAFETY BELT USE REQUIRED IN THIS VEHICLE." The percentage of passengers who wore seat belts doubled—from about 35% to 70%. When the signs were removed for two weeks, seat belt use dropped to near the original level but rose to over 70% when the signs were reintroduced. Something as simple as a sign reminding passengers to wear seat belts can have a *powerful* effect on safety.

Geller and others (1989) also studied the use of pledges to wear seat belts. In this study, the participants were students, faculty, and staff at Virginia Polytechnic Institute and State University. During the fall and spring quarters, over 10,000 pledge cards were made available throughout campus. Individuals who signed the pledge to wear seat belts could drop part of the card into a box, making them eligible for a lottery in which they could win prizes donated by local merchants. The top half of the card was designed to be hung from the car's rearview mirror. Observers at the entrance to university parking lots recorded whether the driver was wearing a seat belt and used parking decals to link the car to the driver's name. Among drivers who signed the pledges, use of seat belts increased from about 50% to about 65% after they pledged. This level of seat belt use was approximately twice as high as those who did not pledge.

Driving while intoxicated is a major cause of death and injury, both to the driver and to others involved in the accident. Geller and associates (1987) evaluated a program in which servers in bars frequented by college students were trained to reduce excessive drinking by their customers. The servers were given information about the effects of alcohol and the risks of excessive drinking. In addition, instruction and role plays were used to teach servers techniques for reducing the drinking of customers who were beginning to drink excessively. These techniques included such things as offering food, suggesting nonalcoholic drinks, and slowing service. The intervention was evaluated by sending 32 college-aged research assistants to two bars in a college town where they posed as regular customers who tried to drink excessively. Half of the servers in each bar had been trained, but the research assistants did not know which servers had been trained. The servers who were trained were much more likely to limit drinking, and the blood alcohol levels of the research assistants who were served by the untrained servers was almost twice as high as that of research assistants served by trained servers! A brief training program for servers in bars can make a huge difference in reducing excessive drinking in college students.

Furthermore, Ryan Smith and Scott Geller (2010) conducted an evaluation of laws that prohibit advertising alcohol in ways that target minors. In the United States, states with such laws had 33% few alcohol-related single-vehicle fatalities involving young drivers.

Many studies have looked at simple but effective ways to reduce accidental injury and death in the workplace (Geller, 1996). Careless behavior on the job is common in many dangerous workplaces. In particular, failure to use necessary protective gear is the cause of approximately 40% of work-related accidents (National Safety Council, 1998). Supervisors sometimes contribute to unsafe practices, both because they, like their workers, minimize the dangers and because they believe that working safely requires working at a slower pace, making it difficult to meet production demands. Setting aside the enormous human costs of workplace injuries, it is generally cost-efficient to work more safely than more quickly (because worker deaths and injuries are extremely expensive to industries in many ways). Moreover, it is not impossible to improve quality and safety at the same time (Geller, 2005).

Not surprisingly, Scott Geller, the author of many of these studies received the Gold Medal Award for Life Achievement in Psychology in the Public Interest in 2009 (Geller, 2009). Many of us applauded this recognition for psychological research that literally saves lives.

Review

Psychological methods have been successfully used in the prevention and treatment of medical problems. Methods have been developed to help people drink less alcohol, exercise regularly, stop smoking, lose excess weight, and make other behavioral changes that reduce the risk of heart attack and other serious diseases. Progressive relaxation training and other treatment techniques have also been successful in treating problems such as high blood pressure, headaches, epilepsy, and diabetes. The more that we are willing to apply to our lives the advances from the field of health psychology in understanding illness, the more we will be able to prevent unnecessary disease and control the cost of health care.

Check Your Learning

To be sure that you have learned the key points from the preceding section, cover the list of correct answers and try to answer each question. If you give an incorrect answer to any question, return to the page given next to the correct answer to see why your answer was not correct.

1. _____ refers to a method of learning to deeply relax the muscles of your body.

   a) Psychoanalysis   c) Aerobics

   b) Cognitive therapy   d) Progressive relaxation training

2. A surprisingly difficult and widespread problem in health care delivery is the lack of _____.

   a) pharmacies   c) medical schools

   b) drugs   d) medical compliance

3. Changes in lifestyle could produce considerable improvements in health and longevity in North America.

   a) true   b) false

Thinking Critically about Psychology

There are no right or wrong answers to the following questions. They are presented to help you become an active reader and think critically about what you have just read.

1. Do the members of your family exercise enough? If not, do you think there is any way that you could convince them to change?

2. Do you think you eat a reasonable amount of complex carbohydrates? If not, what could you do to eat less?

Correct Answers: 1. d (p. 448), 2. d (p. 450–451), 3. a (p. 448–454)

Application of Psychology

Prevention and Management of AIDS

Twenty years ago, the brother of one of my colleagues died of *acquired immune deficiency syndrome,* or AIDS. This tragedy brought the specter of AIDS very much closer to home for me. He was a decent and talented man who died unnecessarily in his 20s.

As we are all well aware, our planet is in the midst of an epidemic of AIDS. This disease, which is caused by the *human immunodeficiency virus (HIV),* has already killed over 25 million men, women, and children worldwide (World Health Organization, 2009). At the end of 2009, a total of 33 million children and adults were infected with HIV. Obviously, an epidemic of this magnitude demands our attention, but why bring up a medical disease in a psychology textbook? The answer is that, as with most other physical diseases, there are important *psychological* aspects to the transmission and treatment of AIDS. It is extremely important that you, as an educated person, understand this important point: each individual's *behavior* determines his or her risk for AIDS.

To explain the role of psychological factors in AIDS, we look first at the physical nature of the disease. AIDS is a disease that impairs the ability of the body's immune system to fight bacteria, viruses, and cancer. HIV has many effects on the immune system, but most important, the virus results in mass destruction of the immune cells known as *lymphocytes* and, indirectly, leaves the important *B-cells* of the immune system useless. HIV disables the B-cells by invading the nucleus of another type of immune cell known as *T-4 Helper cells.* The T-4 Helper cells help the B-cells identify hostile bacteria and viruses and signal the B-cells to destroy them. Unfortunately, HIV either destroys the T-4 cells or deactivates them, making the B-cells useless and leaving the body vulnerable to disease. The person with AIDS does not actually die from the AIDS but from the other diseases, such as pneumonia and cancer, that flourish because of the weakened immune system.

AIDS is the direct result of patterns of behavior that bring persons into contact with the AIDS virus. The rates of new cases of HIV in North America have declined slightly in recent years because people are engaging in somewhat less high-risk behavior. What are these *high-risk behaviors* that increase risk for AIDS? If we know what the high-risk behaviors are, it may be possible for us all to help *prevent* AIDS by reducing high-risk behaviors.

HIV is spread through body fluids—especially blood and semen, but also by saliva and other fluids. The most common means of transmission is all forms of sexual intercourse—vaginal (contact of penis and vagina), oral (contact of penis and mouth), and anal (contact of penis and anus). Although anal intercourse is believed to create an especially high risk of transmission, vaginal intercourse is actually a more common source of transmission, because it is practiced more widely. Although AIDS was first spread among homosexual men in the United States and is still more common among them, the spread of HIV by sexual acts is certainly not limited to homosexuals today. Engaging in intercourse with an HIV-infected partner of either the same or the opposite sex is equally likely to result in the spread of AIDS.

Recent evidence indicates that circumcision of the penis reduces HIV infection by 60% (Auvert & others, 2005). This

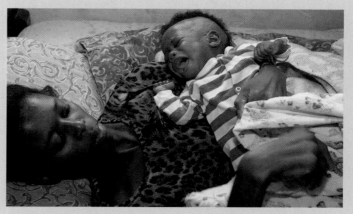

AIDS is a major source of misery and death all over the world, but particularly in Africa.

is extremely important information, but circumcised males should not think that their risk is low enough to engage in unprotected sex.

The next most frequent mode of transmission is intravenous drug use (Centers for Disease Control and Prevention, 2005). Persons who use drugs that are injected are at high risk for acquiring HIV through the blood if they share a needle with someone infected with HIV; such drugs themselves also suppress the functioning of the immune system.

AIDS is much more common in some sociocultural groups than others. In the United States, males are three times more likely to have AIDS than women are (Centers for Disease Control and Prevention, 2005). As shown in figure 13.9, AIDS can be found in every part of the world, but it is far less common in some countries than others (World Health Organization, 2009). AIDS is relatively uncommon in Arabic countries and in Australia and New Zealand, but it is very common in Africa south of the Sahara desert, where HIV was first transmitted from monkeys to humans. In the United States, AIDS is found in all ethnic groups, but rates are higher among African Americans.

Prevention of AIDS Through Behavior Change. New cases of HIV infection can be prevented through programs that change high-risk sexual behaviors (Carey & others, 2004; Schmiege & others, 2009). What behaviors need to be changed? First, persons have virtually no chance of acquiring AIDS if (a) they are not sexually active or are involved in a monogamous sexual relationship with a partner who is not infected with HIV and (b) they do not use intravenous drugs. AIDS is not a difficult disease to avoid if one completely avoids high-risk behaviors. Indeed, the risk of AIDS can be greatly reduced just by having fewer sex partners, engaging in "safer sex" practices such as the use of condoms, avoiding the use of needle drugs, and avoiding sex with persons who may have been exposed to HIV.

As simple as this sounds, however, it is very difficult to convince people to change their behavior—especially their sexual behavior. College students currently have low rates of HIV infection, but because they have been slow to adopt safe sex practices, they are at risk. Needle drug users continue to share needles because it is difficult to obtain new needles, and some

Figure 13.9 Adults and children estimated to be living with HIV, 2008.

North America
1.4 million
(1.2–1.6 million)

Western and
Central Europe
850,000
(710,000–970,000)

Eastern Europe and
Central Asia
1.5 million
(1.4–1.7 million)

East Asia
850,000
(700,000–1 million)

Caribbean
240,000
(220,000–260,000)

Middle East and
North Africa
310,000
(250,000–380,000)

South and
Southeast Asia
3.8 million
(3.4–4.3 million)

Latin America
2 million
(1.8–2.2 million)

Sub-Saharan Africa
22.4 million
(20.8–24.1 million)

Oceania
59,000
(51,000–68,000)

Total: **33.4 million** (31.1–35.8 million)

women who know they have HIV infection become pregnant in spite of the high risk of transmission to their own infants.

Psychological Factors in the Management of AIDS.
AIDS is currently a disease with no cure, but new medical treatments greatly slow the progress of the HIV infection. A great deal of research is currently under way to find ways in which psychological interventions might be useful in helping persons with HIV adjust emotionally to their disease and even slow the progression of HIV infection. Persons who are HIV positive progress to AIDS faster if they experience more negative life events, are depressed, and cope by means of denial (Leserman & others, 2000, 2007). It may be possible, however, to develop psychological interventions that help to strengthen the immune system and to slow the progression of AIDS by changing health-related behavior and managing stress (Moskowitz & others, 2009). Some very promising progress has been made in this area. For example, both regular aerobic exercise and stress-reduction therapy have been shown to buffer the detrimental effects of HIV on key aspects of immune functioning (Antoni & others, 1990, 2002). Unfortunately, the beneficial effects of aerobic exercise are only modest.

Summary

Chapter 13 describes the relationship between stress and mental and physical health.

I. Health psychology attempts to prevent health problems by helping individuals cope with stress and change health-related behavior.

II. There are many sources of stress in our lives, some obvious and some hidden.

A. Frustration is the result of failure to satisfy a motive.

B. Conflict is the result of two or more incompatible motives. The four major types of conflict are

1. Approach-approach conflict

2. Avoidance-avoidance conflict

3. Approach-avoidance conflict

4. Multiple approach-avoidance conflict

C. Pressure is the stress that arises from the threat of negative events.

D. Both positive and negative life events can lead to stressful changes and the need for readjustment.

E. Environmental conditions such as heat, cold, and pollution can be stressful.

III. We react to stress in relatively predictable ways.

A. Reactions to stress involve both psychological and physiological reactions.

B. Some important general aspects of stress reactions are the same regardless of the source of stress.

1. The fact that the body reacts to stress with an alarm reaction, a phase of resistance to the stress, and a stage of exhaustion if coping is not successful has been termed the general adaptation syndrome.

2. Stress mobilizes the body's resources to fight or flee but suppresses the immune system and increases risk factors for heart disease (blood pressure, cholesterol, and blood-clotting factors).

3. Common psychological reactions to stress are anxiety; depression; decreased ability to think, concentrate, and make decisions; and changes in motives, such as increased hunger and decreased interest in sex.

IV. We do not just react passively to stress; we actively attempt to cope with it.

A. Effective coping strategies involve either removing the source of the stress or managing the degree of the stress reactions.

B. Ineffective coping strategies do not help in the long run, either because they create more stress (such as aggression) or because they distort reality (defense mechanisms).

V. The harmful effects of stress are greater under some circumstances than others.

A. Stressful events are more stressful when we have no prior experience with them.

B. Stressful events are more stressful when they are unpredictable and when we have no control over them.

C. Stress creates more severe reactions when we have little effective social support.

D. Some stressors are easier to deal with when we are younger, and some are easier when we are older.

VI. Characteristics of the person also influence the magnitude of stress reactions in a person x situation interaction.

A. Differences in intellectual ability and cognitive appraisal of potential stress events influence stress reactions.

B. Persons who are higher in neuroticism respond more to stress.

C. The Type A behavior pattern, including hostile reaction to competitive pressure, is a risk factor for heart disease.

D. Women respond more strongly to traumatic stress, on average.

VII. Several aspects of our behavior are related to our health.

A. Learning to relax deeply can reduce health risks.

B. Health psychologists also seek to reduce health risks by helping individuals exercise properly, control their weight, not smoke, and follow medical treatments properly.

C. Simple interventions can greatly improve transportation safety and safety in the workplace.

D. Because AIDS is usually acquired from high-risk behaviors, and because factors are intimately related to immune system functioning, the science of psychology is playing a key role in the fight against the AIDS epidemic.

chapter **fourteen**
Abnormal behavior

Prologue

Does giving a speech make you nervous? How about meeting people? If they do, you're not alone; anxiety is quite common in these and other social situations. But for some people, the level of anxiety is so intense that it significantly disrupts their ability to function in important social situations. Let's use Carol, an intelligent, attractive woman who is successful in her professional career, as an example. Carol went to a university psychological clinic specializing in anxiety disorders to learn more about her intense anxiety in social situations. The psychologist observed Carol in three different anxiety-provoking social situations. In the first situation, a stranger played the role of a man on a first date with Carol at a restaurant. In the second scene, a woman pretended to be a new neighbor of Carol. In the third situation, Carol delivered a brief, impromptu speech to two psychologists. During these three tests, Carol wore sensors that monitored her heart rate and blood pressure. After each test, she was asked to choose statements that reflected her thoughts and feelings about her performance during the tests, what she thought the other people thought about her, and her ability to cope.

Carol acted very nervously in each situation. She rarely made eye contact, spoke very little, and frequently shifted her posture. Her blood pressure and her heart rate rose dramatically, particularly during the speech, but was almost as high during the simulated first date. She felt nervous in all situations and thought that she behaved in ways that no one would like.

Carol's social anxiety was intense enough that it caused her to turn down dates and other social invitations, and even led her to change her college major to avoid taking a course in which she would have to give speeches. Because her anxiety was serious enough to cause a problem, she was considered by the psychologist to have a social phobia—one of the forms of abnormal behavior that we will study in this chapter.

Does it surprise you to learn that something as understandable as exaggerated social anxiety would be considered to be "abnormal"? Actually, most forms of abnormal behavior aren't very different from what we would consider to be normal. Abnormal behavior is a pattern of acting, thinking, or feeling that is distressing or harmful to the person or others. Some patterns of abnormal behavior are quite unusual, but it most often is only an exaggeration of normal behavior.

Abnormal behavior takes many forms. Excessive anxiety and depression are the most common types of abnormal behavior. Other psychological disorders involve false beliefs and hallucinations that result in the individual's being "out of touch with reality." Other forms involve symptoms of health problems that have no known physical cause.

What causes abnormal behavior? Many answers have been given to this question throughout history. The earliest answer was that evil spirits caused it, but that view is uncommon today. Today most psychologists believe that abnormal behavior results from a combination of biological factors and psychological and social causes.

Definition of Abnormal Behavior

Abnormal behavior refers to actions, thoughts, and feelings that are distressing or harmful. This harm may take many forms, including not being able to function in a job, not being able to relate to people well enough to have enduring friendships or family relationships, and resulting in physical health problems (as when a person is too frightened of dental procedures to have necessary oral surgery).

Most of us believe that behavior is abnormal only if it is very strange and unusual. That is not how psychologists and psychiatrists use the term *abnormal*, however. Mental health experts define the term *abnormal* broadly to include far more problems in living than most persons think of as "abnormal." As the term is defined by the mental health community today, 18% to 20% of all persons in the United States are considered to exhibit actions, thoughts, or feelings that are harmful enough to be considered to be abnormal during any 12-month period (Narrow & others, 2002). Indeed,

Key Terms

cont'd on pg. 260

abnormal behavior Actions, thoughts, and feelings that are harmful to the person or to others.

cont'd from pg. 259

syndrome A pattern of symptoms that appear together, which represents a disorder.

continuity hypothesis The view that abnormal behavior is just a more severe form of normal psychological problems.

discontinuity hypothesis The view that abnormal behavior is fundamentally different from normal psychological problems.

Abnormal behavior was once explained as demonic possession. Here St. Catherine exorcises a demon from a woman.

46% of Americans will experience a mental disorder at some time during their life (Kessler & others, 2005). Thus, the term *abnormal behavior* does not refer only to rare and strange problems but also to the common problems in negotiating life that are experienced by *many* people.

Most diagnoses of abnormal behavior do not reflect a single problem or symptom. Rather, a pattern of actions, thoughts, or feelings that represent a disorder, a **syndrome,** need to appear together. And, abnormality is defined in terms of *distress* and *harm* to the individual or others. Even if a pattern of behavior is very unusual (statistically uncommon for that group of people), it would not necessarily be considered abnormal. Extreme intellectual abilities and total honesty are unusual, but they hardly are considered abnormal. But some patterns of behavior that are quite common are clearly abnormal, because they are harmful. For example, nearly all contemporary psychologists consider dependence on nicotine, which is still common in our culture today, to be abnormal behavior because of the serious health problems that it causes.

The definition of abnormality requires subjective judgments in two ways. First, even though abnormality is defined in terms of harm rather than unusualness, one must decide whether an individual's problems are *severe enough* to be considered "harmful." For example, people experience some discomfort at times from shyness. How shy does a person have to be to be considered abnormally shy? Shyer than 90% of other people? More than 95% of others? Clearly, psychologists must make somewhat arbitrary decisions about what is abnormal.

Second, subjectivity is also a problem in defining what is *harmful.* That decision reflects the values of the person making the determination, and values differ greatly from one culture to another. For example, in the past, the Zuñi Indians of the southwestern United States believed it was good to be able to have hallucinations without taking drugs, for it meant that the gods were blessing you with visits. Nearly all psychologists in the United States today consider hallucinations harmful. But, differences of opinion exist on other issues in our culture, such as the normality or abnormality of some forms of sexual behavior. There is no complete solution to the problem of subjectivity. The best we can do is to be aware of the problem and try to minimize the role of our personal values in making subjective judgments about the behavior of others.

The concept of abnormal behavior is difficult to use not only because of its inherent subjectivity but also because psychologists have been unable to agree on how abnormal behavior differs from normal behavior. The **continuity hypothesis** of abnormal behavior states that abnormal behavior is just a more severe form of normal psychological problems. The **discontinuity hypothesis,** in contrast, suggests that abnormal behavior is entirely different from normal psychological problems. Advocates of the continuity hypothesis argue that such terms as *insanity* and *mental illness* should not be used because they imply that the individuals have sick minds that separate them from the rest of society. Advocates of the discontinuity hypothesis believe that only such strong terms can accurately portray the true nature of abnormal behavior. Research suggests that most, if not all, abnormal behavior is a severe form of normal problems, supporting the continuity hypothesis (Kraemer, 2008).

Historical Views of Abnormal Behavior

Before we discuss contemporary views of the causes of abnormal behavior, it's instructive to look back through history at beliefs about its cause. This historical perspective makes the important point that our ideas about the causes of abnormal behavior are greatly influenced by cultural expectations and determine what we do to help those who experience it.

Supernatural Theories. The oldest writings about behavior—including those of Plato, the Bible, and the tablets of Babylonian King Hammurabi (1750 B.C.E.)—indicate that our earliest belief was that abnormal behavior was caused by evil spirits. Although there were always some who disagreed with this notion throughout history, the idea that people with psychological problems are possessed by evil spirits was the most influential view throughout the entire 3,500-year period of history stretching from Hammurabi to shortly before the American Revolution.

During most of the time that the supernatural theory held sway, the consequences for those with psychological problems were not too severe. Treatment mostly took the form of prayer, with the most unpleasant treatment being purgatives—foul liquids that were supposed to help the person vomit out the evil spirit. During the Middle Ages (500–1500), however, these supernatural beliefs were translated into far more harmful forms of "treatment."

In medieval Europe, people believed that abnormal behavior "revealed" possession by the devil. Treatment began with a stiff regimen of prayer, fasting, and purgatives, but people who could not stop acting in deviant ways were considered to be witches or warlocks (male witches). It was believed that the only way to save their souls was to destroy their bodies to drive out Satan. As a result, half a million so-called witches, mostly women, were put to death in Europe alone (Loftus, 1993). Even as late as 1692, 20 individuals were put to death as witches in Salem, Massachusetts. Nineteen were hanged for "witchcraft," whereas the twentieth victim died as a result of heavy rocks being placed on him in an effort to force him to confess (Phillips, 1933).

Biological Theories. An ancient voice that argued against the supernatural theory of abnormal behavior was 5th-century B.C.E. Greek physician Hippocrates. He believed that biological disorders of the body caused abnormal behavior. According to Hippocrates' view, the body contains four important fluids, or *humors:* blood, phlegm, black bile, and yellow bile. If these fluids get out of balance, illness and abnormal behavior is the result. An excess of black bile, for example, leads to depression; an excess of yellow bile causes irritability.

Hippocrates' theory was inaccurate, of course. But, he set the stage for later developments by suggesting that abnormal behavior might have *natural* rather than supernatural causes. During the 2,000 years after Hippocrates, a number of scientists searched in vain for a biological cause of abnormal behavior. Finally, in the 1800s, medical researchers, such as German physician Richard von Krafft-Ebing, made a discovery that led to a resurgence of biological theory.

Krafft-Ebing was working with a now rare form of severe psychological disturbance called *paresis.* He and a number of independent researchers discovered that paresis was actually an advanced stage of the venereal disease *syphilis.* Syphilis is a bacterial infection that begins with a sore, or chancre, on the genitals or other point of entry. The untreated disease then goes through a long "invisible" period, which eventually leads to the rotting or destruction of more organs. If the bacteria destroy brain cells, paresis is the result. Because of the long period of time between the original infection and the later paresis, it was not known that the two conditions were related until Krafft-Ebing conducted inoculation tests and found that all of the men with paresis he tested also had syphilis.

The discovery that paresis had a biological cause sent shock waves through the medical community. Soon physicians—who up to this time had little to do with people with abnormal behavior—were placed in charge of mental institutions, and the medical specialty of psychiatry was created. There were high expectations that the biological causes for all the other forms of abnormal behavior would soon be discovered. But, although the discovery of penicillin and its use in the treatment of syphilis almost totally eradicated paresis, few other biological causes of abnormal behavior were discovered for many years. In recent years, however, major advances in the effective drug therapies and brain imaging techniques have led to an acceptance of the view that biological factors contribute to abnormal behavior.

Psychological Theories. Hippocrates was not the only ancient Greek to suggest a *natural* explanation for abnormal behavior. Pythagoras, who also gave us geometry, was very active in the treatment of psychological problems around 500 B.C.E. He believed that psychological problems are caused by *psychological* factors such as stress. He placed individuals with problems in "temples," where they received rest, exercise, a good diet, an understanding person to talk to, and practical advice on how to straighten out their lives. Records from his temples suggest that Pythagoras' methods were highly successful.

Unfortunately, the ideas of Pythagoras were ignored or suppressed for over 1500 years. Psychological explanations of abnormal behavior did not become popular again until the very different psychological views of Sigmund Freud were published, but many different psychological theories of abnormal behavior are influential today.

Contemporary Views of Abnormal Behavior

Today, abnormal behavior is widely believed to be a natural phenomenon with biological, psychological, and social causes (Cicchetti, 2006; Rutter, 2010; Rutter, Moffitt, & Caspi, 2006; Walker & others, 2010). Inherited predispositions to certain kinds of problems and abnormal functioning of neural systems in the brain are some of the biological factors that play a role in psychological disorders. The psychological factors that interact with biological predispositions include stress and abnormal social learning histories. Social factors, such as inadequate social support, also influence abnormal behavior (Mineka & Zinbarg, 2006).

The *Diagnostic and Statistical Manual of Mental Disorders*

Mental health professionals in the United States usually use the definitions of abnormal behavior and terminology of the American Psychiatric Association's (2000) *Diagnostic and Statistical Manual of Mental Disorder*. The current version is the Fourth Edition (text revision), widely known as the *DSM-IV-TR*. The first edition of the *DSM* was published in 1952 to give mental health professionals a common set of definitions of mental disorders. Since that time, the number of disorders and the complexity of their diagnostic criteria has increased enormously. The second edition of the *DSM* (published in 1968) is 119 pages long, but the *DSM-IV-TR* is 886 pages long! Critics of the *DSM-IV-TR* see it as expanding to include many human problems that should not be considered to be mental disorders. Others see the *DSM-IV-TR* as reflecting the rich imagination of psychiatrists more than good research, which has limited our ability to more precisely define different forms of abnormal behavior (Hyman, 2010). I served on the Child Disorders Work Group for *DSM-IV*. My perspective from the inside of the process is that empirical evidence was carefully considered in all cases and influenced diagnostic decisions in many cases. Although the mental disorders defined in *DSM-IV-TR* may be too much the result of committees making decisions based on their own clinical experience, one advantage of the *DSM-IV-TR* is undeniable. It makes the diagnostic criteria specific and public, which gives psychologists and other scientists an opportunity to evaluate them (Lahey & others, 2004).

The *DSM-IV-TR* is a *multi-axial* system, which means that the mental health professional can give more than one diagnosis and provide additional relevant information. The five axes of the *DSM-IV-TR* are these:

I. Clinical disorders (most mental disorders fall in this category)

II. Personality disorders and mental retardation (this encourages clinicians to think about possible abnormal personality and low intelligence in the individual)

III. General medical conditions (this encourages the clinician to consider medical conditions that may be relevant to the mental health problem)

IV. Psychosocial and environmental problems (this allows the clinician to indicate adverse living conditions or stressful circumstances that may be relevant)

V. Global assessment of functioning (the clinician uses a standard scale to indicate how well the person is functioning in life to allow appropriate treatment choices)

As this chapter was being prepared, the next version of the *DSM,* the *DSM 5,* was being fiercely debated. Revising the *DSM* has important implications for the way we view and treat mental illness. What we, as a culture, consider to be abnormal has changed across time. For instance, the early editions of the *DSM* included homosexuality as a mental disorder, but subsequent editions removed homosexuality from the *DSM.* The fact that revising the *DSM* is controversial further emphasizes the importance of both culture and science to our understanding of abnormal behavior.

Public Health Burden of Abnormal Behavior

How harmful are abnormal psychological problems? In the mid 1990s the World Health Organization conducted a ground-breaking study on the public health burden related to medical and psychological problems in developed countries (Murray & Lopez, 1996). The researchers considered the impact of diseases on both fatal and nonfatal health outcomes. They revealed that nine of the top ten leading causes of disability were either psychological disorders (e.g., depression, schizophrenia, obsessive-compulsive disorder) or strongly associated with such disorders (e.g., alcohol and drug use and suicide). In fact, roughly 50% of all disability experience by people in the study was related to the those conditions! Thus, the abnormal behavior leads to great suffering, lost opportunities, and economic costs (Costello, Egger, & Angold, 2005).

The Problem of Stigma

One of the great problems of abnormal behavior is that we *stigmatize* it. This means that we have very negative perceptions of people with such problems. People with mental health problems make us uncomfortable, and sometimes even frightened. Unfortunately, the stigmatization of people with mental disorders is still quite common (Thornicroft & others, 2009) and has actually increased recently (Pescosolido & others, 2010). Such stigma has two very unfortunate and unnecessary consequences (Corrigan, 2004; Hinshaw & Stier, 2008).

1. Stigma may make mental health problems worse. If friends and family members shun the person who has developed fears or depression, they will be stressed by the rejection and lose valuable social support. This can easily make their emotional problems worse.

2. Stigma may prevent persons with mental health problems from seeking help. Imagine that you go to a doctor's office for a first appointment. The person at the desk who checks you in turns out to be a friend from high school. Would you be embarrassed if the doctor was a physician specializing in sports medicine? What if the doctor was a psychologist or psychiatrist specializing in anxiety—how would you feel then? Most of us would be embarrassed. Unfortunately, that stigma keeps millions of us from seeking needed mental health care (Corrigan, 2004).

Why do we stigmatize abnormal behavior? Partly it is our unwillingness to let others see us as flawed (Corrigan, 2004). Many experts believe that we are embarrassed asking for help with our emotions because of our history of viewing mental "illness" as fundamentally different (discontinuous) from mental "health." If we continue to think that some people have "healthy" minds and others have "sick" minds, we will never be able to deal sensibly with abnormal behavior.

How can we fight this stigma? The continuity hypothesis of mental health problems provides a more constructive viewpoint. It is much easier to seek help if we think that people's emotions often just get out of hand than if we think we may have become "mentally ill" or "lost our mind." One of the best solutions for stigma is education. When we learn that mental health problems are extremely common, that many people that we respect have them, and that many common beliefs about mental health problems are incorrect (Corrigan, 2004), we can more easily view mental health problems simply as problems in living life that could benefit from professional help. This will require changes in social policy, portrayals in the media, and practices by mental health professionals (Hinshaw & Stier, 2008).

The Concept of Insanity

insanity A legal definition concerning a person's inability to tell right from wrong, ability to understand the trial proceedings, or whether the person is a direct danger to self or others.

Now that we have closely examined the term *abnormal behavior,* let's turn to the concept of **insanity.** What does it mean to be insane? It is important to understand that *insanity* is not a psychological term but a legal term that refers to rare and unusual conditions. Insanity has three different legal meanings, depending on the circumstances:

1. *Not guilty by reason of insanity.* In many states, individuals cannot be convicted of a crime if they were legally "insane" at the time the crime was committed. The most influential definition of insanity was proposed by the American Law Institute in the 1970s. It states: "A person is not responsible for criminal conduct if at the time of such conduct, as a result of mental disease or defect, he lacks substantial capacity either to appreciate the wrongfulness of his conduct or to conform his conduct to the requirements of the law." This definition means that people committing crimes are considered "not guilty by reason of insanity" if they could not tell right from wrong or could not control their actions at the time of the crime because of serious psychological problems. Generally, juries will consider only persons with severe psychotic or severe mental retardation to be insane. Because individuals with these problems rarely commit crimes, it's rarely a successful legal defense.

Juries in a number of states can now find defendants "guilty but mentally ill." In this case, the person receives a prison sentence but is also given mental health treatment.

2. *Competence to stand trial.* The term *insanity* is also used in hearings to determine whether the individuals are competent to stand trial. In this sense, the question is whether the persons are able to understand the proceedings of the trial sufficiently to aid in their own defense. Again, it's primarily persons with severe psychosis and mental retardation who are considered incompetent in this sense.

3. *Involuntary commitment.* A third meaning of the term *insanity* arises in hearings on the involuntary commitment of individuals to mental institutions. It's legal in most states to commit people to an institution against their will if a court finds them to be insane. The courts generally interpret this as meaning that the individuals are a direct danger—usually meaning a physical danger—to themselves or to others.

John Hinckley, Jr., was found not guilty (by reason of insanity) of his attempted assassination of President Ronald Reagan.

Review

Actions, thoughts, and feelings that are harmful to the individual or to others are considered to be abnormal. This definition is complicated by the subjectivity involved. How severe must an individual's problem be before he or she is considered harmful? And by whose cultural standards should harmfulness be defined? Moreover, psychologists have not been able to agree on how abnormal behavior differs from normal psychological problems. Is abnormal behavior just a more severe version of normal problems, or is it fundamentally different? Advocates of the continuity hypothesis take the former view, whereas advocates of the discontinuity hypothesis take the latter view.

Differences in perspectives among contemporary psychologists seem minor, however, when compared with the differing views of abnormal behavior throughout history. Abnormal behavior has been thought to result from supernatural causes or from biological abnormalities, as well as from psychological causes. The supernatural theory is of little importance in today's psychology, but the biological and psychological perspectives have largely merged today.

Abnormal behavior is not rare, and it is associated with enormous suffering and economic costs. Although much has been learned about abnormal behavior, misunderstandings and prejudice still stigmatize it. This can complicate mental disorders and discourage people from seeking necessary help.

In legal terms, persons are considered to be insane if they lack the capacity to deal with the demands of life in significant ways, either to avoid danger to themselves or others, to understand the difference between right and wrong and to behave accordingly, or to safeguard themselves or others. Legal decisions concerning insanity are made in the context of trials (Is a person not guilty by reason of insanity? Is a person competent to stand trial?) and in hearings concerning involuntary commitment to mental institutions.

Check Your Learning

To be sure that you have learned the key points from the preceding section, cover the list of correct answers and try to answer each question. If you give an incorrect answer to any question, return to the page given next to the correct answer to see why your answer was not correct. Remember that these questions cover only some of the important information in this section; it is important that you make up your own questions to check your learning of other facts and concepts.

1. _____ is defined as those actions, thoughts, and feelings that are harmful to the person or to others.

2. The discovery that paresis developed from syphilis gave support to the theories of _____ abnormal behavior.

   a) supernatural   c) psychological

   b) biological   d) cognitive

3. The writings by Sigmund Freud helped popularize _____ theories.

   a) supernatural   c) psychological

   b) biological   d) cognitive

4. Research supports the view that both biological factors and psychological factors are involved in the origins of many psychological disorders.

   a) true   b) false

Thinking Critically about Psychology

There are no right or wrong answers to the following questions. They are presented to help you become an active reader and think critically about what you have just read.

1. How could biological and psychological theories of abnormal behavior both be correct?

2. Do you think smoking cigarettes should be considered to be abnormal? How might psychologists who hold either the continuity hypothesis or discontinuity hypothesis differ on this question?

Anxiety Disorders

anxiety disorders Psychological disorders that involve excessive levels of negative emotions, such as nervousness, tension, worry, fright, and anxiety.

phobia An intense, irrational fear.

specific phobia A phobic fear of one relatively specific thing.

social phobia A phobic fear of social interactions, particularly those with strangers and those in which the person might be viewed negatively.

agoraphobia (ag˝o-rah-fō´bē-ah) An intense fear of leaving one's home or other familiar places.

Life is a mixture of positive and negative emotions for everyone. But many people experience high levels of the negative emotions that we identify as being *nervous, tense, worried, scared,* and *anxious.* These terms all refer to anxiety. During any 12-month period, 18% of Americans experience enough distressing and impairing anxiety that they are said to have an **anxiety disorder** (Kessler, Chiu, & others, 2005). Indeed, 29% of Americans will experience an anxiety disorder at some time in their life, more women than men (Kessler, Berglund, & others, 2005). The kinds of anxiety disorders vary considerably, but all share heightened reactivity to anxiety-provoking events and increased vigilance (scanning and monitoring) for those events (Mineka & Zinbarg, 2006).

Phobias

A **phobia** is an intense, unrealistic fear. In this case, the anxiety is focused on some object or situation that the individual will often go to great pains to avoid. There are three types of phobias: (a) *specific phobia,* (b) *social phobia,* and (c) *agoraphobia.* In most cases, the individual realizes that his or her phobia is irrational but usually cannot control his fear.

Specific phobia is the most common phobia. Examples include intense fears of heights, dogs, blood, hypodermic injections, and being in closed spaces (Ost, 1992). Individuals with specific phobias often have no other psychological problems, and their lives are disrupted only if the phobia creates a direct problem in daily living. For example, a fear of elevators would be highly disruptive for a person who works in a skyscraper, but it might not be for a vegetable farmer.

The term **social phobia** refers to extreme anxiety in social interactions, particularly those with strangers and those in which the person might be scrutinized and evaluated negatively. Job interviews, public speaking, and first dates are extremely uncomfortable for individuals with social phobia (Stein, Torgrud, & Walker, 2000). Persons with social phobia usually have unrealistically negative views of their social skills (Hirsch & Clark, 2004). Because social phobia hampers, or even limits, social interactions, it can seriously disrupt the individual's social and occupational life.

Agoraphobia literally means "fear of open spaces." Agoraphobia involves an intense fear of leaving one's home or other familiar places. In extreme cases, the person with agoraphobia can be totally homebound, finding even a trip to the mailbox an almost intolerable experience. Other agoraphobic individuals are able to travel freely in their neighborhood but cannot venture beyond it. A 30-year-old German man recounts his experience with agoraphobia in the following passage.

This child's fear of animals may be serious enough to be considered a specific phobia, but only if it causes problems in his life.

> The brief trips to Bonn filled me with a surging sense of the impossible and the far . . . a feeling, especially as to distance, that could convert a half mile, or even five blocks from home, in terms of subjective need and cowardice, into an infinity of remoteness. . . . I start a little walk down the street about a hundred feet from the house, I am compelled to rush back, in horror of being so far away . . . a hundred feet away . . . from home and security. I have never walked or ridden, alone or with others, as a normal man, since that day. . . . (Leonard, 1928, pp. 238, 278)

Generalized and Panic Anxiety Disorders

generalized anxiety disorder An uneasy sense of general tension and apprehension for no apparent reason that makes the individual highly uncomfortable because of its prolonged presence.

Whereas phobias are linked to specific stimulus situations, the other anxiety disorders involve anxiety that is less dependent on environmental triggers. Individuals with **generalized anxiety disorder** experience a vague, uneasy sense of tension and apprehension, sometimes referred to as *free-floating anxiety.* Generalized anxiety makes the individual highly uncomfortable because of its long duration. The person with generalized anxiety disorder does experience periods of calm, but they can be few and far between.

In contrast, the individual with **panic anxiety disorder** is seized by sharp, intensely uncomfortable attacks of anxiety that are not tied to a specific situation. Respiration increases and sudden rapid heartbeats can be felt pounding with such intensity that the individual often feels that he or she is having a heart attack or is going crazy. About 5% of the population experience panic attacks that are frequent and severe enough to qualify as panic disorder at some point in their lifetime, with rates being higher in females (Kessler, Berglund, & others, 2005), but a surprisingly high percentage of adults experience occasional attacks of panic. In fact, approximately 28% of adults have had a panic attack at some point in their life, most of whom do not have panic anxiety disorder (Kessler, Tat Chiu, & others, 2006). It is important to know that such uncomfortable events are relatively common and that they should not be a source of serious concern unless they are severe or frequent enough to disrupt the individual's functioning or well-being.

Persons with panic anxiety disorders are extremely sensitive to small changes in the functioning of their autonomic nervous system, especially their heart rate (Schmidt, Lerew, & Trakowski, 1997), and small changes in the level of carbon dioxide in their blood (Bellodi & others, 1998; Gorman & others, 2001). More important, they interpret these minor normal fluctuations in "catastrophic" ways. That is, their attacks of anxiety are exaggerated reactions to normal body stimuli that most persons ignore.

Persons who develop panic disorder first experience spontaneous panic attacks. Current theory suggests that these are nonspecific responses to stress, but some individuals come to experience repeated panic attacks because of classical conditioning (Bouton, Mineka, & Barlow, 2001; Roy-Byrne, Craske, & Stein, 2006). Typically, the conditioned stimulus is a stimulus from within the body that is part of the panic attack, such as increased heart rate or shortness of breath. According to this theory, when the internal stimulus is experienced again in another context, the individual will be more likely to respond with a full-blown panic attack because of classical conditioning.

The fact that panic attacks involve a sudden and intense increase in sympathetic autonomic arousal was demonstrated by British psychiatrist Michael Lader (Lader & Mathews, 1970). While he was studying the autonomic activity of a woman who was prone to panic attacks, she spontaneously experienced an attack in his laboratory. Figure 14.1 graphically shows the sudden changes in three measures of autonomic arousal that took place during the panic attack.

The case of Richard Benson further illustrates the experience of panic anxiety disorder:

> Richard Benson, age 38, applied to a psychiatrist for therapy because he was suffering from severe and overwhelming anxiety which sometimes escalated to a panic attack. . . . During the times when he was experiencing intense anxiety, it often seemed as if he were having a heart seizure. He experienced chest pains and heart palpitations, numbness, shortness of breath, and he felt a strong need to breathe in air. He reported that in the midst of the anxiety attack, he developed a feeling of tightness over his eyes and he could only see objects directly in front of him (tunnel vision). He further stated that he feared that he would not be able to swallow. (Leon, 1977, p. 113)

panic anxiety disorder A pattern of anxiety in which long periods of calm are broken by an intensely uncomfortable attack of anxiety.

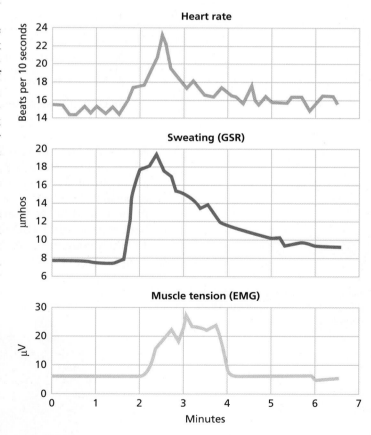

Figure 14.1

Changes in three measures of sympathetic autonomic arousal that occurred when an individual experienced a panic attack while being studied in a laboratory.

Source: Data from M. Lader and A. Mathews, "Changes in Autonomic Arousal in a Woman Undergoing a Spontaneous Panic Attack," *Journal of Psychosomatic Research,* 14:377–382. Copyright 1970, Pergamon Press, Ltd.

Post-Traumatic Stress Disorder

Once begun, wars are never over for those who fight them. World War II ended 60 years ago, the last soldiers returned from Vietnam more than 25 years ago, and many U.S. soldiers are home from tours of duty in Afghanistan and Iraq. Still, hundreds of thousands of veterans continue to fight the psychological aftereffects of these. Their continuing agony has been given the unwieldy name of **post-traumatic stress disorder (PTSD).** In simple terms, they are still suffering severe stress reactions years after the traumatic stress of combat ended. Many persons who experience PTSD recover from it, but for many others it is chronic (Axelrod & others, 2005; Benotsch & others, 2000) and leads to serious problems, such as increased risk for alcohol problems (Thomas & others, 2010) and suicide (Wilcox, Storr, & Breslau, 2009). Indeed, nearly one-third of the men who were prisoners of war of the Japanese during World War II still experience PTSD (Engdahl & others, 1997). Similarly, many Jewish survivors of Nazi concentration camps in World War II still suffer from PTSD (Kuch & Cox, 1992; Yehuda & others, 1995).

PTSD in persons who experienced highly stressful events is defined as following:

1. Recollections of the stressful event that intrude into their waking consciousness and fill their dreams with horror. At times, the person feels and acts as if the stressful event was happening again.

2. Intense emotional and autonomic reactions to stimuli that remind them of the event.

3. An avoidance of stimuli associated with the event.

4. Feeling numbed to the ordinary emotions and pleasures of life.

5. Difficulty sleeping, hyperarousal, irritability, and difficulty concentrating.

Stressors That Cause PTSD. Our understanding of PTSD initially grew out of the efforts of the Veteran's Administration to assist veterans coping with the emotional aftermath of war. Psychologists soon realized, however, that PTSD is not limited to persons who have experienced war. A large national study of 8,000 adults living in the United States found that 5% of all adult males and 10% of all adult females have experienced PTSD for at least a month during their lifetimes (Kessler & others, 1995). Among men, combat-related stress is the most common cause of PTSD, but even for men, PTSD is more often the result of other kinds of traumatic stress, such

Many Iraq War veterans suffer serious symptoms of post-traumatic stress disorder.

as being physically assaulted, being in an automobile accident, or witnessing violence and disasters (Andrews & others, 2000; Breslau & others, 1998; Kassam-Adams & Winston, 2004; O'Donnell & others, 2004). Among women, physical assault, rape and sexual molestation, and the witnessing of violence are the leading causes of PTSD (Breslau & others, 1997; Kessler & others, 1995). The type and amount of stress encountered in everyday life depends in part on our living circumstances. Residents along the Atlantic Coast are more likely to experience hurricanes, residents of California are more likely to experience earthquakes, and residents of inner cities are more likely to be assaulted, to be raped, or to witness violence (Breslau & others, 1997).

Terrorism and PTSD. People in many countries around the world have long been victimized by terrorism, and terrorism came to the United States with the bombing of the Oklahoma Federal Building in 1995 and the destruction of the World Trade Center on September 11, 2001. Unfortunately, some of the survivors of these events suffer PTSD (Verger & others, 2004). In addition, firefighters, police officers, and other disaster workers who witnessed the devastation firsthand are also subject to PTSD (Fullerton & others, 2004).

Who Develops PTSD? The good news is that most persons who experience traumatic stress do not develop PTSD. Indeed, nearly half of North American adults will experience at least one traumatic event in their lives, but less than 10% will develop PTSD. What determines who develops PTSD following stress? At least four factors are involved (Mineka & Zinbarg, 2006):

1. *Severity of stress.* The percent of traumatized persons who develop PTSD depends in part on the type and severity of stress. Soldiers who are directly exposed to combat or atrocities are more likely to experience PTSD than soldiers exposed to less stressful combat (Grieger & others, 2006). And exposure to more severe physical trauma, such as torture, greatly increases the risk for PTSD (Steel & others, 2009). Yet, it is important to note that even exposure to events considered to be low-magnitude stressors can lead to PTSD (Copeland & others, 2010).

2. *Characteristics of the person before the traumatic event.* When the level of exposure to combat was controlled statistically, soldiers with lower intelligence and more previous mental health problems are more likely to experience PTSD (Macklin & others, 1998). Similarly, civilians with higher levels of anxiety before the stress (Breslau & others, 1997, 1998; Kessler & others, 1995) or exposure to previous trauma (Copeland and others, 2010) are more likely to experience PTSD. Recent research also suggests genetic predispositions make some individuals more susceptible to trauma (Kilpatrick & others, 2007).

3. *Social support.* Persons with greater social support after traumatic stress are less likely to experience PTSD (Brewin, Andrews, & Valentine, 2000; Kilpatrick & others, 2007). This is particularly important, given that PTSD does not always develop immediately following exposure to traumatic events, such as combat (Grieger & others, 2006; Thomas & others, 2010).

4. *Sex of the victim.* Although most women and men are resilient in the face of stress, women who experience

Firefighters and police officers who help others during devastating events such as terrorist attacks sometimes later experience post-traumatic stress disorder.

traumatic events are more likely than men to develop PTSD (Olff & others, 2007). This may partly reflect differences in the types of stress experienced by women and men. A U.S. national study found that 75% of women who have been raped experience PTSD for at least six months (Kessler & others, 1995). However, there is some evidence that women are more likely to develop PTSD even when the type of stress is the same (Breslau & others, 1997, 1998).

The negative emotional consequences of traumatic stress are absolutely undeniable. It is important, however, also to note the findings of research on resilience following trauma. Most victims of trauma do not develop PTSD. And, psychologist Patricia Frazier and others (2004) have found that half of women who have experienced sexual assault report positive life changes after their trauma. These include improved relationships with others, a greater sense of purpose in life, and greater empathy for others. It is essential that we do everything we can to prevent rape, terrorism, automobile accidents, and other sources of trauma, of course. It is important, however, not to assume that all victims of trauma are psychologically damaged by it.

Obsessive-Compulsive Disorders

obsessive-compulsive disorders
Disorders that involve obsessions (anxiety-provoking thoughts that will not go away) and/or compulsions (irresistible urges to engage in specific irrational behaviors).

Also classified with anxiety disorders are the **obsessive-compulsive disorders.** Obsessions and compulsions are two separate problems, but they often occur together in the same individuals (Torres & others, 2006). *Obsessions* are anxiety-provoking thoughts that will not go away. They seem uncontrollable and even alien, as if they do not belong to the individual's mind. Thoughts such as a recurrent fear of losing control and killing someone or of having an incestuous sexual relationship can cause extreme anxiety.

Compulsions are irresistible urges to engage in behaviors such as repeatedly touching a spot on one's shoulder, washing one's hands, or checking the locks on doors. If the individual tries to stop engaging in the behavior, she or he experiences an urgent anxiety until the behavior is resumed. Obsessions and compulsions are often found in the same person, such as the person who compulsively washes his hands because he is obsessed with thoughts about germs. Most people with obsessive-complusive disorders experience both obsessions and compulsions (Fullana & others, 2009). It is important to note that roughly 21% of adults experience a compulsion or obsession by the age of 32. But, only 2% of people have obsessive-compulsive disorders (Fullana & others, 2009).

Somatoform Disorders

somatoform disorders
(sōma´to-form) Disorders in which the individual experiences the symptoms of physical health problems that have psychological rather than physical causes.

Somatoform disorders are conditions in which the individual experiences the symptoms of physical health problems that have psychological rather than physical causes. *Soma* is the Latin word for body—hence, somatoform disorders are thought to be disorders in which psychological problems "take the form" of physical problems. Although these symptoms of health problems are not physically caused, they are very real and uncomfortable to the individual (Witthoft & Hiller, 2010). In other words, they are not faked. Somatoform disorders are more prevalent in people who report that they were sexually abused (Paras & others, 2009), which could mean that the disorders may be a psychological reaction to trauma. There are four types of somatoform disorders: *somatization disorders, hypochondriasis, conversion disorders,* and *somatoform pain disorders.* Because of similarities among them, we will discuss these four disorders in pairs.

Somatization Disorders and Hypochondriasis

Somatization disorders take the form of chronic and recurrent aches, pains, tiredness, and other symptoms of somatic (body) illness in the absence of a known medical cause. Individuals with somatization problems also typically experience other psychological difficulties, particularly anxiety and depression. The greatest concern related to somatization disorders concerns the measures that affected individuals take to find relief from their discomfort (Witthoft & Hiller, 2010). Many become addicted to alcohol or tranquilizers and often take medications prescribed by many different physicians, whom they are seeing simultaneously (without telling the other physicians), thus increasing the risk of dangerous chemical interactions among the drugs. Worse still, because of their frequent complaints to physicians, many receive expensive medical assessments and eventually are the recipients of unnecessary medical procedures, including surgeries (Barsky, Orav, & Bates, 2005).

Hypochondriasis can be thought of as a milder form of somatization disorder with some special features of its own. People with hypochondriasis experience somatic symptoms, but they are not as pervasive or as intense as in somatization disorders. Their lives can be dominated by their concerns about their health, however. They show a preoccupation with health, overreact with concern to minor coughs and pains, and go to unreasonable lengths to avoid germs and cancer-causing agents (Witthoft & Hiller, 2010).

"He was a dreadful hypochondriac."

© Punch/Rothco.

somatization disorders
(sō´´mah-ti-zā´shun) Intensely and chronically uncomfortable psychological conditions that involve numerous symptoms of somatic (body) illnesses without physical cause.

hypochondriasis (hī´pō-kon-drī´ ah-sis) A mild form of somatization disorder characterized by excessive concern about one's health.

Conversion Disorders and Somatoform Pain Disorders

Conversion disorders are the most dramatic but rarest of the somatoform disorders. The name comes from the Freudian theory that anxiety has been "converted" into serious somatic symptoms in this condition rather than being directly experienced as anxiety. Individuals with this problem experience functional blindness, deafness, paralysis, fainting, seizures, inability to speak, or other serious impairments in the absence of any physical cause. In addition, these individuals appear to be generally ineffective and dependent on others. These symptoms understandably impair the individuals' lives. Conversion disorders can usually be distinguished easily from medical problems. For example, in conversion disorders the areas of paralysis and loss of sensation are not shaped in the way they would be if there were actual nerve damage (see figure 14.2). Similarly, people with conversion paralysis of the legs can be observed to move their legs normally when sleeping.

Perhaps the most interesting characteristic of conversion disorders is known as *la belle indifference,* "beautiful indifference." Individuals with conversion disorders often are not upset by their condition. The individual with conversion disorders who wakes up paralyzed one morning may show some emotional response, but not nearly to the extent that a person who is physically paralyzed

conversion disorders Somatoform disorders in which individuals experience serious somatic symptoms such as functional blindness, deafness, and paralysis.

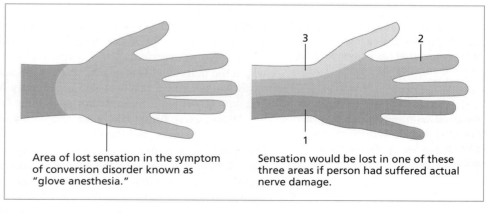

Area of lost sensation in the symptom of conversion disorder known as "glove anesthesia."

Sensation would be lost in one of these three areas if person had suffered actual nerve damage.

Figure 14.2
Because of the pattern in which the sensory nerves serve the skin surface, it would only be medically possible to experience anesthesia within any of the shaded areas shown on the hand on the right. Typical conversion anesthesias do not conform to these patterns, however.

would—for example, in an automobile accident. Some psychologists believe that the conversion symptoms are welcome, in a sense, as they get these people out of responsibilities or force others to take care of them.

Somatoform pain disorders are very similar to conversion disorders, except that the primary symptom is *pain* that has no physical cause. Sometimes somatoform pain can be distinguished from physically caused pain because it does not follow nerve pathways. But in the case of low back pain, joint pains, and chest pains, a diagnosis of somatoform pain disorder can be made only after all possible physical causes have been carefully ruled out. Like conversion disorders, somatoform pain usually occurs at times of high stress and may be beneficial to the individual in some way.

Dissociative Disorders

Dissociative disorders cover a broad category of loosely related rare conditions involving sudden alterations in cognition. The various types of dissociative disorders are characterized by a change in memory, perception, or "identity." These experiences are most common under intense stress (Morgan & others, 2001). There are four kinds of dissociative disorders: *depersonalization, dissociative amnesia, dissociative fugue,* and *dissociative identity disorder.*

Depersonalization

The term **depersonalization** refers to experiences in which the individual feels that he or she has become distorted or "unreal," or that distortions have occurred in one's surroundings. The individual might feel that his hands have become enlarged or out of control. Or the individual might feel like a robot—even though she knows she is a real person—or that her parents are not real people. The individual knows that these feelings are not accurate, although they have an eerie reality to them. One of the more common experiences of depersonalization is the sense of leaving one's body and being able to look back at it from the ceiling. Isolated experiences of depersonalization are rather common, especially in young adults. Unless they are recurrent and cause distress or other problems, these unsettling experiences are not considered abnormal.

Dissociative Amnesia and Fugue

Dissociative amnesia is a kind of memory loss that is psychologically caused. It most often occurs after a period of intense stress and involves loss of memory for all or part of the stressful experience itself, such as loss of memory for an automobile accident in which the individual was responsible for the death of another person. Individuals who suffer amnesia as a result of stress generally have no other psychological problems and typically recover their memories in time.

Dissociative fugue states are rare conditions that resemble amnesia in that there is a loss of memory, but the loss is so complete that the individual cannot remember his or her identity or previous life. The fugue episode also can include a period of "wandering" that may take the individual around the corner or across the continent. In many instances, the individual takes on a new "personality" during the fugue episode, usually one that is more sociable, more fun-loving, and less conventional than the previous one. Generally these changes are transient. Consider the following case:

> When Mrs. Y. was brought to the hospital by her husband, she was dazed, confused, and weeping. Apparently aware of her surroundings and able to answer brief questions in filling out the admitting form, she could not, at the time, discuss any of her problems with the admitting physician. Her husband reported that she had left their

---

somatoform pain disorders (sō-ma´to-form) Somatoform disorders in which the individual experiences a relatively specific and chronic pain that has a psychological rather than a physical cause.

dissociative disorders (dis-sō´sē-a-tiv) A category of conditions involving sudden cognitive changes, such as a sudden loss of memory or loss of one's identity.

depersonalization (de-per´sun-al-i-zā´shun) The perceptual experience of one's body or surroundings becoming distorted or unreal in some way.

dissociative amnesia A dissociative disorder that involves a loss of memory and that has a psychological rather than a physical cause.

dissociative fugue states (fūg) A period of "wandering" that involves a loss of memory and a change in identity.

home two weeks previously while he was at work. All the efforts of her husband and the police to trace her had failed until approximately 24 hours prior to her admission to the hospital, when Mr. Y. received a report that a woman of her description had been arrested in a nearby city. When he arrived and identified her, she did not at first recognize him, did not know her own name, and could not remember what had happened to her or anything about her past. The police informed Mr. Y. that she had been arrested for "resorting" after a motel owner had called the police to complain that several different men had visited the motel room she had rented three days before in the company of a sailor. Mrs. Y. seemed unable to remember any of these alleged events. Gradually she came to recognize her husband as he talked anxiously with her whereupon she began to weep and requested to be brought home. (Goldstein & Palmer, 1963, pp. 71–72)*

---

*From *The Experience of Anxiety: A Casebook, Expanded Edition,* by Michael J. Goldstein and James O. Palmer. Copyright 1975 by Michael J. Goldstein and James O. Palmer. Reprinted by permission of Oxford University Press, Inc.

As will be obvious in the next section, dissociative fugue is quite similar to dissociative identity disorder. For that reason, all of the controversy surrounding that diagnosis applies to dissociative fugue.

Dissociative Identity Disorder (Multiple Personality)

Individuals who exhibit **dissociative identity disorder** (formerly known as *multiple personality*) appear to shift abruptly from one "personality" to another—as if more than one person were inhabiting the same body. Generally, the two or more personalities are quite different from one another. The individual's original personality is often conventional, moralistic, and unhappy, whereas the alternative personalities tend to be quite the opposite. At least one other personality is usually sensual, uninhibited, and rebellious. In most cases, the individual reports that he or she is not aware of the other personalities when they are "in" their original personality but say that the alternative personalities "know about" their rival personalities and are often antagonistic toward the original one.

dissociative identity disorder
A dissociative disorder in which the individual appears to shift abruptly and repeatedly from one "personality" to another.

In 1977, Chris Sizemore published an autobiography revealing that she was the case of dissociative identity disorder made famous in the 1950s movie *The Three Faces of Eve.* Initially, she appeared to manifest two distinctly different personalities, referred to in the movie as Eve White and Eve Black. Eve White was depressive, anxious, conventional, and inhibited, whereas Eve Black was seductive, uninhibited, and wild. In her autobiography, Chris Sizemore reveals that she eventually went through 22 separate personalities but that in recent years she feels she has a single, well-adjusted personality. A similar pattern was reported for the case of "Sybil," a woman who believed that she had developed 16 personalities over the course of 42 years (Schreiber, 1973).

Dissociative identity disorder is a very controversial disorder. Although there is little doubt that some people *behave* as if they have multiple personalities, there is great deal of debate about *why* they behave this way. Some mental health experts believe that dissociative identity disorder is an effort to cope with painful memories from physical or sexual abuse during childhood (Gleaves, 1996). Other psychologists believe that dissociative identity disorder is the result of social learning (Lilienfeld & others, 1999). Sometimes, highly suggestible persons are exposed, through books or movies, to persons who are models of "multiple personalities." If they imitate these models and begin to act as if they have more than one personality, they may behave in previously unacceptable ways that are reinforced (brash, rule-breaking, or promiscuous behavior), but attribute the new behavior to "another personality" rather than

Chris Sizemore, the woman who was the subject of the book and film *The Three Faces of Eve.* Ms. Sizemore reported that she exhibited a total of 22 distinct personalities before achieving her final, permanent personality.

accepting responsibility for the actions. Thus, in the social learning view, multiple personalities are no more than unconscious enactments of roles.

In most cases, however, social learning theorists believe that so-called multiple personalities are inadvertently taught to patients by their psychotherapists (Lilienfeld & others, 1999). This surprising assertion may seem far-fetched at first, but it simply means that when some well-intentioned therapists begin to notice that the patient sometimes acts in ways that are inconsistent with his or her usual behavior, they may suggest to the patient that he or she has one or more "hidden personalities." A patient who is highly suggestible may accept this idea and begin to act more and more as if he or she has multiple personalities. Lilienfeld and colleagues (1999) cite evidence that most people with dissociative identity did not believe that they had multiple personalities until they began seeing a therapist who raised this possibility. Thus, therapists who look for hints of dissociative identity disorder in their patients may unwittingly teach their patients to have dissociative identity disorder.

Review

Anxiety disorders are common problems characterized by anxiety that may be experienced as low and relatively constant levels of generalized anxiety, as sharp and intense attacks of anxiety, or as focalized phobias of various sorts, or that may be linked to obsessive thoughts or compulsive actions.

In somatoform disorders, the individual experiences the symptoms of medical conditions that have psychological rather than physical causes. In some types of somatoform disorders, the symptoms are dramatic and clear-cut, such as blindness and paralysis. In other cases, the individual experiences multiple aches, pains, and maladies or is just excessively concerned with health.

Dissociative disorders are rare psychological problems involving sudden alterations in cognition. These may take the form of memory loss, changes of identity, or feelings of unreality. In rare cases, the alteration of identity is so dramatic that the individual appears to possess more than a single personality. Social learning theorists have raised concerns that dissociative disorders may often be created by the actions of well-intentioned therapists with their highly suggestible patients.

Check Your Learning

To be sure that you have learned the key points from the preceding section, cover the list of correct answers and try to answer each question. If you give an incorrect answer to any question, return to the page given next to the correct answer to see why your answer was not correct.

1. Psychological disorders that involve excessive levels of nervousness, tension, worry, fright, and anxiety are termed _____ disorders.

   a) mood

   b) somatoform

   c) behavior

   d) anxiety

2. Individuals with _____ experience a vague, uneasy sense of tension and apprehension, sometimes referred to as free-floating anxiety, that makes the individual uncomfortable because of its prolonged presence.

   a) panic disorder

   b) dissociative identity disorder

   c) generalized anxiety disorder

   d) agoraphobia

3. _____ are conditions in which the individual experiences the symptoms of physical health problems that have psychological rather than physical causes.

   a) Anxiety disorders

   b) Dissociative disorders

   c) Somatoform disorders

   d) Social phobias

4. _____ disorders are a category of conditions involving sudden cognitive changes, such as a change in memory, perception, or identity.

   a) Panic

   c) Obsessive-compulsive

   b) Conversion

   d) Dissociative

There are no right or wrong answers to the following questions. They are presented to help you become an active reader and think critically about what you have just read.

1. How would a social learning theorist account for a phobic fear of snakes? How might a psychoanalyst account for the same phobia?

2. Our news media seem to highlight cases of dissociative identity disorder even though they are very rare. What role do you think the media play in our society's understanding of abnormal behavior?

Correct Answers: 1. d (p. 466), 2. c (p. 466), 3. c (p. 470), 4. d (p. 472)

Mood Disorders

There are two primary forms of **mood disorders,** depression and mania. Depression can occur alone (a condition known as *major depression*), but mania usually alternates with periods of depression (*bipolar disorder*). Both conditions can produce great misery for the individual.

mood disorders Psychological disorders involving depression and/or abnormal elation.

Major Depression

The individual experiencing **major depression** is deeply unhappy and finds little pleasure in life, but major depression is more than just intense sadness. The person with major depression believes that the future is bleak, holds a negative opinion of self and others, and often sees no reason to live. This is accompanied by at least some of the following: increased or decreased sleep, increased or decreased appetite, loss of interest in sex, loss of energy or excessive energy, and difficulties concentrating and making decisions. Persons who are depressed also often think about death and are far more likely than persons who are not depressed to engage in self-injury, such as cutting one's skin (Nock, 2010), and to commit suicide (Oquendo & others, 2001, 2007).

About 7% of people in the United States experience major depression during any 12-month period, which is more than 13 million persons (Scott & Dicky, 2003; Kessler, Chiu, & others, 2005). In total, 17% of Americans will experience major depression at some time during their lives (Kessler, Berglund, & others, 2005). Worldwide, as many as 100 million persons experience major depression (Scott & Dickey, 2003). Because major depression is common, costly to treat, and causes a considerable loss of productive work, the World Health Organization views it as the most costly of all physical and mental disorders (Scott & Dickey, 2003). Health economists estimated that the financial burden of depression was over $83 billion dollars in 2000 alone (Greenberg & others, 2003)! Unfortunately, there is evidence that rates of depression are increasing (Compton & others, 2006).

As shown in figure 14.3, the probability that an individual will develop major depression for the first time is very low until puberty, rises until a peak is reached between 45 and 55 years of age, then declines again in old age. Overall, the risk for major depression is twice as high for women than for men, particularly during middle age (Kessler, Merikangas, & Wang, 2007; Scott & Dickey, 2003).

major depression An affective disorder characterized by episodes of deep unhappiness, loss of interest in life, and other symptoms.

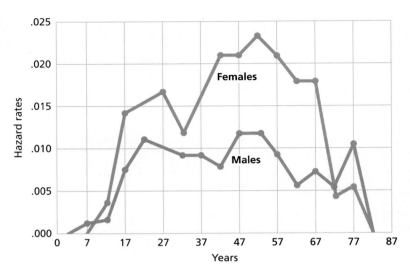

Figure 14.3

The probability that an individual will develop major depression for the first time during a given year of life changes over the life span.

Source: Data from P. M. Lewinsohn, et al., "Age at First Onset for Nonbipolar Depression," *Journal of Abnormal Psychology, 95*:378–383, 1986. Copyright 1986 by the American Psychological Association.

Fortunately, major depression is usually an *episodic* disorder. This means that, in 80% of cases, the individual experiences the symptoms for a period of time and then recovers, often returning to her or his normal self (Grilo & others, 2005). The duration of episodes varies widely, but half of all persons with major depression recover in 12 weeks from the beginning of the depressive episode (Eaton & others, 1997; Solomon & others, 1997; Spijker & others, 2002). About one-third of all individuals who experience an episode of major depression will experience only one episode, but others will be depressed— sometimes repeatedly—during their lifetimes if not properly treated (Scott & Dickey, 2003). In these cases, the depression comes in recurrent episodes, which last from several weeks to many months, followed by periods of relatively normal mood (Scott & Dickey, 2003).

In rare but important cases, major depression is accompanied by bizarre beliefs and perceptions that represent a psychotic distortion of reality. The following excerpt describes a case of severe depression that required the individual to be hospitalized.

At 51 the patient suffered from a depression and was obliged to resign his position. This depression continued for about 9 months, after which he apparently fully recovered. He resumed his work but after 2 years suffered from a second depression. Again he recovered after several months and returned to a similar position and held it until 2 months before his admission. At this time he began to worry lest he was not doing his work well, talked much of his lack of fitness for his duties, and finally resigned. He spent Thanksgiving Day at his son's in a neighboring city, but while there he was sure that the water pipes in his own house would freeze during his absence and that he and his family would be "turned out into the street." A few days later he was found standing by a pond, evidently contemplating suicide. He soon began to remain in bed and sometimes wrapped his head in the bed clothing to shut out the external world. (Kolb, 1977, p. 455)*

---

*From L. C. Kolb, *Modern Clinical Psychiatry,* 9th ed. Copyright 1977. Used by permission of the author.

Causes of Major Depression. The risk for major depression is significantly elevated in persons who have experienced high levels of stress (Lewinsohn, Hoberman, & Rosenbaum, 1988; Mazure, 1998; Steel & others 2009). In particular, events involving loss (of a job or a romantic partner) and personal humiliation are related to episodes of major depression. However, there is also clear evidence that some people are somewhat more vulnerable than others to depression for genetic reasons (Kendler & others, 2006).

Cognitive Factors in Depression. Aaron T. Beck (1976) and others believe that our *cognitions* are an important factor in emotional problems. For example, Beck has suggested that negative views of oneself, the world in which we live, and the future lead some persons to experience life in such negative terms that they develop depression. Much evidence is consistent with this view, particularly Beck's theory that negative views of oneself are a critical component of depression. Many studies (Alloy & others, 1999; Alloy & others, 2006) show that people who believe that they fall far short of being the persons they would like to be or who cope with stress ineffectively are more likely to experience depression. Conversely, having a positive opinion of yourself makes depression less likely following stressful life events (Dozois & Dobson, 2001; Robinson, Garber, & Hilsman, 1995; Stewart & others, 2004).

Thus, our beliefs about ourselves and coping skills make us more or less vulnerable to depression when buffeted by life's inevitable stress (Lewinsohn, Joiner, & Rohde, 2001; Stewart & others, 2004). Interestingly, a classic study by Peter Lewinsohn and his associates (1980) suggests that at least some aspects of the "distorted" cognitions that are characteristic of depressed individuals are not distortions at all. Lewinsohn asked individuals who were experiencing major depression to participate in a group discussion for approximately 20 minutes. During this time, they were rated by a group of judges on their friendliness, assertiveness, warmth, and other social qualities. After the group discussion, each participant also rated himself or herself on the same dimensions. Another group of people who were not depressed went through exactly the same procedure.

As would have been predicted by Beck, the depressed group rated their social skills as being less adequate than did the nondepressed participants. Is this evidence that depressed individuals distort their view of themselves? Actually, it turns out that the self-ratings of the depressed group were *quite accurate* when compared with the ratings of the judges. It was the *normal* participants whose view of themselves was distorted! The nondepressed persons rated themselves as being significantly more socially skilled than the judges did. Furthermore, when the depressed individuals were given treatment and became less depressed, their self-perceptions became more like the normal group: They, too, began to rate themselves in unrealistically positive terms. Perhaps having this kind of "distorted" perception of ourselves is a good thing. Maybe we would all be depressed if we saw ourselves in the realistic terms in which others see us!

When asked to rate their participation after a group discussion, people with major depression give more accurate ratings than do people who aren't depressed. It seems some positive "distortion" of our self-perception can be healthy.

Human Diversity
Ethnic and Gender Differences in Depression and Suicide

Depression afflicts every group of human beings. It is an all-too-common problem for men and women, and it is found in every ethnic group. Likewise, no human group is completely immune to the threat of suicide. There is growing evidence, however, of large differences in rates of depression and suicide between the genders and among ethnic groups. This evidence is inherently important and offers the hope of providing clues to the causes of these disorders.

Maria Oquendo and colleagues (2001, 2007) used data from two epidemiologic studies of some 20,000 adults in the United States to examine gender and ethnic differences in depression and suicide. As previously found in many studies, the likelihood of depression was approximately twice as high in women as in men. In sharp contrast, men were four to five times more likely to commit suicide than women were. Although depressed individuals are far more likely to commit suicide than are individuals who are not depressed (Osby & others, 2001), Oquendo found that depressed women are far less likely to commit suicide than depressed men are. Something about being female generally protects depressed individuals from taking their own lives.

Oquendo and colleagues (2001) also found considerable differences among a number of ethnic groups in the United States in their rates of depression and suicide. As shown in figure 14.4 on p. 478, there are large differences in the percent of deaths each year that are caused by suicide among different race-ethnic **Continued on pg. 478**

Human Diversity

Ethnic and Gender
Differences in
Depression and Suicide

cont'd from pg. 477

Figure 14.4

Percent of deaths due to suicide among different race-ethnic groups living in the United States. National Center for Health Statistics. *National Vital Statistics Report* Vol. 53, Number 7, March 7, 2005.

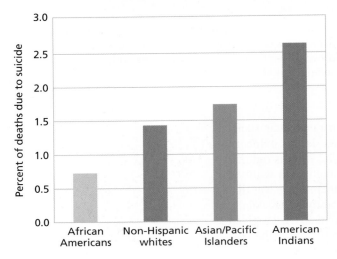

Continued from pg. 477 groups. African Americans are half as likely to die from suicide as are Asian Americans, Pacific Islanders, and Non-Hispanic whites. American Indians have the highest percentage of deaths due to suicide.

An important feature of the study by Oquendo and her colleagues (2001) was that they distinguished among a number of different Hispanic groups. Americans whose ancestry is in Cuba, Mexico, Puerto Rico, and other countries tend to describe themselves in distinct terms. Racially, many Cuban Americans view themselves as white descendants of Spaniards, and many Mexican Americans report that they are a blend of Spanish and native peoples. In cultural terms, too, these groups are quite different from one another.

Oquendo and colleagues (2001) found that among men, Mexican Americans had lower rates of depression than non-Hispanic whites, but Puerto Rican Americans had higher rates of depression than non-Hispanic whites. Among women, Puerto Rican Americans had higher rates of depression than non-Hispanic whites, but there were no other differences among ethnic groups. Among men, non-Hispanic whites had the highest suicide rates, and Mexican Americans had the lowest suicide rates. Among women, non-Hispanic whites had the highest rates of suicide, and Mexican American and Puerto Rican women had the lowest rates.

Finally, Oquendo and colleagues (2001) compared rates of suicide among depressed individuals. When depressed, Mexican Americans and Puerto Rican Americans of both genders had lower rates of suicide than non-Hispanic whites of both genders. In addition, depressed African American women had lower than expected rates of suicide compared to non-Hispanic white women.

What is it about these U.S. ethnic and gender groups that makes their rates of depression and suicide so different? Why are rates of depression higher among Puerto Rican American women and men than other groups in the United States? One important piece of information is that rates of depression among Puerto Ricans living in Puerto Rico are no higher than overall U.S. population rates (Oquendo & others, 2001); the increased risk for depression is found only among Puerto Ricans living in the United States. This could be the result of characteristics of the individuals who migrate to the United States. Perhaps people who are happy in their lives and not prone to depression are less likely to migrate to the United States. Alternatively, the higher rates of depression among Puerto Ricans in the United States could reflect the discrimination and hardship faced by some immigrants.

There are many other questions we might ask as we consider these ethnic and gender differences. Why are depressed white women more likely than the other ethnic groups to commit suicide? Are there cultural factors that protect African American and Hispanic women from taking their lives when depressed? Are there differences in the rates at which depressed women of different cultures turn to drugs and alcohol (see chapter 6 for an overview of alcohol and drug problems)? If so, does this play a role in rates of suicide?

Before the complex relationships among culture, gender, and mental health can be fully understood, however, information is needed on the mental health of Asian Americans and other sizable groups living in the United States that have been understudied. In addition, future studies should take into account the fact that people of western European and African ancestry are not all the same ethnically and may differ in their rates of mental health problems as much as different Hispanic groups. For example, we know little about possible differences in the challenges faced by former slaves living in the United States compared to African Americans who are recent immigrants from Africa or the Caribbean.

Bipolar Disorder

In the condition known as **bipolar disorder** (formerly called *manic-depressive psychosis*), periods of mania usually alternate irregularly with periods of severe depression. **Mania** is a disturbance of mood that can be quite enjoyable to the individual in the short run but is usually damaging both to the person and to others in the long run. During the manic episode, the individual experiences a remarkable "high"—an intense euphoria in which sensory pleasures are heightened, one's self-esteem is very high, thoughts race, little sleep is needed, and unrealistic optimism prevails. Grandiose and financially damaging schemes and buying sprees are common during these periods, as are quitting jobs, getting a divorce, and engaging in sexual promiscuity. Psychotic distortions of reality are also common during manic periods. When well-meaning friends and family members try to control the manic individual, they are often rebuffed in sharp anger. Although an intensely pleasurable state, mania can be quite harmful to the person's finances, health, and personal relationships. This harm can be clearly seen in the case of "Mrs. M.":

> At 17 she suffered from a depression . . . for several months, although she was not hospitalized. At 33, shortly before the birth of her first child, the patient was greatly depressed. For a period of four days she appeared in a coma. About a month after the birth of the baby she "became excited" and was entered as a patient in an institution for neurotic and mildly psychotic patients. As she began to improve, she was sent to a shore hotel for a brief vacation. The patient remained at the hotel for one night and on the following day signed a year's lease on an apartment, bought furniture, and became heavily involved in debt. Shortly thereafter Mrs. M. became depressed and returned to the hospital. . . . After several months she recovered and, except for relatively mild fluctuations of mood, remained well for approximately 2 years.
>
> She then became overactive and exuberant in spirits and visited her friends, to whom she outlined her plans for reestablishing different forms of lucrative business. She purchased many clothes, bought furniture, pawned her rings, and wrote checks without funds. She was returned to a hospital. Gradually her manic symptoms subsided, and after four months she was discharged. For a period thereafter she was mildly depressed. In a little less than a year Mrs. M. again became overactive, played her radio until late in the night, smoked excessively, and took out insurance on a car that she had not yet bought. Contrary to her usual habits, she swore frequently and loudly . . . and instituted divorce proceedings. On the day prior to her second admission to the hospital, she purchased 57 hats. (Kolb, 1977, pp. 455–456)*

*From L. C. Kolb, *Modern Clinical Psychiatry,* 9th ed. Copyright 1977. Used by permission of the author.

Mania usually returns in multiple episodes (Halgin & Whitbourne, 2000; Judd & others, 2002). When mania is recurrent, it usually alternates irregularly with episodes of depression. Some affected individuals shift frequently between mania and depression, whereas others shift infrequently. In a few cases, persons experience episodes of mania over many years without periods of depression (Solomon & others, 2003). The average number of shifts from mania to depression among persons with bipolar disorder is three to four times per year (Judd & others, 2002), but some individuals show an even more serious "rapid cycling" form, with much more frequent shifts from mania to depression (Schneck & others, 2004). Most people with bipolar disorder, however, are more often depressed than manic (Judd & Akiskal, 2003). Bipolar disorder is a relatively uncommon problem occurring in only about 1% of the population and is equally common among women and men (Merikangas & others, 2007).

The causes of bipolar disorder are not currently known, but it appears to be one of the most heritable of all mental disorders (Kieseppa & others, 2004). It is not known if specific environmental events interact with the genetic predisposition to cause bipolar disorder, however. Interestingly, there is credible evidence that the countries in which people eat the lowest amounts of seafood (Germany, Hungary, and

bipolar disorder (bī-pō'lar) A condition in which the individual experiences periods of mania that alternate irregularly with periods of severe depression.

mania (mā'nē-ah) A disturbance of mood in which the individual experiences a euphoria without cause that is characterized by unrealistic optimism and heightened sensory pleasures.

Switzerland) have rates of bipolar disorder that are five times higher than in Taiwan, Korea, and Iceland—the countries in which the most seafood is consumed (Noaghiul & Hibbeln, 2003). This and other evidence (Hirashima & others, 2004; Stoll & others, 1999) suggest that omega-3 fatty acids, which are abundant in fish, may play a beneficial role in neural transmission and protect against bipolar disorder. These new findings may lead to a breakthrough in our understanding of bipolar disorder, but should we take them seriously at this point? This is a good opportunity to use the scientific critical thinking skills that you learned in chapter 2. Can you think of alternative explanations for the differences in rates of bipolar disorder in these countries? What other evidence would you want to see before you accept that omega-3 fats protect against bipolar disorder?

Schizophrenia

Psychologist: "Why do you think people believe in God?"
Patient: Uh, let's, I don't know why, let's see, balloon travel. He holds it up for you, the balloon. He don't let you fall out, your little legs sticking out down through the clouds. He's down to the smokestack, looking through the smoke trying to get the balloon gassed up you know. Way they're flying on top that way, legs sticking out, I don't know, looking down on the ground, heck, that'd make you so dizzy you just stay and sleep you know, hold down and sleep there. The balloon's His home you know up there. I used to sleep outdoors, you know, sleep outdoors instead of going home. He's had a home but His not tell where it's at you know. (Chapman & Chapman, 1973, p. 3)

schizophrenia (skiz″o-fren′-ē-ah) A psychological disorder involving cognitive disturbance (delusions and hallucinations), disorganization, and reduced enjoyment and interests.

The person giving this confused and confusing answer has **schizophrenia.** Schizophrenia is an uncommon disorder that affects about 1% of the general population. Men are approximately 30% more likely than women to be affected by schizophrenia (Aleman & others, 2003). Schizophrenia is usually preceded by a long period of gradual decline in social functioning and intellectual performance during childhood or adolescence (Jobe & Harrow, 2010; Woodberry, Giuliano, Seidman, 2008). The more dramatic and impairing cognitive and emotional features of schizophrenia appear either gradually over time or in a distinct "break" in which these symptoms begin quite suddenly, usually during late adolescence or early adulthood (Jobe & Harrow, 2010; Walker & others, 2010). A small percentage of individuals who experience an episode of schizophrenia recover completely, and as many as 30% return to relatively normal lives for varying lengths of time (Jobe & Harrow, 2010). But more than half experience repeated episodes of schizophrenia or unrelenting cognitive and emotional disturbance throughout their lives (Harvey, 2010; Jobe & Harrow, 2010; Walker & others, 2004; Walker & Tessner, 2008). Schizophrenia is also associated with increased risk of early mortality (Saha, Chant, & McGrath, 2007) and is very costly to society, costing over $23 billion a year in the U.S. (Wu & others, 2005).

Schizophrenia is characterized by three types of serious problems:

1. ***Delusions and hallucinations.*** The central feature of schizophrenia is distortions of cognition that put the individual "out of touch with reality." Persons with schizophrenia often hold strange false beliefs (**delusions**) and have distorted and bizarre false perceptual experiences (**hallucinations**).

delusions False beliefs that distort reality.

2. ***Disorganized thinking, emotions, and behavior.*** Persons with schizophrenia often think in fragmented and disorganized ways. Their emotions and behavior are similarly disorganized and illogical at times. A person with schizophrenia might laugh when told sad news or shift rapidly from happiness to sadness and back again for no apparent reason. As a result, most of us find it very difficult to have conversations with persons with schizophrenia.

hallucinations False perceptual experiences that distort reality.

3. ***Reduced enjoyment and interests.*** Persons with schizophrenia say that they experience less pleasure in life than most persons and have fewer interests and goals that are important to them (known as "blunted affect"). Both their positive and their negative emotions lack normal intensity, including not being as interested in having close friendships.

Causes of Schizophrenia. It is clear that schizophrenia is caused by the interaction of both genetic and environmental factors. Schizophrenia is strongly influenced by genetic factors, but inheritance is hardly destiny in the case of any mental disorder (Pogue-Geile & Yokley, 2010; Walker & Tessner, 2008). Although the risk of schizophrenia is 10 times greater among the children of a schizophrenic parent, that means that only 10% of the children of a schizophrenic will develop schizophrenia (as opposed to a risk of 1% in the general population). Indeed, monozygotic (identical) twins of persons with schizophrenia develop schizophrenia only 25–50% of the time, even though monozygotic twins share all of their genes. This means that environmental factors that interact with genetic influences are also important in causing schizophrenia. One likely environmental cause of schizophrenia are pregnancy complications that cause abnormal brain development (Walker & others, 2010). It appears that the brains of individuals with chronic early onset schizophrenia "shrink"—become increasing smaller during adolescence (Hubl & others, 2004). In addition, childhood head injuries and viral infections of the brain appear to increase risk for schizophrenia (Dalman & others, 2008), perhaps particularly in genetically predisposed individuals. As a result of abnormal brain growth and brain injuries, schizophrenic adults have reduced numbers of neurons (Davatzikos & others, 2005), especially in the hippocampus (Grace, 2010). In addition, living in stressful urban environments (Veling & others, 2008) and families characterized by high levels of discord are associated with increased rates of schizophrenia (Hooley, 2007; Walker & others, 2010). These findings suggest that stress increases the risk of schizophrenia in genetically predisposed individuals.

paranoid schizophrenia
(par´-ah-noid) A subtype of schizophrenia in which the individual holds delusions of persecution and grandeur that seriously distort reality.

Subtypes of Schizophrenia. Schizophrenia is not a single mental disorder but is a broad class of psychotic disorders that is broken down into three major subtypes in the 2000 edition of the American Psychiatric Association's *Diagnostic and Statistical Manual of Mental Disorders (DSM-IV-TR): paranoid, disorganized,* and *catatonic schizophrenia.* A fourth category, *undifferentiated schizophrenia,* is used to classify individuals who do not fit into the other three categories.

Paranoid Schizophrenia. A person with **paranoid schizophrenia** holds *false beliefs,* or *delusions,* that seriously distort reality. Most often, these are beliefs in the exceptional importance of oneself, so-called *delusions of grandeur*—such as being Jesus Christ, a CIA agent, or the inventor of a cure for war. These are often accompanied by delusions that, because one is so important, others are "out to get me" in attempts to thwart the individual's important mission. These are known as *delusions of persecution,* or *paranoia.*

If I were schizophrenic and believed that I were an agent of the CIA who alone had the ability to save the president from assassination by terrorists, I might also believe

German psychiatrist Hans Prinzhorn has assembled the most extensive collection of artwork by mental patients available. This painting from the collection, by August Neter, illustrates the hallucinations and the paranoid fantasies from which many schizophrenic patients suffer. In reviewing a showing of artwork by schizophrenic patients, such as the painting shown here, poet John Ashby wrote: "The lure of the work is strong, but so is the terror of the unanswerable riddles it proposes."

that my students were terrorists who were trying to confuse and poison me. Think for a moment how bizarre I would seem to others who learned of my paranoid delusions. Think, too, about the terrifying, bewildering existence I would live if I believed those things. It would be small wonder that my emotions would seem unpredictable and strange and that I would withdraw from social contact.

Unfortunately, the cognitive disturbances of the paranoid schizophrenic do not stop with delusions. Many individuals with this disorder also experience false perceptual experiences, or *hallucinations.* Their perceptions are either strangely distorted or they may hear, see, or feel things that are not there. These bizarre experiences further add to the terrifying, perplexing unreality of the paranoid schizophrenic's existence.

disorganized schizophrenia A subtype of schizophrenia characterized by shallow silliness, extreme social withdrawal, and fragmented delusions and hallucinations.

catatonic schizophrenia (kat˝ah-ton´ik) A subtype of schizophrenia in which the individual spends long periods in an inactive, statue-like state.

Catatonic individuals sometimes exhibit a state of catatonic stupor, during which they may maintain a single posture for several hours.

attention-deficit/hyperactivity disorder (ADHD) ADHD is defined by serious problems sustaining attention and completing tasks, or by high levels of motor activity and impulsivity, or both. The diagnosis is made only if these symptoms result in serious impairment in functioning in two or more areas of life (e.g., home and school).

Disorganized Schizophrenia. **Disorganized schizophrenia** resembles paranoid schizophrenia in that delusions and hallucinations are present, but the speech and other cognitive processes of the disorganized schizophrenic, as the name implies, are so disorganized and fragmented that the delusions and hallucinations have little recognizable meaning. The central features of this type of schizophrenia are extreme withdrawal from normal human contact and a shallow "silliness" of emotion. The disorganized schizophrenic acts in childlike ways, reacts inappropriately to both happy and sad events, and generally presents a highly bizarre picture to others.

Catatonic Schizophrenia. **Catatonic schizophrenia** is quite different in appearance from other forms of schizophrenia. Although catatonics sometimes experience delusions and hallucinations, their most obvious abnormalities are in social interaction, posture, and body movement. There are long periods of catatonic stupor, an inactive, statue-like state in which the individuals seem locked into a posture. Persons with catatonic schizophrenia are often said to exhibit "waxy flexibility" during these stupors—they passively let themselves be placed into any posture and maintain it. Often the individual ceases to talk, appears not to hear what is spoken to him or her, and may no longer eat without being fed (Fink & Tayor, 2009). Frequently, however, the stupor is abruptly broken by periods of agitation. The person may pace and fidget nervously or may angrily attack others. Both of these patterns may alternate with periods of relative normality.

Attention-Deficit/ Hyperactivity Disorder

The mental health problems described in this textbook are disorders commonly found in adults. Although there are a number of other mental disorders that begin in childhood, these are not addressed in this book, as they tend to be covered in a separate course. The one exception is **attention-deficit/hyperactivity disorder,** commonly known as ADHD. This is a disorder that always begins in childhood, but in the last decade it has become clear that it does not always end in childhood. Although children who meet criteria for ADHD tend to become less active and impulsive as they grow older, researchers have learned that they often retain their difficulties in sustaining attention. Therefore, more and more adults are now being treated for ADHD. Because ADHD is often a concern for college students, I have decided to add a brief discussion of it.

In *DSM-IV-TR,* two kinds of symptoms of ADHD are distinguished, inattention and hyperactivity-impulsivity:

Inattention:

1. Cannot sustain attention

2. Often fails to attend to details or makes careless mistakes

3. Highly distractible

4. Does not follow through and complete tasks

5. Disorganized

6. Often loses pencils, paper, and assignments at school or work

7. Often does not seem to listen when being spoken to

8. Dislikes or avoids tasks that require sustained attention

9. Often forgetful

Hyperactivity-impulsivity:

1. Often fidgets and squirms when seated

2. Often leaves seat when should remain seated

3. Often runs or climbs excessively (or subjective feelings of restlessness in adolescents or adults)

4. Often has difficulty quietly engaging in play or leisure activities

5. Is often "on the go" or acts like he or she is "driven by a motor"

6. Often talks excessively

7. Often blurts out answers before the question has been completed

8. Often has difficulty awaiting her or his turn

9. Often interrupts or intrudes on others

According to the *DSM-IV-TR,* the diagnosis is given when the individual exhibits at least six of *either* list of symptoms. Adolescents and adults tend to meet criteria for inattention, but not hyperactivity-impulsivity.

ADHD can be a very serious problem that is associated with difficulties in school and work, difficulties in social relationships, and increased rates of accidental injuries (Biederman & others, 2010; Lahey & Willcutt, 2002). Indeed, the diagnosis is given only if the symptoms cause difficulties in at least two areas of life (for example, school and peer problems).

It is difficult to diagnose ADHD properly for two reasons. First, the symptoms are variations on normal behavior and it takes an expert to see the subtle but important differences. Second, many kinds of mental health problems, including depression, anxiety, and schizophrenia, are characterized by restlessness and problems in sustaining attention, so a skilled mental health professional must consider many alternatives.

When an adult thinks he or she may have ADHD, the key question is whether he or she had a clear history of ADHD as a child. If not, his or her current difficulties are more likely due to some other problem, or perhaps to a different kind of mental disorder. It is even possible for an adult with a clear history of ADHD to have other mental health problems as an adult that require a different approach to treatment. In my opinion, psychologists and psychiatrists who work with children are actually best able to diagnose ADHD in adults, because they have seen it so often in children and adolescents.

Personality Disorders

Except for ADHD, which begins in childhood, we have been talking about psychological problems that develop in individuals who were once considered to be normal. These are the disorders that are diagnosed on Axis I of the *DSM-IV-TR.* To

personality disorders Psychological disorders that are believed to result from personalities that developed improperly during childhood.

oversimplify the case, schizophrenia, major depression, and the other disorders that we have considered are "breakdowns" in relatively normal persons. In contrast, the **personality disorders** discussed in this section are believed to result from personalities that developed improperly in the first place. These are the Axis II disorders.

A number of different personality disorders differ considerably from one another but share several characteristics: (a) All personality disorders begin early in life; (b) they are disturbing to the person or to others; and (c) they are very difficult to treat. Personality disorders tend to be long-lasting but are not always chronic (Lenzenweger & others, 2009). We will first look at two very different personality disorders to provide examples of this type of problem, then we will provide brief descriptions of the other personality disorders.

Schizoid Personality Disorder

schizoid personality disorder (skiz´oid) A personality disorder characterized by blunted emotions, lack of interest in social relationships, and withdrawal into a solitary existence.

The suffix *-oid* means "like"—hence, *schizoid personality disorder* is like schizophrenia, particularly in that blunted emotions and social withdrawal are exhibited. Unlike true schizophrenia, however, this condition is not characterized by serious cognitive disturbances.

Individuals with **schizoid personality disorder** have little or no desire to have friends and indeed are not interested in even casual social contact. They are classic "loners." Usually, they are very shy as children but are not abnormally withdrawn until later childhood or adolescence. Gradually, they seem to lose interest in friends, family, and social activities and retreat more and more into a solitary existence.

antisocial personality disorder A personality disorder characterized by smooth social skills and a lack of guilt about violating social rules and laws and taking advantage of others.

They display little emotion and appear cold and aloof. Later in life, people with schizoid personality disorder often lose interest in personal appearance, hygiene, and other polite social conventions. Often they do not work, and they may even fall into homelessness or work as streetwalking prostitutes.

Antisocial Personality Disorder

People with antisocial personality disorder frequently violate social laws and rules, while feeling little guilt about it. The disorder has its origins in childhood, when the person is usually highly aggressive and engages in multiple forms of antisocial behavior.

Individuals with **antisocial personality disorder** have a personality disorder quite different from the schizoid group. They frequently violate social rules and laws, take advantage of others, and feel little guilt about it. These individuals often have smooth social skills: They are sweet-talking con artists who are very likable at first, but they experience great difficulties in maintaining close personal relationships. They enter easily into marriages and other intimate relationships, but these tend to break up quickly.

People with antisocial personalities have a low tolerance for frustration. They act on impulse, lose their tempers quickly, and lie easily and skillfully. They are often hardened criminals. In childhood, they are often bullies who fight, lie, cheat, steal, and are truant from school. They blame others for their misdeeds, feel picked on by their parents and teachers, and never seem to learn from their mistakes.

Individuals with antisocial personality disorder are often unemotional and guiltless—they are calm, cool characters. They are highly uncomfortable, however, when they are kept from excitement. They have an abnormal need for stimulation, novelty, and thrills. Because many turn to alcohol and drugs for excitement, they frequently become addicts. The primary harmfulness of the antisocial personality disorder is in the damage that is done to others. Individuals with antisocial personality disorder often leave a trail of victims—victims of their lies, their crimes, their violent outbursts, and their broken intimate relationships. The case of antisocial personality disorder described next illustrates these problems well:

Donald's misbehavior as a child took many forms including lying, cheating, petty theft, and the bullying of smaller children. As he grew older he became more and more interested in sex, gambling, and alcohol. When he was 14 he made crude sexual advances toward a younger girl, and when she threatened to tell her parents he locked her in a shed. It was about 16 hours before she was found. Donald at first denied knowledge of the incident, later stating that she had seduced him and that the door must have locked itself. He expressed no concern for the anguish experienced by the girl and her parents, nor did he give any indication that he felt morally culpable for what he had done.

When he was 17, Donald left the boarding school, forged his father's name to a large check, and spent about a year traveling around the world. He apparently lived well, using a combination of charm, physical attractiveness, and false pretenses to finance his way. During subsequent years he held a succession of jobs, never staying at any one for more than a few months. Throughout this period he was charged with a variety of crimes, including theft, drunkenness in a public place, assault, and many traffic violations. In most cases he was either fined or given a light sentence.

His sexual experiences were frequent, casual, and callous. When he was 22 he married a 41-year-old woman whom he had met in a bar. Several other marriages followed, all bigamous. In each case the pattern was the same: He would marry someone on impulse, let her support him for several months, and then leave. (Lahey & Ciminero, 1980, pp. 326–327)

Other Personality Disorders

The following are brief descriptions of the other eight types of personality disorders listed in *DSM-IV-TR*. Be careful not to diagnose yourself or your friends while reading this list. The pattern must be extreme and consistent to qualify for a diagnosis.

1. Schizotypal personality disorder: few friendships, suspiciousness, strange ideas, such as belief that her or his mind can be read by others and that messages are being received in strange ways

2. Paranoid personality disorder: high degree of suspiciousness and mistrust of others, extreme irritability and sensitivity, coldness and lack of tender feelings

3. Histrionic personality disorder: self-centered, frequently seeking to be the center of attention, manipulating others through exaggerated expression of emotions and difficulties, superficially charming and seductive but lacking genuine concern for others, frequent angry outbursts

4. Narcissistic personality disorder: unrealistic sense of self-importance, preoccupied with fantasies of future success, requires constant attention and praise, reacts very negatively to criticism or is indifferent to criticism, exploits others, feels entitled to special consideration, lack of genuine concern for others

5. Borderline personality disorder: impulsive and unpredictable, unstable personal relationships, angry, almost constantly needs to be with others, lack of clear identity, feelings of emptiness

6. Avoidant personality disorder: extreme shyness or social withdrawal in spite of a desire for friendships, extremely sensitive to rejection, very low self-esteem

7. Dependent personality disorder: passive dependence on others for support and decisions; has low self-esteem, and puts needs of others before self

8. Obsessive-compulsive personality disorder: perfectionistic, dominating, poor ability to express affection, excessive devotion to work, indecisive when faced with major decisions

Review

Major depression involves one or more episodes of this negative mood state and associated feature. Depressive episodes range from mild to severe, with severe episodes sometimes being accompanied by bizarre perceptions and beliefs that distort reality. In bipolar disorder, the episodes of depression alternate irregularly with periods of the mood disturbance known as mania. Although this is an intensely pleasurable state, it's harmful in that it can lead to financial difficulties, can destroy personal relationships, and can often be accompanied by reality-distorting perceptions and beliefs.

Schizophrenia is a broad range of psychotic disorders characterized by disturbances of cognition that grossly distort reality, by distortions of emotions, and by withdrawal from social relationships. There are three major subtypes of schizophrenia. Paranoid schizophrenia is characterized by delusions of grandeur and persecution, often accompanied by hallucinations. Disorganized schizophrenia resembles paranoid schizophrenia but is typified by even more fragmented cognition and by shallow, silly emotions. Catatonic schizophrenia is quite different from the other types, being marked by stupors in which the individual may maintain postures for long periods of time. Biological factors—genetics, cortical deterioration, and abnormal prenatal development—are believed to be important in the origins of schizophrenia, but stress may be the immediate cause that triggers episodes.

ADHD is a disorder that begins in childhood and is characterized by high levels of inattention or high levels of hyperactivity-impulsivity, or both kinds of symptoms. Over time, most children outgrow their overactivity and impulsivity, but attention problems often last into adulthood.

Whereas most kinds of psychological disorders are thought to result from the "breakdown" of a normal personality, personality disorders are thought to result from faulty personality development during childhood. These disorders begin early in life, are disturbing to the individual or to others, and are difficult to treat. For example, individuals with schizoid personality disorder are very shy children who increasingly lose interest in social relationships as they grow older. Eventually, they lose interest in proper dress and social conditions, display little emotion, and rarely hold regular jobs. Antisocial personality disorder is characterized by rule-violating behavior as a child that develops into irresponsibility, dishonesty, and violence as an adult. Such individuals are sometimes con artists who are smooth and likable at first but who have great difficulties maintaining normal relationships. They also have an abnormal need for stimulation and do not seem to learn from punishment.

Check Your Learning

To be sure that you have learned the key points from the preceding section, cover the list of correct answers and try to answer each question. If you give an incorrect answer to any question, return to the page given next to the correct answer to see why your answer was not correct.

1. The individual experiencing _____ is deeply unhappy, finds little pleasure in life, and experiences other symptoms such as sleeping and eating problems and loss of energy.

     a) hypochondriasis   c) delusional disorder

     b) major depression   d) somatoform pain disorders

2. In the condition known as _____, periods of mania alternate irregularly with periods of severe depression.

     a) major depression   c) unipolar depression

     b) mania disorder   d) bipolar disorder

3. The three major areas of abnormality in schizophrenia are (a) _____; (b) _____; and (c) _____.

4. Strange and false perceptual experiences are termed _____.

     a) delusions   c) hallucinations

     b) paranoia   d) social withdrawal

5. The type of schizophrenia characterized by stupor and "waxy flexibility" is called _____.

   a) catatonic   c) disorganized

   b) paranoid   d) stuporous

6. _____ personality disorder is similar to schizophrenia, particularly in that blunted emotions and social withdrawal are exhibited, but unlike true schizophrenia, this condition is not characterized by serious cognitive disturbances.

   a) Antisocial   c) Dependent

   b) Schizoid   d) Histrionic

Thinking Critically about Psychology

There are no right or wrong answers to the following questions. They are presented to help you become an active reader and think critically about what you have just read.

1. What are some possible explanations for the higher incidence of major depression in women?

2. Why do you think personality disorders are generally difficult to treat?

Correct Answers: 1. b (p. 475), **2.** d (p. 479), **3.** delusions and hallucinations; disorganized thinking, emotions, and behavior; and reduced enjoyment and interests (pp. 480–481), **4.** c (p. 480), **5.** a (p. 482), **6.** b (p. 484)

Sexual and Gender Identity Disorders

Human beings differ widely in their sexual preferences and practices. In the sections that follow, we will look at the range of unusual, or **atypical, sexual behavior.** The text first reviews atypical patterns of sexuality that are considered abnormal only if the individuals who engage in the sexual practices consider them harmful for themselves. We will then examine patterns of sexuality that are usually considered to be abnormal (fetishism, sexual sadism, and masochism) or always considered to be abnormal (voyeurism, exhibitionism, and forced sex). In the next section of the chapter, we will review problems with sexual desire and the sexual response cycle.

atypical sexual behavior Sexual practice that differs considerably from the norm.

Transvestism and Gender Identity Disorder

These two superficially similar patterns of sexuality are often confused because they both involve dressing in the clothing of the other sex. But they have little else in common except that they are rarely harmful to anyone. **Transvestism** refers to the practice of dressing in the clothes of the other sex. Transvestites often state that they cross-dress because it is sexually stimulating, but many transvestites say they cross-dress to free themselves from confining sexual stereotypes. Transvestites are almost always males who have relatively well-adjusted sex lives.

    Gender identity disorder (sometimes referred to as Transsexualism), in contrast, refers to a condition in which the individual feels trapped in a body of the wrong sex. For example, a person who is anatomically male feels that he is actually a woman who somehow was given the wrong body. Transsexuals may occasionally or permanently dress in clothes of the other anatomical sex, but this cross-sex dressing has nothing to do with sexual arousal. These individuals merely feel that they are dressing

transvestism (trans-vesˊtizm) The practice of obtaining sexual pleasure by dressing in the clothes of the opposite sex.

gender identity disorder A condition, sometimes referred to as transsexualism (trans-seksˊu-ah-lizm), in which an individual feels trapped in the body of the wrong sex.

in the clothes of their true sex. For example, Mike Penner, a well-known sports writer for the *Los Angeles Times,* revealed that he was transsexual in a 2007 column.

In some instances, these individuals undergo hormone injections and plastic surgery to change their sex organs to those of the desired sex. A famous example is that of physician Richard Raskins, who in 1975 had a sex-change operation because he felt like a female trapped in a male body. After the operation, he adopted the name Renée Richards and briefly played on the women's professional tennis circuit. Male-to-female sex-change operations are much more common than the opposite, probably in part because surgically created penises are less satisfactory than surgically created vaginas (for example, they yield less genital sexual pleasure).

The sex-change clinic at Johns Hopkins Medical Center stopped doing sex-change operations during the 1970s because follow-up studies showed that their patients were no happier with their lives after surgery than before. Follow-up studies of patients from other centers, however, have shown that the patients were generally happy with their new bodies if properly selected for surgery and counseled on what to expect from it (Baker, 1969; Pauly, 1968).

Although many authorities consider transvestism and transsexualism to be normal under most circumstances, the following patterns range from ones that are *usually* considered to be abnormal to ones that are *always* considered to be abnormal because of the harm caused to the individual and/or others.

Fetishism

fetishism (fet´ish-izm) The practice of obtaining sexual arousal primarily or exclusively from specific objects.

Fetishism refers to the fact that some individuals are primarily or exclusively aroused by specific physical objects or types of material (such as leather or lace). In some cases, the fetish is only an exaggeration of normal interest in specific body parts. For example, some individuals are only or primarily aroused by breasts, buttocks, blue eyes, and so on. But the term *fetish* is usually reserved for cases involving inanimate objects, such as panties, shoes, or stockings. A fetish is considered to be abnormal if it interferes with the sexual adjustment of the person or his or her partner. Often, the fetishist (who is usually a male) is aroused only by "used" articles and is sexually aroused by the act of stealing them from an unknowing woman. Because this can be frightening to the victim and is dangerous and illegal, fetishism is considered abnormal when practiced in this manner.

Sexual Sadism and Masochism

sexual sadism (sād´izm) The practice of obtaining sexual pleasure by inflicting pain on others.

sexual masochism (mas´-o-kizm) A condition in which receiving pain is sexually exciting.

Sexual sadism is the practice of receiving sexual pleasure from inflicting pain on others. **Sexual masochism** is the condition in which receiving pain is sexually exciting. Sometimes verbal abuse or "degradation" is substituted for physical pain. Approximately 5% to 10% of men and women find giving or receiving pain to be sexually exciting at times, but this is the preferred or only method of sexual arousal for very few individuals. Many individuals who practice sadism and masochism, or *S&M,* do so with a consenting partner who also enjoys the practice, and they do not inflict pain that is severe or medically dangerous—for example, mild spankings, pinching, and so on. In such cases, S&M may be considered normal if care is taken to avoid accidental harm and one's partner is *truly* willing. In some cases, however, the partner is unwillingly coerced into participation in S&M activities. In other cases, S&M involves intense pain (such as whipping, burning, and kicking). S&M is always considered abnormal if there is any question about voluntary participation by both partners or if intense pain or physical harm is inflicted. In rare cases, the sadist mutilates or even murders the victim to receive pleasure. Such practices are unquestionably abnormal.

Voyeurism and Exhibitionism

Voyeurism is the practice of obtaining sexual pleasure by watching others undressing or engaging in sexual activities. Voyeurs generally find this exciting only when the person they are watching is unaware of their presence and when there is an element of danger involved. They are no more aroused than the average person while at a nudist camp, but they become very excited peeping into windows (Tollison & Adams, 1979). Because they often frighten the person they are watching, and because the activity is illegal, voyeurism is considered to be abnormal. The voyeur is generally a hetero-sexual male who has trouble establishing a normal sexual relationship. Some voyeurs commit rape and other serious crimes, but most are not physically dangerous.

Individuals who practice **exhibitionism** obtain sexual pleasure from exposing their genitals to others. Almost all exhibitionists are heterosexual males who typically are married but who are shy and have inhibited sex lives. Exhibitionists generally want to shock their victims but rarely are dangerous in other ways (Tollison & Adams, 1979). Because such behavior is illegal and frightening, however, exhibitionism is considered abnormal.

voyeurism (voi′yer-izm) The practice of obtaining sexual pleasure by watching members of the opposite sex undressing or engaging in sexual activities.

exhibitionism (ek″sĭ-bish′ŭ-nizm″) The practice of obtaining sexual pleasure by exposing one's genitals to others.

Forced Sexual Behavior

Several other forms of deviant sexual behavior are clearly abnormal because they involve actual, threatened, or implied force to the victim. These acts include rape, sexual abuse of children, incest, and sexual harassment. It is important to note that the definitions of these behaviors are based on legal classifications. The behaviors are not specific mental diagnoses, although the acts may be related to psychological problems.

Rape.

In **rape,** an individual forces another person to engage in a sexual act. In the vast majority of cases, the rapist is a male and the victim is a female—one in every six women has been raped (Tjaden & Thoennes, 2006). Thus, approximately 18 million women have been raped. American Indian/Alaska Native women and mixed-race women reported higher rates of rape than other racial/ethnic groups. Most rapes occurred before the victims were 18 years old. Almost 2.8 million men have been raped, as well. Regardless of their age at victimization, males were most frequently raped by an acquaintance. Contrary to expectations, the person who forced the women to do something sexual usually was not a stranger.

rape The act of forcing sexual activity on an unwilling person.

As discussed earlier in the chapter, rape is traumatic and can precipitate PTSD. Many communities have established rape crisis centers, which provide ongoing support for victims throughout the reporting, investigation, and prosecution processes. Rape crisis centers also provide information and counseling to rape victims to assist them in readjusting after their victimization. See table 14.1 on p. 490 for a summary of rape myths and facts.

There is no single psychological profile for rapists (Kalichman, 1990). Theories of rape, however, have stated that most men who rape are driven by aggressive impulses or the need to feel powerful and dominating rather than by sexual desire (Ellis, 1989; Groth, 1979). Many rapists will have raped numerous women before they are finally apprehended (Abel & others, 1977).

Sexual Abuse of Children.

Many children are sexually assaulted and exploited. In a large survey (Kohn, 1987), 27% of women and 16% of men reported having been sexually violated during childhood. Some statistics suggest that as many as 40 million persons in the United States were sexually victimized as children. There are a variety of types of child sexual abuse. When the sexual contact is perpetrated by a family

Table 14.1
Rape Myths and Rape Facts

Myth	Fact
Myth: A woman who goes to the home of a man on their first date implies she is willing to have sex.	*Fact:* Rapes are brutal and violent acts that may be worse with resistance.
Myth: One reason that women falsely report a rape is that they have a need to call attention to themselves.	*Fact:* It is very rare for a woman to report a rape falsely. Reporting a rape is a traumatic experience.
Myth: Any healthy woman can resist a rapist if she really wants to.	*Fact:* A person going anywhere does not imply that he or she wants to do anything. Rapists distort their perceptions to fit their beliefs.
Myth: Women who go around braless or wearing short skirts are asking for trouble.	*Fact:* No victim has ever asked to be raped. Rapists are responsible for their actions.

incest (in´sest) Sexual relations between relatives.

child molestation Sexual behavior with a child without force or direct threat of force.

member, the sexual abuse is termed **incest.** When there is force or threat of force used, the sexual assault is child rape. When there is no clear threat of force, the sexual abuse of children is referred to as **child molestation.** Even child molestation is considered to be a form of forced sexual behavior, however, because the child cannot consent in any meaningful way to the sexual behavior.

Children who have been sexually violated demonstrate a wide range of emotional and behavioral reactions. If the sexual contact is not threatening to the child, such as in sexual exploration by an older child, there are rarely serious psychological effects for the child if the parents calmly handle the occurrence with love and understanding. When the sexual abuse is upsetting to the child, as is almost invariably the case when the perpetrator is an adult or when threat of force is involved, the psychological effects on the victim can be serious.

Many of the effects of child sexual abuse are believed to be long term. Indeed, the aftermath of child sexual abuse may be similar to that of adult sexual assault, in that children tend to be traumatized and suffer traumatic reactions (Finkelhor, 1990). Children are likely to act out sexually in response to sexual victimization, experience a sense of personal betrayal by the person who violated them, feel that they are powerless and lack control, and feel stigmatized because they were assaulted (Finkelhor & Browne, 1985).

pedophilia (pe´´do-fil´ē-ah) The persistent sexual interest in children who have not reached puberty.

Pedophilia refers to persistent sexual interest in children who have not yet reached puberty (Seto, 2009). Not all individuals with pedophilia engage in child sexual abuse, but most individuals who engage in these illegal acts have pedophilia. Most child molesters and rapists are usually known and trusted by the child victim. Indeed, the molester or rapist is a neighbor, a family member, or someone who knows the child before the incident in over 90% of cases (Tjaden & Thoennes, 2006). The child molester is typically a male heterosexual and the victim is usually a young girl. In some cases, the molester is a male homosexual or a heterosexual female and the victim is a young boy. Tragically, many child molesters will have violated hundreds of children before they are caught. Like persons who rape adults, men who rape or molest children tend to be highly heterogeneous in their psychological makeup (Finkelhor & Browne, 1985).

sexual harassment Unwanted sexual advances, comments, or any other form of coercive sexual behavior by others.

Sexual Harassment. Unwanted sexual advances; requests for sexual favors; unwanted touching of the legs, breasts, or buttocks; sexually suggestive comments; and any other form of coercive sexual behavior by others constitute **sexual harassment.** As many as 60% of women in the United States have been subjected to one or more of these forms of sexual harassment (Hotelling, 1991). But sexual harassment also includes the leering looks and suggestive remarks that men often foist on women on the street, which have made nearly every woman uncomfortable (angry, frightened, disgusted) at one time or another. Although it is less common, men are also the victims of sexual harassment in colleges and in the workplace.

A key component of sexual harassment is that it occurs between persons with different amounts of power, often in schools or the workplace. For example, a woman who is sexually harassed by her boss may think that she cannot report the situation without risking the loss of her job. But differences in power can exist even between two students or two employees with the same job if the person engaging in the harassment is physically stronger than the other (even if no explicit threat of force is made). There are laws, regulations, and policies that guarantee every person's right to attend school and work in a nonhostile environment. Every victim of sexual harassment suffers in the sense of becoming less comfortable and relaxed at school or work. In some cases, however, sexual harassment can provoke serious levels of anxiety and depression.

Review

Atypical patterns of sexual behavior that involve no harm to the individual or others are considered to be normal, even though they are unusual and perceived as immoral by some members of society. Other forms of deviant sexual behavior are considered abnormal if they result in harm to anyone. The transvestite obtains sexual pleasure from dressing in the clothing of the other sex. Transsexualism is the condition in which individuals consider themselves to be trapped within bodies of the other sex. Unless the individual is troubled by the condition, transvestism and transsexualism are generally not harmful to anyone. Fetishism—obtaining sexual pleasure from specific objects—need not be harmful but can be if the objects are stolen or the preference causes trouble in some other way. Sadism—sexual arousal from inflicting pain—may be harmless if practiced in a mild way with a completely willing partner but is generally considered abnormal because of the pain and medical risk involved. Masochism—sexual arousal from receiving pain—is generally considered abnormal for the same reason. Voyeurism is the practice of obtaining sexual pleasure by peeping at nude or sexually involved individuals. Exhibitionism is the practice of obtaining sexual excitement by exposing one's genitals to an unwilling person. Because of the frightening nature and illegality of these activities, both exhibitionism and voyeurism are considered abnormal. Forced sexual behaviors—including rape, sexual abuse of children, incest, and sexual harassment—are always considered abnormal because of the inherent psychological and physical harm they are likely to cause.

Check Your Learning

To be sure that you have learned the key points from the preceding section, cover the list of correct answers and try to answer each question. If you give an incorrect answer to any question, return to the page given next to the correct answer to see why your answer was not correct.

1. Sexual behavior is considered to be abnormal if it is _____.

   a) atypical   c) harmful

   b) strange or bizarre   d) infrequent

2. A person who obtains sexual pleasure from dressing in the clothing of the other sex is said to be _____.

   a) a transvestite   c) a Transylvanian

   b) a transsexual   d) all of the above

3. A person who obtains sexual pleasure by watching others undressing or engaging in sexual activities is said to be _____.

   a) an exhibitionist   c) a masochist

   b) a pedophile   d) a voyeur

Check Your Learning (cont.)

4. Most persons who commit child molestation are _____.

   a) homosexual females   c) homosexual males

   b) heterosexual females   d) heterosexual males

Thinking Critically about Psychology

There are no right or wrong answers to the following questions. They are presented to help you become an active reader and think critically about what you just read.

1. Have you ever experienced, engaged in, or witnessed sexual harassment? What do you think can be done to reduce the frequency of this problem?

2. Some people believe that those who practice transvestism are not psychologically healthy. What do you think, and why?

Correct Answers: 1. c (p. 487), 2. a (p. 487), 3. d (p. 489), 4. d (p. 490)

Sexual Dysfunction and Sexual Health

Several types of problems can interfere with successful and pleasurable sexual intercourse. These problems, in fact, are common (Herbenick & others, 2010; Michael & others, 1995; Shifren, 2008) and should be considered abnormal only when they are prolonged. Even when prolonged, however, they do not mean that the individual has "psychological problems." Sexual problems are highly associated with relationship difficulties, and sexual problems often have medical causes rather than psychological causes.

sexual dysfunction A persistent inability to engage successfully or comfortably in normal sexual activities.

     Sexual dysfunctions are disturbances in any phase of the sexual response cycle. Different dysfunctions may have several different potential causes, both physical and psychological in origin. The most common physical causes of sexual dysfunction are drug or alcohol abuse, side effects of some medications, and some forms of illness (Bhasin & others, 2007). It is important, therefore, that all persons with problems with sexual functioning first be evaluated by a physician who specializes in the sexual-reproductive system, such as a gynecologist or urologist. Fortunately, solutions are available for sexual difficulties caused by medical problems. Many sexual dysfunctions are caused by psychological factors, however (Zemishlany & Weizman, 2008).

     Sexual dysfunctions are classified according to the phases of sexual response within which they occur: sexual desire, sexual arousal, and orgasm.

Dysfunctions of Sexual Desire

Among the most common sexual dysfunctions are those involving interest and desire in sexual relations. It is important not to confuse sexual desire with sexual frequency, because a person can have frequent sexual encounters to please his or her partner but have very little desire for these sexual interactions. In contrast, a person may have strong sexual desire but not engage in sex for any number of reasons.

inhibited sexual desire A condition in which a person desires sex rarely or not at all.

sexual aversion disorder A condition in which a person fearfully avoids sexual behavior.

     It is also important to note that everyone has a different level of sexual motivation (Bancroft & others, 2009). A person is said to have a disorder of sexual desire only if she or he lacks almost all desire for sexual contact and is troubled by the lack of desire. Two specific types of dysfunctions involve sexual desire. First, **inhibited sexual desire** occurs when a person has sexual desire very infrequently or not at all. The second desire problem is called **sexual aversion disorder** and is characterized by a nearly complete fearful avoidance of sexual contact with others (American Psychiatric Association, 2000).

Both men and women experience disorders of sexual desire. There are numerous possible causes of these problems, including extreme anxiety about sexual intimacy or having had a sexually traumatic experience. In other cases, the person may not have a general lack of desire but may lack interest in his or her sexual partner because of problems in that relationship (Beck, 1995; Kaplan, 1983; LoPiccolo & Friedman, 1988).

Therapists who work with sexual desire problems first examine the person's health and overall relationship with his or her partner. If there are few relationship problems, therapy for sexual desire problems tends to focus on the anxiety that the person may experience in relation to sexual intimacy. Anxieties may block desires for sexual contact and interfere with sexual interest. Sexual inhibitions may result from experiences and characteristics of the person. These issues are examined in the context of sex therapy, where persons evaluate their anxieties and employ strategies to reduce them. Often therapy will involve both members of a couple to address specific aspects of their sexual interactions (Rosen & Leiblum, 1995).

Dysfunctions of Sexual Arousal

Sexual arousal disorders occur when there is a lack of sufficient sexual arousal—including erection of the penis for the male and lubrication of the vagina for the female—during the excitement phase of sexual response. Note, however, that a person is said to have a disorder of sexual arousal only if this failure to respond occurs consistently, occurs even with adequate levels of sexual stimulation, and interferes with sexual pleasure or causes discomfort. Thus, in sexual arousal dysfunctions, an interruption of the physical processes occurs in the excitement phase of sexual response—namely, blood flow to the genital region and muscle tension.

Women may develop **female sexual arousal disorder,** which is characterized by a lack of vaginal lubrication and a minimal subjective experience of sexual excitement (American Psychiatric Association, 2000). Because many women occasionally experience transient forms of these difficulties when circumstances do not lend themselves to sexual arousal, the lack of arousal must be persistent even under favorable circumstances to be considered a sexual dysfunction.

Other less common female dysfunctions are vaginismus and dyspareunia. **Vaginismus** refers to involuntary contractions of the walls of the vagina that make it too narrow to allow the penis to enter for sexual intercourse. In **dyspareunia,** the woman experiences pain during intercourse. Often, but not always, these conditions are accompanied by orgasmic dysfunction and anxiety associated with sex. Like the male dysfunctions, the female dysfunctions can usually be eliminated with professional help.

Similar to sexual arousal disorder in women, **male sexual arousal disorders** directly reflect the physiological process of sexual excitement in the male sexual response cycle. In men, the most common sexual arousal disorder is **erectile dysfunction** (previously called "impotence"). In spite of high levels of sexual stimulation, there is insufficient arousal to result in the penis's gaining an erection suitable for sexual penetration. Anyone who has watched television recently knows that medications are now available that help many men who were not able to have erections.

There are many potential causes of dysfunctions of sexual arousal, most of which represent a complex interaction between physical and psychological processes (Bancroft & others, 2009). Anxiety, fear, distractions, fatigue, relationship problems, depression, and substance abuse can all cause sexual arousal disorders. Even just worrying about having an erection can sometimes lead to prolonged erectile failure. Sex therapy, therefore, usually addresses these issues in counseling. However, specific sex therapy techniques can be used to reduce sexual anxieties and increase subjective experiences of sexual sensation. For example, a couple may be instructed in how to pay maximum attention to their senses during sexual contact to increase their pleasure experience (Wincze & Carey, 2001).

female sexual arousal disorder A condition in which sexual arousal does not occur in appropriate circumstances in a female.

vaginismus (vaj″i-niz′mus) A female sexual dysfunction in which the individual experiences involuntary contractions of the vaginal walls, making the vagina too narrow to allow the penis to enter comfortably.

dyspareunia (dis″pah-roo′nē-ah) A sexual dysfunction in which the individual experiences pain during intercourse.

male sexual arousal disorders Conditions in which sexual arousal does not occur in appropriate circumstances in a male.

erectile dysfunction A condition in which the penis does not become erect enough for intercourse under sexually arousing circumstances.

Orgasm Dysfunctions

Orgasm dysfunctions involve the disruption of the climax phase of the sexual response cycle. Thus, although the person has a sufficient level of desire and arousal, the sexual response cycle does not progress to orgasm. In women, sexual dysfunctions of orgasm are referred to as **female orgasmic disorder.** This is defined as a persistent absence or prolonged delay of orgasm, despite sufficient sexual stimulation and arousal (American Psychiatric Association, 2000). Note the important phrase at the end of this definition, "despite sufficient sexual stimulation and arousal." The term *female orgasmic disorder* should not be used if, for example, the sex partners do not fully understand what constitutes adequate stimulation for the woman, or the partner is not caring enough to provide sufficient stimulation. In addition, because women experience many different normal patterns of sexual response and orgasm, the delay or absence of orgasm must be dissatisfying to the woman before it is thought to be a sexual dysfunction. Still, inhibited orgasm is a common reason for women to seek sex therapy from psychologists (Wincze & Carey, 2001).

Inhibited orgasm has many potential causes, including performance anxiety, relationship difficulties, fear of abandonment, and depression. Like other sexual dysfunctions, orgasmic disorder may be the result of sexually traumatic experiences. However, failure to achieve orgasm is commonly the result of a lack of adequate clitoral stimulation (Goldsmith, 1988). Many of the sex therapy techniques used to reduce fears and anxieties discussed earlier may be used to treat female inhibited orgasm. In addition, orgasmic disorder may be caused by specific aspects of a relationship or situation that can become the focus of counseling.

In men, the most common orgasm dysfunction involves ejaculating as a result of minimal levels of sexual stimulation, usually just after or even before penetration occurs. When this problem persists over time and becomes distressful, it is considered a sexual dysfunction referred to as **premature ejaculation** (American Psychiatric Association, 2000). There are many causes of premature ejaculation, including inexperience, performance anxiety, fears, and unfortunate learning experiences early in one's sexual history (Wincze & Carey, 2001). A variety of potential treatments for premature ejaculation can lengthen the period of time before ejaculation occurs. One method, called the squeeze technique, requires either the man or his partner to apply a comfortable but firm squeeze to the penis (either just below its head or at its base) to stop the impending orgasm. The pressure from the squeeze causes a delay of ejaculation when applied several times before ejaculation occurs. With repeated use, this can be an effective treatment for premature ejaculation, as the need for squeezing diminishes over time (Wincze & Carey, 2001).

Some men, in contrast, have an orgasm dysfunction known as **male orgasmic disorder.** In this case, the man is rarely able to have an orgasm in spite of adequate sexual stimulation or is able to reach orgasm only after very long periods of stimulation (American Psychiatric Association, 2000).

All sexual dysfunctions share several things in common. First, because they involve sexual behavior, it is often difficult and embarrassing to seek help or to discuss the problem. Society sometimes places unrealistic and demanding expectations on the sexual performance of women and men. Second, people with sexual problems may believe that they are the only persons who have such difficulties, leading them to believe that they are psychologically abnormal. Again, experiencing sexual difficulties is actually common (Herbenick & others, 2010; Michael & others, 1995; Shifren, 2008). Finally, because society places limitations on discussing sexual matters, people often believe that when they do have a sexual problem they have nowhere to turn for help. This, too, is incorrect—there are many sources of help for sexual dysfunctions.

female orgasmic disorder A condition in which a female has a persistent delay or absence of an orgasm.

premature ejaculation A male sexual dysfunction in which the individual reaches orgasm and ejaculates sperm too early.

male orgasmic disorder A condition in which a male has a persistent delay or absence of an orgasm.

A number of sexual dysfunctions interfere with pleasurable and successful sexual intercourse. Problems in sexual desire, sexual arousal, and orgasm occur in both men and women. When the cause of sexual dysfunction is not physical, the problem commonly stems from lack of information, anxiety, or relationship difficulties. For this reason, sex therapists specialize in addressing psychological issues that can lead to sexual difficulties.

Review

To be sure that you have learned the key points from the preceding section, cover the list of correct answers and try to answer each question. If you give an incorrect answer to any question, return to the page given next to the correct answer to see why your answer was not correct.

Check Your Learning

1. Involuntary contractions of the walls of the vagina that make it too narrow to allow the penis to enter for sexual intercourse are called _____.

   a) orgasm dysfunction   c) vaginismus

   b) dyspareunia   d) chlamydia

2. The squeeze technique can be an effective treatment for _____.

   a) erectile dysfunction   c) orgasmic disorder

   b) dyspareunia   d) premature ejaculation

There are no right or wrong answers to the following questions. They are presented to help you become an active reader and think critically about what you just read.

Thinking Critically about Psychology

1. In addition to the loss of sexual pleasure, how would a sexual dysfunction interfere with an individual's quality of life?

2. How could problems of sexual desire be caused by marital problems?

Correct Answers: 1. c (p. 493), 2. d (p. 494)

Summary

Chapter 14 describes the wide range of thoughts, feelings, and actions that are considered to be abnormal because they cause distress or harm.

I.   Abnormal behavior includes those actions, thoughts, and feelings that are harmful to the person and/or others.

   A. Our ideas about the causes of abnormal behavior determine what we do to help those who experience it.

   B. Abnormal behavior is viewed today as a natural, rather than a supernatural, phenomenon. Both biological and psychological factors are thought to play a role in the origins of abnormal behavior.

II. Anxiety disorders are characterized by excessive anxiety.

   A. Intense, unrealistic fears are called *phobias*.

   B. Generalized anxiety disorder is characterized by free-floating anxiety.

   C. Panic anxiety disorder involves attacks of intense anxiety.

   D. Obsessions are anxiety-provoking thoughts that will not go away; compulsions are urges to repeatedly engage in a behavior.

   E. Emotional problems and related problems that persist long after a traumatic stress event are called post-traumatic stress disorder (PTSD).

III. Somatoform disorders are conditions in which an individual experiences symptoms of health problems that are psychological rather than physical in origin.

   A. Somatization disorders are a type of somatoform disorder that involves multiple symptoms of illness that indirectly create a high risk of medical complications; hypochondriasis is characterized by excessive concern with health.

B. Conversion disorders are a type of somatoform disorder that involves serious specific somatic symptoms in the absence of any physical cause. Somatoform pain disorders involve pain without physical cause.

IV. In the various types of dissociative disorders, there is a change in memory, perception, or identity.

A. Dissociative amnesia and fugue states involve memory loss that has psychological rather than physical causes.

B. In depersonalization, individuals feel that they or their surroundings have become distorted or unreal.

C. Individuals who exhibit dissociative identity disorder act as if they possess more than one personality in the same body.

V. Mood disorders are disturbances of positive or negative moods.

A. The individual experiencing major depression is deeply unhappy and lethargic and shows other characteristic symptoms.

B. In the condition known as bipolar disorder, periods of mania alternate irregularly with periods of severe depression.

VI. Schizophrenia involves three major areas of abnormality: (a) delusions and hallucinations; (b) disorganized thinking, emotions, and behavior; and (c) reduced enjoyment and interests.

A. The paranoid schizophrenic holds false beliefs, or delusions—usually of grandeur and persecution—that seriously distort reality.

B. Disorganized schizophrenia is characterized by extreme withdrawal from normal human contact, fragmented delusions and hallucinations, and a shallow "silliness" of emotion.

C. Catatonic schizophrenia is marked by stupors in which the individual may maintain postures for long periods of time.

VII. Attention-deficit/hyperactivity disorder (ADHD) is characterized by high levels of problems in paying attention or by extreme levels of hyperactivity and impulsivity, or both kinds of symptoms.

VIII. Personality disorders are thought to result from personalities that developed improperly during childhood, rather than from breakdowns under stress.

A. Schizoid personality disorders are characterized by a loss of interest in proper dress and social contact, a lack of emotion, and an inability to hold regular jobs.

B. The antisocial personality frequently violates social rules and laws, is often violent, takes advantage of others, and feels little guilt about it.

IX. A number of uncommon patterns of sexual behavior are considered to be normal, even though they are unusual, unless they cause distress in the person. Transvestism and gender identity disorder are atypical sexual patterns that deviate considerably from the norm but are not considered to be abnormal unless the individual is unhappy with her or his sexual pattern.

X. Other uncommon patterns of sexuality are usually or always harmful to the person and his or her partner.

A. Abnormal patterns of atypical sexual behavior include voyeurism, exhibitionism, fetishism, sadism, masochism, rape, incest, pedophilia, and sexual harassment.

B. Sexual violence (including rape and the sexual assault and molestation of children) and sexual harassment are important social problems.

C. Sexual dysfunctions are problems that can interfere with successful and pleasurable sexual intercourse. These include:

1. Disorders of desire

2. Disorders of arousal

3. Orgasmic disorders

chapter **fifteen**
Therapies

Chapter Outline

Prologue

David had always been a neat and orderly person. During his first session with the therapist, he described with a half-hearted smile an incident in which he slipped and fell in mud on the way to elementary school and returned home sobbing. David's cleanliness caused only minor problems until he was an adult and his daughter was diagnosed with pinworms. David became intensely anxious when the doctor told him to boil the clothing of everyone in the family to kill any pinworm eggs. After he finished boiling the clothes, he washed his hands. But, he thought that there might still be pinworm eggs on them and he washed them again. Soon David began worrying about germs, dirt, and feces that might be on his hands. Within days, he was washing his hands 200 times a day. When his wife became worried about his sanity, and his hands began to crack and bleed because of the constant washing, he decided to contact a therapist (based on Prochaska, 1984, pp. 268–271).

David had developed the form of abnormal behavior called *obsessive-compulsive disorder.* We will see in this chapter that, fortunately, several forms of treatment are effective for this and other psychological problems. Medication is often an effective remedy for obsessive-compulsive disorder, but a simple form of psychological therapy also is very effective. In this therapy, the person agrees to be prevented from washing and to endure the anxiety that not washing creates. In time, the anxiety typically drops to normal levels if the individual does not give in to the urge to wash (Piacentini, 1999; Williams & others, 2010).

Psychotherapy is a process of people helping people. In psychotherapy, a trained professional seeks to help a person with a psychological problem by using methods based on psychological theories of the nature of the problem. Several different forms of psychotherapy are based on the theories of personality discussed in chapter 12.

Therapists who follow the psychoanalytic perspective see abnormal behavior as the result of unconscious conflicts among the id, ego, and superego. These conflicts remain hidden from consciousness, because the ego and superego block them out. Psychoanalysis is an attempt to relax the censorship exerted by the conscious mind and bring unconscious conflicts into awareness, where they can be resolved. Because the contents of the unconscious are revealed only in disguised, symbolic ways, the psychoanalyst helps the individual interpret glimpses of the hidden side of the mind.

Humanistic psychologists also believe that the goal of psychotherapy is to help the person achieve greater awareness of the unconscious, but in ways that differ from those of psychoanalysts. Humanists believe that feelings that conflict with a person's idealized self-concept are often denied conscious awareness. The humanistic psychotherapist seeks to help the person allow this information into his or her consciousness and thus achieve fuller self-awareness and a more accurate self-concept.

Cognitive-behavior therapy is an approach to psychotherapy that is associated with the social learning view of personality. Because psychological problems are believed to be the result of unfortunate learning experiences, the behavior therapist plays the role of a teacher who helps the person *unlearn* abnormal ways of behavior. In addition, cognitive-behavior therapists believe that illogical ways of thinking often cause abnormal behavior. They attempt to change these faulty cognitions by pointing out their irrationality.

Help for abnormal behavior is not delivered only in one-to-one psychotherapy, however. It's sometimes provided in the form of group or family therapy. In addition, therapy often takes the form of medication or—in some cases—other kinds of medical treatment.

Definition of Psychotherapy

People with the serious kinds of psychological problems described in the previous chapter need professional help, and a great many "normal" people encounter difficulties at one time or another for which they need more help than family and friends can provide. Many forms of help are available for psychological disorders from psychologists, psychiatrists, clinical social workers, and counselors. In this chapter, we describe the major forms of therapy.

In general terms, **psychotherapy** can be defined as a process in which a trained professional uses psychological methods to help a person with psychological problems. The term *psychological methods* can refer to almost any kind of human interaction (such as talking or demonstrating) that is based on a psychological theory of the problem, but it does not include medical treatment methods such as medication. Different forms of psychotherapy associated with psychoanalytic, humanistic, and social learning theories of personality involve very different psychological methods. In the *Application of Psychology* section at the end of this chapter, we present evidence on the effectiveness of these various forms of psychotherapy.

psychotherapy (sī-kō-ther′ah-pē) A form of therapy in which a trained professional uses methods based on psychological theories to help a person with psychological problems.

Ethical Standards for Psychotherapy

The relationship between client and psychotherapist is a unique one. The patient divulges highly personal information in an emotion-laden setting and places her or his future in the hands of the psychotherapist. Because this places the therapist in a position of power relative to the client, it's essential that the highest ethical standards be followed in the practice of psychotherapy. The following discussion of ethical principles is based on the policies developed by the American Psychological Association (2002) and the Association for Advancement of Behavior Therapy (1978).

Psychotherapy is considered to be ethical only under the following circumstances:

1. The goals of treatment must be carefully considered with the client. These goals should be in the best interest of the client and society and they must be fully understood by the client.

2. The choices for alternative treatment methods should be carefully considered.

3. The therapist must only treat problems that she or he is qualified to treat. No therapist is trained to use all forms of therapy or to handle all types of problems (adults, children, marital problems, and so on), the therapist must refer cases that fall outside his or her expertise to qualified therapists.

4. The effectiveness of treatment must be evaluated in some way. The best way of doing this is to use meaningful measures of the problem and progress in treating it.

5. The rules and laws regarding the confidentiality of all information obtained about the client during treatment must be fully explained to the client. Under most circumstances it is unethical and illegal for the therapist to reveal any information about the person (even the fact that a person is a client in therapy) to anyone without the written permission of the client. However, there are exceptions to that rule. First, other psychologists in a practice may sometimes cover for the therapist in emergencies and will need to learn about the client. Second, if the therapist is still in training and being supervised by a licensed therapist, it is essential that the client be told of that fact and the name of the supervisor. Third, in some circumstances regarding court matters, the courts can require the therapist to reveal confidential information. Fourth, if the therapist learns that the client is in immediate danger of harm or of harming anyone else, the therapist is obligated to report that information to the proper authorities.

6. The therapist must not use the power of the intense relationship with the client to exploit the client in sexual or other ways. Sexual or romantic intimacies with clients have long been strictly forbidden. In fact—in contrast to novels and movies in which therapists and current or former clients fall in love and

Psychotherapists must respect the rules and laws regarding the confidentiality of information about their clients.

psychoanalysis (sī´kō-ah-nal´i-sis) A method of psychotherapy developed by Freud based on his belief that the root of all psychological problems is unconscious conflicts among the id, the ego, and the superego.

marry—ethical regulations forbid romantic or sexual relationships even with *former* clients under virtually all circumstances. Sexual harassment of clients is similarly strictly forbidden.

7. The therapist must treat human beings with dignity and must understand and respect differences based on gender, ethnicity, sexual orientation, and other sociocultural factors. To the greatest extent possible, therapists must understand and respect human differences and not try to sway clients to their own beliefs and ways. For example, this means that a traditional male therapist must not try to influence a woman who identifies with the feminist philosophy to adopt a more subservient feminine role. Similarly, a therapist who believes that homosexuality is immoral must not attempt to convince a homosexual who is comfortable with her or his sexual orientation to change. If the therapist cannot respect the beliefs and ways of a particular client, the therapist must refer that person to another therapist.

Psychoanalysis

Psychoanalysis is the approach to psychotherapy founded by Sigmund Freud. It is based on Freud's belief that the root of all psychological problems is unconscious conflicts among the id, ego, and superego. Conflicts inevitably exist among these three competing forces, but they can cause problems if they get out of hand. If too much of the energy of the superego and ego is devoted to holding the selfish desires of the id in check, or, if these prohibitions are weak and the id threatens to break free, psychological disturbances result. According to Freud, these conflicts must be brought into consciousness if they are to be solved.

Bringing unconscious conflicts into consciousness is not an easy matter, though. Recall from chapter 12 that the id is completely unconscious. Even the sexual and aggressive motives that we consciously experience have been transformed by the ego into safe and socially acceptable versions of the id's true desires. According to Freud, the ego operates as if the raw, selfish desires of the id were too dangerous to allow into consciousness, so it works diligently to dam up the id in the recesses of our unconscious mind. Special therapy methods must be used, therefore, to allow information about unconscious id conflicts to slip past the censorship of the ego.

It's generally possible to bring information out of the unconscious only when the ego's guard is temporarily relaxed, and even then, the id is able to reveal itself only in disguised, symbolic forms. Thus, the job of the psychoanalyst is (a) to create conditions in which the censorship of the ego is relaxed and (b) to interpret the disguised, symbolic revelations of the unconscious mind to the patient.

Techniques of Psychoanalytic Psychotherapy

Most contemporary psychoanalysts do not practice an orthodox version of psychoanalysis but, rather, practice versions based on the revisions of Jung, Adler, Horney, and more contemporary psychoanalysts. Still, many of the specific techniques of therapy used by Freud are still in use today. These include free association, dream interpretation, interpretation of resistance, and interpretation of transference.

free association A tool used by Freud in which the patient is encouraged to talk about whatever comes to mind, allowing the contents of the unconscious mind to slip past the censorship of the ego.

Free Association. Freud's primary tool of therapy was the method of **free association.** In this method, the individual is encouraged to talk about whatever comes to mind. No thought or feeling is to be withheld, no matter how illogical, trivial, unpleasant, or silly it might seem. Freud hoped that this technique would lead to a "turning off" of the intellectual control of the ego and allow glimpses of the unconscious. To make

In traditional psychoanalysis, the therapist sits out of the patient's sight. Freud had his patients lie on a couch while he sat in a chair to the left.

A patient and therapist in a session of orthodox psychoanalysis.

this more likely to happen, Freud had his patients lie on a couch, facing the ceiling. He sat out of sight, behind them, so they would feel as though they were talking to themselves rather than revealing forbidden information to another person.

Dream Interpretation.

Dream interpretation was used by Freud in much the same manner as free association. As discussed in chapter 6, the obvious, or manifest, content of dreams is believed by psychoanalysts to symbolically mask the true, or latent, content of dreams. By asking patients to recall dreams, Freud believed he had another "window" on the unconscious.

For example, a recurrent dream of an adolescent boy in which he was drifting through a slimy swamp on a raft, reaching down repeatedly into the dirty water and pulling up shoes, might have no meaning at all to the adolescent. The psychoanalyst might translate it to mean that the boy was experiencing conflicts over his heterosexual desires. Shoes are commonly taken to symbolize vaginas in psychoanalytic thinking, and the dirty, forbidding water from which he was attempting to possess these vaginas might represent his guilt feelings about sex.

dream interpretation A method developed by Freud in which the symbols of the manifest content of dreams that are recalled by the patient are interpreted to reveal their latent content.

Interpretation of Resistance.

Freud also placed heavy emphasis on the interpretation of what he called *resistance in therapy.* Resistance is any form of opposition of the patient to the process of psychoanalysis. **Resistance** can occur in two ways. It might take vague forms, such as missing appointments with the therapist or questioning the value of psychoanalysis. Or it might be a specific resistance to the interpretations of the therapist. In either case, resistance meant to Freud that he had located a conflict in the patient that was so laden with anxiety that the patient wanted to avoid talking about it. This avoidance of a topic made Freud all the more interested in pursuing it.

resistance Any form of patient opposition to the process of psychoanalysis.

Interpretation of Transference.

The relationship that forms between patient and therapist can also be a source of information about the unconscious to the psychoanalyst. Because the patient comes to the therapist in need of help, reveals a great deal of private information, and receives acceptance and support, it's not surprising that a rather intense relationship often develops. This relationship is not like the one you have with, say, your dentist, but more like a close relationship with a parent.

Because of the intensity of the relationship in therapy, psychoanalysts believe that the kind of relationship the patient has with the therapist reveals a great deal about

transference (trans-fer´ens) The phenomenon in psychoanalysis in which the patient comes to feel and act toward the therapist in ways that resemble how he or she feels and acts toward other significant adults.

the way the patient relates to her or his parents and other significant authority figures. Psychoanalysts call this phenomenon **transference.** When patients repeatedly ask for reassurance that they will not be dropped as clients, argue about fees, or make sexual advances, they are believed to be transferring to the therapist feelings that they have for other significant adults in their lives. That is, they are feeling and acting toward the therapist in the same basic ways that they feel and act toward their parents, employers, and so on. When interpreted to the patients, psychoanalysts believe that transference can serve as another valuable source of insight.

Catharsis. In addition to the interpretation of symbolic revelations of unconscious conflicts, psychoanalysis allows the patient to release some of the emotion that is pent up with unconscious conflicts. All forms of psychotherapy can be very emotional experiences that at times involve talking about highly upsetting topics. Letting these emotions out—a process psychoanalysts call **catharsis**—appears to be important to the success of psychotherapy (Diener & others, 2007).

catharsis The release of emotional energy related to unconscious conflicts.

Excerpt from Psychoanalytic Psychotherapy

In the following excerpt from a session of psychoanalytic psychotherapy, the therapist attempts to get the client to reinterpret his anxiety:

Client: We had a salesmen's meeting, and a large group of us were cramped together in a small room and they turned out the lights to show some slides, and I got so jumpy and anxious I couldn't stand it.
Therapist: So what happened?
C: I just couldn't stand it. I was sweating and shaking, so I got up and left, and I know I'll be called on the carpet for walking out.
T: You became so anxious and upset that you couldn't stand being in the room even though you knew that walking out would get you into trouble.
C: Yeah. . . . What could have bothered me so much to make me do a dumb thing like that?
T: You know, we've talked about other times in your life when you've become upset in close quarters with other men, once when you were in the army and again in your dormitory at college.
C: That's right, and it was the same kind of thing again.
T: And, if I'm correct, this has never happened to you in a group of men and women together, no matter how closely you've been cramped together.
C: Uh. . . . Yes, that's right.
T: So it appears that something especially about being physically close to other men, and especially in the dark, makes you anxious, as if you're afraid bad things might happen in that kind of situation.
C: (Pause) I think you're right about that . . . and I know I'm not physically afraid of other men. Do you think I might get worried about something homosexual taking place?

*Source: I. B. Weiner, *Principles of Psychotherapy.* Copyright 1975 John Wiley & Sons. This material is used by permission of John Wiley & Sons, Inc.

interpersonal psychotherapy A form of psychological therapy, based on the theories of neo-Freudian Harry Stack Sullivan, that focuses on the accurate identification and communication of feelings and the improvement of current social relationships.

Interpersonal Psychotherapy for Depression

In recent years, a new form of neo-Freudian psychotherapy, known as **interpersonal psychotherapy,** has emerged from the psychoanalytic tradition (Frank & others, 2007; Klerman & Weissman, 1993; Luty & others, 2007; Poleshuck & others, 2010). As discussed in chapter 12, contemporary neo-Freudian theories emphasize the importance of interpersonal relationships in our lives more than unconscious sexual motivation. Therefore, interpersonal therapy, often referred to as IPT, is quite different from classical Freudian psychoanalysis. IPT ignores unconscious motivation, minimizes discussion of the past, and does not involve interpretation of the individual's relationship with the therapist (transference). Instead, IPT focuses on the "here and now." IPT is a brief form of psychotherapy that is usually completed in 12 to 16 weeks. Unlike other forms of Freudian therapies, interpersonal therapy is highly focused and structured, with therapists following detailed treatment manuals.

Originally, interpersonal therapy was developed to treat depression. Interpersonal therapists believe that depression can be treated by improving our understanding of our feelings and improving how we relate and communicate to the important people in our lives. Interpersonal therapists believe that there are *four kinds of problems that cause depression:*

1. Grief over the loss of an important relationship through the breakup of a relationship, a divorce, or the death of a loved one

2. Conflicts with people who are significant to us

3. Life events that are stressful or that create threats to our self-esteem

4. Lack of social skills for establishing healthy interpersonal relationships

How does interpersonal therapy attempt to deal with depression created by these four causes? In IPT, therapists attempt to reach *seven goals* to treat depression:

1. Help the individual feel that the therapist understands her or his feelings and considers them to be important

2. Help the individual understand how his or her feelings are related to what is going on in his or her life, particularly to his or her current social relationships. The interpersonal therapist allows discussion of past social relationships (for example, relationships with parents, former romantic partners, and so on) only to reach an understanding of how "emotional baggage" from past relationships can influence current relationships

3. Help the individual learn to express her or his feelings to other persons in constructive ways

4. Identify relationships that are too unhealthy to fix, end them appropriately, and move on to healthier relationships with others

5. Help the individual develop a sense of mastery of the new roles that are created by life events, such as dating again after divorce or entering a new occupation

6. Improve the individual's skills for creating healthy new relationships and maintaining them

7. Help the individual develop an optimistic focus on current opportunities for change instead of on the past

To reach these goals, the therapist keeps every session focused on the individual's feelings, his or her current life circumstances, and current options for change. For example, Charles has felt very depressed for the past few months. He has a stable job as a waiter, and he has many friends and a long-term relationship with a woman whom he hopes to marry. For the past few months, he has been having many fights with his girlfriend, who recently entered college. The IPT sessions may reveal that Charles feels unimportant to his girlfriend, now that she studies during most evenings and weekends and has less time for him than in the past. In addition, he may feel threatened now that his girlfriend is a college student, because he never attended college. When they do have time to spend together, they often fight because Charles treats her with anger and sarcasm. The therapist would first help Charles see that his feelings involve worry that he is no longer important to her, rather than anger that she has entered college. Then the therapist would help Charles learn to express his feelings of worry to his girlfriend calmly, without anger or sarcasm. This would make it easier for her to respond with nurturing and reassurance. These changes, in turn, could be expected to help reduce his feelings of depression.

The most important thing to know about IPT is that a number of studies have suggested it is quite effective for depression (de Mello & others, 2005) either by itself or combined with medication (Frank & others, 2007; Schramm & others, 2007; Shedler, 2010). Recently, interpersonal psychotherapy has been used with personality disorders and eating disorders (Constantino & others, 2005), but less is known about its effectiveness with these problems.

Review

Psychoanalysis is the method of psychotherapy based on Freud's theory of personality. The therapist attempts to help the patient by bringing unconscious conflicts into consciousness so that she or he can intelligently resolve them. Because the ego works to block from consciousness the contents of the unconscious mind (including conflicts among the id, ego, and superego), the psychoanalyst must create conditions to relax the censorship of the ego. Even when the unconscious mind reveals itself at these times, however, it does so in disguised, symbolic ways. This means that a second function of the psychoanalyst is to interpret the disguised information revealed during psychoanalysis to the patient. The method most commonly used by the psychoanalyst to relax the ego's censorship is free association. Comments made by the patient during these wandering, unguided conversations are believed to symbolically reveal hidden conflicts. In addition, the psychoanalyst interprets information from dreams, resistance to the process of therapy, and the way the patient acts toward the psychoanalyst (transference) to reveal further the unconscious mind to the patient. Psychoanalysis is believed to provide temporary relief by allowing the patient to vent some of the emotion tied up in unconscious conflicts (catharsis). A new form of neo-Freudian psychodynamic psychotherapy, called *interpersonal therapy,* has been found to be effective in the treatment of depression. Unlike classical psychoanalysis, this form of psychotherapy focuses on the "here and now" and helps the individual accurately identify feelings, communicate feelings constructively, and improve social relationships.

Check Your Learning

To be sure that you have learned the key points from the preceding section, cover the list of correct answers and try to answer each question. If you give an incorrect answer to any question, return to the page given next to the correct answer to see why your answer was not correct. Remember that these questions cover only some of the important information in this section; it is important that you make up your own questions to check your learning of other facts and concepts.

1. In general terms, _____ can be defined as a specialized process in which a trained professional uses psychological methods to help a person with psychological problems.

2. _____ is based on Freud's belief that the root of all psychological problems is unconscious conflicts among the id, ego, and superego that must be brought into conscious awareness.

   a) Behavior therapy   c) Psychoanalysis

   b) Client-centered therapy   d) Cognitive therapy

3. Freud's primary tool of therapy was the method of _____, in which the individual talks in a loose and undirected way about whatever comes to mind.

   a) free association   c) dream interpretation

   b) transference   d) resistance

Check Your
Learning (cont.)

4. _____ describes the release of emotional energy related to unconscious
conflicts.

a) Emotional cleansing

c) Liberation

b) Catharsis

d) Outletting

5. The new form of psychotherapy based on neo-Freudian theories that avoids focus
on the past and emphasizes the accurate identification of feelings, constructive
communication, and improvement of social relationships is called _____.

Thinking Critically
about Psychology

There are no right or wrong answers to the following questions. They are presented to help
you become an active reader and think critically about what you have just read.

1. Give a brief personality description of the type of patients who you believe would
benefit most from psychoanalysis. Do you think most women would be comfortable
with psychoanalysis? How about members of ethnic groups different from Freud's?

2. What would you consider to be the strengths of interpersonal therapy? What might
be its weaknesses?

Correct Answers: 1. psychotherapy (p. 499), **2.** c (p. 500), **3.** a (p. 500), **4.** b (p. 502), **5.** interpersonal
psychotherapy (pp. 502–503)

Humanistic Psychotherapy

The humanistic school of thought, like the psychoanalytic school, believes that the
primary goal of therapy is to bring feelings of which the individual is unaware into
conscious awareness. Recall from chapter 12 that Carl Rogers, who was one of the
originators of humanistic psychotherapy, gives us an alternative way of thinking
about feelings and information of which are not consciously aware. Unlike Freud,
Rogers does not believe that we are born with an unconscious mind. Rather, we deny
awareness to information and feelings that differ too much from our concepts of self
and ideal self (by not symbolizing them).

Using the same example that we used to illustrate Freud's concept of the unconscious, suppose you were a person who wanted casual sex. If your ideal self (the one
you think you should ideally be) were the kind of person who would never have casual
sex, you might deny conscious awareness to that desire. The desire for casual sex did
not arise from an unconscious id, according to Rogers, but the end result is the same:
when a feeling is denied awareness, it can create anxiety until it's brought into the
open. That is, it creates trouble until the individual achieves full awareness of his or
her feelings. Because humanists view full self-awareness as necessary for the complete realization of our inner-directed potential, they speak of the process of therapy in
terms of "growth in awareness" rather than insight.

The methods used by humanistic therapists differ considerably from those used
in psychoanalytic psychotherapy. A description of methods of humanistic therapy is
complicated by the fact that a number of different approaches are grouped together
under the name of humanism. We can get a perspective on these therapies, however,
by looking at the methods of two leaders of the humanistic psychotherapy movement,
Carl Rogers and Frederick S. ("Fritz") Perls.

Client-Centered Psychotherapy

Rogers refers to his humanistic approach as **client-centered psychotherapy** (he prefers
the term *client* to the more medically oriented term *patient*) because the client, not the
therapist, is at the center of the process of psychotherapy (Rogers, 1951). More recently,

client-centered psychotherapy
Carl Rogers' approach to humanistic
psychotherapy, in which the therapist
creates an atmosphere that
encourages clients to discover feelings
of which they were unaware.

Carl Rogers (top right) facilitating the discussion during a group therapy session.

reflection (re-flek´shun) A technique in humanistic psychotherapy in which the therapist reflects the emotions of the client to help clients clarify their feelings.

the term *person-centered psychotherapy* has come into use. The emphasis is on the ability of clients to help themselves rather than on the ability of the therapist to help the clients. The job of the therapist in client-centered therapy is not to employ specific therapy techniques or to interpret the client's behavior, but to create an atmosphere that is so emotionally safe for the clients that they will feel free to express to the therapist (and to themselves) the feelings they have denied awareness. Growth in awareness comes not from interpretations but from the client's feeling safe enough to explore hidden emotions in the therapy sessions. Rogers believes that the creation of this safe atmosphere requires three elements from the therapist. The therapist (a) must be warm; (b) must genuinely be able to like the clients and unconditionally accept everything they think, feel, or do without criticism; and (c) must have empathy—an accurate understanding and sharing of the emotions of the client. A number of studies have shown that the degree of warmth and empathy of the therapist is an important determinant of the effectiveness of psychotherapy, even when the method of psychotherapy is not client-centered therapy (Brent & Kolko, 1998; Miller & Rose, 2009).

The closest thing to a specific "technique" in client-centered therapy is the process of **reflection.** The therapist helps the clients clarify the feelings expressed in their statements by reflecting back the emotions of the client. Sometimes the therapists ask questions, but, other than reflections, client-centered therapists say relatively little in therapy. In particular, they strictly avoid giving advice to clients. They feel that clients can easily learn to solve their own problems after they have gained awareness, but that they will remain dependent on the therapist if the therapist solves their problems for them.

Excerpt from Client-Centered Psychotherapy

The following is an excerpt from a conversation between humanistic psychologist Carl Rogers and a depressed young man. Note the complete, nonjudgmental acceptance of the client's feelings.

Rogers: Everything's lousy, huh? You feel lousy? (Silence of 39 seconds)
Rogers: Want to come in Friday at 12 at the usual time?
Client: [Yawns and mutters something unintelligible.] (Silence of 48 seconds)
Rogers: Just kind of feel sunk way down deep in these lousy, lousy feelings, hm? Is that something like it?
Client: No.
Rogers: No? (Silence of 20 seconds)
Client: No. I just ain't no good to nobody, never was, and never will be.
Rogers: Feeling that now, hm? That you're just no good to yourself, no good to anybody. Just that you're completely worthless, huh? Those really are lousy feelings. Just feel that you're no good at all, hm?
[From a session three days later]
Client: I just want to run away and die.
Rogers: M-hm, m-hm, m-hm. It isn't even that you want to get away from here to something. You just want to leave here and go away and die in a corner, hm? (Silence of 30 seconds)
Rogers: I guess as I let that soak in I really do sense how, how deep that feeling sounds, that you—I guess the image that comes to my mind is sort of a—wounded animal that wants to crawl away and die. It sounds as though that's kind of the way you feel that you just want to get away from here and vanish. Perish. Not exist. (Silence of 1 minute)

Client: [almost inaudibly] All day yesterday and all morning I wished I were dead. I even prayed last night that I could die.

Rogers: I think I caught all of that, that for a couple of days now you've just wished you could be dead and you've even prayed for that, I guess that. One way this strikes me is that to live is such an awful thing to you, you just wish you could die, and not live. (Silence of 1 minute, 12 seconds)

Rogers: So that you've been just wishing and wishing that you were not living. You wish that life would pass away from you. (Silence of 30 seconds)

Client: I wish it more'n anything else I've ever wished around here.

Rogers: M-hm, m-hm, m-hm. I guess you've wished for lots of things but boy! It seems as though this wish to not live is deeper and stronger than anything you ever wished before. (Silence of 1 minute, 36 seconds)

---

*Reproduced by permission of the publisher, F. E. Peacock Publishers, Inc., Itasca, Illinois. From Raymond J. Corsini & Contributors, *Current Psychotherapies,* 2nd edition. Copyright 1979, pp. 155–159.

Gestalt Psychotherapy

Humanistic psychologist Fritz Perls named his approach to humanistic psychotherapy Gestalt therapy (Perls, Hefferline, & Goodman, 1951). The term *gestalt* was chosen to emphasize a point first made by the Gestalt psychologists (whom we initially encountered in chapter 1). Writing in the early 1900s, this group pointed out that sensations have no meaning unless they are organized into "whole" perceptions. In an analogous way, Fritz Perls wanted to help his clients perceive themselves in a whole, or complete way, by admitting conflicting information into awareness.

The goal of **Gestalt therapy** is essentially the same as that of client-centered therapy—namely, creating a therapeutic experience that will help the client achieve greater self-awareness. But the kinds of therapeutic experiences created by Gestalt and client-centered psychotherapists are as different as night and day.

Gestalt psychologists are actively involved in the conversations of therapy sessions. In particular, they challenge their clients' statements when they think the statements do not reflect their clients' true feelings, and they point out revealing inconsistencies in the present. For example, if a client claimed to never feel anxious about her performance on the job, she might get a reply like, "Oh, come now, Mary, everyone gets anxious about job performance sometime. And what do you think it means that you start nervously tapping your fingers and squirming in your seat every time I bring up the subject? I think your denials of anxiousness cover up your true feelings."

The emotional atmosphere of Gestalt therapy is also quite different from client-centered therapy. Although Gestalt therapists show concern for their clients, they often deal with them in a confrontational, challenging manner. They are far from warm and accepting in their pushing, prodding, and questioning. Perls refers to this confrontation as a "safe emergency": although it's upsetting to the clients, it occurs in the safe environment of therapy. He feels that the safe emergency of confrontation with the therapist is necessary to shake loose feelings that have been denied awareness.

In recent years, a combination of client-centered therapy and Gestalt therapy has been refined and appears to be effective (Ellison & others, 2009).

Gestalt therapy A humanistic therapy in which the therapist takes an active role (questioning and challenging the client) to help the client become more aware of her or his feelings.

Fritz Perls (1893–1970).

Review

Humanistic psychotherapy strives to help clients achieve fuller self-awareness. Humanists believe that information about individuals that differs too much from their concept of self—both the selves they think they are and the selves they think they should be—is denied awareness. This lack of awareness is harmful both because it keeps the individual from having an accurate view of self to use in making decisions and because the unsymbolized information threatens the person's inaccurate self-image and creates anxiety. Different

Review (cont.)

approaches to humanistic psychotherapy use different methods to bring un-symbolized information into the open and give the person self-awareness. Client-centered psychotherapists create a safe emotional environment in therapy that they believe will allow clients to grow in self-awareness. This is accomplished through the therapist's warmth, empathy, and unconditional acceptance. In addition, the therapist uses the technique of reflection; the humanistic therapist repeats the message that she hears in the client's statements to help the client clarify what he is feeling. Gestalt therapists take a very different approach to humanistic therapy. They actively confront clients about inconsistencies in their statements, as well as between their statements and non-verbal behavior, that they feel reveal conflicting information and feelings. By pointing out these inconsistencies, they hope to help the clients achieve greater self-awareness.

Check Your Learning

To be sure that you have learned the key points from the preceding section, cover the list of correct answers and try to answer each question. If you give an incorrect answer to any question, return to the page given next to the correct answer to see why your answer was not correct.

1. Humanists view full *self-awareness* as necessary for the complete realization of our inner-directed potential.

    a) true   b) false

2. Rogers refers to his humanistic approach to psychotherapy as _____ because the emphasis is on the ability of the clients to help themselves rather than on the ability of therapists to help clients.

3. The process of _____ describes a technique used in client-centered psychotherapy in which the therapist restates the clients' emotions to help clients clarify their feelings.

    a) mimicking   c) repetition

    b) reflection   d) recapitulation

4. A humanistic therapy in which the therapist takes an active role (questioning and challenging) to help the client become more aware of her or his feelings is referred to as _____ therapy.

    a) client-centered   c) Gestalt

    b) confrontational   d) trial

Thinking Critically about Psychology

There are no right or wrong answers to the following questions. They are presented to help you become an active reader and think critically about what you have just read.

1. How can client-centered therapy and Gestalt therapy both be consistent with the views of humanistic therapy when they are so different?

2. What would you describe as the key difference between humanistic psychotherapy and psychoanalysis? How significant is this difference?

Correct Answers: 1. a (p. 505), 2. client-centered (p. 505), 3. b (p. 506), 4. c (p. 507)

cognitive-behavior therapy
Psychotherapy based on social learning theory in which the therapist helps the client unlearn abnormal ways of behaving, learn more adaptive ways of behaving, and change maladaptive cognitions.

Cognitive-Behavior Therapy

Cognitive-behavior therapy, often referred to as CBT, is the approach to psychotherapy that is associated with the social learning theory of personality. Recall from chapter 12 that abnormal behavior is viewed by social learning theorists as *learned* behavior. Rather than being the result of lack of conscious awareness, abnormal behavior simply is learned from inappropriate experiences of classical conditioning, operant conditioning, and modeling. In other words, individuals are abnormal because their environment taught them to be. For example, a young man who was nervous during a social encounter might be reinforced for withdrawing from that social situation by the reduction in anxiety (negative reinforcement) that it produced. If so, social learning theorists would predict that this individual would learn to withdraw from social situations more and more.

Because of this view of the origins of abnormal behavior, it's natural that behavior therapists would see the process of learning as central to the process of therapy as well. The behavior therapist plays the role of a teacher who helps the client *unlearn* abnormal ways of behaving and *learn* more adaptive ways to take their place.

As we will see later in this section, some methods within the CBT approach include methods for teaching both more adaptive and realistic cognitions. We will survey a few of the major techniques of CBT. As you read about each of them, note how they teach adaptive behavior and cognitions.

Fear Reduction Methods

Several CBT methods are used to treat phobias by extinguishing the fear response. The first CBT methods to be developed allowed the person to *imagine* being in the presence of whatever caused the fear (the phobic stimulus). It is now clear that extinction is more effective when conducted in real life settings, a technique known as **graded exposure.**

In graded exposure, the therapist typically accompanies the patient through a series of gradually increasingly fearful situations, beginning with mildly fearful ones. For a person with an intense phobia of heights, the therapist might accompany the client as he or she first walks to the edge of a second-story balcony. After the client has mastered that first situation and feels calm, he or she would walk to the railing of a third-story balcony, then a fourth-story balcony, and so on, until he or she can be in high places with little anxiety (Chambless & Ollendick, 2001; Nathan & Gorman, 2007).

Modern technology has made graded exposure more convenient for both clients and therapists by safely exposing the client to a graded series of highly realistic frightening situations in the therapist's office using computer-generated virtual reality techniques (Powers & Emmelkamp, 2008; Rothbaum, 2004).

graded exposure A behavior therapy technique in which a person with a phobia is first exposed to a stimulus that is mildly fear provoking. Once the client has mastered his or her anxiety in that situation, he or she is exposed to a graded series of more fearful situations.

A person with a fear of elevators might be treated by asking him or her to ride in elevators all day—perhaps for several days in a row—until the anxiety was reduced. This is an example of the behavior therapy technique of flooding.

Behavioral Activation and Social Skills Training

One goal of CBT is to teach the client adaptive skills that lead to a more enjoyable life using methods. For example, people who are depressed typically do not engage in meaningful work or potentially enjoyable activities. In the CBT technique known as **behavioral activation,** the therapist helps the client begin (or return to) activities that have naturally "anti-depressant" qualities (Dimidjian & others, 2006; Kanter & others, 2010). The activities that are encouraged depend on the individual's needs and preferences, and include anything from getting a new job, joining a group that volunteers to help people in need, to resuming piano lessons. A positive activity that often is effective in combating depression is regular physical exercise (Stathopoulou & others, 2006).

behavioral activation A therapeutic approach based on social learning theory in which the therapist teaches the client to engage in activities that have reinforcing consequences to treat depression.

In some cases, depressed individuals are reluctant or unable to begin to engage in positive activities and require considerable coaching and support in the beginning. There is now strong evidence that behavioral activation therapy is effective in the treatment of depression (Dobson & others, 2008 ; Kanter & others, 2010).

People with severe anxiety disorders and schizophrenia frequently have difficulties interacting with other people. They tend to appear shy, awkward, and "odd" and have difficulties expressing their feelings. Most of us experience similar difficulties in interacting with others in some situations (such as first dates and job interviews), but for some people this is a pervasive experience coloring nearly all of their social encounters and requiring a form of therapy.

social skills training The use of techniques of operant conditioning to teach social skills to persons who lack them.

role playing A therapeutic technique in which the therapist and client act as if they were people in problematic situations.

In the CBT technique of **social skills training,** the therapist uses *shaping* and *positive reinforcement* to teach persons with these social deficiencies to speak more often in social situations, to speak in a voice that is loud enough to be heard, to make appropriate eye contact, and to make fewer odd comments (Kurtz & Mueser, 2008). This is usually accomplished by **role playing,** whereby the therapist and clients act as if they were people in problematic social situations. For example, if the client has great difficulties on job interviews and will soon be seeking a job, the therapist might role-play hypothetical job interviews. The therapist might first take the role of the client and model appropriate social behavior. Then, the client would play the role of herself in the next hypothetical job interview. The therapist would then provide positive reinforcement in the form of praise for the good aspects of the client's social behavior and suggest ways of improving the inappropriate aspects. Over a number of role-play sessions, the client usually improves enough to be able to try role-played job interviews with other people, and eventually to interview with actual prospective employers.

Cognitive-behavior therapists have paid particular attention to the widespread social skill problem of unassertiveness. Many people—both "normal" individuals and people with problems—have a difficult time expressing their true feelings, asking questions, disagreeing, and standing up for their rights. Sometimes these individuals continuously hold their feelings in and let others take advantage of them, partly because other people do not know what they want. In most cases, however, unassertive people keep their feelings inside until they become so angry that they pour them out in an angry outburst.

A goal of social skills training is often to teach assertive rather than angry ways of expressing feelings to others. This is usually done by role playing. For example, the client might initially take the role of a friend who asks the therapist for a loan of $50 even though he knows that the therapist is short on money and that he has owed the therapist $60 for the past three months. The therapist would model an assertive way of handling the request ("I wish I could help you, but I don't have enough money to do it, and I really don't think it would be a good idea for me to lend you more money until you're able to pay me back what you already owe me"). Then they would reverse roles and let the client try to handle a similarly difficult situation. After considerable practice with the therapist, the client should possess enough skills and feel comfortable enough to handle real-life situations in an assertive way.

Excerpt from Social Skills Training

In the following excerpt from a session of CBT social skills training, the therapist is persuading the client to practice behaving in more effective ways in a role-playing session in the therapist's office, so that the therapist can shape and reinforce the more effective behavior. The statements in brackets are unstated thoughts of the therapist that were not stated during the therapy session.

Client: The basic problem is that I have the tendency to let people step all over me. I don't know why, but I just have difficulty in speaking my mind.

Therapist: [My immediate tendency here is to reflect and clarify what the client said, adding a behavioral twist. In paraphrasing what she has already said, I can cast it within a behavioral framework by introducing such terms as situation, respond, and learn.] So you find yourself in a number of different situations where you don't respond the way you would really like to. And if I understand correctly, you would like to learn how to behave differently.

C: Yes. But you know, I have tried to handle certain situations differently, but I just don't seem to be able to do so.

T: [Not a complete acceptance of my conceptualization, seemingly because she has tried to behave differently in the past and nothing has happened. What I should do, then, is somehow provide some explanation of why previous attempts may have failed, and use this to draw a contrast with a potentially more effective treatment strategy that we'll be using in our sessions.] It's almost as if there is a big gap between the way you react and the way you would like to react.

C: It seems that way, and I don't know how to overcome it.

T: Well, maybe you've tried to do too much too fast in the past, and consequently weren't very successful. Maybe a good way to look at the situation is to imagine yourself at the bottom of a staircase, wanting to get to the top. It's probably too much to ask to get there in one gigantic leap. Perhaps a better way to go about changing your reaction in these situations is to take it one step at a time.

C: That would seem to make sense, but I'm not sure if I see how that could be done.

T: Well, there are probably certain situations in which it would be less difficult for you to assert yourself such as telling your boss that he forgot to pay you for the past four weeks.

C: (Laughing.) I guess in that situation, I would say something. Although I must admit, I would feel uneasy about it.

T: But not as uneasy as if you went in and asked him for a raise.

C: No. Certainly not.

T: So, the first situation would be low on the staircase, whereas the second would be higher up. If you can learn to handle easier situations, then the more difficult ones would present less of a problem. And the only way you can really learn to change your reactions is through practice.

C: In other words, I really have to go out and actually force myself to speak up more, but taking it a little bit at a time?

T: [This seems like an appropriate time to introduce the function of behavior rehearsal. I won't say anything about the specific procedure yet, but instead will talk about it in general terms and maybe increase its appeal by explaining that any failures will not really "count." If the client goes along with the general description of the treatment strategy, she should be more likely to accept the details as I spell them out.] Exactly. And as a way of helping you carry it off in the real-life situation, I think it would be helpful if we reviewed some of these situations and your reactions to them beforehand. In a sense, going through a dry run. It's safer to run through some of these situations here, in that it really doesn't "count" if you don't handle them exactly as you would like to. Also, it can provide you an excellent opportunity to practice different ways of reacting to these situations, until you finally hit on one which you think would be best.

C: That seems to make sense.

T: In fact, we could arrange things so that you can actually rehearse exactly what you would say, and how you would say it.

C: That sounds like a good idea.

---

*Excerpt reprinted by permission of the authors from *Clinical Behavior Therapy* by M. R. Goldfried and G. C. Davison. Copyright(©) 1994 John Wiley & Sons, Inc.

Cognitive Restructuring

cognitive restructuring A CBT method in which faulty cognitions—maladaptive beliefs, expectations, and ways of thinking—are changed by pointing out their irrationality.

Aaron T. Beck.

Albert Ellis (1913–2007).

Cognitive restructuring is an important CBT method that rests on the assumption that faulty cognitions—maladaptive beliefs, expectations, and ways of thinking—are the cause of abnormal behavior. Cognitive therapy originated both in the cognitive emphasis of contemporary social learning theorists (Bandura, 1977; Ellis, 1962) and contemporary neo-Freudian theorists (Kelly, 1955). Because a great deal of carefully designed research has supported the effectiveness of cognitive therapy for anxiety and depression, it has become one of the most widely used therapy approaches.

Cognitive-behavior therapists believe that problems do not always stem from inappropriate overt actions. For example, some socially anxious people behave in appropriate, even charming ways in social situations, but they experience anxiety because they inaccurately think of themselves as dull, awkward, and unlikable. Trying to modify their already appropriate social behavior would be fruitless in such cases. Instead, it's necessary to modify their maladaptive cognitions—the inaccurate ways in which they think about themselves and others.

Psychologist Albert Ellis (1962, 1999) and psychiatrist Aaron T. Beck (Beck, 1976, 1999; Beck & others, 1979) have described a number of patterns of cognition that they believe contribute to emotional distress and inappropriate behavior. To better understand the CBT method of cognitive restructuring, we should look more closely at one of the most widely used versions for depression. Aaron Beck believes that depression is caused primarily by the following erroneous patterns of thinking (do not be upset if you see some of your own ways of thinking here—we all think in these erroneous ways to some extent):

1. *Selective abstraction.* Let's say you ask the woman with whom you have had a committed relationship for three years if she has kissed another man since she started dating you. She answers, "Never, not once. I've never even flirted with another man. I'm not blind and I can still tell that a guy is cute, but I'm not romantically interested in anybody but you." Most persons would be reassured by the message of commitment in that statement, but would you go into a raging fit because she said she notices that some other men are attractive? If so, that is selective abstraction—basing your thinking on a small detail taken out of context and given an incorrect meaning.

2. *Overgeneralization.* This is the process of reaching a general conclusion based on a few specific bits of evidence. The young scientist who gets a harsh rejection of the first article she submits to a scientific journal is overgeneralizing if she concludes that no journal will ever publish her research.

3. *Arbitrary inference.* This is the error of reaching a conclusion based on little or no logical evidence—as the name says, the conclusion is arbitrary. For example, if you were to receive an invitation to have lunch with your boss, would you conclude that the boss was gently going to break the news to you that you will be fired? Some people reason in this arbitrary way, concluding that just about everything means something bad.

4. *Magnification/minimization.* When the guy sitting next to you says that your ears have an interesting point at the top, do you magnify this statement out of proportion? ("No wonder everybody hates me—I have grotesque Mr. Spock ears!") Or, if you receive a heartfelt compliment from a friend, do you minimize it to nothing? ("Lynne just says nice things to me because she feels sorry for me.") These examples illustrate the process of magnification/minimization.

5. *Personalization.* Suppose you drove to the beach with your friends and it rained all weekend. Did you become gloomy and really mean it when you complained to your friends, "Nothing ever works out for me—every time I try to have fun it turns into a nightmare!" Some people would falsely conclude that it rained just

because they were at the beach. Personalization is the erroneous pattern of reasoning in which external events are seen as being related to you when there is no logical reason for doing so.

6. Absolutistic thinking. The person who did not have good enough grades to get into medical school, but who has a thriving career as a highly respected hospital administrator, tells a former classmate at his 25-year high school reunion, "Ever since college, my life has been a total failure." Although it might be realistic to say that he failed in an important arena, he certainly has not been a total failure. His absolutistic thinking in all-or-nothing terms—either everything is absolutely wonderful or everything is absolutely terrible—is erroneous and maladaptive.

In cognitive restructuring, the therapist uses a variety of techniques of persuasion to help the client change these faulty patterns of thinking. There is strong evidence that cognitive restructuring can be an effective form of therapy for anxiety and depression, particularly when combined with techniques such as behavioral activation and social skills training (Greeven & others, 2007; Hofmann & others, 2007; Stewart & Chambless, 2009; Stice & others, 2008; Vittengl & others, 2007).

Recently, mindfulness training (p. 000) has been incorporated into some forms of cognitive therapy. Evaluations have indicated that it can be effective in reducing anxiety and depression (Hofmann & others, 2010; Kuyken & others, 2008).

Excerpt from Cognitive Restructuring

In the following excerpt from a session of cognitive therapy, see how the therapist uses a series of probing questions to get the client to contradict her own absolutistic thinking and arbitrary inference.

Therapist: Why do you want to end your life?
Patient: Without Raymond, I am nothing . . . I can't be happy without Raymond . . . But I can't save our marriage.
T: What has your marriage been like?
P: It has been miserable from the very beginning . . . Raymond has always been unfaithful . . . I have hardly seen him in the past five years.
T: You say that you can't be happy without Raymond . . . Have you found yourself happy when you are with Raymond?
P: No, we fight all the time and I feel worse.
T: Then why do you feel that Raymond is essential for your living?
P: I guess it's because without Raymond I am nothing.
T: Would you please repeat that?
P: Without Raymond I am nothing.
T: What do you think of that idea?
P: . . . Well, now that I think about it, I guess it's not completely true.
T: You said you are "nothing" without Raymond. Before you met Raymond, did you feel you were "nothing"?
P: No, I felt I was somebody.
T: Are you saying then that it's possible to be something without Raymond?
P: I guess that's true. I can be something without Raymond.
T: If you were somebody before you knew Raymond, why do you need him to be somebody now?
P: (puzzled) Hmmm . . .
T: You seemed to imply that you couldn't go on living without Raymond.
P: Well, I just don't think that I can find anybody else like him.
T: Did you have male friends before you knew Raymond?
P: I was pretty popular then.

T: If I understand you correctly then, you were able to fall in love before with other men and other men have fallen in love with you.

P: Uh huh.

T: Why do you think you will be unpopular without Raymond now?

P: Because I will not be able to attract any other man.

T: Have any men shown an interest in you since you have been married?

P: A lot of men have made passes at me but I ignore them.

T: If you were free of the marriage, do you think that men might be interested in you—knowing that you were available?

P: I guess that maybe they would be.

T: Is it possible that you might find a man who would be more constant than Raymond?

P: I don't know, . . . I guess it's possible.

T: Do you think there are other men as good as Raymond around?

P: I guess there are men who are better than Raymond because Raymond doesn't love me.

*From A. T. Beck & others, *Cognitive Theory of Depression.* Copyright 1979 The Guilford Press, New York, NY. Reprinted by permission of the authors.

Review

The approach to psychotherapy associated with the social learning theory of personality is known as cognitive-behavior therapy, or CBT. Abnormal behavior is viewed as learned behavior. It's simply behavior that results from inappropriate learning experiences. The role of the behavior therapist is to serve as a teacher who helps the client unlearn abnormal behavior and learn adaptive ways of behaving to take its place. The techniques of behavioral activation and social skills training have been shown to be effective in treating anxiety, depression, and other mental health problems. In some cases, the person's problem is not his or her behavior, but his or her ways of thinking about themselves and others. Consequently, CBT often involves cognitive restructuring, which is a method in which the therapist attempts to change cognitions by demonstrating their irrationality. CBT also have been shown to be effective in treating anxiety and particularly depression.

Check Your Learning

To be sure that you have learned the key points from the preceding section, cover the list of correct answers and try to answer each question. If you give an incorrect answer to any question, return to the page given next to the correct answer to see why your answer was not correct.

1. A _____ plays the role of teacher, a person who helps the client unlearn abnormal ways of thinking and behaving and learn more adaptive ways to take their place.

   a) psychoanalyst

   b) cognitive-behavior therapist

   c) humanistic therapist

   d) group therapist

2. _____ refers to the cognitive distortion of basing your thinking on a small detail taken out of context and given an incorrect meaning.

   a) Selective abstraction

   b) Overgeneralization

   c) Personalization

   d) Absolutistic thinking

3. The CBT method of graduated exposure involves treating phobias by guiding the person through exposure to a graduated series of situations that more strongly evoke the fear response. It is based on the principle of learning known as _____.

   a) positive reinforcement

   b) negative reinforcement

   c) extinction

   d) stimulus discrimination

4. If a person loses her job because the company has laid off a thousand workers and then gets depressed because "I knew they thought I was awful at my job," she is engaging in _____.

a) selective abstraction

c) personalization

b) overgeneralization

d) absolutistic thinking

Thinking Critically about Psychology

There are no right or wrong answers to the following questions. They are presented to help you become an active reader and think critically about what you have just read.

1. Could behavioral activation, social skills training, and graded exposure be used together to treat someone with both social anxiety and depression?

2. Think about each of Aaron Beck's list of erroneous thinking patterns associated with depression. Can you think of any characters in novels or on television who think in these ways?

Correct Answers: 1. b (p. 509), **2. a** (p. 512), **3. c** (p. 509), **4. c** (p. 512)

Group and Family Therapy

Therapy is not always conducted on an individual basis. Rather some methods of therapy are carried out with groups or entire families.

Group Therapy

Psychotherapy is usually conducted on a one-to-one basis, but sometimes it's carried out with groups of clients in **group therapy.** One or two therapists typically work with four to eight clients at a time. Group therapy is cost-effective and is believed to offer therapeutic experiences that cannot be obtained in individual therapy (Clarke & others, 2001; Piper & others, 2007; Yalom, 1995). Some of these experiences are (a) receiving encouragement from other group members, (b) learning that one is not alone in one's problems, (c) learning from the advice offered by others, and (d) learning new ways to interact with others. In addition, providing therapy in a group can sometimes make more efficient use of the therapist's time.

group therapy Psychotherapy conducted in groups, typically of four to eight clients at a time.

The format of group therapy differs widely, depending on the approach taken by the therapist (psychoanalytic, humanistic, cognitive, or behavioral), but all provide an opportunity for the client to interact with other clients and to learn from these interactions with the help of the therapist. Each approach to psychotherapy has adapted its own methods for use in groups. Psychoanalysts play the role of interpreter in group therapy, just as they do in individual therapy. They avoid becoming part of the interactions of the group members, except to offer interpretations of what these interactions reveal. Humanists use group interactions to help clients develop more accurate self-perceptions through the actions and reactions of other

An advantage of group therapy is the opportunity for clients to learn from interacting with other members of the group.

Family therapy emphasizes an understanding of the roles of each of the members of the family system.

group members toward them. Cognitive-behavior therapists use groups to facilitate the teaching of adaptive behavior and cognitions. For example, groups of individuals with problems in social interactions are given instructions in how to relate more effectively, are allowed to practice interacting with one another, and are then given feedback and reinforcement from the therapist and other group members.

Psychotherapists from all of these orientations generally believe that interaction with other group members offers special therapeutic advantages to some clients. But individuals with complex problems that require the full attention of the therapist, or who do not wish to discuss their personal problems in front of others, will benefit more from individual psychotherapy.

Family Therapy

family therapy An approach to psychotherapy that emphasizes an understanding of the roles of each of the members of the family system, usually conducted with all members of the family present.

Another important variation of psychotherapy in which the therapist works with groups of individuals is **family therapy.** In this case, the group is the family composed of parents, children, and any other family members. Although family therapy is conducted by therapists who take psychoanalytic, humanistic, and behavioral approaches, the approach that we most often associate with family therapy is the family systems approach of Jay Haley (1976) and Salvador Minuchin (1974).

The family systems view takes the position that it's not possible to understand adequately the psychological problems of an individual without knowing the role of that individual in the family system. There are two reasons why family systems practitioners believe this. First, the problem of the individual is often caused by problems within the family. For example, a depressed mother or an aggressive child may be reacting to the unhappy, conflict-laden relationship of the mother and father. Although the mother or child may be brought to the clinic identified as "the problem," and no mention is initially made of the marital problems, neither the depression nor the aggression can be helped until the marriage problems are resolved.

The second reason that Haley and Minuchin give for needing to understand the operation of the entire family system in order to understand the problems of an individual family member is that the individual's problems may serve a *function* in the family system. For example, the teenage girl who refuses to eat until she has reached a dangerously low weight may be doing so (consciously or unconsciously) to focus concern on her and keep her parents from divorcing. Similarly, parents who blame all of the family's problems on the supposedly wild behavior of their son may be using him as a scapegoat to shift attention away from the fact that they are both unemployed alcoholics. Without working with all of the members of the family system, these factors in the origins of the problems of the individual would be difficult, if not impossible, to uncover.

The family therapist attempts to solve the problems of all of the family members by improving the functioning of the family system as a whole. The therapist attempts to reach this goal in four primary ways. The family therapist works (a) to give the family members insights into the workings of family systems in general and to correct any dysfunctions in their family, (b) to increase the amount of warmth and intimacy among family members, (c) to improve communication among family members, and (d) to help family members establish a reasonable set of rules for the regulation of the family. In this way, it's hoped that the family will become a system that provides each member with an accurate view of self, a positive opinion of self, and a sense of belonging.

Does your ethnicity matter in seeking psychological help? Sadly to say, it does. The United States has one of the most advanced mental health systems in the world, but it cannot be said to fully meet the needs of all of our citizens. Much has been written about inequities in the receipt of psychological services in the United States. Among persons with mental disorders, far fewer Hispanics and African Americans receive adequate mental health treatment as non-Hispanic whites (Hough & others, 1987; Neighbors & others, 2007). Researchers also have raised concerns that African Americans may be more likely than whites to be committed to psychiatric hospitals, often involuntarily, when they have a mental disorder (Lindsey & Paul, 1989; Snowden & Cheung, 1990). In addition, when people of color do receive mental health treatment, it is not always from individuals with an adequate understanding of the culture of the client (Hwang, 2006; Whaley & Davis, 2007). Thus, much remains to be done to ensure that we have not only an effective mental health system but a fair one as well.

How about gender? Are women and men both provided appropriate psychological services? Nancy Felipe Russo (1990) has pointed out probable inequities in mental health services provided to women. Over the past 50 years, an approach to providing effective treatment for women has evolved from the philosophical foundations of feminism. The fundamental concepts of the **feminist psychotherapy** movement are the following (based on Worrell, 1980):

1. Feminist psychotherapy advocates an equal relationship between the client and therapist. The therapist avoids treating the client as someone who must be told what is best for her and instead empowers the client to trust her own ability to make good decisions. This therapy is designed to counteract the sexist view of women as needing guidance from their fathers and husbands. Sometimes this is aided by conducting therapy with groups of similar women to empower them to make constructive suggestions to one another and minimize the role of the therapist.

2. Women clients are encouraged to see the ways in which society has limited their development and has pushed them into dependent roles. To counter these forces, women are encouraged to view themselves as powerful human beings who can effectively use their power in the personal, economic, and political spheres of life.

3. Another goal of feminist psychotherapy is to encourage women to become aware of the anger that they feel over living as second-class citizens in a sexist society and to find constructive ways of expressing that anger.

4. Feminist psychotherapy helps women define themselves in ways that are independent of their roles as wife, mother, and daughter. It also seeks to assist women in dealing with the natural anxiety that they may experience about leaving or redefining these expected traditional roles.

5. Women are encouraged to consider their own needs to be as valid and as worthy of being met as those of others. The goal is to help women increase their sense of worth and self-esteem.

6. Finally, women are empowered to develop skills that are not traditionally encouraged in women. These include assertiveness, career skills, and the skills to deal effectively with tradition-bound persons who oppose such changes.

Continued on pg. 518

Human Diversity
Ethnic, Gender, and Sexual Issues in Psychotherapy

Over the past 25 years, feminist psychotherapy has evolved as an approach to understanding and treating the psychological problems of women. It has increasingly been integrated into broader views of psychotherapy.

feminist psychotherapy An approach to psychotherapy that encourages women to confront issues created by living in a sexist society as part of their psychotherapy.

Continued from pg. 517 It is important to understand that feminist psychotherapy isn't just for women. Its guiding principles of equality, independence, and assertiveness can be helpful for everyone. As a result, the concepts of feminist psychotherapy are increasingly integrated into all forms of psychotherapy rather than considered as a separate approach to therapy.

What about sexual orientation? Does that require special consideration in psychotherapy? Psychologists Catherine Eubanks-Carter, Lisa Burckell, and Marvin Goldfried (2005) have argued cogently that is does. They believe that many psychotherapists view homosexuality and bisexuality as "pathological" to some extent, even if they consciously disavow such attitudes and beliefs and are trying to be accepting. It may be essential for gays, lesbians, and bisexuals to seek psychotherapy from therapists whose attitudes do not complicate the process of psychotherapy.

Medical Therapies

In addition to psychotherapy, medical therapies are commonly used in the treatment of abnormal behavior. **Medical therapies** are generally designed to directly change brain functioning to treat a psychological disorder. There are four types of medical therapy in use today: drug therapy, electroconvulsive therapy, transcranial magnetic stimulation, and psychosurgery.

Drug Therapy

medical therapies Those therapies—including drug therapy, electroconvulsive therapy, and psychosurgery—generally designed to correct a physical condition that is believed to be the cause of a psychological disorder.

drug therapy A medical therapy that uses medications to treat abnormal behavior.

By far, the most widely used medical treatment for abnormal behavior is **drug therapy,** in which medications are used to treat abnormal behavior. The idea that chemicals can be used to treat abnormal behavior dates back at least to the special diets used by Pythagoras around 490 B.C. But the widespread use of effective psychiatric drugs has come about only in the past 40 years. The era of modern drug therapy began in 1954 with the introduction of drugs such as Thorazine for the treatment of schizophrenia. Thorazine gave physicians a tool that for the first time in history substantially improved the lives of schizophrenic persons. Other drugs were also introduced soon after that are also effective in the treatment of depression (antidepressants) and anxiety (tranquilizers).

How do medications help persons with psychological problems? Recall from chapter 3 that our biology and our psychological lives are intimately related. Modern psychiatric medications are designed to improve psychological functioning by influencing a specific neurotransmitter in the brain. For example, selective serotonin-reuptake inhibitors (SSRIs) cause axons that secrete serotonin to reabsorb the serotonin more slowly. This keeps the serotonin active in the synapse longer, giving it more time to stimulate the dendrite of the next neuron. Because neural transmission using serotonin is believed not to operate optimally in individuals with high levels of anxiety, depression, and other problems, these medications often helps "normalize" serotonin transmission in the brain.

Although many people view psychiatric medications as a way of "drugging" people with psychological problems to keep them quiet, the goal is to help their brains operate more *normally.* Because most medications do not influence only one neurotransmitter, however, and because most neurotransmitters play other roles in the brain unrelated to emotional problems, psychiatric medications often have side effects that result from their impact on other neural systems. For example, prolonged use of some antipsychotic medications can cause weight gain and can result in impaired control of the body's muscles if not carefully monitored. Similarly, some antidepressant medications cause the individual to have a dry mouth and gain weight.

Table 15.1
Some Commonly Used Psychiatric Drugs

Physicians have a variety of medications at their disposal for use in the treatment of temporary stress reactions and psychological disorders. Some examples of these medications and their benefits are given here. Some of these medications have several uses and may be prescribed by a physician for reasons other than psychological problems.

Trade Name	Generic Name	For Relief of
Lexapro	escitalopram	Depression and anxiety
Paxil	paroxetine	Depression and anxiety
Prozac	fluoxetine	Depression and anxiety
Zoloft	sertraline	Depression and anxiety
Xanax	alprazolam	Anxiety
Geodon	ziprasidone	Psychotic symptoms
Haldol	haloperidol	Psychotic symptoms
Navane	thiothixene	Psychotic symptoms
Risperdal	risperidone	Psychotic symptoms
Zyprexa	olanzapine	Psychotic symptoms
Depakote	dicalproex	Bipolar disorder
Epilim	valproate	Bipolar disorder
Eskalith	lithium	Bipolar disorder

Today the use of these drugs is widespread. Some examples of the most commonly used psychiatric drugs are given in table 15.1. There is evidence that these medications are effective for many people (Donovan & others, 2010; Leonard & Taylor, 2010; Levine & others, 2010), but they are not without serious shortcomings. In some persons, psychiatric medications can cause serious side effects, such as heart problems, diabetes, or complications of pregnancy (Coccurello & Moles, 2010; Toh & others, 2009).

Dietary Therapies

Increased interest in the role of nutrition in physical and mental health has led to some very encouraging studies. The best evidence that improved nutrition can lead to better mental health comes from studies of omega-3 fatty acids. These are essential to the normal functioning of the brain and circulatory system, but they are not manufactured by the body. Therefore, we need a regular supply of omega-3 fatty acids from our diets. The best source of omega-3 fatty acids is salt-water fish, but most of us primarily consume less healthy fatty acids from red meat and plants. There is now credible evidence that persons who are low in omega-3 fatty acids are more likely to be depressed (Parker & others, 2006) and that depressed persons who are low in omega-3 fatty acids are more likely to attempt suicide (Sublette & others, 2006). Furthermore, there is growing evidence that increasing consumption of omega-3 fatty acids appears to reduce depression (Martins, 2009; Nemets & others, 2006; Parker & others, 2006). Dietary therapies should not replace other forms of therapy for depression, but under the guidance of a physician, they may play an important supplementary role in the treatment of depression.

Electroconvulsive Therapy

The idea that people can be "shocked" out of their psychological problems has been around in one form or another for 2,400 years. Hippocrates recommended the use of the herb hellebore to induce seizures that supposedly restored balance to the body's

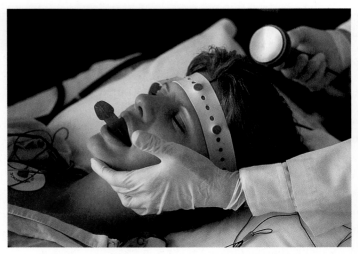

Although electroconvulsive therapy, which was introduced in the 1930s, continues to be used with some severely depressed individuals, it's not endorsed universally by the mental health profession.

electroconvulsive therapy (ECT)
(e-lektro-con-vulsiv) A medical therapy that uses electrical current to induce controlled convulsive seizures that alleviate some types of mental disorders.

four humors. Several different kinds of "shock" treatment were popular in mental institutions during the 1800s: patients were thrown in tubs full of eels, spun in giant centrifuges, and nearly drowned by being dropped into lakes through trapdoors in bridges, a treatment known as "surprise baths" (Altschule, 1965).

Other forms of shock therapy have also been used, particularly ones in which seizures are intentionally induced. In the 1930s, it was noticed that people with epilepsy rarely developed schizophrenia. Several psychiatrists experimented with chemicals that caused seizures to see if they would cure schizophrenia, but camphor, insulin, and other chemicals were found to be of little use with schizophrenics. Italian physicians first used the method of passing an electric current through two metal plates held to the sides of the head to induce convulsive brain seizures. This method, known as **electroconvulsive therapy (ECT),** continues in use today. Although ineffective with most disorders, it's believed by many psychiatrists to be useful with severely depressed individuals. ECT is believed to alter the same neurotransmitters as those affected by antidepressants, but to this day no one knows for sure how ECT works.

Although ECT has been used successfully for 50 years, the procedure is surrounded by considerable controversy. In large part, this controversy is a holdover from the primitive methods that were used when the procedure was first introduced. The shocks were given without anesthesia, and the seizures were so violent that broken bones were not uncommon. Today, the use of anesthesia and muscle relaxants makes ECT a far less unpleasant experience, but mild temporary or permanent memory loss (mostly for relatively unimportant facts) is still a relatively common side effect (Campbell, 1961; Lisanby & others, 2000). Despite the ongoing controversy over ECTs drawbacks, however, many well-designed studies suggest that it is effective in treating both major depression and bipolar disorder (Bailine & others, 2010; Carney & others, 2003; McCall & others, 2004).

Transcranial Stimulation

Transcranial stimulation is similar to ECT, but it stimulates the brain without causing full seizures. A strong magnetic field is passed through part of the frontal cortex. This causes the neurons to fire in mass and is believed to alter the sensitivity of the neurons (Gershon & others, 2003). This treatment is typically repeated over several weeks. There is evidence that transcranial stimulation is more effective than placebo in the treatment of depression, PTSD, and some symptoms of schizophrenia (Cohen & others, 2004; Fitzgerald & others, 2006; Slotema & others, 2010), but much remains to be learned about this treatment. Currently, it is primarily used with seriously depressed individuals who have not responded to other forms of treatment.

Psychosurgery

psychosurgery (sī´´kō-ser´jer-ē)
A medical therapy that involves operating on the brain in an attempt to alleviate some types of mental disorders.

By far the most controversial medical treatment for abnormal behavior is **psychosurgery,** a therapy in which the brain is operated on to try to alleviate the behavior. Archaeologists have found Stone Age skulls in which holes called *trephines* had been "surgically" cut with crude stone knives. These trephining operations—signs of healing indicate that some of these poor souls actually survived the procedure—may have been performed in an attempt to treat abnormal behavior.

Surgical operations on the brain to treat psychological disorders came into vogue in the 1940s and 1950s. In the most original version, the *prefrontal lobotomy,* a double-edged, butter-knife-shaped instrument was inserted through holes drilled in the temple region of the skull. Neural fibers that connect the frontal region of the cerebral cortex with the limbic system were cut. The theory was that the operation would prevent disturbing thoughts and perceptions from reaching the subcortical brain structures, where they would be translated into emotional outbursts. Prefrontal lobotomies were not successful, however, and loss of intellectual functioning and seizures were common side effects (Barahal, 1958). Because of their ineffectiveness and because of the success of drug therapies with schizophrenics, the use of lobotomies and other forms of psychosurgery has declined considerably (Swayze, 1995).

More recently, however, the development of more precise methods of operating on the brain with needle-thin electrical instruments has revived psychosurgery (Martuza & others, 1990). Lobotomies are now being performed under the name of capsulotomy, in spite of causing serious side effects, such as apathy and difficulties in planning (Ruck & others, 2003). Another modern type of psychosurgery is known as **cingulotomy.** In cingulotomy, the part of the limbic system called the *cingulate cortex* (chapter 3, page 63) is partially destroyed by electrical probes. Such operations are performed infrequently and are used only as a last resort (Read & Greenburg, 2009).

Trephining operations were apparently performed in the Middle Ages to treat abnormal behavior.

cingulotomy A type of psychosurgery for severe and otherwise untreatable obsessive-compulsive disorder; it involves surgical destruction of part of the cingulate cortex.

Review

One-to-one psychotherapy is not the only approach taken to solve psychological problems. For one thing, each method of psychotherapy is sometimes practiced with groups of clients rather than individual clients. Group therapy is practiced primarily because the presence of other people with problems offers advantages to some clients. Other clients provide encouragement, give advice, show the client that she or he is not alone in having problems, and provide opportunities for learning new ways of interacting with others. Group therapy also often makes efficient use of the therapist's time. However, individuals with complex problems, or who have sensitive problems that they do not want to discuss in front of others, may be better served by individual psychotherapy. Entire families also often work as a group with therapists who believe that the faulty operation of some family systems can cause psychological problems. Family therapy seeks to reestablish proper functioning in these families.

In addition to psychological treatments for psychological problems, physicians often use biological methods. The most widely used medical treatments are drugs. Drugs introduced since the 1950s have been partially responsible for the progress in treating psychological problems, which has resulted in a decrease in the number of institutionalized mental patients in the United States. There is credible evidence that dietary supplements may be effective in the treatment of some mental health problems, but it should not be used by itself at present. Electroconvulsive therapy—in which an electric current produces controlled brain seizures—is sometimes used in the treatment of severe depression. The controversial method of psychosurgery in which parts of the brain are destroyed to prevent excessive emotional reactions is no longer widely used in the United States, but newer, more precise methods are still used in some cases as a last resort.

Check Your Learning

To be sure that you have learned the key points from the preceding section, cover the list of correct answers and try to answer each question. If you give an incorrect answer to any question, return to the page given next to the correct answer to see why your answer was not correct.

1. _____, or psychotherapy conducted in groups, is believed to offer therapeutic experiences that cannot be obtained in individual therapy, such as learning from the advice offered by others.

2. _____ emphasizes an understanding of the roles of each of the members of a family system with the hope that the family will become a system that provides each member with an accurate view of self, a positive opinion of self, appropriate behavioral guidelines, and a sense of belonging.

3. _____, such as drug treatment or psychosurgery, is generally designed to correct a physical condition that is believed to be the cause of the psychological disorder.

Thinking Critically about Psychology

There are no right or wrong answers to the following questions. They are presented to help you become an active reader and think critically about what you have just read.

1. Which type of therapy for depression makes the most sense to you? Why?

2. If you were seeking treatment for a psychological problem, would you be more likely to try group therapy or individual psychotherapy? Why?

Correct Answers: 1. Group therapy (p. 515), 2. Family therapy (p. 516), 3. Medical therapy (p. 518)

Application of Psychology

What to Do If You Think You Need Help

All of us face difficult and painful times at one time or another in our lives. Sometimes we choose to struggle through these stressful periods on our own; sometimes we ask for the support and advice of friends; and at times, we may decide to seek professional help. If you, or someone close to you, are among the many millions of Americans who will use professional mental health services this year, please consider these thoughts.

First you may need to overcome the issue of *stigma*—the implication that seeking professional help means that you are not a normal or even fully competent person. If you believe that myth, then it will be very difficult indeed for you to lift the telephone and make the first appointment. You should know, however, that mental health professionals do *not* believe there is something fundamentally wrong with people who ask for help. They know that a large portion of their clients are completely normal people who are simply asking for assistance in the tricky business of avoiding—or crawling out of—life's pitfalls. So do not be ashamed to ask for help if you think you need it.

Once you have decided to seek help, where do you look for it? There are many different mental health professions that operate through a number of different kinds of mental health facilities. The challenge is in deciding which kind of professional or facility would be best for you. Most colleges and universities have a student counseling or mental health center that provides high-quality services at little or no cost. The professionals who work in these centers are experienced in meeting the mental health needs of students.

In addition, most psychology departments in larger universities operate their own psychology clinics that provide services both to students and to people in the general community. And most cities have a community mental health center that provides a wide range of services. Both university psychology clinics and community mental health centers often charge fees that are based on your ability to pay. Many of these centers operate 24 hours a day, providing suicide prevention telephone lines that are listed under such titles as "help line" or "crisis line" or that can be reached through the 411 telephone operator or 911.

Services are also provided by professionals in private practice. Like a physician or an attorney, these individuals provide services for a fee. Psychiatrists, psychologists, and other professionals in private practice are listed in the telephone book under titles such as "Physicians—Psychiatrists" and "Psychologists." You might want to turn back to chapter 1, page 18 to familiarize yourself with the differences between these and other mental health professions. In most states, only licensed individuals can list their names in the telephone directory as psychiatrists, psychologists, psychotherapists, counselors, or marriage counselors. In some states, however, some of these titles (except for psychologist and psychiatrist) are not regulated by law. This means that anyone—qualified or not—can set up a private practice in many states under one of these titles. You should be careful, therefore, to ask for a referral to one of these professionals from a qualified physician or psychologist if you choose their services.

Referrals are the best guide to choosing the services of a licensed psychologist or psychiatrist. Like other professionals,

There are many ways to find help with psychological problems if you feel that you need it.

some are better than others—or are better in dealing with certain kinds of problems—and the advice of someone who knows both you and the professionals in the community could be very helpful. If you do not have access to someone to refer you, it would be wise to ask the psychologist or psychiatrist about "board certification." It's legal in most states for a physician to practice psychiatry without having had specific training in that field, but a board-certified psychiatrist has met the criteria of a national board for competence in psychiatry. In psychology, board certification means something different. Only a small proportion of experienced psychologists take and pass a special examination of their skills. They are awarded a diploma by the American Board of Professional Psychology, which is designated in their listing in the telephone directory as "Diplomate in Clinical (or Counseling) Psychology, ABPP." Board-certified psychiatrists and psychologists are not necessarily more competent than those who are not, but it's another way of reducing the uncertainty in choosing a therapist.

Which Is the Most Effective Form of Psychotherapy?

We have seen that there are many different approaches to psychotherapy—which one is the most effective? This seems like a simple question that psychologists should be able to answer, but it is actually quite complicated.

To help consumers make more informed choices among methods of psychotherapy that are based on solid research evidence, the American Psychological Association and other organizations have made efforts to identify the best treatment methods for each kind of mental health problem. Teams of researchers have adopted a strict set of standards for determining that a treatment was effective and systematically combed through the massive number of published studies. The results have been published in an important paper (Chambless & Ollendick, 2001) and in the book *A Guide to Treatments That Work* (Nathan & Gorman, 2007). The psychological treatments that have been shown to be effective for each of a number of kinds of common mental health problems are shown in table 15.2 on p. 524. Other therapies may be effective as well, but to date these are the only psychological therapies that meet

Application of Psychology cont'd

Table 15.2 Psychological Treatments That Have Met Rigorous Scientific Standards of Effectiveness.

Kind of Problem	Effective Method of Treatment
Anxiety Disorders	
Specific phobias	Graduated exposure
Social phobia	Graduated exposure
	Cognitive restructuring
Agoraphobia	Graduated exposure
	Cognitive restructuring
Panic disorder	Cognitive restructuring
Generalized anxiety disorder	Cognitive restructuring
Obsessive-compulsive disorder	Graduated exposure and ritual prevention
Major Depression	Cognitive restructuring
	Interpersonal psychotherapy
Eating Disorders	
Bulimia	Cognitive restructuring
	Interpersonal psychotherapy
Anorexia	Cognitive restructuring

Figure 15.1 Persons with post-traumatic stress disorder (PTSD) showed greater improvement in symptoms when treated with CBT than left untreated or given a self-help booklet.

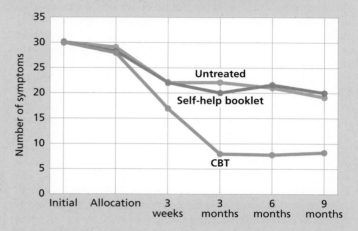

the high standards of evidence-based treatment. Note that the most effective methods are CBT and interpersonal psychotherapy. When you seek a psychotherapist, therefore, the current evidence strongly suggests that you should seek one who was actually trained by experts in the use of these methods, not just someone who read a book about them.

Additional studies conducted since these reviews were published have substantiated their conclusions regarding the effectiveness of interpersonal psychotherapy for depression (Cuijpers & others, 2008; Mufson & others, 2004) and the effectiveness of CBT for major depression (Miranda & others, 2006; Tolin, 2010), panic disorder (Addis & others, 2004), social phobia (Hofmann & others, 2007; Tolin, 2010), insomnia (Bastien & others, 2004), and personality disorder (Verheul & others, 2003). The results of a study of CBT in the treatment of post-traumatic stress disorder (PTSD) in survivors of motor vehicle accidents (Ehlers & others, 2003) provides a good example of such effectiveness data. As shown in figure 15.1, scores on a measure of symptoms of PTSD declined considerably over three months (and stayed low over 9 months) in the group treated with CBT, but declined little in an untreated group and in a group that read a self-help booklet.

Psychotherapy and Medication. Is it better to seek psychotherapy or take medication? The answer depends on the kind of problem that the person has. CBT has been shown to be more effective in treating social phobia than the medication, fluoxetine, that is often prescribed for this disorder (Clark

& others, 2003). Psychotherapy is also more effective than clomipramine in the treatment of obsessive-compulsive disorder (Foa & others, 2005). In addition, there is some evidence that combining medication and CBT in the treatment of anxiety disorders may make CBT *less* effective in the long run (Otto & others, 2005).

In the case of depression, there is evidence that cognitive therapy is just as effective as antidepressant medications (DeRubeis & others, 1999). And cognitive therapy has been shown to be more than twice as effective as medication in preventing *future* episodes of depression (Fava & others, 2004; Jarrett & others, 2001; Teasdale & others, 2001). The combination of medication and CBT for the treatment of depression appears to be slightly more effective than CBT alone, however (Friedman & others, 2004; Pampallona & others, 2004), particularly for persons with chronic or severe depression (Friedman & others, 2004). For schizophrenia and bipolar disorder, cognitive therapy combined with medication is clearly superior to either treatment alone (Lam & others, 2005; Otto, Smits, & Reese, 2005; Scott & others, 2003).

How Effective Can Mental Health Treatment Be?
There is still a great deal to be learned about the treatment of mental health problems. The existing treatments clearly do not help everyone, but there is now strong evidence that psychotherapy and medication (and often the combination of both) can greatly reduce the burden of mental health and increase the happiness and productivity of people with mental health problems. Furthermore, the cost of mental health treatment is more than repaid by the economic contributions to society by treated individuals (Simon & others, 2006, 2007; Vos & others, 2004; Wang & others, 2007). In addition, it is now clear that effective treatment for mental health improves the physical health of treated persons (de Jonge & others, 2007; Taylor & others, 2005).

Summary

Chapter 15 outlines the major forms of therapy through which individuals are helped with psychological problems.

I. Psychotherapy is the use of methods, such as talking, demonstrating, and reinforcing, that are based on a theory of psychological disorders to solve human problems.

   A. Freud is the founder of the form of psychotherapy known as *psychoanalysis,* which helps the patient bring unconscious conflict into consciousness. The principal techniques of psychoanalysis are

      1. Free association, which is used to relax the censorship of the ego.

      2. Dream interpretation, which allows the therapist to obtain another "window" on the unconscious.

      3. Resistance, which is any form of opposition of the patient to the process of psychoanalysis.

      4. Transference, which occurs when there is a relatively intense relationship between patient and therapist during therapy; this can be interpreted to give insights to the patient.

   B. Catharsis is the release of emotion that is pent up with unconscious conflicts in psychoanalysis.

   C. A new form of psychotherapy based on neo-Freudian theories, called *interpersonal psychotherapy,* has been found to be effective in treating depression.

II. Humanistic psychotherapies strive to help the person achieve full self-awareness, so that the person's inner-directed tendency to growth can be realized. Client-centered psychotherapy and Gestalt therapy are two major types of humanistic psychotherapy.

   A. Client-centered psychotherapy helps the client explore unsymbolized feelings and information by providing a safe emotional climate. Self-awareness, in turn, is thought to promote healthy growth.

   B. Gestalt therapy helps the individual achieve greater self-awareness by techniques, such as pointing out inconsistencies in behavior.

III. Cognitive-behavior therapists use a form of psychotherapy in which they help the client unlearn abnormal behavior and learn adaptive ways of thinking, feeling, and acting.

   A. Graduated exposure is widely used for fear reduction.

   B. In behavioral activation therapy, the therapist helps depressed persons engage in constructive and enjoyable activities, including physical exercise, that reduce depression.

   C. Social skills training is an example of teaching new adaptive skills using methods derived from operant conditioning.

   D. Cognitive restructuring rests on the assumption that the faulty cognitions that cause abnormal emotions and actions can be changed in therapy.

IV. Some methods of therapy are carried out with groups or entire families.

   A. Group therapy makes efficient use of therapists' time, and the presence of other people with problems offers advantages to some clients.

   B. Family therapy seeks to reestablish proper functioning within families.

V. Medical therapies are designed to directly change the functioning of the brain to treat a psychological disorder.

chapter **sixteen**
Social psychology

Chapter Outline

Prologue

Human beings are social animals. We enjoy people, we need people, and we are profoundly influenced by people. Indeed, we sometimes behave a bit like sheep in a flock. We are likely to dress and act like other people even when we are not asked to conform, and our beliefs and attitudes are often influenced by others. At times, being in a group can lead to harmful behavior, such as making illogical decisions or failing to help someone in need when it is not clear who is responsible for helping. At other times, however, we accomplish far more and act more humanely in groups than as individuals.

For most of us, our most important interactions are with the people we like and love. We like to walk with them, talk with them, and snuggle with them. Whom do you like and why? Why do you fall in love with one person and not another? Other things being equal, we are attracted to people who are similar to us (or whose opposite characteristics complement us), who are reasonably competent (but not perfect), who are physically attractive, and who like us, too. Once mutual attraction leads to a relationship, our likelihood of staying in that relationship is determined by how closely our expectations for the relationship are met and how fairly balanced the relationship is.

But, we do not only like or love other people. Sadly, we dislike or even hate other people or groups of people. Understanding why we feel intensely—either positively or negatively—about other people or groups of people is an essential part of understanding what it means to be a person.

In this chapter, we discuss the effects of being in a group on the individual. We discuss the origins of our attitudes and their effects on our behavior. We particularly focus on stereotypes and prejudiced attitudes about others, such as prejudice against members of different ethnic groups or against persons with different sexual orientations. The chapter ends with a discussion of what causes us to perceive other people in the way we do and to like or love some of them.

Definition of Social Psychology

Social psychology is a branch of psychology that studies individuals as they interact with others. Up to this point in this course, we have studied people as individuals removed from the social context in which they live. But people live with other people. Their most important learning comes from others, their most important motives are social motives, and so on.

People are almost always with others. It's part of human nature to be social. Social psychologist Elliot Aronson (1995) reminds us that this insight is among the oldest in psychology. In 328 B.C., Aristotle wrote: "Man is by nature a social animal. . . . Anyone who either cannot lead the common life or is so self-sufficient as not to need to, and therefore does not partake of society, is either a beast or a god." People need, like, and are profoundly influenced by people. Social psychologists study these attractions, needs, and influences.

It is not sufficient to study human beings in isolation; we must examine the psychology of the individual in the context of the social situations in which they live. To fully understand people, we must see how they are influenced by their social context.

Groups and Social Influence

Let's begin our study of social influence with a look at the effects of being a member of a group. Although some of what you will learn may make you embarrassed to be a member of the human race, you can understand the power of social influence only by looking at both its negative and positive faces.

Key Terms

attitudes 538

attribution 549

attribution theory 544

cognitive dissonance 542

companionate love 557

conformity 532

deindividuation 528

diffusion of responsibility 529

dispositional attribution 549

equity theory 558

fundamental attribution error 549

groupthink 531

obedience 534

passionate love 557

person perception 549

persuasion 538

polarization 531

prejudice 543

primacy effect 550

situational attribution 549

sleeper effects 538

social facilitation 529

social loafing 529

social norms 533

social psychology 527

social roles 533

stereotype 543

social psychology The branch of psychology that studies individuals as they interact with others.

Social psychology is the branch of psychology that studies individuals as they interact with others.

Deindividuation

Near the start of the 20th century, an African American man named William Carr was arrested and charged with killing the cow of a white family in southern Louisiana. A lynch mob took Carr from the sheriff, who did not resist them, and hanged him without a trial. During the era in which this hanging took place, an average of two African Americans were lynched *each week* in the United States. These lynchings say much about racial prejudice—a topic we will turn to later in the chapter—but they also say a great deal about the effects of groups on the behavior of individuals. The members of lynch mobs were almost never people who had murdered before when alone or who would murder alone afterward. Something about being in a group transformed individuals who were incapable of murder into a mob that was very capable of murder (Postmes & Spears, 1998). An analysis of lynchings over a 47-year period found that the worst atrocities occurred when the mobs were larger and each individual presumably felt more anonymous (Mullen, 1986).

The process of feeling anonymous and unidentifiable in a group is known as **deindividuation** (Zimbardo, 1969). In this state, people are less aware of their own behavior and less concerned with what others think of their behavior. The result can be an increased likelihood of performing actions that you typically wouldn't do. Being in a group in which everyone's appearance is uniform—like wearing a uniform or similar clothing—and stimulating environmental factors like heat and noise increase the likelihood of deindividuation. Think about your own behavior at a crowded ball game, dressed in team colors. You might have screamed vulgar insults at the opposing team or been more aggressive than usual. As research on lynch mobs shows, weakened restraints that result from deindividuation can have more serious effects, such as people being more aggressive when they are unidentifiable (Zimbardo, 1969).

deindividuation State in which people in a group can feel anonymous and unidentifiable and therefore feel less concerned with what others think of their behavior.

Uninvolved Bystanders

In April 2010 a homeless man who had just saved a woman from being mugged was stabbed. He lay dying as dozens of people walked on by without assisting the fallen hero. Hundreds of thousands of people viewed the video on YouTube, were stunned, but to psychologists this was yet another chilling example of what is known as "the bystander effect." The bystander effect was made famous in an incident many years before. In 1964, the newspapers and magazines were filled with stories about the death of Kitty Genovese. The stories described how she had been beaten and stabbed to death in a residential area of New York City over the course of 30 minutes while 38 of her neighbors came to their windows and watched. Incredibly, no one went out to help her or even called the police. How could such a thing have happened? Did Kitty just happen to live in a neighborhood of uncaring cowards? Psychologists didn't think that was the answer and launched a number of studies of why being in an unstructured group often makes each individual less likely to help someone in need. Interestingly, the news accounts of the death of Ms. Genovese turned out to be largely inaccurate. A review of the transcripts of the trial of her assailant did not support the idea that 38 people actually witnessed the event and did nothing to help (Manning, Levine, & Collins, 2007). Nonetheless, this "urban myth" stimulated some very solid research.

Bibb Latané, John Darley, and Judith Rodin carried out a series of experiments in an attempt to understand the lack of action by bystanders when they are in groups. In one experiment (Latané & Rodin, 1969), a female experimenter asked college students to fill out a questionnaire, and while they worked, she went behind a curtain and staged a fake accident. The students heard her climbing and then falling from a chair. She moaned as if in great pain and begged for someone to help her get her foot out from under a heavy object. When students were alone in the other part of the room,

People who feel unidentifiable, or deindividuated, because they are in a large group are more likely to behave aggressively or in other unacceptable ways.

70% went to help her. But when they were paired with one other student who did not respond to the woman's pleas, only 7% tried to help.

In a similar experiment (Darley & Latané, 1968), college students "overheard" a staged epileptic seizure through an intercom. Eighty-five percent of the students tried to find help for the seizure victim when they thought they alone had heard it, but when they thought that others were also listening, only 30% sought help. Social psychologists do not think that bystanders who fail to help in an emergency are lacking in some personal quality; rather, they are influenced by being in a *group*. Many studies have shown that the larger the group, the less likely any particular person is to offer to help a person in distress (Garcia-Herrero & others, 2002; Latané & Nida, 1981).

Why are we less likely to help when we are in an unstructured group? Latané and Darley (1970) have suggested that being in the presence of others influences our perception of the need for help and our assuming responsibility for helping. When we notice an event, we look to others for information. If nobody else is making an effort to help, then it's less likely that we will help because it looks as if there is no reason to help: "No one looks worried, so there must not be a problem." As mentioned in the Latané and Rodin "woman in distress" experiment, 70% of the individuals who were alone went to find help for the person who had fallen, but that number was reduced to 7% when they were paired with another person (actually a confederate of the experimenter) who made no effort at all to offer help. In other bystander experiments in which the confederate tried to find a way to help, the research participants were more likely to help, too.

The presence of other bystanders also makes us less likely to assume responsibility for helping. Unstructured groups create a **diffusion of responsibility.** If everyone in the group is responsible for a lynching, then no one person is individually responsible. In emergencies, a person who is alone is clearly responsible for helping the person in need; however, in a group of bystanders the responsibility can be diffused, with no one person feeling accountable.

Working and Solving Problems in Groups

We humans often gather together to work in groups. We study together, raise barns together, and hold meetings to solve problems in our colleges, businesses, and cities. Does working together in groups bring out the best in us? Sometimes yes, and sometimes no.

In some cases, being in a group improves the performance of the individual members of the group. When this is the case, **social facilitation** is said to occur (Levine & others, 1993). In one of the earliest experiments in social psychology, Triplett (1898) found that teenagers wound fishing reels faster in the presence of other teenagers doing the same thing than when they were alone. This phenomenon also explains why we often eat more when in the company of others (Clendenen & others, 1994), particularly if surrounded by family or friends (DeCastro, 1994). Have you noticed this happening to you?

Sometimes, being in a group results in reduced effort by individual group members. We may applaud enthusiastically as a member of the audience, but is everyone clapping as hard as they can, or are we slacking off a bit? Research shows that if you are asked to clap as loudly as you can, you will make more noise if you think your clap is being measured individually than if you think the loudness of a group of clappers is being measured together (Latané, Williams, & Harkins, 1979). This phenomenon is called **social loafing.**

diffusion of responsibility
The effect of being in a group that apparently reduces the sense of personal responsibility of each group member to act appropriately.

social facilitation An effect in which working in a group improves one's performance on individual projects.

social loafing The tendency of members of groups to work less hard when group performance is measured than when individual performance is measured.

Working as part of a group can affect how hard we work and how well we get the job done.

Suppose you convince your instructor to use the next class period to have a tug-of-war among members of your class. Do you think that you would pull harder on the rope if you were tugging alone against one classmate, or if you were part of a team of four persons tugging against four classmates? As the number of people involved in a tug-of-war increases, the average amount of force exerted by each person actually *declines* (Kravitz & Martin, 1986)! The diminished effort of each individual in a tug-of-war group is partly the result of lack of coordination among members of the group—some rest while others pull, resulting in less average effort. But even persons who are blindfolded and led to believe that others are pulling with them exert less effort than when they think they are pulling alone (Ingham & others, 1974).

Two key variables that influence social loafing are (1) the size of the group and (2) the nature of the task. The larger the group, the more likely individual members are to reduce their individual contributions to the group effort (Sorkin & others, 2001). They may loaf in larger groups because they believe that other people can make better contributions, because other members do not respond positively to their initial attempts to contribute, or because they feel that no one would notice if they slacked off.

Why do I sing when I'm in the car alone more often than when there are friends in the car with me? Perhaps you have experienced a time when you had to speak in front of an audience, and felt that you didn't do your best. The term for this is **social inhibition**—when performance suffers as a result of the presence of others. This is the opposite of social facilitation. What is going on here? Why does the presence of others sometimes inhibit performance and sometimes facilitate it? It turns out that the nature of the task is an important factor. Being in the presence of others activates the sympathetic nervous system, and some tasks are performed better at higher levels of sympathethic arousal while other tasks are performed better at lower levels of such arousal (Zajonc, 1965).

Hazel Markus (1978) asked research participants to dress in preparation for a later phase in an experiment. This task was either easy—putting on everyday shoes and socks—or difficult—dressing in strange and unfamiliar clothes. Participants either dressed alone or with another person in the room. When individuals performed the easy dressing task, they dressed *more quickly* when there was another person in the room, compared with when they dressed alone. When the research participants had to perform the difficult dressing task, they dressed *more slowly* in the presence of another person than they did when they were alone.

Recall the discussion of *optimal levels of arousal* in chapter 11. Easy tasks are easier to perform when people are more highly aroused, but difficult tasks are more difficult when people are aroused. High levels of arousal, such as that produced by performing in front of an audience, may promote social facilitation for easy or skilled tasks and social impairment for difficult or unfamiliar tasks. Professional athletes, musicians, and even instructors who lecture in front of classes often do their best work in the presence of an audience, because they are performing skills that have been practiced over and over again. But amateur athletes and performers (like students speaking in front of a class, or new performers at open mic nights) lack the practiced skills. For them, the task is harder, and they are likely to perform poorly when an audience is present. The familiar phenomenon known as "choking" under pressure often occurs when the outcome is important to us and we are in the presence of others (Baumeister, 1984). Even skilled practitioners can choke when doing something well-practiced and routine, if they focus their attention too much on what they are trying to do (Beilock & Carr, 2001).

social inhibition When the presence or expectations of others inhibits performance of a task.

Group Problem Solving. In general, small groups of people solve complex intellectual problems better in groups than they do when working alone (Laughlin & others, 2006; Sorkin & others, 2001). Even if the individual members of the group engage in some degree of social loafing, it is true that "two heads are better than one" and that the knowledge and skills of more than one person may be needed to solve a complex problem. The exception, however, is during brainstorming. Brainstorming in groups seems to be associated with loss of productivity, and each group member working independently yields more possibilities, and more creative options (Taylor, Berry, and Block, 1958; Mullen and Johnson, 1991). If you have a group project to work on, it might be best for each person to work alone generating a list of ideas before the group meets to review them together.

Sometimes, however, working in a group results in bad decisions that none of the participants would have made alone. Maintaining consensus and cohesion in the group gets in the way of the task at hand, leading to worse decisions. How does this happen? Psychologist Irving Janis (1982) studied the factors involved in group problem solving by knowledgeable and sophisticated decision makers. He proposed that some of the most significant and disastrous decisions made in history—such as President Kennedy's ill-fated decision to send Cuban expatriots to defeat in the Bay of Pigs invasion of Castro's Cuba and NASA's fatal decision in 1986 to launch the space shuttle *Challenger* despite warnings from engineers about defective O-rings (Kruglanski, 1986)—were the result of faulty group decision making. Janis calls the faulty decision-making processes that occur in these groups **groupthink.**

groupthink The faulty decision-making processes that may occur in groups.

What causes group decision making to result in groupthink? There are three key factors: (1) the process of polarization, (2) the cohesiveness of the members of the group, and (3) the size of the group. Suppose a friend asks you for advice about the following dilemma:

> I want to go to graduate school in filmmaking, but to get in I have to make an impressive grade in undergraduate scriptwriting. I could take the course from a famous instructor who is respected by the graduate school, but the famous instructor has such high standards that hardly anyone gets an A or a B. Or I could take the course from an easier, less famous instructor that the graduate school might not be impressed by. What should I do?

What would you recommend? Would you tell your friend to go for broke and take the course from the famous but tough instructor, even though the chances of getting a good grade are very low? Studies have shown that most of us do *not* recommend such risky options *when we are alone with the person asking for advice.* However, when *groups* of persons discuss such dilemmas, they are much more likely to take extreme positions and recommend risky options (Stoner, 1961). The discussion of issues in groups often leads to the **polarization** of thinking, pushing our opinions toward one extreme "pole" of the issue. Groupthink is more likely to occur in tightly knit, cohesive groups. The members of cohesive groups generally prefer to agree with one another and discourage dissent. For that reason, contradictory evidence and opinions often are not presented, leaving the group with a false sense of the correctness of their decision. It is easy to see how unsound decisions could be made under these conditions. To guard against groupthink, at least one member of the group should be asked to take the role of the "devil's advocate," regularly challenging the group's thinking. Even one dissenting opinion or minority view can sometimes break the spell.

polarization The tendency for group discussion to make beliefs and attitudes more extreme.

Finally, the size of the group is important, because the nature of interactions among group members changes as the size of the group increases (Fay & others, 2000). In small groups, people influence one another's ideas through a process of *interactive dialogues.* They speak to one another and ask questions in reciprocal and connected ways. In larger groups, however, members are more likely to engage in *serial monologues.* They take turns giving "speeches" that present their views, and in these monologues they do not integrate or respond to the views of their fellow group members. As a result, there is less constructive give-and-take in larger groups, and the opinion held by the dominant member of the group before the discussion began is likely to prevail (Fay & others, 2000). If the dominant person's opinion is incorrect, it is less likely to get corrected in large groups. A leader that does not support a particular view helps prevent groupthink. Much remains to be learned about the conditions under which group decision-making leads to bad decisions (Kerr & Tindale, 2004), and research continues. For example, it has been found that weaker members of a group may not speak up if a poor decision is about to be made, but stronger members may be vigilant and dissent, to protect the well-being of the group (Packer, 2009).

Conformity, Social Roles, and Obedience

I hope that you are beginning to have a new appreciation for the powerful influence of social situations on the behavior of the individual. Clearly, social situations influence us every day in important ways. But there is still a great deal more to the story of social influence. Why does groupthink occur, if it only takes one person speaking up to prevent it? Next, we consider our tendency to conform to the expectations of our peer groups and our cultures, the influence of socially prescribed roles and norms on our behavior, and our tendency to obediently follow the instructions of authority figures.

conformity Yielding to group pressure even when no direct request to comply has been made.

Conformity. Humans are social creatures, so we tend to behave as others in the group do—that is, we typically conform. **Conformity** is yielding to group pressure to act as everyone else does, even when no direct request has been made. A famous study of conformity was conducted by Solomon Asch (1956). He asked college students to serve as research participants in an experiment that he said concerned visual perception. Each student participated in a group with other "research participants," all of whom were actually confederates of the experimenter. The group was shown four straight lines, depicted in figure 16.1. The task was to tell which of the three lines on the right side of the figure was the same length as line A.

The task was intentionally made easy, with line Y being the obvious correct choice. But the real participant was the last one in line as each student was asked to state his or her choice out loud. The first few rounds were played as expected, but then things changed. One by one, the confederates playing the part of real research participants chose line X. The distress of the real participant was immediately apparent. Participants often initially stuck to the correct answer, but eventually conformed. In an amazing 74% of the cases, the participants conformed to the pressure of the group, giving the wrong answer at least part of the time.

How "deep" was this conformity? Did the research participants know that they were just going along with the group's opinion, or did the group actually change their judgment? People may conform for two reasons: to gain rewards and avoid punishments (such as social approval or disapproval) or to gain information. In the Asch situation, people seemed to conform for the former reason, to seek approval and avoid disapproval. We know this because when the same task was conducted in a slightly different way that allowed the research participants to make their judgments privately, almost no conformity to the erroneous judgments of other individuals occurred. Apparently, we are able to make up our minds privately even in the face of pressure from others, but we often go along with the crowd in terms of outward behavior. To gain social approval, or to remain a part of the group, we conform. We also conform because we look to others as sources of information. For example, at a fancy dinner you may check to see where other people are putting their napkins, which fork they are using for the salad, and where to rest the butter knife. Research suggests this is the reason we conform when the "correct" judgment is less clear than in Asch's line-judging experiment. Sherif (1936) conducted a study that took advantage of a perceptual phenomenon called the *autokinetic effect*. When a person is placed in a completely darkened room with no reference points, a fixed point of light on a wall will appear to move. Because the movement of light is not real, and the distance that it seems to move differs from person to person, this is an extremely ambiguous situation (as compared with Asch's line-judging task, which was very clear-cut). Sherif placed individuals in a room with confederates and asked them to estimate the distance that a fixed light had

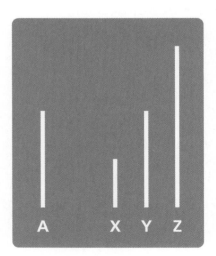

Figure 16.1
Stimuli like those used in Asch's study of conformity.

moved. The confederates gave either extremely low or extremely high estimates of movement, and the research participants tended to agree with the confederates. In this ambiguous situation, however, they still tended to agree with the confederates even when they could report their estimates of the movement of the light in private. When the appropriate response in a situation is not clear, we look to others for information and will not only go along with them but may actually change our judgments to conform.

Several factors increase the likelihood of conformity to the group:

1. *Size of the group.* Up to a point, the more people there are in a group, the more likely we are to go along. As the group gets larger, however, conforming behaviors level off.

In terms of outward behavior, we tend to conform to group norms.

2. *Unanimous groups.* Conformity is highest when we face a group who all feel the same way about a topic—the group is unanimous. But conformity is greatly reduced when even one other person in the group feels as we do (Nail & others, 2000).

3. *Culture and conformity.* Solomon Asch's (1956) experiment showing conformity in the judgment of the length of lines has been replicated in 17 different cultures around the world (Bond & Smith, 1996). Conformity occurs in all cultures, but persons from individualistic cultures, which place an emphasis on the welfare of the individual—as in North America—are less conforming on the Asch task than are persons from collectivistic cultures, which emphasize the welfare of society as a whole rather than the individual (Bond & Smith, 1996).

"All those in favor say 'Aye.'"
"Aye."　　　"Aye."　　　"Aye."
"Aye."　　　"Aye."

© The New Yorker Collection 1979 Henry Martin from cartoonbank.com. All Rights Reserved.

Social Roles and Social Norms. When people work together in groups, the efforts of each individual need to be coordinated with those of others to avoid chaos. In response to this need, **social roles** and **social norms** evolve, to give guidelines as to what is expected of us (Levine & others, 1993). Just like actors in a play who have scripts for their roles, social roles tell us how we are expected to behave. In this course, you play the role of the student, and the nice person who tells you interesting things about psychology plays the role of the instructor. Each social role gives the person a set of expectations for appropriate behavior in a situation. You are not surprised when the person in the role of instructor stands in the front of the classroom and lectures, but you would be surprised if the student sitting next to you were to stand up and deliver a 45-minute lecture on the importance of classical conditioning to our understanding of romantic love.

Social roles have a powerful impact on the behavior of individuals. When we are placed in a new role, our behavior often changes to fit the role. In a dramatic example of the power of social roles in influencing behavior, social psychologist Philip Zimbardo of Stanford University looked at the social roles that exist in prisons. Zimbardo was interested in these particular roles because he felt that they lead to the mistreatment of convicts in a way that worsens their behavior (Haney & Zimbardo, 1998). The following is Zimbardo's description of what was learned:

> We carefully screened over 70 volunteers who answered an ad in a Palo Alto city newspaper and ended up with about two dozen young men who were selected to be part of this study. Half were arbitrarily designated as prisoners by a flip of a coin, the others as guards. These were the roles they were to play in our simulated prison. The guards

social roles Culturally determined guidelines that tell people what behavior is expected of them.

social norms Guidelines provided by every culture for judging acceptable and unacceptable behavior.

In Zimbardo's prison experiment, volunteers assigned to the social roles of guard and prisoner dramatically conformed to those roles.

were made aware of the potential seriousness and danger of the situation and their own vulnerability. They made up their own formal rules for maintaining law, order, and respect, and were generally free to improvise new ones during their eight-hour, three-man shifts. The prisoners were unexpectedly picked up at their homes by a city policeman in a squad car, searched, handcuffed, fingerprinted, booked at the Palo Alto station house, and taken blindfolded to our jail. There they were stripped, deloused, put into a uniform, given a number, and put into a cell with two other prisoners where they expected to live for the next two weeks. The pay was good . . . and their motivation was to make money. . . . At the end of only six days we had to close down our mock prison because what we saw was frightening. It was no longer apparent to most of the subjects (or to us) where reality ended and their roles began. The majority had indeed become prisoners or guards, no longer able to clearly differentiate between role playing and self. There were dramatic changes in virtually every aspect of their behavior, thinking, and feeling. In less than a week the experience of imprisonment undid (temporarily) a lifetime of learning; human values were suspended, self-concepts were challenged, and the ugliest, most base, pathological side of human nature surfaced. We were horrified because we saw some boys (guards) treat others as if they were despicable animals, taking pleasure in cruelty, while other boys (prisoners) became servile, dehumanized robots who thought only of escape, of their own individual survival, and of their mounting hatred for the guards. We had to release three prisoners in the first four days because they had such acute situational traumatic reactions as hysterical crying, confusion in thinking, and severe depression. Others begged to be paroled, and all but three were willing to forfeit all the money they had earned if they could be paroled.

Is this what happened during the Iraq war? Did the social roles that were given to the military prison guards and CIA interrogators lead them to sometimes torture prisoners at Abu Ghraib and other facilities? It is very difficult to understand specific events that cannot be studied scientifically, but social roles and the combination of fear, anger, fatigue, and intense prejudice may have been behind such behavior (Fiske & others, 2004). Don't forget the phenomenon of deindividuation mentioned earlier in this chapter. Zimbardo believed this was an important factor, too. In addition to conforming to our many social roles (student, employee, friend, etc.), which may sometimes conflict, we also behave according to the spoken and unspoken rules known as *social norms.* The social norms of our culture tell us how we should behave in particular situations. We face forward and avoid making eye contact with others in an elevator, and don't pick our noses in public because these are widely held social norms for North Americans. Most people conform to the social norms of their culture most of the time. We sometimes experience "culture-shock" when we are surprised by different norms when we travel, or when people from other cultures visit us.

Understanding our roles, and those of others, greatly facilitates our ability to work together in society for the common good. Without social roles and norms, you would not know what to expect of your psychology instructor, to take but one example. Being a student would be much more difficult if you did not know that the person who plays the role of the instructor will give lectures on which you, in the student role, are presumed to be taking notes and studying, and that the student will be tested and assigned a grade by the instructor. Roles and norms are sources of influence that must be understood, as examples such as the prison experiment and the tragedy of the Abu Ghraib military prison in Iraq dramatically demonstrate (Zimbardo, 2007).

Obedience: Direct Influence by Authority Figures. One of the most fascinating, and often frightening, lines of inquiry in social psychology has been research on **obedience,** doing what we are told to do by people in authority. This research was prompted in part by the behavior of soldiers in World War II and other wars, who committed unthinkable atrocities when ordered to do so. What kind of person would

obedience Doing what one is told to do by people in authority.

cooperate in abusing and murdering 6 million Jews during the Holocaust of World War II? What kind of person would not refuse to obey such an order? The disturbing answer from research is that most of us are that kind of person.

Stanley Milgram (1963, 1965) conducted a series of studies that cast a glaring light on the subject of obedience. To get the full impact of his findings, try to imagine that you are a research participant in one of his experiments. You have volunteered for a study of memory. When you arrive at the appointed time, you and another person, a middle-aged man, meet a somewhat stern, authoritarian experimenter wearing a white lab coat. The experimenter chooses you to be the "teacher" in the experiment and the other participant to be the "learner." The learner will have to memorize a list of word pairs, but you have to test him and operate the equipment. The "equipment" is a console labeled "SHOCK GENERATOR" with a bank of switches marked from 15 to 450 volts.

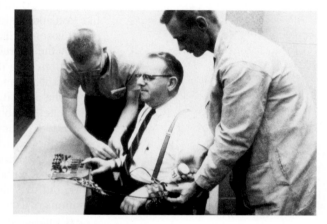

You help strap the learner into something that looks like an electric chair, and you attach electrodes to him that are connected to the shock generator in the other room. The learner asks whether the experiment could be dangerous to his heart condition, but the experimenter assures him that, although the shocks could be extremely painful, they should cause no physical harm. You return to the next room, take your seat at the console, and are told how you should use the shocks to "help" the learner memorize the list.

You are to listen to him attempt to recite the list over the intercom and shock him by throwing one of the switches after each error. You are to begin with the weakest shock and increase the intensity each time he makes a mistake. You are even given a 45-volt shock so you can see what it feels like (it's unpleasant), and the experiment begins. The learner recalls the list fairly accurately but makes a few mistakes, and you shock him for each mistake as you have been instructed to do.

What you do not know is that the learner is not really getting shocked. He is a confederate of the experimenter who is acting a role. He is not even talking over the intercom; you are hearing a tape recording instead. But the important thing is that you *believe* that a man with a heart condition is strapped into an electric chair in the next room and that you are giving him shocks every time he makes a mistake.

The learner groans after an intensity of 75 volts has been reached. At 150 volts, he says that his heart is bothering him and asks to be let out of the experiment. The experimenter denies the request and tells you to give him the shock when he makes a mistake. When the learner has been given the 180-volt shock, the learner screams that he cannot stand the pain, and, as you are told, you turn the shock apparatus to 300 volts—the level marked "DANGER: EXTREME SHOCK." The learner stops responding, but when you look at the experimenter, expecting him to stop the proceedings, he firmly tells you to administer the next shock.

In Milgram's classic obedience experiments, the "learner" was strapped to a chair while participants were instructed to use what they believed was an electric shock generator to shock him after errors in learning.

What would you do? Would you give the extremely dangerous shock, even though the learner is begging you to stop? Or would you refuse to continue? Milgram asked a panel of psychiatrists how many research participants they thought would continue giving shocks at this point, and they predicted that less than 5% would continue. What percentage would you predict? Milgram found that an incredible 65% not only gave the next shock but also continued participating until they had given the highest shock (450 volts).

Milgram's findings were astonishing, even to other social psychologists who understood the power of social situations. Could his results have been a fluke? Did Milgram just happen to recruit a group of sadistic individuals? To find out, Milgram repeated his study and found the same results with men and women from many different walks of life: students, blue-collar workers, white-collar workers, and professionals. He conducted his study in laboratories at prestigious Yale University and in an office space in downtown Bridgeport, Connecticut. This study has been replicated in other countries as well. The results of these studies are a painful reminder of the power of social situations and a warning of the ease with which misguided authorities can use ordinary people like you and me to obediently carry out their wishes.

It is somewhat comforting that later studies found that individuals were less likely to obey the instruction to give the high-voltage shocks when their "victim" was in the same room with them, acting distressed by the shocks. In addition, when the prestige of the experimenter was reduced, the percentage of obedient persons fell to about 50%. When the experimenter gave instructions by telephone rather than in person, the percentage fell to about 25%. Furthermore, when the research participant was in the presence of two other participants who refused to give the high-intensity shocks, only 10% obeyed the experimenter's instructions to the end. Obedience is also reduced when individuals are led to feel more personal responsibility for their actions and when it is obvious that authorities have self-serving goals. These last facts are somewhat encouraging, but they do not lessen the impact of Milgram's findings: The power of social situations over human behavior can be terrifying and must be guarded against.

A final comment is in order about Milgram's study of obedience. Although this study was of great value in exploring an important aspect of human nature, this study would not be considered ethical by today's standards. At a minimum, the experimenter would not be allowed to command the research participant to continue against her or his will—participants may choose to discontinue an experiment at any time. Still, partial replications of this study conducted under today's ethical guidelines have yielded similar results, supporting Milgram's conclusions (Slater & others, 2006).

The Positive Side of Groups

Has this discussion of social loafing, polarization, and groupthink convinced you that people should never work together on anything, or that the only way to remain a good person is to live in a cave as a hermit? It shouldn't at all. Groups allow us to achieve great things. There are many things that a single person working alone could not accomplish. Although it is true that people pull harder alone than when pulling in a group, four people working together could pull hard enough to pull a heavy boat ashore that a single person could never pull. In Milgram's obedience study, you saw that the presence of people who refused to obey the experimenter's instructions made others more likely to refuse to give shocks, as well.

Groups also can be therapeutic—think of support groups and group therapies—and can provide emotional support and comfort. Recall that you learned in chapter 13 that the effects of stress can be reduced considerably by strong social support (page 438). Being aware of the negative effects of groups on our behaviors can help us make the best advantage of being in them.

Review   We are social animals, so we are almost always in the company of others. This is a fundamentally important observation because people can be fully understood only if our social nature is understood. Other people influence our behavior and we must understand that process of influence. We need to be more aware of the power of social situations in influencing behavior.

The very fact of being with others can influence behavior; people often behave differently when they are in groups than when they are alone. Mobs commit crimes that the individuals alone would not commit, and groups of bystanders fail to help people in distress even though most members of that group would have done so if alone.

Groups influence individual behavior through our strong tendency to conform with the group even when not asked to do so. We may conform in terms of outward behavior and, in some instances, may change our inner judgments and attitudes as well. Groups also influence us through the expectations for our behavior that are inherent in social roles and social norms. Frighteningly, we are likely to be persuaded to obey even inappropriate requests from a prestigious authority figure, especially when we face the authority figure alone. When working in groups, individual effort declines under some circumstances and group problem solving can become distorted.

Despite these negative effects, groups can accomplish what an individual could never do when working alone; individual performance improves under some conditions; and the impact of stress can be softened by social support. The effects of our tendency to band together in groups can be positive, especially if we are aware of the potentially negative effects of groups on individual behavior. We are social animals whether we like it or not; as such we must understand the influence of groups on our behavior.

Review (cont.)

Check Your Learning

To be sure that you have learned the key points from the preceding section, cover the list of correct answers and try to answer each question. If you give an incorrect answer to any question, return to the page given next to the correct answer to see why your answer was not correct. Remember that these questions cover only some of the important information in this section; it is important that you make up your own questions to check your learning of other facts and concepts.

1. Social psychology is the branch of psychology that studies _____.

2. People may behave as they do in lynch mobs and at ball games because of a process called _____.

3. In a situation where the solution is not obvious, we are most likely to conform to the group's opinion _____.

   a) publicly in terms of outward behaviors

   b) privately in terms of judgments and attitudes

   c) neither a nor b

   d) both a and b

4. When workers exert less effort in a group than they would when working alone, the result is called _____.

   a) social loafing   c) groupthink

   b) group polarization   d) social facilitation

Thinking Critically about Psychology

There are no right or wrong answers to the following questions. They are presented to help you become an active reader and think critically about what you have just read.

1. How much do you conform to others? When are you most likely to conform?

2. What do you think is the significance of Stanley Milgram's studies? What does it say about individual responsibility to behave ethically in a society?

Attitudes and Persuasion

Attitudes are of special interest, because they are often learned from other people and our attitudes are often reflected in our behavior toward others. Social psychologists define **attitudes** as evaluations that predispose us to act and feel in certain ways. Note that this definition has three components: (1) *beliefs,* such as the belief that door-to-door salespeople are generally dishonest; (2) *feelings,* such as a strong dislike for door-to-door salespeople; and (3) *dispositions to behave,* such as a readiness to be rude to them when they come to the door. Where do our attitudes come from, and what causes them to change?

attitudes Evaluations that predispose one to act and feel in certain ways.

Origins of Attitudes

Some of our attitudes are learned from firsthand experience. Children who are bitten by dogs sometimes carry negative attitudes toward dogs for the rest of their lives, especially toward the kind of dog that bit them. That is, some attitudes appear to be *classically conditioned.* If a stimulus (for example, Pekinese dogs) is paired with a positive or negative experience, the attitude will be similarly positive or negative (Hofman & others, 2010).

Attitudes are also commonly learned from observing the behavior of others (Hilmert & others, 2006). Parents who model positive attitudes toward their Hispanic neighbors are likely to have children who have positive attitudes toward Hispanics. Children whose best friends think baseball is boring may pick up this attitude through modeling.

Persuasion and Attitude Change

Attitudes are not chiseled in granite; they can change after they have been formed. Indeed, the earliest known writings on social psychology were about changing people's attitudes through **persuasion.** Aristotle's *Rhetoric,* which was written 2,500 years ago, was an essay on factors that make for persuasive arguments when orators debate. You probably do not listen to many orators debate, but you are on the receiving end of other kinds of persuasive communications nearly every day. Commercials on the radio and television and advertisements in newspapers and magazines are designed to change your attitudes about the sponsors' products. Political speeches and billboards are intended to persuade you how to vote. Charities hope to persuade you to contribute. Your friends try to persuade you to help them move.

persuasion The process of changing another person's attitudes through arguments and other related means.

Persuasion is a natural and necessary part of our interactions with other members of society. But because of the potentially important consequences of persuasive communications (your friend might actually talk you into lending her your car!), it's important to know something about their nature. The persuasiveness of a communication is not determined merely by the logical quality of the argument. Logic may, in fact, be one of the *least important* factors. Notice that the qualities of persuasive communication fall into three general categories: characteristics of the *speaker,* of the *communication* itself, and of the *people who hear it.*

Characteristics of the Speaker.
Characteristics of the speaker are one factor in determining how persuasive a communication will be. There are a number of characteristics that have been shown to be important for persuasion. In general, the more credible the speaker, the more persuasive the message. But Carl Hovland has qualified this conclusion with the identification of what he called **sleeper effects** (Hovland & Weiss, 1951). Although attempts at persuasion by speakers who are low in credibility

sleeper effects According to Hovland, the potential for low-credibility speakers to influence opinion after a period of time.

Attractive, popular, or famous speakers tend to be more persuasive than unattractive speakers. However, their persuasiveness seems to be limited to relatively unimportant issues.

are ineffective at first, their messages may have an effect later. This is because people tend to forget what speaker presented what message. If you forget that a low-credibility speaker presented a certain message, then later that message will not seem so unbelievable. Unfortunately, even if we later learn that a criminal charge against someone was dropped, we frequently remember only the initial charges, forgetting that it wasn't true! Other things being equal, a speaker who is attractive, popular, famous, and likable will be more effective in changing our opinions than an unattractive speaker. Fortunately, the persuasiveness of attractive speakers seems to be limited to relatively unimportant issues—but that includes almost everything that advertisers want us to buy (Myers, 2005)!

Speakers are generally less persuasive if they obviously intend to change your opinion, particularly if the speaker has something to gain by changing your opinion (Aronson, 1995). This is the rationale behind the "hidden camera" testimonials that are included in some television commercials. Since the people supposedly do not know they are on camera, they do not seem to be trying to sell us anything.

Characteristics of the Message. In addition to the qualities of the speaker, the characteristics of the message have an impact on how persuasive the message is. Considerable evidence suggests that communications that arouse fear can enhance the persuasiveness of a communication, but only under certain circumstances (Mewborn & Rogers, 1979). Fear-inducing, persuasive communication can be effective if (a) the emotional appeal is a relatively strong one (but not too strong), (b) the listeners think that the fearful outcome (such as rotten teeth or lung cancer) is likely to happen to them, and (c) the message offers an effective way of avoiding the fearful outcome (such as an easy way to stop smoking) (Witte and Allen, 2000).

There are two sides to most arguments. If the audience is leaning in your favor or has information only about your position, your message will be more persuasive if you just tell them both sides of the argument. It may lose you some supporters, but if audience members are initially unfavorable to your position or are knowledgeable about both sides of the issue, it's generally better to give them both sides of the argument, as this makes the source appear more credible and less biased (Baron & Byrne, 1982). So the next time somebody does an admirable job of presenting both sides of an issue, you may be dealing with a strong believer in honesty and the democratic process, or you may just be listening to a shrewd operator who is trying to change your mind.

Recall from chapter 9 on cognition, the way in which problems are presented to us in words—or *framed*—strongly influences how we solve those problems (Lee & Aakers, 2004; Rothman & Salovey, 1997). Humans are so influenced by the wording of problems that we often reach very different solutions to exactly the same problem if it is framed differently. New research suggests that the same appears to be true of

Breast Health Action Plan

Mammography:

Annual mammograms are the best way to find breast cancer early.

Have a mammogram every year if you are age 40 or older.

If you have a history of breast cancer in your family, discuss a personal mammography screening schedule with your health care provider.

Clinical Breast Examination:

After age 40, have a clinical breast exam by your health care provider every year.

Between ages 20 and 39, have a clinical breast exam by your health care provider at least every three years.

Breast Self-Examination:

Ask your health care provider to teach you the proper way to do a thorough breast self-exam.

Beginning at age 20, examine your own breasts monthly.

Do messages persuade women to conduct breast self-examinations? It depends on how the message is framed.

persuasive communications: Framing the same message in different ways can sometimes make all the difference.

An excellent and inherently important example has been provided by psychologists Beth Meyerowitz and Shelly Chaiken (1987). They compared the persuasiveness of two messages designed to encourage college-age women to conduct breast self-examinations. Two groups of women read a three-page pamphlet on breast cancer and self-examinations. Their pamphlets were identical, except for several statements. One group read statements framed to emphasize the *gains* of breast self-examination:

> By doing breast self-examination now, you can learn what your normal healthy breasts feel like so that you will be better prepared to notice any small, abnormal changes that might occur as you get older. Research shows that women who do breast self-examination have an increased chance of finding a tumor in the early, more treatable stage of the disease. (p. 504)

The other group read statements framed to emphasize the *loss* involved in not conducting breast self-examination:

> By not doing breast self-examination you will not learn what your normal, healthy breasts feel like so that you will be ill-prepared to notice any small, abnormal changes that might occur as you get older. Research shows that women who do not do breast self-examination have a decreased chance of finding a tumor in the early, more treatable stage of the disease. (p. 504)

Four months later, the women were interviewed to determine if the messages had had any positive effects. The results showed that the second message, framed in terms of potential loss, was more effective than the first version. Women reading the loss-framed message had much more positive attitudes toward breast self-examination and were almost twice as likely to have practiced it, while those reading the potential gains message were no more likely to engage in breast self-examination than was a group who had read neither pamphlet. We cannot conclude that this is just another example of the greater effects of fear-arousing communications, because the two pamphlets did not arouse different amounts of fear. Although a great deal has been learned about the best ways to frame messages to encourage breast self-examination in recent years, health professionals infrequently frame appeals in the most effective ways (Kline & Mattson, 2000). Understanding framing helps us make the point that effective persuasion is not just the result of *what* you say but also *how* you say it.

Finally, repetition of a message increases the persuasiveness of strong arguments (Moons & others, 2009). That is why political candidates repeat the same statements over and over during campaigns.

Characteristics of the Listeners. In addition to qualities of the speaker and the message, certain characteristics of the listeners help determine how persuasive an argument will be. Less intelligent people are generally easier to persuade. The exception is when the message is complex and difficult to understand; under this condition, more intelligent listeners are easier to persuade (Rhodes & Wood, 1992). Some people have a greater need for social approval (a need to be approved of or liked by others) than other people do. People with a high need for social approval are generally easier to persuade than people who are low in this need (Baron & Byrne, 1982). People with high self-esteem are generally very confident of their opinions and difficult to influence, while those with low self-esteem tend not to pay enough attention to the communication to be swayed. For example, a person with a very low opinion of himself might hear a speech on financing public schools and become lost in his own thoughts about his own poor educational performance (Rhodes & Wood, 1992). People whose self-esteem is moderate (who have opinions of themselves that are about as positive as most people's) are generally easier to convince than people with either high or low self-esteem (Rhodes & Wood, 1992; Zellner, 1970). People are also generally easier to persuade when they are listening to the message in a group rather than alone, with bigger crowds leading to greater persuasion than smaller ones (Newton & Mann, 1980). Finally, social support for an attitude is important, and people with a network of friends and acquaintances who share their attitudes are more difficult to persuade to change those attitudes than people whose friends and acquaintances have diverse attitudes (Visser & Mirabile, 2004).

Techniques of Social Influence. Some people are better than others at influencing people to change their attitudes. This is partly because they have the characteristics of persuasive speakers, and partly because they understand the characteristics of the message and the audience—they know how to pitch the most persuasive argument to their audience. But many persuasive people—from politicians to salespeople—also know and use some simple *techniques of social influence* (Cialdini and Goldstein, 2004). As you read, try to recognize examples of these techniques in your own life.

A classic technique of social influence is the *foot-in-the-door technique* (Freedman & Fraser, 1966; Burger, 1999). A small, reasonable request is made first, and you comply with that. Then there is a follow-up with a larger request. If someone were to call you at home and say that she was a researcher at another university who would like to come over and inspect your home, would you agree to let her in? Most people would be reluctant to agree, but people who first agree to answer a few questions over the telephone are more likely to allow researchers to inspect their homes. Agreeing to one small request makes us more likely to agree to a second, larger request (Myers, 2005).

The *low-ball technique* (Cialdini & Goldstein, 2004) is a notorious car dealer tactic, similar to the foot-in-the-door in that you initially agree to a reasonable deal. However, then the deal is changed (additional charges are added in, etc.), yet still people typically complete the transaction, even though they didn't agree to this new deal. Most people don't walk away from the deal, even when the price goes up (Burger, 1986).

Believe it or not, people are more likely to comply with a request for a small favor if first they are asked for a bigger favor to which they initially say no. This is known as the "door in the face" technique (Cialdini & others, 1975). Imagine that you are asked to contribute $100 to a charitable organization that you do, in principle, support. Probably you would say no—that's a lot of money, right? But what if you are then asked if you have some spare change to contribute? Would you be more likely to contribute something than you would have been if you had only been asked for a big contribution? Maybe now you would give dollar or two. Try this next time you are fund-raising for a worthy cause.

Behavior and Attitude Change: Cognitive Dissonance Theory

As we have seen, persuasion is an important source of attitude change, but the discrepancy that often exists between our attitudes and behavior is another cause of changed attitudes. Even though attitudes are partially defined in terms of a disposition to behave, there is sometimes a great difference between our attitudes and our behavior. For example, during the Vietnam War, many men who held attitudes strongly opposed to the war obeyed their draft orders and became a part of the war. Similarly, opinion pollsters know that not everyone who has a favorable attitude toward a product will actually buy it.

cognitive dissonance (dis´so-nans) The discomfort that results from inconsistencies between attitudes and behavior.

An interesting point is that when behavior and attitudes are inconsistent, the attitudes often change to match the behavior *rather than the other way around.* Leon Festinger (1957) proposed the theory of **cognitive dissonance** to explain the tendency of attitudes to sometimes shift to be consistent with behavior. This theory, which has sparked some of the greatest controversy and most interesting research in social psychology, states that inconsistencies between attitudes and behavior are uncomfortable. This discomfort motivates people to do what they can to reduce the discomfort, or *dissonance.*

For example, if you smoke cigarettes (behavior), and you know that cigarette smoking is harmful because it is the leading cause of lung cancer and other diseases (attitude), your behavior and attitude are inconsistent, which produces an uncomfortable state of dissonance. Dissonance theory predicts that either your attitude or your behavior often will change to reduce the dissonance (Gibbons, Eggleston, & Benthin, 1997; Hoshino-Browne & others, 2005) (see figure 16.2). You could change the behavior and quit smoking, but that is often very difficult for smokers. Unfortunately, human beings usually reduce dissonance in the easiest way possible. In this case, it might be easier to change the attitude toward smoking, rather than to change the behavior and quit! How many smokers do you know who say, "So what if smoking causes cancer; I'll die of something anyway"? Irrational and self-defeating arguments are still effective at reducing dissonance.

Festinger and other social psychologists have tested the theory of cognitive dissonance in a large number of experiments. One of the best-known classic studies (Festinger & Carlsmith, 1959) involved asking research participants to perform a boring spool-stacking and peg-turning task for an hour. Afterward, the participants were each asked to tell the next participant that the task was an interesting one. Half of the individuals were offered $20 to say that the task was interesting, and half were offered $1. A third group of individuals stacked spools but were not asked to say anything to the next research participant. Later, all of the participants were asked how interesting they really thought the task was.

Which group do you think reported the most favorable attitude toward the task? Perhaps surprisingly—but just as predicted by the cognitive dissonance theory—the most positive attitudes were expressed by the group offered only $1. The group offered $20 was not placed in a state of dissonance: "The task was really boring, but I'll lie to the next person to get the $20." The group offered $1 was placed in a state of dissonance, however; there was no good explanation for their stating an opinion about the task that was inconsistent with their attitudes, so their attitudes improved to be more consistent with their behavior.

Cognitive dissonance is relevant to more than just our attitudes about stacking spools (Myers, 2005). A study of fund managers found that, when faced with losing investments, they justified their behavior in holding the investments by changing previously held beliefs about the funds (Goetzmann & Peles, 1997).

An interesting study was conducted following the 1980 presidential election, in which Ronald Reagan ran against Jimmy Carter. University students who supported Ronald Reagan in the election were the research participants in this experiment. They were asked to write an essay favoring an issue that Republican Ronald Reagan opposed (federally sponsored health care) or an essay supporting the candidacy of Reagan's Democratic opponent, Jimmy Carter. Half of the students were given very little choice about writing the essays. This group could be expected to experience little cognitive dissonance ("I wrote an essay that was contrary to what I believe, but I had to do it"). The other group of students was given much more choice as to whether or not to write the essay. These students were likely to

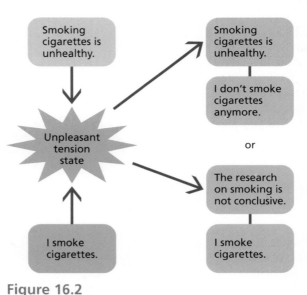

Figure 16.2

If attitudes and behavior are inconsistent, cognitive dissonance is created. To reduce this unpleasant state, either attitudes or behaviors change to be consistent with one another.

experience considerable cognitive dissonance, because they wrote an essay favoring something that they opposed, even though they did not have to do so. As Festinger would have predicted, attitudes toward Jimmy Carter and federally sponsored health care changed very little in the low-cognitive dissonance group (the individuals given little choice about writing the essays) but changed significantly more in the high-cognitive dissonance group (the ones given more choice). When the behavior of writing the essays created cognitive dissonance, attitudes changed to be more consistent with the behavior.

It's a little scary, isn't it? You probably thought your attitudes were always thoughtfully arrived at and based on reality. If Festinger is right, they may sometimes reflect nothing more than an escape from cognitive dissonance.

Prejudice and Stereotypes

Of all the attitudes that we hold about other people, the kind that is most worthy of improved understanding is prejudice. **Prejudice** is a harmful attitude based on inaccurate generalizations about a group of people based on their skin color, religion, sex, age, or any other noticeable difference. The difference is believed by the prejudiced person to imply something negative about the entire group. They're all lazy, or hysterical, or pushy.

It is important to differentiate prejudice, which is an attitude, from discrimination, which is a behavior. Fortunately, as a classic study shows (LaPiere, 1934) even those who hold negative attitudes or are prejudiced may not actually engage in discriminatory behavior. I say fortunately, because research reveals that many of us hold negative attitudes about other races or ethnicities of which we are not explicitly aware (Greenwald & others, 1998).

The generalization on which the prejudice is based is called a **stereotype.** We all hold stereotypes of other groups of people. How does a "rock star" look and act? If you were producing a movie, would you cast former first lady Laura Bush in the role of a rock star? You wouldn't, because she doesn't fit the stereotyped image of rock stars. What are Russians like? Do you have a stereotyped view of them? Think about it for a second. Do you hold stereotypes of women, men, Iraqis, African Americans, old people, Cubans?

Stereotypes can be negative or positive (you might believe that all psychology textbook authors are charming, witty, and attractive), but all stereotypes are inherently harmful for three reasons:

1. *Stereotypes reduce our ability to treat each member of a group as an individual.* When we hold a stereotyped view of a group, we tend to treat each member of that group as if the person has the exact characteristics of the stereotype, whether or not he or she really has those characteristics. Even when the stereotype is partially based on fact, many members of the group will differ from the stereotype in significant ways. Consider the stereotype that many of us hold that Chinese Americans are highly intelligent and good students. Although it's true that, *on the average,* Chinese Americans score slightly higher than whites on some measures of intelligence, not all Chinese Americans are highly intelligent. If a teacher's expectations for a Chinese child of below-average intelligence were based on this stereotype, the child might be criticized for not living up to her or his supposed high intelligence when the child is, in fact, performing up to her or his ability. Stereotyped beliefs that an ethnic group is *low* in intelligence can have even more serious consequences in limiting the educational and occupational opportunities of members of that group.

Stereotypes can be self-limiting, as well, posing a threat when we find ourselves in situations where we are reminded of negative stereotypes. For example, women scored worse on math tests when they were reminded of the gender difference in

prejudice A harmful attitude based on inaccurate generalizations about a group of people.

stereotype An inaccurate generalization on which a prejudice is based.

math performance, even though they were good at math, compared to a situation in which this wasn't an issue (Spencer & others, 1999).

2. *Stereotypes lead to narrow expectations for behavior.* Our stereotypes lead us to expect the members of the stereotyped group to behave in certain ways (Biernat, 2003). For example, we may expect women to be gentle, nurturing, caring, and cooperative, but we expect men to be competitive, ambitious, aggressive, and strong. Individuals of either sex who do not conform to these expectations are viewed as abnormal and are often the objects of anger or ridicule. Thus, stereotypes can be a limiting force for persons who do not conform to the narrow expectations for their group (gender, ethnicity, age, and so on).

3. *Stereotypes lead to faulty attributions.* One of the things that we are most fond of doing is explaining behavior, both others' and our own. Someone has just invited himself over for dinner for the third time this month. Why? Is he broke? Is he just a mooch? Does he just really like you? **Attribution theory** is based on the idea that humans tend to try to explain why things happen. According to attribution theory, we tend to attribute all behavior to a cause.

Our stereotypes influence the attributions that we make about other people's behavior. As Elliot Aronson (1995) points out, if a prejudiced white man sees an overturned trash can and garbage strewn around the yard of a white family, he is apt to attribute the mess to a stray dog looking for food. But, if he sees the same thing in the yard of an African American family, he would more likely attribute it to their supposedly lazy ways. Faulty attributions deepen and strengthen our prejudices as we keep "seeing" evidence that "supports" our stereotypes, rejecting evidence that is contrary to them.

attribution theory (ah-tri-bu´shun) The theory that people tend to look for explanations for their own behavior and that of others.

Automatic Prejudice. Although most of us do not want to admit it, most of us are prejudiced at some level. We think of ourselves as fair-minded people who judge everyone as an individual, but growing up in a prejudiced world affects nearly all of us. A considerable amount of evidence shows that most people—even people who believe that they are not prejudiced—react differently to people of different groups in an instantaneous, automatic way (Greenwald & others, 1998; Baron & Banaji, 2006). Such implicit or automatic prejudice can be seen in such things as differences in neural responses in the limbic system, sympathetic autonomic response, and contraction of facial muscles to people of different races (Wheeler & Fiske, 2005).

In many instances we can consciously control prejudicial responses and not discriminate, but sometimes our automatic prejudice causes real harm in a heartbeat. In one study, students played a video game that simulated the rapid decisions police officers must make to shoot or not shoot suspects. Images of suspects appeared quickly and the participant had to decide whether or not to shoot. White participants were slower to shoot unarmed white suspects than African American suspects (Correll & others, 2002). Unfortunately, it appears to be much harder to change automatic prejudicial attitudes than more explicit and conscious attitudes (Gregg & others, 2006; Rydell & McConnell, 2006).

Causes of Stereotypes and Prejudice. To reduce prejudice, it helps to understand the causes of these harmful attitudes. Social psychologists have proposed three explanations for why prejudice arises:

1. *Realistic conflict.* The *realistic conflict theory* suggests that people who are frustrated and angry because they are competing

Stereotyping people, such as the "typical" salesperson, detracts from our ability to treat members of a group as individuals and leads to faulty attributions.

with another group for scarce resources, such as jobs, food, and territory, come to view the other group in increasingly negative ways (Myers, 2005). This is particularly true when one group is stronger than the other (Guimond & others, 2003). When prejudiced people are made angry, prejudice is strengthened, even if the other group was not the direct source of the anger (DeSteno & others, 2004).

2. *Us versus them.* Another source of prejudice is the tendency people have to divide the world into two groups—*us versus them.* Our group becomes the "in-group," and those who are excluded become the "out-group" (DeSteno & others, 2004). In a classic study at a summer camp, Sherif and Sherif (1953) randomly divided middle-class 11- and 12-year-old boys of the same race into two groups: the Rattlers and the Eagles. After a series of activities designed to promote in-group solidarity and between-group competition, the rival groups began to engage in fighting and name calling—they developed prejudices about one another, even though the groups had been created randomly. It doesn't take much to activate prejudice and cause us to have an emotional response—even a T-shirt, picture, or song reminding us of our in-group membership can evoke feelings of anger about out-groups (Seger & others, 2009).

3. *Social learning.* Like any other kind of attitude, prejudice clearly can be learned from others. When we observe the stereotypes and prejudices expressed by parents, friends, teachers, and the media, we are likely to adopt the same prejudices.

Combating Prejudice. Prejudice is harmful to the human race. But is there anything that can be done about it? There are some effective antidotes:

1. *Recognize prejudice.* Most people believe that they are not prejudiced. The first and most important step in reducing prejudice is to become aware of our own prejudices and the subtle ways in which people of one group put down members of other groups in their daily behavior (Aronson, 1995; Sue & others, 2007).

2. *Control automatic prejudice.* We cannot easily rid ourselves of implicit prejudices that took a lifetime to acquire, but we may be able to consciously control our prejudicial reactions (Dasgupta & Rivera, 2006; Payne, 2005; Wheeler & Fiske, 2005). Imagine that a classmate asks you if she can borrow your notes from the last class. She says that she missed the class because she was sick. If she were a member of an ethnic group that your parents always said was lazy, you might immediately think, "I'll bet she was just too lazy to come to class." People who are genuinely trying to reject prejudice, however, control those immediate prejudice reactions and deal with others on their own merits—not on the basis of automatic prejudice.

3. *Increase contact among prejudiced groups.* Prejudice can often be reduced by increasing direct contact with people from other groups (Turner & others, 2008; Pettigrew & Tropp, 2006). Even a slight, unnoticed touch was enough to reduce prejudicial attitudes at the implicit, automatic level in one study, even though more obvious explicit measures of prejudice remained unchanged (Smith, 2008). A meta-analysis of 515 research studies looking at intergroup contact (Pettigrew & Tropp, 2008) found contact with other groups reduces prejudice by (1) enhancing knowledge about the out-group, (2) reducing anxiety about contact with the other group, and (3) increasing empathy, and the ability to take the perspective of the others. The greatest effects, however, were for the changes in peoples' feelings from interacting with people from the other group (reduced anxiety, increased empathy), rather than thoughts (enhanced knowledge).

Direct contact works best under certain conditions (Pettigrew & Tropp, 2006):

First, the two groups must be approximately *equal in status,* and the environment in which the two groups interact should be one that encourages group equality. Interactions between managers of one race and employees of another race do not decrease prejudice.

Although prejudice can sometimes be reduced through increasing contact among ethnic groups, simple direct contact, such as attending a multiethnic school, is not enough.

Second, prejudice between groups will decline if the group members *view each other as typical of their respective groups*—not as exceptions to the rule. There will be no improvement in relations if the members of one group think, "This person is pretty darn smart—not like the others."

Third, when two groups who are prejudiced against one another interact, their prejudice will decrease if they are engaged in *cooperative rather than competitive tasks*. If a city is trying to decrease prejudice among teenagers of two different ethnic groups by bringing them together in a basketball league, the ethnic groups should be mixed on the same teams, not put on opposing teams. Cooperation builds respect; competition maintains prejudice.

Fourth, *the contact should be informal*, so that there are one-on-one interactions. Formal interactions among employees of different ethnic groups are not as beneficial as informal time spent together on breaks or after work.

Human Diversity
Stereotypes about College Students with Physical Challenges

Most of us are "able-bodied" persons with no serious limitations on our ability to see, hear, speak, or move about. Some of us, however, are challenged by physical conditions that make these everyday activities more difficult or impossible. Like any group that is *different* from most of the people in society, persons with physical challenges are the subject of stereotypes, prejudices, limitations, and stigma. These factors can profoundly influence their lives.

An important study by Catherine Fichten and her colleagues at Dawson College found that able-bodied students' perceptions of peers with disabilities are quite different from these students' perceptions of themselves (Fichten & others, 1989). Three groups of students participated in the study: wheelchair users, students with visual impairment, and able-bodied students. They completed several questionnaires that measured self-concept, dating behavior, and anxiety in social situations. First, they completed these questionnaires about themselves and then they completed the same measures in the way that they thought the other groups would respond.

What are your stereotyped views of classmates with physical challenges?

Fichten and her colleagues found that able-bodied students and students with physical challenges viewed each other in stereotyped ways. For example, able-bodied students believed that students with physical challenges were more anxious about dating and dated less frequently than able-bodied students. The able-bodied students also viewed the students who had physical challenges as nervous, unaggressive, insecure, dependent, and unhappy. The stereotyping was not all negative, however. Able-bodied students also viewed students with physical challenges as quiet, honest, softhearted, non-egotistical, and undemanding. The students with physical challenges held stereotypes about able-bodied students, too, viewing the able-bodied students as demanding, argumentative, overconfident, phony, and complaining.

In most instances, however, the stereotyped perceptions were based on myths. For example, Fichten and her colleagues found no differences in either the number of dates or anxiety about dating reported by students with physical challenges and able-bodied students, even though the able-bodied students thought that students with physical challenges were less satisfied with their dating. Similarly, although able-bodied students believed that the self-esteem **Continued on pg. 547**

Continued from pg. 546 scores of students with physical challenges were lower than their own, there were no actual differences in the self-esteem of able-bodied students, students who were visually impaired, and students who used wheelchairs. Even the students with physical challenges themselves sometimes believed the same myths about students with other physical challenges! Both able-bodied students and students with physical challenges attributed more "handicapped" stereotypes to students with physical challenges than to able-bodied students.

The Americans with Disabilities Act of 1990, designed to enable persons with physical challenges to gain access to public facilities and to the workplace, brought the needs of persons with physical challenges into the consciousness of people in the United States. But societal changes require more than just the passage of laws. As in the civil rights movement, if stereotypes are to be reduced, both groups must learn more about each other through extended contact under conditions of equal status. Laws are passed to create conditions under which members of each group can get to know each other as individuals. In time, such interactions may improve the degree to which people with disabilities will be able to participate fully in society without stereotypes and discrimination.

Whether physically challenged or not, what kinds of exposure have you had to those who are? As you go about your campus and community today, notice how you react when you see someone with physical challenges. Do you react in the same way to able-bodied persons? Can you see the influence of stereotypes in these reactions? How could you make it easier for persons with physical challenges at your school to interact with able-bodied students on an equal basis?

The use of the term *physical disability* has been discouraged to emphasize the fact that the physical condition often does not disable the person in any absolute sense. Many persons prefer the more neutral term of *physically challenged*. But some persons reject the newer term *physically challenged* as well, stating that they alone should decide whether or not their physical condition is "challenging" (Bregante & others, 1993).

Human Diversity
Stereotypes about College Students with Physical Challenges
cont'd from pg. 546

Review

Attitudes are a focus of research for social psychologists because they are influenced by others and they play a key role in our interactions with other people. Attitudes are defined in terms of three components: beliefs, feelings, and dispositions to behave. Attitudes are learned through both direct experience and from what we hear and observe in others.

Attitudes are distinct from behaviors, and may change after they are formed. Nearly every day someone tries to persuade us to change our attitudes or behavior. The effectiveness of these attempts depends on qualities of the speaker, the message, and the listener. Speakers are more influential when they appear credible, are attractive, and do not appear to be trying to influence us for their own personal gain.

We are most likely to be influenced by fear-inducing messages if the fear appeal is moderately strong, if the listener thinks the fearful outcome is likely, and if reasonable ways of avoiding the fearful outcome are presented. Messages that present some information favoring both sides of the argument are more persuasive to listeners who are knowledgeable about both sides of the issue and are initially opposed to the message. The way that a message is framed can affect persuasion. And listeners tend to be more easily persuaded if they are less intelligent, have a high need for social approval, are somewhat low in self-esteem, and are in large groups.

Discrepancies between our behavior and attitudes provide another potent source of attitudes. Sometimes there is a big difference between the attitudes we express and the ways we behave. Under some circumstances, changes in behavior that create a discrepancy

Review (cont.)

between behavior and attitudes are followed by a change in attitudes that makes the attitudes consistent with behavior again. This is most likely to occur when there is no obvious external cause for the change in behavior. Cognitive dissonance theory explains this change in attitude by stating that the discrepancy between behavior and attitudes creates an uncomfortable state. This discomfort is reduced when the attitudes change to fit the behavior.

Prejudice is a negative attitude based on inaccurate generalizations about a group of people, and is distinct from discrimination, which is a behavior. Inaccurate generalizations, called stereotypes, are inherently harmful because they make it difficult to evaluate members of that group on an individual basis and lead to faulty generalizations about their behavior. People can often reduce their prejudices if they become aware of them, control automatic prejudicial reactions, and interact more under positive conditions with members of groups against whom they are prejudiced. Increased interaction will decrease prejudice only when the interactions are among persons of equal status, when those involved in the interactions view each other as typical of their respective groups, when the interactions are cooperative rather than competitive, and when the interactions are informal.

Check Your Learning

To be sure that you have learned the key points from the preceding section, cover the list of correct answers and try to answer each question. If you give an incorrect answer to any question, return to the page given next to the correct answer to see why your answer was not correct.

1. Attitudes consist of three components: _____, _____, and _____.

2. Which of the following speakers would be the least persuasive?

   a) a speaker who intends to persuade you, and you know it

   b) a credible speaker

   c) an attractive speaker

3. Two-sided arguments are most persuasive when _____.

   a) the audience knows only one side of the issue

   b) the audience knows both sides of the issue

   c) the audience is unfavorable to your side of the argument

   d) both b and c

4. Prejudices are harmful attitudes based on inaccurate generalizations known as _____.

   a) attributions   c) discrimination

   b) stereotypes   d) all of these

Thinking Critically about Psychology

There are no right or wrong answers to the following questions. They are presented to help you become an active reader and think critically about what you have just read.

1. How could you use the information contained in this section to convince others to drive automobiles that cause less air pollution?

2. Design a program to effectively reduce racial prejudice in the high school you attended.

Correct Answers: **1.** beliefs, feelings, dispositions to behave (p. 538), **2.** a (p. 538–539), **3.** d (p. 539), **4.** b (p. 543)

Processes of Person Perception

What variables influence our perception of others, and whether we like them, other than attitudes? Attribution processes play a role in the psychological processes involved in **person perception.**

Attribution Processes in Person Perception

We evaluate other people on the basis of *what* they do, and *why* we think they do it. In simple terms, **attribution** is the process of making judgments about what causes people to behave the way they do. One aspect of the attribution process is deciding whether a person is behaving in a particular way because of some external cause (**situational attribution**) or because of his or her disposition, personality, or trait (**dispositional attribution**).

First impressions are often given greater weight than later information in the person perception process.

Social psychologist Fritz Heider (1958) hypothesized that we evaluate people in a systematically biased way, making accurate person perception difficult. He believed we tend to *underestimate* the effects of the temporary situational influences, while *overestimating* the importance of personal characteristics, when accounting for behavior. Heider termed this bias the **fundamental attribution error.** By contrast, when explaining our own behavior, it seemed we were more likely to make situational attributions. This is known as the actor-observer effect (Jones & Nisbett, 1972). For example, seeing someone driving aggressively typically leads us to think "what a jerk!," yet if we are rushing to get somewhere and are driving aggressively, we understand that it is because we have an emergency, or are in danger of being late. Although the behavior may be the same (aggressive driving—not recommended!) the difference in attribution depends on whether we are the actor (running late!) or the observer (cut off in traffic).

Psychologist Betram Malle (2006) of the University of Oregon reviewed 173 published studies using a sophisticated quantitative method combining the results of many studies called *meta-analysis,* He found no overall support, confirming the results in an earlier study of the actor-observer effect (Robins & others, 1996) that also failed to fully support these long-held beliefs. Studies such as these make us reconsider long-accepted simple hypotheses regarding person perception. Actor-observer asymmetries do seem to exist, but they are not as simple as initially proposed (Malle & others, 2007). Even the emotions showing on the face of someone we see influences our impressions of them (Ames & Johar, 2009).

Recent theories look beyond psychological processes in person perception, including the social networks in which they occur (Smith & Collins, 2009). We experience not only our own responses, but also those of the groups with which we identify (Mackie & others, 2008). After all, don't our friends' opinions matter, too? And we all listen to gossip!

person perception The process of forming impressions of others.

attribution The process of trying to explain why things happen—that is, attribute them to some cause.

situational attribution An explanation for behavior that is based on an external cause.

dispositional attribution (dis´po-zish´un-al) An explanation for behavior that is based on a personal characteristic of the individual.

fundamental attribution error The tendency to underestimate the impact of situations on others while overestimating the impact on oneself.

Negative Information: The Bad Outweighs the Good. We seem to go through a complex process of "cognitive algebra" in our perceptions of others—with some factors contributing more to the average than others. Other things being equal, we give greater weight to negative than to positive information (Hamilton & Zanna, 1972). Put yourself in this situation: Imagine that you value warmth, physical attractiveness, and honesty in others. You meet a person in class whom you find extremely warm and attractive; you have an enjoyable conversation with him after class, but during the course of the conversation he asks you to help him think of a lie to tell his girlfriend explaining where he has been. Your opinion of him will probably become quite negative if honesty is really important to you. The fact that he is being dishonest with his girlfriend will overshadow his positive characteristics. In this way, a small amount of negative information often outweighs a considerable amount of positive information—most of us will pass up a delicious-looking cake if we know it contains even a small amount of rat poison.

Primacy Effects: The Importance of First Impressions. Some factors that play a role in person perception have little to do with the person, but rather are related to the circumstances when we meet. Would others perceive us differently if their first impression came from meeting us when we were having a particularly good or bad day? Unfortunately, first impressions are usually very important in the person perception process. A factor that is irrelevant to the nature of the person we are perceiving—the order in which we learn information about that person—can greatly influence our perception of that person. All of us have our good days and bad days, and it's a shame that the perception that others form of us is influenced so much by whether they form their first impression of us on a good or a bad day.

The first information that we are exposed to about a person tends to be given greater weight than later information (Asch, 1946; Belmore, 1987; Hovland, 1957). This is called the **primacy effect.** If you were introduced to Barbara right after you heard her deliver a polished and interesting talk to your sales group on the importance of ethics in business, your impression would probably be quite positive. Later, if you were to run into her in a bar, sitting alone, looking forlorn, disheveled, and half-drunk, you would be seeing a very different side of Barbara. But because your initial impression of her was favorable, there would be a strong tendency for you to ignore or "explain away" this new information ("Something awful must have happened to Barbara to make her act this way").

Suppose, however, that seeing Barbara in the bar was your *first* exposure to her. In that case, your first impression of her would be negative and would tend to dominate your perception of her, even after you were exposed to more positive information about her later. If your second meeting with her was hearing her lecture on business ethics, you would tend to discount the positive impression she was giving in that encounter ("She's holding herself together pretty well today—I bet most people here don't know she's really a drunken slob.").

First impressions (primacy effects) are not always of overriding importance, however. Their impact is greatly reduced under three conditions:

1. *Prolonged exposure.* Prolonged exposure to a person tends to reduce the importance of your first impression of that person. It is important to make a favorable first impression in your new job, but do not worry too much about it if you do not. Eventually, your fellow employees will get to know the real you. Information gathered over a long period of time will erase any first impressions. In fact, we are more likely to notice and remember information that is inconsistent with our first impression of a person (Belmore, 1987; Belmore & Hubbard, 1987).

2. *Passage of time.* Like anything else, first impressions tend to be forgotten over time. If a substantial period of time passes between first and subsequent impressions, the more recent impression will be of greater importance. Thus, if you flubbed your first attempt to favorably impress that gorgeous person, wait awhile and try again later.

primacy effect The tendency for first impressions to heavily influence opinions about other people.

3. *Knowledge of primacy effects.* When people are warned to avoid being influenced by first impressions, the primacy effect can be reduced (Hovland, 1957). Personnel managers and others to whom accurate person perception is important are educated to the dangers of primacy effects and may be able to reduce the importance of primacy in their perceptions.

Review

Our perceptions of others can be thought of as being based on a complex cognitive algebra in which we reach a weighted average of all of the positive and negative characteristics we see in others. Person perception is complicated by several factors, however: Different people evaluate the same characteristics in a person in different ways; our emotional state influences person perception; negative information about a person carries more weight than positive information; and first impressions usually are more important than later impressions.

Check Your Learning

To be sure that you have learned the key points from the preceding section, cover the list of correct answers and try to answer each question. If you give an incorrect answer to any question, return to the page given next to the correct answer to see why your answer was not correct.

1. The process of forming impressions of others is known as _____.

   a) person perception   c) attribution theory

   b) the primacy effect   d) the fundamental attribution error

2. The impact of the primacy effect can be reduced under three conditions: _____, _____, and _____.

Thinking Critically about Psychology

There are no right or wrong answers to the following questions. They are presented to help you become an active reader and think critically about what you have just read.

1. Can you think of an example in which "first impressions are lasting impressions" was true in your life?

2. Do you think we tend to explain other people's behavior in terms of dispositions ("he is clumsy, so he fell"), and our own in terms of situations ("the sidewalk was slippery, so I fell")?

Correct Answers: 1. a (p. 549), 2. prolonged exposure, passage of time, knowledge of primacy effects (p. 550–551).

Interpersonal Attraction: Friendship and Love

Are you in love with someone, or have you ever been in love? What attracted you to him or her and made you experience such intense feelings? Friendship and love are powerful social phenomena that touch all of our lives in one way or another. As such, they have been of special interest to social psychologists. In this section, we look at the qualities of others that make them attractive to us, and the factors involved in maintaining personal relationships.

"Chemistry" of Love and Social Bonding

When we speak of "chemistry" in love, we are usually referring to something about a person, or the process of falling in love, that is powerful but that we cannot quite put our finger on. A considerable amount of research, however, tells us that there is an important chemical side of love—truly, there is "chemistry."

There is strong evidence that a peptide chemical found in the brain and bloodstream, *oxytocin,* plays an important role in the creation of bonds of love, whether it be between parent and child or between romantic partners (Young & Wang, 2004). Closeness and physical touch, like hugs, massages, and breast-feeding in the case of infants, releases oxytocin in the brain. Oxytocin, in turn, creates a sense of calmness, safety, and well-being, and reduces the response of the central and peripheral nervous branches of the nervous system to stress. This positive physical and emotional response can become conditioned to the other person and promote a bond between the two persons. The positive state elicited by oxytocin makes the person conducive to further physical closeness, which further strengthens the bond (Curtis & Wang, 2003). Oxytocin even enhances positive communication and reduces conflict when couples argue (Ditzen et al, 2009). An aspect of what we experience as love has some basis in a chemical that soothes brain, body, and mood.

Characteristics of the Other Person in Interpersonal Attraction

While there is a chemical basis for attraction, there is more to it than that. Whom do we find attractive? What are the characteristics that we like in others?

Similar and Complementary Characteristics. In terms of interpersonal attraction, do "birds of a feather flock together" or do "opposites attract"? Are you more likely to be attracted to someone as a friend or lover who is similar to you in many ways or quite different from you? The answer is *both,* in different ways (Bem, 1996).

Maybe you value people who have an interest in exercise, nutrition, and philosophy because you are also interested in those things. It's enjoyable to have a friend who jogs with you, who pats you on the back for the healthy way you eat, and who shares long, delicious philosophical discussions with you. In general, similarity is highly important in attractiveness. We tend to be most attracted to those people who have similar values, interests, and attitudes (Caspi & Herbener, 1990; Feingold, 1988).

Opposites can also attract, however. Sometimes the attractiveness of persons unlike us is purely erotic (Bem, 1996). But opposites also attract when the opposite characteristic *complements,* or advantageously "fits" with, one of our own characteristics. Maybe you are attracted to the "life of the party" because you are more reserved. Perhaps good listeners gets along better with talkative people than with those who are similarly quiet. Maybe having a partner who is outgoing at social gatherings makes things easier and more fun! Similarly, a dominant person might prefer a submissive person, and a person who likes to "take care of" others might prefer someone who likes to be taken care of (Winch, 1958).

Another condition under which opposites attract is when people who are different from you *like* you (Aronson, 1995). It's often more flattering and attractive to be liked by someone who holds opposite values and opinions than by someone who holds similar ones (Jones, Bell, & Aronson, 1971). But take note that opposites usually do not attract; instead, opposites usually repel in personal relationships. A person who intensely advocates liberal causes probably would not like a person who vocally supports conservative causes. And a highly religious person probably would not be attracted to someone who disdains religion.

Competence and Our "Ideal Self." We tend to be more attracted to competent people. Intelligence, strength, social skill, education, and athletic prowess are generally thought of as attractive qualities. But people who are seen as *too* competent may suffer a loss in attractiveness, perhaps because it makes us uncomfortable to compare ourselves unfavorably with them. Elliot Aronson and associates conducted a clever experiment that demonstrates that it's best to be a *little* less than perfect (Aronson, Willerman, & Floyd, 1966). Participants listened to one of four audiotapes of people who were supposedly trying out to be members of their university's College Bowl quiz team. Two of the people scored over 90% correct on difficult questions and were portrayed as being honor students, athletes, and people active in student activities. The other two answered 30% of the questions correctly and were portrayed as average, unathletic students. Near the end of the tape, one of the superior students and one of the average students blundered—each spilled a cup of coffee on himself. Which one from this group do you think the participants rated as most attractive? The two superior students were rated higher than the two average students, but the superior student who committed the blunder was rated as most attractive of all. Apparently, the slightly clumsy pratfall made him more endearing!

We generally tend to be attracted to people who have the same qualities that we would ideally like to have—people who resemble our "ideal self." On the other hand, we tend to like people who are not *too* perfect because we tend not to like people who are closer to our ideal self than we are (Herbst & others, 2003).

Self-Disclosure We tend to like people who confide in us, and reveal personal information, perhaps because it signifies closeness and liking. A meta-analysis of studies into this well-documented phenomenon found that the more intimate the disclosure was, the greater the liking was (Collins & Miller, 1994). There is speculation that online self-disclosure over the Internet might be an important factor in the development of adolescent friendships today (Valkenburg & Peter, 2009).

Friendships can develop using social media, particularly for those who may not develop social relationships in other ways, but there are potential consequences, as well. People who text a lot seem to feel that they can disclose more of their "real self" via texting, but they tend to be lonelier and more socially anxious, and have smaller social networks compared with those who talk with friends (Reid and Reid, 2004). People with poorer social skills are more likely to prefer online social interaction because it safer, but they are then more likely to develop compulsive use, with negative consequences (Caplan, 2005).

Physical Attractiveness. Although it may vary by culture (Anderson & others, 2008), in general people tend to be more attracted to physically beautiful people Not only do we like beautiful people more; there is also a "halo effect"—we tend to think beautiful people are nicer, better adjusted, more sexual, and more intelligent (Langlois & others, 2000; Maner & others, 2005). Not only is physical attractiveness important, but it also seems to be the *most* important factor in the early stages of attraction (Myers, 2005). This is based on a snap decision, too. Research shows we decide if someone's face is attractive in under 13 milliseconds (Olson and Marshuetz, 2005).

In a classic study, Elaine Walster and colleagues randomly paired male and female college students for blind dates. They rated each student's physical attractiveness and gave her or him tests to measure attitudes, intelligence, and personality characteristics. After the blind dates, the students were asked how much they liked each other and whether they intended to go out on other dates with one another. The overwhelmingly important variable in determining attraction was physical attractiveness—more so than intelligence, personality, and attitudes. The couples who were most likely to like each other well enough to continue dating were the ones in which both the male and the female rated each other as attractive (Walster, Aronson, & Abrahams, 1966).

Physical attractiveness if often the most important factor in the early stages of attraction between people.

One of the key ways that physical attractiveness influences interpersonal attraction was demonstrated in an ingenious experiment (Snyder & others, 1977). Males were asked to participate in a study of how people get acquainted and were asked to speak to a woman over a telephone (to rule out nonverbal communication). Each male was given written information describing the woman he was speaking to and a photograph of her.

Females were paired randomly with males on the other end of the telephone, but the information sheets and pictures had nothing to do with them. All of the information sheets seen by the males were the same, but half of the males saw a picture of a very attractive woman and half saw a picture of a much less attractive woman. After they had talked on the telephone, the men who thought they were talking to a beautiful woman rated her as being more sociable, poised, and humorous than did the men who thought they were talking to an unattractive woman. As in previous studies, greater physical attractiveness led to greater likeability. But that's not the only interesting finding of this study.

When observers rated tape recordings of the males' conversations, they found that males who *thought* they were talking to a beautiful woman spoke to her in a more sociable way (for example, warm, outgoing, interesting) and were rated as enjoying themselves more in the conversation. Perceiving the woman as beautiful led the men to be more charming to her!

The females' recorded conversations were even more interesting. The women knew nothing about the pictures that the men were seeing, but when the men thought that the women were beautiful, the women spoke in a more charming, confident manner and were rated as seeming to like the men more. Apparently, thinking the woman was beautiful led the man to treat her in a way that *induced her to act in a more likable way*. If Alan thinks he will like Eileen because she is pretty, he will probably speak to her in ways that will bring out her most likable side, which will work out well for them (Langlois & others, 2000).

What physical characteristics do we find attractive? In North America, most men find women most attractive when the waist measures 70% of the hip measurement (Singh, 1993; Braun & Brian, 2006; Platek & Singh, 2010). Women find men attractive with a waist measuring about 70% of the shoulder circumference (Singh, 1995; Braun & Brian, 2006). These proportions are not far from the average in North America, and some studies show that we actually tend to find faces and body proportions more attractive when they are average for our cultures (Donahoe & others, 2009). It is possible that these average proportions are preferred because they are good predictors of fertility in both sexes. We also tend to prefer symmetrical faces, which relates to overall health and well-being (Thorrthill & Gangestad, 1993). On the other hand, we do tend to find faces that slightly accentuate the characteristics of the sex—soft skin, fuller lips, bigger eyes, and smaller chins in women, and strong jaws and brows in men—more attractive (Cornwell, & others 2006; Johnston & others, 2001).

But don't despair! Even if we lack these attractive characteristics, there is hope for the rest of us! We seem to want two things in a mate (Penke & others, 2007): physical attractiveness and someone dependable, kind, and trustworthy (women also prefer someone who can provide resources). So it's not all about looks—being nice and reliable is important, too. Besides, people's looks can grow on us. The more we see someone's face, the more we like it (Harmon-Jones & Allen, 2001). We might prefer to be dating someone who looks like Johnny Depp or Beyonce, but we tend to choose dates and mates who closely match our own level of physical attractiveness (Penke & others, 2007; Berscheid & others, 1971).

Perhaps most importantly, the relationship between physical attractiveness and liking goes both ways. We like people better when we think they are beautiful, but as we get to like people better, we begin to think they are more beautiful (Langlois & Stephan, 1981). Thus, to a considerable extent, love is blind and beauty is in the eye of the beholder—and nothing could be nicer.

Characteristics of the Perceiver

We have just noted some qualities of other people that make them more or less attractive to us. But, it takes two to become friends or fall in love. What is our part in person perception? Do our characteristics influence person perception?

Personality and Interpersonal Attraction. There is evidence that our personality traits, which describe how we typically are over time, influence person perception. For example, men and women who are high in the trait of neuroticism tend not to marry (Johnson & others, 2004) or, if they do marry, to be unhappy in their marriages (Robins, & others, 2000). It may surprise you to learn that getting married is strongly influenced by heredity. How could something as uniquely human as marriage be influenced by our genes? The answer seems to be that genes influence personality, and personality influences marrying or not (Johnson & others, 2004).

Emotions and Person Perception. There is also evidence that our moods at the time we meet a person influence person perception (Foster & others, 1998). Positive emotional states lead to greater attraction to others than negative emotions do. William Griffith and Russell Veitch (1971) had a radio news broadcast playing as individuals waited for an experiment in interpersonal attraction to begin. The broadcast was actually taped beforehand. Half of the participants heard a depressing broadcast and half heard happy news. Afterward, the participants hearing the sad news did not like the strangers they had met in the experiment as well as did those who had heard the good news. A well-designed study by Joseph Forgas and Gordon Bower (1987) confirmed these findings. They also found that we are better able to remember positive information about another person when we meet him or her while we are in a good mood, and we are better able to remember negative information when we meet another person while we are in a bad mood. The effects of mood on person perception are likely, then, to be relatively enduring.

Gender Differences in Interpersonal Attraction. Today, the great majority of both women and men feel that being in love is necessary for marriage. This does not mean that men and women fall in love for all the same reasons, however. The evidence is clear that women place more emphasis on their romantic partner's intelligence, character, education, occupational status, ambition, and income than do men (Feingold, 1990, 1992a; Myers, 1999). These qualities are not unimportant to men, but they are comparatively more important to women. Both genders similarly value a sense of humor and a pleasant personality in romantic relationships, but men place considerably greater emphasis on physical attractiveness than do women. Interestingly, these same results have been found in different generations in the United States and across a number of cultures (Feingold, 1992a).

It is important to keep in mind, however, that these things vary widely among members of both genders. Perhaps the most striking thing about the cognitive algebra of person perception is that different people often seem to be using different equations! Whether a characteristic is considered positive or negative and how much weight it will carry in person perception differ markedly from individual to individual. Gloria may feel that an interest in exercise, nutrition, and philosophy and an outgoing personality are all highly positive characteristics. Tanika may feel that these characteristics are not very important one way or another. And Lydia might find them all to be highly negative characteristics. If Gloria, Tanika, and Lydia were to meet a man with these characteristics at a party, each would form a very different perception of him. It's like that for everyone. Because different people evaluate the same characteristics in different ways, some people are going to love you, some are going to dislike you, and the rest will find you so-so.

Proximity. One important, but not very romantic, cause of attraction is proximity, or geographical closeness. You are more friendly with people who live next door to you than with people who live farther away. Physical proximity increases interactions, and repeated exposure to people tends to increase liking (Zajonc, 1968; Harmon-Jones & Allen, 2001). Just like a song on the radio can grow on you—it's the same with people.

Mutual Liking. Let's end this discussion of factors involved in interpersonal attractiveness on an upbeat note. Liking often leads to liking in return. If Vicki likes Neal, she has made herself more attractive to Neal simply by liking him. Neal, if he is like almost everyone else, will be more attracted to people who like him than to people who do not like him. Liking someone will not turn you into an irresistible beauty, but it will help.

One reason this seems to be so is that liking someone actually makes you seem more *physically* attractive, especially if a little lust is thrown in. You have heard people say that a person is more beautiful when in love, and it's true. Your eyes are more attractive. The pupils are more dilated (opened) when you look at someone you find sexually attractive, and others find large pupils more attractive sexually (Hess, 1975). And your posture and movements are more attractive and seductive. In subtle ways, you are more physically alluring when you are attracted to another person.

Another reason that liking tends to lead to liking is that you are nicer to the people whom you like, and being nicer makes you more attractive to them. A number of studies show, for example, that we tend to like people more when they praise us or when they have done favors for us. Favors and praise feel nice, and we like the giver better for having given them to us. So send flowers or create a music mix—it might just tip the balance of love in your favor. As you might expect, there are limits on the impact of praise and favors. If they are excessive, and especially if the other person thinks you are insincere and have selfish motives for giving them, praise and gifts will not lead to increased liking and may even lessen the liking (Aronson, 1995).

Maintaining Relationships

We have talked about some of the factors that determine whether you will be attracted to another person. But what about the factors involved in maintaining relationships? Assuming that one of the people to whom you are attracted becomes your friend, lover, or spouse, what things determine whether you and your partner will stay in the relationship? So many relationships that begin in joy end in a long cry. Why? Two of the major factors are (1) the difference between what you expect to find in a relationship and what you actually find and (2) the degree to which the relationship is fairly balanced or equitable.

Expectations Versus Reality in Relationships. When you begin a relationship with someone you do not know very well, part of what you fall in love with is what you *expect* the person to be like. Some of these expectations may be based on good evidence. One of his friends has told you that he is an especially nice and fair person, so it's reasonable to expect him to be fair and nice to you. You know that he is in the same profession as you, so you can expect to be able to share your workday experiences easily with him. Other expectations are based on less evidence. He has behaved in a strong, self-assured way so far, so you assume that he will always be this way, even though the biggest challenge you have seen him handle is the waiter's mistake of bringing tomato soup instead of minestrone. You *know* that he is a wonderful lover, even though he has only kissed you goodnight once. He dresses like an outdoorsman, so you expect him to love backpacking as much as you do. And he is well-educated, so you feel sure he will share your love of serious literature.

The point is that, even when your expectations are fairly well grounded, some of them will turn out to be incorrect. He will not be exactly as you expect him to be before the relationship begins. This is one primary reason relationships end. If the other person turns out to be significantly different from the person you expected, you may be unwilling to stay in the relationship (Neff & Karney, 2005). This is especially true when a person is disappointed by his or her partner's actual level of caring and responsiveness (Huston, Niehuis, & Smith, 2001).

Even when you know a person well before beginning a serious relationship, differences between expectations and reality can be a problem. A famous theory of love (Sternberg, 1986) proposes that love relationships have three components: intimacy (feelings of closeness), passion (including romance and sexual attraction), and commitment (short-term and long-term). There are different kinds of love relationships, varying by the relative strength of each component, and our experiences vary over the course of a relationship, but love relationships are most satisfactory when partners match on them. One common source of unfulfilled expectations is the predictable shift from **passionate love** to **companionate love** (Hatfield, 1988; Reis & Aron, 2008). When two people first fall in love, they often feel intense passions that are a heady and magnificent mixture of romantic, sexual, and other feelings. Even in the most healthy and enduring relationships, however, passionate love gradually becomes companionate love—a less intense but often wonderful blend of friendship, intimacy, commitment, and security. Although romantic and sexual emotions often continue to be an important part of companionate love, they often do not continue at the initial levels.

If one or both of the partners does not expect passionate love to change, the reality of passionate love's blending into companionate love can be difficult. But if both partners truly want a long-term relationship (many people stay in relationships only as long as the passionate love remains, then leave feeling unfulfilled or hurt), and if the disappointment that often surrounds the lessening of romantic love is handled with compassion on both sides, the couple can usually manage the transition.

Finally, expectations about a love relationship can fail to match its reality, because partners change over time. Sometimes the rugged outdoor person becomes a happy couch potato, and the party animal becomes a health-conscious, jogging vegetarian. If children arrive, and if career promotions are received (or not received), these and other changes can alter the reality of the relationship as well. If these changes in one's partner are not welcome, the reality of the changed relationship can be upsetting. Sometimes, however, a change in a partner can make a good relationship even better.

Equity in Relationships. Relationships are more likely to endure when the good things that we give to our partner are about equal to what our partner gives us. These good "things" that partners give to one another are many and varied. They include compliments, back rubs, help with homework, a day off

passionate love The mixture of romantic, sexual, and other feelings of love.

companionate love The blend of friendship, intimacy, commitment, and security that generally develops after passionate love.

Relationships that last tend to be based on realistic expectations and on the perception of equity in the relationship.

without the kids, flowers, jokes, lovemaking, a willingness to listen about a bad day, interesting meals, kisses, and interesting conversations. They also include things like physical attractiveness (a nice-looking person is enjoyable to look at), honesty, faithfulness, and integrity.

The commonsense idea that enduring relationships are ones in which the partners give and receive in equal proportion has been formalized and improved by social psychologists (Adams, 1965; Myers, 1999; Walster & Walster, 1978) under the name of **equity theory.** Equity theory states that partners will be comfortable in their relationship only when the ratio between their perceived contributions and benefits is equal. Equity theory is often summarized by the following equation:

$$\frac{\text{Perceived benefits of person X}}{\text{Perceived contributions of person X}} = \frac{\text{Perceived benefits of person Y}}{\text{Perceived contributions of person Y}}$$

These benefits and contributions cannot be easily translated into numerical terms, but suppose for a moment that person X perceives that she "gives" 10 things to the relationship, whereas person Y gives only 5 things. Is this an equitable relationship? It is if person X perceives 10 benefits from the relationship whereas person Y perceives benefits, because the equation is in balance:

$$\frac{10}{10} = \frac{5}{5}$$

There are two important points to notice in the equity theory equation. First, the benefits that the two people receive from one another do not have to be equal, but the *ratio* between their benefits and contributions must be equal. A person who both gives and receives a lot can be in an equitable relationship with a person who doesn't give much to the relationship but doesn't receive much from the relationship either. Each person just needs to have a balance in what they personally give and receive.

Second, note that the equation is written in terms of *perceived* benefits and contributions. The only person who can judge how much she or he is giving and receiving is that person. An outside observer might see a relationship as being highly inequitable when the partners themselves are very happy with it. Tender lovemaking might be highly important to one person but much less important than good cooking to someone else.

If either member of a relationship perceives the relationship to be inequitable, that partner will either take steps to restore equity or will leave the relationship. Interestingly, we become uncomfortable in relationships either when we feel that we receive *too little* compared with what we give or when we receive *too much* compared with what we give. In either case, we will be motivated to restore equity by giving more or less or by asking (or in some other way inducing) the other person to give more or less.

One form of "giving" to a relationship is making sacrifices. Sacrifices, such as going to his family's home for Thanksgiving or having sex only as often as the partner with less frequent desire wants it, are inevitable in relationships. Sacrifices can contribute to or harm relationships depending on the motivation for making them, however. Sacrifices generously made out of a wish to make the partner happy are constructive, whereas sacrifices to avoid upsetting the partner can be destructive (Impett & others, 2005).

equity theory The theory that partners will be comfortable in their relationship only when the ratio between their perceived contributions and benefits is equal.

Review

What determines which people we will like or love? Our perceptions of others can be thought of as being based on a complex cognitive algebra in which we reach a weighted average of all of the positive and negative characteristics we see in others. Person perception is complicated by several factors, however: Different people evaluate the same characteristics in a person in different ways, our emotional state influences person perception,

Review (cont.)

negative information about a person carries more weight than positive information, and first impressions usually are more important than later impressions.

Although person perception is a highly complex and personal process, some general factors determine whether one person will be attracted to another. Other things being equal, you are more likely to be attracted to a person who has characteristics similar to yours or who has opposite characteristics that complement your own. Other factors in attractiveness include the other person's being competent (but not excessively competent), looking physically attractive, and their liking, disclosing, and being nice to you.

Once two people are attracted to each other, a number of other factors are involved in whether the relationship will endure. We enter into relationships partly because of our expectations as to what the other person will be like. Because those expectations are generally based on partial information, they are sometimes not met and the relationship fails. Relationships generally fail, too, when they are not equitable. In happy relationships, each person perceives a balance between what each person puts into the relationship and what each person gets out of it, and sacrifices are made altruistically to please the partner rather than to avoid trouble.

Check Your Learning

To be sure that you have learned the key points from the preceding section, cover the correct answer and try to answer the question. If you give an incorrect answer to the question, return to the page given next to the correct answer to see why your answer was not correct.

1. _____ theory states that partners will be comfortable in their relationship only when the ratio between their perceived contributions and benefits is equal.

Thinking Critically about Psychology

There is no right or wrong answer to the following question. It is presented to help you become an active reader and think critically about what you have just read.

1. What have you learned in this chapter that could help you enhance and prolong the important relationships in your life?

Correct Answer: 1. Equity (p. 557)

Summary

Chapter 16 defines social psychology and explores the influence people have on other people, the nature of attitudes and persuasion, and interpersonal attraction.

I. Social psychology is the branch of psychology that studies individuals as they interact with others.

II. Behavior is often influenced powerfully by its social context.

   A. Deindividuation may be responsible for some behavior in mob situations.

   B. The failure to help when in a group is a complex process. The presence of others affects the interpretation of an event as an emergency and creates a diffusion of responsibility.

   C. Individual effort may decline when people work in groups, group problem solving may lead to bad

decisions when opinions become polarized, and even groups of sophisticated decision makers may be susceptible to the effects of groupthink.

   D. Conformity is yielding to group pressure even when no direct request to comply has been made. Conformity can be seen in outward behavior only or can be seen in actual changes in beliefs.

   E. Social roles and social norms are important ways in which social factors can influence the behavior of individuals.

   F. Research by Stanley Milgram indicates that authority figures can command substantial obedience from individuals.

      1. Obedience is greatest when we are instructed to do something by a person who is high in status and who is physically present.

2. Obedience is less likely to occur when we are in the presence of other disobedient individuals.

G. Although groups can have a harmful effect, it is important to remember that groups can sometimes accomplish what no single person can and that social support can soften the impact of stress.

III. Attitudes are beliefs that predispose us to act and feel in certain ways.

A. Attitudes are learned from direct experience and from others.

B. Attitude change through persuasion is determined by the characteristics of the speaker, the communication itself, and the people who hear it.

1. Three characteristics of the speaker are important: credibility, attractiveness, and intent.

2. Characteristics of the message that are important determinants of persuasiveness are fear appeals and message framing. Sometimes it helps to present both sides of the argument.

3. Characteristics of listeners that help determine how persuasive an argument will be include their intelligence, their need for social approval, their self-esteem, and the size of the audience.

4. Effective techniques of persuasion include "foot-in-the-door" and "low-balling."

C. Attitudes sometimes change to become more consistent with our behavior, according to Leon Festinger's cognitive dissonance theory.

D. Prejudice is a harmful attitude based on inaccurate generalizations about a group of people. These generalizations are called stereotypes.

E. Stereotypes are harmful because they take away our ability to treat each member of a group as an individual and lead to faulty attributions.

IV. Friendship and love are social phenomena based on the process of person perception.

A. The process of person perception can be said to involve a "complex algebra" in which we combine and evaluate information about others to form an impression.

1. Negative information is generally weighted more than positive information in person perception.

2. First impressions (the primacy effect) generally influence person perception more than information learned later. The primacy effect is lessened under three conditions.

a. The person has prolonged exposure to the individual about whom the first impression was formed.

b. Time has passed since the first impression was formed, even if there has been no further exposure.

c. The person who formed the first impression understands the primacy effect and tries to minimize it.

3. Person perception is influenced by the emotional state of the perceiver.

B. Although many factors ensure that each individual's perception of another individual will be unique, some general factors partly determine to whom we will be attracted.

1. In general, we tend to be attracted to persons who

a. Have characteristics that are similar or complementary to our own

b. Are competent but not perfect

c. Are physically attractive

d. Also like us

2. Women are more likely to be attracted to a person's intelligence, character, education, occupational status, ambition, and income than are men.

3. Men are more likely to be attracted by physical attractiveness than are women.

4. Within each gender, however, different people perceive the same individual differently because of differences in the weight assigned to the same characteristics and even the perception of them as positive or negative.

C. Two major factors in determining if a relationship will last are the difference between what you expect to find in a relationship and what you actually find, and the degree to which the relationship is fairly balanced or equitable. The most enduring love relationships are able to make the transition from primarily passionate love to primarily companionate love.

chapter **seventeen**

Psychology applied to the environment and to professions

Chapter Outline

Prologue

For many reasons, the earth's environment is changing rapidly in ways that will mean that our children and grandchildren will live in a world that is far more dangerous and unpleasant than our own. In most countries, the degraded environment has already begun to claim lives (e.g., by air pollution increasing deaths due to respiratory and heart disease) and will do so at an increasingly rapid pace in the future. Most of the causes of negative climate change are the result of human behavior—from energy use to poor farming practices—which makes global warming and the sustainability of our planet a hugely important topic for psychology (Kazdin, 2009; Newell & Pitman, 2010). Indeed, it is hard to argue that the sustainability of the planet is not

Key Terms

the most important goal for psychology right now. Psychologists must play an increasingly active role in helping people change their behavior in ways that will create a sustainable world environment.

The difficulty is that it is difficult to get people to change the kinds of behaviors that use energy. Unfortunately, energy use makes us comfortable and happy! That is, as each of us follows our own self-interests in using energy, we are causing damage to everyone, including ourselves (Van Vugt, 2009). To change the behaviors that threaten world sustainability, we will need to use our understanding of human behavior in many different ways. Some of the energy-change solutions are not complicated, however. Sometimes people need just a little help that is easy and economical to give.

For example, a team of Dutch psychologists at the University of Groningen developed a method of using the Internet to help people reduce the amount of energy that their households use (Abrahamse & others, 2007). These psychologists conducted an experiment using volunteer families that consumed experimental method to a control group, which was given information on the environment and the importance of reducing energy use, but no help in reducing energy consumption.

Families in both experimental groups were asked to set a goal of reducing their household energy use by 5% over 5 months. These families began by filling out an interactive Internet-based questionnaire on their living conditions and current energy use. The program then gave each family tailored suggestions for exactly how they could reach the goal. For example, if a family entered that they set the thermostat on their heater at 73°F during the winter, reducing the thermostat was suggested as an energy-saving option. If they already set the thermostat at 65°F, however, they were not given this advice. In this way, the program provided tailored information on how much each of many kinds of such changes in behavior would save in energy, but each family was told that they were free to decide how to reach the goal of a 5% reduction in energy on their own. The families in the experimental groups also were given feedback over time about the amount of energy they were saving and the amount of reduction in their gas and electricity bills. One experimental group was also told that they were working with a group of other households in Groningen in trying to reach the goal.

Families in the two experimental groups reduced their direct household energy use by an average of 8.3% after 5 months, while families in the control group increased their energy use by about 1%. The group that was told that they were part of a group of cooperating households reduced their energy use by slightly more than the other experimental group. Together, the families in the two experimental groups reduced their use of gas and electrical energy by 9,143 megajoules per household (Abrahamse & others, 2007). How much is that? One megajoule is equal to the amount of motion energy of a one-ton truck moving at 100 mph, and each household saved over 9,000 times that amount of energy.

To reverse the warming and degradation of the planet, we will need to make far more such changes using a wide variety of behavior-change methods (Kazdin, 2009). First, however, we must make the decision to save Earth.

Applied Fields of Psychology

Now that you have reached the last chapter of this text, take a moment to think back to chapter 1. We noted on page 3 that the four goals of psychology are to *describe, predict, understand,* and *influence* behavior and mental processes. This chapter focuses on the last of these goals—the use of psychological principles to influence and improve the lives of human beings. In other words, it is about the *application* of psychology to the solution of human concerns. Most of our attention until now has been on the basic principles of psychology—facts and concepts about perception, learning, memory, problem solving, emotion, and many other topics. But we have already covered a great deal of information about the applications of psychology. Within each chapter, many examples of new concepts were illustrated by describing applications of those ideas. Moreover, the chapters on abnormal behavior and therapies covered the heart of the applied fields of clinical and counseling psychology, and the chapter on stress and health gave us a description of the field of health psychology.

We turn now to other important applications of psychology—to both the environment and the worlds of business, architecture, law, and education. Fewer psychologists are employed in these applied settings than in clinical, counseling, and health psychology, but they are significant and growing fields of application.

Environmental Psychology and Sustainability

Environmental psychologists study two important and fascinating topics: (1) the effects of the environment on our behavior and mental processes, and (2) the effects of our behavior on the environment. We begin by summarizing what has been learned about the ways in which our physical environments influence us and then move to the effects of human behavior on the global environment.

environmental psychologists Psychologists who study the effects of the environment on our behavior and mental processes, and the effects of our behavior on the environment.

Architects and interior designers strive to create environments where people can live and work more happily, healthfully, and productively. Environmental psychologists are actively involved in the study of psychological reactions to different aspects of the physical environment. Most findings to date have been interesting but perhaps not surprising. For example, people perceive others in less positive ways and are less interested in socializing in drab, ugly rooms than in attractive rooms (Maslow & Mintz, 1956; Russell & Mehrabian, 1978). Adding touches such as potted plants and an aquarium to professors' offices makes students feel more welcome (Campbell, 1978). And people are less positive toward others in hot rooms than in comfortable rooms (Griffith & Veitch, 1971). Other findings have been less expected and have contributed more to architecture and interior design.

Architectural Design of Workspace and Living Units

A great deal of effort has gone into the design of workspaces to make them enjoyable and safe for employees and to promote productive performance. For example, many offices use the so-called *office landscape* format. In this format, offices are laid out in large open spaces and separated from one another only by low movable partitions, desks, and file cabinets. This creates a space that can be flexibly rearranged, is inexpensive to construct, and is attractive in appearance. Contrary to expectation, however, studies of the psychological effects of office landscapes have not painted a positive picture. One study was conducted after a number of workers moved from a building with traditional separate offices into a new building that was equally divided into traditional offices and an office landscape area. After six months, workers who

Psychologists have helped architects design workspaces that are conducive to both job satisfaction and productivity. Do these workers have enough private space?

had moved into the office landscape area were considerably less satisfied with their surroundings. They reported that they interacted more with one another, but they cooperated less. In addition, they found the new office area less private and noisier and reportedly accomplished less work (Hundert & Greenfield, 1969).

Psychologists have increasingly played a role in the design of living units. Perhaps because psychologists tend to work in universities, college residence halls have been a frequent subject of such research. Traditional residence halls are laid out in one long corridor into which a number of small rooms open. Typically, the residents of these rooms share a single common lounge and bathroom, which are also located off the corridor. In contrast to this traditional single-corridor design is the suite design. In this concept, three or four rooms are clustered around a small lounge and bathroom shared only by the residents of that one suite. Proponents of the suite-design concept suggest that although the same number of people can be housed per square foot in this design (see figure 17.1), it's a far more "human" approach to dense housing. In this case, psychological studies have rather strongly supported the suite-design concept. Residents of single-corridor dorms spend less time in the residence hall, express greater desire to avoid interaction with other residents, and feel that they have less control over what happens in their hall than do residents of suite-design halls (Baum & Valins, 1977).

Even more impressive is the finding that the effects of living in a single-corridor residence hall extend outside the residence setting. Freshmen living in both types of halls were taken to a laboratory, where they were asked to wait with other students in a waiting room. Residents of single-corridor halls initiated fewer conversations, sat at greater physical distance from the other students, and spent less time looking at the faces of other students. Apparently, their unsatisfactory living environment led them to be somewhat less sociable even outside of the residence hall (Baum, Harpin, & Valins, 1975). If you live in a single-corridor hall, you should not be concerned about lasting damage to your social life, but it may have some minor effect on your current behavior.

Duncan Case (1981) has also provided evidence that the architecture of college residence halls influences friendship patterns over long periods of time. According to Case, the key element in residences is "shared required paths"—shared elevators, drinking fountains, and the like. Case found that during their sophomore year, over 80% of the students he studied shared a room with someone with whom they had shared a required path during their freshman year. Even during their senior year, 50% of the roommates had met through shared required paths during their freshman year. Because the students reported that their best friend was one of their roommates 73% of the time, it is clear that friendships are dictated in part by architecture.

Sustainability and Environmental Protection

The life-support system that we call *earth* is in serious jeopardy. It is very likely that future generations will face miserable and stark living conditions. It is even possible that the earth will no longer be able to sustain human life at some point in the future (Oskamp, 2000). There are three reasons for this dire situation: (1) overpopulation, (2) resource depletion, and (3) pollution and climate change. It has been clear for some time now that the earth is headed for disaster. In 1993, 1,600 members of the Union of Concerned Scientists endorsed this statement: "A great change in our stewardship of the earth and the life on it is required, if vast human misery is to be avoided and our global home on this planet is not to be irretrievably mutilated" (p. 1).

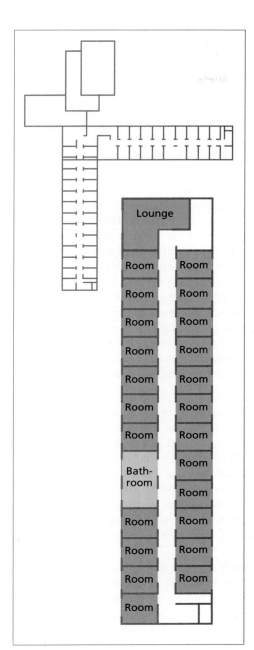
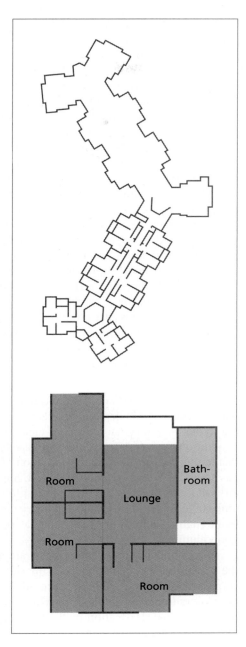

Figure 17.1

Examples of the single corridor and suite design floor plans for college dormitories.

Why is the sustainability of human life a topic for a course in psychology? The answer is that it is *people* who overpopulate, deplete resources, and pollute. Making life on earth sustainable will require *changing the behavior of people.* The people whose behavior must be changed are the people in government, the people who own and operate businesses, and the people who are consumers (Geller, 1995; Koger & Scott, 2007). All of us, in other words.

Overpopulation. It took about 3 million years to reach a population of 1 billion people on the planet. Now, with the addition of approximately 97 million people to the planet every year, another billion of us are added every 8 years. The current population of over 6 billion will *double* in about 47 years, putting the world's population at 10 to 12 billion near the middle of the 21st century! At the current rate, we are adding close

Mismanagement of the earth's resources can have tragic effects for both the environment and the people of the world. Approximately one-fifth of the world's population lives in extreme poverty, which puts them at risk for death and disease. Every day, more than 50,000 infants and children die of starvation or nutrition-related problems.

to 184 additional mouths to feed every minute! There is no question that the human behavior of reproducing at these high rates is a major threat to the environment.

Of the over 6 billion people currently on earth, over 1 billion of them live in absolute poverty, which puts them at high risk of death or serious health problems due to malnutrition and disease. Each day an average of 50,000 infants and children die as a result of starvation and nutrition-related illness. Many of these people live in nonindustrialized countries. Not surprisingly, people living in poverty may show little concern for preserving the environment when daily survival of self and family is in jeopardy. As a result, people in many nonindustrialized countries are forced into behaviors that are harmful to the environment. Examples include exhausting natural resources for export to industrial nations (such as the ongoing destruction of the hardwood forests of Indonesia and South America), degrading the soil through poor farming techniques, and polluting water supplies through poor agricultural, industrial, and sanitation practices. In developing nations throughout the world, these problems are multiplied as the increasing populations become concentrated in large cities.

Although it is still possible to find experts who deny it, the earth's carrying capacity for human beings is quickly reaching its limit, and many say that it has already been surpassed (Oskamp, 2000). How will we know when there are too many people on the planet? Unless we make choices to avoid it, the human population will probably "self-correct." Populations that are too dense will die off through disease or through wars fought over limited resources. Could this in fact already be happening—are the millions of people who have died from AIDS and genocidal wars in recent years in Africa the result of the overpopulation of areas with limited resources? (Oskamp, 2000)

Resource Depletion. A second major environmental problem involves the rate at which humankind is depleting the earth's natural resources. Some resources are essential to our very survival (clean air, clean water, topsoil that can be farmed, and so on). In addition, we consume millions of barrels of oil each day to fuel our lifestyles, a thirst that has already resulted in the depletion of half of the earth's total oil supply. America has about 200 years' worth of coal left, but its use creates other problems (for example, air pollution, mercury poisoning and global warming) that will make this alternative unfeasible. If we are to continue our electrified existence, we will have to turn rapidly to alternative sources of energy such as solar and wind power that are sustainable and nonpolluting.

Water and soil are resources that are already in short supply throughout much of the world. In our own country, primarily in the West and Southwest, demands have surpassed the region's ability to provide adequate amounts of fresh water. Amazingly, the Colorado River, the great provider of water for the Southwest, no longer reaches its former final destination of the Gulf of California—it is completely exhausted by humanity along the way! In nonindustrialized nations, only about half the people have access to safe drinking water today, and the problem will only grow worse in the future. As the population continues to increase, more and more water will be needed for agricultural, industrial, and personal uses. It is essential that ways be found to preserve and protect the earth's limited water resources. In addition, the amount of land that is available for agriculture is diminishing. Each year, erosion, urban sprawl, and other factors create a net loss of tillable land for growing crops.

Similar stories could be told about the loss of other resources such as the oceans' supply of fish, the forests, the rapid extinction of plants and animal species, and numerous other gifts that are supplied by earth's life-support system. They all point to a pattern of excessive consumption that is surpassing the earth's ability to sustain itself.

Pollution and Climate Change. The third major insult to the environment comes from the pollution of earth's air, soil, and water and the difficulties of disposing of both routine and hazardous waste. We have all heard about the problems of acid rain; smog; toxic waste; and polluted rivers, lakes, and saltwater bays. These are much more than threats to the beauty of the environment. They are literally a matter of life and death. Smog from automobiles, trucks, buses, and factories, for example, are a major cause of death from lung cancer, asthma, and other respiratory diseases. One route for the fatal effects of air pollution is through human behavior. People with asthma are twice as likely to commit suicide (even though the vast majority of people with asthma do not even consider suicide) (Kuo & others, 2010). Even small increases in the pollution of the air by fine particles from burning oil and coal increase complications of asthma and increase suicide rates (Kim & others, 2010). The World Health Organization estimates that in many areas of Europe more people are killed by air pollution than by automobile accidents (Oskamp, 2000), and the problem is even worse in some areas of the United States. Pollution of the soil, water, and food supply are equally serious problems.

Our electrified and automobile-driven way of life is fast depleting the earth's irreplaceable resources.

In addition, it is now clear that air pollution is leading to *global warming*. What is global warming and why is it a threat to the sustainability of human life? The increasing amount of pollutants that we release into the air by burning oil and coal (primarily carbon dioxide and methane) eventually reach the upper atmosphere. There they act like the glass roof of a greenhouse, allowing heat from the sun to enter, but trapping the reflected heat and not letting it escape into space. This *greenhouse effect* is causing massive climate change around the world. In most areas, average temperatures are increasing because of the greenhouse effect. For example, in Alaska, average temperatures are now 10° Farenheit warmer than they were in the 1960s. Similar changes in other polar areas are melting the polar ice caps and causing rises in ocean levels. It is just a matter of time until the oceans rise enough to make huge areas of the mostly densely populated areas of the world, such as Bangladesh, Nigeria, and Louisiana, even more vulnerable to massive loss of life and soil from flooding (Oskamp, 2000). In other areas of the world, temperatures are falling because global warming is changing major sea currents. Severe weather events are also expected. In many ways, global warming will have devastating effects on the earth's ability to sustain its current population. For example, it is likely that the great American "breadbasket" in the Midwest could become unsuitable for agriculture. The climate most appropriate for farming would move north to Canada. This would allow that country to become the new "breadbasket," were it not for the fact that it generally lacks the topsoil necessary for the task.

In addition, our pollution of the atmosphere with various chemicals is causing the destruction of the ozone layer of the atmosphere. This layer reflects most of the ultraviolet radiation from the sun away from the earth. Growing holes in the ozone layer have appeared in several parts of the world, particularly over Antarctica, Australia, and New Zealand. This has resulted in marked increases in skin cancer and cataracts of the eye (Oskamp, 2000). Pollution of our freshwater resources is another urgent problem that must be addressed soon. Not only are some of our aquifers (underground water supplies) shrinking, but our waters are being polluted by numerous sources such as industrial and mining wastes, agricultural pesticides and fertilizers, prescription drugs flushed down toilets, and acid rain. Even now, it is estimated that more than 25 million people die in third world countries each year as a result of polluted water. As with other environmental problems, the extent of humankind's polluting behaviors is surpassing the earth's ability to clean and renew itself.

The effects of these assaults on the earth work together to threaten the sustainability of human life. In just over a decade from now, the United Nations estimates that nearly 2 billion people will become "environmental refugees" because the soil, water, and air where they live can no longer sustain the population (Oskamp, 2000).

Psychological Aspects of Sustainability. Part of the solution to these dire environmental problems will come from technological innovations, such as the development of automobiles that create less air pollution. The primary hope for preserving our global life-support system, however, is that we will *all* change our environmentally destructive behavior. Staying within the earth's carrying capacity to sustain human life will require us to control population growth, reduce pollution, and reduce our rate of depleting natural resources. Because the people of the United States consume *vastly* more than our fair share of natural resources (we make up approximately 5% of the world's population but consume 25% of its resources), changes in our behavior are particularly important (Jucker, 2002). There are two theoretical approaches to changing environmentally destructive behavior: the behavioral approach and an approach derived from humanistic and cognitive psychology. As you will see, however, the current approach is to combine both.

Behavioral Approach. The behavioral approach to changing behavior to protect the environment is defined by two key characteristics:

1. The behavioral approach mostly uses the principles of learning to change behavior. After all, learning is a change in behavior due to experience (chapter 7, page 000). Therefore, it is natural to attempt to change behavior using the principles of learning.

2. Behaviorists are careful to gather data to evaluate everything they do. When they attempt to use what they have learned in the laboratory to solve problems in the real world, they evaluate the effectiveness of their real-world solutions as rigorously as they would if it were a laboratory experiment. This "experimental approach" to real-world problems allows psychologists to quickly abandon ineffective strategies and adopt more effective solutions. Sometimes, the experimental approach means adopting methods that someone else suggested but that we were sure would not work. Data should provide the ultimate checks and balances on psychologists' theories.

An excellent example of a behavioral approach to changing the behavior of consumers is provided by Van Houwelingen and Van Raaij (1989). They tested a method based on operant conditioning (chapter 7, page 000) for reducing the burning of natural gas in the home. The principle of operant conditioning states that behavior that is reinforced by its consequences will be more likely, whereas behavior that is punished by its consequences will decrease in frequency. These researchers installed special gas meters in 50 homes so the occupants could easily see how much gas they were using (and how much it cost). If feedback on the amount and costs of gas use "punishes" excessive gas consumption, it should decline. Van Houwelingen and Van Raaij (1989) found that providing the meters reduced gas consumption by about 10%. They further found that having immediate feedback was essential, because gas consumption went back to its original wasteful levels when the meters were removed. The consumers had not permanently learned more economical behavior. This finding suggests that operant feedback must be kept in place to yield long-term changes in behavior. Another similar, successful application of operant feedback is increasing the number of miles that truck drivers achieve per gallon of fuel by publicly displaying each driver's miles per gallon figures (Geller, 1995).

Cognitive and Humanistic Approaches. Many psychologists attempt to change environmentally relevant behavior by changing people's cognitions (beliefs and attitudes about sustainability) or by appealing to their "higher motives" (Schultz & others, 2007). According to these approaches, we must use persuasion to solve five problems if we are to avoid environmental destruction:

1. ***We are in denial.*** Unfortunately, we humans have a tendency to deny or "shut out" threatening information (see chapter 13, page 446). Because it is easier

Reminders to engage in pro-environmental behavior can help improve people's habits, but rewards for appropriate behavior have a stronger effect.

and more comfortable to continue in our environmentally destructive ways, we tend to deny the validity and importance of the kinds of information summarized above.

2. *We have bad habits.* Stern (2000) points to the negative impact of habit on environmentally destructive behavior. It is difficult to motivate people to change their habitual ways of doing things, even when it is clear to them that the world can no longer tolerate the levels of pollution and waste that it could in the past.

3. *We act like helpless "bystanders."* In the previous chapter you learned that people in crowds often do not act to help people in need. There are many reasons for this, including the belief that someone else will solve the problem. Unfortunately, we citizens of the world are in the ultimate "crowd" (6 billion inhabitants of earth and still counting). We need to realize that we must *all* act to save the planet.

4. *We do not believe that we are efficacious.* Social learning theorist Albert Bandura suggests that we only act when we believe in our own self-efficacy (see chapter 12, page 412). Most of us believe that we cannot solve the problem of environmental destruction, no matter how hard we try. Unfortunately, the planet cannot be saved unless we *all* act. We can literally change the world if we act together.

5. *We are guided by short-term self-interest.* At present, we are making decisions about the environment that satisfy our current self interests (it is warm, so turn up the air conditioning) rather than thinking of the future welfare of others. After you graduate, some of you will make decisions that will create profit in the short run at the expense of damaging the environment. You may do so by deciding to burn soft coal in your factory because it is cheap, even though it is highly polluting. Or you may vote for a politician whose platform promises financial advantages to you, even though he or she favors lax regulations that support polluting industries. Even more of us will choose to live in comfort, even though we know that our lifestyles are literally killing people in the world who are less able to protect themselves from pollution and resource depletion. We will even choose these lifestyles at the expense of the welfare of our own children and grandchildren. If we are to solve the problem of environmental destruction, we must begin to act on higher motives.

Integrating the Behavioral, Cognitive, and Humanistic Approaches to Environmental Protection. Psychologists E. Scott Geller (1995) and Paul Stern (2000) argued for an integration of the various approaches to environmental protection. One reason for such an integration is that the most effective interventions come from a range of theoretical perspectives and our efforts should not be limited by our theoretical blinders. A second reason is that the techniques derived from different theoretical perspectives often work best in combination.

Consider the following combination of behavioral and attitude change techniques: In some cases, power companies have an economic incentive to help consumers reduce energy consumption. For example, in some parts of the country, it is very costly to electric companies to have residential electric use increase dramatically in the summer, because they either need to invest in generating capacity that is unneeded during most of the year or to buy electricity at inflated prices from the power grid during times of high demand. What if an electric company offered to pay most of the cost of improving the insulation of existing homes? That offer would provide a strong economic incentive to homeowners to reinsulate, because a small investment in insulation would save them a considerable amount on their future electric bills. Such incentives are helpful but are dramatically more effective when combined with informative and persuasive communications from the power company (Stern, 2000). See chapter 16, page 538, for a refresher on what constitutes persuasive communication.

Review

Environmental psychologists conduct research on the psychological impact of our physical environment. They have found that some aspects of the interior design of rooms, such as the drabness of colors or the presence of plants, influence the mood of the persons in those rooms and their interest in socializing. Similarly, the physical characteristics of the room also influence emotions and social behavior. Friendship patterns have been found to be affected by the architecture of living units in that individuals who share "required paths" are more likely to develop friendships in a dormitory than those who do not. By studying environments such as these and the environments of workspaces, environmental psychologists can offer information to architects and interior designers that helps them design spaces with optimal psychological impact.

The earth's environment has been seriously, and perhaps catastrophically, damaged by overpopulation, resource depletion, and pollution. Ultimately, the cause of environmental damage is the behavior of humans. Psychologists must play a major role in changing human behavior to sustain life on the planet. Techniques for changing environmentally sensitive behavior have come from two broad traditions within psychology. The behavioral approach is characterized mostly by the use of principles of learning to change behavior and the rigorous evaluation of the effectiveness of techniques in the real world. The second approach is based on cognitive and humanistic traditions and focuses on changing attitudes, values, beliefs, and circumstances. In addition, this approach draws heavily on social psychology research on persuasive communication to change attitudes and beliefs. Recently, psychologists from both traditions have recognized the importance of combining the best of both approaches.

Check Your Learning

To be sure that you have learned the key points from the preceding section, cover the list of correct answers and try to answer each question. If you give an incorrect answer to any question, return to the page given next to the correct answer to see why your answer was not correct.

1. A(n) _____ studies the effects of the physical environment on behavior and mental processes and studies ways to protect the environment.

   a) developmental psychologist   c) clinical psychologist

   b) environmental psychologist   d) psychoanalyst

2. College students who live in residence halls tend to meet other students with whom they have _____.

3. The two main psychological approaches to changing behavior that impacts the natural environment are _____ and _____.

4. The behavioral approach is characterized by a focus on (select two):

   a) attitudes, values, beliefs, circumstances   c) persuasive communication

   b) principles of learning   d) rigorous testing of methods

5. The cognitive and humanistic approach is characterized by a focus on (select two):

   a) attitudes, values, beliefs, and circumstances   c) persuasive communication

   d) principles of learning   d) rigorous testing of methods

Thinking Critically about Psychology

Correct Answers: **1. b** (p. 563), **2.** shared required paths (p. 565), **3.** behavioral approach; cognitive and humanistic approach (pp. 568, 569), **4. b** and **d** (p. 569), **5. a** and **c** (p. 569).

Psychology and Work

When you think of the word *work,* do the words *happiness* and *quality of life* come to mind? They should, because work is linked to the quality of our lives in important ways. The standard of living that we enjoy in terms of material goods and services is the product of business. Your car, clothes, haircut, compact discs, and newspaper would not exist without the multifaceted business sector. Moreover, our quality of life is also linked to the satisfaction that comes from our work. Our sense of well-being depends in part on whether our jobs are boring and demeaning or meaningful and rewarding.

Psychologists who work with businesses are known as **industrial-organizational (I/O) psychologists.** They attempt to improve the human benefits of work in a number of ways. For example, they seek ways to help businesses and government organizations produce more and better goods and services, to increase job satisfaction by changing methods of management and training, and to find "the right person for the right job" by improving methods of employee selection (Landy & Conte, 2004). To be sure, psychological principles are sometimes used to improve profits rather than human lives—such as by developing advertisements that are more persuasive than informative—but this is the exception rather than the rule for professional psychologists in business today.

Personnel departments are where industrial-organizational psychologists can be found most frequently, because employee selection and training is the primary responsibility of these departments. Some large companies employ one or more psychologists to work in personnel. Other companies use the services of industrial-organizational psychologists who work for independent consulting firms. They teach both personnel and general managers to put the principles of psychology to work in helping people contribute more effectively and happily to the goals of the business.

Other industrial-organizational psychologists work on behalf of consumers or workers rather than businesses. They are employed by government or public-interest groups performing such jobs as helping consumers make more informed choices in their purchases; or by organizations dedicated to protecting the rights of workers.

industrial-organizational (I/O) psychologists Psychologists who study organizations and seek ways to improve the functioning and human benefits of business.

Employee Selection and Evaluation

Recall from chapters 1 and 9 that Alfred Binet gave us the first practical way of measuring intelligence at the start of the twentieth century. Since Binet's time, numerous useful ways of measuring intelligence and other psychological attributes have been used in applied settings. In business, the most significant uses of psychological measurements have been in selecting and hiring new employees and in evaluating the performance of current employees. The measures most commonly used in employee decisions include interviews, paper-and-pencil tests, performance tests, job performance ratings, and the evaluation of simulated job performance. Employee selection

Psychologists have learned that applicants with average qualifications are rated higher if they are interviewed after two poorly qualified candidates than if they are interviewed after two highly qualified candidates.

and evaluation is an essential part of business because finding the person that best fits the job not only improves employee morale and productivity but also decreases employee turnover and absenteeism as well.

Interviews. Interviews are the heart of the process of evaluating job applicants and play a significant role in considering current employees for possible promotion. Interviews are more or less structured conversations in which the employee or job applicant is questioned about her or his training, experience, and future goals. The suitability of the individual for the job is evaluated partly in terms of factual answers to questions, but also in terms of the individual's personality, spoken language, potential for leadership, and other personal factors.

Unstructured interviews generally are not good predictors of future job performance (Schmidt & Hunter, 1998), unless multiple unstructured interviews are conducted (Sackett & Lievens, 2008). Structured employment interviews, in which every job applicant is asked the same questions, are more efficient and somewhat more valid (Huffcutt & others, 2001; Schmidt & Hunter, 1998). But the other methods of assessing job candidates discussed in this chapter tend to be even more useful in selecting employees than even structured interviews.

Tests of Intelligence. Tests of general intelligence, such as those discussed in chapter 9, are frequently used to select employees, especially for complex jobs (Gottfredson, 1997). Intellectual tests are used for this purpose by governments, the military, and private industry. Furthermore, because tests of intellectual ability are used to select applicants to medical school, law school, and graduate school, they also play a key role in determining who enters such professions. As a result, persons holding different kinds of jobs tend to be highly segregated in North America and other industrialized societies (Gottfredson, 1997). Figure 17.2 shows the range of intelligence test

Figure 17.2

The range of intelligence scores of the middle half of applicants for various occupations (25 percent had intelligence scores above each range and 25 percent had intelligence scores lower than each range).

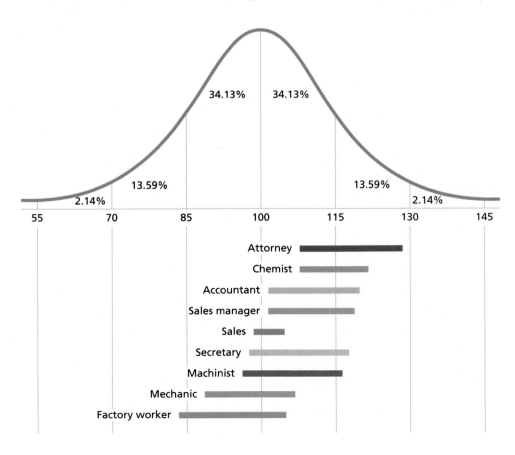

scores of the middle half of applicants for a wide range of jobs. Note that a person with an intelligence score of 115 would have many choices: she or he could be a competitive applicant for any type of job. In contrast, a person with an intelligence score below 80 would not be competitive for any type of position (Gottfredson, 1997). This raises questions of fairness that are discussed later in the chapter, after we have considered other methods of selecting employees.

Tests of Specific Abilities, Skills, and Job Knowledge. Employers use a variety of measures of specific abilities, job skills, and job knowledge to evaluate potential employees. For example, spelling and reading tests are often given to applicants for secretarial and clerical jobs because applicants who are more skilled in these areas generally perform better on jobs such as word processing and proofreading. Applicants for mechanical and engineering jobs are given tests such as those pictured in figures 17.3 and 17.4. These tests tap a person's abilities to mentally visualize

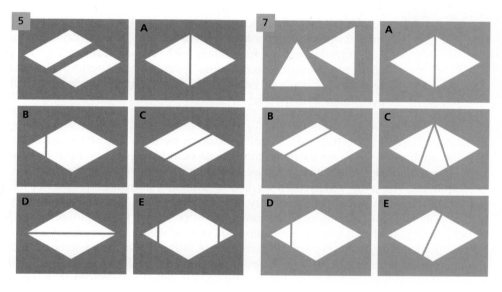

Figure 17.3

Sample items from a test designed to measure an individual's ability to visualize spatial relationships. Which form (A through E) can be constructed from the shapes in the upper left-hand corner (marked 5 and 7)?

Sample item from the Raven's Standard Progressive Matrices. Copyright © 2005 by Harcourt Assessment, Inc. Reproduced with permission. All rights reserved.

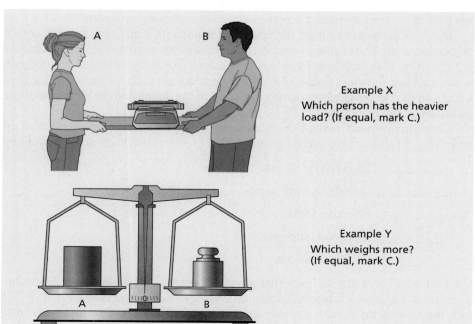

Example X

Which person has the heavier load? (If equal, mark C.)

Example Y

Which weighs more? (If equal, mark C.)

Figure 17.4

Sample items from a paper-and-pencil test designed to measure an individual's mechanical comprehension.

Sample item from the *Differential Aptitude Tests: Fourth Edition.* Copyright © 1972, 1982 by Harcourt Assessment, Inc. Reproduced with permission. All rights reserved.

Figure 17.5
An example of a performance test that might be used to select employees for a job assembling small machine parts.

performance tests Employee selection tests that resemble the actual manual performance required on a job.

job performance ratings Ratings of the actual performance of employees in their jobs by supervisors.

spatial relationships and to understand mechanical concepts. And applicants for sales positions are frequently given tests of sales aptitude. These tests describe problematic situations that often arise in sales work and require the applicant to choose the best course of action from a number of options.

Performance Tests. Tests that measure actual manual performance are often used in selecting employees such as assembly-line workers or equipment repair specialists. **Performance tests** are based on the assumption that the only valid way to find out if applicants can work with their hands is to evaluate them while they are actually working. The Purdue Pegboard is an example of this kind of performance test (see figure 17.5). In this test, pins, collars, and washers are fitted together in ways specified by the tester to evaluate the applicant's manual speed and accuracy. Other types of performance tests more closely resemble the job to be performed. Applicants for word processing jobs are asked to type in timed tests; forklift operators are asked to drive forklifts in a prescribed path; and potential recruits for professional baseball teams are given a chance to bat against professional pitchers. Each performance test provides a sample of behavior that can be used to predict actual performance on the job.

Ratings of Job Performance. Not all evaluation methods are used to select the best job applicants; some are designed to evaluate current employees. Such evaluations determine raises, promotions, and even whether the individual will continue to be employed. The most widely used method of assessing current employees is **job performance ratings.** Ratings are usually done by supervisors, but information may also be obtained from subordinates, customers, coworkers, and the employee himself or herself. If you fill out student evaluations of your professor at the end of a term, you are participating in one type of job performance rating. There are a number of different types of performance ratings, but each is designed by industrial-organizational psychologists to transform a rating of the employee's actual job performance into a numerical evaluation. This numerical information is used to track an employee's progress over time, or to compare the performances of multiple employees.

In job performance ratings, the employee is rated on a number of dimensions of job performance. The evaluator checks the statement from most to least desirable that best describes the employee. Three job dimensions from a hypothetical multiple-step rating scale are shown in figure 17.6. The statements are each assigned a value (5, 4, 3, 2, 1), so the ratings can be summed across all of the dimensions to obtain an overall evaluation of the employee.

Checklists provide numerical evaluations of job performance in a somewhat different way. Evaluators are asked to read a series of statements such as the following:

_____ Doesn't repeat same mistakes

_____ Orderly in work habits

_____ Effective leader

_____ Has good judgment

_____ Has creative ideas

The evaluator checks those items that are characteristic of the employee. Each characteristic is assigned a numerical value according to how important it is for the job, with the sum of these values giving the overall evaluation of the employee. Many

Figure 17.6   Examples of items from a multiple-step rating scale like those used to evaluate employee performance. The rater marks one category for each item.

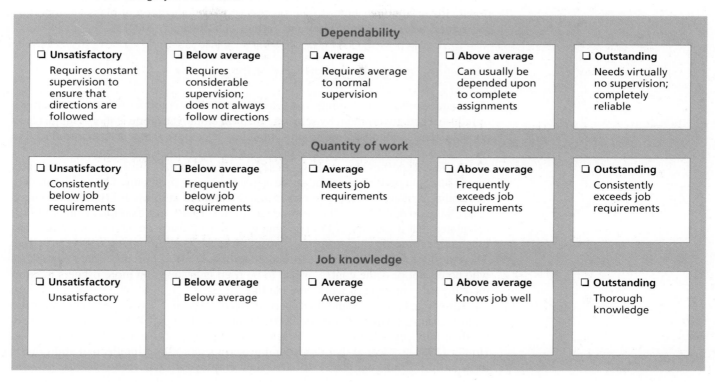

varieties of job performance ratings are used to assess different types of employees when numerical evaluations are needed.

Assessment Centers. Decisions on the hiring or promotion of managers in large companies are often based in part on evaluations made in **assessment centers.** Assessment centers are usually staffed by a team of upper managers and outside psychological consultants. Several candidates for the same position are brought together in the assessment center, so they can be intensively evaluated outside of the usual work environment. This technique was developed during World War II to evaluate candidates for undercover spy assignments and has continued to be a popular method of management selection (Bray, Campbell, & Grant, 1974). Assessment centers use traditional methods of evaluating the candidates for promotion, such as interviews and tests, but the distinctive feature of the approach is the evaluation of candidates while they are carrying out a **simulated management task** (Arthur & others, 2003; Thornton & Cleveland, 1990). For example, a frequently used simulation is the **in-basket exercise.** The candidate is given a problem that might show up in the "in-basket" of the new management position. Candidates would be asked to indicate the actions they would take, such as calling a meeting, obtaining additional information, and communicating a decision. Ratings of the candidate's performance in these simulation exercises would be used in the hiring or promotion decision.

Evaluation of Organizational Citizenship. In recent years, employers have begun to evaluate employees on the basis of more than just task performance. They seek employees who display good **organizational citizenship.** This means contributing to the social and psychological welfare of the organization by actively supporting

assessment centers Programs for the evaluation of employees that use simulated management tasks as their primary method of evaluation.

simulated management task A contrived task requiring managerial skills that is given to candidates for management positions to evaluate their potential as managers.

in-basket exercise A type of management simulation task in which the individual attempts to solve a problem that is typical of the ones that appear in a manager's "in-basket."

organizational citizenship Contributing to the organization by supporting its goals, cooperating with and helping fellow employees, and going beyond the requirements of the job to help the organization.

the organization, cooperating with and helping other employees, and going beyond the requirements of the job to help the organization (Borman, 2004). Because organizational citizenship contributes to the success of the organization, it plays an important role in decisions regarding raises and promotions (Borman, 2004).

Validity of Job Selection Measures

One major purpose of all employee selection measures is to increase the productivity of industry and government by selecting the best employees for each job. But just how good are these methods in improving employee selection? To use a term introduced in our discussion of intelligence tests in chapter 9, how *valid* are these measures?

A great deal of evidence shows that tests of intellectual ability are the best predictors of later job performance and success in job-training programs. The use of intellectual ability tests considerably improves the selection of employees (Higgins & others, 2007; Salgado & others, 2003; Schmidt & Hunter, 1998). For example, Hunter (1979) calculated that if the city of Philadelphia were to stop using an intellectual ability test for the selection of police officers, it would lose $170 million over a 10-year period. These dollar losses would result from the increased cost of training officer candidates who could not pass the course or had to be fired later, needing more officers to complete the same amount of work, and the like.

Researchers also found that performance tests and assessment centers were valid measures (Arthur & others, 2003; Hunter & Hunter, 1984), but were less useful than intellectual ability tests in selecting employees for most jobs. For example, Hunter (1981) indicated that the federal government's use of intellectual ability tests in its hiring of approximately 460,000 new employees each year saves the government $15.6 billion compared with hiring at random. Finally, of the methods that we discussed, unstructured interviews have been found to be the least valid method of selecting more productive employees, and projective personality tests and handwriting analyses have been found not to be valid at all for employee selection (Schmidt & Hunter, 1998).

Why is intellectual ability important to job performance? The prevailing view of why higher intellectual ability and other factors lead to superior job performance (Hough & Oswald, 2000; Schmidt & Hunter, 1992) is based on Earl Hunt's (1995) views on intelligence that we discussed in chapter 9. In this model, knowledge of the job is the most important factor in job performance. Job knowledge, in turn, is the result of both the employee's job experience and intellectual ability (see figure 17.7). Schmidt and Hunter (1992) found that employees steadily gain job knowledge over the first five years; then the benefits of on-the-job experience level off. Intellectual ability mostly influences how quickly the employee gains this job knowledge when he or she starts the job. Higher intellectual ability does improve job performance somewhat after it has been learned (by leading to better solutions to complex problems that arise on the job), but the main reason that more intelligent employees perform better is that they learn the job more quickly. Therefore, the benefits of high intelligence are most obvious in the first five years on the job, when job knowledge is still being learned. After five years on the job, that advantage of higher intelligence declines, because experience tends to equalize the job knowledge of employees. For this reason, tests of job knowledge are as valid as tests of intelligence in selecting experienced workers (Hough & Oswald, 2000; Schmidt & Hunter, 1998).

Intellectual ability tests are the most valid method of selecting new workers for a wide range of jobs, but they are less useful for some jobs than others (Schmidt & Hunter, 1992). Intellectual ability tests are very useful in selecting employees for more complex jobs (sales, managerial, and so on) but less useful when the job is less complex (vehicle operator, semiskilled factory worker, and so on). For these jobs, performance tests of job knowledge are more useful than intellectual ability tests.

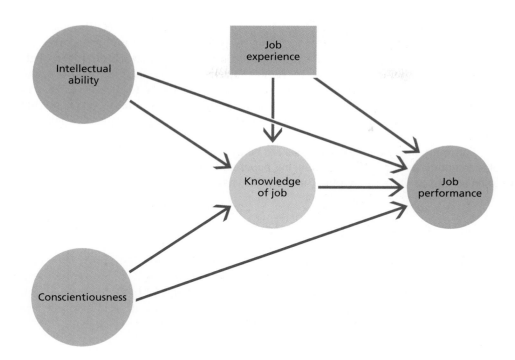

Figure 17.7
Employees who know the skills and information needed to perform a job well tend to perform their jobs better. Employees with higher intellectual ability perform their jobs better mostly because they learn job knowledge faster. Similarly, more experienced employees perform better mostly because they have greater job knowledge. Employees who are higher on the personality trait of conscientiousness also tend to learn job knowledge better. To a smaller extent, all three factors (high intelligence, experience, and conscientiousness) also directly contribute to better job performance in ways that are unrelated to the learning of job knowledge.

One of the "big five" personality traits that we discussed in chapter 12 (page 000) also is useful in predicting job success in many occupations. Employees who are more conscientious learn job knowledge more quickly and perform their jobs better (Barrick, Mount, & Judge, 2001; Higgins & others, 2007). In part, this is because employees who are low in conscientiousness are more likely to miss work and to develop conflicts with supervisors and other employees. Thus, intelligence is not the only psychological dimension that is associated with good job performance; conscientiousness is important as well.

Currently many employment tests are being conducted using web-based methods at a computer terminal rather than using paper and pencil. Web-based testing appears to be at least as valid as the older method (Ployhart & others, 2003).

Fairness in Employee Selection

Some kinds of jobs are more prestigious, lucrative, and influential than others. One important role of the industrial-organizational psychologist is to alert employers to the many possible biases in employee selection. Knowledge of these biases may promote greater fairness in the selection of employees for the most desirable jobs. These are highly complicated issues, however, with no easy solutions.

Gender Biases in Employee Selection. Psychologist Felicia Pratto and her colleagues (1997) at Stanford University have studied differences in the numbers of women and men who work in occupations that give the individual high financial rewards, power over others, or both (attorneys, politicians, business executives, police officers, and military officers). Approximately two-thirds of such occupations in the United States are filled by men (Pratto & others, 1997). In contrast, jobs that involve helping others (psychologists, social workers, and teachers) are mostly held by women. What forces contribute to men's holding most of the more powerful jobs?

Pratto and her colleagues propose that two factors are involved in this unequal distribution of powerful occupations. First, women and men in United States tend to want different kinds of jobs. In particular, women are more likely than men to seek jobs that involve helping other people (Pratto & others, 1997). Second, when women do seek powerful jobs, they are less likely to be hired. According to Pratto and her colleagues, this is because potential employers tend to view female applicants as not holding the values consistent with working in powerful occupations, mostly based on prejudicial views of women (Konrad & others, 2000; Pratto & others, 1997). It has long been known that female applicants for managerial positions tend to be rated lower than male applicants with equal qualifications (Dipboye, Fromkin, & Wilback, 1975). Such prejudice tends to unfairly exclude women from the most powerful occupational roles.

Race-Ethnic Biases in Employee Selection. Just as the most powerful and highly paid occupations tend to be held by men rather than women, they also tend to be held by members of the majority culture rather than members of racial and ethnic minority groups. The huge disparities in occupational achievement among ethnic groups in the United States are surely the result, in large part, of prejudice. Clearly, the majority group has tended directly and indirectly to exclude minority groups from positions of power.

Psychologists John Dovidio and Samuel Gaertner (2000) studied changes both in the expression of racial prejudice and in the biased selection of minority employee applicants over a 10-year period. In studies conducted in 1989 and 1999, samples of college students were studied using the same procedures. In one part of the studies, the participants were asked about racial attitudes. Consistent with trends in the United States over this period, the participants were less likely to express racial prejudice in 1999 than in 1989. In another part of the studies, the participants chose among applicants in a simulated employee selection exercise. In both 1989 and 1999, there was no racial bias in the selection of applicants whose credentials were clearly strong or clearly weak. At both times, however, members of racial minority groups were less likely to be selected for the job than whites when both applicants had average credentials. These findings suggest that although the overt expression of racial prejudice is declining, prejudice remains an important barrier to fair employment for members of some race-ethnic groups.

A great deal of attention has been focused on the unintended role of intelligence tests in possibly continuing to exclude members of ethnic minority groups from prestigious occupations. Because African Americans and Hispanics, on the average, still score somewhat lower on intellectual ability tests than whites, the use of such tests in employee selection means that a smaller proportion of applicants from these ethnic groups are selected on the basis of the test (Sackett & others, 2001; Schmidt & Ones, 1992; Wagner, 1997). For example, if an intellectual ability test were used that selects 50% of the white applicants, it would select an average of only 16% of African American applicants (Hunter & Hunter, 1984; Wagner, 1997).

Some psychologists have argued that some ethnic minority groups score, on the average, lower than whites on intelligence tests because intelligence tests are biased against minority groups (e.g., Williams, 1972). They believe that the bias results from basing test items on information and skills that are prevalent only in the majority culture. Other psychologists have argued that intelligence tests are equally valid for all groups (e.g., Schmidt & Hunter, 1998). In their view, the differences in intelligence test scores reflect the disadvantages and prejudice faced by ethnic minority groups in our society more than cultural bias in the tests.

Richard Wagner (1997) of Florida State University has used data to point out a serious flaw in the argument that intelligence tests are equally valid predictors of future job performance for whites and people of color. The actual size of differences between ethnic groups in actual job performance is noticeably *smaller* than their difference in intelligence scores. This means that a smaller percentage of people of color with good job potential would be selected at every level of intelligence than whites. If Wagner's (1997) interpretation of the data is correct—and it appears to be—then intelligence tests are biased against people of color when used in employee selection.

How should we, the members of a democratic society, respond to this potential ethnic bias inherent in the use of intelligence tests for employee selection? One obvious solution would be to place greater emphasis on tests of job knowledge and skills, which allow each person to demonstrate directly her or his fitness for the job. However, one can use such tests only with *experienced* workers who have already learned the information and skills required by the job. For the selection of *new* employees, tests of intelligence are usually the best predictor of job success. One could minimize the ethnic bias inherent in intelligence tests by setting different minimum qualifying scores for different ethnic groups, but the 1991 U.S. Civil Rights Act made this practice illegal. It may be very difficult for our society to find a fair and acceptable solution to this problem. Richard Wagner (1997) pointed out that banning intelligence tests from employee selection might only make matters worse. If we were to substitute a less valid employee selection test, it would be

Job satisfaction is directly related to productivity. In addition, it's good for both the business and the employees because it reduces employee turnover and absenteeism.

more biased against ethnic minorities (Wagner, 1997). The better a measure predicts future job performance, the less biased it is against ethnic minority groups. And for the selection of new workers for complex jobs, intelligence tests are still the most valid employee selection measure for all groups. Thus, until more valid methods of selecting new employees that are not biased against ethnic minorities are found, we must work to find ways to use intelligence tests in ways that are fairer to everyone.

Job Satisfaction, Happiness, and Productivity

Psychologists working in business have two inherently important goals: to improve the happiness and satisfaction of employees and to improve their productive contributions to the business. The goals of improving job satisfaction and productivity can be met in two principal ways. As we have just discussed, one is to use methods of employee selection to match the right person with the right job. The other way is to improve working conditions, including the ways in which employees are managed and supervised. We will first look at the relationship among job satisfaction, happiness, and productivity; then we will examine the ways in which supervisory style and managerial, organizational, and physical conditions are related to these goals.

It is important to note that the goals of productivity and employee satisfaction are not mutually exclusive. More satisfied employees are more productive, miss less work, have fewer accidents, and are less likely to resign (Harrison & others, 2006). Perhaps most convincing to employers, business units with more satisfied employees have more satisfied customers and make more profit (Harter, Schmidt, & Hayes, 2002). Fortunately, what's good for the employee is good for the employer.

Management Strategies to Improve Job Satisfaction, Happiness, and Productivity.
Three major management strategies are widely used to improve job satisfaction, happiness, and productivity:

1. *Improving management supervisory style.* The most effective managers and supervisors believe that their employees can perform better in the right conditions (Heslin & VandeWalle, 2008). They manage employees in ways that are *considerate* (warm, friendly, and concerned in dealing with employees) and *communicative* (can clearly tell employees what is expected of them and how they will be evaluated on their performance). In addition, the most effective supervisors are also often high in **structuring** (spending a great deal of time organizing and directing the work of their employees). However, being high in structuring is an advantage only when the supervisor is also highly considerate. It may even be a disadvantage when less considerate supervisors closely structure their employees' activities (Anastasi, 1987).

2. *Improving managerial organization.* A great deal of attention has been paid to how the efforts of management are organized. Do messages always come down from top management, or are employees involved in decision making to some extent? Are employees told specifically how to work, or are they best organized in teams that are given specific production goals but allowed freedom in the ways they meet those goals? Does it make any difference? Two strategies of managerial organization that appear to make a significant difference in promoting job satisfaction and productivity are *participative management* and *management by objectives.*

In the **participative management** method, teams of employees at every level of the organization are actively involved in decision making (Hollander & Offermann, 1990; Ilgen, 1999; Turnage, 1990). For instance, when a dressmaking plant must change over to making a new line of clothes, teams of sewing machine operators work out the most efficient ways to do this in discussions with their supervisors. The supervisors link this decision-making process to higher management by participating

structuring The activities of managers that organize and direct the work of employees.

participative management The practice of involving employees at all levels in management decisions.

in decision-making conferences with their supervisors, who then participate in decisions with the next level of management, and so on up to the top. In a classic example of the benefits of participative management, employees of the Weldon Pajama Factory showed an almost 50% increase in productivity and earning when such a system was introduced (Likert, 1967).

Another effective strategy of managerial organization is **management by objectives** (Locke & Latham, 1990; 2006). The key element in this approach is *goal setting*. Employees (or teams or employees) are given a specific goal to accomplish—anything from producing 1,000 dishes per month, to reducing air pollution from the factory by 80 percent, to reducing corporate taxes by 20%—but the teams are given considerable freedom in *how* they meet those objectives. This method benefits the company because it ensures that management focuses on what is really important to the company (its goals). But management by objectives also gives employees a greater sense of independence and an easier way to tell whether they are doing a good job of meeting their goals. A large body of research shows that setting goals for employees that are high but realistic increases employee motivation and improves productivity. When employees are given feedback on their progress and the organization provides the resources to allow high goals to be attained, success in attaining those goals leads to higher job satisfaction (Latham & Pinder, 2005; Locke & Latham, 2006). Management by objectives is often used along with a participative management strategy, allowing employees to participate in the setting of goals.

management by objectives The strategy of giving employees specific goals but giving them considerable freedom in deciding how to reach those goals.

3. *Improving physical conditions.* Considerable research has been done by industrial-organizational psychologists on the influence of physical conditions (such as lighting, noise, and temperature) on productivity and job satisfaction. For example, psychologists have found that working in 95-degree temperatures produces significant increases in perceptual and decision-making errors after four to five hours on the job (Fine & Kobrick, 1978). Considerable attention has also been paid to the design of machines that fit well with the psychological characteristics of the human beings who will be operating them.

Management Strategies to Minimize Social Loafing. Recall from chapter 16 that when people work together on a joint project some people usually work less hard than they would if they were working on an individual project—termed *social loafing* (Latané & others, 1979). Because organizations often need their employees to work together as a group—on group projects ranging from building automobiles to writing governmental regulations—it is important to understand what encourages social loafing and what minimizes it. University of Florida psychologist James Shepard (1995) has summarized research on this topic. According to Shepard, social loafing is the result of low motivation to work on the group project. Low motivation, in turn, results from individuals' perceiving their contributions to be unrewarded, unnecessary, or too costly to the individual.

Social loafing can be minimized, therefore, by reducing its causes:

1. If the individual believes that his or her contribution to the group effort will not be recognized or rewarded even if the group goal is met, the solution is to provide clear incentives to each individual's contribution to the group effort. This incentive could be anything from a good performance evaluation to bonuses that are tied *not to the effort of the group as a whole* but to the effort of the individual.

2. If the individual mistakenly believes that the group goal will be achieved just as well, regardless of how much she or he contributes as an individual, the solution is to show the individual that her or his contribution is indispensable. This can be accomplished by dividing up the task so that each individual contributes something that is both unique and important.

3. Sometimes individuals feel that their contributions to the group effort will cost more than they are worth. For example, a young salesperson might feel that time spent working on a new group retirement plan could be better devoted to earning commissions from sales.

These causes of social loafing can be combated by making the task easier (for example, by getting a consultant to write the first draft of a new retirement plan).

Interestingly, studies of social loafing in different cultures have found that social loafing is universal—it happens in all cultures to some extent (Shepard, 1995). Group effort seems to be motivated by different factors in different cultures, however. The Japanese tend to motivate contributions to group work by mutually monitoring the performance of group members and responding positively to good effort and shaming poor effort. Americans, in contrast, comment less on one another's performance and rely more on each individual's sense of duty to the group. As a result, Japanese workers are more likely than American workers are to withdraw from groups in which social loafing is going on (Shepard, 1995).

transformational management A style in which the manager attempts to positively transform employees for the better by setting a good example, clearly stating goals and helping employees achieve them, seeking innovative solutions, and mentoring and empowering employees.

Human Diversity
Gender Differences in Leadership

Female managers are more likely to use the transformational management style.

The success of any organization also depends on the quality of its leaders. Leadership is the influence of one group member on the others as they work toward shared goals. Psychologists have studied the *traits* of successful leaders. Traits such as drive, honesty, flexibility, leadership motivation, intelligence, and creativity contribute to a person's leadership potential. Effective leaders understand that leadership styles must be adapted to each situation (Zaccaro, 2007). Effective leaders also often share the traits of charisma, clear vision, inspiration, expertise, and personalized attention to the people they lead (Chemers, 1997; Northouse, 1997; Shamir & Howell, 1999).

Overall, men and women tend to behave similarly when they are in leadership positions in business and government (Eagly & others, 2003). There are some differences between female and male leaders, however, that are very important to understand. On average, female managers are more likely to adopt the style of **transformational management.** This means that they seek to transform, or change, their employees for the better. Transformational managers inspire their employees to reach their full potential by setting a good example, clearly stating future goals and helping employees attain them, seeking innovative solutions to problems, and mentoring and empowering employees. In addition, female leaders are more likely to reward employees for a job well done (Eagly, Johannesen-Schmidt, & van Engen, 2003). Although these average differences between female and male managers are small, they are important. All of the leadership characteristics on which females excel are positively related to leadership effectiveness. In contrast, the management characteristics that are more typical of male managers are either unrelated to effectiveness or negatively related to it (Eagly, Johannesen-Schmidt, & van Engen, 2003).

Because businesses, governments, and universities have learned that good leaders make for successful outcomes, regardless of the gender of the leader, women have increasingly found success in senior leadership positions. Nonetheless, there is still evidence of a "glass ceiling" for women in American organizations. Women can rise to a certain level of leadership, but the top positions often elude them (Fernandez, 1998; Lovoy, 2001).

Human Factors Engineering

The first psychologist to use psychological methods to improve productivity in the workplace and to enhance the lives of workers was Lillian Gilbreth. She received her Ph.D. from Brown University in 1915 and began a series of studies in which she used slow-motion photography to analyze the movements of factory workers known as "time and motion" studies. These analyses were then used to devise more efficient ways of performing tasks at work. Gilbreth also conducted time and motion studies in the home. To improve the efficiency of household tasks she designed many kitchen appliances, including trash cans with foot-pedal lid openers and an electric food mixer. Her own family may have motivated her to develop these time-saving devices for the home, as Gilbreth managed both to have a successful career and to raise 12 children. Two of her children drew on their family experiences to write the book *Cheaper By The Dozen* (1949), which was later made into a classic movie.

Gilbreth's pioneering studies laid the foundation for the modern field of **human factors engineering** (sometimes called *ergonomics*). The goal of human factors engineering is the design of machines that can be more easily and efficiently operated by human beings (Karwowski, 2005). For example, airplane pilots must operate a number of different manual controls while their eyes are occupied looking at radar, reading gauges, and watching where the plane is going. The job of the human factors engineer is to design manual controls in a way that will make them easier and safer to use. In this case, the controls would probably be designed in a way that makes use of the pilot's sense of touch, because pilots may need to use the controls in the dark or while their eyes are focused elsewhere. Controls of different shapes can be easily distinguished by touch and are particularly easy to use if their shape is related to their function, as shown in figure 17.8. Human factors research has also found that controls are more easily operated when they are located next to the dial that they influence rather than in separate clusters (see figure 17.9) and when the direction of turning a control matches the direction of the corresponding dial (see figure 17.10 on p. **584**).

Much of current human factors engineering focuses on the design of computers. Over the past 25 years, the educated workforce has gone from the occasional use of computers to almost daily use in their occupations, at home, and even when moving about. As shown in figure 17.11, psychologists who specialize in human factors work with computer scientists to design computers that can be used efficiently by taking into consideration what psychology has learned about attention, cognition, vision, hearing, speech, and motor control (Proctor & Vu, 2010).

Lillian Gilbreth (1878–1972) pioneered the field of human factors engineering.

human factors engineering The branch of industrial-organizational psychology interested in the design of machines to be operated by human beings.

Landing flap   Landing gear

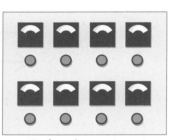

Acceptable arrangement   Preferred arrangement

Figure 17.8

An example of controls that are designed to be easily distinguished by touch and related in form to their function.

Figure 17.9

Examples of controls and dials arranged to fit the cognitive characteristics of human operators.

Figure 17.10

Examples of controls designed to operate in a way that is compatible with the direction of operation of the corresponding dial.

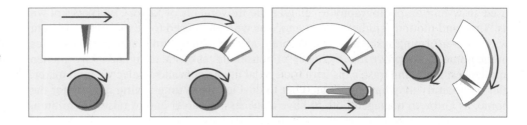

Figure 17.11   Human factors psychologists work with computer scientists to design computers that can be used efficiently by taking into consideration what psychology has learned about attention, cognition, vision, hearing, speech, and motor control.

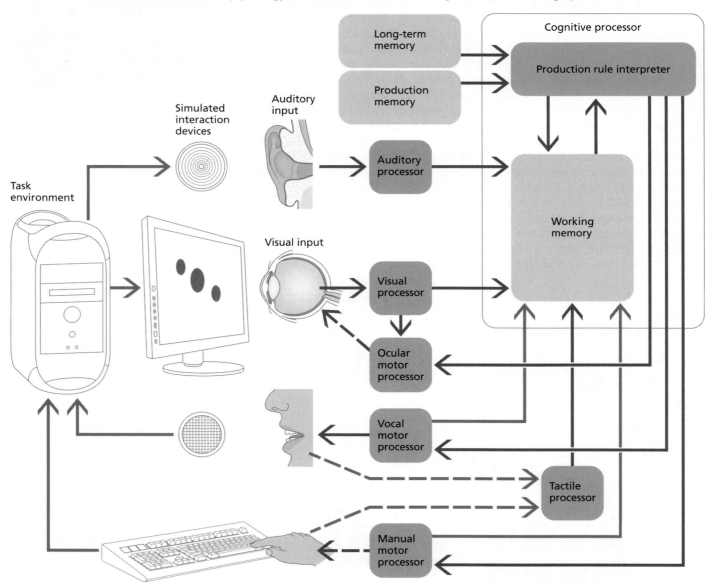

Olson, G. M., & Olson, J. S. (2003). Human-computer interaction: Psychological aspects of the human use of computing. *Annual Review of Psychology, 54,* 491–516.

Human factors engineering was in the spotlight after serious accidents at nuclear power plants at Three Mile Island and Chernobyl in the 1970s and 80s released radioactive debris. Although the causes of these accidents were complex, investigations suggested that the plant operators were asked to deal with too much information that was presented in confusing ways. The design of the operating system and its computer displays of information overloaded the cognitive capacities of the operators, and fatal mistakes were made (Wickens, 1992). Human factors engineers have been working to simplify computer displays of information in many work settings (Howell, 1993).

As more is learned about both biology and psychology, a future direction for human factors engineering is in the development of ways to overcome human frailties. The largest market for such innovative human engineering is older persons. Of all humans aged 65 years or older who have ever lived, half of them are alive today! As these individuals grow older, they will be increasingly likely to make errors and experience limitations owing to their growing motor, sensory, and memory limitations. In most cases, these problems will be minor—forgetting to watch a television program—but in other cases, the errors will be serious, as in taking too few or too many doses of medication each day. In other cases, the elderly will experience unnecessary restrictions on the quality of their lives, such as not being able to learn to use e-mail to keep up with their grandchildren. Psychologists Arthur Fisk and Wendy Rogers (2002) suggest that research could lead to small changes in instruction manuals, operating controls, medicine labels, and the like that could make huge differences to older people. But it is not just the elderly that need help with these things. Fisk and Rogers report that the majority of diabetics make errors in monitoring their glucose levels. This kind of simple human engineering of labels and instructions through research that is based in an understanding of human perception and memory could make an enormous difference.

Health Psychology in the Workplace

We first discussed the field of *health psychology* in chapter 13. We learned about the growing awareness among both medical professionals and the general public that stress and unhealthy patterns of behavior (such as overwork, poor diet, and lack of exercise) are extremely important threats to good health. There is an increasing understanding in the business world, too, that good health among employees is good business (Eby & others, 2010). Healthy employees are more productive, miss fewer days of work, make fewer claims for health benefits, and are less likely to die or become disabled during their most valuable and productive years. The cost of poor health to business is enormous.

Fortunately, many American businesses have concluded that programs to improve employee health are good for everyone—and profitable as well. Consider, for example, programs to increase the cardiovascular fitness of employees. The Centers for Disease Control and Prevention have determined that the risk of cardiovascular disease is twice as high for sedentary persons as for persons who exercise regularly—making it a risk factor as important as high blood pressure, high serum cholesterol, and smoking (Powell & others, 1987). Thus, some 50,000 businesses in the United States have instituted some type of program to increase the fitness of their employees.

Suppose you are offered two jobs after graduation with identical work requirements, salaries, and opportunities for advancement—but one gives you the option of a free membership in the health club of your choice or a locker in the company gym (and time

The risk of cardiovascular disease is twice as high for people with sedentary lifestyles as for those who exercise regularly.

during the day to take an exercise break). The same company prohibits smoking in the workplace and has fruit juice rather than soft drinks in the vending machines. Assuming you are health conscious, which job would you take?

If you took the job with the company that makes exercise easy, would you be working for a company that made a profitable decision in this case? Yes, indeed. First, your company would tend to attract healthier employees who would appreciate the opportunity to exercise and who would likely incur fewer health-related costs. Second, the company would likely save money by *keeping* its employees healthy through exercise. For example, the Johnson & Johnson Corporation studied the costs of such a health plan for 11,000 of its employees and found that it saved the company almost a quarter of a million dollars per year in direct health care claims (Bly, Jones, & Richardson, 1986). In these and other ways, psychologists are beginning to show business that a healthy work environment yields not only employee well-being, but healthy profits, too.

Review

The quality of our lives is linked to business in terms of both our enjoyment of the goods and services that business produces and the satisfaction that we derive from our jobs. Industrial-organizational psychologists help business improve its productivity, improve worker safety and health, and help workers obtain more meaning and enjoyment from their jobs. Psychologists most frequently work through personnel departments because they have responsibility for selecting and training employees.

Industrial-organizational psychologists also help managers improve managerial style (how they relate to their employees), the organizational structure of management (such as through participative management or management by objectives), and the physical and health conditions of work. Through these and many other methods, psychologists are able to contribute to worker satisfaction, happiness, and productivity.

Check Your Learning

To be sure that you have learned the key points from the preceding section, cover the list of correct answers and try to answer each question. If you give an incorrect answer to any question, return to the page given next to the correct answer to see why your answer was not correct. Remember that these questions cover only some of the important information in this section; it is important that you make up your own questions to check your learning of other facts and concepts.

1. A(n) _____ is a psychologist who seeks ways to improve the functioning and human benefits of business.

   a) developmental psychologist

   c) clinical psychologist

   b) industrial-organizational psychologist

   d) Gestalt psychologist

2. One of the "big five" personality factors that has been shown to predict job performance in a variety of types of jobs is _____.

3. _____ are the most valid selection measures for most complex jobs.

   a) Projective tests

   c) Biodata

   b) Performance tests

   d) Intellectual ability tests

4. _____, or spending a great deal of time organizing and directing the work of employees, is most effective when the supervisor is also considerate of others.

   a) Structuring

   c) Decentralizing

   b) Authoritative direction

   d) Categorizing

5. _____ refers to the branch of industrial-organizational psychology interested in the design of machines to be operated by human beings.

a) Mechanical engineering

c) Graphic design

b) Architectural engineering

d) Human factors engineering

There are no right or wrong answers to the following questions. They are presented to help you become an active reader and think critically about what you just read.

1. If unstructured interviews are the least valid method for selecting employees, why do they continue to be widely used?

2. What questions might you ask a potential employer about working conditions to determine your likelihood of achieving a high level of job happiness?

Correct Answers: 1. b (p. 571), 2. conscientiousness (p. 578), 3. d (p. 576), 4. a (p. 580), 5. d (p. 583)

Psychology and Law

Psychology and the legal profession have been working together for many years. Psychologists frequently testify regarding an individual's sanity at the time of the crime or competency to stand trial. Moreover, attorneys are necessarily involved in hearings on the involuntary commitment of patients to mental hospitals and in the protection of the rights of psychiatric patients. In recent years, psychologists have also begun to apply their methods and principles to the *practice* of law in the courtroom. When you think about it, this application of psychology to the practice of law is not surprising. The administration of justice is a process that involves *people*—attorneys, defendants, witnesses, and judges. Any understanding of the profession of law that ignores the human element—the psychology of the people involved—would be an incomplete understanding.

To date, the most extensive psychological study of the legal process has focused on the criminal trial. The findings suggest that, unless they are better understood and controlled, psychological factors in the trial process pose a serious threat to our constitutional guarantee of a fair trial. In addition to the quality of the evidence, the likelihood of conviction depends in part on personal characteristics of the defendant and on characteristics of the jury members. Psychological factors can even influence the quality and convincingness of the evidence itself. Psychologists are increasingly serving the role of consultant on procedures such as jury selection and the presentation of evidence.

Characteristics of Defendants and Plaintiffs

Although we would like to believe that all of us would be treated equally in court, it is not always the case. Your chance of being acquitted in a criminal trial in the United States is better if you are physically attractive, wealthy, and white. Poor people are more likely than affluent ones to be convicted of crimes when charged with similar assault and larceny charges (Haney, 1980). Physically attractive defendants are less likely to be convicted than unattractive ones—unless the attractiveness seemed to play a part in the crime, such as in a swindle (Nemeth, 1981). In addition, white jury members are more likely to vote to convict African Americans than whites (Haney, 1980). The same characteristics of the defendants also play a role in the harshness of the sentence. Persons with facial features that are thought to be typical of African Americans receive longer prison sentences, even when their criminal histories are statistically controlled (Blair & others, 2004). In first-degree murder cases, blue-collar workers are more likely to be sentenced to death than white-collar workers are. And from 1930 to 1979, 2,066 African Americans were executed, compared with 1,751 whites, even though there are four times as many whites in the United States as African Americans (Haney, 1980). These findings suggest that justice is not equal for different kinds of defendants in criminal cases, probably because of prejudices and stereotypes held by jury members about different groups of people. Since characteristics such as income, attractiveness, and race have nothing to do with one's guilt or innocence, these irrelevant factors make it difficult for all people to receive equal protection under the law.

Psychologists have also studied the behavior of juries in civil suits, in which monetary damage awards are sought to compensate for injuries caused by alleged negligence or other wrongdoing. Do the characteristics of the plaintiff (the person seeking a damage award) and the defendant influence the financial awards made by jurors— independently of the facts of the case? The answer is yes. In mock trials, younger plaintiffs and male plaintiffs were awarded much larger financial settlements when injured than older and female plaintiffs were (Greene & Loftus, 1998). Participants on the mock juries explained that these prejudicial differences in sizes of awards were made because they believed that younger males who were injured would have made more money in their careers than older or female plaintiffs, placing less emphasis on their needs for compensation. Juries also awarded larger settlements when the defendant was a corporation rather than an individual, independently of the other facts of the case (Greene & Loftus, 1998). As in criminal cases, irrelevant psychological factors influence the decisions of jurors in civil cases.

Characteristics of Jury Members

Certain types of jury members are more likely to vote for conviction and recommend harsher sentences than other types. Jurors who are more conviction-prone and punitive in sentencing are those who are white, older, better educated, higher in social status, and more conservative and who believe more strongly that authority and law should be respected (Nemeth, 1981). There is mixed evidence as to whether men are more likely than women to vote for conviction, but there is clear-cut evidence of gender differences in cases of rape. Women are more likely to convict and to be harsher in sentencing than male jurors, whereas males are more likely to believe that the female victim encouraged the rapist (Nemeth, 1981). Overall, juries tend to be "kinder to their own kind." Affluent, educated, white jurors tend to be harsher in their treatment of less affluent, less educated, minority defendants.

There is also evidence that jurors who believe in the death penalty are more likely to convict than those who do not. Prior to 1968, individuals who had strong objections to the death penalty were routinely barred from serving on juries in cases involving a possible death penalty. In a landmark ruling in 1968, however, an appeals judge commuted a death penalty to life imprisonment in the case of *Witherspoon* v. *Illinois* on the grounds that the jury was composed only of persons who favored the death penalty and was not, therefore, a fair and "representative" jury. In making this ruling, the judge cited a Gallup poll conducted at that time that found only about 55% of the people surveyed favored the death penalty. The judge ruled that prospective jurors could be excluded only when they were so opposed to the death penalty that they would vote against it regardless of the evidence.

Was this a good decision? Was the judge in *Witherspoon* v. *Illinois* correct in assuming that a jury composed only of individuals who favor the death penalty—a "death-qualified" jury—might not give the defendant a fair trial? Actually, a number of studies support the judge's decision (Nemeth, 1981). For example, a classic study was conducted on the relationship between attitudes toward the death penalty and the tendency to convict in a sample of 207 industrial workers. They were initially asked to fill out a number of questionnaires including the following:

Capital Punishment Attitude Questionnaire

Directions. Assume you are on a jury to determine the sentence for a defendant who has already been convicted of a very serious crime. If the law gives you a choice of death or life imprisonment, or some other penalty: (check one only)

1. I could not vote for the death penalty regardless of the facts and circumstances of the case.

2. There are some kinds of cases in which I know I could not vote for the death penalty even if the law allowed me to, but others in which I would be willing to consider voting for it.

3. I would consider all of the penalties provided by the law and the facts and circumstances of the particular case.

4. I would usually vote for the death penalty in a case where the law allows me to.

5. I would always vote for the death penalty in a case where the law allows me to.

From G. L. Jurow, "New Data on the Effects of a 'Death-Qualified' Jury on the Guilt Determination Process," *Harvard Law Review 84:*59, 1971 Harvard Law Review Association. Used by permission.

As these workers did, try to imagine that you have been selected to serve on the jury in a murder trial in a state that imposes the death penalty. Which alternative would you choose? All of the participants were shown two videotapes of mock murder trials that contained all of the standard elements of procedure and evidence. The first concerned a robbery of a liquor store in which the proprietor of the store was killed in the process. The second case was of a man charged with robbing, raping, and killing a college student in her apartment. After each videotaped trial, the "jurors" voted to convict or acquit the defendant.

The jurors in this experiment were divided into three groups on the basis of their responses to the questionnaire concerning capital punishment. Jurors scoring low in willingness to impose the death penalty (who checked item 1 or 2) were far more likely to vote for acquittal than conviction in the first trial (see table 17.1). Conversely, jurors who were high in willingness to impose the death penalty (who checked item 4 or 5) were much more likely to vote for conviction. The same pattern was shown in the voting after the second trial, although not as strongly.

Thus, this and other studies finding similar differences suggest that juries composed only of jurors who are in favor of the death penalty (who are also more likely to be conservative, high status, authoritarian males) are biased in favor of conviction

	Number Voting to	
Willingness to Impose Death Penalty If Serving as a Juror	Convict	Acquit
Low (1 and 2)	19	40
Medium (3)	59	73
High (4 and 5)	14	2

From G. L. Jurow, "New Data on the Effects of a 'Death-Qualified' Jury on the Guilt Determination Process," *Harvard Law Review 84:*59. 1971 Harvard Law Review Association. Used by permission.

Table 17.1

Number of Jurors in a Simulated Trial Who Voted to Convict or Acquit, Divided According to Their Willingness to Impose the Death Penalty

of defendants (Nemeth, 1981). This means that the current practice of excluding only those jurors who are most strongly opposed to the death penalty or of using separate juries for the trial and the sentencing may make good psychological sense.

Psychological Factors in Presenting Evidence

It's somewhat reassuring to learn that several studies have suggested that although characteristics of the defendants and jurors are important in determining conviction or acquittal, the evidence is several times more important (Nemeth, 1981). Unfortunately, facts are not the only important aspect of courtroom evidence; psychological factors in *presenting* the facts are involved as well.

Criminal trials are "adversarial proceedings." The attorneys for the prosecution and defense attempt to convince the jury of the guilt or innocence of the defendant as if they were competing in a debate. Because both attorneys cannot talk at the same time, they obviously must make their presentations one at a time. Unfortunately, the order in which evidence is presented appears to make a difference in the outcome of the trial. One study investigated the effect of order of presentation in a simulated trial in which law students played the roles of attorneys for the defense and prosecution and undergraduate students served as jurors. The simulated case concerned a man who was charged with murder but claimed he had acted in self-defense. Half of the time, the prosecutor went first, and half of the time the defense attorney went first. The results showed that the attorney who went second held a decided advantage (Thibaut & Walker, 1975). This is not good news if you are falsely accused of a crime, because traditionally the prosecutor is allowed to make the last statement to the jury.

Recall from chapter 16 that information you encounter first when getting to know a stranger ("first impressions") is stronger in determining your overall impression of that person *unless* a relatively long time elapses between the first and subsequent information. That last qualification may help explain the findings about the order of presentation of courtroom evidence. It may be that, because courtroom arguments are lengthy and complex, recently presented information is more easily remembered and potent. This interpretation is strengthened by the finding that the advantage of presenting in the second position is increased further if an attorney states the most convincing points at the very end of the second presentation rather than at the beginning (Thibaut & Walker, 1975).

As you consider the importance of psychological factors involved in the presentation of evidence, do not forget the important research on the fallibility of eyewitness testimony (Wells & Olson, 2003) presented in chapter 8 (pages 000–000).

Interrogating Criminal Suspects

Police use a number of psychological techniques to increase the probability of a confession. Sometimes these lead to good outcomes and sometimes they do not.

Interrogation Techniques. Imagine that you have been taken to a barren interrogating room. You are alone with the interrogators—the room does not even have a telephone—giving you a feeling of being completely cut off from the outside world. The interrogator often stands very close to you, violating your personal space, and giving you a feeling of powerlessness.

The interrogator begins the questioning by pointing out your apparent guilt. But the crime is discussed in such a way as to make it seem so understandable—almost morally justifiable—that you feel that the interrogator would not shame you if you were to confess. If the crime is not a big deal, why not just admit to doing it? But the interrogator soon grows impatient with you for not admitting to the crime and storms out of the room. A second officer in the room steps over, though, and asks you to excuse the behavior of the first interrogator—it's been a long and frustrating day. This second officer is very sympathetic to your situation and emphasizes how much easier the court would be on you if you were to confess. This officer really seems to feel genuine concern for you. Just then, the first interrogator enters the room again and asks you for a confession. You see anger beginning to build, and you blurt out a confession just to avoid the angry outburst. This kind of scene is repeated many times a day in police stations across the country, although not always with favorable results. Individuals who have been interrogated many times by the police know the routine as well as the police and tend not to be influenced by it.

False Confessions. Sometimes people confess to crimes they did not commit. Indeed, in over 20% of the cases in which convicted persons were exonerated based on DNA evidence, they had been convicted on the basis of a false confession (Kassin, 2008). Persons with poor intellectual and emotional resources are particularly likely to make false confessions under pressures from police interrogations (Gudjonsson, 2001; Kassin & others, 2010; Russano & others, 2005). Recent research on police interrogations of suspects has looked for ways to help police investigators detect lying by suspects. All such methods are far from perfectly reliable, but may help investigators in their work. For example, these studies do not support the notion that people who are lying fidget nervously or fail to make eye contact with their interrogator; but they suggest that liars blink less often and pause their speech longer than persons telling the truth (Kassin, 2008; Mann, Vrij, & Bull, 2002).

Review

Criminal trials are conducted by people, so it's not surprising to learn that psychological factors play a role. What may be more surprising—and disturbing—is to see how strong a role they can play. Having different types of people involved in the trial process is likely to produce different outcomes. Poor, uneducated, minority defendants are more likely to be convicted and receive harsher sentences. Jurors who are white, older, higher in social status, more conservative, and more authoritarian than average, as well as those who believe in capital punishment, are more likely to vote for conviction and impose harsh punishments. The quality of the evidence presented in criminal trials is more important in determining the jury's decision than the psychological characteristics of the defendant and jurors, but psychological factors are also involved in courtroom evidence. Even the order in which evidence is presented can influence the outcome of a trial. Obviously, these factors must be understood and controlled as much as possible if the judicial system is to be fair for all concerned.

Check Your Learning

To be sure that you have learned the key points from the preceding section, cover the list of correct answers and try to answer each question. If you give an incorrect answer to any question, return to the page given next to the correct answer to see why your answer was not correct.

Answer each question with True or False.

1. Other things being equal, you have a greater chance of being acquitted in a criminal trial by a white, middle-class jury if you are physically attractive, high in social status, and white.

2. Jurors who believe in the death penalty are less likely to vote for the conviction of a defendant.

3. The attorney who speaks last in a trial has an advantage in persuading the jury.

Psychology and Education

educational psychology The field in which principles of learning, cognition, and other aspects of psychology are applied to improve education.

Like industrial-organizational psychology, **educational psychology** is almost as old as the discipline of psychology itself. Binet's development of a useful intelligence test for schoolchildren laid the foundation for educational testing. Others, such as Edward Lee Thorndike of Columbia University, conducted research during the early 1900s on factors that influence school learning and memory. But although educational psychology is an old field, its current excitement stems from relatively new developments. These innovations show particular promise in improving the education of people of all ages and abilities. Psychologists serve education as professors who help train teachers, as designers of school curricula, as consultants on the development of testing programs, and as specialists employed by school systems (**school psychologists**) to consult with teachers and to test children who may need special educational programs. Public education was established to implement Thomas Jefferson's philosophy that every American citizen should have equal educational as well as political opportunities. Because citizens need an education to govern themselves through democratic institutions, it was decided that education should be available to every American child rather than as a privilege of the rich. The most important recent innovations in educational psychology have been ones that help more children benefit fully from their time in school: the mastery learning approach, effective methods of educating economically disadvantaged children, the development of more meaningful tests of achievement, and the integration of children with psychological and physical challenges into the normal classroom environment, known as mainstreaming or inclusion.

school psychologists Psychologists who aid schools by testing children to determine eligibility for placement in special education programs and who consult with teachers and parents.

Direct Instruction

The direct instruction approach to education is based on an idea as simple and profoundly important as that of mastery learning, about which you will learn in the following section. According to the direct instructional approach the best way to teach a subject is to use what is known about the principles of learning and memory to directly teach that subject (Magliaro & others, 2005; McCrudden, Schraw, & Kambe, 2005; Reis & others, 2007). In particular, the direct instruction approach advocates the following strategies:

1. Children are guided in their learning, rather than being left to discover new concepts and ideas on their own.

2. The new information and skills that students are expected to learn are highlighted for them.

3. New information is presented to students in small easily understood amounts.

4. Students are frequently asked to perform what they are learning—to read or to solve problems—so the teacher can evaluate their progress in real time, rather than just on tests.

5. The teacher frequently provides positive reinforcement for accurate performance, or gentle corrective feedback for inaccurate performance.

In the mid-1960s, the largest and most expensive study of teaching methods was conceived by the U.S. Office of Education to test new ways of educating economically disadvantaged children. Nine groups of researchers were given funds to design and implement what they thought would be ideal educational programs, and independent research organizations were contracted to evaluate their effectiveness. This massive educational experiment, which involved tens of thousands of children across the country, was named **Project Follow Through.** The nine Follow Through projects differed considerably in educational philosophy, and most were clearly unsuccessful in improving educational progress. The most successful projects, which were based on the direct instruction model, were consistently able, however, to bring disadvantaged children to the national average or above. The success of the direct instruction approach is an impressive testimony to the accumulated knowledge of educational psychology (Doernberger & Zigler, 1993; Morrell, 1998; Tucci, Hursh, & Laitinen, 2004).

Project Follow Through A federally sponsored program designed to help educate economically disadvantaged children.

Mastery Learning and Intelligent Tutoring Systems

mastery learning The concept that children should never progress from one learning task to another until they have mastered the more basic one.

If you were a teacher, would you try to teach a child to add and subtract before she had learned to count? Would you teach trigonometry to a child before he had mastered the basics of plane geometry? It does not make much sense to try to teach a child a new skill before she or he has learned the basic skills that are the foundation for further learning, yet this happens every day in American education—children are pushed from one subject to another before they are ready to progress. Why? The reason is that, in many schools, education is conducted according to group schedules. A certain amount of time is allotted for the group to learn to count, and then the group moves on to addition. Students take plane geometry in the fall semester and then trigonometry in the spring. If an individual child is not ready to progress, he or she must usually move on with the group anyway.

Educational psychologist Benjamin Bloom was an outspoken critic of this approach and proposed the **mastery learning** concept to take its place (Bloom, 1974). The mastery learning approach simply insists that children should never progress from one learning task to another until they have fully mastered the first one (Peladeau, Forget, & Gagne, 2003; Zimmerman & Dibenedetto, 2008). For example, a group of high school students who were enrolled in a course on automobile mechanics took part in an evaluation of the mastery learning approach. The course was divided into eight units that built on one another in succession. Half of the students progressed through the units as a group according to a prearranged schedule. The other students—the mastery learning group—moved at their own pace and did not begin the next unit until they had passed a test on the previous unit. At the end of the course, the mastery learning group had learned far more in the same amount of time (Wentling, 1973).

The mastery learning approach is particularly effective for students with less aptitude, but it does not penalize brighter children (Ironsmith & Eppler, 2007). In the traditional approach of group scheduling, the top fifth of American students learns three times as much as the bottom fifth by the

The availability of affordable classroom computers lets intelligent tutoring systems tailor lessons to each student's level of mastery.

time they graduate from high school. When students use a mastery learning approach, however, the learning of the bottom fifth improves so much as to cut this difference in half (Bloom, 1974).

More recently, the availability of inexpensive computers that can be used in the classroom has made possible an improvement on the mastery learning approach called **intelligent tutoring systems** (or ITS) (Atkinson, 2002; Butz & others, 2006). In the ITS approach, a computer is programmed to serve as an individualized tutor to the student. In the case of arithmetic, the animated computer program would tell the student about a new rule of, say, subtraction (visually on the screen and orally through headphones) and then ask the student to solve some problems based on the new rule. As in mastery learning, the computer does not allow the student to progress to the next rule until the current one is mastered. But ITS can also respond to any errors that the student makes and adapt the instruction accordingly. Let's say the student is learning to "borrow" when subtracting two-digit numbers and makes a mistake. The computer might see that the mistake was based on a misunderstanding of the rule for borrowing and would then repeat the rule—possibly in simpler language. However, the computer might detect that the mistake was based on forgetting how to subtract single-digit numbers and go back to a brief review of that material. Not only does ITS make it easier for teachers to work with children who are at different levels of mastery in the same classroom, but it also allows individual remediation of any "gaps" in the learning process. Increasingly, ITS programs are available to students even after school over the Internet (Dedic & others, 2001). ITS can even incorporate virtual reality projections in science activities that, for example, "place" the child in the rain forest when studying deforestation (Moreno & Mayer, 2004).

intelligent tutoring systems
An approach to learning in which computers provide tutoring to students.

Motivating Learning in the Classroom

In chapter 11 you learned the distinction between intrinsic and extrinsic motivation. Although rewards for learning such as praise from the teacher (extrinsic motivation) are effective in motivating learning, increasing student interest in the material to be learned (intrinsic motivation) also is an important aspect of effective teaching. For example, when teachers emphasize the intrinsic importance of the content that can be learned from books, rather than the good grades that students will earn if they read carefully, their students learn much more (Guthrie & others, 2004). Similarly, students who are allowed to choose among several interesting texts are more motivated to read and to learn more from their reading (Guthrie & others, 2004). Thus, educational programs that achieve the right balance between intrinsic and extrinsic motivation differ considerably in their effectiveness.

Criterion-Referenced Testing

The renewed interest in finding better ways to prepare students to lead successful adult lives has also led to the development of an approach to evaluating how much students have learned in school. In traditional approaches to educational testing, children are compared with one another. For example, a traditional test of computational skills in arithmetic would require children to work a large number of problems. A child who correctly solved the same number of problems as the average for children in her or his grade would be considered to be "on grade level." The goal of **criterion-referenced testing,** however, is not to compare children but to determine whether a given child can meet the minimum criteria for a specific educational objective (Sprinthall, Sprinthall, & Oja, 1998). These are usually practical objectives. For example, one criterion-referenced test asks children to fill in a personal information form like the

criterion-referenced testing
Testing designed to determine whether a child can meet the minimum standards of a specific educational objective.

ones required by most employment applications. The issue in this kind of testing is not how well a child can fill in the form compared with other children but simply whether the child can do it appropriately. This is a skill well worth teaching to students, because adults who cannot fill out employment forms stand little chance of being hired.

Criterion-referenced testing provides the kind of information that teachers need to improve education. If the items accurately reflect the goals of education, then criterion-referenced test scores can provide feedback to teachers on how well they are teaching. If Mary cannot fill out a personal information blank, then the teacher knows that Mary needs more instruction on that skill. If most of the students in a school cannot fill out such forms, then the school administration knows that a better teaching method must be implemented. Thus, criterion-referenced tests play an important role in evaluating and improving teaching methods.

Mainstreaming provides children with special needs a public education in the least restrictive environment. Public Law 94-142 helped get many such children into regular classrooms.

Mainstreaming: Education for Persons with Special Needs

During the 1970s, enormous strides were made in the legal standing of children with challenging conditions such as mental retardation, emotional problems, and physical challenges. Federal legislation—famous as Public Law 94-142—established that *every* child has a *right* to a public education, regardless of her or his special needs. This means that many more children with severe challenges are being served by public schools than ever before.

Furthermore, federal law states that the child is entitled to receive her or his education in the *least restrictive environment*. This legal phrase means that children must receive educational and psychological assistance in circumstances that are as similar as possible to the normal day-to-day environment of nonhandicapped children. Thus, it's no longer legal to isolate children with special needs in separate schools if it's possible to educate them in regular schools and allow them to interact with other children. Whenever possible, in fact, children with special needs must be kept in the regular classroom for as large a part of the school day as possible and removed for special assistance only when necessary. This practice is known as **mainstreaming,** because it keeps such children within the mainstream of normal social and educational development.

mainstreaming The practice of integrating children with special needs into regular classrooms.

In addition to protecting the legal rights of people with special needs, federal law offers some important benefits to all concerned. First, it gives students with special needs an opportunity to learn how to fit into the world of youngsters without disabilities. Second and equally important, it gives children without special needs a chance to learn firsthand that children with special needs are fully human and well worth having as friends (Augustine, Gruber, & Hanson, 1990; Sprinthall, Sprinthall, & Oja, 1998).

Review

Educational psychologists have long sought to improve ways of teaching and testing schoolchildren, but the recent excitement in educational psychology stems from new concepts and methods of teaching and testing that promise to help more children benefit fully from the opportunities offered by the educational system. The mastery learning approach provides a way to both enhance learning and decrease the gap between the most and

Review (cont.)	least successful learners. The direct instruction approach has developed effective methods based on the principles of learning for teaching. Other methods for increasing learning in the classroom focus on ways for teachers to increase their students' intrinsic motivation to learn. The shift toward criterion-referenced testing provides us with a more meaningful way of evaluating success in teaching necessary skills and knowledge to children. In a different way, the mainstreaming approach assures children with special needs of their place in the educational system.

Check Your Learning

To be sure that you have learned the key points from the preceding section, cover the list of correct answers and try to answer each question. If you give an incorrect answer to any question, return to the page given next to the correct answer to see why your answer was not correct.

1. _____ psychology is the field in which principles of learning, cognition, and other aspects of psychology are applied to improve teaching and learning.

   a) Developmental   c) Environmental

   b) School   d) Educational

2. _____ is the concept that children should never progress from one learning task to another until they have mastered the more basic one.

   a) Stage theory   c) Step learning

   b) Mastery learning   d) Progression theory

3. _____ testing is designed to determine whether a child has met the minimum standards of a specific educational program.

   a) Intelligence   c) Criterion-referenced

   b) Aptitude   d) Personality

4. The practice of integrating children with special needs into regular classrooms is called _____.

   a) integration   c) combining

   b) assimilation   d) mainstreaming

Thinking Critically about Psychology

There are no right or wrong answers to the following questions. They are presented to help you become an active reader and think critically about what you just read.

1. How could the mastery learning approach provide a greater degree of equality of opportunity to all people?

2. This textbook was designed to increase your ease of learning. What could be done to make it better?

Correct Answers: 1. d (p. 592), **2. b** (p. 593), **3. c** (p. 594), **4. d** (p. 595)

Summary

Chapter 17 describes the applications of psychology to the environment, business, architecture, law, and education.

I. The field of environmental psychology uses the methods of psychology to evaluate human reactions to architectural spaces and to study the effects of our behavior on the environment.

II. The behavior of humans has created overpopulation, resource depletion, and pollution that seriously threaten the planet's ability to sustain life.

A. Saving the environment from catastrophic damage will require changes in behavior at the level of the individual, the business, and the government.

B. Psychologists working in two theoretical traditions have developed techniques for changing environmentally destructive behavior.

1. The behavioral approach is characterized by the use of principles of learning to change behavior and the rigorous evaluation of the effectiveness of techniques in the real world.

2. The cognitive and humanistic approach focuses on changing attitudes, values, beliefs, and circumstances.

3. Recently, psychologists from both traditions have recognized the importance of combining the best of both the behavior and cognitive-humanistic approaches.

III. Psychologists who work for businesses are known as industrial-organizational psychologists. They help businesses design better methods of selecting and promoting employees, help managers organize and manage employees more effectively, and design machines that can be used more efficiently and safely by employees (human factors engineering).

A. The best predictor of the success of new employees in complex jobs is intelligence, but it is less valid for less complex jobs. Over time, the advantage of high intelligence in less complex jobs declines as employees acquire job knowledge and skills.

B. Structured interviews are more valid for the selection of employees than unstructured interviews are.

C. Tests of job knowledge and performance tests are valid methods for hiring experienced workers.

D. The dimension of personality known as conscientiousness is an important nonintellectual predictor of job success.

E. Several methods exist for assessing performance of currently employed workers.

1. Worker performance is evaluated using job performance ratings, such as multiple-step rating scales and checklists.

2. Assessment centers are frequently used to evaluate applicants or currently employed candidates for management positions in companies.

G. The overall goals of psychologists working in business are to improve the satisfaction of employees and to improve their productivity. They can accomplish these goals by

1. Selecting the right person for the job

2. Improving supervisory style

3. Improving managerial organization

4. Improving physical conditions

H. Employee health programs can also improve job satisfaction while reducing both the direct costs of health benefits and the indirect costs due to poor health and premature death of valuable employees.

IV. Psychologists apply their methods to the practice of the law in the courtroom.

A. They have found that the characteristics of defendants affect the likelihood of conviction and the harshness of the sentence. The characteristics of plaintiffs and defendants also affect the decisions of juries in civil cases independently of the merits of the case.

B. They have also found that certain types of jury members are more likely than other types to vote for conviction and to recommend harsher sentences.

C. The order in which evidence is presented appears to affect the outcome of the trial.

V. Psychologists serve the field of education as professors who help train teachers, as consultants on testing programs, and as school psychologists employed by school systems.

A. One successful approach to improving school learning is mastery learning, based on Benjamin Bloom's belief that children should never progress from one learning task to another until they have fully mastered the previous one. Mastery learning approaches are easily implemented using computerized intelligent tutoring systems.

B. The direct instruction approach has led to improved learning in the classroom by focusing on:

1. Actively guiding learning

2. Highlighting the new information or skills that students are expected to learn

3. Presenting new information in small amounts that are easily understood

4. Asking students to perform what they are learning frequently

5. Providing frequent positive reinforcement for accurate performance, or gentle corrective feedback for inaccurate performance

C. Research also shows that students learn more when teachers give them choices among interesting materials and point out the intrinsic importance of what they are asked to learn.

D. Criterion-referenced testing is a form of testing designed to determine if a given child can meet the minimum criteria for a specific educational objective.

E. Federal law states that every child has a right to public education, regardless of his or her disability. The law states that the education must take place in the least restrictive environment possible.

Glossary

A

abnormal behavior: Actions, thoughts, and feelings that are harmful to the person or to others. (p. 459)

absolute threshold: The smallest magnitude of a stimulus that can be detected half the time. (p. 122)

achievement motivation: The psychological need in humans for success. (p. 360)

action potential: Brief electrical signal that travels the length of the axon. (p. 50)

adolescence: The period from the onset of puberty until the beginning of adulthood. (p. 325)

adolescent egocentrism: The quality of thinking that leads some adolescents to believe that they are the focus of attention in social situations, to believe that their problems are unique, to be unusually hypocritical, and to be "pseudostupid." (p. 327)

adolescent growth spurt: The rapid increase in weight and height that occurs around the onset of puberty. (p. 326)

adrenal glands (ah-drē´nal): Two glands on the kidneys that are involved in physical and emotional arousal. (p. 77)

afferent neurons (af´er-ent): Neurons that transmit messages from sense organs to the central nervous system. (p. 57)

agoraphobia (ag´´o-rah-fō´bē-ah): An intense fear of leaving one's home or other familiar places. (p. 466)

algorithms (al´go-rith´mz): Systematic patterns of reasoning that guarantee finding a correct solution to a problem. (p. 271)

all-or-none principle: Law that states that once a neural action potential is produced, its magnitude is always the same. (p. 51)

amphetamine psychosis (sī-kō´sis): Prolonged reaction to the excessive use of stimulants, characterized by disordered thinking, confused and rapidly changing emotions, and intense suspiciousness. (p. 183)

amphetamines (am-fet´ah-minz): Powerful stimulants that produce a conscious sense of increased energy and euphoria. (p. 183)

amygdala (ah-mig´dah-lah): A part of the limbic system that plays a role in emotion. (p. 63)

anal expulsive: A personality type based on anal fixation in which the person is cruel, pushy, messy, and disorderly. (p. 405)

anal retentive: A personality type based on anal fixation, in which the person is stingy, obstinate, stubborn, and compulsive. (p. 405)

anal stage: According to Freud, the second psychosexual stage (from 1 to 3 years), in which gratification is focused on the anus. (p. 405)

androgynous: Having both typically female and male psychological characteristics. (p. 104)

angiotensin (an´´jē-ō-ten´sin): A substance in the blood that signals the hypothalamus that the body needs water. (p. 355)

animism (a´-n-mizm): The egocentric belief of preoperational children that inanimate objects are alive, as children are. (p. 322)

anterograde amnesia (an´-terō-grād): Disorder of memory characterized by an inability to store and/or retrieve new information in long-term memory. (p. 254)

antidiuretic hormone (ADH) (an´´tī-di´´u-ret´ik): A hormone produced by the pituitary that causes the kidneys to conserve water in the body by reabsorbing it from the urine. (p. 355)

antisocial personality disorder: A personality disorder characterized by smooth social skills and a lack of guilt about violating social rules and laws and taking advantage of others. (p. 484)

anxiety disorders: Psychological disorders that involve excessive levels of negative emotions, such as nervousness, tension, worry, fright, and anxiety. (p. 466)

applied psychologists: Psychologists who use knowledge of psychology to solve and to prevent human problems. (p. 17)

approach-approach conflict: Conflict in which the individual must choose between two positive goals of approximately equal value. (p. 429)

assessment centers: Programs for the evaluation of employees that use simulated management tasks as their primary method of evaluation. (p. 575)

association areas: Areas within each lobe of the cerebral cortex believed to play general rather than specific roles. (p. 68)

astral projection (as´tral): Depersonalization that includes the illusion that the mind has left the body. (p. 180)

attachments: The psychological bonds between infants and caregivers. (p. 321)

attention: Selective focus on some things in the environments to the exclusion of others. (p. 163)

attention-deficit/hyperactivity disorder (ADHD): ADHD is defined by serious problems sustaining attention and completing tasks, or by high levels of motor activity and impulsivity, or both. The diagnosis is made only if these symptoms result in serious impairment in functioning in two or more areas of life (e.g., home and school). (p. 482)

attitudes: Evaluations that predispose one to act and feel in certain ways. (p. 583)

attribution: The process of trying to explain why things happen—that is, attribute them to some cause. (p. 549)

attribution theory (ah-tri-bu´shun): The theory that people tend to look for explanations for their own behavior and that of others. (p. 544)

atypical sexual behavior: Sexual practice that differs considerably from the norm. (p. 487)

audition (aw-dish´-un): Sense of hearing. (p. 132)

autonomic nervous system (aw´´to-nom´ik): The part of the peripheral nervous system that regulates the actions of internal body organs, such as heartbeat. (p. 57)

avoidance-avoidance conflict: Conflict in which the individual must choose between two negative outcomes of approximately equal value. (p. 429)

avoidance conditioning: Operant conditioning in which the behavior is reinforced, because it prevents something negative from happening (a form of negative reinforcement). (p. 208)

axons (ak´sonz): Neuron branches that transmit messages to other neurons. (p. 49)

B

basilar membrane (bas´-ĭ-lar): One of the membranes that separate the two tubes of the cochlea and on which the organ of Corti rests. (p. 134)

basket cells: Sensory receptor cells at the base of hairs that detect pressure. (p. 138)

behavior: Directly observable and measurable actions. (p. 2)

behavioral activation: A therapeutic approach based on social learning theory in which the therapist teaches the client to engage in activities that have reinforcing consequences to treat depression. (p. 509)

behaviorism (be-hāv´yor-izm): School of psychology that emphasizes the process of learning and the measurement of overt behavior. (p. 8)

binocular cues (bīn-ok´ū-lar): Two visual cues that require both eyes to allow us to perceive depth. (p. 151)

bipolar disorder (bī-pō´lar): A condition in which the individual experiences periods of mania that alternate irregularly with periods of severe depression. (p. 479)

blind experiment: Formal experiment in which the researcher who measures the dependent variable does not know which participants are in the experimental group or the control group. In double-blind experiments, the participants also do not know if they are in the experimental or the control group. (p. 35)

blind spot: Spot where the optic nerve attaches to the retina; it contains no rods or cones. (p. 127)

body mass index: The ratio of a person's weight to that person's height. (p. 448)

brain: The complex mass of neural cells and related cells encased in the skull. (p. 48)

Broca's area: Area of the frontal lobe of the left cerebral hemisphere that plays a role in speaking language. (p. 66)

C

Cannon-Bard theory of emotion: The theory that conscious emotional experiences and physiological reactions and behavior are relatively independent events. (p. 379)

castration anxiety (kas-trā´shun): According to Freud, the fear of a young boy that his father will punish his sexual desire for his mother by removing his genitals. (p. 406)

catatonic schizophrenia (kat´´ah-ton´ik): A subtype of schizophrenia in which the individual spends long periods in an inactive, statuelike state. (p. 482)

catharsis: The release of emotional energy related to unconscious conflicts. (p. 386)

cell body: The central part of the neuron that includes the nucleus. (p. 49)

cell membrane: The covering of a neuron or another cell. (p. 50)

central nervous system: The brain and the spinal cord. (p. 56)

cerebellum (ser´´e-bel´um): Two rounded structures behind the pons involved in the coordination of muscle movements, learning, and memory. (p. 61)

cerebral cortex (sere-bral): The largest structure in the forebrain, controlling conscious experience and intelligence and being involved with the somatic nervous system. (p. 64)

cerebral hemispheres: The two main parts of the cerebral cortex, divided into left and right hemispheres. (p. 70)

child molestation: Sexual behavior with a child without force or direct threat of force. (p. 490)

chromosomes (krō´mō-somz): Strands of DNA (deoxyribonucleic acid) in cells. (p. 94)

chunks: Units of memory. (p. 233)

ciliary muscle (sil´ē-ar´´e): Muscle in the eye that controls the shape of the lens. (p. 126)

cingulate cortex: A part of the limbic system, lying in the cerebral cortex, that processes cognitive information in emotion. (p. 63)

cingulotomy: A type of psychosurgery for severe and otherwise untreatable obsessive-compulsive disorder; it involves surgical destruction of part of the cingulate cortex. (p. 521)

circadian rhythm (sur-kā´dē-un): Internally generated cycles lasting about 24 hours a day that regulate sleepiness and wakefulness, body temperature, and the secretion of some hormones. (p. 170)

classical conditioning: Form of learning in which a previously neutral stimulus (CS) is paired with an unconditioned stimulus (UCS) to elicit a conditioned response (CR) that is identical to or very similar to the unconditioned response (UCR). (p. 198)

client-centered psychotherapy: Carl Rogers' approach to humanistic psychotherapy, in which the therapist creates an atmosphere that encourages clients to discover feelings of which they were unaware. (p. 505)

climacteric (klī-mak´ter-ik): The period between about ages 45 and 60 in which there is a loss of capacity to sexually reproduce in women and a decline in the reproductive capacity of men. (p. 334)

clinical method: Method of studying people while they are receiving psychological help from a mental health professional. (p. 29)

closure principle (klo´zhur): Gestalt principle of perception that states that incomplete figures of familiar objects tend to be perceived as wholes. (p. 149)

cochlea (cok´lē-ah): Spiral structure of the inner ear that is filled with fluid and contains the receptors for hearing. (p. 134)

cognition (kog-nish´un): Mental processes of perceiving, believing, thinking, remembering, knowing, deciding, and so on. (p. 8)

cognitive dissonance (dis´so-nans): The discomfort that results from inconsistencies between attitudes and behavior. (p. 542)

cognitive-behavior therapy: Psychotherapy based on social learning theory in which the therapist helps the client unlearn abnormal ways of behaving, learn more adaptive ways of behaving, and change maladaptive cognitions. (p. 508)

cognitive map (kog´ni-tiv): Inferred mental awareness of the structure of a physical space or related elements. (p. 218)

cognitive psychology: Viewpoint in psychology that emphasizes the importance of cognitive processes, such as perception, memory, and thinking. (p. 8)

cognitive restructuring: A CBT method in which faulty cognitions—maladaptive beliefs, expectations, and ways of thinking—are changed by pointing out their irrationality. (p. 512)

cognitive theory of emotion: The theory that the cognitive interpretation of events in the outside world and stimuli from our own bodies is the key factor in emotions. (p. 379)

collective unconscious: According to Jung, the content of the unconscious mind with which all humans are born. (p. 407)

companionate love: The blend of friendship, intimacy, commitment, and security that generally develops after passionate love. (p. 557)

concepts (kon´septs): Categories of things, events, and qualities that are linked together by a common feature or features in spite of their differences. (p. 265)

concrete operational stage: In Piaget's theory, the period of cognitive development from ages 7 to 11. (p. 323)

conditioned response (CR): Response that is similar or identical to the unconditioned response that comes to be elicited by a conditioned stimulus. (p. 198)

conditioned stimulus (CS): Stimulus that comes to elicit responses as a result of being paired with an unconditioned stimulus. (p. 197)

conditions of worth: The standards used by others or ourselves in judging our worth. (p. 415)

cones: The 6 million receptor cells located mostly in the center of the retina that transduce light waves into neural impulses, thereby coding information about light, dark, and color. (p. 127)

conflict: The state in which two or more motives cannot be satisfied because they interfere with one another. (p. 428)

conformity: Yielding to group pressure even when no direct request to comply has been made. (p. 532)

conjunctive concepts (kon-junk´´tiv´): Concepts defined by the simultaneous presence of two or more common characteristics. (p. 266)

conscience: According to Freud, the moral inhibitions of the superego. (p. 404)

conscious mind: That portion of the mind of which one is presently aware. (p. 402)

consciousness (kon´shus-nes): A state of awareness. (p. 164)

conservation: The concept understood by concrete operational children that quantity (number, mass, etc.) does not change just because shape or other superficial features have changed. (p. 323)

consolidation (kon sol´ ah day´´ shun): The gradual strengthening of chemical changes in synapses following learning experiences. (p. 252)

continuity hypothesis: The view that abnormal behavior is just a more severe form of normal psychological problems. (p. 460)

continuity principle (kon´ti-noo´´i-tee): Gestalt principle of perception that states that lines or patterns that follow a smooth contour are perceived as part of a single unit. (p. 149)

control group: Group in simple experiments that is not exposed to any level of the independent variable and is used for comparisons with the treatment group. (p. 33)

convergent thinking: Thinking that is logical and conventional and that focuses on a problem. (p. 273)

conversion disorders: Somatoform disorders in which individuals experience serious somatic symptoms such as functional blindness, deafness, and paralysis. (p. 471)

cooperative play: Play that involves cooperation between two or more children. (p. 323)

coping: Attempts by individuals to deal with the source of stress and/or control their reactions to it. (p. 443)

cornea (kor´nē-ah): Protective coating on the surface of the eye through which light passes. (p. 126)

corpus callosum (kor´pus kah-lo´-sum): The major neural structure connecting the left and the right cerebral hemispheres. (p. 70)

correlation coefficient: The numerical expression of the strength and the direction of a relationship between two variables. (p. 30)

correlational method (kor´´ĕ-lā´shun-al): Research method that measures the strength of the relation between variables. (p. 29)

cortisol: Stress hormone produced by the adrenal glands. (p. 78)

counterconditioning: Process of eliminating a classically conditioned response by pairing the conditioned stimulus (CS) with an unconditioned stimulus (UCS) for a response that is stronger than the conditioned response (CR) and that cannot occur at the same time as the CR. (p. 201)

creativity: The ability to make human products and ideas (such as symphonies or solutions to social problems) that are both novel and valued by others. (p. 273)

cretinism (krē´tin-izm): Type of mental retardation in children caused by a deficiency of thyroxin. (p. 80)

criterion-referenced testing: Testing designed to determine whether a child can meet the minimum standards of a specific educational objective. (p. 594)

critical period: A biologically determined period in the life of some animals during which certain forms of learning can take place most easily. (p. 307)

criticism trap: An increase in the frequency of a negative behavior that often follows the use of criticism, reinforcing the behavior it is intended to punish. (p. 209)

crystallized intelligence: The ability to use previously learned information and skills to solve familiar problems. (p. 286)

cultural relativity: Perspective that promotes thinking of different cultures in relative terms rather than judgmental terms. (p. 14)

culture: Patterns of behavior, beliefs, and values shared by a group of people. (p. 99)

cupula (ku´-pu-lah): Gelatin-like structure containing a tuft of hairlike sensory receptor cells in the semicircular canals. (p. 137)

D

dark adaptation: Increased sensitivity of the eye in semidarkness following a reduction in overall illumination. (p. 127)

day residue: Dream content that is similar to events in the person's waking life. (p. 174)

daydreams: Relatively focused thinking about fantasies. (p. 173)

decay theory: The theory that forgetting occurs as the memory trace fades over time. (p. 243)

decenter (dĕ-sen´ter): To think about more than one characteristic of a thing at a time; a capacity of concrete operational children. (p. 324)

decibel (db) (des´i-bel): Measurement of the intensity of perceived sound. (p. 132)

declarative memory: Semantic and episodic memory. (p. 235)

deep structure: The underlying structure of a statement that holds its meaning. (p. 277)

defense mechanisms: According to Freud, the unrealistic strategies used by the ego to discharge tension. (p. 445)

deindividuation: State in which people in a group can feel anonymous and unidentifiable and therefore feel less concerned with what others think of their behavior. (p. 528)

delay of reinforcement: The passage of time between the response and the positive reinforcement that leads to reduced efficiency of operant conditioning. (p. 204)

delusions: False beliefs that distort reality. (p. 480)

dendrites (den´ drīts): Extensions of the cell body that usually serve as receiving areas for messages from other neurons. (p. 49)

dependent variable: Variable whose quantitative value is expected to depend on the effects of the independent variable. (p. 33)

depersonalization (de-per´´sun-al-i-zā´shun): The perceptual experience of one's body or surroundings becoming distorted or unreal in some way. (p. 180)

depolarization: Process during which positively charged ions flow into the axon, making it less negatively charged inside. (p. 50)

depressants: Drugs that reduce the activity of the central nervous system, leading to a sense of relaxation, drowsiness, and lowered inhibitions. (p. 182)

descriptive statistics: Statistics such as the mean and standard deviation that summarize the numerical results of studies. (p. 36)

descriptive studies: Methods of observation used to describe predictable behavior and mental processes. (p. 27)

development: The more-or-less predictable changes in behavior associated with increasing age. (p. 304)

developmental origins hypothesis: The belief that prenatal factors influence the development of physical and psychological health. (p. 317)

developmental psychology: The field of psychology that focuses on development across the life span. (p. 304)

deviation IQ: The intelligence quotient based on the degree of deviation from average of the person's score on an intelligence test. (p. 287)

difference threshold: The smallest difference between two stimuli that can be detected half the time. (p. 122)

diffusion of responsibility: The effect of being in a group that apparently reduces the sense of personal responsibility of each group member to act appropriately. (p. 529)

discontinuity hypothesis: The view that abnormal behavior is fundamentally different from normal psychological problems. (p. 460)

disinhibition (dis''in-hi-bish'un): Temporary increase in the strength of an extinguished response caused by an unrelated stimulus event. (p. 216)

disjunctive concepts (dis-junk''tiv'): Concepts defined by the presence of one of two common characteristics or both. (p. 266)

disorganized schizophrenia: A subtype of schizophrenia characterized by shallow silliness, extreme social withdrawal, and fragmented delusions and hallucinations. (p. 482)

displacement (dis-plās'ment): A defense mechanism in which the individual directs aggressive or sexual feelings away from the primary object to someone or something safe. (p. 404)

dispositional attribution (dis''po-zish'un-al): An explanation for behavior that is based on a personal characteristic of the individual. (p. 549)

dissociative amnesia: A dissociative disorder that involves a loss of memory and that has a psychological rather than a physical cause. (p. 472)

dissociative disorders (dis-sō''sē-a-tiv): A category of conditions involving sudden cognitive changes, such as a sudden loss of memory or loss of one's identity. (p. 472)

dissociative fugue states (fūg): A period of "wandering" that involves a loss of memory and a change in identity. (p. 472)

dissociative identity disorder: A dissociative disorder in which the individual appears to shift abruptly and repeatedly from one "personality" to another. (p. 473)

divergent thinking: Thinking that is loosely organized, only partially directed, and unconventional. (p. 273)

divided consciousness: The splitting off of two conscious activities that occur simultaneously. (p. 164)

dizygotic twins (dī''zī-got'ik): Twins formed from the fertilization of two ova by two sperm. (p. 93)

dominant gene: Version of a polymorphic gene that produces a trait in an individual even when paired with a recessive gene. (p. 93)

Down syndrome: Abnormality caused by the presence of an additional 21st chromosome. (p. 97)

dream interpretation: A method developed by Freud in which the symbols of the manifest content of dreams that are recalled by the patient are interpreted to reveal their latent content. (p. 501)

dreaming: Conscious awareness during sleep that primarily occurs during rapid-eye-movement (REM) sleep. (p. 168)

drug therapy: A medical therapy that uses medications to treat abnormal behavior. (p. 518)

dyspareunia (dis''pah-roo'nē-ah): A sexual dysfunction in which the individual experiences pain during intercourse. (p. 493)

E

eardrum: Thin membrane that sound waves cause to vibrate; a structure of the middle ear. (p. 133)

early experiences: Experiences occurring very early in development, believed by some to have lasting effects. (p. 307)

educational psychology: The field in which principles of learning, cognition, and other aspects of psychology are applied to improve education. (p. 592)

efferent neurons (ef'er-ent): Neurons that transmit messages from the central nervous system to organs and muscles. (p. 57)

ego (ē'go): According to Freud, that part of the mind that uses the reality principle to satisfy the id. (p. 403)

ego ideal: According to Freud, the standard of perfect conduct of the superego. (p. 404)

egocentric (e''gō-sen'trik): The self-oriented quality in the thinking of preoperational children. (p. 322)

elaboration (e-lab''or-rā'shun): The process of creating associations between a new memory and existing memories. (p. 241)

Electra complex (e-lek'-trah): According to Freud, the transfer of a young girl's sexual desires from her mother to her father after she discovers she has no penis. (p. 406)

electroconvulsive therapy (ECT) (e-lektro-con-vulsiv): A medical therapy that uses electrical current to induce controlled convulsive seizures that alleviate some types of mental disorders. (p. 520)

electroencephalogram (EEG) (e-lek''trō-en-sef'ah-lo-gram): A measure of electrical brain activity; recording of the electrical activity of the brain obtained through electrodes placed on the scalp. (p. 69)

electromagnetic radiation (e-lek''trō-mag-net'ik): Form of energy including electricity, radio waves, and X rays, of which visible light is a part. (p. 125)

embryonic stage: The second period of prenatal development during which organs start to form. (p. 317)

emotion: Positive or negative feelings generally in reaction to stimuli that are accompanied by physiological arousal and related behavior. (p. 351)

empirical evidence: Evidence based on observations of publicly observable phenomena, such as behavior, that can be confirmed by other observers. (p. 25)

encode (en'cōd): To represent information in some form in the memory system. (p. 230)

endocrine system (en'dō-krin): The system of glands that secretes hormones. (p. 77)

engram (en'gram): The partially understood memory trace in the brain that is the biological basis of memory. (p. 251)

environmental psychologists: Psychologists who study the effects of the environment on our behavior and mental processes, and the effects of our behavior on the environment. (p. 563)

ephedra: Herbal stimulant that may suppress appetite but may cause serious emotional disturbance. (p. 184)

epinephrine (ep''i-nef'rin): Hormone produced by the adrenal glands. (p. 78)

episodic memory (epĭ-sodik): Memory for specific experiences that can be defined in terms of time and space. (p. 235)

equity theory: The theory that partners will be comfortable in their relationship only when the ratio between their perceived contributions and benefits is equal. (p. 558)

erectile dysfunction: A condition in which the penis does not become erect enough for intercourse under sexually arousing circumstances. (p. 493)

erogenous zones: A part of the body that releases sexual energy when stimulated. (p. 405)

escape conditioning: Operant conditioning in which the behavior is reinforced, because it causes a negative event to cease (a form of negative reinforcement). (p. 208)

estrogen (es'tro-jen): A female sex hormone. (p. 79)

ethnic group: Group of persons who are descendants of a common group of ancestors. (p. 99)

ethnic identity: Each person's sense of belonging to a particular ethnic group. (p. 99)

evolutionary psychology: The perspective in psychology that the psychological characteristics of human and nonhuman animals arose through natural selection. (p. 111)

excitement phase: The first stage of the sexual response cycle, during which the penis becomes erect and the vagina lubricates. (p. 367)

exhibitionism (ek´´sĭ-bish´ŭ-nizm´´): The practice of obtaining sexual pleasure by exposing one's genitals to others. (p. 489)

experimental control: Requirement that all explanations for differences in the dependent variable are controlled in formal experiments, except for differences in conditions of the independent variable. (p. 34)

experimental group: Group in an experiment that receives some value of the independent variable. (p. 35)

experimenter bias: Subtle but potentially powerful unintentional influences on the dependent variable caused by experimenters' interacting differently with participants in the experimental and the control groups. (p. 35)

expressive aphasia (ah-fā´ze-ah): Impairment of the ability to generate spoken language but not to comprehend of language. (p. 66)

external auditory canal: Tube connecting the pinna to the middle ear. (p. 133)

extinction (eks-tink´-shun): Process of unlearning a learned response because of the removal of the original source of learning. (p. 214)

extraversion (eks´´tro-ver´zhun): According to Jung, the tendency of some individuals to be friendly and open to the world. (p. 407)

extrinsic motivation (eks-trin´sik): Human motives activated by external rewards. (p. 363)

F

false memory: Remembering an event that did not occur or that occurred in a way that was substantially different from the memory of the event. (p. 248)

family therapy: An approach to psychotherapy that emphasizes an understanding of the roles of each of the members of the family system, usually conducted with all members of the family present. (p. 516)

feelings of inferiority: According to Adler, the feelings that result from children being less powerful than adults that must be overcome during the development of the healthy personality. (p. 408)

female orgasmic disorder: A condition in which a female has persistent delayed or absence of an orgasm. (p. 494)

female sexual arousal disorder: A condition in which sexual arousal does not occur in appropriate circumstances in a female. (p. 493)

feminist psychotherapy: An approach to psychotherapy that encourages women to confront issues created by living in a sexist society as part of their psychotherapy. (p. 517)

fertilization (fer´tĭ-li-zā´shun): The uniting of sperm and ovum, which produces a zygote. (p. 94)

fetal stage The final stage of prenatal development during which the organs mature. (p. 317)

fetishism (fet´ish-izm): The practice of obtaining sexual arousal primarily or exclusively from specific objects. (p. 488)

figure-ground principle: Gestalt principle of perception that states that part of a visual stimulus will be the center of our attention (figure) and the rest will be the indistinct ground. In many cases, the figure and ground can be reversed in our perception of the same stimulus. (p. 149)

fixed interval schedule: Reinforcement schedule in which the reinforcer is given following the first response occurring after a predetermined period of time. (p. 206)

fixed ratio schedule: Reinforcement schedule in which the reinforcer is given only after a specified number of responses. (p. 205)

fluid intelligence: The ability to learn or invent new strategies to deal with new problems. (p. 285)

forebrain: The parts of the brain, including the thalamus, hypothalamus, and cerebral cortex, that cover the hindbrain and midbrain and fill much of the skull. (p. 62)

formal experiment: Research method that allows the researcher to manipulate the independent variable to study its effect on the dependent variable. (p. 32)

formal operational stage: Period characterized by an ability to use abstract concepts. (p. 327)

fovea (fō´vē-ah): Central spot of the retina, which contains the greatest concentration of cones. (p. 127)

free association: A tool used by Freud in which the patient is encouraged to talk about whatever comes to mind, allowing the contents of the unconscious mind to slip past the censorship of the ego. (p. 500)

free nerve endings: Sensory receptor cells in the skin that detect pressure, temperature, and pain. (p. 138)

frequency of cycles: Rate of vibration of sound waves; determines pitch. (p. 132)

Freud's instinct theory: The theory that aggression is caused by an inborn aggressive instinct. (p. 386)

frontal lobes: The part of the cerebral cortex in the front of the skull involved in planning, organization, thinking, decision making, memory, voluntary motor movements, and speech. (p. 64)

frustration: The result of being unable to satisfy a motive. (p. 428)

frustration-aggression theory: The theory that aggression is a natural reaction to the frustration of important motives. (p. 386)

functional MRI: Type of MRI that measures the activity of parts of the brain by measuring the use of oxygen by groups of neurons. (p. 69)

functionalism (funk´shun-al-izm): 19th-century school of psychology that emphasized the useful functions of consciousness. (p. 6)

fundamental attribution error: The tendency to underestimate the impact of situations on others while overestimating the impact on oneself. (p. 549)

G

ganglia (gang´glē-ah): Clusters of cell bodies of neurons outside the central nervous system. (p. 59)

gender: The psychological experience of being male or female. (p. 104)

gender identity: One's view of oneself as male or female. (p. 104)

Gender Identity Disorder (trans-seks´u-ah-lizm): A condition, sometimes referred to as transsexualism, in which an individual feels trapped in the body of the wrong sex. (p. 487)

gender role: The typical behaviors consistent with being male or female within a given culture. (p. 104)

gene expression: The physical chain effects through which genes determine which proteins are synthesized to create the structure of neurons, glands, and other bodily structures. (p. 103)

gene-environment interaction: The phenomenon in which genes influence how environments influence us and environments influence how genes influence us. (p. 102)

general adaptation syndrome (GAS): According to Selye, the mobilization of the body to ward off threats, characterized by a three-stage pattern of the alarm reaction, the resistance stage, and the exhaustion stage. (p. 432)

generalized anxiety disorder: An uneasy sense of general tension and apprehension for no apparent reason that makes the individual highly uncomfortable because of its prolonged presence. (p. 466)

generative (jen´e-ra´´tiv): The ability to create an infinite set of utterances using a finite set of elements and rules. (p. 278)

genes (jēnz): Segments of chromosomes made up of sequences of base pairs of adenine, thymine, guanine, and cystine, which are the basic biological units of inheritance, because they contain all the coded genetic information needed to influence some aspect of a structure or function of the body. (p. 94)

genital stage (jen´i-tal): According to Freud, the psychosexual stage (from 11 years through adulthood) in which sexual and romantic interest is directed toward one's peers. (p. 406)

germinal stage: The period of development right after conception, which lasts about two weeks. (p. 317)

Gestalt (ges-tawlt´): Organized or unified whole. (p. 6)

Gestalt psychology: School of thought based on the belief that human consciousness cannot be broken down into its elements. (p. 6)

Gestalt therapy: A humanistic therapy in which the therapist takes an active role (questioning and challenging the client) to help the client become more aware of her or his feelings. (p. 507)

glands: The structures in the body that secrete substances. (p. 77)

glial cells (glee-uhl): Cells that assist neurons by transporting nutrients to them, producing myelin sheath, and regulating the likelihood of transmission of messages across the synaptic gap. (p. 52)

glucagon (gloo´kah-gon): Hormone produced by the islets of Langerhans that causes the liver to release sugar into the bloodstream. (p. 79)

gonads (gō´nadz): Glands that produce sex cells and hormones important in sexual arousal and that contribute to the development of secondary sex characteristics. (p. 79)

graded exposure: A behavior therapy technique in which a person with a phobia is first exposed to a stimulus that is mildly fear provoking. Once the client has mastered his or her anxiety in that situation, he or she is exposed to a graded series of more fearful situations. (p. 509)

group therapy: Psychotherapy conducted in groups, typically of four to eight clients at a time. (p. 515)

groupthink: The faulty decision-making processes that may occur in groups. (p. 531)

gustation (gus-tā´-shun): Sense of taste. (p. 144)

H

hair cells: Receptor neuron cells for hearing located in the organ of Corti. (p. 134)

hallucinations: False perceptual experiences that distort reality. (p. 480)

hallucinogens (hah-lū´si´´no-jenz): Drugs that alter perceptual experiences. (p. 181)

hammer, anvil, stirrup: Three linked bones of the middle ear, which pass sound waves to the inner ear. (p. 133)

health psychology: The field of psychology that uses psychological principles to encourage healthy lifestyles and to minimize the impact of stress. (p. 447)

hertz (Hz): Measurement of the frequency of sound waves in cycles per second. (p. 132)

heterosexuality: Romantic and sexual attraction to those of the different sex. (p. 372)

heuristic reasoning: Way of thinking based on strategies that increase the probability of finding a correct solution but do not guarantee it. (p. 271)

hindbrain: The lowest part of the brain, located at the base of the skull. (p. 61)

hippocampus (hip´o-kam´pus): The part of the limbic system that plays a role in memory and the processing of emotion. (p. 63)

homeostatic mechanisms (hō´´mē-ō-stat´ik): Internal body mechanisms that sense biological imbalances and stimulate actions to restore the proper balance. (p. 352)

homosexuality: Romantic and sexual attraction to those of the same sex, as distinguished from heterosexual. (p. 372)

hormones (hor´mōnz): Chemical substances, produced by endocrine glands, that influence internal organs. (p. 77)

human factors engineering: The branch of industrial-organizational psychology interested in the design of machines to be operated by human beings. (p. 582)

humanistic psychology: Psychological view that human beings possess an innate tendency to improve and determine their lives by the decisions they make. (p. 10)

humanistic theory: The psychological view that human beings possess an innate tendency to improve and to determine their lives through the decisions they make. (p. 414)

hyperphagia (hī´´per-fā´jē-ah): Excessive overeating that results from the destruction of the satiety center of the hypothalamus. (p. 353)

hypnagogic state (hip´´nah-goj´ik): Relaxed state of dreamlike awareness between wakefulness and sleep. (p. 166)

hypnosis (hip-nō´sis): Altered state of consciousness in which the individual is highly relaxed and susceptible to suggestions. (p. 179)

hypochondriasis (hī´-pō-kon-drī´ōah-sis): A mild form of somatization disorder characterized by excessive concern about one's health. (p. 471)

hypothalamus (hī´´-pō-thal´ah-mus): The small part of the forebrain involved with motives, emotions, and the functions of the autonomic nervous system. (p. 62)

hypothesis: Prediction based on a theory that is tested in a study. (p. 26)

I

id: According to Freud, the inborn part of the unconscious mind that uses the primary process to satisfy its needs and that acts according to the pleasure principle. (p. 403)

ideal self: According to humanists, the person one wishes one were. (p. 414)

identification: The tendency to base one's identity and actions on individuals who are successful in gaining satisfaction from life. (p. 404)

immune system: The complex body system of defenses to illness, such as white cells and natural killer cells of the blood. (p. 434)

imprinting (im´print-ing): A form of early learning that occurs in some animals during a critical period. (p. 307)

in-basket exercise: A type of management simulation task in which the individual attempts to solve a problem that is typical of the ones that appear in a manager's "in-basket." (p. 575)

incentives: External cues that activate motives. (p. 354)

incest (in´sest): Sexual relations between relatives. (p. 489)

independent variable: Variable whose quantitative value is independently controlled by the researcher. (p. 33)

individual differences The variations in development that make people different. (p. 339)

industrial-organizational (I/O) psychologists: Psychologists who study organizations and seek ways to improve the functioning and human benefits of business. (p. 571)

inhalants (in-hā´lants): Toxic substances that produce a sense of intoxication when inhaled. (p. 182)

inhibited female orgasm: A female sexual dysfunction in which the individual is unable to experience orgasm. (p. 494)

inhibited sexual desire: A condition in which a person desires sex rarely or not at all. (p. 492)

inner-directedness: A force that humanists believe all people possess that internally leads them to grow and improve. (p. 414)

insanity: A legal definition concerning a person's inability to tell right from wrong, ability to understand the trial proceedings, or whether the person is a direct danger to self or others. (p. 464)

insight (in´sīt): Form of cognitive change that involves recognition of previously unseen relationships. (p. 220)

insomnia: Sleep disorder in which the person has difficulty falling asleep or staying asleep. (p. 176)

insulin (in´su-lin): Hormone produced by the islets of Langerhans that reduces the amount of sugar in the bloodstream. (p. 79)

intelligence (in-tel´i-jens): The cognitive abilities of an individual to learn from experience, to reason well, and to cope with the demands of daily living. (p. 282)

intelligence quotient (IQ): A numerical value of intelligence derived from the results of an intelligence test. (p. 287)

intelligent tutoring systems: An approach to learning in which computers provide tutoring to students. (p. 594)

intensity: Density of vibrating air molecules, which determines the loudness of sound. (p. 132)

interference theory: The theory that forgetting occurs because similar memories interfere with the storage or retrieval of information. (p. 244)

interneurons: Neurons in the central nervous system that connect other neurons. (p. 56)

interpersonal psychotherapy: A form of psychological therapy, based on the theories of neo-Freudian Harry Stack Sullivan, that focuses on the accurate identification and communication of feelings and the improvement of current social relationships. (p. 502)

interview: A subjective method of personality assessment that involves questioning techniques designed to reveal the personality of a client. (p. 419)

intrinsic motivation (in-trin´sik): Human motives stimulated by the inherent nature of the activity or its natural consequences. (p. 362)

introspection (in´´tro-spek´shun): The process of looking inward at one's own consciousness. (p. 5)

introversion (in-tro-ver´zhun): According to Jung, the tendency of some individuals to be shy and to focus their attention on themselves. (p. 407)

ions (i´ons): Electrically charged particles. (p. 50)

iris (i´ris): Colored part of the eye behind the cornea that regulates the amount of light that enters. (p. 126)

islets of Langerhans (i´lets of lahng´er-hanz): Endocrine cells in the pancreas that regulate the level of sugar in the blood. (p. 79)

J

James-Lange theory of emotion: The theory that conscious emotional experiences are caused by feedback to the cerebral cortex from physiological reactions and behavior. (p. 377)

job performance ratings: Ratings of the actual performance of employees in their jobs by supervisors. (p. 574)

K

kinesthetic receptors (kin´es-thet´ik): Receptors in the muscles, joints, and skin that provide information about movement, posture, and orientation. (p. 137)

Korsakoff's syndrome (Kor-sak´ofs): A disorder involving both anterograde and retrograde amnesia caused by excessive use of alcohol. (p. 255)

L

language: A symbolic code used in communication. (p. 277)

latency stage: According to Freud, the fourth psychosexual stage (from about 6 to 11 years), during which sexual energy is sublimated and converted into socially valued activities. (p. 406)

latent content: According to Freud, the true meaning of dreams that is found in the symbols in their manifest content. (p. 175)

lateral hypothalamus: A portion of the hypothalamus involved in feeling hungry and starting to eat (the feeding center). (p. 353)

learned taste aversion (ah-ver´shun): Negative reaction to a particular taste that has been associated with nausea or other illness. (p. 223)

learning: Any relatively permanent change in behavior brought about through experience. (p. 194)

learning set: Improvement in the rate of learning to solve new problems through practice solving similar problems. (p. 222)

lens: Transparent portion of the eye that adjusts to focus light on the retina. (p. 126)

leptin (lep´tin): A hormone that plays a role in regulating hunger and metabolism. (p. 353)

levels of processing model: An alternative to the stage theory of memory stating that the distinction between short-term and long-term memory is a matter of degree rather than different kinds of memory and is based on how incoming information is processed. (p. 240)

libido: The energy of the life instincts of sex, hunger, and thirst. (p. 403)

life events: Psychologically significant events that occur in a person's life, such as divorce, childbirth, or change in employment. (p. 426)

light adaptation: Regaining sensitivity of the eye to bright light following an increase in overall illumination. (p. 128)

limbic system: A complex brain system, composed of the amygdala, hippocampus, and cingulate cortex, that works with the hypothalamus in emotional arousal. (p. 63)

linguistic relativity hypothesis: The idea that the structure of a language may influence the way individuals think. (p. 279)

long-term memory (LTM): The third stage of memory, involving the storage of information that is kept for long periods of time. (p. 230)

M

magnetic resonance imaging (MRI): Imaging technique using magnetic resonance to obtain detailed views of the brain structure and function. (p. 69)

mainstreaming: The practice of integrating children with special needs into regular classrooms. (p. 595)

major depression: An affective disorder characterized by episodes of deep unhappiness, loss of interest in life, and other symptoms. (p. 475)

male orgasmic disorder: A condition in which a male has persistent delayed or absence of an orgasm. (p. 494)

male sexual arousal disorders: Conditions in which sexual arousal does not occur in appropriate circumstances in a male. (p. 493)

management by objectives: The strategy of giving employees specific goals but giving them considerable freedom in deciding how to reach those goals. (p. 581)

mania (mā´nē-ah): A disturbance of mood in which the individual experiences a euphoria without cause that is characterized by unrealistic optimism and heightened sensory pleasures. (p. 479)

manifest content: According to Freud, the literal meaning of dreams. (p. 175)

mantras (man´trahz): Words or sounds containing religious meaning that are used during meditation. (p. 178)

Maslow's hierarchy of motives: The concept that more basic needs must be met before higher-level motives become active. (p. 364)

mastery learning: The concept that children should never progress from one learning task to another until they have mastered the more basic one. (p. 593)

maturation (mach´´u-rā´shun): Systematic physical growth of the body, including the nervous system. (p. 305)

mean: The average of a set of scores. (p. 36)

median: The middle of a set of scores that are ordered from smallest to largest where 50% have higher and 50% have lower scores. (p. 36)

medical therapies: Those therapies— including drug therapy, electroconvulsive therapy, and psychosurgery—generally designed to correct a physical condition that is believed to be the cause of a psychological disorder. (p. 518)

meditation (med´´i-tā-shun): Several methods of focusing concentration away from thoughts and feelings and generating a sense of relaxation. (p. 178)

medulla (mě-dula´h): The swelling just above the spinal cord within the hindbrain responsible for controlling breathing and a variety of reflexes. (p. 61)

menarche (mě-nar´kē): The first menstrual period. (p. 326)

menopause (men´o-pawz): The cessation of menstruation and the capacity to reproduce in women. (p. 334)

mental processes: Private psychological activities that include thinking, perceiving, and feeling. (p. 2)

mental set: A habitual way of approaching or perceiving a problem. (p. 271)

metabolism (me-tab´o-lizm): Process through which the body uses energy. (p. 80)

midbrain: The small area at the top of the hindbrain that serves primarily as a reflex center for orienting the eyes and ears. (p. 61)

mindfulness: The state of focusing conscious awareness completely on what is going on at the present moment. (p. 178)

mode: The most common score in a set of scores. (p. 37)

modeling: Learning based on observation of the behavior of another. (p. 222)

monocular cues (mon-ok´ū-lar): Eight visual cues that can be seen with one eye and that allow us to perceive depth. (p. 150)

monozygotic twins (mon´´ō-zī-got´ik): Twins formed from a single ovum; they are identical in appearance because they have the same genetic structure. (p. 93)

mood disorders: Psychological disorders involving depression and/or abnormal elation. (p. 475)

morphemes (mor´fēm): The smallest units of meaning in a language. (p. 278)

motivated forgetting: Forgetting that is believed to be based on the upsetting or threatening nature of the information that is forgotten. (p. 248)

motivation: The internal state or condition that activates and gives direction to our thoughts, feelings, and actions. (p. 351)

motive for affiliation: The need to be with other people and to have personal relationships. (p. 358)

motives: Internal states or conditions that activate behavior and give it direction. (p. 9)

multiple approach-avoidance conflict: Conflict that requires the individual to choose between two alternatives, each of which contains both positive and negative consequences. (p. 430)

myelin sheath (mī´e-lin): Insulating fatty covering wrapped around the axon that speeds the transmission of neural messages. (p. 51)

myoclonia (mi´´o-klō´nē-ah): An abrupt movement that sometimes occurs during the hypnagogic state in which the sleeper often experiences a sense of falling. (p. 166)

N

narcolepsy: Sleep disorder in which the person suddenly falls asleep during activities usually performed when fully awake, even when the person has had adequate sleep. (p. 176)

narcotics: Powerful and highly addictive depressants. (p. 184)

naturalistic observation: Research method based on recording behavior as it occurs in natural life settings. (p. 28)

negative reinforcement: Reinforcement that occurs when (1) a behavior is followed by the removal or the avoidance of a negative event, and (2) the probability that the behavior will occur in the future increases as a result. (p. 208)

neonatal period (ne´´ō-nā´tal): The first two weeks of life following birth. (p. 318)

nerve: Bundle of long neurons outside the brain and spinal cord. (p. 50)

neural pruning: Normal process of selective loss of gray matter in the brain over time, which is thought to improve the efficiency of neural systems by eliminating unnecessary cells. (p. 74)

neurogenesis (nu´rō jen´´i sis): Hypothesized growth of new neurons in adult mammals. (p. 75)

neuron (nuron): Individual nerve cell. (p. 49)

neuropeptides (nur-o-pep-tidz): Large group of neurotransmitters sometimes referred to as neuromodulators, because they appear to broadly influence the action of the other neurotransmitters. (p. 54)

neuroscience perspective: Viewpoint in psychology that focuses on the nervous system in explaining behavior and mental processes. (p. 10)

neurotransmitters (nu´rō-tranz´-mit-erz): Chemical substances, produced by axons, that transmit messages across the synapse. (p. 52)

night terrors: Upsetting nocturnal experiences that occur most often in preschool-age children during deep non-REM sleep. (p. 175)

nightmares: Dreams that occur during REM sleep and whose content is exceptionally frightening, sad, angry, or in some other way uncomfortable. (p. 175)

nocioceptors (nō´´-see-oh-sep´-turs): Receptors for stimuli that are experienced as painful. (p. 139)

norepinephrine (nor´ep-i-nef´rin): Hormone produced by the adrenal glands; neurotransmitter believed to be involved in vigilance and attention and released by sympathetic autonomic neurons and the adrenal glands. (p. 54)

normal distribution: Symmetrical pattern of scores on a scale in which a majority of the scores are clustered near the center and a minority are at the extremes. (p. 37)

norms: Standards (created by the scores of a large group of individuals) used as the basis of comparison for scores on a test. (p. 288)

novel stimulation: New or changed experiences. (p. 357)

nucleotides (noo´kli-uh-tīds): The four chemical compounds (adenine, thymine, guanine, and cystine) located on the double helix of DNA. (p. 94)

O

obedience: Doing what one is told to do by people in authority. (p. 534)

object permanence: The understanding that objects continue to exist when they are not in view. (p. 319)

objectivity: Lack of subjectivity in a test question so that the same score is given regardless of who does the scoring. (p. 288)

observational methods: Methods of personality assessment that involve watching a person's actual behavior in a natural or simulated situation. (p. 419)

obsessive-compulsive disorders: Disorders that involve obsessions (anxiety-provoking thoughts that will not go away) and/or compulsions (irresistible urges to engage in specific irrational behaviors). (p. 470)

occipital lobes (ok-sip´ī-tal): The part of the cerebral cortex, located at the base of the back of the head, that plays an essential role in the processing of sensory information from the eyes. (p. 68)

Oedipus complex (ed´i-pus): According to Freud, the unconscious wish of all male children to kill their fathers and sexually possess their mothers. (p. 405)

olfaction (ōl-fak´-shun): Sense of smell. (p. 144)

olfactory epithelium (ōl-fak´to-rē ep´´i-thē´lē-um): Sheet of receptor cells at the top of the nasal cavity. (p. 145)

operant conditioning (op´e-rant): Learning in which the consequences of behavior lead to changes in the probability of its occurrence. (p. 203)

operational definition: Definition used in science that is explicitly based on the procedures, or operations, used to measure a scientific phenomenon, including behavior. (p. 26)

opiates (ō´pē-ats): Narcotic drugs derived from the opium poppy. (p. 185)

opponent-process theory of motivation: Solomon's theory of the learning of new motives based on changes over time in contrasting feelings; theory of color vision contending that the visual system has two kinds of color processors, which respond to light in either the red-green or yellow-blue ranges of wavelength. (p. 361)

optic chiasm: Area in the brain where half of the optic nerve fibers from each eye cross to the opposite side of the brain. (p. 127)

optic nerve: Nerve that carries neural messages about vision to the brain. (p. 127)

optimal level of arousal: The apparent human need for a comfortable level of stimulation, achieved by acting in ways that increase or decrease it. (p. 357)

oral aggressive personality: A personality type in which the person seeks pleasure by being verbally hostile to others. (p. 405)

oral dependent personality: A personality type in which the person seeks pleasure through overeating, smoking, and other oral means. (p. 405)

oral stage: According to Freud, the first psychosexual stage (from birth to 1 year), in which id gratification is focused on the mouth. (p. 405)

organ of Corti (kor´tē): Sensory receptor in the cochlea that transduces sound waves into coded neural impulses. (p. 134)

organizational citizenship: Contributing to the organization by supporting its goals, cooperating with and helping fellow employees, and going beyond the requirements of the job to help the organization. (p. 575)

orgasm: The reflexive phase of the sexual response cycle accompanied by peak levels of arousal and pleasure and usually by ejaculation in males. (p. 367)

oval window: Membrane of the inner ear that vibrates in response to movement of the stirrup, creating waves in the fluid of the cochlea. (p. 134)

ovaries (o´vah-rēz): Female endocrine glands that secrete sex-related hormones and produce ova, or eggs. (p. 79)

P

pancreas (pan´krē-as): Organ near the stomach that contains the islets of Langerhans. (p. 79)

panic anxiety disorder: A pattern of anxiety in which long periods of calm are broken by an intensely uncomfortable attack of anxiety. (p. 467)

papillae (pah-pil´ē): Clusters of taste buds on the tongue. (p. 144)

parallel play: Playing near but not with another child. (p. 323)

paranoid schizophrenia (par´´ah-noid): A subtype of schizophrenia in which the individual holds delusions of persecution and grandeur that seriously distort reality. (p. 481)

parasympathetic nervous system (par´´uh-sim´´pa-thet´ik): The part of the autonomic nervous system that promotes bodily maintenance and energy conservation and storage under nonstressful conditions. (p. 58)

parathormone (par´´ah-thor´mōn): Hormone that regulates ion levels in neurons and controls excitability of the nervous system. (p. 80)

parathyroid glands (par´´ah-thī´roid): Four glands embedded in the thyroid that produce parathormone. (p. 80)

paraventricular nucleus: A part of the hypothalamus that plays a role in the motive of hunger by regulating the level of blood sugar. (p. 353)

parietal lobes (pah-rī´e-tal): The part of the cerebral cortex that is behind the frontal lobes at the top of the skull and that contains the somatosensory area. (p. 67)

partial reinforcement effect: Phenomenon whereby responses that have been reinforced on variable ratio or variable interval schedules are more difficult to extinguish than responses that have been continuously reinforced. (p. 215)

participative management: The practice of involving employees at all levels in management decisions. (p. 580)

passionate love: The mixture of romantic, sexual, and other feelings of love. (p. 557)

pedophilia (pe´´do-fil´ē-ah): The practice of obtaining pleasure from sexual contact with children. (p. 490)

penis envy: According to Freud, the desire of a girl to possess a penis. (p. 406)

perception (per-sep´-shun): Process of organizing and interpreting information received from the outside world. (p. 121)

perceptual constancy: Tendency for perceptions of objects to remain relatively unchanged in spite of changes in raw sensations. (p. 148)

performance tests: Employee selection tests that resemble the actual manual performance required on a job. (p. 574)

peripheral nervous system (pĕ-rif´´er-al): The network of nerves that branches from the brain and the spinal cord to all parts of the body. (p. 56)

person perception: The process of forming impressions of others. (p. 549)

person variables: All characteristics of an individual that are relatively enduring, such as ways of thinking, beliefs, or physiological reactivity to stress. (p. 438)

person × situation interactionism (in´´ter-ak´shun-izm): The view that behavior is influenced by a combination of the characteristics of both the person and the situation. (p. 412)

personal unconscious: According to Jung, the motives, conflicts, and information that are repressed by a person because they are threatening to that individual. (p. 407)

personality: The sum total of the typical ways of acting, thinking, and feeling that makes each person different from other people. (p. 395)

personality disorders: Psychological disorders that are believed to result from personalities that developed improperly during childhood. (p. 483)

persuasion: The process of changing another person's attitudes through arguments and other related means. (p. 539)

phallic personality (fal´ik): Personality type caused by fixation in the phallic stage in which the person is selfish, impulsive, and lacking in genuine feeling for others. (p. 406)

phallic stage (fal´ik): According to Freud, the third psychosexual stage (from 3 to 6 years), in which gratification is focused on the genitals. (p. 405)

pheromones: Chemicals that stimulate receptors in the vomeronasal organ in some animals, influencing some aspects of reproductive behavior. (p. 145)

phi phenomenon (fī fe-nom´ĕ-nom): Perception of apparent movement between two stationary stimuli. (p. 6)

phobia: An intense, irrational fear. (p. 466)

phonemes (fō´nēm): The smallest units of sound in a language. (p. 278)

pineal gland (pin´e-al): The endocrine gland that is largely responsible for the regulation of biological rhythms. (p. 80)

pinna (pin´nah): External part of the ear. (p. 133)

pitch: Experience of sound vibrations sensed as high or low. (p. 133)

pituitary gland (pǐ-tu´i-tār´´ē): The body's master gland, located near the bottom of the brain, whose secretions help regulate the activity of the other glands in the endocrine system. (p. 77)

placebo effect: Changes in behavior produced by a condition in a formal experiment thought to be inert or inactive, such as an inactive pill. (p. 35)

placenta: The organ that connects the fetus and the mother during prenatal development. (p. 317)

plasticity: Ability of parts of the brain, particularly the cerebral cortex, to acquire new functions that partly or completely replace the functions of a damaged part of the brain. (p. 73)

plateau phase: High levels of sexual arousal and pleasure that are maintained for variable periods of time. (p. 367)

pleasure principle: According to Freud, the attempt of the id to seek immediate pleasure and avoid pain, regardless of how harmful it might be to others. (p. 403)

polarization: The tendency for group discussion to make beliefs and attitudes more extreme. (p. 531)

polarized (-pō′lar-īz′d): Resting state of a neuron, when more negative ions are inside and more positive ions are outside the cell membrane. (p. 50)

polymorphic gene (pah′lī mor′fik): Gene that has more than one different version. (p. 94)

pons (ponz): The part of the hindbrain that is involved in balance, hearing, and some parasympathetic functions. (p. 61)

positive reinforcement (rē′′in-fors′ment): Any consequence of behavior that leads to an increase in the probability of its occurrence. (p. 204)

positron emission tomography (PET): Imaging technique that reveals the functions of the brain. (p. 69)

post-traumatic stress disorder (PTSD): Severe anxiety and distress that persists long after traumatic stress. (p. 468)

preconscious mind: That portion of the mind containing information that is not presently conscious but can be easily brought into consciousness. (p. 402)

prejudice: A harmful attitude based on inaccurate generalizations about a group of people. (p. 543)

premature ejaculation: A male sexual dysfunction in which the individual reaches orgasm and ejaculates sperm too early. (p. 494)

prenatal period: The time between conception and birth. (p. 317)

preoperational stage: In Piaget's theory, the period of cognitive development from ages 2 to 7. (p. 322)

pressure: Stress that arises from the threat of negative events. (p. 430)

primacy effect: The tendency for first impressions to heavily influence opinions about other people. (p. 550)

primary motives: Human motives for things that are necessary for survival, such as food, water, and warmth. (p. 351)

primary process thinking: According to Freud, the attempt by the id to satisfy its needs by forming a wish-fulfilling mental image of the desired object. (p. 403)

primary reinforcers: Innate positive reinforcers that do not have to be acquired through learning. (p. 205)

primary sex characteristics: Ovulation and menstruation in females and production of sperm in males. (p. 325)

proactive interference (pro-aktiv): Interference created by memories from prior learning. (p. 245)

problem solving: The cognitive process through which information is used to reach a goal that is blocked by some obstacle. (p. 269)

procedural memory: Memory for motor movements and skills. (p. 235)

progressive relaxation training: A method of learning to deeply relax the muscles of the body. (p. 447)

Project Follow Through: A federally sponsored program designed to help educate economically disadvantaged children. (p. 593)

projective test: A test that uses ambiguous stimuli designed to reveal the contents of the client's unconscious mind. (p. 419)

proximity principle (prok′sim′′-i-tee): Gestalt principle of perception that states that parts of a visual stimulus that are close together are perceived as belonging together. (p. 149)

psychoanalysis (sī′kō-ah-nal′i-sis): A method of psychotherapy developed by Freud based on his belief that the root of all psychological problems is unconscious conflicts among the id, the ego, and the superego. (p. 9)

psychoanalytic theory: Freud's theory that the origin of personality lies in the balance among the id, the ego, and the superego. (p. 407)

psychological motives: Motives related to the individual's happiness and well-being, but not to survival. (p. 357)

psychology: Science of behavior and mental processes. (p. 2)

psychometrics: Perspective in psychology founded by Binet that focuses on the measurement of mental functions. (p. 10)

psychophysics (sī′′kō-fiz′iks): Specialty area of psychology that studies sensory limits, sensory adaptation, and related topics. (p. 123)

psychosexual stages: In the personality theory of Sigmund Freud, developmental periods during which the sexual energy of the id finds different sources of satisfaction. (p. 405)

psychosurgery (sī′′kō-ser′jer-ē): A medical therapy that involves operating on the brain in an attempt to alleviate some types of mental disorders. (p. 520)

psychotherapy (sī-kō-ther′ah-pē): A form of therapy in which a trained professional uses methods based on psycho-

logical theories to help a person with psychological problems. (p. 499)

psychotropic drugs (sī′′ko-trōp′pik): The various classes of drugs, including stimulants, depressants, and hallucinogens, that alter conscious experience. (p. 181)

puberty (pū′ber-tē): The point in development at which the individual is first physically capable of sexual reproduction. (p. 325)

punishment: A negative consequence of a behavior, which leads to a decrease in the frequency of the behavior that produces it. (p. 209)

pupil (pyoo′pil): Opening of the iris. (p. 126)

Q

quantitative measures (kwon′ti-tā-tiv): Units of measure expressed in numerical terms. (p. 29)

R

random assignment: Requirement that participants be assigned randomly to experimental conditions in formal experiments rather than in a systematic way. (p. 34)

rape: The act of forcing sexual activity on an unwilling person. (p. 489)

ratio IQ: The intelligence quotient based on the ratio between the person's mental age and chronological age. (p. 287)

reality principle: According to Freud, the attempt by the ego to find safe, realistic ways of meeting the needs of the id. (p. 404)

reappraisal: Changing how a person thinks about or interprets a potentially stressful event to reduce its stressfulness. (p. 444)

recall method: A measure of memory based on the ability to retrieve information from long-term memory with few cues. (p. 238)

receptor sites: Sites on the neuron that receive the neurotransmitter substance. (p. 52)

recessive gene: Version of a polymorphic gene that produces a trait in an individual only when the same recessive gene has been inherited from both parents. (p. 96)

reciprocal determination (re-sip′′ro-kal): Bandura's observation that the individual's behavior and the social learning environment continually influence one another. (p. 411)

recognition method: A measure of memory based on the ability to select correct information from among the options provided. (p. 238)

reconstruction (schema) theory: The theory that information stored in LTM sometimes changes over time to become more consistent with our beliefs, knowledge, and expectations. (p. 245)

reflection (re-flek´shun): A technique in humanistic psychotherapy in which the therapist reflects the emotions of the client to help clients clarify their feelings. (p. 506)

refractory period: The period of time following orgasm during which males are incapable of sexual arousal. (p. 367)

rehearsal: Mental repetition of information to retain it longer in short-term memory. (p. 231)

relearning method: A measure of memory based on the length of time it takes to relearn forgotten material. (p. 238)

reliability: A test's ability to produce similar scores if the test is administered on different occasions or by different examiners. (p. 288)

REM sleep: Rapid-eye-movement sleep, characterized by movement of the eyes under the lids; often accompanies dreams. (p. 169)

replication: Repeating studies based on the scientific principle that the results of studies should be doubted until the same results have been found in similar studies by other researchers. (p. 27)

representativeness heuristic: The strategy of making judgments about the unknown on the assumption that it is similar to what we know. (p. 272)

repression: Sigmund Freud's theory that unpleasant information is often pushed into unconsciousness without our being aware of it. (p. 402)

resistance: Any form of patient opposition to the process of psychoanalysis. (p. 501)

resolution phase: The stage in the sexual response cycle following orgasm when arousal and pleasure diminish. (p. 367)

response prevention: Prevention of avoidance responses to ensure that the individual sees that the negative consequence will not occur to speed up the extinction of avoidance responses. (p. 215)

retarded ejaculation: A condition in which a male does not ejaculate despite adequate sexual stimulation. (p. 494)

reticular formation (reh-tik´ū-lar): Sets of neurons in the medulla and pons from which neurons project down the spinal cord to play a role in maintaining muscle tone and cardiac reflexes and upward throughout the cerebral cortex where they influence wakefulness, arousal level, and attention. (p. 61)

retina (ret´i-nah): Area at the back of the eye on which images are formed and that contains the rods and cones. (p. 127)

retroactive interference (ret´´rō-ak´tiv): Interference created by memories from later learning. (p. 245)

retrograde amnesia (ret´rō-grād): A memory disorder characterized by an inability to retrieve old long-term memories, generally for a specific period of time extending back from the beginning of the disorder. (p. 254)

reversibility (re-ver´sbil—tē): The concept understood by concrete operational children that logical propositions can be reversed (if 2 + 3 = 5, then 5 − 3 = 2). (p. 323)

rods: The 125 million cells located outside the center of the retina that transduce light waves into neural impulses, thereby coding information about light and dark. (p. 127)

role playing: A therapeutic technique in which the therapist and client act as if they were people in problematic situations. (p. 510)

rooting reflex: An automatic response in which an infant turns its head toward stimulation on the cheek. (p. 318)

round window: Membrane that relieves pressure from the vibrating waves in the cochlear fluid. (p. 134)

S

saccule, utricle (sak´ūl ū´tre-k´l): Fluid-filled sacs of the vestibular organ that inform the brain about the body's orientation. (p. 137)

sample: Group of human or nonhuman research participants studied to learn about an entire population of human beings or animals. (p. 26)

schizoid personality disorder (skiz´oid): A personality disorder characterized by blunted emotions, lack of interest in social relationships, and withdrawal into a solitary existence. (p. 483)

schizophrenia (skiz´´o-fren´-ē-ah): A psychological disorder involving cognitive disturbance (delusions and hallucinations), disorganization, and reduced enjoyment and interests. (p. 480)

school psychologists: Psychologists who aid schools by testing children to determine eligibility for placement in special education programs and who consult with teachers and parents. (p. 592)

science: Approach to knowledge based on systematic observation. (p. 2)

scientific method: Method of studying nature based on systematic observation and rules of evidence. (p. 25)

secondary reinforcers: Learned positive reinforcers. (p. 205)

secondary sex characteristics: Development of the breasts and hips in females; growth of the testes, broadening of the shoulders, lowered voice, and growth of the penis and facial hair in males; and growth of pubic and other body hair in both sexes. (p. 326)

sedatives: Depressants that in mild doses produce a state of calm relaxation. (p. 184)

self: According to humanists, the person one thinks one is. (p. 414)

self-actualization: According to Maslow, the seldomly reached full result of the inner-directed drive of humans to grow, improve, and use their potential to the fullest. (p. 365)

self-concept: Our subjective perception of who we are and what we are like. (p. 414)

self-efficacy: According to Bandura, the perception of being capable of achieving one's goals. (p. 411)

self-regulation: According to Bandura, the process of cognitively reinforcing and punishing our own behavior, depending on whether it meets our personal standards. (p. 412)

semantic content: The meaning in symbols, such as language. (p. 277)

semantic memory (se-man´tik): Memory for meaning without reference to the time and place of learning. (p. 235)

semicircular canals (sem´´ē-ser´kū-lar): Three nearly circular tubes in the vestibular organ that inform the brain about tilts of the head and body. (p. 137)

semipermeable (sem´´ē-pe´r-mē-ah-b´l): Surface that allows some, but not all, particles to pass through. (p. 50)

sensation (sen-sā´-shun): Process of receiving, translating, and transmitting messages from the outside world to the brain. (p. 121)

sense organs: Organs that receive stimuli. (p. 121)

sensorimotor stage: In Piaget's theory, the period of cognitive development from birth to 2 years. (p. 319)

sensory adaptation: Weakened magnitude of a sensation resulting from prolonged presentation of the stimulus. (p. 122)

sensory receptor cells: Cells in sense organs that translate messages into neural impulses that are sent to the brain. (p. 121)

sensory register: The first stage of memory, in which an exact image of each sensory experience is held briefly until it can be processed. (p. 230)

separation anxiety: The distress experienced by infants when they are separated from their caregivers. (p. 321)

serial position effect: The finding that immediate recall of items listed in a fixed order is often better for items at the beginning and end of the list than for those in the middle. (p. 239)

sex: The distinction between males and females based on biological characteristics. (p. 104)

sexual aversion disorder: A condition in which a person fearfully avoids sexual behavior. (p. 492)

sexual dysfunction: An inability to engage successfully or comfortably in normal sexual activities. (p. 492)

sexual harassment: Unwanted sexual advances, comments, or any other form of coercive sexual behavior by others. (p. 490)

sexual masochism (mas´-o-kizm): A condition in which receiving pain is sexually exciting. (p. 488)

sexual sadism (sād´izm): The practice of obtaining sexual pleasure by inflicting pain on others. (p. 488)

shaping: Strategy of positively reinforcing behaviors that are successively more similar to desired behaviors. (p. 207)

short-term memory (STM): The second stage of memory, in which five to nine bits of information can be stored for brief periods of time. (p. 231)

simulated management task: A contrived task requiring managerial skills that is given to candidates for management positions to evaluate their potential as managers. (p. 575)

similarity principle: Gestalt principle of perception that states that parts of a visual stimulus that are similar are perceived as belonging together. (p. 149)

situationism (sit´´ū-ā´shun-izm): The view that behavior is not consistent but is strongly influenced by different situations. (p. 412)

situational attribution: An explanation for behavior that is based on an external cause. (p. 549)

Skinner box: Cage for animals, equipped with a response lever and a food tray dispenser, used in research on operant conditioning. (p. 207)

sleep apnea: Sudden interruption of breathing during sleep. (p. 176)

sleep disorders: Disturbances of sleep. (p. 175)

sleeper effects: According to Hovland, the potential for low-credibility speakers to influence opinion after a period of time. (p. 538)

sleeptalking: Talking during any phase of the sleep cycle. (p. 175)

sleepwalking: Waking and carrying on complicated activities during the deepest part of non-REM sleep. (p. 175)

social anthropology (an´ thro¯pol´´e gee): Field of social science that studies the ways in which cultures are both similar and different from one another and how cultures influence human behavior. (p. 14)

social facilitation: An effect in which working in a group improves one's performance on individual projects. (p. 529)

social learning theory: The viewpoint that the most important parts of our behavior are learned from other persons in society—family, friends, and culture. (p. 8)

social loafing: The tendency of members of groups to work less hard when group performance is measured than when individual performance is measured. (p. 529)

social norms: Guidelines provided by every culture for judging acceptable and unacceptable behavior. (p. 533)

social phobia: A phobic fear of social interactions, particularly those with strangers and those in which the person might be viewed negatively. (p. 466)

social psychology: The branch of psychology that studies individuals as they interact with others. (p. 527)

social roles: Culturally determined guidelines that tell people what behavior is expected of them. (p. 533)

social skills training: The use of techniques of operant conditioning to teach social skills to persons who lack them. (p. 510)

social support: The role played by friends and relatives in providing advice, assistance, and someone in whom to confide private feelings. (p. 438)

sociocultural perspective: Theory of psychology that states it is necessary to understand a person's culture and other social influences to fully understand him/her. (p. 14)

solitary play: Playing alone. (p. 323)

somatic nervous system (sō-mat´ik): The part of the peripheral nervous system that carries messages from the sense organs to the central nervous system and from the central nervous system to the skeletal muscles. (p. 57)

somatization disorders (sō´´mah-ti-zā´shun): Intensely and chronically uncomfortable psychological conditions that involve numerous symptoms of somatic (body) illnesses without physical cause. (p. 471)

somatoform disorders (sōma´to-form): Disorders in which the individual experiences the symptoms of physical health problems that have psychological rather than physical causes. (p. 470)

somatoform pain disorders (sō-ma´to-form): Somatoform disorders in which the individual experiences a relatively specific and chronic pain that has a psychological rather than a physical cause. (p. 472)

somatosensory area: The strip of parietal cortex running parallel to the motor area of the frontal lobes that plays a role in body senses. (p. 67)

sound waves: Cyclical changes in air pressure that constitute the stimulus for hearing. (p. 132)

specialized end bulbs: Sensory receptor cells that detect pressure. (p. 138)

specific phobia: A phobic fear of one relatively specific thing. (p. 466)

spinal cord: The nerve fibers in the spinal column. (p. 48)

spontaneous recovery: Temporary increase in the strength of a conditioned response, which is likely to occur during extinction after the passage of time. (p. 216)

stage: One of several time periods in development that is qualitatively distinct from the periods that come before and after. (p. 310)

stage theory of memory: A model of memory based on the idea that we store information in three separate but linked memories. (p. 230)

standard deviation: Mathematical measure of how spread out scores are from the mean score. (p. 37)

standardization: Administering a test in the same way to all individuals. (p. 288)

statistical significance: Decision based on statistical calculations that a finding was unlikely to have occurred by chance. (p. 38)

stereotype: An inaccurate generalization on which a prejudice is based. (p. 543)

stimulants: Drugs that increase the activity of motivational centers in the brain, providing a sense of energy and well-being. (p. 182)

stimulus (stim´ ū-lus): Any aspect of the outside world that directly influences our behavior or conscious experience. (p. 121)

stimulus discrimination: Tendency for responses to occur more often in the presence of one stimulus than others. (p. 212)

stimulus generalization: Tendency for similar stimuli to elicit the same response. (p. 212)

stress: Any event or circumstance that strains or exceeds an individual's ability to cope. (p. 425)

structuralism (struk´tūr-al-izm): 19th-century school of psychology that sought to determine the structure of the mind through controlled introspection. (p. 5)

structuring: The activities of managers that organize and direct the work of employees. (p. 580)

subjective reality: Each person's unique perception of reality that, according to humanists, plays a key role in organizing our personalities. (p. 414)

sublimation (sub´´li-mā´shun): According to Freud, a form of displacement in which a socially desirable goal is substituted for a socially harmful goal; the best form of displacement for society as a whole. (p. 404)

superego: According to Freud, that part of the mind that opposes the desires of the id by enforcing moral restrictions and by striving to attain perfection. (p. 403)

surface structure: The superficial spoken or written structure of a statement. (p. 277)

survey method: Research method that uses interviews and questionnaires with individuals. (p. 27)

symbolization: In Rogers' theory, the process of representing experience, thoughts, or feelings in mental symbols of which we are aware. (p. 415)

sympathetic nervous system (sim´´pa-thet´ik): The part of the autonomic nervous system that prepares the body to respond to psychological or physical stress. (p. 58)

synapse (sin-aps´): Space between the axon of one neuron and another neuron. (p. 52)

synaptic facilitation: The process by which neural activity causes structural changes in the synapses that facilitate more efficient learning and memory. (p. 251)

synaptic gap: The small space between two neurons at a synapse. (p. 52)

synaptic terminal (si-nap´tik): The knoblike tips of axons. (p. 52)

synaptic vesicles: Tiny vessels containing stored quantities of the neurotransmitter substance held in the synaptic terminals of the axon. (p. 52)

syntax (sin´taks): The grammatical rules of a language. (p. 278)

T

tacit intelligence: The practical knowledge and skills needed to deal with everyday problems that are usually not taught in school. (p. 289)

tactile discs (tak´til): Sensory receptor cells that detect pressure. (p. 138)

taste cells: Sensory receptor cells for gustation located in the taste buds. (p. 144)

telegraphic speech: The abbreviated speech of 2-year-olds. (p. 320)

temporal lobes: The part of the cerebral cortex that extends back from the area of the temples beneath the frontal and parietal lobes and that contains areas involved in the sense of hearing and understanding language. (p. 67)

testes (tes´tēz): Male endocrine glands that secrete sex-related hormones and produce sperm cells. (p. 79)

testosterone (tes-tos´ter-ōn): A male sex hormone. (p. 79)

thalamus (thal´-a-mus): The part of the forebrain that primarily routes sensory messages to appropriate parts of the brain. (p. 62)

theories: Tentative explanations of facts and relationships in sciences. (p. 3)

thyroid gland (thī´roid): Gland below the voice box that regulates metabolism. (p. 80)

thyroxin (thīrok´sin): Hormone produced by the thyroid that is necessary for proper mental development in children and helps determine weight and level of activity in adults. (p. 80)

timbre (tam´br): Characteristic quality of a sound as determined by the complexity of the sound wave. (p. 133)

traits: Relatively enduring patterns of behavior (thinking, acting, and feeling) that are relatively consistent across situations. (p. 396)

transcendental state: Altered state of consciousness, sometimes achieved during meditation, that is said to transcend normal human experience. (p. 178)

transduction (trans-duk´shun): Translation of energy from one form to another. (p. 122)

transductive reasoning (trans-duk´tiv): Errors in understanding cause-and-effect relationships that are commonly made by preoperational children. (p. 322)

transference (trans-fer´ens): The phenomenon in psychoanalysis in which the patient comes to feel and act toward the therapist in ways that resemble how he or she feels and acts toward other significant adults. (p. 502)

transformational management: A style in which the manager attempts to positively transform employees for the better by setting a good example, clearly stating goals and helping employees achieve them, seeking innovative solutions, and mentoring and empowering employees. (p. 582)

transsexualism (trans-seks´u-ah-lizm): A condition in which an individual feels trapped in the body of the wrong sex. (p. 487)

transvestism (trans-ves´tizm): The practice of obtaining sexual pleasure by dressing in the clothes of the opposite sex. (p. 487)

trichromatic theory (trī´´krō-mat´ik): Theory of color vision contending that the eye has three different kinds of cones, each of which responds to light of one range of wavelength. (p. 128)

Type A personality: The pattern of behavior characterized most by intense competitiveness, hostility, overwork, and a sense of time urgency. (p. 439)

U

unconditioned response (UCR): Unlearned, inborn reaction to an unconditioned stimulus. (p. 197)

unconditioned stimulus (UCS): Stimulus that can elicit a response without any learning. (p. 197)

unconscious mind: The part of the mind of which we can never be directly aware; the storehouse of primitive instinctual motives and of memories and emotions that have been repressed. (p. 8)

V

vaginismus (vaj´´i-niz´mus): A female sexual dysfunction in which the individual experiences involuntary contractions of the vaginal walls, making the vagina too narrow to allow the penis to enter comfortably. (p. 493)

validity: The extent to which a test measures what it's supposed to measure. (p. 289)

variable: A factor that can be assigned a numerical value. (p. 29)

variable interval schedule: Reinforcement schedule in which the reinforcer is given following the first response occurring after a variable amount of time. (p. 206)

variable ratio schedule: Reinforcement schedule in which the reinforcer is given after a varying number of responses have been made. (p. 205)

ventromedial hypothalamus: A part of the hypothalamus involved in inhibiting eating when sufficient food has been consumed (the satiety center). (p. 353)

vestibular organ (ves-tib´ū-lar): Sensory structures in the inner ear that provide the brain with information about orientation and movement of the head and body. (p. 137)

vicarious punishment: Observed punishment of the behavior of a model, which also decreases the probability of the same behavior in the observer. (p. 222)

vicarious reinforcement (vī-kar´ē-us): Observed reinforcement of the behavior of a model, which also increases the probability of the same behavior in the observer. (p. 222)

visual acuity (vizh´u-al ah-ku´i-tē): Clarity and sharpness of vision. (p. 126)

visual illusion: Visual stimuli in which the cues used in visual perception create a false perception. (p. 153)

voyeurism (voi´yer-izm): The practice of obtaining sexual pleasure by watching members of the opposite sex undressing or engaging in sexual activities. (p. 489)

W

wavelength: The frequency of light waves, which determines the hue we perceive. (p. 125)

Weber's law: Law stating that the amount of change in a stimulus needed to detect a difference is in direct proportion to the intensity of the original stimulus. (p. 123)

Wernicke's aphasia: Form of aphasia in which persons can speak fluently (but nonsensically) and cannot make sense out of language spoken to them by others. (p. 68)

Wernicke's area: The language area of the cortex that plays an essential role in understanding spoken language. (p. 68)

Y

Yerkes-Dodson law: A law stating that effective performance is more likely if the level of arousal is suitable for the activity. (p. 358)

Z

zygote (zī′gōt): The stable cell resulting from fertilization; in humans, it has 46 chromosomes—23 from the sperm and 23 from the ovum. (p. 94)

References

A

Abbey, A. (1982). Sex differences in attributions for friendly behavior: Do males misperceive females' friendliness? *Journal of Personality and Social Psychology, 42,* 830–838.

Abbey, A., & Melby, C. (1986). The effects of nonverbal cues on gender differences in perceptions of sexual intent. *Sex Roles, 15,* 283–298.

Abbott, B. B., Schoen, L. S., & Badia, P. (1984). Predictable and unpredictable shock: Behavioral measures of aversion and physiological measures of stress. *Psychological Bulletin, 96,* 45–71.

Abe, O., Yamasue, H., Yamada, H., Masutani, Y., Kabasawa, H., Sasaki, H., et al. (2010). Sex dimorphism in gray/white matter volume and diffusion tensor during normal aging. *NMR Biomed, 23*(5), 446–458.

Abel, G., Barlow, D., Blanchard, E., & Guild, D. (1977). Components of rapists' arousal. *Archives of General Psychiatry, 34,* 895–908.

Abele, A. E. (2003). The dynamics of masculine-agentic and feminine-communal traits: Finding from a prospective study. *Journal of Personality and Social Psychology, 85,* 768–776.

Abhold, J. (1992). Unpublished doctoral dissertation, University of Arkansas, cited in Loftus, E. F. (1993). The reality of repressed memories. *American Psychologist, 48,* 518–537.

Aboa-Éboulé, C., Brisson, C., Maunsell, E., Mâsse, B., Bourbonnais, R., Vézina, M., et al. (2007). Job strain and risk of acute recurrent coronary heart disease events. *JAMA, 298,* 1652–1660.

Abrahamse, W., Steg, L., Vlek, C., & Rothengatter, T. (2007). The effect of tailored information, goal setting, and tailored feedback on household energy use, energy-related behaviors, and behavioral antecedents. *Journal of Environmental Psychology, 27,* 265–276.

Ackerman, D. (1991). *A natural history of the senses.* New York: Vintage Books.

Acocella, J. (1999). Creating hysteria: Women and multiple personality disorder. San Francisco: Jossey-Bass.

Adams, J. (1965). Inequity in social exchange. In L. Berkowitz (Ed.), *Advances in experimental social psychology* (Vol. 2). New York: Academic Press.

Adams, P. R., & Adams, G. R. (1984). Mount Saint Helens' ashfall: Evidence for a disaster stress reaction. *American Psychologist, 39,* 252–260.

Addis, M. E., Hatgis, C., Krasnow, A. D., Jacob, K., Bourne, L., & Mansfield, A. (2004). Effectiveness of cognitive-behavioral treatment for panic disorder versus treatment as usual in a managed care setting. *Journal of Consulting and Clinical Psychology, 72,* 625–635.

Ader, R. (Ed.). (1981). *Psychoneuroimmunology.* New York: Academic Press.

Ader, R., & Cohen, N. (1981). Conditioned immunopharmacologic responses. In R. Ader (Ed.), *Psychoneuroimmunology.* New York: Academic Press.

Ader, R., & Cohen, N. (1993). Psychoneuroimmunology: Conditioning and stress. *Annual Review of Psychology, 44,* 53–85.

Adolph, K. E., & Berger, S. A. (2006). Motor development. In W. Damon & R. Lerner (Series Eds.) & D. Kuhn & R. S. Siegler (Vol. Eds.), *Handbook of child psychology: Vol 2: Cognition, perception, and language* (6th ed.), 161–213. New York: Wiley.

Agumadu, C. O., Yosufufi, S. M., et al. (2004). Seasonal variation in mood in African American college students in the Washington, D.C., metropolitan area. *Archives of General Psychiatry, 161,* 1084–1089.

Ainsworth, M. D. S. (1979). Infant-mother attachment. *American Psychologist, 34,* 932–937.

Alaimo, K., Olson, C., & Frongillo, E. A. (2001). Food insufficiency and American school-aged children's cognitive, academic, and psychological development. *Pediatrics, 108,* 44–53.

Albert, K. A., Hemmings, H. C., Adamo, A. I. B., Potkin, S. G., Akbarian, S., Sandman, C. A., Cotman, C. W., Bunney, W. E., & Greengard, P. (2002). Evidence for decreased darpp-32 in the prefrontal cortex of patients with schizophrenia. *Archives of General Psychiatry, 59,* 705–712.

Aleman, A., Kahn, R. S., & Selten, J. (2003). Sex differences in the risk of schizophrenia: evidence from meta-analysis. *Archives of General Psychiatry, 60,* 565–571.

Allen, J. J., Iacono, W. G., Laravuso, J. J., & Dunn, L. A. (1995). An event-related potential investigation of posthypnotic recognition amnesia. *Journal of Abnormal Psychology, 104,* 421–430.

Allen, K. E., Hart, R. M., Buell, J. S., Harris, F. R., & Wolf, M. M. (1964). Effects of social reinforcement on isolate behavior of a nursery school child. *Child Development, 35,* 511–518.

Allen, L. S., & Gorski, R. A. (1992). Sexual orientation and the size of the anterior commissure in the human brain. *Proceedings of the National Academy of Sciences USA, 89,* 7199–7202.

Alloy, L. B., Abramson, L. Y., & Francis, E. L. (1999). Do negative cognitive styles confer vulnerability to depression? *Current Directions in Psychological Science, 8,* 128–132.

Alloy, L. B., Abramson, L. Y., Whitehouse, W. G., Hogan, M. E., Panzarella, C., & Rose, D. T. (2006). Prospective incidence of first onsets and recurrences of depression in individuals at high and low cognitive risk for depression. *Journal of Abnormal Psychology, 115,* 145–156.

Allport, G. W. (1937). *Personality: A psychological interpretation.* New York: Holt, Rinehart & Winston.

Allport, G. W. (1961). *Pattern and growth in personality.* New York: Holt, Rinehart & Winston.

Allport, G. W., & Odbert, H. S. (1936). Trait names: A psycholexical study. *Psychological Monographs, 47* (211), 1–171.

Altschule, M. D. (1965). *Roots of modern psychiatry* (2nd ed.). New York: Grune & Stratton.

Alvarez, G. A., & Cavanaugh, P. (2004). The capacity of visual short-term memory is set by both visual information load and by number of objects. *Psychological Science, 15,* 106–118.

Amato, P. (2010). Research on divorce: Continuing trends and new developments. *Journal of Marriage and Family, 72,* 650–666.

Amedi, A., Stern, W. M., Camprodon, J. A., Bermpohl, F., Merabet, L., Rotman, S., Hemond, C., Meijer, P., & Pascual-Leone, A. (2007). Shape conveyed by visual-to-auditory sensory substitution activates the lateral occipital complex. *Nature Neuroscience, 10,* 687–689.

American Psychiatric Association. (2000a). *Diagnostic and statistical manual of mental disorders (Fourth Edition-Text Revision).* Washington, DC: American Psychiatric Press.

American Psychiatric Association. (2000b). *Diagnostic and statistical manual of mental disorders* (4th ed.). Washington, DC: Author.

Ames, D. R., & Johar, G. V. (2009). I'll know what you're like when I see how you feel: How and when affective displays adjust behavior-based impressions. *Psychological Science, 20*(5), 586–593.

Amoore, J. E., Johnston, J. W., & Rubin, M. (1964, February). The stereo-chemical theory of odor. *Scientific American.*

Amso, D., & Casey, B. J. (2006). Beyond what develops when: Neuroimaging may inform how cognition changes with development. *Current Directions in Psychological Science, 15,* 24–29.

Anastasi, A. (1987). *Psychological testing* (6th ed.). New York: Macmillan.

Anderson, C. A. (1989). Temperature and aggression: Ubiquitous effects of heat on occurrence of human violence. *Psychological Bulletin, 106,* 74–96.

Anderson, C. A. (2001). Heat and violence. *Psychological Science, 10,* 33–38.

Anderson, C. A., Berkowitz, L., et al. (2003). The influence of media violence on youth. *Psychological Science in the Public Interest, 4,* 81–110.

Anderson, C. A., & Bushman, B. J. (2001). Effects of violent video games on aggressive behavior, aggressive cognition, aggressive affect, physiological arousal, and prosocial behavior: A meta-analytic review of the scientific literature. *Psychological Science, 12,* 353–359.

Anderson, C. A., Bushman, B. J., & Groom, R. W. (1997). Hot years and serious and deadly assault: Empirical tests of the heat hypothesis. *Journal of Personality and Social Psychology, 73,* 1213–1223.

Anderson, C. A., Ihori, N., Bushman, B. J., Rothstein, H. R., Shibuya, A., Swing, E. L., et al. (2010). Violent video game effect on aggression, empathy, and prosocial behavior in eastern and western countries: A meta-analytic review. *Psychological Bulletin, 136*(2), 151–173.

Anderson, C. A., Lindsay, J. J., & Bushman, B. J. (1999). Research in the psychological laboratory: Truth or triviality? *Current Directions in Psychological Science, 8,* 3–9.

Anderson, D., Huston, A., Althea, C., Schmitt, K., Linebarger, D., & Wright, J. (2001). Early childhood television viewing and adolescent behavior: The recontact study. *Monographs of the Society for Research in Child Development, 66,* 1–158.

Anderson, K. E., Lytton, H., & Romney, D. M. (1986). Mother's interactions with normal and conduct-disordered boys: Who affects whom? *Developmental Psychology, 22,* 604–609.

Anderson, M. (2001). Annotation: Conceptions of intelligence. *Journal of Child Psychology and Psychiatry, 42,* 287–298.

Anderson, S. L., Adams, G., & Plaut, V. (2008). The cultural grounding of personal relationship: The importance of attractiveness in everyday life. *Journal of Personality and Social Psychology, 95*(2), 352–368.

Andreasen, N. C. (1999). A unitary model of schizophrenia: Bleuler's "fragmented phrene" as schizoencephaly. *Archives of General Psychiatry, 56,* 781–787.

Andrews, B., Brewin, C. R., Rose, S., & Kirk, M. (2000). Predicting PTSD symptoms in victims of violent crime: The role of shame, anger, and childhood abuse. *Journal of Abnormal Psychology, 109,* 69–73.

Angoff, W. H. (1988). The nature-nurture debate, aptitudes, and group differences. *American Psychologist, 43,* 713–720.

Annon, J. (1984). Simple behavioral treatment of sexual problems. In J. M. Swanson & K. Forrect (Eds.), *Men's reproductive health.* New York: Springer.

Antoni, M. H., & others. (1990). Psychoneuroimmunology and HIV-1. *Journal of Consulting and Clinical Psychology, 58,* 38–49.

Antoni, M. H., Cruess, D. G., Cruess, S., Lutgendorf, S., Kumar, M., Ironson, G., Klimas, N., Fletcher, M. A., & Schneiderman, N. (2002). Cogitive-behavioral stress management intervention effects on anxiety, 24-hr urinary norepinephrine output, and T-cytotoxic suppressor cells over time among symptomatic HIV-infected gay men. *Journal of Consulting and Clinical Psychology, 68,* 31–45.

APA. (2009). Gold medal award for life achievement in psychology in the public interest. *American Psychologist, 64*(5), 363–365.

Aral, S. O., & Holmes, K. K. (1991). Sexually transmitted diseases in the AIDS era. *Scientific American,* pp. 62–70.

Ardrey, R. (1966). *The territorial imperative.* New York: Atheneum.

Arndt, S., Andreasen, N. C., Flaum, M., Miller, D., & Nopoulos, P. (1995). A longitudinal study of symptom dimensions in schizophrenia: Prediction and patterns of change. *Archives of General Psychiatry, 52,* 352–360.

Arnett, J. J. (1999). Adolescent storm and stress, reconsidered. *American Psychologist, 54,* 317–326.

Arnetz, B., & others. (1987). Immune function in unemployed women. *Psychosomatic Medicine, 49,* 3–18.

Arnold, M. B. (1960). *Emotion and personality* (2 Vols.). New York: Columbia University Press.

Aronson, E. (1995). *The social animal* (6th ed.). San Francisco: W. H. Freeman.

Aronson, E., Willerman, B., & Floyd, J. (1966). The effect of a pratfall on increasing interpersonal attractiveness. *Psychonomic Science, 4,* 227–228.

Arsenault, L. & others (2004). Causal association between cannabis and psychosis: An examination of the evidence. *British Journal of Psychiatry, 184,* 110–117.

Arthur, W., Jr., Day, E. A., McNelly, T. L., & Edens, P. S. (2003). A meta-analysis of the criterion-related validity of assessment center dimensions. *Personnel Psychology, 56,* 125–154.

Asakawa, K., & Csikszentmihalyi, M. (1998). Feelings of connectedness and internalization of values in Asian American adolescents. *Journal of Youth and Adolescence, 29,* 121–145.

Asarnow, J., Glynn, S., Pynoos, R. S., Nahum, J., Guthrie, D., Cantwell, D. P., & Franklin, B. (1999). When the earth stops shaking: Earthquake sequelae among children diagnosed for pre-earthquake psychopathology. *Journal of the American Academy of Child and Adolescent Psychiatry, 38,* 1016–1023.

Asch, S. (1946). Forming impressions of personality. *Journal of Abnormal and Social Psychology, 41,* 258–290.

Asch, S. (1956). Studies of independence and conformity. A minority of one against a unanimous majority. *Psychological Monographs, 70* (9, Whole No. 416).

Aschoff, J. (1981). *Handbook of behavioral neurobiology: Vol. 4. Biological rhythms.* New York: Plenum.

Ashby, F. G., & Maddox, W. T. (2005). Human category learning. *Annual Review of Psychology, 56,* 149–178.

Ashton, M. C., Lee, K., & Goldberg, L. R. (2004). A hierachical analysis of 1,710 English personality-descriptive adjectives. *Journal of Personality and Social Psychology, 87,* 707–721.

Association for Advancement of Behavior Therapy. (1978). *Ethical issues for human services* (pamphlet). New York: Author.

Astin, A. W., Korn, W. S., & Berz, E. R. (1991). *The American freshman: National norms for 1990.* Los Angeles: American Council on Education.

Atkinson, R. C., & Shiffrin, R. M. (1968). Human memory: A proposed system and its control processes. In K. W. Spence & J. T. Spence (Eds.), *The psychology of learning and motivation* (Vol. 2). New York: Academic Press.

Atkinson, R. K. (2002). Optimizing learning from examples using animated pedagogical agents. *Journal of Educational Psychology, 94,* 416–427.

Atlantis, E., Chow, C.-M., Kirby, A., & Singh, M. F. (2004). An effective exercise-based intervention for improving mental health and quality of life measures: A randomized controlled trial. *Preventive Medicine, 39,* 424–434.

Augustine, D. K., Gruber, K. D., & Hanson, L. R. (1990). Cooperation works. *Educational Leadership, 47,* 4–11.

Ausubel, D. P. (1960). The use of advance organizers in the learning and retention of meaningful verbal material. *Journal of Educational Psychology, 51,* 267–272.

Auvert, B., Taljaard, D., Lagarde, E., Sobngwi-Tambekou, J., Sitta, R., & Puren, A. (2005). Randomized, controlled intervention trial of male circumcision for reduction of HIV infection risk: The ANRS 1265 Trial. *PLoS Medicine, 2,* 1112–1122.

Axelrod, S. R., Morgan, C. A., & Southwick, S. M. (2005). Symptoms of post-traumatic stress disorder and borderline personality disorder in veterans of Operation Desert Storm. *American Journal of Psychiatry, 162,* 270–275.

B

Baddeley, A. (1992). Working memory. *Science, 255,* 556–559.

Baddeley, A. D. (1999). *Essentials of human memory.* Hove, England: Psychology Press/Taylor & Francis.

Bahrick, H. P. (1984). Semantic memory content in permastore: 50 years of memory for Spanish learned in school. *Journal of Experimental Psychology: General, 113,* 1–29.

Bahrick, H. P., Bahrick, P. O., & Wittlinger, R. P. (1975). Fifty years of memory for names and faces: A cross-sectional approach. *Journal of Experimental Psychology, 104,* 54–75.

Bailine, S., Fink, M., Knapp, R., Petrides, G., Husain, M. M., Rasmussen, K., & others. (2010). Electroconvulsive therapy is equally effective in unipolar and bipolar depression. *Acta Psychiatrica Scandinavica, 121*(6), 431–436.

Ball, K., MacFarlane, A., Crawford, D., Savige, G., Andrianopoulos, N., & Worsley, A. (2009). Can social cognitive theory constructs explain socio-economic variations in adolescent eating behaviours? A mediation analysis. *Health Education Research, 24*(3), 496–506.

Baker, H. (1969). Transsexualism: Problems in treatment. *American Journal of Psychiatry, 125,* 118–124.

Baker, T. B. (2004). Motivational influences on cigarette smoking. *Annual Review of Psychology, 55,* 463–491.

Baker, T. B., Japuntich, S. J., Hogle, J. M., McCarthy, D. E., & Curtin, J. J. (2006). Pharmacologic and behavioral withdrawal from addictive drugs. *Current Directions in Psychological Science, 15,* 232–236.

Baker, T. B., Piper, M. E., et al. (2004). Addiction motivation reformulated: An affective processing model of negative reinforcement. *Psychological Review, 111,* 33–51.

Balsam, K. F., Beauchaine, T. P., Mickey, R. M., & Rothblum, E. D. (2005). Mental health of lesbian, gay, bisexual, and heterosexual siblings: Effects of gender, sexual orientation, and family. *Journal of Abnormal Psychology, 114,* 471–476.

Baltes, P. B., & Staudinger, U. M. (1993). The search for a psychology of wisdom. *Current Directions in Psychological Science, 2,* 75–80.

Banaji, M. R., & Bhaskar, R. (1999). Implicit stereotypes and memory: The bounded rationality of social beliefs. In D. L. Schachter & E. Scarry (Eds.), *Memory, brain, and belief.* Cambridge, MA: Harvard University Press.

Bancroft, J., Graham, C. A., Janssen, E., & Sanders, S. A. (2009). The dual control model: Current status and future directions. *Journal of Sex Research, 46,* 121–142.

Bandelow, B., Wedekind, D., Pauls, J., Broocks, A., Hajak, G., & Ruther, E. (2000). Salivary cortisol in panic attacks. *American Journal of Psychiatry, 157,* 454–456.

Bandura, A. (1969). *Principles of behavior modification.* New York: Holt, Rinehart & Winston.

Bandura, A. (1973). *Aggression: A social learning analysis.* Englewood Cliffs, NJ: Prentice Hall.

Bandura, A. (1977). *Social learning theory.* Englewood Cliffs, NJ: Prentice Hall.

Bandura, A. (1982). Self-efficacy mechanism in human agency. *American Psychologist, 37,* 122–147.

Bandura, A. (1989). Human agency in social cognitive theory. *American Psychologist, 44,* 1175–1184.

Bandura, A. (1999a). Social cognitive theory of personality. In D. Cervone & others (Eds.), *The coherence of personality: Social cognitive bases of consistency, variability, and organization* (pp. 185–241). New York: Guilford Press.

Bandura, A. (1999b). Social cognitive theory of personality. In L. A. Pervin & O. P. John (Eds.), *Handbook of personality: Theory and research* (2nd ed., pp. 154–196). New York: Guilford.

Bandura, A., Blanchard, E. B., & Ritter, B. (1969). The relative efficacy of desensitization and modeling approaches for inducing behavioral, affective, and attitudinal changes. *Journal of Personality and Social Psychology, 13,* 173–199.

Bandura, A., & Bussey, K. (2004). On broadening the cognitive, motivational, and socio-structural scope of theorizing about gender development and functioning: Comment on Martin, Ruble, and Szkrybalo. *Psychological Bulletin, 130,* 691–701.

Bandura, A., Ross, D., & Ross, S. A. (1963). Imitation of film-mediated aggressive models. *Journal of Abnormal and Social Psychology, 66,* 3–11.

Banich, M. T. (1998). Integration of information between the two cerebral hemispheres. *Current Directions in Psychological Science, 7,* 32–37.

Banich, M. T., & Heller W. (1998). Evolving perspectives on lateralization of function.

Current Directions in Psychological Science, 7, 1–2.

Banks, M., & Salapatek, P. (1981). Infant pattern vision: A new approach based on the contrast sensitivity function. *Journal of Experimental Child Psychology, 31,* 1–45.

Barahal, H. S. (1958). 1000 prefrontal lobotomies. Five- to ten-year follow-up study. *Psychiatric Quarterly, 32,* 653–678.

Barber, T. X., & Wilson, S. C. (1977). Hypnosis, suggestions, and altered states of consciousness. Experimental evaluation of the new cognitive behavioral theory and the traditional trancestate theory of hypnosis. In W. E. Edmundson (Ed.), *Conceptual and investigative approaches to hypnosis and hypnotic phenomena.* New York: New York Academy of Sciences.

Bard, P. (1934). Emotion I: The neurohumoral basis of emotional reactions. In C. Murchison (Ed.), *Handbook of general experimental psychology.* Worcester, MA: Clark University Press.

Bargh, J. A., & Morsella, E. (2008). The unconscious mind. *Perspectives on Psychological Science, 3*(1), 73–79.

Barker, D. J. P. (Ed.) (1992). *Fetal and infant origins of adult disease.* New York: Wiley.

Barnes, D. E., Alexopoulos, G. S., Lopez, O. L., Williamson, J. D., & Yaffe, K. (2006). Depressive symptoms, vascular disease, and mild cognitive impairment: Findings from the Cardiovascular Health Study. *Archives of General Psychiatry, 63,* 273–280.

Barnes, K. E. (1971). Preschool play norms: A replication. *Developmental Psychology, 5,* 99–103.

Baron, A. S., & Banaji, M. R. (2006). The development of implicit attitudes: Evidence of race evaluations from ages 6 and 10 and adulthood. *Psychological Science, 17,* 53–58.

Baron, R., & Byrne, D. (1982). *Exploring social psychology* (2nd ed.). Boston: Allyn & Bacon.

Baron, R. A., & Ramsberger, V. M. (1978). Ambient temperature and the occurrence of collective violence: The "long hot summer" revisited. *Journal of Personality and Social Psychology, 36,* 351–360.

Barr, C. E., Mednick, S. A., & Munk-Jorgensen, P. (1990). Exposure to influenza epidemics during gestation and adult schizophrenia. *Archives of General Psychiatry, 47,* 869–874.

Barrett, L. F., Mesquita, B., Ochsner, K. N., & Gross, J. J. (2007). The experience of emotion. *Annual Review of Psychology, 58,* 373–403.

Barrick, M. R., Mount, M. K., & Judge, T. A. (2001). Personality and performance at the beginning of the new millennium: What do we know and where do we go next? *International Journal of Selection and Assessment, 9,* 9–30.

Barsky, A. J., Orav, E. J., & Bates, D. W. (2005). Somatization increases medical utilization and costs independent of psychiatric and medical comorbidity. *Archives of General Psychiatry, 62,* 903–910.

Bartels, M., van Beijsterveldt, C. E. M., & Boomsma, D. I. (2009). Breastfeeding, maternal education and cognitive function: A prospective study in twins. *Behavior Genetics, 39*(6), 616–622.

Bartlett, F. C. (1932). *Remembering: A study in experimental and social psychology.* New York: Cambridge University Press.

Bartoshuk, L. (1988). Taste. In R. C. Atkinson, R. J. Herrnstein, G. Lindzey, & R. D. Luce (Eds.), *Stevens' handbook of experimental psychology: Vol. 1. Perception and motivation.* New York: Wiley-Interscience.

Bartzokis, G., Beckson, M., Lu, P., Nuechterlein, K., Edwards, N., & Mintz, J. (2001). Age-related changes in frontal and temporal lobe volumes in men. *Archives of General Psychiatry, 58,* 461–465.

Basoglu, M., Marks, I., Livanou, M., & Swinson, R. (1997). Double-blindness procedures, rater blindness, and ratings of outcome: Observations from a controlled trial. *Archives of General Psychiatry, 54,* 744–748.

Bastien, C. H., Morin, C. M., Ouellet, M. C., Blais, F. C., & Bouchard, S. (2004). Cognitive-behavioral therapy for insomnia: Comparison of individual therapy, group therapy, and telephone consultations. *Journal of Consulting and Clinical Psychology, 72,* 653–659.

Batsell, W. (2000). Augmentation: Synergistic conditioning in taste-aversion learning. *American Psychological Society, 9,* 164–168.

Baum, A., Harpin, R. E., & Valins, S. (1975). The role of group phenomena in the experience of crowding. *Environment and Behavior, 7,* 185–198.

Baum, A., & Valins, S. (1977). *Architecture and social behavior: Psychological studies of social density.* Hillsdale, NJ: Erlbaum.

Baumeister, R. F. (1984). Choking under pressure: Self-consciousness and paradoxical effects of incentives on skillful performance. *Journal of Personality and Social Psychology, 46*(3), 610–620.

Baumeister, R. F., & Masicampo, E. J. (2010). Conscious thought is for facilitating social and cultural interactions: How mental simulations serve the animal-culture interface. *Psychological Review,* (3), 945–971.

Baumrind, D. (1983). Rejoinder to Lewis's reinterpretation of parental firm control effects: Are authoritative families really harmonious? *Psychological Bulletin, 94,* 132–142.

Baumrind, D. (1991). Parenting styles and adolescent development. In J. Brooks-Gunn, R. Lerner, & A. Peterson (Eds.), *The encyclopedia of adolescence.* New York: Garland.

Baxter, L. C., Saykin, A. J., Flashman, L. A., Johnson, S. C., Guerin, S. J., Babcock, D.R., & Wishart, H. A. (2003). Sex differences in semantic language processing: A functional MRI study. *Brain and Language, 84,* 264–272.

Bayer, C. P., Klasen, F., & Adam, H. (2007). Association of trauma and PTSD symptons with openness to reconciliation and feelings of revenge among former Ugandan and Congolese child soldiers. *JAMA, 298,* 555–559.

Bean, B. P. (2007). The action potential in mammalian central neurons. *Nature Reviews Neuroscience, 8,* 451–465.

Beatty, J. (1995). *Principles of behavioral neuroscience.* Madison, WI: Brown & Benchmark.

Beck, A. T. (1976). *Cognitive therapy and the emotional disorders.* New York: International Universities Press.

Beck, A. T. (1999). *Prisoners of hate: The cognitive basis of anger, hostility, and violence.* New York: HarperCollins.

Beck, A. T. (2008). The evolution of the cognitive model of depression and its neurobiological correlates. *American Journal of Psychiatry, 165*(8), 969–977.

Beck, A. T., Rush, A. J., Shaw, B. F., & Emery, G. (1979). *Cognitive therapy of depression.* New York: Guilford Press.

Beck, J. G. (1995). Hypoactive sexual desire disorder: An overview. *Journal of Consulting and Clinical Psychology, 63*, 919–927.

Becker, C. B., Smith, L. M., & Ciao, A. C. (2006). Peer-facilitated eating disorder prevention: A randomized effectiveness trial of cognitive dissonance and media advocacy. *Journal of Counseling Psychology, 53*(4), 550–555.

Beeman, M. J., & Chiarello, C. (1998). Complementary right- and left-hemisphere language comprehension. *Current Directions in Psychological Science, 7*, 2–8.

Beilock, S. L., & Carr, T. H. (2001). On the fragility of skilled performance: What governs choking under pressure? *Journal of Experimental Psychology, 130*(4), 701–725.

Beiman, I., Majestic, H., Johnson, S. A., Puente, A., & Graham, L. (1976). *Transcendental meditation versus behavior therapy: A controlled investigation.* Paper presented to the Association for the Advancement of Behavior Therapy.

Bellodi, L., Perna, G., Caldirola, D., Arancio, C., Bertani, A., & Di Bella, D. (1998). CO_2–induced panic attacks: A twin study. *American Journal of Psychiatry, 155*(9), 1184–1188.

Belmore, S. M. (1987). Determinants of attention during impression formation. *Journal of Experimental Psychology: Learning, Memory, and Cognition, 13*, 480–489.

Belmore, S. M., & Hubbard, M. L. (1987). The role of advance expectancies in person memory. *Journal of Personality and Social Psychology, 53*, 61–70.

Belzer, E. G. (1981). Orgasmic expulsions of women: A review and heuristic inquiry. *Journal of Sex Research, 17*, 1–12.

Bem, D. J. (1996). Exotic becomes erotic: A developmental theory of sexual orientation. *Psychological Review, 103*, 320–335.

Bem, S. (1974). The measurement of psychological androgyny. *Journal of Consulting and Clinical Psychology, 42*, 155–162.

Ben-Ari, A., & Lavee, Y. (2004). Cultural orientation, ethnic affiliation, and negative daily occurrences: A multidimensional cross-cultural analysis. *American Journal of Orthopsychiatry, 74*, 102–111.

Benbow, C. Persson., Lubinski, D., Shea, D. L., & Eftekhari-Sanjani, H. (2000). Sex differences in mathematical reasoning ability at age 13: Their status 20 years later. *Psychological Science, 11*, 474–480.

Benedict, R. F. (1934). *Patterns of culture.* Boston: Houghton Mifflin.

Benes, F. M. (1998). Images in neuroscience: Brain development, VIII. *American Journal of Psychiatry, 155*, 1489.

Benham, G., Woody, E. Z., Wilson, K. S., & Nash, M. R. (2006). Expect the unexpected: ability, attitude, and responsiveness to hypnosis. *Journal of Personality and Social Psychology, 91*, 342–350.

Benotsch, E. G., Brailey, K., Vasterling, J. J., & Sutker, P. B. (2000). War zone stress, personal and environmental resources, and PTSD symptoms in Gulf War veterans: A longitudinal perspective. *Journal of Abnormal Psychology, 109*, 205–213.

Benson, H. (1975). *The relaxation response.* New York: Morrow.

Ben-Zur, H. (2002). Associations of Type A behavior with the emotional traits of anger and curiosity. *Anxiety, Stress, and Coping, 15*, 95–104.

Berkowitz, L. (1989). Frustration-aggression hypothesis: Examination and reformulation. *Psychological Bulletin, 106*, 59–73.

Berkowitz, L. (1993). *Aggression: Its causes, consequences, and control.* New York: McGraw-Hill.

Bermant, G. (1976). Sexual behavior: Hard times with the Coolidge effect. In M. H. Siegel & H. P. Ziegler (Eds.), *Psychological research: The inside story.* New York: Harper & Row.

Bernstein, I. L. (1978). Learned taste aversions in children receiving chemotherapy. *Science, 200*, 1302–1309.

Bernstein, I. L. (1985). Learned food aversions in the progression of cancer and its treatment. In N. S. Braverman & P. Bernstein (Eds.), *Experimental assessments and clinical applications of conditioned food aversions. Annals of the New York Academy of Sciences, 443.*

Bernstein, I. L., Webster, M. M., & Bernstein, P. (1982). Food aversions in children receiving chemotherapy for cancer. *Cancer, 50*, 2961–2963.

Berscheid, E., Dion, K. K., Walster, E., & Walster, G. W. (1971). Physical attractiveness and dating choice: A test of the matching hypothesis. *Journal of Experimental Social Psychology, 7*, 173–189.

Berthoud, H. R., & Morrison, C. (2008). The brain, appetite, and obesity. *Annual Review of Psychology, 59*, 55–92.

Betancourt, H., & Lopez, S. R. (1993). The study of culture, ethnicity, and race in American psychology. *American Psychologist, 48* (6), 629.

Bettencourt, B. A., & Miller, N. (1996). Gender differences in aggression as a function of provocation: A meta-analysis. *Psychological Bulletin, 119*, 422–447.

Bhasin, S., Enzlin, P., Coviello, A., & Basson, R. (2007). Sexual dysfunction in men and women with endocrine disorders. *Lancet, 369*, 597–611.

Bianchi, S. M. & Milkie, M. A. (2010). Work and family research in the first decade of the 21st century. *Journal of Marriage and Family, 72*, 705–725.

Biederman, J., Petty, C. R., Monuteaux, M. C., Fried, R., Byrne, D., Mirton, T, Spencer, T., Wilens, T. E., & Faraone, S. V. (2010). Adult psychiatric outcomes of girls with attention deficit hyperactivity disorder: 11-year follow-up in a longitudinal case-control study. *American Journal of Psychiatry, 167*, 409–417.

Biernat, M. (2003). Toward a broader view of social stereotyping. *American Psychologist, 58*(12), 1019–1027.

Bigelow, H. J. (1850). Dr. Harlow's case of recovery from the passage of an iron bar through the head. *American Journal of Medical Science, 20*, 13–22.

Birch, H. C. (1945). The relation of previous experience to insightful problem solving. *Journal of Comparative Psychology, 38*, 367–383.

Bjorklund, D. F., & Green, B. L. (1992). The adaptive nature of cognitive immaturity. *American Psychologist, 47*, 46–54.

Bjorklund, D. F., & Kipp, K. (1996). Parental investment theory and gender differences in the evolution of inhibition mechanisms. *Psychological Bulletin, 120*, 163–188.

Bjorklund, D. F., & Shackleford, T. K. (1999). Differences in parental investment contribute to differences between men and women. *Current Directions in Psychological Science, 8*, 86–89.

Blair, I. V., Judd, C. M., & Chapleau, K. M. (2004). The influence of Afrocentric facial features in criminal sentencing. *Psychological Science, 15*(10), 674–679.

Blanchard, R., & others. (1996a). Birth order and sibling sex ratio in homosexual male adolescents and probably pre-homosexual feminine boys. *Developmental Psychology, 31*, 22–30.

Blanchard, R., & others. (1996b). Birth order and sibling sex ratio in two samples of Dutch gender-dysphoric homosexual males. *Archives of Sexual Behavior, 25*, 495–514.

Blanchard-Fields, F. (2007). Everyday problem solving and emotion. *Current Directions in Psychological Science, 16*, 26–31.

Blanchette, I., & Richards, A. (2004). Reasoning about emotional and neutral materials: Is logic affected by emotion? *Psychological Science, 15*, 745–752.

Blaustein, J. D. (2008). Neuroendocrine regulation of feminine sexual behavior: Lessons from rodent models and thoughts about humans. *Annual Review of Psychology, 59*, 93–118.

Blonder, L. X., Bowers, D., & Heilman, K. M. (1991). The role of the right hemisphere in emotional communication. *Brain, 114*, 1115–1127.

Bloom, B. S. (1974). Time and learning. *American Psychologist, 29*, 681–688.

Blum, D. (2002). *Love at Goon Park: Harry Harlow and the Science of Affection.* New York: Perseus Publishing.

Bly, J., Jones, R., & Richardson, T. (1986). Impact of worksite health promotion on healthcare costs and utilization: Evaluation of Johnson and Johnson's Life for Life program. *Journal of the American Medical Association, 256*, 3235–3240.

Bock, M. (1986). The influence of emotional meaning on the recall of words processed for form or self-reference. *Psychological Research, 48*, 107–112.

Bock, M., & Klinger, E. (1986). Interaction of emotion and cognition in word recall. *Psychological Research, 48*, 99–100.

Bogaert, A. F. (1998). Birth order and sibling sex ratio in homosexual and heterosexual nonwhite men. *Archives of Sexual Behavior, 27*, 467–473.

Bogaert, A. F. (2003). Number of older brothers and sexual orientation: New tests and the attraction/behavior distinction in two national probability samples. *Journal of Personality and Social Psychology, 84* (3), 644–652.

Bohman, M. (1996). Predispositions to criminality: Swedish adoption studies in retrospect. In G. R. Bock & J. A. Goode (Eds.), *Genetics of criminal and antisocial behavior.* Chichester, England: Wiley.

Bolger, N., & Amarel, D. (2007). Effects of social support visibility on adjustment to stress: Experimental evidence. *Journal of Personality and Social Psychology, 92,* 458–475.

Bolm-Andorff, U., Schwämmle, J., Ehlenz, K., Koop, H., & Kaffarnik, H. (1986). Hormonal and cardiovascular variations during a public lecture. *European Journal of Applied Physiology, 54,* 669–674.

Bonanno, G. A., Galea, S., Bucciarelli, A., & Vlahov, D. (2006). Psychological resilience after disaster: New York City in the aftermath of the September 11th terrorist attack. *Psychological Science, 17,* 181–186.

Bond, R., & Smith, P. B. (1996). Culture and conformity: A meta-analysis of studies using Asch's (1952b, 1956) line judgment task. *Psychological Bulletin, 119,* 111–137.

Bondareff, W., Raval, J., Woo, B., Hauser, D. L., & Colletti, P. M. (1990). Magnetic resonance imaging and the severity of dementia in older adults. *Archives of General Psychiatry, 47,* 47–51.

Borman, W. C. (2004). The concept of organizational citizenship. *Current Directions in Psychological Science, 13,* 238–241.

Bornstein M. H., Cote L. R., Maital S., Painter K., Park S. Y., Pascual L., Pecheux M. G., Ruel J., Venuti P., & Vyt A. (2004). Cross-linguistic analysis of vocabulary in young children: Spanish, Dutch, French, Hebrew, Italian, Korean, and American English. *Child Development. 75,* 1115–1139.

Bosmans, J. C., Geertzen, J. H., Post, W. J., van der Schans, C. P., & Dijkstra, P. U. (2010). Factors associated with phantom limb pain: A 3½-year prospective study. *Clinical Rehabilitation, 24*(5), 444–453.

Bostwick, W. B., Boyd, C. J., Hughes, T. L., & McCabe, S. E. (2010). Dimensions of sexual orientation and the prevalence of mood and anxiety disorders in the United States. *American Journal of Public Health, 100*(3), 468–475.

Bouchard, T. J. (2004). Genetic influences in human psychological traits: A survey. *Current Directions in Psychological Science, 13,* 148–151.

Bouchard, T. J., Jr. (2009). Genetic influence on human intelligence (Spearman's g): how much? *Annals of Human Biology, 36*(5), 527–544.

Bouchard, T. J., & McGue, M. (1981). Familial studies of intelligence: A review. *Science, 212,* 1055–1059.

Bousfield, W. A. (1953). The occurrence of clustering in recall of randomly arranged associates. *Journal of General Psychology, 49,* 229–240.

Bouton, M. E., Mineka, S., & Barlow, D. H. (2001). A modern learning theory perspective on the etiology of panic disorder. *Psychological Review, 108,* 4–32.

Bovbjerg, D. H. (2003). Conditioning, cancer, and immune regulation. *Brain, Behavior, and Immunity, 17,* S58–S61.

Bower, G. H. (1973). Educational applications of mnemonic devices. In K. O. Doyle (Ed.), *Interaction: Readings in human psychology.* Boston: D. C. Heath.

Bower, G. H., & Clark, M. C. (1969). Narrative stories as mediators for serial learning. *Psychonomic Science, 14,* 181–182.

Bowers, K. S. (1976). *Hypnosis for the seriously curious.* Monterey, CA: Brooks/Cole.

Boyce, C. J., Brown, G. D. A., & Moore, S. C. (2010). Money and happiness: Rank of income, not income, affects life satisfaction. *Psychological Science, 21,* 471–475.

Brainerd, C. J., Holliday, R. E., Reyna, V. F., Yang, Y., & Toglia, M. P. (2008). Developmental reversals in false memory: Effects of emotional valence and arousal. *Journal of Experimental Child Psychology, 107*(2), 137–154.

Brainerd, C. J., Reyna, V. F., Wright, R., & Mojardin, A. H. (2003). Recollection rejection: False-memory editing in children and adults. *Psychological Review, 110,* 762–784.

Brainerd, C. J., Stein, L. M., Silveira, R. A., Rohenkohl, G., & Reyna, V. F. (2008). How does negative emotion cause false memories? *Psychological Science, 19*(9), 919–925.

Bratzke, D., Rolke, B., Ulrich, R., & Peters, M. (2007). Central slowing during the night. *Psychological Science, 18,* 456–461.

Braun, M. F., & Bryan, A. (2006). Female waist-to-hip and male waist-to-shoulder ratios as determinants of romantic partner desirability. *Journal of Social and Personal Relationships, 23*(5), 805–819.

Bray, D. W., Campbell, R. J., & Grant, D. L. (1974). *Formative years in business: A long-term AT&T study of managerial lives.* New York: Wiley.

Bregante, J. L., Martinez, K., & O'Toole, C. J. (1993). *New bridges: Building community between disabled and nondisabled women.* Presentation at the Fifth International Interdisciplinary Conference on Women.

Brent, D. A., & Kolko, D. J. (1998). Psychotherapy: Definitions, mechanisms of action, and relationship to etiological models. *Journal of Abnormal Child Psychology, 26,* 17–25.

Breslau, N., Davis, G. C., Peterson, E. L., & Schultz, L. (1997). Psychiatric sequelae of posttraumatic stress disorder in women. *Archives of General Psychiatry, 54,* 81–87.

Breslau, N., Johnson, E., Hiripi, E., & Kessler, R. (2001). Nicotine dependence in the United States—prevalence, trends, and smoking persistence. *Archives of General Psychiatry, 58,* 810–816.

Breslau, N., Kessler, R. C., Chilcoat, H. D., Schultz, L. R., Davis, G. C., & Andreski, P. (1998). Trauma and posttraumatic stress disorder in the community. *Archives of General Psychiatry, 55,* 626–632.

Breslau, N., Lucia, V. C., & Alvarado, G. F. (2006). Intelligence and other predisposing factors in exposure to trauma and posttraumatic stress disorder: A follow-up study at age 17 years. *Archives of General Psychiatry, 63,* 1238–1245.

Breslow, L., & Enstrom, J. E. (1980). Persistence of health habits and their relationship to mortality. *Preventive Medicine, 9,* 469–483.

Brewin, C. R., Andrews, B., & Valentine, J. D. (2000). Meta-analysis of risk factors for posttraumatic stress disorder in trauma-exposed adults. *Journal of Consulting and Clinical Psychology, 68,* 748–766.

Briere, J., Downes, A., & Spensley, J. (1983). Summer in the city: Urban weather conditions and psychiatric emergency-room visits. *Journal of Abnormal Psychology, 92,* 77–80.

Briggs, G. C., Freeman, R. K., & Yaffe, S. J. (1986). *Drugs in pregnancy and lactation.* Baltimore: Williams & Wilkins.

Brody, A. L., Mandelkern, M. A., London, E. D., Olmstead, R. E., Farahi, J., Scheibal, D., et al. (2006). Cigarette smoking saturates brain and nicotinic acetycholine receptors. *Archives of General Psychiatry, 63,* 907–915.

Brody, N. (1997). Intelligence, schooling, and society. *American Psychologist, 52.*

Brown, A. S., Begg, M. D., Gravenstein, S., Schaefer, C. A., Wyatt, R. J., Bresnahan, M., Babulas, V. P., & Susser, E. S. (2004). Serologic evidence of prenatal influenza in the etiology of schizophrenia. *Archives of General Psychiatry, 61,* 774–780.

Brown, A. S., & Derkits, E. J. (2010). Prenatal infection and schizophrenia: A review of epidemiologic and translational studies. *American Journal of Psychiatry, 167,* 261–280.

Brown, K. W., & Ryan, R. M. (2003). The benefits of being present: Mindfulness and its role in psychological well-being. *Journal of Personality and Social Psychology, 84,* 822–848.

Brown, R., & Kulik, J. (1977). Flashbulb memories. *Cognition, 5,* 73–99.

Brown, R. W., & McNeil, D. (1966). The "tip of the tongue" phenomenon. *Journal of Verbal Learning and Verbal Behavior, 5,* 325–337.

Brownlee-Dufek, M., Peterson, L., Simonds, J. F., Goldstein, D., Kilo, C., & Hoette, S. (1987). The role of health beliefs in the regimen adherence and metabolic control of adolescents and adults with diabetes mellitus. *Journal of Consulting and Clinical Psychology, 55,* 139–144.

Bruck, M., & Ceci, S. (2004). Forensic developmental psychology. *Current Directions in Psychological Science, 13,* 229–232.

Bruner, J. S. (Ed.). (1974). *The growth of competence.* New York: Academic Press.

Bruner, J. S., & Goodman, C. C. (1947). Value and need as organizing factors in perception. *Journal of Abnormal and Social Psychology, 42,* 33–44.

Brunstein, J. C., & Maier, G. W. (2005). Implicit and self-attributed motives to achieve: Two separate but interacting needs. *Journal of Personality and Social Psychology, 89,* 205–222.

Bryant, R. A., & Guthrie, R. M. (2005). Maladaptive appraisals as a risk factor for posttraumatic stress: A study of trainee firefighters. *Psychological Science, 16,* 749–752.

Buchanan, T. W. (2007). Retrieval of emotional memories. *Psychological Bulletin, 133,* 761–779.

Buchert, R., Thomasius, R., et al. (2004). A voxel-based PET investigation of the long-term effects of ecstasy consumption on brain serotonin transporters. *American Journal of Psychiatry, 161,* 1181–1189.

Buchsbaum, M. (1983). The mind readers. *Psychology Today,* pp. 58–62.

Buck, L. B. (1996). Information coding in the vertebrate olfactory system. *Annual Review of Neuroscience, 19,* 517–544.

Buckhout, R. (1974). Eyewitness testimony. *Scientific American,* pp. 23–33.

Buckner, R. L., & Barch, D. (1999). Memory, 1: Episodic memory retrieval. *American Journal of Psychiatry, 156,* 1311.

Budney, A., Hughes, J., Moore, B., & Novy, P. (2001). Marijuana abstinence effects in marijuana smokers maintained in their environment. *Archives in General Psychiatry, 58,* 917–924.

Bullock, T., Bennett, M. V., Johnston, D., Josephson, R., Marder, E., & Fields, R. D. (2005). The neuron doctrine redux. *Science 310,* 791–793.

Burchinal, M. R., Campbell, F. A., Bryant, D. M., Wasik, B. H., & Ramey, C. T. (1997). Early intervention and mediating processes in cognitive performance of children of low-income African American families. *Child Development, 68,* 935–954.

Burger, J. M. (1986). Temporal effects on attributions: Actor and observer differences. *Social Cognition, 4,* 377–387.

Burger, J. M. (1999). The foot-in-the-door compliance procedure: A multiple-process analysis and review. *Personality and Social Psychology Review, 3*(4), 303–325.

Burgess, A. W., & Holstrom, K. L. (1974). Rape trauma syndrome. *American Journal of Psychiatry, 131,* 981–986.

Burt, S. A., McGue, M., DeMarte, J. A., Krueger, R. F., & Iacono, W. G. (2006). Timing of menarche and the origins of conduct disorder. *Archives of General Psychiatry, 63,* 890–896.

Bushman, B. J., Ridge, R. D., Das, E., Key, C. W., & Busath, G. L. (2007). When God sanctions killing: Effect of scriptural violence on aggression. *Psychological Science, 18,* 204–207.

Buss, D. M. (1995). Psychological sex differences: Origins through sexual selection. *American Psychologist, 50,* 164–168.

Buss, D. M. (1999). Human nature and individual differences: The evolution of human personality. In L. A. Pervin & O. P. John (Eds.), *Handbook of personality: Theory and research* (2nd ed.), (pp. 31–56). New York: Guilford.

Buss, D. M. (2001). Cognitive biases and emotional wisdom in the evolution of conflict between the sexes. *Psychological Science, 10,* 219–223.

Bussey, K., & Bandura, A. (1999). Social cognitive theory of gender development and differentiation. *Psychological Review, 106,* 676–713.

Butcher, H. J. (1968). *Human intelligence: Its nature and assessment.* New York: Harper Torchbooks.

Butler, R. A. (1953). Discrimination learning by rhesus monkey by visual-exploration motivation. *Journal of Comparative and Physiological Psychology, 46,* 95–98.

Butz, B. P., Duarte, M., & Miller, S. M. (2006). An intelligent tutoring system for circuit analysis. *IEEE Transactions on Education, 49,* 216–223.

Byne, W., Buchsbaum, M., Kemether, E., Hazlett, E., Shinwari, A., Mitropoulou, V., & Siever, L. (2001). Magnetic resonance imaging of the thalamic mediodorsal nucleus and pulvinar in schizophrenia and schizotypal personality disorder. *Archives in General Psychiatry, 58,* 133.

Byrnes, J. P., Miller, D. C., & Schafer, W. D. (1999). Gender differences in risk taking: A meta-analysis. *Psychological Bulletin, 125,* 367–383.

C

Cacioppo, J. T., Gardner, W. L., & Berntson, G. G. (1999). The affect system has parallel and integrative processing components: Form follows functions. *Journal of Personality and Social Psychology, 76,* 839–855.

Cadoret, R. J., Yates, W. R., Troughton, E., Woodward, G., & Stewart, M. A. (1995). Genetic-environmental interaction in the genesis of aggressivity and conduct disorders. *Archives of General Psychiatry, 52,* 916–924.

Cahn, B. R., & Polich, J. (2006). Meditation states and traits: EEG, ERP, and neuroimaging studies. *Psychological Bulletin, 132,* 180–211.

Calabrese, E. J. (2008). Stress biology and hormesis: The Yerkes-Dodson law in psychology—a special case of the hormesis dose response. *Critical Reviews in Toxicology, 38*(5), 453–462.

Calahan, D., & Room, R. (1974). *Problem drinking among American men.* New Brunswick, NJ: Rutgers Center of Alcohol Studies.

Caldwell, T. (2010). Academic performance in African American undergraduates: Effects of cultural mistrust, educational value, and achievement motivation. *Journal of Career Development, 36*(4), 348–369.

Calhoun, K. S., & Atkeson, B. M. (1989). *Treatment of rape victims.* New York: Pergamon Press.

Calkins, M. W. (1893). Statistics of dreams. *American Journal of Psychology, 5,* 311–343.

Campbell, D. E. (1961). The psychological effects of cerebral electroshock. In H. J. Eysenck (Ed.), *Handbook of abnormal psychology.* New York: Basic Books.

Campbell, D. E. (1978). *Interior office design and visitor response.* Paper presented to the American Psychological Association, Toronto.

Campbell, F. A., & Ramey, C. T. (1994). Effects of early intervention on intellectual and academic achievement: A follow-up study of children from low-income families. *Child Development, 65,* 684–698.

Campbell, F. A., & Ramey, C. T. (1995). Cognitive and school outcomes for high-risk African American students at middle adolescence: Positive effects of early intervention. *American Educational Research Journal, 32,* 743–772.

Cannon, T. D., Mednick, S. A., Parnas, J., Schulsinger, F., Praestholm, J., & Vestergaard, A. (1993). Developmental brain abnormalities in the offspring of schizophrenic mothers: I. Contributions of genetic and perinatal factors. *Archives of General Psychiatry, 50,* 551–564.

Cannon, T. D., van Erp, T. G. M., Huttunen, M., Lonnqvist, J., Salonen, O., Valanne, L., Poutanen, V. P., StandertskjoldNordenstam, C. G., Gur, R. E., & Yan, M. (1998). Regional gray matter, white matter, and cerebrospinal fluid distributions in schizophrenic patients, their siblings, and controls. *Archives of General Psychiatry, 55,* 1084–1091.

Cannon, W. B. (1927). The James-Lange theory of emotions: A critical examination and an alternative theory. *American Journal of Psychology, 39,* 106–124.

Cannon, W. B., & Washburn, A. L. (1912). An explanation of hunger. *American Journal of Physiology, 29,* 441–454.

Cano, A., & O'Leary, K. D. (2000). Infidelity and separations precipitate major depressive episodes and symptoms of nonspecific depression and anxiety. *Journal of Consulting and Clinical Psychology, 68,* 774–781.

Caplan, S. E. (2005). A social skill account of problematic Internet use. *Journal of Communication, 55*(4), 721–736.

Cappuccio, F. P., D'Elia, L., Strazzullo, P., & Miller, M. A. (2010). Sleep duration and all-cause mortality: a systematic review and meta-analysis of prospective studies. *Sleep, 33*(5), 585–592.

Carey, M. P., Carey, K. B., Maisto, S. A., Gordon, C. M., Schroder, KEE, & Vanable, P. A. (2004). Reducing HIV-risk behavior among adults receiving outpatient psychiatric treatment: Results from a randomized controlled trial. *Journal of Consulting and Clinical Psychology, 72* (2): 252–268.

Carmichael, L., Hogan, H. P., & Walter, A. A. (1932). An experimental study of the effect of language on the reproduction of visually perceived form. *Journal of Experimental Psychology, 15,* 73–86.

Carnagey, N. L., & Anderson, C. A. (2005). The effects of reward and punishment in violent video games on agressive affect, cognition, and behavior. *Psychological Science, 16,* 882–889.

Carney, S., Cowen, P., Geddes, J., Goodwin, G., Rogers, R., Dearness, K., & others. (2003). Efficacy and safety of electroconvulsive therapy in depressive disorders: A systematic review and meta-analysis. *LANCET, 361*(9360), 799–808.

Carpenter, P. A., Just, M. A., & Shell, P. (1990). What one intelligence test measures: A theoretical account of the processing in the Raven Progressive Matrices Test. *Psychological Review, 97,* 404–431.

Carroll, C. R. (1989). *Drugs in modern society* (2nd ed.). Dubuque, IA: Wm. C. Brown.

Carroll, C. R. (2000). *Drugs in modern society* (5th ed.). Boston: McGraw-Hill.

Carstensen, L. L., & Charles, S. T. (1998). Emotion in the second half of life. *Current Directions in Psychological Science, 7,* 144–149.

Carstensen, L. L., Isaacowitz, D. M., & Charles, S. T. (1999). Taking time seriously. A theory of socioemotional selectivity. *American Psychologist, 54,* 165–181.

Case, F. D. (1981). Dormitory architecture influences: Patterns of student social relations over time. *Environment and Behavior, 13,* 23–41.

Casey, B. J., Jones, R. M., Hare, T. A. (2008). The adolescent brain. *Annals of the New York Academy of Sciences, 1124,* 111–126.

Casey, M. B., Nuttall, R., & Pezaris, E. (1997). Mediators of gender differences in mathematics college entrance test scores: A comparison of spatial skills with internalized beliefs and anxieties. *Developmental Psychology, 33,* 669–680.

Casey, M. B., Nuttall, R., Pezaris, E., & Benbow, C. P. (1995). The influence of spatial ability on gender differences in mathematics college entrance test scores across diverse samples. *Developmental Psychology, 31,* 697–705.

Casper, L. M., & Bianchi, S. M. (2002). *Continuity and change in the American family.* Thousand Oaks, CA: Sage.

Caspi, A., & Herbener, E. S. (1990). Continuity and change: Assortative marriage and the consistency of personality in adulthood. *Journal of Personality and Social Psychology, 58,* 250–258.

Caspi, A., McClay, J., Moffitt, T. E., Mill, J., Martin, J., Craig, I. W., Taylo, A., & Poulton, R. (2002). Role of genotype in the cycle of violence in maltreated children. *Science, 297*(5582), 851–854.

Caspi, A., & Moffitt, T. E. (2006). Gene-environment interactions in psychiatry: Joining forces with neuroscience. *Nature Reviews Neuroscience, 7,* 583–590.

Caspi, A., Roberts, B. W., & Shiner, R. L. (2005). Personality development: Stability and change. *Annual Review of Psychology, 56,* 453–484.

Cassia, V. M., Turati, C., & Simion, F. (2004). Can a nonspecific bias toward top-heavy patterns explain newborns' fame preference? *Psychological Science, 15*(6), 379–383.

Cassidy, J., & Shaver, P. R. (Eds.) (2008). *Handbook of attachment: Theory, research and clinical applications* (2nd ed.). New York: Guilford Publications.

Castelluci, V., & Kandel, E. R. (1976). Presynaptic facilitation as a mechanism for behavioral sensitization in *Aplysia. Science, 194,* 1176–1178.

Ceci, S. J., & Williams, W. M. (1997). Schooling, intelligence, and income. *American Psychologist, 52,* 1051–1058.

Ceci, S. J., Williams, W. M., & Barnett, S. M. (2009). Women's underrepresentation in science: Sociocultural and biological considerations. *Psychological Bulletin, 135*(2), 218–261.

Center for Disease Control and Prevention (2005). A glance at the AIDS epidemic. www .cdc.gob/hiv/PUBS/Facts/At-AGlance.htm.

Cepeda-Benito, A., Reynoso, J. T., & Erath, S. (2004). Meta-analysis of the efficacy of nicotine replacement therapy for smoking cessation: Differences between men and women. *Journal of Consulting and Clinical Psychology, 72,* 712–722.

Cervone, D. (2004). The architecture of personality. *Psychological Review, 111,* 183–204.

Chambers, R., Lo, B. C. Y., & Allen, N. B. (2008). The impact of intensive mindfulness training on attentional control, cognitive style, and affect. *Cognitive Therapy and Research, 32*(3), 303–322.

Chambless, D. L., & Ollendick, T. H. (2001). Empirically supported psychological interventions: controversies and evidence. *Annual Review of Psychology, 52,* 685–716

Chapman, L. J., & Chapman, J. P. (1973). *Disordered thought in schizophrenia.* New York: Appleton-Century-Crofts.

Chemers, M. M. (1997). *An integrative theory of leadership.* Mahwah, NJ: Lawrence Erlbaum.

Chida, Y., & Hamer, M. (2008). Chronic psychosocial factors and acute physiological responses to laboratory-induced stress in healthy populations: A quantitative review of 30 years of investigations. *Psychological Bulletin, 134*(6), 829–885.

Chien, L., Ko, H., & Wu, J. Y. (2007). The five-factor model of personality and depressive symptoms: One-year follow-up. *Personality and Individual Differences, 43,* 1013–1023.

Chivers, M. L., Rieger, G., Latty, E., & Bailey, J. M. (2004). A sex difference in the specificity of sexual arousal. *Psychological Science, 15,* 736–744.

Choi, I., Nisbett, R. E., & Norenzayan, A. (1999). Causal attribution across cultures: Variation and universality. *Psychological Bulletin, 125,* 47–63.

Chomsky, N. (1957). *Syntactic structures.* The Hague: Mouton.

Christie, M. J., & Mallet, C. (2009). Endocannabinoids can open the pain gate. *Science Signaling, 2*(88).

Chruschel, T. L. (1982). General pharmacology and toxicology of alcohol. In F. Hoffmeister & G. Stille (Eds.), *Psychotropic agents. Part III: Alcohol and Psychotomimetics* (Vol. 55). New York: Springer-Verlag.

Chu, L.-W., Ma, E. S. K., Lam, K. K. Y., Chan, M. F., & Lee, D. H. S. (2005). Increased alpha 7 nicotinic acetylcholine receptor protein levels in Alzheimer's disease patients. *Dementia and Geriatric Cognitive Disorders. Vol. 19(2–3)* Feb., 106–112.

Chun, W. Y., & Kruglanski, A. W. (2006). The role of task demands and processing resources in the use of base-rate and individuating information. *Journal of Personality and Social Psychology, 91,* 205–217.

Church, R. M. (1969). Response suppression. In B. A. Campbell & R. M. Church (Eds.), *Punishment and aversive behavior.* New York: Appleton-Century- Crofts.

Cialdini, R. B., Bassett, R., Cacioppo, J. T., & Miller, J. A. (1978). Low-ball procedure for producing compliance: Commitment then cost. *Journal of Personality and Social Psychology, 36*(5), 463–476.

Cialdini, R. B., & Goldstein, N. J. (2004). Social influence: Compliance and conformity. *Annual Review of Psychology, 55,* 591–621.

Cialdini, R. B., Vincent, J. E., Lewis, S. K., Catalan, J., Wheeler, D., & Darby, B. L. (1975). Reciprocal concessions procedure for inducing compliance: The door-in-the-face technique. *Journal of Personality and Social Psychology, 31*(2), 206–215.

Cicchetti, D. (2006). Development and psychopathology. In Cicchetti & Cohen (2006) *Handbook of Developmental Psychopathology Volume 1,* pps. 1–18. NY: Wiley.

Clark, D. M., Ehlers, A., McManus, F., Hackmann, A., Fennell, M., Campbell, H., et al. (2003). Cognitive therapy versus fluoxetine in generalized social phobia: A randomized placebo-controlled trial. *Journal of Consulting and Clinical Psychology, 71,* 1058–1067.

Clark, K. B., & Clark, M. P. (1939). The development of self and the emergence of racial identification in Negro preschool children. *Journal of Social Psychology, 10,* 591–599.

Clark, R. D., & Hatfield, E. (1989). Gender differences in receptivity to sexual offers. *Journal of Psychology & Human Sexuality, 2,* 39–55.

Clarke, A. M., & Clarke, A. B. D. (Eds.). (1976). *Early experience: Myth and science.* New York: Appleton-Century-Crofts.

Clarke, G. N., Hornbrook, M., Lynch, F., Polen, M., Gale, J., Beardslee, W., O'Connor, E., & Seeley, J. (2001). A randomized trial of a group cognitive intervention for preventing depression in adolescent offspring of depressed parents. *Archives of General Psychiatry, 58,* 1127–1134.

Clendenen, V. I., Herman, C. P., & Polivy, J. (1994). Social facilitation of eating among friends and strangers. *Appetite, 23,* 1–13.

Clifford-Walton, V. A. (1998). Feminist perspectives on women's health research. In S. E. Romans & others (Eds.), *Folding back the shadows: A perspective on women's mental health.* Dunedin, New Zealand: University of Otago Press.

Cling, B. J. (2004). *Sexualized violence against women and children.* New York: Guilford Press.

Coccurello, R., & Moles, A. (2010). Potential mechanisms of atypical antipsychotic-induced metabolic derangement: Clues for understanding obesity and novel drug design. *Pharmacology & Therapeutics, 127*(3), 210–251.

Coe, C. L. & Lubach, G. R. (2008). Fetal programming: Prenatal origins of health and illness. *Current Directions in Psychological Science, 17,* 36–41.

Cohen, H., Kaplan, Z., Kotler, M., Kouperman, I., Moisa, R., & Grisaru, N. (2004). Repetitive transcranial magnetic stimulation of the right dorsolateral prefrontal cortex in post-traumatic stress disorder: A double-blind, placebo-controlled study. *American Journal of Psychiatry, 161,* 515–524.

Cohen, L. G., Celnik, P., Pascual-Leone, A., Corwell, B., Falz, L., Dambroasia, J., Honda, M., Sadato, N., Gerloff, C., & Catala, M. D. (1997). Functional relevance of cross-model plasticity in blind humans. *Nature, 389,* 180–183.

Cohen, S. (1996). Psychological stress, immunity, and upper respiratory infections. *Current Directions in Psychological Science, 5,* 86–90.

Cohen, S. (2004). Social relationships and health. *American Psychologist.* 676–684.

Cohen, S., Doyle, W. J., Turner, R., Alper, C. M., & Skoner D. P. (2003). Sociability and susceptibility to the common cold. *Psychological Science, 14* (5): 389–395.

Cohen, S., Janicki-Deverts, D., & Miller, G. E. (2007). Psychological stress and disease. *JAMA, 298,* 1685–1687.

Cohen, S., & Pressman, S. D. (2006). Positive affect and health. *Current Directions in Psychological Science, 15,* 122–125.

Cohn, E. G., & Rotton, J. (1997). Assault as a function of time and temperature: A moderator-variable time-series analysis. *Journal of Personality and Social Psychology, 72,* 1322–1334.

Coifman, K. G., Bonanno, G. A., Ray, R. D., & Gross, J. J. (2007). Does repressive coping promote resilience? Affective-autonomic response discrepancy during bereavement. *Journal of Personality and Social Psychology, 92,* 745–758.

Collins, N. L., & Miller, L. C. (1994). Self-disclosure and liking: A meta-analytic review. *Psychological Bulletin, 116*(3), 457–475.

Colby, C. Z., Lanzetta, J. T., & Kleck, R. E. (1977). Effects of the expression of pain on autonomic and pain tolerance responses to subject controlled pain. *Psychophysiology, 14,* 537–540.

Collaer, M. L., & Hines, M. (1995). Human behavioral sex differences: A role for gonadal hormones during early development? *Psychological Bulletin, 118,* 55–107.

Collins, A. M., & Loftus, E. F. (1975). A spreading activation theory of semantic processing. *Psychological Review, 82,* 407–428.

Coman, A., Manier, D., & Hirst, W. (2009). Forgetting the unforgettable through conversation: Socially shared retrieval-induced forgetting of September 11 memories. *Psychological Science, 20*(5), 627–633.

Comas-Díaz, L. (2000). An ethnopolitical approach to working with people of color. *American Psychologist, 55,* 1319–1325.

Compton, M. T., Kelley, M. E., Ramsay, C. E., Pringle, M., Goulding, S. M., Esterberg, M. L., Stewart, T., & Walker, E. F. (2009). Association of pre-onset cannabis, alcohol, and tobacco use with age at onset of prodrome and age at onset of psychosis in first-episode patients. *American Journal of Psychiatry,166,* 1251–1257.

Compton, W. M., Conway, K. P., Stinson, F. S., & Grant, B. F. (2006). Changes in the prevalence of major depression and comorbid substance use disorders in the United States between 1991–1992 and 2001–2002. *American Journal of Psychiatry, 163,* 2141–2147.

Confer, J. C., Easton, J. A., Fleischman, D. S., Goetz, C. D., Lewis, D. M., Perilloux, C., & others. (2010). Evolutionary psychology. Controversies, questions, prospects, and limitations. *American Psychologist, 65*(2), 110–126.

Conklin, H. M., & Iacono, W. G. (2002). Schizophrenia: A neurodevelopmental perspective. *Psychological Science, 11,* 33–37.

Constantino, M. J., Arnow, B. A., Blasey, C., & Agras, W. S. (2005). The association between patient characteristics and the therapeutic alliance in cognitive-behavioral and interpersonal therapy for bulimia nervosa. *Journal of Consulting and Clinical Psychology.* 73: 2, 203–11.

Contrada, R. J., Ashmore, R. D., Gary, M. L., Coups, E., Egeth, J. D., Sewell, A., Ewell, K., Goyal, T. M., & Chasse, V. (2000). Ethnicity-related sources of stress and their effects on well-being. *Psychological Science, 9,* 136–143.

Cook, E. W., Hodes, R. L., & Lang, P. (1986). Preparedness and phobia: Effects of stimulus content on human visceral learning. *Journal of Abnormal Psychology, 95,* 195–207.

Cooper, J. R., Blum, F. E., & Roth, R. H. (2003). *The biochemical basis of neuropharmacology* (8th ed.). New York: Oxford University Press.

Cooper, M. L. (2006). Does drinking promote risky sexual behavior? *Current Directions in Psychological Science, 15,* 19–23.

Copeland, W. E., Keeler, G., Angold, A., & Costello, E. (2010). Posttraumatic stress without trauma in children. *American Journal of Psychiatry.*

Corballis, M. C. (2004). The origins of modernity: Was autonomous speech the critical factor? *Psychological Review, 111,* 543–552.

Coren, S. (1996). Accidental death and the shift to daylight savings time. *Perceptual and Motor Skills, 83,* 921–922.

Coren, S. (2004). *The clocks within us.* Washington, DC: American Psychological Association.

Coren, S., & Girgus, J. S. (1978). *Seeing is deceiving: The psychology of visual illusions.* Hillsdale, NJ: Erlbaum.

Cornwell, R. E., Smith, M. J. L., Boothroyd, L. G., Moore, F. R., Davis, H. P., Stirrat, M., Tiddeman, B., & Perrett, D. I. Reproductive strategy, sexual development and attraction to facial characteristics. Philosophical Transactions of the Royal Society. *Biological Sciences, 361,* 2143–2154.

Correll, J., Park, B., Judd, C. M., & Wittenbrink, B. (2002). The police officer's dilemma: Using ethnicity to disambiguate potentially threatening individuals. *Journal of Personality and Social Psychology, 83,* 1314–1329.

Corrigan, P. (2004). How stigma interferes with mental health care. *American Psychologist, 5,* 614–625.

Costello E. J., Egger H. L., & Angold A. (2005). 10-year research update review: The epidemiology of child and adolescent psychiatric disorders: I. Methods and public health burden. *Journal of the American Academy of Child & Adolescent Psychiatry, 44*(10):972–986.

Cowan, N. (1987). Auditory sensory storage in relation to the growth of sensation and acoustic information extraction. *Journal of Experimental Psychology, 13,* 204–215.

Cowan, N. (1988). Evolving conceptions of memory storage, selective attention, and their mutual constraints within the human information-processing system. *Psychological Bulletin, 104,* 163–191.

Cowan, N., Chen, Z., & Rouder, J. N. (2004). Constant capacity in an immediate serial-recall task: A logical sequel to Miller (1956). *Psychological Science, 15,* 634–640.

Cox, M. G., & Geller, E. S. (2010). Prompting safety belt use: Comparative impact on the target behavior and relevant body language. *Journal of Applied Behavior Analysis, 43*(2), 321–325.

Craik, F., Moroz, T. M., Moscovitch, M., Stuss, D. T., Winocur, G., Tulving, E., & Kapur, J. (1999). In search of the self: A positron emission tomography study. *Psychological Science, 10,* 26–34.

Craik, F. I. M., & Lockhart, R. S. (1972). Levels of processing. A framework for memory research. *Journal of Verbal Learning and Verbal Behavior, 11,* 671–684.

Cromberg, H. S., & Robinson, T. E. (2004). Drugs, environment, brain, and behavior. *Current Directions in Psychological Science, 13,* 107–110.

Crosnoe, R., & Elder, G. H. (2004). From childhood to the later years: Pathways of human development. *Research on Aging, 26,* 623–654.

Cross, S. E., & Markus, H. R. (1999). The cultural constitution of personality. In L. A. Pervin & O. P. John (Eds.), *Handbook of personality: Theory and research* (2nd ed., pp. 378–396). New York: Guilford.

Crowley, S. J., Acebo, C., & Carskadon, M. A. (2007). Sleep, circadian rhythms, and delayed phase in adolescence. *Sleep Medicine, 8,*(6), 602–612.

Cuijpers, P., Straten, A. V., Andersson, G., & Oppen, P. V. (2008). Psychotherapy for depression in adults: A meta-analysis of comparative outcome studies. *Journal of Consulting and Clinical Psychology, 76*(6), 909–922.

D

Dale, N., & Kandel, E. R. (1990). Facilitatory and inhibitory transmitters modulate spontaneous transmitter release at cultured Aplysia sensorimotor synapses. *Journal of Physiology, 421,* 203–222.

Dalman, C., Allebeck, P., Cullberg, J., Grunewald, C., & Köster, M. (1999). Obstetric complications and the risk of schizophrenia. *Archives of General Psychiatry, 56,* 234–240.

Dalman, C., Allebeck, P., Gunnell, D., Harrison, G., Kristensson, K., Lewis, G., et al. (2008). Infections in the CNS during childhood and the risk of subsequent psychotic illness: a cohort study of more than one million Swedish subjects. *American Journal of Psychiatry, 165,* 59–65.

Damasio, A. (2001). Fundamental feelings. *Nature, 413,* 781.

Darley, J., & Latané, B. (1968). Bystander intervention in emergencies. Diffusion of responsibility. *Journal of Personality and Social Psychology, 8,* 377–383.

Darwin, C. (1871). *The descent of man and selection in relation to sex* (Vols. 1 and 2). London: Murray.

Darwin, C. (1899). *The expression of the emotions in man and animals.* New York: Appleton.

Dasgupta, N., & Rivera, L. M. (2006). From automatic antigay prejudice to behavior: The moderating role of conscious beliefs about gender and behavioral control. *Journal of Personality and Social Psychology, 91,* 268–280.

Davatzikos, C., Shen, D., Gur, R. C., Wu, X., Liu, D., Fan, Y., et al. (2005). Whole-brain morphometric study of schizophrenia revealing a spatially complex set of focal abnormalities. *Archives of General Psychiatry, 62,* 1218–1227.

Davidson, R. J. (1992). Emotion and affective style: Hemispheric substrates. *Psychological Science,* 39–43.

Davidson, R. J., Ekman, P., Saron, C. D., Senulis, J. A., & Friesen, W. V. (1990). Approach-withdrawal and cerebral asymmetry: Emotional expression and brain physiology. *Journal of Personality and Social Psychology, 58,* 330–341.

Davis, M., Myers, K. M., Ressler, K., & Rothbaum, B. O. (2005). Facilitation of extinction of conditioned fear by d-cycloserine. *Current Directions in Psychological Science, 14,* 214–219.

Davis, S., & Mirick, D. K. (2006). Circadian disruption, shift work and the risk of cancer: A summary of the evidence and studies in Seattle. *Cancer Causes Control, 17,* 539–545.

Davydov, D. M., Stewart, R., Ritchie, K., & Chaudieu, I. (2010). Resilience and mental health. *Clinical Psychology Review, 30,* 479–495.

de Bruin, W. B., Fischhoff, B., & Parker, A. M. (2007). Individual differences in adult decision making competence. *Journal of Personality and Social Psychology, 92,* 938–956.

De Castro, J. M. (1994). Family and friends produce greater social facilitation of food intake than other companions. *Physiology & Behavior, 56*(3), 445–455.

de Jonge, P., Honig, A., van Melle, J. P., Schene, A. H., Kuyper, A. M. G., Tulner, D., et al. (2007). Nonresponse to treatment for depression following myocardial infarction: Association with subsequent cardiac events. *American Journal of Psychiatry, 164,* 1371–1378.

de Mello, M. F., de Jesus Mari, J., Bacaltchuk, J., Verdeli, H., & Neugebauer, R. (2005). A systematic review of research findings on the efficacy of interpersonal therapy for depressive disorders. *European Archives of Psychiatry and Clinical Neuroscience, 255,* 75–82.

De Rooij, S. R., Wouters, H., Yonker, J. E., Painter, R. C., & Roseboom, T. J. (2010). Prenatal undernutrition and cognitive function in late adulthood. *Proceedings of the National Academy of Sciences, 107,* 16881–16886.

de Vries, G. J., & Sodersten, P. (2009). Sex differences in the brain: The relation between structure and function. *Hormones and Behavior, 55*(5), 589–596.

de Waal, F. B. M. (2002). Evolutionary psychology: The wheat and the chaff. *Current Directions in Psychological Science,* 187–191.

Deary, I. J., Batty, G. D., & Gale, C. R. (2008). Bright children become enlightened adults. *Psychological Science, 19*(1), 1–6.

Dedic, H., Rosenfield, S., Cooper, M., & Fuchs, M. (2001). "Do I really hafta?"; Webcal, a look at the use of livemath software in Web-based materials that provide interactive engagement in a collaborative learning environment for differential calculus. *Educational Research and Evaluation, 7,* 285–312.

Deese, J., & Deese, E. K. (1979). *How to study* (3rd ed.). New York: McGraw-Hill.

Deikman, A. J. (1980). De-automization and the mystic experience. In J. R. Tisdale (Ed.), *Growing edges in the psychology of religion* (pp. 201–217). Chicago: Nelson-Hall.

Dember, W. N. (1965). The new look in motivation. *American Scientist, 53,* 409–427.

Denson, T. F., Spanovic, M., & Miller, N. (2009). Cognitive appraisals and emotions predict cortisol and immune responses: A meta-analysis of acute laboratory social stressors and emotion inductions. *Psychological Bulletin, 135*(6), 823–853.

DeRubeis, R. J., Gelfand, L. A., Tang, T. Z., & Simons, A. D. (1999). Medications versus cognitive behavior therapy for severely depressed outpatients: Mega-analysis of four randomized comparisons. *American Journal of Psychiatry, 156,* 1107–1013.

D'Esposito, M. (2000). Functional imaging of neurocognition. *Seminars in Neurology, 20,* 487–498.

DeSteno, D., Dasgupta, N., Bartlett, M. Y., & Cajdric, A. (2004). Prejudice from thin air: The effect of emotions on automatic intergroup attitudes. *Psychological Science, 15,* 319–324.

Devan, B. D., Petri, H. L., Mishkin, M., Stouffer, E. M., Bowker, J. L., Yin, P.-B., Buffalari, D. M., & Olds, James L. (2002). A room with a view and a polarizing cue: Individual differences in the stimulus control of place navigation and passive latent learning in the water maze. *Neurobiology of Learning and Memory, 78,* 79–99.

Devine, P. G. (1996, January/February). Breaking the prejudice habit. *Psychological Science Agenda,* 10–11.

Dew, M. A., Ragni, M. V., & Nimorwicz, P. (1990). Infection with human immuno-deficiency virus and vulnerability to psychological distress. *Archives of General Psychiatry, 47,* 437–445.

Dewsbury, D. A. (1990). Early interactions between animal psychologists and animal activists and the founding of the APA Committee on Precautions in Animal Experimentation. *American Psychologist, 45,* 315–327.

Diamond, E. L. (1982). The role of anger and hostility in essential hypertension and coronary heart disease. *Psychological Bulletin, 92,* 410–433.

Diamond, L. M. (2007). A dynamical systems approach to the development and expression of female same-sex sexuality. *Perspectives on Psychological Science, 2,* 142–161.

Diamond, L. M., Fagundes, B. P., & Butterworth, M. R. (2010). Intimate relationships across the life span. Temperament and personality through the life span. In M. Lamb & A. Freund (Eds). *The handbook of life-span development: Social and emotional development: Vol. 2.* 379–433. Hoboken, NJ: Wiley.

Dickens, W. T., & Flynn, J. R. (2006). Black Americans reduce the racial IQ gap. *Psychological Science, 17,* 913–920.

Dickerson, C. A., Thibodeau, R., Aronson E., & Miller, D. (1992). Using cognitive dissonance to encourage water conservation. *Journal of Applied Social Psychology, 22*(11), 841–854.

Diekman, A. B., Brown, E. R., Johnston, A. M., & Clark, E. K. (2010). Seeking congruity between goals and roles: a new look at why women opt out of science, technology, engineering, and mathematics careers. *Psychological Science.*

Diener, E., Oishi, S., & Lucas, R. E. (2003). Personality, culture, and subjective well-being: Emotional and cognitive evaluations of life. *Annual Review of Psychology, 54,* 403–425.

Diener, E., & Seligman, M. E. P. (2002). Very happy people. *Psychological Science, 13,* 81–84.

Diener, E., & Seligman, M. E. P. (2004). Beyond money. *Psychological Science in the Public Interest, 5,* 1–31.

Diener, M. J., Hilsenroth, M. J., & Weinberger, J. (2007). Therapist affect focus and patient outcomes in psychodynamic psychotherapy: A meta-analysis. *American Journal of Psychiatry, 164,* 936–941.

Dijksterhuis, A., & Aarts, H. (2010). Goals, attention, and (un)consciousness. *Annual Review of Psychology, 61,* 467–490.

Dijksterhuis, A., & Nordgren, L. F. (2006). A theory of unconscious thought. *Perspectives on Psychological Science, 1,* 95–108.

Dindia, K., & Allen, M. (1992). Sex differences in self-disclosure: A meta-analysis. *Psychological Bulletin, 112,* 106–124.

Dipboye, R. L., Fromkin, H. L., & Wilback, K. (1975). The importance of applicant sex, attractiveness, and scholastic standing in evaluation of job application resumes. *Journal of Applied Psychology, 60,* 39–43.

Dishman, R. K. (1982). Compliance/adherence in health-related exercise. *Health Psychology, 1,* 237–267.

Ditzen, B., Schaer, M., Gabriel, B., Bodenmann, G., Ehlert, U., & Heinrichs, M. (2009). Intranasal oxytocin increases positive communication and reduces cortisol levels during couple conflict. *Biological Psychiatry, 65,* 728–731.

Dobson, K. S., Dimidjian, S., Kohlenberg, R. J., & others. (2008). Randomized trial of behavioral activation, cognitive therapy, and antidepressant medication in the prevention of relapse and recurrence in major depression. *Journal of Consulting and Clinical Psychology, 76*(3), 468–477.

Doernberger, C., & Zigler, E. (1993). Project Follow Through: Intent and reality. In E. Zigler & S. J. Styfco (Eds.), *Head Start and beyond: A national plan for extended childhood intervention* (p. 155). New Haven, CT: Yale University Press.

Dohanich, G. (2003). Ovarian steroids and cognitive function. *Current Directions in Psychological Science, 22,* 57–61.

Dohr, K. B., Rush, A. J., & Bernstein, I. H. (1989). Cognitive biases and depression. *Journal of Abnormal Psychology, 98,* 263–267.

Dohrenwend, B. (2006). Inventorying stressful life events as risk factors for psychopathology: Toward resolution of the problem of intracategory variability. *Psychological Bulletin, 132,* 477–495.

Dollard, J., Doob, L. W., Miller, N. E., Mowrer, O. H., & Sears, R. R. (1939). *Frustration and aggression.* New Haven, CT: Yale University Press.

Dolnick, E. (1993). Deafness as culture. *Atlantic Monthly, 272,* 37–53.

Domjan, M. (2005). Pavlovian conditioning: A functional perspective. *Annual Review of Psychology, 56,* 179–206.

D'Onofrio, B. M., Van Hulle, C. A., Waldman, I. D., Rodgers, J. L., Rathouz, P. J., & Lahey, B. B. (2007). Causal inferences regarding prenatal alcohol exposure and childhood externalizing problems. *Archives of General Psychiatry, 64,* 1296–1304.

Donohoe, M. L., Von Hippel, W., & Brooks, R. C. (2009). Beyond waist-hip ratio: Experimental multivariate evidence that average women's torsos are most attractive. *Behavioral Ecology, 20*(4), 716–721.

Donovan, M. R., Glue, P., Kolluri, S., & Emir, B. (2010). Comparative efficacy of antidepressants in preventing relapse in anxiety disorders—a meta-analysis. *Journal of Affective Disorders, 123*(1–3), 9–16.

Dovidio, J. F., & Gaertner, S. L. (1999). Reducing prejudice: Combating intergroup biases. *Current Directions in Psychological Science 8,* 101–105.

Dovidio, J. F., & Gaertner, S. L. (2000). Aversive racism and selection decisions: 1989 and 1999. *American Psychological Society, 11,* 315–319.

Dozois, D. J. A., & Dobson, K. S. (2001). Information processing and cognitive organization in unipolar depression: Specificity and comorbidity issues. *Journal of Abnormal Psychology, 110,* 236–246.

Draganski, B. (2004). Changes in grey matter induced by training. *Nature 247,* 311–312.

Dragoi, V., & Staddon, J. E. R. (1999). The dynamics of operant conditioning. *Psychological Review, 106,* 20–61.

Dravnieks, A. (1983). Odor character profiling. *Journal of the Air Pollution Control Association, 33,* 752–755.

Druss B. G., & Marcus S. C. (2004). Use of psychotropic medications before and after Sept. 11, 2001. *American Journal of Psychiatry. 161* (8): 1377–1382.

Dudai, Y. (2004). The neurobiology of consolidation, or, how stable is the engram? *Annual Review of Psychology, 55,* 51–86.

Dulac, C. & Axel, R. (1998). Expression of candidate pheromone receptor genes in vomeronasal neurons. *Chemical Senses, 23,* 467–475.

Duncker, K. (1945). On problem solving. *Psychological Monographs, 58*(5).

Dunlosky, J., Rawson, K. A., & Hacker, D. J. (2002). Metacomprehension of science text: Investigating the levels-of-disruption hypothesis. In J. Otero, Leon J. A., & Graesser A. C. (Eds.). *The psychology of science text comprehension.* (pp. 255–279). Mahwah, NJ: Lawrence Erlbaum Associates.

Durston, S., Hulshoff, H., Casey, B. J., Giedd, J., Buitelaar, J., & van Engeland, H. (2001). Anatomical MRI of the developing human brain: What have we learned? *Journal of American Academy of Child & Adolescent Psychiatry, 40,* 1012–1019.

Dutton, D. G., & Aron, A. P. (1974). Some evidence for heightened sexual attraction under conditions of high anxiety. *Journal of Personality and Social Psychology, 30,* 510–517.

E

Eagly, A. H. (1978). Sex differences in influence-ability. *Psychological Bulletin, 85,* 86–116.

Eagly, A. H. (1995). The science and politics of comparing women and men. *American Psychologist, 50,* 145–158.

Eagly, A. H. (2009). The his and hers of prosocial behavior: An examination of the social psychology of gender. *American Psychologist, 64*(8), 644–658.

Eagly, A. H., Diekman, A. B., Johannesen-Schmidt, M. C., & Koenig, A. M. (2004). Gender gaps in sociopolitical attitudes: A social psychological analysis. *Journal of Personality and Social Psychology, 87,* 796–816.

Eagly, A. H., Johannesen-Schmidt, M. C., & van Engen. (2003). Transformational, transactional, and laissez-faire leadership styles: A meta-analysis comparing women and men. *Psychological Bulletin, 129,* 569–591.

Eagly, A. H., & Wood, W. (1999). The origins of sex differences in human behavior: Evolved dispositions versus social roles. *American Psychologist, 54,* 408–423.

Eastwick, P. W. (2009). Beyond the pleistocene: Using phylogeny and constraint to inform the evolutionary psychology of human mating. *Psychological Bulletin, 135,* 794–821.

Eaton, W. W., Anthony, J. C., Gallo, J., Cai, G., Tien, A., Romanoski, A., Lyketsos, C., & Chen, L. (1997). Natural history of diagnostic interview schedule/DSM-IV major depression. *Archives of General Psychiatry, 54,* 993–999.

Ebert, P. D., & Hyde, J. S. (1976). Selection for agonistic behavior in wild female *Mus musculus. Behavior Genetics, 6,* 291–304.

Eby, L. T., Maher, C. P., & Butts, M. M. (2010). The intersection of work and family life: The role of affect. *Annual Review of Psychology, 61,* 599–622.

Eckhardt, C. I. (2007). Effects of alcohol intoxication on anger experience and expression among partner assaultive men. *Journal of Consulting and Clinical Psychology, 75,* 61–71.

Ehlers, A., Clark, D. M., Hackmann, A., & others. (2003). A randomized controlled trial of cognitive therapy, a self-help booklet, and repeated assessments as early interventions for posttraumatic stress disorder. *Archives of General Psychiatry, 60*(10), 1024–1032.

Eibl-Eibesfeldt, I. (1968). Ethology of human greeting behavior. *Zeitschrift fuer Tierpsychologie, 25,* 727–744.

Eibl-Eibesfeldt, I. (1973). The expressive behavior of the deaf and blind-born. In M. von Cranach & I. Vine (Eds.), *Social communication and movement.* New York: Academic Press.

Eidelson R. J., & Eidelson J. I. (2003). Dangerous ideas: Five beliefs that propel groups toward conflict. *American Psychologist,* 182–192.

Ekman, P. (1992). Facial expressions of emotion: New findings, new questions. *Psychological Science, 3,* 34–38.

Elkind, D. (1967). *Children and adolescents: Interpretive essays on Jean Piaget.* New York: Oxford University Press.

Elkind, D. (1981). Understanding the young adolescent. In L. D. Steinberg (Ed.), *The life cycle: Readings in human development.* New York: Columbia University Press.

Elkind, D., & Bowen, R. (1979). Imaginary audience behavior in children and adolescents. *Developmental Psychology, 15,* 38–44.

Ellegren, H., & Parsch, J. (2007). The evolution of sex-biased genes and sex biased gene expression. *Nature Reviews Genetics 8,* 689–698.

Elliot, A. J., & Church, M. A. (1997). A hierarchical model of approach and avoidance achievement motivation. *Journal of Personality and Social Psychology, 72,* 218–232.

Elliott, W. J. (2001). Cyclic and circadian variations in cardiovascular events. *American Journal of Hypertension,14*(9), S291–S295 .

Ellis, A. (1962). *Reason and emotion in psychotherapy.* New York: Lyle Stuart.

Ellis, A. (1999). *How to make yourself happy and remarkably less disturbable.* Atascadero, CA: Impact.

Ellis, B. (2004). Timing of pubertal maturation in girls: an integrated life history approach. *Psychological Bulletin, 130,* 920–958.

Ellis, B. J., & Boyce, W. T. (2008). Biological sensitivity to context. *Current Directions in Psychological Science, 17*(3), 183–187.

Ellis, H. C. (1987). Recent developments in human memory. In V. Mokosky (Ed.), *The G. Stanley Hall Series.* Washington, DC: American Psychological Association.

Ellis, H. C., & Hunt, R. R. (1993). *Fundamentals of cognitive psychology.* Madison, WI: Brown & Benchmark.

Ellis, L. (1989). *Theories of rape: Inquiries into causes of sexual aggression.* New York: Hemisphere.

Ellison, J. A., Greenberg, L. S., Goldman, R. N., & Angus, L. (2009). Maintenance of gains following experiential therapies for depression. *Journal of Consulting and Clinical Psychology, 77*(1), 103–112.

Else-Quest, N. M., Hyde, J. S., & Linn, M. C. (2010). Cross-national patterns of gender differences in mathematics: A meta-analysis. *Psychological Bulletin, 136*(1), 103–127.

Emery, V. O., & Oxmans, T. E. (1992). Update on the dementia spectrum of depression. *American Journal of Psychiatry, 149,* 305–317.

Engdahl, B., Dikel, T. N., Eberly, R., & Blank, A. (1997). Posttraumatic stress disorder in a community group of former prisoners of war: A normative response to severe trauma. *American Journal of Psychiatry, 154*(11), 1576–1581.

Engle, S. A. (1999). Using neuroimaging to measure mental representations: Finding color-opponent neurons in visual cortex. *Current Directions in Psychological Science, 8,* 23–27.

Epstein, S. (1982). Conflict and stress. In L. Goldberger & S. Breznitz (Eds.), *Handbook of stress.* New York: Free Press.

Epstein, S., & Roupenian, A. (1970). Heart rate and skin conductance during experimentally induced anxiety. *Journal of Personality and Social Psychology, 16,* 20–28.

Erikson, E. (1963). *Childhood and society.* New York: Norton.

Erlenmeyer-Kimling, L., & Jarvik, L. F. (1963). Genetics and intelligence: A review. *Science, 142,* 1477–1479.

Ernst, M. O., & Bulthoff, H. H. (2004). Merging the senses into a robust percept. *Trends In Cognitive Sciences, 8,* 162–169.

Erren, T. C., Pape, H. G., Reiter, R. J., & Piekarsk, C. (2008). Chronodisruption and cancer. *Naturwissenschaften, 95,* 367–382.

Eubanks-Carter, C., Burckell, L. A., & Goldfried, M. R. (2005). Enhancing therapeutics effectiveness with lesbian, gay, and bisexual clients. *Clinical Psychology: Science and Practice, 12,* 1–18.

Eulenburg, V., & Gomeza, J. (2010). Neurotransmitter transporters expressed in glial cells as regulators of synapse function. *Brain Research Reviews, 63,* 103–112.

Evans, J. S. T., & Thompson, V. A. (2004). Informal reasoning: Theory and method. *Canadian Journal of Experimental Psychology, 58,* 69–74.

Evers, S. E., Bass, M., Donner, A., & McWhinney, I. R. (1987). Lack of impact on salt restriction advice on hypertensive patients. *Preventive Medicine, 16,* 213–220.

Exline, J. J., & Lobel, M. (1999). The perils of outperformance: Sensitivity about being the target of a threatening upward comparison. *Psychological Bulletin, 125,* 307–337.

Exner, J. (1986). *The Rorschach: A comprehensive system: Vol. 2. Current research and advanced interpretation.* New York: Wiley.

Eyal, T., Liberman, N., Trope, Y., Walther, E., & Liberman, N. (2004). The pros and cons of temporally near and distant action. *Journal of Personality and Social Psychology, 86,* 781–795.

Ezell, C. (1994). The long and short of short- and long-term memory. *Journal of NIH Research, 6,* 56–61.

Ezell, C. (1995). Fat times for obesity research: Tons of new information, but how does it all fit together? *Journal of NIH Research, 7,* 39–43.

F

Fabricatore, A. N., & Wadden, T. A. (2006). Obesity. *Annual Review of Clinical Psychology, 2,* 357–377.

Fagot, B. I. (1974). Sex differences in toddlers' behavior and parental reaction. *Developmental Psychology, 10,* 554–558.

Fan, W., & Williams, C. M. (2010). The effects of parental involvement on students' academic self-efficacy, engagement and intrinsic motivation. *Educational Psychology, 30*(1), 53–74.

Farooqi, I. S., Bullmore, E., Keogh, J., Gillard, J., O'Rahilly, S., & Fletcher, P. C. (2007). Leptin regulates striatal regions and human eating behavior. *Science, 317,* 1355.

Farrell, M. P., & Rosenberg, S. D. (1981). *Men at midlife.* Boston: Auburn House.

Fava, G. A., Ruini, C., Rafanelli, C., Finois, L., Conti, S., & Grandi, S. (2004). Six-year outcome of cognitive behavior therapy for prevention of recurrent depression. *American Journal of Psychiatry, 161,* 1872–1876.

Fawzi, F. I., & others. (1990). A structured psychiatric intervention for cancer patients: 2. Changes over time in immunological measures. *Archives of General Psychiatry, 47,* 729–736.

Fay, N., Garrod, S., & Carletta, J. (2000). Group discussion as interactive dialogue. *Psychological Science, 11,* 481–486.

Feifel, H. (1990). Psychology and death: Meaningful rediscovery. *American Psychologist, 45,* 537–543.

Fein, S., & Spencer, S. J. (1997). Prejudice as self-image maintenance: Affirming the self through derogating others. *Journal of Personality and Social Psychology, 73,* 31–44.

Feingold, A. (1988). Matching for attractiveness in romantic partner and same-sex friends: A meta-analysis and theoretical critique. *Psychological Bulletin, 104,* 226–235.

Feingold, A. (1990). Gender differences in effects of physical attractiveness on romantic attraction: A comparison across five research paradigms. *Journal of Personality and Social Psychology, 59,* 981–993.

Feingold, A. (1992). Gender differences in mate selection processes: A test of the parental investment model. *Psychological Bulletin, 112,* 125–139.

Feingold, A. (1994). Gender differences in personality: A meta-analysis. *Psychological Bulletin, 116,* 429–456.

Feldman, J. (2003). The simplicity principle in human concept learning. *Current Directions in Psychological Science, 12,* 227–232.

Feldman, R., Weller, A., Zagoory-Sharon, O., & Levine, A. (2007). Evidence for a neuroendocrinological foundation of human affiliation. *Psychological Science, 18,* 965–970.

Fergusson, D. M., Horwood, L. J., Ridder, E. M., & Beautrais, A. L. (2005). Sexual orientation and mental health in a birth cohort of young adults. *Psychological Medicine, 35,* 971–981.

Fernandez, M. (1998). Asian Indian Americans in the Bay area and the glass ceiling. *Sociological Perspectives, 41,* 119–149.

Ferster, C. B., & Skinner, B. F. (1957). *Schedules of reinforcement.* New York: Appleton-Century-Crofts.

Festinger, L. A. (1957). *A theory of cognitive dissonance.* Evanston, IL: Harper & Row, Peterson.

Festinger, L. A., & Carlsmith, L. M. (1959). Cognitive consequences of forced compliance. *Journal of Abnormal and Social Psychology, 58,* 203–210.

Fichten, C. S., Robillard, K., Judd, D., & Amsel, R. (1989). College students with physical disabilities: Myths and realities. *Rehabilitation Psychology, 34,* 243–257.

Fields, R. D. (2004). The other half of the brain. *Scientific American,* April, 55–61.

Findley, L. J., Unverzagt, M. E., & Suratt, P. M. (1988). Automobile accidents involving patients with obstructive sleep apnea. *American Review of Respiratory Diseases, 138*(2), 337–340.

Fine, B. J., & Kobrick, J. L. (1978). Effects of altitude and heat on complex cognitive tasks. *Human Factors, 20,* 115–122.

Fink, M., & Taylor, M. A. (2009). The catatonia syndrome forgotten but not gone. *Archives of General Psychiatry, 66*(11), 1173–1177.

Finkel, E. J., & Eastwick, P. W. (2009). Arbitrary social norms influence sex differences in romantic selectivity. *Psychological Science, 20*(10), 1290–1295.

Finkelhor, D. (1990). Early and long-term effects of child sexual abuse: An update. *Professional Psychology: Research and Practice, 21,* 325–330.

Finkelhor, D., & Browne, A. (1985). The traumatic impact of child sexual abuse. *American Journal of Orthopsychiatry, 55,* 530–541.

Fisk, A. D., & Rogers, W. A. (2002). Psychology and aging: Enhancing the lives of an aging population. *American Psychological Society, 11,* 107–110.

Fiske, S. T., Harris, L. T., & Cuddy, A. J. C. (2004). Why ordinary people torture enemy prisoners. *Science, 306,* 1482–1483.

Fitzgerald, P. B., Benitez, J., de Castella, A., Daskalakis, Z. J., Brown, T. L., & Kulkarni, J. (2006). A randomized, controlled trial of sequential bilateral repetitive transcranial magnetic stimulation for treatment-resistant depression. *American Journal of Psychiatry, 163,* 88–94.

Flint, M. S., Baum, A., Chambers, W. H., & Jenkins, F. J. (2007). Inductions of DNA damage, alteration of DNA repair and transcriptional activation by stress hormones. *Psychoneuroendocrinology, 32,* 470–479.

Flor, H., Elbert, T., Knecht, S., Wienbruch, C., Pantev, C., Birbaumer, N., Larbig, W., & Taub, E. (1995). Phantom-limb pain as a perceptual correlate of cortical reorganization following arm amputation. *Nature, 375,* 482–490.

Flynn, J. R. (1998). IQ gains over time: Towards finding the causes. In U. Neisser (Ed.), *The rising curve: Long-term gains in IQ and related measures* (pp. 25–66). Washington, DC: American Psychological Association.

Flynn, J. R. (1999). Searching for justice: The discovery of IQ gains over time. *American Psychologist, 54,* 5–20.

Flynn, J. R. (2003). Movies about intelligence: The limitations of *g. Current Directions in Psychological Science, 12,* 95–99.

Flynn, J. R. (2007). *What is intelligence?* New York: Cambridge University Press.

Foa, E. B., Liebowitz, M. R., Kozak, M. J., Davies, S., Campeas, R., Franklin, M. E., et al. (2005). Randomized, placebo-controlled trial of exposure and ritual prevention, clomipramine, and their combination in the treatment of obsessive-compulsive disorder. *American Journal of Psychiatry, 162,* 151–161.

Foa, E. B., & Riggs, D. S. (1995). Posttraumatic stress disorder following assault: Theoretical considerations and empirical findings. *Current Directions in Psychological Science, 4,* 61–65.

Folkman, S., & Moskowitz, J. T. (2000). Coping: Pitfalls and promise. *Annual Review of Psychology, 55,* 745–774.

Forbes, E. E., & Dahl, R. E. (2010). Pubertal development and behavior: Hormonal activation of social and motivational tendencies. *Brain and Cognition, 72*(1), 66–72.

Foreyt, J. P., Scott, L. W., Mitchell, R. E., & Gotto, A. M. (1979). Plasma lipid changes in the normal population following behavioral treatment. *Journal of Consulting and Clinical Psychology, 47,* 440–452.

Forgas, J. P., & Bower, G. H. (1987) Mood effects on person-perception judgments. *Journal of Personality and Social Psychology, 53,* 53–60.

Forster, J. L., Jeffrey, R. W., & Snell, M. K. (1988). One-year follow-up study to a work-site weight control program. *Preventive Medicine, 17,* 129–133.

Foster, C. A., Witcher, B. S., Campbell, W. K., & Green, J. D. (1998). Arousal and attraction: Evidence for automatic and controlled processes. *Journal of Personality and Social Psychology, 74,* 86–101.

Fosse, R., Stickgold, R., & Hobson, J. A. (2001). The mind in REM sleep: Reports of emotional experience. *Sleep, 24*(8), 947–955.

Fougnie, D., & Marois, R. (2006). Distinct capacity limits for attention and working memory. *Psychological Science, 17,* 526–534.

Foulkes, D. (1989, December). Understanding our dreams. *Natural Science,* pp. 296–301.

Fouts, R. (1997). *Next of kin: What chimpanzees have taught me about who we are.* New York: William Morrow.

Frank, E., Kupfer, D. J., Buysse, D. J., Swartz, H. A., Pilkonis, P. A., Houck, P. R., et al. (2007). Randomized trial of weekly, twice-monthly, and monthly interpersonal psychotherapy as maintenance treatment for women with recurrent depression. *American Journal of Psychiatry, 164,* 761–767.

Frankel, F. H. (1995). Discovering new memories in psychotherapy—Childhood revisited, fantasy, or both? *New England Journal of Medicine,* 591–594.

Franz, E. A., Waldie, K. E., & Smith, M. J. (2000). The effect of callostomy on novel versus familiar bimanual actions: A neural dissociation between controlled and automatic processes? *Psychological Science, 11,* 82–85.

Frazier, J. A., & Morrison, F. J. (1998). The influence of extended-year schooling on growth of achievement and perceived competence in early elementary school. *Child Development, 69,* 495–517.

Frazier, P. A., Tix, A. P., & Barron, K. E. (2004). Testing moderator and mediator effects in counseling psychology research. *Journal of Counseling Psychology, 51*(1), 115–134.

Freedman, J. L., & Fraser, J. L. (1966). Compliance without pressure: The foot-in-the-door technique. *Journal of Personality and Social Psychology, 4*(2), 155–202.

Freeman, L. (1972). *The story of Anna O.* New York: Walker.

French, E. G. (1956). Motivation as a variable in work-partner selection. *Journal of Abnormal and Social Psychology, 53,* 96–99.

French, S. E., Seidman, E., Allen, L., & Aber, L. (2006). The development of ethnic identity during adolescence *Developmental Psychology 42,* 1–10.

Frezza, M., di Padova, C., Pozzato, G., Terpin, M., Baraona, E., & Lieber, C. S. (1990). High blood alcohol levels in women: The role of decreased gastric alcohol dehydrogenase activity and first-pass metabolism. *New England Journal of Medicine, 322,* 95–99.

Friedman, H. S., Tucker, J. S., Schwartz, J. E., Tomlinson-Keasey, C., Martin, L. R., Wingard, D. L., & Criqui, M. H. (1995). Psychosocial and behavioral predictors of longevity: The aging and death of the "termites." *American Psychologist, 50,* 69–78.

Friedman, J. M. (2004). Modern science versus the stigma of obesity. *Nature Medicine, 10,* 563–569.

Friedman, M. A., Detweiler-Bedell, J. B., Leventhal, H. E., Horne, R., Keitner, G. I., & Miller, I. W. (2004). Combined psychotherapy and pharmacotherapy for the treatment of major depressive disorder. *Clinical Psychology: Science and Practice, 11,* 47–68.

Friedman, M., & Rosenman, R. H. (1974). *Type A behavior and your heart.* New York: Knopf.

Fry, A. F., & Hale, S. (1996). Processing speed, working memory, and fluid intelligence: Evidence for a developmental cascade. *Psychological Science, 7,* 237–241.

Fullana, M. A., Mataix-Cols, D., Caspi, A., Harrington, H., Grisham, J. R., Moffitt, T. E., & Poulton, R. (2009). Obsessions and compulsions in the community: Prevalence, interference, help-seeking, developmental stability, and co-occurring psychiatric conditions. *American Journal of Psychiatry, 166,* 329–336.

Fullerton, C. S., Ursano, R. J., Epstein, R. S., Crowley, B., Vance, K., Kao, T. C., Dougall, A., & Baum, A. (2001). Gender differences in posttraumatic stress disorder after motor vehicle accidents. *American Journal of Psychiatry, 158,* 1486–1491.

Fullerton, C. S., Ursano, R. J., & Wang, L. M. (2004). Acute stress disorder, posttraumatic stress disorder, and depression in disaster or rescue workers. *American Journal of Psychiatry, 161*(8), 1370–1376.

Furomoto, L., & Scarborough, E. (1986). Placing women in the history of psychology: The first women psychologists. *American Psychologist, 41,* 35–42.

Fuster, J. M. (1995). *Memory in the cerebral cortex.* Cambridge, MA: MIT Press.

G

Galambos, N. L. (1992). Parent-adolescent relations. *Current Directions in Psychological Science, 1,* 146–149.

Galanter, E. (1962). *New directions in psychology.* New York: Holt, Rinehart & Winston.

Galea, S., Brewin, C. R., Gruber, M., Jones, R. T., King, D. W., King, L. A., et al. (2007). Exposure to hurricane-related stressors and mental illness after hurricane Katrina. *Archives of General Psychiatry, 64,*1427–1434.

Gallo, L. C., & Matthews, K. A. (2003). Understanding the association between socioeconomic status and physical health: Do negative emotions play a role? *Psychological Bulletin, 129,* 10–51.

Galotti, K. (1990). Approaches to studying formal and everyday reasoning. *Psychological Bulletin, 105,* 331–351.

Galotti, K. (2007). Decision structuring in important real life choices. *Psychological Science, 18,* 320–324.

Ganger J., & Brent M. R. (2004). Reexamining the vocabulary spurt. *Developmental Psychology, 40,* 621–632.

Gangestad, S. W., Garver-Apgar, C. E., Simpson, J. A., & Cousins, A. J. (2007). Changes in women's mate preferences across the ovulatory cycle. *Journal of Personality and Social Psychology, 92,* 151–163.

Gangestad, S. W., Thornhill, R., & Garver-Apgar, C. E. (2005). Adaptations to ovulation. *Current Directions in Psychological Science, 14,* 312–316.

Ganzel, B. L., Morris, P. A., & Wethington, E. (2010). Allostasis and the human brain: Integrating models of stress from social and life sciences. *Psychological Review, 117*(1), 134–174.

Garb, H. N., Florio, C. M., & Grove, W. M. (1998). The validity of the Rorschach and Minnesota Multiphasic Personality Inventory: Results from meta-analyses. *Psychological Science, 9,* 402–404.

Garcia, J., Hankins, W. G., & Rusiniak, K. W. (1974). Behavioral regulation of the *milieu interne* in man and rat. *Science, 185,* 824–831.

Garcia-Herrero, S., Saldana, M. A. M., Manzanedo del Campo, M. A., & Ritzed, D. O. (2002). From the traditional concept of safety management to safety integrated with quality. *Journal of Safety Research, 33,* 1–20.

Gardner, B. T., & Gardner, R. A. (1971). Twoway communication with an infant chimpanzee. In A. M. Schrier & F. Stollnitz (Eds.), *Behavior of nonhuman primates* (Vol. 4). New York: Academic Press.

Gardner, H. (2000). *Intelligence reframed: Multiple intelligences for the 21st century.* New York: Basic Books.

Gariepy, J. L., Bauer, D. J., & Cairns, R. B. (2001). Selective breeding for differential aggression in mice provides evidence for heterochrony in social behaviours. *Animal Behaviour, 61,* 933–947.

Garlick, D. (2002). Understanding the nature of the general factor of intelligence: The role of individual differences in neural plasticity as an explanatory mechanism. *Psychological Review, 109,* 116–136.

Garro, L. C. (1990). Culture, pain and cancer. *Journal of Palliative Care, 6,* 34–44.

Garver-Apgar, C. E., Gangestad, S. W., Thornhill, R., Miller, R. D., & Olp, J. J. (2006). Major histocompatibility complex alleles, sexual responsivity, and unfaithfulness in romantic couples. *Psychological Science, 17,* 830–834.

Gazzaniga, M. (1992). *Nature's mind: The biological roots of thinking, emotion, sexuality, language, and intelligence.* Boston: Houghton Mifflin.

Gazzaniga, M. S. (1967). The split brain in man. *Scientific American,* pp. 24–29.

Gazzaniga, M. S. (1998, July). The split brain revisited. *Scientific American,* pp. 50–55.

Gazzaniga, M. S. (2000). *Cognitive neuroscience: A reader.* Malden, MA: Blackwell.

Geary, D. C. (1998). *Male, female: The evolution of human sex differences.* Washington, DC: American Psychological Association.

Geary, D. C. (1999). Evolution and developmental sex differences. *Current Directions in Psychological Science, 8,* 115–120.

Geary, D. C. (2005). *The origin of mind: Evolution of brain, cognition, and general intelligence.* Washington, DC: American Psychological Association Press.

Geer, J., Heiman, J., & Leitenberg, H. (1984). *Human sexuality.* Englewood Cliffs, NJ: Prentice Hall.

Gegenfurtner, K. R. (2003). Cortical mechanisms of colour vision. *Nature Reviews–Neuroscience, 4,* 563–572.

Geier, A. B., Rozin, P., & Doros, G. (2006). Unit bias: A new heuristic that helps explain the effect of portion size on food intake. *Psychological Science, 17,* 521–525.

Geller, E. S. (1988). A behavioral science approach to transportation safety. *Bulletin of the New York Academy of Medicine, 64,* 632–661.

Geller, E. S. (1995). Integrating behaviorism and humanism for environmental protection. *Journal of Social Issues, 51,* 179–195.

Geller, E. S. (1996). *The psychology of safety: How to improve behaviors and attitudes on the job.* Boca Raton, FL: CLC Press.

Geller, E. S. (2005). Behavior-based safety and occupational risk management. *Behavior Modification, 29,* 539–561.

Geller, E. S., Kalsher, M. J., Rudd, J. R., & Lehman, G. R. (1989). Promoting safety belt use on a university campus: An integration of commitment and incentive strategies. *Journal of Applied Social Psychology, 19,* 3–19.

Geller, E. S., Ross, N. W., & Delphos, W. A. (1987). Does server intervention training make a difference: An empirical field evaluation. *Alcohol, Health & Research World,* 64–69.

Gellis, L. A., Lichstein, K. L., Scarinci, I. C., Durrence, H. H., Taylor, D. J., Bush, A. J., et al. (2005). Socioeconomic status and insomnia. *Journal of Abnormal Psychology, 114,* 111–118.

Gentile, D. A. (1993). Just what are sex and gender, anyway? A call for a new terminological standard. *Psychological Science, 4,* 120–126.

Geraerts, E., Bernstein, D. M., Merckelbach, H., Linders, C., Raymaekers, L., & Loftus, E. F. (2008). Lasting false beliefs and their behavioral consequences. *Psychological Science, 19*(8), 749–753.

Gershon, A. A., Dannon, P. N., & Grunhaus, L. (2003). Trancranial magnetic stimulation in the treatment of depression. *American Journal of Psychiatry, 160,* 835–845.

Gershon, E. S., & Rieder, R. O. (1992, September). Major disorders of mind and brain. *Scientific American,* pp. 126–133.

Gibbons, F. X., Eggleston, T. J., & Benthin, A. C. (1997). Cognitive reactions to smoking relapse: The reciprocal relation between dissonance and self-esteem. *Journal of Personality and Social Psychology, 72,* 184–195.

Gibson, E., & Walk, R. (1960). The "visual cliff." *Scientific American,* pp. 64–71.

Giedd, J. N., Castellanos, F. X., Rajapakse, J. C., Vaituzis, A. C., & Rapoport, J. L. (1997). Sexual dimorphism of the developing human brain. *Progress in Neuro-Psychopharmacology & Biological Psychiatry, 21,* 1185–1201.

Giedd, J. N., Schmitt, J. E., & Neale, M. C. (2007). Structural brain magnetic resonance imaging of pediatric twins. *Human Brain Mapping, 28,* 474–481.

Gigerenzer, G. (2004). Dread risk, September 11, and fatal traffic accidents. *Psychological Science, 15,* 286–287.

Gilbertini, M., Graham, C., & Cook, M. R. (1999). Self-report of circadian type reflects phase of the melatonin rhythm. *Biological Psychology, 50,* 19–33.

Gildea, W. (1993, August 29). Seeing pride in his accomplishments. *Washington Post,* pp. 7, 2.

Gilligan, C. (1982). *In a different voice.* Cambridge, MA: Harvard University Press.

Glanzer, M., & Cunitz, A. R. (1966). Two storage mechanisms in free recall. *Journal of Verbal Learning and Verbal Behavior, 5,* 351–360.

Gleaves, D. H. (1996). The sociocognitive model of dissociative identity disorder: A reexamination of the evidence. *Psychological Bulletin, 120,* 42–59.

Gleaves, D. H., Smith, S. M., Butler, L. D., & Spiegel, D. (2004). False and recovered memories in the laboratory and clinic: A review of experimental and clinical evidence. *Clinical Psychology: Science and Practice, 11,* 3–28.

Goetzmann, W. N., & Peles, N. (1997). Cognitive dissonance and mutual fund investors. *The Journal of Financial Research, XX*(2), 145–158.

Golay, A., Buclin, S., Ybarra, J., Toti, F., Pichard, C., Picco, N., de Tonnac, N., Allaz, A. F., & Golay, A. (2004). New interdisciplinary cognitive-behavioural-nutritional approach to obesity treatment: A 5-year follow-up study. *Eating & Weight Disorders, 9,* 29–34.

Goldfried, M., & Davison, G. (1976). *Clinical behavior therapy.* New York: Holt, Rinehart & Winston.

Goldman, N., Chen, M., Fujita, T., Xu, Q., Peng, W., Liu, W., & others. (2010). Adenosine A1 receptors mediate local anti-nociceptive effects of acupuncture. *Nature Neuroscience, 13*(7), 883–888.

Goldman-Rakic, P. S. (1992). Working memory and the mind. *Scientific American,* pp. 111–117.

Goldsmith, H. H., & Alansky, J. A. (1987). Maternal and infant temperamental predictors of attachment: A meta-analytic review. *Journal of Consulting and Clinical Psychology, 55,* 805–816.

Goldsmith, L. (1988). Treatment of sexual dysfunction. In E. Weinstein & E. Rosen (Eds.), *Sexuality counseling: Issues and implications.* Monterey, CA: Brooks/Cole.

Goldstein, M. J., & Palmer, J. O. (1963). *The experience of anxiety.* New York: Oxford University Press.

Gorman, J. M., Kent, J., Martinez, J., Browne, S., Coplan, J., & Papp, L. A. (2001). Physiological changes during carbon dioxide inhalation in patients with panic disorder, major depression, and premenstrual dysphoric disorder. *Archives of General Psychiatry, 58,* 125–131.

Gosling, S. D., Kwan, V. S. Y., & John, O. P. (2003). A dog's got personality: A cross-species comparative approach to personality judgments in dogs and humans. *Journal of Personality and Social Psychology, 85,* 1161–1169.

Gottesman, I. I. (2001). Psychopathology through a life span-genetic prism. *American Psychologist, 56,* 861–878.

Gottesman, I. I., & Hanson, D. R. (2005). Human development: Biological and genetic processes. *Annual Review of Psychology, 56,* 263–286.

Gottfredson, L. S. (1997). Why g matters: The complexity of everyday life. *Intelligence, 24,* 79–132.

Gottfredson, L. S., & Deary, I. (2004). Intelligence predicts health and longevity, but why? *Current Directions in Psychological Science, 13,* 1–4.

Gottfried, A. E., Fleming, J. S., & Gottfried, A. W. (1998). Role of cognitively stimulating home environment in children's academic intrinsic motivation: A longitudinal study. *Child Development, 69,* 1448–1460.

Gould, E. (2007). How widespread is adult neurogenesis in mammals? *Nature Reviews Neuroscience, 8,* 481–487.

Gould, E., Tanapat, P., Rydel, T., & Hastings, N. (2000). Regulation of hippocampal neurogenesis in adulthood. *Biological Psychiatry, 48,* 715–720.

Grace, A. A. (2010). Ventral hippocampus, interneurons, and schizophrenia: A new understanding of the pathophysiology of schizophrenia and its implications for treatment and prevention. *Current Directions in Psychological Science, 19,* 232–237.

Grady, C. L., McIntosh, A. R., Horwitz, B., Maisog, J. M., Ungerleider, L. G., Mentis, M. J., Pietrini, P., Schapiro, M. B., & Haxby, J. V. (1995). Age-related reductions in human recognition memory due to impaired encoding. *Science, 269,* 218–220.

Graf, M. (2006). Coordinate transformations in object recognition *Psychological Bulletin, 132,* 920–945.

Grandner, M. A., Hale, L., Moore, M., & Patel, N. P. (2010). Mortality associated with short sleep duration: The evidence, the possible mechanisms, and the future. *Sleep Medicines Reviews, 14*(3), 191–203.

Granic, I., & Patterson, G. R. (2006). Toward a comprehensive model of antisocial development: A dynamic systems approach. *Psychological Review, 113,* 101–131.

Grant, B. F., Hasin, D., Chou, P., Stinson, F. S., & Dawson, D. A. (2004). Nicotine dependence and psychiatric disorders in the United States. *Archives of General Psychiatry, 61,* 1107–1114.

Gray, J. (1998). Caffeine, coffee and health. *Nutrition and Food Sciences, 6,* 314–319.

Gray, J. A. (1988). The neuropsychological basis of anxiety. In C. G. Last & M. Hersen (Eds.), *Handbook of anxiety disorders.* Elmsford, NY: Pergamon Press.

Gray, J. R., & Thompson, P. M. (2004). Neurobiology of intelligence: Science and ethics. *Neuroscience, 5,* 471–482.

Gray, R. A. (2008). Multisensory information in the control of complex motor actions. *Current Directions in Psychological Science, 17,* 244–248.

Graziano, W. G., & Habashi, M. M. (2010). Motivational processes underlying both prejudice and helping. *Personality and Social Psychology Review, 14,* 313–331.

Greenberg, P. E., Kessler, R. C., Birnbaum, H. G., Leong, S. A., Lowe, S. W., Berglund, P. A., & Corey-Lile, P. K. (2003). The economic burden of depression in the United States: How did it change between 1990 and 2000? *Journal of Clinical Psychiatry, 64,* 1465–1475.

Greene, E., & Loftus, E. F. (1998). Psycholegal research on jury damage awards. *Current Directions in Psychological Science 7,* 50–54.

Greenfield, P. (1998). The cultural evolution of IQ. In U. Neisser (Ed.), *The rising curve: Long-term gains in IQ and related measures* (pp. 81–124). Washington, DC: American Psychological Association.

Greenwald, A. G., McGhee, D. E., & Schwartz, J. L. K. (1998). Measuring individual differences in implicit cognition: The implicit association test. *Journal of Personality and Social Psychology, 74*(6), 1464–1480.

Greeven, A., van Balkom, A. J. L. M., Visser, S., Merkelbach, J. W. v. R., Y. R., van Dyck, R., Van der Does, A. J. W., et al. (2007). Cognitive behavior therapy and paroxetine in the treatment of hypochondriasis: A randomized controlled trial. *American Journal of Psychiatry, 164,* 91–99.

Gregg, A. P., Seibt, B., & Banaji, M. R. (2006). Easier done than undone: Asymmetry in the malleability of implicit preferences. *Journal of Personality and Social Psychology, 90,* 1–20.

Grieger, T. A., Cozza, S. J., Ursano, R. J., Hoge, C., Martinez, P. E., Engel, C. C., & Wain, H. J. (2006). Posttraumatic stress disorder and depression in battle-injured soldiers. *American Journal of Psychiatry, 163,* 1777–1783.

Griffith, W., & Veitch, R. (1971). Influences of population density on interpersonal affective behavior. *Journal of Personality and Social Psychology, 17,* 92–98.

Grilo, C. M., Sanislow, C. A., Shea, M. T., & others. (2005). Two-year prospective naturalistic study of remission from major depressive disorder as a function of personality disorder comorbidity. *Journal of Consulting and Clinical Psychology, 73*(1), 78–85.

Grissmer, Williamson, Kirby, & Berends. (1998). Exploring the rapid rise in Black achievement scores in the United States (1970–1990). In U. Neisser (Ed.), *The rising curve: Long-term gains in IQ and related measures* (pp. 251–286). Washington, DC: American Psychological Association.

Grossman, S. P. (1960). Eating and drinking elicited by direct adrenergic and cholinergic stimulation of hypothalamus. *Science, 132,* 301–302.

Groth, N. (1979). Men who rape: The psychology of the offender. New York: Plenum.

Groves, A. K. (2010). The challenge of hair cell regeneration. *Experimental Biology and Medicine, 235*(4), 434–446.

Groves, P. M., & Rebec, C. V. (1988). *Introduction to biological psychology* (3rd ed.). Dubuque, IA: Wm. C. Brown.

Gruskin, E. P. (1999). *Treating lesbians and bisexual women: Challenges and strategies for health professionals.* Thousand Oaks, CA: Sage.

Gubernator, N. G., Zhang, H., Staal, R. G., Mosharov, E. V., Pereira, D. B., Yue, M., & others. (2009). Fluorescent false neurotransmitters visualize dopamine release from individual presynaptic terminals. *Science, 324*(5933), 1441–1444.

Gudjonsson, G. (2001). False confessions. *Psychologist, 14,* 588–591.

Guilford, J. P. (1950). Creativity. *American Psychologist, 5,* 444–454.

Guilford, J. P. (1967). *The nature of human intelligence.* New York: McGraw-Hill.

Guillery, R, W., & Harting, J. K. (2003). Structure and connections of the thalamic reticular nucleus: Advancing views over half a century. *Journal of Comparative Neurology, 463,* 360–371.

Guimond, S., Dambrun, M., Michinov, N., & Duarte, S. (2003). Does social dominance generate prejudice? Integrating individual and contextual determinants of intergroup cognitions. *Journal of Personality and Social Psychology, 84,* 697–721.

Gujar, N., Yoo, S-S, Hu, P., & Walker, M. P. (2010). The unrested resting brain: Sleep deprivation alters activity within the default-mode network. *Journal of Cognitive Neuroscience, 22*(8),1637–1648.

Gustavson, C. R., Garcia, J., Hankins, W. G., & Rusiniak, K. W. (1974). Coyote predation control by aversive conditioning. *Science, 184,* 581–584.

Guthrie, J. T., Wigfield, A., Barbosa, P., Perencevich, K. C., Taboada, A., Davis, M. H., Scafiddi, N. T., & Tonks, S. (2004). Increasing reading comprehension and engagement through concept-oriented reading instruction. *Journal of Educational Psychology, 96,* 403–423.

H

Hafer, J. C., & Richmond, E. D. (1988). What hearing parents should learn about deaf culture. *Perspectives for Teachers of the Hearing Impaired, 7,* 2–5.

Hahn, U., & Oaksford, M. (2007). The rationality of informal argumentation: A Bayesian approach to reasoning fallacies. *Psychological Review, 114,* 704–732.

Haimov, I., & Lavie, P. (1996). Melatonin—A soporific hormone. *Current Directions in Psychological Science, 5,* 106–111.

Haley, J. (1976). *Problem-solving therapy.* San Francisco: Jossey-Bass.

Halgin, R., & Whitbourne, S. K. (2000). *Abnormal psychology: Clinical perspectives on psychological disorders.* Boston: McGraw-Hill.

Hall, C. S. (1951). What people dream about. *Scientific American,* pp. 60–63.

Halpern, D. (1992). *Sex differences in cognitive abilities* (2nd ed.). Hillsdale, NJ: Erlbaum.

Halpern, D. F. (1997). Sex differences in intelligence: Implications for education. *American Psychologist, 52,* 1091–1102.

Halpern, D. F. (1998). Teaching critical thinking for transfer across domains: Dispositions, skills, structure training, and metacognitive monitoring. *American Psychologist, 53,* 449–455.

Halpern, D. F. (2004). A cognitive-process taxonomy for sex differences in cognitive abilities. *Current Directions in Psychological Science, 13,* 135–139.

Hamilton, D. L., & Zanna, M. P. (1972). Differential weighting of favorable and unfavorable attributes in impressions of personality. *Journal of Experimental Research in Personality, 6,* 204–212.

Hampson, S. E. (2008). Mechanisms by which childhood personality traits influence adult well-being. *Current Directions in Psychological Science, 17*(4), 264–268.

Hanawalt, H. F., & Demarest, I. H. (1939). The effect of verbal suggestion in the recall period upon the reproduction of visually perceived forms. *Journal of Experimental Psychology, 25,* 159–174.

Haney, C. (1980). Social psychology and the criminal law. In P. W. Middlebrook (Ed.), *Social psychology and modern life* (2nd ed.). New York: Knopf.

Haney, C., & Zimbardo, P. (1998). The past and future of U.S. prison policy: Twenty-five years after the Stanford prison experiment. *American Psychologist, 53,* 709–727.

Harkness, K. L., Frank, E., Anderson, B., Houck, P. R., Luther, J., & Kupfer, D. J. (2002). Does interpersonal psychotherapy protect women from depression in the face of stressful life events? *Journal of Consulting and Clinical Psychology, 70,* 908–915.

Harlow, H. F. (1949). The formation of learning sets. *Psychological Review, 56,* 51–56.

Harlow, H. F., & Harlow, M. K. (1965). The affectional systems. In A. M. Schrier, H. F. Harlow, & F. Stollnitz (Eds.), *Behavior of nonhuman primates* (Vol. 2). London: Academic Press.

Harlow, H. F., Harlow, M. K., & Meyer, D. R. (1950). Learning motivated by a manipulation drive. *Journal of Experimental Psychology, 40,* 228–234.

Harlow, H. F., & Novak, M. A. (1973). Psychopathological perspectives. *Perspectives in Biology and Medicine, 16,* 461–478.

Harmon, T. M., Hyan, M. T., & Tyre, T. E. (1990). Improved obstetric outcomes using hypnotic analgesia and skill mastery combined with childbirth education. *Journal of Consulting and Clinical Psychology, 58,* 525–530.

Harmon-Jones, E., & Allen, J. J. B. (2001). The role of affect in the mere exposure effect: Evidence from psychophysiological and individual differences approaches. *Personality and Social Psychology Bulletin, 27*(7), 889–898.

Harris, A. H. S. (2006). Does expressive writing reduce health care utilization? A meta-analysis of randomized trials. *Journal of Consulting and Clinical Psychology, 74,* 243–252.

Harris, C. R. (2002). Sexual and romantic jealousy in heterosexual and homosexual adults. *Psychological Science, 13,* 7–12.

Harris, T. G. (1973, July). As far as heroin is concerned, the worst is over. *Psychology Today,* pp. 68–79.

Harrison, D. A., Newman, D. A., & Roth, P. L. (2006). How important are job attitudes? Meta-analytic comparisons of integrative behavioral outcomes and time sequences. *Academy of Management Journal, 49,* 305–325.

Harrison, S. A., & Tong, F. (2009). Decoding reveals the contents of visual working memory in early visual areas. *Nature, 458*(7238), 632–635.

Harte, J. L., Eifert, G. H., & Smith, R. (1995). The effects of running and meditation on beta-endorphin, corticotropin-releasing hormone and cortisol in plasma, and on mood. *Biological Psychology, 40,* 251–265.

Harter, J. K., Schmidt, F. L., & Hayes, T. L. (2002). Business-unit-level relationship between employee satisfaction, employee engagement and business outcomes: A meta-analysis. *Journal of Applied Psychology, 87,* 268–279.

Hartmann, E., Russ, D., Oldfield, M., Sivian, I., & Cooper, S. (1987). Who has nightmares? The personality of the lifelong nightmare sufferer. *Archives of General Psychiatry, 44,* 49–56.

Harvey, P. D. (2010). Cognitive functioning and disability in schizophrenia. *Current Directions in Psychological Science, 19,* 249–254.

Hatfield, E. (1988). Passionate and companionate love. In R. J. Sternberg & M. L. Barnes (Eds.), *The psychology of love.* New Haven: Yale University Press.

Hauser, R. M. (1998). Trends in Black-White test-score differentials: I. Uses and misuses of NAEP/SAT data. In U. Neisser (Ed.), *The rising curve: Long-term gains in IQ and related measures* (pp. 219–249). Washington, DC: American Psychological Association.

Hazlett, E. A., & others. (1999). Three-dimensional analysis with MRI and PET of the size, shape, and function of the thalamus in the schizophrenia spectrum. *American Journal of Psychiatry, 156,* 1190–1199.

Heald, A. (2010). Physical health in schizophrenia: A challenge for antipsychotic therapy. *European Psychiatry, 25 Suppl 2,* S6–11.

Hebb, D. O. (1949). *Organization of behavior.* New York: Wiley.

Hedges, L. V., & Nowell, A. (1995). Sex differences in mental test scores, variability, and numbers of high-scoring individuals. *Science, 269,* 41–45.

Hedtke, K. A., Ruggiero, K. J., Fitzgerald, M. M., Zinzow, H. M., Saunders, B. E., Resnick, H. S., & others. (2008). A longitudinal investigation of interpersonal violence in relation to mental health and substance use. *Journal of Consulting and Clinical Psychology, 76*(4), 633–647.

Heider, F. (1958). *The psychology of interpersonal relations.* New York: Wiley.

Heien, D. M., & Pittman, D. J. (1993). The external costs of alcohol abuse. *Journal of Studies on Alcohol, 54,* 302–307.

Heine, S. J., & Norenzayan, A. (2006). Toward a psychological science for a cultural species. *Perspectives on Psychological Science, 1*(3), 251–269.

Held, R., & Hein, A. (1963). Movement-produced stimulation in the development of visually guided behavior. *Journal of Comparative and Physiological Psychology, 56,* 23–44.

Helie, S., & Sun, R. (2010). Incubation, insight, and creative problem solving: A unified theory and a connectionist model. *Psychological Review, 117*(3), 994–1024.

Heller, D., Ilies, R., & Watson, D. (2004). The role of person versus situations in life satisfaction: A critical examination. *Psychological Bulletin, 130,* 574–600.

Heller, K., Swindle, R. W., & Dusenbury, L. (1986). Components of social support processes. *Journal of Consulting and Clinical Psychology, 54,* 466–470.

Heller, W., Nitscke, J. B., & Miller, G. A. (1998). Lateralization in emotion and emotional disorders. *Current Directions in Psychological Science, 7,* 26–32.

Helson, R., Kwan, V. S. Y., John, O. P., & Jones, C. (2002). The growing evidence for personality change in adulthood: Findings from research with personality inventories. *Journal of Research in Personality, 36,* 287–306.

Hempel, A., Giesel, F., Caraballo, N. M. G. et al. (2004). Plasticity of cortical activation related to working memory during training. *American Journal of Psychiatry, 161,* 745–747.

Henderlong, J., & Lepper, M. R. (2002). The effects of praise on children's intrinsic motivation: A review and synthesis. *Psychological Bulletin, 128,* 774–795.

Hennekens, C. H., Rosner, B., & Cole, D. S. (1978). Daily alcohol consumption and fatal coronary heart disease. *American Journal of Epidemiology, 107,* 196–200.

Henquet, C., Krabbendam, L., de Graaf, R., ten Have, M., & van Os, J. (2006). Cannabis use and expression of mania in the general population. *Journal of Affective Disorders, 95,* 103–110.

Henseler, I., Falkai, P., & Gruber, O. (2010). Disturbed functional connectivity within brain networks subserving domain-specific subcomponents of working memory in schizophrenia: Relation to performance and clinical symptoms. *Journal of Psychiatric Research, 44*(6), 364–372.

Herbenick, D., Reece, M., Schick, V., Sanders, S. A., Dodge, B., & Fortenberry, J. D. (2010). An event-level analysis of the sexual characteristics and composition among adults ages 18 to 59: Results from a national probability sample in the United States. *Journal of Medicine, 7 (Supplement 5),* 346–361.

Herbst, K. C., Gaertner, L., & Insko, C. A. (2003). My head says "yes," but my heart says "no": Cognitive and affective attraction as a function of similarity to the ideal self. *Journal of Personality and Social Psychology, 84,* 1206–1219.

Herdt, G. (1984). *Ritualized homosexuality in Melanesia.* Berkeley: University of California Press.

Herek, G. M. (2000). The psychology of sexual prejudice. *Psychological Science, 9,* 19–22.

Herlitz, A., & Rehnman, J. (2008). Sex differences in episodic memory. *Psychological Science, 71*(1).

Heslin, P. A., & Vande Walle, D. (2008). Managers' implicit assumptions about personnel. *Current Directions in Psychological Science, 17,* 219–222.

Hess, E. H. (1975, November). The role of pupil size in communication. *Scientific American,* pp. 110–119.

Hetherington, M. (1979). Divorce: A children's perspective. *American Psychologist, 34,* 851–858.

Hickok, G., & Poeppel, D. (2007). The cortical organization of speech processing. *Nature Reviews Neuroscience, 8,* 393–401.

Higgins, D. M., Pihl, R. O., Peterson, J. B., & Lee, A. G. M. (2007). Prefrontal cognitive ability, intelligence, big five personality, and the prediction of advanced academic and workplace performance. *Journal of Personality, 93,* 298–319.

Hilgard, E. R. (1975). Hypnosis. *Annual Review of Psychology, 26,* 19–44.

Hilmert, C. J., Kulik, J. A., & Christenfeld, N. J. S. (2006). Positive and negative opinion modeling: The influence of another's similarity and dissimilarity. *Journal of Personality and Social Psychology, 90,* 440–452.

Hinshaw, S .P. & Stier, A. (2008). Stigma as related to mental disorders. *Annual Review of Clinical Psychology, 4,* 367–393.

Hipp, J. R., Bauer, D. J., Curran, P. J., & Bollen, K. A. (2004). Crimes of opportunity or crimes of emotion? Testing two explanations of seasonal change in crime. *Social Forces, 82,* 1333–1372.

Hirashima, F., Parow, A. M., Stoll, A. L., Demopulos, C. M., Damico, K. E., Rohan, M. L., Eskesen, J. G., Zuo, C. S., Cohen, B. M., & Renshaw, P. F. (2004). Omega-3 Fatty Acid Treatment and T-sub-2 whole brain relaxation times in Bipolar Disorder. *American Journal of Psychiatry, 161,* 1922–1924.

Hirsch, C. R. & Clark, D. M. (2004). Information-processing bias in social phobia. *Clinical Psychology Review, 24,* 799–825.

Hirst, W. (1982). The amnesic syndrome: Descriptions and explanations. *Psychological Bulletin, 91,* 435–460.

Hobson, J. A. (1989). *Sleep.* New York: Scientific American Library.

Hobson, J. A., & McCarley, R. W. (1977). The brain as a dream state generator: An activation-synthesis hypothesis of the dream process. *The American Journal of Psychiatry, 134*(12), 1335–1348.

Hochberg, J. (1988). Visual perception. In R. C. Atkison, R. J. Herrnstein, G. Lindzey, & R. D. Luce (Eds.), *Stevens' handbook of experimental psychology: Vol. 1. Perception and motivation.* New York: Wiley-Interscience.

Hofmann, S. G., Meuret, A. E., Rosenfield, D., Suvak, M. K., Barlow, D. H., Gorman, J. M., et al. (2007). Preliminary evidence for cognitive mediation during cognitive-behavioral therapy of panic disorder. *Journal of Consulting and Clinical Psychology, 75,* 374–379.

Hofmann, S. G., Sawyer, A. T., Witt, A. A., & Oh, D. (2010). The effect of mindfulness-based therapy on anxiety and depression: A meta-analytic review. *Journal of Consulting and Clinical Psychology, 78*(2), 169–183.

Hofmann, W., De Houwer, J., Perugini, M., Baeyens, F., & Crombez, G. (2010). Evaluative conditioning in humans: A meta-analysis. *Psychological Bulletin, 136*(3), 390–421.

Hogan, R., Mankin, D., Conway, J., & Fox, S. (1970). Personality correlates of undergraduate marijuana use. *Journal of Consulting and Clinical Psychology, 35,* 58–63.

Hogarth, R. M., & Karelaia, N. (2007). Heuristic and linear models of judgement: Matching rules and environments. *Psychological Review, 114,* 733–758.

Hokanson, J. E., DeGood, D. E., Forrest, M. S., & Brittain, T. M. (1963). Availability of avoidance behaviors for modulating vascular-stress responses. *Journal of Personality and Social Psychology, 67,* 60–68.

Holahan, C. J., & Moos, R. H. (1987). Risk, resistance, and psychological distress: A longitudinal analysis with adults and children. *Journal of Abnormal Psychology, 96,* 3–13.

Holahan, C. K., Holahan, C., & Wonacott, N. L. (1999). Self-appraisal, life satisfaction, and retrospective life choices across one and three decades. *Psychology & Aging, 14,* 238–244.

Holden, R. J., & Pakula, I. (1998). Marijuana, stress and suicide: A neuroimmunological

explanation. *Australian & New Zealand Journal of Psychiatry, 32,* 465–466.

Hole, J. W. (1990). *Human anatomy and physiology* (5th ed.). Dubuque, IA: Wm. C. Brown.

Holinger, P. C., & Offer, D. (1993). *Adolescent suicide.* New York: Guilford Press.

Hollander, E. P., & Offermann, L. R. (1990). Power and leadership in organizations: Relations in transition. *American Psychologist, 45,* 179–189.

Holman, E. A., Silver, R. C., Poulin, M., Andersen, J. A., Gil-Rivas, V., & McIntosh, D. N. (2008). Terrorism, acute stress, and cardiovascular health: A 3-year national study following the September 11th attacks. *Archives of General Psychiatry, 65,* 73–80.

Holmes, T. H., & Rahe, R. H. (1967). The social readjustment rating scale. *Journal of Psychosomatic Research, 11,* 213–218.

Hong, S. W., & Shevell, S. K. (2004). Brightness contrast and assimilation from patterned inducing backgrounds. *Vision Research, 44,* 35–43.

Hong, Y., Morris, M. W., Chiu, C., & Benet-Martinez, V. (2000). Multicultural minds: A dynamic constructivist approach to culture and cognition. *American Psychologist, 55,* 709–720.

Hooley, J. M. (2007). Expressed emotion and relapse of psychopathology. *Annual Review of Clinical Psychology, 3,* 329–352.

Hopkin, K. (1995). Sugar 'n spice vs. puppy-dog tails: Sex differences in the brain. *Journal of NIH Research, 7,* 39–43.

Hopkins, K. (1997). Show me where it hurts: Tracing the pathways of pain. *Journal of NIH Research, 9,* 37–43.

Hopkins, W. D., & Cantalupo, C. (2010). Theoretical speculations on the evolutionary origins of hemispheric specializations. *Psychological Science, 17*(3), 233–237.

Horgan, J. (1993, June). Eugenics revisited. *Scientific American,* pp. 122–131.

Horne, J. (1988). *Why we sleep: The functions of sleep in humans and other mammals.* New York: Oxford University Press.

Hoshino-Browne, E., Zanna, A. S., Spencer, S. J., Zanna, M. P., & Kitayama, S. (2005). On the cultural guises of cognitive dissonance: The case of Easterners and Westerners. *Journal of Personality and Social Psychology, 89,* 294–310.

Hotelling, K. (1991). Sexual harassment: A problem shielded by silence. *Journal of Consulting and Clinical Psychology, 69,* 487–501.

Hough, L. M. & Oswald, F. L. (2000). Personnel selection: Looking toward the future—remembering the past. *Annual Review of Psychology, 51,* 631–664.

Hough, R. L., & others. (1987). Utilization of health and mental health services by Los Angeles Mexican-Americans and non-Hispanic whites. *Archives of General Psychiatry, 44,* 702–709.

Houston, J. P. (1985). *Motivation.* New York: Macmillan.

Hovland, C. I. (Ed.). (1957). *The order of presentation in persuasion.* New Haven, CT: Yale University Press.

Hovland, C. I., & Weiss, W. (1951). The influence of source credibility on communication effectiveness. *The Public Opinion Quarterly, 15,* 635–650.

Howell, W. C. (1993). Engineering psychology in a changing world. *Annual Review of Psychology, 44,* 231–263.

Hu, P., Stylos-Allan, M., & Walker, M. P. (2006). Sleep facilities consolidation of emotional declartive memory. *Psychological Science, 17,* 891–898.

Huang, M., & Hauser, R. M. (1998). Trends in Black-White test-score differentials: II. The WORDSUM Vocabulary Test. In U. Neisser (Ed.), *The rising curve: Long-term gains in IQ and related measures* (pp. 303–334). Washington, DC: American Psychological Association.

Hubbs-Tait, L., Kennedy, T. S., Droke, E. A., Belanger, D. M., & Parker, J. R. (2007). Zinc, iron, and lead: Relations to Head Start children's cognitive scores and teachers' ratings of behavior. *Journal of the American Dietetic Association, 107*(1), 128–133.

Hubbs-Tait, L., Nation, J. R., Krebs, N. F., & Bellinger, D. C. (2005). Neurotoxicants, micronutrients, and social environments: Individual and combined effects on children's development. *Psychological Science in the Public Interest, 8,* 57–121.

Hubl, D., Koenig, T., Strik, W., & others. (2004). Pathways that make voices—White matter changes in auditory hallucinations. *Archives of General Psychiatry, 61*(7), 658–668.

Huddy, L., Billig, J., Bracciodieta, J., Heoffler, L., Moynihan, P. J., & Pugliani, P. (1997). The effect of interviewer gender on the survey response. *Political Behavior, 19,* 197–220.

Huesmann, L. R., Moise, J. F., & Podolski, C. L. (1997). The effects of media violence on the development of antisocial behavior. In D. M. Stoff, J. Breiling, & J. D. Maser (Eds.), *Handbook of antisocial behavior* (pp. 181–193). New York: John Wiley.

Huffcutt, A. I., Conway, J. M., Roth, P. L., & Stone, N. J. (2001). Identification and meta-analytic assessment of psychological constructs measured in employment interviews. *Journal of Applied Psychology, 86,* 897–913.

Hugdahl, K., & Karker, A. C. (1981). Biological versus experiential factors in phobic conditioning. *Behaviour Research and Therapy, 16,* 315–321.

Hughes, J. R., Oliveto, A. H., Helzer, J., Higgins, S. R., & Bickel, W. K. (1992). Should caffeine abuse, dependence, or withdrawal be added to *DSM-IV* and *ICD-10*? *American Journal of Psychiatry, 149,* 33–40.

Hummer, T. A., & McClintock, M. K. (2009). Putative human pheromone androstadienone attunes the mind specifically to emotional information. *Hormones and Behavior, 55*(4), 548–559.

Hundert, A. J., & Greenfield, N. (1969). *Physical space and organizational behavior: A study of an office landscape.* Paper presented to the American Psychological Association, Los Angeles.

Hunt, E. (1995). The role of intelligence in modern society. *American Scientist, 83,* 356–368.

Hunter, J. E. (1979). *An analysis of the validity, test fairness, and utility for the Philadelphia Police Officers Selection Examination prepared by Educational Testing Service.* Report to the Philadelphia Federal District Court, Alvarez v. City of Philadelphia.

Hunter, J. E. (1981). *The economic benefits of personnel selection using ability tests: A state-of-the-art review including a detailed analysis of the dollar benefit of U.S. Employment Office placements and a critique of the low-cutoff method of test use.* Washington, DC: U.S. Employment Service, U.S. Department of Labor.

Hunter, J. E., & Hunter, R. F. (1984). Validity and utility of alternative predictors of job performance. *Psychological Bulletin, 96,* 72–98.

Huntsinger, C. S., Jose, P. E., & Larson, S. L. (1998). Do parent practices to encourage academic competence influence the social adjustment of young European American and Chinese American children? *Developmental Psychology, 34,* 747–756.

Huston, T. L., Niehuis, S., & Smith, S. E. (2001). The early marital roots of conjugal distress and divorce. *Current Directions in Psychological Science, 10,* 116–119.

Hwang, W. (2006). The psychotherapy adaptation and modification framework: Application to Asian Americans. *American Psychologist, 61,* 702–715.

Hyde, J. S. (1985). *Half the human experience: The psychology of women.* Lexington, MA: D. C. Heath.

Hyde, J. S. (2007). New directions in the study of gender similarities and differences. *Current Directions in Psychological Science, 16,* 259–263.

Hyde, J. S., Lindberg, S. M., Linn, M. C., Ellis, A. B., & Williams, C. C. (2008). Diversity: Gender similarities chracterize math performance. *Science, 321,* 494–495.

Hyde, J. S., & Plant, E. A. (1995). Magnitude of psychological gender differences: Another side to the story. *American Psychologist, 50,* 159–161.

Hyman, I. E., & Billings, F. J. (1998). Individual differences in the creation of false childhood memories. *Memory, 6,* 1–20.

Hyman, I. E., & Loftus, E. F. (1998). Errors in autobiographical memory. *Clinical Psychology Review, 18,* 933–947.

Hyman, I. E., & Pentland, J. (1996). The role of mental imagery in the creation of false memories. *Journal of Memory and Language, 35,* 101–117.

Hyman, Jr., I. E., Boss, S. M., Wise, B. M., McKenzie, K. E., & Caggiano, J. M. (2009). Did you see the unicycling clown? Inattentional blindness while walking and talking on a cell phone. *Applied Cognitive Psychology.*

Hyman, S. E. (2010). The diagnosis of mental disorders: The problem of reification. *Annual Review of Clinical Pscyhology, 6,* 155–179.

I

Ilgen, D. R. (1999). Teams embedded in organizations: Some implications. *American Psychologist, 54,* 129–139.

Impett, E. A., Gable, S. L., & Peplau, L. A. (2005). Giving up and giving in: The costs and benefits of daily sacrifice in intimate relationships. *Journal of Personality and Social Psychology, 89,* 327–344.

Ingham, A. G., Levinger, B., Graves, J., & Peckham, V. (1974). The Ringelmann effect: Studies of group size and group performance. *Journal of Experimental Social Psychology, 10,* 371–384.

Inhelder, B., & Piaget, J. (1958). *The growth of logical thinking from childhood to adolescence.* New York: Basic Books.

Irons, E. D., & Moore, G. W. (1985). *Black managers: The case of the banking industry.* New York: Praeger.

Ironsmith, M., & Eppler, M. A. (2007). Mastery learning benefits low-aptitude students. *Teaching of Psychology, 34,* 28–31.

Irving, G. A., Bor, R., & Catalan, J. (1995). Psychological distress among gay men supporting a lover or partner with AIDS: A pilot study. *AIDS Care, 7,* 605–617.

Irwin, M. R., & Miller, A. H. (2007). Depressive disorders and immunity: 20 years of progress and discovery. *Brain, Behavior, and Immunity, 21,* 374–383.

Iyengar, S. S., & Lepper, M. R. (1999). Rethinking the value of choice: A cultural perspective on intrinsic motivation. *Journal of Personality and Social Psychology, 76,* 349–366.

Izard, C. E. (1972). *Patterns of emotions: A new analysis of anxiety and depression.* New York: Academic Press.

Izard, C. E. (1977). *Human emotions.* New York: Plenum.

Izard, C. E. (1991). *The psychology of emotions.* New York: Plenum Press.

Izard, C. E. (1997). Emotions and facial expressions: A perspective from Differential Emotions Theory. In J. A. Russell & others, (Eds.), *The psychology of facial expression: Studies in emotion and social interaction* (pp. 57–77). New York: Cambridge University Press.

Izard, C. E., & others. (1997). The ontogeny and significance of infants' facial expressions in the first 9 months of life. *Developmental Psychology, 31,* 997–1013.

J

Jabbi, M., Korf, J., Kema, I. P., Hartman, C., van der Pompe, G., Minderaa, R. B., et al. (2007). Convergent genetic modulation of the endocrine stress response involves polymorphic variations of 5-HTT, COMT, MAOA. *Molecular Psychiatry, 12,* 483–490.

Jacob, O., Kinnunen, L., Metz, J., Cooper, M., & McClintock, M. (2007). Sustained human chemosignal unconsciously alters brain function. *Neuroreport: An International Journal for the Rapid Communication of Research in Neuroscience, 12,* 2391–2394.

Jacobs, L. F., & Schenck, F. (2003). Unpacking the cognitive map: The parallel map theory of hippocampal function. *Psychological Review, 110,* 285–315.

Jaffee, S., & Shibley-Hyde, J. (2000). Gender differences in moral orientation: A meta-analysis. *Psychological Bulletin, 126,* 703–726.

Jaffee, S. R., Caspi, A., Moffitt, T. E., Polo-Tomas, M., Price, T. S., & Taylor, A. (2004). The limits of child effects: Evidence for genetically mediated child effects on corporal punishment but not on physical maltreatment. *Developmental Psychology, 40,* 1047–1058.

James, W. (1890). *The principles of psychology.* New York: Holt, Rinehart & Winston.

Janis, I. L. (1982). *Groupthink: Psychological studies of policy decisions and fiascoes.* Boston: Houghton Mifflin.

Janis, I. L. (1983). The role of social support in adherence to stressful decisions. *American Psychologist, 38,* 143–160.

Jarrett, R. B., Kraft, D., Doyle, J., Foster, B. M., Eaves, G. G., & Silver, P. C. (2001). Preventing recurrent depression using cognitive therapy with and without a continuation phase. *Archives of General Psychiatry, 58,* 381–388.

Jeffrey, K. J., & Reid, I. A. (1997). Modifiable neuronal connections: An overview of psychiatrists. *American Journal of Psychiatry, 154,* 156–164.

Jenkins, C. D. (1988). Dietary risk factors and their modification in cardiovascular disease. *Journal of Consulting and Clinical Psychology, 56,* 350–357.

Jenkins, R. W. (1988). Epidemiology of cardiovascular diseases. *Journal of Consulting and Clinical Psychology, 56,* 324–332.

Ji, L.-I., Zhang, Z., & Nisbett, R. E. (2004). Is it culture or is it language? Examination of language effects in cross-cultural research on categorization. *Journal of Personality and Social Psychology, 87,* 57–65.

Jobe, T. H. & Harrow, M. (2010). Schizophrenia course, long-term outcome, recovery, and prognosis. *Current Directions in Psychological Science, 19,* 220–225.

Johnson, M. K., Bransford, J. P., & Solomon, S. (1973). Memory for tacit implications of sentences. *Journal of Experimental Psychology, 98,* 203–205.

Johnson, M. K., Mitchell, K. J., Raye, C. L., & Greene, E. J. (2004). An age-related deficit in prefrontal cortical function associated with refreshing information. *Psychological Science, 15,* 127–132.

Johnson, W., & Krueger, R. F. (2006). How money buys happiness: Genetic and environmental processes linking finances and life satisfaction. *Journal of Personality and Social Psychology, 90,* 680–691.

Johnston, T. D., & Edwards, L. (2002). Genes, environments, and the development of behavior. *Psychological Review, 109,* 26–34.

Johnston, V. S., Hagela, R., Franklin, M., Fink, B., & Grammar, K. (2001). Male facial attractiveness: Evidence for hormone-mediated adaptive design. *Evolution and Human Behavior, 22*(4), 251–267.

Joiner, T. E., & Schmidt, N. B. (1998). Excessive reassurance-seeking predicts depressive but not anxious reactions to acute stress. *Journal of Abnormal Psychology, 107,* 533–537.

Jones, E., Bell, L., & Aronson, E. (1971). The reciprocation of attraction from similar and dissimilar others: A study in person perception and evaluation. In C. McClintock (Ed.), *Experimental social psychology.* New York: Holt, Rinehart & Winston.

Jones, E. E., & Nisbett, R. E. (1972). The actor and the observer: Divergent perceptions of the causes of behavior. In E. E. Jones, D. E. Kanouse, H. H. Kelley, Richard E. Nisbett, S. Valins, & B. Weiner (Eds.), *Attribution: Perceiving the causes of behavior* (pp. 79–94). Morristown, NJ: General Learning Press.

Jones, G. V. (1983). Identifying basic categories. *Psychological Bulletin, 94,* 423–428.

Jones, M. C. (1924). A laboratory study of fear: The case of Peter. *Pedagogical Seminary, 31,* 308–315.

Jorgensen, R. S., Nash, J. K., Lasser, N. L., Hymowitz, N., & Langer, A. W. (1988). Heart rate acceleration and its relationship to total serum cholesterol, triglycerides, and blood pressure. *Psychophysiology, 25,* 39–44.

Josephson, W. L. (1987). Television violence and children's aggression: Testing the priming, social script, and disinhibition predictions. *Journal of Personality and Social Psychology, 53,* 882–890.

Jucker, R. (2002). Sustainability? Never heard of it!: Some basics we shouldn't ignore when engaging in education for sustainability. *International Journal of Sustainability in Higher Education, 3,* 8–18.

Judd, L. L., & Akiskal, H. S. (2003). Depressive episodes and symptoms dominate the longitudinal course of bipolar disorder. *Current Psychiatry Reports, 5,* 417–418.

Judd, L. L., Akiskal, H. S., Schettler, P. J., Endicott, J., Maser, J., Solomon, D. A., Leon, A., Rice, J. A., & Keller, M. B. (2002). The long-term natural history of the weekly symptomatic status of bipolar I disorder. *Archives of General Psychiatry, 59,* 530–537.

Juliano, L. M., & Griffiths, R. R. (2004). A critical review of caffeine withdrawal: Empirical validation of symptoms and signs, incidence, severity, and associated features. *Psychopharmacology, 176,* 1–29.

K

Kagan, J. (1984). *The nature of the child.* New York: Basic Books.

Kahneman, D., & Tversky, A. (1982). The psychology of preferences. *Scientific American,* pp. 160–173.

Kahneman, D., & Tversky, A. (1996). On the reality of cognitive illusions. *Psychological Review, 103,* 582–591.

Kalichman, S. C. (1989). Sex roles and sex differences in adult spatial performance. *Journal of Genetic Psychology, 150,* 93–100.

Kalichman, S. C. (1990). Affective and personality characteristics of replicated MMPI profile subgroups of incarcerated adult rapists. *Archives of Sexual Behavior, 19,* 443–459.

Kalichman, S. C., Rompa, D., & Coley, B. (1996). Experimental component analysis of a behavioral HIV-AIDS prevention intervention for inner-city women. *Journal of Consulting and Clinical Psychology, 64* (4), 687–693.

Kalish, R. A., & Reynolds, D. K. (1976). *Death and ethnicity: A psychocultural study.* Los Angeles: University of Southern California Press.

Kameda, T., Takezawa, M., & Hastie, R. (2005). Where do social norms come from? The example of communal sharing. *Current Directions in Psychological Science, 14*(6), 331–334.

Kanaya, T., Scullin, M. H., & Ceci, S. J. (2003). The Flynn effect and U.S. policies: The impact of rising IQ scores on American policy. *American Psychologist, 58,* 778–790.

Kandel, E., & Abel, T. (1995). Neuropeptides, adenyl cyclase, and memory storage. *Science, 268,* 825–826.

Kandel, E. R. (1999). Biology and the future of psychoanalysis: A new intellectual framework for psychiatry revisited. *American Journal of Psychiatry, 156,* 505–524.

Kandel, E. R. (2009). The biology of memory: A forty-year perspective. *Journal of Neuroscience, 29*(41), 12748–12756.

Kandel, E. R., & Hawkins, R. D. (1992). The biological basis of learning and individuality. *Scientific American,* pp. 79–86.

Kandel, E. R., & Schwartz, J. H. (1982). Molecular biology of learning: Modulation of transmitter release. *Science, 218,* 433–443.

Kandel, E. R., Schwartz, J. H., & Jessel, T. M. (1995). *Essentials of neural science and behavior.* East Norwalk, CT: Appleton & Lange.

Kaniasty, K., & Norris, F. H. (1995). Mobilization and deterioration of social support following natural disasters. *Current Directions in Psychological Science, 4,* 94–98.

Kanter, J. W., Manos, R. C., Bowe, W. M., Baruch, D. E., Busch, A. M., & Rusch, L. C. (2010). What is behavioral activation? A review of the empirical literature. *Clinical Psychology Review, 30*(6), 608–620.

Kaplan, H. S. (1983). *The evaluation of sexual disorders.* New York: Brunner/Mazel.

Kaplan, R. M. (2000). Two pathways to prevention. *American Psychologist, 55,* 382–396.

Kapur, N. (1999). Syndromes of retrograde amnesia: A conceptual and empirical synthesis. *Psychological Bulletin, 125,* 800–825.

Karwowski, W. (2005). Ergonomics and human factors: the paradigms for science, engineering, design, technology and management of human-compatible systems. *Ergonomics, 48,* 436–463.

Kasper, S., Wehr, T. A., Bartko, J. J., Gaist, P. A., & Rosenthal, N. E. (1989). Epidemiological findings of seasonal changes in mood and behavior. *Archives of General Psychiatry, 46,* 823–833.

Kassam-Adams, & N., Winston, F. K. (2004). Predicting Child PTSD: the relationship between acute stress disorder and PTSD in injured children. External Website. *Journal of Academic Child and Adolescent Psychology,* 43:403–11.

Kasser, T., & Ryan, R. M. (1993). A dark side of the American dream: Correlates of financial success as a central life aspiration. *Journal of Personality and Social Psychology, 65,* 410–422.

Kassin, S., Tubb, V., Hosch, H., & Memon, A. (2001). On the general acceptance of eyewitness testimony research. *American Psychologist, 56,* 405–416.

Kassin, S. M. (2008). False confessions: causes, consequences, and implications for reform. *Current Directions in Psychological Science, 17*(4), 249–252.

Kassin, S. M., Drizin, S. A., Grisso, T., & others. (2010). Police-induced confessions: Risk factors and recommendations. *Law and Human Behavior, 34*(1), 3–38.

Kassin, S. M., Ellsworth, P. C., & Kassin, S. M. (1989). The "general acceptance" of psychological research on eyewitness testimony: A survey of experts. *American Psychologist, 44,* 1089–1098.

Kaufman, A. S., Kaufman, J. C., Chen, T. H., & Kaufman, N. L. (1996). Differences on six horn abilities for 14 age groups between 15–16 and 75–94 years. *Psychological Assessment, 8,* 161–171.

Kawada, C. L. K., Oettingen, G., Gollwitzer, P. M., & Bargh, J. A. (2004). The projection of implicit and explicit goals. *Journal of Personality and Social Psychology, 86,* 545–559.

Kazdin, A. E. (2009). Psychological science's contributions to a sustainable environment: extending our reach to a grand challenge of society. *American Psychologist, 64*(5), 339–356.

Kearins, J. (1986). Visual spatial memory in aboriginal and white Australian children. *Australian Journal of Psychology, 38*(3), 203–214.

Keefe, F. J., & France, C. R. (1999). Pain: Biopsychosocial mechanisms and management. *Current Directions in Psychological Science, 5,* 137–141.

Keenan, K., & Shaw, D. (1997). Developmental and social influences on young girls' early problem behavior. *Psychological Bulletin, 121,* 95–113.

Kehoe, P., & Bass, E. M. (1986). Conditioned aversions and their memories in 5-day-old rats during suckling. *Journal of Experimental Psychology: Animal Behavior Processes, 12,* 40–47.

Keller, M., Fredrickson, B., Ybarra, O., Cote, S., Johnson, K., Mikels, J., et al. (2005). A warm heart and a clear head. *American Psychological Society, 16,* 724.

Kelley, H. H. (1973). The processes of causal attribution. *American Psychologist, 28,* 107–128.

Kellman, P., Garrigan, P., & Shipley, T. (2005). Object interpolation in three dimensions. *Psychological Review, 112,* 586–609.

Kelly, A. E. (1999). Revealing personal secrets. *Current Directions in Psychological Science, 8,* 105–109.

Kelly, G. A. (1955). *The psychology of personal constructs.* New York: Norton.

Kelly, J. A., St. Lawrence, J. S., Hood, H. V., & Brasfield, T. L. (1989). Behavioral intervention to reduce AIDS risk activities. *Journal of Consulting and Clinical Psychology, 57,* 60–67.

Kelly, J. B., & Emery, R. E. (2003). Children's adjustment following divorce: Risk and resilience perspectives. *Family Relations, 52,* 352–362.

Kendall-Tackett, K. A., Williams, L. M., & Finkelhor, D. (1993). Impact of sexual abuse on children: A review and synthesis of recent empirical studies. *Psychological Bulletin, 113,* 164–180.

Kendler, K. (2001). Twin studies of psychiatric illness. *Archives of General Psychiatry, 58,* 1005–1014.

Kendler, K. S., Gardner, C. O., & Prescott, C. A. (2006). Toward a comprehensive developmental model for major depression in men. *American Journal of Psychiatry, 163,* 115–124.

Kendler, K. S., Thornton, L. M., Gilman, S. E., & Kessler, R. C. (2000). Sexual orientation in U.S. national sample of twin and nontwin sibling pairs. *American Journal of Psychiatry, 157,* 1843–1846.

Kennedy, Q., Mather, M., & Carstensen, L. L. (2004). The role of motivation in the age-related positivity effect in autobiographical memory. *Psychological Science, 15,* 208–214.

Kerr, N. L., & Tindale, R. S. (2004). Small group decision making and performance. *Annual Review of Psychology, 55,* 623–656.

Kessler, R. C., Berglund, P., Demler, O., Jin, R., & Walters, E. E. (2005). Lifetime prevalence and age-of-onset distributions of *DSM-IV* disorders in the National Comorbidity Survey Replication. *Archives of General Psychiatry, 62.*

Kessler, R. C., Chiu, W. T., Demler, O., & Walters, E. E. (2005). Prevalence, severity, and comorbidity of 12-month DSM-IV disorders in the National Comorbidity Survey Replication. *Archives of General Psychiatry, 62,* 617–627.

Kessler, R. C., McGonagle, Z. S., Nelson, C. B., Hughes, M., Eshelman, S., Wittchen, H. U., & Kendler, K. S. (1993). Lifetime and 12-month prevalence of *DSM-III-R* psychiatric disorders in the United States: Results from the National Comorbidity Survey. *Archives of General Psychiatry, 51,* 8–19.

Kessler, R. C., Merikangas, K. R., & Wang, P. S. (2007). Prevalence, comorbidity and service utilization for mood disorders in the United States at the beginning of the twenty-first century. *Annual Review of Clinical Psychology, 3,* 137–158.

Kessler, R. C., Sonnega, A., Bromet, E., Hughes, M., & Nelson, C. B. (1995). Posttraumatic stress disorder in the national comorbidity survey. *Archives of General Psychiatry, 52,* 1048–1060.

Kessler, R. C., Tat Chiu, W., Jin, R., Ruscio, A. M., Shear, K., & Walters, E. E. (2006). The epidemiology of panic attacks, panic disorder, and agoraphobia in the National Comorbidity Survey Replication. *Archives of General Psychiatry, 63,* 415–424.

Kiecolt-Glaser, J. K., Fisher, L. D., Orgrocki, P., Stout, J. C., Speicher, C. E., & Glaser, R. (1987). Marital quality, marital disruption, and immune function. *Psychosomatic Medicine, 49,* 13–30.

Kiecolt-Glaser, J. K., & Newton, T. L. (2001). Marriage and health: His and hers. *Psychological Bulletin, 127,* 472–503.

Kieseppa, T., Partonen, T., Haukka, J., Kaprio, J., & Lonnqvist, J. (2004). High concordance of bipolar I disorder in a nationwide sample of twins. *American Journal of Psychiatry, 161,* 1814–1821.

Kilpatrick, D. G., Koenen, K. C., Ruggiero, K. J., Acierno, R., Galea, S., Resnick, H. S., Roitzsch, J., Boyle, J., & Gelernter, J. (2007). The serotonin transporter genotype and social support and moderation of posttraumatic stress disorder and depression in hurricane-exposed adults. *American Journal of Psychiatry, 164,* 1693–1699.

Kim, C., Jung, S. H., Kang, D. R., Kim, H. C., Moon, K. T., Hur, N. W., & others. (2010). Ambient particulate matter as a risk factor for suicide. *American Journal of Psychiatry, 167*(9), 1100–1107.

Kim, J. E., & Moen, P. (2001). Is retirement good or bad for subjective well-being? *Current Directions in Psychological Science, 10,* 83–86.

Kimball, M. M. (1989). A new perspective on women's math achievement. *Psychological Bulletin, 105,* 198–214.

Kim-Cohen, J., Caspi, A., Taylor, A., Williams, B., Newcombe, R., Craig, I. W., et al. (2006). MAOA, maltreatment, and gene-environment interaction predicting children's mental health: New evidence and a meta-analysis. *Molecular Psychiatry, 11,* 903–913.

King, A. J., & Nelken, I. (2009). Unraveling the principles of auditory cortical processing: Can we learn from the visual system? *Nature Neuroscience, 12*(6), 698–701.

King, C. R., Knutson, K. L., Rathouz, P. J., Sidney, S., Liu, K., & Lauderdale, D. S. (2008). Short sleep duration and incident coronary artery calcification. *JAMA, 300*(24), 2859–2866.

King, L. A., Hicks, J. A., Krull, J. L., & Del Gaiso, A. K. (2006). Positive affect and the experience of meaning in life. *Journal of Personality and Social Psychology, 90,* 179–196.

Kinney, D. K., Levy, D. L., Todd-Yurgelun, D. A., Tramer, S. J., & Holzman, P. S. (1998). Inverse relationship of perinatal complications and eye tracking dysfunction in relatives of patients with schizophrenia: Evidence of a two-factor model. *American Journal of Psychiatry, 15,* 976–978.

Kinsbourne, M. (1988). *Cerebral dysfunction in depression.* Washington, DC: American Psychiatric Association Press.

Kirkpatrick, B., Ran, R., Amador, X. F., Buchanan, R. W., McGlashan, T., Tohen, M., & Bromet, E. (1998). Summer birth and the deficit syndrome of schizophrenia. *American Journal of Psychiatry, 155,* 1221–1226.

Kirsch, I., & Braffman, W. (2001). Imaginative suggestibility and hypnotizability. *American Psychological Society, 10,* 57–61.

Kirsch, I., & Lynn, S. J. (1995). The altered state of hypnosis: Changes in the theoretical landscape. *American Psychologist, 50,* 846–858.

Klatzky, R. L. (1980). *Human memory: Structures and processes.* San Francisco: W. H. Freeman.

Kleitman, N. (1960). The nature of dreaming. In G. E. W. Wolstenholme & M. O'Connor (Eds.), *Ciba Foundation symposium on the nature of sleep.* Boston: Little, Brown.

Klerman, G. L., & Weissman, M. M. (1993). *New applications of interpersonal psychotherapy.* Washington DC: American Psychiatric Press.

Kline, K. N., & Mattson, M. (2000). Breast self-examination pamphlets: A content analysis grounded in fear appeal research. *Health Communication, 12,* 1–21.

Kling, K. C., Hyde, J. S., Showers, C. J., & Buswell, B. N. (1999). Gender differences in self-esteem. *Psychological Bulletin, 125,* 470–500.

Knight, G. P., Fabes, R. A., & Higgins, D. A. (1996). Concerns about drawing causal inferences from meta-analyses: An example in the study of gender differences in aggression. *Psychological Bulletin, 119,* 410–421.

Knutson, K. L., Van Cauter, E., Rathouz, P. J., DeLeire, T., & Lauderdale, D. S. (2010). Trends in the prevalence of short sleepers in the USA: 1975–2006. *Sleep, 33*(1), 37–45.

Knutson, K. L., Van Cauter, E., Rathouz, P. J., Yan, L. L., Hulley, S. B., Liu, K., & Lauderdale, D. S. (2009). Association between sleep and blood pressure in midlife: the CARDIA sleep study. *Archives of Internal Medicine, 169*(11), 1055–1061.

Kobayashi, Y., Sekiguchi, M., Konno, S., & Kikuchi, S. (2010). Increased intramuscular pressure in lumbar paraspinal muscles and low back pain: Model development and expression of substance P in the dorsal root ganglion. *Spine, 35*(15), 1423–1428.

Koenigs, M., Young, L., Adolphs, R., Tranel, D., Cushman, F., Hauser, M., et al. (2007). Damage to the prefontal cortex increases utilitarian moral judgements. *Nature, 446,* 908–911.

Koger, S. M., & Scott, B. A. (2007). Psychology and environmental sustainability: A call for integration. *Teaching of Psychology, 34,* 10–18.

Kohlberg, L. (1964). The development of moral character. In M. L. Hoffman & L. W. Hoffman (Eds.), *Review of child development research* (Vol. I, p. 400). New York: Russell Sage Foundation.

Kohlberg, L. (1969). Stage and sequence: The cognitive-developmental approach to socialization. In D. A. Goslin (Ed.), *Handbook of socialization theory and research.* Chicago: Rand McNally.

Kohn, A. (1987). Shattered innocence. *Psychology Today,* pp. 54–58.

Kolb, L. C. (1977). *Modern clinical psychiatry* (9th ed.). Philadelphia: W. B. Saunders.

Konjin, E. A., Bijvank, M. N., & Bushman, B. J. (2007). I wish I were a warrior: The role of wishful identification in the effects of violent video games on aggression in adolescent boys. *Developmental Psychology, 43,* 1038–1044.

Konrad, A. M., Ritchie Jr., J. E., Lieb, P., & Corrigall, E. (2000). Sex differences and similarities in job attribute preferences: A meta-analysis. *American Psychological Association, Inc., 126,* 593–641.

Korman, A. K. (1974). *The psychology of motivation.* Englewood Cliffs, NJ: Prentice Hall.

Koss, M., Leonard, K., Beezley, D., & Oros, C. (1985). Nonstranger sexual aggression: A discriminant analysis of the psychological characteristics of undetected offenders. *Sex Roles, 12,* 981–992.

Koss, M., & Oros, C. (1982). Sexual experiences survey: A research instrument investigating sexual aggression and victimization. *Journal of Consulting and Clinical Psychology, 50,* 455–457.

Kosslyn, S., Thompson, W., Costantini-Ferrando, M., Alpert, N., & Spiegel, D. (2000). Hypnotic visual illusion alters color processing in the brain. *American Journal of Psychiatry, 157,* 1279–1285.

Kotov, R., Gamez, W., Schmidt, F., & Watson, D. (2010). Linking "big" personality traits to anxiety, depressive, and substance use disorders: A meta-analysis. *Psychological Bulletin, 136*(5), 768–821.

Kraemer, H. C. (2008). DSM categories and dimensions in clinical and research contexts. In J. E. Helzer, H. C. Kraemer, R. F. Krueger, H. Wittchen, P. J. Sirovotka et al. (Eds.), *Dimensional approaches in diagnostic classification: Refining the research agenda for SDM-V,* 5–17. Washington, DC: American Psychiatric Publishing.

Kramer, U. (2010). Coping and defence mechanisms: What's the difference?—second act. *Psychology and Psychotherapy, 83*(2), 207–221.

Kravitz, D. A., & Martin, B. (1986). Ringelmann rediscovered: The original article. *Journal of Personality and Social Psychology, 50,* 936–941.

Krawcyzk, D. C. (2002). Contributions of the prefrontal cortex to the neural basis of decision making. *Neuroscience and Biobehavioral Reviews, 26,* 631–664.

Kreider, R. M., & Elliott, D. B. (2009). *America's families and living arrangements: 2007.* Current Population Reports, P20–561. U.S. Census Bureau: Washington, DC.

Kripke, D., Garfinkel, L., Wingard, D., Klauber, M., & Marler, M. (2002). Mortality associated with sleep duration and insomnia. *Archives of General Psychiatry, 59,* 131–136.

Kübler-Ross, E. (1969). *On death and dying.* New York: Macmillan.

Kübler-Ross, E. (1974). *Questions and answers on death and dying.* Englewood Cliffs, NJ: Prentice Hall.

Kubzansky, L. D., Koenen, K. C., Spiro III, A., Vokonas, P. S., & Sparrow, D. (2007). Prospective study of posttraumatic stress disorder symptoms and coronary heart disease in the normative aging study. *Archives of General Psychiatry, 64,* 109–116.

Kuch, K., & Cox, B. J. (1992). Symptoms of PTSD in 124 survivors of the Holocaust. *American Journal of Psychiatry, 149,* 337–340.

Kuhl, J., & Kazen, M. (2008). Motivation, affect, and hemispheric asymmetry: Power versus affiliation. *Journal of Personality and Social Psychology, 95*(2), 456–469.

Kuncel, N. R., Hezlett, S. A., & Ones, D. S. (2004). Academic performance, career potential, creativity, and job performance: Can one construct predict them all? *Journal of Personality and Social Psychology, 86,* 148–161.

Kunugi, H., & others. (1995). Schizophrenia following in utero exposure to the 1957 influenza epidemics in Japan. *American Journal of Psychiatry, 152,* 450–452.

Kuo, C. J., Chen, V. C., Lee, W. C., Chen, W. J., Ferri, C. P., Stewart, R., & others. (2010). Asthma and suicide mortality in young people: a 12-year follow-up study. *American Journal of Psychiatry, 167*(9), 1092–1099.

Kurtz, M. M., & Mueser, K. T. (2008). A meta-analysis of controlled research on social skills training for schizophrenia. *Journal of Consulting and Clinical Psychology, 76*(3), 491–504.

Kuyken, W., Byford, S., Taylor, R. S., Watkins, E., Holden, E., White, K., & others. (2008). Mindfulness-based cognitive therapy to prevent relapse in recurrent depression. *Journal of Consulting and Clinical Psychology, 76*(6), 966–978.

Kwon, H., Menon, V., Eliez, S., White, C., Dyer-Friedman, J., Taylor, A., Glover, G., & Reiss, A. (2001). Functional neuro-anatomy of visuospatial working memory in fragile X syndrome: Relation to behavioral and molecular measures. *American Journal of Psychiatry, 158,* 1040–1051.

L

La Greca, A. M., Silverman, W. K., & Wasserstein, S. B. (1998). Children's predisaster functioning as a predictor of posttraumatic stress following Hurricane Andrew. *Journal of Consulting and Clinical Psychology, 66,* 883–892.

Lackner, J. R., & DiZio, P. (2005). Vestibular, proprioceptive, and haptic contributions to spatial orientation. *Annual Review of Psychology, 56,* 115–147.

LaCroix, A. Z., Mead, L. A., Liang, K., Thomas, C. B., & Pearson, T. P. (1986). Coffee consumption and the incidence of coronary heart disease. *New England Journal of Medicine, 315,* 977–982.

Lader, M. H., & Mathews, A. (1970). Physiological changes during spontaneous panic attacks. *Journal of Psychosomatic Research, 14,* 377–382.

Lahey, B. B. (2009). Public health significance of neuroticism. *American Psychologist, 64*(4), 241–256.

Lahey, B. B., Applegate, B., Waldman, I. D., Loft, J. D., Hankin, B. L., & Rick, J. (2004). The structure of child and adolescent psychopathology: Generating new hypotheses. *Journal of Abnormal Psychology, 113,* 358–385.

Lahey, B. B., & Ciminero, A. R. (1980). *Maladaptive behavior.* Glenview, IL: Scott, Foresman.

Lahey, B. B., Hartdagen, S. E., Frick, P. J., McBurnett, K., Connor, R., & Hyrd, G. W. (1988). Conduct disorder: Parsing the confounded relation to parental divorce and antisocial personality. *Journal of Abnormal Psychology, 97,* 334–337.

Lahey, B. B., Loeber, R., Quay, H. C., Applegate, B., Shaffer, D., Waldman, I., Hart, E. L., McBurnett, K., Frick, P. J., Jensen, P., Dulcan, M., Canino, G., & Bird, H. (1998). Validity of DSM-IV subtypes of conduct disorder based on age of onset. *Journal of the American Academy on Child and Adolescent Psychiatry, 37,* 435–442.

Lahey, B. B., & Willcutt, E. (2002). The validity of attention-deficit/ hyperactivity disorder among children and adolescents. In P. S. Jensen & J. Cooper (Eds.), *Attention deficit hyperactivity disorder: State of the science, best practices.* pp. 1–1 – 1–23. Kingston, NJ: Civic Research Institute (based on NIH Consensus Development Conference presentation).

Lam, D. H., Hayward, P., Watkins, E. R., Wright, K., & Sham, P. (2005). Relapse prevention in patients with bipolar disorder: Cognitive therapy outcome after 2 years. *American Journal of Psychiatry, 162,* 324–329.

Laming, D. (2010). Serial position curves in free recall. *Psychological Review, 117*(1), 93–133.

Landy, F. J., & Conte, J. M. (2004), *Work in the 21st century.* New York: McGraw-Hill.

Lang, P. J. (1995). The emotion probe: Studies of motivation and attention. *American Psychologist, 5,* 372–385.

Langan-Fox, J., Waycott, J. L., & Albert, K. (2000). Linear and graphic advance organizers: Properties and processing. *International Journal of Cognitive Ergonomics, 4,* 19–34.

Lange, C. G. (1922). *The emotions.* Baltimore: Williams & Williams.

Langlois, J. H., Kalakanis, L., Rubenstein, A. J., Larson, A., Hallam, M., & Smoot, M. (2000). Maxims or myths of beauty? A meta-analytic and theoretical review. *Psychological Bulletin, 126,* 390–423.

Langlois, J. H., & Stephan, C. W. (1981). Beauty and the beast: The role of physical attractiveness in the development of peer relations and social behavior. In S. S. Brehm, S. M.

Kassin, & F. X. Gibbons (Eds.), *Developmental social psychology*. New York: Oxford University Press.

Lanphear, B. P., Hornung, R., Khoury, J., Yolton, K., Baghurst, P., Bellinger, D. C., et al. (2005). Low-level environmental lead exposure and children's intellectual function: An international pooled analysis. *Environmental Health Perspectives 113*, 894–899.

LaPiere, R. T. (1934). Attitudes vs actions. *Social Forces,13*(2).

Latané, B., & Darley, J. (1970). *The unresponsive bystander: Why doesn't he help?* New York: Appleton-Century-Crofts.

Latané, B., & Nida, S. (1981). Ten years of research on group size and helping. *Psychological Bulletin, 89*, 308–324.

Latané, B., & Rodin, J. (1969). A lady in distress: Inhibiting effects of friends and strangers on bystander intervention. *Journal of Experimental Social Psychology, 5*, 189–202.

Latané, B., Williams, K., & Harkins, S. (1979). Too many hands make light the work: The causes and consequences of social loafing. *Journal of Personality and Social Psychology, 37*, 822–832.

Latham, G. P., & Pinder, C. C. (2005). Work motivation theory and research at the dawn of the twenty-first century. *Annual Review of Psychology, 56*, 485–516.

Laudenslager, M. L., Ryan, S. M., Drugan, R. C., Hyson, R. L., & Maier, S. F. (1983). Coping and immunosuppression: Inescapable but not escapable shock suppresses lymphocyte proliferation. *Science, 221*, 568–570.

Lauer, C., Riemann, D., Lund, D., & Berger, M. (1987). Shortened REM latency: A consequence of psychological strain? *Psychophysiology, 24*, 263–271.

Laughlin, P. R., Hatch, E. C., Silver, J. S., & Boh, L. (2006). Groups perform better than the best individuals on letters-to-numbers problems: Effects of group size. *Journal of Personality and Social Psychology, 90*, 644–651.

Laumann, E. O., Gagnon, J. H., Michael, R. T., & Michaels, S. (1994). *The social organization of sexuality: Sexual practices in the United States*. Chicago: University of Chicago Press.

Lazarov, O., & Marr, R. A. (2010). Neurogenesis and Alzheimer's disease: At the crossroads. *Experimental Neurology, 223*(2), 267–281.

Lazarus, J. (2000). *Stress relief and relaxation techniques*. Lincolnwood, IL: Keats.

Lazarus, R. S. (1991). *Emotion and adaptation*. New York: Oxford University Press.

Lazarus, R. S. (1999). *Stress and emotion: A new synthesis*. New York: Springer.

LeBar, K. S. (2007). Beyond fear emotional memory mechanisms in the human brain. *Current Directions in Psychological Science 16*(4), 173–177.

LeDoux, J. (1996). *The emotional brain*. New York: Simon & Schuster.

Lee, A., & Aaker, J. (2004). Bringing the frame into focus: The influence of regulatory fit on processing fluency and persuasion. *Journal of Personality and Social Psychology, 86*, 205–218.

Lee, E., & Son, H. (2009). Adult hippocampal neurogenesis and related neurotrophic factors. *BMB Reports, 42*(5), 239–244.

Leenstra, T., Petersen, L. T., Kariuki, S. K., Oloo, A. J., Kager, P. A., & ter Kuile, F. O. (2005). Prevalence and severity of malnutrition and age at menarche; cross-sectional studies in adolescent schoolgirls in western Kenya. *European Journal of Clinical Nutrition, 59*, 41–8.

Lehman, D. R., Chiu, C.-Y. & Schaller, M. (2004). Psychology and culture. *Annual Review of Psychology, 55*, 689–714.

Lenneberg, E. H. (1967). *Biological foundations of language*. New York: Wiley.

Lenroot, R. K., & Giedd, J. N. (2006). Brain development in children and adolescents: Insights from anatomical magnetic resonance imaging. *Neuroscience and Biobehavioral Reviews, 30*, 718–729.

Lenroot, R. K., & Giedd, J. N. (2010). Sex differences in the adolescent brain. *Brain and Cognition, 72*(1), 46–55.

Lenzenweger, M. F. (2008). Epidemiology of personality disorders. *Psychiatric Clinics of North America, 31*(3), 395–.

Leon, A. S. (1983). Exercise and coronary heart disease. *Hospital Medicine, 19*, 38–59.

Leon, G. R. (1977). *Case histories of deviant behavior: An interactional perspective* (2nd ed.). Boston: Holbrook Press.

Leonard, B., & Taylor, D. (2010). Escitalopram—translating molecular properties into clinical benefit: Reviewing the evidence in major depression. *Journal of Psychopharmacology, 24*(8), 1143–1152.

Leonard, W. E. (1928). *The locomotive god*. London: Chapman & Hall.

Lepper, M. R., Greene, D., & Nisbett, R. E. (1973). Undermining children's intrinsic interest with extrinsic reward: A test of the "overjustification" hypothesis. *Journal of Personality and Social Psychology, 28*, 129–137.

Lerner, J. S., Small, D. A., & Lowenstein, G. (2004). Heart strings and purse strings: Carryover effects of emotions on economic decisions. *Psychological Science, 15*, 337–340.

Leserman, J., Pence, B. W., Whetten, K., Mugavero, M. J., Thielman, N. M., Swartz, M. S., & others. (2007). Relation of lifetime trauma and depressive symptoms to mortality in HIV. *American Journal of Psychiatry, 164*(11), 1707–1713.

Leserman, J., Petitto, J. M., Golden, R. N., Gaynes, B. N., Gu, H., Perkins, D. O., Silva, S. G., Folds, J. D., & Evans, D. L. (2000). Impact of stressful life events, depression, social support, coping and cortisol on progression to AIDS. *American Journal of Psychiatry, 157*, 1221–1228.

LeVay, S. (1991). A difference in hypothalamic structure between heterosexual and homosexual men. *Science, 253*, 1034–1037.

Levenson, J. M., & Sweatt, D. W. (2005). Epigenetic mechanisms in memory formation. *Nature Reviews Neuroscience, 6*, 108–118.

Leventhal, H., & Tomarken, A. J. (1986). Emotion: Today's problem. *Annual Review of Psychology, 37*, 565–610.

Levin, B. E. (2010). Developmental gene × environment interactions affecting systems regulating energy homeostasis and obesity. *Frontiers in Neuroendocrinology, 31*(3), 270–283.

Levin, R., & Nielson, T. A. (2007). Distributed dreaming, posttraumatic stress disorder, and affect distress: A review and neurocognitive model. *Psychological Bulletin, 133*, 482–528.

Levine, C., Kohlberg, L., & Hewer, A. (1985). The current formulation of Kohlberg's theory in response to critics. *Human Development, 28*, 94–100.

Levine, J. D., Gordon, N. C., & Fields, H. C. (1979). The role of endorphin in placebo analgesia. In J. J. Bonica, J. G. Liebeskind, & D. Albe-Fressard (Eds.), *Advances in pain research and therapy* (Vol. 3). New York: Raven Press.

Levine, J. M., Resnick, L. B., & Higgins, E. T. (1993). Social foundations of cognition. *Annual Review of Psychology, 44*, 585–612.

Levine, S. Z., Rabinowitz, J., Case, M., & Ascher-Svanum, H. (2010). Treatment response trajectories and their antecedents in recent-onset psychosis: A 2-year prospective study. *Journal of Clinical Psychopharmacology, 30*(4), 446–449.

Levinson, D. J. (1978). *The seasons of a man's life*. New York: Knopf.

Levinson, D. J. (1986). A conception of adult development. *American Psychologist, 41*, 3–13.

Lewin, K. (1931). Environmental forces in child behavior and development. In C. Murchison (Ed.), *A handbook of child psychology*. Worcester, MA: Clark University Press.

Lewinsohn, P. M., Hoberman, H. M., & Rosenbaum, M. (1988). A prospective study of risk factors for major depression. *Journal of Abnormal Psychology, 97*, 251–264.

Lewinsohn, P. M., Joiner, T. E., & Rohde, P. (2001). Evaluation of cognitive diathesis-stress models in predicting major depressive disorder in adolescents. *Journal of Abnormal Psychology, 110*, 203–215.

Lewinsohn, P. M., Mischel, W., Chaplin, W., & Barton, R. (1980). Social competence and depression: The role of illusory self-perceptions. *Journal of Abnormal Psychology, 89*, 203–212.

Lewis, D. A. (1997). Development of the prefrontal cortex during adolescence: Insights into vulnerable neural circuits in schizophrenia. *Neuropsycho-pharmacology, 16*, 385–398.

Lewis, M., & Rosenblum, L. A. (Eds.). (1978). *The development of affect*. New York: Plenum.

Lewontin, R. (1982). *Human diversity*. New York: Scientific American Library.

Leyens, J. P., Camino, L., Parke, R. D., & Berkowitz, L. (1975). Effects of movie violence on aggression in a field setting as a function of group dominance and cohesion. *Journal of Personality and Social Psychology, 32*, 346–360.

Li, S. C. (2002). Connecting the many levels and facets of cognitive aging. *Psychological Science, 11*, 38–43.

Li, S. C., Lindenberger, U., Hommel, B., Aschersleben, G., Prinz, W., & Battes, P. B. (2004). Lifespan transformations in the couplings of mental abilities and underlying cognitive processes. *Psychological Science, 15*, 153–163.

Li, R., Polat, U., Makous, W., & Bavelier, D. (2009). Enhancing the contrast sensitivity function through action video game training. *Nature Neuroscience, 12*(5), 549–551.

Li, X., Staszewski, L., Xu, H., Durick, K., Zoller, M., & Adler, E. (2002). Human receptors for sweet and unami taste. *PNAS, 99*, 4692–4696.

Liberles, S. D., Horowitz, L. F., Kuang, D. H., Contos, J. J., Wilson, K. L., Siltberg-Liberles, J., Liberles, D. A., & Buck, L. B. (2009). Formyl peptide receptors are candidate chemosensory receptors in the vomeronasal organ. *Proceedings of the National Academy of Sciences of the United States of America, 106*(24), 9842–9847.

Lieberman, M., Eisenberger, N., Crockett, M., Tom, S., Pfeifer, J., & Way, B. M. (2007). Putting feelings into words. *Psychological Science 18*, 421–428.

Liebert, R. M., Neale, J. M., & Davidson, E. S. (1983). *The early window: The effects of television on children and youth.* New York: Pergamon Press.

Likert, R. (1967). *The human organization: Its management and value.* New York: McGraw-Hill.

Lilienfeld, S. O., Kirsch, I., Sarbin, T. R., Lynn, S. J., Chaves, J. F., Ganaway, G. K., & Powell, R. A. (1999). Dissociative identity disorder and the sociocognitive model: Recalling the lessons of the past. *Psychological Bulletin, 125,* 507–523.

Lilienfeld, S. O., Wood, J. M., & Garb, H. N. (2000). The scientific status of projective techniques. *Journal of the American Psychological Society, 1,* 27–66.

Lim, J., & Dinges, D. F. (2008). Sleep deprivation and vigilant attention. *Annals of the New York Academy of Sciences,1129,* Issue Molecular and Biophysical Mechanisms of Arousal, Alertness, and Attention, 305–322.

Lim, J., & Dinges, D. F. (2010). A meta-analysis of the impact of short-term sleep deprivation on cognitive variables. *Psychological Bulletin,136*(3), 357–389.

Lin, Lin, (2009). Breadth-biased versus focused cognitive control in media multitasking behaviors. Proceedings of the National Academy of Sciences, September 15, 2009, 106 (37), 15521–15522.

Lindberg, S. M., Hyde, J. S., Petersen, J. L., & Linn, M. C. (2010). New trends in gender and mathematics performance: A meta-analysis. *Psychological Bulletin, 136,* 1123–1135.

Lindsey, K. P., & Paul, G. L. (1989). Involuntary commitment to public mental institutions: Issues involving the overrepresentation of Blacks as assessment of relevant functioning. *Psychological Bulletin, 106,* 171–183.

Lippa, R. A. (2003). Are 2d:4d finger-length ratios related to sexual orientation? Yes for men, no for women. *Journal of Personality and Social Psychology, 85,* 179–188.

Lippa, R. A. (2006). Is high sex drive associated with increased sexual attraction to both sexes? It depends on whether you are male or female. *Psychological Science, 17,* 46–52.

Lipsitt, L. P. (2003). Crib death: A biobehavioral phenomenon? *Current Directions in Psychological Science, 12*(5), 164–170.

Lisanby, S. H., Maddox, J. H., Prudic, J., Devanand, D. P., & Sackeim, H. A. (2000). The effects of electro-convulsive therapy on memory of autobiographical and public events. *Archives of General Psychiatry, 57,* 581–590.

Locke, E. A., & Latham, G. P. (1990). *A theory of goal setting and task performance.* Englewood Cliffs, NJ: Prentice Hall.

Locke, E. A., & Latham, G. P. (2006). New directions in goal-setting theory. *Current Directions in Psychological Science, 15,* 265–268.

Loftus, E. F. (1993). The reality of repressed memories. *American Psychologist, 48,* 518–537.

Loftus, E. F. (1997). Creating false memories. *Scientific American,* pp. 70–75.

Loftus, E. F. (2004). Memories of things unseen. *Current Directions in Psychological Science, 13,* 145–147.

Loftus, E. F., & Davis, D. (2006). Recovered memories. *Annual Review of Psychology, 2,* 469–498.

Loftus, E. F., & Palmer, J. C. (1974). Reconstruction of automobile destruction: An example of the interaction between language and memory. *Journal of Verbal Learning and Verbal Behavior, 13,* 585–589.

Loftus, E. F., Polonsky, S., & Fullilove, M. T. (1993). *Memories of childhood sexual abuse: Remembering and repressing.* Unpublished manuscript, Columbia University, cited in E. F. Loftus, The reality of repressed memories. *American Psychologist, 48,* 518–537.

London, E. D., & others. (1990). Morphine-induced metabolic changes in the human brain: Studies with positron emission tomography and [fluorine 18] fluorodeoxyglucose. *Archives of General Psychiatry, 47,* 73–81.

Long, G. M., & Toppino, T. C. (2004). Enduring interest in perceptual ambiguity: Alternating views of reversing figures. *Psychological Bulletin, 130,* 748–768.

Longo, M. R., Betti, V., Aglioti, S. M., & Haggard, P. (2009). Visually induced analgesia: Seeing the body reduces pain. *Journal of Neuroscience, 29*(39), 12125–12130.

LoPiccolo, J. (1985). Diagnosis and treatment of male sexual dysfunction. *Journal of Sex and Marital Therapy, 11,* 215–232.

LoPiccolo, J., & Friedman, J. M. (1988). Blood-spectrum treatment of low sexual desire: Integration of cognitive, behavioral, and systematic therapy. In S. R. Leiblum & R. C. Rosen (Eds.), *Sexual desire disorders.* New York: Guilford.

Lorenz, K. (1937). The companion in the bird's world. *Auk, 54,* 245–273.

Lorenz, K. (1967). *On aggression.* New York: Bantam.

Lovden, M., Backman, L., Lindenberger, U., Schaefer, S., & Schmiedek, F. (2010). A theoretical framework for the study of adult cognitive plasticity. *Psychological Bulletin, 136*(4), 659–676.

Love, B. C., Medin, D. L., & Gureckis, T. M. (2004). SUSTAIN: A network model of category learning. *Psychological Review, 111,* 309–332.

Lovoy, L. (2001). A historical survey of the glass ceiling and the double bind faced by women in the workplace: Options for avoidance. *Law & Psychology Review, 25,* 179–203.

Low, B. S. (1989). Cross-cultural patterns in the training of children: An evolutionary perspective. *Journal of Comparative Psychology, 103,* 311–319.

Lubinski, D., Benbow, C. P., Webb, R. M., & Rechek, A. B. (2006). Tracking exceptional human capital over two decades. *Psychological Science, 17,* 194–199.

Lubinski, D., & Humphreys, L. G. (1997). Incorporating general intelligence into epidemiology and the social sciences. *Intelligence, 24,* 159–202.

Luborsky, L., & Barrett, M. S. (2006). The history and empirical status of key psychoanalytic concepts. *Annual Review of Clinical Psychology, 2,* 1–19.

Lucas, R. E. (2007). Long-term disability is associated with lasting changes in subjective well-being: Evidence from two nationally representative longitudinal studies. *Journal of Personality and Social Psychology, 92,* 717–730.

Lucas, R. E., Clark, A. E., Georgellis, Y., & Diener, E. (2003). Reexamining adaption and the set point model of happiness: Reactions to changes in marital status. *Journal of Personality and Social Psychology, 84,* 527–539.

Lucas R. E., Clark, A. E., Georgellis Y., & Diener E. (2004). Unemployment alters the set point for life satisfaction. *Psychological Science, 15,* 8–12.

Lucassen, P. J., Meerlo, P., Naylor, A. S., van Dam, A. M., Dayer, A. G., Fuchs, E., & others. (2010). Regulation of adult neurogenesis by stress, sleep disruption, exercise and inflammation: Implications for depression and antidepressant action. *European Neuropsychopharmacology, 20*(1), 1–17.

Luchins, K. S. (1942). Mechanization in problem solving: The effects of "Einstellung." *Psychometric Monographs, 54*(6).

Luders, E., Narr, K. L., Thompson, P. M., Rex, D. E., Jancke, L., Steinmetz, H., & Toga, A. W. (2004). Gender differences in cortical complexity. *Nature Neuroscience, 7,* 799–800.

Luty, S. E., Carter, J. D., McKenzie, J. M., Rae, A. M., Frampton, C. M. A., Mulder, R. T., et al. (2007). Randomised controlled trial of interpersonal psychotherapy and cognitive-behavioural therapy for depression. *British Journal of Psychiatry, 190,* 496–502.

Lykken, D., & Tellegen, A. (1996). *Happiness is a stochastic phenomenon* (Vol. 7): Blackwell Publishers.

Lynskey, M. T., & others (2004). Major depressive disorder, suicidal ideation, and suicide attempt in twins discordant for cannabis dependence and early-onset cannabis use. *Archives of General Psychiatry, 61,* 1026–1032.

Lyubomirsky, S. (2001). Why are some people happier than others? *American Psychologist, 56,* 239–249.

Lyubomirsky, S., King, L., & Diener, E. (2005). The benefits of frequent positive affect: Does happiness lead to success? *Psychological Bulletin, 131,* 803–855.

Lyubomirsky, S., Sousa, L., & Dickerhoof, R. (2006). The costs and benefits of writing, talking, and thinking about life's triumphs and defeats. *Journal of Personality and Social Psychology, 90,* 692–708.

M

Ma, S. H., & Teasdale, J. D. (2003). Mindfulness-based cognitive therapy for depression: Replication and exploration of differential relapse prevention effects. *Journal of Consulting and Clinical Psychology, 72,* 31–40.

Maass, A., Karasawa, M., Politi, F., & Suga, S. (2006). Do verbs and adjectives play different roles in different cultures? A cross-linguistic analysis of person representation. *Journal of Personality and Social Psychology, 90,* 734–750.

Mackie, D. M., Smith, E. R., & Ray, D. G. (2008). Intergroup emotions and intergroup relations. *Social and Personality Psychology Compass, 2*(5),1866–1880.

Macklin, M. L., Metzger, L. J., Litz, B. T., McNally, R. J., Lasko, N. B., Orr, S. P., & Pitman, R. K. (1998). Lower precombat intelligence is a risk factor for post-traumatic stress disorder. *Journal of Consulting and Clinical Psychology, 66,* 323–326.

Madsen, C. H., Becker, W. C., & Thomas, D. R. (1968). Rules, praise, and ignoring: Elements of elementary classroom control. *Journal of Applied Behavioral Analysis, 1,* 139–150.

Magliaro, S. G., Lockee, B. B., & Burton, J. K. (2005). Direct instruction revisited: A key model for instructional technology. *Educational Technology Research and Development, 53,* 41–55.

Maglione, M., Miotto, K., Iguchi, M., Jungvig, L., Morton, S. C., & Shekelle, P. G. (2005). Psychiatric effects of ephedra use: An analysis of Food and Drug Administration reports of adverse events. *American Journal of Psychiatry, 162,* 189–191.

Maguire, E. A., Spiers, H. J., Good, C. D., Hartley, T., Frackowiak, R. S. J., & Burgess, N. (2003). Navigation expertise and the human hippocampus: A structural brain imaging analysis. *Hippocampus, 13,* 250–259.

Maier, S. F., & Watkins, L. R. (2000). The immune system as a sensory system: Implications for psychology. *Psychological Science, 9,* 98–102.

Malatesta, P., Appolloni, I., & Calzolari, F. (2008). Radial glia and neural stem cells. *Cell Tissue Research, 331*(1), 165–178.

Malle, B. F. (2006). The actor-observer asymmetry in attribution: A (suprising) meta-analysis. *Psychological Bulletin, 132,* 895–919.

Malle, B. F., Knobe, J. M., & Nelson, S. E. (2007). Actor-observer asymmetries in explanations of behavior: New answers to an old question. *Journal of Personality and Social Psychology, 93*(4), 491–514.

Mancuso, K., Hauswirth, W. W., Li, Q., Connor, T. B., Kuchenbecker, J. A., Mauck, M. C., & others. (2009). Gene therapy for red-green colour blindness in adult primates. *Nature, 461*(7265), 784–787.

Mandara, J., Varner, F., Greene, N., & Richman, S. (2009). Intergenerational family predictors of the black-white achievement gap. *Journal of Educational Psychology, 101*(4), 867–878.

Mandel, D. R., Jusczyk, P. W., & Pisoni, D. B. (1995). Infants recognition of the sound patterns of their own names. *Psychological Science, 6,* 314–317.

Mandel, D., Zimlichman, E., Mimouni, F. B., Grotto, I., & Kreiss, Y. (2004). Age at menarche and body mass index: A population study. *Journal of Pediatric Endocrinology, 17,* 1507–1510.

Maner, J. K., Kenrick, D. T., Becker, D., Robertson, T. E., Hofer, B., Neuberg, S. L., Delton, A. W., Butner, J., & Schaller, M. (2005). Functional projection: How fundamental social motives can bias interpersonal perception. *Journal of Personality and Social Psychology, 88,* 63–78.

Mann, S., Vrij, A., & Bull, R. (2002). Suspects, lies and videotape: An analysis of authentic high-stake liars. *Lay and Human Behavior, 26,* 365–376.

Mann, T., Tomiyama, A. J., Westling, E., Lew, A., Samuels, B., & Chatman, J. (2007). Medicare's search for effective obesity treatments. *American Psychologist, 62,* 220–223.

Manne, S., Alfieri, T., Taylor, K., & Dougherty, J. (1999). Preferences for spousal support among individuals with cancer. *Journal of Applied Social Psychology, 29,* 722–749.

Manning, R., Levine, M., & Collins, A. (2007). The Kitty Genovese murder and the social psychology of helping: The parable of the 38 witnesses. *American Psychologist, 62,* 555–562.

Markus, H. (1978). The effect of mere presence on social facilitation: An unobtrusive test. *Journal of Experimental Social Psychology, 14,* 389–397.

Marlatt, G. A., & Rose, F. (1980). Addictive disorders. In A. E. Kazdin, A. S. Bellack, & M. Hersen (Eds.), *New perspectives in abnormal psychology* (pp. 298–324). New York: Oxford University Press.

Marshall, N. L. (2004). The quality of early child care and children's development. *Current Directions in Psychological Science, 13,* 165–168.

Martin, R. C. (2005). Components of short term memory and their relation to language processing. *Current Directions in Psychological Science, 14,* 204–208.

Martin, R. J., White, B. D., & Hulsey, M. G. (1991). The regulation of body weight. *American Scientist, 79,* 528–541.

Martinez, D., Narendran, R., Foltin, R. W., Hwang, D. R., Slifstein, M., Broft, A., et al. (2007). Amphetamine-induced dopamine release: Markedly blunted in cocaine dependence and predictive of the choice to self administer cocaine. *American Journal of Psychiatry, 164,* 622–629.

Martino, S. C., Collins, R. L., Kanouse, D. E., Elliot, M., & Berry, S. H. (2005). Social cognitive processes mediating the relationship between exposure to television's sexual content and adolescents' sexual behavior. *Journal of Personality and Social Psychology, 89,* 914–924.

Martins, J. G. (2009). EPA but not DHA appears to be responsible for the efficacy of omega-3 long chain polyunsaturated fatty acid supplementation in depression: Evidence from a meta-analysis of randomized controlled trials. *Journal of the American College of Nutrition, 28*(5), 525–542.

Martins, Y., Preti, G., Crabtree, C. R., Runyan, T., Vainius, A. A., & Wysocki, C. J. (2005). Preference for human body odors is influenced by gender and sexual orientation. *Psychological Science, 16,* 694–700.

Martorell, R. (1998). Nutrition and the worldwide rise in IQ scores. In U. Neisser (Ed.), *The rising curve: Long-term gains in IQ and related measures* (pp. 183–206). Washington, DC: American Psychological Association.

Martuza, R. L., Chiocca, E. A., Jenike, M. A., Giriunas, I. E., & Ballantine, H. T. (1990). Stereotactic radiofrequency thermal cingulotomy for obsessive compulsive disorder. *Journal of Neuropsychiatry, 2,* 331–336.

Maslow, A. (1967). A theory of meta-motivation: The biological rooting of the value-life. *Journal of Humanistic Psychology, 7,* 93–127.

Maslow, A. (1970). *Motivation and personality* (2nd ed.). New York: Harper & Row.

Maslow, A. H., & Mintz, N. L. (1956). Effects of aesthetic surroundings: I. Initial effects of three aesthetic conditions upon perceiving "energy" and "well-being" in faces. *Journal of Psychology, 41,* 247–254.

Mason, C. (2009). The development of developmental neuroscience. *Journal of Neuroscience, 29*(41), 12735–12747.

Massimini, F., & Fave, A. D. (2000). Individual development in a biocultural perspective. *American Psychologist, 55,* 24–33.

Masters, W. H., & Johnson, V. E. (1966). *Human sexual response.* Boston: Little, Brown.

Mata, I., Perez-Iglesias, R., Roiz-Santianez, R., Tordesillas-Gutierrez, D., Gonzalez-Mandly, A., Vazquez-Barquero, J. L., & others. (2009). A neuregulin 1 variant is associated with increased lateral ventricle volume in patients with first-episode schizophrenia. *Biological Psychiatry, 65*(6), 535–540.

Matchock, R. L., Susman, E. J., & Brown, F. M. (2004). Seasonal rhythms of menarche in the United States: Correlates to menarcheal age, birth age, and birth month. *Women's Health Issues, 14,* 184–192.

Matefy, R. E., & Kroll, R. G. (1974). An initial investigation of psychedelic drug flashback phenomena. *Journal of Consulting and Clinical Psychology, 42,* 854–860.

Mathalon, D., Sullivan, E., Lim, K., & Pfefferbaum, A. (2001). Progressive brain volume changes and the clinical course of schizophrenia in men. *Archives in General Psychiatry, 58,* 148–157.

Mather, M., Canli, T., English, T., Whitfield, S., Wais, P., Ochsner, K., Gabrieli, J. D. E., & Carstensen, L. L. (2004). Amygdala responses to emotionally valenced stimuli in older and younger adults. *Psychological Science, 15*(4), 259–263.

Mathews, A., & MacLeod, C. (1986). Discrimination of threat cues without awareness in anxiety states. *Journal of Abnormal Psychology, 95,* 131–138.

Matlin, M. (1983). *Cognition.* New York: Holt, Rinehart & Winston.

Matlin, M. W. (1988). *Sensation and perception* (2nd ed.). Boston: Allyn & Bacon.

Matthews, D. B., Best, P. J., White, A. M., Vandergriff, L., & Simpson, P. E. (1996). Ethanol impairs spatial cognitive processing: New behavioral and electrophysiological findings. *Current Directions in Psychological Science, 5,* 111–115.

Matthews, E. L. (1982). Psychological perspectives on the Type A behavior pattern. *Psychological Bulletin, 91,* 293–323.

Matthews, K. A. (2005). Psychological perspectives on the development of coronary heart disease. *American Psychologist, 60,* 783–796.

Matusek, J. A., Wendt, S. J., & Wiseman, C. V. (2004). Dissonance, thin-ideal and didactic healthy behavior eating disorder prevention programs: Results from a controlled trial. *International Journal of Eating Disorders, 36*(4), 376–388.

Mays, V. M., Cochran, S. D., & Barnes, N. W. (2007). Race, race-based discrimination, and health outcomes among African Americans. *Annual Review of Clinical Psychology, 58,* 201–225.

Mazure, C. M. (1998). Life stressors as risk factors in depression. *Clinical Psychology: Science and Practice, 5,* 291–313.

McAdams, D. P., & Vaillant, G. E. (1982). Intimacy motivation and psychosocial adjustment: A longitudinal study. *Journal of Personality Assessment, 46,* 586–593.

McCall, R. B. (1979). *Infants.* Cambridge, MA: Harvard University Press.

McCall, W. V., Dunn, A., & Rosenquist, P. B. (2004). Quality of life and function after electroconvulsive therapy. *British Journal of Psychiatry, 185,* 405–409.

McConaghy, M. J. (1979). Gender permanence and the genital basis of gender: Stages in the development of constancy of gender identity. *Child Development, 50,* 1223–1226.

McCormick, E. J., & Ilgen, D. (1980). *Industrial psychology* (7th ed.). Englewood Cliffs, NJ: Prentice Hall.

McCrae, R. R., & Costa, P. T. (1987). Validation of the five-factor model of personality across instruments and observers. *Journal of Personality and Social Psychology, 52,* 81–90.

McCrae, R. R., & Costa, P. T., Jr. (1994). The stability of personality: Observations and evaluations. *Current Directions in Psychological Science, 3,* 173–175.

McCrae, R. R., & Costa, P. T. (1997). Personality trait structure as a human universal. *American Psychologist, 52,* 509–516.

McCrae, R. R., & Costa, P. T. (1999). A five-factor theory of personality. In L. A. Pervin & O. P. John (Eds.), *Handbook of personality: Theory and research* (2nd ed., pp. 139–153). New York: Guilford.

McCrae, R. R., Costa, P. T., Jr., de Lima, M. P., Simones, A., Ostendorf, F., Angleitner, A., Marusic, I., Bratko, D., Caprara, G. V., Barbaranelli, C., Chae, J. H., & Piedmont, R. L. (1999). Age differences in personality across the adult life span: Parallels in five cultures. *Developmental Psychology, 35,* 466–477.

McCrae, R. R., & Terracciano, A. (2005). Universal features of personality traits from the observer's perspective: Data from 50 cultures. *Journal of Personality of Social Psychology, 88,* 547–561.

McCrudden, M. T., Schraw, G., & Kambe, G. (2005). The effect of relevance instructions on reading time and learning. *Journal of Educational Psychology, I 97,* 88–102.

McDermott, K. B., Watson, J. M., & Ojemann, J. G. (2005). Presurgical language mapping. *Current Directions in Psychological Science, 14,* 291–295.

McEwen, B. S. (1998). Protective and damaging effects of stress mediators. *The New England Journal of Medicine, 338,* 171–179.

McFarlane, A. C., & Van Hooff, M. (2009). Impact of childhood exposure to a natural disaster on adult mental health: 20-year longitudinal follow-up study. *British Journal of Psychiatry, 195*(2), 142–148.

McGaugh, J. L. (1983). Preserving the presence of the past. Hormonal influences on memory storage. *American Psychologist, 38,* 161–174.

McGowan, S., Lawrence, A. D., Sales, T., Quested, D., & Grasby, P. (2004). Presynaptic dopaminergic dysfunction in schizophrenia: A positron emission [18fluorodpa] study. *Archives of General Psychiatry, 61,* 134–142.

McGraw, M. B. (1940). Neural maturation as exemplified in achievement of bladder control. *Journal of Pediatrics, 16,* 580–590.

McGregor, A., Hayward, A. J., Pearce, J. M., & Good, M. A. (2004). Hippocampal lesions disrupt navigation based on the shape of the environment. *Behavioral Neuroscience, 118,* 1011–1021.

McNamara, P., McLaren, D., Smith, D., Brown, A., & Stickgold, R. (2005). A Jekyll and Hyde within: Aggressive versus friendly interactions in REM and non-REM dreams. *Psychological Science, 16,* 130–136.

McWilliams, S. A., & Tuttle, R. J. (1973). Long-term psychological effects of LSD. *Psychological Bulletin, 79,* 341–351.

Mead, M. (1935). *Sex and temperament in three primitive societies.* New York: Morrow.

Mednick, S. A., Machon, R. A., Huttunen, M. O., & Bonett, D. (1988). Adult schizophrenia following prenatal exposure to an influenza epidemic. *Archives of General Psychiatry, 45,* 189–192.

Megdal, S. P., Kroenke, C. H., Laden, F., Pukkalae, E., & Schernhammer, E. S. (2005). Night work and breast cancer risk: A systematic review and meta-analysis. *European Journal of Cancer, 41*(13), 2023–2032.

Melamed, S., Shirom, A., Toker, S., Berliner, S., & Shapira, I. (2006). Burnout and risk of cardiovascular disease: Evidence, possible causal paths, and promising research directions. *Psychological Bulletin, 132,* 327–353.

Mellon, J. C. (1975). *National assessment and the teaching of English.* Urbana, IL: National Council of Teachers of English.

Melzack, R. (1992, April). Phantom limbs. *Scientific American,* pp. 120–126.

Melzack, R. (1999). From the gate to the neuromatrix. *Pain. Supplement 6,* S121–S126.

Melzack, R., & Wall, P. D. (1983). *The challenge of pain.* New York: Basic Books.

Mendle, J., Turkheimer, E., & Emery, R. E. (2007). Detrimental psychological outcomes associated with early pubertal timing in adolescent girls. *Developmental Review, 27,* 151–171.

Mercklebach, H., van den Hout, M., Jansen, A., & van der Molen, G. M. (1988). Many stimuli are frightening, but some are more frightening: The contributions of preparedness, dangerousness, and unpredictability to making a stimulus fearful. *Journal of Psychopathology and Behavioral Assessment, 10,* 355–366.

Merikangas, K. R., Akiskal, H. S., Angst, J., Greenberg, P. E., Hirschfeld, R. M. A., Petukhova, M., & Kessler, R. C. (2007). Lifetime and 12-month prevalence of bipolar spectrum disorder in the National Comorbidity Survey Replication. *Archives of General Psychiatry, 64,* 543–552.

Mesulam, M. M. (1995). Cholinergic pathways and the ascending reticular activating system of the human brain. *Annals of the New York Academy of Sciences, 757,* 169–179.

Mewborn, C. R., & Rogers, R. W. (1979). Effects of threatening and reassuring components of fear appeals on physiological and verbal measures of emotion and attitudes. *Journal*

of Experimental Social Psychology, 15, 242–253.

Meyer, A. C., Frank, T., Khimich, D., Hoch, G., Riedel, D., Chapochnikov, N. M., et al. (2009). Tuning of synapse number, structure and function in the cochlea. *Nature Neuroscience, 12*(4), 444–453.

Meyer, D. E., & Schvaneveldt, R. W. (1971). Facilitation in recognizing pairs of words: Evidence of a dependence between retrieval operations. *Journal of Experimental Psychology, 90,* 227–234.

Meyer, U., & Feldon, J. (2010). Epidemiology-driven neurodevelopmental animal models of schizophrenia. *Progress in Neurobiology, 90*(3), 285–326.

Meyer-Bahlburg, H. F. L., & others. (1995). Prenatal estrogens and the development of homosexual orientation. *Developmental Psychology, 31,* 12–21.

Meyerowitz, B. E., & Chaiken, S. (1987). The effect of message framing on breast self-examination attitudes, intentions, and behavior. *Journal of Personality and Social Psychology, 52,* 500–510.

Meyerowitz, B. E., Richardson, J., Hudson, S., & Leedham, B. (1998). Ethnicity and cancer outcomes: Behavioral and psychosocial considerations. *Psychological Bulletin, 123,* 47–70.

Meyers, C. A., Berman, S. A., Scheibel, R. S. & Hayman, A. (1992). Case report: Acquired antisocial personal disorder associated with unilateral left orbital frontal lobe damage. *Journal of Psychiatry and Neuroscience, 17,* 121–125.

Michael, R. T., Gagnon, J. H., Laumann, E. O., & Kolata, G. (1994). *Sex in America: A definitive survey.* Boston: Little, Brown.

Michael, R. T., Gagnon, J. H., Laumann, E. O., & Kolata, G. (1995). *Sex in America: A definitive survey.* Boston: Little, Brown.

Milgram, S. (1963). Behavioral study of obedience. *Journal of Abnormal and Social Psychology, 67,* 371–378.

Milgram, S. (1965). Some conditions of obedience and disobedience to authority. *Human Relations, 18,* 57–76.

Miller, C. A., & Sweatt, D. W. (2007). Covalent modification of DNA regulates memory formation. *Neuron, 53,* 857–869.

Miller, G. A. (1956). The magic number seven, plus or minus two. Some limits on our ability to process information. *Psychological Review, 63,* 81–97.

Miller, J. G. (1999). Cultural psychology: Implications for basic psychological theory. *Psychological Science, 10,* 85–91.

Miller, L. C., Putcha-Bhagavatula, A., & Pedersen, W. C. (2002). Men's and women's mating preferences: Distinct evolutionary mechanisms? *Psychological Science, 11,* 88–93.

Miller, N. E. (1944). Experimental studies of conflict. In J. McV. Hunt (Ed.), *Personality and the behavior disorders* (Vol. 1). New York: Ronald Press.

Miller, S. L., & Maner, J. K. (2010). Scent of a woman: Men's testosterone responses to olfactory ovulation cues. *Psychological Science, 21*(2), 276–283.

Miller, W. R., & Rose, G. S. (2009). Toward a theory of motivational interviewing. *American Psychologist, 64*(6), 527–537.

Milling, L. S., Reardon, J. M., & Carosella, G. M. (2006). Meditation and moderation of psychological pain treatments: Repsonse expectancies and hypnotic suggestibility. *Journal of Consulting and Clinical Psychology, 74,* 253–262.

Mills, T. C., Paul, J., Stall, R., Pollack, L., Canchola, J., Chang, Y. J., et al. (2004). Distress and depression in men who have sex with men: The urban men's health study. *American Journal of Psychiatry, 161,* 278–285.

Milner, B., Corkin, S., & Teuber, H. L. (1968). Further analysis of the hippocampal amnesic syndrome: 14-year follow-up study of H. M. *Neuropsychologia, 6,* 215–234.

Milner, B., Squire, L. R., & Kandel, E. R. (1998). Cognitive neuroscience and the study of memory. *Neuron, 20,* 445–468.

Mineka, S., & Zinbarg, R. (2006). A contemporary learning theory perpective on the etiology of anxiety disorders: It's not what you thought it was. *American Psychologist, 61,* 10–26.

Mingroni, M. A. (2007). Resolving the IQ paradox: Heterosis as a cause of the Flynn effect and other trends. *Psychological Review, 114,* 806–829.

Minton, H. (2000). Psychology and gender at the turn of the century. *American Psychologist, 55,* 613–615.

Minuchin, S. (1974). *Families and family therapy.* Cambridge, MA: Harvard University Press.

Miranda, J., Green, B. L., Krupnick, J. L., Chung, J., Siddique, J., Belin, T., et al. (2006). One-year outcomes of a randomized clinical trial treating depression in low-income minority women. *Journal of Consulting and Clinical Psychology, 74,* 99–111.

Mirescu, C., Peters, J. D., Noiman, L., & Gould, E. (2006). Sleep deprivation inhibits adult neurogenesis in the hippocampus by elevating glucocorticoids. *Proceedings of the National Academy of Sciences of the United States of America, 103*(50), 19170–19175.

Mischel, W. (1968). *Personality and assessment.* New York: Wiley.

Mischel, W., & Shoda, Y. (1999). Integrating dispositions and processing dynamics within a unified theory of personality: The cognitive-affective personality system. In L. A. Pervin & O. P. John (Eds.), *Handbook of personality: Theory and research* (2nd ed., pp. 197–218). New York: Guilford.

Modigliani, V., & Hedges, D. G. (1987). Distributed rehearsals and the primacy effect in single-trial free recall. *Journal of Experimental Psychology: Learning, Memory, and Cognition, 13,* 426–436.

Moffitt, T. E. (1993). Adolescence-limited and life-course-persistent antisocial behavior: A developmental taxonomy. *Psychological Review, 100,* 674–701.

Mogil, J. S., Sternberg, W. F., Kest, B., Marek, P., & Liebeskind, J. C. (1993). Sex differences in the antagonism of swim-stress induced analgesia: Effects of gonadectomy and estrogen replacement. *Pain, 53,* 17.

Mohs, R. C., Breitner, J. C. S., Silverman, J. M., & Davis, K. L. (1987). Alzheimer's disease: Morbid risk among first-degree relatives. *Archives of General Psychiatry, 44,* 405–408.

Mölle, M., & Born, J. (2009). Hippocampus whispering in deep sleep to prefrontal cortex—for good memories? *Neuron, 61*(4), 496–498.

Money, J. (1987). Sin, sickness, or status: Homosexual gender identity and psycho-neuroendocrinology. *American Psychologist, 42,* 384–389.

Money, J. (1988). *Gay, straight, and in-between.* New York: Oxford University Press.

Monroe, S. M., Slavich, G. M., Torres, L. D., & Gotlib, I. H. (2007). Major life events and major chronic difficulties are differentially associated with history of major depressive episodes. *Journal of Abnormal Psychology, 116,* 116–124.

Moons, W. G., Mackie, D. M., & Garcia-Marques, T. (2009). The impact of repetition-induced familiarity on agreement with weak and strong arguments. *Journal of Personality and Social Psychology, 96*(1), 32–44.

Moore, M. K., & Meltzoff, A. N. (2004). Object permanence after a 24–hour delay and leaving the locale of disappearance: The role of memory, space and identity. *Developmental Psychology, 40,* 606–620.

Moore-Ede, M. C., Sulzman, F. M., & Fuller, C. A. (1982). *The clocks that time us.* Cambridge: Harvard University Press.

Morell, P., & Norton, W. T. (1980, May). Myelin. *Scientific American,* pp. 88–118.

Moreno, R., & Mayer, R. E. (2004). Personalized messages that promote science learning in virtual environments. *Journal of Educational Psychology, 96,* 165–173.

Morgan, C. A., Hazlett, M. G., Wang, S., Richardson, E. G., Schnurr, P., & Southwick, S. M. (2001). Symptoms of dissociation in humans experiencing acute, uncontrollable stress: A prospective investigation. *American Journal of Psychiatry, 158,* 1239–1247.

Morissette, S. B., Tull, M. T., Gulliver, S. B., Kamholz, B. W., & Zimering, R. T. (2007). Anxiety, anxiety disorders, tobacco use, and nicotine: A critical review of interrelationships. *Psychological Bulletin, 133,* 245–272.

Morrell, R. F. (1998). Project Follow Through: Still ignored. *American Psychologist, 53,* 318.

Morris, M. W., & Peng, K. (1994). Culture and cause: American and Chinese attributions for social physical events. *Journal of Personality and Social Psychology, 67,* 949–971.

Morris, N. (1986). A working memory, 1974–1984. A review of a decade of research. *Current Psychological Research and Reviews, 5,* 281–295.

Moscowitz, D. S., Brown, K. W., & Cote, S. (1997). Reconceptualizing stability: Using time as a psychological dimension. *Current Directions in Psychological Science, 6,* 127–132.

Moskowitz, J. T., Hult, J. R., Bussolari, C., & Acree, M. (2009). What works in coping with HIV? A meta-analysis with implications for coping with serious illness. *Psychological Bulletin, 135*(1), 121–141.

Motivala, S. J., & Irwin, M. R. (2007). Sleep and immunity: Cytokine pathways linking sleep and health outcomes. *Current Directions in Psychological Science, 16,* 21–25.

Muehlenhard, C., & Hollabaugh, L. (1988). Do women sometimes say no when they mean yes? The prevalence and correlates of women's token resistance to sex. *Journal of Personality and Social Psychology, 54,* 872–879.

Mufson, L., Dorta, K. P., Wickramaratne, P., Nomura, Y., Olfson, M., & Weissman, M. M. (2004). A randomized effectiveness trial of interpersonal psychotherapy for depressed adolescents. *Archive of General Psychiatry, 61,* 577–584.

Mullen, B. (1986). Atrocity as a function of lynch mob composition: A self-attention perspective. *Personality and Social Psychology Bulletin, 12,* 187–197.

Mullen, B., & Johnson, C. (1991). Productivity loss in brainstorming groups: A meta-analytic integration. *Basic and Applied Social Psychology, 72*(1), 3–23.

Mumford, E., Schlesinger, H. J., & Glass, G. V. (1981). Reducing medical cost through mental health treatment: Research problems and recommendations. In A. Broskowski, E. Marks, & S. H. Budman (Eds.), *Linking health and mental health.* Beverly Hills, CA: Sage.

Murray, C. L., & Lopez, A. D. (Eds.). (1996). *The global burden of diseases: A comprehensive assessment of mortality and disability from diseases injuries, and risk factors in 1990 and projected to 2020.* Cambridge, MA: Harvard University Press.

Murray, H. (1938). *Exploration in personality.* New York: Oxford University Press.

Murray, H. (1951). Uses of the T.A.T. *American Journal of Psychiatry, 107,* 577–581.

Myers, D. G. (1999). *Social psychology* (6th ed.). New York: McGraw-Hill.

Myers, D. G. (2000). The funds, friends, and faith of happy people. *American Psychologist, 55,* 56–67.

Myers, D. G. (2005). *Social psychology* (8th ed.). New York: McGraw-Hill.

Myers, D. G., & Diener, E. (1995). Who is happy? *Psychological Science, 6,* 10–18.

Myers, D. H., & Grant, G. A. (1972). A study of depersonalization in students. *British Journal of Psychiatry, 121,* 59–65.

Mykletun, A., Bjerkeset, O., Overland, S., Prince, M., Dewey, M., & Stewart, R. (2009). Levels of anxiety and depression as predictors of mortality: The HUNT study. *British Journal of Psychiatry, 195*(2), 118–125.

N

Nadel, L., & Jacobs, W. J. (1998). Traumatic memory is special. *Current Directions in Psychological Science, 7,* 154–157.

Nail, P. R., MacDonald, G., & Levy, D. (2000). Proposal of a four-dimensional model of social response. *Psychological Bulletin, 126,* 454–470.

Nairne, J. S., & Pandeirada, J. N. (2010). Adaptive memory: Ancestral priorities and the mnemonic value of survival processing. *Cognitive Psychology, 61*(1), 1–22.

Nairne, J. S., & Pandeirada, J. N. S. (2008). Adaptive memory: Remembering with a stone-age brain. *Current Directions in Psychological Science, 17*(4), 239–243.

Nairne, J. S., Pandeirada, J. N., & Thompson, S. R. (2008). Adaptive memory: The comparative value of survival processing. *Psychological Science, 19*(2), 176–180.

Naqvi, N., Shiv, B., & Bechara, A. (2006). The role of emotion in decision making. *Current Directions in Psychological Science, 15,* 260–264.

Narrow, W. E., Rae, D. S., Robins, L. N., & Reiger, D. A. (2002). Revised prevalence estimates of mental disorders in the United States. *Archives of General Psychiatry, 59,* 115–123.

Nash, S. C. (1975). The relationship among sex-role stereotyping, sex-role performance, and sex differences in spatial visualization. *Sex Roles, 1,* 15–32.

Nathan, P. E., & Gorman, J. M. (2007). *A guide to treatments that work* (2nd ed.). New York: Oxford University Press.

National Advisory Mental Health Council. (1995a). *Basic behavioral research for mental health: A national investment.* Rockville, MD: National Institute of Mental Health.

National Advisory Mental Health Council. (1995b). Basic behavioral science research for mental health: A national investment (emotion and motivation). *American Psychologist, 50,* 838–845.

National Center for Health Statistics. (2009). *Causes of death in the United States.* http://www.cdc.gov/nchs/

National Institute on Alcohol Abuse and Alcoholism. (1987). *Report.* Washington, DC: U.S. Government Printing Office.

National Safety Council. (1998). *Accident facts.* Itasca, IL: National Safety Council.

National Victim Center. (1992). *Rape in America: A report to the nation.* Fort Worth, TX: Author.

Nee, D. E., Berman, M. G., Moore, K. S., & Jonides, J. (2008). Neuroscientific evidence about the distinction between short- and long-term memory. *Current Directions in Psychological Science, 17*(2), 102–106.

Neff, L. A., & Karney, B. R. (2005). To know you is to love you: The importance of global adoration and specific understanding for close relationships. *Journal of Personality and Social Psychology, 88,* 480–497.

Neighbors, H. W., Caldwell, C., Williams, D. R., Nesse, R., Taylor, R. J., Bullard, K. M., et al. (2007). Race, ethnicity, and the use of services for mental disorders: Results from The National Survey of American Life. *Archives of General Psychiatry, 64,* 485–494.

Neisser, U. (1998). Rising test scores and what they mean. In U. Neisser (Ed.), *The rising curve: Long-term gains in IQ and related measures* (pp. 3–24). Washington, DC: American Psychological Association.

Nelson, K., & Fivush, R. (2004). The emergence of autobiographical memory: A social cultural developmental theory. *Psychological Review, 111,* 486–511.

Nelson, L. P., & Nelson, V. (1973). *Religion and death anxiety.* Paper presented at the Society for the Scientific Study of Religion, San Francisco.

Nemeth, C. J. (1981). Jury trials. Psychology and law. In L. Berkowitz (Ed.), *Advances in experimental social psychology* (Vol. 14). New York: Academic Press.

Nemets, H., Nemets, B., Apter, A., Bracha, Z., & Belmaker, R. H. (2006). Omega-3 treatment of childhood depression: A controlled, double-blind pilot study. *American Journal of Psychiatry, 163,* 1098–1100.

Nesselroade, J. R. & Molenaar, P. C. M. (2010). Emphasizing intraindividual variability in the study of development over the life span: Concepts and issues. In W. F. Overton (Ed)., *The handbook of life-span development: Social and emotional development: Vol. 1.* 30–54. Hoboken, NJ: Wiley.

Neugarten, B. L., & Hagestad, G. O. (1976). Age and the life course. In R. H. Binstock & E. Shanas (Eds.), *Handbook of aging and the social sciences.* New York: Van Nostrand Reinhold.

Neuner, F., Onyut, P. L., Ertl, V., Odenwald, M., Schauer, E., & Elbert, T. (2008). Treatment of posttraumatic stress disorder by trained lay counselors in an African refugee settlement: A randomized controlled trial. *Journal of Consulting and Clinical Psychology, 76*(4), 686–694.

Newell, B. R., & Pitman, A. J. (2010). The psychology of global warming improving the fit between the science and the message. *American Meteorological Society,* 1003–1014.

Newman, M. L, & Josephs, R. A. (2009). Testosterone as a personality variable. *Journal of Research in Personality, 43,* 258–259.

Newton, J. W., & Mann, L. (1980). Crowd size as a factor in the persuasion process: A study of religious crusade meetings. *Journal of Personality and Social Psychology, 39,* 874–883.

Neyland, T. C., & others. (1998). Sleep disturbances in the Viet Nam generation: Findings from a nationally representative sample of male veterans. *American Journal of Psychiatry, 155,* 929–933.

NICHD Early Child Care Research Network. (2002). Child care structure, process, outcome: Direct and indirect effects of child care quality on young children's development. *Psychological Science, 13,* 199–206.

Nickerson, C., Schwarz, N., Diener, E., & Kahneman, D. (2003). Zeroing in on the dark side of the American dream: A closer look at the negative consequences of the goal for financial success. *Psychological Science, 14,* 531–536.

Niedenthal, P. M. (2007). Embodying emotion. *Science, 316,* 1002–1005.

Nijenhuis, J., & van der Flier, H. (2007). The secular rise in IQs in the Netherlands: Is the Flynn effect on g? *Personality and Individual Differences 43,* 1259–1265.

Niparko, J. K. (Ed.) (2009). *Cochlear implants: Principles and practices* (2nd Ed.). Philadelphia, PA: Lippincott Williams & Wilkins.

Niparko, J. K., Tobey, E. A., Thal, D. J., Eisenberg, L. S., Wang, N., Quittner, A. L., Fink, N. E., & the CDaCI Investigative Team. (2010). Spoken language development in children following cochlear implantation. *JAMA, 303,* 1498–1506.

Nithianantharajah, J., & Hannan, A. J. (2009). The neurobiology of brain and cognitive reserve: Mental and physical activity as modulators of brain disorders. *Progress in Neurobiology, 89*(4), 369–382.

Niwano, Y., Adachi, T., Kashimura, J., & others. (2009). Is glycemic index of food a feasible predictor of appetite, hunger, and satiety? *Journal of Nutritional Science and Vitaminology, 55*(3), 201–207.

Noaghiul, S., & Hibbeln, J. R. (2003). Cross-national comparisons of seafood consumption and rates of bipolar disorders. *American Journal of Psychiatry, 160,* 2222–7.

Nock, M. K. (2010). Self-injury. *Annual Review of Clinical Psychology, 6,* 339–363.

Norman, J. F., Todd, J. T., & Orban, G. A. (2004). Perception of three-dimensional shape form specular highlights, deformation of shading, and other types of visual information. *Psychological Science, 15,* 565–570.

Northouse, P. G. (1997). *Leadership: Theory and practice.* Thousand Oaks, CA: Sage.

Nosek, B. A., Banaji, M. R., & Greenwald, A. G. (2002). Math [H11005] Male, Me [H11005] Female, Therefore Math [H11005]/ Me. *Journal of Personality and Social Psychology, 83,* 44–59.

Nunes, E. V., Frank, K. A., & Kornfeld, D. S. (1987). Psychologic treatment for the Type A behavior pattern and for coronary heart disease: A meta-analysis of the literature. *Psychosomatic Medicine, 48,* 159–166.

Nyman, L. (2010). Documenting history: An interview with Kenneth Bancroft Clark. *History of Psychology, 13*(1), 74–88.

O

Oberauer, K., & Lewandowsky, S. (2008). Forgetting in immediate serial recall: Decay, temporal distinctiveness, or interference? *Psychological Review, 115*(3), 544–576.

O'Connor, M. C., & Paunonen, S. V. (2007). Big Five personality predictors of post-secondary academic performance. *Personality and Individual Differences, 43,* 971–990.

O'Donnell, M. L., Creamer, M., & Pattison, P. (2004). Posttraumatic Stress Disorder and Depression Following Trauma: Understanding Comorbidity. *American Journal of Psychiatry,* 161, 1390–1396.

Öhman, A., Erixon, G., & Löfberg, I. (1975). Phobias and preparedness: Phobic versus neutral pictures as conditioned stimuli for human autonomic responses. *Journal of Abnormal Psychology, 84,* 41–45.

Öhman, A., & Mineka, S. (2001). Fears, phobias, and preparedness: Toward an evolved module of fear and fear learning. *Psychological Review, 108,* 483–522.

Oishi, S. (2001). Culture and memory for emotional experiences: On-line versus retrospective judgments of subjective well-being. *Dissertation Abstracts International, 61* (10–B): 5625.

Olds, J., & Milner, P. (1954). Positive reinforcement produced by electrical stimulation of septal area and other regions of rat brain. *Journal of Comparative and Physiological Psychology, 47,* 419–427.

O'Leary, S. G. (1995). Parental discipline mistakes. *Current Directions in Psychological Science, 4,* 11–13.

Olff, M., Langeland, W., Draijer, N., & Gersons, B. P. R. (2007). Gender differences in posttraumatic stress disorder. *Psychological Bulletin, 133,* 183–204.

Oliver, M. B., & Hyde, J. S. (1993). Gender differences in sexuality: A meta-analysis. *Psychological Bulletin, 114,* 29–51.

Olson, I. R., & Marshuetz, C. (2005). Facial attractiveness is appraised in a glance. *Emotion, 5*(4), 498–502.

Ophira, E., Nass, C., & Wagner, A. D. (2009). Cognitive control in media multitaskers. Proceedings of the National Academy of

Sciences, September 15, 2009,106(37),15583–15587.

Oquendo, M. A., Bongiovi-Garcia, M. E., Galfalvy, H., Goldberg, P. H., Grunebaum, M. F., Burke, A. K., et al. (2007). Sex differences in clinical predictors of suicidal acts after major depression: a prospective study. *American Journal of Psychiatry, 164*, 134–141.

Oquendo, M. A., Ellis, S. P., Greenwald, S., Malone, K. M., Weissman, M. M., & Mann, J. J. (2001). Ethnic and sex differences in suicide rates relative to major depression in the United States. *American Journal of Psychiatry, 158*, 1652–1658.

Ornstein, P. A., & Haden, C. A. (2002). Memory development or the development of memory. *Psychological Science, 10*, 202–205.

Osby, U., Brandt, L., Correia, N., Ekbom, A., & Sparen, P. (2001). Excess mortality in bipolar and unipolar disorder in Sweden. *Archives in General Psychiatry, 58*, 844–850.

Oskamp, S. (2000). A sustainable future for humanity? How can psychology help? *American* Psychologist, 55, 496–508.

Ost, L. G. (1992). Blood and injection phobia: Background and cognitive, physiological, and behavioral variables. *Journal of Abnormal Psychology, 101*, 68–74.

Ostro, B., Lipsett, M., Reynolds, P., Goldberg, D., Hertz, A., Garcia, C., & others. (2010). Long-term exposure to constituents of fine particulate air pollution and mortality: Results from the California teachers study. *Environmental Health Perspectives, 118*(3), 363–369.

Otto, M. W., Smits, J. A. J., & Reese, H. E. (2005). Combined psychotherapy and pharmacotherapy for mood and anxiety disorders in adults: Review and analysis. *Clinical Psychology: Science and Practice, 12*, 72–82.

P

Packer, D. J. (2009). Avoiding groupthink: Whereas weakly identified members remain silent, strongly identified members dissent about collective problems. *Psychological Science, 20*, 546–548.

Padmos, R. C., Hillegers, M. H., Knijff, E. M., Vonk, R., Bouvy, A., Staal, F. J., & others. (2008). A discriminating messenger RNA signature for bipolar disorder formed by an aberrant expression of inflammatory genes in monocytes. *Archives of General Psychiatry, 65*(4), 395–407.

Pahnke, W. N. (1980). Drugs and mysticism. In J. R. Tisdale (Ed.), *Growing edges in the psychology of religion* (pp. 183–200). Chicago: Nelson-Hall.

Paik, H., & Comstock, G. (1994). The effects of television violence on antisocial behavior: A meta-analysis. *Communication Research, 21*, 516–546.

Palmer, S. E. (2002). Perceptual grouping: It's later than you think. *Psychological Science, 11*, 101–106.

Pampallona, S., Bollini, P., Tibaldi, G., Kupelnick, B., & Munizza, C. (2004). Combined pharmacotherapy and psychological treatment for depression. *Archive of General Psychiatry, 61*, 714–718.

Pansky, A., & Koriat, A. (2004). The basic-level convergence effect in memory distortions. *Psychological Science, 15*, 52–59.

Paras, M. L., Murad, M. H., Chen, L. P., & others. (2009). Sexual abuse and lifetime diagnosis of somatic disorders: A systematic review and meta-analysis. *JAMA, 302*, 550–661.

Parker, A. (2007). Binocular depth perception and the cerebral cortex. *Nature Reviews Neuroscience, 8*, 379–391.

Parker, G., Barrett, E. A., & Hickie, I. B. (1992). From nurture to network: Examining links between perceptions of parenting received in childhood and social bonds in adulthood. *American Journal of Psychiatry, 149*, 877–885.

Parker, G., Gibson, N. A., Brotchie, H., Heruc, G., Rees, A., & Hadzi-Pavlovic, D. (2006). Omega-3 fatty acids and mood disorders. *American Journal of Psychiatry, 163*, 969–978.

Parker, K. J., Buckmaster, C. L., Schatzberg, A. F., & Lyons, D. M. (2004). Prospective investigation of stress inoculation in young monkeys. *Archive of General Psychiatry. 61*: 933–940.

Parrott, A. C. (1999). Does cigarette smoking cause stress? *American Psychologist, 54*, 817–820.

Passe, T. J., Rajagopalan, P., Tupler, L. A., Byrum, C. E., MacFall, J. R., & Krishnan, K. R. R. (1997). Age and sex effects on brain morphology. *Progress in NeuroPsychopharmacology & Biological Psychiatry, 21*, 1231–1237.

Pates, J., Oliver, R., & Maynard, I. (2001). The effects of hypnosis on flow states and golf-putting performance. *Journal of Applied Sport Psychology,13*, 341–354.

Patterson, D. R. (2004). Treating pain with hypnosis. *Current Directions in Psychological Science, 13*, 252–255.

Patterson, D. R., Hoffman, H. G., Palacios, A. G., & Jensen, M. J. (2006). Analgesic effects of posthypnotic suggestions and virtual reality distraction on thermal pain. *Journal of Abnormal Psychology, 115*, 834–841.

Patterson, F. (1977). The gestures of a gorilla: Language acquisition in another primate species. In J. Hambrug, J. Goodall, & L. McCown (Eds.), *Perspectives in human evolution* (Vol. 4). Menlo Park, CA: W. A. Benjamin.

Pauly, I. (1968). The current status of the change of sex operation. *Journal of Nervous and Mental Disorders, 147*, 460–471.

Payne, B. K. (2005). Conceptualizing control in social cognition: How executive functioning modulates the expression of automatic stereotyping. *Journal of Personality and Social Psychology, 89*, 488–503.

Payne, J. D., Stickgold, R., Swanberg, K., & Kensinger, E. A. (2008). Sleep preferentially enhances memory for emotional components of scenes. *Psychological Science,19*(8), 781–788.

Pedersen, W. C., Miller, L. C., Putcha-Bhagavatula, A. D., & Yang, Y. (2002). Evolved sex differences in the number of partners desired? The long and short of it. *Psychological Science, 13*, 157–161.

Peladeau, N., Forget, J., & Gagne, F. (2003). Effect of paced and unpaced practice on skill application and retention: How much is enough? *American Educational Research Journal, 40*, 769–801.

Pelphrey, K. A., Reznick, J. S., Goldman, B. D., Sasson, N., Morrow, J., Donahoe, A., & Hodgson, K. (2004). Development of visuospatial short-term memory in the second half of the 1st year. *Developmental Psychology, 40*, 836–851.

Penke, L., Todd, P. M., Lenton, A. P., & Fasolo, B. (2007). How self-assessments can guide human mating decisions. In G. Geher & G. F. Miller (Eds.), *Mating intelligence: New insights into intimate relationships, human sexuality, and the mind's reproductive system*. Mahwah: Lawrence Erlbaum.

Pennebaker, J. W., & Beall, J. K. (1986). Confronting a traumatic event: Toward an understanding of inhibition and disease. *Journal of Abnormal Psychology, 95*, 274–281.

Peplau, L. A. (2003). Human sexuality: How do men and women differ? *Current Directions in Psychological Science*, 37–40.

Peplau, L. A., & Fingerhut, A. W. (2007). The close relationships of lesbians and gay men. *Annual Review of Psychology, 58*, 405–424.

Pepperberg, I. M. (2002). Cognitive and communicative abilities of grey parrots. *Psychological Science, 11*, 83–87.

Perl, E. R. (2007). Ideas about pain, a historical view. *Nature Reviews Neuroscience, 8*, 71–80.

Perls, F. S., Hefferline, R. F., & Goodman, P. (1951). *Gestalt Therapy*. New York: Julian Press.

Pescosolido, B. A., Martin, J. K., Long, J. S., Medina, T. R., Phelan, J. C., & Link, B. G. (2010). "A disease like any other"? A decade of change in public reactions to schizophrenia, depression, and alcohol dependence. *American Journal of Psychiatry, 167*, 1321–1330.

Petersen, J. L., & Hyde, J. S. (2010). A meta-analytic review of research on gender differences in sexuality, 1993–2007. *Psychological Bulletin, 136*(1), 21–38.

Petersen, R. C., & Stillman, R. C. (1978). *Phencyclidine (PCP) abuse: An appraisal* (National Institute on Drug Abuse Monograph No. 21). Washington, DC: U.S. Government Printing Office.

Peterson, L., Brown, D., & Aronson, H. (1998). Faculty gender, status, roles, and privileges in applied doctoral programs. *The Clinical Psychologist, 51*, 11–16.

Peterson, L. R., & Peterson, M. J. (1959). Short-term retention of individual items. *Journal of Experimental Psychology, 58*, 193–198.

Petitto, J. M., Gariepy, J.-L., Gendreau, P. L., Rodriguez, R., & Lewis, M. H. (1999). Differences in NK cell function in mice bred for high and low aggression: Genetic linkage between complex behavioral and immunological traits. *Brain, Behavior, and Immunity, 13*, 175–186.

Petri, H. L. (1986). *Motivation: Theory and research* (3rd ed.). Belmont, CA: Wadsworth.

Petrill, S. A., Lipton, P. A., Hewitt, J. K., Plomin, R., Cherny, S. S., Corley, R., & DeFries, J. C. (2004). Genetic and environmental contributions to general cognitive ability through the first 16 years of life. *Developmental Psychology, 40*, 805–812.

Pettigrew, T. F., & Tropp, L. R. (2006). A meta-analytic test of intergroup contact theory. *Journal of Personality and Social Psychology, 90*, 751–783.

Pettigrew, T. F., & Tropp, L. R. (2008). How does intergroup contact reduce prejudice? Meta-analytic tests of three mediators. *European Journal of Social Psychology 38,* 922–934.

Pevtsova, E. I., Tolpygo, S. M., Obukhova, M. F., & Kotov, A. V. (2009). Complexes of angiotensin IV with functionally different proteins in the regulation of drinking behavior and hemodynamics in rats. *Bulletin of Experimental Biology and Medicine, 148*(5), 738–741.

Phelps, E. A. (2006). Emotion and cognition: Insights from studies of the human amygdala. *Annual Review of Psychology 57,* 27–53.

Phillips, A. C., Batty, G. D., Weiss, A., Deary, I., Gale, C. R., Thomas, G. N., & others. (2010). Neuroticism, cognitive ability, and the metabolic syndrome: The Vietnam experience study. *Journal of Psychosomatic Research, 69*(2), 193–201.

Phillips, J. D. (1933). *Salem in the seventeenth century.* Cambridge, MA: Riverside Press.

Piacentini, J. (1999). Cognitive behavioral therapy of childhood OCD. *Child and Adolescent Psychiatric Clinics of North America, 8,* 599–616.

Piaget, J. (1972). Intellectual development from adolescence to adulthood. *Human Development, 15,* 1–12.

Piaget, J., & Inhelder, B. (1963). *The child's conception of space.* London: Routledge and Paul.

Picotte, D. M., Strong, D. R., Abrantes, A. M., Tarnoff, G., Ramsey, S. E., Kazura, A. N., et al. (2006). Family and peer influences on tobacco use among adolescents with psychiatric disorders. *Journal of Nervous and Mental Disease, 194,* 518–523.

Pincomb, G. A., Lovallo, W. R., Passey, R. B., Brackett, D. J., & Wilson, M. F. (1987). Caffeine enhances the physiological response to occupational stress in medical students. *Health Psychology, 6,* 101–112.

Piper, M. E., & Curtin, J. J. (2006). Tobacco withdrawal and negative affect: An analysis of initial emotional response intensity and voluntary emotion regulation. *Journal of Abnormal Psychology, 115,* 96–102.

Piper, W. E., Ogrodniczuk, J. S., Joyce, A. S., Weideman, R., & Rosie, J. S. (2007). Group composition and group therapy for complicated grief. *Journal of Consulting and Clinical Psychology, 75,* 116–125.

Pizzagalli, D. A., Sherwood, R. J., Henriques, J. B., & Davidson, R. J. (2005). Frontal brain asymmetry and reward responsiveness: A source-localization study. *Psychological Science, 16,* 805–813.

Platek, S. M., & Singh, D. (2010). Optimal waist-to-hip ratios in women activate neural reward centers in men. *PLoS One, 5*(2), 9042.

Plaut, V. C., Markus, H. R., & Lachman, M. E. (2002). Place matters: Consensual features and regional variation in American well-being and self. *Journal of Personality and Social Psychology, 83,* 160–184.

Plomin, R. (1989). Environment and genes: Determinants of behavior. *American Psychologist, 44,* 105–111.

Plomin, R. (1999). Genetics of childhood disorders: III. Genetics and intelligence. *Journal of the American Academy of Child and Adolescent Psychiatry, 38,* 786–788.

Plomin, R., DeFries, J. C., & Loehlin , J. C. (1977). Genotype-environment interaction and correlation in the analysis of human behavior. *Psychological Bulletin 84,* 309–322.

Plomin, R., & Spinath, F. M. (2004). Intelligence: Genetics, genes, and genomics. *Journal of Personality and Social Psychology, 86,* 112–129.

Ployhart, R. E., Weekley, J. A., Holtz, B. C. & Kemp, C. (2003). Web-based and paper-and-pencil testing of applicants in a proctored setting: Are personality, biodata, and situational judgment tests comparable? *Personnel Psychology, 56,* 733–752.

Pogue-Geile, M. F., & Yokley, J. L. (2010). Current research on genetic contributors to schizophrenia. *Current Directions in Psychological Science, 19,* 214–219.

Poleshuck, E. L., Gamble, S. A., Cort, N., Hoffman-King, D., Cerrito, B., Rosario-McCabe, L. A., & others. (2010). Interpersonal psychotherapy for co-occurring depression and chronic pain. *Professional Psychology Research and Practice, 41*(4), 312–318.

Pollard, J., Shepherd, J., & Shepherd, J. (1999). Average faces are average faces. *Current Psychology: Developmental • Learning • Personality • Social, 18*(1), 98–103.

Pope, H., Gruber, A., Hudson, J., Huestis, M., & Yurgelun-Todd, D. (2001). Neuropsychological performance in long-term cannabis users. *Archives in General Psychiatry, 58,* 909–915.

Poropat, A. E. (2009). A meta-analysis of the five-factor model of personality and academic performance. *Psychological Bulletin, 135*(2), 322–338.

Porter, S., Birt, A., Yuille, J., & Lehman, D. (2000). Negotiating false memories: Interviewer and rememberer characteristics related to memory distortion. *Psychological Science, 11,* 507–510.

Posner, M. I. (1973). *Cognition: An introduction.* Glenview, IL: Scott, Foresman.

Postmes, T., & Spears, R. (1998). Deindividuation and anti-normative behavior: A meta-analysis. *Psychological Bulletin, 123,* 238–259.

Powell, L. H., Calvin III, J. E., & Calvin Jr., J. E. (2007). Effective obesity treatments. *American Psychologist, 62,* 234–246.

Powell, K. E., Thompson, P. D., Caspersen, C. J., & Kendrick, J. S. (1987). Physical activity and incidence of coronary heart disease. *American Review of Public Health, 8,* 253–287.

Powers, M. B., & Emmelkamp, P. M. (2008). Virtual reality exposure therapy for anxiety disorders: A meta-analysis. *Journal of Anxiety Disorders, 22*(3), 561–569.

Pratto, F., Stallworth, L. M., Sidanius, J., & Siers, B. (1997). The gender gap in occupational role attainment: A social dominance approach. *Journal of Personality and Social Psychology, 72,* 37–53.

Prescott, J., & Wilkie, J. (2007). Pain tolerance selectively increased by a sweet-smelling odor. *Psychological Science, 16,* 308–311.

Pressman, S. D., & Cohen, S. (2005). Does positive affect influence health? *Psychological Bulletin, 131,* 925–971.

Preston, S. H. (1998). Differential fertility by IQ and the IQ distribution of a population. In U. Neisser (Ed.), *The rising curve: Long-term gains in IQ and related measures* (pp. 377–388). Washington, DC: American Psychological Association.

Price, D. D. (1988). *Psychological and neural mechanisms of pain.* New York: Raven Press.

Price, D. D., & Barber, J. (1987). An analysis of factors that contribute to the efficiency of hypnotic analgesia. *Journal of Abnormal Psychology, 96,* 46–51.

Primack, B. A., Aronson, J. D., & Agarwal, A. A. (2006). An old custom, a new threat to tobacco control. *American Journal of Public Health, 96,* 1339.

Prinzmetal, W. (1995). Visual feature integration in a world of objects. *Current Directions in Psychological Science, 4,* 90–94.

Prochaska, J. O. (1984). *Systems of psychotherapy: A transtheoretical analysis* (2nd ed.). Pacific Grove, CA: Brooks/Cole.

Proctor, R. W., & Vu, K. P. L. (2010). Cumulative knowledge and progress in human factors. *Annual Review of Psychology, 61,* 623–651.

Proffitt, D. R. (2006). Embodied perception and the economy of action. *Perspectives on Psychological Science 1,* 110–122.

Pugh, E. N. (1988). Vision: Physics and retinal physiology. In R. C. Atkinson, R. J. Herrnstein, G. Lindzey, & R. D. Luce (Eds.), *Stevens' handbook of experimental psychology: Vol. 1. Perception and Motivation.* New York: Wiley Interscience.

Puts, D. A. (2010). Beauty and the beast: Mechanisms of sexual selection in humans. *Evolution and Human Behavior, 31*(157), 157–175.

Q

Querido, J. G., Warner, T. D., & Eyberg, S. M. (2002). Parenting styles and child behavior in African American families of preschool children. *Journal of Clinical Child Psychology, 31,* 272–277.

R

Raaheim, K., & Kaufmann, G. (1972). Level of activity and success in solving an unfamiliar task. *Psychological Reports, 30,* 271–274.

Raaijmakers, J. G. W., & Shiffrin, R. M. (1992). Models for recall and recognition. *Annual Review of Psychology, 43,* 205–234.

Rachman, S. (1966). Sexual fetishism: An experimental analogue. *Psychological Record, 16,* 293–296.

Ramchand, R., Marshall, G. N., Schell, T. L., & Jaycox, L. H. (2008). Posttraumatic distress and physical functioning: A longitudinal study of injured survivors of community violence. *Journal of Consulting and Clinical Psychology, 76*(4), 668–676.

Ranganath, C. (2010). Binding items and contexts: The cognitive neuroscience of episodic memory. *Current Directions in Psychological Science, 19*(3), 131–137.

Ranken, H. B. (1963). Language and thinking: Positive and negative effects of naming. *Science, 141,* 48–50.

Rasch, B., & Born, J. (2008). Reactivation and consolidation of memory during sleep. *Current Directions in Psychological Science, 17*(3), 188–192.

Ray, O. (2004). How the mind hurts and heals the body. *American Psychologist. 59* (1): 29–40.

Raynor, H. A., & Epstein, L. H. (2001). Dietary variety, energy regulation, and obesity. *Psychological Bulletin, 127,* 325–341.

Read, C. N., & Greenberg, B. D. (2009). Psychiatric neurosurgery 2009: Review and perspective. *Seminars in Neurology, 29*(3), 256–265.

Recanzone, G. H., & Cohen, Y. E. (2010). Serial and parallel processing in the primate auditory cortex revisited. *Behavioural brain research, 206*(1), 1–7.

Rechtschaffen, A., & Bergmann, B. M. (1995). Sleep deprivation in the rat by the disk-over-water method. *Behavioural Brain Research, 69,* Issues 1-2, 55–63.

Rechtschaffen, A., & Buchignami, C. (1983). Visual dimensions and correlates of dream images. *Sleep Research, 12,* 189.

Redd, W. H., Jacobsen, P. B., Die-Trill, M., Dermatis, H., McEvoy, M., & Holland, J. C. (1987). Cognitive/attentional distraction in the control of conditioned nausea in pediatric cancer patients receiving chemotherapy. *Journal of Consulting and Clinical Psychology, 55,* 391–395.

Redish, A. D., Jensen, S., Johnson, A., & Nelson, Z. K. (2007). Reconciling reinforcement learning models with behavioral extinction and renewal: Implication for addiction, relapse, and problem gambling. *Psychological Review, 114,* 784–805.

Reed, C. F. (1984). Terrestrial passage theory of the moon illusion. *Journal of Experimental Psychology: General, 113,* 489–516.

Reeves, A., & Plumb, F. (1969). Hyperphagia, rage, and dementia accompanying a ventromedial hypothalamic neoplasm. *Archives of Neurology, 20,* 616–624.

Reichle, E. D., Reineberg, A. E., & Schooler, J. W. (2010). Eye movements during mindless reading. *Psychological Sciences, 21*(9), 1300.

Reid, D., & Reid, F. (2004). Insights into the social and psychological effects of SMS text messaging. www.160characters.org/documents/SocialEffectsOfTextMessaging.pdf

Rhodes, G., Sumich, A., & Byatt, G. (1999). Are average facial configurations attractive only because of their symmetry? *Psychological Science,* 10(1), 52–58.

Rhodes, G., & Tremewan, T. (1996). Averageness, exaggeration, and facial attractiveness. *Psychological Science, 7*(2), 105–110.

Reis, H. T., & Aron, A. (2008). Love: What is it, why does it matter, and how does it operate? *Perspectives on Psychological Science, 3,* 80–86.

Reis, S. M., McCoach, D. B., Coyne, M., Schreiber, F. J., Eckert, R. D., & Gubbins, E. J. (2007). Using planned enrichment strategies with direct instruction to improve reading fluency, comprehension, and attitude toward reading: An evidence-based study. *Elementary School Journal, 108,* 3–23.

Reiss, A. L., & others. (1996). Brain development, gender and IQ in children: A volumetric imaging study. *Brain, 119,* 1763–1774.

Reneman, L., Lavalaye, J., Schmand, B., de Wolff, F., van den Brink, W., den Heeten, G., & Booij, J. (2001). Cortical serotonin transporter density and verbal memory in individuals

who stopped using 3, 4-ethylenedioxymeth-amphetamine (MDMA or "Ecstasy"). *Archives in General Psychiatry, 58,* 901–906.

Reynolds, A. G., & Flagg, P. W. (1983). *Cognitive psychology* (2nd ed.). Boston: Little, Brown.

Rhee, S. H., & Waldman, I. D. (2002). Genetic and environmental influences on antisocial behaivor: A meta-analysis of twin and adoption studies. *Psychological Bulletin 128(3),* 490–529.

Rhodes, G., Sumich, A., & Byatt, G. (1999). Are average facial configurations attractive only because of their symmetry? *Psychological Science,* 10(1), 52–58.

Rhodes, N., & Wood, W. (1992). Self-esteem and intelligence affect influenceability: The mediating role of message reception. *Psychological Bulletin, 111,* 156–171.

Ribeiro, A. C., LeSauter, J., Dupre, C., & Pfaff, D. W. (2009). Relationship of arousal to circadian anticipatory behavior: Ventromedial hypothalamus: One node in a hunger-arousal network. *The European Journal of Neuroscience, 30*(9), 1730–1738.

Ribeiro, S., Goyal, V., Mello, C., & Pavlides, C. (1999). Constantine. Brain gene expression during REM sleep depends on prior waking experience. *Learning and Memory, 6,* 500–508.

Ribeiro, S., Mello, C., Velho, T., Gardner, T. J., Jarvis, E. D., & Pavlides, C. (2002). Induction of hippocampal long-term potentiation during the waking leads to increased extrahippocampal zif-268 expression during rapid-eye-movement sleep. *Journal of Neuroscience, 22,* 10914–10923.

Riccio, D. C., Millin, P. M., & Gisquet-Verrier, P. (2003). Retrograde amnesia: Forgetting back. *Current Directions in Psychological Science, 12,* 41–44.

Richards, J. M. (2004). The cognitive consequences of concealing feelings. *Current Directions in Psychological Science.* 13(4): 131–134.

Richards, J. M., Beal, W. E., Seagal, J. D., & Pennebaker, J. W. (2000). Effects of disclosure of traumatic events on illness behavior among psychiatric prison inmates. *Journal of Abnormal Psychology, 109,* 156–160.

Richter, L. M. (2006). Studying adolescence. *Science, 312,* 1902–1905.

Roberts, B. W., Caspi, A., & Moffitt, T. E. (2001). The kids are alright: Growth and stability in personality development from adolescence to adulthood. *Journal of Personality and Social Psychology, 81,* 670–683.

Roberts, B. W., Kuncel, N. R., Shiner, R., Caspi, A., & Goldberg, L. R. (2007). The power of personality: The comparative validity of personality traits, socioeconomic status, and cognitive ability for predicting important life outcomes. *Perspectives on Psychological Science, 2,* 313–344.

Roberts, B. W., Smith, J., Jackson, J. J., & Edmonds, G. (2009). Compensatory conscientiousness and health in older couples. *Psychological Science, 20*(5), 553–559.

Roberts, P., & Newton, P. M. (1987). Levinsonian studies of women's adult development. *Psychology and Aging, 2,* 154–163.

Robins, R. W., Caspi, A., & Moffitt, T. E. (2000). Two personalities, one relationship: Both partners' personality traits shape the quality

of their relationship. *Journal of Personality and Social Psychology, 79*(2), 251–259.

Robins, R. W., Mendelsohn, G. A., & Spranca, M. D. (1996). The actor-observer effect revisited: Effects of individual differences and repeated social interactions on actor and observer attributions. *Journal of Personality and Social Psychology, 71*(2), 375–389.

Robinson, N. S., Garber, J., & Hilsman, R. (1995). Cognitions and stress: Direct and moderating effects on depressive versus externalizing symptoms during the junior high school transition. *Journal of Abnormal Psychology, 104,* 3.

Robinson, R. G., & Starkstein, S. E. (1990). Current research in affective disorders following stroke. *Journal of Neuropsychiatry and Clinical Neurosciences, 2,* 1–14.

Robles, T. F., Glaser, R., & Kiecolt-Glaser, J. (2005). Out of balance: A new look at chronic stress, depression, and immunity. *Current Directions in Psychological Science, 14,* 111–115.

Rock, I., & Kaufman, L. (1972). The moon illusion. In R. Held & W. Richards (Eds.), *Perception: Mechanisms and models.* San Francisco: W. H. Freeman.

Rodgers, J., & Ashton, C. H. (2004). Liquid ecstasy: A new kid on the dance floor. *British Journal of Psychiatry, 184,* 104–106.

Rodin, J., & Ickovics, R. (1990). Women's health: Review and research agenda as we approach the 21st century. *American Psychologist, 45,* 1018–1034.

Roe, A. (1946). The personality of artists. *Educational Psychology Measurement, 6,* 401–408.

Roe, A. (1953). *The making of a scientist.* New York: Dodd, Mead.

Roedieger, H., & McDermott, K. (2000). Tricks of memory. *American Psychological Society, 9,* 123–127.

Rogers, C. R. (1951). *Client-centered therapy: Its current practice, implications, and theory.* Boston: Houghton Mifflin.

Rohan, K. J., Roecklein, K. A., Lacy, T. J., & Vacek, P. M. (2009). Winter depression recurrence one year after cognitive-behavioral therapy, light therapy, or combination treatment. *Behavior Therapy, 40,* 225–238.

Roisman, G. I., Masten, A. S., Coatsworth, J. D., & Tellegen, A. (2004). Salient and emerging developmental tasks in the transition to adulthood. *Child Development, 75,* 123–133.

Rolls, E. T., Burton, M. J., & Mora, F. (1976). Hypothalamic neuronal responses associated with the sight of food. *Brain Research, 111,* 53–66.

Rorschach, H. (1953). *Psychodiagnostics* (5th ed.). New York: Grune & Stratton.

Rosch, E. (1973). Natural categories. *Cognitive Psychology, 4,* 328–350.

Rosch, E. (1975). Cognitive representations of semantic categories. *Journal of Experimental Psychology: General, 104,* 192–233.

Rosch, E. H., Mervis, C. B., Gray, W. B., Johnson, D. M., & Boyes-Braem, P. (1976). Basic objects in natural categories. *Cognitive Psychology, 8,* 382–439.

Rose, A. J., Carlson, W., & Waller, E. M. (2007). Prospective associations of corumination with friendship and emotional adjustment:

Considering the socioemotional trade-offs of corumination. *Developmental Psychology, 43,* 1019–1031.

Rose, J. E., & others (2003). PET studies of the influences of nicotine on neural systems in cigarette smokers. *American Journal of Psychiatry, 160,* 323–333.

Rosen, R. C., & Leiblum, S. R. (1995). Treatment of sexual disorders in the 1990s: An integrated approach. *Journal of Consulting and Clinical Psychology, 63,* 877–890.

Rosenkranz, M. A. (2007). Substance P at the nexus of mind and body in chronic inflammation and affective disorders. *Psychological Bulletin, 133,* 1007–1037.

Ross, M., & Wilson, A. E. (2003). Autobiographical memory and conceptions of self: Getting better all the time. *Current Directions in Psychological Science, 12*(2), 66–69.

Rossi, A. S. (1980). Aging and parenthood in the middle years. In P. B. Balter & O. G. Brim (Eds.), *Life-span development and behavior* (Vol. 3). New York: Academic Press.

Rossi, E. A., & Roorda, A. (2010). The relationship between visual resolution and cone spacing in the human fovea. *Nature Neuroscience, 13*(2), 156–157.

Rothbaum, B. O. (2004). Technology and manual-based therapies. *Clinical Psychology: Science and Practice, 11,* 339–341.

Rothman, A. J., & Salovey, P. (1997). Shaping perceptions to motivate healthy behavior: The role of message framing. *Psychological Bulletin, 121,* 3–19.

Roussos, A., Goenjian, A. K., Steinberg, A. M., Sotiropoulou, C., Kakaki, M., Kabakos, C., Karagianni, S., & Manouras, V. (2005). Posttraumatic stress and depressive reactions among children and adolescents after the 1999 earthquake in Ano Liosia, Greece. *American Journal of Psychiatry, 162,* 530–537.

Rovee-Collier, C. (1999). The development of infant memory. *Current Directions in Psychological Science, 8,* 80–85.

Roy, M., & Steptoe, A. (1991). The inhibition of cardiovascular responses to mental stress following aerobic exercise. *Psychophysiology, 28,* 689–700.

Roy-Byrne, P. P., Craske, M. G., & Stein, M. B. (2006). Panic disorder. *Lancet, 368,* 1023–1032.

Roysamb, E., Tambs, K., Reichborn-Kjennerud, T., Neale, M. C., & Harris, J. R. (2003). Happiness and health: Environmental and genetic contributions to the relationship between subjective well-being, perceived health, and somatic illness. *Journal of Personality and Social Psychology, 85* (6): 1136–1146.

Rozin, P. (1996). Towards a psychology of food and eating: From motivation to model to marker, morality, meaning, and metaphor. *Current Directions in Psychological Science, 5,* 18–24.

Rubin, D. C. (2006). The basic systems model of episodic memory. *Perspectives on Psychological Science, 1,* 277–310.

Rubin, K. H. (1998). Social and emotional development from a cultural perspective. *Developmental Psychology, 34,* 611–615.

Ruble, D. N., & Ruble, T. L. (1980). Sex stereotypes. In A. G. Miller (Ed.). *In the eye of the beholder: Contemporary issues in stereotyping.* New York: Holt, Rinehart & Winston.

Ruck, C., Andreewitch, S., Flyckt, K., Edman, G., Nyman, H., Meyerson, B. A., et al. (2003). Capsulotomy for refractory anxiety disorders: Long-term follow-up of 26 patients. *American Journal of Psychiatry, 160,* 513–521.

Rudman, L. A., & Goodwin, S. A. (2004). Gender differences in automatic in-group bias: Why do women like women more than men like men? *Interpersonal relations and group processes, 87,* 494–509.

Rumbaugh, D. M., & Gill, T. V. (1976). The mastery of language-type skills by the chimpanzee (*Pan*). In S. Harnad, H. Steklis, & J. Lancaster (Eds.), *Origins and evolution of language and speech.* New York: New York Academy of Sciences.

Rumelhart, D. E., & McClelland, J. L. (Eds.). (1986). *Parallel distributed processing: Explorations in the microstructure of cognition, Vol. 1: Foundations.* Cambridge, MA: MIT Press.

Russano, M. B., Meissner, C. A., Nardnet, F. M. & Kassings, M. (2005). *Psychological Science, 16,* 481–486.

Russell, J. A., & Mehrabian, A. (1978). Approach-avoidance and affiliation as functions of the emotion-eliciting equality of an environment. *Environment and Behavior, 10,* 355–387.

Russo, N. F. (1990). Overview: Forging research priorities for women's mental health. *American Psychologist, 45,* 368–373.

Rutherford, S. D. (1988). The culture of American deaf people. *Sign Language Studies, 59,* 129–147.

Rutter, M. (2006). *Genes and behavior.* Malden, MA: Wiley-Blackwell.

Rutter, M. (2010). Gene-environment interplay. *Depression and Anxiety, 27,* 1–4.

Rutter, M., Moffitt, T. E., & Caspi, A. (2006). Gene–environment interplay and psychopathology: Multiple varieties but real effects. *Journal of Child Psychology and Psychiatry, 47,* 226–261.

Rutter, M., Sonuga-Barke, E. J., Beckett, C., Castle, J., Kreppner, J., Kumsta, R., Scholtz, W., Stevens, S., & Bell, C. A. (2010). Deprivation-specific psychological patterns: Effects of institutional deprivation. *Monographs of the Society for Research in Child Development, 75.*

Ryan, R. M., & Deci, E. L. (2000). Self-determination theory and the facilitation of intrinsic motivation, social development, and well-being. *American Psychologist, 55,* 68–78.

Rydell, R. J., & McConnell, A. R. (2006). Understanding implicit and explicit attitude change: A systems of reasoning analysis. *Journal of Personality and Social Psychology, 91,* 995–1008.

S

Sachs, J. D. S. (1967). Recognition memory for syntactic and semantic aspects of connected discourse. *Perception and Psychophysics, 2,* 437–442.

Sackett, P. R., Kuncel, N. R., Arneson, J. J., Cooper, S. R., & Walters, S. D. (2009). Does socioeconomic status explain the relationship between admissions tests and post-secondary academic performance? *Psychological Bulletin, 135*(1), 1–22.

Sackett, P. R., & Lievens, F. (2008). Personnel selection. *Annual Review of Psychology, 59,* 419–450.

Sackett, P. R., Schmitt, N., Ellingson, J. E., & Kabin, M. B. (2001). High-stakes testing in employment, credentialing, and higher education: Prospects in a post-affirmative-action world. *American Psychologist, 56,* 302–318.

Saha, S., Chant, D., & McGrath, J. (2007). A systematic review of mortality in schizophrenia: Is the differential mortality gap worsening over time? *Archives of General Psychiatry, 64,* 1123–1131.

Sakurai, T. (2007). The neural circuit of orexin (hypocretin): maintaining sleep and wakefulness. *Nature Reviews Neuroscience, 8,* 171–180.

Salgado, J. F., Anderson, N., Moscoso, S., Bertua, C., de Fruyt, F., & Rolland, J. P. (2003). A meta-analytic study of general mental ability validity for different occupations in the European community. *Journal of Applied Psychology, 88,* 1068–1081.

Salomoni, P., & Calegari, F. (2010). Cell cycle control of mammalian neural stem cells: Putting a speed limit on G1. *Trends in Cell Biology, 20*(5), 233–243.

Salthouse, T. A. (2004). What and when of cognitive aging. *Current Directions in Psychological Science, 13*(4), 140–144.

Sandfort, T. G. M., de Graaf, R., Bijl, R. V., & Schnabel, P. (2001). Same-sex sexual behavior and psychiatric disorders. *Archives of General Psychiatry, 58,* 85–91.

Santtila, P., Sandnabba, N. K., Harlaar, N., & others. (2008). Potential for homosexual response is prevalent and genetic. *Biological Psychology, 77,* 102–105.

Santrock, J. W. (1998). *Children* (5th ed.). Boston: McGraw-Hill.

Sargent, C. (1984). Between death and shame: Dimensions of pain in Bariba culture. *Social Science and Medicine, 19,* 1299–1304.

Savic, I. (2002). Sex differeniated hypothalamic activation by putative phermones. *Molecular Psychiatry, 7,* 335–336.

Savin-Williams, R. C. (2006). Who's gay? Does it matter? *Current Directions in Psychological Science, 15,* 40–44.

Scarr, S., & Eisenberg, M. (1993). Child care research: Issues, perspectives, and results. *Annual Review of Psychology, 44,* 613–644.

Scarr, S., Philips, D., & McCartney, K. (1990). Facts, fantasies, and the future of childcare in the United States. *Psychological Science, 1,* 26–35.

Scarr, S., & Salapatek, P. (1970). Patterns of fear development during infancy. *Merrill-Palmer Quarterly, 16,* 53–90.

Schachter, D. L. (1999). The seven sins of memory: Insights from psychology and cognitive neuroscience. *American Psychologist, 54,* 182–203.

Schachter, S. (1959). *The psychology of affiliation. Experimental studies of sources of gregariousness.* Stanford, CA: Stanford University Press.

Schachter, S., & Singer, J. E. (1962). Cognitive, social and physiological determinants of emotional state. *Psychological Review, 69,* 379–399.

Scherer, K. R. (1997). The role of culture in emotion-antecedent appraisal. *Journal of Personality Assessment, 73,* 902–922.

Schermerhorn, A. C., Cummings, E. M., & Davies, P. T. (2008). Children's representations of multiple family relationships: Organizational structure and development in early childhood. *Journal of Family Psychology, 22,* 89–101.

Schermerhorn, A. C., Cummings, E. M., DeCarlo, C. A., & Davies, P. T. (2007). Children's influence in marital relationship. *Journal of Family Psychology, 21,* 259–269.

Schiff, M., & Lewontin, R. (1986). *Education and class: The irrelevance of IQ genetic studies.* Oxford, England: Clarendon.

Schiffman, H. R. (1976). *Sensation and perception. An integrated approach.* New York: Wiley.

Schiffman, S. S., Graham, B. G., Sately-Miller, E. A., & Warwick, Z. S. (1998). *Current Directions in Psychological Science, 7,* 137–143.

Schilt, T., de Win, M. M. L., Koeter, M., Jager, G., Korf, D. J., ven den Brink, W., et al. (2007). Cognition in novice ecstasy users with minimal exposure to other drugs. *Archives of General Psychiatry 64,* 728–736.

Schimmack, U., Oishi, S., Radhakrishnan, P., & Dzokoto, V. (2002). Culture, personality, and subjective well-being: Integrating process models of life satisfaction. *Journal of Personality and Social Psychology, 82,* 582–593.

Schlehofer, M. M., Thompson, S. C., Ting, S., Ostermann, S., Nierman, A., & Skenderian, J. (2010). Psychological predictors of college students' cell phone use while driving. *Accident Analysis and Prevention, 42*(4), 1107–1112.

Schlottman, A. (2001). Perception versus knowledge of cause and effect in children: When seeing is believing. *Psychological Science, 10,* 111–115.

Schmidt, F. L., & Hunter, J. E. (1992). Development of a causal model of processes determining job performance. *Current Directions in Psychological Science, 1,* 89–92.

Schmidt, F. L., & Hunter, J. E. (1993). Tacit knowledge, practical intelligence, general mental ability, and job knowledge. *Current Directions in Psychological Science, 2,* 8–9.

Schmidt, F. L., & Hunter, J. E. (1998). The validity and utility of selection methods in personnel psychology: Practical and theoretical implications of 85 years of research findings. *Psychological Bulletin, 124,* 262–274.

Schmidt, F. L., & Ones, D. S. (1992). Personnel selection. *Annual Review of Psychology, 43,* 627–670.

Schmidt, N. B., Lerew, D. R., & Trakowski, J. H. (1997). Body vigilance in panic disorder: Evaluating attention to bodily perturbations. *Journal of Consulting and Clinical Psychology, 65*(2), 214–220.

Schmiege, S. J., Broaddus, M. R., Levin, M., & Bryan, A. D. (2009). Randomized trial of group interventions to reduce HIV/STD risk and change theoretical mediators among detained adolescents. *Journal of Consulting and Clinical Psychology, 77*(1), 38–50.

Schmitt, D. P. (2003). Universal sex differences in the desire for sexual variety: Tests from 52 nations, 6 continents, and 13 islands. *Journal of Personality and Social Psychology, 85,* 85–104.

Schmitz, N., Kruse, J., & Kugler, J. (2003). Disabilities, quality of life, and mental disorders associated with smoking and nicotine dependence. *American Journal of Psychiatry, 160,* 1670–1676.

Schneck, C. D., Miklowitz, D. J., Calabrese, J. R., et al. (2004). Phenomenology of rapid cycling bipolar disorder: Data from the first 500 participants in the Systematic Treatment Enhancement Program. *American Journal of Psychiatry, 161,* 1902–1908.

Schneiderman, N. (2004). Psychosocial, behavioral, and biological aspects chronic diseases. *Current Directions in Psychological Science, 13* (6): 247–250.

Schramm, E., van Calker, D., Dykierek, P., Lieb, K., Kech, S., Zobel, I., et al. (2007). An intensive treatment program of interpersonal psychotherapy plus pharmacotherapy for depressed inpatients: Acute and long-term results. *American Journal of Psychiatry, 164,* 768–777.

Schreiber, F. R. (1973). *Sybil.* New York: Henry Regnery.

Schulkin, J. (1999). *The neuroendocrine regulation of behavior.* New York: Cambridge University Press.

Schultz, P. W., Nolan, J. M., Cialdini, R. B., Goldstein, N. J., & Griskevicius, V. (2007). The constructive, destructive, and reconstructive power of social norms. *Psychological Science, 18,* 429–434.

Schultz, W. (2006). Behavioral theories and the neurophysiology of reward. *Annual Review of Psychology, 57,* 87–115.

Schwarz, N. (1999). Self-reports: How the questions shape the answer. *American Psychologist, 54,* 93–105.

Schwarzer, R. (2001). Social-cognitive factors in changing health-related behaviors. *Psychological Science, 10,* 47–51.

Scott, J., Dickey, B. (2003). Global burden of depression: the intersection of culture and medicine. *British Journal of Psychiatry, 183,* 92–94.

Scott, J., Palmer, S., Paykel, E., Teasdale, J., & Hayhurst, H. (2003). Use of cognitive therapy for relapse prevention in chronic depression. *The British Journal of Psychiatry, 182,* 221–227.

Scoville, W. B., & Milner, B. (1957). Loss of recent memory after bilateral hippocampal lesions. *Journal of Neurology, Neurosurgery, and Psychiatry, 20,* 11–21.

Scullin, M. K., & McDaniel, M. A. (2010). Remembering to execute a goal: Sleep on it! *Psychological Science, 21*(7), 1028–1035.

Seckl, J. R. (2008). Glucocorticoids, developmental 'programming' and the risk of affective dysfunction. *Progress in Brain Research, 167,* 17–34.

Seeley, R. J., & Schwartz, M. W. (1997). The regulation of energy balance: Peripheral hormonal signals and hypothalamic neuropeptides. *Current Directions in Psychological Science, 6,* 39–44.

Seger, C. R., Smith, E. R., & Mackie, D. M. (2009). Subtle activation of a social categorization triggers group-level emotions. *Journal of Experimental Social Psychology, 45,* 460–467.

Segerstrom, S. C., & Miller, G. E. (2004). Psychological stress and the human immune system: A meta-analytic study of 30 years of inquiry. *Psychological Bulletin, 130* (4): 601–630.

Seidlitz, L., & Diener, E. (1998). Sex differences in the recall of affective experiences. *Journal of Personality and Social Psychology, 74,* 262–271.

Seitz, H. K., Egerer, G., Simanowski, U. A., Waldherr, R., Eckey, R., Agarwal, D. P., Goedde, H. W., & von Wartburg, J. P. (1993). Effect of age, sex, and alcoholism. Human gastric alcohol dehydrogenase activity: effect of age, sex, and alcoholism. *Gut,* (34),1433–1437.

Self, D. (2004). Drug dependence and addiction. *American Journal of Psychiatry, 161,* 223.

Selye, H. (1976). *The stress of life.* New York: Knopf.

Seto, M. C. (2009). Pedophilia. *Annual Review of Clinical Psychology, 5,* 391–407.

Shaffer, D., Fisher, P., Dulcan, M., Davies, M., Piacentini, J., Schwab-Stone, M., Lahey, B.B., Bourdon, K., Jensen, P., Bird, H., Canino, G., & Regier, D. (1996). The NIMH Diagnostic Interview Schedule for Children (DISC 2.3): Description, acceptability, prevalences, and performance in the MECA study. *Journal of the American Academy of Child and Adolescent Psychiatry, 35,* 865–877.

Shamir, B., & Howell, J. M. (1999). Organizational and contextual influences on the emergency and effectiveness of charismatic leadership. *Leadership Quarterly, 10,* 257–283.

Shamloo, Z. S., & Cox, W. M. (2010). The relationship between motivational structure, sense of control, intrinsic motivation and university students' alcohol consumption. *Addictive Behaviors, 35*(2):140–146.

Shaywitz, B. A., Shaywitz, S. E., Pugh, K. R., Constable, R. T., et al. (1995). Sex differences in the functional organization of the brain for language. *Nature, 373,* 607–609.

Shaywitz, B. A., Shaywitz, S. E., Pugh, K. R., Constable, R. T., Skudlarski, P., Fulbright, R. K., Bronen, R. A., Fletcher, J. M., Shankweiler, D. P., Katz, L., & Gores, J. C. (1995). Sex differences in the functional organization of the brain for language. *Nature, 373,* 607–609.

Shedler, J. (2010). The efficacy of psychodynamic psychotherapy. *American Psychologist, 65*(2), 98–109.

Sheese, B. E., & Graziano, W. G. (2005). Deciding to defect. *American Psychological Society, 16,* 354–357.

Sheldon, K. M., & Kasser, T. (2001). Getting older, getting better? Personal strivings and psychological maturity across the life span. *Developmental Psychology, 37,* 491–501.

Shelton, J. T., Elliott, E. M., Eaves, S. D., & Exner, A. L. (2009). The distracting effects of a ringing cell phone: An investigation of the laboratory and the classroom setting. *Journal of Environmental Psychology, 29*(4), 513–521.

Shepard, J. A. (1995). Remedying motivation and productivity losses in collective settings. *Current Directions in Psychological Science, 4,* 131–139.

Sheppard, L. C., & Teasdale, J. D. (2000). Dysfunctional thinking in major depressive disorder: A deficit in metacognitive monitoring. *Journal of Abnormal Psychology, 109,* 768–776.

Sheppard, W. C., & Willoughby, R. H. (1975). *Child behavior.* Chicago: Rand McNally.

Sherif, M. (1936). *The psychology of social norms.* New York: Harper.

Sherif, M., & Sherif, C. W. (1953). *Groups in harmony and tension; An integration of studies of intergroup relations.* New York: Harper.

Shifren, J. L. (2008). Sexual problems and distress in United States women prevalence and correlates. *Obstetrics & Gynecology, 112,* 970–978.

Shih, R. A., Glass, T. A., Bandeen-Roche, K., Carlson, M. C., Bolla, K. I., Todd, A. C., et al. (2006). Environmental lead exposure and cognitive function in community-dwelling older adults. *Neurology 67,* 1556–1562.

Shihadeh, A. (2003). Investigation of the mainstream smoke aerosol of the argileh water pipe. *Food and Chemical Toxicology, 41,* 143–152.

Shimamura, A. P., Berry, J. M., Mangels, J. A., Rusting, C. L., & Jurica, P. J. (1995). Memory and cognitive abilities in university professors: Evidence for successful aging. *Psychological Science, 6,* 271–277.

Shimizu, M., & Pelham, B. W. (2004). The unconscious cost of good fortune: Implicit and explicit self-esteem, positive life events, and health. *Health Psychology, 23*(1), 101–105.

Shin, L. M., Wright, C. I., Cannistraro, P. A., Wedig, M. M., et al. (2005). A functional magnetic resonance imaging study of amygdala and medial prefrontal cortex responses to overtly presented fearful faces in posttraumatic stress disorder. *Archives of General Psychiatry, 62,* 273–281.

Shirtcliff, E. A., Coe, C. L., & Pollak, S. D. (2009). Early childhood stress is associated with elevated antibody levels to herpes simplex virus type 1. *Proceedings of the National Academy of Sciences, 106,* 2963–2967.

Sholl, M. J. (2008). Human allocentric heading orientation and ability. *Current Directions in Psychological Science, 17*(4), 275–280.

Siegel, S. (2004). Intra-administrations and withdrawal symptoms: Morphine-elicited morphine withdrawal. *Experimental and Clinical Psychopharmacology, 12,* 3–11.

Siegler, R. S. (2000). Unconscious insights. *Psychological Sciences, 9,* 79–83.

Sigman, M., & Whaley, S. E. (1998). In U. Neisser (Ed.), *The rising curve: Long-term gains in IQ and related measures* (pp. 155–182). Washington, DC: American Psychological Association.

Signorella, M., & Jamison, W. (1986). Masculinity, femininity, androgyny, and cognitive performance: A meta-analysis. *Psychological Bulletin, 100,* 207–228.

Silventoinen, K., Magnusson, P.K.E., Tynelius, P., Kaprio, J., & Rasmussen, F. (2008). Heritability of body size and muscle strength in young adulthood: A study of one million Swedish men. *Genetic Epidemiology, 32*(4), 341–349.

Silventoinen, K., Posthuman, D., van Beijsterveldt, T., Bartels, M., & Boomsma, D. I. (2006). Genetic contributions to the association between height and intelligence: Evidence from dutch twin data from childhood to middle age. *Genes, Brain, and Behavior, 5,* 585–595.

Silverstein, L. B. (1991). Transforming the debate about child care and maternal employment. *American Psychologist, 46,* 1025–1032.

Simmon, D., Krawczyk, D. C., & Holyonak, K. J. (2004). Construction of preferences by constraint satisfaction. *Psychological Science. 15*(5): 331–336.

Simon, G. E., Katon, W. J., Lin, E. H. B., Rutter, C., Manning, W. G., Von Korff, M., et al. (2007). Cost-effectiveness of systematic depression treatment among people with diabetes mellitus. *Archives of General Psychiatry, 64,* 65–72.

Simon, G. E., Ludman, E. J., Bauer, M. S., Unutzer, J., & Operskalski, B. (2006). Long-term effectiveness and cost of a systematic care program for bipolar disorder. *Archives of General Psychiatry, 63,* 500–508.

Simons, D. J., & Chabris, C. F. (2009). Gorillas in our midst: sustained inattentional blindness for dynamic events. *Perception, (28),*1059–1074.

Simons-Morton, B., Chen, R., Abroms, L., & Haynie, D. L. (2004). Growth curve analyses of peer and parent influences on smoking progression among early adolescents. *Health Psychology, 23,* 612–621.

Singh, D. (1993). Adaptive significance of female physical attractiveness: Role of waist-to-hip ratio. *Journal of Personality and Social Psychology, 65*(2), 293–307.

Singh, D. (1995). Female judgment of male attractiveness and desirability for relationships: Role of waist-to-hip ratio and financial status. *Journal of Personality and Social Psychology, 69*(6),1089–110.

Sio, U. N., & Ormerod, T. C. (2009). Does incubation enhance problem solving? A meta-analytic review. *Psychological Bulletin, 135*(1), 94–120.

Skinner, B. F. (1953). *Science and human behavior.* New York: Macmillan.

Skosnik, P. D., Krishnan, G. P., Aydt, E. E., Kuhlenshmidt, H. A., & O'Donnell, B. F. (2006). Psychophysiological evidence of altered neural syncronization in cannabis use: Relationship to schizotypy. *American Journal of Psychiatry, 163,* 1798–1804.

Skuse, D. H., & Gallagher, L. (2009). Dopaminergic-neuropeptide interactions in the social brain. *Trends in Cognitive Science, 13*(1), 27–35.

Slater, M., Antley, A., Davison, A., & others. (2006). A virtual reprise of the Stanley Milgram obedience experiments, *Plos One, 1*(1), e39.

Slavich, G. M., Way, B. M., Eisenberger, N. I., & Taylor, S. E. (2010). Neural sensitivity to social rejection is associated with inflammatory responses to social stress. *Proc Natl Acad Sci USA, 107*(33), 14817–14822.

Sloan, D. M., Marx, B. P., & Epstein, E. M. (2005). Further examination of the exposure model underlying the efficacy of written emotional disclosure. *Journal of Consulting and Clinical Psychology, 73,* 549–554.

Slobin, D. I. (1979). *Psycholinguistics.* Glenview, IL: Scott, Foresman.

Slotema, C. W., Blom, J. D., Hoek, H. W., & Sommer, I. E. (2010). Should we expand the toolbox of psychiatric treatment methods to include Repetitive Transcranial Magnetic Stimulation (rTMS)? A meta-analysis of the efficacy of rTMS in psychiatric disorders. *Journal of Clinical Psychiatry, 71*(7), 873–884.

Sluyter, F., Van der Vlugt, J. J., van Oortmerssen, G. A., Koolhaas, J. M., van der Hoeven, F., & de Boer, P. (1996). Studies on wild house mice: VII. Prenatal maternal environment and aggression. *Behavior Genetics, 26,* 513–518.

Smith, D. M., Langa, K. M., Kabeto, M. U., & Ubel, P. A. (2005). Health, wealth, and happiness: Financial resources buffer subjective well-being after the onset of a disability. *Psychological Science, 16,* 663–666.

Smith, E. (2000). Neural bases of human working memory. *American Psychological Society, 9,* 45–49.

Smith, E. R. (2008). An embodied account of self-other "overlap" and its effects. In G. R. Semin & E. R. Smith (Eds.), *Embodied grounding: Social, cognitive, affective, and neuroscientific approaches* (pp. 148–159). New York: Cambridge University Press.

Smith, E. R., & Collins, E. C. (2009). Contextualizing person perception: Distributed social cognition. *Psychological Review, 116*(2), 343–364.

Smith, L. B., & Thelen, E. (Eds.). (1993). *A dynamic systems approach to development.* Cambridge, MA: MIT Press.

Smith, R. C., & Geller, E. S. (2009). Marketing and alcohol-related traffic fatalities: Impact of alcohol advertising targeting minors. *Journal of Safety Research, 40*(5), 359–364.

Smith, T. W. (2006). Personality as risk and resilience in physical health. *Current Directions in Psychological Science, 15,* 227–231.

Smith, V. L., & Ellsworth, P. C. (1987). The social psychology of eyewitness accuracy: Misleading questions and communicator expertise. *Journal of Applied Psychology, 72,* 294–300.

Smyth, J. M., Soefer, M. H., Hurewitz, A., & Stone, A. A. (1999). The effect of tape recorded relaxation training on well-being, symptoms, and peak expiratory flow rate in adult asthmatics: A pilot study, *Psychology and Health, 14,* 487–501.

Snowden, L. R., & Cheung, F. K. (1990). Use of inpatient mental health services by members of ethnic minority groups. *American Psychologist, 45,* 347–355.

Snyder, M., Tauke, E. D., & Berscheid, E. (1977). Social perception and interpersonal behavior: On the self-fulfilling nature of social stereotypes. *Journal of Personality and Social Psychology, 35,* 656–666.

Snyder, S. H. (1974). *Madness and the brain.* New York: McGraw-Hill.

Snyder, S. H. (2009). Neurotransmitters, receptors, and second messengers galore in 40 years. *Journal of Neuroscience, 29*(41), 12717–12721.

Solomon, D. A., Keller, M. B., Leon, A. C., Mueller, T. I., Lavori, P. W., Shea, T., Coryell, W., Warshaw, M., Turvey, C., Maser, J. D., & Endicott, J. (2000). Multiple recurrences of major depressive disorder. *American Journal of Psychiatry, 157,* 229–233.

Solomon, D. A., Keller, M. B., Leon, A. C., Mueller, T. I., Shea, M. T., Warshaw, M., Maser, J. D., Coryell, W., & Endicott, J. (1997). Recovery from major depression. *Archives of General Psychiatry, 54,* 1001–1006.

Solomon, D. A., Leon, A. C., Endicott, J., & others. (2003). Unipolar mania over the course of a 20-year follow-up study. *American Journal of Psychiatry, 160*(11), 2049–2051.

Solomon, R. L. (1980). The opponent-process theory of acquired motivation. *American Psychologist, 35,* 691–712.

Solomon, S., & Lennie, P. (2007). The machinery of colour vision. *Nature Reviews Neuroscience, 8,* 276–286.

Sorensen, H. J., Mortensen, E. L., Reinisch, J. M., & Mednick, S. A. (2003). Do hypertension and diuretic treatment in pregnancy increase the risk of schizophrenia in offspring? *American Journal of Psychiatry, 160,* 464–468.

Sorkin, R. D., Hays, C. J., & West, R. (2001). Signal-detection analysis of group decision making. *Psychological Review, 108,* 183–203.

Sowell, E. R., Peterson, B. S., Thompson, P. M., Welcome, S. E., Henkenius, A. L., & Toga, A. W. (2003). Mapping cortical change across the human life span. *Nature Neuroscience, 6,* 309–315.

Spanos, N. P. (1996). *Multiple identities and false memories: A sociocognitive perspective.* Washington, DC: American Psychological Association Press.

Spear, L. P. (2000). Neurobehavioral changes in adolescence. *Psychological Science, 9,* 111–114.

Spearman, C. E., & Wynn-Jones, L. (1950). *Human ability.* London: Macmillan.

Speck, O., Ernst, T., Braun, J., Koch, C., Miller, E., & Chang, L. (2000). Gender differences in the functional organization of the brain for working memory. *Neuroreport, 11,* 2581–2585.

Speisman, J. C., Lazarus, R. S., Mordokoff, A. M., & Davison, L. (1964). Experimental reduction of stress based on ego-defense theory. *Journal of Abnormal and Social Psychology, 68,* 367–380.

Spence, C. & Read, L. (2003). Speech shadowing while driving: On the difficulty of splitting attention between eye and ear. *Psychological Science, 14,* 251–256.

Spence, J. T., & Helmreich, R. L. (1978). *Masculinity and femininity: Their psychological dimensions, correlates, and antecedents.* Austin: University of Texas Press.

Spencer, N. A., McClintock, M. K., Sellergren, S. A., Bullivant, S., Jacob, S., & Mennella, J. A. (2004). Social chemosignals from breast-feeding women increase sexual motivation. *Hormones and Behavior, 46,* 362–370.

Spencer, S. J., Steele, C. M., & Quinn, D. M. (1999). Stereotype threat and women's math performance. *Journal of Experimental Social Psychology, 35*(1), 4–28.

Sperling, G. (1960). The information available in brief visual presentations. *Psychological Monographs, 74,* 1–29.

Spiegler, M. D., & Guevremont, D. C. (1998). *Contemporary behavior therapy* (3rd ed.). Pacific Grove, CA: Brooks/Cole.

Spijker, J., De Graaf, R., Bijl, R. V., Beekman, A. T. F., Ormel, J., & Nolen, W. A. (2002). Duration of major depressive episodes in the general population: Results from the Netherlands Mental Health Survey and Incidence Study (NEMESIS). *British Journal of Psychiatry, 181,* 208–213.

Spillane, N. S., & Smith, G. T. (2007). A theory of reservation: Dwelling American Indian alcohol use risk. *Psychological Bulletin, 133,* 395–418.

Spiteri, T., Musatov, S., Ogawa, S., Ribeiro, A., Pfaff, D. W., & Agmo, A. (2010). Estrogen-induced sexual incentive motivation, proceptivity and receptivity depend on a functional estrogen receptor alpha in the ventromedial nucleus of the hypothalamus but not in the amygdala. *Neuroendocrinology, 91*(2), 142–154.

Sprinthal, R. C., Sprinthal, N. A., & Oja, S. N. (1998). *Educational psychology: A developmental approach* (7th ed.). Boston: McGraw-Hill.

Squire, L. R. (1987). *Memory and the brain.* New York: Oxford University Press.

Squire, L. R. (2009). Memory and brain systems: 1969–2009. *Journal of Neuroscience 29*(41), 12711–12716.

Squire, L. R., Knowlton, B., & Musen, G. (1993). The structure and organization of memory. *Annual Review of Psychology, 44,* 453–495.

Staples, S. L. (1996). Human response to environmental noise: Psychological research and public policy. *American Psychologist, 51,* 143–150.

Starkstein, S. E., Robinson, R. G., & Price, T. R. (1988). Comparison of patients with and without poststroke major depression matched for size and the location of lesion. *Archives of General Psychiatry, 45,* 247–252.

Stathopoulou, G., Powers, M. B., Berry, A. C., Smits, J. A. J., & Otto, M. W. (2006). Exercise interventions for mental health: A quantitative and qualitative review. *Clinical Psychology: Science and Practice, 13,* 179–193.

Staub, E. (1996). Cultural-societal roots of violence: The examples of genocidal violence and of contemporary youth violence in the United States. *American Psychologist, 51,* 117–132.

Steel, Z., Chey, T., Silove, D., Marnane, C., Bryant, R. A., & van Ommeren, M. (2009). Association of torture and other potentially traumatic events with mental health outcomes among populations exposed to mass conflict and displacement: A systematic review and meta-analysis. *JAMA, 302,* 537–549.

Steele, C. M. (1997). A threat in the air: How stereotypes shape intellectual identity and performance. *American Psychologist, 52,* 613–629.

Steele, C. M., & Josephs, R. A. (1990). Alcohol myopia: Its prized and dangerous effects. *American Psychologist, 45,* 921–933.

Stein, E. A., & others. (1998). Nicotine-induced activation in the human brain: A functional MRI study. *American Journal of Psychiatry, 155,* 1009–1015.

Stein, M. B., Torgrud, L. J., & Walker, J. R. (2000). Social phobia symptoms, subtypes, and severity. *Archives of General Psychiatry, 57,* 1046–1052.

Steinberg, J. (1995). The graying of the senses. *Journal of NIMH Research, 7,* 32–33.

Steinberg, L. (2009). Should the science of adolescent brain development inform public policy? *American Psychologist, 64*(8), 739–750.

Steketee, G., & Cleere, L. (1990). Obsessive-compulsive disorders. In A. S. Bellack, M. Hersen, & A. E. Kazdin (Eds.), *International handbook of behavior modification and therapy* (2nd ed., pp. 307–332). New York: Plenum.

Stephan, W., Berscheid, E., & Walster, E. (1971). Sexual arousal and heterosexual perception. *Journal of Personality and Social Psychology, 20,* 93–101.

Stern, K., & McClintock, M. K. (1998). Regulation of ovulation by human pheromones. *Nature, 392,* 177–179.

Stern, P. C. (2000). Toward a coherent theory of environmentally significant behavior. *Journal of Social Issues, 56,* 407–424.

Stern, R. M., & Koch, K. L. (1996). Motion sickness and differential susceptibility. *Current Directions in Psychological Science, 4,* 115–120.

Sternbach, R. A. (Ed.). (1978). *The psychology of pain.* New York: Raven Press.

Sternberg, R. J. (1979). The nature of mental abilities. *American Psychologist, 34,* 214–230.

Sternberg, R. J. (1981). Testing and cognitive psychology. *American Psychologist, 36,* 1181–1189.

Sternberg, R. J. (1986). A triangular theory of love. *Psychological Review, 93*(2), 119–135.

Sternberg, R. J. (2004). Culture and intelligence. *American Psychologist, 5,* 325–338.

Sternberg, R. J., & Gardner, M. K. (1982). A componential interpretation of the general factor in human intelligence. In J. J. Eysenck (Ed.), *A model for intelligence.* Berlin: Springer.

Sternberg, R. J., & Wagner, R. K. (1993). The egocentric view of intelligence and job performance is wrong. *Current Directions in Psychological Science, 2,* 1–5.

Sternberg, S. (1969). Memory scanning: Mental processes revealed by reaction time experiments. *Acta Psychologica, 30,* 276–315.

Stewart, A. J., & Ostrove, J. M. (1998). Women's personality in middle age: Gender, history, and midcourse corrections. *American Psychologist, 55,* 1185–1194.

Stewart, A. J., & Vadewater, E. A. (1999). "If I had it to do over again . . .": Midlife review, midcourse corrections, and women's well-being in midlife. *Journal of Personality and Social Psychology, 76,* 270–283.

Stewart, J. L., Bismark, A. W., Towers, D. N., Coan, J. A., & Allen, J. J. (2010). Resting frontal EEG asymmetry as an endophenotype for depression risk: Sex-specific patterns of frontal brain asymmetry. *Journal of Abnormal Psychology, 119*(3), 502–512.

Stewart, R. E., & Chambless, D. L. (2009). Cognitive-behavioral therapy for adult anxiety disorders in clinical practice: A meta-analysis of effectiveness studies. *Journal of Consulting and Clinical Psychology, 77*(4), 595–606.

Stewart, S. M., Kennard, B. D., Lee, P.W.H., & others. (2004). A cross-cultural investigation of cognitions and depressive symptoms in adolescents. *Journal of Abnormal Psychology, 113*(2), 248–257.

Stice, E., Rohde, P., Seeley, J. R., & Gau, J. M. (2008). Brief cognitive-behavioral depression prevention program for high-risk adolescents outperforms two alternative interventions: A randomized efficacy trial. *Journal of Consulting and Clinical Psychology, 76*(4), 595–606.

Stiggelbout, M., Popkema, D. Y., Hopman-Rock, M., de Greef, M., & van Mechelen, W. (2004). Once a week is not enough: Effects of a widely implemented group based exercise programme for older adults; A randomised controlled trial. *Journal of Epidemiology & Community Health, 58,* 83–88.

Stoll, A. L., Severus, E., Freeman, M. P., Rueter, S., Zboyan, H. A., Diamond, E.; Cress, K. K., & Marangell, L. B. Omega 3 fatty acids in bipolar disorder: A preliminary double-blind, placebo-controlled trial. *Archives of General Psychiatry. 56* (5) May 1999, 407–412.

Stone, A. A., Schwartz, J. E., Broderick, J. E., & Deaton, A. (2010). A snapshot of the age distribution of psychological well-being in the United States. *Proceedings of the National Academy of Sciences, 107,* 9985–9990.

Stoner, J. A. F. (1961). *A comparison of individual and group decisions involving risk.* Unpublished master's thesis, Massachusetts Institute of Technology, Cambridge.

Storandt, M. (2008). Cognitive deficits in the early stages of Alzheimer's disease. *Current Directions in Psychological Science, 17*(3), 198–202.

Strauch, I., & Meier, B. (1996). *In search of dreams: Experimental dream research.* Albany: State University of New York Press.

Strauman, T. J. (1992). Self-guides, autobiographical memory, and anxiety and dysphoria: Toward a cognitive model of vulnerability to emotional distress. *Journal of Abnormal Psychology, 101,* 87–95.

Strayer, D. L., & Johnston, W. A. (2001). Driven to distraction: Dual-task studies of simulated driving and conversing on a cellular phone. *American Psychological Society, 12,* 462–466.

Stumpf, H., & Stanley, J. C. (1998). Stability and change in gender-related differences on the College Board Advanced Placement and Achievement Tests. *Current Directions in Psychological Science, 7,* 192–196.

Stuss, D. T., & Levine, B. (2002). Adult clinical neuropsychology: Lessons from studies of the frontal lobes. *Annual Review of Psychology, 53,* 401–433.

Su, R., Rounds, J., & Armstrong, P. I. (2009). Men and things, women and people: A meta-analysis of sex differences in interests. *Psychological Bulletin, 135*(6), 859–884.

Sublette, M. E., Hibbeln, J. R., Galfalvy, H., Oquendo, M. A., & Mann, J. J. (2006). Omega-3 polyunsaturated essential fatty acid status as a predictor of future suicide risk. *American Journal of Psychiatry, 163,* 1100–1102.

Subotnik, R., Kassan, L., Summers, E., & Wasser, A. (1993). *Genius revisited: High IQ children grown up.* Norwood, NJ: Ablex.

Sue, D. W., Capodilupo, C. M., Torino, G. C., Bucceri, J. M., Holder, A. M. B., Nadal, K. L., et al. (2007). Racial microaggressions in everyday life: Implications for clinical practice. *American Psychologist, 62,* 271–286.

Suinn, R. M. (2001). The terrible twos—anger and anxiety. *American Psychologist, 56,* 27–36.

Sulloway, F. J. (2007). Birth order and intelligence. *Science, 316,* 1711–1712.

Suomi, S. (1988). *Genetic and environmental influences on social-emotional development in rhesus monkeys.* Presentation to the Fourth Annual Colloquium of the Center of Family Research, University of Georgia.

Susser, E., & others. (1996). Schizophrenia after prenatal famine: Further evidence. *Archives of General Psychiatry, 53,* 25–31.

Susser, E., Struening, E. L., & Conner, S. (1989). Psychiatric problems in homeless men. *Archives of General Psychiatry, 46,* 845–850.

Swaab, D. F., & Hofman, M. A. (1990). An enlarged superchiasmatic nucleus in homosexual men. *Brain Research, 537,* 141.

Swaab, D. F., & Hofman, M. A. (1995). Sexual differentiation of the human hypothalamus in relation to gender and sexual orientation. *Trends in Neurosciences, 18,* 264–270.

Swayze, V. W. (1995). Frontal leukotomy and related psychosurgical procedures in the era before antipsychotics (1935–1954): A historical overview. *American Journal of Psychiatry, 152,* 505–515.

Swendsen, J. D., Tennen, H., Carney, M. A., Affleck, G., Willard, A., & Hromi, A. (2000). Mood and alcohol consumption: An experience sampling test of the self-medication hypothesis. *Journal of Abnormal Psychology, 109,* 198–204.

Symons, C. S., & Johnson, B. T. (1997). The self-reference effect in memory: A meta-analysis. *Psychological Bulletin, 121,* 371–394.

Szyszkowicz, M., Rowe, B. H., & Colman, I. (2009). Air pollution and daily emergency department visits for depression. *International Journal of Occupational Medicine and Environmental Health, 22*(4), 355–362.

T

Takahashi, K., Honda, Y., & Emori, S. (2007). Assessing mortality risk from heat stress due to global warming. *Journal of Risk Research, 10*(3), 339–354.

Talarico, J. M., & Rubin, D. C. (2003). Confidence, not consistency, characterizes flashbulb memories. *Psychological Science, 14,* 455–461.

Tamminga, C. A. (2006). The anatomy of fear extinction. *American Journal of Psychiatry, 163,* 961.

Tang, S.-H., & Hall, V. C. (1995). The overjustification effect: A meta-analysis. *Applied Cognitive Psychology, 9,* 365–404.

Tanner, J. M. (1970). Physical growth. In P. H. Mussen (Ed.), *Carmichael's manual of child psychology* (Vol. 1). New York: Wiley.

Tarpy, R. M., & Mayer, R. E. (1978). *Foundations of learning and memory.* Glenview, IL: Scott, Foresman.

Tart, C. T. (1975). *States of consciousness.* New York: Dutton.

Tauer, J. M., & Harackiewicz J. M. (2004). The effects of cooperation and competition on intrinsic motivation and performance. *Journal of Personality and Social Psychology, 86,* 849–861.

Taylor, C. B., Youngblood, M. E., Catellier, D., Veith, R. C., Carney, R. M., Burg, M. M., et al. (2005). Effects of anti-depressant medication on morbidity and mortality in depressed patients after myocardial infarction. *Archives of General Psychiatry, 62,* 792–798.

Taylor, D. W., Berry, P. C., & Block, C. H. (1958). Does group participation when using brainstorming facilitate or inhibit creative thinking? *Administrative Science Quarterly, 3*(1), 23–47.

Taylor, M., Carlson, S. M., Maring, B. L., Gerow, L., & Charley, C. M. (2004). The characteristics and correlates of fantasy in school-age children: Imaginary comparisons, impersonation, and social understanding. *Developmental Psychology, 40,* 1173–1187.

Taylor, S. E. (1986). *Health psychology.* New York: Random House.

Taylor, S. E. (1999). *Health psychology* (4th ed.). Boston: McGraw-Hill.

Taylor, S. E. (2002). *The tending instinct.* Times Books.

Taylor, S. E. (2010). Inaugural article: Mechanisms linking early life stress to adult health outcomes. *Proc Natl Acad Sci USA, 107*(19), 8507–8512.

Taylor, S. E., Burklund, L. J., Eisenberger, N. I., Lehman, B. J., Hilmert, C. J., & Lieberman, M. D. (2008). Neural bases of moderation of cortisol stress responses by psychosocial resources. *Journal of Personality and Social Psychology, 95*(1), 197–211.

Taylor, S. E., Cousino Klein, L., Lewis, B. P., Gruenewald, T. L., Gurung, R. A. R., & Updegraff, J. A. (2000). Biobehavioral responses to stress in females: Tend-and-befriend, not fight-or-flight. *Psychological Review, 107,* 411–429.

Taylor, S. E., Pham, L. B., Rivkin, I. D., & Armor, D. A. (1998). Harnessing the imagination, mental simulation, self-regulation, and coping. *American Psychologist, 53,* 429–439.

Taylor, S. E., & Stanton, A. L. (2007). Coping resources, coping processes, and mental health. *Annual Review of Clinical Psychology, 3,* 377–401.

Taylor, S. E., Welch, W. T., Kim, H. S., & Sherman, D. K. (2007). Cultural differences in the impact of social support on psychological and biological stress responses. *Psychological Bulletin, 18,* 831–837.

Teasdale, J. D., Scott, J., Moore, R. G., Hayhurst, H., Pope, M., & Paykel, E. S. (2001). How does cognitive therapy prevent relapse in residual depression? Evidence from a controlled trial. *Journal of Consulting and Clinical Psychology, 69,* 347–357.

Tellegen, A., Watson, D., & Clark, L. A. (1999). On the dimensional and hierarchical structure of affect. *Psychological Science, 10,* 297–303.

Terman, L. M. (1925). Mental and physical traits of a thousand gifted children. In M. Terman (Ed.), *Genetic studies of genius.* Palo Alto, CA: Stanford University Press.

Terrace, H. (1987). *Nim.* New York: Columbia University Press.

Thapar, A., & Rutter, M. (2009). Do prenatal risk factors cause psychiatric disorder? Be wary of causal claims. *British Journal of Psychiatry, 195,* 100–101.

Theyel, B. B., Llano, D. A., & Sherman, M. (2010). The corticothalamocortical circuit drives higher-order cortex in the mouse. *Nature Neuroscience, 13,* 84–246.

Thibaut, J., & Walker, L. (1975). *Procedural justice: A psychological analysis.* Hillsdale, NJ: Erlbaum.

Thomas, J. L., Wilk, J. E., Riviere, L. A., McGurk, D., Castro, C. A., & Hoge, C. W. (2010). Prevalence of mental health problems and functional impairment among active component and national guard soldiers 3 and 12 months following combat in Iraq. *Archives of General Psychiatry, 67,* 614–623.

Thompson, J. K., Jarvie, G. J., Lahey, B. B., & Cureton, K. J. (1982). Exercise and obesity: Etiology, physiology, and intervention. *Psychological Bulletin, 91,* 55–79.

Thompson, R. A., & Nelson, C. A. (2001). Developmental science and the media. *American Psychologist, 56,* 5–15.

Thompson, R. F. (2005). In search of memory traces. *Annual Review of Psychology, 56,* 1–23.

Thompson, R. J., Mata, J., Jaeggi, S. M., Buschkuehl, M., Jonides, J., & Gotlib, I. H. (2010). Maladaptive coping, adaptive coping, and depressive symptoms: Variations across age and depressive state. *Behaviour Research and Therapy, 48*(6), 459–466.

Thomson, D. M. (1988). Context and false recognition. In G. M. Davies & D. M. Thomson (Eds.), *Memory in context: Context in memory* (pp. 285–304). Chichester, England: Wiley.

Thorndike, E. L. (1911). *Animal intelligence: Experimental studies.* New York: Macmillan.

Thornhill, R., & Gangestad, S. W. (1993). Human facial beauty: Averageness, symmetry, and parasite resistance. *Human Nature, 4*(3).

Thornicroft, G., Brohan, E., Rose, D., Sartorius, N., Leese, M., & INDIGO Study Group. (2009). Global pattern of experienced and anticipated discrimination against people with schizophrenia: A cross-sectional survey. *Lancet, 373,* 1335–1337.

Thornton, G. C., & Cleveland, J. N. (1990). Developing managerial talent through simulation. *American Psychologist, 45,* 190–199.

Thurstone, L. L. (1938). Primary mental abilities. *Psychometric Monographs* (1).

Thyer, B. A., & Geller, E. S. (1987). The "buckle-up" dashboard sticker: An effective environmental intervention for safety belt promotion. *Environment and Behavior, 19,* 484–494.

Tjaden, P., & Thoennes, N. (2006). *Extent, nature, and consequences of rape victimization: Findings from the national violence against women survey.* Department of Justice. www.ncjrs.gov/pdffiles1/nij/210346.pdf

Todd, J. T., Oomes, A. H. J., Koenderink, J. J., & Kappers, A. M. L. (2004). The perception of doubly curved surfaces from anistropic textures. *Psychological Science, 15,* 40–46.

Toh, S., Mitchell, A. A., Louik, C., Werler, M. M., Chambers, C. D., & Hernandez-Diaz, S. (2009). Selective serotonin reuptake inhibitor use and risk of gestational hypertension. *American Journal of Psychiatry, 166*(3), 319–320.

Tolin, D. F. (2010). Is cognitive-behavioral therapy more effective than other therapies? A meta-analytic review. *Clinical Psychology Review, 30*(6), 710–720.

Tolin, D. F., & Foa, E. B. (2006). Sex differences in trauma and posttraumatic stress disorder: A quantitative review of 25 years of research. *Psychological Bulletin, 132,* 959–992.

Tollison, C. D., & Adams, H. E. (1979). *Sexual disorders: Treatments, theory, research.* New York: Gardner Press.

Tolman, E. C., & Honzik, C. H. (1930). Introduction and removal of reward, and maze performance in rats. *University of California Publications in Psychology, 4,* 257–276.

Tolman, E. C., Ritchie, B. F., & Kalish, D. (1946). Studies in spatial learning. I: Orientation and the shortcut. *Journal of Experimental Psychology, 36,* 13–25.

Tomiyama, A. J., Mann, T., Vinas, D., Hunger, J. M., Dejager, J., & Taylor, S. E. (2010). Low calorie dieting increases cortisol. *Psychosomatic Medicine, 72*(4), 357–364.

Torres, A. R., Prince, M. J., Bebbington, P. E., Bhugra, D., Brugha, T. S., Farrell, M., et al. (2006). Obsessive-compulsive disorder: prevalence, comorbidity, impact, and help-seeking in the British National Psychiatry Morbidity Survey of 2000. *American Journal of Psychiatry, 163,* 1978–1985.

Triandis, H. (1991). *Training for diversity.* Paper presented to the annual meeting of the American Psychological Association, San Francisco.

Triandis, H. C., & Suh, E. M. (2002). Cultural influences on personality. *Annual Review of Psychology, 53,* 133–160.

Triplett, N. (1898). The dynamogenic factors in peacemaking and competition. *American Journal of Psychology, 9,* 507–533.

Tronson, N. C., & Taylor, J. R. (2007). Molecular mechanisms of memory reconsolidation. *Nature Reviews Neuroscience, 8,* 262–275.

Tsai, J. L., Knutson, B., & Fung, H. H. (2006). Cultural variation in affect valuation. *Journal of Personality and Social Psychology, 90,* 288–307.

Tsien, J. Z. (2007). The memory. *Scientific American July* 52–59.

Tucci, V., Hursh, D. E., & Laitinen, R. E. (2004). The competent learner model: A merging of applied behavior analysis, direct instruction, and precision teaching. In D. J. Moran & R. W. Malott (Eds) (2004). *Evidence-Based Educational Methods.* (pp. 109–123). Amsterdam: Elsevier.

Tulving, E. (1972). Episodic and semantic memory. In E. Tulving & W. Donaldson (Eds.), *Organization and memory.* New York: Academic Press.

Tulving, E. (2002). Episodic memory: From mind to brain. *Annual Review of Psychology, 53,* 1–25.

Turkat, I. D., & Calhoun, J. F. (1980). The problem-solving flow chart. *The Behavior Therapist, 3,* 21.

Turnage, J. J. (1990). The challenge of new workplace technology for psychology. *American Psychologist, 45,* 171–178.

Turnbull, C. (1962). *The forest people.* New York: Simon & Schuster.

Turner, R. N., Hewstone, M., Voci, A., & Vonofakou, C. (2008). A test of the extended intergroup contact hypothesis: The mediating role of intergroup anxiety, perceived ingroup and outgroup norms, and inclusion of the outgroup in the self. Journal of *Personality and Social Psychology, 95*(4), 843–860.

Tversky, A., & Kahneman, D. (1974). Judgment under uncertainty: Heuristics and biases. *Science, 185,* 1124–1131.

Tyler, L. E. (1965). *The psychology of human differences.* New York: Appleton-Century-Crofts.

Unsworth, N., & Engle, R. W. (2007). On the division of short-term and working memory: An examination of simple and complex span and their relation to higher order abilities. *Psychological Bulletin, 133,* 1038–1066.

Urry, H. L., Nitschke, J. B., Dolski, I., Jackson, D. C., Dalton, K. M., Mueller, C. J., Rosenkranz, M. A., Ryff, C. D., Singer, B. H., & Davidson, R. J. (2004). Making a life worth living: Neural correlates of well-being. *Psychological Science, 15,* 367–372.

Vaidya, J. G., Gray, E. K., Haig, J., & Watson, D. (2002). On the temporal stability of personality: Evidence for differential stability and the role of life experiences. *Journal of Personality and Social Psychology, 83,* 1469–1484.

Vaillant, G. E., & Mukamal, K. (2001). Successful aging. *American Journal of Psychiatry, 158,* 839–847.

Vaitl, D., Birbaumer, N., Gruzelier, J., Jamieson, G. A., Kotchoubey, B., Kubler, A., Lehmann, D., Miltner, W. H. R., Ott, U., Putz, P., Sammer, G., Strauch, I., Strehl, U., Wackermann, J., & Weiss, T. (2005). Psychobiology of altered states of consciousness. *Psychological Bulletin, 131,* 98–127.

Valkenburg, P. M., & Peter, J. (2009). Social consequences of the Internet for adolescents. *Current Directions in Psychological Science, 18*(1), 1–5.

van der Maas, H. L. J., Dolan, C. V., Grasman, R. P. P. P., Wicherts, J. M., Huizenga, H. M., & Raijmakers, M. E. J. (2006). A dynamical model of general intelligence: The positive manifold of intelligence by mutualism. *Psychological Review, 113,* 842–861.

Van Duuren, F., & DiGiacomo, J. P. (1997). Degrading situations, affiliation, and social dependency. *European Journal of Social Psychology, 27,* 495–510.

Van Erp, T. G. M., Saleh, P. A., Rosso, I. M. R., Huttunen, M., Lonnqvist, J., Pirkola, T., Salonen, O., Valanne, L., Poutanen, V. P., Stanertskjold- Nordenstam, C. G., & Cannon, T. D. (2002). Contributions of genetic risk and fetal hypoxia to hippocampal volume in patients with schizophrenia or schizo-affective disorder, their unaffected siblings and healthy unrelated volunteers. *American Journal of Psychiatry, 159,* 1514–1520.

Van Houwelingen, J. H., & Van Raaij, W. F. (1989). The effect of goal-setting and daily electronic feedback on in-home energy use. *Journal of Consumer Research, 16,* 98–105.

Van Vugt, M. (2009). Averting the tragedy of the commons. *Current Directions in Psychological Science, 18*(3), 169–173.

Vandell, D. L., Belsky, J., Burchinal, M., Steinberg, L.,Vandergrift, N. & the NICHD Early Child Care Research Network (2010). Do effects of early child care extend to age 15 years? *Child Development, 81,* 737–756.

Vasquez, M. J., Lott, B., Garcia-Vazquez, E., Grant, S. K., Iwamasa, G. Y., Molina, L. E., & others. (2006). Personal reflections: Barriers and strategies in increasing diversity in psychology. *American Psychologist, 61*(2), 157–172.

Vataja, R., Pohjasvaara, T., Leppavuoir, A., Mantyla, R., Aronen, H., Salonen, O., Kaste, M., & Erkinjuntti, T. (2001). Magnetic resonance imaging correlates of depression after ischemic stroke. *Archives in General Psychiatry, 58,* 925–931.

Veen, N. D., & others (2004). Cannabis use and age at onset of schizophrenia. *American Journal of Psychiatry, 161,* 501–506.

Veleber, D. M., & Templer, D. I. (1984). Effects of caffeine on anxiety and depression. *Journal of Abnormal Psychology, 93,* 120–122.

Veling, W., Susser, E., van Os, J., Mackenbach, J. P., Selten, J. P., & Hoek, H. W. (2008). Ethnic density of neighborhoods and incidence of psychotic disorders among immigrants. *American Journal of Psychiatry, 165,* 66–73.

Ventura, J., Neuchterlein, K. H., Lukoff, D., & Hardesty, J. P. (1989). A prospective study of stressful life events and schizophrenic relapse. *Journal of Abnormal Psychology, 98,* 407–411.

Verger, P., Dab, W., Lamping, D. L., Loze, J. Y., Deschaseaux-Voinet, C., Abenhaim, L., & Rouillon F. (2004). The psychological impact of terrorism: An epidemiologic study of post-traumatic stress disorder and associated factors in victims of the 1995–1996 bombings in France. *American Journal of Psychiatry,* 161:1384–1389.

Verheul, R., Van Den Bosch, L. M. C., Koeter, M. W. J., De Ridder, M. A. J., Stijnen, T., & Van Den Brink, W. (2003). Dialectical behavior therapy for women with borderline personality disorder. *The British Journal of Psychiatry, 182,* 135–140.

Verona, E., Sadeh, N., & Curtin, J. J. (2009). Stress-induced asymmetric frontal brain activity and aggression risk. *Journal of Abnormal Psychology, 118*(1), 131–145.

Vervliet, B., Vansteenwegen, D., & Eelen, P. (2004). Generalization of extinguished skin conductance responding in human fear conditioning. *Learning and Memory, 11,* 555–558.

Vikas, M., & Ross, W. T. (1998). The impact of positive and negative affect and issue framing on issue interpretation and risk taking. *Organizational Behavior and Human Decision Processes, 76,* 298–324.

Vinck, P., Pham, P. N., Stover, E., & Weinstein, H. M. (2007). Exposure to war crimes and implications for peace building in Northern Uganda. *JAMA, 298,* 543–554.

Visitainer, M. A., Volpicelli, J. R., & Seligman, M. E. P. (1982). Tumor rejection in rats after inescapable or escapable shock. *Science, 216,* 437–439.

Visser, P. S., & Mirabile, R. R. (2004). Attitudes in the social context: The impact of social network composition on individual-level attitude strength. *Journal of Personality and Social Psychology, 87,* 779–795.

Vitaliano, P. P., Young, H. M., & Zhang, J. (2004). Is caregiving a risk factor for illness? *Current Directions in Psychological Science. 13* (1): 13–16.

Vittengl, J. R., Clark, L. A., Dunn, T. W., & Jarrett, R. B. (2007). Reducing relapse and recurrence in unipolar depression: a comparative meta-analysis of cognitive-behavioral therapy's effects. *Journal of Consulting and Clinical Psychology, 75,* 475–488.

von Frisch, K. (1953). *The dancing bees: An account of the life and senses of the honey-bee.* New York: Harcourt, Brace, & World.

Vos, T., Haby, M. M., Barendregt, J. J., Kruijshaar, M., Corry, J., & Andrews, G. (2004). The burden of major depression avoidable by longer-term treatment strategies. *Archives of General Psychiatry, 61,* 1097–1103.

Votruba-Drzal, E., Coley, R. L., & Chase-Lansdale, P. L. (2004). Child care and low-income children's development: Direct and moderated effects. *Child Development, 75,* 196–312.

W

Wadden, T. A., Vogt, R. A., Anderson, R. E., Bartlett, S. J., Foster, G. D., Kuehnel, R. H., Wilk, J., Weinstock, R., Buckenmeyer, P., Berkowitz, R. I., & Steen, S. N. (1997). Exercise in the treatment of obesity: Effect of four interventions on body composition, resting energy expenditure, appetite, and mood. *Journal of Consulting and Clinical Psychology, 65,* 269–277.

Waenke, M., Schwarz, N., & Noelle-Neumann, E. (1995). Asking comparative questions: The impact of the direction of the comparison. *Public Opinion Quarterly, 59,* 347–372.

Wagner, R. K. (1997). Intelligence, training, and employment. *American Psychologist, 52,* 1059–1069.

Waldron, I. (1991). Gender and health-related behavior. In D. S. Goodman (Ed.), *Health behavior: Emerging research perspectives.* New York: Plenum.

Walker, E., Shapiro, D., Esterberg, M., & Trotman, H. (2010). Neurodevelopment and schizophrenia: Broadening the focus. *Current Directions in Psychological Science, 19,* 204–208.

Walker, E., & Tessner, K. (2008). Schizophrenia. *Perspectives on Psychological Science, 3,* 30–37.

Walker, L. (1986). Cognitive processes in moral development. In G. L. Sapp (Ed.), *Handbook of moral development: Models processes, techniques, and research.* Birmingham: Religious Education Press.

Walker, M. P. (2009). The role of sleep in cognition and emotion. *The Year in Cognitive Neuroscience 2009: Annals of the New York Academy of Science,1156,* 168–197.

Walker, M. P., & Stickgold, R. (2006). Sleep, memory, and plasticity. *Annual Review of Psychology, 57,* 139–166.

Walker, M. P., & van der Helm, E. (2009). Overnight therapy? The role of sleep in emotional brain processing. *Psychological Bulletin, 135*(5), 731–748.

Wallace, B., & Fisher, L. E. (1983). *Consciousness and behavior.* Boston: Allyn & Bacon.

Wallace, R. K., & Benson, H. (1972). The physiology of meditation. *Scientific American,* pp. 85–90.

Wallas, G. (1926). *The art of thought.* New York: Harcourt Brace.

Walsh, R., & Shapiro, S. L. (2006). The meeting of meditative disciplines and western psychology. *American Psychologist, 61,* 227–239.

Walster, E., Aronson, V., & Abrahams, D. (1966). On increasing the persuasiveness of a low prestige communicator. *Journal of Experimental Social Psychology, 2,* 325–343.

Walster, E. W., & Walster, G. W. (1978). *Equity: Theory and research.* Boston: Allyn & Bacon.

Wandell, B. A., & Smirnakis, S. M. (2009). Plasticity and stability of visual field maps in adult primary visual cortex. *Nature Reviews Neuroscience, 10*(12), 873–884.

Wang, J. S., Estevez, M. E., Cornwall, M. C., & Kefalov, V. J. (2009). Intra-retinal visual cycle required for rapid and complete cone dark adaptation. *Nature Neuroscience, 12*(3), 295–302.

Wang, P. S., Simon, G. E., Avorn, J., Azocar, F., Ludman, E. J., McCulloch, J., et al. (2007). Telephone screening, outreach, and care management for depressed workers and impact on clinical and work productivity outcomes: A randomized controlled trial. *JAMA, 298,* 1401–1411.

Watkins, L. R., & Maier, S. F. (2003). When good pain turns bad. *Current Directions in Psychological Science, 12,* 232–235.

Watson, D., & Tellegen, A. (1985). Toward a consensual structure of mood. *Psychological Bulletin, 98,* 219–235.

Watson, J. B., & Rayner, R. (1920). Conditioned emotional reactions. *Journal of Experimental Psychology, 3,* 1–4.

Watson, R. I. (1971). *The great psychologists* (4th ed.). Philadelphia: J. B. Lippincott.

Webb, W. B. (1968). *Sleep: An experimental approach.* New York: Macmillan.

Webb, W. B. (1982). Sleep and biological rhythms. In W. B. Webb (Ed.), *Biological rhythms, sleep, and performance* (pp. 87–110). New York: Wiley.

Webb, W. B., & Bonnet, M. H. (1979). Sleep and dreams. In M. E. Meyer (Ed.), *Foundations of contemporary psychology.* New York: Oxford University Press.

Weddington, W. W., & others. (1990). Changes in mood, craving, and sleep during short-term abstinence reported by male cocaine addicts. *Archives of General Psychiatry, 47,* 861–868.

Wells, G. L., & Olson, E. A. (2003). Eyewitness testimony. *Annual Review of Psychology, 54,* 277–295.

Wells, G. L., Small, M., Penrod, S., Malpass, R. S., Fulero, S. M., & Brimacombe, C. A. E. (1998). Eyewitness identification procedures: Recommendations for lineups and photospreads. *Law and Human Behavior, 22,* 603–647.

Wentling, T. (1973). Mastery versus nonmastery instruction with varying test item feedback treatments. *Journal of Educational Psychology, 65,* 50–58.

Westen, D. (1998). The scientific legacy of Sigmund Freud: Toward a psychodynamically informed psychological science. *Psychological Bulletin, 124,* 333–371.

Westen, D., & Gabbard, G. O. (1999). Psychoanalytic approaches to personality. In L. A. Pervin & O. P. John (Eds.), *Handbook of personality: Theory and research* (2nd ed., pp. 57–101). New York: Guilford.

Westover, A., McBride, S., & Haley, R. W. (2007). Stroke in young adults who abuse amphetamines or cocaine. *Archives of General Psychiatry, 64,* 495–502.

Whaley, A. L., & Davis, K. E. (2007). Cultural competence and evidence-based practice in mental health services: A complementary perspective. *American Psychologist, 62,* 563–574.

Wheeler, M. A., Stuss, D. T., & Tulving, E. (1997). Toward a theory of episodic memory: The frontal lobes and autonoetic consciousness. *Psychological Bulletin, 121,* 331–354.

Wheeler, M. E., & Fiske, S. T. (2005). Controlling racial prejudice: Social-cognitive goals affect amygdala and stereotype activation. *Psychological Science, 16,* 56–63.

White, K. G. (2002). Psychophysics of remembering: The discrimination hypothesis. *Current Directions in Psychological Science, 11,* 141–145.

Whitlock, J. R., Heynen, A. J., Shuler, M. G., & Bear, M. F. (2006). Learning induces long-term potentiation in the hippocampus. *Science, 313,* 1093–1097.

Whorf, B. L. (1956). Science and linguistics. In J. B. Carroll (Ed.), *Language, thought and reality: Selected writings of Benjamin Lee Whorf.* Cambridge, MA: MIT Press.

Wickens, C. D. (1992). *Engineering psychology and human performance.* New York: HarperCollins.

Wickens, D. D., Born, D. G., & Allen, C. K. (1963). Proactive inhibition item similarity in short-term memory. *Journal of Verbal Learning and Verbal Behavior, 2,* 440–445.

Widom, C. S. (1989). The cycle of violence. *Science,* 160–166.

Wilcox, H. C., Storr, C. L., & Breslau, N. (2009). Posttraumatic stress disorder and suicide attempts in a community sample of urban American young adults. *Archives of General Psychiatry, 66,* 305–311.

Wilk, S. L., Desmarais, L. B., & Sackett, P. R. (1995). Gravitation to jobs commensurate with ability: Longitudinal and cross-sectional tests. *Journal of Applied Psychology, 80,* 79–85.

Wilkinson, R., Allison, S., Feeney, M., & Kaminska, Z. (1989). Alertness of night nurses: Two shift systems compared. *Ergonomics, 32,* 281–292.

Williams, G. V., & Goldman-Rakic, P. S. (1995). Modulation of memory fields by dopamine D1 receptors in prefrontal cortex. *Nature, 376,* 572–575.

Williams, J. M., & Hall, D. W. (1988). Use of single session hypnosis for smoking cessation. *Addictive Behaviors, 13,* 205–208.

Williams, R. B., Lane, J. D., Kunn, C. M., Melosh, W., White, A. D., & Schanberg, S. M. (1982). Type A behavior and elevated physiological and neuroendocrine responses to cognitive tasks. *Science, 218,* 483–485.

Williams, R. L. (1972). Abuses and misuses in testing black children. *Journal of Black Psychology, 4,* 77–92.

Williams, T. I., Salkovskis, P. M., Forrester, L., Turner, S., White, H., & Allsopp, M. A. (2010). A randomised controlled trial of cognitive behavioural treatment for obsessive compulsive disorder in children and adolescents. *European Child and Adolescent Psychiatry, 19*(5), 449–456.

Williams, W. M. (1998). Are we raising smarter children today? School- and home-related influences on IQ. In U. Neisser (Ed.), *The rising curve: Long-term gains in IQ and related measures* (pp. 125–154). Washington, DC: American Psychological Association.

Williams, W. M., & Ceci, S. J. (1997). Are Americans becoming more or less alike? Trends in race, class, and ability differences in intelligence. *American Psychologist, 52,* 1126–1235.

Wilson, R. S., & Bennett, D. A. (2003). Cognitive activity and risk of Alzheimer's disease. *Current Directions in Psychological Science, 12,* 87–91.

Wilson, T. D., & Gilbert, D. T. (2008). Explaining away a model of affective adaption. *Perspectives on Psychological Science, 3*(5), 370–386.

Winch, R. F. (1958). *Mate-selection.* New York: Harper & Row.

Wincze, J., & Carey, M. P. (2001). *Sexual dysfunction.* New York: Guilford Press.

Winett, R. A. (1995). A framework for health promotion and disease prevention programs. *American Psychologist, 50,* 341–350.

Winkielman, P. & Berridge, K. C. (2004). Unconscious emotion. *Current Directions in Psychological Science, 13,* 120–123.

Winner, E. (2000). Giftedness: Current theory and research. *Psychological Science, 9,* 153–156.

Winter, W. C., Hammond, W. R., Green, N. H., Zhang, Z., & Bliwise, D. L. (2009). Measuring circadian advantage in major league baseball: A 10-year retrospective study. *International Journal of Sports Physiology and Performance, 4,* 394–401.

Wisniewski, A. B. (1998). Sexually dimorphic patterns of cortical asymmetry, and the role for sex steroid hormones in determining cortical patterns of lateralization. *Psychoneuroendocrinology, 23,* 519–547.

Witte, K., & Allen, M. (2000). A meta-analysis of fear appeals: Implications for effective public health campaigns. *Health, Education and Behavior, 27,* 591–615.

Witthoft, M., & Hiller, W. (2010). Psychological approaches to the origins and treatments of somatoform disorders. *Annual Review of Clinical Psychology, 6,* 257–283.

Wixted, J. T. (2004). The psychology and neuroscience of forgetting. *Annual Review of Psychology, 55,* 235–269.

Wong, W. C. (2009). Retracing the footsteps of Wilhelm Wundt: Explorations in the disciplinary frontiers of psychology and in Volkerpsychologie. *History of Psychology, 12*(4), 229–265.

Wood, J. M., Bootzin, R. R., Rosenhan, D., Nolen-Hoeksema, S., & Jourdon, F. (1992). Effects of the 1989 San Francisco earthquake on frequency and content of nightmares. *Journal of Abnormal Psychology, 101,* 219–224.

Wood, W., Christensen, P. N., Hebl, M. R., & Rothgerber, H. (1997). Conformity to sex-typed norms, affect, and the self-concept. *Journal of Personality and Social Psychology, 73,* 523–535.

Wood, W., & Eagly, A. H. (2002). A cross-cultural analysis of the behavior of women and men: Implications for the origins of sex differences. *Psychological Bulletin, 128,* 699–727.

Woodberry, K. A., Giuliano, A. J., & Seidman, L. J. (2008). Premorbid IQ in schizophrenia: A meta-analytic review. *American Journal of Psychiatry, 165,* 579–587.

Woodhill, B. M., & Samuels, C. A. (2004). Desirable and undesirable androgyny: A prescription for the twenty-first century. *Journal of Gender Studies, 13,* 15–28.

Woodruff-Pak, D. S. (1999). New directions for a classical paradigm: Human eyeblink conditioning. *Psychological Science, 10,* 1–3.

World Health Organization. (2009). *Current and future directions of the HIV/AIDS pandemic.* Geneva.

Worrell, J. (1980). New directions in counseling women. *Personnel and Guidance Journal, 58,* 477–484.

Wright, D. B., Memon, A., Skagerberg, E. M., & Gabbert, F. (2009). When eyewitnesses talk. *Current Directions in Psychological Science, 18*(3), 174–178.

Wright, J. W., & Harding, J. W. (2010). The brain RAS and Alzheimer's disease. *Experimental Neurology, 223*(2), 326–333.

Wu, E. Q., Birnbaum, H. G., Shi, L., Ball, D. E., Kessler, R. C., Moulis, M., & Aggarwal, J. (2005). The economic burden of schizophrenia in the United States in 2002. *Journal of Clinical Psychiatry, 66,* 1122–1129.

Wyatt, R. J. (1996). Neurodevelopment abnormalities and schizophrenia: A family affair. *American Journal of Psychiatry, 53,* 11–15.

Y

Yalom, I. D. (1995). *The theory and practice of group psychotherapy* (4th ed.). New York: Basic Books.

Yeates, G. N., Gracey, F., & McGrath, J. C. (2008). A biopsychosocial deconstruction of "personality change" following acquired brain injury. *Neuropsychological Rehabilitation, 18,* 566–589.

Yehuda, R., Kahana, B., Schmeidler, J., Southwick, S. M., Wilson, S., & Giller, E. L. (1995). Impact of cumulative lifetime trauma and recent stress on current post-traumatic stress disorder symptoms in Holocaust survivors. *American Journal of Psychiatry, 152,* 12.

Young, L. J., & Wang, Z. (2004). The neurobiology of pair bonding. *Nature Neuroscience, 7*(10), 1048–1052.

Z

Zaccaro, S. J. (2007). Trait-based perspective. *American Psychologist, 62,* 7–16.

Zajonc, R. B. (1965). Social facilitation. *Science, 149,* 269–274.

Zajonc, R. B. (1968). Attitudinal effects of mere exposure. *Journal of Personality and Social Psychology Monograph Supplement, 9,* 1–27.

Zajonc, R. B., & Mullally, P. R. (1997). Birth order: Reconciling conflicting effects. *American Psychologist, 52,* 685–699.

Zamble, E., Mitchell, J. B., & Findlay, H. (1986). Pavlovian conditioning of sexual arousal: Parametric and background manipulations. *Journal of Experimental Psychology: Animal Behavior Processes, 12,* 403–411.

Zaragoza, M. S., & Mitchell, K. J. (1996). Repeated exposure to suggestion and the creation of false memories. *Psychological Science, 1,* 294–300.

Zellner, M. (1970). Self-esteem, reception, and influenceability. *Journal of Personality and Social Psychology, 15,* 87–93.

Zemishlany, Z., & Weizman, A. (2008). The impact of mental illness on sexual dysfunction. *Advances in Psychosomatic Medicine, 29,* 89–106.

Zimbardo, P. (1969). The human choice: Individuation, reason, and order versus deindividuation, impulse, and chaos. In W. Arnold and D. Levine (Eds.), *Nebraska Symposium on Motivation, 17,* 237–307.

Zimbardo, P. (1972). The pathology of imprisonment. *Society, 9*(6), 4.

Zimbardo, P. (2004). Does psychology make a significant difference in our lives? *American Psychologist, 59,* 339–351.

Zimbardo, P. (2007). *The Lucifer effect: Understanding how good people turn evil.* Random House Publishing Group.

Zimmerman, B. J., & Dibenedetto, M. K. (2008). Mastery learning and assesment: implications for students and teachers in an era of high-stakes testing. *Psychology in the Schools, 45,* 206–210.

Zisook, S., & Shuchter, S. R. (1991). Depression through the first year after the death of a spouse. *American Journal of Psychiatry, 148,* 1346–1352.

Zubieta, J.-K., Heitzeg, M. M., Xu, Y., Koeppe, R. A., Ni, L., Guthrie, S., & Domino, E. F. (2005). Regional cerebral blood flow responses to smoking in tobacco smokers after overnight abstinence. *American Journal of Psychiatry, 162,* 567–577.

Zubieta, J.-K., Ketter, T. A., Bueller, J. A., Xu, J., Kilbourn, M. R., Young, E. A., & Koeppe, R. A. (2003). Regulation of human affective responses by anterior cingulated and limbic m-opioid neurotransmission. *Archives of General Psychiatry, 60,* 1145–1153.

Zverev, Y. P. (2004). Effects of caloric deprivation and satiety on sensitivity of the gustatory system. *BMC Neuroscience, 5,* 1–5.

Zvolensky, M. J., & Bernstein, A. (2005). Cigarette smoking and panic psychopathology. *Current Directions in Psychological Science, 14,* 301–305.

Credits

NAME INDEX

A

Aaker, J. L., 539
Aarts, H., 163
Abbey, A., 390
Abbot, B. B., 437
Abe, O., 74, 75
Abel, G., 489
Abel, T., 77
Abele, A. E., 114
Aber, L., 100
Abhold, J., 258
Aboa-Éboulé, C., 425
Abrahams D., 538, 553
Abrahamse, W., 562
Acebo, C., 170
Ackerman, D., 145
Adams, D. B., 368, 370
Adams, G. R., 427
Adams, H. E., 489
Adams, J., 558
Adams, P. R., 427
Addis, M. E., 524
Ader, R., 201, 202
Adler, Alfred, 408, *408*, 409, 422, 500
Adolph, K. E., 319
Agumadu, C. O., 27
Ainsworth, M. D. S., 341
Akiskal, H. S., 479
Alaimo, K., 293
Alansky, J. A., 341
Albert, K. A., 83
Aleman, A., 480
Alfieri, T., 360
Allen, C. K., 244*f*
Allen, J. J., 180
Allen, J. J. B., 554, 556
Allen, K. E., 204, 204*f*
Allen, L., 100
Allen, L. S., 374
Allen, M., 107*t*, 539
Allison, K. C., 354
Alloy, L. B., 476
Allport, G. W., 259, 259*f*, 396, 396*f*, 397
Alou, Felipe, 91
Alou, Jesús, 91
Alou, Matty, 91
Alou, Moisés, 91
Alston, J. Henry, *5*, 5–6
Altschule, M. D., 520
Alvarez, G. A., 232
Amarel, D., 438
Amato, P., 343, 344
Amedi, A., 68
Ames, D. R., 549

Amoore, J. E., 145
Anastasi, A., 580
Anderson, C. A., 30, 31, 32, 33, 222, 223, 387
Anderson, K. E., 342
Anderson, M., 284
Anderson, S. L., 553
Andreasen, N. C., 61, 82, 83
Andrews, B., 469
Angoff, W. H., 94, 99
Angold, A., 463
Antoni, M. H., 456
Archimedes, 274
Ardrey, R., 386
Aristotle, 1, 2, 2, 21, 527, 528, 538
Arnett, J. J., 328, 329
Arnetz, B., 425
Arnold, M. B., 379
Aron, A., 380, 557
Aronson, E., 527, 539, 544, 545, 552, 553, 555, 556
Aronson, H., 16
Aronson, V., 538, 553
Arsenault, L., 186
Arthur, W., 575
Asakawa, K., 384
Asarnow, J., 427, 439
Asch, S., 532, 533, 550
Aschersleben, G., 331*f*
Aschoff, J., 171
Aserinsky, E., 168
Ashby, F. G., 266, 268
Ashby, John, 481*f*
Ashton, C. H., 186
Ashton, M. C., 397
Astin, A. W., 390
Atkinson, R. C., 230
Atkinson, R. K., 594
Atlantis, E., 450
Augustine, D. K., 595
Auvert, B., 455
Axel, R., 145
Axelrod, S. R., 468

B

Baddeley, A. D., 230, 232, 234
Badia, P., 437
Baer, L., 521
Bahrick, H. P., 234, 238
Bahrick, P. O., 238
Bailine, S., 520
Baker, H., 488
Baker, T. B., 187, 190
Ball, K., 354

Balsam, K. F., 373
Baltes, P. B., 331, 331*f*, 335
Banaji, M. R., 259, 544
Bancroft, J., 492, 493
Bandelow, B., 78
Bandura, Albert, 9, 114, 221, 222, 222*f*, 382, 387, *410*, 410–411, 412, 413, 417, 422, 512, 569
Banich, M. T., 70, 109
Banks, M., 318
Barahal, H. S., 521
Barber, J., 179
Barber, T. X., 180
Barch, D., 234
Bard, P., 379
Bargh, J. A., 165
Barker, D. J. P., 317
Barlow, D. H., 467
Barnes, D. E., 435
Barnes, K. E., 323
Baron, A. S., 544
Baron, R., 539, 540
Baron, R. A., 431
Barr, C. E., 84
Barrett, E. A., 307
Barrett, L. F., 377
Barrett, M. S., 407, 409
Barrick, M. R., 578
Barrymore, Drew, *255*
Barsky, A. J., 471
Bartels, M., 95, 293
Bartlett, F. C., 245, 248
Bartoshuk, L., 144
Bartzokis, G., 74
Basoglu, M., 35
Bass, E. M., 223
Bastien, C. H., 524
Bates, D. W., 471
Batsell, W., 224
Baum, A., 564
Baumeister, R. F., 163, 530
Baumrind, D., 342
Baxter, L. C., 69, 74
Baxter, L. R., 498
Bayer, C. P., 426
Beach, F. A., 368
Beall, J. K., 438
Bean, B. P., 50
Beck, A. T., 435, 476, 477, 512, *512*, 514
Beck, J. G., 493
Beeman, M. J., 70
Beethoven, Ludwig van, 416, *416*
Beilock, S. L., 530
Beiman, I., 178
Bell, L., 552
Bell, R., 342

SUBJECT INDEX

A

A. *See* adenine
abnormal behavior, 458–496. *See also*
 schizophrenia
 ADHD, **482**–483, 496
 anxiety disorders, **466**–470, 495
 atypical sexual behavior, **487**–491, 496
 biological theories, 461
 CBT and, 508–509
 contemporary views of, 462, 495
 defined, **459**
 definition of, 459–460
 dissociative disorders, **472**–474, 495
 DSM-IV and, 462–463
 historical views of, 460–462
 insanity and, **464**
 mood disorders, **475**–480, 495
 personality disorders, **483**–485, 496
 psychological theories of, 462
 public health burden of, 463
 sexual dysfunction, **492**–494, 496
 somatoform disorders, **470**–472, 495
 stigma and, 373, 463–464, 523
 supernatural theories, 460–461
abnormalities, chromosome, 97
absolute threshold, **122**
 difference threshold *v.*, **122**, 123
 of human hearing, 133
absolutist thinking, 513
Abu Ghraib incident, 534
abuse
 alcohol, 182*t*, 187, 190–191, 297
 drug, 186–187
 sexual/physical, repressed memories of,
  259–260
acceptance stage, 339
accidents, safety management and, 452–453
accommodation, **150**
acetone, 182*t*. *See also* inhalants
acetylcholine, **54**, 54*t*
achievement motivation, **360**–361, 391
achievement/cognitive ability, gender differences
 in, 106, 106*t*
acquired immune deficiency syndrome. *See* AIDS
action potential, **50**, 51
active gene-environment correlation, 102, 118
acupuncture, *140*, 140–141
adaptive behavior, 21
addiction, drug, 186
adenine (A), 94, 95*f*
adequate debriefing, 41
ADH. *See* antidiuretic hormone
ADHD. *See* attention-deficit/hyperactivity
 disorder

Adlerian preschools, 408
adolescence, **325**, 345
 mood changes in, 328
 parent-child conflicts in, 328
 peers and, 328, 345
 risky behavior in, 329
adolescent development, 325–329, 345
 cognitive development, 326–327
 emotional/social development, 328–329
 formal operational stage, 311*f*, 326–**327**, 345
 physical development, 325–326
adolescent egocentrism, **327**
adolescent growth spurt, **326**, 326*f*
adopted children, studies of, 94, 117
adrenal glands, **77**–79, 78*f*, 86
 cortisol and, **78**, 79*f*, 170, 170*f*, 171, 433*f*
 epinephrine and, 58, 59*f*, **78**, 79*f*, 80, 433*f*
 norepinephrine and, **54**, 54*t*, **78**, 79*f*, 80, 433*f*
 stress and, 78–79, 79*f*, 80, 433*f*
ads, personal, 399–400
adulthood, 330–339, 345
 aging, 336–338, 347
 cognitive development, 330–331
 crystallized intelligence and, 331, 331*f*
 death/dying, 337–338
 development, historical change and,
  335–336
 early, 332
 emotional/social development, 331–332
 fluid intelligence and, 331, 331*f*
 later, 333*f*, 334–335
 Levinson's periods of adult development,
  332–334, 333*f*
 longevity and, 336–337
 middle, 332–334, 333*f*, 345
 personality changes in, 331, *331*
 physical development, 330
 stage theories, evaluation of, 335–337
 stages, 332–339, 345–347
aerial perspective, **150**, *151*
aerobic exercise, 448, *449*, 449–451
afferent neurons, **57**, 57*f*
affiliation motivation, 358–360, 391
afterimages, color, 129–130, 129*f*
aggression, 385–388, *386*, 392
 animals and, 41
 cognitive theory of, 387–388, 392
 evolutionary selection of, 112
 Freud's instinct theory of, **386**, 392
 frustration-aggression theory, **386**–387, 392
 genes' influence on, 92, 92*f*
 ineffective coping and, 445
 social learning theory and, 386–387, 392
 violent youth gangs and, 388
aging, 336–338, 347

agoraphobia, **466**, 524*t*
agreeableness, 397, 397*t*
AIDS (acquired immune deficiency syndrome), 3,
 373, 455–456, 456*f*, 458
 cancer and, 455
 denial and, 456
 high-risk behavior and, 455
 HIV and, 186, 455–456, 458
 management, psychological factors in, 456
 overpopulation and, 566
 prevention, behavior change and, 455
 social support and, 438
 women and, 451–452
air pollution
 behavior/mental processes and, 99
 deaths from, 450, 561, 567
 depression study and, 431, 431*f*
airplane design, ergonomics and, 583*f*
alarm reaction (GAS), 432–433, 433*f*
alcohol abuse, 182*t*, 187, 190–191, 297
Alcohol Abuse and Alcoholism, National Institute
 on, 191
alcohol-blood levels, 190, 191, 191*f*
alcoholism, 191, 297
algorithms, **271**
all-or-none principle, **51**
Allport's trait theory, 396
alprazolam (Xanax), 182*t*, 184, 519*t*
altered states of consciousness, 177–187
 characteristics of, 177–178
 depersonalization, **181**, 191
 drugs and, 181–191, 191
 hypnosis, **179**–180
 meditation, *178*, **178**
 mindfulness, **178**–179
Alzheimer's disease, 54, 62, *85*, **85**, 85*f*, 330
 brain and, 54, 62, 85, *85*, 85*f*
 MRI of brain, 85, 85*f*
 schizophrenia *v.*, 85
Ambien, 184
American Law Institute, 464
American Psychiatric Association, 462, 481, 492,
 493, 494
American Psychological Association (APA)
 Clark as president of, 16
 Committee on Precautions in Animal
  Experimentation, 42
 effective psychotherapies and, 523
 ethical research on humans, 41
 ethical standards for psychotherapy,
  499–500
 website, 41
American Sign Language (ASL), 281
Americans with Disabilities Act, 547
Ames room, 154, 155*f*

5 VALUES IN PSYCHOLOGY
Value empirical evidence, tolerate ambiguity, act ethically, and reflect other values that are the underpinnings of psychology as a science.

5.1 Recognize the necessity for ethical behavior in all aspects of the science and practice of psychology.

5.2 Demonstrate reasonable skepticism and intellectual curiosity by asking questions about causes of behavior.

5.3 Seek and evaluate scientific evidence for psychological claims.

5.4 Tolerate ambiguity and realize that psychological explanations are often complex and tentative.

5.5 Recognize and respect human diversity and understand that psychological explanations may vary across populations and contexts.

5.6 Assess and justify their engagement with respect to civic, social, and global responsibilities.

5.7 Understand the limitations of their psychological knowledge and skills.

- **Ch 1**: Goals of Psychology, p. 3; Contemporary Perspectives and Specialty Areas in Psychology, p. 13-8; What We Know about Human Behavior: Some Starting Places, p. 19-21
- **Ch 2**: Basic Concepts of Research, p. 25-7; Research Methods, p. 27-39; Ethical Principles of Research, p. 40-2
- **Ch 7**: Operant Conditioning: Learning from the Consequences of Your Behavior, p. 203-13; Application of Psychology, p. 226
- **Ch 10**: Stage Theories of Development, p. 310-4; Variations in Development that Make Us Unique, p. 339-40
- **Ch 11**: Primary Motives: Biological Needs, p. 351-6; Psychological Motives, p. 357-65
- **Ch 14**: Definition of Abnormal Behavior, p. 459-64
- **Ch 15**: Ethical Standards for Psychotherapy, p. 499-500; Human Diversity: Ethnic, Gender, and Sexual Issues in Psychotherapy, p. 517-8; Application of Psychology: What To Do If You Think You Need Help, p. 523-4
- **Ch 17**: Environmental Psychology and Sustainability, p. 563-70

6 INFORMATION AND TECHNOLOGICAL LITERACY
Demonstrate information competence and the ability to use computers and other technology for many purposes.

6.1 Demonstrate information competence at each stage in the following process: formulating a researchable topic, choosing relevant and evaluating relevant resources, and reading and accurately summarizing scientific literature that can be supported by database search strategies.

6.2 Use appropriate software to produce understandable reports of the psychological literature, methods, and statistical and qualitative analyses in APA or other appropriate style, including graphic representations of data.

6.3 Use information and technology ethically and responsibly.

6.4 Demonstrate basic computer skills, proper etiquette, and security safeguards.

- **Ch 2**: Basic Concepts of Research, p. 25-7; Research Methods; p. 27-39; Application of Psychology: Design Your Own Formal Experiment, p. 44-5
- **Ch 9**: Thinking and Problem Solving: Using Information to Reach Goals, p. 269-76
- **Ch 11**: Emotions, p. 375-84
- **Ch 16**: Attitudes and Persuasion, p. 538-46
- **Ch 17**: Psychology and Education, p. 592-5

7 COMMUNICATION SKILLS
Communicate effectively in a variety of formats.

7.1 Demonstrate effective writing skills in various formats (e.g., essays, correspondence, technical papers, note taking) and for various purposes (e.g., informing, defending, explaining, persuading, arguing, teaching).

7.2 Demonstrate effective oral communication skills in various formats (e.g., group discussion, debate, lecture) and for various purposes (e.g., informing, defending, explaining, persuading, arguing, teaching).

7.3 Exhibit quantitative literacy.

7.4 Demonstrate effective interpersonal communication skills.

7.5 Exhibit the ability to collaborate effectively.

- **Ch 2**: Basic Concepts of Research, p. 25-7
- **Ch 8**: Application of Psychology: Eyewitness Testimony and Memory, p. 257-61
- **Ch 9**: Language: Symbolic Communication, p. 277-81
- **Ch 10**: Human Diversity: Raising a Child Who Cannot Hear, p. 308-9
- **Ch 11**: Application of Psychology: Date Rape, p. 390-1
- **Ch 15**: Psychoanalysis, p. 500-4; Humanistic Psychotherapy, p. 505-507; Cognitive Behavior Therapy, p. 508-14
- **Ch 16**: Groups and Social Influence, p. 527-36; Attitudes and Persuasion, p. 538-46
- **Ch 17**: Psychology and Work, p. 571-86; Psychology and Law, p. 587-9